Trade Mark Law in Europe

Trade Mark Law in Europe

Case Law of the Court of Justice of the European Union

Fourth Edition

Ulrich Hildebrandt

Wolters Kluwer

Published by:
Kluwer Law International B.V.
PO Box 316
2400 AH Alphen aan den Rijn
The Netherlands
E-mail: lrs-sales@wolterskluwer.com
Website: www.wolterskluwer.com/en/solutions/kluwerlawinternational

Sold and distributed by:
Wolters Kluwer Legal & Regulatory U.S.
920 Links Avenue
Landisville, PA 17538
United States of America
E-mail: customer.service@wolterskluwer.com

ISBN 978-94-035-4127-3

e-Book: ISBN 978-94-035-4137-2
web-PDF: ISBN 978-94-035-4147-1

About the Author

Ulrich Hildebrandt studied Music and Law. He is a founding partner of the German law firm Hildebrandt. Rechtsanwälte. He has been active in the field of trade mark law since the year 2000. Additionally, he is a professor at the Heinrich-Heine-University Dusseldorf, Germany, and the author of several books, especially the German standard reference work 'Marken und andere Kennzeichen' (Trade Marks and Other Signs) and the commentary *Hildebrandt/Sosnitza*, EU Trade Mark Regulation (EUTMR). He is a member of the Special Committee for Unfair Competition and Trade Mark Law of the German GRUR-Association, a member of the Working Committee for Trade Mark Law at the Markenverband (German Trade mark Association), and Correspondent for the Dutch journal *Berichten Industriële Eigendom*.

Notes to the user

1. The material provisions of the **Directive** are reproduced with their original wording. Major changes to previous versions of the Directive are expressly marked. The author tries a prediction whether case law concerning the previous version may also be relevant for the actual version.

2. The **appendixes** 1, 2, and 3 enable the finding of the relevant provision of the actual Directive and the relevant case law.

3. An unofficial full text of the decisions of the European Court of Justice is available on the **Internet** at curia.europa.eu. Both numerical access to the case law and a search form are provided. In some instances, decisions may be found by using one of the search methods, but not the other.

4. The **citation** goes by the schema 'file number, date of the decision – catchword, paragraph'. Since there are no official catchwords, reference is made to the designation found in the numerical list of case law on the Court's Internet page. These catchwords may differ from familiar catchwords used by certain journals. Appendix 3 compiles the decisions sorted by catchword.

5. Wherever no official translation of a decision exists in the English language, a translation by the author is provided, followed by a **footnote**. Sections that contain unavoidable variances from the original wording are identified.

6. **Quotations** in the case law sections are adopted from the wording of the decision.

7. **Bold type** inside the case law sections was supplied by the author for purposes of emphasis and clarity.

8. The **case law until September 2023** has been taken into account.

Table of Contents

List of Abbreviations

CDR	Council Regulation (EC) No 6/2002 of 12 December 2001 on Community Designs
CJEU	Court of Justice of the European Union
CTMIR	Commission Regulation (EC) No. 2868/95 of 13 December 1995 implementing Council Regulation (EC) No 40/94 on the Community Trade Mark
CTMR	Council Regulation (EC) No. 207/2009 of 26 February 2009 on the Community Trade Mark (OJ L 78, 24.3.2009, p. 1) [references to the Council Regulation (EC) No 40/94 of 20 December 1993 on the Community Trade Mark (OJ Nr. L 11 of 14 January 1994, p. 1) have been adopted]
EC	European Community / Treaty establishing the European Community (consolidated text)
ECR	European Court Reports
EEA	European Economic Area
EEC Treaty	Treaty establishing the European Community of 25 March 1957
EUIPO	European Intellectual Property Office
et seq.	and the following
et seqq.	and the following
EUTMR	Regulation (EU) 2017/1001 of the European Parliament and of the Council of 14 June 2017 on the European Union Trade Mark (Codification) (OJ L 154, 16.6.2017, p. 1–99)
No.	Number
OHIM	Office for Harmonization in the Internal Market / European Union Intellectual Property Office
OJ	*Official Journal of the European Community*

OJ-OHIM	*Official Journal of the Office for Harmonization in the Internal Market*
p.	Page
para.	Paragraph
TMD	Directive (EU) 2015/2436 of the European Parliament and of the Council to Approximate the Laws of the Member States Relating to Trade Marks (OJ L 336, 23.12.2015, p. 1)
TMD2008	Directive 2008/95/EC of the European Parliament and of the Council of 22 October 2008 to Approximate the Laws of the Member States Relating to Trade Marks (OJ L 299, 8.11.2008, p. 25) [references to the First Directive 89/104/EEC of the Council, of 21 December 1988, to Approximate the Laws of the Member States Relating to Trade Marks (OJ EC No L 40 of 11.2.1989, p. 1) have been adopted]
Treaty	Treaty establishing the European Community of 25 March 1957
TRIPS	Agreement on Trade Related Aspects of Intellectual Property Rights of April 15, 1994

Foreword

The book you are holding in your hand (or reading from your screen) is a valuable tool for any trade mark professional, be it in academia or in practice.

The trade mark system as such is already somewhat complicated, but in a long string of decisions, starting around 1997, the Court of Justice of the European Union (CJEU) has made this even more complex, and sometimes even incomprehensible for those who have not studied the field in detail. Just as examples, one can look at the interpretation that the CJEU gives to Trade mark Law concepts, how it tries to harmonize Trade Mark Law with other laws an fundamental rights or the legal construct of the 'function theory', which is essential to trade mark protection, but in no way is defined or delineated in the text of the Trade marks Directive or Community Trade mark Regulation. Also, other rights and limitations have been created by the case law of the CJEU, and I have yet to meet a trade mark professional that has not been taken by surprise by a CJEU decision at some point. Each time we have to recalibrate, consider how the decision fits into the trade mark system (or how it could be fitted into it). As such, in-depth knowledge of the CJEU case law is essential.

This is not easy to gain, for anybody. It requires an overview of the subject matter and knowledge of previous decisions. This is what Ulrich Hildebrandt has, and he takes the reader along the winding path that the CJEU case law has taken. He does so on the basis of some key basic principles, followed by an overview of what the CJEU decision teaches us, following the structure of the Trade marks Directive.

Those who read or study this book – even if it is just on a specific topic or article – will feel less lost in a thick forest that European Trade mark Law has become, and may well find that open spot where things are clarified and answers can be found.

I, for one, always keep this book within reach.

Prof. Dr Tobias Cohen Jehoram
Amsterdam, 16 November 2023

Directive (EU) 2015/2436 of the European Parliament and of the Council to approximate the laws of the Member States relating to trade marks (Recast)

THE EUROPEAN PARLIAMENT AND THE COUNCIL OF THE EUROPEAN UNION,

Having regard to the Treaty on the Functioning of the European Union, and in particular Article 114(1) thereof,

Having regard to the proposal from the European Commission,

After transmission of the draft legislative act to the national parliaments,

Having regard to the opinion of the European Economic and Social Committee[1]*, Acting in accordance with the ordinary legislative procedure*[2]*,*

Whereas:

(1) A number of amendments should be made to Directive 2008/95/EC of the European Parliament and of the Council[3]*. In the interests of clarity, that Directive should be recast.*
(2) Directive 2008/95/EC has harmonised central provisions of substantive trade mark law which at the time of adoption were considered as most directly affecting the functioning of the internal market by impeding the free movement of goods and the freedom to provide services in the Union.

1. OJ C 327, 12.11.2013, p. 42.
2. Position of the European Parliament of 25 Feb. 2014 (not yet published in the Official Journal) and position of the Council at first reading of 10 Nov. 2015 (not yet published in the Official Journal). Position of the European Parliament of 15 Dec. 2015.
3. Directive 2008/95/EC of the European Parliament and of the Council of 22 Oct. 2008 to approximate the laws of the Member States relating to trade marks (OJ L 299, 8.11.2008, p. 25).

(3) Trade mark protection in the Member States coexists with protection available at Union level through European Union trade marks ('EU trade marks') which are unitary in character and valid throughout the Union as laid down in Council Regulation (EC) No 207/2009.[4] *The coexistence and balance of trade mark systems at national and Union level in fact constitutes a cornerstone of the Union's approach to intellectual property protection.*

(4) Further to the Commission's Communication of 16 July 2008 on an Industrial Property Rights Strategy for Europe, the Commission carried out a comprehensive evaluation of the overall functioning of the trade mark system in Europe as a whole, covering Union and national levels and the interrelation between the two.

(5) In its conclusions of 25 May 2010 on the future revision of the trade mark system in the European Union, the Council called on the Commission to present proposals for the revision of Regulation (EC) No 207/2009 and Directive 2008/95/EC. The revision of that Directive should include measures to make it more consistent with Regulation (EC) No 207/2009, which would thus reduce the areas of divergence within the trade mark system in Europe as a whole, while maintaining national trade mark protection as an attractive option for applicants. In this context, the complementary relationship between the EU trade mark system and national trade mark systems should be ensured.

(6) The Commission concluded in its Communication of 24 May 2011 entitled 'A Single Market for Intellectual Property Rights' that in order to meet increased demands from stakeholders for faster, higher quality, more streamlined trade mark registration systems, which are also more consistent, user friendly, publicly accessible and technologically up-to-date, there is a necessity to modernise the trade mark system in the Union as a whole and adapt it to the internet era.

(7) Consultation and evaluation for the purpose of this Directive has revealed that, in spite of the previous partial harmonisation of national laws, there remain areas where further harmonisation could have a positive impact on competitiveness and growth.

(8) In order to serve the objective of fostering and creating a well-functioning internal market and to facilitate acquiring and protecting trade marks in the Union to the benefit of the growth and the competitiveness of European businesses, in particular small and medium-sized enterprises, it is necessary to go beyond the limited scope of approximation achieved by Directive 2008/95/EC and extend approximation to other aspects of substantive trade mark law governing trade marks protected through registration pursuant to Regulation (EC) No 207/2009.

(9) For the purpose of making trade mark registrations throughout the Union easier to obtain and administer, it is essential to approximate not only provisions of substantive law but also procedural rules. Therefore, the principal procedural rules in the area of trade mark registration in the Member States and in the EU trade mark system should be aligned. As regards procedures under national law, it is sufficient to lay down general principles, leaving the Member States free to establish more specific rules.

(10) It is essential to ensure that registered trade marks enjoy the same protection under the legal systems of all the Member States. In line with the extensive protection granted

4. Council Regulation (EC) No. 207/2009 of 26 Feb. 2009 on the Community trade mark (OJ L 78, 24.3.2009, p. 1).

to EU trade marks which have a reputation in the Union, extensive protection should also be granted at national level to all registered trade marks which have a reputation in the Member State concerned.

(11) This Directive should not deprive the Member States of the right to continue to protect trade marks acquired through use but should take them into account only with regard to their relationship with trade marks acquired by registration.

(12) Attainment of the objectives of this approximation of laws requires that the conditions for obtaining and continuing to hold a registered trade mark be, in general, identical in all Member States.

(13) To this end, it is necessary to list examples of signs which are capable of constituting a trade mark, provided that such signs are capable of distinguishing the goods or services of one undertaking from those of other undertakings. In order to fulfil the objectives of the registration system for trade marks, namely to ensure legal certainty and sound administration, it is also essential to require that the sign is capable of being represented in a manner which is clear, precise, self-contained, easily accessible, intelligible, durable and objective. A sign should therefore be permitted to be represented in any appropriate form using generally available technology, and thus not necessarily by graphic means, as long as the representation offers satisfactory guarantees to that effect.

(14) Furthermore, the grounds for refusal or invalidity concerning the trade mark itself, including the absence of any distinctive character, or concerning conflicts between the trade mark and earlier rights, should be listed in an exhaustive manner, even if some of those grounds are listed as an option for the Member States which should therefore be able to maintain or introduce them in their legislation.

(15) In order to ensure that the levels of protection afforded to geographical indications by Union legislation and national law are applied in a uniform and exhaustive manner in the examination of absolute and relative grounds for refusal throughout the Union, this Directive should include the same provisions in relation to geographical indications as contained in Regulation (EC) No 207/2009. Furthermore, it is appropriate to ensure that the scope of absolute grounds is extended to also cover protected traditional terms for wine and traditional specialties guaranteed.

(16) The protection afforded by the registered trade mark, the function of which is in particular to guarantee the trade mark as an indication of origin, should be absolute in the event of there being identity between the mark and the sign and the goods or services. The protection should apply also in the case of similarity between the mark and the sign and the goods or services. It is indispensable to give an interpretation of the concept of similarity in relation to the likelihood of confusion. The likelihood of confusion, the appreciation of which depends on numerous elements and, in particular, on the recognition of the trade mark on the market, the association which can be made with the used or registered sign, the degree of similarity between the trade mark and the sign and between the goods or services identified, should constitute the specific condition for such protection. The ways in which a likelihood of confusion can be established, and in particular the onus of proof in that regard, should be a matter for national procedural rules which should not be prejudiced by this Directive.

(17) In order to ensure legal certainty and full consistency with the principle of priority, under which a registered earlier trade mark takes precedence over later registered trade marks, it is necessary to provide that the enforcement of rights which are conferred by a trade mark should be without prejudice to the rights of proprietors acquired prior to the filing or priority date of the trade mark. Such an approach is in conformity with Article 16(1) of the Agreement on trade related aspects of intellectual property rights of 15 April 1994 ('TRIPS Agreement').

(18) It is appropriate to provide that an infringement of a trade mark can only be established if there is a finding that the infringing mark or sign is used in the course of trade for the purposes of distinguishing goods or services. Use of the sign for purposes other than for distinguishing goods or services should be subject to the provisions of national law.

(19) The concept of infringement of a trade mark should also comprise the use of the sign as a trade name or similar designation, as long as such use is made for the purposes of distinguishing goods or services.

(20) In order to ensure legal certainty and full consistency with specific Union legislation, it is appropriate to provide that the proprietor of a trade mark should be entitled to prohibit a third party from using a sign in comparative advertising where such comparative advertising is contrary to Directive 2006/114/EC of the European Parliament and of the Council[5]*.*

(21) In order to strengthen trade mark protection and combat counterfeiting more effectively, and in line with international obligations of the Member State under the World Trade Organization (WTO) framework, in particular Article V of the General Agreement on Tariffs and Trade on freedom of transit and, as regards generic medicines, the 'Declaration on the TRIPS Agreement and Public Health' adopted by the Doha WTO Ministerial Conference on 14 November 2001, the proprietor of a trade mark should be entitled to prevent third parties from bringing goods, in the course of trade, into the Member State where the trade mark is registered without being released for free circulation there, where such goods come from third countries and bear without authorisation a trade mark which is identical or essentially identical with the trade mark registered in respect of such goods.

(22) To this effect, it should be permissible for trade mark proprietors to prevent the entry of infringing goods and their placement in all customs situations, including, in particular transit, transhipment, warehousing, free zones, temporary storage, inward processing or temporary admission, also when such goods are not intended to be placed on the market of the Member State concerned. In performing customs controls, the customs authorities should make use of the powers and procedures laid down in Regulation (EU) No 608/2013 of the European Parliament and of the Council[6]*, also at*

5. Directive 2006/114/EC of the European Parliament and of the Council of 12 Dec. 2006 concerning misleading and comparative advertising (OJ L 376, 27.12.2006, p. 21).
6. Regulation (EU) No. 608/2013 of the European Parliament and of the Council of 12 Jun. 2013 concerning customs enforcement of intellectual property rights and repealing Council Regulation (EC) No. 1383/2003 (OJ L 181, 29.6.2013, p. 15).

the request of the right holders. In particular, the customs authorities should carry out the relevant controls on the basis of risk analysis criteria.

(23) In order to reconcile the need to ensure the effective enforcement of trade mark rights with the necessity to avoid hampering the free flow of trade in legitimate goods, the entitlement of the proprietor of the trade mark should lapse where, during the subsequent proceedings initiated before the judicial or other authority competent to take a substantive decision on whether the registered trade mark has been infringed, the declarant or the holder of the goods is able to prove that the proprietor of the registered trade mark is not entitled to prohibit the placing of the goods on the market in the country of final destination.

(24) Article 28 of Regulation (EU) No 608/2013 provides that a right holder is to be liable for damages towards the holder of the goods where, inter alia, the goods in question are subsequently found not to infringe an intellectual property right.

(25) Appropriate measures should be taken with a view to ensuring the smooth transit of generic medicines. With respect to international non-proprietary names (INN) as globally recognised generic names for active substances in pharmaceutical preparations, it is vital to take due account of the existing limitations on the effect of trade mark rights. Consequently, the proprietor of a trade mark should not have the right to prevent a third party from bringing goods into a Member State where the trade mark is registered without being released for free circulation there based upon similarities between the INN for the active ingredient in the medicines and the trade mark.

(26) In order to enable proprietors of registered trade marks to combat counterfeiting more effectively, they should be entitled to prohibit the affixing of an infringing trade mark to goods, and certain preparatory acts carried out prior to the affixing.

(27) The exclusive rights conferred by a trade mark should not entitle the proprietor to prohibit the use of signs or indications by third parties which are used fairly and thus in accordance with honest practices in industrial and commercial matters. In order to create equal conditions for trade names and trade marks against the background that trade names are regularly granted unrestricted protection against later trade marks, such use should only be considered to include the use of the personal name of the third party. Such use should further permit the use of descriptive or non-distinctive signs or indications in general. Furthermore, the proprietor should not be entitled to prevent the fair and honest use of the mark for the purpose of identifying or referring to the goods or services as those of the proprietor. Use of a trade mark by third parties to draw the consumer's attention to the resale of genuine goods that were originally sold by or with the consent of the proprietor of the trade mark in the Union should be considered as being fair as long as it is at the same time in accordance with honest practices in industrial and commercial matters. Use of a trade mark by third parties for the purpose of artistic expression should be considered as being fair as long as it is at the same time in accordance with honest practices in industrial and commercial matters. Furthermore, this Directive should be applied in a way that ensures full respect for fundamental rights and freedoms, and in particular the freedom of expression.

(28) It follows from the principle of free movement of goods that the proprietor of a trade mark should not be entitled to prohibit its use by a third party in relation to goods which have been put into circulation in the Union, under the trade mark, by him or with his

consent, unless the proprietor has legitimate reasons to oppose further commercialisation of the goods.

(29) It is important, for reasons of legal certainty to provide that, without prejudice to his interests as a proprietor of an earlier trade mark, the latter may no longer request a declaration of invalidity or oppose the use of a trade mark subsequent to his own trade mark of which he has knowingly tolerated the use for a substantial length of time, unless the application for the subsequent trade mark was made in bad faith.

(30) In order to ensure legal certainty and safeguard legitimately acquired trade mark rights, it is appropriate and necessary to provide that, without prejudice to the principle that the later trade mark cannot be enforced against the earlier trade mark, proprietors of earlier trade marks should not be entitled to obtain refusal or invalidation or to oppose the use of a later trade mark if the later trade mark was acquired at a time when the earlier trade mark was liable to be declared invalid or revoked, for example because it had not yet acquired distinctiveness through use, or if the earlier trade mark could not be enforced against the later trade mark because the necessary conditions were not applicable, for example when the earlier mark had not yet obtained a reputation.

(31) Trade marks fulfil their purpose of distinguishing goods or services and allowing consumers to make informed choices only when they are actually used on the market. A requirement of use is also necessary in order to reduce the total number of trade marks registered and protected in the Union and, consequently, the number of conflicts which arise between them. It is therefore essential to require that registered trade marks actually be used in connection with the goods or services for which they are registered, or, if not used in that connection within five years of the date of the completion of the registration procedure, be liable to be revoked.

(32) Consequently, a registered trade mark should only be protected in so far as it is actually used and a registered earlier trade mark should not enable its proprietor to oppose or invalidate a later trade mark if that proprietor has not put its trade mark to genuine use. Furthermore, Member States should provide that a trade mark may not be successfully invoked in infringement proceedings if it is established as a result of a plea that the trade mark could be revoked or, when the action is brought against a later right, could have been revoked at the time when the later right was acquired.

(33) It is appropriate to provide that, where the seniority of a national mark or a trade mark registered under international arrangements having effect in the Member State has been claimed for an EU trade mark and the mark providing the basis for the seniority claim has thereafter been surrendered or allowed to lapse, the validity of that mark can still be challenged. Such a challenge should be limited to situations where the mark could have been declared invalid or revoked at the time it was removed from the register.

(34) For reasons of coherence and in order to facilitate the commercial exploitation of trade marks in the Union, the rules applicable to trade marks as objects of property should be aligned to the extent appropriate with those already in place for EU trade marks, and should include rules on assignment and transfer, licensing, rights in rem and levy of execution.

(35) Collective trade marks have proven a useful instrument for promoting goods or services with specific common properties. It is therefore appropriate to subject national

collective trade marks to rules similar to the rules applicable to European Union collective marks.

(36) In order to improve and facilitate access to trade mark protection and to increase legal certainty and predictability, the procedure for the registration of trade marks in the Member States should be efficient and transparent and should follow rules similar to those applicable to EU trade marks.

(37) In order to ensure legal certainty with regard to the scope of trade mark rights and to facilitate access to trade mark protection, the designation and classification of goods and services covered by a trade mark application should follow the same rules in all Member States and should be aligned to those applicable to EU trade marks. In order to enable the competent authorities and economic operators to determine the extent of the trade mark protection sought on the basis of the application alone, the designation of goods and services should be sufficiently clear and precise. The use of general terms should be interpreted as including only goods and services clearly covered by the literal meaning of the term. In the interest of clarity and legal certainty, the offices should, in cooperation with each other, endeavour to compile a list reflecting their respective administrative practices with regard to the classification of goods and services.

(38) For the purpose of ensuring effective trade mark protection, Member States should make available an efficient administrative opposition procedure, allowing at least the proprietor of earlier trade mark rights and any person authorised under the relevant law to exercise the rights arising from a protected designation of origin or a geographical indication to oppose the registration of a trade mark application. Furthermore, in order to offer efficient means of revoking or declaring invalid trade marks, Member States should provide for an administrative procedure for revocation or declaration of invalidity within the longer transposition period of seven years, after the entry into force of this Directive.

(39) It is desirable that Member States' central industrial property offices and the Benelux Office for Intellectual Property cooperate with each other and with the European Union Intellectual Property Office in all fields of trade mark registration and administration in order to promote convergence of practices and tools, such as the creation and updating of common or connected databases and portals for consultation and search purposes. The Member States should further ensure that their offices cooperate with each other and with the European Union Intellectual Property Office in all other areas of their activities which are relevant for the protection of trade marks in the Union.

(40) This Directive should not exclude the application to trade marks of provisions of law of the Member States other than trade mark law, such as provisions relating to unfair competition, civil liability or consumer protection.

(41) Member States are bound by the Paris Convention for the Protection of Industrial Property ('the Paris Convention') and the TRIPS Agreement. It is necessary that this Directive be entirely consistent with that Convention and that Agreement. The obligations of the Member States resulting from that Convention and that Agreement should not be affected by this Directive. Where appropriate, the second paragraph of Article 351 of the Treaty on the Functioning of the European Union should apply.

(42) Since the objectives of this Directive, namely to foster and create a well-functioning internal market and to facilitate the registration, administration and protection of trade

marks in the Union to the benefit of growth and competitiveness, cannot be sufficiently achieved by the Member States but can rather, by reason of their scale or effects, be better achieved at Union level, the Union may adopt measures, in accordance with the principle of subsidiarity as set out in Article 5 of the Treaty on European Union. In accordance with the principle of proportionality as set out in that Article, this Directive does not go beyond what is necessary in order to achieve those objectives.

(43) Directive 95/46/EC of the European Parliament and of the Council[7] *governs the processing of personal data carried out in the Member States in the context of this Directive.*

(44) The European Data Protection Supervisor was consulted in accordance with Article 28(2) of Regulation (EC) No. 45/2001 of the European Parliament and of the Council[8] *and delivered an opinion on 11 July 2013.*

(45) The obligation to transpose this Directive into national law should be confined to those provisions which represent a substantive amendment as compared with the earlier Directive. The obligation to transpose the provisions which are unchanged arises under the earlier Directive.

(46) This Directive should be without prejudice to the obligations of the Member States under Directive 2008/95/EC relating to the time limit for transposition of Directive 89/104/EEC into national law as set out in Part B of Annex I to Directive 2008/95/EC,

HAVE ADOPTED THIS DIRECTIVE:

[A] Principles

As a preliminary point, it should be borne in mind that the protection of trade marks is characterized, within the European Union (EU), by the **coexistence of several systems of protection**.[9]

Member States must take measures which are sufficiently effective to **achieve the aim of the directive,** and they must ensure that the rights conferred by it can be effectively relied upon before the national courts by the persons concerned.[10]

TMD2008, which applies, in accordance with Article 1, in particular to trade marks for goods or services which are the subject of registration or of an application in a Member State for registration, approximates, as stated in recitals 4, 6, 8 and 10, those national provisions of law which most directly affect the functioning of the internal market. According to those recitals, it is fundamental, for that purpose, to ensure that registered trade marks enjoy the same protection under the legal systems of all the

7. Directive 95/46/EC of the European Parliament and of the Council of 24 Oct. 1995 on the protection of individuals with regard to the processing of personal data and on the free movement of such data (OJ L 281, 23.11.1995, p. 31).
8. Regulation (EC) No. 45/2001 of the European Parliament and of the Council of 18 Dec. 2000 on the protection of individuals with regard to the processing of personal data by the Community institutions and bodies and on the free movement of such data (OJ L 8, 12.1.2001, p. 1).
9. CJEU C-190/10 of 22.3.2012 – Génesis, para. 30; C-196/11 P of 24.5.2012 – Formula One Licensing/OHIM, paras 38 et seq.; C-149/11 of 19.12.2012 – Leno Merken, para. 26.
10. CJEU C-145/05 of 27.4.2006 – Levi Strauss, para. 16.

Member States and that the conditions for obtaining a registered trade mark are, in general, identical in all Member States while leaving the Member States free to fix the procedural provisions concerning *inter alia* the registration of those trade marks.[11]

It follows from the need for **uniform application of EU law** and from the principle of equality that the terms of a provision of EU law which makes no express reference to the law of the Member States for the purpose of determining its meaning and scope must normally be given an autonomous and uniform interpretation throughout the European Union, having regard not only to its wording but also to the context of the provision and the objective pursued by the legislation in question.[12]

Where a national court is called upon to **interpret national law**, whether the provisions in question were adopted before or after the directive concerned, it is required to do so, so far as possible, in the light of the wording and the purpose of the directive in order to achieve the result pursued by the latter and thereby comply with the third paragraph of Article 249 EC. That applies notwithstanding any contrary interpretation which may arise from the *travaux préparatoires* for the national rule.[13]

According to settled case law, in a field which has been exhaustively harmonized at Community level, a national measure must be assessed in the light of the provisions of that harmonizing measure and not of those of primary law.[14]

[B] The guarantee of origin

Trade mark rights, the Court has held, constitute an essential element in the system of undistorted competition which the Treaty is intended to establish. In such a system, undertakings must be able to attract and retain customers by the quality of their products or services, which is possible only, thanks to the existence of distinctive signs allowing them to be identified. For the trade mark to be able to fulfil that function, it must constitute a guarantee that all products which bear it have been manufactured under the control of a single undertaking to which responsibility for their quality may be attributed.[15]

11. CJEU C-705/17 of 12.6.2019 – Patent- och registreringsverket/Hansson, para. 32.
12. CJEU C-617/15 of 18.5.2017 – Hummel Holding/Nike a.o., para. 22, with further proof; C-571/22 P of 5.12.2022 – Unite the Union/EUIPO, para. 20; *see also* CJEU C-172/18 of 5.9.2019 – AMS Neve a.o./Heritage Audio a.o., para. 52.
13. CJEU C-408/01 of 23.10.2003 – Adidas-Salomon and Adidas Benelux, para. 21; C-371/02 of 29.4.2004 – Björnekulla Fruktindustrier, para. 13; C-245/02 of 16.11.2004 – Anheuser-Busch, para. 56; *see also* CJEU C-320/12 of 27.6.2013 – Malaysia Dairy Industries, para. 28.
14. CJEU C-421/04 of 9.3.2006 – Matratzen Concord, para. 20.
15. CJEU C-71 to 73/94 of 11.7.1996 – Eurim-Pharm Arzneimittel/Beiersdorf and Others, para. 30; C-427/93, C-429/93 and C-436/93 of 11.7.1996 – Bristol-Myers Squibb and Others/Paranova, para. 43; C-232/94 of 11.7.1996 – MPA Pharma/Rhône-Poulenc Pharma, para. 16; C-349/95 of 11.11.1997 – Loendersloot/Ballantine & Son and Others, para. 22; C-517/99 of 4.10.2001 – Merz & Krell, para. 21; C-206/01 of 12.11.2002 – Arsenal Football Club, para. 47; C-228/03 of 17.3.2005 – Gillette Company and Gillette Group Finland, para. 25; C-202/08 and C-208/08 of 16.7.2009 – American Clothing Associates/OHIM, para. 41; C-48/09 P of 14.9.2010 – Lego Juris/OHIM, para. 38; C-337/12 P to C-340/12 P of 6.3.2014 – Pi-Design/OHIM, para. 42; C-30/15 P of 10.11.2016 – Simba Toys/EUIPO, para. 36; C-291/16 of 20.12.2017 – Schweppes/Red Paralela, para. 36; C-129/17 of 25.7.2018 – Mitsubishi Shoji Kaisha a.o./Duma Forklifts a.o.,

In relation to trade marks, the specific subject matter is in particular to guarantee to the proprietor of the trade mark that he has the exclusive right to use that trade mark for the purpose of putting a product into circulation for the first time and therefore to protect him against competitors wishing to take advantage of the status and reputation of the trade mark by selling products illegally bearing that trade mark. In order to answer the question of whether that exclusive right involves the right to prevent the trade mark being affixed by a third person after the product has been repackaged, regard must be had to the essential function of the trade mark, which is to guarantee the identity of the origin of the trade marked product to the consumer or ultimate user, by enabling him without any possibility of confusion to distinguish that product from products which have another origin. This guarantee of origin means that the consumer or ultimate user can be certain that a trade marked product which is sold to him has not been subject at a previous stage of marketing to interference by a third person, without the authorization of the proprietor of the trade mark, such as to affect the original condition of the product. The right attributed to the proprietor of preventing any use of the trade mark which is likely to impair the guarantee of origin so understood is therefore part of the specific subject matter of the trade mark right.[16]

The tenth recital in the preamble to the directive emphasizes that the protection afforded by the registered trade mark has the aim of guaranteeing the trade mark as an indication of origin and that in the case of similarity between the mark and between the sign and goods or services, the likelihood of confusion constitutes the specific condition for protection.[17]

In order that a trade mark may achieve that essential function, the TMD2008 confers on the proprietor of the mark a set of rights while limiting them to what is strictly necessary for the performance of that function.[18]

---

para. 30; *see also* CJEU C-10/89 of 17.10.1990 – CNL-SUCAL/HAG, para. 13; C-690/17 of 11.4.2019 – Oko-Text Verlag/Dr. Rudolf Liebe Nachf., para. 40; C-104/18 P of 12.9.2019 – Koton Mağazacilik Tekstil Sanayi ve Ticaret/EUIPO, para. 45.

16. CJEU 102/77 of 23.5.1978 – Hoffmann-La Roche/Centrafarm, para. 7; *see also* CJEU C-299/99 of 18.7.2002 – Philips, para. 30; C-329/02 P of 16.9.2004 – SAT.1 SATELLITENFERNSEHEN/OHIM, para. 23; C-16/03 of 30.11.2004 – Peak Holding, para. 38; C-206/01 of 12.11.2002 – Arsenal Football Club, para. 48; C-228/03 of 17.3.2005 – Gillette Company and Gillette Group Finland, para. 26; C-37/03 P of 15.9.2005 – BioID/OHIM, para. 27; C-120/04 of 6.10.2005 – Medion, para. 23; C-348/04 of 26.4.2007 – Boehringer Ingelheim and Others (II), para. 14; C-412/05 P of 26.4.2007 – Alcon/OHIM (II), para. 53; C-59/08 of 23.4.2009 – Copad, para. 22; C-236/08 to C-238/08 of 23.3.2010 – Google France, para. 82; C-324/09 of 12.7.2011 – L'Oréal, para. 80; C-90/11 and C-91/11 of 15.3.2012 – Strigl and Securvita, para. 30; C-12/12 of 18.4.2013 – Colloseum Holding, para. 26; C-409/12 of 6.3.2014 – Backaldrin Österreich The Kornspitz Company, para. 20; C-379/14 of 16.7.2015 – TOP Logistics, para. 47; C-215/14 of 16.9.2015 – Société des Produits Nestlé, para. 59; C-297/15 of 10.11.2016 – Ferring Lægemidler/Orifarm, para. 14; C-673/15 P to C-676/15 P of 20.9.2017 – The Tea Board/EUIPO, para. 52; *see also* CJEU C-642/16 of 17.5.2018 – Junek Europ-Vertrieb/Lohmann & Rauscher International, para. 23; C-129/17 of 25.7.2018 – Mitsubishi Shoji Kaisha a.o./Duma Forklifts a.o., para. 35.
17. CJEU C-120/04 of 6.10.2005 – Medion, para. 24.
18. CJEU C-714/18 P of 16.7.2020 – ACTC/EUIPO, para. 36.

[C] Balance between the interests

While Article 5 TMD2008 confers certain rights on the proprietor of a trade mark, the directive requires consequences to be drawn from the proprietor's conduct in determining the scope of protection of those rights.[19]

Thus, Article 9(1) TMD2008 provides that where, in a Member State, the proprietor of an earlier trade mark has acquiesced, for a period of five successive years, in the use of a later trade mark registered in that Member State while being aware of such use, he is in principle no longer entitled on the basis of the earlier trade mark either to apply for a declaration that the later trade mark is invalid or to oppose the use of the later trade mark in respect of the goods or services for which the later trade mark has been used. By the same token, Article 10 TMD2008 provides that if, following completion of the registration procedure, the proprietor has not put the trade mark to genuine use in the Member State concerned in connection with the goods or services in respect of which it is registered, or if such use has been suspended during an uninterrupted period of five years, that trade mark is to be subject to the sanctions provided for in the directive, unless there are proper reasons for non-use. Finally, under Article 12(1) and (2) TMD2008, a trade mark is to be liable to revocation if it has not been put to genuine use within a continuous period of five years or if it has become, in consequence of its proprietor's conduct, the common name for a product or service.[20]

Those provisions indicate that the purpose of the directive is generally to strike a balance between the interest of the proprietor of a trade mark to safeguard its essential function, on the one hand, and the interests of other economic operators in having signs capable of denoting their products and services.[21]

It follows that the protection of rights that the proprietor of a trade mark derives under the directive in question is not unconditional since in order to maintain the balance between those interests, that protection is limited in particular to those cases in which the proprietor shows himself to be sufficiently vigilant by opposing the use of signs by other operators likely to infringe his mark.[22]

[D] Paris Convention

All Member States of the Community are bound by the Paris Convention for the Protection of Industrial Property. It is necessary that the provisions of the Directive are entirely consistent with those of the Paris Convention.[23]

19. CJEU C-145/05 of 27.4.2006 – Levi Strauss, para. 27.
20. CJEU C-145/05 of 27.4.2006 – Levi Strauss, para. 28.
21. CJEU C-145/05 of 27.4.2006 – Levi Strauss, para. 29.
22. CJEU C-145/05 of 27.4.2006 – Levi Strauss, para. 30, *see also* CJEU C-466/20 of 19.5.2022 – HEITEC/HEITECH Promotion, para. 47.
23. CJEU C-40/01 of 11.3.2003 – Ansul, para. 32; C-363/99 of 12.2.2004 – Koninklijke KPN Nederland, para. 29 f.; C-442/07 of 9.12.2008 – Verein Radetzky-Orden, para. 15.

The provisions of the Paris Convention also cannot be relied on directly in the present case.[24]

First of all, the Community is not a party to the Paris Convention, in contrast in fact to the TRIPS Agreement.[25]

Second, when the Community legislature considered it necessary to give some provisions of the Paris Convention direct effect, it expressly referred to them in the CTMR, in particular, in relation to absolute grounds for refusal, in Article 7(1)(h) and (i) of that regulation. By contrast, Article 7(1) makes no such reference in relation to the distinctive character of trade marks, and the Community legislature has in this respect created a separate provision in Article 7(1)(b) CTMR.[26]

Third, while the direct effect of the Paris Convention could flow from the cross-reference made to it by Article 2(1) of the TRIPS Agreement, such a cross-reference cannot, in the absence of the direct applicability of the TRIPS Agreement, render the Paris Convention directly applicable.[27]

[E] TRIPS Agreement

It is apparent from its case law that **the Court has jurisdiction** to interpret a provision of the TRIPS Agreement for the purpose of responding to the needs of the judicial authorities of the Member States where they are called upon to apply their national rules with a view to ordering measures for the protection of rights created by Community legislation which fall within the scope of that agreement.[28]

Since the Community is a party to the TRIPS Agreement, it is indeed under an obligation to interpret its trade mark legislation, as far as possible, in the light of the wording and purpose of that agreement.[29]

The Court has already held that, having regard to their nature and structure, the provisions of the TRIPS Agreement do not have a direct effect. Those provisions are not, in principle, among the rules in the light of which the Court is to review the legality of measures of the Community institutions under the first paragraph of Article 230 EC and are not such as to create rights upon which individuals may rely directly before the courts by virtue of Community law.[30]

It is settled case law that a provision of an agreement entered into by the Community with non-member countries must be regarded as being directly applicable when, regard being had to the wording, purpose and nature of the agreement, it may

24. CJEU C-238/06 P of 25.10.2007 – Develey Holding/OHIM, para. 40.
25. CJEU C-238/06 P of 25.10.2007 – Develey Holding/OHIM, para. 41.
26. CJEU C-238/06 P of 25.10.2007 – Develey Holding/OHIM, para. 42.
27. CJEU C-238/06 P of 25.10.2007 – Develey Holding/OHIM, para. 43.
28. CJEU C-245/02 of 16.11.2004 – Anheuser-Busch, para. 41; *see also* CJEU C-53/96 of 16.6.1998 – Hermès International/FHT Marketing Choice BV, para. 29; C-89/99 of 13.9.2001 – Schieving-Nijstad and Others, para. 30.
29. CJEU C-245/02 of 16.11.2004 – Anheuser-Busch, paras 42 and 55; C-809/18 P of 11.11.2020 – EUIPO/John Mills, para. 64; *see also* CJEU C-246/05 of 14.6.2007 – Häupl, para. 48; C-414/11 of 18.7.2013 – Daiichi Sankyo, para. 80.
30. CJEU C-300/98 and C-392/98 of 14.12.2000 – Dior and Others, para. 44; C-245/02 of 16.11.2004 – Anheuser-Busch, para. 54; C-238/06 P of 25.10.2007 – Develey Holding/OHIM, para. 39.

be concluded that the provision contains a clear, precise and unconditional obligation which is not subject, in its implementation or effects, to the adoption of any subsequent measure.[31]

The primary objective of TRIPS is to strengthen and harmonize the protection of intellectual property on a worldwide scale.[32]

According to its preamble, the object of TRIPS is to reduce distortions and impediments to international trade, and taking into account the need to promote effective and adequate protection of intellectual property rights, and to ensure that measures and procedures to enforce intellectual property rights do not themselves become barriers to legitimate trade. Those objectives are also set out in Article 41(1) and (2) of TRIPS.[33]

It is therefore for the judicial authorities, when called upon to apply national rules with a view to ordering provisional measures, to take into account all the circumstances of the case before them so as to ensure that a balance is maintained between the competing rights and obligations of the right holder and of the defendant.[34]

The **TRIPS Agreement** applies in the event of a conflict between a trade mark and a sign alleged to infringe that trade mark where that conflict arose before the **date of application** of the TRIPS Agreement but continued beyond that date.[35]

If the alleged infringement of a trade mark arose before the date of application of the TRIPS Agreement to the Community and the Member States – that is to say, prior to 1 January 1996 – this does not necessarily mean that such acts 'occurred' before that date within the meaning of Article 70(1) of the TRIPS Agreement. Where the acts which the third party is alleged to have committed continued up to the date on which a ruling was given – which, in the case giving rise to the above-mentioned judgment, occurred after the date of application of the TRIPS Agreement – the relevant provision of that agreement is temporally relevant to the settlement of the dispute in the main case.[36]

The effect of Article 70(1) of the TRIPS Agreement is merely to exclude the imposition of obligations under that agreement in respect of 'acts which occurred' before its date of application, but it does not exclude such obligations in respect of situations which continue beyond that date. By contrast, Article 70(2) of the TRIPS Agreement states that the obligations arising from that agreement apply in respect of 'all subject-matter existing ... and which is protected' on the date of application of that Agreement to a member of the World Trade Organization ('the WTO'), so that, from that date, such a member is required to fulfil all the obligations arising from that agreement in respect of that existing subject matter (*see also*, to that effect, the Report

31. CJEU C-300/98 and C-392/98 of 14.12.2000 – Dior and Others, para. 42.
32. CJEU C-89/99 of 13.9.2001 – Schieving-Nijstad and Others, para. 36; C-245/02 of 16.11.2004 – Anheuser-Busch, para. 65.
33. CJEU C-89/99 of 13.9.2001 – Schieving-Nijstad and Others, para. 37; C-245/02 of 16.11.2004 – Anheuser-Busch, para. 66.
34. CJEU C-89/99 of 13.9.2001 – Schieving-Nijstad and Others, para. 38.
35. CJEU C-245/02 of 16.11.2004 – Anheuser-Busch, para. 53.
36. CJEU C-245/02 of 16.11.2004 – Anheuser-Busch, para. 48.

of the WTO Appellate Body, issued on 18 September 2000, Canada – Term of Patent Protection (AB-2000-7), WT/DS170/AB/R, paragraphs 69, 70 and 71).[37]

Furthermore, Article 70(4) of the TRIPS Agreement applies to acts in respect of specific objects embodying protected subject matter which become infringing under the terms of legislation in conformity with that agreement, and which were commenced, or in respect of which a significant investment was made, before the date of acceptance of the WTO Agreement. In such a situation, Article 70(4) allows the members to provide for limitations of the remedies available to the holder of the right against continued performance of such acts after the date of application of the TRIPS Agreement to the WTO member concerned.[38]

In the present case, it is apparent from the decision to refer that the acts which Budvar is alleged to have committed in Finland certainly commenced before the date of application of the TRIPS Agreement but that they continued after that date. Moreover, it is undisputed that the proceedings alleging infringement concern signs which were protected as trade marks in Finland on the date of application of the TRIPS Agreement, that is to say, in respect of that Member State, 1 January 1996, and that those proceedings were brought on 11 October 1996, that is to say, after that date.[39]

It follows that, in accordance with Article 70(1) and (2), the TRIPS Agreement applies to that situation.[40]

It should be noted that the WTO Agreement was concluded in the **English, French and Spanish languages** and that those three versions alone are authentic (*see* the closing wording of the WTO Agreement).[41]

[F] Relevant classes of persons

[1] Examination of the relevant classes of persons

In general, the **perception of consumers or end users** will play a decisive role. The whole aim of the commercialization process is the purchase of the product by those persons, and the role of the intermediary consists as much in detecting and anticipating the demand for that product as in increasing or directing it.[42]

Accordingly, the relevant classes of persons comprise principally consumers and end users. However, depending on the features of the product market concerned, the influence of **intermediaries** on decisions to purchase, and thus their perception of the trade mark, must also be taken into consideration.[43]

It is true, as the Court highlighted in that interpretation, that whether a trade mark has become the common name in the trade for a product or service in respect of

37. CJEU C-245/02 of 16.11.2004 – Anheuser-Busch, para. 49.
38. CJEU C-245/02 of 16.11.2004 – Anheuser-Busch, para. 50.
39. CJEU C-245/02 of 16.11.2004 – Anheuser-Busch, para. 51.
40. CJEU C-245/02 of 16.11.2004 – Anheuser-Busch, para. 52.
41. CJEU C-89/99 of 13.9.2001 – Schieving-Nijstad and Others, para. 44.
42. CJEU C-371/02 of 29.4.2004 – Björnekulla Fruktindustrier, para. 24.
43. CJEU C-371/02 of 29.4.2004 – Björnekulla Fruktindustrier, para. 25; C-412/05 P of 26.4.2007 – Alcon/OHIM (II), para. 56.

which it is registered must be assessed not only in the light of the perception of consumers or end users but also, depending on the features of the market concerned, in the light of the perception of those in the trade, such as sellers.[44]

However, as the Court pointed out in paragraph 24 of the judgment in *Björnekulla Fruktindustrier*, in general, the perception of consumers or end users will play a decisive role. It must be held that in a case such as that at issue in the main proceedings, which is, subject to verification by the referring court, characterized by the loss of distinctive character of the trade mark concerned from the point of view of the end users, that loss may result in the revocation of that trade mark. The fact that the sellers are aware of the existence of that trade mark and of the origin which it indicates cannot, on its own, preclude such revocation.[45]

The healthcare **professional** at issue must be included in the relevant public for the purposes of the application of Article 8(1)(b) CTMR, the function of the trade mark as an indication of origin being also relevant to intermediaries who deal with the goods commercially in so far as it will tend to influence their conduct in the market.[46]

The fact that intermediaries such as healthcare professionals are liable to influence or even to determine the choice made by the end users is not, in itself, capable of excluding all likelihood of confusion on the part of those consumers as regards the origin of the goods at issue.[47]

In so far as it is found, in its definitive assessment of the facts, that the products at issue are sold in pharmacies to the end users, the Court of First Instance was fully entitled to infer therefrom that, even though the choice of those products is influenced or determined by intermediaries, such a likelihood of confusion also exists for those consumers since they are likely to be faced with those products, even if that takes place during separate purchasing transactions for each of those individual products, at various times.[48]

Furthermore, since it is undisputed that the whole process of marketing the goods at issue is aimed at the end user's acquisition of them, the Court of First Instance was entitled to hold that the role played by intermediaries, even if they are healthcare professionals whose prior intervention is required in order to sell those goods to end users, must be in part balanced against the high degree of attentiveness which may be shown by those users, in the light of the fact that the goods at issue are pharmaceutical products, when they are prescribed and, consequently, against those users' ability to make those professionals take into account their perception of the trade marks at issue and, in particular, their requirements or preferences.[49]

As regards the case which gave rise to the judgment of the Court of First Instance in *Alcon v. OHIM – Dr Robert Winzer Pharma (BSS)*,[50] that case concerned a trade mark application which related not to goods sold to end users in pharmacies but to

44. CJEU C-409/12 of 6.3.2014 – Backaldrin Österreich The Kornspitz Company, para. 28.
45. CJEU C-409/12 of 6.3.2014 – Backaldrin Österreich The Kornspitz Company, para. 29.
46. CJEU C-412/05 P of 26.4.2007 – Alcon/OHIM (II), para. 56.
47. CJEU C-412/05 P of 26.4.2007 – Alcon/OHIM (II), para. 57.
48. CJEU C-412/05 P of 26.4.2007 – Alcon/OHIM (II), para. 58.
49. CJEU C-412/05 P of 26.4.2007 – Alcon/OHIM (II), para. 61.
50. CJEU C-192/03 P of 5.10.2004 – ALCON/OHIM (I).

'ophthalmic pharmaceutical preparations; sterile solutions for ophthalmic surgery' in respect of which the Court of First Instance was entitled to hold without erring in law that the customary nature of the trade mark at issue should be assessed from the point of view of the medical specialists for whom it was intended, namely ophthalmologists and ophthalmic surgeons practising in the EU.[51]

[2] Perception

If the relevant goods and services are intended for all consumers, the relevant public must be deemed to be composed of the **average consumer, reasonably well informed and reasonably observant and circumspect.**[52]

The average consumer normally perceives a **mark as a whole** and does not proceed to analyse its various details.[53]

However, account should be taken of the fact that the average consumer only rarely has the chance to make a direct comparison between the different marks but must place his trust in the **imperfect picture** of them that he has kept in his mind.[54]

It should also be borne in mind that the average consumer's **level of attention** is likely to vary according to the category of goods or services in question.[55]

The finding of the level of attention paid by the average consumer is a finding of fact, which is not subject to review by the Court of Justice on appeal, where it does not entail a distortion of the factual evidence produced to the Court of First Instance.[56]

51. CJEU C-412/05 P of 26.4.2007 – Alcon/OHIM (II), para. 66.
52. CJEU C-104/01 of 6.5.2003 – Libertel, para. 46; C-456/01 P and C-457/01 P of 29.4.2004 – Henkel/OHIM, para. 35; C-468/01 P to C-472/01 P of 29.4.2004 – Procter & Gamble/OHIM (three-dimensional form of tablet I), para. 33; C-473/01 P and C-474/01 P of 29.4.2004 – Procter & Gamble/OHIM (three-dimensional form of tablet II), para. 33; C-329/02 P of 16.9.2004 – SAT.1 SATELLITENFERNSEHEN/OHIM, para. 24; C-107/03 P of 23.9.2004 – Procter & Gamble/OHIM (form of a soap), paras 30 and 39; C-136/02 P of 7.10.2004 – Mag Instrument/OHIM, para. 19; C-37/03 P of 15.9.2005 – BioID/OHIM, para. 68; C-412/05 P of 26.4.2007 – Alcon/OHIM (II), para. 59, 62; *see also* CJEU C-323/09 of 22.9.2011 – Interflora, para. 50; C-494/08 P of 9.12.2009 – Prana Haus/HABM, para. 26; C-541/18 of 12.9.2019 – AS/Deutsches Patent- und Markenamt, para. 20; C-456/19 of 8.10.2020 – Aktiebolaget Östgötatrafiken/Patent- och registreringsverket, para. 32.
53. CJEU C-251/95 of 11.11.1997 – SABEL/Puma, Rudolf Dassler Sport, para. 23; C-342/97 of 22.6.1999 – Lloyd Schuhfabrik Meyer, para. 25; C-3/03 P of 28.4.2004 – Matratzen Concord/OHIM, para. 29; C-286/04 P of 30.6.2005 – Eurocermex/OHIM, para. 22; C-252/12 of 18.7.2013 – Specsavers International Healthcare, para. 35; C-445/13 P of 7.5.2015 – Voss of Norway/OHIM, para. 105; C-705/17 of 12.6.2019 – Patent- och registreringsverket/Hansson, para. 45; C-328/18 P of 4.3.2020 – EUIPO/Equivalenza Manufactory, para. 58.
54. CJEU C-342/97 of 22.6.1999 – Lloyd Schuhfabrik Meyer, para. 26; C-412/05 P of 26.4.2007 – Alcon/OHIM (II), para. 60.
55. CJEU C-342/97 of 22.6.1999 – Lloyd Schuhfabrik Meyer, para. 26; C-291/00 of 20.3.2003 – LTJ Diffusion, para. 52; C-104/01 of 6. 5. 2003 – Libertel, para. 64; C-107/03 P of 23.9.2004 – Procter & Gamble/OHIM (form of a soap), para. 44; C-361/04 P of 12.1.2006 – Ruiz-Picasso and Others/OHIM, para. 38.
56. CJEU C-456/01 P and C-457/01 P of 29.4.2004 – Henkel/OHIM, para. 56; C-468/01 P to C-472/01 P of 29.4.2004 – Procter & Gamble/OHIM (three-dimensional form of tablet I), para. 53; C-473/01 P and C-474/01 P of 29.4.2004 – Procter & Gamble/OHIM (three-dimensional form of tablet II), para. 53.

It is **when making his choice** between different products in the category concerned that the average consumer exhibits the highest level of attention.[57]

The fact that the relevant public is also likely to perceive such goods and the marks relating to them in circumstances unconnected with any act of purchase and to display, where appropriate, a lower level of attention on such occasions does not prevent the taking into account of the particularly high level of attention exhibited by the average consumer when he prepares and makes his choice between different goods in the category concerned.[58]

First, it is clear that, whatever the goods and marks at issue, there will always be situations in which the public faced with them will grant them only a low degree of attention. However, to require that account be taken of the lowest degree of attention which the public is capable of displaying when faced with a product and a mark would amount to denying all relevance, for the purpose of an assessment of the likelihood of confusion, to the criterion relating to the variable level of attention according to the category of goods.[59]

Second, the authority called upon to assess whether there is a likelihood of confusion cannot reasonably be required to establish, for each category of goods, the consumer's average amount of attention on the basis of the level of attention which he is capable of displaying in different situations.[60]

Nor does *Arsenal Football Club*[61] militate against the foregoing analysis.[62]

Some consumers, in particular if they come across the goods after they have been sold and taken away from the stall where the notice appears, may interpret the sign as designating Arsenal FC as the undertaking of origin of the goods.[63]

It must be noted that in that judgment, the Court was called upon to rule on whether Article 5(1)(a) TMD2008 was to be interpreted as precluding the sale and offer for sale of goods when they were marked with a sign identical to a mark registered by a third party in respect of the same goods.[64]

After concluding that that was indeed the case, the Court stated that the fact that a sign to be found at the place of sale of the goods at issue drew consumers' attention to the fact that those goods did not come from the proprietor of the mark did not affect such a conclusion. It is against that particular background that the Court, in paragraph 57 of *Arsenal Football Club*, referred in particular to the fact that even on the assumption that that type of notice may be relied upon by the interested party as a defence, it was possible, in the case which gave rise to that judgment, that some consumers, in particular if they came across the goods after they had been sold and taken away from the place of sale, might interpret the sign affixed to those goods as

57. CJEU C-361/04 P of 12.1.2006 – Ruiz-Picasso and Others/OHIM, para. 41; C-24/05 P of 22.6.2006 – Storck/OHIM (light-brown sweet), para. 72.
58. CJEU C-361/04 P of 12.1.2006 – Ruiz-Picasso and Others/OHIM, para. 41.
59. CJEU C-361/04 P of 12.1.2006 – Ruiz-Picasso and Others/OHIM, para. 42.
60. CJEU C-361/04 P of 12.1.2006 – Ruiz-Picasso and Others/OHIM, para. 43.
61. CJEU C-206/01 of 12.11.2002 – Arsenal Football Club.
62. CJEU C-361/04 P of 12.1.2006 – Ruiz-Picasso and Others/OHIM, para. 44.
63. CJEU C-206/01 of 12.11.2002 – Arsenal Football Club, para. 57.
64. CJEU C-361/04 P of 12.1.2006 – Ruiz-Picasso and Others/OHIM, para. 45.

designating the proprietor of the mark concerned as the undertaking of origin of the goods.[65]

In doing so, the Court did not in any way express a general rule from which it could be inferred that, for the purposes of an assessment of the likelihood of confusion within the meaning of Article 5(1)(b) TMD2008 or Article 8(1)(b) CTMR, there is no need to refer specifically to the particularly high level of attention displayed by consumers when purchasing a certain category of goods.[66]

Finally, it must be stated that, by asserting that the question of the degree of attention of the relevant public to be taken into account for assessing the likelihood of confusion is different from the question of whether circumstances subsequent to the purchase situation may be relevant for assessing whether there has been a breach of trade mark rights, as was accepted, as regards the use of a sign identical to the trade mark, in *Arsenal Football Club*, the Court of First Instance did not in any way hold that the concept of likelihood of confusion under Articles 8(1)(b) and 9(1)(b) CTMR must be interpreted differently.[67]

[3] National trade usage

The distinctive character of a trade mark within the meaning of Article 3(1)(b) TMD2008 may be assessed solely on the basis of national trade usage, without any need for other administrative investigations to be undertaken in order to determine whether and to what extent identical trade marks have been registered or have been refused registration in other Member States of the EU.[68]

Article 3(1)(b) and (c) TMD2008 does not preclude the registration in a Member State, as a national trade mark, of a term borrowed from the language of another Member State in which it is devoid of distinctive character or descriptive of the goods or services in respect of which registration is sought, unless the **relevant parties** in the Member State in which registration is sought are **capable of identifying the meaning of the term.**[69]

Article 3 TMD2008 does not include any ground for refusal to register specifically aimed at trade marks constituted by a term borrowed from the language of a Member State other than the State of registration in which it is devoid of distinctive character or descriptive of the goods or services in respect of which registration is sought.[70]

Moreover, such a trade mark does not necessarily fall within the grounds for refusal to register relating to the lack of distinctive character or the descriptive character of the trade mark, referred to in points (b) and (c) respectively of Article 3(1) TMD2008.[71]

65. CJEU C-361/04 P of 12.1.2006 – Ruiz-Picasso and Others/OHIM, para. 46.
66. CJEU C-361/04 P of 12.1.2006 – Ruiz-Picasso and Others/OHIM, para. 47.
67. CJEU C-361/04 P of 12.1.2006 – Ruiz-Picasso and Others/OHIM, para. 48.
68. CJEU C-218/01 of 12.2.2004 – Henkel, para. 65; similar CJEU C-445/02 P of 28.6.2004 – Glaverbel/OHIM, para. 20.
69. CJEU C-421/04 of 9.3.2006 – Matratzen Concord, para. 26.
70. CJEU C-421/04 of 9.3.2006 – Matratzen Concord, para. 22.
71. CJEU C-421/04 of 9.3.2006 – Matratzen Concord, para. 23.

In fact, to assess whether a national trade mark is devoid of distinctive character or is descriptive of the goods or services in respect of which its registration is sought, it is necessary to take into account the perception of the relevant parties, that is to say in trade and/or amongst average consumers of the said goods or services, reasonably well informed and reasonably observant and circumspect, in the territory in respect of which registration is applied for.[72]

It is possible not only that, because of linguistic, cultural, social and economic differences between the Member States, a trade mark which is devoid of distinctive character or descriptive of the goods or services concerned in one Member State is not so in another Member State[73] but also that a mark devoid of distinctive character at Community level is not so in a Member State.[74]

This interpretation of the Directive is in accordance with the Treaty requirements, and in particular those of Articles 28 EC and 30 EC.[75]

According to settled case law, in the context of the application of the principle of the free movement of goods, the Treaty does not affect the existence of rights recognized by the legislation of a Member State in matters of intellectual property, but only restricts, depending on the circumstances, the exercise of those rights.[76]

Applying that case law, the Court ruled that the principle of the free movement of goods does not prohibit a Member State from registering as a national trade mark a sign which, in the language of another Member State, is descriptive of the goods or services concerned.[77]

That also applies if the sign in question is, in the language of a Member State other than that of registration, devoid of distinctive character with regard to the goods or services covered by the application for registration.[78]

It should be added that registration in a Member State of a trade mark does not prohibit all use of the term constituting the trade mark by other traders in the said Member State.[79]

[G] Community trade mark

[1] Material law concerning the Community trade mark

Article 1(2) CTMR specifies that a Community trade mark has a unitary character. Subject to certain exceptions (*see* in that regard Article 106, on the prohibition of use of Community trade marks, and Article 107, on prior rights applicable to particular localities, CTMR), the Community trade mark 'shall have equal effect throughout the

72. CJEU C-421/04 of 9.3.2006 - Matratzen Concord, para. 24, wording slightly changed.
73. CJEU C-421/04 of 9.3.2006 - Matratzen Concord, para. 25; C-238/06 P of 25.10.2007 - Develey Holding/OHIM, para. 58.
74. CJEU C-238/06 P of 25.10.2007 - Develey Holding/OHIM, para. 58.
75. CJEU C-421/04 of 9.3.2006 - Matratzen Concord, para. 27.
76. CJEU C-421/04 of 9.3.2006 - Matratzen Concord, para. 28.
77. CJEU C-421/04 of 9.3.2006 - Matratzen Concord, para. 29.
78. CJEU C-421/04 of 9.3.2006 - Matratzen Concord, para. 30.
79. CJEU C-421/04 of 9.3.2006 - Matratzen Concord, para. 31.

Community: it shall not be registered, transferred or surrendered or be the subject of a decision revoking the rights of the proprietor or declaring it invalid, nor shall its use be prohibited, save in respect of the whole Community'.[80]

Under Article 8(1)(b) and (2) CTMR, in the case where the earlier mark relied on in support of opposition proceedings is a Community trade mark, the trade mark in respect of which registration is sought will not be registered if because of its identity with or similarity to the earlier trade mark and the identity or similarity of the goods or services covered by the trade marks there exists a likelihood of confusion on the part of the public in the Community territory.[81]

For a Community trade mark to be refused registration under Article 8(1)(b) CTMR, the likelihood of confusion does not have to exist in the whole territory of the Member State concerned and in all its linguistic areas. In fact, an earlier national mark can be relied on in opposition proceedings against any application for registration of a Community trade mark which would adversely affect the protection of the first mark, even if only in relation to the perception of consumers in part of the territory in which the earlier trade mark is protected.[82]

It does **not** follow from Article 8(1)(b) CTMR that, for a Community trade mark to be refused registration under that provision, the likelihood of confusion must exist in **all Member States** and in all linguistic areas of the Community.[83]

In fact, the unitary character of the Community trade mark means that an earlier Community trade mark can be relied on in opposition proceedings against any application for registration of a Community trade mark which would adversely affect the protection of the first mark, even if only in relation to the perception of consumers in part of the Community.[84]

If visual or phonetic similarities between the signs at issue exist for a substantial part of the relevant public, for which conceptual differences between those signs, liable to counteract those similarities, have not been proved, the General Court must carry out a global assessment of the likelihood of confusion.[85]

The argument taking into account the possibility of conversion of the Community trade mark application to a national trade mark application must also be rejected.[86]

---

80. CJEU C-514/06 of 18.9.2008 – Armacell Enterprise/OHIM, para. 54.
81. CJEU C-514/06 of 18.9.2008 – Armacell Enterprise/OHIM, para. 55; C-254/09 P of 2.9.2010 – Calvin Klein/OHIM, para. 43; C-581/13 P and C-582/13 P of 20.11.2014 – Intra-Presse/OHIM, para. 48.
82. CJEU C-394/08 P of 3.6.2009 – Zipcar/OHIM, para. 49.
83. CJEU C-514/06 of 18.9.2008 – Armacell Enterprise/OHIM, para. 56; C-223/15 of 22.9.2016 – combit Software/Commit Business Solutions, para. 26; C-662/16 P of 20.6.2017 – Laboratoire de la mer/EUIPO, paras 6/10 and 7.
84. CJEU C-514/06 of 18.9.2008 – Armacell Enterprise/OHIM, para. 57; C-223/15 of 22.9.2016 – combit Software/Commit Business Solutions, para. 26; C-662/16 P of 20.6.2017 – Laboratoire de la mer/EUIPO, paras 6/10 and 7; C-714/18 P of 16.7.2020 – ACTC/EUIPO, para. 76.
85. CJEU C-714/18 P of 16.7.2020 – ACTC/EUIPO, para. 77, with reference to CJEU C-328/18 P of 4.3.2020 – EUIPO/Equivalenza Manufactory, paras 74-76.
86. CJEU C-514/06 of 18.9.2008 – Armacell Enterprise/OHIM, para. 59.

Admittedly, as follows from Article 108(2)(b) CTMR, the grounds for refusal of the registration of the Community trade mark determine whether that trade mark can be registered at the national level.[87]

However, the purpose of opposition proceedings is to provide undertakings with an opportunity to oppose, by way of a single procedure, applications for Community trade marks which might create a likelihood of confusion with their earlier marks or rights, and not to resolve in advance possible conflicts at the national level.[88]

It must be pointed out, at the outset, that the provisions of Article 8(1)(b) and Article 8(5) CTMR reproduce identically those of Article 8(1)(b) and Article 8(5) of Council Regulation (EC) No. 40/94 of 20 December 1993 on the Community trade mark.[89] Consequently, the case law of the Court of Justice relating to Article 8(1)(b) and Article 8(5) of Regulation No. 40/94 must be regarded as relevant with regard to the interpretation of Article 8(1)(b) and Article 8(5) CTMR.[90]

Article 8(2) of Regulation No. 864/2007[91] must be interpreted as meaning that the 'country in which the act of infringement was committed' within the meaning of that provision refers to the country where the event giving rise to the damage occurred. Where the same defendant is accused of various acts of infringement committed in various Member States, the correct approach for identifying the event giving rise to the damage is not to refer to each alleged act of infringement but to make an overall assessment of that defendant's conduct in order to determine the place where the initial act of infringement at the origin of that conduct was committed or threatened by it.[92]

The **EUIPO Guidelines** are not binding legal acts for the purpose of interpreting provisions of EU law.[93]

[2] Community trade mark system

The Community trade mark regime is an autonomous system with its own set of objectives and rules peculiar to it, and that system applies independently of any national system.[94]

87. CJEU C-514/06 of 18.9.2008 – Armacell Enterprise/OHIM, para. 60.
88. CJEU C-514/06 of 18.9.2008 – Armacell Enterprise/OHIM, para. 61.
89. OJ 1994 L 11, p. 1.
90. CJEU C-603/14 P of 10.12.2015 – El Corte Inglés/OHIM, para. 37.
91. Regulation (EC) No 864/2007 of the European Parliament and of the Council of 11 July 2007 on the law applicable to non-contractual obligations (Rome II) (OJ L 199, 31.7.2007, p. 40–49).
92. CJEU C-24/16 and C-25/16 of 27.9.2017 – Nintendo, para. 111.
93. CJEU C-149/11 of 19.12.2012 – Leno Merken, para. 48; C-445/12 P of 12.12.2013 – Rivella International/OHIM, para. 42; C-162/17 P of 16.1.2019 – Republic of Poland/EUIPO, para. 59; C-223/18 P of 6.6.2019 – Deichmann/EUIPO, para. 49; *see also* CJEU C-560/17 P of 13.3.2018 – Mediaexpert/EUIPO, para. 3/4; C-236/21 P of 1.9.2021 – sprd.net/EUIPO, para. 19.
94. CJEU C-238/06 P of 25.10.2007 – Develey Holding/OHIM, para. 65; C-488/06 P of 17.7.2008 – L & D/OHIM, para. 58; C-202/08 and C-208/08 of 16.7.2009 – American Clothing Associates/ OHIM, para. 58; C-479/09 P of 30.9.2010 – Evets/OHIM, para. 49 [concerning EPO]; C-482/09 of 22.9.2011 – Budějovický Budvar, para. 36; C-190/10 of 22.3.2012 – Génesis, para. 36; C-307/11 P of 26.4.2012 – Deichmann/OHIM, para. 57; C-354/11 P of 22.3.2012 – Emram/OHIM, para. 93; C-379/12 P of 16.5.2013 – Arav Holding/OHIM, para. 70; C-357/12 P of 30.5.2013 – Wohlfahrt/ OHIM, para. 33; C-320/12 of 27.6.2013 – Malaysia Dairy Industries, para. 33; C-445/12 P of

The system is uniform and exhaustive.[95]

Consequently, the mark applied for must be assessed only on the basis of relevant Community rules, and the national decision can under no circumstances call into question the legality of either the contested decision or the judgment under appeal.[96]

It follows that OHIM is under no obligation to follow the assessment of the authority with jurisdiction over trade marks in the country of origin or to lay down the same requirements, or to register the mark applied for on the basis that that national authority considered it to be merely suggestive rather than directly descriptive.[97]

In the light of the exclusive competence of EUIPO's adjudicating bodies to authorize or refuse the registration of an EU trade mark, the subject matter of any proceedings before EUIPO relating to registration of an EU trade mark or **opposition** to that registration necessarily is **different to any proceedings before a national court**, even where that court acts as an EU trade marks court.[98]

No provision of the CTMR envisages the procedural situation of the present case, namely the interplay between an infringement action before an EU trade mark court concerning an earlier EU trade mark and a national trade mark, on the one hand, and opposition proceedings before EUIPO invoking the same earlier EU trade mark and the same sign as the national trade mark for which registration is sought on the EU level, on the other. More specifically, the CTMR does not contain any provision by which EUIPO is bound by a decision, even now definitive, by an EU trade mark court delivered in an action for infringement, in the context of the exercise of its exclusive jurisdiction over registration of EU trade marks and, in particular, when, in so doing, it examines oppositions lodged against applications to register EU trade marks.[99]

12.12.2013 – Rivella International/OHIM, para. 48; C-325/13 P and C-326/13 P of 10.7.2014 – Peek & Cloppenburg/OHIM, para. 55; C-141/13 P of 17.7.2014 – Reber Holding/OHIM, para. 36; C-466/13 P of 22.10.2014 – Repsol YPF/OHIM, para. 89; C-190/15 P of 19.11.2015 – Fetim/OHIM, para. 24; C-536/17 P of 17.1.2018 – Josel/EUIPO, paras 5/4 and 7; C-655/17 P of 31.5.2018 – Berliner Stadtwerke/EUIPO, paras 3/16 and 6; C-656/17 P of 31.5.2018 – Berliner Stadtwerke/EUIPO, paras 3/20 and 6; C-32/17 P of 6.6.2018 – Apcoa Parking Holdings/EUIPO, para. 31; C-118/18 P of 28.6.2018 – Hochmann Marketing/EUIPO, paras 5/21 and 7; C-488/16 P of 6.9.2018 – Bundesverband – Souvenir – Geschenke – Ehrenpreise/EUIPO, para. 72; C-744/18 P of 21.5.2019 – Volkswagen/EUIPO, para. 31; C-285/19 P of 6.11.2019 – Geske/EUIPO, paras 5/15 and 6; C-61/20 P of 28.5.2020 – Billa/EUIPO, para. 20.

95. CJEU C-478/07 of 8.9.2009 – Budějovický Budvar, para. 114; *see also* CJEU C-56/16 P of 14.9.2017 – EUIPO/Instituto dos Vinhos do Douro e do PortoIP, para. 52.
96. CJEU C-238/06 P of 25.10.2007 – Develey Holding/OHIM, para. 66; C-202/08 and C-208/08 of 16.7.2009 – American Clothing Associates/OHIM, para. 58; C-307/11 P of 26.4.2012 – Deichmann/OHIM, para. 57; C-354/11 P of 22.3.2012 – Emram/OHIM, para. 93; C-466/13 P of 22.10.2014 – Repsol YPF/OHIM, para. 90; C-32/17 P of 6.6.2018 – Apcoa Parking Holdings/EUIPO, para. 32; C-488/16 P of 6.9.2018 – Bundesverband – Souvenir – Geschenke – Ehrenpreise/EUIPO, para. 72; C-744/18 P of 21.5.2019 – Volkswagen/EUIPO, para. 31; C-285/19 P of 6.11.2019 – Geske/EUIPO, paras 5/15 and 6.
97. CJEU C-238/06 P of 25.10.2007 – Develey Holding/OHIM, para. 73; C-202/08 and C-208/08 of 16.7.2009 – American Clothing Associates/OHIM, para. 58; C-98/11 P of 24.5.2012 – Chocoladefabriken Lindt & Sprüngli/OHIM, para. 50; C-307/11 P of 26.4.2012 – Deichmann/OHIM, para. 57; C-32/17 P of 6.6.2018 – Apcoa Parking Holdings/EUIPO, para. 34.
98. CJEU C-226/15 P of 21.7.2016 – Apple and Pear Australia a.o./EUIPO, para. 62.
99. CJEU C-226/15 P of 21.7.2016 – Apple and Pear Australia a.o./EUIPO, para. 48.

That said, it follows in particular from recitals 16 and 17 of the CTMR that the EU legislature has established mechanisms to ensure the uniform protection of the EU trade mark throughout the European Union, accordingly confirming the unitary character of the EU trade mark. The EU legislature created, in that context, the EU trade mark courts having jurisdiction to order the cessation of acts of infringement or threatened infringement of an EU trade mark extending throughout the territory of the Union.[100]

In contrast, it follows from the CTMR, and, in particular, Title IV thereof, relating to the procedure for registration of an EU trade mark, that EUIPO has exclusive jurisdiction over registration and opposition to such registration of an EU trade mark. EUIPO is the only body empowered by the Union legislature to examine registration applications and, accordingly, authorize or refuse registration of an EU trade mark. The absence of provisions laying down that EUIPO's adjudicating bodies, when exercising their competence concerning the registration of an EU trade mark or the opposition to such registration, are bound by a final decision of an EU trade mark court is therefore the consequence of the exclusive nature of EUIPO's competence in that area.[101]

Moreover, attention should be drawn to the importance, both in the legal order of the European Union and in national legal systems, of the principle of res judicata. In order to ensure both stability of the law and legal relations and the sound administration of justice, it is important that decisions of courts or tribunals which have become definitive after all rights of appeal have been exhausted or after expiry of the time limits provided for in that connection can no longer be called into question.[102]

In that regard, it should be noted that, although the CTMR does not explicitly define the concept of 'res judicata', it follows, in particular, from Article 56(3) and Article 100(2) CTMR that, in order that decisions of a court of a Member State or EUIPO which have become final are res judicata and can therefore be binding on such a court or EUIPO, it is required that parallel proceedings before them have the same parties, the same subject matter and the same cause of action.[103]

As regards the registration of a mark as an EU trade mark, its purpose is, as is clear from Article 6 CTMR, to obtain such an EU trade mark. Accordingly, the opposition to such registration is intended to prevent the applicant for that registration from obtaining the mark in question. In that regard, in accordance with Article 42(5) of that regulation, following the examination of the opposition to the registration, either the application for registration of the mark is refused in respect of all or part of the goods or services for which that mark is sought, or the opposition is rejected.[104]

As regards the infringement action brought before a national court acting as an EU trade marks court, the proprietor of the earlier EU trade mark asks, in the context of such an action, that court to prohibit the use of a sign creating a likelihood of

100. CJEU C-226/15 P of 21.7.2016 – Apple and Pear Australia a.o./EUIPO, para. 49.
101. CJEU C-226/15 P of 21.7.2016 – Apple and Pear Australia a.o./EUIPO, para. 50, *see also* CJEU C-256/21 of 13.10.2022 – KP/TV a.o., para. 42.
102. CJEU C-226/15 P of 21.7.2016 – Apple and Pear Australia a.o./EUIPO, para. 51, with further proof.
103. CJEU C-226/15 P of 21.7.2016 – Apple and Pear Australia a.o./EUIPO, para. 52.
104. CJEU C-226/15 P of 21.7.2016 – Apple and Pear Australia a.o./EUIPO, para. 56.

confusion with that of the earlier EU trade mark. The proprietor of the EU trade mark accordingly seeks to render the infringer liable for infringement of its exclusive rights.[105]

It should be noted, moreover, that the Court of Justice has already distinguished between the subject matter of infringement proceedings, actions for a declaration of invalidity and proceedings concerning registration, under the CTMR, to the effect that the possibility for the proprietor of an earlier EU trade mark to bring infringement proceedings against the proprietor of a later registered EU trade mark cannot render either the bringing of an application for a declaration of invalidity before EUIPO or the mechanisms for prior control available under the procedure for registering EU trade marks devoid of all purpose.[106]

[3] Registration

If the examiner based the refusal to register the sign as a Community trade mark on Article 7(1)(b) CTMR alone, the Court of First Instance is entitled to confine itself in the contested judgment to a consideration of the dispute in the light of that provision, and to hold that there is no need to rule on the plea of infringement of Article 7(1)(c), since for registration to be refused it is sufficient that one of the grounds listed in Article 7(1) applies.[107]

If the dispute before the Court of First Instance concerned the refusal to register the sign Companyline on the ground that that lacked distinctiveness, the Court of First Instance is entitled to confine itself to considering that question, and is under no obligation to rule on the possible dividing line between the concept of lack of distinctiveness and that of minimum distinctiveness.[108]

Under Article 74(1) CTMR, OHIM examiners and, on appeal, the Boards of Appeal of OHIM are required to examine the facts of their own motion in order to determine whether the mark registration of which is sought falls under one of the grounds for refusal of registration laid down in Article 7 of that regulation. It follows that the competent bodies of OHIM may be led to base their decisions on **facts which have not been alleged by the applicant** for the mark.[109]

Whilst it is in principle the task of those bodies to establish in their decisions the accuracy of such facts, such is not the case where they allege **facts** which are **well known**.[110]

105. CJEU C-226/15 P of 21.7.2016 – Apple and Pear Australia a.o./EUIPO, para. 58.
106. CJEU C-226/15 P of 21.7.2016 – Apple and Pear Australia a.o./EUIPO, para. 61, with reference to CJEU C-561/11 of 21.2.2013 – Fédération Cynologique Internationale, para. 48.
107. CJEU C-104/00 P of 19.9.2002 – DKV/OHIM, para. 28; C-369/10 P of 14.3.2011 – Ravensburger/OHIM, para. 63.
108. CJEU C-104/00 P of 19.9.2002 – DKV/OHIM, para. 20.
109. CJEU C-25/05 P of 22.6.2006 – Storck/OHIM (gold-coloured sweet wrapper), para. 50; C-273/05 P of 19.4.2007 – OHIM/Celltech, para. 38; C-88/11 P of 10.11.2011 – LG Electronics/OHIM, para. 26.
110. CJEU C-25/05 P of 22.6.2006 – Storck/OHIM (gold-coloured sweet wrapper), para. 51; C-273/05 P of 19.4.2007 – OHIM/Celltech, para. 39; C-394/08 P of 3.6.2009 – Zipcar/OHIM, para. 42; C-88/11 P of 10.11.2011 – LG Electronics/OHIM, para. 27.

In that regard, an applicant for a trade mark against whom OHIM relies on such well-known facts may challenge their accuracy before the Court of First Instance.[111]

In such a situation, pursuant to the principle of equality of arms, OHIM has a right to present documents to the General Court in order to support the accuracy of such a known fact which has not been established in OHIM's decision as contested before the General Court; this would thus permit the latter to examine this fact and its accuracy on the basis of concrete elements and to make a decision on the applicant's opposition. If this were not so, the OHIM organs would be forced to establish, in their decisions, the accuracy of a known fact in order to prevent every revocation of these in the case of opposition of such a fact by the applicant.[112]

OHIM argues that the expression 'cell technology' is sufficiently self-explanatory and, therefore, that any additional explanation, and, in particular, a scientific explanation, was superfluous. However, in deciding that the existence and nature of cell technology is not a well-known fact and that it was therefore for the Board of Appeal to establish the correctness of its findings in that regard, the Court of First Instance made a finding of fact.[113]

The finding, by the Court of First Instance, as to whether the facts on which the Board of Appeal of OHIM has based its decision are well known or not is a factual assessment which, save where the facts or evidence are distorted, is not subject to review by the Court of Justice on appeal.[114]

[4] Brexit

The mere communication by a Member State of its intention to leave the European Union in accordance with Article 50 TEU does not have the effect of suspending the application of EU law in that Member State, and consequently, EU law continues in full force and effect in that Member State until the time of its actual withdrawal from the European Union.[115]

[5] Seniority

Article 14 TMD2008, read in conjunction with Article 34(2) CTMR, must be interpreted as precluding an interpretation of national legislation according to which the invalidity or revocation of an earlier national mark, the seniority of which is claimed for an EU mark, may be established a posteriori only if the conditions for that invalidity or that revocation were met, not only on the date on which that earlier national mark was

111. CJEU C-25/05 P of 22.6.2006 – Storck/OHIM (gold-coloured sweet wrapper), para. 52; C-88/11 P of 10.11.2011 – LG Electronics/OHIM, para. 28.
112. CJEU C-88/11 P of 10.11.2011 – LG Electronics/OHIM, para. 29; unofficial translation.
113. CJEU C-273/05 P of 19.4.2007 – OHIM/Celltech, paras 44 et seq.
114. CJEU C-25/05 P of 22.6.2006 – Storck/OHIM (gold-coloured sweet wrapper), para. 53; C-273/05 P of 19.4.2007 – OHIM/Celltech, para. 45.
115. CJEU C-340/17 P of 29.11.2018 – Alcohol Countermeasure Systems/EUIPO, para. 89, with further proof.

surrendered or the date on which it lapsed but also on the date on which the judicial decision-making that finding is taken.[116]

[6] Rules governing the burden of proof in the registration proceeding

First of all, as the Court of First Instance recalled in paragraphs 15 and 16 of the judgment under appeal, in the context of an examination of the existence of absolute grounds for refusal under Article 7(1) CTMR, the role of OHIM is to decide whether the application for registration of the trade mark falls under an absolute ground for refusal.[117]

Further, it must be added that, under Article 74(1) CTMR, OHIM must examine of its own motion the relevant facts that could lead it to apply an absolute ground for refusal.[118]

Finally, if an applicant claims that a trade mark applied for is distinctive, despite OHIM's analysis, it is for that applicant to provide specific and substantiated information to show that the trade mark applied for has either an intrinsic distinctive character or a distinctive character acquired by usage.[119]

[7] Common rules for opposition and invalidity proceedings

In any event, for reasons of legal certainty and proper administration, it is necessary to ensure that **trade marks whose use could successfully be challenged before the courts are not registered.**[120]

It results from a reading of Rule 16 in conjunction with Rule 20 CTMIR (1995), first, that **OHIM is entitled to require proof that an earlier mark has been renewed** where that mark expires after the notice of opposition has been filed and, second, that those provisions do not require an opposing party, on its own initiative, to submit such proof.[121]

It should be added that the power thus conferred on OHIM to require proof that an earlier mark has been renewed can also be founded on Article 76 CTMR.[122]

116. CJEU C-148/17 of 19.4.2018 – Peek & Cloppenburg/Peek & Cloppenburg, para. 32.
117. CJEU C-238/06 P of 25.10.2007 – Develey Holding/OHIM, para. 48; C-97/12 P of 15.5.2014 – Louis Vuitton Malletier/OHIM, para. 70.
118. CJEU C-238/06 P of 25.10.2007 – Develey Holding/OHIM, para. 49; C-265/09 P of 9.9.2010 – OHIM/BORCO-Marken-Import Matthiesen, para. 57; C-97/12 P of 15.5.2014 – Louis Vuitton Malletier/OHIM, para. 71.
119. CJEU C-238/06 P of 25.10.2007 – Develey Holding/OHIM, para. 50; C-265/09 P of 9.9.2010 – OHIM/BORCO-Marken-Import Matthiesen, para. 59; C-97/12 P of 15.5.2014 – Louis Vuitton Malletier/OHIM, para. 72; C-67/21 P of 12.5.2021 – BSH Hausgeräte/EUIPO, para. 18.
120. CJEU C-39/97 of 29.9.1998 – Canon Kabushiki Kaisha/Metro-Goldwyn-Mayer, para. 21; C-104/01 of 6.5.2003 – Libertel, para. 59; C-29/05 P of 13.3.2007 – OHIM/Kaul, para. 48.
121. CJEU C-214/09 P of 29.7.2010 – Anheuser-Busch/OHIM, para. 69.
122. CJEU C-214/09 P of 29.7.2010 – Anheuser-Busch/OHIM, para. 70.

Neither Article 42(3) CTMR nor Rules 16(1) and (3) and 20(2) CTMIR (1995) specify the facts, evidence and arguments which must be submitted in support of the opposition within the period fixed under Article 42(3) CTMR.[123]

In particular, those provisions contain nothing to suggest that an opponent should automatically provide, within the period fixed by OHIM, evidence of renewal of the earlier mark relied on where the renewal is to occur after notice of opposition has been filed.[124]

Furthermore and in any event, such an interpretation does not follow either from the case law of the General Court or from any consistent practice of OHIM prior to adoption of CTMIR (2005).[125]

In any event, nor is it apparent that, prior to adoption of CTMIR (2005), a consistent practice had developed at OHIM whereby an opponent was required to furnish, automatically, evidence of renewal of the earlier mark with the other facts, evidence and arguments to be submitted in support of the opposition within the period fixed by OHIM to that end under Article 42(3) CTMR.[126]

It thus also follows that nor is it apparent that the provisions of Rule 19(2) and (4) CTMIR (2005) may be taken into account in this instance on the ground that they represent no more than a codification of the interpretation developed by the General Court, on the basis of OHIM's consistent practice, of Article 42(3) CTMR and Rules 16(1) and (3) and 20(2) CTMIR (1995).[127]

In any event, while the above-mentioned provisions of CTMIR (2005) now impose, within certain limits, an express obligation on an opponent to produce proof of renewal of the earlier trade mark within the period referred to in Article 42(3) CTMR, they thereby clarify the general rule laid down by Article 42(3) CTMR, which is intended to afford greater legal certainty to operators engaged in opposition proceedings before OHIM. In those circumstances, the new rules laid down in CTMIR (2005) cannot be applied with retroactive effect in the present case.[128]

Therefore, if there has been an assignment of the sign on which the opposition was based without that assignment being taken into account during the procedure before the Opposition Division of OHIM, the assignee must adduce, within the four-month period provided for in Article 59 CTMR, before the Board of Appeal of OHIM the necessary proof that he became the owner of that sign by transfer in order to show that he has *locus standi*; otherwise, the appeal will be declared inadmissible.[129]

It follows from the coexistence of Community trade marks and **national trade marks**, and from the fact that the registration of the latter does **not** fall **within the sphere of competence of OHIM**, and that judicial review in respect of them does not fall within the jurisdiction of the General Court, that in proceedings opposing the

123. CJEU C-214/09 P of 29.7.2010 – Anheuser-Busch/OHIM, para. 57.
124. CJEU C-214/09 P of 29.7.2010 – Anheuser-Busch/OHIM, para. 58.
125. CJEU C-214/09 P of 29.7.2010 – Anheuser-Busch/OHIM, para. 59.
126. CJEU C-214/09 P of 29.7.2010 – Anheuser-Busch/OHIM, para. 64.
127. CJEU C-214/09 P of 29.7.2010 – Anheuser-Busch/OHIM, para. 67.
128. CJEU C-214/09 P of 29.7.2010 – Anheuser-Busch/OHIM, para. 68.
129. CJEU C-53/11 P of 19.1.2012 – OHIM/Nike International, para. 55.

registration of a Community trade mark, the validity of national trade marks may not be called into question.[130]

Therefore, in such opposition proceedings, it is not possible to find, with regard to a sign identical to a trade mark protected in a Member State, an absolute ground for refusal, such as the lack of distinctive character, provided by Article 7(1)(b) CTMR and Article 3(1)(b) TMD2008. In this respect, it should be noted that the characterization of a sign as descriptive or generic is equivalent to denying its distinctive character.[131]

It is true that where an opposition, based on the existence of an earlier national trade mark, is filed against the registration of a Community trade mark, OHIM and, consequently, the General Court must verify the way in which the relevant public perceives the sign which is identical to the national trade mark in the mark applied for and evaluate, if necessary, the degree of distinctiveness of that sign.[132]

However, their verification has limits.[133]

Their verification may not culminate in a finding of the lack of distinctive character of a sign identical to a registered and protected national trade mark since such a finding would not be compatible with the coexistence of Community trade marks and national trade marks or with Article 8(1)(b) CTMR, read in conjunction with Article 8(2)(a)(ii).[134]

Such a finding would be detrimental to national trade marks identical to a sign considered as being devoid of distinctive character, as the registration of such a Community trade mark would bring about a situation likely to eliminate the national protection of those marks. Hence, such a finding would not respect the system established by the CTMR, which is based on the coexistence of Community trade marks and national trade marks as stated by the fifth recital in the preamble to that regulation, given that the validity of an international or national trade mark may be called into question for lack of distinctive character only in cancellation proceedings brought in the Member State concerned by virtue of Article 3(1)(b) TMD2008.[135]

It should be noted that Article 8(2)(a)(ii) CTMR expressly provides, in opposition proceedings, for trade marks registered in a Member State to be taken into consideration as earlier trade marks.[136]

It follows that, in order to avoid infringing Article 8(1)(b) CTMR, it is **necessary to acknowledge a certain degree of distinctiveness of an earlier national mark** on which an opposition against the registration of a Community trade mark is based.[137]

---

130. CJEU C-196/11 P of 24.5.2012 – Formula One Licensing/OHIM, para. 40; C-357/12 P of 30.5.2013 – Wohlfahrt/OHIM, para. 46; C-410/12 P of 16.10.2013 – medi/OHIM, para. 34; C-43/15 P of 8.11.2016 – BSH Bosch und Siemens Hausgeräte/EUIPO, para. 66.
131. CJEU C-196/11 P of 24.5.2012 – Formula One Licensing/OHIM, para. 41; C-410/12 P of 16.10.2013 – medi/OHIM, para. 34; C-43/15 P of 8.11.2016 – BSH Bosch und Siemens Hausgeräte/EUIPO, para. 66.
132. CJEU C-196/11 P of 24.5.2012 – Formula One Licensing/OHIM, para. 42.
133. CJEU C-196/11 P of 24.5.2012 – Formula One Licensing/OHIM, para. 43.
134. CJEU C-196/11 P of 24.5.2012 – Formula One Licensing/OHIM, para. 44.
135. CJEU C-196/11 P of 24.5.2012 – Formula One Licensing/OHIM, para. 45; C-43/15 P of 8.11.2016 – BSH Bosch und Siemens Hausgeräte/EUIPO, para. 68.
136. CJEU C-196/11 P of 24.5.2012 – Formula One Licensing/OHIM, para. 46.
137. CJEU C-196/11 P of 24.5.2012 – Formula One Licensing/OHIM, para. 47; C-33/15 P of 15.10.2015 – Cantina Broglie 1, para. 50; C-34/15 P of 15.10.2015 – Cantina Broglie 1, para. 50; C-43/15 P of 8.11.2016 – BSH Bosch und Siemens Hausgeräte/EUIPO, para. 67.

On the one hand, the **opponent is free to choose** the form of evidence which it considers appropriate to submit to the EUIPO in the context of an opposition based on an **earlier right**, within the meaning of Article 8(4) CTMR, and, on the other hand, the EUIPO is required to analyse the evidence submitted by the opponent, without being able from the outset to refuse a type of evidence on the ground of its form.[138]

As regards the **burden of proof** and the taking of evidence, where the proprietor of a mark wishes to rely on the ground for refusing registration referred to in Article 8(5) CTMR, Rule 19(1) and (2)(c) CTMIR provides that EUIPO must give the opposing party the opportunity to present the facts, evidence and arguments in support of its opposition, in particular evidence that the **earlier mark has a reputation**, or to complete any facts, evidence or arguments that have already been submitted. Since CTMR and CTMIR do not list the forms of evidence which the opponent may present in order to demonstrate the existence of the earlier mark's reputation, the opponent is free, in principle, to choose the form of evidence which it considers useful to submit to EUIPO in opposition proceedings based on an earlier right; EUIPO is obliged to examine the evidence submitted by the opponent, and cannot reject out of hand a type of evidence on the basis of its form.[139]

Furthermore, Article 76(1) CTMR provides that, in proceedings before EUIPO, the latter must, in principle, examine the facts of its own motion. However, that provision provides that, in proceedings relating to relative grounds for refusal of registration, such as the ground provided for in Article 8(5) CTMR, the examination is to be restricted to the facts, evidence and arguments provided by the parties and the relief sought.[140]

In circumstances where an opponent relies on earlier EUIPO decisions relating to the reputation of a mark, in a precise manner, before the Opposition Division, as evidence of the reputation, for the purposes of Article 8(5) CTMR, of the same earlier mark relied on in support of its opposition, it is incumbent on the competent EUIPO bodies to take into account the decisions which they have already adopted and to consider with especial care whether it should decide in the same way or not, in accordance with the case law cited above. Where those bodies decide to take a different view from the one adopted in those previous decisions, they should, having regard to the context in which they adopt their new decision, since reliance on those previous decisions forms part of that text, provide an explicit statement of their reasoning for departing from those decisions.[141]

It must be noted, in that regard, that the oppositions at issue are based on Article 8(1)(b) CTMR and Article 8(5) CTMR. For the purposes of the application of each of those provisions, the opposing party must duly rely on an earlier trade mark, within the meaning of Article 8(2) CTMR. However, in the present case, having withdrawn all lines of argument based on other marks, the Republic of Cyprus **relies only on the**

138. CJEU C-478/16 P of 19.4.2018 – EUIPO/Group, para. 58, inofficial translation.
139. CJEU C-564/16 P of 28.6.2018 – EUIPO/Puma, para. 58, with reference to CJEU C-478/16 P of 19.4.2018 – EUIPO/Group, para. 57-59.
140. CJEU C-564/16 P of 28.6.2018 – EUIPO/Puma, para. 59.
141. CJEU C-564/16 P of 28.6.2018 – EUIPO/Puma, para. 66.

mark which has been definitively cancelled with ex tunc effect. In such circumstances, it must be held that those oppositions have definitively become ineffective.[142]

The **withdrawal of the opposition**, following a transaction between the parties, has the effect of putting an end to the dispute concerning the rejection of that application, with the result that that appeal has become devoid of purpose.[143]

[8] Invalidity proceedings

The right to apply to OHIM for a declaration of invalidity of a Community trade mark is **not subject to the rules of admissibility applicable to judicial proceedings** and specific thereto. In that regard, the application for a declaration of invalidity under Article 55(1)(a) CTMR is an administrative procedure and not a court action, and the case law concerning Article 230 EC is not relevant to such a case before it either directly or by analogy.[144]

First of all, it is not disputed that Article 55(1)(a) CTMR makes no reference to an interest in bringing proceedings.[145]

Next, Article 55(1)(a) CTMR provides that an application for a declaration of invalidity based on an absolute ground for invalidity may be submitted by any natural or legal person and any group or body set up for the purpose of representing the interests of manufacturers, producers, suppliers of services, traders or consumers, which has the capacity in its own name to sue and be sued, whereas Article 55(1)(b) and (c) CTMR, concerning applications for a declaration of invalidity based on a relative ground for invalidity, reserves the right to make such an application to certain specific persons who have an interest in bringing proceedings. It is apparent from the scheme of that article that the legislature intended to restrict the group of persons able to apply for a declaration of invalidity in the latter case but not in the former.[146]

Finally, whereas relative grounds for refusal of registration protect the interests of proprietors of certain earlier rights, the absolute grounds for refusal of registration aim to protect the general interest underlying them, which explains why Article 55(1)(a) CTMR does not require the applicant to show an interest in bringing proceedings.[147]

Moreover, there is no basis for the claim that Article 55(1)(a) CTMR must be interpreted as requiring there to be an actual or potential economic interest in

142. CJEU C-608/18 P, C-609/18 P and C-767/18 P of 30.4.2020 – Republic of Cyprus/EUIPO, para. 32.
143. CJEU C-565/07 P of 19.5.2009 – AMS/OHIM, paras 14 et seq.; C-587/11 P of 18.9.2012 – Omnicare/OHIM, para. 11; C-588/11 P of 18.9.2012 – Omnicare/OHIM, para. 11; C-170/19 P of 10.7.2019 – CheapFlights International/EUIPO, paras 5/11 and 6.
144. CJEU C-408/08 P of 25.2.2010 – Lancôme parfums et beauté & Cie/OHIM, para. 36; *see also* CJEU C-450/13 P of 19.6.2014 – Donaldson Filtration Deutschland/OHIM, paras 37–50; C-622/13 P of 30.4.2015 – Castel Frères/EUIPO, paras 42-47.
145. CJEU C-408/08 P of 25.2.2010 – Lancôme parfums et beauté & Cie/OHIM, para. 38.
146. CJEU C-408/08 P of 25.2.2010 – Lancôme parfums et beauté & Cie/OHIM, para. 39.
147. CJEU C-408/08 P of 25.2.2010 – Lancôme parfums et beauté & Cie/OHIM, para. 40; *see also* CJEU C-654/21 of 8.6.2023 – LM/KP, para. 40.

cancellation of a contested mark in order for it to be possible to apply to OHIM for a declaration of invalidity of that mark.[148]

First, such an interpretation is not borne out by the reference made in Article 55(1)(a) CTMR to groups or bodies set up for the purpose of representing the interests of manufacturers, producers, suppliers of services, traders or consumers, which under the terms of the law governing them have the capacity to sue and be sued. That list, which also contains consumers to whom an economic interest cannot generally be attributed, seeks merely to include, on the list of persons who may apply to OHIM for a declaration of invalidity under that provision, groups and bodies of that nature which, although they have the capacity to bring proceedings in accordance with the law governing them, do not have legal personality.[149]

Second, such an interpretation does not follow from Joined Cases *Windsurfing Chiemsee*.[150] In paragraph 25 of that judgment, the Court held that the general interest requires that descriptive signs or indications relating to the goods or services in respect of which registration is sought may be freely used by all. It can be inferred from this that the general interest underlying the ground for refusal of registration of a mark because of its descriptiveness is not exclusively the interest of the trade mark applicant's or proprietor's competitors (who may be subject to some form of constraint and who, on that basis, have an actual or potential economic interest in having the contested mark declared invalid), but a common interest.[151]

[9] Older rights under Article 8(4) CTMR

Under Article 53(1)(c) of Regulation No. 207/2009, read in conjunction with Article 8(4) thereof, the proprietor of an unregistered trade mark or other sign used in the course of trade may obtain a declaration of invalidity of a European Union trade mark if that sign cumulatively satisfies **four conditions**, namely, the sign must be used in the course of trade, it must have a scope which is not merely local, the right to the sign must have been acquired in accordance with the law of the Member State in which the sign was used prior to the date of filing of the EU trade mark application and, finally, the right to the sign must entitle its proprietor to prohibit the use of a more recent trade mark. While the first two conditions must be interpreted in the light of Union law, the last two must be assessed in the light of the law governing the sign concerned.[152]

If an opponent is to be able, on the basis of Article 8(4) CTMR, to prevent registration of a Community trade mark, it is necessary – and sufficient – that, at the **date** on which OHIM determines whether all the conditions for opposition are met, an

148. CJEU C-408/08 P of 25.2.2010 – Lancôme parfums et beauté & Cie/OHIM, para. 41.
149. CJEU C-408/08 P of 25.2.2010 – Lancôme parfums et beauté & Cie/OHIM, para. 42.
150. CJEU C-108/97 and C-109/97 of 4.5.1999 – Windsurfing Chiemsee.
151. CJEU C-408/08 P of 25.2.2010 – Lancôme parfums et beauté & Cie/OHIM, para. 43, *see also* CJEU C-654/21 of 8.6.2023 – LM/KP, para. 40.
152. CJEU C-325/13 P and C-326/13 P of 10.7.2014 – Peek & Cloppenburg/OHIM, paras 46 et seq.; C-75/17 P of 19.4.2018 – Fiesta Hotels & Resorts/EUIPO, para. 34.

earlier right may be claimed which has not been declared invalid by a judicial decision that has become final.[153]

In those circumstances, although it is for OHIM, when it decides upon an opposition based on Article 8(4) CTMR, to take into account decisions of the courts of the relevant Member States concerning the validity or classification of the earlier rights claimed to ensure that those rights continue to produce the effects required by that provision, it is not for it to substitute its assessment for that of the competent national courts – a power which, in any event, the CTMR does not confer on it.[154]

Furthermore, it is necessary to apply to the requirement for use in the course of trade of the sign relied on in opposition the same temporal condition as that expressly laid down in Article 8(4)(a) CTMR with regard to acquisition of the right to the sign, that is to say, that of the date of application for registration of the Community trade mark.[155]

In view, in particular, of the considerable period of time which may elapse between the filing of an application for registration and its publication, applying that temporal condition provides a better guarantee that the use claimed for the sign concerned is real and not an exercise whose sole aim has been to prevent registration of a new trade mark.[156]

Furthermore, as a general rule, where the sign concerned is used exclusively or to a large extent during the period between filing of the application for a Community trade mark and publication of the application, that will not be sufficient to establish that the use of the sign in the course of trade has been such as to prove that the sign is of sufficient significance.[157]

Whilst it is true that the **words 'used in the course of trade'** in Article 8(4) CTMR do not necessarily have to be interpreted in the same way as they are in relation to Article 9(1) CTMR or Articles 5(1) and 6(1) TMD2008 since account must be taken of the purpose of each of those provisions, the fact remains that if those words are interpreted as meaning, in essence, that the sign need only be put to some commercial use, such an interpretation is consistent with their usual meaning.[158]

Article 8(4) CTMR **does not concern the 'genuine' use** of a sign relied on in support of an opposition, and there is nothing in the wording of Article 43(2) and (3) CTMR to suggest that the requirement for proof of genuine use applies to such a sign.[159]

If the requirement for genuine use were imposed on the signs covered by Article 8(4) CTMR on the same conditions as those set out in Article 43(2) and (3) CTMR, such an interpretation would impose on those signs requirements specific to oppositions based on earlier trade marks, and that, by contrast with those oppositions, in

153. CJEU C-96/09 P of 29.3.2011 – Anheuser-Busch, para. 94; C-75/17 P of 19.4.2018 – Fiesta Hotels & Resorts/EUIPO, para. 49.
154. CJEU C-96/09 P of 29.3.2011 – Anheuser-Busch, para. 95; C-75/17 P of 19.4.2018 – Fiesta Hotels & Resorts/EUIPO, para. 50.
155. CJEU C-96/09 P of 29.3.2011 – Anheuser-Busch, para. 166.
156. CJEU C-96/09 P of 29.3.2011 – Anheuser-Busch, para. 167.
157. CJEU C-96/09 P of 29.3.2011 – Anheuser-Busch, para. 168.
158. CJEU C-96/09 P of 29.3.2011 – Anheuser-Busch, para. 144; *see also* CJEU C-376/11 of 19.7.2012 – Pie Optiek, para. 45.
159. CJEU C-96/09 P of 29.3.2011 – Anheuser-Busch, para. 143.

oppositions under Article 8(4) CTMR the opponent must also show that the sign concerned gives him the right, according to the law of the Member State concerned, to prohibit use of a subsequent trade mark.[160]

Moreover, if the requirement for genuine use laid down for earlier trade marks were applied by analogy to the earlier rights referred to in Article 8(4) CTMR, that would also be contrary to the, in principle, autonomous nature of that relative ground for refusal, which is made apparent by conditions specific to that ground and which must also be interpreted in the light of the very wide variety of earlier rights that may be covered by that ground.[161]

The words 'used in the course of trade' mean that use of a geographical indication relied on under Article 8(4) CTMR must be made in accordance with the essential **function of the sign.**[162]

For Article 8(4) CTMR to apply, it is sufficient to find that the sign relied on in support of the opposition is used in the course of trade and that the fact that that sign is identical to a trade mark does not mean that it is not used in the course of trade.[163]

As regards the function to be performed by use of the sign, the latter must be used as a distinctive element in that it must serve to identify an economic activity engaged in by its proprietor.[164]

Deliveries made without charge could be taken into account in order to ascertain whether the requirement for use of the earlier right in the course of trade was met since those deliveries could have been made in the context of a commercial activity with a view to economic advantage, namely to acquire new outlets.[165]

It follows that, in order to be capable of preventing registration of a new sign, the sign relied on in opposition **must** actually be **used in a sufficiently significant manner in the course of trade, and its geographical extent must not be merely local**, which implies, where the territory in which that sign is protected may be regarded as other than local, that the sign must be used in a substantial part of that territory.[166]

In order to ascertain whether that is the case, account must be taken of the duration and intensity of the use of that sign as a distinctive element vis-à-vis its addressees, namely purchasers and consumers as well as suppliers and competitors. In that regard, the use made of the sign in advertising and commercial correspondence is of particular relevance.[167]

Where the **geographical extent of the protection** of a sign is merely local, the sign must indeed be regarded as of mere local significance. However, it does not follow that the condition laid down in Article 8(4) CTMR is met in every case simply because

160. CJEU C-96/09 P of 29.3.2011 - Anheuser-Busch, para. 145.
161. CJEU C-96/09 P of 29.3.2011 - Anheuser-Busch, para. 146.
162. CJEU C-96/09 P of 29.3.2011 - Anheuser-Busch, para. 147.
163. CJEU C-96/09 P of 29.3.2011 - Anheuser-Busch, para. 148.
164. CJEU C-96/09 P of 29.3.2011 - Anheuser-Busch, para. 149.
165. CJEU C-96/09 P of 29.3.2011 - Anheuser-Busch, para. 152.
166. CJEU C-96/09 P of 29.3.2011 - Anheuser-Busch, para. 159; C-325/13 P and C-326/13 P of 10.7.2014 - Peek & Cloppenburg/OHIM, para. 52; C-75/17 P of 19.4.2018 - Fiesta Hotels & Resorts/EUIPO, para. 39.
167. CJEU C-96/09 P of 29.3.2011 - Anheuser-Busch, para. 160; C-75/17 P of 19.4.2018 - Fiesta Hotels & Resorts/EUIPO, para. 39.

the sign in question is protected in a territory which cannot be regarded as merely local, in the present case because the territory of protection extends beyond the territory of origin.[168]

The common purpose of the two conditions laid down in Article 8(4) CTMR is to limit conflicts between signs by preventing an earlier right which is not sufficiently definite – that is to say, important and significant in the course of trade – from preventing registration of a new Community trade mark. A right of opposition of that kind must be reserved to signs which actually have a real presence on their relevant market.[169]

Accordingly, the significance of a sign cannot be a function of the mere geographical extent of its protection since, if that were the case, a sign whose protection is not merely local could, by virtue of that fact alone, prevent registration of a Community trade mark – and could do so even though the sign is used only to a very limited extent in the course of trade.[170]

In the wording of Article 8(4) CTMR, there is nothing to indicate the fact that more strict requirements should be applied if two identical signs are protected in the same national territory. To demand in this case that the right granted in a respective **Member State** to prohibit the use of a younger mark should apply to the whole national sovereign territory concerned would prevent the respective owners from prohibiting the registration of a Community trade mark not only by one of their own but also by any third party, irrespective of whether the signs in question were really and effectively present in their relevant market. The independent requirement that the respective mark should be commercially used in a significant manner would thus be stripped of its effectiveness.[171]

Regarding the argument that the distinction made in Articles 110 and 111 CTMR had the consequence that signs which possess more than mere local significance must provide entitlement to prohibit the use of a younger mark in the whole area of the Member State covered by protection, it must be ascertained that Article 110 CTMR refers to 'older rights in the meaning of Article 8' of this Regulation, so that the requirements provided for in Article 8 determine the meaning of these rights. Incidentally, an overall view of Articles 8, 110 and 111 CTMR permits the conclusion that this regulation differentiates between two categories of signs according to whether they are of local significance or not, whereby only signs of more than mere local significance allow, according to Article 8(4) CTMR, both the prevention of the registration of a younger Community mark and the prohibition of its use according to national law.[172]

The condition relating to **use in the course of trade** must be assessed **separately for each of the territories** in which the right relied on in support of the opposition is

168. CJEU C-96/09 P of 29.3.2011 – Anheuser-Busch, para. 156.
169. CJEU C-96/09 P of 29.3.2011 – Anheuser-Busch, para. 157; C-325/13 P and C-326/13 P of 10.7.2014 – Peek & Cloppenburg/OHIM, para. 53; C-75/17 P of 19.4.2018 – Fiesta Hotels & Resorts/EUIPO, para. 35.
170. CJEU C-96/09 P of 29.3.2011 – Anheuser-Busch, para. 158.
171. CJEU C-325/13 P and C-326/13 P of 10.7.2014 – Peek & Cloppenburg/OHIM, para. 54.
172. CJEU C-325/13 P and C-326/13 P of 10.7.2014 – Peek & Cloppenburg/OHIM, para. 56.

protected. The significance of the sign cannot therefore be inferred from a cumulative assessment of the use of the sign in more than one relevant territory.[173]

Article 8(4)(b) CTMR lays down the **condition** that, pursuant to the law of the Member State governing the sign relied on under Article 8(4), that sign confers on its proprietor the **right to prohibit the use of a subsequent trade mark.**[174]

Since one of the purposes of Article 8(4) CTMR is to ensure protection for signs which are actually and genuinely present on the relevant market, the concept of 'the right to prevent use of a more recent trade mark', within the meaning of that provision, must be understood as encompassing the situation in which the proprietor of a sign is, under the applicable national law, able to prevent such use by means of an action for a declaration of invalidity brought against a more recent trade mark.[175]

Furthermore, in accordance with Article 74(1), the burden of proving that that condition is met lies with the opponent before OHIM.[176]

On the contrary, the opponent cannot be required to establish that that right has been used, in other words, that the opponent has actually been able to prohibit such use.[177]

The condition for the application of Article 8(4) CTMR that the earlier right relied on must relate to a 'sign used in the course of trade of more than mere local significance' is assessed in the light of EU law.[178]

[10] Older rights under Article 53(2) CTMR

The wording and structure of Article 52(2) CTMR do not, where a **right to a name** is asserted, allow application of that provision to be restricted merely to situations where the registration of a Community trade mark conflicts with a right intended exclusively to protect a name as an attribute of the personality of the person concerned.[179]

As regards the wording of that provision, it should be noted that the words 'right to a name' do not provide any support for the restrictive interpretation proposed by the appellant, to the effect that the provision concerns only that right as an attribute of personality and does not cover commercial exploitation of a name.[180]

The structure of Article 52(2) CTMR, for its part, is inconsistent with such an interpretation. According to that provision, a Community trade mark may be declared

173. CJEU C-96/09 P of 29.3.2011 – Anheuser-Busch, para. 163.
174. CJEU C-96/09 P of 29.3.2011 – Anheuser-Busch, para. 188; *see also* CJEU C-76/11 P of 29.11.2011 – Tresplain Investments/OHIM, para. 56; C-325/13 P and C-326/13 P of 10.7.2014 – Peek & Cloppenburg/OHIM, para. 47; C-75/17 P of 19.4.2018 – Fiesta Hotels & Resorts/EUIPO, para. 56.
175. CJEU C-75/17 P of 19.4.2018 – Fiesta Hotels & Resorts/EUIPO, para. 60.
176. CJEU C-96/09 P of 29.3.2011 – Anheuser-Busch, para. 189; *see also* CJEU C-76/11 P of 29.11.2011 – Tresplain Investments/OHIM, para. 56; C-325/13 P and C-326/13 P of 10.7.2014 – Peek & Cloppenburg/OHIM, para. 47.
177. CJEU C-96/09 P of 29.3.2011 – Anheuser-Busch, para. 191; C-325/13 P and C-326/13 P of 10.7.2014 – Peek & Cloppenburg/OHIM, para. 48.
178. CJEU C-76/11 P of 29.11.2011 – Tresplain Investments/OHIM, para. 56; C-325/13 P and C-326/13 P of 10.7.2014 – Peek & Cloppenburg/OHIM, para. 51.
179. CJEU C-263/09 P of 5.7.2011 – Edwin/OHIM, para. 36.
180. CJEU C-263/09 P of 5.7.2011 – Edwin/OHIM, para. 33.

invalid on application by a person concerned claiming 'another earlier right'. In order to clarify the nature of such an earlier right, that provision lists four rights, while indicating, by the use of the adverb 'in particular', that that list is not exhaustive. The examples given include, besides the right to a name and the right of personal portrayal, a copyright and an industrial property right.[181]

It is apparent from that non-exhaustive list that the rights cited by way of examples are intended to protect interests of different types. It should be noted that for some of them, such as **copyright** and **industrial property rights**, the economic aspects are protected, both under the national legal systems and under EU law, against commercial infringements.[182]

[11] National law applicable by the reference in a provision of European Union law

It is apparent from the wording of Article 52(2) CTMR that when that provision refers to the situation in which the existence of an earlier right makes it possible to prohibit the use of a Community trade mark, it distinguishes clearly between two situations, depending on whether the earlier right is protected under the Community legislation 'or' under national law.[183]

As regards the procedural arrangements laid down by the implementing regulation in the case of an application pursuant to Article 52(2) CTMR, based on an earlier right protected under national law, Rule 37 CTMIR provides that the applicant must provide particulars showing that he is entitled under the national law applicable to lay claim to that right.[184]

That rule requires the applicant to provide OHIM **not only** with particulars showing that he satisfies **the necessary conditions**, in accordance with the national law of which he is seeking application, in order to be able to have the use of a Community trade mark prohibited by virtue of an earlier right, **but also particulars establishing the content of that law**.[185]

Where an application for a Community trade mark to be declared invalid is based on an earlier right protected by a rule of national law, the competent **OHIM** bodies must first assess the authority and scope of the particulars submitted by the applicant in order to establish the content of that rule.[186]

---

181. CJEU C-263/09 P of 5.7.2011 – Edwin/OHIM, para. 34.
182. CJEU C-263/09 P of 5.7.2011 – Edwin/OHIM, para. 35; *see also* Directive 2004/48/EC of the European Parliament and of the Council of 29 Apr. 2004 on the enforcement of intellectual property rights (OJ 2004 L 157, p. 45).
183. CJEU C-263/09 P of 5.7.2011 – Edwin/OHIM, para. 48.
184. CJEU C-263/09 P of 5.7.2011 – Edwin/OHIM, para. 49; C-598/14 P of 5.4.2017 – EUIPO/Szajner a.o., para. 35; *see also* CJEU C485/16 P of 31.1.2017 – Universal Protein Supplements, paras 21 et seq.
185. CJEU C-263/09 P of 5.7.2011 – Edwin/OHIM, para. 50; C-530/12 P of 27.3.2014 – OHIM/National Lottery Commission, para. 34; C-301/13 P of 6.2.2014 – El Corte Inglés, para. 49; C-598/14 P of 5.4.2017 – EUIPO/Szajner a.o., para. 35; C-478/16 P of 19.4.2018 – EUIPO/Group, para. 46.
186. CJEU C-263/09 P of 5.7.2011 – Edwin/OHIM, para. 51; C-530/12 P of 27.3.2014 – OHIM/National Lottery Commission, para. 35; C-598/14 P of 5.4.2017 – EUIPO/Szajner a.o., para. 36.

Second, according to Article 63(2) CTMR, actions may be brought before the **General Court** against decisions of the Boards of Appeal on grounds of infringement of the Treaty, of the CTMR or of any rule of law relating to their application. It follows from this that the General Court has jurisdiction to conduct a full review of the legality of OHIM's assessment of the particulars submitted by an applicant in order to establish the content of the national law whose protection he claims.[187]

It is not apparent from paragraphs 50–52 of *Edwin v. OHIM* that a rule of national law, made applicable by a reference such as that in Article 52(2) CTMR, should be treated as a purely factual matter, the existence of which OHIM and the Court merely establish on the basis of the evidence before them.[188]

It is apparent, by contrast, from those paragraphs that the Court intended to emphasize the scope of the review that is required, both before the competent bodies of **OHIM and** before the **General Court**, regarding the application of national law in a dispute arising from an application for annulment of a Community trade mark.[189]

It is in the light of those considerations that it must be examined whether OHIM and the General Court, in such a procedural context, should do no more than examine the documents submitted by the applicant in order to establish the content of the applicable national law or whether they may exercise a power of verification regarding the relevance of the law invoked that involves, if necessary, obtaining information of their own motion on the conditions of application and the scope of the rules of national law relied upon.[190]

In that regard, it should be noted that the review by OHIM and by the General Court must be conducted in the light of the requirement of ensuring the practical effect of the CTMR, which is to protect the Community mark.[191]

In view of the above, since the application of national law can lead to a finding that there is a ground for invalidation of a duly registered Community trade mark, it seems necessary for OHIM and the General Court to be able, before granting the application for a declaration of invalidity of such a mark, to ascertain the relevance of the evidence produced by the applicant with regard to the taking of evidence, which is incumbent upon it, concerning the content of that national law.[192]

If the General Court were to restrict itself to applying the national law as it was interpreted by the national courts at the time of the decision by the Board of Appeal of EUIPO, this could result in the refusal to register an EU trade mark or its revocation, even though the relevant national law does not provide, as of the time at which the General Court issues its decision, any basis for so doing.[193]

187. CJEU C-263/09 P of 5.7.2011 – Edwin/OHIM, para. 52; C-530/12 P of 27.3.2014 – OHIM/National Lottery Commission, para. 36; C-598/14 P of 5.4.2017 – EUIPO/Szajner a.o., paras 37 and 45.
188. CJEU C-530/12 P of 27.3.2014 – OHIM/National Lottery Commission, para. 37.
189. CJEU C-530/12 P of 27.3.2014 – OHIM/National Lottery Commission, para. 38.
190. CJEU C-530/12 P of 27.3.2014 – OHIM/National Lottery Commission, para. 39.
191. CJEU C-530/12 P of 27.3.2014 – OHIM/National Lottery Commission, para. 40; C-598/14 P of 5.4.2017 – EUIPO/Szajner a.o., para. 39.
192. CJEU C-530/12 P of 27.3.2014 – OHIM/National Lottery Commission, para. 41.
193. CJEU C-598/14 P of 5.4.2017 – EUIPO/Szajner a.o., para. 40.

That result would run counter not only to the requirement of ensuring the practical effect of the CTMR but also, by depriving the General Court of the real possibility of conducting in an effective manner the full review of legality, to the principle of effective judicial protection.[194]

It follows that, in assessing the protection granted by national law, the General Court must apply a rule of national law as interpreted by the national courts at the time at which it issues its decision. It must therefore also be able to take into consideration a decision originating from a national court, issued after the adoption of the decision of the Board of Appeal of EUIPO.[195]

It is true that the taking into consideration of a decision of a national court issued after the adoption of the decision of the Board of Appeal of EUIPO could lead the General Court to undertake an assessment of a rule of national law which differs from that of that Board of Appeal. However, since the judicial review of the assessment of national law by that Board of Appeal, conducted by the General Court, would be a full review of legality, the fact – revealed after the adoption of the decision of the same Board of Appeal – that that decision was based on an incorrect interpretation of national law cannot prevent that error from being corrected.[196]

This conclusion is not called into question by the case law according to which, first, the General Court must, in principle, confine itself to finding the decision that the Board of Appeal of EUIPO should have reached on the basis of the particulars underlying the Board of Appeal's decision; second, the General Court may annul or alter a decision against which an action has been brought only if, at the date on which that decision was adopted, it was vitiated by one of those grounds for annulment or alteration referred to in Article 65(2) CTMR; and, third, it may not annul or alter that decision on grounds which come into existence subsequent to its adoption.[197]

While it is true that that principle has a broad scope and prohibits, *inter alia*, the General Court from annulling or altering the decision of the Board of Appeal of EUIPO by taking into account facts which came into existence after that decision had been adopted or by applying substantive legal provisions which were not yet in force at the time of that adoption, it does not, by contrast, prohibit the General Court from taking into account, in disputes concerning the application of Article 8(4) CTMR, an evolution in the interpretation, by the national courts, of the rule of national law examined by the Board of Appeal of EUIPO. That rule of national law was one of the particulars subject to assessment by that Board of Appeal, and the application of that rule by the same

194. CJEU C-598/14 P of 5.4.2017 – EUIPO/Szajner a.o., para. 41.
195. CJEU C-598/14 P of 5.4.2017 – EUIPO/Szajner a.o., para. 42; C-307/20 P of 29.10.2020 – Peek & Cloppenburg/EUIPO, para. 18; C-308/20 P of 29.10.2020 – Peek & Cloppenburg/EUIPO, para. 18; C-309/20 P of 29.10.2020 – Peek & Cloppenburg/EUIPO, para. 18; C-310/20 P of 29.10.2020 – Peek & Cloppenburg/EUIPO, para. 18; C-311/20 P of 29.10.2020 – Peek & Cloppenburg/EUIPO, para. 18; C-312/20 P of 29.10.2020 – Peek & Cloppenburg/EUIPO, para. 18.
196. CJEU C-598/14 P of 5.4.2017 – EUIPO/Szajner a.o., para. 43.
197. CJEU C-598/14 P of 5.4.2017 – EUIPO/Szajner a.o., para. 44, with reference to CJEU C-263/09 P of 5.7.2011 – Edwin/OHIM, paras 71 et seq.; C-482/15 P of 26.10.2016 – Westermann Lernspielverlage/EUIPO, para. 27.

Board of Appeal is subject, pursuant to Article 65(2) CTMR, to a full review of legality by the General Court.[198]

However, in accordance with the principle that the parties should be heard, which comes under the right to a fair trial laid down in Article 47 of the Charter of Fundamental Rights of the European Union, the taking into consideration by the General Court of a decision of a national court issued after the adoption of the decision of the Board of Appeal of EUIPO is subject to the condition that, as in the present case, the parties have had, before the General Court, the opportunity to submit observations on the relevant national decision (*see*, to that effect, judgment of 27 March 2014, OHIM v National Lottery Commission, C-530/12 P, EU:C:2014:186, paragraphs 52 to 54).[199]

The review conducted by the competent OHIM bodies and by the General Court must also meet the requirements of the role performed by them in disputes relating to Community trade marks.[200]

Where the competent OHIM bodies are called upon to rule, initially, on an application for a declaration of invalidity of a Community mark based on an earlier copyright protected by a rule of national law, their decision may have the effect of depriving the proprietor of the Community trade mark of a right that has been granted to him. The scope of such a decision necessarily implies that the authority which takes it is not limited to the role of mere validation of the national law as submitted by the applicant for a declaration of invalidity.[201]

As regards the judicial review conducted, subsequently, by the General Court, it should be noted that that review must meet the requirements of the principle of effective judicial protection. In so far as the application of national law, in the procedural context in question, may have the effect of depriving the proprietor of a Community trade mark of his right, it is essential that that Court is not deprived, due to possible lacunae in the documents submitted as evidence of the applicable national law, of the real possibility of exercising an effective review. To that end, it must therefore be able to confirm, beyond the documents submitted, the content, the conditions of application and the scope of the rules of law relied upon by the applicant for a declaration of invalidity.[202]

As regards the examination, in the context of an appeal, of the findings made by the General Court with regard to that national law, the **Court of Justice** has jurisdiction to determine, first of all, whether the General Court, on the basis of the documents and

198. CJEU C-598/14 P of 5.4.2017 – EUIPO/Szajner a.o., para. 45, with reference to CJEU C-530/12 P of 27.3.2014 – OHIM/National Lottery Commission, paras 36 to 38.
199. CJEU C-598/14 P of 5.4.2017 – EUIPO/Szajner a.o., para. 46, with reference to CJEU C-530/12 P of 27.3.2014 – OHIM/National Lottery Commission, paras 52 to 54.
200. CJEU C-530/12 P of 27.3.2014 – OHIM/National Lottery Commission, para. 42.
201. CJEU C-530/12 P of 27.3.2014 – OHIM/National Lottery Commission, para. 43; C-598/14 P of 5.4.2017 – EUIPO/Szajner a.o., para. 36.
202. CJEU C-530/12 P of 27.3.2014 – OHIM/National Lottery Commission, para. 44; C-598/14 P of 5.4.2017 – EUIPO/Szajner a.o., para. 38; *see also* CJEU C-307/20 P of 29.10.2020 – Peek & Cloppenburg/EUIPO, para. 20; C-308/20 P of 29.10.2020 – Peek & Cloppenburg/EUIPO, para. 20; C-309/20 P of 29.10.2020 – Peek & Cloppenburg/EUIPO, para. 20; C-310/20 P of 29.10.2020 – Peek & Cloppenburg/EUIPO, para. 20; C-311/20 P of 29.10.2020 – Peek & Cloppenburg/EUIPO, para. 20; C-312/20 P of 29.10.2020 – Peek & Cloppenburg/EUIPO, para. 20.

other evidence submitted to it, distorted the wording of the national provisions at issue or of the national case law relating to them, or of the academic writings concerning them; second, whether the General Court, as regards those particulars, made findings that were manifestly inconsistent with their content; and, lastly, whether the General Court, in examining all the particulars, attributed to one of them, for the purpose of establishing the content of the national law at issue, a significance which is not appropriate in the light of the other particulars, where that is manifestly apparent from the documentation in the case-file.[203]

The General Court erred in law in holding that the protection conferred on **protected designations of origin and geographical indications** under Regulation No. 1234/2007,[204] provided that they are 'earlier rights' within the meaning of Article 53(1)(c) CTMR, read in conjunction with Article 8(4) and Article 53(2)(d) CTMR, 'may be supplemented by the relevant national law granting additional protection'.[205]

[12] Proof of genuine use

Where a request for proof of genuine use of the earlier marks is not submitted in due time, for the purposes of the comparison of the goods concerned, all the goods and services for which the Community trade mark and the earlier trade marks had been registered, and on which the application for a declaration of invalidity was based, should be taken into account.[206]

[13] Restriction of the list of goods or services

Under Article 44(1) CTMR, the applicant may at any time restrict the list of goods or services contained in the application. A request to amend an application submitted under that provision must comply with the detailed rules established by Rule 13 CTMIR.[207]

The applicant is not disputing that it failed to lodge such a request. It maintains however that in the absence of any oral proceedings before the Board of Appeal, an express proposal for restriction of the specification of goods, such as that set out in this instance in its pleading before that board, should have been taken into account where the Board intended to uphold the opposition.[208]

However, no such obligation is laid down either in the CTMR or in the CTMIR. Any request for restriction of the specification of goods must be submitted, pursuant to

203. CJEU C-263/09 P of 5.7.2011 – Edwin/OHIM, para. 53; C-468/17 P of 13.12.2017 – Morton's of Chicago/EUIPO, paras 5/7 and 6.
204. Council Regulation (EC) No 1234/2007 of 22 October 2007 establishing a common organization of agricultural markets and on specific provisions for certain agricultural products.
205. CJEU C-56/16 P of 14.9.2017 – EUIPO/Instituto dos Vinhos do Douro e do PortoIP, para. 108.
206. CJEU C-353/09 P of 15.2.2011 – Perfetti Van Melle/OHIM, paras 45 and 46.
207. CJEU C-412/05 P of 26.4.2007 – Alcon/OHIM (II), para. 107; C-388/10 P of 24.3.2011 – Muñoz Arraiza/OHIM, para. 72.
208. CJEU C-412/05 P of 26.4.2007 – Alcon/OHIM (II), para. 108.

those regulations, in the form of a request for amendment which complies with certain detailed rules. Such a request must be made expressly and unconditionally.[209]

Consequently, since it is undisputed in this case that the proposal set out by the applicant in its pleading before the Board of Appeal did not comply with those requirements, the Court of First Instance was entitled to hold that the Board of Appeal cannot be criticized for failing to take that proposal into account.[210]

[14] Amendment of an application

Under Article 26(3) CTMR, an application for a Community trade mark must comply 'with the conditions laid down in the Implementing Regulation referred to in Article 162(1)' CTMR, that is to say, the conditions laid down in the CTMIR. Therefore, such an application **must indicate the categories** mentioned in Rule 3 CTMIR into which the mark in question falls.[211]

Moreover, Rule 9 CTMIR is applicable for deficiencies, that concerning formal requirements in connection with the application but not for the amendment of the application.[212]

Accordingly, the CFI was right in holding that the applicant's request to modify the indication of the application's category from 'colour mark *per se*' to 'figurative colour mark' constituted a request to amend the Community trade mark application in the sense of Article 43(2) CTMR.[213]

It is apparent from the very wording of Article 43(2) CTMR that a Community trade mark application may be amended, upon request of the applicant, only by 'correcting the name and address of the applicant, errors of wording or of copying, or obvious mistakes', and that such a correction may only be possible, 'provided that [it] does not substantially change the trade mark or extend the list of goods or services'. Therefore, this amendment is only valid if the request for amendment is justified by one of the reasons expressly mentioned in this provision. Otherwise, the request must be rejected without examining whether the requested correction would substantially change the trade mark or extend the list of goods or services.[214]

Article 43(2) CTMR does not authorize the category of EU trade mark chosen by the applicant in its application to be changed to another category of mark.[215]

If the General Court were required to examine the distinctiveness of a mark applied for, not only in the light of the category chosen by the applicant in its application but also in the light of all other potentially relevant categories, that

209. CJEU C-412/05 P of 26.4.2007 – Alcon/OHIM (II), para. 109; C-388/10 P of 24.3.2011 – Muñoz Arraiza/OHIM, para. 72.
210. CJEU C-412/05 P of 26.4.2007 – Alcon/OHIM (II), para. 110.
211. CJEU C-170/15 P of 21.1.2016 – Enercon/OHIM, para. 17; unofficial translation; C-433/17 P of 25.10.2018 – Enercon/EUIPO, para. 24.
212. CJEU C-170/15 P of 21.1.2016 – Enercon/OHIM, para. 18; unofficial translation.
213. CJEU C-170/15 P of 21.1.2016 – Enercon/OHIM, para. 19; unofficial translation.
214. CJEU C-170/15 P of 21.1.2016 – Enercon/OHIM, para. 21; unofficial translation.
215. CJEU C-170/15 P of 21.1.2016 – Enercon/OHIM, para. 28; unofficial translation; C-433/17 P of 25.10.2018 – Enercon/EUIPO, para. 25.

applicant's obligation to indicate the category of mark applied for and the impossibility pursuant to Article 43(2) CTMR of subsequently amending that category would be deprived of all practical effect.[216]

[15] Linguistic solution

In determining the official languages of the Community which may be used as languages of proceedings in opposition, revocation and invalidity proceedings, where the parties cannot agree on which language to use, the Council was pursuing the legitimate aim of seeking an appropriate linguistic solution to the difficulties arising from such a failure to agree.[217]

Even if the Council did treat the official languages of the Community differently, its choice to limit the languages to those which are most widely known in the European Community is appropriate and proportionate.[218]

Since the proceedings comprise all such acts as must be carried out in processing an application, it follows that the term **'procedural documents'** covers any document that is required or prescribed by the Community legislation for the purposes of processing an application for a Community trade mark or necessary for such processing, be they notifications, requests for correction, clarification or other documents. Contrary to the Office's submissions, all such documents must therefore be drawn up by it in the language used for filing the application.[219]

In contrast to procedural documents, written communications, as referred to in the second sentence of Article 115(4) CTMR, are any communications which, from their content, cannot be regarded as amounting to procedural documents, such as letters under cover of which the Office sends procedural documents, or by which it communicates information to applicants.[220]

It is settled law that the rule according to which the **evidence** submitted in support of an opposition or of an application for invalidity or revocation of the trade mark must be submitted in the language of the proceedings or be accompanied by a translation into that language is justified by the need to observe the principle of the right to be heard and to ensure equality of arms between the parties in *inter partes* proceedings.[221]

216. CJEU C-170/15 P of 21.1.2016 – Enercon/OHIM, para. 29; unofficial translation; C-433/17 P of 25.10.2018 – Enercon/EUIPO, para. 26.
217. CJEU C-361/01 P of 9.9.2003 – KIK/OHIM, para. 93.
218. CJEU C-361/01 P of 9.9.2003 – KIK/OHIM, para. 94.
219. CJEU C-361/01 P of 9.9.2003 – KIK/OHIM, para. 46.
220. CJEU C-361/01 P of 9.9.2003 – KIK/OHIM, para. 47.
221. CJEU C-100/11 P of 10.5.2012 – Helena Rubinstein and L'Oréal/OHIM, para. 102.

[16] *Right to be heard*

According to the second sentence of Article 73 CTMR, decisions of the Office may be based only on reasons or evidence on which the parties concerned have had an opportunity to present their comments.[222]

In accordance with that provision, a Board of Appeal of the Office may base its decision only on matters of fact or of law on which the parties have been able to set out their views.[223]

Consequently, in the case in which the Board of Appeal assembles of its own motion facts intended to serve as a basis for its decision, it is under an obligation to notify the parties of those facts in order that the parties may submit their views thereon.[224]

It is therefore necessary to examine whether or not, in the present case, the parties had the opportunity in the course of the proceedings before the General Court to submit their observations on that [Italian] **judgment**.[225]

The right to be heard does not require that, before taking a final position on the assessment of the evidence submitted by a party, the Board of Appeal of OHIM must offer that party a further opportunity to comment on that evidence.[226]

In addition, a party which itself submitted the facts and evidence in question was by definition in a position to state their possible relevance to the resolution of the dispute at the time when it submitted them.[227]

[17] *Obligation to state reasons*

The first sentence of Article 75 CTMR provides that '[d]ecisions of the Office shall state the reasons on which they are based'.[228]

The obligation on OHIM, referred to in Article 75 CTMR, to state reasons for its decisions has the **dual purpose** of enabling interested parties to know the purported justification for the measure taken so as to be able to defend their rights and of enabling the Courts of the EU to exercise their jurisdiction to review the legality of the decision.[229]

---

222. CJEU C-447/02 P of 21.10.2004 – KWS Saat/OHIM, para. 41; C-193/09 P of 4.3.2010 – Kaul/OHIM, para. 58; C-96/11 P of 6.9.2012 – Storck/OHIM, para. 74; *see also* CJEU C-530/12 P of 27.3.2014 – OHIM/National Lottery Commission, para. 54.
223. CJEU C-447/02 P of 21.10.2004 – KWS Saat/OHIM, para. 42; C-155/18 P to C-158/18 P of 4.3.2020 – Tulliallan Burlington/EUIPO, para. 94.
224. CJEU C-447/02 P of 21.10.2004 – KWS Saat/OHIM, para. 43.
225. CJEU C-530/12 P of 27.3.2014 – OHIM/National Lottery Commission, para. 56.
226. CJEU C-53/11 P of 19.1.2012 – OHIM/Nike International, para. 53; C-62/15 P of 8.9.2015 – DTL Corporatión/OHIM, para. 45; C-155/18 P to C-158/18 P of 4.3.2020 – Tulliallan Burlington/EUIPO, para. 94.
227. CJEU C-155/18 P to C-158/18 P of 4.3.2020 – Tulliallan Burlington/EUIPO, para. 94, with reference to C-193/09 P of 4.3.2010 – Kaul/OHIM, para. 66.
228. CJEU C-447/02 P of 21.10.2004 – KWS Saat/OHIM, para. 63; C-20/08 P of 9.12.2008 – Enercon/OHIM, para. 28.
229. CJEU C-100/11 P of 10.5.2012 – Helena Rubinstein and L'Oréal/OHIM, para. 111; C-96/11 P of 6.9.2012 – Storck/OHIM, para. 86; C-17/15 P of 26.10.2015 – Popp and Zech/OHIM, para. 26;

The obligation to state reasons, as thus laid down, has the same scope as that which derives from Article 296(2) TFEU.[230]

The scope of the obligation to state reasons depends on the nature of the measure in question and that, in the case of measures of general application, the statement of reasons may be confined to indicating the general situation which led to its adoption, on the one hand, and the general objectives which it is intended to achieve, on the other. If the contested measure clearly discloses the essential objective pursued by the institution, it would be excessive to require a specific statement of reasons for the various technical choices made.[231]

It is settled case law that the statement of reasons required by Article 296 TFEU must disclose in a clear and unequivocal manner the reasoning followed by the institution which adopted the measure in question in such a way as to enable the persons concerned to ascertain the reasons for the measure and to enable the competent Community Court to exercise its power of review. It is not necessary for the reasoning to go into all the relevant facts and points of law since the question of whether the statement of reasons meets the requirements of Article 253 EC must be assessed with regard not only to its wording but also to its context and to all the legal rules governing the matter in question.[232]

---

see also CJEU C-320/14 P of 13.1.2015 – Asos/OHIM, para. 36; C-252/15 P of 17.3.2016 – Naazneen/OHIM, para. 29; C-474/15 P of 7.4.2016 – Harper Hygienics/EUIPO, para. 25; C-475/15 P of 7.4.2016 – Harper Hygienics/EUIPO, para. 28; C-480/15 P of 14.4.2016 – KS Sports IPCo/EUIPO, para. 32; C-537/14 P of 27.10.2016 – Debonair Trading Internacional/EUIPO, para. 32; C-655/15 P of 2.3.2017 – Panrico/EUIPO, para. 72; C-71/16 P of 4.5.2017 – Comercializadora Eloro/EUIPO, para. 41; C-50/17 P of 1.6.2017 – Universidad Internacional de la Rioja/EUIPO, paras 5/12 and 6; C-84/16 P of 26.7.2017 – Continental Reifen Deutschland/EUIPO, para. 83; C-471/16 P of 26.7.2017 – Staatliche Porzellan-Manufaktur Meissen/EUIPO, para. 28; C-520/17 P of 30.11.2017 – C-cen-tek/EUIPO, paras 6/9 and 7; C-139/17 P of 25.7.2018 – QuaMa Quality Management/EUIPO, para. 59; C-488/16 P of 6.9.2018 – Bundesverband – Souvenir – Geschenke – Ehrenpreise/EUIPO, para. 63; C-564/16 P of 28.6.2018 – EUIPO/Puma, para. 64; C-340/17 P of 29.11.2018 – Alcohol Countermeasure Systems/EUIPO, para. 89; C-463/18 P of 15.1.2019 – CeramTec/EUIPO, paras 5/33 and 15; C-553/18 P of 15.1.2019 – Lion's Head Global Partners/EUIPO, paras 5/10 and 6; C-554/18 P of 15.1.2019 – Lion's Head Global Partners/EUIPO, paras 5/10 and 6; C-162/17 P of 16.1.2019 – Republic of Poland/EUIPO, para. 78; C-194/17 P of 31.1.2019 – Pandalis/EUIPO, para. 67; C-505/17 P of 28.2.2019 – Groupe Léa Nature/EUIPO, para. 54; C-739/18 P of 2.5.2019 – Chefaro Ireland/EUIPO, paras 5/11 and 6; C-780/18 P of 22.5.2019 – Cuervo y Sobrinos 1882/EUIPO, paras 5/12 and 7; C-822/18 P of 4.6.2019 – Aldo Supermarkets/EUIPO, paras 5/18 and 8; C-31/19 P of 2.7.2019 – Seven/EUIPO, paras 5/7 and 6; C-99/18 P of 4.7.2019 – FTI Touristik/EUIPO, para. 17; C-819/18 P of 11.7.2019 – Next design + produktion/EUIPO, paras 5/13 and 6; C-728/18 P of 25.9.2019 – EM Research Organization/EUIPO, paras 4/21 and 5; C-278/19 P of 25.9.2019 – Mas Que Vinos Global/EUIPO, paras 5/10 and 6; C-783/18 P of 12.12.2019 – EUIPO/Wajos, para. 39; C-115/19 P of 11.6.2020 – China Construction Bank/EUIPO, para. 67; C-702/18 P of 18.6.2020 – Przedsiębiorstwo Produkcyjno-Handlowe 'Primart' Marek Łukasiewicz/EUIPO, para. 61; C-142/19 P of 18.6.2020 – Dovgan/EUIPO, para. 63; C-245/22 P(I) of 12.7.2022 – Cipla Europe/EUIPO, para. 29.

230. CJEU C-447/02 P of 21.10.2004 – KWS Saat/OHIM, para. 64; C-20/08 P of 9.12.2008 – Enercon/OHIM, para. 29; C-45/11 P of 7.12.2011 – Deutsche Bahn/OHIM, para. 56; C-480/15 P of 14.4.2016 – KS Sports IPCo/EUIPO, para. 32; C-564/16 P of 28.6.2018 – EUIPO/Puma, para. 65.

231. CJEU C-361/01 P of 9.9.2003 – KIK/OHIM, para. 102; *see also* C-68/19 P of 11.9.2019 – Camomilla/EUIPO, paras 3/9 and 4.

232. CJEU C-447/02 P of 21.10.2004 – KWS Saat/OHIM, para. 65; C-20/08 P of 9.12.2008 – Enercon/OHIM, para. 31; C-45/11 P of 7.12.2011 – Deutsche Bahn/OHIM, para. 58; *see also*

It is for the Court of First Instance alone to assess the value to be attached to the evidence adduced before it, and it cannot be required to give express reasons for its assessment of the value of each piece of evidence presented to it. The Court of First Instance is obligated to **provide reasons** which will allow the Court of Justice to exercise its judicial review; in particular, they must make it possible for the Court to consider whether there has been any distortion of the evidence submitted to the Court of First Instance.[233]

The obligation to state reasons is an essential procedural requirement which must be distinguished from **the question of whether the reasons given are correct**, the latter being a matter going to the substantive legality of the contested measure.[234]

The reasoning of a decision consists in a formal statement of the grounds on which that decision is based. If those grounds are vitiated by errors, the latter will vitiate the substantive legality of the decision, but not the statement of reasons in it, which may be adequate even though it sets out reasons which are incorrect.[235]

It is a settled case law of the Court of Justice that the General Court cannot - subject to the obligation: (i) to observe the general principles and the rules of procedure relating to the burden of proof and the taking of evidence and (ii) not to distort the clear sense of the evidence - be required to give express reasons for its assessment of the value of each piece of evidence presented to it, in particular where it considers that that **evidence is unimportant or irrelevant** to the outcome of the dispute.[236]

The reasoning may therefore be **implicit**, on condition that it enables the persons concerned to know the grounds on which the General Court has based its findings and provides the Court of Justice with sufficient material for it to exercise its appellate jurisdiction.[237]

CJEU C-263/09 P of 5.7.2011 - Edwin/OHIM, para. 64; C-670/13 P of 19.6.2014 - The Cartoon Network/OHIM, para. 27; C-62/15 P of 8.9.2015 - DTL Corporatión/OHIM, para. 48; C-342/16 P of 6.12.2016 - Novomatic/EUIPO, paras 4/13 and 5; *see also* CJEU C-252/15 P of 17.3.2016 - Naazneen/OHIM, paras 31 et seq.; C-499/17 P of 14.12.2017 - Miguel Torres/EUIPO, paras 7/11 and 8.

233. CJEU C-214/05 P of 18.7.2006 - Rossi/OHIM, para. 22; C-461/09 P of 9.7.2010 - The Wellcome Foundation, para. 30; *see also* CJEU C-96/11 P of 6.9.2012 - Storck/OHIM, paras 87 et seq.; C-450/13 P of 19.6.2014 - Donaldson Filtration Deutschland/OHIM, para. 48; C-642/15 of 1.12.2016 - Klement, para. 24.

234. CJEU C-535/14 P of 18.6.2015 - Ipatau/Council, para. 37; C-442/15 P of 22.9.2016 - Pensa Pharma/EUIPO, para. 35.

235. CJEU C-413/06 P of 10.7.2008, Bertelsmann and Sony Corporation of America/Impala, para. 181; C-442/15 P of 22.9.2016 - Pensa Pharma/EUIPO, para. 35.

236. CJEU C-50/15 P of 21.1.2016 - Hesse/OHIM, para. 24; C-479/15 P of 14.4.2016 - Nanu-Nana Joachim Hoepp/EUIPO, para. 26; *see also* CJEU C-237/98 P of 15.6.2000 - Dorsch Consult/ Council and Commission, para. 51.

237. CJEU C-597/12 P of 17.10.2013 - Isdin/OHIM, para. 21; C-581/13 P and C-582/13 P of 20.11.2014 - Intra-Presse/OHIM, para. 53; C-374/14 P of 12.2.2015 - Walcher Meßtechnik/ OHIM, para. 29; C-33/15 P of 15.10.2015 - Cantina Broglie 1, para. 35; C-34/15 P of 15.10.2015 - Cantina Broglie 1, para. 35; C-351/16 P of 10.11.2016 - 100 % Capri Italia/EUIPO, paras 8/9 and 9; *see also* CJEU C-182/14 P of 19.3.2015 - MEGA Brands International/OHIM, para. 54; C-84/16 P of 26.7.2017 - Continental Reifen Deutschland/EUIPO, para. 83; C-162/17 P of 16.1.2019 - Republic of Poland/EUIPO, para. 79.

The Court of Justice will reject outright complaints directed against grounds of a judgment of the Court of First Instance **included purely for the sake of completeness** since they cannot lead to the judgment being set aside and are therefore nugatory.[238]

The plea of lack to state reasons is a plea that is purely a matter of law; the Court may remedy the omission of the Court of First Instance.[239]

Alleging absence of reasons or inadequacy of the reasons stated goes to an issue of infringement of essential procedural requirements and, involving a matter of public policy, must be raised **by the Community judicature of its own motion.**[240]

If the General Court did not respond to the complaint that the EUIPO based its decision on an error in the application of the principles of the case law relating to the overall assessment of trade marks and the General Court did not give reasons for its assertion, the plea of lack to state reasons is founded.[241]

[18] General principle of community law under which the parties delimit the subject matter of a case

The Court of First Instance is in no way bound by the agreement between the applicant and OHIM as to the similarity or even the likelihood of confusion between the conflicting marks. The Court is therefore correct to consider whether the contested decision infringed the concept of likelihood of confusion.[242]

[19] Time limits

According to settled case law, no derogation from the application of the Community rules on procedural time limits may be made, save where the circumstances are quite exceptional, in the sense of being unforeseeable or amounting to force majeure, in accordance with the second paragraph of Article 45 of the Statute of the Court of Justice, since the strict application of those rules services the requirements of legal certainty and the need to avoid any discrimination or arbitrary treatment in the administration of justice.[243]

---

238. CJEU C-184/01 P of 7.11.2002 – Hirschfeld, para. 48, with further proof; C-515/15 P of 14.4.2016 – Roland/EUIPO, para. 28; C-655/15 P of 2.3.2017 – Panrico/EUIPO, para. 92; *see also* CJEU C-31/14 P of 11.12.2014 – OHIM/Kessel medintim, para. 53; C-104/18 P of 12.9.2019 – Koton Mağazacilik Tekstil Sanayi ve Ticaret/EUIPO, para. 65; C-281/18 P of 31.10.2019 – Repower/EUIPO, para. 37; C-142/19 P of 18.6.2020 – Dovgan/EUIPO, para. 92; C-121/19 P of 16.9.2020 – Edison/EUIPO, para. 44.
239. CJEU C-361/01 P of 9.9.2003 – KIK/OHIM, para. 101; C-412/05 P of 26.4.2007 – Alcon/OHIM (II), paras 97 et seq.; *see also* CJEU C-611/11 P of 10.10.2012 – ara/OHIM, para. 35.
240. CJEU C-265/97 P of 30.3.2000 – Coöperatieve Vereniging De Verenigde Bloemenveilingen Aalsmeer/Florimex, para. 114; C-20/08 P of 9.12.2008 – Enercon/OHIM, para. 30.
241. CJEU C-519/17 P and C-522/17 P to C-525/17 P of 30.5.2018 – L'Oréal/EUIPO, para. 80-82, unofficial transcription.
242. CJEU C-106/03 P of 12.10.2004 – VEDIAL/OHIM, para. 37.
243. CJEU C-325/03 P of 18.1.2005 – Zuazaga Meabe/OHIM, para. 16; translation according to CJEU C-369/03 P of 19.2.2004 – Crama/Commission, para. 16.

According to the sixth paragraph of Article 43 of the rules of the procedure of the Court of First Instance, the date on which a copy of the signed original of a pleading is received at the Registry by telefax shall only be deemed to meet a time limit, provided that the signed original of the pleading is lodged at the Registry no later than ten days thereafter.[244]

Therefore, an interpretation cannot apply according to which the said term begins to run as of the date of expiration of a term of two months and ten days due to the combined application of the fifth paragraph of Article 63 CTMR and the second paragraph of Article 102 of the rules of the procedure of the Court of First Instance, whichever is the date of reception of the fax. It is necessary to emphasize that the sixth paragraph of Article 43 of the rules of the procedure of the Court of First Instance does not have the effect to extend the term, provided that the fax is received more than ten days before.[245]

Has an application been sent by telefax on 3 January 2003, the original of the pleading has to be received by the Registry no later than 13 January 2003, for the telefax to be considered.[246]

[20] Unforseeable circumstances and force majeure

The concept of 'unforseeable circumstances' has an objective element, relating to abnormal circumstances beyond the control of the operator, and a subjective element, relating to the obligation on the party concerned to protect itself against the consequences of the abnormal event by taking appropriate measures without making excessive sacrifices. In particular, the operator must carefully monitor the progress of the proceedings initiated and, in particular, show diligence in order to comply with the time limits laid down.[247]

The concept of force majeure in the meaning of Article 45 of the Statute of the Court of Justice contains an objective element relating to abnormal circumstances unconnected with the trader in question and a subjective element involving the obligation, on his part, to guard against the consequences of the abnormal event by taking appropriate steps without making unreasonable sacrifices. In particular, the trader must pay close attention to the course of the procedure set in motion and, in particular, demonstrate diligence in order to comply with the prescribed time limits.[248] Consequently, the concept of force majeure does not apply to a situation in which,

244. CJEU C-325/03 P of 18.1.2005 – Zuazaga Meabe/OHIM, para. 17; unofficial translation; *see also* CJEU C-181/15 P of 6.10.2015 – Marpefa/OHIM, paras 16 et seq.; C-602/15 P of 4.5.2016 – Monster Energy/EUIPO, paras 38 et seq.; C-603/15 P of 4.5.2016 – Monster Energy/EUIPO, paras 38 et seq.
245. CJEU C-325/03 P of 18.1.2005 – Zuazaga Meabe/OHIM, para. 18; unofficial translation.
246. CJEU C-325/03 P of 18.1.2005 – Zuazaga Meabe/OHIM, para. 19; unofficial translation.
247. CJEU C-399/15 P of 12.7.2016 – Vichy Catelán, para. 24, with further proof, unofficial translation; C-245/22 P(I) of 12.7.2022 – Cipla Europe/EUIPO, para. 35.
248. Translation according to CJEU C-195/91 P of 15.12.1994 – Bayer/Commission, para. 32.

objectively, a diligent and prudent person would have been able to take the necessary steps before the expiry of the period prescribed for instituting proceedings.[249]

Therefore, errors committed by an applicant's employees or by service providers used by the applicant in the conduct of its business cannot, in so far as they do not constitute circumstances unconnected with the applicant, be relied on to demonstrate the existence of unforeseeable circumstances or of force majeure.[250]

A party may not rely on the inadequate functioning of its internal organization or on a failure to apply its internal instructions in support of the existence of unforeseeable circumstances or of force majeure.[251]

Is the original of a pleading given, not directly to the post, but to a private forwarder, four days after the sending of the telefax, and does the forwarder wait further two days before sending the document by post, the risk that the pleading reaches the Court late is increased; the expected diligence of a normally careful plaintiff to meet time limits is not shown.[252]

Such missing diligence excludes to approve force majeure.[253]

[21] New facts and evidence given before the Board of Appeal

First, it must be found that, as is apparent from the wording of Article 74(2) CTMR, **OHIM may disregard facts** which were **not submitted or evidence** which was **not produced in due time** by the parties.[254]

It results from such wording that, as a general rule and unless otherwise specified, the submission of facts and evidence by the parties remains possible after the expiry of the time limits to which such submission is subject under the provisions of the CTMR and that OHIM is in no way prohibited from taking account of facts and evidence which are submitted or produced late.[255]

---

249. CJEU C-325/03 P of 18.1.2005 – Zuazaga Meabe/OHIM, para. 25; unofficial translation; also CJEU C-602/15 P of 4.5.2016 – Monster Energy/EUIPO, paras 35; C-603/15 P of 4.5.2016 – Monster Energy/EUIPO, para. 35; C-103/22 P(I) of 17.5.2022 – Shanghai Panati/EUIPO, para. 51.
250. CJEU C-245/22 P(I) of 12.7.2022 – Cipla Europe/EUIPO, para. 36; C-103/22 P(I) of 17.5.2022 – Shanghai Panati/EUIPO, para. 52.
251. CJEU C-245/22 P(I) of 12.7.2022 – Cipla Europe/EUIPO, para. 37.
252. CJEU C-325/03 P of 18.1.2005 – Zuazaga Meabe/OHIM, para. 26; unofficial translation.
253. CJEU C-325/03 P of 18.1.2005 – Zuazaga Meabe/OHIM, para. 27; unofficial translation.
254. CJEU C-29/05 P of 13.3.2007 – OHIM/Kaul, para. 41; C-16/06 P of 18.12.2008 – Les Éditions Albert René/OHIM, para. 141.
255. CJEU C-29/05 P of 13.3.2007 – OHIM/Kaul, para. 42; C-621/11 P of 18.7.2013 – New Yorker SHK Jeans/OHIM, para. 22; C-610/11 P of 26.9.2013 – Centrotherm Systemtechnik/OHIM, para. 77; C-120/12 P of 3.10.2013 – Rintisch/OHIM, para. 22; C-121/12 P of 3.10.2013 – Rintisch/OHIM, para. 23; C-122/12 P of 3.10.2013 – Rintisch/OHIM, para. 23; C-611/15 P of 16.6.2016 – L'Oréal/EUIPO, para. 24; C-71/16 P of 4.5.2017 – Comercializadora Eloro/EUIPO, para. 55; C-478/16 P of 19.4.2018 – EUIPO/Group, para. 34; C-634/16 P of 24.1.2018 – EUIPO/European Food, para. 55; C-418/16 P of 28.2.2018 – mobile.de/EUIPO, para. 48; C-150/18 P of 6.9.2018 – El Corte Inglés/EUIPO, paras 6/17 and 7; C-151/18 P of 6.9.2018 – El Corte Inglés/EUIPO, paras 6/16 and 7.

Article 76(2) CTMR, read in conjunction with Rule 37(b)(iv) CTMIR, does not imply that evidence submitted for the first time before the Board of Appeal must be regarded by the Board as belated.[256]

However, it is equally apparent from that wording that a party has no unconditional right to have facts and evidence submitted out of time taken into consideration by OHIM. In stating that the latter 'may', in such a case, decide to disregard facts and evidence, Article 74(2) CTMR grants **OHIM a wide discretion to decide** while giving reasons for its decision in that regard, whether or not to take such information into account.[257]

General, categorical assertions do not establish that the Board of Appeal effectively exercised the discretion conferred on it by Article 76(2) CTMR, in order to decide, in giving proper reasons and taking account of all relevant facts, whether or not to take into account the additional evidence submitted to it in order to make the decision it is called upon to give.[258]

It must be emphasized at the outset that any taking into account by OHIM of that additional evidence is in no way a 'favour' granted to one party or the other, but rather must result from an objective, reasoned exercise of the discretion conferred on OHIM by Article 76(2) CTMR.[259]

It should also be borne in mind that the statement of reasons thus required is all the more necessary when OHIM decides to reject the evidence submitted out of time.[260]

Where OHIM is called upon to give judgment in the context of opposition proceedings, taking such facts or evidence into account is particularly likely to be justified where OHIM considers, first, that the material which has been produced late is, on the face of it, likely to be relevant to the outcome of the opposition brought before it and, second, that the stage of the proceedings at which that late submission takes place and the circumstances surrounding it do not argue against such matters being taken into account.[261]

256. CJEU C-634/16 P of 24.1.2018 – EUIPO/European Food, para. 35.
257. CJEU C-29/05 P of 13.3.2007 – OHIM/Kaul, para. 43; C-216/10 P of 25.11.2010 – Lufthansa AirPlus Servicekarten/OHIM, para. 45; C-308/10 P of 19.5.2011 – Union Investment Privatfonds/OHIM, para. 42; C-621/11 P of 18.7.2013 – New Yorker SHK Jeans/OHIM, para. 23; C-610/11 P of 26.9.2013 – Centrotherm Systemtechnik/OHIM, para. 78; C-120/12 P of 3.10.2013 – Rintisch/OHIM, para. 23; C-121/12 P of 3.10.2013 – Rintisch/OHIM, para. 24; C-122/12 P of 3.10.2013 – Rintisch/OHIM, para. 24; C-71/16 P of 4.5.2017 – Comercializadora Eloro/EUIPO, para. 56; C-478/16 P of 19.4.2018 – EUIPO/Group, para. 35; C-634/16 P of 24.1.2018 – EUIPO/European Food, para. 56; C-418/16 P of 28.2.2018 – mobile.de/EUIPO, para. 49; C-150/18 P of 6.9.2018 – El Corte Inglés/EUIPO, paras 6/17 and 7; C-151/18 P of 6.9.2018 – El Corte Inglés/EUIPO, paras 6/16 and 7.
258. CJEU C-610/11 P of 26.9.2013 – Centrotherm Systemtechnik/OHIM, para. 110; *see* CJEU C-120/12 P of 3.10.2013 – Rintisch/OHIM, para. 37; C-121/12 P of 3.10.2013 – Rintisch/OHIM, para. 38; C-122/12 P of 3.10.2013 – Rintisch/OHIM, para. 38.
259. CJEU C-610/11 P of 26.9.2013 – Centrotherm Systemtechnik/OHIM, para. 111; C-634/16 P of 24.1.2018 – EUIPO/European Food, para. 58.
260. CJEU C-610/11 P of 26.9.2013 – Centrotherm Systemtechnik/OHIM, para. 112; C-71/16 P of 4.5.2017 – Comercializadora Eloro/EUIPO, para. 60.
261. CJEU C-29/05 P of 13.3.2007 – OHIM/Kaul, para. 44; C-308/10 P of 19.5.2011 – Union Investment Privatfonds/OHIM, para. 43; C-621/11 P of 18.7.2013 – New Yorker SHK Jeans/OHIM, para. 33; C-610/11 P of 26.9.2013 – Centrotherm Systemtechnik/OHIM, para. 113; C-120/12 P of 3.10.2013 – Rintisch/OHIM, para. 38; C-121/12 P of 3.10.2013 – Rintisch/OHIM,

Similarly and *mutatis mutandis*, such considerations are particularly likely to justify OHIM's taking into account, when it is called upon to rule on an application for revocation, evidence of use of the mark which, although not submitted within the time limit set under Rule 40(5) CTMR, is submitted at a later stage of the proceedings by way of complement to the evidence submitted within that time limit.[262]

Moreover, it is **not necessary** that the party concerned be **unable to submit evidence** within the time limit in order for additional evidence of use of the mark submitted after expiry of the time limit referred to in Rule 40(5) CTMR to be taken into account.[263]

As rightly submitted by OHIM, if it were compelled to take into consideration, in all circumstances, the facts and evidence produced by the parties to opposition proceedings outside of the time limits set to that end under the provisions of the CTMR, those provisions would be rendered redundant.[264]

However, the interpretation set out in paragraphs 42–44 of this judgment in respect of Article 74(2) CTMR is capable of preserving the effectiveness of those provisions while making it possible to reconcile various imperatives.[265]

It is consistent with the principle of sound administration and the need to ensure the proper conduct and effectiveness of proceedings that the parties have an incentive to respect the time limits imposed on them by OHIM when hearing a case. The fact that the latter may, if necessary, decide to disregard facts and evidence produced by the parties outside the time limits prescribed should, in itself, have such an incentive effect.[266]

By preserving, nevertheless, the possibility for the department called upon to make a decision in a dispute of taking into account facts and evidence submitted late by the parties, that interpretation is, at least in respect of opposition proceedings, likely to contribute to ensuring that marks whose use could later successfully be challenged by means of annulment or infringement proceedings are not registered. As the Court has already held, reasons of legal certainty and sound administration speak in favour of that approach.[267]

Second, no reason of principle related to the nature of the proceedings under way before the Board of Appeal or to the jurisdiction of that department precludes it, for the purpose of giving judgment on the appeal before it, from taking into account **facts and evidence produced for the first time at the appeal stage.**[268]

para. 39; C-122/12 P of 3.10.2013 – Rintisch/OHIM, para. 39; C-71/16 P of 4.5.2017 – Comercializadora Eloro/EUIPO, para. 59; C-634/16 P of 24.1.2018 – EUIPO/European Food, para. 57; C-418/16 P of 28.2.2018 – mobile.de/EUIPO, para. 63.

262. CJEU C-610/11 P of 26.9.2013 – Centrotherm Systemtechnik/OHIM, para. 114.
263. CJEU C-610/11 P of 26.9.2013 – Centrotherm Systemtechnik/OHIM, para. 117.
264. CJEU C-29/05 P of 13.3.2007 – OHIM/Kaul, para. 45.
265. CJEU C-29/05 P of 13.3.2007 – OHIM/Kaul, para. 46.
266. CJEU C-29/05 P of 13.3.2007 – OHIM/Kaul, para. 47.
267. CJEU C-29/05 P of 13.3.2007 – OHIM/Kaul, para. 48.
268. CJEU C-29/05 P of 13.3.2007 – OHIM/Kaul, para. 49; C-634/16 P of 24.1.2018 – EUIPO/European Food, para. 36.

In that regard, disputes arising from an opposition to the registration of a trade mark are potentially subject to a four-tier review system.[269]

A procedure is, initially, a matter for OHIM, its Opposition Divisions first of all and, then, on appeal, its Boards of Appeal which, in spite of the independence enjoyed by those departments and their members, remain none the less departments of OHIM. Subsequent to that procedure, there exists the possibility of judicial review by the Court of First Instance and, if necessary, on appeal by the Court of Justice.[270]

As stated in Article 63(2) CTMR, the Court of First Instance may annul or alter a decision of a Board of Appeal of OHIM only 'on grounds of lack of competence, infringement of an essential procedural requirement, infringement of the Treaty, of [the] Regulation or of any rule of law relating to their application or misuse of power'.[271]

It follows, in particular, from that provision that the Court of First Instance may annul or alter a decision against which an action has been brought only if, at the time the decision was adopted, it was vitiated by one of those grounds for annulment or alteration. The Court of First Instance may not annul or alter that decision on grounds which come into existence subsequent to its adoption.[272]

It is also apparent from that provision that facts not submitted by the parties before the departments of OHIM cannot be submitted at the stage of the appeal brought before that Community court. The Court of First Instance is called upon to assess the legality of the decision of the Board of Appeal by reviewing the application of Community law made by that board, particularly in the light of facts which were submitted to the latter. By contrast, that Court cannot carry out such a review by taking into account matters of fact newly produced before it.[273]

In accordance with the logic of the institutional architecture referred to in paragraphs 50 and 51 of this judgment, the judicial review thus exercised by the Court of First Instance cannot consist of a mere repetition of a review previously carried out by the Board of Appeal of OHIM.[274]

It follows, in that regard, from Article 62(1) CTMR that, following the examination as to the merits of the appeal, the Board of Appeal is to decide it and that, in doing so, it may 'exercise any power within the competence of the department which was responsible for the decision appealed', that is to say, in the present case, give judgment

269. CJEU C-29/05 P of 13.3.2007 – OHIM/Kaul, para. 50.
270. CJEU C-29/05 P of 13.3.2007 – OHIM/Kaul, para. 51.
271. CJEU C-29/05 P of 13.3.2007 – OHIM/Kaul, para. 52; C-482/15 P of 26.10.2016 – Westermann Lernspielverlage/EUIPO, para. 27; *see also* C-311/05 P of 4.10.2007 – Naipes Heraclio Fournier/OHIM, para. 39; C-598/14 P of 5.4.2017 – EUIPO/Szajner a.o., para. 44.
272. CJEU C-29/05 P of 13.3.2007 – OHIM/Kaul, para. 53; C-311/05 P of 4.10.2007 – Naipes Heraclio Fournier/OHIM, para. 37; C-482/15 P of 26.10.2016 – Westermann Lernspielverlage/EUIPO, para. 27; C-598/14 P of 5.4.2017 – EUIPO/Szajner a.o., para. 44.
273. CJEU C-29/05 P of 13.3.2007 – OHIM/Kaul, para. 54; C-131/06 P of 24.4.2007 – Castellblanch/OHIM, para. 21; C-311/05 P of 4.10.2007 – Naipes Heraclio Fournier/OHIM, para. 38; C-442/15 P of 22.9.2016 – Pensa Pharma/EUIPO, para. 47; C-75/17 P of 19.4.2018 – Fiesta Hotels & Resorts/EUIPO, para. 68.
274. CJEU C-29/05 P of 13.3.2007 – OHIM/Kaul, para. 55; also CJEU C-442/15 P of 22.9.2016 – Pensa Pharma/EUIPO, para. 25.

itself on the opposition by either rejecting it or declaring it to be founded, thereby either upholding or reversing the contested decision.[275]

It thus follows from Article 62(1) CTMR that, through the effect of the appeal brought before it, the Board of Appeal is called upon to carry out a new, full examination of the merits of the opposition, in terms of both law and fact.[276]

It also follows from Articles 61(2) and 76 CTMR that, for the purposes of the examination as to the merits of the appeal brought before it, the Board of Appeal is to invite the parties, as often as necessary, to file observations on communications issued by itself and that it may also order preliminary measures, among which feature the submission of matters of fact or evidence. Article 62(2) CTMR states that if the Board of Appeal remits the case for further prosecution to the department whose decision was appealed against, that department is to be bound by the *ratio decidendi* of the Board of Appeal, 'in so far as the facts are the same'. In turn, such provisions demonstrate the possibility of seeing the underlying facts of a dispute multiply at various stages of the proceedings before OHIM.[277]

Third, it is apparent from Article 42(3) CTMR that a person who brings an opposition against the registration of a mark on the ground that that mark should be rejected on the basis of Article 8(1) of that regulation may submit facts, evidence and arguments in **support of that opposition within the time limit** set to that end by OHIM.[278]

Unlike Article 42(3), Article 59 CTMR, which lays down the conditions for bringing an appeal before the Board of Appeal, does not refer to the submission of facts or evidence, but only to the filing, within a time limit of four months, of a written statement setting out the grounds of appeal.[279]

It follows that Article 59 of the regulation cannot be interpreted as starting a new time limit for the person bringing such an appeal in which to submit facts and evidence in support of his opposition.[280]

Consequently, the Court of First Instance erred in law in finding in that paragraph that the facts and evidence were submitted 'in due time' within the meaning of Article 74(2) and in inferring therefrom that the Board of Appeal was required to take that

275. CJEU C-29/05 P of 13.3.2007 – OHIM/Kaul, para. 56; C-402/11 P of 18.10.2012 – Jager & Polacek/OHIM, para. 66.
276. CJEU C-29/05 P of 13.3.2007 – OHIM/Kaul, para. 57; C-418/10 P of 28.3.2011 – Herhof-Verwaltungsgesellschaft/OHIM, para. 79; C-349/10 P of 2.3.2011 – Claro/OHIM, para. 44; C-308/10 P of 19.5.2011 – Union Investment Privatfonds/OHIM, para. 40; C-581/13 P and C-582/13 P of 20.11.2014 – Intra-Presse/OHIM, para. 83; C-62/15 P of 8.9.2015 – DTL Corporatión/OHIM, para. 35; C-442/15 P of 22.9.2016 – Pensa Pharma/EUIPO, para. 24; C-634/16 P of 24.1.2018 – EUIPO/European Food, para. 37; C-155/18 P to C-158/18 P of 4.3.2020 – Tulliallan Burlington/EUIPO, para. 97.
277. CJEU C-29/05 P of 13.3.2007 – OHIM/Kaul, para. 58; C-16/06 P of 18.12.2008 – Les Éditions Albert René/OHIM, para. 139; C-581/13 P and C-582/13 P of 20.11.2014 – Intra-Presse/OHIM, para. 84; C-634/16 P of 24.1.2018 – EUIPO/European Food, para. 38; C-564/16 P of 28.6.2018 – EUIPO/Puma, para. 98; C-418/16 P of 28.2.2018 – mobile.de/EUIPO, para. 57.
278. CJEU C-29/05 P of 13.3.2007 – OHIM/Kaul, para. 59.
279. CJEU C-29/05 P of 13.3.2007 – OHIM/Kaul, para. 60; C-634/16 P of 24.1.2018 – EUIPO/European Food, para. 39.
280. CJEU C-29/05 P of 13.3.2007 – OHIM/Kaul, para. 61; C-634/16 P of 24.1.2018 – EUIPO/European Food, para. 39.

information into consideration in the decision which it was called upon to give on the appeal brought before it.[281]

Where such facts and evidence have not been submitted and produced by the party concerned within the time limit set to that end under the provisions of the CTMR, and thus not 'in due time' within the meaning of Article 74(2) of that regulation, that party does not enjoy an unconditional right to have such information taken into account by the Board of Appeal. On the contrary, that board has a discretion as to whether or not to take such information into account when making the decision which it is called upon to give.[282]

It follows from all the foregoing that, in finding that the Board of Appeal is required to take account of the facts and evidence submitted for the first time by the party opposing an application for registration of a mark in the written statement lodged in support of its appeal before that board against a decision given by an Opposition Division, and in annulling the contested decision merely because the Board of Appeal refused, in this instance, to take account of such information, the Court of First Instance infringed the combined provisions of Articles 42(3), 59 and 74(2) CTMR.[283]

However, it **cannot be inferred** from the *Kaul* judgment **that all the evidence** adduced before the Board of Appeal must be regarded as **belated** in all circumstances.[284]

First, it is clear that, unlike in the present case, the case that gave rise to the *Kaul* judgment concerned proceedings for opposition to registration of a trade mark. In accordance with the third subparagraph of Rule 50(1) CTMIR, where an appeal is directed against a decision of an Opposition Division, the Board of Appeal is to limit its examination of the appeal to facts and evidence presented within the time limits set or specified by the Opposition Division. Therefore, in that context, the evidence submitted before the Board of Appeal is regarded as being belated but may, nevertheless, be taken into account, where appropriate, pursuant to Article 76(2) CTMR.[285]

Second, without prejudice to the special rule applicable to opposition proceedings referred to in Rule 50(1)(3) CTMIR, it is always possible to submit evidence in time for the first time before the Board of Appeal in so far as such evidence is intended to challenge the reasons given by the Cancellation Division in the contested decision. That evidence is, therefore, either evidence supplementary to that submitted in the proceedings before the Cancellation Division or evidence on a new matter which could not be raised during those proceedings.[286]

Moreover, it should be noted that it is for the party presenting the evidence for the first time before the Board of Appeal to justify why that evidence is being submitted at

281. CJEU C-29/05 P of 13.3.2007 – OHIM/Kaul, para. 62.
282. CJEU C-29/05 P of 13.3.2007 – OHIM/Kaul, para. 63; C-16/06 P of 18.12.2008 – Les Éditions Albert René/OHIM, para. 142; C-308/10 P of 19.5.2011 – Union Investment Privatfonds/OHIM, para. 49.
283. CJEU C-29/05 P of 13.3.2007 – OHIM/Kaul, para. 64.
284. CJEU C-634/16 P of 24.1.2018 – EUIPO/European Food, para. 40.
285. CJEU C-634/16 P of 24.1.2018 – EUIPO/European Food, para. 41.
286. CJEU C-634/16 P of 24.1.2018 – EUIPO/European Food, para. 42.

that stage of the proceedings and demonstrate that submission during the proceedings before the Cancellation Division was impossible.[287]

Finally, the evidence submitted for the first time before the Board of Appeal may be delivered to it on its request, as measures of enquiry and within the time limits imposed on the parties.[288]

Although the first subparagraph of Rule 50(1) CTMIR lays down the principle that the provisions relating to proceedings before the department which has made the decision against which the appeal is brought are to be applicable to appeal proceedings *mutatis mutandis*, the third subparagraph of Rule 50(1) constitutes a special rule derogating from that principle. That special rule is specific to the appeal proceedings brought against the **Opposition Division's decision** and specifies the rules, before the Board of Appeal, governing the facts and evidence submitted after the expiry of the time limits set or specified at first instance.[289]

The third subparagraph of Rule 50(1) CTMIR must therefore be applied, at this particular stage of the appeal proceedings against the Opposition Division's decision, in place of the provisions relating to the proceedings before that division, which include Rule 20(1) CTMIR.[290]

It must be emphasized here that that special rule was introduced in the Implementing Regulation when it was amended by Regulation No. 1041/2005, which, according to recital 7 thereof, seeks to specify clearly the legal consequences of procedural deficiencies in the opposition proceedings. That statement confirms that the consequences, before the Board of Appeal, of the delay in the submission of evidence before the Opposition Division must be determined on the basis of that rule.[291]

Under the third subparagraph of Rule 50(1) CTMIR, where the appeal is directed against a decision of an Opposition Division, the Board of Appeal must limit its examination of the appeal to facts and evidence presented within the time limits set in or specified by the Opposition Division, unless the Board considers that additional or supplementary facts and evidence must be taken into account pursuant to Article 74(2) CTMR.[292]

The CTMIR therefore expressly provides that the Board of Appeal enjoys, when examining an appeal directed against a decision of the Opposition Division, the discretion deriving from Rule 50(1)(3) CTMIR and from Article 74(2) CTMR to decide whether or not to take into account additional or supplementary facts and evidence

287. CJEU C-634/16 P of 24.1.2018 – EUIPO/European Food, para. 43.
288. CJEU C-634/16 P of 24.1.2018 – EUIPO/European Food, para. 44.
289. CJEU C-120/12 P of 3.10.2013 – Rintisch/OHIM, para. 28; C-121/12 P of 3.10.2013 – Rintisch/OHIM, para. 29; C-122/12 P of 3.10.2013 – Rintisch/OHIM, para. 29; CJEU C-634/16 P of 24.1.2018 – EUIPO/European Food, para. 48.
290. CJEU C-120/12 P of 3.10.2013 – Rintisch/OHIM, para. 29; C-121/12 P of 3.10.2013 – Rintisch/OHIM, para. 30; C-122/12 P of 3.10.2013 – Rintisch/OHIM, para. 30.
291. CJEU C-120/12 P of 3.10.2013 – Rintisch/OHIM, para. 30; C-121/12 P of 3.10.2013 – Rintisch/OHIM, para. 31; C-122/12 P of 3.10.2013 – Rintisch/OHIM, para. 31.
292. CJEU C-120/12 P of 3.10.2013 – Rintisch/OHIM, para. 31; C-121/12 P of 3.10.2013 – Rintisch/OHIM, para. 32; C-122/12 P of 3.10.2013 – Rintisch/OHIM, para. 32.

which were not presented within the time limits set or specified by the Opposition Division.[293]

Consequently, in finding that Rule 20(1) CTMIR constituted a provision to the contrary which prevented evidence submitted late to OHIM by the appellant from being taken into account by the Board of Appeal, with the result that the Board of Appeal did not have any discretion under Article 74(2) CTMR for the purposes of taking into account that evidence, the General Court committed an error of law which vitiates its judgment.[294]

As regards the submission of evidence of genuine use of the mark in the context of revocation proceedings brought on the basis of Article 51(1)(a) CTMR, it should be noted, first of all, that that regulation does not contain any provisions specifying the time period in which such evidence must be adduced.[295]

By contrast, Rule 40(5) CTMIR provides in that regard that OHIM is to invite the proprietor of the Community trade mark to furnish proof of genuine use of the mark within such period as it may specify.[296]

Next, it should be borne in mind that Rule 40(5) CTMIR further states, in the second sentence, that if the proof of use of the mark is not provided within the time limit set by OHIM, it is to be revoked.[297]

In that regard, although it does follow from the wording of that provision that where no proof of the use of the mark in question is produced within the time period set by OHIM, it must, as a rule, revoke the mark of its own motion, this is not required where evidence of that use is produced within that time.[298]

In that case, unless it emerges that that evidence is entirely irrelevant for the purpose of establishing genuine use of the mark, the proceedings must take their course. OHIM must, *inter alia*, as provided for by Article 57(1) CTMR, invite the parties, as often as necessary, to file observations on communications from the other parties or issued by OHIM itself. Should those proceedings subsequently lead to revocation of the mark, it will not be as a result of the application of Rule 40(5) CTMIR, which is an essentially procedural provision, but solely of the application of the substantive provisions in Articles 51(1) and 57 CTMR.[299]

293. CJEU C-120/12 P of 3.10.2013 – Rintisch/OHIM, para. 32; C-121/12 P of 3.10.2013 – Rintisch/OHIM, para. 33; C-122/12 P of 3.10.2013 – Rintisch/OHIM, para. 33; C-418/16 P of 28.2.2018 – mobile.de/EUIPO, para. 60; C-85/16 P and C-86/16 P of 30.5.2018 – Kenzo Tsujimoto/EUIPO, para. 44.
294. CJEU C-120/12 P of 3.10.2013 – Rintisch/OHIM, para. 33; C-121/12 P of 3.10.2013 – Rintisch/OHIM, para. 34; C-122/12 P of 3.10.2013 – Rintisch/OHIM, para. 34.
295. CJEU C-621/11 P of 18.7.2013 – New Yorker SHK Jeans/OHIM, para. 24; C-610/11 P of 26.9.2013 – Centrotherm Systemtechnik/OHIM, para. 79; C-597/14 P of 21.7.2016 – EUIPO/Grau Ferrer, para. 26; C-71/16 P of 4.5.2017 – Comercializadora Eloro/EUIPO, para. 57.
296. CJEU C-621/11 P of 18.7.2013 – New Yorker SHK Jeans/OHIM, para. 25; C-610/11 P of 26.9.2013 – Centrotherm Systemtechnik/OHIM, para. 80; C-71/16 P of 4.5.2017 – Comercializadora Eloro/EUIPO, para. 57.
297. CJEU C-621/11 P of 18.7.2013 – New Yorker SHK Jeans/OHIM, para. 27; C-610/11 P of 26.9.2013 – Centrotherm Systemtechnik/OHIM, para. 82.
298. CJEU C-621/11 P of 18.7.2013 – New Yorker SHK Jeans/OHIM, para. 28; C-610/11 P of 26.9.2013 – Centrotherm Systemtechnik/OHIM, para. 86.
299. CJEU C-621/11 P of 18.7.2013 – New Yorker SHK Jeans/OHIM, para. 29; C-610/11 P of 26.9.2013 – Centrotherm Systemtechnik/OHIM, para. 87; C-418/16 P of 28.2.2018 – mobile.de/EUIPO, para. 54.

It follows *inter alia* from the foregoing that it remains **possible to submit evidence of use** of the mark in addition to the evidence adduced within the time period set by OHIM under Rule 40(5) CTMIR after expiry of that time limit and that OHIM is in no way prohibited from taking account of additional evidence which is submitted after that time.[300]

Article 76(2) CTMR should be interpreted in the same way in relation to **proof of the existence, validity and scope of protection of a trade mark** since that provision contains a rule which applies horizontally within the scheme of that regulation, inasmuch as it applies irrespective of the nature of the proceedings concerned. It follows that Rule 50 CTMIR cannot be interpreted as meaning that it extends the discretion of the Boards of Appeal to new evidence.[301]

There may be revocation under that provision only when **no proof of the use** of the mark at issue is produced **within the time period** set by OHIM, or it emerges that that evidence is entirely irrelevant for the purpose of establishing genuine use of the mark.[302]

As regards the submission of proof of genuine use of the earlier mark pursuant to Article 57(2) or (3) CTMR, in the context, as in the present case, of **invalidity proceedings** brought on the basis of Article 53(1)(a) CTMR, Rule 40(6) CTMIR provides that EUIPO is to invite the proprietor of the earlier mark to prove the use of that mark during a period which it is to specify.[303]

In that regard, the first subparagraph of Rule 50(1)(1) CTMIR provides that, unless otherwise provided, the provisions relating to proceedings before the department which made the contested decision are to be applicable to appeal proceedings *mutatis mutandis*.[304]

[22] Intervention

Article 134(1) and (2) of the Rules of Procedure of the **General Court** provides that the parties to the proceedings before the Board of Appeal other than the applicant may participate, as interveners, in the proceedings before the General Court and may, in that capacity, apply for a form of order and put forward pleas in law independently of those applied for and put forward by the main parties. Article 134(3) of the Rules of Procedure adds, in that regard, that such an intervener may, in his response, seek an

300. CJEU C-621/11 P of 18.7.2013 – New Yorker SHK Jeans/OHIM, para. 30; C-610/11 P of 26.9.2013 – Centrotherm Systemtechnik/OHIM, para. 88; C-611/15 P of 16.6.2016 – L'Oréal/ EUIPO, para. 25 and 27; C-597/14 P of 21.7.2016 – EUIPO/Grau Ferrer, para. 26; C-71/16 P of 4.5.2017 – Comercializadora Eloro/EUIPO, para. 58; C-478/16 P of 19.4.2018 – EUIPO/Group, para. 37; C-564/16 P of 28.6.2018 – EUIPO/Puma, para. 91; C-418/16 P of 28.2.2018 – mobile.de/EUIPO, paras 53 and 55 et seq.
301. CJEU C-597/14 P of 21.7.2016 – EUIPO/Grau Ferrer, para. 27, *see also* CJEU C-478/16 P of 19.4.2018 – EUIPO/Group, para. 37; C-418/16 P of 28.2.2018 – mobile.de/EUIPO, para. 61.
302. CJEU C-610/11 P of 26.9.2013 – Centrotherm Systemtechnik/OHIM, para. 98.
303. CJEU C-418/16 P of 28.2.2018 – mobile.de/EUIPO, para. 52.
304. CJEU C-418/16 P of 28.2.2018 – mobile.de/EUIPO, para. 51.

order annulling or altering the decision of the Board of Appeal on a point not raised in the application and put forward pleas in law not raised in the application.[305]

It follows from the foregoing that, in its capacity as intervener in the proceedings for partial annulment of the contested decision brought by the claimant before the General Court, the intervener could have applied for annulment or alteration of that decision.[306]

Yet the very wording of Article 134(2) and (3) of the Rules of Procedure of the General Court makes it clear that an intervener may put forward, in its statement in response, independent 'forms of order' seeking annulment or alteration of the contested decision. It follows that, in principle, what an intervener intends to seek on the basis of that provision must be clear from the forms of order sought in its statement in response.[307]

It follows from the wording of Article 134(1) of the Rules of Procedure of the General Court that, in order to be considered an intervener before the General Court, a party to the proceedings before the Board of Appeal of OHIM other than the applicant before the General Court **must have responded to the application** in the manner and within the period prescribed.[308]

Pursuant to Article 135(1) of the Rules of Procedure of the General Court, OHIM and the parties to the proceedings before the Board of Appeal other than the applicant are to lodge their responses to the application within a period of two months from the service of the application.[309]

In the present case, it is undisputed that Enercon did not submit a response to the application before the General Court, although that application was served on it, and that it merely sent the General Court the power of attorney given to its lawyer and a letter accepting the language of the case. It cannot therefore be regarded as having responded to the application in the manner and within the period prescribed. Moreover, in the judgment of the General Court, it is referred to only as 'the other party to the proceedings before the Board of Appeal of OHIM'.[310]

It must therefore be held that Enercon did not participate in the proceedings before the General Court within the meaning of Article 134(1) of the Rules of Procedure of the General Court, particularly since it neither proposed its own form of order nor stated that it was supporting the form of order sought by either of the other parties. Accordingly, it was not an intervener in the proceedings before the General Court and cannot, therefore, bring an appeal against the judgment of the General Court under the second paragraph of Article 56 of the Statute of the Court of Justice. In that respect, it must be emphasized that an exchange of correspondence between the services of the

305. CJEU C-609/11 P of 26.9.2013 – Centrotherm Systemtechnik/OHIM, para. 38.
306. CJEU C-609/11 P of 26.9.2013 – Centrotherm Systemtechnik/OHIM, para. 39.
307. CJEU C-609/11 P of 26.9.2013 – Centrotherm Systemtechnik/OHIM, para. 43.
308. CJEU C-35/14 P of 12.2.2015 – Enercon/OHIM, para. 22; C-206/15 P of 24.11.2015 – Sun Mark and Bulldog Energy Drink/HABM, para. 30.
309. CJEU C-35/14 P of 12.2.2015 – Enercon/OHIM, para. 23; C-206/15 P of 24.11.2015 – Sun Mark and Bulldog Energy Drink/HABM, para. 31.
310. CJEU C-35/14 P of 12.2.2015 – Enercon/OHIM, para. 24; *see also* CJEU C-206/15 P of 24.11.2015 – Sun Mark and Bulldog Energy Drink/HABM, paras 32 et seq.

Court and an applicant cannot in any way prejudge the admissibility of the action brought by it.[311]

According to Articles 93 and 123 of the Rules of Procedure of the **Court of Justice**, the application to intervene must be made on the basis of the second paragraph of Article 40 of the Statute of the Court of Justice.[312]

According to the latter provision, anyone who is able to **establish an interest** in the result of any case submitted to the Court has the right to intervene in that case. Pursuant to the fourth paragraph of Article 40 of the Statute of the Court of Justice, the application to intervene shall be limited to supporting the form of order sought by one of the parties.[313]

The concept of an 'interest in the result of a case', within the meaning of that provision, must be defined in the light of the precise subject matter of the dispute and be understood as meaning a direct, existing interest in the ruling on the forms of order sought, and not as an interest in relation to the pleas in law or arguments raised. The words 'result of a case' refer to the final decision sought, as set out in the operative part of the future judgment.[314]

In that regard, it must, in particular, be ascertained whether the applicant for leave to intervene is directly affected by the contested measure and whether its interest in the result of the case is established. In principle, an interest in the result of the case can be considered to be sufficiently direct only to the extent to which that result is likely to alter the legal position of the person seeking leave to intervene.[315]

In accordance with that latter provision, the right to intervene in a case before the Court is open to any person establishing an interest in the result of the case. In particular, the Court allows intervention by **representative associations** whose object is to protect their members in cases raising questions of principle liable to affect those members.[316]

INTA has established an interest in intervening in the present case in support of the form of order sought by the applicant.[317]

It must be noted in that regard that INTA is a not-for-profit association of more than six thousand undertakings in all the Member States and worldwide. Further, it is apparent from its statutes that the object of INTA – which has, *inter alia*, observer status at the World Intellectual Property Organization (WIPO) and with the Administrative Board of OHIM – is, in particular, to promote the interests of its members in the uses of their trade marks.[318]

---

311. CJEU C-35/14 P of 12.2.2015 – Enercon/OHIM, para. 25; *see also* CJEU C-206/15 P of 24.11.2015 – Sun Mark and Bulldog Energy Drink/HABM, para. 34.
312. CJEU C-301/05 P of 9.2.2007 – Wilfer/OHIM, para. 4; unofficial translation.
313. CJEU C-301/05 P of 9.2.2007 – Wilfer/OHIM, para. 5; unofficial translation.
314. CJEU C-301/05 P of 9.2.2007 – Wilfer/OHIM, para. 6; C-337/22 P of 27.4.2023 – EUIPO a.o./Nowhere, para. 7.
315. CJEU C-337/22 P of 27.4.2023 – EUIPO a.o./Nowhere, para. 8.
316. CJEU C-151/98 P of 28.9.1998 – Pharos/Commission, para. 6; C-445/13 P of 25.3.2014 – Voss of Norway/OHIM, para. 7; C-337/22 P of 27.4.2023 – EUIPO a.o./Nowhere, para. 9.
317. CJEU C-445/13 P of 25.3.2014 – Voss of Norway/OHIM, para. 11; C-337/22 P of 27.4.2023 – EUIPO a.o./Nowhere, para. 21.
318. CJEU C-445/13 P of 25.3.2014 – Voss of Norway/OHIM, para. 8; C-337/22 P of 27.4.2023 – EUIPO a.o./Nowhere, para. 13.

It must also be noted that some of the questions raised in the present case may be considered to be questions of principle concerning the assessment of the validity of three-dimensional marks, and thus liable to affect the interests of INTA's members who are proprietors of such Community trade marks.[319]

At issue, first, is the question of to what extent there is a presumption of validity in respect of a registered Community trade mark, so that the burden of proof as to the lack of distinctive character of that trade mark falls on the person contesting validity, and, secondly, the definition of the 'norms or customs of the relevant sector' in the context of the assessment of the distinctive character of a three-dimensional sign.[320]

The **Austrian Association of Patent Attorneys**, however, founds its application to intervene on the assertion that the case at hand raises a fundamental question that could harm the interests of its members, the Austrian patent attorneys. The Austrian Association of Patent Attorneys claims that it has the duty to protect said members. In particular, it alleges that Article 19 of the Statute of the Court of Justice creates a right for it to represent its members before the Community Courts.[321]

Thus, the Austrian Association of Patent Attorneys submits that it has an interest in respect of the first ground of appeal. With the ground of appeal in question, it is submitted that the Court misinterpreted Article 19 of the Statute of the Court when it declared that Mr Zech as a German patent attorney could not represent Mr Wilfer together with the latter's attorney. This interest in a ground of appeal, however, cannot be put on a level with an interest in the success of the first plea of the applicant, namely that number one of the tenor of the judgment appealed against be overturned. That part of the judgment rejected the application he made in the first instance to overturn the decision of the First Board of Appeal of the OHIM on the rejection of the registration of the Community Trade Mark 'Rockbass'.[322]

Under these circumstances, the application to intervene must be rejected.[323]

[23] Notifications

Rule 61 of Regulation No. 2868/95, headed 'General provisions on notifications', gives an exhaustive list of the means by which OHIM is to notify, *inter alia*, its decisions. Thus, paragraph 2 of that rule states that notifications are to be made by post, by hand delivery, by deposit in a post box at OHIM, by telecopier or other technical means or by public notification.[324]

In addition, where notification is by post, Rule 62(1) of that regulation provides that decisions subject to a time limit for appeal, such as the disputed decision, are to be notified by registered letter with advice of delivery.[325]

319. CJEU C-445/13 P of 25.3.2014 – Voss of Norway/OHIM, para. 9.
320. CJEU C-445/13 P of 25.3.2014 – Voss of Norway/OHIM, para. 10.
321. CJEU C-301/05 P of 9.2.2007 – Wilfer/OHIM, para. 7; unofficial translation.
322. CJEU C-301/05 P of 11.10.2007 – Wilfer/OHIM, para. 8; unofficial translation.
323. CJEU C-301/05 P of 11.10.2007 – Wilfer/OHIM, para. 9; unofficial translation.
324. CJEU C-144/07 P of 2.10.2008 – K-Swiss/OHIM, para. 19.
325. CJEU C-144/07 P of 2.10.2008 – K-Swiss/OHIM, para. 20.

However, where OHIM is unable to prove that a document has been duly notified, or if provisions relating to its notification have not been observed, but that document has reached the addressee, it follows from Rule 68 of Regulation No. 2868/95 that OHIM may produce proof of the date of receipt and that the document is deemed to have been notified on that date.[326]

The existence of valid notice is in no way subject to effective knowledge actually being acquired by the person who, according to the internal rules of the undertaking to which the decision is addressed, is competent to deal with the matter and that a decision is duly notified once it has been communicated to the person to whom it is addressed and the latter is in a position to take cognizance of it.[327]

[24] Representatives

It is apparent from Rule 76(1)–(3) CTMIR, headed 'Authorisations', that the authorization of the representative of a trade mark proprietor before OHIM covers all procedural steps relating to trade marks, including the procedural steps relating to the renewal of registration of a Community trade mark.[328]

Pursuant to Rule 77 CTMIR, headed 'Representation', any notification or other communication addressed by OHIM to a duly authorized representative is to have the same effect as if it had been addressed to the represented person. The same is true of any communication addressed to OHIM by the duly authorized representative, which is to have the same effect as if it originated from the represented person.[329]

It must be pointed out that Rule 77 CTMIR does not lay down any distinction between a notification or communication which has the effect of causing a period to start to run and one which does not have such an effect, with the result that that rule applies irrespective of the effect produced by that notification or communication.[330]

It therefore follows from the rules of representation in the context of the CTMR that what matters with regard to OHIM are the communications and notifications exchanged between it and the representative of the proprietor of the trade mark in question and not those exchanged between the representative of the proprietor of that mark and that proprietor.[331]

Rule 76(6) CTMIR provides that any representative who has ceased to be authorized is to continue to be regarded as the representative until the termination of his authorization has been communicated to OHIM.[332]

Where the proprietor of a Community trade mark expressly appoints a third party to carry out the procedural requirements for renewal of registration of that mark, pursuant to Article 47 CTMR, that third party does not have capacity, under the scheme

326. CJEU C-144/07 P of 2.10.2008 – K-Swiss/OHIM, para. 23.
327. CJEU C-36/19 P of 4.7.2019 – Daico International/EUIPO, para. 5/9 and 6.
328. CJEU C-479/09 P of 30.9.2010 – Evets/OHIM, para. 38.
329. CJEU C-479/09 P of 30.9.2010 – Evets/OHIM, paras 39 and 45.
330. CJEU C-479/09 P of 30.9.2010 – Evets/OHIM, para. 40.
331. CJEU C-479/09 P of 30.9.2010 – Evets/OHIM, para. 41.
332. CJEU C-479/09 P of 30.9.2010 – Evets/OHIM, para. 46.

established by that regulation, to receive a notification or communication from OHIM unless he has also been appointed as a representative before OHIM.[333]

What is more, in a situation where that third party is appointed as a representative before OHIM, it is apparent from Rule 67(2) CTMR that if several representatives have been appointed for a single interested party, notification to any one of them is to be sufficient.[334]

[25] Decisions as subject of appeal

The EU legislature has provided, first, **two separate stages in the opposition proceedings and**, second, **mechanisms to** enable the defendant in the opposition proceedings to **contest** the decision by which OHIM incorrectly finds the opposition admissible.[335]

First, it is apparent from Title II of the CTMIR that proceedings to oppose registration of a trade mark comprise **two separate stages**. Rule 17 CTMIR sets out the conditions under which the opposition may be regarded as admissible and states, at paragraph 5 of that rule, that the decision which establishes that the opposition is deemed not to have been entered or that it must be declared inadmissible is to be notified to the applicant. It follows that the stage at which admissibility is examined may lead to the adoption of a decision terminating the proceedings, which, as such, is subject to appeal, pursuant to Article 57(1) CTMR.[336]

Moreover, Rule 18(1) CTMIR states that '[w]hen the opposition is found admissible pursuant to Rule 17, [OHIM] shall send a communication to the parties informing them that the opposition proceedings shall be deemed to commence two months after receipt of the communication'. It is apparent from the very wording of Rule 18 that the opposition proceedings themselves, that is, the *inter partes* stage, commence only when OHIM has verified that the opposition is admissible and that none of the grounds set out in Rule 17 precludes admissibility.[337]

The use of the words 'jugée recevable' (found admissible) in the French version of the Implementing Regulation indicates that the EU legislature intended that OHIM should examine, at that stage in the proceedings, whether the opposition is admissible and satisfy itself that the opposition fee has been duly paid.[338]

The other language versions of the Implementing Regulation use the words 'se considere admisible' in Spanish, 'gilt' in German, 'found admissible' in English and 'considerata ammissibile' in Italian. The examination of those different versions – with the exception of the German version, in which the word 'gilt' does not have the same force as the words used in the other language versions – shows that the opposition must be found admissible before the *inter partes* proceedings can commence.[339]

333. CJEU C-479/09 P of 30.9.2010 – Evets/OHIM, para. 47.
334. CJEU C-479/09 P of 30.9.2010 – Evets/OHIM, para. 48.
335. CJEU C-402/11 P of 18.10.2012 – Jager & Polacek/OHIM, para. 69.
336. CJEU C-402/11 P of 18.10.2012 – Jager & Polacek/OHIM, para. 48.
337. CJEU C-402/11 P of 18.10.2012 – Jager & Polacek/OHIM, para. 49.
338. CJEU C-402/11 P of 18.10.2012 – Jager & Polacek/OHIM, para. 50.
339. CJEU C-402/11 P of 18.10.2012 – Jager & Polacek/OHIM, para. 51.

Lastly, it follows from Article 57(2) CTMR that there may be measures which, while they are adopted in the course of the proceedings and do not terminate them, nevertheless constitute decisions.[340]

The **rights of the defendant** in the opposition proceedings are ensured protection by the withdrawal mechanism provided for in Article 77a CTMR and the appeal mechanism in Article 57 CTMR.[341]

First, the opposing party has no interest in bringing an action against a measure by which OHIM finds its opposition admissible.[342]

Second, if OHIM errs in its assessment of the admissibility of the opposition by declaring, incorrectly, that it is admissible and thus initiates the *inter partes* proceedings, the defendant in the opposition proceedings is not deprived of the opportunity to assert its rights.[343]

The defendant in the opposition proceedings may, first of all, submit to OHIM that an error has been made concerning the admissibility of the opposition and request that it withdraw the decision by which it found the opposition to be admissible, on the basis of Article 77a CTMR.[344]

On that point, it is apparent from the Court's case law that, in principle, the withdrawal of an unlawful measure is permissible, even though the principles of legal certainty and the protection of legitimate expectations require that the withdrawal should occur within a reasonable time and that regard be had to how far the person concerned might have been led to rely on the lawfulness of the measure.[345]

As regards OHIM, the EU legislature has regulated the procedure for the withdrawal of unlawful measures adopted by that body. In that regard, Article 77a(1) CTMR states that where OHIM has taken a decision which contains an obvious procedural error attributable to it, it is to ensure that the decision is revoked.[346]

Article 77a(2) CTMR provides that revocation of the incorrect decision may be determined, ex officio or at the request of one of the parties, and must be effected within six months from the date on which the decision was taken, after consultation with, *inter alia*, the parties to the proceedings. It is therefore apparent that the withdrawal procedure may be initiated by the defendant in the opposition proceedings.[347]

Lastly, Article 77a(3) CTMR provides that the revocation procedure is without prejudice to the rights of the parties to submit an appeal under, *inter alia*, Article 57 CTMR.[348]

Second, it is open to the defendant in the opposition proceedings to **seek annulment** of the measure finding the opposition admissible. Such an application for

340. CJEU C-402/11 P of 18.10.2012 – Jager & Polacek/OHIM, para. 52.
341. CJEU C-402/11 P of 18.10.2012 – Jager & Polacek/OHIM, para. 68.
342. CJEU C-402/11 P of 18.10.2012 – Jager & Polacek/OHIM, para. 56.
343. CJEU C-402/11 P of 18.10.2012 – Jager & Polacek/OHIM, para. 57.
344. CJEU C-402/11 P of 18.10.2012 – Jager & Polacek/OHIM, para. 58.
345. CJEU C-402/11 P of 18.10.2012 – Jager & Polacek/OHIM, para. 59; *see also* CJEU C-508/03 of 4.5.2006 – Commission/United Kingdom, para. 68.
346. CJEU C-402/11 P of 18.10.2012 – Jager & Polacek/OHIM, para. 60.
347. CJEU C-402/11 P of 18.10.2012 – Jager & Polacek/OHIM, para. 61.
348. CJEU C-402/11 P of 18.10.2012 – Jager & Polacek/OHIM, para. 62.

annulment may be made in the appeal against the decision adopted at the conclusion of the *inter partes* proceedings. In so far as that measure does not terminate the proceedings, it can be appealed together with the final decision on the substance of the opposition, in accordance with Article 57(2) CTMR.[349]

It is apparent from the examination of all those provisions that, where OHIM finds that the opposition is admissible, the *inter partes* stage of the proceedings commences. For a period of six months, where the decision by which opposition was found to be admissible contains an obvious procedural error, it may be withdrawn ex officio or at the request of one of the parties, which has the effect of terminating the opposition proceedings. Once that period has expired, the *inter partes* stage of the proceedings must be pursued and a decision must be given.[350]

In the latter instance, the defendant to the opposition proceedings may bring an appeal before the Board of Appeal and argue that the opposition was inadmissible.[351]

The Court has already held that it follows from Article 62(1) CTMR that, following the examination as to the merits of the appeal, the Board of Appeal is to decide on it and that, in doing so, it may 'exercise any power within the competence of the department which was responsible for the contested decision', that is to say, in the present case, give a decision itself on the opposition by either rejecting it or declaring it to be founded, thereby either upholding or reversing the contested decision.[352]

Those powers on the part of the Board of Appeal also include the power to review the admissibility of the opposition in order to enable the defendant in the opposition proceedings, where appropriate, to challenge the finding of admissibility in the appeal which is available to it under Article 57(2) CTMR.[353]

OHIM cannot seek the annulment or alteration of the Board of Appeal's decision on a point not raised in the application initiating proceedings.[354]

However, in accordance with Article 176 of the Rules of Procedure of the Court of Justice, OHIM may bring a cross-appeal before the Court of Justice. Under Article 178(1) of those Rules, that cross-appeal must seek to have set aside, in whole or in part, the decision of the General Court.[355]

[26] Appeal and deadlines

Regarding the notion of 'submission', according to the text of Article 59 CTMR, an appeal must be made in writing to OHIM. The presentation of a brief exposing the motifs of the appeal constitutes a precondition for the admissibility of the appeal.[356]

349. CJEU C-402/11 P of 18.10.2012 – Jager & Polacek/OHIM, para. 63.
350. CJEU C-402/11 P of 18.10.2012 – Jager & Polacek/OHIM, para. 64.
351. CJEU C-402/11 P of 18.10.2012 – Jager & Polacek/OHIM, para. 65.
352. CJEU C-402/11 P of 18.10.2012 – Jager & Polacek/OHIM, para. 66.
353. CJEU C-402/11 P of 18.10.2012 – Jager & Polacek/OHIM, para. 67.
354. CJEU C-106/03 P of 12.10.2004 – VEDIAL/OHIM, para. 34; C-97/12 P of 15.5.2014 – Louis Vuitton Malletier/OHIM, para. 81.
355. CJEU C-97/12 P of 15.5.2014 – Louis Vuitton Malletier/OHIM, para. 82.
356. CJEU C-324/13 P of 30.1.2014 – Fercal – Consultadoria e Serviços/OHIM, para. 42; unofficial translation.

First of all it must be emphasized that the respective provisions of the CTMR clear up the question of the 'notification' of decisions and documents in the procedure before OHIM. Similarly, it can be deduced from logic and from the structure of the CTMR that the underlying principle is precisely the principle of the reception of such by the recipient. It can be deduced from the general economy of the respective regulations, as also from the text of the relevant provisions, that the principle of reception of the documents is that which governs the procedures before the OHIM.[357]

This conclusion is similarly confirmed by the text of section 2, B, of the decision of the Presidium, applicable in virtue of Article 1(6) of Regulation No. 216/96, as modified by Regulation No. 2082/2004,[358] which uses the expressions 'to communicate the act of appeal' and 'to present the writ exposing the grounds for appeal'. It is necessary to add that recital 9 of the aforementioned section clearly stipulates that it is recommended that the parties do not wait for the end of the prescribed period of four months in order to present the writ exposing the motifs of appeal, but to submit it at the beginning of the procedure.[359]

It can be deduced from Rule 62(3) CTMIR that when the notification has been effected by registered mail, with or without advice of delivery, this will be deemed to have been delivered to the recipient on the tenth day after sending by post, unless the document has not reached the recipient or has only reached the recipient on a later day. It thus follows that the date of sending is not the relevant date for determining the admissibility of the documents concerned. The relevant date is the tenth day after sending or, in the case of alternative reception, the date on which the letter has been received by the recipient.[360]

Concerning the method of determining the day on which the time limit began, it is necessary to remember that Rule 70(2) CTMIR provides that the time limit shall begin on the day following the date on which the relevant event took place. The same provision provides in its paragraph 4 that if a time limit has been set for one or several months, it expires in the month in consideration, on the day on which the event in question took place.[361]

First, it is necessary to emphasize that, in virtue of Article 59 CTMR, the prescribed period for the submission of the grounds of appeal is expressed in terms of months, namely four months counting from the date of notification of the decision. In accordance with Rule 70(4) CTMIR, the time limit expires on the same day of the respective month, as the day on which the event in question took place.[362]

357. CJEU C-324/13 P of 30.1.2014 – Fercal – Consultadoria e Serviços/OHIM, para. 43; unofficial translation.
358. Commission Regulation (EC) No. 2082/2004 of 6 Dec. 2004 amending Regulation (EC) No. 216/96 laying down the rules of procedure of the Boards of Appeal of the Office for Harmonization in the Internal Market (Trade Marks and Designs).
359. CJEU C-324/13 P of 30.1.2014 – Fercal – Consultadoria e Serviços/OHIM, para. 44; unofficial translation.
360. CJEU C-324/13 P of 30.1.2014 – Fercal – Consultadoria e Serviços/OHIM, para. 45; unofficial translation.
361. CJEU C-324/13 P of 30.1.2014 – Fercal – Consultadoria e Serviços/OHIM, para. 47; unofficial translation.
362. CJEU C-324/13 P of 30.1.2014 – Fercal – Consultadoria e Serviços/OHIM, para. 48; unofficial translation.

Finally, concerning the prescribed means of communication according to Rules 61–65 CTMIR, the interpretation made by the applicant is without particular relevance. Even if the parties were free to choose the means of communication, this does not mean that the time limits would be modified in conformity with their choice.[363]

Provisions 61(1) and 65 CTMIR, taken in conjunction, prescribe that the parties can use facsimiles and other means in order to communicate with OHIM. Copies of documents produced by the parties must not be certified. It therefore results that the parties dispose of several means of communication for transmitting documents to OHIM within the prescribed time limits and that they are repeatedly instructed of their obligation to submit these documents within these time limits.[364]

While a party may choose to submit their writ on the last day of a set time limit by means of a registered letter which will be deemed to have been received by the recipient by the tenth day after sending, and while the party is not obliged to use a means of communication which is faster, none the less their choice does not cause modification of the date of expiry of this period or of their obligation to communicate their writ within the same period.[365]

[27] Appeal to the General Court

Under Article 21 of the Statute of the Court of Justice of the European Union and Article 76(d) of the Rules of Procedure of the General Court, the application at first instance must contain a brief statement of the pleas in law on which the application is based. According to consistent case law, in order to guarantee legal certainty and the sound administration of justice, that summary of the applicant's pleas in law must be sufficiently clear and precise to enable the defendant to prepare its defence and the competent Court to rule on the action.[366]

Under Article 135(4) of the Rules of Procedure of the General Court, the parties' pleadings may not change the subject matter of the proceedings before the Board of Appeal. Moreover, according to the case law of the Court of Justice, the purpose of an action before the General Court is to review the lawfulness of decisions of the Boards of Appeal of OHIM within the meaning of Article 65(2) CTMR.[367]

The General Court can carry out a **full review of the legality of the decisions of OHIM's Boards of Appeal**, if necessary examining whether those boards have made a

363. CJEU C-324/13 P of 30.1.2014 – Fercal – Consultadoria e Serviços/OHIM, para. 50; unofficial translation.
364. CJEU C-324/13 P of 30.1.2014 – Fercal – Consultadoria e Serviços/OHIM, para. 51; unofficial translation.
365. CJEU C-324/13 P of 30.1.2014 – Fercal – Consultadoria e Serviços/OHIM, para. 52; unofficial translation.
366. CJEU C-728/18 P of 25.9.2019 – EM Research Organization/EUIPO, paras 4/8 and 5, with further proof.
367. CJEU C-414/14 P of 26.2.2015 – Fundação Calouste Gulbenkian/OHIM, para. 38; *see also* CJEU C-440/15 P of 3.3.2016 – AgriCapital/OHIM, paras 22 et seq.; C-471/16 P of 26.7.2017 – Staatliche Porzellan-Manufaktur Meissen/EUIPO, paras 24 et seq.; C-678/19 P of 20.11.2019 – Retail Royalty/EUIPO, para. 22.

correct legal classification of the facts of the dispute or whether their assessment of the facts submitted to them was flawed.[368]

It does not follow from the Court of First Instance's case law that it is required to ascertain whether, at the time it rules on an action against a decision of the OHIM Board of Appeal, it may lawfully adopt a new decision with the same operative part as the decision appealed against. The Court of First Instance merely stated that that obligation applies to the OHIM Boards of Appeal because of the principle of continuity, in terms of their functions, as between the OHIM adjudicating bodies deciding on the application at first instance - such as the examiners, the Opposition Division and the Cancellation Division - and those boards.[369]

Under Article 63 of the CTMR, the Court of First Instance may annul or alter a decision of an OHIM Board of Appeal only 'on grounds of lack of competence, infringement of an essential procedural requirement, infringement of the Treaty, of Regulation [CTMR] or of any rule of law relating to [its] application or misuse of power'.[370]

It follows that the Court of First Instance may annul or alter a decision against which an action has been brought only if, at the time the decision was adopted, it was vitiated by one of those grounds for annulment or alteration. The Court of First Instance may not, however, annul or alter that decision on **grounds which come into existence subsequent** to its adoption.[371]

The expiry of an earlier mark after the action had been brought before the General Court did not deprive the decision of the Board of Appeal of EUIPO of its purpose or of its effects. The assessment in that decision that there was a likelihood of confusion between the marks at issue therefore continued to produce its effects at the time the General Court delivered its judgment.[372]

By contrast, that Court cannot carry out such a review by taking into account matters of fact newly produced before it.[373]

However, the appellant had to be in a position to criticize those findings of the Board of Appeal [the assessment of the inherent distinctive character of the earlier mark on its own motion] before the General Court, as, under Article 263 TFEU, when read in the light of Article 47 of the Charter of Fundamental Rights of the European

368. CJEU C-16/06 P of 18.12.2008 - Les Éditions Albert René/OHIM, para. 39; C-418/10 P of 28.3.2011 - Herhof-Verwaltungsgesellschaft/OHIM, para. 48; C-396/15 P of 17.2.2016 - Shoe Branding Europe/OHIM, para. 41.
369. CJEU C-416/04 P of 11.5.2006 - Sunrider/OHIM, para. 53.
370. CJEU C-416/04 P of 11.5.2006 - Sunrider/OHIM, para. 54; C-214/05 P of 18.7.2006 - Rossi/OHIM, para. 50; C-412/05 P of 26.4.2007 - Alcon/OHIM (II), para. 44; *see also* CJEU C-29/05 P of 13.3.2007 - OHIM/Kaul, para. 54.
371. CJEU C-416/04 P of 11.5.2006 - Sunrider/OHIM, para. 55; C-29/05 P of 13.3.2007 - OHIM/Kaul, para. 53; C-482/15 P of 26.10.2016 - Westermann Lernspielverlage/EUIPO, para. 28; C-340/17 P of 29.11.2018 - Alcohol Countermeasure Systems/EUIPO, para. 116; *see also* CJEU C-795/18 P of 20.6.2019 - FCA US/EUIPO paras 9; C-449/18 P and C-474/18 P of 17.9.2020 - EUIPO/Messi Cuccittini, para. 71.
372. CJEU C-482/15 P of 26.10.2016 - Westermann Lernspielverlage/EUIPO, para. 29, with reference to CJEU C-268/12 P of 8.5.2013 - Cadila Healthcare/OHIM, para. 31-34.
373. CJEU C-29/05 P of 13.3.2007 - OHIM/Kaul, para. 54; C-412/05 P of 26.4.2007 - Alcon/OHIM (II), para. 38, 44.

Union, an applicant must be able to contest before the EU Courts each and every issue of fact and law on which an EU body bases its decisions.[374]

The line of argument which states that the conditions required for the earlier mark to be regarded as having been put to genuine use are not satisfied logically falls under the plea alleging that there is no evidence of such genuine use in respect of ophthalmic products. That line of argument, apart from being based on the infringement of the same provision of the CTMR as that submitted in the plea in question, seeks, like that plea, to dispute that the earlier mark was actually used in the course of trade. Consequently, it may be regarded as amplifying that plea and must be held to be admissible.[375]

It follows from Article 74(1) CTMR that, in proceedings relating to refusal of registration, such as those in this case, OHIM is restricted in its examination to the facts, evidence and arguments provided by the parties and the relief sought.[376]

Since OHIM could not take into account facts which were not put forward before it by the parties, the lawfulness of its decisions cannot be challenged on the basis of such facts. It follows that the Court of First Instance, likewise, cannot take account of evidence intended to prove those facts.[377]

Evidence which has never been produced before OHIM has not, in any event, been produced in due time and cannot be used as a criterion with which to assess the legality of the decision of the Board of Appeal.[378]

For the purposes of examining the distinctive character of a trade mark, the bodies of the EUIPO may base their decisions on **well-known facts**. In such circumstances, the EUIPO bodies do not have to establish, in their decisions, the accuracy of such facts. However, an applicant who is confronted with well-known facts by the EUIPO may challenge their correctness before the Court of First Instance, which must then examine the fact and its correctness. Finally, for the purposes of that examination, the EUIPO may put forward arguments and submit evidence in order to demonstrate the accuracy of the alleged well-known facts.[379]

By recognizing the right of an applicant against whom the EUIPO relies on such facts to challenge their accuracy before the Court of First Instance and the right of the EUIPO to submit arguments and evidence in order to establish the accuracy of those facts, the Court of Justice has made it clear that the EUIPO is not entitled to challenge the accuracy of the facts before the Court of First Instance.[380]

---

374. CJEU C-702/18 P of 18.6.2020 – Przedsiębiorstwo Produkcyjno-Handlowe 'Primart' Marek Łukasiewicz/EUIPO, para. 46.
375. CJEU C-412/05 P of 26.4.2007 – Alcon/OHIM (II), para. 40.
376. CJEU C-214/05 P of 18.7.2006 – Rossi/OHIM, para. 51.
377. CJEU C-214/05 P of 18.7.2006 – Rossi/OHIM, para. 52; C-414/14 P of 26.2.2015 – Fundação Calouste Gulbenkian, para. 38.
378. CJEU C-16/06 P of 18.12.2008 – Les Éditions Albert René/OHIM, para. 143; *see also* CJEU C-351/16 P of 10.11.2016 – 100 % Capri Italia/EUIPO, paras 8/5 and 9; C-433/17 P of 25.10.2018 – Enercon/EUIPO, para. 35.
379. CJEU C-461/19 P of 30.9.2019 – All Star/EUIPO, para. 18 (unofficial translation), with reference to CJEU C-88/11 P of 10.11.2011 – LG Electronics/OHIM, para. 27-31; *see also* CJEU C-162/17 P of 16.1.2019 – Republic of Poland/EUIPO, para. 69.
380. CJEU C-461/19 P of 30.9.2019 – All Star/EUIPO, para. 19.

[28] Appeal to the CJEU

It should be noted at the outset that, in the field of Community marks, the **CJEU's jurisdiction** is provided for by Article 65 CTMR.[381]

Under Article 225 EC, the first paragraph of Article 58 of the Statute of the Court of Justice and Article 112(1)(c) of the Rules of Procedure of the Court of Justice, an **appeal must indicate precisely the contested elements** of the judgment which the appellant seeks to have set aside and also the legal arguments specifically advanced in support of the appeal.[382]

381. CJEU C-396/15 P of 17.2.2016 – Shoe Branding Europe/OHIM, para. 65.
382. CJEU C-286/04 P of 30.6.2005 – Eurocermex/OHIM, paras 42, 49, 50; C-25/05 P of 22.6.2006 – Storck/OHIM (gold-coloured sweet wrapper), para. 47; C-325/06 P of 20.3.2007 – Galileo International Technology and Others/Commission, para. 36; C-234/06 P of 13.9.2007 – Il Ponte Finanziaria/OHIM, para. 44; C-488/08 P and C-489/08 P of 4.12.2009 – Rath/OHIM, para. 44; C-23/09 P of 22.1.2010 – ecoblue/OHIM, para. 41; C-559/08 P of 16.9.2010 – Deepak Rajani/OHIM, paras 40 et seq.; C-22/10 P of 27.10.2010 – Rewe-Zentral/OHIM, para. 36; C-316/11 P of 21.9.2011 – Longevity Health Products/OHIM, para. 16; C-378/11 P of 21.9.2011 – Longevity Health Products/OHIM, para. 16; C-222/11 P of 1.12.2011 – Longevity Health Products/OHIM, para. 24; C-21/12 P of 17.1.2013 – Abbott Laboratories/OHIM, paras 84 et seq.; C-120/12 P of 3.10.2013 – Rintisch/OHIM, para. 49; C-121/12 P of 3.10.2013 – Rintisch/OHIM, para. 50; C-122/12 P of 3.10.2013 – Rintisch/OHIM, para. 50; C-422/12 P of 30.1.2014 – Industrias Alen/OHIM, para. 39; C-324/13 P of 30.1.2014 – Fercal – Consultadoria e Serviços/OHIM, para. 36; C-412/13 P of 10.4.2014 – Franz Wilhelm Langguth Erben/OHIM, para. 50; C-43/15 P of 8.11.2016 – BSH Bosch und Siemens Hausgeräte/EUIPO, para. 51; *see also* CJEU C-388/10 P of 24.3.2011 – Muñoz Arraiza/OHIM, para. 74; C-532/10 P of 29.6.2011 – adp Gauselmann/OHIM, paras 37 et seq.; C-87/11 P of 21.3.2012 – Fidelio/OHIM, para. 47; C-624/11 P of 27.9.2012 – Brighton Collectibles/OHIM, para. 34; C-611/11 P of 10.10.2012 – ara/OHIM, para. 46; C-42/12 P of 29.11.2012 – Hrbek/OHIM, para. 53; C-266/12 P of 7.2.2013 – Majczak/OHIM, para. 24; C-341/12 P of 21.3.2013 – Mizuno/OHIM, para. 27; C-381/12 P of 6.6.2013 – I Marchi Italiani/OHIM, paras 46 and 60; C-70/13 P of 12.12.2013 – Getty Images (US)/OHIM, para. 21; C-159/13 P of 12.12.2013 – Fercal – Consultadoria e Serviços/OHIM, para. 20; C-177/13 P of 13.2.2014 – Marszałkowski/OHIM, para. 64; C-608/12 P of 8.5.2014 – Greinwald/HABM, paras 26 and 31; C-374/13 P of 10.4.2014 – Metropolis Inmobiliarias y Restauraciones/OHIM, paras 50 and 51; C-521/13 P of 11.9.2014 – Think Schuhwerk/OHIM, paras 27 and 28; C-320/14 P of 13.1.2015 – Asos/OHIM, paras 25 and 26; C-311/14 P of 20.1.2015 – Longevity Health Products/OHIM, paras 31 and 32; C-370/14 P of 12.2.2015 – Argo Group International Holdings/OHIM, paras 32 and 33; C-531/14 P of 2.9.2015 – Giorgis/OHIM, paras 37 et seq.; C-29/15 P of 3.12.2015 – Verband der Kölnisch-Wasser Hersteller, Köln/OHIM, paras 27 et seq.; C-396/15 P of 17.2.2016 – Shoe Branding Europe/OHIM, para. 21; C-346/15 P of 25.2.2016 – Steinbeck/OHIM, para. 27; C-487/15 P of 25.2.2016 – Deutsche Rockwool Mineralwoll/OHIM, para. 30; C-440/15 P of 3.3.2016 – AgriCapital/OHIM, para. 53; C-252/15 P of 17.3.2016 – Naazneen/OHIM, paras 22 et seq.; C-577/14 P of 16.2.2017 – Brandconcern/EUIPO, para. 37; C-576/16 P of 2.3.2017 – TVR Italia/EUIPO, paras 3/1 and 4; C-687/16 P of 7.6.2017 – Capella/EUIPO, paras 4/6 and 5; C-224/17 P of 19.10.2017 – Hernández Zamora/EUIPO, paras 5/3 and 6; C-520/17 P of 30.11.2017 – C-cen-tek/EUIPO, paras 6/13 and 7; C-570/17 P of 16.1.2018 – Lackmann Fleisch- und Feinkostfabrik/EUIPO, paras 5/11 and 6; C-678/16 P of 18.1.2018 – Monster Energy/EUIPO, para. 44; C-634/16 P of 24.1.2018 – EUIPO/European Food, para. 63; C-560/17 P of 13.3.2018 – Mediaexpert/EUIPO, paras 3/8 and 5; C-642/17 P of 22.3.2018 – Arrigoni/EUIPO, paras 4/2 and 5; C-651/17 of 12.4.2018 – Grupo Osborne/EUIPO, paras 6/5 and 7; C-652/17 of 12.4.2018 – Grupo Osborne/EUIPO, paras 6/5 and 7; C-519/17 P and C-522/17 P to C-525/17 P of 30.5.2018 – L'Oréal/EUIPO, para. 67; C-655/17 P of 31.5.2018 – Berliner Stadtwerke/EUIPO, paras 3/30 and 6; C-656/17 P of 31.5.2018 – Berliner Stadtwerke/EUIPO, paras 3/34 and 6; C-62/18 P of 31.5.2018 – Merck/EUIPO, paras 5/3 and 6; C-32/17 P of 6.6.2018 – Apcoa Parking Holdings/EUIPO, para. 38; C-136/18 P of 6.9.2018 – Hansen/EUIPO, paras 6/18 and 19; C-246/18 P of

It is settled case law that if the grounds of a judgment of the Court of First Instance reveal an infringement of Community law but the operative part appears well founded on other legal grounds, the appeal must be dismissed.[383]

An **argument** put forward for the first time before the Court of Justice must be declared **inadmissible** because, in so far as it was **raised for the first time** at the stage of the appeal, it is not directed at seeking to establish that the Court of First Instance erred in law.[384]

It follows from that provision [Article 63 CTMR] that facts not submitted by the parties before the departments of OHIM cannot be submitted at the stage of the appeal brought before the Court of First Instance.[385]

It is also apparent from that provision that the Court of First Instance cannot re-evaluate the factual circumstances in the light of evidence adduced for the first time before it. The legality of a decision of a Board of Appeal of OHIM must be assessed in the light of the information available to it when it adopted that decision.[386]

6.9.2018 – Dochirnie pidpryiemstvo Kondyterska korporatsiia 'Roshen'/EUIPO, paras 5/14 and 6; C-463/18 P of 15.1.2019 – CeramTec/EUIPO, paras 5/28 and 15; C-698/17 P of 23.1.2019 – Klement/EUIPO, para. 28; C-733/18 P of 19.3.2019 – Sevenfriday/EUIPO, paras 5/6 and 6; C-734/18 P of 19.3.2019 – Sevenfriday/EUIPO, paras 5/6 and 6; C-68/19 P of 11.9.2019 – Camomilla/EUIPO, paras 3/30 and 4; C-162/19 P of 5.9.2019 – Iceland Foods/EUIPO, paras 5/6 and 6; C-124/19 P of 11.9.2019 – Vitromed/EUIPO, paras 5/5 and 6; C-121/19 P of 16.9.2020 – Edison/EUIPO, para. 37.

383. CJEU C-64/02 P of 21.10.2004 – OHIM/ERPO MÖBELWERK, para. 52; C-447/02 P of 21.10.2004 – KWS Saat/OHIM, para. 51.

384. CJEU C-361/01 P of 9.9.2003 – KIK/OHIM, para. 77; C-456/01 P and C-457/01 P of 29.4.2004 – Henkel/OHIM, para. 49 f.; C-24/05 P of 22.6.2006 – Storck/OHIM (light-brown sweet), para. 45; C-25/05 P of 22.6.2006 – Storck/OHIM (gold-coloured sweet wrapper), para. 61; C-104/05 P of 28.9.2006 – El Corte Inglés/OHIM, para. 40; C-273/05 P of 19.4.2007 – OHIM/Celltech, para. 21; C-408/08 P of 25.2.2010 – Lancôme parfums et beauté & Cie/OHIM, para. 53; C-214/09 P of 29.7.2010 – Anheuser-Busch/OHIM, para. 100; C-559/08 P of 16.9.2010 – Deepak Rajani/OHIM, paras 66 and 97; C-92/10 P of 13.1.2011 – Media-Saturn-Holding/OHIM, para. 39; C-308/10 P of 19.5.2011 – Union Investment Privatfonds/OHIM, para. 31; C-546/10 P of 13.9.2011 – Wilfer/OHIM, para. 44; C-76/11 P of 29.11.2011 – Tresplain Investments/OHIM, para. 53; C-307/11 P of 26.4.2012 – Deichmann/OHIM, para. 65; C-624/11 P of 27.9.2012 – Brighton Collectibles/OHIM, para. 53; C-611/11 P of 10.10.2012 – ara/OHIM, para. 58; C-249/14 P of 9.7.2015 – Pêra-Grave/OHIM, para. 24; *see also* CJEU C-70/13 P of 12.12.2013 – Getty Images (US)/OHIM, para. 23; C-412/13 P of 10.4.2014 – Franz Wilhelm Langguth Erben/OHIM, para. 41; C-308/13 P and C-309/13 P of 18.9.2014 – Società Italiana Calzature/OHIM, para. 50; C-370/14 P of 12.2.2015 – Argo Group International Holdings/OHIM, para. 28; C-414/14 P of 26.2.2015 – Fundação Calouste Gulbenkian, para. 52; C-62/15 P of 8.9.2015 – DTL Corporatión/OHIM, para. 51; C-43/15 P of 8.11.2016 – BSH Bosch und Siemens Hausgeräte/EUIPO, para. 43; C-501/16 P of 16.2.2017 – Monster Energy/EUIPO, paras 5/4 and 6; C-502/16 P of 16.2.2017 – Monster Energy/EUIPO, paras 5/4 and 6; C-655/15 P of 2.3.2017 – Panrico/EUIPO, para. 46; C-421/15 P of 11.5.2017 – Yoshida Metal Industry/EUIPO, para. 46; C-139/17 P of 25.7.2018 – QuaMa Quality Management/EUIPO, para. 44; C-340/17 P of 29.11.2018 – Alcohol Countermeasure Systems/EUIPO, para. 77; C-505/17 P of 28.2.2019 – Groupe Léa Nature/EUIPO, para. 31; C-124/18 P of 29.7.2019 – Red Bull/EUIPO, para. 94; C-728/18 P of 25.9.2019 – EM Research Organization/EUIPO, paras 4/14 and 5.

385. CJEU C-16/06 P of 18.12.2008 – Les Éditions Albert René/OHIM, para. 137; C-461/09 P of 9.7.2010 – The Wellcome Foundation, para. 26; C-546/10 P of 13.9.2011 – Wilfer/OHIM, para. 41; C-88/11 P of 10.11.2011 – LG Electronics/OHIM, para. 25; C-81/11 P of 8.3.2012 – Longevity Health Products/OHIM, para. 34; C-248/18 P of 11.9.2018 – Moscow Confectionery Factory 'Krasnyiy oktyabr'/EUIPO, paras 6/26 and 7.

386. CJEU C-16/06 P of 18.12.2008 – Les Éditions Albert René/OHIM, para. 138; C-461/09 P of 9.7.2010 – The Wellcome Foundation, para. 27; C-546/10 P of 13.9.2011 – Wilfer/OHIM, para.

According to the settled case law of the Court of Justice, grounds of appeal which merely **repeat** or reproduce verbatim the grounds of appeal and the arguments put forward before the Court of First Instance, without indicating precisely the points criticized in the judgment whose setting aside is sought and the specific legal arguments in support of that application, are manifestly inadmissible.[387]

By contrast, provided that the appellant challenges the interpretation or application of Community law by the Court of First Instance, the points of law examined at first instance may be **discussed again** in the course of an appeal. Indeed, if an appellant could not thus base his appeal on pleas in law and arguments already relied on before the Court of First Instance, an appeal would be deprived of part of its purpose.[388]

It must be pointed out that Article 42(2) of the Rules of Procedure provides that no new plea in law may be introduced in the course of proceedings unless it is based on matters of law or of fact which come to light in the course of the procedure.[389]

It follows that the power of the General Court to alter decisions does not have the effect of conferring on that Court the power to substitute its own reasoning for that of a Board of Appeal or to carry out an assessment on which that Board of Appeal has not yet adopted a position. Exercise of the power to alter decisions must therefore, in principle, be limited to situations in which the General Court, after reviewing the assessment made by the Board of Appeal, is in a position to determine, on the basis of the matters of fact and of law as established, what decision the Board of Appeal was required to take.[390]

However, it must also be pointed out that a plea which may be regarded as amplifying a plea made previously, whether directly or by implication, in the original application must be considered admissible.[391]

41; C-88/11 P of 10.11.2011 – LG Electronics/OHIM, para. 25; C-266/12 P of 7.2.2013 – Majczak/OHIM, para. 45; C-294/12 P of 14.5.2013 – You-Q/OHIM, para. 63; C-414/14 P of 26.2.2015 – Fundação Calouste Gulbenkian, para. 38; C-248/18 P of 11.9.2018 – Moscow Confectionery Factory 'Krasnyiy oktyabr'/EUIPO, paras 6/26 and 7.

387. CJEU C-547/17 P of 6.9.2018 – Basic Net/EUIPO, para. 43, with further proof; C-733/18 P of 19.3.2019 – Sevenfriday/EUIPO, paras 5/6 and 6; C-734/18 P of 19.3.2019 – Sevenfriday/EUIPO, paras 5/14 and 6; C-795/18 P of 20.6.2019 – FCA US/EUIPO paras 5/14 and 21; C-281/18 P of 31.10.2019 – Repower/EUIPO, para. 44; C-714/18 P of 16.7.2020 – ACTC/EUIPO, para. 83; C-121/19 P of 16.9.2020 – Edison/EUIPO, para. 54.

388. CJEU C-25/05 P of 22.6.2006 – Storck/OHIM (gold-coloured sweet wrapper), para. 48; C-324/13 P of 30.1.2014 – Fercal – Consultadoria e Serviços/OHIM, para. 39; *see also* CJEU C-273/05 P of 19.4.2007 – OHIM/Celltech, paras 22 et seq.; C-42/12 P of 29.11.2012 – Hrbek/OHIM, para. 54.

389. CJEU C-66/02 of 15.12.2005 – Italian Republic/Commission, para. 85; C-311/05 P of 4.10.2007 – Naipes Heraclio Fournier/OHIM, para. 58; *see also* CJEU C-16/06 P of 18.12.2008 – Les Éditions Albert René/OHIM, paras 122 et seq.; C-263/09 P of 5.7.2011 – Edwin/OHIM, para. 71; C-342/16 P of 6.12.2016 – Novomatic/EUIPO, paras 4/11 and 5; C-48/18 P of 13.11.2018 – Toontrack Music/EUIPO, para. 42.

390. CJEU C-263/09 P of 5.7.2011 – Edwin/OHIM, para. 72; C-371/16 P of 8.12.2016 – L'Oréal/EUIPO, paras 4/7 and 5; *see also* CJEU C-418/10 P of 28.3.2011 – Herhof-Verwaltungsgesellschaft/OHIM, paras 47 et seq.; C-609/11 P of 26.9.2013 – Centrotherm Systemtechnik/OHIM, para. 48.

391. CJEU 306/81 of 19.5.1983 – Verros/Parliament, para. 9; C-301/97 of 22.11.2001 – Netherlands/Council, para. 169; C-66/02 of 15.12.2005 – Italian Republic/Commission, para. 86; C-311/05 P of 4.10.2007 – Naipes Heraclio Fournier/OHIM, para. 59.

Arguments in an appeal which criticize the decision whose annulment was applied for before the General Court, rather than the judgment delivered by the General Court following that application for annulment, are inadmissible.[392]

An appeal that does not seek to have the judgment under appeal, that is to say the operative part thereof, set aside, even in part, but **merely to amend some of the grounds** of that judgment, is **inadmissible**.[393]

The **Court of First Instance** has **exclusive jurisdiction to find the facts**, save where a substantive inaccuracy in its findings is attributable to the documents submitted to it, and to appraise those facts. That appraisal thus does not, save where the clear sense of the evidence before it has been distorted, constitute a point of law which is subject, as such, to review by the Court of Justice on appeal.[394]

---

392. CJEU C-462/10 P of 13.1.2012 - Evropaïki Dynamiki/EEA, para. 36; C-21/12 P of 17.1.2013 - Abbott Laboratories/OHIM, para. 86; C-70/13 P of 12.12.2013 - Getty Images (US)/OHIM, para. 38; C-521/13 P of 11.9.2014 - Think Schuhwerk/OHIM, para. 29; C-531/14 P of 2.9.2015 - Giorgis/OHIM, para. 39; C-684/17 P of 17.5.2018 - Banca Monte dei Paschi di Siena/EUIPO, paras 4/4 and 5; C-685/17 P of 17.5.2018 - Banca Monte dei Paschi di Siena/EUIPO, paras 4/4 and 5; *see also* CJEU C-141/13 P of 17.7.2014 - Reber Holding/OHIM, para. 54; C-687/16 P of 7.6.2017 - Capella/EUIPO, paras 4/4 and 5; C-139/17 P of 25.7.2018 - QuaMa Quality Management/EUIPO, para. 39.
393. CJEU C-84/17 P, C-85/17 P and C-95/17 P of. 25.7.2018 - Société des produits Nestlé/EUIPO, para. 42.
394. CJEU C-104/00 P of 19.9.2002 - DKV/OHIM, para. 22; C-144/06 P of 4.10.2007 - Henkel/ OHIM, para. 49; C-212/07 P of 13.2.2008 - Indorata-Serviços e Gestão, para. 38; C-243/07 P of 15.2.2008 - Brinkmann/OHIM, para. 34; C-344/07 P of 11.4.2008 - Focus Magazin Verlag/ OHIM, para. 49; C-497/07 P of 27.6.2008 - Philip Morris Products/OHIM, para. 29; C-514/06 of 18.9.2008 - Armacell Enterprise/OHIM, para. 69; C-513/07 P of 17.10.2008 - AGC Flat Glass Europe/OHIM, para. 29; C-81/08 P of 13.11.2008 - Cabrera Sánchez/OHIM, para. 24; C-494/08 P of 9.12.2009 - Prana Haus/HABM, para. 36; C-57/08 P of 11.12.2008 - Gateway/OHIM, para. 38; C-197/07 P of 12.12.2008 - Aktieselskabet af 21. Nov. 2001/OHIM, para. 15; C-16/06 P of 18.12.2008 - Les Éditions Albert René/OHIM, para. 68; C-17/08 P of 6.2.2009 - MPDV Mikrolab, para. 27; C-136/08 P of 30.4.2009 - Japan Tobacco/OHIM, para. 32; C-398/07 P of 7.5.2009 - Waterford Wedgwood/OHIM, para. 40; C-394/08 P of 3.6.2009 - Zipcar/OHIM, para. 39; C-300/08 P of 11.6.2009 - Leche Celta/OHIM, para. 35; C-416/08 P of 10.7.2009 - Apple Computer/OHIM, para. 22; C-202/08 and C-208/08 of 16.7.2009 - American Clothing Associates/OHIM, para. 53; C-481/08 P of 24.9.2009 - Alcon/OHIM, para. 18; C-520/08 P of 24.9.2009 - HUP Uslugi Polska, para. 35; C-78/09 P of 24.9.2009 - Compagnie des bateaux mouches/OHIM, para. 21; C-488/08 P and C-489/08 P of 4.12.2009 - Rath/OHIM, para. 37; C-579/08 P of 15.1.2010 - Messer Group/OHIM, para. 54; C-23/09 P of 22.1.2010 - ecoblue/ OHIM, para. 51; C-80/09 P of 5.2.2010 - Mergel a. o./OHIM, para. 25; C-193/09 P of 4.3.2010 - Kaul/OHIM, para. 75; C-282/09 P of 18.3.2010 - CFCMCEE/OHIM, para. 47; C-461/09 P of 9.7.2010 - The Wellcome Foundation, para. 21; C-254/09 P of 2.9.2010 - Calvin Klein/OHIM, para. 49; C-559/08 P of 16.9.2010 - Deepak Rajani/OHIM, paras 78 and 88; C-84/10 P of 22.10.2010 - Longevity Health Products/OHIM, para. 30; C-342/09 P of 27.10.2010 - Victor Guedes/OHIM, para. 20; C-22/10 P of 27.10.2010 - Rewe-Zentral/OHIM, paras 32 and 43; C-92/10 P of 13.1.2011 - Media-Saturn-Holding/OHIM, para. 27; C-353/09 P of 15.2.2011 - Perfetti Van Melle/OHIM, para. 40; C-552/09 P of 24.3.2011 - Ferrero/OHIM, para. 73; C-388/10 P of 24.3.2011 - Muñoz Arraiza/OHIM, para. 31; C-418/10 P of 28.3.2011 - Herhof-Verwaltungsgesellschaft/OHIM, para. 66; C-5/10 P of 16.5.2011 - Torresan/OHIM, para. 85; C-429/10 P of 16.5.2011 - X Technology Swiss/OHIM, para. 41; C-54/10 P and C-55/10 P of 22.6.2011 - Agencja Wydawnicza Technopol/HABM, para. 31; C-56/10 P of 22.6.2011 - Agencja Wydawnicza Technopol/HABM, para. 56; C-532/10 P of 29.6.2011 - adp Gauselmann/OHIM, para. 31; C-536/10 P of 7.7.2011 - MPDV Mikrolab/OHIM, para. 37; C-546/10 P of 13.9.2011 - Wilfer/OHIM, para. 62; C-88/11 P of 10.11.2011 - LG Electronics/ OHIM, para. 36; C-45/11 P of 7.12.2011 - Deutsche Bahn/OHIM, para. 46; C-81/11 P of

8.3.2012 - Longevity Health Products/OHIM, para. 27; C-87/11 P of 21.3.2012 - Fidelio/OHIM, para. 59; C-354/11 P of 22.3.2012 - Emram/OHIM, para. 48; C-307/11 P of 26.4.2012 - Deichmann/OHIM, para. 58; C-100/11 P of 10.5.2012 - Helena Rubinstein and L'Oréal/OHIM, paras 74 and 84; C-198/11 P of 11.5.2012 - LAN Airlines/OHIM, para. 33; C-453/11 P of 14.5.2012 - Timehouse/OHIM, para. 35; C-306/11 P of 28.6.2012 - XXXLutz Marken/OHIM, para. 51; C-311/11 P of 12.7.2012 - Smart Technologies/OHIM, para. 52; C-327/11 P of 6.9.2012 - United States Polo/OHIM, para. 62; C-624/11 P of 27.9.2012 - Brighton Collectibles/ OHIM, para. 43; C-649/11 P of 3.10.2012 - Cooperativa Vitivinícola Arousana, S. Coop. Galega/OHIM, para. 39; C-611/11 P of 10.10.2012 - ara/OHIM, para. 41; C-42/12 P of 29.11.2012 - Hrbek/OHIM, para. 44; C-21/12 P of 17.1.2013 - Abbott Laboratories/OHIM, para. 53; C-261/12 P of 17.1.2013 - Annunziata Del Prete/OHIM, para. 27; C-266/12 P of 7.2.2013 - Majczak/OHIM, para. 31; C-171/12 P of 28.2.2013 - Carrols/OHIM, para. 35; C-341/12 P of 21.3.2013 - Mizuno/OHIM, para. 26; C-393/12 P of 21.3.2013 - Foundation for the Protection of the Traditional Cheese of Cyprus named Halloumi/OHIM, para. 38; C-354/12 P of 11.4.2013 - ASA/OHIM, para. 28; C-268/12 P of 8.5.2013 - Cadila Healthcare/OHIM, para. 41; C-294/12 P of 14.5.2013 - You-Q/OHIM, para. 59; C-379/12 P of 16.5.2013 - Arav Holding/OHIM, para. 41; C-14/12 P of 30.5.2013 - Shah/OHIM, para. 24; C-357/12 P of 30.5.2013 - Wohlfahrt/OHIM, para. 58; C-381/12 P of 6.6.2013 - I Marchi Italiani/OHIM, para. 73; C-346/12 P of 13.6.2013 - DMK Deutsches Milchkontor, para. 41; C-410/12 P of 16.10.2013 - medi/OHIM, para. 24; C-524/12 P of 14.11.2013 - TeamBank/OHIM, para. 36; C-70/13 P of 12.12.2013 - Getty Images (US)/OHIM, para. 20; C-159/13 P of 12.12.2013 - Fercal - Consultadoria e Serviços/OHIM, para. 23; C-193/13 P of 16.1.2014 - nfon/OHIM, para. 26; C-422/12 P of 30.1.2014 - Industrias Alen/OHIM, para. 37; C-301/13 P of 6.2.2014 - El Corte Inglés, para. 41; C-177/13 P of 13.2.2014 - Marszałkowski/OHIM, para. 40; C-374/13 P of 10.4.2014 - Metropolis Inmobiliarias y Restauraciones/OHIM, para. 39; C-608/12 P of 8.5.2014 - Greinwald/HABM, para. 36; C-97/12 P of 15.5.2014 - Louis Vuitton Malletier/OHIM, para. 61; C-414/13 P of 20.5.2014 - Reber Holding/OHIM, para. 31; C-150/14 P of 4.9.2014 - Goldsteig Käsereien Bayerwald/OHIM, para. 23; C-509/13 P of 4.92014 - Metropolis Inmobiliarias y Restauraciones/OHIM, para. 38; C-669/13 P of 21.10.2014 - Mundipharma/OHIM, para. 28; C-521/13 P of 11.9.2014 - Think Schuhwerk/OHIM, para. 43; C-466/13 P of 22.10.2014 - Repsol YPF/OHIM, para. 54; C-170/14 P of 6.11.2014 - Big Line Sas di Graziani Lorenzo/OHIM, para. 31; C-581/13 P and C-582/13 P of 20.11.2014 - Intra-Presse/OHIM, para. 38; C-368/14 P of 11.12.2014 - Compagnie des bateaux mooches/OHIM, para. 24; C-320/14 P of 13.1.2015 - Asos/OHIM, para. 19; C-311/14 P of 20.1.2015 - Longevity Health Products/ OHIM, para. 33; C-494/13 P of 22.1.2015 - GRE Grand River Enterprises Deutschland/OHIM, para. 35; C-495/13 P of 22.1.2015 - GRE Grand River Enterprises Deutschland/OHIM, para. 35; C-496/13 P of 22.1.2015 - GRE Grand River Enterprises Deutschland/OHIM, para. 33; C-370/14 P of 12.2.2015 - Argo Group International Holdings/OHIM, para. 24; C-374/14 P of 12.2.2015 - Walcher Meßtechnik/OHIM, para. 26; C-182/14 P of 19.3.2015 - MEGA Brands International/ OHIM, para. 47; C-445/13 P of 7.5.2015 - Voss of Norway/OHIM, para. 97; C-579/14 P of 4.6.2015 - Junited Autoglas Deutschland/OHIM, para. 25; C-531/14 P of 2.9.2015 - Giorgis/ OHIM, para. 32; C-548/14 P of 17.9.2015 - Arnoldo Mondadori Editore/OHIM, para. 38; C-33/15 P of 15.10.2015 - Cantina Broglie 1, para. 51; C-34/15 P of 15.10.2015 - Cantina Broglie 1, para. 51; C-17/15 P of 26.10.2015 - Popp and Zech/OHIM, para. 56; C-190/15 P of 19.11.2015 - Fetim/OHIM, para. 30; C-29/15 P of 3.12.2015 - Verband der Kölnisch-Wasser Hersteller, Köln/OHIM, para. 33; C-603/14 P of 10.12.2015 - El Corte Inglés/OHIM, para. 31; C-374/15 P of 28.1.2016 - Harper Hygienics/OHIM, para. 32; C-251/15 P of 4.2.2016 - Emsibeth/OHIM, para. 28; C-440/15 P of 3.3.2016 - AgriCapital/OHIM, para. 32; C-252/15 P of 17.3.2016 - Naazneen/OHIM, para. 59; C-295/15 P of 22.6.2016 Matratzen Concord/EUIPO, para. 28; C-87/16 P of 21.7.2016 - Tsujimoto/EUIPO, paras 5/7 and 6; C-224/14 P of 6.9.2016 - Lidl/EUIPO, para. 27; C-237/14 P of 6.9.2016 - Lidl/EUIPO, para. 27; C-309/15 P of 8.9.2016 - Real Express/EUIPO, para. 56; C-442/15 P of 22.9.2016 - Pensa Pharma/EUIPO, para. 59; C-43/15 P of 8.11.2016 - BSH Bosch und Siemens Hausgeräte/EUIPO, para. 50; C-351/16 P of 10.11.2016 - 100 % Capri Italia/EUIPO, paras 8/13 and 9; C-389/16 P of 15.11.2016 - BSH Hausgeräte/EUIPO, paras 6/3 and 7; C-371/16 P of 8.12.2016 - L'Oréal/EUIPO, paras 4/2 and 5; C-501/16 P of 16.2.2017 - Monster Energy/EUIPO, paras 5/5 and 6; C-502/16 P of 16.2.2017 - Monster Energy/EUIPO, paras 5/5 and 6; C-655/15 P of 2.3.2017 - Panrico/EUIPO, para. 67;

C-421/15 P of 11.5.2017 – Yoshida Metal Industry/EUIPO, para. 22; C-639/16 P of 11.5.2017 – Foodcare/EUIPO, paras 5/19 and 6; C-37/17 P of 31.5.2017 – Keil/EUIPO, paras 4/2 and 5; C-86/17 P of 7.6.2017 – Redpur/EUIPO, paras 4/4 and 5; C-84/16 P of 26.7.2017 – Continental Reifen Deutschland/EUIPO, para. 35; C-182/16 P of 26.7.2017 – Meica Ammerländische Fleischwarenfabrik Fritz Meinen/EUIPO, para. 33; C-158/17 P of 20.9.2017 – Anton Riemerschmid Weinbrennerei und Likörfabrik/EUIPO, paras 6/3 and 7; C-501/15 P of 11.10.2017 – EUIPO/Cactus, para. 60; C-559/17 P of 11.1.2018 – Cafés Pont/EUIPO, paras 4/3 and 5; C-570/17 P of 16.1.2018 – Lackmann Fleisch- und Feinkostfabrik/EUIPO, paras 5/6 and 6; C-529/17 P of 22.2.2018 – Martín Osete/EUIPO, paras 6/9 and 7; C-412/16 P and 413/16 P of 1.3.2018 – Ice Mountain Ibiza/EUIPO, para. 45; C-651/17 of 12.4.2018 – Grupo Osborne/EUIPO, paras 6/10 and 7; C-652/17 of 12.4.2018 – Grupo Osborne/EUIPO, paras 6/10 and 7; C-85/16 P and C-86/16 P of 30.5.2018 – Kenzo Tsujimoto/EUIPO, para. 42; C-655/17 P of 31.5.2018 – Berliner Stadtwerke/EUIPO, paras 3/11 and 6; C-656/17 P of 31.5.2018 – Berliner Stadtwerke/EUIPO, paras 3/15 and 6; C-62/18 P of 31.5.2018 – Merck/EUIPO, paras 5/2 and 6; C-73/18 P of 7.6.2018 – Cotécnica/EUIPO, paras 5/6 and 6; C-139/17 P of 25.7.2018 – QuaMa Quality Management/EUIPO, para. 33; C-488/16 P of 6.9.2018 – Bundesverband – Souvenir – Geschenke – Ehrenpreise/EUIPO, para. 29; C-136/18 P of 6.9.2018 – Hansen/EUIPO, paras 6/22 and 19; C-246/18 P of 6.9.2018 – Dochirnie pidpryiemstvo Kondyterska korporatsiia 'Roshen'/EUIPO, paras 5/5 and 6; C-248/18 P of 11.9.2018 – Moscow Confectionery Factory 'Krasnyiy oktyabr'/EUIPO, paras 6/5 and 7; C-26/17 P of 13.9.2018 – Birkenstock Sales/EUIPO, para. 29; C-48/18 P of 13.11.2018 – Toontrack Music/EUIPO, para. 28; C-340/17 P of 29.11.2018 – Alcohol Countermeasure Systems/EUIPO, para. 40; C-408/18 P of 13.12.2018 – Senetic/EUIPO, paras 5/10 and 6; C-409/18 P of 13.12.2018 – Senetic/EUIPO, paras 5/10 and 6; C-463/18 P of 15.1.2019 – CeramTec/EUIPO, paras 5/22 and 15; C-162/17 P of 16.1.2019 – Republic of Poland/EUIPO, para. 36; C-194/17 P of 31.1.2019 – Pandalis/EUIPO, para. 51; C-505/17 P of 28.2.2019 – Groupe Léa Nature/EUIPO, para. 62; C-733/18 P of 19.3.2019 – Sevenfriday/EUIPO, paras 5/12 and 6; C-734/18 P of 19.3.2019 – Sevenfriday/EUIPO, paras 5/12 and 6; C-653/17 P of 15.5.2019 – VM Vermögens-Management/EUIPO, para. 68; C-780/18 P of 22.5.2019 – Cuervo y Sobrinos 1882/EUIPO, paras 5/4 and 7; C-31/19 P of 2.7.2019 – Seven/EUIPO, paras 5/4 and 6; C-99/18 P of 4.7.2019 – FTI Touristik/EUIPO, para. 39; C-819/18 P of 11.7.2019 – Next design + produktion/EUIPO, paras 5/9 and 6; C-795/18 P of 20.6.2019 – FCA US/EUIPO paras 5/17 and 21; C-124/19 P of 11.9.2019 – Vitromed/EUIPO, paras 5/18 and 6; C-728/18 P of 25.9.2019 – EM Research Organization/EUIPO, paras 4/33 and 5; C-278/19 P of 25.9.2019 – Mas Que Vinos Global/EUIPO, paras 5/15 and 6; C-293/19 P of 2.10.2019 – Et Djili Soy Dzhihangir Ibryam/EUIPO, paras 7/8 and 8; C-285/19 P of 6.11.2019 – Geske/EUIPO, paras 5/10 and 6; C-528/18 P of 13.11.2019 – Outsource Professional Services/EUIPO, para. 47; C-155/18 P to C-158/18 P of 4.3.2020 – Tulliallan Burlington/EUIPO, para. 101; C-449/18 P and C-474/18 P of 17.9.2020 – EUIPO/Messi Cuccittini, para. 55; C-818/18 P and C-6/19 P of 3.6.2021 – The Yokohama Rubber/EUIPO, para. 49; C-529/18 P and 531/18 P of 24.3.2022 – PJ/EUIPO, para. 55; *see also* CJEU C-326/01 P of 5.2.2004 – Telefon & Buch/OHIM, para. 35; C-150/02 P of 5.2.2004 – Streamserve/OHIM, para. 30; C-456/01 P and C-457/01 P of 29.4.2004 – Henkel/OHIM, para. 56 f.; C-468/01 P to C-472/01 P of 29.4.2004 – Procter & Gamble/OHIM (three-dimensional form of tablet I), para. 53 f.; C-473/01 P and C-474/01 P of 29.4.2004 – Procter & Gamble/OHIM (three-dimensional form of tablet II), para. 53 f.; C-3/03 P of 28.4.2004 – Matratzen Concord/OHIM, para. 34; C-445/02 P of 28.6.2004 – Glaverbel/OHIM, paras 31, 53; C-107/03 P of 23.9.2004 – Procter & Gamble/OHIM (form of a soap), para. 17 f.; C-192/03 P of 5.10.2004 – ALCON/OHIM (I), para. 33; C-136/02 P of 7.10.2004 – Mag Instrument/OHIM, para. 39, 76, 88; C-447/02 P of 21.10.2004 – KWS Saat/OHIM, paras 35, 85; C-206/04 P of 23.3.2006 – Mülhens/OHIM, paras 28, 41; C-286/04 P of 30.6.2005 – Eurocermex/OHIM, para. 43; C-37/03 P of 15.9.2005 – BioID/OHIM, para. 43; C-416/04 P of 11.5.2006 – Sunrider/OHIM, para. 49; C-324/05 P of 1.6.2006 – Plus Warenhandelsgesellschaft/OHIM, para. 28; C-24/05 P of 22.6.2006 – Storck/OHIM (light-brown sweet), para. 36; C-25/05 P of 22.6.2006 – Storck/OHIM (gold-coloured sweet wrapper), para. 40; C-314/05 P of 29.6.2006 – Creative Technology/OHIM, para. 35; C-92/06 P of 13.7.2006 – Soffass/OHIM, para. 17; C-214/05 P of 18.7.2006 – Rossi/OHIM, para. 26; C-104/05 P of 28.9.2006 – El Corte Inglés/OHIM, para. 45; C-196/06 P of 9.3.2007 – Alecansan/OHIM, para. 31; C-245/06 P of 9.3.2007 – Saiwa/OHIM, para. 33; C-171/06 P of 15.3.2007 – T.I.M.E.

It must be pointed out that the assessment, which relates to the **definition of the relevant public**, constitutes an assessment of a factual nature.[395]

Findings relating to the **characteristics of the relevant public and its degree of attention, perception or attitude** represent appraisals of fact.[396]

ART/OHIM, para. 51; C-325/06 P of 20.3.2007 – Galileo International Technology and Others/Commission, para. 60; C-312/05 P of 27.3.2007 – TeleTech/OHIM, para. 67; C-131/06 P of 24.4.2007 – Castellblanch/OHIM, paras 32, 60; C-412/05 P of 26.4.2007 – Alcon/OHIM (II), para. 71; C-334/05 P of 12.6.2007 – OHIM/Shaker, para. 28; C-234/06 P of 13.9.2007 – Il Ponte Finanziaria/OHIM, para. 38; C-193/06 P of 20.9.2007 – Nestlé/OHIM, para. 53; C-405/06 P of 24.9.2007 – Torres/OHIM, para. 32; C-238/06 P of 25.10.2007 – Develey Holding/OHIM, para. 92; C-512/06 P of 26.10.2007 – PTV Planung Transport Verkehr/OHIM, para. 39; C-108/07 P of 17.4.2008 – Ferrero Deutschland/OHIM, para. 30; C-304/06 P of 8.5.2008 – Eurohypo/OHIM, para. 33; C-488/06 P of 17.7.2008 – L & D/OHIM, para. 40; C-20/08 P of 9.12.2008 – Enercon/OHIM, para. 53; C-498/07 P of 3.9.2009 – Aceites del Sur-Coosur/OHIM, para. 78; C-204/10 P of 23.11.2010 – Enercon/OHIM, para. 28; C-263/09 P of 5.7.2011 – Edwin/OHIM, para. 46; C-76/11 P of 29.11.2011 – Tresplain Investments/OHIM, para. 73; C-222/11 P of 1.12.2011 – Longevity Health Products/OHIM, para. 29; C-655/11 P of 21.2.2013 – Seven for all mankind/OHIM, para. 79; C-411/13 P of 8.5.2014 – OHIM/Sanco, paras 56 and 57; C-374/15 P of 28.1.2016 – Harper Hygienics/OHIM, para. 47; C-346/15 P of 25.2.2016 – Steinbeck/OHIM, para. 33; C-396/15 P of 17.2.2016 – Shoe Branding Europe/OHIM, para. 67; C-487/15 P of 25.2.2016 – Deutsche Rockwool Mineralwoll/OHIM, paras 28 et seq.; C-474/15 P of 7.4.2016 – Harper Hygienics/EUIPO, para. 56; C-475/15 P of 7.4.2016 – Harper Hygienics/EUIPO, para. 58; C-479/15 P of 14.4.2016 – Nanu-Nana Joachim Hoepp/EUIPO, para. 14; C-515/15 P of 14.4.2016 – Roland/EUIPO, para. 26; C-232/15 P of 21.4.2016 – ultra air/EUIPO, paras 42 and 49; C-482/15 P of 26.10.2016 – Westermann Lernspielverlage/EUIPO, para. 35; C-30/15 P of 10.11.2016 – Simba Toys/EUIPO, para. 34; C-642/15 of 1.12.2016 – Klement, para. 18; C-10/17 P of 1.6.2017 – Polo Club/EUIPO, paras 4/4 and 5; C-468/17 P of 13.12.2017 – Morton's of Chicago/EUIPO, paras 5/4 and 6; C-101/17 P of 14.12.2017 – Verus/EUIPO, para. 28; C-536/17 P of 17.1.2018 – Josel/EUIPO, paras 5/15 and 7; C-75/17 P of 19.4.2018 – Fiesta Hotels & Resorts/EUIPO, para. 41; C-150/18 P of 6.9.2018 – El Corte Inglés/EUIPO, paras 6/9 and 7; C-151/18 P of 6.9.2018 – El Corte Inglés/EUIPO, paras 6/8 and 7; C-542/17 P of 11.9.2018 – Allstate Insurance/EUIPO, para. 23; C-411/18 P of 3.10.2018 – Romantik Hotels & Restaurants/ EUIPO, paras 4/12 and 5; C-326/18 P of 4.10.2018 – Safe Skies/EUIPO, paras 5/21 and 6; C-48/18 P of 13.11.2018 – Toontrack Music/EUIPO, para. 29; C-553/18 P of 15.1.2019 – Lion's Head Global Partners/EUIPO, paras 5/3 and 6; C-554/18 P of 15.1.2019 – Lion's Head Global Partners/EUIPO, paras 5/3 and 6; C-744/18 P of 21.5.2019 – Volkswagen/EUIPO, para. 49; C-68/19 P of 11.9.2019 – Camomilla/EUIPO, paras 3/8 and 4; C-228/19 P of 24.9.2019 – ETI Gıda Sanayi ve Ticaret/EUIPO, paras 5/11 and 6; C-858/19 P of 6.2.2020 – NHS/EUIPO, para. 14.

395. CJEU C-57/08 P of 11.12.2008 – Gateway/OHIM, para. 39; *see also* CJEU C-17/08 P of 6.2.2009 – MPDV Mikrolab, para. 28; C-416/08 P of 10.7.2009 – Apple Computer/OHIM, para. 34; C-481/08 P of 24.9.2009 – Alcon/OHIM, para. 16.

396. CJEU C-461/09 P of 9.7.2010 – The Wellcome Foundation, para. 20; C-84/10 P of 22.10.2010 – Longevity Health Products/OHIM, para. 29; C-353/09 P of 15.2.2011 – Perfetti Van Melle/ OHIM, para. 51; C-546/10 P of 13.9.2011 – Wilfer/OHIM, para. 61; C-81/11 P of 8.3.2012 – Longevity Health Products/OHIM, para. 26; C-87/11 P of 21.3.2012 – Fidelio/OHIM, para. 58; C-354/12 P of 11.4.2013 – ASA/OHIM, para. 31; C-294/12 P of 14.5.2013 – You-Q/OHIM, para. 60; C-14/12 P of 30.5.2013 – Shah/OHIM, para. 28; C-581/13 P and C-582/13 P of 20.11.2014 – Intra-Presse/OHIM, para. 62; C-311/14 P of 20.1.2015 – Longevity Health Products/OHIM, para. 34; C-374/14 P of 12.2.2015 – Walcher Meßtechnik/OHIM, para. 23; C-33/15 P of 15.10.2015 – Cantina Broglie 1, para. 52; C-34/15 P of 15.10.2015 – Cantina Broglie 1, para. 52; C-251/15 P of 4.2.2016 – Emsibeth/OHIM, para. 29; C-396/15 P of 17.2.2016 – Shoe Branding Europe/OHIM, para. 15; *see also* CJEU C-655/11 P of 21.2.2013 – Seven for all mankind/OHIM, para. 78; C-410/12 P of 16.10.2013 – medi/OHIM, para. 25; C-177/13 P of 13.2.2014 – Marszałkowski/OHIM, para. 42; C-411/13 P of 8.5.2014 – OHIM/Sanco, para. 55; C-414/13 P of 20.5.2014 – Reber Holding/OHIM, para. 52; C-150/14 P of 4.9.2014 – Goldsteig Käsereien

The same is true as regards the relevant public's **understanding of** the meanings of different **languages**.[397]

The findings, first, that some of the **goods in question** are likely to be bought and used by end-consumers and, second, that, even where the goods are bought by a **professional** employed to carry out the work, the **end consumer** has an interest in being involved in the choice of a design such as that comprising the trade mark applied for, and therefore such a choice is also made, in large part, by the end consumer, are findings of a factual nature.[398]

The question of whether a mark is **distinctive** is factual in nature.[399]

The question of whether a mark is **descriptive** is factual in nature.[400]

The identification of the **essential characteristics of a sign and the assessment of its function** is factual.[401]

The question of what an applicant's intentions were in filing a potentially **bad faith** trade mark application is factual.[402]

Bayerwald/OHIM, para. 27; C-509/13 P of 4.92014 - Metropolis Inmobiliarias y Restauraciones, para. 39; C-669/13 P of 21.10.2014 - Mundipharma/OHIM, para. 30; C-170/14 P of 6.11.2014 - Big Line Sas di Graziani Lorenzo/OHIM, para. 42; C-368/14 P of 11.12.2014 - Compagnie des bateaux mooches/OHIM, para. 23; C-232/15 P of 21.4.2016 - ultra air/EUIPO, para. 41; C-94/16 P of 15.6.2016 - LTJ Diffusion/EUIPO, paras 6/9 and 7; C-619/15 P of 21.6.2016 - Mocek a.o./EUIPO, paras 4/22 and 5; C-401/16 P 1.12.2016 - Market Watch Franchise & Consulting/EUIPO, paras 5/6 and 6; C-402/16 P 1.12.2016 - Market Watch Franchise & Consulting/EUIPO, paras 5/6 and 6; C-587/16 P of 28.2.2017 - Skylotec/EUIPO, paras 4/7 and 5; C-417/16 P of 4.5.2017 - August Storck/EUIPO, para. 52; C-50/17 P of 1.6.2017 - Universidad Internacional de la Rioja/EUIPO, paras 5/4 and 6; C-662/16 P of 20.6.2017 - Laboratoire de la mer/EUIPO, paras 6/3 et seq. and 7; C-182/16 P of 26.7.2017 - Meica Ammerländische Fleischwarenfabrik Fritz Meinen/EUIPO, para. 32; C-501/15 P of 11.10.2017 - EUIPO/Cactus, para. 61; C-570/17 P of 16.1.2018 - Lackmann Fleisch- und Feinkostfabrik/EUIPO, paras 5/5 and 6; C-726/17 P of 11.7.2018 - Tetra Pharm (1997)/EUIPO, paras 5/8 and 7; *see also* CJEU C-412/16 P and 413/16 P of 1.3.2018 - Ice Mountain Ibiza/EUIPO, para. 78; C-139/17 P of 25.7.2018 - QuaMa Quality Management/EUIPO, para. 55; C-150/18 P of 6.9.2018 - El Corte Inglés/EUIPO, paras 6/8 and 7; C-151/18 P of 6.9.2018 - El Corte Inglés/EUIPO, paras 6/7 and 7; C-124/19 P of 11.9.2019 - Vitromed/EUIPO, paras 5/19 and 6; C-728/18 P of 25.9.2019 - EM Research Organization/EUIPO, paras 4/30 and 5.

397. CJEU C-532/10 P of 29.6.2011 - adp Gauselmann/OHIM, para. 51; C-581/13 P and C-582/13 P of 20.11.2014 - Intra-Presse/OHIM, para. 62.
398. CJEU C-513/07 P of 17.10.2008 - AGC Flat Glass Europe/OHIM, para. 30.
399. CJEU C-476/15 P of 15.3.2016 - Grupo Bimbo/OHIM, para. 18, unofficial transcription; C-351/16 P of 10.11.2016 - 100 % Capri Italia/EUIPO, paras 8/19 and 9, unofficial translation; C-520/17 P of 30.11.2017 - C-cen-tek/EUIPO, paras 6/6 and 7, unofficial transcription; C-417/16 P of 4.5.2017 - August Storck/EUIPO, para. 44, unofficial transcription.
400. CJEU C-487/15 P of 25.2.2016 - Deutsche Rockwool Mineralwoll/OHIM, para. 34, unofficial transcription; *see also* CJEU C-63/16 P of 24.5.2016 - Actega Terra/EUIPO, paras 5/9 and 6; C-285/16 P of 13.10.2016 - Grupo Bimbo/EUIPO, paras 5/5 and 6, unofficial transcription; C-232/15 P of 21.4.2016 - ultra air/EUIPO, para. 40; C-488/16 P of 6.9.2018 - Bundesverband - Souvenir - Geschenke - Ehrenpreise/EUIPO, para. 30; C-285/19 P of 6.11.2019 - Geske/EUIPO, paras 5/11 and 6.
401. CJEU C-893/19 P of 12.3.2020 - Roxtec/EUIPO, para. 17.
402. CJEU C-639/16 P of 11.5.2017 - Foodcare/EUIPO, paras 5/16 et seq. and 6, unofficial transcription.

The assessment of the **extent and sufficiency of genuine use** is an assessment of the facts.[403]

The **determination of the criteria** to be employed for the assessment of genuine use of the earlier mark is a **question of law** and thus falls within the Court's jurisdiction.[404]

The assessment of whether an element added to the trade mark **alters the distinctive character** of the trade mark within the meaning of Article 15 CTMR is of a factual nature.[405]

However, the determination of the criteria to be employed for the global assessment of equivalence of signs from the perspective of their distinctiveness is a question of law falling within the Court of Justice's jurisdiction.[406]

The assessment of whether there are **proper reasons for non-use** is an assessment of the facts.[407]

Whereas the evaluation of the factors assessing the **likelihood of confusion** is an issue of fact that cannot be reviewed by the Court.[408]

Failure to take all of those factors into account, on the other hand, constitutes an error of law.[409]

---

403. CJEU C-295/15 P of 22.6.2016 Matratzen Concord/EUIPO, para. 28, unofficial transcription; C-575/15 P of 26.10.2016 – Industria de Diseño Textil/EUIPO, para. 22, unofficial transcription; *see also* CJEU C-252/15 P of 17.3.2016 – Naazneen/OHIM, paras 60 et seqq.; C-278/19 P of 25.9.2019 – Mas Que Vinos Global/EUIPO, paras 5/16 and 6.
404. CJEU C-340/17 P of 29.11.2018 – Alcohol Countermeasure Systems/EUIPO, para. 76, with reference to CJEU C-501/15 P of 11.10.2017 – EUIPO/Cactus, para. 64; also CJEU C-714/18 P of 16.7.2020 – ACTC/EUIPO, para. 29.
405. CJEU C-611/15 P of 16.6.2016 – L'Oréal/EUIPO, para. 18, unofficial transcription; *see also* CJEU C-94/16 P of 15.6.2016 – LTJ Diffusion/EUIPO, paras 6/9 and 7; C-224/14 P of 6.9.2016 – Lidl/EUIPO, paras 44 et seq.; C-237/14 P of 6.9.2016 – Lidl/EUIPO, paras 44 et seq.; C-587/16 P of 28.2.2017 – Skylotec/EUIPO, paras 4/12 and 5.
406. CJEU C-501/15 P of 11.10.2017 – EUIPO/Cactus, para. 64; C-143/19 P of 12.12.2019 – Der Grüne Punkt – Duales System Deutschland /EUIPO, para. 51.
407. CJEU C-529/17 P of 22.2.2018 – Martín Osete/EUIPO, paras 6/15 and 7; *see also* C-246/05 of 14.6.2007 – Häupl, para. 55.
408. CJEU C-317/10 P of 16.6.2011 – Union Investment Privatfonds/OHIM, para. 45; C-354/11 P of 22.3.2012 – Emram/OHIM, para. 40; C-193/13 P of 16.1.2014 – nfon/OHIM, para. 52; C-177/13 P of 13.2.2014 – Marszałkowski/OHIM, para. 52; C-414/13 P of 20.5.2014 – Reber Holding/OHIM, para. 33; C-466/13 P of 22.10.2014 – Repsol YPF/OHIM, para. 63; C-311/14 P of 20.1.2015 – Longevity Health Products/OHIM, para. 39; C-370/14 P of 12.2.2015 – Argo Group International Holdings/OHIM, para. 26; C-343/14 P of 7.5.2015 – Adler Modemärkte/OHIM, para. 32; C-190/15 P of 19.11.2015 – Fetim/OHIM, para. 37; C-639/15 P of 26.5.2016 – Gat Microencapsulation/EUIPO, para. 4/7 and 5; C-371/16 P of 8.12.2016 – L'Oréal/EUIPO, paras 4/10 and 5; C-501/16 P of 16.2.2017 – Monster Energy/EUIPO, paras 5/8 et seq. and 6; C-502/16 P of 16.2.2017 – Monster Energy/EUIPO, paras 5/8 et seq. and 6; C-553/18 P of 15.1.2019 – Lion's Head Global Partners/EUIPO, paras 5/6 and 6; C-554/18 P of 15.1.2019 – Lion's Head Global Partners/EUIPO, paras 5/6 and 6, unofficial transcription; C-780/18 P of 22.5.2019 – Cuervo y Sobrinos 1882/EUIPO, paras 5/8 and 7; C-99/18 P of 4.7.2019 – FTI Touristik/EUIPO, para. 13; C-228/19 P of 24.9.2019 – ETI Gıda Sanayi ve Ticaret/EUIPO, paras 5/15 and 6; *see also* CJEU C-320/14 P of 13.1.2015 – Asos/OHIM, paras 20–23.
409. CJEU C-317/10 P of 16.6.2011 – Union Investment Privatfonds/OHIM, para. 45; C-354/11 P of 22.3.2012 – Emram/OHIM, para. 40; C-193/13 P of 16.1.2014 – nfon/OHIM, para. 52; C-177/13 P of 13.2.2014 – Marszałkowski/OHIM, para. 52; C-414/13 P of 20.5.2014 – Reber Holding/OHIM, para. 33; C-466/13 P of 22.10.2014 – Repsol YPF/OHIM, para. 63; C-311/14 P of 20.1.2015 – Longevity Health Products/OHIM, para. 39; C-43/15 P of 8.11.2016 – BSH Bosch

The question whether **qualities conveyed by a trade mark** are capable of being transferred to the whole body of services for which registration is, is a question of factual assessment.[410]

The assessment of the **similarities between the signs** at issue is of a factual nature.[411]

The assessment of the degree of similarity of the signs is a question of fact.[412]

The weighting of all these factors of visual, aural and conceptual similarity is a matter for the Court of First Instance to decide on the facts on a case-by-case basis.[413]

In so far as the Court has decided that there are phonetic or conceptual differences between the application mark and the older mark, it has made a finding of facts.[414]

---

und Siemens Hausgeräte/EUIPO, para. 52; C-158/17 P of 20.9.2017 - Anton Riemerschmid Weinbrennerei und Likörfabrik/EUIPO, paras 6/14 and 7; C-780/18 P of 22.5.2019 - Cuervo y Sobrinos 1882/EUIPO, paras 5/8 and 7; C-99/18 P of 4.7.2019 - FTI Touristik/EUIPO, para. 13; CJEU C-766/18 P of 5.3.2020 - Foundation for the Protection of the Traditional Cheese of Cyprus named Halloumi/EUIPO, para. 61.

410. CJEU C-673/15 P to C-676/15 P of 20.9.2017 - The Tea Board/EUIPO, para. 72, unofficial transcription.

411. CJEU C-254/09 P of 2.9.2010 - Calvin Klein/OHIM, para. 50; C-388/10 P of 24.3.2011 - Muñoz Arraiza/OHIM, para. 32; C-14/12 P of 30.5.2013 - Shah/OHIM, para. 25; C-346/12 P of 13.6.2013 - DMK Deutsches Milchkontor, paras 44 and 45; C-422/12 P of 30.1.2014 - Industrias Alen/OHIM, para. 38; C-150/14 P of 4.9.2014 - Goldsteig Käsereien Bayerwald/OHIM, para. 24; C-311/14 P of 20.1.2015 - Longevity Health Products/OHIM, para. 34; C-343/14 P of 7.5.2015 - Adler Modemärkte/OHIM, para. 32; C-251/15 P of 4.2.2016 - Emsibeth/OHIM, para. 30; C-442/15 P of 22.9.2016 - Pensa Pharma/EUIPO, para. 60; *see also* CJEU C-16/06 P of 18.12.2008 - Les Éditions Albert René/OHIM, para. 91; C-354/11 P of 22.3.2012 - Emram/OHIM, para. 85; C-466/13 P of 22.10.2014 - Repsol YPF/OHIM, para. 53; C-182/14 P of 19.3.2015 - MEGA Brands International/OHIM, para. 48; C-619/15 P of 21.6.2016 - Mocek a.o./EUIPO, paras 4/8 and 5; C-401/16 P 1.12.2016 - Market Watch Franchise & Consulting/EUIPO, paras 5/6 and 6; C-402/16 P 1.12.2016 - Market Watch Franchise & Consulting/EUIPO, paras 5/6 and 6; C-655/15 P of 2.3.2017 - Panrico/EUIPO, para. 68; C-158/17 P of 20.9.2017 - Anton Riemerschmid Weinbrennerei und Likörfabrik/EUIPO, paras 6/4 and 7; C-499/17 P of 14.12.2017 - Miguel Torres/EUIPO, paras 7/4 and 8; C-678/16 P of 18.1.2018 - Monster Energy/EUIPO, para. 49; C-651/17 of 12.4.2018 - Grupo Osborne/EUIPO, paras 6/21 and 7, unofficial transcription; C-652/17 of 12.4.2018 - Grupo Osborne/EUIPO, paras 6/21 and 7, unofficial transcription; C-553/18 P of 15.1.2019 - Lion's Head Global Partners/EUIPO, paras 5/5 and 6; C-554/18 P of 15.1.2019 - Lion's Head Global Partners/EUIPO, paras 5/5 and 6, unofficial transcription; *see also* CJEU C-86/17 P of 7.6.2017 - Redpur/EUIPO, paras 4/4 and 5; C-733/18 P of 19.3.2019 - Sevenfriday/EUIPO, paras 5/15 and 6; C-734/18 P of 19.3.2019 - Sevenfriday/EUIPO, paras 5/15 and 6; C-124/19 P of 11.9.2019 - Vitromed/EUIPO, paras 5/21 and 6; C-228/19 P of 24.9.2019 - ETI Gıda Sanayi ve Ticaret/EUIPO, paras 5/13 and 6; C-293/19 P of 2.10.2019 - Et Djili Soy Dzhihangir Ibryam/EUIPO, paras 7/9 and 7/17 and 8; C-887/19 P of 11.2.2020 - Rutzinger-Kurpas/EUIPO, para. 14; C-328/18 P of 4.3.2020 - EUIPO/Equivalenza Manufactory, para. 40; C-714/18 P of 16.7.2020 - ACTC/EUIPO, para. 67.

412. CJEU C-479/15 P of 14.4.2016 - Nanu-Nana Joachim Hoepp/EUIPO, para. 15.

413. CJEU C-474/15 P of 7.4.2016 - Harper Hygienics/EUIPO, para. 70, unofficial transcription; C-475/15 P of 7.4.2016 - Harper Hygienics/EUIPO, para. 72, unofficial transcription; C-182/16 P of 26.7.2017 - Meica Ammerländische Fleischwarenfabrik Fritz Meinen/EUIPO, para. 25, unofficial transcription; C-50/17 P of 1.6.2017 - Universidad Internacional de la Rioja/EUIPO, paras 5/17 and 6, unofficial transcription.

414. CJEU C-3/03 P of 28.4.2004 - Matratzen Concord/OHIM, para. 34; C-324/05 P of 1.6.2006 - Plus Warenhandelsgesellschaft/OHIM, para. 26; C-312/05 P of 27.3.2007 - TeleTech/OHIM, para. 66, unofficial transcription.

The analysis of the General Court, according to which, in essence, the word signs at issue are visually and phonetically similar and the alleged dissimilarity on the conceptual level is insufficient to counteract that similarity, is such an appraisal of facts.[415]

The assessment of the **overall impression** of the signs at issue is of a factual nature.[416]

The assessment of which element of a complex sign is the **dominant element** is of a factual nature.[417]

The assessment of which element of a complex sign is a **descriptive element** is of a factual nature.[418]

The **determination of distinctive character**, or lack of distinctive character, **of the various elements** of a sign, their importance in the overall impression given by the sign as well as the finding of conceptual similarity in relation to another sign involves a weighing up of those criteria which entails an analysis of a factual nature.[419]

The assessment of the comparison of the **conflicting goods** is factual in nature.[420]

---

415. CJEU C-23/09 P of 22.1.2010 – ecoblue/OHIM, para. 52, unofficial transcription; C-412/16 P and 413/16 P of 1.3.2018 – Ice Mountain Ibiza/EUIPO, para. 94, unofficial transcription; *see also* CJEU C-669/13 P of 21.10.2014 – Mundipharma/OHIM, para. 53.
416. CJEU C-655/15 P of 2.3.2017 – Panrico/EUIPO, para. 68, unofficial transcription; C-651/17 of 12.4.2018 – Grupo Osborne/EUIPO, paras 6/11 and 7, unofficial transcription; C-652/17 of 12.4.2018 – Grupo Osborne/EUIPO, paras 6/11 and 7, unofficial transcription.
417. CJEU C-488/06 P of 17.7.2008 – L & D/OHIM, paras 82 et seq.; C-388/10 P of 24.3.2011 – Muñoz Arraiza/OHIM, para. 66; C-379/12 P of 16.5.2013 – Arav Holding/OHIM, paras 40–42; C-494/13 P of 22.1.2015 – GRE Grand River Enterprises Deutschland/OHIM, paras 38 and 39; C-495/13 P of 22.1.2015 – GRE Grand River Enterprises Deutschland/OHIM, paras 38 and 39; C-496/13 P of 22.1.2015 – GRE Grand River Enterprises Deutschland/OHIM, paras 35 and 36; C-579/14 P of 4.6.2015 – Junited Autoglas Deutschland/OHIM, paras 26 and 27; C-619/15 P of 21.6.2016 – Mocek a.o./EUIPO, para. 4/11 and 5; *see also* CJEU C-224/14 P of 6.9.2016 – Lidl/EUIPO, para. 53; C-237/14 P of 6.9.2016 – Lidl/EUIPO, para. 58; C-412/16 P and 413/16 P of 1.3.2018 – Ice Mountain Ibiza/EUIPO, para. 80; C-651/17 of 12.4.2018 – Grupo Osborne/EUIPO, paras 6/11 and 7; C-652/17 of 12.4.2018 – Grupo Osborne/EUIPO, paras 6/11 and 7; C-726/17 P of 11.7.2018 – Tetra Pharm (1997)/EUIPO, para. 6; C-553/18 P of 15.1.2019 – Lion's Head Global Partners/EUIPO, paras 5/4 and 6; C-554/18 P of 15.1.2019 – Lion's Head Global Partners/EUIPO, paras 5/4 and 6; C-510/18 P of 14.2.2019 – Prada/EUIPO, paras 5/4 and 6; C-733/18 P of 19.3.2019 – Sevenfriday/EUIPO, paras 5/14 and 6; C-734/18 P of 19.3.2019 – Sevenfriday/EUIPO, paras 5/14 and 6; C-780/18 P of 22.5.2019 – Cuervo y Sobrinos 1882/EUIPO, paras 5/4 and 7; C-124/19 P of 11.9.2019 – Vitromed/EUIPO, paras 5/20 and 6; C-228/19 P of 24.9.2019 – ETI Gıda Sanayi ve Ticaret/EUIPO, paras 5/12 and 6; C-52/20 P of 28.5.2020 – K.A. Schmersal Holding/EUIPO, para. 18.
418. CJEU C-361/16 P of 8.11.2016 – Franmax/EUIPO, para. 5/24 and 6.
419. CJEU C-655/11 P of 21.2.2013 – Seven for all mankind/OHIM, para. 85; C-193/13 P of 16.1.2014 – nfon/OHIM, para. 28; C-190/15 P of 19.11.2015 – Fetim/OHIM, para. 33; *see also* CJEU C-327/11 P of 6.9.2012 – United States Polo/OHIM, paras 59 and 61; C-354/12 P of 11.4.2013 – ASA/OHIM, para. 32; C-193/13 P of 16.1.2014 – nfon/OHIM, para. 58; C-17/15 P of 26.10.2015 – Popp and Zech/OHIM, para. 57; C-251/15 P of 4.2.2016 – Emsibeth/OHIM, para. 37; C-278/15 P of 14.1.2016 – Royal County of Berkshire Polo Club/OHIM, para. 36; C-84/16 P of 26.7.2017 – Continental Reifen Deutschland/EUIPO, para. 70.
420. CJEU C-591/12 P of 8.5.2014 – Bimbo/OHIM, para. 24; C-494/13 P of 22.1.2015 – GRE Grand River Enterprises Deutschland/OHIM, para. 37; C-495/13 P of 22.1.2015 – GRE Grand River Enterprises Deutschland/OHIM, para. 37; C-548/14 P of 17.9.2015 – Arnoldo Mondadori Editore/OHIM, para. 39; C-479/15 P of 14.4.2016 – Nanu-Nana Joachim Hoepp/EUIPO, para. 28; C-480/15 P of 14.4.2016 – KS Sports IPCo/EUIPO, para. 73; C-655/15 P of 2.3.2017 – Panrico/EUIPO, para. 68; C-224/17 P of 19.10.2017 – Hernández Zamora/EUIPO, paras 5/4

The assessment of the **reputation of the earlier marks and of the link which the public may make** between the mark applied for and the earlier marks constitutes a matter of fact.[421]

The finding, by the General Court, as to whether the **facts** on which the Board of Appeal of OHIM based its decision were **well known or not** is a factual assessment.[422]

The **assessment of the link between the marks at issue**, for the purpose of Article 8(5) CTMR, is a factual finding regarding the degree of similarity between the marks and their degree of respective distinctiveness.[423]

The **assessment of the facts and evidence** and, in particular, the probative weight to be given to the **sworn statement** produced by a party, conducted by the General Court for that purpose, comes within the scope of the facts of the case.[424]

The assessment of **EUIPO's notifications** is factual in nature.[425]

However, provided that the appellant challenges the interpretation or the application of EU law by the General Court, the **points of law** examined at first instance may be discussed again in the context of an appeal.[426]

The question of whether the **grounds** of a judgment of the General Court are **contradictory** is a question of law which is, as such, amenable to judicial review on appeal.[427]

The question of whether the grounds of a judgment of the General Court are inadequate is a question of law which, as such, is amenable to review on appeal.[428]

The issue of whether the evidence presented in support of the reputation was properly obtained and whether the general principles of law and the rules of procedure

---

and 6; C-684/17 P of 17.5.2018 - Banca Monte dei Paschi di Siena/EUIPO, paras 4/23 and 5; C-685/17 P of 17.5.2018 - Banca Monte dei Paschi di Siena/EUIPO, paras 4/23 and 5; C-228/19 P of 24.9.2019 - ETI Gıda Sanayi ve Ticaret/EUIPO, paras 5/14 and 6.

421. CJEU C-294/12 P of 14.5.2013 - You-Q/OHIM, para. 61; *see also* CJEU C-548/14 P of 17.9.2015 - Arnoldo Mondadori Editore/OHIM, para. 57; C-50/15 P of 21.1.2016 - Hesse/OHIM, para. 29; C-505/17 P of 28.2.2019 - Groupe Léa Nature/EUIPO, para. 75.
422. CJEU C-579/08 P of 15.1.2010 - Messer Group/OHIM, para. 37; C-449/18 P and C-474/18 P of 17.9.2020 - EUIPO/Messi Cuccittini, para. 57.
423. CJEU C-499/17 P of 14.12.2017 - Miguel Torres/EUIPO, paras 7/7 and 8, unofficial transcription.
424. CJEU C-610/11 P of 26.9.2013 - Centrotherm Systemtechnik/OHIM, para. 44; C-414/13 P of 20.5.2014 - Reber Holding/OHIM, para. 32; *see also* CJEU C-234/06 P of 13.9.2007 - Il Ponte Finanziaria/OHIM, para. 75.
425. CJEU C-902/19 P of 3.3.2020 - Esim Chemicals/EUIPO, para. 13, unofficial transcription.
426. CJEU C-488/06 P of 17.7.2008 - L & D/OHIM, para. 43; C-552/09 P of 24.3.2011 - Ferrero/OHIM, para. 74.
427. CJEU C-14/12 P of 30.5.2013 - Shah/OHIM, para. 30; C-97/12 P of 15.5.2014 - Louis Vuitton Malletier/OHIM, para. 93; C-343/14 P of 7.5.2015 - Adler Modemärkte/OHIM, para. 51; *see also* CJEU C-446/00 P of 13.12.2001 - Cubero Vermurie/Commission, para. 20; C-54/09 P of 29.7.2010 - Greece/Commission, para. 87; C-642/15 of 1.12.2016 - Klement, para. 25; C-586/19 P of 7.10.2019 - L'Oréal/EUIPO, para. 10; C-587/19 P of 7.10.2019 - L'Oréal/EUIPO, para. 10; C-588/19 P of 7.10.2019 - L'Oréal/EUIPO, para. 10; C-589/19 P of 7.10.2019 - L'Oréal/EUIPO, para. 10; C-590/19 P of 7.10.2019 - L'Oréal/EUIPO, para. 10; C-328/18 P of 4.3.2020 - EUIPO/Equivalenza Manufactory, para. 25.
428. CJEU C-97/12 P of 15.5.2014 - Louis Vuitton Malletier/OHIM, para. 84; C-586/19 P of 7.10.2019 - L'Oréal/EUIPO, para. 10; C-587/19 P of 7.10.2019 - L'Oréal/EUIPO, para. 10; C-588/19 P of 7.10.2019 - L'Oréal/EUIPO, para. 10; C-589/19 P of 7.10.2019 - L'Oréal/EUIPO, para. 10; C-590/19 P of 7.10.2019 - L'Oréal/EUIPO, para. 10.

in relation to the burden of proof and the taking of evidence were observed constitutes a point of law which is subject to review by the Court of Justice.[429]

Distortion of the content of an act also constitutes an error of law.[430]

The **withdrawal**, after delivery of the Advocate General's Opinion, **of the application** for registration as a Community trade mark does not render the present appeal entirely devoid of purpose.[431]

That withdrawal does not, in itself, have any impact on the judgment under appeal. That judgment produced legal effects, and OHIM could still demonstrate that it has an interest in taking action to call into question those effects and the interpretation of Article 7(1)(b) and (c) CTMR which the Court of First Instance considered itself entitled to adopt in this case. Moreover, that judgment upheld the applicant's claims and could be helpful to that company in the context of other proceedings for registration of those words.[432]

Under the circumstances that it is common ground that that withdrawal has the effect of bringing to an end the dispute concerning the refusal of registration of those words as a Community trade mark, that the parties thus coincide in the view that the dispute is now settled, and that OHIM considers, in particular, that the withdrawal of the application for registration is 'valid' and considers that its claim for the judgment under appeal to be set aside no longer has any purpose, it is now unnecessary to give judgment in the present appeal.[433]

If the two parties to the proceedings have never pleaded that they have any interest whatsoever in the proceedings being continued after the application to register has been withdrawn, and if they agree that the case has been settled by withdrawing the application, granting any legal remedy would be irrelevant. Thus, a decision on the merits of the case is unnecessary.[434]

In **fixing the recoverable costs**, the Court takes account of all the circumstances of the case up to the making of the order on taxation of the costs, including the expenses necessarily incurred in relation to the taxation of costs proceedings.[435]

In the absence of provisions of EU law laying down fee scales, the Court must make an unfettered assessment of the facts of the case, taking into account the purpose and nature of the proceedings, their significance from the point of view of EU law, the difficulties presented by the case, the amount of work generated by the case for the agents or counsel involved and the economic interests which the parties had in the proceedings.[436]

---

429. CJEU C-564/16 P of 28.6.2018 – EUIPO/Puma, para. 57, with further proof.
430. CJEU C-164/98 P of 27.1.2000 – DIR International Film and Others/Commission, para. 48; C-317/10 P of 16.6.2011 – Union Investment Privatfonds/OHIM, para. 46; C-251/15 P of 4.2.2016 – Emsibeth/OHIM, para. 44.
431. CJEU C-498/01 P of 1.12.2004 – OHIM/Zapf, para. 10.
432. CJEU C-498/01 P of 1.12.2004 – OHIM/Zapf, para. 11.
433. CJEU C-498/01 P of 1.12.2004 – OHIM/Zapf, paras 12 et seq.
434. CJEU C-82/04 P of 19.1.2006 – Audi/OHIM, paras 22 et seq.; unofficial translation.
435. CJEU C-30/15 P-DEP2 of 30.5.2018 – Simba Toys/EUIPO, para. 25.
436. CJEU C-309/15 P-DEP of 14.12.2017 – MIP Metro Group Intellectual Property/Real Express, para. 10, with further proof.

An application for costs shall be admissible only if, on the date of the application, there was a dispute as to the recoverable costs and whether the parties have attempted to agree on any disputed amounts.[437]

[29] Request that the appeal be allowed

Take care: Appeals lodged after 1.5.2019 are subject to a procedure of admission on application – Article 58a I of the Statute of the Court of Justice of the European Union/Article 170a(1) of the Rules of Procedure.

Article 58a:

An appeal brought against a decision of the General Court concerning a decision of an independent board of appeal of one of the following offices and agencies of the Union shall not proceed unless the Court of Justice first decides that it should be allowed to do so:

(a) the European Union Intellectual Property Office;
(b) the Community Plant Variety Office;
(c) the European Chemicals Agency;
(d) the European Union Aviation Safety Agency.

The procedure referred to in the first paragraph shall also apply to appeals brought against decisions of the General Court concerning a decision of an independent board of appeal, set up after 1 May 2019[438] *within any other office or agency of the Union, which has to be seised before an action can be brought before the General Court.*

An appeal shall be allowed to proceed, wholly or in part, in accordance with the detailed rules set out in the Rules of Procedure, where it raises an issue that is significant with respect to the unity, consistency or development of Union law.

The decision as to whether the appeal should be allowed to proceed or not shall be reasoned, and it shall be published.

Article 170a Request that the appeal be allowed to proceed:

1. *In the situations referred to in the first and second paragraphs of Article 58a of the Statute, the appellant shall annex to the appeal a request that the appeal be allowed to proceed, setting out the issue raised by the appeal that is significant with respect to the unity, consistency or development of European Union law and containing all the information necessary to enable the Court of Justice to rule on that request. If there is no such request, the Vice-President of the Court shall declare the appeal inadmissible.*
2. *The request that the appeal be allowed to proceed shall not exceed seven pages and shall be drawn up taking into account all the formal requirements contained in the Practice Directions to parties concerning cases brought before the Court, adopted on the basis of these Rules.*
3. *If the request that the appeal be allowed to proceed does not comply with the requirements set out in the preceding paragraph, the Registrar shall prescribe a reasonable time limit within which the appellant is to put the request in*

437. CJEU C-586/15 P-DEP of 9.11.2017 – Nestlé Unternehmungen Deutschland/EUIPO, para. 9, with further proof.
438. *See* CJEU C-499/19 P of 5.9.2019 – Lupu/EUIPO, para. 7.

> *order. If the appellant fails to put the request in order within the time limit prescribed, the Vice-President of the Court shall decide, on a proposal from the Judge-Rapporteur and after hearing the Advocate General, whether the non-compliance with that formal requirement renders the appeal formally inadmissible.*

Since the requirement laid down in Article 170a(2) of the Rules of Procedure, according to which the application for leave to appeal may **not exceed seven pages**, has not been complied with and the appellant has not remedied the defect in its application for leave to appeal within the time limit laid down, the appeal must be dismissed pursuant to Article 170a(3) of the Rules of Procedure.[439]

The applicant submitted that seven pages were not sufficient to satisfy the requirements for leave to appeal arising from Article 58a of the Statute of the Court of Justice of the EU and Article 170a of the Rules of Procedure, as interpreted by the Court, where, as in the present case, the appeal is based on several grounds. Since it is necessary to indicate, in relation to each of those grounds of appeal, the reasons why the issue raised is important for the unity, consistency or development of European Union law, the maximum length of the application for leave to appeal laid down in Article 170a(2) of the Rules of Procedure must be multiplied by the number of grounds of appeal relied on.[440]

In that regard, it must be stated that such an interpretation is in any event contrary to the clear wording of that provision, according to which the application for leave to appeal may not exceed seven pages. The appellant's application for leave to appeal, which runs to sixteen pages, is manifestly excessive in the present case.[441]

It is **for the appellant to demonstrate** that the issues raised by its appeal are significant with respect to the unity, consistency or development of EU law.[442]

439. CJEU C-575/22 P of 10.10.2022 – Hochmann Marketing/EUIPO, para. 11, unofficial translation.
440. CJEU C-575/22 P of 10.10.2022 – Hochmann Marketing/EUIPO, para. 9, unofficial translation.
441. CJEU C-575/22 P of 10.10.2022 – Hochmann Marketing/EUIPO, para. 10, unofficial translation.
442. CJEU C-461/19 P of 30.9.2019 – All Star/EUIPO, para. 10; C-460/19 P of 1.10.2019 – Stada Arzneimittel/EUIPO, para. 10; C-577/19 P of 10.10.2019 – KID-Systeme/EUIPO, para. 11; C-582/19 P of 22.10.2019 – Holzer y Cia/EUIPO, para. 9; C-613/19 P of 24.10.2019 – Porsche/EUIPO, para. 13; C-622/19 P of 5.11.2019 – Luz Saúde/EUIPO, para. 10; C-659/19 P of 19.11.2019 – Nonnemacher/EUIPO, para. 11; C-660/19 P of 19.11.2019 – Nonnemacher/EUIPO, para. 11; C-678/19 P of 20.11.2019 – Retail Royalty/EUIPO, para. 13; C-664/19 P of 5.12.2019 – Agencja Wydawnicza Technopol/EUIPO, para. 13; C-713/19 P of 12.12.2019 – Guiral Broto/EUIPO, para. 9; C-714/19 P of 12.12.2019 – Guiral Broto/EUIPO, para. 9; C-715/19 P of 12.12.2019 – Guiral Broto/EUIPO, para. 9; C-696/19 P of 19.12.2019 – Hauzenberger/EUIPO, para. 13; C-858/19 P of 6.2.2020 – NHS/EUIPO, para. 10; C-887/19 P of 11.2.2020 – Rutzinger-Kurpas/EUIPO, para. 9; C-823/19 P of 13.2.2020 – ruwido austria/EUIPO, para. 12; C-867/19 P of 13.2.2020 – Confédération nationale du Crédit Mutuel/EUIPO, para. 10; C-902/19 P of 3.3.2020 – Esim Chemicals/EUIPO, para. 8; C-893/19 P of 12.3.2020 – Roxtec/EUIPO, para. 11; C-908/19 P of 18.3.2020 – European Food/EUIPO, para. 12; C-26/20 P of 21.4.2020 – Rezon/EUIPO, para. 10; C-936/19 P of 23.4.2020 – Rubik's Brand/EUIPO, para. 12; C-14/20 P of 23.4.2020 – Neoperl/EUIPO, para. 9; C-52/20 P of 28.5.2020 – K.A. Schmersal Holding/EUIPO, para. 12; C-61/20 P of 28.5.2020 – Billa/EUIPO, para. 11; C-74/20 P of 28.5.2020 – Hänstens Sängar/EUIPO, para. 15; C-101/20 P of 28.5.2020 – Currency One/EUIPO, para. 12; C-72/20 P of 4.6.2020 – Refan Bulgaria/EUIPO, para. 9; C-97/20 P of 4.6.2020 – Société des produits Nestlé/EUIPO, para. 13; C-239/20 P of 30.9.2020 – Giorgio

Armani/EUIPO, para. 14; C-240/20 P of 30.9.2020 – Giorgio Armani/EUIPO, para. 13; C-313/20 P of 13.10.2020 – Abarca/EUIPO, para. 10; C-386/20 P of 21.10.2020 – eSky Group IP/EUIPO, para. 9; C-307/20 P of 29.10.2020 – Peek & Cloppenburg/EUIPO, para. 12; C-308/20 P of 29.10.2020 – Peek & Cloppenburg/EUIPO, para. 12; C-309/20 P of 29.10.2020 – Peek & Cloppenburg/EUIPO, para. 12; C-310/20 P of 29.10.2020 – Peek & Cloppenburg/EUIPO, para. 12; C-311/20 P of 29.10.2020 – Peek & Cloppenburg/EUIPO, para. 12; C-312/20 P of 29.10.2020 – Peek & Cloppenburg/EUIPO, para. 12; C-446/20 P of 12.11.2020 – Katjes Fassin/EUIPO, para. 8; C-418/20 P of 26.11.2020 – Scorify/EUIPO, para. 17; C-400/20 P of 3.12.2020 – Dermavita/EUIPO, para. 10; C-404/20 P of 17.12.2020 – Brands Up/EUIPO, para. 14; C-401/20 P of 19.1.2021 – Leinfelder Uhren München/EUIPO, para. 13; C-626/20 P of 28.1.2021 – Kaminski/EUIPO, para. 10; C-600/20 P of 11.2.2021 – Klose/EUIPO, para. 11; C-667/20 P of 18.3.2021 – Laboratorios Ern/EUIPO, para. 13; C-678/20 P of 18.3.2021 – Laboratorios Ern/EUIPO, para. 13; C-639/20 P of 23.3.2021 – CEDC International/EUIPO, para. 16; C-681/20 P of 24.3.2021 – smart things solutions/EUIPO, para. 11; C-722/20 P of 25.3.2021 – Ultrasun/EUIPO, para. 11; C-41/21 P of 29.4.2021 – Allergan Holdings France/EUIPO, para. 11; C-26/21 P of 4.5.2021 – Dermavita/EUIPO, para. 11; C-5/21 P of 5.5.2021 – Deutsche Post/EUIPO, para. 13; C-143/21 P of 5.5.2021 – Production Christian Gallimard/EUIPO, para. 11; C-48/21 P of 12.5.2021 – Topcart/EUIPO, para. 14; C-49/21 P of 12.5.2021 – Topcart/EUIPO, para. 14; C-67/21 P of 12.5.2021 – BSH Hausgeräte/EUIPO, para. 10; C-59/21 P of 18.5.2021 – Embutidos Monells/EUIPO, para. 11; C-93/21 P of 20.5.2021 – easyCosmetic Swiss/EUIPO, para. 9; C-109/21 P of 2.6.2021 – H.R. Participations/EUIPO, para. 13; C-114/21 P of 22.6.2021 – Cinkciarz.pl/EUIPO, para. 10; C-219/21 P of 24.6.2021 – Olimp Laboratories/EUIPO, para. 13; C-185/21 P of 29.6.2021 – Turk Hava Yollari/EUIPO, para. 13; C-236/21 P of 1.9.2021 – sprd.net/EUIPO, para. 14; C-417/21 P of 8.9.2021 – repowermap.org/EUIPO, para. 14; C-369/21 P of 22.9.2021 – Apologistics/EUIPO, para. 13; C-360/21 P of 6.10.2021 – FCA Italy/EUIPO, para. 12; C-415/21 P of 10.11.2021 – Comercializadora Eloro/EUIPO, para. 12; C-424/21 P of 11.11.2021 – Sun Stars & Sons/EUIPO, para. 12; C-425/21 P of 11.11.2021 – Sun Stars & Sons/EUIPO, para. 12; C-465/21 P of 12.11.2021 – König Ludwig International/EUIPO, para. 12; C-498/21 P of 22.11.2021 – Birkenstock IP a.o./EUIPO, para. 12; C-345/21 P of 23.11.2021 – Foundation for the Protection of the Traditional Cheese of Cyprus named Halloumi/EUIPO, para. 12; C-327/21 P of 26.11.2021 – Giro Travel Company/EUIPO, para. 11; C-483/21 P of 30.11.2021 – Health Product Group/EUIPO, para. 17; C-373/21 P of 1.12.2021 – Hasbro/EUIPO, para. 13; C-462/21 P of 1.12.2021 – Puma/EUIPO, para. 17; C-473/21 P of 8.12.2021 – Franz Schröder/EUIPO, para. 11; C-474/21 P of 8.12.2021 – Franz Schröder/EUIPO, para. 11; C-475/21 P of 8.12.2021 – Franz Schröder/EUIPO, para. 11; C-476/21 P of 10.12.2021 – Rezon/EUIPO, para. 10; C-387/21 P of 13.12.2021 – Asolo a.o./EUIPO, para. 20; C-589/21 P of 13.12.2021 – Abitron Germany/EUIPO, para. 14; C-619/21 P of 13.12.2021 – Cora/EUIPO, para. 12; C-523/21 P of 16.12.2021 – Innovative Cosmetic Concepts/EUIPO, para. 9; C-538/21 P of 21.12.2021 – Republic of Cyprus/EUIPO, para. 15; C-599/21 P of 17.1.2022 – AM.VI. a.o./EUIPO, para. 14; C-557/21 P of 27.1.2022 – Acciona/EUIPO, para. 13; C-672/21 P of 4.2.2022 – Eos Products/EUIPO, para. 11; C-674/21 P of 22.2.2022 – Residencial Palladium/EUIPO, para. 11; C-678/21 P of 24.2.2022 – Sony Interactive Entertainment Europe/EUIPO, para. 14; C-679/21 P of 24.2.2022 – Sony Interactive Entertainment Europe/EUIPO, para. 12; C-730/21 P of 23.3.2022 – Collibra/EUIPO, para. 13; C-781/21 P of 28.3.2022 – Daw/EUIPO, para. 15; C-743/21 P of 31.3.2022 – Marina Yachting Brand Management/EUIPO, para. 12; C-744/21 P of 31.3.2022 – Henry Cotton's Brand Management/EUIPO, para. 12; C-761/21 P of 31.3.2022 – St. Hippolyt Holding/EUIPO, para. 13; C-762/21 P of 31.3.2022 – St. Hippolyt Holding/EUIPO, para. 13; C-784/21 P of 5.4.2022 – Kappes/EUIPO, para. 14; C-785/21 P of 5.4.2022 – Kappes/EUIPO, para. 14; C-801/21 P of 7.4.2022 – EUIPO/Indo European Foods, para. 24; C-65/22 P of 6.5.2022 – Industria de Diseño Textil/EUIPO, para. 11; C-194/22 P of 7.6.2022 – Magic Box Int. Toys/EUIPO, para. 13; C-120/22 P of 15.6.2022 – Republic of Cyprus/EUIPO, para. 12; C-121/22 P of 15.6.2022 – Foundation for the Protection of the Traditional Cheese of Cyprus named Halloumi/EUIPO, para. 12; C-145/22 P of 17.6.2022 – Lück/EUIPO, para. 13; C-253/22 P of 6.7.2022 – Rice/EUIPO, para. 11; C-187/22 P of 11.7.2022 – Laboratorios Ern/EUIPO, para. 11; C-247/22 P of 14.7.2022 – Ignacio Carrasco/EUIPO, para. 10; C-233/22 P of 15.7.2022 – Meta Cluster/EUIPO, para. 10; C-338/22 P of 22.9.2022 – Hrebenyuk/EUIPO, para. 9; C-320/22

As is apparent from the third paragraph of Article 58a of the Statute of the Court, read together with Article 170b(4) of the Court's Rules of Procedure, the request that an appeal be allowed to proceed must **contain all the information necessary** to enable the Court to give a ruling on whether the appeal should be allowed to proceed and to specify, where the appeal is allowed to proceed in part, the pleas in law or parts of the appeal to which the response must relate. Given that the objective of the mechanism provided for in Article 58a of the Statute of the Court whereby the Court determines whether an appeal should be allowed to proceed is to restrict review by the Court to issues that are significant with respect to the unity, consistency or development of EU law, only grounds of appeal that raise such issues and that are established by the appellant are to be examined by the Court in an appeal.[443]

P of 28.9.2022 – the airscreen company/EUIPO, para. 11; C-342/22 P of 28.9.2022 – Laboratorios Ern/EUIPO, para. 9; C-383/22 P of 17.10.2022 – SFC/EUIPO, para. 10; C-446/22 P of 20.10.2022 – Fidelity National Information Services/EUIPO, para. 11; C-405/22 P of 8.11.2022 – Mandeley/EUIPO, para. 12; C-337/22 P of 16.11.2022 – EUIPO/Nowhere, para. 23; C-577/22 P of 29.11.2022 – Munich/EUIPO, para. 10; C-571/22 P of 5.12.2022 – Unite the Union/EUIPO, para. 14; C-594/22 P of 5.12.2022 – Gugler France/EUIPO, para. 8; C-612/22 P of 5.12.2022 – Tigercat International/EUIPO, para. 10; C-702/22 P of 1.2.2023 – Balaban/EUIPO, para. 10; C-681/22 P of 27.2.2023 – Olimp Laboratories/EUIPO, para. 11; C-605/22 P of 8.3.2023 – Hijos de Moisés Rodríguez González/EUIPO, para. 15; C-788/22 P of 21.3.2023 – Louis Vuitton Malletier/EUIPO, para. 11; C-732/22 P of 23.3.2023 – G-Core Innovations/EUIPO, para. 10; C-735/22 P of 24.3.2023 – Primagran/EUIPO, para. 9; C-42/23 P of 19.4.2023 – Mendes/EUIPO, para. 11; C-15/23 P of 11.5.2023 – Heinze/EUIPO, para. 14; C-38/23 P of 13.6.2023 – Grupa 'Lew'/EUIPO, para. 13; C-199/23 P of 15.6.2023 – Zielonogórski Klub Żużlowy Sportowa/EUIPO, para. 10; C-77/23 P of 27.6.2023 – Haskovo Chamber of Commerce and Industry/EUIPO, para. 21; C-120/23 P of 5.7.2023 – Suicha/EUIPO, para. 11; C-64/23 P of 11.7.2023 – Neoperl/EUIPO, para. 10; C-142/23 P of 13.7.2023 – Hecht Pharma/EUIPO, para. 14; C-94/23 P of 17.7.2023 – Puma/EUIPO, para. 15; C-145/23 P of 17.7.2023 – Puma/EUIPO, para. 16; C-280/23 P of 17.7.2023 – Canai Technology/EUIPO, para. 9.

443. CJEU C-577/19 P of 10.10.2019 – KID-Systeme/EUIPO, para. 12; C-582/19 P of 22.10.2019 – Holzer y Cia/EUIPO, para. 10; C-613/19 P of 24.10.2019 – Porsche/EUIPO, para. 14; C-622/19 P of 5.11.2019 – Luz Saúde/EUIPO, para. 11; C-659/19 P of 19.11.2019 – Nonnemacher/EUIPO, para. 12; C-660/19 P of 19.11.2019 – Nonnemacher/EUIPO, para. 12; C-678/19 P of 20.11.2019 – Retail Royalty/EUIPO, para. 14; C-664/19 P of 5.12.2019 – Agencja Wydawnicza Technopol/EUIPO, para. 14; C-713/19 P of 12.12.2019 – Guiral Broto/EUIPO, para. 10; C-714/19 P of 12.12.2019 – Guiral Broto/EUIPO, para. 10; C-715/19 P of 12.12.2019 – Guiral Broto/EUIPO, para. 10; C-696/19 P of 19.12.2019 – Hauzenberger/EUIPO, para. 14 C-858/19 P of 6.2.2020 – NHS/EUIPO, para. 11; C-887/19 P of 11.2.2020 – Rutzinger-Kurpas/EUIPO, para. 10; C-823/19 P of 13.2.2020 – ruwido austria/EUIPO, para. 13; C-867/19 P of 13.2.2020 – Confédération nationale du Crédit Mutuel/EUIPO, para. 11; C-902/19 P of 3.3.2020 – Esim Chemicals/EUIPO, para. 9; C-893/19 P of 12.3.2020 – Roxtec/EUIPO, para. 12; C-908/19 P of 18.3.2020 – European Food/EUIPO, para. 13; C-26/20 P of 21.4.2020 – Rezon/EUIPO, para. 11; C-14/20 P of 23.4.2020 – Neoperl/EUIPO, para. 10; C-936/19 P of 23.4.2020 – Rubik's Brand/EUIPO, para. 13; C-52/20 P of 28.5.2020 – K.A. Schmersal Holding/EUIPO, para. 13; C-61/20 P of 28.5.2020 – Billa/EUIPO, para. 12; C-74/20 P of 28.5.2020 – Hänstens Sängar/EUIPO, para. 16; C-101/20 P of 28.5.2020 – Currency One/EUIPO, para. 13; C-72/20 P of 4.6.2020 – Refan Bulgaria/EUIPO, para. 10; C-97/20 P of 4.6.2020 – Société des produits Nestlé/EUIPO, para. 14; C-239/20 P of 30.9.2020 – Giorgio Armani/EUIPO, para. 15; C-240/20 P of 30.9.2020 – Giorgio Armani/EUIPO, para. 14; C-313/20 P of 13.10.2020 – Abarca/EUIPO, para. 11; C-386/20 P of 21.10.2020 – eSky Group IP/EUIPO, para. 10; C-307/20 P of 29.10.2020 – Peek & Cloppenburg/EUIPO, para. 13; C-308/20 P of 29.10.2020 – Peek & Cloppenburg/EUIPO, para. 13; C-309/20 P of 29.10.2020 – Peek & Cloppenburg/EUIPO, para. 13; C-310/20 P of 29.10.2020 – Peek & Cloppenburg/EUIPO, para. 13; C-311/20 P of 29.10.2020 – Peek & Cloppenburg/EUIPO, para. 13; C-312/20 P of 29.10.2020 – Peek & Cloppenburg/EUIPO, para. 13; C-446/20 P of 12.11.2020

– Katjes Fassin/EUIPO, para. 9; C-418/20 P of 26.11.2020 – Scorify/EUIPO, para. 18; C-400/20 P of 3.12.2020 – Dermavita/EUIPO, para. 11; C-404/20 P of 17.12.2020 – Brands Up/EUIPO, para. 15; C-401/20 P of 19.1.2021 – Leinfelder Uhren München/EUIPO, para. 14; C-626/20 P of 28.1.2021 – Kaminski/EUIPO, para. 11; C-600/20 P of 11.2.2021 – Klose/EUIPO, para. 12; C-667/20 P of 18.3.2021 – Laboratorios Ern/EUIPO, para. 14; C-678/20 P of 18.3.2021 – Laboratorios Ern/EUIPO, para. 14; C-639/20 P of 23.3.2021 – CEDC International/EUIPO, para. 17; C-681/20 P of 24.3.2021 – smart things solutions/EUIPO, para. 12; C-722/20 P of 25.3.2021 – Ultrasun/EUIPO, para. 12; C-41/21 P of 29.4.2021 – Allergan Holdings France/EUIPO, para. 12; C-26/21 P of 4.5.2021 – Dermavita/EUIPO, para. 12; C-5/21 P of 5.5.2021 – Deutsche Post/EUIPO, para. 14; C-143/21 P of 5.5.2021 – Production Christian Gallimard/EUIPO, para. 12; C-48/21 P of 12.5.2021 – Topcart/EUIPO, para. 15; C-49/21 P of 12.5.2021 – Topcart/EUIPO, para. 15; C-67/21 P of 12.5.2021 – BSH Hausgeräte/EUIPO, para. 11; C-59/21 P of 18.5.2021 – Embutidos Monells/EUIPO, para. 12; C-93/21 P of 20.5.2021 – easyCosmetic Swiss/EUIPO, para. 10; C-109/21 P of 2.6.2021 – H.R. Participations/EUIPO, para. 14; C-114/21 P of 22.6.2021 – Cinkciarz.pl/EUIPO, para. 11; C-219/21 P of 24.6.2021 – Olimp Laboratories/EUIPO, para. 14; C-185/21 P of 29.6.2021 – Turk Hava Yollari/EUIPO, para. 14; C-211/21 P of 1.9.2021 – 12seasons/EUIPO, para. 12; C-236/21 P of 1.9.2021 – sprd.net/EUIPO, para. 15; C-417/21 P of 8.9.2021 – repowermap.org/EUIPO, para. 15; C-369/21 P of 22.9.2021 – Apologistics/EUIPO, para. 14; C-360/21 P of 6.10.2021 – FCA Italy/EUIPO, para. 13; C-415/21 P of 10.11.2021 – Comercializadora Eloro/EUIPO, para. 13; C-424/21 P of 11.11.2021 – Sun Stars & Sons/EUIPO, para. 13; C-425/21 P of 11.11.2021 – Sun Stars & Sons/EUIPO, para. 13; C-465/21 P of 12.11.2021 – König Ludwig International/EUIPO, para. 13; C-498/21 P of 22.11.2021 – Birkenstock IP a.o./EUIPO, para. 13; C-345/21 P of 23.11.2021 – Foundation for the Protection of the Traditional Cheese of Cyprus named Halloumi/EUIPO, para. 13; C-327/21 P of 26.11.2021 – Giro Travel Company/EUIPO, para. 12; C-483/21 P of 30.11.2021 – Health Product Group/EUIPO, para. 18; C-373/21 P of 1.12.2021 – Hasbro/EUIPO, para. 14; C-462/21 P of 1.12.2021 – Puma/EUIPO, para. 18; C-473/21 P of 8.12.2021 – Franz Schröder/EUIPO, para. 12; C-474/21 P of 8.12.2021 – Franz Schröder/EUIPO, para. 12; C-475/21 P of 8.12.2021 – Franz Schröder/EUIPO, para. 12; C-476/21 P of 10.12.2021 – Rezon/EUIPO, para. 11; C-387/21 P of 13.12.2021 – Asolo a.o./EUIPO, para. 21; C-589/21 P of 13.12.2021 – Abitron Germany/EUIPO, para. 15; C-619/21 P of 13.12.2021 – Cora/EUIPO, para. 13; C-523/21 P of 16.12.2021 – Innovative Cosmetic Concepts/EUIPO, para. 10; C-538/21 P of 21.12.2021 – Republic of Cyprus/EUIPO, para. 16; C-599/21 P of 17.1.2022 – AM.VI. a.o./EUIPO, para. 15; C-557/21 P of 27.1.2022 – Acciona/EUIPO, para. 14; C-672/21 P of 4.2.2022 – Eos Products/EUIPO, para. 12; C-674/21 P of 22.2.2022 – Residencial Palladium/EUIPO, para. 12; C-678/21 P of 24.2.2022 – Sony Interactive Entertainment Europe/EUIPO, para. 15; C-679/21 P of 24.2.2022 – Sony Interactive Entertainment Europe/EUIPO, para. 13; C-730/21 P of 23.3.2022 – Collibra/EUIPO, para. 14; C-781/21 P of 28.3.2022 – Daw/EUIPO, para. 16; C-743/21 P of 31.3.2022 – Marina Yachting Brand Management/EUIPO, para. 13; C-744/21 P of 31.3.2022 – Henry Cotton's Brand Management/EUIPO, para. 13; C-761/21 P of 31.3.2022 – St. Hippolyt Holding/EUIPO, para. 14; C-762/21 P of 31.3.2022 – St. Hippolyt Holding/EUIPO, para. 14; C-784/21 P of 5.4.2022 – Kappes/EUIPO, para. 15; C-785/21 P of 5.4.2022 – Kappes/EUIPO, para. 15; C-801/21 P of 7.4.2022 – EUIPO/Indo European Foods, para. 25; C-65/22 P of 6.5.2022 – Industria de Diseño Textil/EUIPO, para. 12; C-194/22 P of 7.6.2022 – Magic Box Int. Toys/EUIPO, para. 14; C-120/22 P of 15.6.2022 – Republic of Cyprus/EUIPO, para. 13; C-121/22 P of 15.6.2022 – Foundation for the Protection of the Traditional Cheese of Cyprus named Halloumi/EUIPO, para. 13; C-145/22 P of 17.6.2022 – Lück/EUIPO, para. 14; C-253/22 P of 6.7.2022 – Rice/EUIPO, para. 12; C-187/22 P of 11.7.2022 – Laboratorios Ern/EUIPO, para. 12; C-247/22 P of 14.7.2022 – Ignacio Carrasco/EUIPO, para. 11; C-233/22 P of 15.7.2022 – Meta Cluster/EUIPO, para. 11; C-338/22 P of 22.9.2022 – Hrebenyuk/EUIPO, para. 10; C-320/22 P of 28.9.2022 – the airscreen company/EUIPO, para. 12; C-342/22 P of 28.9.2022 – Laboratorios Ern/EUIPO, para. 10; C-383/22 P of 17.10.2022 – SFC/EUIPO, para. 11; C-446/22 P of 20.10.2022 – Fidelity National Information Services/EUIPO, para. 12; C-405/22 P of 8.11.2022 – Mandeley/EUIPO, para. 13; C-337/22 P of 16.11.2022 – EUIPO/Nowhere, para. 24; C-577/22 P of 29.11.2022 – Munich/EUIPO, para. 11; C-571/22 P of 5.12.2022 – Unite the Union/EUIPO, para. 15; C-594/22 P of 5.12.2022 – Gugler France/EUIPO, para. 9; C-612/22 P of 5.12.2022 – Tigercat International/EUIPO, para. 11; C-702/22 P of 1.2.2023 – Balaban/

Accordingly, a request that an appeal be allowed to proceed must, in any event, set out **clearly and in detail the grounds** on which the appeal is based, identify with equal clarity and detail the issue of law raised by each ground of appeal; specify whether that issue is significant with respect to the unity, consistency or development of EU law; and set out the specific reasons why that issue is significant according to that criterion. As regards, in particular, the grounds of appeal, the request that an appeal be allowed to proceed must specify the provision of EU law or the case law that has been infringed by the judgment under appeal, explain succinctly the nature of the error of law allegedly committed by the General Court, and indicate to what extent that error had an effect on the outcome of the judgment under appeal.[444]

EUIPO, para. 11; C-681/22 P of 27.2.2023 – Olimp Laboratories/EUIPO, para. 12; C-605/22 P of 8.3.2023 – Hijos de Moisés Rodríguez González/EUIPO, para. 16; C-788/22 P of 21.3.2023 – Louis Vuitton Malletier/EUIPO, para. 12; C-732/22 P of 23.3.2023 – G-Core Innovations/EUIPO, para. 11; C-735/22 P of 24.3.2023 – Primagran/EUIPO, para. 10; C-42/23 P of 19.4.2023 – Mendes/EUIPO, para. 12; C-15/23 P of 11.5.2023 – Heinze/EUIPO, para. 15; C-38/23 P of 13.6.2023 – Grupa 'Lew'/EUIPO, para. 14; C-199/23 P of 15.6.2023 – Zielonogórski Klub Żużlowy Sportowa/EUIPO, para. 11; C-77/23 P of 27.6.2023 – Haskovo Chamber of Commerce and Industry/EUIPO, para. 22; C-120/23 P of 5.7.2023 – Suicha/EUIPO, para. 12; C-64/23 P of 11.7.2023 – Neoperl/EUIPO, para. 11; C-142/23 P of 13.7.2023 – Hecht Pharma/EUIPO, para. 15; C-94/23 P of 17.7.2023 – Puma/EUIPO, para. 16; C-145/23 P of 17.7.2023 – Puma/EUIPO, para. 17; C-280/23 P of 17.7.2023 – Canai Technology/EUIPO, para. 10.

444. CJEU C-461/19 P of 30.9.2019 – All Star/EUIPO, para. 14; C-577/19 P of 10.10.2019 – KID-Systeme/EUIPO, para. 13; C-582/19 P of 22.10.2019 – Holzer y Cia/EUIPO, para. 11; C-613/19 P of 24.10.2019 – Porsche/EUIPO, para. 15; C-622/19 P of 5.11.2019 – Luz Saúde/EUIPO, para. 12; C-659/19 P of 19.11.2019 – Nonnemacher/EUIPO, para. 13; C-660/19 P of 19.11.2019 – Nonnemacher/EUIPO, para. 13; C-678/19 P of 20.11.2019 – Retail Royalty/EUIPO, para. 15; C-664/19 P of 5.12.2019 – Agencja Wydawnicza Technopol/EUIPO, para. 15; C-713/19 P of 12.12.2019 – Guiral Broto/EUIPO, para. 11; C-714/19 P of 12.12.2019 – Guiral Broto/EUIPO, para. 11; C-715/19 P of 12.12.2019 – Guiral Broto/EUIPO, para. 11; C-696/19 P of 19.12.2019 – Hauzenberger/EUIPO, para. 15; C-858/19 P of 6.2.2020 – NHS/EUIPO, para. 12; C-887/19 P of 11.2.2020 – Rutzinger-Kurpas/EUIPO, para. 11; C-823/19 P of 13.2.2020 – ruwido austria/EUIPO, para. 14; C-867/19 P of 13.2.2020 – Confédération nationale du Crédit Mutuel/EUIPO, para. 12; C-902/19 P of 3.3.2020 – Esim Chemicals/EUIPO, para. 10; C-893/19 P of 12.3.2020 – Roxtec/EUIPO, para. 13; C-908/19 P of 18.3.2020 – European Food/EUIPO, paras 14 et seq.; C-26/20 P of 21.4.2020 – Rezon/EUIPO, para. 12; C-14/20 P of 23.4.2020 – Neoperl/EUIPO, para. 11; C-936/19 P of 23.4.2020 – Rubik's Brand/EUIPO, para. 14; C-52/20 P of 28.5.2020 – K.A. Schmersal Holding/EUIPO, para. 14; C-61/20 P of 28.5.2020 – Billa/EUIPO, para. 13; C-74/20 P of 28.5.2020 – Hänstens Sängar/EUIPO, para. 17; C-101/20 P of 28.5.2020 – Currency One/EUIPO, para. 14 and 18; C-72/20 P of 4.6.2020 – Refan Bulgaria/EUIPO, para. 11; C-97/20 P of 4.6.2020 – Société des produits Nestlé/EUIPO, para. 15; C-239/20 P of 30.9.2020 – Giorgio Armani/EUIPO, para. 16; C-240/20 P of 30.9.2020 – Giorgio Armani/EUIPO, para. 15; C-313/20 P of 13.10.2020 – Abarca/EUIPO, para. 12; C-386/20 P of 21.10.2020 – eSky Group IP/EUIPO, para. 11; C-307/20 P of 29.10.2020 – Peek & Cloppenburg/EUIPO, para. 14; C-308/20 P of 29.10.2020 – Peek & Cloppenburg/EUIPO, para. 14; C-309/20 P of 29.10.2020 – Peek & Cloppenburg/EUIPO, para. 14; C-310/20 P of 29.10.2020 – Peek & Cloppenburg/EUIPO, para. 14; C-311/20 P of 29.10.2020 – Peek & Cloppenburg/EUIPO, para. 14; C-312/20 P of 29.10.2020 – Peek & Cloppenburg/EUIPO, para. 14; C-446/20 P of 12.11.2020 – Katjes Fassin/EUIPO, para. 10; C-418/20 P of 26.11.2020 – Scorify/EUIPO, para. 19; C-400/20 P of 3.12.2020 – Dermavita/EUIPO, para. 12; C-404/20 P of 17.12.2020 – Brands Up/EUIPO, para. 16; C-401/20 P of 19.1.2021 – Leinfelder Uhren München/EUIPO, para. 15; C-626/20 P of 28.1.2021 – Kaminski/EUIPO, para. 12; C-600/20 P of 11.2.2021 – Klose/EUIPO, para. 13; C-667/20 P of 18.3.2021 – Laboratorios Ern/EUIPO, para. 15; C-678/20 P of 18.3.2021 – Laboratorios Ern/EUIPO, para. 15; C-639/20 P of 23.3.2021 – CEDC International/EUIPO, para. 18; C-681/20 P of 24.3.2021 – smart things solutions/EUIPO, para. 13; C-722/20 P of 25.3.2021

– Ultrasun/EUIPO, para. 13; C-41/21 P of 29.4.2021 – Allergan Holdings France/EUIPO, para. 13; C-26/21 P of 4.5.2021 – Dermavita/EUIPO, para. 13; C-5/21 P of 5.5.2021 – Deutsche Post/EUIPO, para. 15; C-143/21 P of 5.5.2021 – Production Christian Gallimard/EUIPO, para. 13; C-48/21 P of 12.5.2021 – Topcart/EUIPO, para. 16; C-49/21 P of 12.5.2021 – Topcart/EUIPO, para. 16; C-67/21 P of 12.5.2021 – BSH Hausgeräte/EUIPO, para. 12; C-59/21 P of 18.5.2021 – Embutidos Monells/EUIPO, para. 13; C-93/21 P of 20.5.2021 – easyCosmetic Swiss/EUIPO, para. 11; C-109/21 P of 2.6.2021 – H.R. Participations/EUIPO, para. 15; C-114/21 P of 22.6.2021 – Cinkciarz.pl/EUIPO, para. 12; C-219/21 P of 24.6.2021 – Olimp Laboratories/EUIPO, para. 15; C-185/21 P of 29.6.2021 – Turk Hava Yollari/EUIPO, para. 15; C-211/21 P of 1.9.2021 – 12seasons/EUIPO, para. 13; C-236/21 P of 1.9.2021 – sprd.net/EUIPO, para. 16; C-417/21 P of 8.9.2021 – repowermap.org/EUIPO, para. 16; C-369/21 P of 22.9.2021 – Apologistics/EUIPO, para. 15; C-360/21 P of 6.10.2021 – FCA Italy/EUIPO, para. 14; C-415/21 P of 10.11.2021 – Comercializadora Eloro/EUIPO, para. 14; C-424/21 P of 11.11.2021 – Sun Stars & Sons/EUIPO, para. 14; C-425/21 P of 11.11.2021 – Sun Stars & Sons/EUIPO, para. 14; C-465/21 P of 12.11.2021 – König Ludwig International/EUIPO, para. 14; C-498/21 P of 22.11.2021 – Birkenstock IP a.o./EUIPO, para. 14; C-345/21 P of 23.11.2021 – Foundation for the Protection of the Traditional Cheese of Cyprus named Halloumi/EUIPO, para. 14; C-327/21 P of 26.11.2021 – Giro Travel Company/EUIPO, para. 13; C-483/21 P of 30.11.2021 – Health Product Group/EUIPO, para. 19; C-373/21 P of 1.12.2021 – Hasbro/EUIPO, para. 15; C-462/21 P of 1.12.2021 – Puma/EUIPO, para. 19; C-473/21 P of 8.12.2021 – Franz Schröder/EUIPO, para. 13; C-474/21 P of 8.12.2021 – Franz Schröder/EUIPO, para. 13; C-475/21 P of 8.12.2021 – Franz Schröder/EUIPO, para. 13; C-476/21 P of 10.12.2021 – Rezon/EUIPO, para. 12; C-387/21 P of 13.12.2021 – Asolo a.o./EUIPO, para. 22; C-589/21 P of 13.12.2021 – Abitron Germany/EUIPO, para. 16; C-619/21 P of 13.12.2021 – Cora/EUIPO, para. 14; C-523/21 P of 16.12.2021 – Innovative Cosmetic Concepts/EUIPO, para. 11; C-538/21 P of 21.12.2021 – Republic of Cyprus/EUIPO, para. 17; C-599/21 P of 17.1.2022 – AM.VI. a.o./EUIPO, para. 16; C-557/21 P of 27.1.2022 – Acciona/EUIPO, para. 15; C-672/21 P of 4.2.2022 – Eos Products/EUIPO, para. 13; C-674/21 P of 22.2.2022 – Residencial Palladium/EUIPO, para. 13; C-678/21 P of 24.2.2022 – Sony Interactive Entertainment Europe/EUIPO, para. 16; C-679/21 P of 24.2.2022 – Sony Interactive Entertainment Europe/EUIPO, para. 14; C-730/21 P of 23.3.2022 – Collibra/EUIPO, para. 15; C-781/21 P of 28.3.2022 – Daw/EUIPO, para. 17; C-743/21 P of 31.3.2022 – Marina Yachting Brand Management/EUIPO, para. 14; C-744/21 P of 31.3.2022 – Henry Cotton's Brand Management/EUIPO, para. 14; C-761/21 P of 31.3.2022 – St. Hippolyt Holding/EUIPO, para. 15; C-762/21 P of 31.3.2022 – St. Hippolyt Holding/EUIPO, para. 15; C-784/21 P of 5.4.2022 – Kappes/EUIPO, para. 16; C-785/21 P of 5.4.2022 – Kappes/EUIPO, para. 16; C-801/21 P of 7.4.2022 – EUIPO/Indo European Foods, para. 26; C-65/22 P of 6.5.2022 – Industria de Diseño Textil/EUIPO, para. 13; C-194/22 P of 7.6.2022 – Magic Box Int. Toys/EUIPO, para. 15; C-120/22 P of 15.6.2022 – Republic of Cyprus/EUIPO, para. 14; C-121/22 P of 15.6.2022 – Foundation for the Protection of the Traditional Cheese of Cyprus named Halloumi/EUIPO, para. 14; C-145/22 P of 17.6.2022 – Lück/EUIPO, para. 15; C-253/22 P of 6.7.2022 – Rice/EUIPO, para. 13; C-187/22 P of 11.7.2022 – Laboratorios Ern/EUIPO, para. 13; C-247/22 P of 14.7.2022 – Ignacio Carrasco/EUIPO, para. 12; C-233/22 P of 15.7.2022 – Meta Cluster/EUIPO, para. 12; C-338/22 P of 22.9.2022 – Hrebenyuk/EUIPO, para. 11; C-320/22 P of 28.9.2022 – the airscreen company/EUIPO, para. 13; C-342/22 P of 28.9.2022 – Laboratorios Ern/EUIPO, para. 11; C-383/22 P of 17.10.2022 – SFC/EUIPO, para. 12; C-446/22 P of 20.10.2022 – Fidelity National Information Services/EUIPO, para. 13; C-405/22 P of 8.11.2022 – Mandeley/EUIPO, para. 14; C-337/22 P of 16.11.2022 – EUIPO/Nowhere, para. 25; C-577/22 P of 29.11.2022 – Munich/EUIPO, para. 12; C-571/22 P of 5.12.2022 – Unite the Union/EUIPO, para. 16; C-594/22 P of 5.12.2022 – Gugler France/EUIPO, para. 10; C-612/22 P of 5.12.2022 – Tigercat International/EUIPO, para. 12; C-702/22 P of 1.2.2023 – Balaban/EUIPO, para. 12; C-681/22 P of 27.2.2023 – Olimp Laboratories/EUIPO, para. 13; C-605/22 P of 8.3.2023 – Hijos de Moisés Rodríguez González/EUIPO, para. 18; C-788/22 P of 21.3.2023 – Louis Vuitton Malletier/EUIPO, para. 13; C-732/22 P of 23.3.2023 – G-Core Innovations/EUIPO, para. 12; C-735/22 P of 24.3.2023 – Primagran/EUIPO, para. 11; C-42/23 P of 19.4.2023 – Mendes/EUIPO, para. 13; C-15/23 P of 11.5.2023 – Heinze/EUIPO, para. 16; C-38/23 P of 13.6.2023 – Grupa 'Lew'/EUIPO, para. 15; C-199/23 P of 15.6.2023 – Zielonogórski Klub

Therefore, a request that an appeal be allowed to proceed which does not contain the mentioned information cannot, from the outset, be capable of demonstrating that the appeal raises an issue that is significant with respect to the unity, consistency or development of EU law that justifies the appeal being allowed to proceed.[445]

Żużlowy Sportowa/EUIPO, para. 12; C-77/23 P of 27.6.2023 – Haskovo Chamber of Commerce and Industry/EUIPO, para. 23; C-120/23 P of 5.7.2023 – Suicha/EUIPO, para. 13; C-64/23 P of 11.7.2023 – Neoperl/EUIPO, para. 12; C-142/23 P of 13.7.2023 – Hecht Pharma/EUIPO, para. 16; C-94/23 P of 17.7.2023 – Puma/EUIPO, para. 17; C-145/23 P of 17.7.2023 – Puma/EUIPO, para. 18; C-280/23 P of 17.7.2023 – Canai Technology/EUIPO, para. 11.

445. CJEU C-577/19 P of 10.10.2019 – KID-Systeme/EUIPO, para. 14; C-582/19 P of 22.10.2019 – Holzer y Cia/EUIPO, para. 13; C-613/19 P of 24.10.2019 – Porsche/EUIPO, para. 16; C-622/19 P of 5.11.2019 – Luz Saúde/EUIPO, para. 13; C-659/19 P of 19.11.2019 – Nonnemacher/EUIPO, para. 14; C-660/19 P of 19.11.2019 – Nonnemacher/EUIPO, para. 14; C-678/19 P of 20.11.2019 – Retail Royalty/EUIPO, para. 16; C-664/19 P of 5.12.2019 – Agencja Wydawnicza Technopol/EUIPO, para. 16; C-696/19 P of 19.12.2019 – Hauzenberger/EUIPO, para. 16; C-858/19 P of 6.2.2020 – NHS/EUIPO, para. 13; C-887/19 P of 11.2.2020 – Rutzinger-Kurpas/EUIPO, para. 12; C-823/19 P of 13.2.2020 – ruwido austria/EUIPO, para. 15; C-867/19 P of 13.2.2020 – Confédération nationale du Crédit Mutuel/EUIPO, para. 13; C-902/19 P of 3.3.2020 – Esim Chemicals/EUIPO, para. 11; C-893/19 P of 12.3.2020 – Roxtec/EUIPO, para. 14; C-908/19 P of 18.3.2020 – European Food/EUIPO, para. 16; C-26/20 P of 21.4.2020 – Rezon/EUIPO, para. 13; C-936/19 P of 23.4.2020 – Rubik's Brand/EUIPO, para. 15; C-14/20 P of 23.4.2020 – Neoperl/EUIPO, para. 12; C-52/20 P of 28.5.2020 – K.A. Schmersal Holding/EUIPO, para. 15; C-61/20 P of 28.5.2020 – Billa/EUIPO, para. 14; C-74/20 P of 28.5.2020 – Hänstens Sängar/EUIPO, para. 18; C-101/20 P of 28.5.2020 – Currency One/EUIPO, para. 15; C-72/20 P of 4.6.2020 – Refan Bulgaria/EUIPO, para. 12; C-97/20 P of 4.6.2020 – Société des produits Nestlé/EUIPO, para. 16; C-239/20 P of 30.9.2020 – Giorgio Armani/EUIPO, para. 17; C-240/20 P of 30.9.2020 – Giorgio Armani/EUIPO, para. 16; C-313/20 P of 13.10.2020 – Abarca/EUIPO, para. 13; C-386/20 P of 21.10.2020 – eSky Group IP/EUIPO, para. 12; C-307/20 P of 29.10.2020 – Peek & Cloppenburg/EUIPO, para. 15; C-308/20 P of 29.10.2020 – Peek & Cloppenburg/EUIPO, para. 15; C-309/20 P of 29.10.2020 – Peek & Cloppenburg/EUIPO, para. 15; C-310/20 P of 29.10.2020 – Peek & Cloppenburg/EUIPO, para. 15; C-311/20 P of 29.10.2020 – Peek & Cloppenburg/EUIPO, para. 15; C-312/20 P of 29.10.2020 – Peek & Cloppenburg/EUIPO, para. 15; C-446/20 P of 12.11.2020 – Katjes Fassin/EUIPO, para. 11; C-418/20 P of 26.11.2020 – Scorify/EUIPO, para. 20; C-400/20 P of 3.12.2020 – Dermavita/EUIPO, para. 13; C-404/20 P of 17.12.2020 – Brands Up/EUIPO, para. 18; C-401/20 P of 19.1.2021 – Leinfelder Uhren München/EUIPO, para. 16; C-626/20 P of 28.1.2021 – Kaminski/EUIPO, para. 13; C-600/20 P of 11.2.2021 – Klose/EUIPO, para. 14; C-667/20 P of 18.3.2021 – Laboratorios Ern/EUIPO, para. 16; C-678/20 P of 18.3.2021 – Laboratorios Ern/EUIPO, para. 16; C-639/20 P of 23.3.2021 – CEDC International/EUIPO, para. 19; C-681/20 P of 24.3.2021 – smart things solutions/EUIPO, para. 14; C-722/20 P of 25.3.2021 – Ultrasun/EUIPO, para. 14; C-41/21 P of 29.4.2021 – Allergan Holdings France/EUIPO, para. 14; C-26/21 P of 4.5.2021 – Dermavita/EUIPO, para. 14; C-5/21 P of 5.5.2021 – Deutsche Post/EUIPO, para. 16; C-143/21 P of 5.5.2021 – Production Christian Gallimard/EUIPO, para. 14; C-48/21 P of 12.5.2021 – Topcart/EUIPO, para. 17; C-49/21 P of 12.5.2021 – Topcart/EUIPO, para. 17; C-67/21 P of 12.5.2021 – BSH Hausgeräte/EUIPO, para. 13; C-59/21 P of 18.5.2021 – Embutidos Monells/EUIPO, para. 14; C-93/21 P of 20.5.2021 – easyCosmetic Swiss/EUIPO, para. 12; C-109/21 P of 2.6.2021 – H.R. Participations/EUIPO, para. 16; C-114/21 P of 22.6.2021 – Cinkciarz.pl/EUIPO, para. 13; C-219/21 P of 24.6.2021 – Olimp Laboratories/EUIPO, para. 16; C-185/21 P of 29.6.2021 – Turk Hava Yollari/EUIPO, para. 16; C-211/21 P of 1.9.2021 – 12seasons/EUIPO, para. 14; C-236/21 P of 1.9.2021 – sprd.net/EUIPO, para. 17; C-417/21 P of 8.9.2021 – repowermap.org/EUIPO, para. 17; C-369/21 P of 22.9.2021 – Apologistics/EUIPO, para. 16; C-360/21 P of 6.10.2021 – FCA Italy/EUIPO, para. 15; C-415/21 P of 10.11.2021 – Comercializadora Eloro/EUIPO, para. 15; C-424/21 P of 11.11.2021 – Sun Stars & Sons/EUIPO, para. 15; C-425/21 P of 11.11.2021 – Sun Stars & Sons/EUIPO, para. 15; C-465/21 P of 12.11.2021 – König Ludwig International/EUIPO, para. 15; C-498/21 P of 22.11.2021 – Birkenstock IP a.o./EUIPO, para. 15; C-345/21 P of 23.11.2021 – Foundation for the Protection of the Traditional Cheese of Cyprus named Halloumi/EUIPO, para. 15; C-327/21

In accordance with the burden of proof which lies with the appellant requesting that the appeal be allowed to proceed, the appellant must demonstrate that, independently of the issues of law raised in its appeal, the appeal raises one or more issues that are significant with respect to the unity, consistency or development of EU law, the scope of that criterion going beyond the judgment under appeal and, ultimately, its appeal. In order to demonstrate that that is the case, it is necessary to establish both the existence and significance of such issues by means of concrete evidence specific to the particular case and not simply arguments of a general nature.[446]

P of 26.11.2021 – Giro Travel Company/EUIPO, para. 14; C-483/21 P of 30.11.2021 – Health Product Group/EUIPO, para. 20; C-373/21 P of 1.12.2021 – Hasbro/EUIPO, para. 16; C-462/21 P of 1.12.2021 – Puma/EUIPO, para. 20; C-473/21 P of 8.12.2021 – Franz Schröder/EUIPO, para. 14; C-474/21 P of 8.12.2021 – Franz Schröder/EUIPO, para. 14; C-475/21 P of 8.12.2021 – Franz Schröder/EUIPO, para. 14; C-476/21 P of 10.12.2021 – Rezon/EUIPO, para. 13; C-387/21 P of 13.12.2021 – Asolo a.o./EUIPO, para. 23; C-589/21 P of 13.12.2021 – Abitron Germany/EUIPO, para. 17; C-619/21 P of 13.12.2021 – Cora/EUIPO, para. 15; C-523/21 P of 16.12.2021 – Innovative Cosmetic Concepts/EUIPO, para. 12; C-538/21 P of 21.12.2021 – Republic of Cyprus/EUIPO, para. 18; C-599/21 P of 17.1.2022 – AM.VI. a.o./EUIPO, para. 17; C-557/21 P of 27.1.2022 – Acciona/EUIPO, para. 16; C-672/21 P of 4.2.2022 – Eos Products/EUIPO, para. 14; C-674/21 P of 22.2.2022 – Residencial Palladium/EUIPO, para. 14; C-678/21 P of 24.2.2022 – Sony Interactive Entertainment Europe/EUIPO, para. 17; C-679/21 P of 24.2.2022 – Sony Interactive Entertainment Europe/EUIPO, para. 15; C-730/21 P of 23.3.2022 – Collibra/EUIPO, para. 16; C-781/21 P of 28.3.2022 – Daw/EUIPO, para. 18; C-743/21 P of 31.3.2022 – Marina Yachting Brand Management/EUIPO, para. 15; C-744/21 P of 31.3.2022 – Henry Cotton's Brand Management/EUIPO, para. 15; C-761/21 P of 31.3.2022 – St. Hippolyt Holding/EUIPO, para. 16; C-762/21 P of 31.3.2022 – St. Hippolyt Holding/EUIPO, para. 16; C-784/21 P of 5.4.2022 – Kappes/EUIPO, para. 17; C-785/21 P of 5.4.2022 – Kappes/EUIPO, para. 17; C-801/21 P of 7.4.2022 – EUIPO/Indo European Foods, para. 27; C-65/22 P of 6.5.2022 – Industria de Diseño Textil/EUIPO, para. 14; C-194/22 P of 7.6.2022 – Magic Box Int. Toys/EUIPO, para. 16; C-120/22 P of 15.6.2022 – Republic of Cyprus/EUIPO, para. 15; C-121/22 P of 15.6.2022 – Foundation for the Protection of the Traditional Cheese of Cyprus named Halloumi/EUIPO, para. 16; C-145/22 P of 17.6.2022 – Lück/EUIPO, para. 16; C-253/22 P of 6.7.2022 – Rice/EUIPO, para. 14; C-187/22 P of 11.7.2022 – Laboratorios Ern/EUIPO, para. 14; C-247/22 P of 14.7.2022 – Ignacio Carrasco/EUIPO, para. 13; C-338/22 P of 22.9.2022 – Hrebenyuk/EUIPO, para. 12; C-320/22 P of 28.9.2022 – the airscreen company/EUIPO, para. 14; C-342/22 P of 28.9.2022 – Laboratorios Ern/EUIPO, para. 12; C-383/22 P of 17.10.2022 – SFC/EUIPO, para. 13; C-446/22 P of 20.10.2022 – Fidelity National Information Services/EUIPO, para. 14; C-405/22 P of 8.11.2022 – Mandeley/EUIPO, para. 15; C-337/22 P of 16.11.2022 – EUIPO/Nowhere, para. 26; C-577/22 P of 29.11.2022 – Munich/EUIPO, para. 13; C-571/22 P of 5.12.2022 – Unite the Union/EUIPO, para. 17; C-594/22 P of 5.12.2022 – Gugler France/EUIPO, para. 11; C-612/22 P of 5.12.2022 – Tigercat International/EUIPO, para. 13; C-702/22 P of 1.2.2023 – Balaban/EUIPO, para. 13; C-681/22 P of 27.2.2023 – Olimp Laboratories/EUIPO, para. 14; C-605/22 P of 8.3.2023 – Hijos de Moisés Rodríguez González/EUIPO, para. 19; C-788/22 P of 21.3.2023 – Louis Vuitton Malletier/EUIPO, para. 14; C-732/22 P of 23.3.2023 – G-Core Innovations/EUIPO, para. 13; C-735/22 P of 24.3.2023 – Primagran/EUIPO, para. 12; C-42/23 P of 19.4.2023 – Mendes/EUIPO, para. 14; C-15/23 P of 11.5.2023 – Heinze/EUIPO, para. 17; C-38/23 P of 13.6.2023 – Grupa 'Lew'/EUIPO, para. 16; C-199/23 P of 15.6.2023 – Zielonogórski Klub Żużlowy Sportowa/EUIPO, para. 13; C-77/23 P of 27.6.2023 – Haskovo Chamber of Commerce and Industry/EUIPO, para. 24; C-120/23 P of 5.7.2023 – Suicha/EUIPO, para. 14; C-64/23 P of 11.7.2023 – Neoperl/EUIPO, para. 13; C-142/23 P of 13.7.2023 – Hecht Pharma/EUIPO, para. 17; C-94/23 P of 17.7.2023 – Puma/EUIPO, para. 18; C-145/23 P of 17.7.2023 – Puma/EUIPO, para. 19; C-280/23 P of 17.7.2023 – Canai Technology/EUIPO, para. 12.

446. CJEU C-61/20 P of 28.5.2020 – Billa/EUIPO, para. 16; C-239/20 P of 30.9.2020 – Giorgio Armani/EUIPO, para. 14; C-240/20 P of 30.9.2020 – Giorgio Armani/EUIPO, para. 20; C-313/20 P of 13.10.2020 – Abarca/EUIPO, para. 15; C-619/21 P of 13.12.2021 – Cora/EUIPO, para. 21;

In accordance with the burden of proof which lies with the appellant requesting that the appeal be allowed to proceed, such arguments are not, in themselves, sufficient to establish that that appeal raises an issue that is significant with respect to the unity, consistency or development of EU law, the appellant having to comply to that end with all the requirements set out.[447]

The claim that the **General Court departed from the Court of Justice's case law** in a given order or judgment is **not, in itself, sufficient** to establish, in accordance with the evidential burden which is borne by the party requesting that an appeal be allowed to proceed, that that appeal raises an issue which is significant with respect to the unity, consistency or development of EU law. For that purpose, the party requesting that its appeal be allowed to proceed must set out, succinctly but clearly and precisely, first, where the conflict which it is invoking lies, identifying both the paragraphs of the judgment or order under appeal which it is calling into question and those of the decision of the Court of Justice which were disregarded, and, second, the specific

C-781/21 P of 28.3.2022 – Daw/EUIPO, para. 21; C-743/21 P of 31.3.2022 – Marina Yachting Brand Management/EUIPO, para. 17; C-744/21 P of 31.3.2022 – Henry Cotton's Brand Management/EUIPO, para. 17; C-801/21 P of 7.4.2022 – EUIPO/Indo European Foods, para. 34; C-65/22 P of 6.5.2022 – Industria de Diseño Textil/EUIPO, paras 16 et seq.; C-253/22 P of 6.7.2022 – Rice/EUIPO, para. 16; C-247/22 P of 14.7.2022 – Ignacio Carrasco/EUIPO, para. 17; C-320/22 P of 28.9.2022 – the airscreen company/EUIPO, para. 16; C-405/22 P of 8.11.2022 – Mandeley/EUIPO, para. 17; C-337/22 P of 16.11.2022 – EUIPO/Nowhere, paras 32 et seq.; C-577/22 P of 29.11.2022 – Munich/EUIPO, para. 15; C-594/22 P of 5.12.2022 – Gugler France/EUIPO, para. 12; C-732/22 P of 23.3.2023 – G-Core Innovations/EUIPO, para. 16; C-120/23 P of 5.7.2023 – Suicha/EUIPO, para. 19; C-142/23 P of 13.7.2023 – Hecht Pharma/ EUIPO, para. 21; C-94/23 P of 17.7.2023 – Puma/EUIPO, para. 20; C-145/23 P of 17.7.2023 – Puma/EUIPO, para. 21; C-280/23 P of 17.7.2023 – Canai Technology/EUIPO, para. 16.

447. CJEU C-613/19 P of 24.10.2019 – Porsche/EUIPO, para. 17; C-887/19 P of 11.2.2020 – Rutzinger-Kurpas/EUIPO, para. 15; C-867/19 P of 13.2.2020 – Confédération nationale du Crédit Mutuel/EUIPO, para. 17; C-902/19 P of 3.3.2020 – Esim Chemicals/EUIPO, para. 12; C-893/19 P of 12.3.2020 – Roxtec/EUIPO, para. 15 and 21; C-74/20 P of 28.5.2020 – Hänstens Sängar/EUIPO, para. 20; C-101/20 P of 28.5.2020 – Currency One/EUIPO, para. 22; C-97/20 P of 4.6.2020 – Société des produits Nestlé/EUIPO, para. 21; C-313/20 P of 13.10.2020 – Abarca/EUIPO, para. 17; C-446/20 P of 12.11.2020 – Katjes Fassin/EUIPO, para. 13; C-400/20 P of 3.12.2020 – Dermavita/EUIPO, para. 22; C-401/20 P of 19.1.2021 – Leinfelder Uhren München/EUIPO, para. 24; C-722/20 P of 25.3.2021 – Ultrasun/EUIPO, para. 16; C-5/21 P of 5.5.2021 – Deutsche Post/EUIPO, para. 18; C-59/21 P of 18.5.2021 – Embutidos Monells/ EUIPO, para. 19; C-345/21 P of 23.11.2021 – Foundation for the Protection of the Traditional Cheese of Cyprus named Halloumi/EUIPO, para. 16; C-327/21 P of 26.11.2021 – Giro Travel Company/EUIPO, para. 15; C-483/21 P of 30.11.2021 – Health Product Group/EUIPO, para. 22; C-373/21 P of 1.12.2021 – Hasbro/EUIPO, para. 19; C-387/21 P of 13.12.2021 – Asolo a.o./EUIPO, para. 24; C-589/21 P of 13.12.2021 – Abitron Germany/EUIPO, para. 19; C-619/21 P of 13.12.2021 – Cora/EUIPO, para. 19; C-679/21 P of 24.2.2022 – Sony Interactive Entertainment Europe/EUIPO, para. 17; C-781/21 P of 28.3.2022 – Daw/EUIPO, para. 20; C-743/21 P of 31.3.2022 – Marina Yachting Brand Management/EUIPO, paras 19 et seq.; C-744/21 P of 31.3.2022 – Henry Cotton's Brand Management/EUIPO, paras 19 et seq.; C-784/21 P of 5.4.2022 – Kappes/EUIPO, para. 18; C-785/21 P of 5.4.2022 – Kappes/EUIPO, para. 18; C-801/21 P of 7.4.2022 – EUIPO/Indo European Foods, para. 33; C-194/22 P of 7.6.2022 – Magic Box Int. Toys/EUIPO, para. 17; C-187/22 P of 11.7.2022 – Laboratorios Ern/EUIPO, para. 17; C-571/22 P of 5.12.2022 – Unite the Union/EUIPO, para. 18; C-594/22 P of 5.12.2022 – Gugler France/EUIPO, para. 13; C-605/22 P of 8.3.2023 – Hijos de Moisés Rodríguez González/ EUIPO, para. 20; C-280/23 P of 17.7.2023 – Canai Technology/EUIPO, para. 13.

reasons for which it takes the view that such a conflict raises an issue which is significant with respect to the unity, consistency or development of EU law.[448]

A plea based on an alleged **distortion of the facts** by the General Court cannot, in principle, be capable of raising in itself, even if it were well founded, a question of importance for the unity, consistency or development of Union law.[449]

Failure to state reasons or an inadequate statement of reasons constitutes an error of law which may be relied on in the context of an appeal; the determination as to whether the appeal is allowed to proceed nevertheless remains subject to specific conditions consisting, for the appellant, in demonstrating that that appeal raises one or more issues that are significant with respect to the unity, consistency or development of EU law.[450]

The claim that the appeal raises an issue that is likely to arise **in all cases** concerning the assessment of genuine use of an EU trade mark is simply an argument

448. CJEU C-586/19 P of 7.10.2019 – L'Oréal/EUIPO, para. 16; C-587/19 P of 7.10.2019 – L'Oréal/EUIPO, para. 16; C-588/19 P of 7.10.2019 – L'Oréal/EUIPO, para. 16; C-589/19 P of 7.10.2019 – L'Oréal/EUIPO, para. 16; C-590/19 P of 7.10.2019 – L'Oréal/EUIPO, para. 16; C-582/19 P of 22.10.2019 – Holzer y Cia/EUIPO, para. 12; C-613/19 P of 24.10.2019 – Porsche/EUIPO, para. 18; C-678/19 P of 20.11.2019 – Retail Royalty/EUIPO, para. 17; C-893/19 P of 12.3.2020 – Roxtec/EUIPO, para. 19; C-418/20 P of 26.11.2020 – Scorify/EUIPO, para. 23; C-67/21 P of 12.5.2021 – BSH Hausgeräte/EUIPO, para. 15; *see also* CJEU C-369/19 P of 15.7.2019 – Herrero Torres/EUIPO, para. 10; C-823/19 P of 13.2.2020 – ruwido austria/EUIPO, para. 18; C-936/19 P of 23.4.2020 – Rubik's Brand/EUIPO, para. 20; C-14/20 P of 23.4.2020 – Neoperl/EUIPO, para. 16; C-97/20 P of 4.6.2020 – Société des produits Nestlé/EUIPO, para. 18 and 20; C-239/20 P of 30.9.2020 – Giorgio Armani/EUIPO, paras 23 et seq.; C-240/20 P of 30.9.2020 – Giorgio Armani/EUIPO, paras 22 et seq.; C-400/20 P of 3.12.2020 – Dermavita/EUIPO, paras 16 et seq.; C-404/20 P of 17.12.2020 – Brands Up/EUIPO, para. 17; C-401/20 P of 19.1.2021 – Leinfelder Uhren München/EUIPO, para. 17; C-626/20 P of 28.1.2021 – Kaminski/EUIPO, paras 14 et seqq.; C-600/20 P of 11.2.2021 – Klose/EUIPO, paras 16 et seqq.; C-667/20 P of 18.3.2021 – Laboratorios Ern/EUIPO, para. 22; C-678/20 P of 18.3.2021 – Laboratorios Ern/EUIPO, para. 22; C-681/20 P of 24.3.2021 – smart things solutions/EUIPO, para. 18; C-722/20 P of 25.3.2021 – Ultrasun/EUIPO, para. 18; C-41/21 P of 29.4.2021 – Allergan Holdings France/EUIPO, para. 15; C-59/21 P of 18.5.2021 – Embutidos Monells/EUIPO, para. 16; C-114/21 P of 22.6.2021 – Cinkciarz.pl/EUIPO, paras 15 et seq.; C-219/21 P of 24.6.2021 – Olimp Laboratories/EUIPO, para. 20; C-236/21 P of 1.9.2021 – sprd.net/EUIPO, para. 20.; C-415/21 P of 10.11.2021 – Comercializadora Eloro/EUIPO, para. 17; C-424/21 P of 11.11.2021 – Sun Stars & Sons/EUIPO, para. 17; C-425/21 P of 11.11.2021 – Sun Stars & Sons/EUIPO, para. 17; C-465/21 P of 12.11.2021 – König Ludwig International/EUIPO, para. 18; C-462/21 P of 1.12.2021 – Puma/EUIPO, para. 23; C-476/21 P of 10.12.2021 – Rezon/EUIPO, para. 16; C-538/21 P of 21.12.2021 – Republic of Cyprus/EUIPO, para. 20; C-446/22 P of 20.10.2022 – Fidelity National Information Services/EUIPO, para. 16; C-612/22 P of 5.12.2022 – Tigercat International/EUIPO, para. 18; C-15/23 P of 11.5.2023 – Heinze/EUIPO, para. 19; C-64/23 P of 11.7.2023 – Neoperl/EUIPO, para. 16; C-142/23 P of 13.7.2023 – Hecht Pharma/EUIPO, para. 19.

449. CJEU C-426/19 P of 24.9.2019 – Hesse/EUIPO, para. 11, unofficial translation; C-307/20 P of 29.10.2020 – Peek & Cloppenburg/EUIPO, para. 21; C-308/20 P of 29.10.2020 – Peek & Cloppenburg/EUIPO, para. 21; C-309/20 P of 29.10.2020 – Peek & Cloppenburg/EUIPO, para. 21; C-310/20 P of 29.10.2020 – Peek & Cloppenburg/EUIPO, para. 21; C-311/20 P of 29.10.2020 – Peek & Cloppenburg/EUIPO, para. 21; C-312/20 P of 29.10.2020 – Peek & Cloppenburg/EUIPO, para. 21; C-599/21 P of 17.1.2022 – AM.VI. a.o./EUIPO, para. 19.

450. CJEU C-696/19 P of 19.12.2019 – Hauzenberger/EUIPO, para. 20; C-26/21 P of 4.5.2021 – Dermavita/EUIPO, para. 21; C-236/21 P of 1.9.2021 – sprd.net/EUIPO, para. 22; C-405/22 P of 8.11.2022 – Mandeley/EUIPO, para. 19; C-605/22 P of 8.3.2023 – Hijos de Moisés Rodríguez González/EUIPO, para. 21; C-94/23 P of 17.7.2023 – Puma/EUIPO, para. 23; C-145/23 P of 17.7.2023 – Puma/EUIPO, para. 24.

of a general nature and, consequently, is not such as to justify the appeal being allowed to proceed. Furthermore, the fact that an issue might concern a large number of cases clearly cannot be regarded as relevant for the purpose of establishing the legal significance of the issue for the unity, consistency or development of EU law.[451]

The fact that a point of law has **not been examined by the Court of Justice** does not mean that that question is necessarily significant for the development of Union law. Indeed, the appellant is always obliged to demonstrate such significance by providing precise information not only on the novelty of that question but also on the reasons why it is significant in the light of that development.[452]

It should be noted, in the first place, that EUIPO **clearly describes its single ground of appeal**, stating that the General Court, first of all, conflated the procedural requirement of an interest in bringing proceedings with the review of the substantive legality of the decision at issue, next, that it did not assess *in concreto* whether Indo European Foods' interest in bringing proceedings continued, as regards the benefit that the annulment of the decision at issue could secure for it, that it, in addition, refused to consider the fact that the latter had not complied with its obligation to show that its interest in bringing proceedings continued even though nothing would suggest that it so continued after the end of the transition period and, lastly, that it held, in essence, that EUIPO was not to take account of the effects flowing from Article 50(3) TEU and from Articles 126 and 127 of the withdrawal agreement, thereby disregarding the relevant provisions of the EUTMR, in particular the principle of territoriality of intellectual property law.[453]

In particular, EUIPO has set out in detail the paragraphs of the grounds of the judgment under appeal which, in its view, are inconsistent with the case law of the Court of Justice relating to the continuation of the interest in bringing proceedings but

451. CJEU C-400/20 P of 3.12.2020 – Dermavita/EUIPO, para. 19; C-26/21 P of 4.5.2021 – Dermavita/EUIPO, para. 20, unofficial comprehension.
452. CJEU C-461/19 P of 30.9.2019 – All Star/EUIPO, para. 16; C-577/19 P of 10.10.2019 – KID-Systeme/EUIPO, para. 19; C-613/19 P of 24.10.2019 – Porsche/EUIPO, para. 19; C-659/19 P of 19.11.2019 – Nonnemacher/EUIPO, para. 17; C-660/19 P of 19.11.2019 – Nonnemacher/EUIPO, para. 17; C-74/20 P of 28.5.2020 – Hänstens Sängar/EUIPO, para. 29; *see also* CJEU C-586/19 P of 7.10.2019 – L'Oréal/EUIPO, para. 11; C-587/19 P of 7.10.2019 – L'Oréal/EUIPO, para. 11; C-588/19 P of 7.10.2019 – L'Oréal/EUIPO, para. 11; C-589/19 P of 7.10.2019 – L'Oréal/EUIPO, para. 11; C-590/19 P of 7.10.2019 – L'Oréal/EUIPO, para. 11; C-867/19 P of 13.2.2020 – Confédération nationale du Crédit Mutuel/EUIPO, para. 15; C-401/20 P of 19.1.2021 – Leinfelder Uhren München/EUIPO, para. 20; C-722/20 P of 25.3.2021 – Ultrasun/EUIPO, para. 17; C-26/21 P of 4.5.2021 – Dermavita/EUIPO, para. 22; C-67/21 P of 12.5.2021 – BSH Hausgeräte/EUIPO, para. 14; C-417/21 P of 8.9.2021 – repowermap.org/EUIPO, para. 22; C-369/21 P of 22.9.2021 – Apologistics/EUIPO, para. 21; C-498/21 P of 22.11.2021 – Birkenstock IP a.o./EUIPO, para. 17; C-373/21 P of 1.12.2021 – Hasbro/EUIPO, para. 17; C-462/21 P of 1.12.2021 – Puma/EUIPO, para. 25; C-387/21 P of 13.12.2021 – Asolo a.o./EUIPO, para. 27; C-619/21 P of 13.12.2021 – Cora/EUIPO, para. 17; C-538/21 P of 21.12.2021 – Republic of Cyprus/EUIPO, para. 22; C-678/21 P of 24.2.2022 – Sony Interactive Entertainment Europe/EUIPO, para. 23; C-781/21 P of 28.3.2022 – Daw/EUIPO, para. 24; C-743/21 P of 31.3.2022 – Marina Yachting Brand Management/EUIPO, para. 21; C-744/21 P of 31.3.2022 – Henry Cotton's Brand Management/EUIPO, para. 21; C-120/22 P of 15.6.2022 – Republic of Cyprus/EUIPO, para. 19; C-233/22 P of 15.7.2022 – Meta Cluster/EUIPO, para. 14; C-199/23 P of 15.6.2023 – Zielonogórski Klub Żużlowy Sportowa/EUIPO, para. 16.
453. CJEU C-801/21 P of 7.4.2022 – EUIPO/Indo European Foods, para. 30; *see also* CJEU C-337/22 P of 16.11.2022 – EUIPO/Nowhere, para. 29.

also with the provisions of the EUTMR relating to the registration of marks, their enforceability and the implementation of the principle of territoriality, and with Article 50(3) TEU and Articles 126 and 127 of the withdrawal agreement, identifying both the paragraphs at issue in the judgment under appeal and the provisions and decisions allegedly infringed.[454]

In the second place, the appellant criticizes the General Court for having held, in paragraph 28 of the judgment under appeal, that the case had not become devoid of purpose and that Indo European Foods' interest in bringing proceedings subsisted. Thus, it is clear from the request that the appeal be allowed to proceed that the allegedly incorrect interpretation of the procedural requirements adopted by the General Court influenced the operative part of the judgment under appeal. In accordance with the case law cited by EUIPO and referred to in paragraph 8 of the present order, the purpose must continue, like the interest in bringing proceedings, until the delivery of the legal decision, failing which there will be no need to adjudicate.[455]

In the present case, EUIPO identifies the issue raised by its single ground of appeal, which consists, in essence, in determining the date and circumstances to be taken into account in order to assess whether the purpose of the dispute and the interest in bringing proceedings subsist where, first, the dispute brought before the General Court relates to a decision adopted following opposition proceedings based on an earlier right protected only in the United Kingdom and, second, the transition period came to an end during the proceedings before the General Court. More generally, according to EUIPO, that issue concerns the impact of the disappearance, in the course of the proceedings, of the earlier right in question on the existence of the purpose of the proceedings and on Indo European Foods' interest in bringing proceedings.[456]

Moreover, EUIPO sets out the specific reasons why such an issue is significant with respect to the unity, consistency and development of EU law.[457]

In particular, EUIPO states that that issue concerns the fundamental procedural requirement of having an interest in bringing proceedings and principles that constitute the pillars of intellectual property law, namely the principle of territoriality, the principle of the unitary character of the EU trade mark and the fundamental concept of the essential function of a trade mark, in the context of the end of the transition period.[458]

In that regard, first of all, it emphasizes the horizontal nature of the requirement that there must be a continuing interest in bringing proceedings and the fact that there is a divergence in the interpretation of that requirement both within the General Court and between the General Court and the Court of Justice.[459]

454. CJEU C-801/21 P of 7.4.2022 – EUIPO/Indo European Foods, para. 31, with further proof.
455. CJEU C-801/21 P of 7.4.2022 – EUIPO/Indo European Foods, para. 32, with further proof.
456. CJEU C-801/21 P of 7.4.2022 – EUIPO/Indo European Foods, para. 35; C-337/22 P of 16.11.2022 – EUIPO/Nowhere, para. 34.
457. CJEU C-801/21 P of 7.4.2022 – EUIPO/Indo European Foods, para. 36; C-337/22 P of 16.11.2022 – EUIPO/Nowhere, para. 35.
458. CJEU C-801/21 P of 7.4.2022 – EUIPO/Indo European Foods, para. 37; C-337/22 P of 16.11.2022 – EUIPO/Nowhere, para. 36.
459. CJEU C-801/21 P of 7.4.2022 – EUIPO/Indo European Foods, para. 38; C-337/22 P of 16.11.2022 – EUIPO/Nowhere, para. 37.

Next, it states that clarification by the Court of Justice is necessary both for the users of the EU trade mark system and for the national courts, in particular in view of the fact that the issue raised concerns not only on the effect of the withdrawal agreement on pending proceedings but also on all situations, frequently regarding intellectual property, where an earlier right ceases to exist during the judicial proceedings, in particular in the event of revocation or expiry of a trade mark. In particular, as regards the matter of the interest in bringing proceedings in the event of an earlier right ceasing to exist during those proceedings, EUIPO sets out the General Court's contradictory case law on the matter. In addition, it notes that the Court of Justice addressed that issue only in a specific context, namely that which led to the delivery of the order *Cadila Healthcare v OHIM*.[460]

Lastly, it observes that the matter of determining what consequences are to be drawn from the rule that the author of the annulled measure must refer back to the date of that act in order to adopt the replacement act, in particular in the context of the withdrawal agreement and the end of the transition period, is an important matter of a procedural nature that is not limited to intellectual property law.[461]

Lastly, it submits, in essence, that the issue which it raises concerns the fundamental principle of the unitary character of the EU trade mark, which the EU legislature sought when that mark was introduced into the EU legal order, in a context in which, in the absence of specific rules laid down by the CTMR or in the Withdrawal Agreement, the General Court, in the judgment under appeal, laid down a rule which, disregarding the effects of Article 50(3) TEU and Articles 126 and 127 of the Withdrawal Agreement, obliges EUIPO to examine a relative ground for refusal in relation to a territory in which, in any event, the EU trade mark applied for will not enjoy any protection. It adds that, in addition to the risks created by that approach in the light of the principle of legal certainty, that approach also poses risks with regard to the principle of reciprocity since it is likely to create an imbalance between the protection of earlier UK rights in the European Union and the protection of EU trade marks in the United Kingdom.[462]

[H] Enforcement of the Community trade mark

[1] Jurisdiction in court actions

Article 22(4) of Regulation No. 44/2001[463] must be interpreted as **not applying** to proceedings to determine whether a person was **correctly registered as the proprietor of a trade mark.**[464]

460. CJEU C-801/21 P of 7.4.2022 – EUIPO/Indo European Foods, para. 39, with reference to CJEU C-268/12 P of 8.5.2013 – Cadila Healthcare/OHIM; also CJEU C-337/22 P of 16.11.2022 – EUIPO/Nowhere, para. 38.
461. CJEU C-801/21 P of 7.4.2022 – EUIPO/Indo European Foods, para. 40.
462. CJEU C-337/22 P of 16.11.2022 – EUIPO/Nowhere, para. 39.
463. Council Regulation (EC) No 44/2001 on jurisdiction and the recognition and enforcement of judgments in civil and commercial matters.
464. CJEU C-341/16 of 5.10.2017 – Hanssen Beleggingen/Prast Knipping, para. 43, with further proof.

Article 97 (1) CTMR must be interpreted as meaning that a legally distinct second-tier subsidiary, with its seat in a Member State, of a parent body that has no seat in the European Union is an '**establishment**', within the meaning of that provision, of that parent body if the subsidiary is a centre of operations which, in the Member State where it is located, has a certain real and stable presence from which commercial activity is pursued, and has the appearance of permanency to the outside world, such as an extension of the parent body.[465]

It follows from the need for uniform application of EU law and from the principle of equality that the terms of a provision of EU law which makes no express reference to the law of the Member States for the purpose of determining its meaning and scope must normally be given an autonomous and uniform interpretation throughout the European Union, having regard not only to its wording but also to the context of the provision and the objective pursued by the legislation in question.[466]

That applies to the concept of 'establishment' within the meaning of Article 97 (1)CTMR since that concept is not defined in that regulation, and the regulation makes no reference to national laws for the purpose of determining its meaning.[467]

First of all, it should be noted that the CTMR provides, subject to the exceptions to which it expressly refers, for the application of Regulation No. 44/2001[468] to proceedings relating to EU trade marks and applications for such trade marks, as is expressly stated in recital 16 and Articles 94 and 97(1) CTMR.[469]

In that regard, although certain provisions of Regulation No. 44/2001, such as Articles 5(5) and 18(2), also refer to the concept of 'establishment', so that it cannot be ruled out that the guidance from the Court's case law on those two provisions may to some extent be relevant for interpreting the concept of 'establishment' within the meaning of the CTMR, it cannot, however, be considered that that concept must necessarily bear the same meaning, whether it is used in one or the other of the two regulations.[470]

Thus, notwithstanding the principle that Regulation No. 44/2001 applies to proceedings relating to an EU trade mark, the application of certain provisions of that regulation, in particular the rules in Articles 4 and 5(1), to proceedings in respect of the actions and claims referred to in Article 96 CTMR is excluded by Article 94(2) CTMR. In the light of that exclusion, the jurisdiction of the EU trade mark courts laid down in Article 95(1) CTMR to hear the actions and claims referred to in Article 96 CTMR results from rules directly provided for by that regulation, which have the character of *lex specialis* in relation to the rules provided for by Regulation No. 44/2001.[471]

465. CJEU C-617/15 of 18.5.2017 – Hummel Holding/Nike a.o., para. 41.
466. CJEU C-617/15 of 18.5.2017 – Hummel Holding/Nike a.o., para. 22.
467. CJEU C-617/15 of 18.5.2017 – Hummel Holding/Nike a.o., para. 23.
468. Council Regulation (EC) No 44/2001 on jurisdiction and the recognition and enforcement of judgments in civil and commercial matters.
469. CJEU C-617/15 of 18.5.2017 – Hummel Holding/Nike a.o., para. 24.
470. CJEU C-617/15 of 18.5.2017 – Hummel Holding/Nike a.o., para. 25.
471. CJEU C-617/15 of 18.5.2017 – Hummel Holding/Nike a.o., para. 26, with reference to CJEU C-360/12 of 5.6.2014 – Coty Germany, paras 26 et seq.; also CJEU C-172/18 of 5.9.2019 – AMS Neve a.o./Heritage Audio a.o., para. 34; C-104/22 of 27.4.2023 – Lännen MCE/Berky a.o., para. 25.

In addition, Regulation No. 44/2001, on the one hand, and the CTMR, on the other, do not pursue the same objectives. Thus, according to recitals 12 and 13 of Regulation No. 44/2001, that regulation aims to lay down, in addition to the defendant's domicile, alternative grounds of jurisdiction based on a close link between the court and the action, or in order to facilitate the sound administration of justice, or, in relation to insurance, consumer and employment contracts, to protect the weaker party by rules of jurisdiction more favourable to his interests than the general rules.[472]

The CTMR for its part aims, according to recitals 15 to 17, to strengthen the protection of EU trade marks, to prevent inconsistent decisions on the part of the courts and to ensure that the unitary character of those trade marks is not undermined, by means of decisions of EU trade mark courts which have effect and cover the entire area of the European Union.[473]

Accordingly, in order to determine the defining characteristics of the concept of 'establishment' within the meaning of Article 97(1) CTMR, it is necessary to take account not only of the wording of that provision but also of its context and objectives.[474]

The wording of Article 97(1) CTMR does not explain the concept of 'establishment' for the purposes of its application. Nevertheless, it is apparent that a defendant who is not domiciled within the European Union is capable of having one or several establishments within the European Union, which a priori appears to suggest that, in such a case, actions may be brought before the courts of the various Member States where those establishments are located.[475]

As regards the context of which Article 97 CTMR forms part, that provision ensures that a court within the European Union always has jurisdiction to hear and determine cases concerning the infringement and validity of an EU trade mark. That article, which provides for several grounds of international jurisdiction, lists in paragraphs 1 to 4 the successive criteria for determining the Member State whose courts have jurisdiction, under Article 98(1)(a) CTMR, in order to ensure effective protection of EU trade marks throughout the entire area of the European Union.[476]

Article 97(1) CTMR provides, as the primary rule, for jurisdiction of the courts of the Member State in which the defendant is domiciled or, if he is not domiciled in any of the Member States, of the Member State in which he has an establishment. Only if the defendant is not domiciled in and has no establishment in a Member State of the European Union does Article 97(2) and (3) provide, as an alternative, for jurisdiction to lie with the courts of the domicile or the establishment of the plaintiff and, as a further alternative, with the courts of the Member State where EUIPO has its seat.[477]

As regards Article 97(5) CTMR, that paragraph provides, *inter alia*, that the courts of the Member State in which the act of infringement has been committed or threatened are to have jurisdiction, although in this case the extent of the jurisdiction

472. CJEU C-617/15 of 18.5.2017 – Hummel Holding/Nike a.o., para. 27.
473. CJEU C-617/15 of 18.5.2017 – Hummel Holding/Nike a.o., para. 28.
474. CJEU C-617/15 of 18.5.2017 – Hummel Holding/Nike a.o., para. 29.
475. CJEU C-617/15 of 18.5.2017 – Hummel Holding/Nike a.o., para. 30.
476. CJEU C-617/15 of 18.5.2017 – Hummel Holding/Nike a.o., para. 31.
477. CJEU C-617/15 of 18.5.2017 – Hummel Holding/Nike a.o., para. 32.

of such courts is limited to the territory of the Member State in which they are located, as appears from Article 98 CTMR.[478]

Article 97(1) CTMR, which provides that the courts of the Member State in which there is an establishment of a company which has no seat within the European Union are to have jurisdiction, far from being an exception to the basic rule of jurisdiction at the domicile of the defendant, which follows from Article 2(1) of Regulation No. 44/2001 read in the light of recital 11 of the regulation, is, rather, an implementation of that principle, which suggests that that concept should be interpreted broadly.[479]

That jurisdictional rule is a general principle, which expresses the maxim *actor sequitur forum rei* because it makes it easier, in principle, for a defendant to defend himself. Such is the case where a party is required to defend itself before the courts of a Member State in which it has an establishment and with which it is therefore more closely linked.[480]

Furthermore, that interpretation does not undermine the objectives of the legislation on the EU trade mark as the decisions of the EU trade mark courts with jurisdiction on the basis of Article 97 CTMR have effect and cover the entire area of the European Union.[481]

It follows from such a broad interpretation that there must be visible signs enabling the existence of an 'establishment' within the meaning of Article 97(1) CTMR to be easily recognized. The existence of an establishment thus requires a certain real and stable presence, from which commercial activity is pursued, as manifested by the presence of personnel and material equipment. In addition, that establishment must have the appearance of permanency to the outside world, such as the extension of a parent body.[482]

In that regard, it is irrelevant whether the establishment on the territory of a Member State of an undertaking whose seat is outside the European Union has legal personality or not. Third parties must thus be able to rely on the appearance created by an establishment acting as an extension of the parent body.[483]

The fact that an undertaking with its seat in a Member State before the courts of which an action is brought is a second-tier subsidiary of the undertaking whose seat is located outside of the European Union and not a direct subsidiary of that undertaking is also irrelevant, provided that the conditions set out above are satisfied.[484]

Furthermore, it is, in principle, irrelevant for the purposes of Article 97(1) CTMR whether the establishment thereby determined has participated in the alleged infringement. Such a requirement, which is not laid down in Article 97(1) CTMR, would, in addition, not be reconcilable with the need for a broad interpretation of the concept of 'establishment'.[485]

478. CJEU C-617/15 of 18.5.2017 – Hummel Holding/Nike a.o., para. 33.
479. CJEU C-617/15 of 18.5.2017 – Hummel Holding/Nike a.o., para. 34.
480. CJEU C-617/15 of 18.5.2017 – Hummel Holding/Nike a.o., para. 35, with further proof.
481. CJEU C-617/15 of 18.5.2017 – Hummel Holding/Nike a.o., para. 36.
482. CJEU C-617/15 of 18.5.2017 – Hummel Holding/Nike a.o., para. 37, with further proof.
483. CJEU C-617/15 of 18.5.2017 – Hummel Holding/Nike a.o., para. 38, with further proof.
484. CJEU C-617/15 of 18.5.2017 – Hummel Holding/Nike a.o., para. 39.
485. CJEU C-617/15 of 18.5.2017 – Hummel Holding/Nike a.o., para. 40.

The concept of the 'Member State in which the act of infringement has been committed' in **Article 93(5) CTMR** must be interpreted as meaning that, in the event of a sale and delivery of a counterfeit product in one Member State, followed by a resale by the purchaser in another Member State, that provision does not allow jurisdiction to be established to hear an infringement action against the original seller who did not himself act in the Member State where the court seized is situated.[486]

Regarding the question of whether the concept of 'Member State in which the act of infringement has been committed' in Article 93(5) CTMR must be interpreted in a manner analogous to that of the 'place where the harmful event occurred' in Article 5(3) of Regulation No. 44/2001,[487] it should be noted that, notwithstanding the principle that Regulation No. 44/2001 applies to court proceedings relating to a Community trade mark, the application of certain provisions of that regulation to proceedings in respect of the actions and claims referred to in Article 92 CTMR is precluded under Article 90(2) of that regulation.[488]

In the light of that exclusion, the jurisdiction of the Community trade mark courts provided for in Article 91(1) CTMR to decide actions and claims referred to in Article 92 CTMR results from rules directly provided for by that regulation, which have the character of *lex specialis* in relation to the rules provided for by Regulation No. 44/2001.[489]

More specifically, under the combined provisions of Articles 90(2) and 92 CTMR, the application of Article 5(3) of the Brussels Convention,[490] to which Article 5(3) of Regulation No. 44/2001 corresponds, to Community trade mark infringement actions is expressly precluded.[491]

In that regard, it should be noted that Article 93 CTMR provides for several grounds of international jurisdiction.[492]

In particular, Article 93(5) CTMR establishes, *inter alia*, jurisdiction in favour of the courts of the Member State in which the infringement was committed or is threatened.[493]

With regard to the interpretation of Article 93(5), the concept of 'the Member State in which the act of infringement has been committed or threatened', referred to in that provision, must be interpreted independently of the concept of 'the place where the harmful event occurred or may occur' referred to in Article 5(3) of Regulation No. 44/2001.[494]

Consequently, the duality of linking factors, namely the place of the event giving rise to the damage and that where the damage occurred, accepted by the Court's case

486. CJEU C-360/12 of 5.6.2014 – Coty Germany, para. 38.
487. Council Regulation (EC) No. 44/2001 of 22 Dec. 2000 on jurisdiction and the recognition and enforcement of judgments in civil and commercial matters (OJ 2001 L 12, p. 1).
488. CJEU C-360/12 of 5.6.2014 – Coty Germany, para. 26.
489. CJEU C-360/12 of 5.6.2014 – Coty Germany, para. 27.
490. Convention of 27 Sep. 1968 on Jurisdiction and the Enforcement of Judgments in Civil and Commercial Matters (OJ 1978 L 304, p. 36).
491. CJEU C-360/12 of 5.6.2014 – Coty Germany, para. 28.
492. CJEU C-360/12 of 5.6.2014 – Coty Germany, para. 29.
493. CJEU C-360/12 of 5.6.2014 – Coty Germany, para. 30.
494. CJEU C-360/12 of 5.6.2014 – Coty Germany, para. 31.

law[495] relating to Article 5(3) of Regulation No. 44/2001, cannot automatically apply to the interpretation of the concept of 'the Member State in which the act of infringement has been committed or threatened' in Article 93(5) CTMR.[496]

In order to determine whether an independent interpretation of the latter provision nevertheless leads to an acknowledgement of such a duality of linking factors, it is necessary, in accordance with the Court's settled case law, to take into account not only the wording of that provision but also its context and purpose.[497]

With regard to the wording of Article 93(5) CTMR, the concept of 'the Member State in which the act of infringement has been committed' implies that that linking factor relates to active conduct on the part of the person causing that infringement. Therefore, the linking factor provided for by that provision refers to the Member State where the act giving rise to the alleged infringement occurred or may occur, not the Member State where that infringement produces its effects.[498]

It should also be noted that the existence of jurisdiction under Article 93(5) based on the place where the alleged infringement produces its effects would conflict with the wording of Article 94(2) CTMR, which limits the jurisdiction of Community trade mark courts under Article 93(5) to acts committed or threatened in the Member State where the court seized is situated.[499]

Furthermore, both the origin and the context of the CTMR confirm the intention of the EU legislature to derogate from the rule on jurisdiction provided for in Article 5(3) of Regulation No. 44/2001 in the light, in particular, of the inability of the rule on jurisdiction to respond to the specific problems relating to the infringement of a Community trade mark.[500]

Consequently, jurisdiction under Article 93(5) CTMR may be established solely in favour of Community trade mark courts in the Member State in which the defendant committed the alleged unlawful act.[501]

Article 125(5) EUTMR states that the applicant may 'also' bring his or her action in the courts of the Member State 'in which the act of infringement has been committed or threatened'.[502]

Article 126(1) EUTMR provides that where an action is brought before an EU trade mark court on the basis of Article 125(1) of that regulation, that court is to have jurisdiction in respect of acts of infringement committed or threatened within the territory of any of the Member States, while Article 126(2) EUTMR provides that where an action is brought before such a court on the basis of Article 125(5) EUTMR, that

495. *See* CJEU 21/76 of 30.10.1976 – Bier, para. 19; C-45/13 of 16.1.2014 – Kainz, para. 23.
496. CJEU C-360/12 of 5.6.2014 – Coty Germany, para. 32.
497. CJEU C-360/12 of 5.6.2014 – Coty Germany, para. 33.
498. CJEU C-360/12 of 5.6.2014 – Coty Germany, para. 34; *see also* CJEU C-172/18 of 5.9.2019 – AMS Neve a.o./Heritage Audio a.o., paras 44 et seqq.
499. CJEU C-360/12 of 5.6.2014 – Coty Germany, para. 35.
500. CJEU C-360/12 of 5.6.2014 – Coty Germany, para. 36.
501. CJEU C-360/12 of 5.6.2014 – Coty Germany, para. 37; *see also* CJEU C-172/18 of 5.9.2019 – AMS Neve a.o./Heritage Audio a.o., para. 45.
502. CJEU C-104/22 of 27.4.2023 – Lännen MCE/Berky a.o., para. 28.

court is to have jurisdiction only in respect of acts committed or threatened within the territory of the Member State in which it is situated.[503]

Article 97(5) CTMR must be interpreted as meaning that the proprietor of an EU trade mark, who considers that his rights have been infringed by the use without his consent, by a third party, of a sign identical to that mark in advertising and offers for sale displayed electronically in relation to products that are identical or similar to the goods for which that mark is registered, may bring an infringement action against that third party before an EU trade mark court of the **Member State within which the consumers or traders to whom that advertising and those offers for sale are directed are located**, notwithstanding that that third party took decisions and steps in another Member State to bring about that electronic display.[504]

With respect to national trade marks, TMD2008 did not establish specific rules in relation to jurisdiction. The same is true of the TMD, which repealed and replaced, with effect from 15 January 2019, TMD2008.[505]

Under Article 97(1) CTMR, where the defendant is domiciled in a Member State, the applicant is to bring its action before the courts of that Member State.[506]

However, Article 97(5) CTMR states that the applicant may 'also' bring its action before the courts of the Member State 'in which the act of infringement has been committed or threatened'.[507]

Article 98(1) CTMR states that where an action is brought before an EU trade mark court on the basis of Article 97(1) CTMR, it has jurisdiction in respect of acts of infringement committed or threatened within the territory of any of the Member States, and Article 98(2) CTMR states that, where an action is brought before such a court on the basis of Article 97(5) CTMR, it has jurisdiction only in respect of acts committed or threatened within the territory of the Member State in which that court is situated.[508]

It follows from that distinction that the applicant, according to whether he chooses to bring infringement proceedings before the EU trade mark court where the defendant is domiciled or before the EU trade mark court of the place where the act of infringement has been committed or threatened, determines the extent of the territorial jurisdiction of the court before which the action is brought. When the infringement action is based on Article 97(1) CTMR, it potentially covers acts of infringement committed throughout the European Union, whereas when the action is based on Article 97(5) CTMR, the action is restricted to acts of infringement committed or threatened within a single Member State, namely the Member State where the court before which the action is brought is situated.[509]

The right conferred on the applicant to choose one or other basis, arising from the use of the word 'also' in Article 97(5) CTMR, cannot be understood as meaning that the

503. CJEU C-104/22 of 27.4.2023 – Lännen MCE/Berky a.o., para. 29.
504. CJEU C-172/18 of 5.9.2019 – AMS Neve a.o./Heritage Audio a.o., para. 65.
505. CJEU C-172/18 of 5.9.2019 – AMS Neve a.o./Heritage Audio a.o., para. 35.
506. CJEU C-172/18 of 5.9.2019 – AMS Neve a.o./Heritage Audio a.o., para. 37.
507. CJEU C-172/18 of 5.9.2019 – AMS Neve a.o./Heritage Audio a.o., para. 38.
508. CJEU C-172/18 of 5.9.2019 – AMS Neve a.o./Heritage Audio a.o., para. 39.
509. CJEU C-172/18 of 5.9.2019 – AMS Neve a.o./Heritage Audio a.o., para. 40; C-104/22 of 27.4.2023 – Lännen MCE/Berky a.o., para. 30.

applicant may, with reference to the same acts of infringement, simultaneously bring actions based on paragraphs (1) and (5) of Article 97 CTMR, but merely reflects the fact that the forum indicated in Article 97(5) is an alternative to the fora indicated in the other paragraphs of that article.[510]

The EU legislature, in providing for such an alternative forum and restricting, in Article 98(2) CTMR, the territorial jurisdiction attached to that forum, enables the proprietor of the EU trade mark to bring, if he wishes, targeted actions each of which relates to acts of infringement committed within a single Member State. As the Court has stated previously, where a number of infringement actions involving the same parties concern the use of the same sign but do not relate to the same territory, they do not have the same subject matter and are therefore not subject to the rules on lis pendens. Accordingly, the courts of the various Member States before which actions are brought in such circumstances cannot deliver 'contradictory judgments', within the meaning of recital 17 of the CTMR, since the actions that the applicant has brought relate to distinct territories.[511]

The foregoing considerations must guide the Court in responding to the concerns of the referring court in relation to the meaning of the wording 'Member State in which the act of infringement has been committed', in Article 97(5) CTMR.[512]

The Court has stated, when called on to provide an interpretation of Article 93(5) of Regulation No. 40/94, that the criterion for jurisdiction expressed in that wording relates to active conduct on the part of the person causing the alleged infringement (judgment of 5 June 2014, Coty Germany, C-360/12, EU:C:2014:1318, paragraph 34).[513]

The Court concluded that, in the event of a sale and delivery of a counterfeit product in one Member State, followed by a resale by the purchaser in another Member State in which the original seller has not himself acted, that criterion is not sufficient to establish the jurisdiction of the EU trade mark court of the latter Member State to hear an infringement action brought against the initial seller. Such jurisdiction would be based on an effect of the infringement committed by the original seller and not on the alleged unlawful act committed by the original seller, which would be contrary to the sense of the wording 'Member State in which the act of infringement has been committed'.[514]

In accordance with that case law and the considerations set out above, an EU trade mark court before which an infringement action on the basis of Article 97(5) CTMR is brought must, when it is called upon to review its jurisdiction to give a ruling on whether there is an infringement in the territory of the Member State where that

510. CJEU C-172/18 of 5.9.2019 – AMS Neve a.o./Heritage Audio a.o., para. 41 C-104/22 of 27.4.2023 – Lännen MCE/Berky a.o., para. 31.
511. CJEU C-172/18 of 5.9.2019 – AMS Neve a.o./Heritage Audio a.o., para. 42, with reference to CJEU C-231/16 of 19.10.2017 – Merck, para. 42; also CJEU C-104/22 of 27.4.2023 – Lännen MCE/Berky a.o., para. 32.
512. CJEU C-172/18 of 5.9.2019 – AMS Neve a.o./Heritage Audio a.o., para. 43.
513. CJEU C-172/18 of 5.9.2019 – AMS Neve a.o./Heritage Audio a.o., para. 44, with reference to CJEU C-360/12 of 5.6.2014 – Coty Germany, para. 34; *see also* CJEU C-104/22 of 27.4.2023 – Lännen MCE/Berky a.o., para. 40.
514. CJEU C-172/18 of 5.9.2019 – AMS Neve a.o./Heritage Audio a.o., para. 45, with reference to CJEU C-360/12 of 5.6.2014 – Coty Germany, para. 34, 37 and 38.

court is situated, be satisfied that the acts allegedly committed by the defendant were committed in that territory.[515]

Where the acts allegedly committed by the defendant consist of advertising and offers for sale displayed electronically with respect to products bearing a sign identical or similar to an EU trade mark without the consent of the proprietor of that mark, it is necessary to hold that those acts, which fall within the scope of Article 9(2)(b) and (d) CTMR, were committed in the territory where the consumers or traders to whom that advertising and those offers for sale are directed are located, notwithstanding the fact that the defendant is established elsewhere, that the server of the electronic network that he uses is located elsewhere, or even that the products that are the subject of such advertising and offers for sale are located elsewhere.[516]

As is apparent from the same paragraph of that judgment, it must be ensured that a third party who directs advertising and offers for sale to EU consumers using a sign identical or similar to an EU trade mark in relation to products that are identical or similar to the goods for which that mark is registered cannot evade the application of Article 9 CTMR and thereby undermine the effectiveness of that provision by relying on the fact that that advertising and those offers for sale were placed online outside the European Union.[517]

Similarly, it must be ensured that a third party who has used a sign identical or similar to an EU trade mark without the consent of the proprietor of that mark in relation to products that are identical or similar to the goods for which that mark is registered cannot contest the application of Article 97(5) CTMR and thereby undermine the effectiveness of that provision by relying on the place where his advertising and those offers for sale were placed online in order to exclude the jurisdiction of any court other than the court of that place and the court with jurisdiction over where he is established.[518]

If the wording 'Member State in which the act of infringement has been committed', in Article 97(5) CTMR, were to be interpreted as meaning that it refers to the Member State in the territory of which the person carrying out those commercial acts set up his website and activated the display of his advertising and offers for sale, parties established within the European Union committing an infringement, operating electronically and seeking to prevent the proprietors of infringed EU marks from resorting to an alternative forum, would have to do no more than ensure that the territory where the advertising and offers for sale were placed online was the same territory as that where those parties are established. In that way, Article 97(5) CTMR would, in the event that the advertising and the offers for sale are directed to consumers

515. CJEU C-172/18 of 5.9.2019 – AMS Neve a.o./Heritage Audio a.o., para. 46; *see also* CJEU C-104/22 of 27.4.2023 – Lännen MCE/Berky a.o., para. 41.
516. CJEU C-172/18 of 5.9.2019 – AMS Neve a.o./Heritage Audio a.o., para. 47, with reference to CJEU C-324/09 of 12.7.2011 – L'Oréal, para. 63; *see also* CJEU C-104/22 of 27.4.2023 – Lännen MCE/Berky a.o., para. 41.
517. CJEU C-172/18 of 5.9.2019 – AMS Neve a.o./Heritage Audio a.o., para. 48.
518. CJEU C-172/18 of 5.9.2019 – AMS Neve a.o./Heritage Audio a.o., para. 49.

of other Member States, be deprived of any scope constituting an alternative to that of the rule on jurisdiction laid down in Article 97(1).[519]

An interpretation of the wording 'Member State in which the act of infringement has been committed' as meaning that it refers to the place where the defendant took decisions and technical measures to activate a display on a website is all the more inappropriate given that it may, in many cases, prove excessively difficult, or even impossible, for the applicant to identify that place. As opposed to situations in which proceedings are already pending, a factor in the situation in which the proprietor of the EU trade mark finds himself before the bringing of court proceedings is that it is impossible to compel the defendant to disclose that place when no action has been brought before any court at that stage.[520]

In order to maintain the effectiveness of the EU legislature's provision of an alternative forum, it is necessary, in accordance with the case law to the effect that the terms of a provision of EU law which makes no express reference to the law of the Member States for the purpose of determining its meaning and scope must be interpreted having regard to the context of the provision and the objectives pursued by the legislation of which it forms part, to give to the wording 'Member State in which the act of infringement has been committed' an interpretation which is consistent with the other provisions of the CTMR with respect to infringement.[521]

One of those provisions is, in particular, Article 9 CTMR, which lists the acts of infringement which the proprietor of an EU trade mark can contest.[522]

Accordingly, the expression 'the act of infringement' must be understood as relating to acts, specified in Article 9, which the applicant claims to have been committed by the defendant, such as, in this case, acts specified in Article 9(2)(b) and (d) of that article, consisting of advertising and offers for sale under a sign identical to the mark at issue, and those acts must be held to have been 'committed' in the territory where they can be classified as advertising or as offers for sale, namely where their commercial content has in fact been made accessible to the consumers and traders to whom it was directed. Whether the result of that advertising and those offers for sale was that, thereafter, the defendant's products were purchased is, however, irrelevant.[523]

Subject to the findings of the referring court, the documents available to the Court and the question referred indicate that the object of the applicants in the main proceedings, by means of the infringement proceedings brought before that court, is the advertising and offers for sale displayed by the defendants on a website and on social media platforms solely to the extent that that advertising and those offers for sale were directed to consumers and/or traders in the United Kingdom.[524]

519. CJEU C-172/18 of 5.9.2019 – AMS Neve a.o./Heritage Audio a.o., para. 50.
520. CJEU C-172/18 of 5.9.2019 – AMS Neve a.o./Heritage Audio a.o., para. 51.
521. CJEU C-172/18 of 5.9.2019 – AMS Neve a.o./Heritage Audio a.o., para. 52, with reference to CJEU C-617/15 of 18.5.2017 – Hummel Holding/Nike a.o., para. 22.
522. CJEU C-172/18 of 5.9.2019 – AMS Neve a.o./Heritage Audio a.o., para. 53.
523. CJEU C-172/18 of 5.9.2019 – AMS Neve a.o./Heritage Audio a.o., para. 54.
524. CJEU C-172/18 of 5.9.2019 – AMS Neve a.o./Heritage Audio a.o., para. 55.

Accordingly, in circumstances such as those at issue in the main proceedings, if it is apparent from the content of the website and the platforms at issue submitted by the applicants in the main proceedings that the advertising and offers for sale which they contained were targeted at consumers or traders situated in the United Kingdom and were entirely accessible by them, which is a finding that it is for the referring court to make on the basis of, *inter alia*, the details contained on that website and those platforms with respect to the geographical areas where the products at issue were to be delivered, those applicants have the right to bring, on the basis of Article 97(5) CTMR, their infringement action before a court of the United Kingdom, seeking a declaration of an infringement of the EU trade mark in that Member State.[525]

That interpretation is supported by the fact that the EU trade mark courts of the Member State where the consumers or traders, to whom such advertising and offers for sale are directed are resident, are particularly suited to assessing whether the alleged infringement exists. In the judgment Wintersteiger,[526] the Court took account of that factor of proximity, interpreting the wording 'the place where the harmful event occurred', in Article 5(3) CTMR, as meaning that the proprietor of a national mark may bring an infringement action before the courts of the Member State in which the national mark is registered, since those courts are, having regard to the criteria for assessing infringement established in the judgments *Google France and Google*,[527] and *L'Oréal and Others*,[528] best able to assess whether the mark has been infringed. The courts of the place where the harmful event occurred are particularly suited to giving a ruling by reason of proximity and ease of taking evidence.[529]

The interpretation of Article 97(5) CTMR, as *lex specialis* with respect to actions alleging infringement of EU marks, must, it is true, be independent of the interpretation of Article 5(3) of Regulation No. 44/2001 adopted by the Court[530] with respect to actions alleging infringement of national marks. None the less, the interpretations of the concepts of 'Member State in which the act of infringement has been committed' and 'the place where the harmful event occurred', in those provisions, must have a degree of consistency in order, in accordance with the objective laid down in recital 17 of the CTMR, to reduce as far as possible cases of lis pendens as a result of the bringing of actions, in different Member States, involving the same parties and the same territory, one brought on the basis of an EU trade mark and another on the basis of parallel national trade marks.[531]

If the rule of jurisdiction laid down in Article 97(5) CTMR were to be interpreted as meaning that that provision did not, unlike Article 5(3) of Regulation No. 44/2001, permit the proprietors of EU marks to bring an infringement action before the courts of

525. CJEU C-172/18 of 5.9.2019 – AMS Neve a.o./Heritage Audio a.o., para. 56, with reference to CJEU C-324/09 of 12.7.2011 – L'Oréal, paras 64 et seq.
526. CJEU C-523/10 of 19.4.2012 – Wintersteiger, paras 28 et seq.
527. CJEU C-236/08 to C-238/08 of 23.3.2010 – Google France.
528. CJEU C-324/09 of 12.7.2011 – L'Oréal.
529. CJEU C-172/18 of 5.9.2019 – AMS Neve a.o./Heritage Audio a.o., para. 57, with further proof; *see also* CJEU C-104/22 of 27.4.2023 – Lännen MCE/Berky a.o., para. 42.
530. CJEU C-360/12 of 5.6.2014 – Coty Germany, para. 31.
531. CJEU C-172/18 of 5.9.2019 – AMS Neve a.o./Heritage Audio a.o., para. 58, with reference to CJEU C-231/16 of 19.10.2017 – Merck, para. 30-32.

the Member State within which they seek a declaration of an infringement, the consequence would be that those proprietors would bring proceedings alleging infringement of an EU trade mark and proceedings alleging infringement of parallel national trade marks before courts of different Member States. Frequent application of the mechanism provided in Article 109 CTMR to resolve cases of lis pendens would, because of such a divergent approach in Article 97(5) CTMR (now Article 125(5) EUTMR) and Article 5(3) of Regulation No. 44/2001 (now Article 7(2) of Regulation No. 1215/2012), be likely, thereby defeating the objective, pursued by those regulations, of reducing cases of lis pendens.[532]

It must, last, be observed that the interpretation adopted in the present judgment is not invalidated by the interpretation deriving from the judgment *Nintendo*,[533] to which the referring court made reference.[534]

In paragraphs 108 and 111 of the judgment *Nintendo*, the Court interpreted the wording 'country in which the act of infringement [of the intellectual property right at issue] was committed', in Regulation No. 864/2007, as referring to the law of the country where the initial act of infringement, at the origin of the allegedly wrongful conduct, was committed or may have been committed, that initial act, in the context of electronic commerce, being the act of activating the process of placing online the offer for sale.[535]

However, the purpose and object of the wording of Article 8(2) of Regulation No. 864/2007 are fundamentally different from that of Article 97(5) CTMR and Article 5(3) of Regulation No. 44/2001.[536]

Article 97(5) CTMR provides an alternative forum of jurisdiction and is intended to enable the proprietor of an EU trade mark to bring one or more actions, each relating specifically to the acts of infringement committed within a single Member State. In contrast, Article 8(2) of Regulation No. 864/2007 does not concern the determination of which court has jurisdiction, but relates to the question of how, in the case of a non-contractual obligation arising from an infringement of a unitary intellectual property right, the law applicable to any question that is not governed by the relevant EU instrument is to be determined.[537]

That determination of the applicable law may become necessary when an infringement action, brought before a court that has jurisdiction to give rulings on acts of infringement committed within any Member State, relates to various acts of infringement, committed in different Member States. In such circumstances, in order to ensure that a court does not have to apply more than one law, one alone of those acts of infringement, namely the initial act of infringement, must be identified as determinative of the law applicable to the proceedings. The need to ensure that only one law is applicable does not exist in the context of rules concerning which court has

532. CJEU C-172/18 of 5.9.2019 – AMS Neve a.o./Heritage Audio a.o., para. 59.
533. CJEU C-24/16 and C-25/16 of 27.9.2017 – Nintendo.
534. CJEU C-172/18 of 5.9.2019 – AMS Neve a.o./Heritage Audio a.o., para. 60.
535. CJEU C-172/18 of 5.9.2019 – AMS Neve a.o./Heritage Audio a.o., para. 61.
536. CJEU C-172/18 of 5.9.2019 – AMS Neve a.o./Heritage Audio a.o., para. 62.
537. CJEU C-172/18 of 5.9.2019 – AMS Neve a.o./Heritage Audio a.o., para. 63, with reference to CJEU C-24/16 and C-25/16 of 27.9.2017 – Nintendo, para. 91.

jurisdiction, such as those contained in Regulation No. 44/2001 and in the CTMR, which provide for more than one forum.[538]

Article 125(5) EUTMR must be interpreted as meaning that the proprietor of an EU trade mark who considers that he or she has been prejudiced by the use, without his or her consent, by a third party, of a sign identical with that mark in online advertisements and offers for sale in respect of goods identical with, or similar to, those for which that mark is registered, may bring an infringement action against that third party before an EU trade mark court of the **Member State in which consumers and traders targeted by those advertisements or offers for sale are located**, notwithstanding the fact that the third party does not expressly and unambiguously list that Member State among the territories to which a supply of the goods in question might be made if that third party has made use of that sign by means of paid referencing on a search engine website which **uses a national top-level domain name of that Member State**. By contrast, that is not the case simply because the third party concerned has used the natural referencing of images of its goods on an online photo-sharing service under a generic top-level domain, having recourse to meta tags using the trade mark concerned as a keyword.[539]

In the present case, it is apparent from the documents before the Court that the acts of infringement alleged by the proprietor of the EU trade mark relate to the online display of content relating to the products of that proprietor's competitors, by means of paid and natural referencing on the basis of a sign identical to that trade mark, only to the extent that that display was directed at consumers or traders located in Finland.[540]

Thus, in order to determine whether that online display was actually directed at consumers or traders located in Finland, the referring court asks, in particular, whether the nature of the products concerned, the scope of the market in question and the fact that that display occurred on the website of a search engine operating under the national top-level domain of that Member State are relevant factors for ascertaining whether it has international jurisdiction under Article 125(5) EUTMR and, if so, whether other factors must be taken into account to that end.[541]

In that regard, although the acts of infringement alleged against each of the defendant companies in the main proceedings, which form part of the same group of undertakings, are different, a single set of judicial proceedings was instituted before the referring court.[542]

It is, therefore, necessary to determine whether the acts of infringement alleged against those two companies make it possible to establish, in both of the two cases, a sufficient connecting factor with the Member State in which the court seised of the infringement action is situated, pursuant to Article 125(5) EUTMR.[543]

538. CJEU C-172/18 of 5.9.2019 – AMS Neve a.o./Heritage Audio a.o., para. 64, with reference to CJEU C-24/16 and C-25/16 of 27.9.2017 – Nintendo, para. 103 and 104.
539. CJEU C-104/22 of 27.4.2023 – Lännen MCE/Berky a.o., para. 54.
540. CJEU C-104/22 of 27.4.2023 – Lännen MCE/Berky a.o., para. 33.
541. CJEU C-104/22 of 27.4.2023 – Lännen MCE/Berky a.o., para. 34.
542. CJEU C-104/22 of 27.4.2023 – Lännen MCE/Berky a.o., para. 35, wording slightly changed.
543. CJEU C-104/22 of 27.4.2023 – Lännen MCE/Berky a.o., para. 36.

Furthermore, it should be borne in mind that the determination of the jurisdiction of the court seised of an infringement action does not amount to an examination of the substance of that action.[544]

It would be excessive to require the court seised of an infringement action to carry out, at the stage of determining whether it has international jurisdiction under Article 125(5) EUTMR, a detailed examination of those complex matters of fact and of law.[545]

Consequently, evidence which gives rise to a reasonable presumption that acts of infringement may have been committed or threatened on the territory of a Member State is sufficient for the EU trade mark court of that Member State to have jurisdiction under Article 125(5) EUTMR.[546]

In that context, it must be observed that, according to the case law of the Court, the criterion for jurisdiction expressed by the words 'Member State in which the act of infringement has been committed or threatened', in Article 125(5) EUTMR, relates to active conduct on the part of the person causing the infringement.[547]

In particular, as regards the duty of an EU trade mark court to be satisfied – pursuant to the review of its jurisdiction to give a ruling on whether there is an infringement in the territory of the Member State where that court is situated, pursuant to Article 125(5) EUTMR – that the acts allegedly committed by the defendant were committed in that territory, the Court has held that where those acts consist in advertising and offers for sale displayed electronically with respect to products bearing a sign identical with, or similar to, an EU trade mark, without the consent of the proprietor of that mark, it is necessary to hold that those acts were committed in the territory where the consumers or traders to whom that advertising and those offers for sale are directed are located.[548]

Thus, where the display of online content is, even if only potentially, directed at consumers or traders located in the territory of a Member State, bearing in mind that details of the geographic areas of supply of the products in question are evidence which is particularly important for the purposes of the aforementioned assessment, the proprietor of an EU trade mark is entitled to bring an action in that Member State, on the basis of Article 125(5) EUTMR, for a declaration that his or her trade mark has been infringed in that Member State. Indeed, the EU trade mark courts of the Member State where the consumers or traders to whom advertising and offers for sale are directed are resident are particularly suited to assessing whether the alleged infringement exists.[549]

In the present case, it must be found, subject to the verification to be carried out by the referring court, that the geographical areas of delivery of the products concerned are not mentioned in the advertisement. Furthermore, the map on Senwatec's website,

544. CJEU C-104/22 of 27.4.2023 – Lännen MCE/Berky a.o., para. 37, with further proof.
545. CJEU C-104/22 of 27.4.2023 – Lännen MCE/Berky a.o., para. 38.
546. CJEU C-104/22 of 27.4.2023 – Lännen MCE/Berky a.o., para. 39.
547. CJEU C-104/22 of 27.4.2023 – Lännen MCE/Berky a.o., para. 40, with reference to CJEU C-172/18 of 5.9.2019 – AMS Neve a.o./Heritage Audio a.o., para. 44.
548. CJEU C-104/22 of 27.4.2023 – Lännen MCE/Berky a.o., para. 41, with reference to CJEU C-172/18 of 5.9.2019 – AMS Neve a.o./Heritage Audio a.o., para. 47.
549. CJEU C-104/22 of 27.4.2023 – Lännen MCE/Berky a.o., para. 42, with reference to CJEU C-324/09 of 12.7.2011 – L'Oréal, para. 65; C-172/18 of 5.9.2019 – AMS Neve a.o./Heritage Audio a.o., para. 57.

which, according to Lännen, proves that Senwatec's market is global, cannot, in itself, establish a connecting factor with Finland since the context of which that map forms part does not support the conclusion that Senwatec directs its activity towards the Finnish market.[550]

In the absence of precise information as to the geographical areas of delivery of the products in question, the connecting factor with the Member State concerned, in this case Finland, must be established in the light of other factors in order for the applicant to be able to bring an infringement action before a court in that Member State on the basis of Article 125(5) EUTMR.[551]

Admittedly, the provisions of the EUTMR relating to actions for infringement of EU trade marks have the character of *lex specialis* in relation to the rules provided for by Regulation No. 1215/2012.[552] This does not, however, deprive Regulation No. 1215/2012 of relevance in terms of clarifying and interpreting the meaning of concepts which are similar to those for which it provides and which, since they are covered by the EUTMR, are necessary for interpreting the latter regulation.[553]

In that connection, as regards the interpretation of Article 17(1)(c) of Regulation No. 1215/2012, the Court has held that various indicia are capable of supporting the conclusion that the trader's activities are directed to the Member State of the consumer's domicile, namely the international nature of the activity, use of a language or a currency other than the language or currency generally used in the Member State in which the trader is established, mention of telephone numbers with an international code, outlay of expenditure on an internet referencing service in order to facilitate access to the trader's site or that of its intermediary by consumers domiciled in other Member States, use of a top-level domain name other than that of the Member State in which the trader is established, and mention of an international clientele composed of customers domiciled in various Member States.[554]

That list, although not exhaustive, contains matters which may be relevant for the purposes of applying Article 125(5) EUTMR. In the present case, the provision of advertisements and offers for sale on a website with a top-level domain other than that of the Member State in which the trader is established is of relevance.[555]

It must, however, be made clear that the mere fact that a website is accessible from the territory covered by the trade mark is not a sufficient basis for concluding that the offers for sale displayed there are targeted at consumers in that territory.[556]

It follows from the foregoing considerations that active conduct of the kind in question includes the fact that an undertaking pays the operator of a search engine website with a national top-level domain of a Member State other than that in which it

550. CJEU C-104/22 of 27.4.2023 – Lännen MCE/Berky a.o., para. 43.
551. CJEU C-104/22 of 27.4.2023 – Lännen MCE/Berky a.o., para. 44.
552. Regulation (EU) No 1215/2012 of the European Parliament and of the Council of 12 December 2012 on jurisdiction and the recognition and enforcement of judgments in civil and commercial matters (OJ 2012 L 351, p. 1).
553. CJEU C-104/22 of 27.4.2023 – Lännen MCE/Berky a.o., para. 45.
554. CJEU C-104/22 of 27.4.2023 – Lännen MCE/Berky a.o., para. 46, with further proof.
555. CJEU C-104/22 of 27.4.2023 – Lännen MCE/Berky a.o., para. 47.
556. CJEU C-104/22 of 27.4.2023 – Lännen MCE/Berky a.o., para. 48, with reference to CJEU C-324/09 of 12.7.2011 – L'Oréal, para. 64.

is established, in order to display, for the public of that Member State, a link to that undertaking's website, thereby enabling a specifically targeted public to access its product offering.[557]

Accordingly, such paid referencing constitutes a sufficient connecting factor, in terms of Article 125(5) EUTMR, with the Member State of which the public is thereby targeted.[558]

As regards the use of the sign registered as a trade mark as a meta tag on an online photo-sharing service under a generic top-level domain, this should be considered as differing from paid referencing for the purposes of assessing the condition relating to the existence of active conduct directed at the territory of the Member State where the act of infringement was committed or threatened. In the case of such natural referencing, that condition does not seem to be capable of being fulfilled in so far as, first, a website with a generic top-level domain is not intended for the public of any specific Member State and, secondly, the meta tag is intended only to enable search engines better to identify the images contained on that website and, in so doing, to increase the accessibility thereof.[559]

In those circumstances, the referring court cannot declare that it has jurisdiction, on the basis of Article 125(5) EUTMR, in the absence of other matters capable of proving that such natural referencing is intended for a public established in Finland.[560]

As regards the nature of the products in question and the extent of the geographical market, it is for the court hearing the infringement action to assess on a case-by-case basis the extent to which those matters are relevant in order to conclude that referencing accessible on the territory covered by the trade mark is targeted at consumers in that territory.[561]

Article 5(3) of Regulation No. 44/2001 must be interpreted as meaning that, in the event of an allegation of **unlawful comparative advertising or unfair imitation** of a sign protected by a Community trade mark, prohibited by the law against unfair competition of the Member State in which the court seized is situated, that provision does not allow jurisdiction to be established, on the basis of the place where the event giving rise to the damage resulting from the infringement of that law occurred, for a court in that Member State where the presumed perpetrator who is sued there did not himself act there. By contrast, in such a case, that provision does allow jurisdiction to be established, on the basis of the place of occurrence of damage, to hear an action for damages based on that national law brought against a person established in another Member State who is alleged to have committed, in that State, an act which caused or may cause damage within the jurisdiction of that court.[562]

557. CJEU C-104/22 of 27.4.2023 – Lännen MCE/Berky a.o., para. 49, with reference to CJEU C-324/09 of 12.7.2011 – L'Oréal, para. 64.
558. CJEU C-104/22 of 27.4.2023 – Lännen MCE/Berky a.o., para. 50.
559. CJEU C-104/22 of 27.4.2023 – Lännen MCE/Berky a.o., para. 51.
560. CJEU C-104/22 of 27.4.2023 – Lännen MCE/Berky a.o., para. 52.
561. CJEU C-104/22 of 27.4.2023 – Lännen MCE/Berky a.o., para. 53, with reference to CJEU C-324/09 of 12.7.2011 – L'Oréal, para. 61.
562. CJEU C-360/12 of 5.6.2014 – Coty Germany, para. 59.

Article 109(1)(a) CTMR must be interpreted as meaning that the condition laid down in that provision as to the existence of the '**same cause of action**' is satisfied where actions for infringement between the same parties, on the basis of a national trade mark and an EU trade mark respectively, are brought before the courts of different Member States, only in so far as those actions relate to an alleged infringement of a national trade mark and an identical EU trade mark in the territory of the same Member States.[563]

Article 109(1)(a) CTMR must be interpreted as meaning that where actions for infringement, the first on the basis of a national trade mark concerning an alleged infringement within the territory of a Member State and the second on the basis of an EU trade mark concerning an alleged infringement in the entire territory of the European Union, are brought before the courts of different Member States between the same parties, the court other than the court first seised must decline jurisdiction in respect of the part of the dispute relating to the territory of the Member State referred to in the action for infringement brought before the court first seised.[564]

Article 109(1)(a) CTMR must be interpreted as meaning that the condition laid down in that provision as to the existence of the '**same cause of action**' is no longer satisfied where, following a partial withdrawal by an applicant, provided that it was properly declared, of an action for infringement on the basis of an EU trade mark seeking initially to prohibit the use of that trade mark in the territory of the European Union, such a withdrawal concerning the Member State referred to in the action brought before the court first seised, on the basis of a national trade mark seeking to prohibit the use of that trade mark within the territory of that Member State, the actions in question no longer relate to an alleged infringement of a national trade mark and an identical EU trade mark in the territory of the same Member States.[565]

Article 109(1)(a) CTMR must be interpreted as meaning that, where the **trade marks are identical**, the court other than the court first seised must decline jurisdiction in favour of the court first seised only in so far as those trade marks are valid for identical goods or services.[566]

[2] Territorial scope of the prohibition

The territorial scope of a prohibition against further infringement or threatened infringement of a Community trade mark, as provided for in Article 98(1) CTMR, is to be determined **both** by the **territorial jurisdiction** of the Community trade mark court issuing that prohibition **and** by the territorial **extent of the Community trade mark proprietor's exclusive right** which is adversely affected by the infringement or threatened infringement, as that extent results from the CTMR.[567]

563. CJEU C-231/16 of 19.10.2017 – Merck, para. 44.
564. CJEU C-231/16 of 19.10.2017 – Merck, para. 53.
565. CJEU C-231/16 of 19.10.2017 – Merck, para. 58.
566. CJEU C-231/16 of 19.10.2017 – Merck, para. 62.
567. CJEU C-235/09 of 12.4.2011 – DHL Express France, para. 33.

As regards, first, the **territorial jurisdiction** of a Community trade mark court, under Article 14(1) and (3) CTMR, infringement of a Community trade mark is to be governed by the national law relating to infringement of a national trade mark in accordance with the provisions of Title X of that regulation. The rules of procedure to be applied are to be determined in accordance with the provisions of Title X, headed 'Jurisdiction and procedure in legal actions relating to Community trade marks' and comprising Articles 90–104 of that regulation.[568]

Article 92(a) CTMR provides that the Community trade mark courts are to have exclusive jurisdiction to adjudicate upon all infringement actions and – if they are permitted under national law – actions in respect of threatened infringement relating to Community trade marks.[569]

Under Article 93(1)–(4) CTMR, read in conjunction with Article 94(1) CTMR, a Community trade mark court, which is established in accordance with Article 91 CTMR in order to protect the rights conferred by a Community trade mark, is to have jurisdiction, in particular, in respect of acts of infringement committed or threatened within the territory of any of the Member States.[570]

Therefore, a Community trade mark court, such as that hearing the case in the main proceedings, has jurisdiction in respect of acts of infringement committed or threatened within the territory of **one or more Member States, or even all the Member States**. Thus, its jurisdiction may extend to the entire area of the EU.[571]

Second, the **exclusive right of a Community trade mark proprietor**, conferred under the CTMR, extends, as a rule, to the entire area of the EU, throughout which Community trade marks enjoy uniform protection and have effect.[572]

In accordance with Article 1(2) CTMR, a Community trade mark is to have a unitary character. Having equal effect throughout the EU, it may not, in accordance with that provision, be registered, transferred or surrendered or be the subject of a decision revoking the rights of the proprietor or declaring it invalid, nor may its use be prohibited, save in respect of the whole of the EU. This principle is to apply unless otherwise provided in that regulation.[573]

In addition, it follows from the second recital in the preamble to the CTMR that the objective pursued by that regulation involves the creation of Community arrangements for trade marks to which uniform protection is given and which produce their effects throughout the entire area of the EU.[574]

The unitary character of the Community trade mark is also apparent from the fifteenth and sixteenth recitals in the preamble to the CTMR. These state, first, that the effects of decisions regarding the validity and infringement of Community trade marks

568. CJEU C-235/09 of 12.4.2011 – DHL Express France, para. 34.
569. CJEU C-235/09 of 12.4.2011 – DHL Express France, para. 35.
570. CJEU C-235/09 of 12.4.2011 – DHL Express France, para. 37.
571. CJEU C-235/09 of 12.4.2011 – DHL Express France, para. 38.
572. CJEU C-235/09 of 12.4.2011 – DHL Express France, para. 39; C-93/16 of 20.7.2017 – Ornua Co-operative/Tindale & Stanton, para. 28.
573. CJEU C-235/09 of 12.4.2011 – DHL Express France, para. 40.
574. CJEU C-235/09 of 12.4.2011 – DHL Express France, para. 41; C-190/10 of 22.3.2012 – Génesis, para. 35.

must cover the entire area of the EU, in order to prevent inconsistent decisions on the part of the courts and OHIM and to ensure that the unitary character of Community trade marks is not undermined, and, second, that contradictory judgments should be avoided in actions which involve the same acts and the same parties and which are brought on the basis of a Community trade mark and parallel national trade marks.[575]

In addition, the Court has already held[576] that the objective of Article 98(1) CTMR is the uniform protection, throughout the entire area of the EU, of the right conferred by the Community trade mark against the risk of infringement.[577]

In order to ensure that uniform protection, a prohibition against further infringement or threatened infringement issued by a competent Community trade mark court must therefore, as a rule, extend to the entire area of the EU.[578]

If the territorial scope of that prohibition were, on the contrary, limited to the territory of the Member State in respect of which that court had found there to be an act of infringement or threatened infringement or to the territory of only the Member States which gave rise to such a finding, there would be a risk that the defendant would begin to exploit the sign at issue afresh in a Member State for which the prohibition had not been issued. In addition, the new judicial proceedings which the Community trade mark proprietor would be compelled to bring would increase, in a manner proportional to those proceedings, the risk of inconsistent decisions relating to the Community trade mark concerned, in particular because of the factual assessment of the likelihood of confusion. Such a consequence runs counter to the objective of the uniform protection of the Community trade mark pursued by the CTMR as well as to the unitary character of that mark.[579]

However, the territorial scope of the prohibition may, in certain circumstances, be restricted. The exclusive right of a Community trade mark proprietor, as provided for under Article 9(1) CTMR, is conferred in order to enable that proprietor to protect his specific interests as such, that is, to ensure that the trade mark is able to fulfil its functions. The exercise of that right must therefore be reserved to cases in which a third party's use of the sign affects or is liable to affect the functions of the trade mark.[580]

It follows that the exclusive right of a Community trade mark proprietor and, hence, the territorial scope of that right may not extend beyond what that right allows its proprietor to do in order to protect his trade mark, that is, to prohibit only uses which are liable to affect the functions of the trade mark. The acts or future acts of a defendant (namely the person whose use of the Community trade mark is complained of) which do not affect the functions of the Community trade mark cannot therefore be prohibited.[581]

575. CJEU C-235/09 of 12.4.2011 – DHL Express France, para. 42.
576. CJEU C-316/05 P of 14.12.2006 – Nokia, para. 60.
577. CJEU C-235/09 of 12.4.2011 – DHL Express France, para. 43.
578. CJEU C-235/09 of 12.4.2011 – DHL Express France, para. 44; C-223/15 of 22.9.2016 – combit Software/Commit Business Solutions, para. 30.
579. CJEU C-235/09 of 12.4.2011 – DHL Express France, para. 45.
580. CJEU C-235/09 of 12.4.2011 – DHL Express France, para. 46; C-223/15 of 22.9.2016 – combit Software/Commit Business Solutions, para. 32.
581. CJEU C-235/09 of 12.4.2011 – DHL Express France, para. 47.

Accordingly, if a Community trade mark court hearing a case finds that the acts of infringement or threatened infringement of a Community trade mark are limited to a single Member State or to part of the territory of the EU, in particular because the applicant for a prohibition order has restricted the territorial scope of its action in exercising its freedom to determine the extent of that action or because the defendant proves that the use of the sign at issue does not affect or is not liable to affect the functions of the trade mark, for example, on linguistic grounds, that court must limit the territorial scope of the prohibition which it issues.[582]

Lastly, it must be stated that the territorial scope of a prohibition against further infringement or threatened infringement of a Community trade mark can extend to the entire area of the EU. That said, in accordance with Article 90 CTMR, which is concerned with the application of the Brussels Convention, read in conjunction with Article 33(1) of Regulation No. 44/2001, the other Member States are, as a rule, required to recognize and enforce the judgment, thereby conferring on it a cross-border effect.[583]

Consequently, Article 98(1) CTMR must be interpreted as meaning that the scope of the prohibition against further infringement or threatened infringement of a Community trade mark, issued by a Community trade mark court whose jurisdiction is based on Articles 93(1)-(4) and 94(1) CTMR, extends, as a rule, to the entire area of the EU.[584]

Article 1(2), Article 9(1)(b) and Article 102(1) CTMR must be interpreted as meaning that where an EU trade mark court finds that the use of a sign creates a **likelihood of confusion with an EU trade mark in one part of the European Union** whilst not creating such a likelihood in another part thereof, that court must conclude that there is an infringement of the exclusive right conferred by that trade mark and issue an order prohibiting the use in question for the entire area of the European Union with the exception of the part in respect of which there has been found to be no likelihood of confusion.[585]

In that regard, it should be stated at the outset that, in a case such as that in the main proceedings, in which the court seised is acting in its capacity as an EU trade mark court to decide on an action brought under Article 97(1) to (4) CTMR, that court, in accordance with Article 98(1) CTMR, has jurisdiction to consider whether acts of infringement have been committed or threatened within the territory of any of the Member States.[586]

When the EU trade mark court finds, in the exercise of that jurisdiction, that the use of a sign creates, in one part of the European Union, a likelihood of confusion with an EU trade mark, whilst, in another part of the Union, that same use does not give rise to such a likelihood of confusion, that court cannot conclude that there is no infringement of the exclusive right conferred by that trade mark. Rather, it must find

582. CJEU C-235/09 of 12.4.2011 - DHL Express France, para. 48.
583. CJEU C-235/09 of 12.4.2011 - DHL Express France, para. 49.
584. CJEU C-235/09 of 12.4.2011 - DHL Express France, para. 50.
585. CJEU C-223/15 of 22.9.2016 - combit Software/Commit Business Solutions, para. 36.
586. CJEU C-223/15 of 22.9.2016 - combit Software/Commit Business Solutions, para. 24.

that the function of the trade mark as an indication of origin is adversely affected and that, as a consequence, there is an infringement of the exclusive right conferred by the mark.[587]

In that context, the Court has already held, in a case concerning the right of the proprietor of an EU trade mark to oppose, pursuant to Article 8(1)(b) CTMR, registration of a similar EU trade mark which would create a likelihood of confusion, that such an opposition must be upheld where it is established that there is a likelihood of confusion in part of the European Union, a Member State, for example, being capable of constituting such a part.[588]

A similar approach is necessary in cases concerning the right of the proprietor of an EU trade mark to prohibit the use of a sign which creates a likelihood of confusion. Article 9(1)(b) CTMR protects the proprietor of an EU trade mark against any use which adversely affects that trade mark's function of indicating origin or is liable to do so.[589] The proprietor is therefore entitled to prohibit such use, even if the latter adversely affects the above-mentioned function only in part of the European Union.[590]

It follows from the foregoing that a likelihood of confusion in the German-speaking part of the European Union, such as the referring court has found to exist in the present case, must lead the EU trade mark court before which the proceedings have been brought to conclude that the exclusive right conferred by the trade mark concerned has been infringed.[591]

Under Article 102(1) CTMR, the court which has made such a finding must issue an order prohibiting the defendant from proceeding with the acts which infringe or would infringe the EU trade mark. Although it is true that, under that provision, the existence of 'special reasons' may justify not issuing such an order, the Court of Justice has already held that that exception must be interpreted strictly and covers only certain exceptional situations, which are not in issue in the case in the main proceedings.[592]

In order to guarantee the uniform protection which EU trade marks are afforded throughout the entire area of the European Union, the prohibition on proceeding with acts which infringe or would infringe an EU trade mark must, as a rule, extend to the whole of that area.[593]

587. CJEU C-223/15 of 22.9.2016 – combit Software/Commit Business Solutions, para. 25, *see also* CJEU C-93/16 of 20.7.2017 – Ornua Co-operative/Tindale & Stanton, para. 33.
588. CJEU C-223/15 of 22.9.2016 – combit Software/Commit Business Solutions, para. 26, with further proof.
589. *See*, as regards Article 5(1)(b) TMD2008, the wording of which corresponds to that of Article 9(1)(b) CTMR, CJEU C-179/15 of 3.3.2016 – Daimler/Együd Garage Gépjárműjavító és Értékesítő, para. 26, and the case law cited.
590. CJEU C-223/15 of 22.9.2016 – combit Software/Commit Business Solutions, para. 27; *see also* CJEU C-93/16 of 20.7.2017 – Ornua Co-operative/Tindale & Stanton, para. 29.
591. CJEU C-223/15 of 22.9.2016 – combit Software/Commit Business Solutions, para. 28.
592. CJEU C-223/15 of 22.9.2016 – combit Software/Commit Business Solutions, para. 29, with reference to CJEU C-316/05 P of 14.12.2006 – Nokia, para. 30; C-280/15 of 22.6.2016 – Nikolajeva/Multi Protect, para. 33.
593. CJEU C-223/15 of 22.9.2016 – combit Software/Commit Business Solutions, para. 30, with reference to CJEU C-235/09 of 12.4.2011 – DHL Express France, para. 39 to 44.

However, as follows from the judgment of *DHL Express France*,[594] in a situation in which - as in the case in the main proceedings - an EU trade mark court finds that the use of the similar sign in question for goods that are identical to those for which the EU trade mark at issue is registered does not, in a given part of the European Union, create any likelihood of confusion, in particular for linguistic reasons, and therefore cannot, in that part of the Union, adversely affect the trade mark's function of indicating origin, that court must limit the territorial scope of the aforementioned prohibition.[595]

Indeed, where an EU trade mark court concludes, on the basis of information which must, as a rule, be submitted to it by the defendant, that there is no likelihood of confusion in a part of the European Union, legitimate trade arising from the use of the sign in question in that part of the European Union cannot be prohibited. Such a prohibition would go beyond the exclusive right conferred by the EU trade mark, as that right merely permits the proprietor of that mark to protect his specific interests as such, that is to say, to ensure that the mark is able to fulfil its functions.[596]

It is also important that the EU trade mark court concerned identifies with precision the part of the European Union in respect of which it finds there to be no actual or potential adverse effect on the functions of the trade mark, so that it is absolutely clear from the order issued under Article 102 CTMR which part of the Union is not covered by the prohibition on using the sign in question. Where, as in the present case, that court intends to exclude from the prohibition on use certain linguistic areas of the European Union such as those designated by the term 'English-speaking', it must state comprehensively which areas it intends that term to cover.[597]

An interpretation whereby a prohibition on the use of a sign creating a likelihood of confusion with an EU trade mark applies to the entire area of the European Union, with the exception of the part of that area for which there has been found to be no such likelihood of confusion, does not undermine the unitary character of the EU trade mark referred to in Article 1(2) CTMR since the right of the proprietor of the trade mark to prohibit all use which adversely affects the functions inherent in that mark is preserved.[598]

[3] Claims for injunctive relief

Article 102(1) CTMR must be interpreted as not precluding an EU trade mark court from refraining, pursuant to certain principles of national procedural law, from issuing an order which prohibits a third party from proceeding with acts of infringement on the

594. CJEU C-235/09 of 12.4.2011 - DHL Express France, para. 48.
595. CJEU C-223/15 of 22.9.2016 - combit Software/Commit Business Solutions, para. 31; C-93/16 of 20.7.2017 - Ornua Co-operative/Tindale & Stanton, para. 36.
596. CJEU C-223/15 of 22.9.2016 - combit Software/Commit Business Solutions, para. 32, with reference to CJEU C-235/09 of 12.4.2011 - DHL Express France, para. 46 and 47.
597. CJEU C-223/15 of 22.9.2016 - combit Software/Commit Business Solutions, para. 34.
598. CJEU C-223/15 of 22.9.2016 - combit Software/Commit Business Solutions, para. 35.

ground that the proprietor of the trade mark concerned has not applied for such an order before that court.[599]

It should be recalled that Article 101(3) CTMR states that, unless otherwise provided in that regulation, an EU trade mark court is to apply the rules of procedure governing the same type of action relating to a national trade mark in the Member State in which the court is located.[600]

Since the CTMR does not provide otherwise, it does not preclude application of the principle that the subject matter of proceedings is determined by the parties and of the principle of ne ultra petita.[601]

Therefore, Article 102(1) CTMR does not preclude an EU trade mark court from refraining, pursuant to those principles of national procedural law, from issuing an order which prohibits a third party from proceeding with acts of infringement on the ground that the proprietor of the trade mark concerned has not applied for such an order.[602]

As the absence of an obligation to issue an order referred to in Article 102(1) CTMR therefore follows from the application, which the regulation does not preclude, of rules of national procedural law, there is no need to examine whether that absence of an obligation is justified on the basis that there is a 'special reason' within the meaning of that provision.[603]

In any event, the fact that, by his action before the EU trade mark court, the proprietor of an EU trade mark has merely applied for a declaration that an act of infringement has occurred, but has not applied for an order that it cease, cannot be classified as a 'special reason' within the meaning of Article 102(1) CTMR.[604]

Article 98(1) CTMR is to be interpreted as meaning that the mere fact that the risk of further infringement or threatened infringement of a Community trade mark is not obvious or is otherwise merely limited does not constitute a special reason for a Community trade mark court not to issue an **order prohibiting the defendant from proceeding with those acts**.[605]

It follows from the need for uniform application of Community law and from the principle of equality that the terms of a provision of Community law which makes no express reference to the law of the Member States for the purpose of determining its meaning and scope must normally be given an autonomous and uniform interpretation throughout the Community, having regard to the context of the provision and the objective pursued by the legislation in question.[606]

That applies to the term 'special reasons' in the first sentence of Article 98(1) CTMR.[607]

599. CJEU C-280/15 of 22.6.2016 – Nikolajeva/Multi Protect, para. 34.
600. CJEU C-280/15 of 22.6.2016 – Nikolajeva/Multi Protect, para. 28.
601. CJEU C-280/15 of 22.6.2016 – Nikolajeva/Multi Protect, para. 29.
602. CJEU C-280/15 of 22.6.2016 – Nikolajeva/Multi Protect, para. 30.
603. CJEU C-280/15 of 22.6.2016 – Nikolajeva/Multi Protect, para. 31.
604. CJEU C-280/15 of 22.6.2016 – Nikolajeva/Multi Protect, para. 32.
605. CJEU C-316/05 P of 14.12.2006 – Nokia, para. 36.
606. CJEU C-316/05 P of 14.12.2006 – Nokia, para. 21.
607. CJEU C-316/05 P of 14.12.2006 – Nokia, para. 22.

It is true that Article 14(1) CTMR provides that 'infringement of a Community trade mark shall be governed by the national law relating to infringement of a national trade mark in accordance with the provisions of Title X'.[608]

However, first, as indicated by the words 'in accordance with the provisions of Title X', that reference to the national law of the Member States does not preclude the establishment, by the Community legislature, of a number of rules to govern uniformly the issue of infringement of Community trade marks.[609]

Second, as is apparent from the second recital in the preamble to the Regulation, the Community arrangements for trade marks established by the Regulation seek, *inter alia*, to allow undertakings to 'obtain Community trade marks to which uniform protection is given and which produce their effects throughout the entire area of the Community'.[610]

It is essential, for the purposes of protecting Community trade marks, to enforce the prohibition against infringement of those marks.[611]

If the condition relating to 'special reasons' were to be interpreted differently in the various Member States, the same circumstances could give rise to prohibitions of further infringement or threatened infringement in some Member States and not in others. Consequently, the protection afforded to Community trade marks would not be uniform throughout the entire area of the Community.[612]

The term 'special reasons' must therefore be given a uniform interpretation within the Community legal order.[613]

In that regard, it must be noted, firstly, that, in the different language versions, the first sentence of Article 98(1) CTMR is drafted in mandatory terms (*see*, *inter alia*, in Spanish, 'dictará providencia para prohibirle'; in German, 'verbietet'; in English, 'shall ... issue an order prohibiting'; in French, 'rend ... une ordonnance lui interdisant'; in Italian, 'emette un'ordinanza vietandogli'; and, in Dutch, 'verbiedt').[614]

It follows that, in principle, a Community trade mark court must issue an order prohibiting further infringement or threatened infringement and, therefore, that the condition relating to 'special reasons for not doing so' – which the wording of Article 98(1) clearly shows is an exception to that obligation (*see*, *inter alia*, in Spanish, '[n]o habiendo'; in German, 'sofern ... nicht ... entgegenstehen'; in English, 'unless there are'; in French, 'sauf s'il y a'; in Italian, 'a meno que esistano'; and in Dutch, 'tenzij er ... zijn') – must be interpreted strictly.[615]

Second, Article 98(1) CTMR is an essential provision for the purposes of achieving the objective pursued by the Regulation of protecting Community trade marks within the Community.[616]

608. CJEU C-316/05 P of 14.12.2006 – Nokia, para. 23.
609. CJEU C-316/05 P of 14.12.2006 – Nokia, para. 24.
610. CJEU C-316/05 P of 14.12.2006 – Nokia, para. 25.
611. CJEU C-316/05 P of 14.12.2006 – Nokia, para. 26.
612. CJEU C-316/05 P of 14.12.2006 – Nokia, para. 27.
613. CJEU C-316/05 P of 14.12.2006 – Nokia, para. 28.
614. CJEU C-316/05 P of 14.12.2006 – Nokia, para. 29.
615. CJEU C-316/05 P of 14.12.2006 – Nokia, para. 30; C-223/15 of 22.9.2016 – combit Software/ Commit Business Solutions, para. 29.
616. CJEU C-316/05 P of 14.12.2006 – Nokia, para. 31.

If the issue of a prohibition against further infringement or threatened infringement of a Community trade mark were conditional on an obvious or not merely limited risk of recurrence of such acts, the applicant would probably be required to furnish evidence of that risk. Such evidence regarding the possible conduct of the defendant in the future would be difficult for the applicant to adduce and risk undermining the exclusive right conferred on him by the Community trade mark.[617]

Third, as was pointed out in paragraph 25 of this judgment, the protection of Community trade marks must be uniform throughout the entire area of the Community.[618]

An interpretation according to which the issue of a prohibition against further infringement or threatened infringement of a Community trade mark was conditional on an obvious or not merely limited risk of recurrence of such acts on the part of the defendant would result in the extent of the protection of that mark varying from one court to another, indeed from one action to another, according to the assessment made of that risk.[619]

The above considerations obviously do not preclude a Community trade mark court from not issuing such a prohibition were it to find that further infringement or threatened infringement on the part of the defendant was no longer possible. That would apply in particular if, after the commission of the acts in question, an action were brought against the proprietor of the mark infringed which culminated in a revocation of his rights.[620]

Article 98(1) CTMR is to be interpreted as meaning that the fact that the national law includes a **general prohibition** of the infringement of Community trade marks and provides for the possibility of penalizing further infringement or threatened infringement, whether intentional or due to gross negligence, **does not constitute a special reason** for a Community trade mark court not to issue an order prohibiting the defendant from proceeding with those acts.[621]

First, as is apparent from the choice of words used by the Community legislature in the first sentence of Article 98(1) CTMR (*see, inter alia*, in Spanish, 'razones especiales'; in German, 'besondere Gründe'; in English, 'special reasons'; in French, 'raisons particulières'; in Italian, 'motivi particolari'; and in Dutch, 'speciale redenen'), the term 'special reasons' relates to factual circumstances specific to a given case.[622]

The fact that the legislation of a Member State provides for a general prohibition of infringement and for the possibility of penalizing further infringement or threatened infringement cannot be regarded as specific to every action for infringement or

617. CJEU C-316/05 P of 14.12.2006 – Nokia, para. 32.
618. CJEU C-316/05 P of 14.12.2006 – Nokia, para. 33.
619. CJEU C-316/05 P of 14.12.2006 – Nokia, para. 34.
620. CJEU C-316/05 P of 14.12.2006 – Nokia, para. 35; C-280/15 of 22.6.2016 – Nikolajeva/Multi Protect, para. 33; CJEU C-223/15 of 22.9.2016 – combit Software/Commit Business Solutions, para. 29.
621. CJEU C-316/05 P of 14.12.2006 – Nokia, para. 45.
622. CJEU C-316/05 P of 14.12.2006 – Nokia, para. 38.

threatened infringement brought before the Community trade mark courts of that State.[623]

Moreover, under Articles 44(1) and 61 of the TRIPS Agreement, all Member States are required to provide for civil and criminal remedies, including prohibition, for infringement of intellectual property rights. The existence of such remedies under national law cannot therefore, *a fortiori*, constitute a special reason within the meaning of the first sentence of Article 98(1) CTMR.[624]

Second, if the fact that the law of a Member State provides for a general prohibition of infringement and for the possibility of a penalty for further infringement or threatened infringement were to be regarded as a special reason, within the meaning of the first sentence of Article 98(1) CTMR, application of the principle - laid down in that provision - that the Community trade mark courts must, subject to exceptions, issue an order prohibiting further infringement or threatened infringement would depend on the content of the national law applicable.[625]

The Community trade mark courts of a Member State whose legislation provides for a statutory general prohibition of infringement and also for the possibility of penalizing further infringement would thus automatically be relieved of the obligation to issue an order prohibiting the defendant from proceeding with the acts in question, without even having to look at the specific facts of each case, and, therefore, Article 98(1) CTMR would be rendered redundant within the territory of that State.[626]

Such an outcome would be incompatible both with the principle of the primacy of Community law and with the requirement that it be uniformly applied.[627]

Lastly, the existence, under the national law applicable, of a general prohibition on infringement and the possibility of a penalty in the event of further acts of infringement do not have the same dissuasive effect as a specific prohibition against the defendant from proceeding with those acts, coupled with measures aimed at ensuring that that prohibition is complied with, that prohibition having already been ordered by means of an enforceable court decision. Consequently, the proprietor of the mark infringed cannot be protected in a comparable way where there is no such specific prohibition.[628]

[4] Claims for compensation

Article 13(1) of Directive 2004/48[629] must be interpreted as permitting a party injured by an intellectual property infringement, who claims compensation for his material damage as calculated, in accordance with heading (b) of the second subparagraph of

623. CJEU C-316/05 P of 14.12.2006 - Nokia, para. 39.
624. CJEU C-316/05 P of 14.12.2006 - Nokia, para. 40.
625. CJEU C-316/05 P of 14.12.2006 - Nokia, para. 41.
626. CJEU C-316/05 P of 14.12.2006 - Nokia, para. 42.
627. CJEU C-316/05 P of 14.12.2006 - Nokia, para. 43.
628. CJEU C-316/05 P of 14.12.2006 - Nokia, para. 44.
629. Directive 2004/48/EC of the European Parliament and of the Council of 29 Apr. 2004 on the enforcement of intellectual property rights (OJ 2004 L 157, p. 45, and corrigendum OJ 2004 L 195, p. 16).

Article 13(1) of that directive, on the basis of the amount of hypothetical royalties, **also** to claim **compensation for the moral prejudice** that he has suffered, as provided for under heading (a) of the second subparagraph of Article 13(1) of that directive.[630]

In that regard, according to the Court's settled case law, for the purpose of interpreting a provision of EU law, it is necessary to consider not only its wording but also the context in which it occurs and the objectives pursued by the rules of which it is part.[631]

With regard, first, to the wording of heading (b) of the second subparagraph of Article 13(1) of Directive 2004/48, it must be noted that, although that provision does not mention moral prejudice as an element which the judicial authorities must take into consideration when setting the amount of damages to be paid to the rightholder, it also does not exclude that type of harm from being taken into account. By providing for the possibility of setting the damages as a lump sum on the basis of, 'at least', the elements referred to therein, that provision allows other elements to be included in that amount, such as, where appropriate, compensation for any moral prejudice caused to the rightholder.[632]

Secondly, it must be pointed out that such a finding is confirmed by an analysis of the context in which that provision features.[633]

On the one hand, the first subparagraph of Article 13(1) of Directive 2004/48 sets out the general rule that the competent judicial authorities must order the infringer to pay the injured rightholder damages that are 'appropriate to the actual prejudice suffered by him as a result of the infringement'. As noted by the Advocate General in point 28 of his Opinion, moral prejudice, such as damage to the reputation of the author of a work, constitutes, provided that it is proven, a component of the prejudice actually suffered by the rightholder.[634]

Consequently, where the rightholder in question has in fact suffered moral prejudice, the actual wording of heading (b) of the second subparagraph of Article 13(1) of Directive 2004/48, read in conjunction with the first subparagraph of Article 13(1) of that directive, precludes the calculation of the amount of damages to be paid to that rightholder from being based exclusively on the amount of hypothetical royalties.[635]

On the other hand, it should be noted that the application, by the competent judicial authorities, of the lump sum calculation method provided for under heading (b) of the second subparagraph of Article 13(1) of Directive 2004/48 is permitted as an alternative only 'in appropriate cases'.[636]

As indicated in recital 26 of that directive, the latter term applies 'for example where it would be difficult to determine the amount of the actual prejudice suffered'. In such circumstances,.the amount of damages may be calculated on the basis of

630. CJEU C-99/15 of 17.3.2016 – Liffers/Producciones Mandarina, para. 27.
631. CJEU C-99/15 of 17.3.2016 – Liffers/Producciones Mandarina, para. 14, with further proof.
632. CJEU C-99/15 of 17.3.2016 – Liffers/Producciones Mandarina, para. 15.
633. CJEU C-99/15 of 17.3.2016 – Liffers/Producciones Mandarina, para. 16.
634. CJEU C-99/15 of 17.3.2016 – Liffers/Producciones Mandarina, para. 17.
635. CJEU C-99/15 of 17.3.2016 – Liffers/Producciones Mandarina, para. 18.
636. CJEU C-99/15 of 17.3.2016 – Liffers/Producciones Mandarina, para. 19.

elements such as the royalties or fees normally due for the use of the intellectual property right, which does not take into account any moral prejudice.[637]

As regards, lastly, the objectives pursued by Directive 2004/48, it must first of all be pointed out that, according to recital 10 thereof, the objective of that directive is to ensure, *inter alia*, a high, equivalent and homogeneous level of intellectual property protection in the internal market.[638]

Next, recital 17 of that directive indicates that the measures, procedures and remedies provided for therein should be determined in each case in such a manner as to take due account of the specific characteristics of that case.[639]

Finally, recital 26 of the directive states, *inter alia*, that, with a view to compensating for the prejudice suffered as a result of an infringement committed by an infringer, the amount of damages awarded to the holder of the intellectual property right should take account of all appropriate aspects, including any moral prejudice caused to the rightholder.[640]

It thus follows from recitals 10, 17 and 26 of Directive 2004/48 that the objective of that directive is to attain a high level of protection of intellectual property rights that takes into account the specific aspects of each given case and is based on a method of calculating damages that addresses those specific aspects.[641]

In the light of the objectives of Directive 2004/48, the first subparagraph of Article 13(1) of that directive must be interpreted as establishing the principle that the calculation of the amount of damages to be paid to the holder of the intellectual property right must seek to ensure that the latter is compensated in full for the 'actual prejudice suffered' by him, which also includes any moral prejudice.[642]

However, as is apparent from paragraph 20 of the present judgment, setting the amount of damages due as a lump sum on the basis of hypothetical royalties alone covers only the material damage suffered by the intellectual property rightholder concerned; consequently, for the purposes of providing compensation in full, that rightholder must be able to seek, in addition to the damages thus calculated, compensation for any moral prejudice which he has suffered.[643]

Article 9(3)(2) CTMR must be interpreted as precluding the proprietor of an EU trade mark from being able to claim **compensation** in respect of acts of third parties occurring **before publication of an application** for registration of a trade mark. In the case of acts of third parties committed during the period after publication of the application for registration of the mark concerned but before publication of its registration, the concept of 'reasonable compensation' in that provision refers to recovery of the profits actually derived by third parties from use of the mark during that period. On the other hand, that concept of 'reasonable compensation' rules out

637. CJEU C-99/15 of 17.3.2016 – Liffers/Producciones Mandarina, para. 20.
638. CJEU C-99/15 of 17.3.2016 – Liffers/Producciones Mandarina, para. 21.
639. CJEU C-99/15 of 17.3.2016 – Liffers/Producciones Mandarina, para. 22.
640. CJEU C-99/15 of 17.3.2016 – Liffers/Producciones Mandarina, para. 23.
641. CJEU C-99/15 of 17.3.2016 – Liffers/Producciones Mandarina, para. 24.
642. CJEU C-99/15 of 17.3.2016 – Liffers/Producciones Mandarina, para. 25.
643. CJEU C-99/15 of 17.3.2016 – Liffers/Producciones Mandarina, para. 26.

compensation for the wider harm which the proprietor of the mark may have suffered, including, as the case may be, moral prejudice.[644]

Under Article 9(3)(1) CTMR, the rights conferred by an EU trade mark are to prevail against third parties from the date of publication of registration of the trade mark concerned.[645]

It follows that the exclusive right which the EU trade mark confers on its proprietor, enabling him, in particular, to prevent third parties from using the mark concerned in infringement actions pursuant to Article 9(1) and (2) CTMR can relate only to acts of third parties occurring after publication of registration of that mark.[646]

However, in order to grant applicants for registration of a trade mark a degree of protection in the period between the date of publication of the application – the date from which the application is deemed to be known to third parties – and the date of publication of the mark's registration, Article 9(3)(2) CTMR lays down a right to 'reasonable compensation' in respect of acts having taken place during that period which, had they occurred after the date of registration of the mark, would have been prohibited.[647]

That protection can be explained by the body of economic rights which the CTMR attaches to an application for registration of an EU trade mark.[648]

Indeed, under Article 24 CTMR, which is in section 4, headed 'EU trade marks as objects of property', applications for registration of EU trade marks can be the subject of various types of legal acts, such as a transfer, the creation of rights in rem, or licences, which possess the common feature that their purpose or effect is to create or transfer a right in respect of the trade mark concerned.[649]

In the present instance, the application for registration of the trade mark at issue in the main proceedings was the subject matter of a licence as soon as it was filed.[650]

The intrinsic economic value of an application for registration of an EU trade mark also stems from other rights attaching to such an application. Thus, by virtue of the CTMR the applicant enjoys in principle a right of priority, from the date on which his application for registration of a mark is filed, over applications filed subsequently.[651]

Furthermore, such considerations relating to the body of economic rights that attach to an application for registration of a trade mark have in particular led the European Court of Human Rights to hold that, in the light of the circumstances of the case considered as a whole, such an application was capable of constituting a substantive interest protected under the fundamental right to property laid down in

644. CJEU C-280/15 of 22.6.2016 – Nikolajeva/Multi Protect, para. 59.
645. CJEU C-280/15 of 22.6.2016 – Nikolajeva/Multi Protect, para. 36.
646. CJEU C-280/15 of 22.6.2016 – Nikolajeva/Multi Protect, para. 37.
647. CJEU C-280/15 of 22.6.2016 – Nikolajeva/Multi Protect, para. 38.
648. CJEU C-280/15 of 22.6.2016 – Nikolajeva/Multi Protect, para. 39.
649. CJEU C-280/15 of 22.6.2016 – Nikolajeva/Multi Protect, para. 40, with reference to CJEU C-163/15 of 4.2.2016 – Hassan, para. 21.
650. CJEU C-280/15 of 22.6.2016 – Nikolajeva/Multi Protect, para. 41.
651. CJEU C-280/15 of 22.6.2016 – Nikolajeva/Multi Protect, para. 42.

Article 1 of Protocol No 1 to the European Convention for the Protection of Human Rights and Fundamental Freedoms, signed in Rome on 4 November 1950.[652]

In the light of those considerations, it must be held that since Article 9(3)(2) CTMR contains a strictly circumscribed exception to the rule that an EU trade mark does not prevail before publication of its registration, no compensation can be claimed under that provision in respect of acts which occurred before publication of the application for registration of such a mark.[653]

Also, as Article 9(3)(2) CTMR makes no express reference to the law of the Member States for the purpose of determining its meaning and scope, it follows, in accordance with the Court's settled case law, that the concept of 'reasonable compensation' in that provision must normally be given an autonomous and uniform interpretation, having regard to the context of that provision and the objective pursued by the legislation concerned.[654]

For the purposes of that interpretation, account should be taken, as the referring court has also observed, of the fact that the protection taking the form of 'reasonable compensation', within the meaning of Article 9(3)(2) CTMR, in respect of the acts referred to in that provision must, by its nature, be more limited than the protection enjoyed by the proprietor of a trade mark for acts occurring after the date of its registration, since the interest to be protected in respect of an application for registration of a mark falls short of the interest to be protected which the mark must possess as a result of its registration.[655]

The acts referred to in Article 9(3)(2) CTMR occur at a time when it is not yet certain that the trade mark whose registration has been applied for will in fact be registered since absolute or relative grounds for refusal of registration may still preclude this in whole or in part.[656]

Thus, the rights conferred by an application for registration of an EU trade mark possess, before registration of the mark concerned, what can be described as a 'conditional' nature.[657]

That conditional nature is indeed clear from Article 9(3)(3) CTMR since it provides that actions founded on Article 9(3)(2) CTMR cannot be brought before an EU trade mark court until after the registration of the trade mark concerned has been published.[658]

It follows that the 'reasonable compensation' that may be claimed in an action founded on Article 9(3)(2) CTMR must be smaller in scope than the damages which the

652. CJEU C-280/15 of 22.6.2016 – Nikolajeva/Multi Protect, para. 43, with reference to EctHR, 11 January 2007, Anheuser-Busch Inc. v. Portugal, CE:ECHR:2007:0111JUD007304901, §§ 73 to 78.
653. CJEU C-280/15 of 22.6.2016 – Nikolajeva/Multi Protect, para. 44.
654. CJEU C-280/15 of 22.6.2016 – Nikolajeva/Multi Protect, para. 45, with reference to CJEU C-316/05 P of 14.12.2006 – Nokia, para. 21.
655. CJEU C-280/15 of 22.6.2016 – Nikolajeva/Multi Protect, para. 46.
656. CJEU C-280/15 of 22.6.2016 – Nikolajeva/Multi Protect, para. 47.
657. CJEU C-280/15 of 22.6.2016 – Nikolajeva/Multi Protect, para. 48.
658. CJEU C-280/15 of 22.6.2016 – Nikolajeva/Multi Protect, para. 49.

proprietor of an EU trade mark may claim in respect of the harm caused by an act of infringement.[659]

The distinction between these two types of actions is also clear from the list, in Article 96 CTMR, of the various areas of exclusive jurisdiction of EU trade mark courts, in that Article 96 mentions separately, in (a), 'infringement actions' and, in (c), 'actions brought as a result of acts referred to in Article 9(3)(2)' CTMR.[660]

In addition, since the CTMR does not contain rules relating to the damages that may be claimed by the proprietor of an EU trade mark for acts of infringement, it follows from Article 101(2) CTMR that, in principle, an EU trade mark court is to apply its national law, including its private international law, on the matter. It is apparent, furthermore, from Article 14(2) CTMR that, in particular, the regulation does not preclude the complementary application of national law relating to infringement and, in particular, national law relating to civil liability.[661]

In this context, Article 13 of Directive 2004/48[662] lays down certain rules which concern damages intended to compensate for the harm caused by acts of infringement, and which differ according to whether or not the third party must be considered to have knowingly – or with reasonable grounds to know – engaged in an infringing activity.[663]

Thus, Article 13(1) of Directive 2004/48 prescribes compensation which is in principle full compensation, for the harm actually suffered, which may include 'moral prejudice', in the event of acts of infringement committed knowingly, whereas Article 13(2) permits only the recovery of profits or the payment of damages, which may be pre-established, where the acts of infringement have not been committed knowingly.[664]

Whilst those provisions apply, in themselves, only to acts of infringement and therefore to acts which have occurred after publication of the registration of the trade mark concerned and not to acts before its publication, such as those referred to in Article 9(3)(2) CTMR, it may, however, be inferred from them that the sum payable by way of 'reasonable compensation' cannot exceed the reduced compensation provided for in Article 13(2) of Directive 2004/48.[665]

Since Article 9(3)(2) CTMR seeks to attach conditional rights to a trade mark from publication of the application for its registration and even before publication of its registration, the 'reasonable compensation', within the meaning of that provision, must have a narrower scope than the damages which may be claimed by the proprietor of an EU trade mark for acts of infringement occurring after publication of the

659. CJEU C-280/15 of 22.6.2016 – Nikolajeva/Multi Protect, para. 50.
660. CJEU C-280/15 of 22.6.2016 – Nikolajeva/Multi Protect, para. 51.
661. CJEU C-280/15 of 22.6.2016 – Nikolajeva/Multi Protect, para. 52.
662. Directive 2004/48/EC of the European Parliament and of the Council of 29 Apr. 2004 on the enforcement of intellectual property rights (OJ 2004 L 157, p. 45, and corrigendum OJ 2004 L 195, p. 16).
663. CJEU C-280/15 of 22.6.2016 – Nikolajeva/Multi Protect, para. 53.
664. CJEU C-280/15 of 22.6.2016 – Nikolajeva/Multi Protect, para. 54.
665. CJEU C-280/15 of 22.6.2016 – Nikolajeva/Multi Protect, para. 55.

registration of that mark and which are intended, in principle, to ensure full compensation for the harm actually suffered, which may, as the case may be, include moral prejudice.[666]

For the purpose of determining 'reasonable compensation', within the meaning of Article 9(3)(2) CTMR, it is therefore appropriate to apply the criterion relating to the recovery of profits and to exclude from that compensation redress for the wider harm that the proprietor of the trade mark concerned may have suffered on account of its use, which may include, in particular, moral prejudice.[667]

The criterion regarding the recovery of profits, in that it relates to recovery of the profits unfairly derived by third parties from use of the trade mark concerned during the period referred to in Article 9(3)(2) CTMR, falls within the scope of the objective pursued by that provision, which consists in preventing third parties from improperly benefiting from the intrinsic economic value constituted by the application for registration of a trade mark, when they are deemed to have had knowledge of that application as a result of its publication.[668]

Article 33(2)(1) CDR must be interpreted as meaning that the licensee may bring proceedings alleging infringement of a registered Community design which is the subject of the licence although that licence has not been entered in the register of Community designs.[669]

Article 32(3) CDR must be interpreted as meaning that the licensee can claim damages for its own loss in proceedings for infringement of a Community design brought by it in accordance with that provision.[670]

On a proper construction of **Article 89(1)(d) of Regulation No. 6/2002,**[671] claims for the destruction of infringing products are governed by the law of the Member State in which the acts of infringement or threatened infringement have been committed, including its private international law. Claims for compensation for damage resulting from the activities of the person responsible for the acts of infringement or threatened infringement and for disclosure, in order to determine the extent of that damage, of information relating to those activities, are governed, pursuant to Article 88(2) of that regulation, by the national law of the Community design court hearing the proceedings, including its private international law.[672]

[5] Claims for ownership of a trade mark

Articles 16 and 18 CTMR must be interpreted as not precluding the application to an EU trade mark of a national provision, such as that at issue in the main proceedings, under which a person harmed, by the trade mark registration which was applied for in fraud of his rights or in breach of a legal or contractual obligation, is entitled to claim

666. CJEU C-280/15 of 22.6.2016 – Nikolajeva/Multi Protect, para. 56.
667. CJEU C-280/15 of 22.6.2016 – Nikolajeva/Multi Protect, para. 57.
668. CJEU C-280/15 of 22.6.2016 – Nikolajeva/Multi Protect, para. 58.
669. CJEU C-419/15 of 22.6.2016 – Thomas Philipps, para. 25.
670. CJEU C-419/15 of 22.6.2016 – Thomas Philipps, para. 32.
671. Council Regulation (EC) No. 6/2002 of 12 Dec. 2001 on Community designs (OJ 2002 L 3, p. 1).
672. CJEU C-479/12 of 13.2.2014 – H. Gautzsch Großhandel, para. 55.

ownership of that trade mark, provided that the situation concerned does not fall within those covered by Article 18 of that regulation.[673]

First of all, it must be borne in mind that Article 16(1) CTMR provides that 'Unless Articles 17 to 24 provide otherwise, [an EU] trade mark as an object of property shall be dealt with in its entirety, and for the whole area of the [European Union], as a national trade mark registered in the Member State in which, according to the Register of [EU] trade marks ... the proprietor has his seat or his domicile [or failing this] an establishment.'[674]

In that regard, it is important to note that Article 18 CTMR entitles the proprietor of an EU trade mark to demand the assignment in his favour of the registration of that mark if it is registered without his authorization in the name of his agent or representative.[675]

It follows that actions for recovery of ownership of an EU trade mark registered in the name of an agent or representative of the proprietor of that trade mark without that proprietor's authorization are governed exclusively by the CTMR.[676]

On the other hand, Article 18 CTMR does not govern actions for recovery of ownership of an EU trade mark in cases other than that of a trade mark registered in the name of an agent or representative of the proprietor of that trade mark without that proprietor's authorization.[677]

Consequently, as provided for in Article 16 CTMR, an EU trade mark as an object of property must, in cases falling outside that envisaged in Article 18 CTMR, be dealt with as a national trade mark registered in the Member State determined in accordance with the criteria set out in Article 16.[678]

Accordingly, provided that a situation does not fall within the scope of Article 18 CTMR, it is the national legislation of the Member State which will apply to actions for the recovery of ownership of an EU trade mark.[679]

[6] Counterclaims

Article 99(1) CTMR must be interpreted as meaning that an **action for infringement** brought before an EU trade mark court in accordance with Article 96(a) CTMR **may not be dismissed on the basis of an absolute ground for invalidity**, such as that provided for in Article 52(1)(b) CTMR, without that court having upheld the counterclaim for a declaration of invalidity brought by the defendant in that infringement action, pursuant to Article 100(1) CTMR, and based on the same ground for invalidity.[680]

673. CJEU C-381/16 of 23.11.2017 – Bravo de Laguna/Torras Ferrazzuolo, para. 38.
674. CJEU C-381/16 of 23.11.2017 – Bravo de Laguna/Torras Ferrazzuolo, para. 32.
675. CJEU C-381/16 of 23.11.2017 – Bravo de Laguna/Torras Ferrazzuolo, para. 33.
676. CJEU C-381/16 of 23.11.2017 – Bravo de Laguna/Torras Ferrazzuolo, para. 34.
677. CJEU C-381/16 of 23.11.2017 – Bravo de Laguna/Torras Ferrazzuolo, para. 35.
678. CJEU C-381/16 of 23.11.2017 – Bravo de Laguna/Torras Ferrazzuolo, para. 36.
679. CJEU C-381/16 of 23.11.2017 – Bravo de Laguna/Torras Ferrazzuolo, para. 37.
680. CJEU C-425/16 of 19.10.2017 – Raimund/Aigner, para. 35.

According to the settled case law of the Court, the interpretation of provisions of EU law requires account to be taken not only of their wording but also of the context in which they occur and the objectives of the rules of which they form part.[681]

As regards the wording of Article 99 CTMR, entitled 'Presumption of validity – Defence as to the merits', which appears in section 2 of Title X of that regulation, relating to disputes concerning the infringement and validity of EU trade marks, that provision states in paragraph 1 that the EU trade mark courts are to treat the EU trade mark as valid unless its validity is put in issue by the defendant with a counterclaim for revocation or for a declaration of invalidity.[682]

Whilst it is thus apparent from that provision that an EU trade mark is presumed to be valid, a presumption which, in the context of infringement proceedings, may be rebutted by a counterclaim for a declaration of invalidity, it cannot be determined on the basis of the wording of that provision alone whether, where a defendant in an infringement action challenges that action on the basis of a ground for invalidity of the mark and, moreover, brings a counterclaim for a declaration of invalidity based on the same ground for invalidity, the EU trade mark court must uphold that counterclaim before it can dismiss the action for infringement.[683]

As regards the context of Article 99(1) CTMR, it must be noted that Article 104(1) CTMR requires an EU trade mark court hearing an action referred to in Article 96 CTMR, unless there are special grounds for continuing the hearing, to stay the proceedings where the validity of the EU trade mark is already in issue before another EU trade mark court or where an application for revocation or for a declaration of invalidity has already been filed at EUIPO.[684]

Accordingly, interpreting Article 99(1) CTMR as meaning that the fact that a counterclaim for a declaration of invalidity has been brought before an EU trade mark court is sufficient for that court to be able, even before ruling on that counterclaim, to rule on the action for infringement brought under Article 96(a) CTMR, in reliance on the same ground for invalidity as that invoked in the counterclaim, would have the illogical effect that the rules in that regulation concerning related actions pending before different EU trade mark courts would be stricter than those concerning related actions pending before the same EU trade mark court.[685]

As to the objective of the CTMR, it must be borne in mind that Article 1(2) CTMR affirms the unitary character of the EU trade mark. Having equal effect throughout the Union, the trade mark may not, in accordance with that provision, be registered, transferred or surrendered or be the subject of a decision revoking the rights of the proprietor or declaring it invalid, nor may its use be prohibited, save in respect of the whole Union.[686]

In that regard, recital 16 of the CTMR states that decisions regarding the validity of EU trade marks must have effect and cover the entire area of the Union, as this is the

681. CJEU C-425/16 of 19.10.2017 – Raimund/Aigner, para. 22, with further reference.
682. CJEU C-425/16 of 19.10.2017 – Raimund/Aigner, para. 23.
683. CJEU C-425/16 of 19.10.2017 – Raimund/Aigner, para. 24.
684. CJEU C-425/16 of 19.10.2017 – Raimund/Aigner, para. 25.
685. CJEU C-425/16 of 19.10.2017 – Raimund/Aigner, para. 26.
686. CJEU C-425/16 of 19.10.2017 – Raimund/Aigner, para. 27.

only way of preventing inconsistent decisions on the part of the courts and EUIPO and of ensuring that the unitary character of EU trade marks is not undermined.[687]

It is thus apparent from the objective of that regulation that, in order to safeguard the unitary character of the EU trade mark, the decision of an EU trade mark court which, in the context of a counterclaim for a declaration of invalidity brought pursuant to Article 100(1) CTMR, declares an EU trade mark to be invalid necessarily has effect erga omnes throughout the Union.[688]

The erga omnes effect of such a decision is, moreover, confirmed both by Article 100(6) CTMR, according to which an EU trade mark court must send EUIPO a copy of the decision which has become final on a counterclaim for revocation or for invalidity of an EU trade mark, and by the rules on related actions set out in Article 104 CTMR.[689]

Conversely, the decision of such a court on an action for infringement has effect only *inter partes*, and, therefore, once such a decision has become final, it is binding only on the parties to that action.[690]

That is the case where the EU trade mark court dismisses the action for infringement because of the existence of an absolute ground for invalidity – such as the applicant's bad faith when he filed the application for the trade mark as provided for in Article 52(1)(b) CTMR – without first having ruled on the counterclaim for a declaration of invalidity brought by the defendant to that action.[691]

However, it must be pointed out that, given the unitary character of the EU trade mark and the objective of preventing inconsistent decisions in such matters, the declaration of invalidity of an EU trade mark based on such an absolute ground for invalidity must have effect throughout the Union and not only vis-à-vis the parties to the infringement action. That requirement means that the EU trade mark court concerned must rule on the counterclaim for a declaration of invalidity before ruling on the action for infringement.[692]

Consequently, the EU trade mark court is required to uphold the counterclaim for a declaration of invalidity of the EU trade mark brought, in accordance with Article 100(1) CTMR, in the context of an action for infringement of that mark, as provided for by Article 96(a) CTMR, before it may dismiss the latter action on the basis of the same ground for absolute invalidity.[693]

The provisions of the CTMR must be interpreted as not precluding an EU trade mark court from being able to dismiss an action for infringement within the meaning of Article 96(a) CTMR on the basis of an absolute ground for invalidity, such as that

687. CJEU C-425/16 of 19.10.2017 – Raimund/Aigner, para. 28.
688. CJEU C-425/16 of 19.10.2017 – Raimund/Aigner, para. 29; C-256/21 of 13.10.2022 – KP/TV a.o., para. 48; C-654/21 of 8.6.2023 – LM/KP, para. 48.
689. CJEU C-425/16 of 19.10.2017 – Raimund/Aigner, para. 30; C-256/21 of 13.10.2022 – KP/TV a.o., para. 49; C-654/21 of 8.6.2023 – LM/KP, para. 49.
690. CJEU C-425/16 of 19.10.2017 – Raimund/Aigner, para. 31; C-256/21 of 13.10.2022 – KP/TV a.o., para. 50.
691. CJEU C-425/16 of 19.10.2017 – Raimund/Aigner, para. 32.
692. CJEU C-425/16 of 19.10.2017 – Raimund/Aigner, para. 33; *see also* CJEU C-256/21 of 13.10.2022 – KP/TV a.o., para. 51.
693. CJEU C-425/16 of 19.10.2017 – Raimund/Aigner, para. 34; *see also* CJEU C-256/21 of 13.10.2022 – KP/TV a.o., para. 51.

provided for in Article 52(1)(b) CTMR, **even though the decision** on the counterclaim for a declaration of invalidity, brought pursuant to Article 100(1) CTMR, and based on the same ground for invalidity, **has not become final**.[694]

By its second question, the referring court asks, in essence, whether the provisions of the CTMR must be interpreted as meaning that the EU trade mark court may dismiss an action for infringement within the meaning of Article 96(a) CTMR on the basis of an absolute ground for invalidity, such as that provided for in Article 52(1)(b) CTMR, even though the decision on the counterclaim for a declaration of invalidity, brought pursuant to Article 100(1) CTMR, and based on the same ground for invalidity, has not become final.[695]

It is apparent from the answer to the first question that, in order to safeguard the unitary character of the EU trade mark and to prevent the risk of inconsistent decisions, Article 99(1) CTMR requires the EU trade mark court to uphold the counterclaim brought pursuant to Article 100(1) CTMR before it may dismiss the infringement action within the meaning of Article 96(a) CTMR.[696]

However, the CTMR does not contain any rule requiring the decision upholding the counterclaim for a declaration of invalidity to have become final in order for the EU trade mark court to be able to dismiss the action for infringement, nor any rule prohibiting that court from waiting until the decision upholding the counterclaim for a declaration of invalidity has become final before dismissing the infringement action.[697]

There is no provision in that regulation that makes the EU trade mark court's ability to dismiss actions for infringement of a trade mark on the basis of a ground for invalidity conditional upon that court's decision upholding the counterclaim for a declaration of invalidity of that mark, on the same ground for invalidity, having become final, whereas such a requirement is provided for in other cases in Article 100 CTMR.[698]

In that context, it must be borne in mind that, in accordance with the Court's settled case law, in the absence of EU rules governing the matter, it is for the domestic legal system of each Member State, in accordance with the principle of procedural autonomy, to designate the courts and tribunals having jurisdiction and to lay down the detailed procedural rules governing actions for safeguarding rights which individuals derive from EU law, the Member States having none the less responsibility for ensuring that those rights are effectively protected in each case.[699]

In this respect, in accordance with the principle of sincere cooperation enshrined in Article 4(3) TEU, the detailed procedural rules governing actions for safeguarding an individual's rights under EU law must be no less favourable than those governing similar domestic actions (principle of equivalence) and must not render impossible in

694. CJEU C-425/16 of 19.10.2017 – Raimund/Aigner, para. 48.
695. CJEU C-425/16 of 19.10.2017 – Raimund/Aigner, para. 36.
696. CJEU C-425/16 of 19.10.2017 – Raimund/Aigner, para. 37.
697. CJEU C-425/16 of 19.10.2017 – Raimund/Aigner, para. 38.
698. CJEU C-425/16 of 19.10.2017 – Raimund/Aigner, para. 39.
699. CJEU C-425/16 of 19.10.2017 – Raimund/Aigner, para. 40, with further proof.

practice or excessively difficult the exercise of rights conferred by EU law (principle of effectiveness).[700]

It follows from the Court's case law that the requirements stemming from the principles of equivalence and effectiveness apply, in particular, to the definition of the procedural rules governing actions based on EU law.[701]

It must be pointed out in that regard that where the same court is required to rule both on an action for infringement of a mark and on a counterclaim for a declaration of invalidity of the same mark, consistency with the decision handed down by that court in the context of the counterclaim will prevent it from delivering an inconsistent ruling in the context of the infringement action.[702]

Admittedly, the EU trade mark court is obliged to await the outcome of the counterclaim for a declaration of invalidity before ruling on the action for infringement. However, as the referring court has correctly pointed out, linking the outcome of the proceedings relating to the infringement action to the conduct of the parties in relation to the appeals against the decision upholding the counterclaim for a declaration of invalidity would in all likelihood involve serious delays to those proceedings. It should be borne in mind in that regard that, in so far as the parties to both sets of proceedings are the same, they have the same grounds of defence and must bear the consequences of their actions. The possibility that one of the parties may seek, through successive appeals, to delay the definitive effect of court decisions cannot therefore prevail over the court's obligation to determine the dispute brought before it.[703]

Accordingly, the fact that the EU trade mark court is dealing with the counterclaim for a declaration of invalidity based on Article 100(1) CTMR and the infringement action brought pursuant to Article 96(a) CTMR together ensures that the principle of effectiveness is observed.[704]

Article 124(a) and (d) and Article 128 EUTMR must be interpreted as meaning that an EU trade mark court hearing an action for infringement based on an EU trade mark the validity of which is challenged by means of a counterclaim for a declaration of invalidity **still has jurisdiction to rule on the validity of that mark, in spite of the withdrawal of the main action.**[705]

In order to answer that question, it is necessary to define the meaning and scope to be given to the term 'counterclaim' within the meaning of that regulation.[706]

According to settled case law, both the uniform application of EU law and the principle of equality require that the terms of a provision of EU law which makes no express reference to the law of the Member States for the purpose of determining its meaning and scope must normally be given an autonomous and uniform interpretation throughout the European Union. In addition, the meaning and scope of terms for which EU law provides no definition must be determined by reference to their usual meaning

700. CJEU C-425/16 of 19.10.2017 – Raimund/Aigner, para. 41, with further proof.
701. CJEU C-425/16 of 19.10.2017 – Raimund/Aigner, para. 42, with further proof.
702. CJEU C-425/16 of 19.10.2017 – Raimund/Aigner, para. 44.
703. CJEU C-425/16 of 19.10.2017 – Raimund/Aigner, para. 45.
704. CJEU C-425/16 of 19.10.2017 – Raimund/Aigner, para. 46.
705. CJEU C-256/21 of 13.10.2022 – KP/TV a.o., para. 58.
706. CJEU C-256/21 of 13.10.2022 – KP/TV a.o., para. 31.

while also taking into account the context in which they occur and the purposes of the rules of which they are part.[707]

The EUTMR makes no express reference to the law of the Member States as regards the meaning and scope to be given to that term. The said term must therefore be regarded as an autonomous concept of EU law and interpreted uniformly throughout the European Union.[708]

The reference made by Article 129(3) EUTMR to national procedural rules 'unless otherwise provided for' in that regulation cannot invalidate that finding.[709]

It cannot be assumed that that regulation does not deal with the question of whether a counterclaim continues to exist in spite of the withdrawal of the action for infringement in response to which that counterclaim was brought. The answer to that question depends specifically on the scope that the EU legislature intended to give to that legal remedy.[710]

It is appropriate, therefore, in the absence of a definition of the term 'counterclaim' in Regulation 2017/1001 to note, in the first place, that that term is usually understood and as is borne out by the terms used, *inter alia*, in the versions of the relevant provisions of that regulation in Danish (Modkrav), in German (Widerklage) and in Greek (ανταγωγή), as referring to a cross-action lodged by the defendant in proceedings brought against him or her by the applicant before the same court.[711]

As regards, in the second place, the context of those provisions, it must, first, be noted that, as recital 32 of the EUTMR states, Article 122 EUTMR makes the EU rules on jurisdiction and the recognition and enforcement of judgments in civil and commercial matters applicable to proceedings relating to EU trade marks. It is therefore appropriate to interpret the term 'counterclaim', within the meaning of the EUTMR, in a manner consistent with those rules and the case law relating thereto.[712]

It follows, in that regard, from the case law on the system created by the Brussels Convention,[713] as amended and subsequently reproduced first in Regulation No. 44/2001[714] and then in Regulation No. 1215/2012, that a counterclaim is not indissociable from a mere defence. Although brought in proceedings initiated by means of another legal remedy, it is a separate and self-standing claim the procedural treatment of which is independent of the main claim and which can thus be proceeded with even if the claim of the principal claimant is dismissed.[715]

In the light of the foregoing, it must be concluded that the **term 'counterclaim'**, within the meaning of the EUTMR, must be understood as a legal remedy which

707. CJEU C-256/21 of 13.10.2022 - KP/TV a.o., para. 32, with further proof.
708. CJEU C-256/21 of 13.10.2022 - KP/TV a.o., para. 33, with further proof.
709. CJEU C-256/21 of 13.10.2022 - KP/TV a.o., para. 34.
710. CJEU C-256/21 of 13.10.2022 - KP/TV a.o., para. 35.
711. CJEU C-256/21 of 13.10.2022 - KP/TV a.o., para. 36; C-654/21 of 8.6.2023 - LM/KP, para. 31.
712. CJEU C-256/21 of 13.10.2022 - KP/TV a.o., para. 37.
713. Convention of 27 September 1968 on jurisdiction and the enforcement of judgments in civil and commercial matters (OJ 1978 L 304, p. 36).
714. Council Regulation (EC) No 44/2001 of 22 December 2000 on jurisdiction and the recognition and enforcement of judgments in civil and commercial matters (OJ 2001 L 12, p. 1).
715. CJEU C-256/21 of 13.10.2022 - KP/TV a.o., para. 38, with further proof; C-654/21 of 8.6.2023 - LM/KP, para. 32.

remains conditional, admittedly, on the bringing of an action for infringement and which is, consequently, linked to that action. Nevertheless, such a legal remedy is intended to extend the subject matter of the dispute and to obtain recognition of a claim which is separate and independent from the main claim, *inter alia* in order to have the mark concerned declared invalid.[716]

Thus, by involving the extension of the subject matter of the dispute and notwithstanding the link between the main action and the counterclaim, the counterclaim becomes independent of the main action and continues to exist in the event of withdrawal of the main action. The counterclaim can therefore be distinguished from a mere defence, and its outcome does not depend on that of the action for infringement on the occasion of which it was brought.[717]

Second, it is apparent from the general scheme of the EUTMR that, by using the expression 'counterclaim' in the context of that regulation, the EU legislature intended to give that expression the same meaning and scope as those specified above.[718]

It is true, as the referring court notes, that the EUTMR reserves exclusive jurisdiction to EUIPO over registration of EU trade marks and opposition to such registration. However, that is not the case as far as concerns the validity of those marks. Although the EUTMR opts, as a rule, for the centralized treatment of applications for a declaration of invalidity or for revocation by EUIPO, that rule is nevertheless tempered and jurisdiction to declare an EU trade mark invalid or to revoke an EU trade mark is shared, pursuant to Articles 63 and 124 EUTMR, between the EU trade mark courts designated by the Member States, in accordance with Article 123(1) EUTMR, and EUIPO.[719]

In that regard, given the doubts expressed by the referring court as to the exact scope of that division of jurisdiction, it should also be noted that the jurisdiction conferred on those trade mark courts constitutes the direct application of a rule conferring jurisdiction laid down in the EUTMR and cannot therefore be considered to constitute an 'exception' to EUIPO's jurisdiction in the matter.[720]

Furthermore, the jurisdictions in question are exercised in accordance with the principle of the priority of the body seised. According to Article 132(1) EUTMR and the first sentence of paragraph 2 thereof, 'unless there are special grounds for continuing the hearing', it is the body first seised of a dispute concerning the validity of an EU trade mark which has jurisdiction in the matter.[721]

The fact that, under Article 128(7) EUTMR, the proprietor of a mark the validity of which is being challenged before an EU trade mark court by means of a counterclaim may arrange for the decision on the validity of that mark to be taken at the end of proceedings before EUIPO does not call into question the priority principle referred to

716. CJEU C-256/21 of 13.10.2022 – KP/TV a.o., para. 39; C-654/21 of 8.6.2023 – LM/KP, para. 33.
717. CJEU C-256/21 of 13.10.2022 – KP/TV a.o., para. 40; C-654/21 of 8.6.2023 – LM/KP, para. 34.
718. CJEU C-256/21 of 13.10.2022 – KP/TV a.o., para. 41.
719. CJEU C-256/21 of 13.10.2022 – KP/TV a.o., para. 42, with reference to CJEU C-226/15 P of 21.7.2016 – Apple and Pear Australia a.o./EUIPO, para. 50 and further proof; also CJEU C-654/21 of 8.6.2023 – LM/KP, para. 51.
720. CJEU C-256/21 of 13.10.2022 – KP/TV a.o., para. 43; C-654/21 of 8.6.2023 – LM/KP, para. 52.
721. CJEU C-256/21 of 13.10.2022 – KP/TV a.o., para. 44; C-654/21 of 8.6.2023 – LM/KP, para. 53.

above. As is apparent from its very wording, that provision grants a mere option of staying the proceedings, as the EU trade mark court can just as well decide to rule on the counterclaim.[722]

The same applies to the situation referred to in the second sentence of Article 132(2) EUTMR. The EU trade mark court is obliged to stay the proceedings pending before it only if an application for revocation or for a declaration of invalidity of the EU trade mark at issue had already been filed before EUIPO before the counterclaim was filed, in accordance with Article 128(4) EUTMR.[723]

Thus, having regard to the system of division of jurisdiction described above, it should be observed that, in the context of the scheme established by the EUTMR, which, in accordance with recital 4 and Article 1(2) EUTMR, enshrines the unitary character of the EU trade mark, the EU legislature intended to confer jurisdiction to review the validity of EU trade marks both on EUIPO and, in respect of their decisions on counterclaims, on EU trade mark courts.[724]

The Court has held that such a court is required to rule on the counterclaim for a declaration of invalidity of an EU trade mark brought, in accordance with Article 128(1) of Regulation 2017/1001, in the context of an action for infringement of that mark, as provided for by Article 124(a) of that regulation, before it may rule on that action, which is challenged on the basis of the same ground for absolute invalidity.[725]

In the light of the specificities of the scheme governing the counterclaim, if that autonomous legal remedy, which is intended to assess the validity of EU trade marks, were to be interpreted as meaning that the proprietor of an EU trade mark could, by withdrawing his or her action for infringement, deprive an EU trade mark court of the possibility of ruling on the counterclaim for a declaration of invalidity brought in the context of that action, the scope of the jurisdiction that the legislature intended to confer on EU trade mark courts would effectively be disregarded. It is therefore apparent from the general scheme of the EUTMR that such a claim continues to exist in the event of withdrawal of the main action.[726]

Last, in the third place, the meaning and scope of the term 'counterclaim' within the meaning of the EUTMR are confirmed by the objectives pursued by the EUTMR.[727]

First, it is apparent from the case law on the system established by the Brussels Convention, as amended and subsequently reproduced first in Regulation No. 44/2001 and then in Regulation No. 1215/2012, that, in the interests of the sound administration of justice, the possibility of bringing a counterclaim enables the parties, in the same proceedings and before the same court, to litigate all their claims against each other that have a common origin and, in so doing, seeks, *inter alia*, to avoid unnecessary multiple proceedings, entailing a risk of contradictory judgments. As is apparent from recital 32 of the EUTMR, such objectives are covered by the scheme

722. CJEU C-256/21 of 13.10.2022 – KP/TV a.o., para. 45.
723. CJEU C-256/21 of 13.10.2022 – KP/TV a.o., para. 46.
724. CJEU C-256/21 of 13.10.2022 – KP/TV a.o., para. 47; C-654/21 of 8.6.2023 – LM/KP, para. 54.
725. CJEU C-256/21 of 13.10.2022 – KP/TV a.o., para. 51, with reference to CJEU C-425/16 of 19.10.2017 – Raimund/Aigner, paras 33 et seq.
726. CJEU C-256/21 of 13.10.2022 – KP/TV a.o., para. 52.
727. CJEU C-256/21 of 13.10.2022 – KP/TV a.o., para. 53.

provided for by that regulation as a whole and, specifically, in Articles 124 and 128 EUTMR.[728]

It follows that, in order to achieve such objectives, an EU trade mark court must be able to rule on the claim brought by the defendant in an action for infringement by means of a counterclaim for a declaration of invalidity of the EU trade mark concerned, in spite of the withdrawal of the main action.[729]

By contrast, compelling the party who filed a counterclaim to initiate proceedings before EUIPO in the event of withdrawal by the principal claimant in order to ensure that he or she no longer has to defend himself or herself in the future against the principal claimant would run counter to the principle of procedural economy.[730]

Second, interpreting the term 'counterclaim' as meaning that, in the event of withdrawal of the main action, it would no longer be possible for an EU trade mark court to give judgment on a counterclaim for a declaration of invalidity would allow the proprietor of an EU trade mark, by withdrawing from infringement proceedings which he or she has himself or herself initiated, to continue to use, as the case may be in bad faith, an EU trade mark that could be registered in disregard of the absolute grounds for refusal of registration referred to in Article 7(1) EUTMR. Such a situation would undermine the effective attainment of the objectives pursued by that regulation.[731]

Article 124(d) EUTMR, read in conjunction with Article 128(1) EUTMR, must be interpreted as meaning that a counterclaim for a declaration of invalidity of an EU trade mark may relate to all the rights which the proprietor of that mark derives from its registration and that the subject matter of that counterclaim is **not restricted by the scope of the dispute** as defined by the action for infringement.[732]

Given the independent nature of the counterclaim provided for in Article 128 EUTMR, the subject matter of that counterclaim cannot be restricted by that of the action for infringement in connection with which that counterclaim is brought.[733]

That conclusion is supported, in the first place, by the provisions of that regulation relating to the grounds for invalidity which may be relied on in support of a counterclaim for a declaration of invalidity brought under Article 128 EUTMR.[734]

It is true that the counterclaim can be distinguished from an application for a declaration of invalidity filed with EUIPO in terms of the persons who may file the former and submit the latter. In accordance with Article 63(1) EUTMR, an application for a declaration of invalidity may, where Articles 58 and 59 EUTMR apply, be submitted 'by any natural or legal person' and any group or body set up for the purpose of representing the interests of manufacturers, producers, suppliers of services, traders or consumers, which, under the terms of the law governing it, has the capacity in its

728. CJEU C-256/21 of 13.10.2022 – KP/TV a.o., para. 54, with further proof.
729. CJEU C-256/21 of 13.10.2022 – KP/TV a.o., para. 55.
730. CJEU C-256/21 of 13.10.2022 – KP/TV a.o., para. 56, *see also* CJEU C-654/21 of 8.6.2023 – LM/KP, para. 44.
731. CJEU C-256/21 of 13.10.2022 – KP/TV a.o., para. 57, with reference to CJEU C-622/13 P of 30.4.2015 – Castel Frères/EUIPO, paras 46 et seq.
732. CJEU C-654/21 of 8.6.2023 – LM/KP, para. 55.
733. CJEU C-654/21 of 8.6.2023 – LM/KP, para. 35.
734. CJEU C-654/21 of 8.6.2023 – LM/KP, para. 36.

own name to sue and be sued. By contrast, the only natural or legal person who may file a counterclaim within the meaning of Article 128 EUTMR is the defendant in the infringement proceedings concerned. However, that restriction as to the persons who may file a counterclaim in no way means that the subject matter of that counterclaim must be restricted so as to cover only what falls within the scope of the claimant's own interests.[735]

It should be recalled in that regard that, under Article 128(1) EUTMR, 'a counterclaim for revocation or for a declaration of invalidity may only be based on the grounds for revocation or invalidity mentioned in this Regulation'. It follows from that provision that although a counterclaim for a declaration of invalidity for the purposes of that regulation may be based only on the grounds for invalidity expressly referred to in that regulation, it may nevertheless be based on any of the grounds provided for therein.[736]

Article 59 EUTMR, entitled 'Absolute grounds for invalidity', provides, in point (a) of paragraph 1 thereof, that an EU trade mark is to be declared invalid on application to EUIPO or on the basis of a counterclaim in infringement proceedings 'where [that mark] has been registered contrary to the provisions of Article 7 [of that regulation]'. Thus, in terms of their scope, the EUTMR equates the application for a declaration of invalidity submitted to EUIPO with the counterclaim for a declaration of invalidity filed in connection with infringement proceedings pending before an EU trade mark court.[737]

In accordance with the case law, the absolute grounds for refusal of registration aim to protect the general interest underlying them and cannot, therefore, necessarily be linked to actual or potential economic interests in having the contested mark declared invalid (*see*, to that effect, judgment of 25 February 2010, Lancôme v OHIM, C-408/08 P, EU:C:2010:92, paragraphs 40 and 43).[738]

Moreover, it is apparent from the wording of Article 7(1) EUTMR that some of the grounds for invalidity referred to in points (a) to (m) of that provision on which a main claim for a declaration of invalidity or a counterclaim for a declaration of invalidity of an EU trade mark may be based are liable, by their nature, to relate to all the goods or services covered by the registration of that mark.[739]

That is the case, in particular, of the ground for invalidity set out in point (f), which refers to 'trade marks which are contrary to public policy or to accepted principles of morality', the ground for invalidity set out in point (g), which refers to 'trade marks which are of such a nature as to deceive the public, for instance as to the nature, quality or geographical origin of the goods or service', or the grounds for invalidity set out in points (j), (k), (l) and (m), which relate to the protection,

735. CJEU C-654/21 of 8.6.2023 – LM/KP, para. 37.
736. CJEU C-654/21 of 8.6.2023 – LM/KP, para. 38.
737. CJEU C-654/21 of 8.6.2023 – LM/KP, para. 39.
738. CJEU C-654/21 of 8.6.2023 – LM/KP, para. 40, with reference to CJEU C-408/08 P of 25.2.2010 – Lancôme parfums et beauté & Cie/OHIM, paras 40 and 43.
739. CJEU C-654/21 of 8.6.2023 – LM/KP, para. 41.

respectively, of designations of origin and geographical indications, traditional terms for wine, traditional specialities guaranteed, and plant variety rights.[740]

Similarly, the absolute ground for invalidity referred to in Article 59(1)(b) EUTMR, namely bad faith on the part of the applicant when filing the application for the trade mark, is also liable to relate to all the rights which the proprietor of an EU trade mark derives from the registration of that mark.[741]

It would run counter to the principle of procedural economy, which is one of the objectives pursued by the counterclaim, to hold that such a counterclaim based on one of the grounds for invalidity may lead only to a declaration of partial invalidity of the trade mark on which the infringement proceedings concerned are based.[742]

Article 59(3) EUTMR, which provides that an EU trade mark is to be declared invalid only as regards the goods or services in respect of which the ground for invalidity relied on exists, constitutes the only restriction laid down in that regulation concerning the scope and outcome of an application for a declaration of invalidity and, accordingly, of a counterclaim for a declaration of invalidity.[743]

It follows that a counterclaim for a declaration of invalidity of an EU trade mark filed pursuant to Article 128 EUTMR may, due to its nature, relate to all the rights which the proprietor of that mark derives from its registration.[744]

In the second place, the rules governing the effects of a counterclaim confirm the conclusion since those effects are the same as the effects reserved for the revocation or declaration of invalidity of an EU trade mark following proceedings brought before EUIPO.[745]

Lastly, the considerations set out above cannot be called into question by the system of the division of jurisdiction between EUIPO and the EU trade mark courts established by that regulation.[746]

[7] Extinction of rights over time

The defences of the extinction of rights over time and of an action being time-barred that may be raised against an action brought on the basis of Articles 19(2) and 89(1)(a) of Regulation No. 6/2002[747] are governed by national law, which must be applied in a manner that observes the principles of equivalence and effectiveness.[748]

740. CJEU C-654/21 of 8.6.2023 – LM/KP, para. 42.
741. CJEU C-654/21 of 8.6.2023 – LM/KP, para. 43.
742. CJEU C-654/21 of 8.6.2023 – LM/KP, para. 44, with reference to CJEU C-256/21 of 13.10.2022 – KP/TV a.o., para. 56.
743. CJEU C-654/21 of 8.6.2023 – LM/KP, para. 45.
744. CJEU C-654/21 of 8.6.2023 – LM/KP, para. 46.
745. CJEU C-654/21 of 8.6.2023 – LM/KP, para. 47.
746. CJEU C-654/21 of 8.6.2023 – LM/KP, para. 50.
747. Council Regulation (EC) No. 6/2002 of 12 Dec. 2001 on Community designs (OJ 2002 L 3, p. 1).
748. CJEU C-479/12 of 13.2.2014 – H. Gautzsch Großhandel, para. 50.

[8] Coercive measures

Article 98(1) CTMR is to be interpreted as meaning that a Community trade mark court which has issued an order prohibiting the defendant from proceeding with infringement or threatened infringement of a Community trade mark is required to take such **measures**, in accordance with its national law, as are aimed at ensuring that that prohibition is complied with, even if the national law includes a general prohibition of infringement of Community trade marks and provides for the possibility of penalizing further infringement or threatened infringement, whether intentional or due to gross negligence.[749]

In that regard, it must be pointed out, firstly, that the second sentence of Article 98(1) CTMR is drafted in mandatory terms (*see, inter alia*, in Spanish, 'adoptará las medidas'; in German, 'trifft ... die ... Maßnahmen'; in English, 'shall ... take ... measures'; in French, 'prend ... les mesures'; in Italian, '[p]rende ... le misure'; and, in Dutch, 'treft ... maatregelen').[750]

Second, unlike the obligation to issue an order prohibiting further infringement or threatened infringement - provided for in the first sentence of Article 98(1) CTMR - which is coupled with a derogation in the event of 'special reasons', the obligation to attach to that prohibition measures aimed at ensuring that it is complied with - provided for in the second sentence of that provision - does not allow for any exception.[751]

It follows that where the Community trade mark court of a Member State has issued an order prohibiting further infringement or threatened infringement, it is required to take, from among the measures provided for under the legislation of that Member State, such as are aimed at ensuring that that prohibition is complied with.[752]

Such an interpretation is moreover consistent with the objective pursued by Article 98(1) CTMR, which is to protect the right conferred by the Community trade mark.[753]

As is apparent from the reply to the second question, the fact that the national legislation applicable includes a general prohibition of the infringement of Community trade marks and provides for the possibility of penalizing further infringement or threatened infringement, whether intentional or due to gross negligence, does not relieve a Community trade mark court of the obligation to issue an order prohibiting the defendant from proceeding with those acts.[754]

Accordingly, that same circumstance likewise does not relieve it of the obligation to take such measures, in accordance with its national law, as are aimed at ensuring that that prohibition is complied with.[755]

749. CJEU C-316/05 P of 14.12.2006 - Nokia, para. 53.
750. CJEU C-316/05 P of 14.12.2006 - Nokia, para. 47.
751. CJEU C-316/05 P of 14.12.2006 - Nokia, para. 48.
752. CJEU C-316/05 P of 14.12.2006 - Nokia, para. 49; C-235/09 of 12.4.2011 - DHL Express France, para. 53.
753. CJEU C-316/05 P of 14.12.2006 - Nokia, para. 50.
754. CJEU C-316/05 P of 14.12.2006 - Nokia, para. 51.
755. CJEU C-316/05 P of 14.12.2006 - Nokia, para. 52.

Article 98(1) CTMR is to be interpreted as meaning that a Community trade mark court which has issued an order prohibiting the defendant from proceeding with infringement or threatened infringement of a Community trade mark is required to take, from among the measures provided for under national law, such as are aimed at **ensuring** that that **prohibition** is complied with, even if those measures could not, under that law, be taken in the case of a corresponding infringement of a national trade mark.[756]

The Community legislature has introduced an obligation on Community trade mark courts, first, to prohibit further infringement or threatened infringement of a Community trade mark unless there are special reasons for not doing so, and, secondly, to take such measures as are aimed at ensuring that that prohibition is complied with.[757]

Under Article 14(1) CTMR, 'infringement of a Community trade mark shall be governed by the national law relating to infringement of a national trade mark in accordance with the provisions of Title X [of the Regulation]'.[758]

Thus, the nature of the measures referred to in the second sentence of Article 98(1) CTMR is to be determined by the national law of the Member State of the Community trade mark court before which the action is brought, as is apparent from the specific reference made by the provision to that law. In this respect, it is for Member States to provide in their national law for effective measures in order to prevent further infringement or threatened infringement of a Community trade mark.[759]

On the other hand, by introducing an absolute requirement for Community trade mark courts to take such measures when they issue an order prohibiting further infringement or threatened infringement, the Community legislature has precluded the national law of a Member State from making such measures contingent on compliance with additional conditions.[760]

Consequently, the second sentence of Article 98(1) CTMR must be interpreted as not referring to national law as regards the conditions for implementing the measures provided for under that law which are aimed at ensuring that the prohibition against further infringement or threatened infringement is complied with, but as requiring that such measures be ordered as soon as an order prohibiting further infringement or threatened infringement has been made. It follows, *inter alia,* that Community trade mark courts are required to take such measures without having regard to the conditions necessary for their implementation under the national law applicable.[761]

If that were not the case, the objective of Article 98(1) CTMR, which is the uniform protection, throughout the entire area of the Community, of the right conferred by the Community trade mark against the risk of infringement, would not be achieved. A prohibition against further infringement or threatened infringement which is not

756. CJEU C-316/05 P of 14.12.2006 – Nokia, para. 62.
757. CJEU C-316/05 P of 14.12.2006 – Nokia, para. 55.
758. CJEU C-316/05 P of 14.12.2006 – Nokia, para. 56.
759. CJEU C-316/05 P of 14.12.2006 – Nokia, para. 57.
760. CJEU C-316/05 P of 14.12.2006 – Nokia, para. 58; C-235/09 of 12.4.2011 – DHL Express France, para. 57.
761. CJEU C-316/05 P of 14.12.2006 – Nokia, para. 59.

coupled with measures aimed at ensuring that it is complied with would, generally speaking, have no dissuasive effect.[762]

It is thus, *a fortiori*, immaterial that, in equivalent factual circumstances, the national law does not allow the national courts to attach such measures to a prohibition against further infringement of a national trade mark. It must be borne in mind in this connection that although the TMD harmonized the content of the rights conferred by national trade marks, it did not harmonize the legal actions intended to ensure that third parties observe those rights.[763]

Article 98(1), second sentence, CTMR must be interpreted as meaning that a coercive measure, such as a periodic penalty payment, ordered by a Community trade mark court by **application of its national law**, in order to ensure compliance with a prohibition against further infringement or threatened infringement which it has issued, has effect in Member States to which the territorial scope of such a prohibition extends other than the Member State of that court, under the conditions laid down in Chapter III of Regulation No. 44/2001 with regard to the recognition and enforcement of judgments. Where the national law of one of those other Member States does not contain a coercive measure similar to that ordered by the Community trade mark court, the objective pursued by that measure must be attained by the competent court of that other Member State by having **recourse to the relevant provisions of its national law** which are such as to ensure that the prohibition is complied with in an equivalent manner.[764]

Coercive measures ordered by a Community trade mark court pursuant to its Member State's national law can achieve the objective for which they were issued – namely, ensuring that a prohibition is complied with so that the right conferred by a Community trade mark against the risk of infringement is actually protected throughout the area of the EU – only if the measures have effect in the same territory as that in which the prohibition order itself has effect.[765]

Where the national law of the Member State in which recognition and enforcement of the decision of a Community trade mark court is sought does not provide for a coercive measure similar to that ordered by the Community trade mark court which issued the prohibition against further infringement or threatened infringement (and coupled that prohibition with such a measure in order to ensure compliance with the prohibition), the court seized of the case in that Member State must attain the objective pursued by the measure by having recourse to the relevant provisions of its national law which are such as to ensure that the prohibition originally issued is complied with in an equivalent manner.[766]

That obligation to attain the objective pursued by the coercive measure constitutes an extension of the obligation on the Community trade mark courts to take

762. CJEU C-316/05 P of 14.12.2006 – Nokia, para. 60; C-235/09 of 12.4.2011 – DHL Express France, paras 46 and 54.
763. CJEU C-316/05 P of 14.12.2006 – Nokia, para. 61.
764. CJEU C-235/09 of 12.4.2011 – DHL Express France, para. 59.
765. CJEU C-235/09 of 12.4.2011 – DHL Express France, para. 54.
766. CJEU C-235/09 of 12.4.2011 – DHL Express France, para. 56.

coercive measures when they issue an order prohibiting further infringement or threatened infringement. Without those related obligations, a prohibition of that kind might not be coupled with measures aimed at ensuring that it is complied with so that it would, to a large extent, have no dissuasive effect.[767]

In that connection, it should be recalled that under the principle of sincere cooperation laid down in Article 4(3), second subparagraph, TEU, it is for the Member States' courts to ensure judicial protection of an individual's rights under EU law.[768] By virtue of that same provision, the Member States are to take any appropriate measure, general or particular, to ensure fulfilment of the obligations arising out of the Treaties or resulting from the acts of the institutions of the Union. In particular, under Article 3 of Directive 2004/48, Member States are to provide for the measures, procedures and remedies necessary to ensure the enforcement of the intellectual property rights covered by that Directive, including, *inter alia*, the rights of trade mark proprietors. In accordance with Article 3(2), those measures, procedures and remedies are to be effective, proportionate and dissuasive and are to be applied in such a manner as to avoid the creation of barriers to legitimate trade and to provide for safeguards against their abuse.[769]

[I] Relation to other intellectual property-related rights

[1] Trade names

A trade name may constitute a sign within the meaning of the first sentence of Article 16(1) of the TRIPS Agreement. That provision is intended to confer on the proprietor of a trade mark the exclusive right to prevent a third party from using such a sign if the use in question prejudices or is liable to prejudice the functions of the trade mark, in particular its essential function of guaranteeing to consumers the origin of the goods.[770]

It follows from Article 8 of the Paris Convention, which must be complied with by virtue of the TRIPS Agreement, that the protection of trade names is to be guaranteed and that such protection may not be made subject to any registration requirement.[771]

As regards any conditions relating to minimum use or minimum awareness of the trade name to which that name may be subject under national law, it should be observed that, in principle, neither Article 16(1) of the TRIPS Agreement nor Article 8 of the Paris Convention precludes such conditions.[772]

767. CJEU C-235/09 of 12.4.2011 – DHL Express France, para. 57.
768. CJEU C-432/05 of 13.3.2007 – Unibet, para. 38.
769. CJEU C-235/09 of 12.4.2011 – DHL Express France, para. 58.
770. CJEU C-245/02 of 16.11.2004 – Anheuser-Busch, para. 85.
771. CJEU C-245/02 of 16.11.2004 – Anheuser-Busch, para. 96; C-112/21 of 2.6.2022 – X/Classic Coach Company a.o., para. 39.
772. CJEU C-245/02 of 16.11.2004 – Anheuser-Busch, para. 97; C-112/21 of 2.6.2022 – X/Classic Coach Company a.o., para. 39.

Articles 30 and 52[773] of the Treaty do not preclude a provision of national law which prohibits, where there is a risk of confusion, the use of a trade name as the specific designation of an undertaking.[774]

[2] Domains

The third subparagraph of Article 12(2) of Regulation No. 874/2004[775] must be interpreted as meaning that, in a situation where the prior right concerned is a trade mark right, the words 'licensees of prior rights' do not refer to a person who has been authorized by the proprietor of the trade mark concerned solely to register, in his own name but on behalf of that proprietor, a domain name identical or similar to that trade mark, but without that person being authorized to use the trade mark commercially in a manner consistent with its functions.[776]

[3] Community designs

Article 14 of Directive 98/71/EC[777] and Article 110 of Regulation (EC) No. 6/2002[778] must be interpreted as meaning that they do not authorize, by way of derogation from the provisions of the TMD2008 and of the CTMR, the producer of vehicle replacement parts and accessories such as wheel caps to apply on his goods a sign which is identical with a trade mark registered by a vehicle manufacture, *inter alia*, for such goods without his authorization, with the argument that the use of the mark thus made is the only possibility to repair the respective vehicle and restore a complex product's original appearance.[779]

[4] Health claims

Article 28(2) of Regulation No. 1924/2006[780] must be interpreted as referring only to foods bearing a trade mark or brand name which must be considered a nutrition or health claim within the meaning of that regulation and which, in that form, existed before 1 January 2005.[781]

773. Articles 28 und 43 EC.
774. CJEU C-255/97 of 11.5.1999 – Pfeiffer, para. 29.
775. Commission Regulation (EC) No. 874/2004 of 28 Apr. 2004 laying down public policy rules concerning the implementation and functions of the.eu Top Level Domain and the principles governing registration (OJ 2004 L 162, p. 40).
776. CJEU C-376/11 of 19.7.2012 – Pie Optiek, para. 53.
777. Directive 98/71/EC of the European Parliament and of the Council of 13 Oct. 1998 on the legal protection of designs (OJ L 289, p. 28).
778. Council Regulation (EC) No. 6/2002 of 12 Dec. 2001 on Community designs (OJ 2002 L 3, p. 1).
779. CJEU C-500/14 of 6.10.2015 – Ford Motor Company, para. 45.
780. Regulation (EC) No. 1924/2006 of the European Parliament and of the Council of 20 Dec. 2006 on nutrition and health claims made on foods (OJ 2006 L 404, p. 9, and corrigendum OJ 2007 L 12, p. 3), as amended by Commission Regulation (EU) No. 116/2010 of 9 Feb. 2010 (OJ 2010 L 37, p. 16) ('Regulation No. 1924/2006').
781. CJEU C-299/12 of 18.7.2013 – Green – Swan Pharmaceuticals CR, para. 37.

Under Article 1(3) of the regulation, a trade mark or brand name appearing in the labelling, presentation or advertising of a food which may be construed as a nutrition or health claim may be used without undergoing the authorization procedures laid down in the regulation, provided that it is accompanied by a related nutrition or health claim in that labelling, presentation or advertising which complies with the provisions of the regulation.[782]

In that context, Article 28(2) of the regulation, which establishes a derogating and transitional measure, only refers to a trade mark or to a brand name which already existed before 1 January 2005 and which can be considered a nutrition or health claim within the meaning of the regulation. Foods bearing such a trade mark or such a brand name may continue to be marketed until 19 January 2022.[783]

[J] Procedural trade mark law

[1] Preliminary ruling

In accordance with settled case law, in the context of the cooperation between the Court and the national courts provided for in Article 234 EC, it is solely for the national court before which a dispute has been brought, and which must assume responsibility for the subsequent judicial decision, to determine in the light of the particular circumstances of the case both the **need for a preliminary ruling** in order to enable it to deliver judgment and the relevance of the questions which it submits to the Court. However, the Court has no jurisdiction to give a preliminary ruling on a question submitted by a national court where it is quite obvious, *inter alia*, that the interpretation of Community law sought by that court bears no relation to the actual facts of the main action or its purpose or where the problem is hypothetical.[784]

In the context of the procedure established by Article 234 EC providing for cooperation between national courts and the Court of Justice, it is for the latter to provide the national court with an **answer** which will be **of use** to it and enable it to determine the case before it. To that end, the Court may find it necessary to consider provisions of Community law to which the national court has not referred in its question.[785]

It is for the Court to provide the national court with **all the elements of interpretation** of Community law which may be of assistance in adjudicating on the case pending before it, whether or not that court specifically refers to them in its questions.[786]

Are the Court of Justice and the Court of First Instance seized of cases raising the same issue of interpretation within the meaning of the third paragraph of Article 54 of

782. CJEU C-299/12 of 18.7.2013 – Green – Swan Pharmaceuticals CR, para. 35.
783. CJEU C-299/12 of 18.7.2013 – Green – Swan Pharmaceuticals CR, para. 36.
784. CJEU C-239/05 of 15.2.2007 – BVBA Management, Training en Consultancy, para. 52.
785. CJEU C-421/04 of 9.3.2006 – Matratzen Concord, para. 18.
786. CJEU C-245/02 of 16.11.2004 – Anheuser-Busch, para. 75; C-321/03 of 25.1.2007 – Dyson, para. 24; C-48/05 of 25.1.2007 – Adam Opel, para. 31; C-17/06 of 11.9.2007 – Céline, para. 29.

the State of the Court of Justice, it is in the interests of the proper administration of justice to stay the proceedings until such time as the Court of First Instance has delivered its final judgment.[787]

The **Appointed Person**, established by the British Trade Marks Act 1994, must be regarded as a court or tribunal within the meaning of Article 234 EC, so that the questions referred for a preliminary ruling are admissible.[788]

The **Oberster Patent- und Markensenat**, established by §§74 and 75 of the Austrian Patent Act, is a court or tribunal within the meaning of Article 234 EC and that the Court therefore has jurisdiction to answer the questions submitted to it by that body.[789]

The Court of Justice has no jurisdiction to answer the questions referred by the **Úřad průmyslového vlastnictví** (Czech Republic).[790]

The jurisdiction of the [Romanian] **Tribunalul de Arbitraj Institutionalizat Galati** is expressly dependent on the consent of the parties to the main proceedings.[791]

It follows that the TAIG does not meet the criterion of the mandatory nature of its jurisdiction and therefore cannot be qualified as a 'court or tribunal' within the meaning of Article 267 TFEU.[792]

[2] Obligation to take into account decisions already taken

Appeal must be assessed **solely on the basis of that regulation**, as interpreted by the Community judicature, and not on the basis of a previous decision-making practice of those boards.[793]

787. CJEU C-321/03 of 12.10.2004 – Dyson, para. 15 f.
788. CJEU C-259/04 of 30.3.2006 – Emanuel, para. 25.
789. CJEU C-246/05 of 14.6.2007 – Häupl, para. 21.
790. CJEU C-49/13 of 14.11.2013 – MF 7, para. 25.
791. CJEU C-370/18 of 13.12.2018 – Uniunea Naţională a Barourilor din România/Holunga, para. 19.
792. CJEU C-370/18 of 13.12.2018 – Uniunea Naţională a Barourilor din România/Holunga, para. 20.
793. CJEU C-37/03 P of 15.9.2005 – BioID/OHIM, para. 47; C-39/08 und C-43/08 of 12.2.2009 – bild digital, para. 13; C-202/08 and C-208/08 of 16.7.2009 – American Clothing Associates/OHIM, para. 40/OHIM, para. 47; C-173/04 P of 12.1.2006 – Deutsche SiSi-Werke/OHIM, para. 48; C-412/05 P of 26.4.2007 – Alcon/OHIM (II), para. 65; C-212/07 P of 13.2.2008 – Indorata-Serviços e Gestão, para. 43; C-243/07 P of 15.2.2008 – Brinkmann/OHIM, para. 39; C-202/08 and C-208/08 of 16.7.2009 – American Clothing Associates/OHIM, para. 57; C-536/10 P of 7.7.2011 – MPDV Mikrolab/OHIM, para. 45; C-53/11 P of 19.1.2012 – OHIM/Nike International, para. 57; C-649/11 P of 3.10.2012 – Cooperativa Vitivinícola Arousana, S. Coop. Galega/OHIM, para. 59; C-354/12 P of 11.4.2013 – ASA/OHIM, para. 34; C-410/12 P of 16.10.2013 – medi/OHIM, para. 32; C-400/14 P of 16.7.2015 – Basic AG Lebensmittelhandel/OHIM, para. 52; C-480/15 P of 14.4.2016 – KS Sports IPCo/EUIPO, para. 36; C-664/19 P of 5.12.2019 – Agencja Wydawnicza Technopol/EUIPO, para. 17; C-404/20 P of 17.12.2020 – Brands Up/EUIPO, para. 21; C-600/20 P of 11.2.2021 – Klose/EUIPO, para. 21; C-219/21 P of 24.6.2021 – Olimp Laboratories/EUIPO, para. 22; C-236/21 P of 1.9.2021 – sprd.net/EUIPO, para. 19.

OHIM is under a duty to exercise its powers in accordance with the general principles of EU law, such as the **principle of equal treatment and the principle of sound administration**.[794]

In the light of those two principles, OHIM must, when examining an application for registration of a Community trade mark, take into account the decisions already taken in respect of similar applications and consider with especial care whether it should decide in the same way or not.[795]

That said, the way in which the principles of equal treatment and sound administration are applied must be consistent with **respect for legality**.[796]

Consequently, a person who files an application for registration of a sign as a trade mark cannot rely, to his advantage and in order to secure an identical decision, on a possibly unlawful act committed to the benefit of someone else.[797]

That examination must be undertaken in each individual case. The registration of a sign as a mark depends on specific criteria, which are applicable in the factual circumstances of the particular case and the purpose of which is to ascertain whether the sign at issue is caught by a ground for refusal.[798]

It cannot be expected that the Board of Appeal take that judgment into account a GC decision that was taken on the same day.[799]

794. CJEU C-51/10 P of 10.3.2011 – Agencja Wydawnicza Technopol/HABM, para. 73; C-70/13 P of 12.12.2013 – Getty Images (US)/OHIM, para. 41; C-521/13 P of 11.9.2014 – Think Schuhwerk/OHIM, para. 57; C-564/16 P of 28.6.2018 – EUIPO/Puma, para. 60; C-150/18 P of 6.9.2018 – El Corte Inglés/EUIPO, paras 6/21 and 7; C-151/18 P of 6.9.2018 – El Corte Inglés/EUIPO, paras 6/20 and 7.

795. CJEU C-51/10 P of 10.3.2011 – Agencja Wydawnicza Technopol/HABM, para. 74; C-70/13 P of 12.12.2013 – Getty Images (US)/OHIM, para. 42; C-521/13 P of 11.9.2014 – Think Schuhwerk/OHIM, para. 57; C-33/15 P of 15.10.2015 – Cantina Broglie 1, para. 49; C-34/15 P of 15.10.2015 – Cantina Broglie 1, para. 49; C-480/15 P of 14.4.2016 – KS Sports IPCo/EUIPO, para. 37; C-681/20 P of 24.3.2021 – smart things solutions/EUIPO, para. 20.

796. CJEU C-51/10 P of 10.3.2011 – Agencja Wydawnicza Technopol/HABM, para. 75; C-54/10 P and C-55/10 P of 22.6.2011 – Agencja Wydawnicza Technopol/HABM, para. 42; C-56/10 P of 22.6.2011 – Agencja Wydawnicza Technopol/HABM, para. 65; C-70/13 P of 12.12.2013 – Getty Images (US)/OHIM, para. 43; C-141/13 P of 17.7.2014 – Reber Holding/OHIM, para. 45; C-521/13 P of 11.9.2014 – Think Schuhwerk/OHIM, para. 57; C-77/16 P of 26.5.2016 – Hewlett Packard Development Company/EUIPO, paras 4/6 and 5; C-564/16 P of 28.6.2018 – EUIPO/Puma, para. 61; C-150/18 P of 6.9.2018 – El Corte Inglés/EUIPO, paras 6/21 and 7; C-151/18 P of 6.9.2018 – El Corte Inglés/EUIPO, paras 6/20 and 7; C-681/20 P of 24.3.2021 – smart things solutions/EUIPO, para. 20.

797. CJEU C-51/10 P of 10.3.2011 – Agencja Wydawnicza Technopol/HABM, para. 76; C-54/10 P and C-55/10 P of 22.6.2011 – Agencja Wydawnicza Technopol/HABM, para. 42; C-56/10 P of 22.6.2011 – Agencja Wydawnicza Technopol/HABM, paras 36 and 65; C-77/16 P of 26.5.2016 – Hewlett Packard Development Company/EUIPO, paras 4/6 and 5.

798. CJEU C-218/01 of 12.2.2004 – Henkel, para. 62; C-39/08 und C-43/08 of 12.2.2009 – bild digital, para. 15; C-51/10 P of 10.3.2011 – Agencja Wydawnicza Technopol/HABM, para. 77; C-70/13 P of 12.12.2013 – Getty Images (US)/OHIM, para. 44; C-77/16 P of 26.5.2016 – Hewlett Packard Development Company/EUIPO, paras 4/6 and 5; C-150/18 P of 6.9.2018 – El Corte Inglés/EUIPO, paras 6/21 and 7; C-151/18 P of 6.9.2018 – El Corte Inglés/EUIPO, paras 6/20 and 7; C-162/17 P of 16.1.2019 – Republic of Poland/EUIPO, para. 60.

799. CJEU C-480/15 P of 14.4.2016 – KS Sports IPCo/EUIPO, para. 39.

The **General Court** is not bound by decisions taken by EUIPO.[800]

Registrations already made in Member States are only one factor which may be taken into account in connection with the registration of a Community trade mark, the mark for which registration is sought having to be assessed on the basis of the relevant EU rules.[801]

There is no provision in the CTMR requiring OHIM to come to the same conclusions as those arrived at by national authorities in similar circumstances. The Court of First Instance cannot therefore be said to have erred in law in that respect.[802]

Decisions concerning registration of a sign as a Community trade mark which the Boards of Appeal are called on to take under the CTMR are **adopted in the exercise of circumscribed powers** and are not a matter of discretion. Accordingly, the legality of the decisions of Boards of Appeal must be assessed solely on the basis of that regulation, as interpreted by the Community judicature, and not on the basis of a previous decision-making practice of those boards.[803]

A Board of Appeal whose task is, *inter alia,* to ensure the proper application of CTMR cannot, in the exercise of this task, in particular in the light of the independence enjoyed by its members be bound by a position allegedly defended by an OHIM official at a hearing before the Community Courts; accordingly, this second limb of the ground of appeal must also be rejected as manifestly unfounded.[804]

It follows that the identity or similarity of the trade mark applied for in relation to another Community trade mark is irrelevant where elements of fact or of law which have been put forward in support of the application for that other mark are not put forward by the appellant for the purpose of showing the distinctive character of the trade mark applied for.[805]

Registrations already made in Member States are only factors which may **merely be taken into consideration**, without being given decisive weight, for the purposes of registering a Community trade mark. There is no provision in the CTMR requiring

800. CJEU C-141/13 P of 17.7.2014 – Reber Holding/OHIM, para. 57; C-728/18 P of 25.9.2019 – EM Research Organization/EUIPO, paras 4/57 and 5; C-619/21 P of 13.12.2021 – Cora/EUIPO, para. 18.
801. CJEU C-98/11 P of 24.5.2012 – Chocoladefabriken Lindt & Sprüngli/OHIM, para. 50; C-354/12 P of 11.4.2013 – ASA/OHIM, para. 43; *see also* CJEU C-173/04 P of 12.1.2006 – Deutsche SiSi-Werke/OHIM, para. 49; C-410/12 P of 16.10.2013 – medi/OHIM, para. 35.
802. CJEU C-104/00 P of 19.9.2002 – DKV/OHIM, para. 39.
803. CJEU C-37/03 P of 15.9.2005 – BioID/OHIM, para. 47; C-202/08 and C-208/08 of 16.7.2009 – American Clothing Associates/OHIM, para. 40/OHIM, para. 47; C-173/04 P of 12.1.2006 – Deutsche SiSi-Werke/OHIM, para. 48; C-412/05 P of 26.4.2007 – Alcon/OHIM (II), para. 65; C-212/07 P of 13.2.2008 – Indorata-Serviços e Gestão, para. 43; C-243/07 P of 15.2.2008 – Brinkmann/OHIM, para. 39; C-202/08 and C-208/08 of 16.7.2009 – American Clothing Associates/OHIM, para. 57; C-536/10 P of 7.7.2011 – MPDV Mikrolab/OHIM, para. 45; C-53/11 P of 19.1.2012 – OHIM/Nike International, para. 57; C-649/11 P of 3.10.2012 – Cooperativa Vitivinícola Arousana, S. Coop. Galega/OHIM, para. 59; C-374/13 P of 10.4.2014 – Metropolis Inmobiliarias y Restauraciones/OHIM, para. 44; C-351/16 P of 10.11.2016 – 100 % Capri Italia/EUIPO, paras 8/22 and 9; *see also* CJEU C-354/12 P of 11.4.2013 – ASA/OHIM, para. 42; C-190/15 P of 19.11.2015 – Fetim/OHIM, para. 24.
804. CJEU C-193/09 P of 4.3.2010 – Kaul/OHIM, para. 72.
805. CJEU C-37/03 P of 15.9.2005 – BioID/OHIM, para. 49.

OHIM or, on appeal, the Court of First Instance, to come to the same conclusions as those arrived at by national authorities in similar circumstances.[806]

These considerations apply even if the sign whose registration is sought as a Community trade mark is composed in a manner identical to that of a mark in respect of which OHIM already approved registration as a Community trade mark and which refers to goods or services identical or similar to those in respect of which registration of the sign in question is sought.[807]

These rules must **also** be applied if the application for a mark in a Member State is based on the fact that **a similar or identical mark has already been registered**.[808]

The competent office of a Member State, which is to make a decision regarding a trade mark registration, is not obliged to ignore the ground for refusal listed in Article 3(1)(b) and (c) TMD2008 and therefore allow the application just because the sign for which registration is being sought is depicted in an identical or comparable way to a sign which it has already allowed to be registered as a sign and which refers to identical or similar goods or services.[809]

Although, within the framework of the assessment of such an application, the national office responsible for the registration must take account of similar applications in as far as it has access to such information, and pay special attention to the question of whether a decision should be reached in the same tenor or not, they are not in any way bound by these decisions.[810]

Furthermore, the principles of equality of treatment must be reconciled with the principle of legality. Pursuant to this, no person may rely, in support of his claim, on an unlawful act committed in favour of another in order to reach an identical decision.[811] Thus a company before the competent office of a Member State cannot invoke the decision-making practice of this office in their own favour which would run contrary to the TMD or would lead to the office making an unlawful decision.[812]

[3] Interim relief

Article 50(6) of **TRIPS** is a procedural provision intended to be applied by Community and national courts in accordance with obligations assumed both by the Community and by the Member States.[813]

---

806. CJEU C-173/04 P of 12.1.2006 – Deutsche SiSi-Werke/OHIM, para. 49; C-39/08 und C-43/08 of 12.2.2009 – bild digital, para. 15; C-118/18 P of 28.6.2018 – Hochmann Marketing/EUIPO, paras 5/21 and 7; C-285/19 P of 6.11.2019 – Geske/EUIPO, paras 5/15 and 6.
807. CJEU C-70/13 P of 12.12.2013 – Getty Images (US)/OHIM, para. 45; *see also* CJEU C-39/08 und C-43/08 of 12.2.2009 – bild digital, paras 15–19.
808. CJEU C-39/08 und C-43/08 of 12.2.2009 – bild digital, para. 16; unofficial translation.
809. CJEU C-39/08 und C-43/08 of 12.2.2009 – bild digital, para. 19; unofficial translation.
810. CJEU C-39/08 und C-43/08 of 12.2.2009 – bild digital, para. 17; unofficial translation.
811. *See* CJEU 188/83 of 9.10.1984 – Witte/Parliament, para. 15; 134/84 of 4.7.1985 – Williams/Rechnungshof, para. 14.
812. CJEU C-39/08 und C-43/08 of 12.2.2009 – bild digital, para. 18; unofficial translation.
813. CJEU C-300/98 and C-392/98 of 14.12.2000 – Dior and Others, para. 46; C-89/99 of 13.9.2001 – Schieving-Nijstad and Others, para. 31.

Where the judicial authorities are called upon to apply national rules with a view to ordering provisional measures for the protection of intellectual property rights falling within a field to which TRIPS applies and in respect of which the Community has already legislated, they are required to do so as far as possible in the light of the wording and purpose of Article 50(6) of TRIPS, taking account, more particularly, of all the circumstances of the case before them, so as to ensure that a balance is struck between the competing rights and obligations of the right holder and of the defendant.[814]

A **measure** whose purpose is to put an end to alleged infringements of a trade mark right and which is adopted in the course of a procedure is distinguished by the following features:

- the measure is characterized under national law as an 'immediate provisional measure', and its adoption must be required 'on grounds of urgency';
- the opposing party is summoned and is heard if he appears before the Court;
- the decision adopting the measure is reasoned and given in writing following an assessment of the substance of the case by the judge hearing the interim application;
- an appeal may be lodged against the decision; and
- although the parties remain free to initiate proceedings on the merits of the case, the decision is usually accepted by the parties as a 'final' resolution of their dispute, is to be regarded as a 'provisional measure' within the meaning of Article 50 of the TRIPS Agreement.[815]

Article 50 of TRIPS does not lay down any detailed rules concerning the procedure to be followed for the enforcement of intellectual property rights.[816]

Article 1(1) of TRIPS, relating to the nature and scope of obligations, provides that members shall be free to determine the appropriate method of implementing the provisions of this agreement within their own legal system and practice.[817]

It follows that, in the absence of any Community rules in the matter, it is for the domestic legal system of each Member State to lay down the detailed procedural rules relating to actions for the enforcement of intellectual property rights.[818]

From the standpoint of the right holder, the mechanism provided for in Article 50 of TRIPS strengthens the right which is to be guaranteed to him pursuant to Article 41(1) of TRIPS, namely the right to obtain expeditious remedies to prevent infringements of those rights and remedies which constitute a deterrent to further infringements.[819]

However, Article 8(2) of TRIPS recognizes that intellectual property rights may be abused and that right holders may resort to practices which unreasonably restrain trade

814. CJEU C-89/99 of 13.9.2001 – Schieving-Nijstad and Others, para. 54.
815. CJEU C-53/96 of 16.6.1998 – Hermès International/FHT Marketing Choice BV, para. 45.
816. CJEU C-89/99 of 13.9.2001 – Schieving-Nijstad and Others, para. 32.
817. CJEU C-89/99 of 13.9.2001 – Schieving-Nijstad and Others, para. 33.
818. CJEU C-89/99 of 13.9.2001 – Schieving-Nijstad and Others, para. 34.
819. CJEU C-89/99 of 13.9.2001 – Schieving-Nijstad and Others, para. 39.

or adversely affect the international transfer of technology. That could be the position, in particular, if provisional measures were prescribed without the defendant being heard.[820]

With a view to preventing such abuse, Article 50(4) of TRIPS provides that where the defendant has not been heard, he is entitled to request an immediate review of the provisional measures ordered.[821]

In addition, whether the defendant has been heard or not, Article 50(6) of TRIPS establishes in his favour a safeguard measure to protect him against any abuse of intellectual property rights, by laying down a simple procedure for setting aside unjustified provisional measures where no substantive proceedings have been instituted within the time limit prescribed.[822]

That mechanism is all the more important where the defendant contests the provisional measures prescribed by the judicial authority concerned and wishes to compel the right holder to bring substantive proceedings in the course of which the defendant will be in a position to put forward his full defence.[823]

It is therefore apparent, both from the wording of the three authentic versions of TRIPS and from the objective of Article 50(6), that the mechanism established by that provision is based on the premises that the intellectual property right holder whose application for provisional measures has been granted will normally institute substantive proceedings seeking a definitive measure with regard to the alleged infringement of those rights, in the course of which the defendant will be in a position to put forward his full defence.[824]

Article 50(6) of TRIPS is to be interpreted as meaning that a request by the defendant is necessary in order for the provisional measures ordered by way of interim relief to lapse on the ground that no substantive action has been brought either within the period prescribed in the provisional measures or, where no period is prescribed, within twenty working days or thirty-one calendar days, whichever is the longer period.[825]

In the absence of any provision in TRIPS concerning the point in time at which the period of twenty working days or thirty-one calendar days prescribed by Article 50(6) of that agreement is to start, it is for each contracting party to determine when that period is to start, provided always that it is 'reasonable having regard to the circumstances of each case and taking into account the balance to be struck between the competing rights and obligations of the intellectual property right holder and of the defendant'.[826]

In the absence of any Community rule on the point and in accordance with Article 1(1) of TRIPS, it is for each Member State to determine the limits of the powers of the judicial authorities in ordering provisional measures. Article 50(6) of TRIPS neither

820. CJEU C-89/99 of 13.9.2001 – Schieving-Nijstad and Others, para. 40.
821. CJEU C-89/99 of 13.9.2001 – Schieving-Nijstad and Others, para. 41.
822. CJEU C-89/99 of 13.9.2001 – Schieving-Nijstad and Others, para. 42.
823. CJEU C-89/99 of 13.9.2001 – Schieving-Nijstad and Others, para. 43.
824. CJEU C-89/99 of 13.9.2001 – Schieving-Nijstad and Others, para. 46.
825. CJEU C-89/99 of 13.9.2001 – Schieving-Nijstad and Others, para. 61.
826. CJEU C-89/99 of 13.9.2001 – Schieving-Nijstad and Others, para. 66.

requires nor forbids the legal order of a Member State to provide, where appropriate, that its judicial authorities are to determine of their own motion the period within which substantive proceedings are to be instituted at the same time as ordering provisional measures, without any request by the defendant being necessary for that purpose.[827]

Article 50(6) of TRIPS neither requires nor forbids the Member States to provide, where appropriate, that its judicial authorities are to determine of their own motion the period within which substantive proceedings are to be instituted. Since the provision in question is silent on that point, the scope of the powers conferred on appellate courts in that regard falls within the competence of each Member State.[828]

Article 90(1) of Regulation No. 6/2002[829] must be interpreted as meaning that the courts and tribunals of the Member States with jurisdiction to order provisional measures, including protective measures, in respect of a national design also have jurisdiction to order such **measures in respect of a Community design**.[830]

[4] Claims for information

Article 8(3)(e) of Directive 2004/48[831] must be interpreted as precluding a national provision, such as that at issue in the main proceedings, which allows, in an unlimited and unconditional manner, a banking institution to invoke banking secrecy in order to refuse to provide, pursuant to Article 8(1)(c) of that directive, information concerning the name and address of an account holder.[832]

Article 8(1) of Directive 2004/48 must be interpreted as applying to a situation, such as that at issue in the main proceedings, in which, after the definitive termination of proceedings in which it was held that an intellectual property right was infringed, the applicant in separate proceedings seeks information on the origin and distribution networks of the goods or services by which that intellectual property right is infringed.[833]

Article 8(1) of Directive 2004/48 must be interpreted as meaning that, in proceedings concerning an infringement of an intellectual property right under that provision, the applicant must, for the purpose of a request for information under Article 8, provide any reasonably available **evidence** enabling the court seised of that request

827. CJEU C-89/99 of 13.9.2001 – Schieving-Nijstad and Others, para. 70.
828. CJEU C-89/99 of 13.9.2001 – Schieving-Nijstad and Others, para. 73.
829. Council Regulation (EC) No 6/2002 of 12 December 2001 on Community designs (OJ 2002 L 3, p. 1).
830. CJEU C-678/18 of 21.11.2019 – Procureur-Generaal bij de Hoge Raad der Nederlanden, para. 44.
831. Directive 2004/48/EC of the European Parliament and of the Council of 29 Apr. 2004 on the enforcement of intellectual property rights (OJ 2004 L 157, p. 45, and corrigendum OJ 2004 L 195, p. 16).
832. CJEU C-580/13 of 16.7.2015 – Coty Germany, para. 43.
833. CJEU C-427/15 of 18.1.2017 – NEW WAVE/ALLTOYS, para. 28.

to satisfy itself with a sufficient degree of certainty **that the applicant is the right-holder**, by submitting evidence appropriate to the nature of that right and any special applicable formalities.[834]

[5] Claims for damages

Article 13 of Directive 2004/48[835] must be interpreted as not precluding national legislation, such as that at issue in the main proceedings, under which the holder of an intellectual property right that has been infringed may demand from the person who has infringed that right either compensation for the damage that he has suffered, taking account of all the appropriate aspects of the particular case, or, without him having to prove the actual loss, payment of a sum corresponding to **twice the appropriate fee** which would have been due if permission had been given for the work concerned to be used.[836]

Article 5(1)(b), the first subparagraph of Article 10(1) and the first subparagraph of Article 12(1) of TMD2008, read in conjunction with recital 6 thereof, must be interpreted as leaving Member States the option of allowing the proprietor of a trade mark whose rights in that mark have been revoked on expiry of the five-year period from its registration because he or she failed to make genuine use of the mark in the Member State concerned in connection with the goods or services for which it was registered to retain the right to claim **compensation for the injury** sustained as a result of the use by a third party, **before the date on which the revocation took effect**, of a similar sign in connection with identical or similar goods or services that is liable to be confused with his or her trade mark.[837]

In that regard, the Court has previously held that Article 15(1) and Article 51(1)(a) CTMR confer on the proprietor of a trade mark a grace period within which to begin to make genuine use of that mark, during which he or she may rely on the exclusive rights which the mark confers, pursuant to Article 9(1) of the regulation, in respect of all the goods or services for which that mark is registered, without having to demonstrate such use.[838]

In determining, under Article 9(1)(b) CTMR, whether the goods or services of the alleged infringer are identical or similar to the goods or services covered by the EU trade mark at issue, the extent of the exclusive right conferred by virtue of that provision should be assessed, during the five-year period following registration of the EU trade mark, by having regard to the goods and services as covered by the mark's registration,

834. CJEU C-628/21 of 27.4.2023 – TB/Castorama Polska a.o., para. 55.
835. Directive 2004/48/EC of the European Parliament and of the Council of 29 Apr. 2004 on the enforcement of intellectual property rights (OJ 2004 L 157, p. 45, and corrigendum OJ 2004 L 195, p. 16).
836. CJEU C-367/15 of 25.1.2017 – Stowarzyszenie 'Oławska Telewizja Kablowa'/Stowarzyszenie Filmowców Polskich, para. 33.
837. CJEU C-622/18 of 26.3.2020 – AR/Cooper International Spirits a.o., para. 48.
838. CJEU C-622/18 of 26.3.2020 – AR/Cooper International Spirits a.o., para. 37, with reference to CJEU C-654/15 of 21.12.2016 – Länsförsäkringar, para. 26.

and not in relation to the use that the proprietor has been able to make of the mark during that period.[839]

As Article 9(1), Article 15(1) and Article 51(1)(a) CTMR correspond, in essence, to Article 5(1), the first subparagraph of Article 10(1) and the first subparagraph of Article 12(1) TMD2008, that case law is entirely applicable by analogy to the interpretation of the latter provisions.[840]

It should be added that the Court has held that, from the time when the five-year period following registration of the EU trade mark expires, the extent of that exclusive right may be affected by the finding - made following a counterclaim, or a defence as to the merits, lodged by the third party in infringement proceedings - that the proprietor had at that time not yet begun to make genuine use of his or her mark in respect of some or all of the goods and services for which it has been registered.[841]

As the referring court observes, the case in the main proceedings can be distinguished from the case that gave rise to the judgment *Länsförsäkringar*, in that, specifically, it concerns the question of the scope of that exclusive right on expiry of the grace period where the trade mark has already been revoked.[842]

It is therefore necessary to examine whether, under the TMD2008, revocation of the rights conferred by the mark concerned may have an effect on whether it is possible for the proprietor to rely, after expiry of the grace period, on infringements of the exclusive rights conferred by that mark which occurred within that period.[843]

In that regard, first, in accordance with recital 6 of TMD2008, which states, *inter alia*, that '[the] Member States should remain free to determine the effects of revocation or invalidity of trade marks', that directive left the national legislature entirely free to determine the date on which revocation of a trade mark takes effect. Secondly, it follows from Article 11(3) TMD2008 that the Member States remain free to decide whether they wish to provide that, where a counter-claim for revocation is made, a trade mark may not be successfully invoked in infringement proceedings if it is established as a result of a plea that the trade mark could be revoked pursuant to Article 12(1) TMD2008.[844]

In the present case, the French legislature chose to have the revocation of a trade mark for non-use take effect on the expiry of a five-year period following registration of the mark. Moreover, there is nothing in the order for reference to suggest that, at the material time in the main proceedings, the French legislature had made use of the option provided for in Article 11(3) TMD2008.[845]

It follows that French legislation maintains the possibility, for the proprietor of the trade mark concerned, of relying, after expiry of the grace period, on infringements

839. CJEU C-622/18 of 26.3.2020 - AR/Cooper International Spirits a.o., para. 38, with reference to CJEU C-654/15 of 21.12.2016 - Länsförsäkringar, para. 27.
840. CJEU C-622/18 of 26.3.2020 - AR/Cooper International Spirits a.o., para. 39.
841. CJEU C-622/18 of 26.3.2020 - AR/Cooper International Spirits a.o., para. 40, with reference to CJEU C-654/15 of 21.12.2016 - Länsförsäkringar, para. 28.
842. CJEU C-622/18 of 26.3.2020 - AR/Cooper International Spirits a.o., para. 41.
843. CJEU C-622/18 of 26.3.2020 - AR/Cooper International Spirits a.o., para. 42.
844. CJEU C-622/18 of 26.3.2020 - AR/Cooper International Spirits a.o., para. 43.
845. CJEU C-622/18 of 26.3.2020 - AR/Cooper International Spirits a.o., para. 44.

of the exclusive rights conferred by that mark which occurred within that period, even if the proprietor has had his or her rights in the mark revoked.[846]

As regards the award of damages, reference must be made to Directive 2004/48,[847] and in particular to the first subparagraph of Article 13(1) thereof, under which such damages must be 'appropriate to the actual prejudice suffered by [the proprietor of the trade mark]'.[848]

Although the fact that a trade mark has not been used does not, in itself, preclude compensation in respect of acts of infringement that have been committed, that remains an important factor to be taken into account in determining the existence and, as the case may be, the extent of the injury sustained by the proprietor and, accordingly, the amount of damages that he or she might claim.[849]

[6] Claims for destruction

In the light of all the foregoing considerations, the answer to the question referred to is that Article 10(1) of Directive 2004/48[850] must be interpreted as **precluding** the interpretation of a provision of **national law** according to which a protective measure in the form of the **destruction of goods may not be applied** to goods which have been manufactured and to which an EU trade mark has been affixed, with the consent of the proprietor of that mark, but which were placed on the market of the EEA without his or her consent.[851]

On a proper construction of **Article 89(1)(d) of Regulation No. 6/2002,**[852] claims for the destruction of infringing products are governed by the law of the Member State in which the acts of infringement or threatened infringement have been committed, including its private international law. Claims for compensation for damage resulting from the activities of the person responsible for the acts of infringement or threatened infringement and for disclosure, in order to determine the extent of that damage, of information relating to those activities, are governed, pursuant to Article 88(2) of that regulation, by the national law of the Community design court hearing the proceedings, including its private international law.[853]

846. CJEU C-622/18 of 26.3.2020 – AR/Cooper International Spirits a.o., para. 45.
847. Directive 2004/48/EC of the European Parliament and of the Council of 29 Apr. 2004 on the enforcement of intellectual property rights (OJ 2004 L 157, p. 45, and corrigendum OJ 2004 L 195, p. 16).
848. CJEU C-622/18 of 26.3.2020 – AR/Cooper International Spirits a.o., para. 46.
849. CJEU C-622/18 of 26.3.2020 – AR/Cooper International Spirits a.o., para. 47.
850. Directive 2004/48/EC of the European Parliament and of the Council of 29 Apr. 2004 on the enforcement of intellectual property rights (OJ 2004 L 157, p. 45, and corrigendum OJ 2004 L 195, p. 16).
851. CJEU C-355/21 of 13.10.2022 – Perfumesco.pl/Procter & Gamble International Operations, para. 55.
852. Council Regulation (EC) No. 6/2002 of 12 Dec. 2001 on Community designs (OJ 2002 L 3, p. 1).
853. CJEU C-479/12 of 13.2.2014 – H. Gautzsch Großhandel, para. 55.

[7] Customs action

The customs regulation[854] must be interpreted as meaning that the holder of an intellectual property right over goods sold to a person residing in the territory of a Member State through an online sales website in a non-member country enjoys the protection afforded to that holder by that regulation at the time when those goods enter the territory of that Member State merely by virtue of the acquisition of those goods. It is not necessary, in addition, for the goods at issue to have been the subject, prior to the sale, of an offer for sale or advertising targeting consumers of that State.[855]

According to the definition of the terms '**counterfeit goods**' and '**pirated goods**' in Article 2(1) of the customs regulation, they cover infringements of a trade mark, copyright, a related right or a design which applies pursuant to EU legislation or pursuant to the domestic law of the Member State in which the application for action by the customs authorities is made. It follows that only infringements of intellectual property rights as conferred by EU law and the national law of the Member States are covered.[856]

The customs regulation introduces **no new criterion** for the purposes of ascertaining the existence **of an infringement** of intellectual property rights.[857] Such an infringement can, therefore, be relied on to justify action by the customs authorities under that regulation only if the sale of the goods concerned is liable to affect the rights conferred under the conditions laid down by the copyright directive, the trade mark directive and the Community trade mark regulation.[858]

Article 5(4) of the customs regulation, read in the light of Article 146 CTMR, is to be interpreted as allowing the holder of an **internationally registered trade mark** to secure action by the customs authorities of one or more other Member States, besides that of the Member State in which it is lodged, just like the proprietor of a Community trade mark.[859]

[8] Reimbursement of costs

National legislation providing for **flat rates** is, in principle, consistent with Article 14 of Directive 2004/48.[860] However, the Court stated that even in such a case, those rates should ensure that the costs which, under that national legislation, may be imposed on the unsuccessful party are reasonable and that the maximum amounts that may be

854. Council Regulation (EC) No. 1383/2003 of 22 Jul. 2003 concerning customs action against goods suspected of infringing certain intellectual property rights and the measures to be taken against goods found to have infringed such rights (OJ 2003 L 196, p. 7).
855. CJEU C-98/13 of 6.2.2014 – Blomqvist, para. 35.
856. CJEU C-98/13 of 6.2.2014 – Blomqvist, para. 24; *see also* CJEU C-446/09 and C-495/09 of 1.12.2011 – Koninklijke Philips Electronics, para. 50.
857. *See* CJEU C-281/05 of 9.11.2006 – Montex Holdings, para. 40.
858. CJEU C-98/13 of 6.2.2014 – Blomqvist, para. 25.
859. CJEU C-302/08 of 2.7.2009 – Zino Davidoff, para. 26.
860. Directive 2004/48/EC of the European Parliament and of the Council of 29 Apr. 2004 on the enforcement of intellectual property rights (OJ 2004 L 157, p. 45, and corrigendum OJ 2004 L 195, p. 16).

claimed under those costs are not too low either in relation to the rates normally charged by a lawyer in the field of intellectual property.[861]

Article 14 of Directive 2004/48 must be interpreted as not precluding national legislation which provides that, where the infringement of an intellectual property right has been committed by a natural person outside his trade, business or profession, the reimbursement of 'other costs' within the meaning of that provision to which the proprietor of that right is entitled is to be calculated as a **lump sum** on the basis of an amount in dispute limited by that legislation, **unless** the national court considers that the application of such a limit would be **inequitable** having regard to the specific features of the case before it.[862]

Article 14 of Directive 2004/48 must be interpreted as not precluding national legislation, such as that at issue in the main proceedings, which provides that the unsuccessful party is to be ordered to pay the legal costs incurred by the successful party, offers the courts responsible for making that order the possibility of taking into account features specific to the case before it, and provides for a **flat-rate scheme** for the reimbursement of costs for the assistance of a lawyer, subject to the condition that those rates ensure that the costs to be borne by the unsuccessful party are reasonable, which it is for the referring court to determine. However, Article 14 of that directive **precludes national legislation providing flat rates which**, owing to the maximum amounts that it contains being too low, do not ensure that, at the very least, a significant and appropriate part of the reasonable costs incurred by the successful party are borne by the unsuccessful party.[863]

Articles 3 and 14 of Directive 2004/48 must be interpreted as **precluding national legislation** or an interpretation thereof **which does not allow the court** before which an action is brought under that directive to take due account, in each case brought before it, of its specific characteristics for the purposes of assessing whether the legal costs incurred by the successful party are **reasonable and proportionate**.[864]

Nor does anything in Directive 2004/48 preclude the costs of a representative, such as a **patent lawyer**, to whom a rightholder has had recourse to individually or jointly with a lawyer, from being regarded, in principle, as being capable of falling within the concept of 'legal costs', in so far as those costs arise immediately and directly from the legal action itself.[865]

Such an origin may be accepted for the costs of a patent adviser authorized under national law to appear in court for the holders of intellectual property rights in proceedings before the competent courts, referred to in Directive 2004/48, relating, *inter alia*, to the establishment, by such an adviser, of pleadings or the appearance of that adviser at the hearings held, where appropriate, in those proceedings. Nor can it be ruled out that such an origin may also be accepted for the costs associated with the

861. CJEU C-57/15 of 28.7.2016 – United Video Properties, paras 25, 26, 30 and 32; C-531/20 of 28.4.2022 – NovaText/Ruprecht-Karls-Universität Heidelberg, para. 50.
862. CJEU C-559/20 of 28.4.2022 – Koch Media/FU, para. 65.
863. CJEU C-57/15 of 28.7.2016 – United Video Properties, para. 32, wording slightly changed.
864. CJEU C-531/20 of 28.4.2022 – NovaText/Ruprecht-Karls-Universität Heidelberg, para. 55.
865. CJEU C-531/20 of 28.4.2022 – NovaText/Ruprecht-Karls-Universität Heidelberg, para. 41.

assistance of such an adviser in the steps seeking an amicable settlement, in particular, in a dispute which is already pending before a court.[866]

Article 14 of Directive 2004/48 must be interpreted as precluding national rules providing that reimbursement of the **costs of a technical adviser** are provided for only in the event of fault on the part of the unsuccessful party, given that those costs are directly and closely linked to a judicial action seeking to have such an intellectual property right upheld.[867]

Article 14 of Directive 2004/48[868] must be interpreted as meaning that the costs incurred by a proprietor of intellectual property rights for the purposes of representation by counsel with a view to the **extra-judicial enforcement** of those rights, such as the costs associated with a warning notice, fall within the concept of 'other costs' within the meaning of that provision.[869]

866. CJEU C-531/20 of 28.4.2022 – NovaText/Ruprecht-Karls-Universität Heidelberg, para. 42.
867. CJEU C-57/15 of 28.7.2016 – United Video Properties, para. 40.
868. Directive 2004/48/EC of the European Parliament and of the Council of 29 Apr. 2004 on the enforcement of intellectual property rights (OJ 2004 L 157, p. 45, and corrigendum OJ 2004 L 195, p. 16).
869. CJEU C-559/20 of 28.4.2022 – Koch Media/FU, para. 45.

CHAPTER 1
General Provisions

Article 1 Scope

This Directive applies to every trade mark in respect of goods or services which is the subject of registration or of an application for registration in a Member State as an individual trade mark, a guarantee or certification mark or a collective mark, or which is the subject of a registration or an application for registration in the Benelux Office for Intellectual Property or of an international registration having effect in a Member State.

[A] General principles

The **registration system for trade marks** constitutes an essential element of their protection, which contributes, in respect of both Community law and the different national laws, to legal certainty and sound administration.[870]

In that regard, it should be noted, first, as is stated in the fourth recital in the preamble to the Directive, that acquisition of the rights in a mark results, on the one hand, from depositing and registering the mark and, on the other, from use. However, Article 1 TMD2008 provides that the Directive is to **apply only to trade marks which are the subject of registration** or of an application for registration in a Member State or in the Benelux Trade mark Office or of an international registration having effect in a Member State. Furthermore, the sixth recital in the preamble to the CTMR also states that the rights in a Community trade mark may not be obtained otherwise than by registration.[871]

Under Articles 4–6 CTMR, a trade mark may be **registered only individually**, and the minimum five-year protection afforded by such registration is conferred on it

870. CJEU C-273/00 of 12.12.2002 – Sieckmann, para. 37.
871. CJEU C-273/00 of 12.12.2002 – Sieckmann, para. 38.

only as an individual trade mark, even where several trade marks having one or more common and distinctive elements are registered at the same time.[872]

[B] Principle of territoriality

National trade mark rights are first of all territorial. This principle of territoriality, which is recognized under international treaty law, means that it is the law of the country where protection of a trade mark is sought which determines the conditions of that protection. Moreover, national law can only provide relief in respect of acts performed on the national territory in question.[873]

Article 36 of the EEC Treaty[874] itself, by allowing certain restrictions on imports on grounds of protection of intellectual property, presupposes that in principle the legislation of the importing State applies to acts performed in that State in relation to the imported product. A restriction on importation permitted by that legislation will of course escape Article 30[875] only if it is covered by Article 36.[876]

National trade mark rights are also independent of each other.[877]

The principle of the independence of trade marks is expressed in Article 6(3) of the Paris Union Convention which provides: 'A mark duly registered in a country of the Union shall be regarded as independent of marks registered in other countries of the Union ... .'[878]

Article 6(1) of the Brussels Convention[879] must be interpreted as meaning that it does not apply in European patent infringement proceedings involving a number of companies established in various Contracting States in respect of acts committed in one or more of those States even where those companies, which belong to the same group, may have acted in an identical or similar manner in accordance with a common policy elaborated by one of them.[880]

Article 16(4) of the Convention[881] is to be interpreted as meaning that the rule of exclusive jurisdiction laid down therein concerns all proceedings relating to the registration or validity of a patent, irrespective of whether the issue is raised by way of an action or a plea in objection.[882]

872. CJEU C-234/06 P of 13.9.2007 – Il Ponte Finanziaria/OHIM, para. 61.
873. CJEU C-9/93 of 22.6.1994 – IHT Internationale Heiztechnik/Ideal-Standard, para. 22.
874. Article 30 EC.
875. Article 28 EC.
876. CJEU C-9/93 of 22.6.1994 – IHT Internationale Heiztechnik/Ideal-Standard, para. 23.
877. CJEU C-9/93 of 22.6.1994 – IHT Internationale Heiztechnik/Ideal-Standard, para. 24.
878. CJEU C-9/93 of 22.6.1994 – IHT Internationale Heiztechnik/Ideal-Standard, para. 25.
879. Convention of 27 Sep. 1968 on Jurisdiction and the Enforcement of Judgments in Civil and Commercial Matters (OJ 1978 L 304, p. 36).
880. CJEU C-539/03 of 13.7.2006 – Roche Nederland and Others, para. 41.
881. Convention of 27 Sep. 1968 on Jurisdiction and the Enforcement of Judgments in Civil and Commercial Matters (OJ 1978 L 304, p. 36).
882. CJEU C-4/03 of 13.7.2006 – GAT, para. 31.

Article 2 Definitions

For the purpose of this Directive, the following definitions apply:

(a) 'office' means the central industrial property office of the Member State or the Benelux Office for Intellectual Property, entrusted with the registration of trade marks;
(b) 'register' means the register of trade marks kept by an office.

CHAPTER 2

Substantive Law on Trade Marks

SECTION 1 SIGNS OF WHICH A TRADE MARK MAY CONSIST

Article 3 Signs of which a trade mark may consist

A trade mark may consist of any signs, in particular words, including personal names, or designs, letters, numerals, colours, the shape of goods or of the packaging of goods, or sounds, provided that such signs are capable of:

(a) distinguishing the goods or services of one undertaking from those of other undertakings; and
(b) being represented on the register in a manner which enables the competent authorities and the public to determine the clear and precise subject matter of the protection afforded to its proprietor.

[A] Principles

It is common ground that **Article 2 of the Directive and Article 4 CTMR**, which are drafted in almost identical terms, must be given and are in fact given the **same interpretation**.[883]

The purpose of Article 2 TMD2008 is to define the types of signs of which a trade mark may consist, irrespective of the goods or services for which protection might be sought. It provides that a trade mark may consist, *inter alia,* of words and letters, provided that they are capable of distinguishing the goods or services of one undertaking from those of other undertakings.[884]

It is clear from the wording of Article 3(1)(a) TMD2008 and the structure of the Directive that that provision is intended essentially to exclude from registration signs which are not generally **capable of being a trade mark** and thus cannot be represented

883. CJEU C-321/03 of 12.10.2004 - Dyson, para. 14.
884. CJEU C-363/99 of 12.2.2004 - Koninklijke KPN Nederland, para. 80.

graphically and/or are not capable of distinguishing the goods or services of one undertaking from those of other undertakings.[885]

Article 15 of the TRIPS Agreement provides, *inter alia*, that any sign, or any combination of signs, capable of distinguishing the goods or services of one undertaking from those of other undertakings is to be capable of constituting a trade mark.[886]

Thus, like Article 2 TMD2008, Article 15 of the TRIPS Agreement lays down a guarantee of origin which is the essential function of a trade mark.[887]

To that end, **three conditions** must be satisfied. First, it must be a sign. Second, that sign must be capable of graphic representation. Third, the sign must be capable of distinguishing the goods or services of one undertaking from those of other undertakings.[888]

Article 2 TMD2008 contains a list, described as a 'list of examples' in the seventh recital in the preamble to that directive, of signs which may constitute a trade mark, provided that such signs are capable of distinguishing the goods or services of one undertaking from those of other undertakings, that is to say, to fulfil the trade mark's function as an indicator of origin. That list expressly includes 'personal names'.[889]

However, as is clear from the language of both Article 2 TMD2008 and the seventh recital in the preamble thereto, which refers to a 'list [of] examples' of signs which may constitute a trade mark, that list is not exhaustive. Consequently, that provision, although it does not mention signs which are not in themselves capable of being perceived visually, such as odours, does not, however, expressly exclude them.[890]

A colour mark per se is capable of constituting, under certain conditions, a trade mark within the meaning of Article 2 TMD2008.[891]

Articles 7 and 51 of Regulation No. 40/94 and Article 3 of First Directive 89/104 must be interpreted as meaning that a Community trade mark or a national trade mark **cannot be declared wholly or partially invalid** on the ground that terms used to designate the **goods and services** in respect of which that trade mark was registered **lack clarity and precision**.[892]

885. CJEU C-299/99 of 18.6.2002 – Philips, para. 37.
886. CJEU C-245/02 of 16.11.2004 – Anheuser-Busch, para. 68.
887. CJEU C-245/02 of 16.11.2004 – Anheuser-Busch, para. 69.
888. CJEU C-104/01 of 6.5.2003 – Libertel, para. 23; C-49/02 of 24.6.2004 – Heidelberger Bauchemie, para. 22; C-321/03 of 25.1.2007 – Dyson, para. 28; C-420/13 of 10.7.2014 – Netto Marken-Discount, para. 31; C-421/13 of 10.7.2014 – Apple, para. 17; *see also* CJEU C-53/01 to C-55/01 of 8.4.2003 – Linde and Others, para. 37; C-191/01 P of 23.10.2003 – OHIM/Wrigley, para. 28.
889. CJEU C-404/02 of 16.9.2004 – Nichols, para. 22; C-259/04 of 30.3.2006 – Emanuel, para. 43.
890. CJEU C-273/00 of 12.12.2002 – Sieckmann, para. 44; C-283/01 of 27.11.2003 – Shield Mark, para. 35; C-321/03 of 25.1.2007 – Dyson, para. 32.
891. CJEU C-217/13 and 218/13 of 19.6.2014 – Oberbank, para. 36; *see also* CJEU C-104/01 of 6.5.2003 – Libertel, paras 27–42; C-49/02 of 24.6.2004 – Heidelberger Bauchemie, para. 42.
892. CJEU C-371/18 of 29.1.2020 – Sky a.o./SkyKick UK a.o., para. 71.

[B] Sign

It must be pointed out that a **colour** per se cannot be presumed to constitute a sign. Normally, a colour is a simple property of things. Yet, it may constitute a sign. That depends on the context in which the colour is used. None the less, a colour per se is capable, in relation to a product or service, of constituting a sign.[893]

A **product's shape** is a sign which may constitute a trade mark.[894]

Article 2 TMD2008 is to be interpreted as meaning that the subject matter of an application for trade mark registration, such as that lodged in the main proceedings, which relates to **all the conceivable shapes of a transparent bin or collection chamber** forming part of the external surface of a vacuum cleaner, is not a 'sign' within the meaning of that provision and therefore is not capable of constituting a trade mark within the meaning thereof.[895]

It should be borne in mind that, according to Article 2 TMD2008, a trade mark may consist of any sign, particularly words, including personal names, designs, letters, numerals, the shape of goods or of their packaging.[896]

Although that provision mentions only signs which are capable of being perceived visually, are two-dimensional or three-dimensional and can thus be represented by means of letters or written characters or by a picture, it is however clear from the language of both Article 2 TMD2008 and the seventh recital in the preamble thereto, which refers to a 'list [of] examples' of signs which may constitute a trade mark, that that list is not exhaustive. Accordingly, the Court has held previously that Article 2 TMD2008, although it does not mention signs which are not in themselves capable of being perceived visually, such as sounds or smells, does not expressly exclude them.[897]

However, if that condition is not to be deprived of all substance, it cannot be accepted that the subject matter of any trade mark application necessarily constitutes a sign within the meaning of Article 2 TMD2008.[898]

The purpose of that requirement is in particular to prevent the abuse of trade mark law in order to obtain an unfair competitive advantage.[899]

In the present case, it is common ground that the subject matter of the application in the main proceedings is not a particular type of transparent collecting bin forming part of the external surface of a vacuum cleaner, but rather, in a general and abstract manner, all the conceivable shapes of such a collecting bin.[900]

In that regard, Dyson cannot maintain that the subject matter of its application in the main proceedings is capable of being perceived visually. What consumers can

---

893. CJEU C-104/01 of 6.5.2003 – Libertel, para. 27; C-49/02 of 24.6.2004 – Heidelberger Bauchemie, para. 23 f.
894. CJEU C-48/09 P of 14.9.2010 – Lego Juris/OHIM, para. 39; *see also* CJEU C-337/12 P to C-340/12 P of 6.3.2014 – Pi-Design/OHIM, para. 43.
895. CJEU C-321/03 of 25.1.2007 – Dyson, para. 40.
896. CJEU C-321/03 of 25.1.2007 – Dyson, para. 31; concerning letters *see also* CJEU C-265/09 P of 9.9.2010 – OHIM/BORCO-Marken-Import Matthiesen, para. 28.
897. CJEU C-321/03 of 25.1.2007 – Dyson, para. 32.
898. CJEU C-321/03 of 25.1.2007 – Dyson, para. 33.
899. CJEU C-321/03 of 25.1.2007 – Dyson, para. 34.
900. CJEU C-321/03 of 25.1.2007 – Dyson, para. 35.

identify visually is not so much the subject matter of the application as two of Dyson's graphic representations as contained in the application. Those representations cannot be assimilated to the subject matter of the application because, as pointed out by Dyson on a number of occasions, they are merely examples of it.[901]

It follows that, unlike the applications which gave rise to the judgments in *Sieckmann* and *Shield Mark*, the subject matter of the application in the main proceedings is capable of taking on a multitude of different appearances and is thus not specific. The shape, the dimensions, the presentation and composition of that subject matter depend both on the vacuum cleaner models developed by Dyson and on technological innovations. Likewise, transparency allows for the use of various colours.[902]

Given the exclusivity inherent in trade mark right, the holder of a trade mark relating to such a non-specific subject matter would obtain an unfair competitive advantage, contrary to the purpose pursued by Article 2 TMD2008, since it would be entitled to prevent its competitors from marketing vacuum cleaners having any kind of transparent collecting bin on their external surface, irrespective of its shape.[903]

It follows that the subject matter of the application at issue in the main proceedings is, in actual fact, a mere property of the product concerned and does not therefore constitute a 'sign' within the meaning of Article 2 TMD2008.[904]

[C] Capability of being represented on the register

> *Take care: There was a major change in the wording of TMD2008 from 'capable of being represented graphically' to 'capable of being represented on the register in a manner which enables the competent authorities and the public to determine the clear and precise subject matter of the protection afforded to its proprietor'.*

Probably inapplicable: A trade mark may consist of a sign which is not in itself capable of being perceived visually, provided that it can be represented graphically, particularly by means of images, lines or characters, and that the representation is clear, precise, self-contained, easily accessible, intelligible, durable and objective.[905]

Inapplicable: First, the function of the graphic representability requirement is, in particular, to define the mark itself in order to determine the precise subject of the protection afforded by the registered mark to its proprietor.[906]

901. CJEU C-321/03 of 25.1.2007 – Dyson, para. 36.
902. CJEU C-321/03 of 25.1.2007 – Dyson, para. 37.
903. CJEU C-321/03 of 25.1.2007 – Dyson, para. 38.
904. CJEU C-321/03 of 25.1.2007 – Dyson, para. 39.
905. CJEU C-273/00 of 12.12.2002 – Sieckmann, para. 55; C-104/01 of 6.5.2003 – Libertel, para. 28 seq.; C-283/01 of 27.11.2003 – Shield Mark, para. 55; C-49/02 of 24.6.2004 – Heidelberger Bauchemie, para. 25 seqq.; C-223/18 P of 6.6.2019 – Deichmann/EUIPO, para. 44.
906. CJEU C-273/00 of 12.12.2002 – Sieckmann, para. 48; *see also* CJEU C-307/10 of 19.6.2012 – Chartered Institute of Patent Attorneys, para. 37.

Probably still applicable: Next, the entry of the mark in a public register has the aim of making it accessible to the competent authorities and the public, particularly to economic operators.[907]

Probably still applicable: On the one hand, the competent authorities must know with **clarity and precision** the nature of the signs of which a mark consists in order to be able to fulfil their obligations in relation to the prior examination of registration applications and to the publication and maintenance of an appropriate and precise register of trade marks.[908]

Probably still applicable: On the other hand, economic operators must, with clarity and precision, be able to find out about registrations or applications for registration made by their current or potential competitors and thus to receive relevant information about the rights of third parties.[909]

Probably still applicable: If the users of that register are to be able to determine the precise nature of a mark on the basis of its registration, its graphic representation in the register must be **self-contained, easily accessible and intelligible**.[910]

Probably still applicable: Furthermore, in order to fulfil its role as a registered trade mark, a sign must always be perceived unambiguously and in the same way so that the mark is guaranteed as an indication of origin. In the light of the duration of a mark's registration and the fact that, as the Directive provides, it can be renewed for varying periods, the representation must be **durable**.[911]

Basically probably still applicable: Finally, the object of the representation is specifically to avoid any element of subjectivity in the process of identifying and perceiving the sign. Consequently, the means of graphic representation must be **unequivocal and objective**.[912]

Articles 2 and 3(1)(b) TMD2008 must be interpreted as meaning that the **classification as a 'colour mark' or 'figurative mark'** given to a sign by the applicant on registration is a relevant factor among others for the purpose of establishing whether that sign can constitute a trade mark within the meaning of Article 2 TMD2008.[913]

In that regard, it should be noted, first of all, that the fact that the registration of a sign is sought as a 'colour mark' or 'figurative mark' is relevant in order to determine the subject matter and scope of the protection conferred by trade mark law for the purpose of applying Article 2 TMD2008. The classification of a sign as a 'colour mark' or 'figurative mark' serves to clarify the subject matter and scope of the protection sought under trade mark law, in that it enables it to be specified whether the contours are part of the subject matter of the application for registration.[914]

907. CJEU C-273/00 of 12.12.2002 – Sieckmann, para. 49; *see also* C-307/10 of 19.6.2012 – Chartered Institute of Patent Attorneys, para. 46.
908. CJEU C-273/00 of 12.12.2002 – Sieckmann, para. 50, *see also* CJEU C-541/18 of 12.9.2019 – AS/Deutsches Patent- und Markenamt, para. 27.
909. CJEU C-273/00 of 12.12.2002 – Sieckmann, para. 51.
910. CJEU C-273/00 of 12.12.2002 – Sieckmann, para. 52; C-337/12 P to C-340/12 P of 6.3.2014 – Pi-Design/OHIM, para. 57.
911. CJEU C-273/00 of 12.12.2002 – Sieckmann, para. 53.
912. CJEU C-273/00 of 12.12.2002 – Sieckmann, para. 54.
913. CJEU C-578/17 of 27.3.2019 – Oy Hartwall/Patentti- ja rekisterihallitus, para. 35.
914. CJEU C-578/17 of 27.3.2019 – Oy Hartwall/Patentti- ja rekisterihallitus, para. 25.

As for the effect of the classification of a sign as a ‘colour mark’ or ‘figurative mark’ on the assessment of distinctive character, it must be held that when a competent authority examines a trade mark application, it must, in order to determine whether the sign in respect of which protection is sought under trade mark law has distinctive character within the meaning of Article 3(1)(b) TMD2008, carry out an examination by reference to the actual situation, taking account of all the circumstances of the case and in particular any use which has been made of the sign.[915]

The examination of the distinctive character of a mark cannot therefore be carried out in the abstract.[916]

Article 2 TMD2008 must be interpreted as **precluding the registration of a sign as a mark**, where the **classification** as a ‘colour mark’ or ‘figurative mark’ is **not clear**, due to an inconsistency in the application for registration, which it is for the referring court to ascertain.[917]

In that regard, it should be noted that, according to the Court’s settled case law, a sign may be registered as a mark only if the applicant provides a graphic representation in accordance with the requirement in Article 2 TMD2008, to the effect that the subject matter and scope of the protection sought are clearly and precisely determined.[918]

The verbal description of the sign serves to clarify the subject matter and scope of the protection sought under trade mark law.[919]

When the trade mark application contains an inconsistency between the sign, protection in respect of which is sought in the form of a drawing, and the classification given to the mark by the applicant, the consequence of which is that it is impossible to determine exactly the subject matter and scope of the protection sought under trade mark law, the competent authority must refuse registration of the mark on account of the lack of clarity and precision of the trade mark application.[920]

915. CJEU C-578/17 of 27.3.2019 – Oy Hartwall/Patentti- ja rekisterihallitus, para. 26, with reference to CJEU C-104/01 of 6.5.2003 – Libertel, para. 76; C-363/99 of 12.2.2004 – Koninklijke KPN Nederland, para. 31-35; C-49/02 of 24.6.2004 – Heidelberger Bauchemie, para. 41; *see also* CJEU C-456/19 of 8.10.2020 – Aktiebolaget Östgötatrafiken/Patent- och registreringsverket, para. 33.
916. CJEU C-578/17 of 27.3.2019 – Oy Hartwall/Patentti- ja rekisterihallitus, para. 27, with reference to CJEU C-363/99 of 12.2.2004 – Koninklijke KPN Nederland, para. 31.
917. CJEU C-578/17 of 27.3.2019 – Oy Hartwall/Patentti- ja rekisterihallitus, para. 43, unofficial transcription.
918. CJEU C-578/17 of 27.3.2019 – Oy Hartwall/Patentti- ja rekisterihallitus, para. 38, with reference to CJEU C-104/01 of 6.5.2003 – Libertel, para. 29; also CJEU C-124/18 P of 29.7.2019 – Red Bull/EUIPO, para. 36.
919. CJEU C-578/17 of 27.3.2019 – Oy Hartwall/Patentti- ja rekisterihallitus, para. 39, with reference to CJEU C-283/01 of 27.11.2003 – Shield Mark, para. 59; C-49/02 of 24.6.2004 – Heidelberger Bauchemie, para. 34; *see also* CJEU C-124/18 P of 29.7.2019 – Red Bull/EUIPO, para. 37.
920. CJEU C-578/17 of 27.3.2019 – Oy Hartwall/Patentti- ja rekisterihallitus, para. 40; C-124/18 P of 29.7.2019 – Red Bull/EUIPO, para. 37.

[1] Odours

Basically still applicable: In respect of the description of an odour, although it is graphic, it is not sufficiently clear, precise and objective.[921]

Basically still applicable: As to the deposit of an odour sample, it does not constitute a graphic representation for the purposes of Article 2 TMD2008. Moreover, an odour sample is not sufficiently stable or durable.[922]

Basically still applicable: If, in respect of an olfactory sign, a chemical formula, a description in words or the deposit of an odour sample are not capable of satisfying, in themselves, the requirements of graphic representability, nor is a combination of those elements able to satisfy such requirements, in particular those relating to clarity and precision.[923]

[2] Sounds

Probably no longer applicable: As regards the representation of a sound sign by a **description using the written language,** it cannot be precluded a priori that such a mode of graphical representation satisfies the requirements. In the case of signs such as those at issue in the main proceedings, a graphical representation such as the first nine notes of Für Elise or a cockcrow at the very least lacks precision and clarity and therefore does not make it possible to determine the scope of the protection sought. Accordingly, it cannot constitute a graphical representation of that sign for the purposes of Article 2 TMD2008.[924]

Basically probably still applicable: As regards, next, an **onomatopoeia**, it must be held that there is a lack of consistency between the onomatopoeia itself, as pronounced, and the actual sound or noise, or the sequence of actual sounds or noises, which it purports to imitate phonetically. Thus, where a sound sign is represented graphically by a simple onomatopoeia, it is not possible for the competent authorities and the public, in particular traders, to determine whether the protected sign is the onomatopoeia itself, as pronounced, or the actual sound or noise. Furthermore, an onomatopoeia may be perceived differently, depending on the individual, or from one Member State to another. That is so in the case of the Dutch onomatopoeia Kukelekuuuuu, which seeks to transcribe a cockcrow, and which is very different from the corresponding onomatopoeia in the other languages used in the Benelux Member States. Consequently, a simple onomatopoeia cannot without more constitute a graphical representation of the sound or noise of which it purports to be the phonetic description.[925]

Still applicable: As regards, last, **musical notes**, which are a common method of representing sounds, a sequence of notes without more, such as E, D#, E, D#, E, B, D,

921. CJEU C-273/00 of 12.12.2002 – Sieckmann, para. 70.
922. CJEU C-273/00 of 12.12.2002 – Sieckmann, para. 71.
923. CJEU C-273/00 of 12.12.2002 – Sieckmann, para. 72.
924. CJEU C-283/01 of 27.11.2003 – Shield Mark, para. 59, *see also* CJEU C-578/17 of 27.3.2019 – Oy Hartwall/Patentti- ja rekisterihallitus, para. 39.
925. CJEU C-283/01 of 27.11.2003 – Shield Mark, para. 60.

C, A, does not constitute a graphical representation for the purposes of Article 2 TMD2008 either. Such a description, which is neither clear nor precise nor self-contained does not make it possible, in particular, to determine the pitch and the duration of the sounds forming the melody in respect of which registration is sought and which constitute essential parameters for the purposes of knowing the melody and, accordingly, of defining the trade mark itself.[926]

Basically still applicable: On the other hand, a stave divided into bars and showing, in particular, a clef (a treble clef, bass clef or alto or tenor clef), musical notes and rests whose form (for the notes: semibreve, minim, crotchet, quaver, semiquaver, etc.; for the rests: semibreve rest, minim rest, crotchet rest, quaver rest, etc.) indicates the relative value and, where appropriate, accidentals (sharp, flat, natural) – all of this notation determining the pitch and duration of the sounds – may constitute a faithful representation of the sequence of sounds forming the melody in respect of which registration is sought. This mode of graphical representation of the sounds meets the requirements of the case law of the Court that such representation must be clear, precise, self-contained, easily accessible, intelligible, durable and objective.[927]

Still applicable: Even if such a representation is not immediately intelligible, the fact remains that it may be easily intelligible, thus allowing the competent authorities and the public, in particular traders, to know precisely the sign whose registration as a trade mark is sought.[928]

[3] ***Colours***

No longer applicable: A **mere sample of a colour** does not, however, satisfy the requirements set out above.[929]

No longer applicable: In particular, a sample of a colour may deteriorate with time. There may be certain media on which it is possible to reproduce a colour in permanent form. However, with other media, including paper, the exact shade of the colour cannot be protected from the effects of the passage of time. In these cases, the filing of a sample of a colour does not possess the durability required by Article 2 TMD2008.[930]

No longer applicable: It follows that filing a sample of a colour does not per se constitute a graphic representation within the meaning of Article 2 TMD2008.[931]

Basically still applicable: On the other hand, a **verbal description of a colour**, in so far as it is composed of words which themselves are made up of letters, does constitute a graphic representation of the colour.[932]

926. CJEU C-283/01 of 27.11.2003 – Shield Mark, para. 61.
927. CJEU C-283/01 of 27.11.2003 – Shield Mark, para. 62.
928. CJEU C-283/01 of 27.11.2003 – Shield Mark, para. 63.
929. CJEU C-104/01 of 6.5.2003 – Libertel, para. 31.
930. CJEU C-104/01 of 6.5.2003 – Libertel, para. 32.
931. CJEU C-104/01 of 6.5.2003 – Libertel, para. 33.
932. CJEU C-104/01 of 6.5.2003 – Libertel, para. 34.

Basically still applicable: A description in words of the colour will not necessarily satisfy the conditions set out in every instance. That is a question which must be evaluated in the light of the circumstances of each individual case.[933]

Basically still applicable: A **sample of a colour, combined with a description in words** of that colour, may therefore constitute a graphic representation within the meaning of Article 2 TMD2008, provided that the description is clear, precise, self-contained, easily accessible, intelligible, and objective.[934]

Basically still applicable: The designation of a colour using an internationally recognized **identification code** may be considered to constitute a graphic representation. Such codes are deemed to be precise and stable.[935]

No longer applicable: Where a sample of a colour, together with a description in words, does not satisfy the conditions laid down in Article 2 TMD2008 in order for it to constitute a graphic representation because, *inter alia*, it lacks precision or durability, that deficiency may, depending on the facts, be remedied by adding a colour designation from an internationally recognized identification code.[936]

Basically still applicable: A graphic representation consisting of **two or more colours, designated in the abstract and without contours**, must be systematically arranged by associating the colours concerned in a predetermined and uniform way.[937]

Basically still applicable: The mere juxtaposition of two or more colours, without shape or contours, or a reference to two or more colours 'in every conceivable form' does not exhibit the qualities of precision and uniformity required by Article 2 TMD2008.[938]

Basically still applicable: Such representations would allow numerous different combinations, which would not permit the consumer to perceive and recall a particular combination, thereby enabling him to make further purchases with certainty, any more than they would allow the competent authorities and economic operators to know the scope of the protection afforded to the proprietor of the trade mark.[939]

[4] Designs

Basically still applicable: It is absolutely plain from the wording of Article 2 TMD2008 that designs are among the categories of signs capable of graphic representation.[940]

Still applicable: It follows that a representation which depicts the **layout of a retail store** by means of an integral collection of lines, curves and shapes may

933. CJEU C-104/01 of 6.5.2003 – Libertel, para. 35.
934. CJEU C-104/01 of 6.5.2003 – Libertel, para. 36; C-49/02 of 24.6.2004 – Heidelberger Bauchemie, para. 36.
935. CJEU C-104/01 of 6.5.2003 – Libertel, para. 37.
936. CJEU C-104/01 of 6.5.2003 – Libertel, para. 38.
937. CJEU C-49/02 of 24.6.2004 – Heidelberger Bauchemie, para. 33; C-578/17 of 27.3.2019 – Oy Hartwall/Patentti- ja rekisterihallitus, para. 33; C-124/18 P of 29.7.2019 – Red Bull/EUIPO, para. 38.
938. CJEU C-49/02 of 24.6.2004 – Heidelberger Bauchemie, para. 34.
939. CJEU C-49/02 of 24.6.2004 – Heidelberger Bauchemie, para. 35; C-124/18 P of 29.7.2019 – Red Bull/EUIPO, para. 38.
940. CJEU C-421/13 of 10.7.2014 – Apple, para. 18.

constitute a trade mark, provided that it is capable of distinguishing the products or services of one undertaking from those of other undertakings. Consequently, such a representation satisfies the first and second conditions of Article 2 TMD2008, without it being necessary either, on the one hand, to attribute any relevance to the fact that the design does not contain any indication as to the size and proportions of the retail store that it depicts, or, on the other hand, to examine whether such a design could equally, as a 'presentation of the establishment in which a service is provided', be treated in the same way as 'packaging' within the meaning of Article 2 TMD2008.[941]

Still applicable: Articles 2 and 3 TMD2008 must be interpreted as meaning that the representation, by a design alone, without indicating the size or the proportions, of the layout of a retail store, may be registered as a trade mark for services consisting in services relating to those goods but which do not form an integral part of the offer for sale thereof, provided that the sign is capable of distinguishing the services of the applicant for registration from those of other undertakings and that registration is not precluded by any of the grounds for refusal set out in that directive.[942]

[D] Capability of distinguishing

Article 3(3) TMD2008 is linked to the concept of '**distinctive character of a sign**' for the purposes of Article 2 TMD2008. According to the wording of Article 3(3) TMD2008, the registration or validity of marks referred to in Article 3(1)(b), (c) or (d) is to be allowed by virtue of the use which has been made of them where, on account of that use, the marks have 'acquired a distinctive character'.[943]

That essential function of trade marks has been incorporated by the EU legislature into Article 2 TMD2008, which provides that signs which are capable of being represented graphically may only constitute a trade mark if they are capable of distinguishing the goods or services of one undertaking from those of other undertakings.[944]

There is no reason to find that a **word** like Postkantoor is not, in respect of certain goods or services, capable of fulfilling the essential function of a trade mark, which is to guarantee the identity of the origin of the marked goods or services to the consumer or end user by enabling him, without any possibility of confusion, to distinguish the goods or services from others which have another origin. Accordingly, an interpretation of Article 2 TMD2008 appears not to be useful for the purposes of deciding the present case.[945]

A trade mark such as 'ELIZABETH EMANUEL' may have that function of distinguishing the goods manufactured by an undertaking, particularly where that

941. CJEU C-421/13 of 10.7.2014 – Apple, para. 19.
942. CJEU C-421/13 of 10.7.2014 – Apple, para. 27.
943. CJEU C-371/06 of 20.9.2007 – Benetton Group, para. 24.
944. CJEU C-409/12 of 6.3.2014 – Backaldrin Österreich The Kornspitz Company, para. 21; *see also* CJEU C-517/99 of 4.10.2001 – Merz & Krell, para. 23; C-371/02 of 29.4.2004 – Björnekulla Fruktindustrier, para. 21.
945. CJEU C-363/99 of 12.2.2004 – Koninklijke KPN Nederland, para. 81.

trade mark has been assigned to that undertaking and the undertaking manufactures the same type of goods as those which initially bore the trade mark in question.[946]

In that connection, it must be borne in mind that, whilst **colours** are capable of conveying certain associations of ideas, and of arousing feelings, they possess little inherent capacity for communicating specific information, especially since they are commonly and widely used, because of their appeal, in order to advertise and market goods or services, without any specific message.[947]

However, that factual finding would not justify the conclusion that colours per se cannot, as a matter of principle, be considered to be capable of distinguishing the goods or services of one undertaking from those of other undertakings. The possibility that a colour per se may in some circumstances serve as a badge of origin of the goods or services of an undertaking cannot be ruled out. It must therefore be accepted that colours per se may be capable of distinguishing the goods or services of one undertaking from those of other undertakings, within the meaning of Article 2 TMD2008.[948]

Save in exceptional cases, colours do not initially have a distinctive character, but may be capable of acquiring such character as the result of the use made of them in relation to the goods or services claimed.[949]

Subject to the above, it must be accepted that for the purposes of Article 2 TMD2008, colours and combinations of colours, designated in the abstract and without contours, may be capable of distinguishing the goods or services of one undertaking from those of other undertakings.[950]

Article 7(1)(b) CTMR does not distinguish between trade marks for services and trade marks for goods for the assessment of distinctiveness. By deducing from existing case law that in the assessment of the distinctiveness of a colour mark for services, no other criteria are to be applied than in the case of colour marks for goods, the General Court applied Article 7(1)(b) CTMR correctly. In its assessment of distinction, the court thus made no difference between trade marks for services and trade marks for goods.[951]

Article 2 TMD2008 makes no distinction between different categories of trade marks. The criteria for assessing the distinctive character of **three-dimensional trade marks** are thus no different from those to be applied to other categories of trade marks.[952]

In particular, the Directive in no way requires that the **shape of the article** in respect of which the sign is registered must include some capricious addition. Under

946. CJEU C-259/04 of 30.3.2006 – Emanuel, para. 45.
947. CJEU C-104/01 of 6.5.2003 – Libertel, para. 40.
948. CJEU C-104/01 of 6.5.2003 – Libertel, para. 41; *see also* CJEU C-49/02 of 24.6.2004 – Heidelberger Bauchemie, para. 37.
949. CJEU C-49/02 of 24.6.2004 – Heidelberger Bauchemie, para. 39; C-170/15 P of 21.1.2016 – Enercon/OHIM, para. 31.
950. CJEU C-49/02 of 24.6.2004 – Heidelberger Bauchemie, para. 40.
951. CJEU C-45/11 P of 7.12.2011 – Deutsche Bahn/OHIM, para. 43; *see also* CJEU C-104/01 of 6.5.2003 – Libertel, para. 41; C-49/02 of 24.6.2004 – Heidelberger Bauchemie, para. 37.
952. CJEU C-299/99 of 18.6.2002 – Philips, para. 48; *see also* CJEU C-456/01 P and C-457/01 P of 29.4.2004 – Henkel/OHIM, para. 31; C-468/01 P to C-472/01 P of 29.4.2004 – Procter & Gamble/OHIM (three-dimensional form of tablet I), para. 29; C-473/01 P and C-474/01 P of 29.4.2004 – Procter & Gamble/OHIM (three-dimensional form of tablet II), para. 29; C-445/02 P of 28.6.2004 – Glaverbel/OHIM, para. 42.

Article 2 TMD2008, the shape in question must simply be capable of distinguishing the product of the proprietor of the trade mark from those of other undertakings and thus fulfil its essential purpose of guaranteeing the origin of the product.[953]

The representation, by a design, of the **layout of a retail store** is also capable of distinguishing the products or services of one undertaking from those of other undertakings and, hence, satisfying the third condition of Article 2 TMD2008. In that regard, it suffices to observe that it cannot be ruled out that the layout of a retail outlet depicted by such a sign may allow the products or the services for which registration is sought to be identified as originating from a particular undertaking. This could be the case when the depicted layout departs significantly from the norm or customs of the economic sector concerned.[954]

SECTION 2 GROUNDS FOR REFUSAL OR INVALIDITY

Article 4 Absolute grounds for refusal or invalidity

1. *The following shall not be registered or, if registered, shall be liable to be declared invalid:*
   - *(a) signs which cannot constitute a trade mark;*
   - *(b) trade marks which are devoid of any distinctive character;*
   - *(c) trade marks which consist exclusively of signs or indications which may serve, in trade, to designate the kind, quality, quantity, intended purpose, value, geographical origin, or the time of production of the goods or of rendering of the service, or other characteristics of the goods or services;*
   - *(d) trade marks which consist exclusively of signs or indications which have become customary in the current language or in the bona fide and established practices of the trade;*
   - *(e) signs which consist exclusively of:*
     - *(i) the shape, or another characteristic, which results from the nature of the goods themselves,*
     - *(ii) the shape, or another characteristic, of goods which is necessary to obtain a technical result,*
     - *(iii) the shape, or another characteristic, which gives substantial value to the goods;*
   - *(f) trade marks which are contrary to public policy or to accepted principles of morality;*
   - *(g) trade marks which are of such a nature as to deceive the public, for instance as to the nature, quality or geographical origin of the goods or service;*

953. CJEU C-299/99 of 18.6.2002 – Philips, para. 49; *see also* CJEU C-456/01 P and C-457/01 P of 29.4.2004 – Henkel/OHIM, para. 31; C-468/01 P to C-472/01 P of 29.4.2004 – Procter & Gamble/OHIM (three-dimensional form of tablet I), para. 29; C-473/01 P and C-474/01 P of 29.4.2004 – Procter & Gamble/OHIM (three-dimensional form of tablet II), para. 29; C-445/02 P of 28.6.2004 – Glaverbel/OHIM, para. 42; C-30/15 P of 10.11.2016 – Simba Toys/EUIPO, para. 37.
954. CJEU C-421/13 of 10.7.2014 – Apple, para. 20; *see also* CJEU C-25/05 P of 22.6.2006 – Storck/OHIM (gold-coloured sweet wrapper), para. 28; C-97/12 P of 15.5.2014 – Louis Vuitton Malletier/OHIM, para. 52; C-456/19 of 8.10.2020 – Aktiebolaget Östgötatrafiken/Patent- och registreringsverket, para. 41.

(h) trade marks which have not been authorised by the competent authorities and are to be refused or invalidated pursuant to Article 6ter of the Paris Convention for the Protection of Industrial Property ('the Paris Convention');
(i) trade marks which are excluded from registration pursuant to Union legislation or the national law of the Member State concerned, or to international agreements to which the Union or the Member State concerned is party, providing for protection of designations of origin and geographical indications;
(j) trade marks which are excluded from registration pursuant to Union legislation or international agreements to which the Union is party, providing for protection of traditional terms for wine;
(k) trade marks which are excluded from registration pursuant to Union legislation or international agreements to which the Union is party, providing for protection of traditional specialities guaranteed;
(l) trade marks which consist of, or reproduce in their essential elements, an earlier plant variety denomination registered in accordance with Union legislation or the national law of the Member State concerned, or international agreements to which the Union or the Member State concerned is party, providing protection for plant variety rights, and are in respect to plant varieties of the same or closely related species.

2. *A trade mark shall be liable to be declared invalid where the application for registration of the trade mark was made in bad faith by the applicant. Any Member State may also provide that such a trade mark is not to be registered.*
3. *Any Member State may provide that a trade mark is not to be registered or, if registered, is liable to be declared invalid where and to the extent that:*
   (a) the use of that trade mark may be prohibited pursuant to provisions of law other than trade mark law of the Member State concerned or of the Union;
   (b) the trade mark includes a sign of high symbolic value, in particular a religious symbol;
   (c) the trade mark includes badges, emblems and escutcheons other than those covered by Article 6ter of the Paris Convention and which are of public interest, unless the consent of the competent authority to their registration has been given in conformity with the law of the Member State.
4. *A trade mark shall not be refused registration in accordance with paragraph 1(b), (c) or (d) if, before the date of application for registration, following the use which has been made of it, it has acquired a distinctive character. A trade mark shall not be declared invalid for the same reasons if, before the date of application for a declaration of invalidity, following the use which has been made of it, it has acquired a distinctive character.*
5. *Any Member State may provide that paragraph 4 is also to apply where the distinctive character was acquired after the date of application for registration but before the date of registration.*

[A] Principles

A trade mark confers on its proprietor an exclusive right, in relation to certain goods and services, that allows him to monopolize the sign registered as a trade mark for an unlimited period.[955]

955. CJEU C-104/01 of 6.5.2003 – Libertel, para. 49.

The possibility of registering a trade mark may be limited for reasons relating to the **public interest**.[956]

In that regard, it is appropriate to observe that although the third recital in the preamble to the Directive states that the full-scale approximation of the trade mark laws of the Member States does not appear necessary at present, the seventh recital makes clear that the conditions for obtaining and continuing to hold a registered trade mark are, in general, identical in all the Member States and that, to that end, the grounds for refusal of registration concerning the trade mark itself are listed exhaustively in the Directive.[957]

According to settled case law, in a field which has been exhaustively harmonized at Community level, a national measure must be assessed in the light of the provisions of that harmonizing measure and not of those of primary law.[958]

Consequently, it is the Directive, and in particular Article 3 TMD2008, on the absolute grounds for refusal or invalidity of registration, and not Articles 28 EC and 30 EC, which must be assessed to determine whether Community law precludes the registration of a national trade mark such as that at issue in the main proceedings.[959]

The Court of Justice has had occasion to find a degree of overlap between the respective scope of the absolute grounds for refusal to register a trade mark set out in Article 7(1)(b)–(d) CTMR.[960]

Each of the **grounds for refusal** to register listed in Article 3(1) TMD2008 is **independent** of the others and calls for a **separate** examination.[961]

In those circumstances, it is important for the correct application of Article 7(1) CTMR to ensure that the ground for refusal set out in Article 7(1)(c) duly continues to be applied only to the situations specifically covered by that ground for refusal.[962]

It follows that if a three-dimensional shape of product trade mark is not refused registration under Article 3(1)(e) TMD2008, registration may still be refused if it falls within one or more of the categories set out in Article 3(1)(b)–(d) TMD2008.[963]

956. CJEU C-104/01 of 6.5.2003 – Libertel, para. 50.
957. CJEU C-363/99 of 12.2.2004 – Koninklijke KPN Nederland, paras 78 and 122; *see also* CJEU C-299/99 of 18.6.2002 – Philips, para. 74; C-371/18 of 29.1.2020 – Sky a.o./SkyKick UK a.o., para. 56.
958. CJEU C-421/04 of 9.3.2006 – Matratzen Concord, para. 20.
959. CJEU C-421/04 of 9.3.2006 – Matratzen Concord, para. 21.
960. CJEU C-304/06 P of 8.5.2008 – Eurohypo/OHIM, para. 54; C-282/09 P of 18.3.2010 – CFCMCEE/OHIM, paras 50 and 52; C-51/10 P of 10.3.2011 – Agencja Wydawnicza Technopol/HABM, para. 47; C-56/10 P of 22.6.2011 – Agencja Wydawnicza Technopol/HABM, para. 29; C-90/11 and C-91/11 of 15.3.2012 – Strigl and Securvita, para. 20; C-307/11 P of 26.4.2012 – Deichmann/OHIM, para. 47.
961. CJEU C-53/01 to C-55/01 of 8.4.2003 – Linde and Others, para. 67; C-363/99 of 12.2.2004 – Koninklijke KPN Nederland, para. 67; C-265/00 of 12.2.2004 – Campina Melkunie, para. 18; C-456/01 P and C-457/01 P of 29.4.2004 – Henkel/OHIM, para. 45; C-329/02 P of 16.9.2004 – SAT.1 SATELLITENFERNSEHEN/OHIM, para. 25; C-64/02 P of 21.10.2004 – OHIM/ERPO MÖBELWERK, para. 39; C-37/03 P of 15.9.2005 – BioID/OHIM, para. 59; C-173/04 P of 12.1.2006 – Deutsche SiSi-Werke/OHIM, para. 59; C-304/06 P of 8.5.2008 – Eurohypo/OHIM, para. 54; C-282/09 P of 18.3.2010 – CFCMCEE/OHIM, para. 50; C-90/11 and C-91/11 of 15.3.2012 – Strigl and Securvita, para. 20.
962. CJEU C-51/10 P of 10.3.2011 – Agencja Wydawnicza Technopol/HABM, para. 48.
963. CJEU C-53/01 to C-55/01 of 8.4.2003 – Linde and Others, paras 68 and 70; C-218/01 of 12.2.2004 – Henkel, para. 39.

It is quite evident from the wording of Article 7(1) CTMR that it is sufficient that **one of the absolute grounds for refusal** listed in that provision applies for the sign at issue not to be registrable as a Community trade mark.[964]

In particular, it is thus not open to the competent authority to conclude that a mark is not devoid of any distinctive character in relation to certain goods or services purely on the ground that it is not descriptive of them.[965]

A word mark which is descriptive of characteristics of goods or services for the purposes of Article 3(1)(c) TMD2008 is, on that account, necessarily devoid of any distinctive character with regard to the same goods or services within the meaning of Article 3(1)(b) TMD2008.[966]

However, that case law on Article 7(1) lit. (c) CTMR is not applicable, *mutatis mutandis*, in the context of Article 7(1)(b) CTMR, where the distinctive character of the trade mark applied for, within the meaning of Article 7(1)(b) CTMR, is called into question for reasons other than its descriptive character.[967]

A sign may be devoid of distinctive character for the purposes of Article 7(1)(b) CTMR for reasons other than the fact that it may be descriptive.[968]

If it is demonstrated that the phrase concerned is commonly used in business communications and, in particular, in advertising, as provided by Article 7(1)(d) CTMR, it follows that that sign is not capable of distinguishing the goods or services of an undertaking from those of other undertakings and does not therefore fulfil the essential function of a trade mark.[969]

While Article 3 TMD2008 specifies the circumstances in which a trade mark is incapable, *ab initio*, of fulfilling its function as an indication of origin, Article 12(2)(a) TMD2008 relates to the situation where the trade mark has become the common name and has therefore lost its distinctive character, with the result that it no longer fulfils that function.[970]

964. CJEU C-104/00 P of 19.9.2002 – DKV/OHIM, para. 29; C-212/07 P of 13.2.2008 – Indorata-Serviços e Gestão, para. 27; C-87/11 P of 21.3.2012 – Fidelio/OHIM, para. 72; C-21/12 P of 17.1.2013 – Abbott Laboratories/OHIM, para. 76; C-70/13 P of 12.12.2013 – Getty Images (US)/OHIM, para. 31; C-126/13 P of 10.7.2014 – BSH Bosch und Siemens Hausgeräte/OHIM, para. 33; C-232/15 P of 21.4.2016 – ultra air/EUIPO, para. 57; C-37/17 P of 31.5.2017 – Keil/EUIPO, paras 4/7 and 5; C-285/19 P of 6.11.2019 – Geske/EUIPO, paras 5/23 and 6.
965. CJEU C-363/99 of 12.2.2004 – Koninklijke KPN Nederland, paras 70 and 86.
966. CJEU C-363/99 of 12.2.2004 – Koninklijke KPN Nederland, para. 86; C-265/00 of 12.2.2004 – Campina Melkunie, para. 19; C-51/10 P of 10.3.2011 – Agencja Wydawnicza Technopol/ HABM, para. 46; C-90/11 and C-91/11 of 15.3.2012 – Strigl and Securvita, paras 21 and 39; C-307/11 P of 26.4.2012 – Deichmann/OHIM, para. 46; C-37/17 P of 31.5.2017 – Keil/EUIPO, paras 4/7 and 5; C-411/18 P of 3.10.2018 – Romantik Hotels & Restaurants/EUIPO, paras 4/6 and 5; C-214/19 P of 3.9.2020 – achtung!/EUIPO, para. 34.
967. CJEU C-214/19 P of 3.9.2020 – achtung!/EUIPO, para. 35.
968. CJEU C-51/10 P of 10.3.2011 – Agencja Wydawnicza Technopol/HABM, para. 46; C-307/11 P of 26.4.2012 – Deichmann/OHIM, para. 46; C-214/19 P of 3.9.2020 – achtung!/EUIPO, para. 36.
969. CJEU C-192/03 P of 5.10.2004 – ALCON/OHIM (I), para. 29; C-64/02 P of 21.10.2004 – OHIM/ERPO MÖBELWERK, para. 38.
970. CJEU C-409/12 of 6.3.2014 – Backaldrin Österreich The Kornspitz Company, para. 22; *see also* CJEU C-371/02 of 29.4.2004 – Björnekulla Fruktindustrier, para. 22.

With the exception of Article 3(1)(e) TMD2008, which exclusively covers signs for which registration is sought consisting of the shape of the goods and is thus irrelevant for the resolution of the dispute in the main proceedings, the provisions of Article 3(1) TMD2008, such as subparagraphs (b) and (c), make no explicit distinction between different categories of trade mark.[971] It follows that the assessment criteria that must be used by the competent authority when it applies the latter provisions to signs consisting of a design depicting the layout of a retail store do not differ from those used for other types of signs.[972]

The General Court rightly held that the removal from the register of a mark which is either descriptive or devoid of distinctive character is **not** the consequence of engaging in **unfair competition** in so far as such a mark should have been refused registration because there are absolute grounds for refusal vitiating it, but a consequence of trade mark law, laid down in Article 57(5) and (6) of CTMR.[973]

[1] Connection with goods or services

The distinctive character of a mark, including that acquired by use, must be assessed in relation to the goods or services in respect of which registration is applied for.[974]

971. *See* CJEU C-53/01 to C-55/01 of 8.4.2003 – Linde and Others, paras 43.
972. CJEU C-421/13 of 10.7.2014 – Apple, para. 24.
973. CJEU C-450/13 P of 19.6.2014 – Donaldson Filtration Deutschland/OHIM, para. 63.
974. CJEU C-299/99 of 18.6.2002 – Philips, para. 59; C-326/01 P of 5.2.2004 – Telefon & Buch/OHIM, para. 29; C-218/01 of 12.2.2004 – Henkel, para. 31; C-363/99 of 12.2.2004 – Koninklijke KPN Nederland, paras 71 and 75; C-456/01 P and C-457/01 P of 29.4.2004 – Henkel/OHIM, para. 35; C-468/01 P to C-472/01 P of 29.4.2004 – Procter & Gamble/OHIM (three-dimensional form of tablet I), para. 33; C-473/01 P and C-474/01 P of 29.4.2004 – Procter & Gamble/OHIM (three-dimensional form of tablet II), para. 33; C-445/02 P of 28.6.2004 – Glaverbel/OHIM, para. 20; C-404/02 of 16.9.2004 – Nichols, para. 23; C-107/03 P of 23.9.2004 – Procter & Gamble/OHIM (form of a soap), para. 29; C-136/02 P of 7.10.2004 – Mag Instrument/OHIM, para. 19; C-64/02 P of 21.10.2004 – OHIM/ERPO MÖBELWERK, para. 43; C-37/03 P of 15.9.2005 – BioID/OHIM, para. 48; C-173/04 P of 12.1.2006 – Deutsche SiSi-Werke/OHIM, para. 25; C-24/05 P of 22.6.2006 – Storck/OHIM (light-brown sweet), para. 23; C-25/05 P of 22.6.2006 – Storck/OHIM (gold-coloured sweet wrapper), para. 25; C-239/05 of 15.2.2007 – BVBA Management, Training en Consultancy, para. 31; C-144/06 P of 4.10.2007 – Henkel/OHIM, para. 35; C-238/06 P of 25.10.2007 – Develey Holding/OHIM, para. 79; C-304/06 P of 8.5.2008 – Eurohypo/OHIM, para. 67; C-17/08 P of 6.2.2009 – MPDV Mikrolab, para. 34; C-398/08 P of 21.1.2010 – Audi/OHIM, para. 34; C-265/09 P of 9.9.2010 – OHIM/BORCO-Marken-Import Matthiesen, paras 32 and 35; C-546/10 P of 13.9.2011 – Wilfer/OHIM, para. 52; C-344/10 P and C-345/10 P of 20.10.2011 – Freixenet/OHIM, para. 43; C-307/11 P of 26.4.2012 – Deichmann/OHIM, para. 50; C-98/11 P of 24.5.2012 – Chocoladefabriken Lindt & Sprüngli/OHIM, para. 41; C-311/11 P of 12.7.2012 – Smart Technologies/OHIM, para. 24; C-21/12 P of 17.1.2013 – Abbott Laboratories/OHIM, para. 69; C-97/12 P of 15.5.2014 – Louis Vuitton Malletier/OHIM, para. 50; C-368/14 P of 11.12.2014 – Compagnie des bateaux mooches/OHIM, para. 19; C-421/13 of 10.7.2014 – Apple, para. 22; C-521/13 P of 11.9.2014 – Think Schuhwerk/OHIM, para. 47; C-445/13 P of 7.5.2015 – Voss of Norway/OHIM, para. 89; C-278/15 P of 14.1.2016 – Royal County of Berkshire Polo Club/OHIM, para. 44; C-232/15 P of 21.4.2016 – ultra air/EUIPO, para. 34; C-417/16 P of 4.5.2017 – August Storck/EUIPO, para. 32; C-437/15 P of 17.5.2017 – EUIPO/Deluxe Entertainment Services Group, para. 28; C-139/16 of 6.7.2017 – Marín a.o./Abadía, para. 24; C-26/17 P of 13.9.2018 – Birkenstock Sales/EUIPO, para. 31; C-541/18 of 12.9.2019 – AS/Deutsches Patent- und Markenamt, para. 20; C-783/18 P of 12.12.2019 – EUIPO/Wajos, para. 23; C-214/19 P of 3.9.2020 – achtung!/EUIPO, para. 25;

It follows that if, on completion of the examination of a trade mark application, the competent authority finds, in the light of all the relevant facts and circumstances, that the average consumer of certain goods or services, reasonably well informed and reasonably attentive, perceives a mark as devoid of any distinctive character with regard to those goods or services, it must refuse to register the mark for those goods or services pursuant to Article 3(1)(b) TMD2008.[975]

However, it is of no relevance that the average consumer of other goods or services, reasonably well informed and reasonably observant, perceives the same mark as descriptive of the characteristics of those other goods or services for the purposes of Article 3(1)(c) TMD2008.[976]

It is correct to take account, for the purposes of assessing whether the goods and services concerned are homogeneous, in particular their characteristics, their essential qualities and their purposes.[977]

The mere fact that the goods and services concerned are within the same class of the **Nice Agreement is not sufficient** for a finding that such homogeneity exists, as those classes often contain a large variety of goods and services which are not necessarily interlinked in a sufficiently direct and specific way.[978]

In order to determine whether the goods and services covered by an application for registration of an EU mark are interlinked in a sufficiently direct and specific way and can be placed in sufficiently homogenous categories and groups, for the purposes of the case law cited in the previous paragraph, account must be taken of the fact that the objective of that exercise is to enable and facilitate the assessment *in concreto* of the question of whether or not the mark concerned by the application for registration comes under one of the absolute grounds for refusal.[979]

Accordingly, the placement of the goods and services at issue in one or more groups or categories must be carried out in particular on the basis of the characteristics which are common to them and which are relevant for the analysis of whether or not a specific absolute ground for refusal may apply to the mark applied for in respect of those goods and services. It follows that such an assessment must be carried out *in concreto* for the examination of each application for registration and, as the case may be, for each of the different absolute grounds for refusal which may apply.[980]

It follows from the foregoing considerations that it cannot be ruled out a priori that the goods and services covered by an application for registration all present a relevant characteristic for the analysis of an absolute ground for refusal and that they can be placed, for the purposes of examining the application for registration at issue in

C-456/19 of 8.10.2020 – Aktiebolaget Östgötatrafiken/Patent- och registreringsverket, para. 32; *see also* CJEU C-115/19 P of 11.6.2020 – China Construction Bank/EUIPO, para. 56.

975. CJEU C-363/99 of 12.2.2004 – Koninklijke KPN Nederland, para. 76.
976. CJEU C-363/99 of 12.2.2004 – Koninklijke KPN Nederland, para. 77.
977. CJEU C-282/09 P of 18.3.2010 – CFCMCEE/OHIM, para. 46.
978. CJEU C-282/09 P of 18.3.2010 – CFCMCEE/OHIM, para. 40; C-597/12 P of 17.10.2013 – Isdin/OHIM, para. 27; C-437/15 P of 17.5.2017 – EUIPO/Deluxe Entertainment Services Group, para. 31.
979. CJEU C-437/15 P of 17.5.2017 – EUIPO/Deluxe Entertainment Services Group, para. 32.
980. CJEU C-437/15 P of 17.5.2017 – EUIPO/Deluxe Entertainment Services Group, para. 33.

relation to that absolute ground for refusal, in a sufficiently homogenous single category or group.[981]

The Directive must be interpreted as meaning that it does not preclude national legislation which prevents the **court reviewing the decision** of the competent authority from ruling on the distinctive character of the mark separately for each of the individual goods and services specified in the trade mark application, where neither that decision nor that application related to categories of goods or services or goods or services considered separately.[982]

By way of a preliminary point, as is apparent from the third recital in the preamble thereto, the Directive is not intended to bring about full-scale approximation of the trade mark laws of the Member States but confines itself to approximating those national provisions of law which most directly affect the functioning of the internal market.[983]

Moreover, as set out in the fifth recital, the Directive gives the Member States extensive freedom to fix the provisions of procedure concerning, *inter alia*, the registration of trade marks, in particular with regard to the form of the registration procedure.[984]

According to settled case law, in the absence of Community legislation governing a particular aspect of a matter falling within the scope of Community law, it is for the domestic legal system of each Member State to lay down the detailed procedural rules governing court actions for safeguarding rights which individuals derive from Community law; such rules must not be less favourable than those governing similar domestic actions (principle of equivalence) and must not render virtually impossible or excessively difficult the exercise of rights conferred by Community law (principle of effectiveness).[985]

With regard to national legislation which prevents the court which is reviewing the decision of the competent authority from ruling on the distinctive character of the mark separately for each of the individual goods and services specified in the application for registration of that mark, where neither that application nor the decision of that authority relates to categories of goods or services or goods or services considered separately, such a limitation on the court's powers cannot be regarded as being contrary to the principle of effectiveness, especially since the party concerned may, following a decision that is wholly or partially unfavourable to that party, make a fresh application for registration of the mark. It is for the referring court, however, to determine whether those principles of equivalence and effectiveness have been observed.[986]

It also follows from the Court's case law that a court asked to review a decision on an application to register a trade mark must also have regard to all the relevant facts

981. CJEU C-437/15 P of 17.5.2017 – EUIPO/Deluxe Entertainment Services Group, para. 34.
982. CJEU C-239/05 of 15.2.2007 – BVBA Management, Training en Consultancy, para. 48.
983. CJEU C-239/05 of 15.2.2007 – BVBA Management, Training en Consultancy, para. 43.
984. CJEU C-239/05 of 15.2.2007 – BVBA Management, Training en Consultancy, para. 44.
985. CJEU C-239/05 of 15.2.2007 – BVBA Management, Training en Consultancy, para. 45.
986. CJEU C-239/05 of 15.2.2007 – BVBA Management, Training en Consultancy, para. 46.

and circumstances, subject to the limits on the exercise of its powers as defined by the relevant national legislation.[987]

It must be pointed out that the fact that a sign is devoid of any distinctive character in relation to **only some of the goods or services** within a category listed as such in the application for registration does not preclude that application from being refused or the sign in question from being declared invalid if it has already been registered, given that, in the opposite situation, nothing would preclude its proprietor from using it also for the goods or services of the category of goods for which its registration is sought, in respect of which it is not distinctive.[988]

[2] Relevant public

For the purposes of determining whether a sign is registrable as a trade mark it is necessary to take as a standpoint that of the relevant public.[989]

The average consumer is deemed to be reasonably well informed and reasonably observant and circumspect.[990]

---

987. CJEU C-239/05 of 15.2.2007 – BVBA Management, Training en Consultancy, para. 47, 58.
988. CJEU C-97/12 P of 15.5.2014 – Louis Vuitton Malletier/OHIM, para. 94.
989. CJEU C-104/01 of 6.5.2003 – Libertel, para. 45; C-456/01 P and C-457/01 P of 29.4.2004 – Henkel/OHIM, para. 35; C-468/01 P to C-472/01 P of 29.4.2004 – Procter & Gamble/OHIM (three-dimensional form of tablet I), para. 33; C-473/01 P and C-474/01 P of 29.4.2004 – Procter & Gamble/OHIM (three-dimensional form of tablet II), para. 33; C-329/02 P of 16.9.2004 – SAT.1 SATELLITENFERNSEHEN/OHIM, para. 24; C-404/02 of 16.9.2004 – Nichols, para. 23; C-107/03 P of 23.9.2004 – Procter & Gamble/OHIM (Form of a soap), para. 29; C-136/02 P of 7.10.2004 – Mag Instrument/OHIM, para. 19; C-64/02 P of 21.10.2004 – OHIM/ERPO MÖBELWERK, para. 43; C-37/03 P of 15.9.2005 – BioID/OHIM, para. 28, 48; C-173/04 P of 12.1.2006 – Deutsche SiSi-Werke/OHIM, para. 25; C-24/05 P of 22.6.2006 – Storck/OHIM (light-brown sweet), para. 23; C-25/05 P of 22.6.2006 – Storck/OHIM (gold-coloured sweet wrapper), para. 25; C-144/06 P of 4.10.2007 – Henkel/OHIM, para. 35; C-238/06 P of 25.10.2007 – Develey Holding/OHIM, para. 79; C-304/06 P of 8.5.2008 – Eurohypo/OHIM, para. 67; C-398/08 P of 21.1.2010 – Audi/OHIM, para. 34; C-265/09 P of 9.9.2010 – OHIM/BORCO-Marken-Import Matthiesen, para. 32; C-546/10 P of 13.9.2011 – Wilfer/OHIM, para. 52; C-307/11 P of 26.4.2012 – Deichmann/OHIM, para. 50; C-98/11 P of 24.5.2012 – Chocoladefabriken Lindt & Sprüngli/OHIM, para. 41; C-311/11 P of 12.7.2012 – Smart Technologies/OHIM, paras 24 and 51; C-21/12 P of 17.1.2013 – Abbott Laboratories/OHIM, para. 69; C-97/12 P of 15.5.2014 – Louis Vuitton Malletier/OHIM, para. 50; C-421/13 of 10.7.2014 – Apple, para. 22; C-521/13 P of 11.9.2014 – Think Schuhwerk/OHIM, para. 47; C-368/14 P of 11.12.2014 – Compagnie des bateaux mooches/OHIM, para. 19; C-445/13 P of 7.5.2015 – Voss of Norway/OHIM, para. 89; C-232/15 P of 21.4.2016 – ultra air/EUIPO, para. 34; C-139/16 of 6.7.2017 – Marín a.o./Abadía, para. 24; C-541/18 of 12.9.2019 – AS/Deutsches Patent- und Markenamt, para. 20; C-783/18 P of 12.12.2019 – EUIPO/Wajos, para. 23; C-214/19 P of 3.9.2020 – achtung!/EUIPO, para. 25; C-456/19 of 8.10.2020 – Aktiebolaget Östgötatrafiken/Patent- och registreringsverket, para. 32; *see also* above Preamble 'Relevant classes of persons'.
990. CJEU C-25/05 P of 22.6.2006 – Storck/OHIM (gold-coloured sweet wrapper), para. 25; C-307/11 P of 26.4.2012 – Deichmann/OHIM, para. 50; also *see* CJEU C-251/95 of 11.11.1997 – SABEL/Puma, Rudolf Dassler Sport, para. 23; C-342/97 of 22.6.1999 – Lloyd Schuhfabrik Meyer, para. 25, 26; C-3/03 P of 28.4.2004 – Matratzen Concord/OHIM, para. 29; C-361/04 P of 12.1.2006 – Ruiz-Picasso and Others/OHIM, para. 36; C-235/05 P of 27.4.2006 – L'Oréal/OHIM, para. 41; C-334/05 P of 12.6.2007 – OHIM/Shaker, para. 35; C-412/05 P of 26.4.2007 – Alcon/OHIM (II), para. 59, 62; C-193/06 P of 20.9.2007 – Nestlé/OHIM, para. 34; C-108/07 P of 17.4.2008 – Ferrero Deutschland/OHIM, para. 46; C-353/09 P of 15.2.2011 – Perfetti Van

[3] Relevant territory

Under Article 7(2) CTMR, paragraph 1 of that article is to apply notwithstanding that the grounds of non-registrability obtain in only part of the European Union. It follows that, *inter alia*, a mark must be refused registration even if it is descriptive of the goods or services concerned only in one of the official languages of the European Union.[991]

The General Court held that the Board of Appeal could not be criticized for having relied on websites from English-speaking countries outside the EU, on the ground that, while there are some differences of vocabulary between United Kingdom and American English, it is well known that words and expressions have identical connotations in these two variants of the English language. The General Court also noted that the appellant had not put forward any valid argument showing that this is not the case for the word 'memory'.[992]

It follows that the General Court referred to that evidence not for territorial reasons or in order to establish the situation of the mark at issue on the English-speaking markets of countries outside the EU, but only for purely linguistic reasons, in order to demonstrate the possible uses of the word 'memory' in English.[993]

In those circumstances, the General Court cannot be validly criticized for having referred to that evidence in order to assess the semantic content of the word 'memory' in the English-speaking territory of the EU.[994]

[4] Overall impression

In order to assess whether or not a trade mark has any distinctive character, the overall impression given by it must be considered.[995]

The descriptive character of a mark comprising **several words**, such as that at issue in the present case, may be assessed, in part, in relation to each of its terms, taken separately, but must, in any event, also be established in relation to the whole which they comprise.[996]

As regards a trade mark comprising words or a word and a digit the distinctiveness of each of those terms or elements, taken separately, may be assessed, in part, but

Melle/OHIM, para. 48; C-421/13 of 10.7.2014 – Apple, para. 22; C-308/13 P and C-309/13 P of 18.9.2014 – Società Italiana Calzature/OHIM, para. 41.

991. CJEU C-104/00 P of 19.9.2002 – DKV/OHIM, para. 40; C-728/18 P of 25.9.2019 – EM Research Organization/EUIPO, paras 4/61 and 5.
992. CJEU C-369/10 P of 14.3.2011 – Ravensburger/OHIM, para. 72.
993. CJEU C-369/10 P of 14.3.2011 – Ravensburger/OHIM, para. 72.
994. CJEU C-369/10 P of 14.3.2011 – Ravensburger/OHIM, para. 72.
995. CJEU C-468/01 P to C-472/01 P of 29.4.2004 – Procter & Gamble/OHIM (three-dimensional form of tablet I), para. 44; C-473/01 P and C-474/01 P of 29.4.2004 – Procter & Gamble/OHIM (three-dimensional form of tablet II), para. 44; C-136/02 P of 7.10.2004 – Mag Instrument/OHIM, para. 20; C-286/04 P of 30.6.2005 – Eurocermex/OHIM, para. 22; C-144/06 P of 4.10.2007 – Henkel/OHIM, para. 39; C-238/06 P of 25.10.2007 – Develey Holding/OHIM, para. 82; C-311/11 P of 12.7.2012 – Smart Technologies/OHIM, para. 49; C-520/17 P of 30.11.2017 – C-cen-tek/EUIPO, paras 6/14 and 7.
996. CJEU C-17/08 P of 6.2.2009 – MPDV Mikrolab, para. 38; C-520/08 P of 24.9.2009 – HUP Uslugi Polska, para. 30; C-494/08 P of 9.12.2009 – Prana Haus/HABM, para. 42.

must, in any event, depend on an appraisal of the whole which they comprise. Indeed, the mere fact that each of those elements, considered separately, is devoid of distinctive character does not mean that their combination cannot present a distinctive character.[997]

It must be borne in mind that the Court has already held, regarding a **three-dimensional sign**, that whether that sign has distinctive character may be assessed, in part, in relation to each of its elements taken separately, but must, in any event, be based on the overall perception of that mark by the relevant public and not on the presumption that elements that are individually devoid of distinctive character cannot, on being combined, have such character.[998]

As regards trade marks composed of words descriptiveness must be determined not only in relation to each word taken separately but also in relation to the whole which they form.[999]

That does not mean, however, that the competent authority, responsible for ascertaining whether the trade mark for which registration is sought is capable of being perceived by the public as an indication of origin, may not first examine each of the individual features of the get-up of that mark in turn. It may be useful, in the course of the competent authority's overall assessment, to examine each of the components of which the trade mark concerned is composed.[1000]

As a general rule, a mere **combination of elements**, each of which is descriptive of characteristics of the goods or services in respect of which registration is sought, itself remains descriptive of those characteristics for the purposes of Article 3(1)(c) TMD2008. Merely bringing those elements together without introducing any unusual variations, in particular as to syntax or meaning, cannot result in anything other than a mark consisting exclusively of signs or indications which may serve, in trade, to designate characteristics of the goods or services concerned.[1001]

---

997. CJEU C-329/02 P of 16.9.2004 - SAT.1 SATELLITENFERNSEHEN/OHIM, para. 28; C-37/03 P of 15.9.2005 - BioID/OHIM, para. 29; C-273/05 P of 19.4.2007 - OHIM/Celltech, para. 79; C-304/06 P of 8.5.2008 - Eurohypo/OHIM, para. 41; C-92/10 P of 13.1.2011 - Media-Saturn-Holding/OHIM, para. 36; C-56/10 P of 22.6.2011 - Agencja Wydawnicza Technopol/HABM, para. 41; C-90/11 and C-91/11 of 15.3.2012 - Strigl and Securvita, para. 23; C-453/11 P of 14.5.2012 - Timehouse/OHIM, para. 40; C-70/13 P of 12.12.2013 - Getty Images (US)/OHIM, para. 24; C-445/13 P of 7.5.2015 - Voss of Norway/OHIM, para. 124.
998. CJEU C-445/13 P of 7.5.2015 - Voss of Norway/OHIM, para. 124.
999. CJEU C-383/99 P of 20.9.2001 - Procter & Gamble/OHIM (baby-dry), para. 40; C-363/99 of 12.2.2004 - Koninklijke KPN Nederland, para. 96; C-265/00 of 12.2.2004 - Campina Melkunie, para. 37; C-329/02 P of 16.9.2004 - SAT.1 SATELLITENFERNSEHEN/OHIM, para. 28; C-273/05 P of 19.4.2007 - OHIM/Celltech, para. 76; C-622/13 P of 30.4.2015 - Castel Frères/EUIPO, paras 71.
1000. CJEU C-468/01 P to C-472/01 P of 29.4.2004 - Procter & Gamble/OHIM (three-dimensional form of tablet I), para. 45; C-473/01 P and C-474/01 P of 29.4.2004 - Procter & Gamble/OHIM (three-dimensional form of tablet II), para. 45; C-329/02 P of 16.9.2004 - SAT.1 SATELLITENFERNSEHEN/OHIM, para. 28; C-286/04 P of 30.6.2005 - Eurocermex/OHIM, para. 23; C-37/03 P of 15.9.2005 - BioID/OHIM, para. 31; C-144/06 P of 4.10.2007 - Henkel/OHIM, para. 39; C-238/06 P of 25.10.2007 - Develey Holding/OHIM, para. 82; C-445/13 P of 7.5.2015 - Voss of Norway/OHIM, para. 106.
1001. CJEU C-363/99 of 12.2.2004 - Koninklijke KPN Nederland, para. 98; C-265/00 of 12.2.2004 - Campina Melkunie, para. 39; C-273/05 P of 19.4.2007 - OHIM/Celltech, para. 77; C-408/08 P

However, such a combination may not be descriptive within the meaning of Article 3(1)(c) TMD2008, provided that it creates an impression which is sufficiently far removed from that produced by the simple combination of those elements.[1002]

It does not follow from the Court's case law that the prior analysis of each of the elements of which a mark is composed is an essential step. On the contrary, OHIM's Boards of Appeal and, where an action is brought, the Court of First Instance are required to assess the descriptiveness of the mark, considered as a whole.[1003]

In *SAT.1 v. OHIM,* concerning an application for a Community trade mark in respect of the term 'SAT.2', the Court set aside the judgment of the Court of First Instance in Case T-323/00 *SAT.1 v. OHIM(SAT.2),* on the ground that, in order to justify refusal of registration of that term, that Court had based itself on the presumption that elements individually devoid of distinctive character cannot, on being combined, present such a character. The Court of First Instance had thus examined the impression as a whole produced by that term only as a secondary matter, refusing to attribute any relevance to aspects such as the existence of a fanciful element, which ought to be taken into account in such an analysis.[1004]

Word combinations like BABY-DRY cannot therefore be regarded as exhibiting, as a whole, descriptive character; they are lexical inventions bestowing distinctive power on the mark so formed and may not be refused registration under Article 7(1)(c) CTMR.[1005]

As it is, that word combination, whilst it does unquestionably allude to the function which the goods are supposed to fulfil, still does not satisfy the disqualifying criteria. Whilst each of the two words in the combination may form part of expressions used in everyday speech to designate the function of babies' nappies, their syntactically unusual juxtaposition is not a familiar expression in the English language, either for designating babies' nappies or for describing their essential characteristics.[1006]

[5] Visual, aural or conceptual impression

However, a combination may not be descriptive within the meaning of Article 3(1)(c) TMD2008, provided that it creates an impression which is sufficiently far removed from that produced by the simple combination of its elements. In the case of a word mark,

of 25.2.2010 – Lancôme parfums et beauté & Cie/OHIM, para. 61; *see also* CJEU C-494/08 P of 9.12.2009 – Prana Haus/HABM, para. 38.

1002. CJEU C-363/99 of 12.2.2004 – Koninklijke KPN Nederland, paras 99 and 104; C-265/00 of 12.2.2004 – Campina Melkunie, para. 43; C-273/05 P of 19.4.2007 – OHIM/Celltech, para. 78; *see also* CJEU C-37/03 P of 15.9.2005 – BioID/OHIM, para. 34; C-408/08 P of 25.2.2010 – Lancôme parfums et beauté & Cie/OHIM, paras 61 et seq.

1003. CJEU C-273/05 P of 19.4.2007 – OHIM/Celltech, para. 80; C-67/21 P of 12.5.2021 – BSH Hausgeräte/EUIPO, para. 17.

1004. CJEU C-37/03 P of 15.9.2005 – BioID/OHIM, para. 30.

1005. CJEU C-383/99 P of 20.9.2001 – Procter & Gamble/OHIM (baby-dry), para. 44.

1006. CJEU C-383/99 P of 20.9.2001 – Procter & Gamble/OHIM (baby-dry), para. 43.

which is intended to be heard as much as to be read, that condition must be satisfied as regards both the aural and the visual impression produced by the mark.[1007]

[6] Public interest

The various grounds for refusal of registration listed in Article 3 TMD2008 must be interpreted in the light of the public interest underlying each of them.[1008]

The public interest taken into account in the examination of each of those grounds for refusal may, or even must, reflect different considerations, depending upon which ground for refusal is at issue.[1009]

It is not Article 8(1)(b) CTMR but Articles 7(1)(b) and (c) and 51 CTMR and Article 3(1)(b) and (c) TMD2008 which are intended to avoid such monopolization.[1010]

[7] Stringent and full examination

The practice of a trade mark registration authority which concentrates solely on refusing to register manifestly inadmissible marks is incompatible with Article 3 TMD2008.[1011]

In that regard, it is appropriate to observe that although the third recital in the preamble to the Directive states that the full-scale approximation of the trade mark laws of the Member States does not appear necessary at present, the seventh recital makes clear that the conditions for obtaining and continuing to hold a registered trade mark are, in general, identical in all the Member States and that, to that end, the grounds for refusal of registration concerning the trade mark itself are listed exhaustively in the Directive.[1012]

1007. CJEU C-363/99 of 12.2.2004 – Koninklijke KPN Nederland, para. 99; C-265/00 of 12.2.2004 – Campina Melkunie, para. 40.
1008. CJEU C-299/99 of 18.6.2002 – Philips, para. 77; C-53/01 to C-55/01 of 8.4.2003 – Linde and Others, para. 71; C-104/01 of 6.5.2003 – Libertel, para. 51; C-363/99 of 12.2.2004 – Koninklijke KPN Nederland, paras 68 and 94; C-265/00 of 12.2.2004 – Campina Melkunie, para. 34; C-456/01 P and C-457/01 P of 29.4.2004 – Henkel/OHIM, para. 45; C-49/02 of 24.6.2004 – Heidelberger Bauchemie, para. 41; C-329/02 P of 16.9.2004 – SAT.1 SATELLITENFERNSEHEN/OHIM, para. 25; C-37/03 P of 15.9.2005 – BioID/OHIM, para. 59; C-173/04 P of 12.1.2006 – Deutsche SiSi-Werke/OHIM, para. 59; C-273/05 P of 19.4.2007 – OHIM/Celltech, para. 74; C-304/06 P of 8.5.2008 – Eurohypo/OHIM, para. 55; C-48/09 P of 14.9.2010 – Lego Juris/OHIM, para. 43; C-51/10 P of 10.3.2011 – Agencja Wydawnicza Technopol/HABM, para. 36; C-90/11 and C-91/11 of 15.3.2012 – Strigl and Securvita, para. 22; C-337/12 P to C-340/12 P of 6.3.2014 – Pi-Design/OHIM, para. 44; C-205/13 of 18.9.2014 – Hauck, para. 17; C-215/14 of 16.9.2015 – Société des Produits Nestlé, para. 43; C-30/15 P of 10.11.2016 – Simba Toys/EUIPO, para. 38.
1009. CJEU C-456/01 P and C-457/01 P of 29.4.2004 – Henkel/OHIM, para. 46; C-329/02 P of 16.9.2004 – SAT.1 SATELLITENFERNSEHEN/OHIM, para. 25; C-37/03 P of 15.9.2005 – BioID/OHIM, para. 59; C-173/04 P of 12.1.2006 – Deutsche SiSi-Werke/OHIM, para. 59; C-304/06 P of 8.5.2008 – Eurohypo/OHIM, para. 55; C-90/11 and C-91/11 of 15.3.2012 – Strigl and Securvita, para. 22.
1010. CJEU C-43/15 P of 8.11.2016 – BSH Bosch und Siemens Hausgeräte/EUIPO, para. 65.
1011. CJEU C-363/99 of 12.2.2004 – Koninklijke KPN Nederland, para. 126.
1012. CJEU C-363/99 of 12.2.2004 – Koninklijke KPN Nederland, para. 122; *see also* CJEU C-421/04 of 9.3.2006 – Matratzen Concord, para. 19.

In addition, the scheme of the Directive is founded on review prior to registration, even though it also makes provision for ex post facto review. The examination of the grounds for refusal listed in Article 3 TMD2008 in particular, which takes place when registration is applied for, must be thorough and full in order to ensure that trade marks are not improperly registered.[1013]

The examination of trade mark applications must **not** be **minimal**, but must be **stringent and full**, in order to prevent trade marks from being improperly registered and, for reasons of legal certainty and good administration, to ensure that trade marks whose use could be successfully challenged before the courts are not registered.[1014]

Therefore, the competent authority within a Member State must refuse to register any mark caught by one of the grounds for refusal laid down by the Directive, in particular in Article 3 TMD2008.[1015]

The very objective of an a priori review would be thwarted if, despite the requirement, recalled in paragraph 39 above, to carry out an examination, based on the facts, of the distinctive character of the mark applied for, it was open to OHIM, without relevant justification, to rely on conjecture or mere doubts.[1016]

Article 3 TMD2008 does not distinguish between marks which cannot be registered and those which manifestly cannot be registered. Consequently, the competent authority cannot register marks caught by one of the grounds for refusal listed in that article on the ground that the marks are not manifestly inadmissible.[1017]

A trade mark registration authority must have regard, in addition to the mark as filed, to **all the relevant facts and circumstances**. It must have regard to all the relevant facts and circumstances before adopting a final decision on an application to register a trade mark. A court asked to review a decision on an application to register a trade mark must also have regard to all the relevant facts and circumstances, subject to the limits on the exercise of its powers as defined by the relevant national legislation.[1018]

As regards the question whether a competent authority must have regard to all the relevant facts and circumstances when examining a trade mark application, it is appropriate to point out, first, that the twelfth recital in the preamble to the Directive

1013. CJEU C-363/99 of 12.2.2004 – Koninklijke KPN Nederland, para. 123; C-64/02 P of 21.10.2004 – OHIM/ERPO MÖBELWERK, para. 45; C-239/05 of 15.2.2007 – BVBA Management, Training en Consultancy, para. 30; C-54/10 P and C-55/10 P of 22.6.2011 – Agencja Wydawnicza Technopol/HABM, para. 42; C-56/10 P of 22.6.2011 – Agencja Wydawnicza Technopol/HABM, paras 36 and 65; *see also* CJEU C-51/10 P of 10.3.2011 – Agencja Wydawnicza Technopol/HABM, paras 61 and 77.

1014. CJEU C-265/09 P of 9.9.2010 – OHIM/BORCO-Marken-Import Matthiesen, para. 45; C-521/13 P of 11.9.2014 – Think Schuhwerk/OHIM, para. 57; C-437/15 P of 17.5.2017 – EUIPO/Deluxe Entertainment Services Group, para. 27, with reference to CJEU C-104/01 of 6.5.2003 – Libertel, para. 59; C-541/18 of 12.9.2019 – AS/Deutsches Patent- und Markenamt, para. 28; *see also* CJEU C-564/16 P of 28.6.2018 – EUIPO/Puma, para. 61.

1015. CJEU C-363/99 of 12.2.2004 – Koninklijke KPN Nederland, para. 124.

1016. CJEU C-265/09 P of 9.9.2010 – OHIM/BORCO-Marken-Import Matthiesen, para. 46.

1017. CJEU C-363/99 of 12.2.2004 – Koninklijke KPN Nederland, para. 125.

1018. CJEU C-363/99 of 12.2.2004 – Koninklijke KPN Nederland, para. 37; C-239/05 of 15.2.2007 – BVBA Management, Training en Consultancy, para. 58; *see also* CJEU C-49/02 of 24.6.2004 – Heidelberger Bauchemie, para. 41.

states that all Member States of the Community are bound by the Paris Convention for the Protection of Industrial Property and that it is necessary that the provisions of this Directive are entirely consistent with those of the Paris Convention.[1019]

Article 6 *quinquies* C(1) of the Paris Convention provides that in determining whether a mark is eligible for protection, all the factual circumstances must be taken into consideration, particularly the length of time the mark has been in use.[1020]

Second, when the competent authority examines a trade mark application and, for that purpose, must determine, *inter alia*, whether or not the mark is devoid of any distinctive character, whether or not it is descriptive of the characteristics of the goods or services concerned and whether or not it has become generic, it **cannot carry out the examination in the abstract**.[1021]

In the course of that examination, it is for the competent authority to have regard to the characteristics peculiar to the mark for which registration is sought, including the type of mark (word mark, figurative mark, etc.) and, in the case of a word mark, its meaning, in order to ascertain whether or not any of the grounds for refusal set out in Article 3 TMD2008 apply to the mark.[1022]

In its assessment, the competent authority has regard to all the relevant facts and circumstances, including, where appropriate, the results of any study submitted by the applicant seeking to establish, for example, that the mark is not devoid of any distinctive character or is not misleading.[1023]

Documents, although published **outside the European Union**, may support the conclusion that the target public regarded a term as having become customary.[1024]

Where the applicable national law provides that the exclusive right conferred by registration, by a competent authority in an area in which **a number of officially recognized languages coexist**, of a word mark expressed in one of those languages extends automatically to its translation in the other languages, the authority must ascertain as regards each of those translations whether the mark actually consists exclusively of signs or indications which may serve, in trade, to designate characteristics of those goods or services.[1025]

The Directive is to be interpreted as meaning that it does not preclude national legislation which prevents the court reviewing a decision of the competent authority from taking account of **facts and circumstances which arose after that decision had been taken**.[1026]

In such proceedings, as the Commission has rightly observed, the national courts must rule on the lawfulness of a given decision of the competent authority. That

1019. CJEU C-363/99 of 12.2.2004 – Koninklijke KPN Nederland, para. 29.
1020. CJEU C-363/99 of 12.2.2004 – Koninklijke KPN Nederland, para. 30.
1021. CJEU C-363/99 of 12.2.2004 – Koninklijke KPN Nederland, para. 31; C-578/17 of 27.3.2019 – Oy Hartwall/Patentti- ja rekisterihallitus, para. 27; *see also* CJEU C-421/13 of 10.7.2014 – Apple, para. 23.
1022. CJEU C-363/99 of 12.2.2004 – Koninklijke KPN Nederland, para. 32; *see also* CJEU C-421/13 of 10.7.2014 – Apple, para. 23.
1023. CJEU C-363/99 of 12.2.2004 – Koninklijke KPN Nederland, para. 35.
1024. CJEU C-192/03 P of 5.10.2004 – ALCON/OHIM (I), para. 42.
1025. CJEU C-363/99 of 12.2.2004 – Koninklijke KPN Nederland, para. 61.
1026. CJEU C-239/05 of 15.2.2007 – BVBA Management, Training en Consultancy, para. 61.

decision could have been taken only on the basis of the facts and circumstances of which it was possible for that authority to be aware at the time when it reached that decision.[1027]

It must therefore be concluded that a national legal order may prevent the court reviewing a decision of the competent authority from taking account of facts and circumstances subsequent to that decision in order to determine whether that decision was lawful.[1028]

[8] Material date

The **date of filing the application** for registration of the Community trade mark is the material date for that examination.[1029]

With regard to a refusal to register a trade mark, the date on which the application for registration of that trade mark was made is determinative for the purposes of identifying the applicable substantive law.[1030]

Regarding the decision *Alcon/OHIM*, it must be stated that the time of registration alone is relevant for the assessment of an application for revocation based on Article 51(1)(a) CTMR.[1031]

In the legal proceedings in which the decision *Alcon/OHIM* was reached, the Court of Justice was namely concerned with a plea for revocation in which it was asserted that, by taking into account evidence from the time after the registration of the Community trade mark in question, the General Court had made an error of law and in so doing, did not rely on the time of registration for the assessment of whether this trade mark was common and, pursuant to this, whether the trade mark could be revoked according to Article 51(1)(a) CTMR. However, in paragraph 40 of this decision, the Court of Justice stated that OHIM had correctly declared that the time of registration of the Community trade mark was the decisive factor for this assessment.[1032]

Moreover, the Court of First Instance could without inconsistency in its reasoning or error of law take account of material which, although subsequent to the date of filing the application, enabled the drawing of conclusions on the situation as it was on that date.[1033]

1027. CJEU C-239/05 of 15.2.2007 – BVBA Management, Training en Consultancy, para. 59.
1028. CJEU C-239/05 of 15.2.2007 – BVBA Management, Training en Consultancy, para. 60.
1029. CJEU C-192/03 P of 5.10.2004 – ALCON/OHIM (I), para. 40; C-78/09 P of 24.9.2009 – Compagnie des bateaux mouches/OHIM, para. 18; C-332/09 P of 23.4.2010 – OHIM/Frosch Touristik, paras 39 et seq.; C-5/10 P of 16.5.2011 – Torresan/OHIM, para. 84; C-337/12 P to C-340/12 P of 6.3.2014 – Pi-Design/OHIM, para. 59.
1030. CJEU C-456/19 of 8.10.2020 – Aktiebolaget Östgötatrafiken/Patent- och registreringsverket, para. 28, with reference to CJEU C-371/18 of 29.1.2020 – Sky a.o./SkyKick UK a.o., para. 49; *see also* CJEU C-21/18 of 14.3.2019 – Textilis a.o./Svenskt Tenn, paras 29 et seqq.
1031. CJEU C-332/09 P of 23.4.2010 – OHIM/Frosch Touristik, para. 41; unofficial translation.
1032. CJEU C-332/09 P of 23.4.2010 – OHIM/Frosch Touristik, para. 42; unofficial translation.
1033. CJEU C-192/03 P of 5.10.2004 – ALCON/OHIM (I), para. 41; C-332/09 P of 23.4.2010 – OHIM/Frosch Touristik, para. 43; C-5/10 P of 16.5.2011 – Torresan/OHIM, para. 84; C-337/12

The fact that the Court of Justice clarified this point in paragraph 41 of the decision confirms that, for the assessment pursuant to Article 51(1)(a) CTMR, the time of registration of the Community trade mark is decisive. For if circumstances after this point in time could be taken into account in the assessment of the absolute grounds for revocation, such a clarification would have been superfluous.[1034]

Second, with respect to the validity of the consideration regarding the duration of the registration process and the parallels between Article 51(1)(a) and Article 7(3) CTMR, only with such an interpretation of Article 51(1)(a) CTMR can it be avoided that a loss of registrability of a trade mark becomes more and more probable, the longer the registration process takes.[1035]

Thus if it is also correct that the duration of the registration process is influenced by numerous factors, then it is dependent above all on the various legal remedies provided in the CTMR such as those of the opposition proceedings, the appeal before the Board of Appeal, the main case proceedings before the European General Court and of the legal remedy before the European Court of Justice. Therefore, by the time these remedies have been completely exhausted and the registration of the Community trade mark has acquired definitive character, the registration proceedings can take several years.[1036]

In this connection, it must be noted that according to Article 9(3) CTMR, the rights from a Community trade mark can only be conferred on third parties after the publication of the registration of the mark, so that until this time, the registrant of the mark has no rights which can be applied to prohibit or hinder the mark from becoming a common generic name.[1037]

Incidentally, in Article 50 CTMR, a mechanism is set up which will provide a legal sanction for any loss of registrability that might have occurred after the application for a trade mark, thereby protecting general interest, namely the declaration of revocation of a Community trade mark. In particular, it must be emphasized that according to Article 50(1)(b) CTMR, a Community trade mark will be declared to be revoked if, due to the behaviour or the inactivity of its owner, it has become a common name for any goods or services for which it has been registered.[1038]

This provision which has been set by the legal entities of the Community makes it possible to stay abreast of changes which could arise during the registration process. OHIM's argument that the Court places the interests of the individual over and above the general interest and disregards any developments occurring after the point of application cannot therefore be accepted.[1039]

P to C-340/12 P of 6.3.2014 – Pi-Design/OHIM, para. 60; C-326/18 P of 4.10.2018 – Safe Skies/EUIPO, paras 5/7 et seq. and 6; *see also* CJEU C-488/06 P of 17.7.2008 – L & D/OHIM, para. 71.

1034. CJEU C-332/09 P of 23.4.2010 – OHIM/Frosch Touristik, para. 44; unofficial translation.
1035. CJEU C-332/09 P of 23.4.2010 – OHIM/Frosch Touristik, para. 47; unofficial translation.
1036. CJEU C-332/09 P of 23.4.2010 – OHIM/Frosch Touristik, para. 48; unofficial translation.
1037. CJEU C-332/09 P of 23.4.2010 – OHIM/Frosch Touristik, para. 49; unofficial translation.
1038. CJEU C-332/09 P of 23.4.2010 – OHIM/Frosch Touristik, para. 50; unofficial translation.
1039. CJEU C-332/09 P of 23.4.2010 – OHIM/Frosch Touristik, para. 51; unofficial translation.

[B] Signs which cannot constitute a trade mark

Under Article 3(1)(a) TMD2008, signs which cannot constitute a trade mark are not to be registered or if registered are liable to be declared invalid. That provision thus precludes the registration of signs which do not meet the conditions imposed by Article 2 TMD2008, the purpose of which is to define the types of signs of which a trade mark may consist.[1040]

[C] No distinctive character

[1] Principles

As the grounds for refusal or invalidity set out in Article 3(1)(b) and (c) **TMD2008** are **identical** to the grounds for refusal referred to in Article 7(1)(b) and (c) **CTMR**, the case law of the Court relating to those regulations is applicable to the provisions of the directive which are at issue in the disputes in the main proceedings.[1041]

The fact that a sign is, in general, capable of constituting a trade mark within the meaning of Article 4 CTMR does not mean that the sign necessarily has distinctive character for the purposes of Article 7(1)(b) CTMR in relation to a specific product or service.[1042]

For a mark to possess **distinctive character** within the meaning of that provision, it must serve to identify the product in respect of which registration is applied for as **originating** from a particular undertaking, and thus to distinguish that product from products of other undertakings.[1043]

1040. CJEU C-321/03 of 25.1.2007 – Dyson, para. 25.

1041. CJEU C-90/11 and C-91/11 of 15.3.2012 – Strigl and Securvita, para. 19; C-541/18 of 12.9.2019 – AS/Deutsches Patent- und Markenamt, para. 32.

1042. CJEU C-456/01 P and C-457/01 P of 29.4.2004 – Henkel/OHIM, para. 32; C-468/01 P to C-472/01 P of 29.4.2004 – Procter & Gamble/OHIM (three-dimensional form of tablet I), para. 30; C-473/01 P and C-474/01 P of 29.4.2004 – Procter & Gamble/OHIM (three-dimensional form of tablet II), para. 30; C-265/09 P of 9.9.2010 – OHIM/BORCO-Marken-Import Matthiesen, para. 29; C-217/13 and 218/13 of 19.6.2014 – Oberbank, para. 37; C-421/13 of 10.7.2014 – Apple, para. 21.

1043. CJEU C-53/01 to C-55/01 of 8.4.2003 – Linde and Others, para. 40; C-104/01 of 6.5.2003 – Libertel, para. 62; C-218/01 of 12.2.2004 – Henkel, para. 48; C-456/01 P and C-457/01 P of 29.4.2004 – Henkel/OHIM, para. 34; C-468/01 P to C-472/01 P of 29.4.2004 – Procter & Gamble/OHIM (three-dimensional form of tablet I), para. 32; C-473/01 P and C-474/01 P of 29.4.2004 – Procter & Gamble/OHIM (three-dimensional form of tablet II), para. 32; C-107/03 P of 23.9.2004 – Procter & Gamble/OHIM (form of a soap), para. 28; C-136/02 P of 7.10.2004 – Mag Instrument/OHIM, paras 29 and 46; C-64/02 P of 21.10.2004 – OHIM/ERPO MÖBELWERK, paras 33 and 42; C-329/02 P of 16.9.2004 – SAT.1 SATELLITENFERNSEHEN/OHIM, para. 23; C-353/03 of 7.7.2005 – Nestlé, para. 22; C-37/03 P of 15.9.2005 – BioID/OHIM, para. 27; C-173/04 P of 12.1.2006 – Deutsche SiSi-Werke/OHIM, para. 45; C-144/06 P of 4.10.2007 – Henkel/OHIM, para. 34; C-238/06 P of 25.10.2007 – Develey Holding/OHIM, para. 79; C-304/06 P of 8.5.2008 – Eurohypo/OHIM, para. 66; C-398/08 P of 21.1.2010 – Audi/OHIM, para. 33; C-265/09 P of 9.9.2010 – OHIM/BORCO-Marken-Import Matthiesen, para. 31; C-546/10 P of 13.9.2011 – Wilfer/OHIM, para. 52; C-344/10 P and C-345/10 P of 20.10.2011 – Freixenet/OHIM, para. 42; C-307/11 P of 26.4.2012 – Deichmann/OHIM, para. 49; C-306/11 P of 28.6.2012 – XXXLutz Marken/OHIM, para. 64; C-311/11 P of 12.7.2012 – Smart

In that connection, regard must be had both to the ordinary use of trade marks as a badge of origin in the sectors concerned and to the perception of the relevant public.[1044]

It is not appropriate to limit the scope of Article 7(1)(b) CTMR to trade marks for which registration is refused on the basis of Article 7(1)(d) thereof by reason of the fact that they are commonly used in business communications and, in particular, in advertising.[1045]

In order to contribute to the assessment of the distinctiveness of a mark for the purposes of Article 7(1)(b) CTMR, that **evidence** must show that consumers did not need to become accustomed to the mark through the use made of it, but that it immediately enabled them to distinguish the goods or services bearing the mark from the goods or services of competing undertakings. Article 7(3) CTMR would be redundant if a mark fell to be registered in accordance with Article 7(1)(b) by reason of its having become distinctive in consequence of the use made of it.[1046]

A **simple departure from the norm or customs of the sector** is not sufficient to render inapplicable the ground for refusal given in Article 3(1)(b) TMD2008. In contrast, a trade mark which **significantly** departs from the norm or customs of the sector and thereby fulfils its essential original function is not devoid of distinctive character.[1047]

Any perceptible difference between the combination of words submitted for registration and the terms used in the common parlance of the relevant class of consumers to designate the goods or services or their essential characteristics is apt to confer distinctive character on the word 'combination', enabling it to be registered as a trade mark.[1048]

Word combinations like BABY-DRY cannot therefore be regarded as exhibiting, as a whole, descriptive character; they are lexical inventions bestowing distinctive

Technologies/OHIM, para. 23; C-553/11 of 25.10.2012 – Rintisch, para. 19; C-12/12 of 18.4.2013 – Colloseum Holding, para. 26; C-252/12 of 18.7.2013 – Specsavers International Healthcare, para. 22; C-97/12 P of 15.5.2014 – Louis Vuitton Malletier/OHIM, para. 50; C-368/14 P of 11.12.2014 – Compagnie des bateaux mooches/OHIM, para. 18; C-445/13 P of 7.5.2015 – Voss of Norway/OHIM, para. 88; C-215/14 of 16.9.2015 – Société des Produits Nestlé, para. 60; C-139/16 of 6.7.2017 – Marín a.o./Abadía, para. 27; C-214/19 P of 3.9.2020 – achtung!/EUIPO, para. 25.

1044. CJEU C-104/01 of 6.5.2003 – Libertel, para. 62.
1045. CJEU C-64/02 P of 21.10.2004 – OHIM/ERPO MÖBELWERK, para. 40.
1046. CJEU C-136/02 P of 7.10.2004 – Mag Instrument/OHIM, para. 50.
1047. CJEU C-218/01 of 12.2.2004 – Henkel, para. 49; C-456/01 P and C-457/01 P of 29.4.2004 – Henkel/OHIM, para. 39; C-468/01 P to C-472/01 P of 29.4.2004 – Procter & Gamble/OHIM (three-dimensional form of tablet I), para. 37; C-473/01 P and C-474/01 P of 29.4.2004 – Procter & Gamble/OHIM (three-dimensional form of tablet II), para. 37; C-144/06 P of 4.10.2007 – Henkel/OHIM, para. 37; C-98/11 P of 24.5.2012 – Chocoladefabriken Lindt & Sprüngli/OHIM, para. 42; C-521/13 P of 11.9.2014 – Think Schuhwerk/OHIM, para. 49; C-445/13 P of 7.5.2015 – Voss of Norway/OHIM, paras 81 and 91; C-456/19 of 8.10.2020 – Aktiebolaget Östgötatrafiken/Patent- och registreringsverket, para. 40.
1048. CJEU C-383/99 P of 20.9.2001 – Procter & Gamble/OHIM (baby-dry), para. 40; *see also* CJEU C-622/13 P of 30.4.2015 – Castel Frères/EUIPO, paras 67.

power on the mark so formed and may not be refused registration under Article 7(1)(c) CTMR.[1049]

[2] *Assessment in concreto*

The distinctive character of the sign must be assessed ***in concreto***.[1050]

Article 3(1)(b) TMD2008 must be interpreted as meaning that in examining the distinctive character of a sign in respect of which registration as a trade mark is sought, **all the relevant facts and circumstances must be taken into account, including all the likely types of use of the mark** applied for. The latter correspond, in the absence of other indications, to the types of use which, in the light of the customs in the economic sector concerned, can be practically significant.[1051]

It should be recalled that, in accordance with Article 2 TMD2008, any sign which is the subject of an application for registration as an individual mark must, in order to be registrable as such, satisfy several conditions, including that of being capable of distinguishing the goods or services of one undertaking from those of other undertakings.[1052]

It cannot a priori be excluded that a sign comprising a hashtag, such as that at issue in the main proceedings, is capable of distinguishing the goods and/or services in respect of which registration is sought as coming from a particular undertaking and therefore satisfies the condition referred to above. It is in fact possible that such a sign be presented to the public in relation to goods or services and be capable of performing the essential function of a mark, which is to indicate the commercial origin of the goods or services covered.[1053]

There may, moreover, be cases in which significant use has also not been made of the sign in respect of which registration as a trade mark is sought prior to the date of the application for registration.[1054]

In such circumstances, the competent authorities which have to determine the distinctive character of a sign in respect of which registration as a trade mark is sought can find themselves in a situation where they do not have at their disposal, with regard to identifying the likely use of the mark applied for and, therefore, the way in which that mark will, if registered, probably be shown to the average consumer, any factor of assessment other than those arising from the customs of the economic sector concerned.[1055]

When it is apparent from those customs that several uses are practically significant in that economic sector, those authorities must, in accordance with their

1049. CJEU C-383/99 P of 20.9.2001 – Procter & Gamble/OHIM (baby-dry), para. 44.
1050. CJEU C-421/13 of 10.7.2014 – Apple, para. 22; C-541/18 of 12.9.2019 – AS/Deutsches Patent- und Markenamt, para. 21, with further proof.
1051. CJEU C-541/18 of 12.9.2019 – AS/Deutsches Patent- und Markenamt, para. 33; C-214/19 P of 3.9.2020 – achtung!/EUIPO, para. 28.
1052. CJEU C-541/18 of 12.9.2019 – AS/Deutsches Patent- und Markenamt, para. 17.
1053. CJEU C-541/18 of 12.9.2019 – AS/Deutsches Patent- und Markenamt, para. 18.
1054. CJEU C-541/18 of 12.9.2019 – AS/Deutsches Patent- und Markenamt, para. 23.
1055. CJEU C-541/18 of 12.9.2019 – AS/Deutsches Patent- und Markenamt, para. 24.

obligation to examine the distinctive character of the sign concerned in the light of all the relevant facts and circumstances, take into consideration those various uses in order to determine whether the average consumer of the goods or services covered will perceive that sign as an indication of the commercial origin of those goods or services.[1056]

By contrast, those authorities must qualify as irrelevant the uses which, whilst being conceivable in that economic sector, are not practically significant and therefore seem unlikely, except where the applicant has provided concrete evidence which, in his case, makes a use which is unusual in that sector more likely.[1057]

It is necessary to prevent the register of trade marks, which must be appropriate and precise, from including signs which serve to distinguish the proprietor's goods or services from those of other undertakings solely in the case of a very specific use which the proprietor is unlikely to make.[1058]

In the present case, the referring court found that, in the clothing sector, it is usual to place the mark on both the exterior of the goods and the labels sewn on the inside of them.[1059]

That court thus identified two types of placement which are practically significant in that sector. In such a situation, the authorities with competence to examine the perception of the average consumer will have to take those uses into consideration and assess whether that consumer, on seeing those two types of placement, or at least one of them on a garment, will perceive the sign at issue as a trade mark.[1060]

It is thus for the national court having jurisdiction to determine whether the average consumer, when he sees the sign #darferdas? on the front of a tee-shirt or the label placed on the inside of it, will perceive that sign as an indication of the commercial origin of the item and not simply as a decorative element or social message.[1061]

The approach taken in the order *Deichmann v. OHIM*[1062] remains relevant only in those cases where it appears that solely one type of use is practically significant in the economic sector concerned.[1063]

[3] Public interest

Article 7(1)(b) CTMR is intended to preclude registration of trade marks which are devoid of distinctive character which alone renders them capable of fulfilling the essential function of a trade mark, which is to guarantee the identity of the origin of the marked product or service to the consumer or end user by enabling him, without any

1056. CJEU C-541/18 of 12.9.2019 – AS/Deutsches Patent- und Markenamt, para. 25.
1057. CJEU C-541/18 of 12.9.2019 – AS/Deutsches Patent- und Markenamt, para. 26.
1058. CJEU C-541/18 of 12.9.2019 – AS/Deutsches Patent- und Markenamt, para. 27, with reference to CJEU C-273/00 of 12.12.2002 – Sieckmann, para. 50.
1059. CJEU C-541/18 of 12.9.2019 – AS/Deutsches Patent- und Markenamt, para. 29.
1060. CJEU C-541/18 of 12.9.2019 – AS/Deutsches Patent- und Markenamt, para. 30.
1061. CJEU C-541/18 of 12.9.2019 – AS/Deutsches Patent- und Markenamt, para. 31.
1062. CJEU C-307/11 P of 26.4.2012 – Deichmann/OHIM, para. 55.
1063. CJEU C-541/18 of 12.9.2019 – AS/Deutsches Patent- und Markenamt, para. 32.

possibility of confusion, to distinguish the product or service from others which have another origin.[1064]

The requirement of availability is the reason underlying certain grounds for refusal of registration set out in Article 3 TMD2008.[1065]

As regards the registration as trade marks of colours per se, not spatially delimited, the Court has ruled that the public interest underlying the provision is aimed at the need not to restrict unduly the availability of colours for the other operators who offer for sale goods or services of the same type as those in respect of which registration is sought.[1066]

There is no public interest in conferring the benefit of the full protection envisaged by CTMR on a trade mark which does not fulfil its essential function, namely that of ensuring that the consumer or the end user can identify the origin of the product or service concerned by allowing him to distinguish that product or service from those emanating from a different origin, without any risk of confusion.[1067]

Furthermore, in view of the extent of the protection afforded to a trade mark by the regulation, the public interest underlying Article 7(1)(b) CTMR is, manifestly, indissociable from the essential function of a trade mark, which is to guarantee the identity of the origin of the marked product or service to the consumer or end user by enabling him, without any possibility of confusion, to distinguish the product or service from others which have another origin.[1068]

The fact that registration as a trade mark of a colour per se is sought for a large number of goods or services, or for a specific product or service or for a specific group of goods or services, is relevant, together with all the other circumstances of the particular case, to assessing both the distinctive character of the colour in respect of which registration is sought and whether its registration would run counter to the general interest in not unduly limiting the availability of colours for the other operators who offer for sale goods or services of the same type as those in respect of which registration is sought.[1069]

The greater the **number of the goods or services** for which the trade mark is sought to be registered, the more excessive the exclusive right which it may confer is likely to be, and, for that very reason, the more likely is that right to come into conflict with the maintenance of a system of undistorted competition, and with the public interest in not unduly restricting the availability of colours for the other traders who

1064. CJEU C-173/04 P of 12.1.2006 – Deutsche SiSi-Werke/OHIM, para. 60; C-304/06 P of 8.5.2008 – Eurohypo/OHIM, para. 56; C-453/11 P of 14.5.2012 – Timehouse/OHIM, para. 39; C-20/14 of 22.10.2015 – BGW Beratungs-Gesellschaft Wirtschaft, para. 25.
1065. CJEU C-102/07 of 10.4.2008 – adidas/Marca Mode, para. 23.
1066. CJEU C-104/01 of 6.5.2003 – Libertel, paras 60 and 71; C-49/02 of 24.6.2004 – Heidelberger Bauchemie, para. 41; C-456/01 P and C-457/01 P of 29.4.2004 – Henkel/OHIM, para. 47; C-329/02 P of 16.9.2004 – SAT.1 SATELLITENFERNSEHEN/OHIM, para. 26; C-578/17 of 27.3.2019 – Oy Hartwall/Patentti- ja rekisterihallitus, para. 31; C-124/18 P of 29.7.2019 – Red Bull/EUIPO, para. 65.
1067. CJEU C-456/01 P and C-457/01 P of 29.4.2004 – Henkel/OHIM, para. 48.
1068. CJEU C-329/02 P of 16.9.2004 – SAT.1 SATELLITENFERNSEHEN/OHIM, para. 27; C-37/03 P of 15.9.2005 – BioID/OHIM, para. 60; C-173/04 P of 12.1.2006 – Deutsche SiSi-Werke/OHIM, para. 61; C-512/06 P of 26.10.2007 – PTV Planung Transport Verkehr/OHIM, para. 24, 26.
1069. CJEU C-104/01 of 6.5.2003 – Libertel, para. 71.

market goods or services of the same type as those in respect of which registration is sought.[1070]

[4] Irrelevant criteria

Registration of a sign as a trade mark is not subject to a finding of a specific **level of linguistic or artistic creativity or imaginativeness** on the part of the proprietor of the trade mark. It suffices that the trade mark should enable the relevant public to identify the origin of the goods or services protected thereby and to distinguish them from those of other undertakings.[1071]

The absence of an **additional element of imagination** or an additional element of originality is an incorrect criterion concerning distinctive character.[1072]

A criterion according to which trade marks which are capable of being **commonly used**, in trade, for the presentation of the goods or services in question may not be registered is relevant in the context of Article 7(1)(c) CTMR, but it is not the yardstick against which Article 7(1)(b) thereof should be judged.[1073]

The fact that it has been shown that the trade mark applied for is commonly used by the public or by competitors is a relevant factor under Article 7(1)(d) CTMR, but not under Article 7(1)(b).[1074]

Article 3 TMD2008 does not include any ground for refusal to register specifically aimed at trade marks constituted by a term borrowed from the language of a Member State other than the State of registration in which it is devoid of distinctive character or descriptive of the goods or services in respect of which registration is sought.[1075]

Moreover, such a trade mark does not necessarily fall within the grounds for refusal to register relating to the lack of distinctive character or the descriptive character of the trade mark, referred to in points (b) and (c) respectively of Article 3(1) TMD2008.[1076]

[5] Different categories of trade marks

Article 3(1)(b) TMD2008 makes no distinction between different categories of trade marks for the purposes of assessing their distinctiveness.[1077]

1070. CJEU C-104/01 of 6.5.2003 – Libertel, para. 56.
1071. CJEU C-329/02 P of 16.9.2004 – SAT.1 SATELLITENFERNSEHEN/OHIM, para. 41.
1072. CJEU C-64/02 P of 21.10.2004 – OHIM/ERPO MÖBELWERK, para. 50.
1073. CJEU C-329/02 P of 16.9.2004 – SAT.1 SATELLITENFERNSEHEN/OHIM, para. 36; C-37/03 P of 15.9.2005 – BioID/OHIM, para. 62; C-173/04 P of 12.1.2006 – Deutsche SiSi-Werke/OHIM, para. 63.
1074. CJEU C-37/03 P of 15.9.2005 – BioID/OHIM, para. 41.
1075. CJEU C-421/04 of 9.3.2006 – Matratzen Concord, para. 22.
1076. CJEU C-421/04 of 9.3.2006 – Matratzen Concord, para. 22.
1077. CJEU C-53/01 to C-55/01 of 8.4.2003 – Linde and Others, paras 42 and 49; C-456/01 P and C-457/01 P of 29.4.2004 – Henkel/OHIM, para. 38; C-468/01 P to C-472/01 P of 29.4.2004 – Procter & Gamble/OHIM (three-dimensional form of tablet I), para. 36; C-473/01 P and C-474/01 P of 29.4.2004 – Procter & Gamble/OHIM (three-dimensional form of tablet II), para. 36; C-445/02 P of 28.6.2004 – Glaverbel/OHIM, para. 21; C-404/02 of 16.9.2004 – Nichols,

Even though there are certain categories of signs which are less likely prima facie to have distinctive character initially, the Court, nevertheless, has not exempted the trade mark authorities from having to carry out an examination of their distinctive character based on the facts.[1078]

Difficulties in establishing distinctiveness which may be associated with certain categories of trade marks because of their very nature, such as those consisting of **advertising slogans** – difficulties which it is legitimate to take into account – do not justify laying down specific criteria supplementing or derogating from the criterion of distinctiveness.[1079]

The criteria for assessment of the distinctive character of trade marks constituted by a **personal name** are therefore the same as those applicable to the other categories of trade mark.[1080]

The criteria for assessing the distinctive character of **three-dimensional trade marks** are no different from those to be applied to other categories of trade marks.[1081]

'**Position marks**' are similar to the categories of figurative and three-dimensional marks as they related to the application of three-dimensional elements to the surface of a product and that when assessing the distinctiveness of a mark, the classification of a 'position mark' as a figurative or three-dimensional mark or as a specific category of marks is irrelevant.[1082]

In the context of that assessment, it may indeed appear that the **perception of the relevant public** is not necessarily the same for each of the categories and that,

para. 24; C-107/03 P of 23.9.2004 – Procter & Gamble/OHIM (form of a soap), para. 48; C-136/02 P of 7.10.2004 – Mag Instrument/OHIM, para. 30; C-447/02 P of 21.10.2004 – KWS Saat/OHIM, para. 78; C-265/09 P of 9.9.2010 – OHIM/BORCO-Marken-Import Matthiesen, para. 33; C-546/10 P of 13.9.2011 – Wilfer/OHIM, para. 53; C-344/10 P and C-345/10 P of 20.10.2011 – Freixenet/OHIM, para. 46; C-97/12 P of 15.5.2014 – Louis Vuitton Malletier/ OHIM, para. 51; C-417/16 P of 4.5.2017 – August Storck/EUIPO, para. 33; *see also* CJEU C-299/99 of 18.6.2002 – Philips, para. 48.

1078. CJEU C-265/09 P of 9.9.2010 – OHIM/BORCO-Marken-Import Matthiesen, para. 37.

1079. CJEU C-64/02 P of 21.10.2004 – OHIM/ERPO MÖBELWERK, para. 36; *see also* CJEU C-398/08 P of 21.1.2010 – Audi/OHIM, para. 38; C-265/09 P of 9.9.2010 – OHIM/BORCO-Marken-Import Matthiesen, para. 34; C-311/11 P of 12.7.2012 – Smart Technologies/OHIM, para. 27; *see also* CJEU C-217/13 and 218/13 of 19.6.2014 – Oberbank, para. 47.

1080. CJEU C-404/02 of 16.9.2004 – Nichols, para. 25.

1081. CJEU C-299/99 of 18.6.2002 – Philips, para. 48; C-53/01 to C-55/01 of 8.4.2003 – Linde and Others, paras 42 and 49; C-456/01 P and C-457/01 P of 29.4.2004 – Henkel/OHIM, para. 38; C-468/01 P to C-472/01 P of 29.4.2004 – Procter & Gamble/OHIM (three-dimensional form of tablet I), para. 36; C-473/01 P and C-474/01 P of 29.4.2004 – Procter & Gamble/OHIM (three-dimensional form of tablet II), para. 36; C-136/02 P of 7.10.2004 – Mag Instrument/ OHIM, para. 30; C-173/04 P of 12.1.2006 – Deutsche SiSi-Werke/OHIM, para. 27; C-24/05 P of 22.6.2006 – Storck/OHIM (light-brown sweet), para. 24; C-25/05 P of 22.6.2006 – Storck/OHIM (gold-coloured sweet wrapper), para. 26; C-238/06 P of 25.10.2007 – Develey Holding/OHIM, para. 80; C-144/06 P of 4.10.2007 – Henkel/OHIM, para. 36 Holding/OHIM, para. 80; C-546/10 P of 13.9.2011 – Wilfer/OHIM, para. 53; C-344/10 P and C-345/10 P of 20.10.2011 – Freixenet/OHIM, para. 45; C-96/11 P of 6.9.2012 – Storck/OHIM, para. 33; C-445/13 P of 7.5.2015 – Voss of Norway/OHIM, para. 90; C-26/17 P of 13.9.2018 – Birkenstock Sales/EUIPO, para. 32; C-783/18 P of 12.12.2019 – EUIPO/Wajos, para. 24.

1082. CJEU C-223/18 P of 6.6.2019 – Deichmann/EUIPO, para. 42.

accordingly, it could prove more difficult to establish the distinctive character of trade marks in certain categories than that of those in other categories.[1083]

[6] *In particular: word marks*

Although the way in which the term 'SAT.2' is made up is not unusual, in particular as regards the perception which the average consumer may have of services falling within the communications industry, and the juxtaposition of a verbal element, such as 'SAT' with a digit such as '2', separated by a '.', does not reflect a particularly high degree of inventiveness, those facts are not sufficient to establish that such a word is devoid of distinctive character within the meaning of Article 7(1)(b) CTMR.[1084]

The frequent use of trade marks consisting of a word and a number in the telecommunications sector indicates that that type of combination cannot be considered to be devoid, in principle, of distinctive character.[1085]

In the same way as a term used in everyday language, a common surname may serve the trade mark function of indicating origin and therefore distinguish the products or services concerned where it is not subject to a ground of refusal of registration other than the one referred to in Article 3(1)(b) TMD2008, such as, for example, the generic or descriptive character of the mark or the existence of an earlier right.[1086]

The registration of a trade mark constituted by a surname cannot be refused in order to ensure that no advantage is afforded to the first applicant since the Directive contains no provision to that effect, regardless, moreover, of the category to which the trade mark whose registration is sought belongs.[1087]

Stricter general criteria of assessment based, for example, on:

- a predetermined number of persons with the same name, above which that name may be regarded as devoid of distinctive character;
- the number of undertakings providing products or services of the type covered by the application for registration; or

1083. CJEU C-53/01 to C-55/01 of 8.4.2003 – Linde and Others, para. 48; C-218/01 of 12.2.2004 – Henkel, para. 52; C-456/01 P and C-457/01 P of 29.4.2004 – Henkel/OHIM, para. 38; C-468/01 P to C-472/01 P of 29.4.2004 – Procter & Gamble/OHIM (three-dimensional form of tablet I), para. 36; C-473/01 P and C-474/01 P of 29.4.2004 – Procter & Gamble/OHIM (three-dimensional form of tablet II), para. 36; C-445/02 P of 28.6.2004 – Glaverbel/OHIM, para. 23; C-404/02 of 16.9.2004 – Nichols, para. 28; C-107/03 P of 23.9.2004 – Procter & Gamble/OHIM (form of a soap), para. 49 f.; C-136/02 P of 7.10.2004 – Mag Instrument/OHIM, para. 30; C-398/08 P of 21.1.2010 – Audi/OHIM, para. 37; C-265/09 P of 9.9.2010 – OHIM/BORCO-Marken-Import Matthiesen, para. 33; C-344/10 P and C-345/10 P of 20.10.2011 – Freixenet/OHIM, para. 46; C-311/11 P of 12.7.2012 – Smart Technologies/OHIM, para. 26; C-96/11 P of 6.9.2012 – Storck/OHIM, para. 34; C-521/13 P of 11.9.2014 – Think Schuhwerk/OHIM, para. 48; C-445/13 P of 7.5.2015 – Voss of Norway/OHIM, para. 90; C-417/16 P of 4.5.2017 – August Storck/EUIPO, para. 33; C-783/18 P of 12.12.2019 – EUIPO/Wajos, para. 24.
1084. CJEU C-329/02 P of 16.9.2004 – SAT.1 SATELLITENFERNSEHEN/OHIM, para. 40.
1085. CJEU C-329/02 P of 16.9.2004 – SAT.1 SATELLITENFERNSEHEN/OHIM, para. 44.
1086. CJEU C-404/02 of 16.9.2004 – Nichols, para. 30, wording corrected.
1087. CJEU C-404/02 of 16.9.2004 – Nichols, para. 31.

- the prevalence or otherwise of the use of surnames in the relevant trade cannot be applied to such trade marks.[1088]

[7] In particular: figurative word marks

The trade mark applied for contains the abbreviation BioID and figurative elements, namely the typographical characteristics of that abbreviation, and two graphic elements placed after the abbreviation BioID, namely a full stop (.) and a sign (®). As regards the said abbreviation, the relevant public will understand BioID, in the light of the goods and services claimed in the trade mark application, as being made up of the abbreviation of an adjective 'biometrical' and of a noun ('identification'), and thus, as a whole, as meaning 'biometrical identification'. Therefore, that abbreviation, which is indistinguishable from the goods and services covered by the trade mark application, is not of a character which can guarantee the identity of the origin of the marked product or service to the consumer or end user from the viewpoint of the relevant public. In addition, in the light of the recurrent nature of the typographical features of the abbreviation BioID and the absence of any particular distinctive element, the characters in 'Arial' typeface and characters of different boldness do not enable the trade mark applied for to guarantee, to the relevant public, the identity of the origin of the goods and services covered by the trade mark application. Furthermore, the two graphic elements placed after the abbreviation BioID, namely a full stop (.) and a sign (®), do nothing to enable the relevant public to distinguish, without any possibility of confusion, the products or services covered by the trade mark application from others which have another origin. It follows that those graphic elements are not capable of fulfilling the essential function of a trade mark in relation to the relevant goods and services. When the overall impression conveyed by the trade mark applied for to the relevant public is examined, the abbreviation BioID, which is devoid of any distinctive character, is the dominant element of that mark. Moreover, the figurative and graphic elements are so minimal in nature that they do not endow the trade mark applied for as a whole with any distinctive character. Those elements do not possess any feature, in particular in terms of fancifulness or as regards the way in which they are combined, allowing that mark to fulfil its essential function in relation to the goods and services covered by the trade mark application. Accordingly, the trade mark applied for is devoid of any distinctive character within the meaning of Article 7(1)(b) CTMR.[1089]

[8] In particular: slogans

The fact that the **term 'slogan' is not expressly used** in the CTMR is not such as to establish that the General Court considered advertising slogans to be a subcategory of trade marks. Article 4 CTMR, in listing the types of signs capable of constituting a trade mark within the meaning of the regulation, in no way had the purpose of establishing

1088. CJEU C-404/02 of 16.9.2004 – Nichols, para. 26.
1089. CJEU C-37/03 P of 15.9.2005 – BioID/OHIM, paras 69 et seq.

or defining different categories of trade marks consisting of signs. The concept of a 'slogan', like that of a 'word sign' or 'word mark', was developed by the case law on the interpretation of that regulation, without such slogans being considered to be a special subcategory of word signs, or even a distinct category thereof. The Court has, on several occasions, classified word signs with a laudatory connotation as slogans.[1090]

The possibility cannot be excluded that the case law mentioned[1091] is also relevant to word marks consisting of advertising slogans. That could be the case in particular if it were established, when assessing the distinctiveness of the trade mark in question, that it served a promotional function consisting, for example, of commending the quality of the product in question and that the importance of that function was not manifestly secondary to its purported function as a trade mark, namely that of guaranteeing the origin of the product. Indeed, in such a case, the authorities may take account of the fact that average consumers are not in the habit of making assumptions about the origin of products on the basis of such slogans.[1092]

The Court of Justice has held that the registration of a mark made up of signs or indications that are also used as advertising slogans, indications of quality or incitements to purchase the goods or services covered by that mark is not excluded as such by virtue of such use.[1093]

As regards the assessment of the distinctive character of such marks, the Court has already held that it is inappropriate to apply to slogans criteria which are stricter than those applicable to other types of signs.[1094]

An advertising slogan **cannot be required** to display '**imaginativeness**' or even '**conceptual** tension which would create surprise and so make a striking impression' in order to have the minimal level of distinctiveness required under Article 7(1)(b) CTMR.[1095]

By holding that a trade mark is not devoid of distinctive character within the meaning of Article 7(1)(b) CTMR unless it is demonstrated that the phrase concerned is commonly used in business communications and, in particular, in advertising the Court of First Instance applied a criterion other than the one laid down by Article 7(1)(b) CTMR.[1096]

However, while it is true that a mark possesses distinctive character only in so far as it serves to identify the goods or services in respect of which registration is applied for as originating from a particular undertaking, it must be held that the mere fact that

1090. CJEU C-311/11 P of 12.7.2012 - Smart Technologies/OHIM, para. 40.
1091. *See* above Art. 4 'No distinctive character/Different categories of trade marks'.
1092. CJEU C-64/02 P of 21.10.2004 - OHIM/ERPO MÖBELWERK, para. 35.
1093. CJEU C-64/02 P of 21.10.2004 - OHIM/ERPO MÖBELWERK, para. 41; C-398/08 P of 21.1.2010 - Audi/OHIM, para. 35; C-311/11 P of 12.7.2012 - Smart Technologies/OHIM, para. 25; C-139/16 of 6.7.2017 - Marín a.o./Abadía, para. 28.
1094. CJEU C-398/08 P of 21.1.2010 - Audi/OHIM, para. 36; C-311/11 P of 12.7.2012 - Smart Technologies/OHIM, para. 25; also CJEU C-636/15 P of 11.5.2016 - August Storck/EUIPO, para. 19; C-139/16 of 6.7.2017 - Marín a.o./Abadía, para. 28.
1095. CJEU C-311/11 P of 12.7.2012 - Smart Technologies/OHIM, para. 28; *see also* CJEU C-64/02 P of 21.10.2004 - OHIM/ERPO MÖBELWERK, paras 31 et seq.; C-398/08 P of 21.1.2010 - Audi/OHIM, para. 39.
1096. CJEU C-64/02 P of 21.10.2004 - OHIM/ERPO MÖBELWERK, para. 46.

a mark is perceived by the relevant public as a promotional formula, and that, because of its laudatory nature, it could in principle be used by other undertakings, is not sufficient, in itself, to support the conclusion that that mark is devoid of distinctive character.[1097]

On that point, it should be noted that the laudatory connotation of a word mark does not mean that it cannot be appropriate for the purposes of guaranteeing to consumers the origin of the goods or services which it covers. Thus, such a mark can be perceived by the relevant public both as a promotional formula and as an indication of the commercial origin of goods or services. It follows that, in so far as the public perceives the mark as an indication of that origin, the fact that the mark is at the same time understood - perhaps even primarily understood - as a promotional formula has no bearing on its distinctive character.[1098]

All marks made up of signs or indications that are also used as advertising slogans, indications of quality or incitements to purchase the goods or services covered by those marks convey by definition, to a greater or lesser extent, an objective message. It is clear, however, that those marks are not, by virtue of that fact alone, devoid of distinctive character.[1099]

Thus, in so far as those marks are not descriptive for the purposes of Article 7(1)(c) CTMR, they can express an objective message, even a simple one, and still be capable of indicating to the consumer the commercial origin of the goods or services in question. That can be the position, in particular, where those marks are not merely an ordinary advertising message, but possess a certain originality or resonance, requiring at least some interpretation by the relevant public, or setting off a cognitive process in the minds of that public.[1100]

As regards the finding that the mark Vorsprung durch Technik can have **a number of meanings, or constitute a play on words or be perceived as imaginative, surprising and unexpected** and, in that way, be easily remembered, it should be noted that, although the existence of such characteristics is not a necessary condition for establishing that an advertising slogan has distinctive character the fact remains that, as a rule, the presence of those characteristics is likely to **endow** that mark **with distinctive character**.[1101]

The expression **'Vorsprung durch Technik'** is a **widely known slogan** which Audi has been using for years to promote the sale of its motor vehicles. It was registered in 2001 as a Community trade mark for goods in Class 12 on the basis of proof that that slogan was widely known in German-speaking regions.[1102]

1097. CJEU C-398/08 P of 21.1.2010 - Audi/OHIM, para. 44; C-311/11 P of 12.7.2012 - Smart Technologies/OHIM, para. 29; C-139/16 of 6.7.2017 - Marín a.o./Abadía, para. 29; C-411/18 P of 3.10.2018 - Romantik Hotels & Restaurants/EUIPO, paras 4/15 and 5.
1098. CJEU C-398/08 P of 21.1.2010 - Audi/OHIM, para. 45; C-311/11 P of 12.7.2012 - Smart Technologies/OHIM, para. 30; *see also* CJEU C-92/10 P of 13.1.2011 - Media-Saturn-Holding/OHIM, para. 52; C-636/15 P of 11.5.2016 - August Storck/EUIPO, para. 19.
1099. CJEU C-398/08 P of 21.1.2010 - Audi/OHIM, para. 56.
1100. CJEU C-398/08 P of 21.1.2010 - Audi/OHIM, para. 57; C-636/15 P of 11.5.2016 - August Storck/EUIPO, para. 21.
1101. CJEU C-398/08 P of 21.1.2010 - Audi/OHIM, para. 47.
1102. CJEU C-398/08 P of 21.1.2010 - Audi/OHIM, para. 53.

Even if it were to be supposed that the slogan 'Vorsprung durch Technik' conveys an objective message to the effect that technological superiority enables the manufacture and supply of better goods and services, that fact would not support the conclusion that the mark applied for is devoid of any inherently distinctive character. However simple such a message may be, it cannot be categorized as ordinary to the point of excluding, from the outset and without any further analysis, the possibility that that mark is capable of indicating to the consumer the commercial origin of the goods or services in question.[1103]

In that context, it should be pointed out that that message does not follow obviously from the slogan in question. As Audi observed, the combination of words 'Vorsprung durch Technik' (meaning, *inter alia*, advance or advantage through technology) suggests, at first glance, only a causal link and accordingly requires a measure of interpretation on the part of the public. Furthermore, that slogan exhibits a certain originality and resonance which makes it easy to remember. Lastly, inasmuch as it is a widely known slogan which has been used by Audi for many years, it cannot be excluded that the fact that members of the relevant public are used to establishing the link between that slogan and the motor vehicles manufactured by that company also makes it easier for that public to identify the commercial origin of the goods or services covered.[1104]

Article 3(1)(c) TMD2008 must be interpreted as meaning that a sign such as 'la Milla de Oro', referring to the characteristic of a product or service which is that such a product or service can be found in abundance in a single place with a high degree of value, is unlikely to have characteristics the use of which as a trade mark would constitute a ground for invalidity within the meaning of that provision.[1105]

[9] In particular: letters

In relation, more particularly, to the fact that the sign at issue consists of a single letter with no graphic modifications, it should be borne in mind that registration of a sign as a trade mark is not subject to a finding of a specific level of linguistic or artistic creativity or imaginativeness on the part of the proprietor of the trade mark.[1106]

It follows that, particularly as it may prove more difficult to establish distinctiveness for marks consisting of a single letter than for other word marks, OHIM is required to assess whether the sign at issue is capable of distinguishing the different goods and services in the context of an examination, based on the facts, focusing on those goods or services.[1107]

1103. CJEU C-398/08 P of 21.1.2010 – Audi/OHIM, para. 58.
1104. CJEU C-398/08 P of 21.1.2010 – Audi/OHIM, para. 59.
1105. CJEU C-139/16 of 6.7.2017 – Marín a.o./Abadía, para. 31.
1106. CJEU C-265/09 P of 9.9.2010 – OHIM/BORCO-Marken-Import Matthiesen, para. 38; *see also* CJEU C-51/10 P of 10.3.2011 – Agencja Wydawnicza Technopol/HABM, para. 31.
1107. CJEU C-265/09 P of 9.9.2010 – OHIM/BORCO-Marken-Import Matthiesen, para. 39.

[10] *In particular: numerals*

First of all, it should be pointed out that the fact that a sign is composed exclusively of numerals is not enough in itself to prevent that sign from being registered as a trade mark.[1108]

That is apparent, so far as concerns Community trade marks, from Article 4 CTMR, which expressly provides that numerals are among the signs of which a mark may consist.[1109]

Furthermore, the fact that a sign is composed of numerals with no graphic modifications and has not therefore been stylized creatively or artistically by the applicant for registration does not as such preclude that sign from being registered as a mark.[1110]

However, as is also apparent from Article 4 CTMR, the registration of a sign as a trade mark is subject to the condition that it is capable of distinguishing the goods or services of one undertaking from those of other undertakings.[1111]

Article 7(1)(c) CTMR does not require the sign at issue to be the usual means of designation. Paragraph 37 of *Procter & Gamble v. OHIM*,[1112] which uses the terms 'no different from the usual way of designating the relevant goods or services or their characteristics', cannot therefore be understood as defining a condition for refusing to register a sign as a Community trade mark.[1113]

[11] *In particular: design marks*

Article 3(1)(b) TMD2008 must be interpreted as meaning that the distinctive character of a sign for which registration as a trade mark in respect of a service is sought, which sign consists of coloured motifs and which is intended to be **affixed exclusively and systematically in a specific manner to a large part of the goods** used for the provision of that service, must be assessed by taking into account the perception of the relevant public of the affixing of that sign to those goods, without it being necessary to examine whether that sign departs significantly from the norm or customs of the economic sector concerned.[1114]

Although the colour motifs to which the applications for registration relate are intended to be affixed in a specific manner to a large part of the goods used for the provision of transport services, the appellant in the main proceedings has expressly

1108. CJEU C-51/10 P of 10.3.2011 – Agencja Wydawnicza Technopol/HABM, para. 29.
1109. CJEU C-51/10 P of 10.3.2011 – Agencja Wydawnicza Technopol/HABM, para. 30.
1110. CJEU C-51/10 P of 10.3.2011 – Agencja Wydawnicza Technopol/HABM, para. 31; *see also* CJEU C-265/09 P of 9.9.2010 – OHIM/BORCO-Marken-Import Matthiesen, para. 38.
1111. CJEU C-51/10 P of 10.3.2011 – Agencja Wydawnicza Technopol/HABM, para. 32.
1112. CJEU C-107/03 P of 23.9.2004 – Procter & Gamble/OHIM (form of a soap), para. 37.
1113. CJEU C-51/10 P of 10.3.2011 – Agencja Wydawnicza Technopol/HABM, para. 40; C-54/10 P and C-55/10 P of 22.6.2011 – Agencja Wydawnicza Technopol/HABM, para. 28; C-56/10 P of 22.6.2011 – Agencja Wydawnicza Technopol/HABM, para. 53.
1114. CJEU C-456/19 of 8.10.2020 – Aktiebolaget Östgötatrafiken/Patent- och registreringsverket, para. 44.

stated that the shape of those goods was not, as such, the object of those applications.[1115]

Consequently, it must be held that, by its two questions, which it is appropriate to consider together, the referring court asks, in essence, whether Article 3(1)(b) TMD2008 must be interpreted as meaning that the distinctive character of a sign for which registration as a trade mark is sought, for a service, which consists of colour motifs and which is intended to be affixed exclusively and systematically in a specific manner to a large part of the goods used for the provision of that service, must be assessed in relation to those goods and by examining whether that sign departs significantly from the norm or customs of the economic sector concerned.[1116]

Furthermore, in order to assess the distinctive character of a sign within the meaning of Article 3(1)(b) TMD2008, the competent authority must carry out an examination by reference to the actual situation, taking into account all the relevant circumstances of the case, including, where appropriate, the use made of that sign.[1117]

Where, as in the main proceedings, the trade mark application concerns a sign intended to be affixed exclusively and systematically in a specific manner to a large part of the goods used to provide the services, the distinctive character of that sign cannot be assessed independently of the perception of the relevant public of the affixing of that sign to those goods.[1118]

Even if the goods which are used to provide the services are not the subject of the trade mark application, the fact remains that the relevant public perceives the colour motifs of which the sign in question consists as being affixed to the goods which serve as their exclusive medium.[1119]

It follows that the assessment of the distinctive character of a sign consisting of coloured motifs which are intended to be applied exclusively and systematically to goods used for the provision of services must, in particular, take account of that perception.[1120]

It will be for the referring court to determine, in the context of its overall analysis by reference to the actual situation in the case, whether the systematically arranged colour combinations, as shown in the applications for registration, are capable of conferring inherent distinctive character on the signs in question. That condition must be regarded as satisfied if it emerges from that analysis that the colour combinations applied to the transport vehicles of the appellant in the main proceedings enable the

1115. CJEU C-456/19 of 8.10.2020 – Aktiebolaget Östgötatrafiken/Patent- och registreringsverket, para. 30.
1116. CJEU C-456/19 of 8.10.2020 – Aktiebolaget Östgötatrafiken/Patent- och registreringsverket, para. 31.
1117. CJEU C-456/19 of 8.10.2020 – Aktiebolaget Östgötatrafiken/Patent- och registreringsverket, para. 33, with reference to CJEU C-578/17 of 27.3.2019 – Oy Hartwall/Patentti- ja rekisterihallitus, para. 26.
1118. CJEU C-456/19 of 8.10.2020 – Aktiebolaget Östgötatrafiken/Patent- och registreringsverket, para. 34.
1119. CJEU C-456/19 of 8.10.2020 – Aktiebolaget Östgötatrafiken/Patent- och registreringsverket, para. 35.
1120. CJEU C-456/19 of 8.10.2020 – Aktiebolaget Östgötatrafiken/Patent- och registreringsverket, para. 36.

average consumer to distinguish, without any confusion, between the transport services provided by that undertaking and those provided by other undertakings.[1121]

If those colour combinations prove not to have intrinsic distinctive character for the services in question, that fact will not be such as to preclude their becoming distinctive after use.[1122]

In the context of that analysis, it is not necessary to examine whether the signs for which registration as a trade mark is sought depart significantly from the norm or customs of the economic sector concerned.[1123]

As is clear from the settled case law of the Court, the criterion for assessment of whether there is a significant departure from the norm or customs of the economic sector concerned applies where the sign consists of the shape of the product for which registration as a trade mark is sought, average consumers not being in the habit of making assumptions about the origin of products on the basis of their shape or the shape of their packaging in the absence of any graphic or word element.[1124]

That criterion for assessment also applies where the sign consists of the representation of the layout of the physical space in which the services in respect of which registration as a trade mark is sought are provided.[1125]

Such a situation does not arise in a case in which, as in the main proceedings, the signs at issue consist of graphic elements intended to be affixed to goods which are used to provide the services designated by the application for registration.[1126]

In that regard, it must be noted that although the goods used for the provision of the services at issue in the main proceedings, namely transport vehicles, are shown in dotted lines in the applications for registration, for the purpose of indicating both the places where the marks applied for are intended to be affixed and the outlines of those marks, the signs in respect of which registration as trade marks is sought are, even so, not indissociable from the shape or packaging of those goods and nor is their purpose to represent the physical space in which the services are provided. Indeed, those signs consist of colour compositions which are systematically arranged and spatially limited. Those applications for registration thus relate to clearly defined graphic elements which, unlike the signs referred to in the case law cited in paragraphs 40 and 41 of this

1121. CJEU C-456/19 of 8.10.2020 – Aktiebolaget Östgötatrafiken/Patent- och registreringsverket, para. 37.
1122. CJEU C-456/19 of 8.10.2020 – Aktiebolaget Östgötatrafiken/Patent- och registreringsverket, para. 38.
1123. CJEU C-456/19 of 8.10.2020 – Aktiebolaget Östgötatrafiken/Patent- och registreringsverket, para. 39.
1124. CJEU C-456/19 of 8.10.2020 – Aktiebolaget Östgötatrafiken/Patent- och registreringsverket, para. 40, with reference to CJEU C-456/01 P and C-457/01 P of 29.4.2004 – Henkel/OHIM, para. 39; C-417/16 P of 4.5.2017 – August Storck/EUIPO, para. 27-29; C-445/13 P of 7.5.2015 – Voss of Norway/OHIM, paras 90 and 91.
1125. CJEU C-456/19 of 8.10.2020 – Aktiebolaget Östgötatrafiken/Patent- och registreringsverket, para. 41, with reference to CJEU C-421/13 of 10.7.2014 – Apple, para. 20.
1126. CJEU C-456/19 of 8.10.2020 – Aktiebolaget Östgötatrafiken/Patent- och registreringsverket, para. 42.

judgment, are not intended to represent goods or an area for the provision of services by the mere reproduction of the lines and the contours thereof.[1127]

[12] In particular: colour trade marks

The perception of the relevant public is not necessarily the same in the case of a sign consisting of a colour per se as it is in the case of a word or figurative mark consisting of a sign that bears no relation to the appearance of the goods it denotes. While the public is accustomed to perceiving word or figurative marks instantly as signs identifying the commercial origin of the goods, the same is not necessarily true where the sign forms part of the look of the goods in respect of which registration of the sign as a trade mark is sought. Consumers are not in the habit of making assumptions about the origin of goods based on their colour or the colour of their packaging, in the absence of any graphic or word element, because as a rule a colour per se is not, in current commercial practice, used as a means of identification. A colour per se is not normally inherently capable of distinguishing the goods of a particular undertaking.[1128]

The number of colours which that public is capable of distinguishing is limited because it is rarely in a position directly to compare products in various shades of colour. It follows that the number of different colours that are in fact available as potential trade marks to distinguish goods or services must be regarded as limited.[1129]

As regards the registration as trade marks of colours per se, not spatially delimited, the fact that the number of colours actually available is limited means that a small number of trade mark registrations for certain services or goods could exhaust the entire range of the colours available. Such an extensive monopoly would be incompatible with a system of undistorted competition, in particular because it could have the effect of creating an unjustified competitive advantage for a single trader. Nor would it be conducive to economic development or the fostering of the spirit of enterprise for established traders to be able to register the entire range of colours that is in fact available for their own benefit, to the detriment of new traders.[1130]

It must therefore be acknowledged that there is, in Community trade mark law, a public interest in not unduly restricting the availability of colours for the other operators who offer for sale goods or services of the same type as those in respect of which registration is sought.[1131]

The **classification as a 'colour mark' or 'figurative mark'** given to a sign by the applicant on registration does not release the competent trade mark authority from its

1127. CJEU C-456/19 of 8.10.2020 – Aktiebolaget Östgötatrafiken/Patent- och registreringsverket, para. 43.
1128. CJEU C-104/01 of 6.5.2003 – Libertel, para. 65; C-107/03 P of 23.9.2004 – Procter & Gamble/OHIM (form of a soap), para. 49 f.; C-447/02 P of 21.10.2004 – KWS Saat/OHIM, para. 78; C-578/17 of 27.3.2019 – Oy Hartwall/Patentti- ja rekisterihallitus, para. 29; *see also* CJEU C-417/16 P of 4.5.2017 – August Storck/EUIPO, para. 34.
1129. CJEU C-104/01 of 6.5.2003 – Libertel, para. 47.
1130. CJEU C-104/01 of 6.5.2003 – Libertel, para. 54.
1131. CJEU C-104/01 of 6.5.2003 – Libertel, para. 55; *see also* CJEU C-49/02 of 24.6.2004 – Heidelberger Bauchemie, para. 41; C-447/02 P of 21.10.2004 – KWS Saat/OHIM, para. 78 f.

obligation to carry out a global assessment of distinctive character by reference to the actual situation of the mark considered, which means that that authority cannot refuse registration of a sign as a mark on the sole ground that that sign has not acquired distinctive character through use in relation to the goods or services claimed.[1132]

In the case of a colour per se, distinctiveness without any prior use is inconceivable save in exceptional circumstances and even if a colour per se does not initially have any distinctive character, it may acquire such character in relation to the goods or services in respect of which registration of the mark is sought following the use made of it.[1133]

The Court's case law does not release competent trade mark authorities from the obligation to carry out an examination of distinctive character by reference to the actual situation, taking account of all the circumstances of the case. Thus, it would run counter to such an examination if those authorities could establish distinctive character of a colour per se or colour combination only on account of such a colour sign being used in relation to the goods or services claimed.[1134]

Moreover, when the sign registration of which as a mark is sought consists of a colour combination designated in the abstract and without contours, it is the Court's settled case law that the graphic representation of those colours must be systematically arranged by associating them in a predetermined and uniform way.[1135]

Thus, in the overall analysis of distinctive character by reference to the actual situation, it is necessary to examine whether and to what extent the systematically arranged colour combination is capable of conferring inherent distinctive character on the sign in question.[1136]

[13] In particular: shape of product mark

The interest that competitors of an applicant for a three-dimensional mark consisting of the product's design may have in being able freely to choose shapes and patterns for their own products is not in itself a ground for refusing registration of such a mark, nor a criterion sufficient in itself for the assessment of the mark's distinctive character.[1137]

In any event, the perception of the average consumer is not necessarily the same in the case of a three-dimensional trade mark, consisting of the **packaging of a product**, as it is in the case of a word or figurative mark which consists of a sign that is independent from the appearance of the goods it denotes. Average consumers are not in the habit of making assumptions about the origin of goods based on the shape of

1132. CJEU C-578/17 of 27.3.2019 – Oy Hartwall/Patentti- ja rekisterihallitus, para. 35.
1133. CJEU C-578/17 of 27.3.2019 – Oy Hartwall/Patentti- ja rekisterihallitus, para. 30, with reference to CJEU C-104/01 of 6.5.2003 – Libertel, paras 66 et seq.
1134. CJEU C-578/17 of 27.3.2019 – Oy Hartwall/Patentti- ja rekisterihallitus, para. 32.
1135. CJEU C-578/17 of 27.3.2019 – Oy Hartwall/Patentti- ja rekisterihallitus, para. 33, with reference to CJEU C-49/02 of 24.6.2004 – Heidelberger Bauchemie, para. 33.
1136. CJEU C-578/17 of 27.3.2019 – Oy Hartwall/Patentti- ja rekisterihallitus, para. 34; *see also* CJEU C-456/19 of 8.10.2020 – Aktiebolaget Östgötatrafiken/Patent- och registreringsverket, para. 37.
1137. CJEU C-173/04 P of 12.1.2006 – Deutsche SiSi-Werke/OHIM, para. 69.

their packaging, in the absence of any graphic or word element, and it could therefore prove more difficult to establish distinctive character in the case of such a three-dimensional trade mark than in the case of a word or figurative mark.[1138]

These considerations are not restricted to mass-produced products.[1139]

The more closely the shape for which registration is sought resembles the shape most likely to be taken by the product in question, the greater the likelihood of the shape being devoid of any distinctive character for the purposes of Article 7(1)(b) CTMR. Only a trade mark which departs significantly from the norm or customs of the sector and thereby fulfils its essential function of indicating origin is not devoid of any distinctive character for the purposes of that provision.[1140]

The court can determine the standard and customary in the industry in such a way that no product of this shape is usually used. In doing so, it does not have to additionally indicate in general and abstract terms everything that corresponds to the norm and customary in the industry concerned and may limit itself to indicating from which customary in the industry the trade mark applied for is to deviate significantly.[1141]

Where a three-dimensional mark is constituted by the shape of the product for which registration is sought, the mere fact that that shape is a 'variant' of a common shape of that type of product is not sufficient to establish that the mark is not devoid of any distinctive character for the purposes of Article 7(1)(b) CTMR. It must always be determined whether such a mark permits the average consumer of that product, who is reasonably well informed and reasonably observant and circumspect, to distinguish

1138. CJEU C-218/01 of 12.2.2004 – Henkel, para. 52; C-173/04 P of 12.1.2006 – Deutsche SiSi-Werke/OHIM, para. 28; C-24/05 P of 22.6.2006 – Storck/OHIM (light-brown sweet), para. 25; C-25/05 P of 22.6.2006 – Storck/OHIM (gold-coloured sweet wrapper), para. 27; C-144/06 P of 4.10.2007 – Henkel/OHIM, para. 36; C-238/06 P of 25.10.2007 – Develey Holding/OHIM, para. 80; C-497/07 P of 27.6.2008 – Philip Morris Products/OHIM, para. 25; C-20/08 P of 9.12.2008 – Enercon/OHIM, para. 49; C-546/10 P of 13.9.2011 – Wilfer/OHIM, para. 53; C-344/10 P and C-345/10 P of 20.10.2011 – Freixenet/OHIM, para. 46; C-96/11 P of 6.9.2012 – Storck/OHIM, para. 34; C-97/12 P of 15.5.2014 – Louis Vuitton Malletier/OHIM, para. 51; C-26/17 P of 13.9.2018 – Birkenstock Sales/EUIPO, para. 32; C-26/17 P of 13.9.2018 – Birkenstock Sales/EUIPO, para. 33; C-783/18 P of 12.12.2019 – EUIPO/Wajos, para. 24.

1139. CJEU C-546/10 P of 13.9.2011 – Wilfer/OHIM, para. 55; unofficial translation.

1140. CJEU C-218/01 of 12.2.2004 – Henkel, para. 49; C-456/01 P and C-457/01 P of 29.4.2004 – Henkel/OHIM, para. 39; C-468/01 P to C-472/01 P of 29.4.2004 – Procter & Gamble/OHIM (three-dimensional form of tablet I), para. 37; C-473/01 P and C-474/01 P of 29.4.2004 – Procter & Gamble/OHIM (three-dimensional form of tablet II), para. 37; C-136/02 P of 7.10.2004 – Mag Instrument/OHIM, para. 31; C-173/04 P of 12.1.2006 – Deutsche SiSi-Werke/OHIM, para. 31; C-24/05 P of 22.6.2006 – Storck/OHIM (light-brown sweet), para. 26; C-25/05 P of 22.6.2006 – Storck/OHIM (gold-coloured sweet wrapper), para. 28; C-144/06 P of 4.10.2007 – Henkel/OHIM, para. 37; C-238/06 P of 25.10.2007 – Develey Holding/OHIM, para. 81; C-546/10 P of 13.9.2011 – Wilfer/OHIM, para. 54; C-344/10 P and C-345/10 P of 20.10.2011 – Freixenet/OHIM, para. 47; C-98/11 P of 24.5.2012 – Chocoladefabriken Lindt & Sprüngli/OHIM, para. 42; C-96/11 P of 6.9.2012 – Storck/OHIM, para. 35; C-97/12 P of 15.5.2014 – Louis Vuitton Malletier/OHIM, para. 52; C-445/13 P of 7.5.2015 – Voss of Norway/OHIM, para. 91; C-417/16 P of 4.5.2017 – August Storck/EUIPO, para. 35; C-783/18 P of 12.12.2019 – EUIPO/Wajos, para. 24; C-698/17 P of 23.1.2019 – Klement/EUIPO, para. 65.

1141. CJEU C-783/18 P of 12.12.2019 – EUIPO/Wajos, para. 31, unofficial translation, with further proof.

the product concerned from those of other undertakings without conducting an analytical examination and without paying particular attention.[1142]

The fact that goods benefit from a **high quality of design** does not necessarily mean that a mark consisting of the three-dimensional shape of those goods enables *ab initio* those goods to be distinguished from those of other undertakings for the purposes of Article 7(1)(b) CTMR.[1143]

It does not follow from that case law that it is necessary systematically to restrict the **sector** for the purposes of comparison to the actual goods in respect of which registration is sought. It cannot be excluded that the consumers of a given product may in certain cases be influenced, in their perception of the trade mark which the product bears, by the marketing methods used for other goods which they also use. Thus, depending on the nature of the goods in question and the trade mark applied for, it may be necessary, for the purposes of assessing whether or not the trade mark is devoid of any distinctive character, to take into consideration a wider sector.[1144]

In particular, when the trade mark for which registration is sought consists of the three-dimensional shape of the packaging of the goods in question – *a fortiori* where the goods, because of their very nature, must be packaged in order to be marketed, so that the packaging chosen imposes its shape on the goods and, for the purposes of examining an application for registration as a mark, must be assimilated to the shape of the product – the relevant norm or customs may be those which apply in the sector of the packaging of goods which are of the same type and intended for the same consumers as those goods in respect of which registration is sought.[1145]

It cannot be excluded that the average consumer, who is accustomed to seeing various products from different undertakings packaged in the same type of packaging, does not at first identify the use of that type of packaging by an undertaking for the marketing of a given product as being, of itself, an indication of origin, when the same product is marketed by competitors of that undertaking in other types of packaging. In that regard, it should be noted that the average consumer, who does not make a study of the market, will not know in advance that only one undertaking markets a given product in a certain type of packaging, whilst its competitors use other types of packaging for that product.[1146]

Restriction of the sector in which the comparison is to be made falls within the appraisal of the facts.[1147]

Goods exist which possess an intrinsic **shape**, in so far as this **necessarily** derives from the features of the goods themselves and it is unnecessary to give them a particular shape to enable them to be marketed. In such cases, there is, in principle, no sufficiently close relationship between the packaging and the goods, with the result that the packaging cannot be assimilated to the shape of the goods for the purposes of

1142. CJEU C-136/02 P of 7.10.2004 – Mag Instrument/OHIM, para. 32; C-445/13 P of 7.5.2015 – Voss of Norway/OHIM, para. 92; C-783/18 P of 12.12.2019 – EUIPO/Wajos, para. 25.
1143. CJEU C-136/02 P of 7.10.2004 – Mag Instrument/OHIM, para. 68.
1144. CJEU C-173/04 P of 12.1.2006 – Deutsche SiSi-Werke/OHIM, para. 32.
1145. CJEU C-173/04 P of 12.1.2006 – Deutsche SiSi-Werke/OHIM, para. 33.
1146. CJEU C-173/04 P of 12.1.2006 – Deutsche SiSi-Werke/OHIM, para. 34.
1147. CJEU C-173/04 P of 12.1.2006 – Deutsche SiSi-Werke/OHIM, para. 35.

examining an application for registration as a mark. This might be the case, for example, of nails, which are, in trade, generally packaged.[1148]

On the other hand, other goods exist which do not possess an intrinsic shape and must be packaged in order to be marketed. The packaging chosen imposes its shape on the goods. In such circumstances, that packaging, for the purposes of examining an application for registration as a mark, must be assimilated to the shape of the product. That applies, for example, to goods manufactured, in particular, in the form of granules, powder or liquid which, because of their very nature, lack a shape of their own.[1149]

With regard, in particular, to three-dimensional trade marks consisting of the packaging of goods, such as **liquids**, which are packaged in trade for reasons linked to the very nature of the product, the Court has held that they must enable average consumers of the goods in question, who are reasonably well informed and reasonably observant and circumspect, to distinguish the product concerned from those of other undertakings without conducting an analytical or comparative examination and without paying particular attention.[1150]

The Court of First Instance did not therefore err in law by holding that the average consumer will see the form of drinks packaging as an indication of the product's commercial origin only if that form may be perceived immediately as such an indication. Moreover, in the same paragraph of the judgment under appeal, the Court of First Instance in no way held that the consumer would, as a matter of principle, be indifferent to the shape as an indication of origin or that the packaging of liquid goods could never have a distinctive character within the meaning of Article 7(1)(b) CTMR.[1151]

The Court of First Instance found that the shape of the wrappers at issue is a normal and traditional shape for a sweet wrapper, that a large number of sweets so wrapped could be found on the market, that the golden colour of the wrappers at issue is not unusual in itself, and it is not rare to see it used for sweet wrappers, that the characteristics of the combination of shape and colour of the mark applied for are not sufficiently different from those of the basic shapes commonly used for sweet wrappers, and that the wrappers in dispute come naturally to mind as a typical wrapper shape for those goods.[1152]

By those findings, the Court of First Instance established to the requisite legal standard that the mark applied for does not depart significantly from the norm or customs of the confectionery sector. Therefore, it did not err in law in finding that the mark is devoid of any distinctive character.[1153]

1148. CJEU C-218/01 of 12.2.2004 – Henkel, para. 32; *see also* CJEU C-408/18 P of 13.12.2018 – Senetic/EUIPO, paras 5/7 and 6; C-409/18 P of 13.12.2018 – Senetic/EUIPO, paras 5/7 and 6.
1149. CJEU C-218/01 of 12.2.2004 – Henkel, para. 33.
1150. CJEU C-173/04 P of 12.1.2006 – Deutsche SiSi-Werke/OHIM, para. 29; C-344/10 P and C-345/10 P of 20.10.2011 – Freixenet/OHIM, para. 48.
1151. CJEU C-173/04 P of 12.1.2006 – Deutsche SiSi-Werke/OHIM, para. 30.
1152. CJEU C-25/05 P of 22.6.2006 – Storck/OHIM (gold-coloured sweet wrapper), para. 32; *see also* CJEU C-24/05 P of 22.6.2006 – Storck/OHIM (light-brown sweet), para. 29.
1153. CJEU C-25/05 P of 22.6.2006 – Storck/OHIM (gold-coloured sweet wrapper), para. 33; *see also* CJEU C-24/05 P of 22.6.2006 – Storck/OHIM (light-brown sweet), para. 30.

That case law, which was developed in relation to three-dimensional trade marks consisting of the appearance of the product itself, also applies where the trade mark applied for is a **figurative mark** consisting of the two-dimensional representation of that product. In such a case, the mark likewise does not consist of a sign unrelated to the appearance of the products it covers.[1154]

That case law also applies where the mark applied for is a sign consisting of a design applied to the surface of a product.[1155]

That case law is also applicable where only a part of the product designated is represented by a mark.[1156]

It is apparent from the foregoing considerations that, where the issue is establishing the distinctive character of a mark consisting of the appearance of the product which it designates, it is necessary to verify whether that mark departs significantly from the standard or customs of the sector, such verification not being reserved solely to three-dimensional marks.[1157]

Where a three-dimensional mark incorporates a figurative element not consisting of a sign which is independent of the appearance of the products, but constitutes, in the mind of the consumer, only a decorative configuration, that mark cannot be assessed under the criteria for word and figurative marks which consist of a sign independent of the appearance of the products which they designate. Such considerations are clearly transposable to two-dimensional marks that have a figurative element.[1158]

The possibility afforded in *Lego Juris v. OHIM* to the competent authority when examining a three-dimensional sign can be extended to the examination of **any sign** constituted by the shape of goods within the meaning of Article 7(1)(e)(ii) CTMR.[1159]

It follows from that latter finding that the case law relating to three-dimensional marks must be applicable also where only part of the product designated is represented by a mark. Such a mark no more consists of a sign independent of the appearance of the product it designates than a figurative mark representing the entire product.[1160]

Even if the application of the case law relating to three-dimensional and figurative marks constituted, respectively, by the shape of the product concerned or by a representation of that shape presupposes the existence of a link between the mark and

1154. CJEU C-25/05 P of 22.6.2006 – Storck/OHIM (gold-coloured sweet wrapper), para. 29; C-144/06 P of 4.10.2007 – Henkel/OHIM, para. 38; C-546/10 P of 13.9.2011 – Wilfer/OHIM, para. 58; C-344/10 P and C-345/10 P of 20.10.2011 – Freixenet/OHIM, para. 48; C-97/12 P of 15.5.2014 – Louis Vuitton Malletier/OHIM, para. 53; C-521/13 P of 11.9.2014 – Think Schuhwerk/OHIM, para. 49; C-417/16 P of 4.5.2017 – August Storck/EUIPO, para. 36; C-26/17 P of 13.9.2018 – Birkenstock Sales/EUIPO, para. 34; *see also* CJEU C-96/11 P of 6.9.2012 – Storck/OHIM, para. 33.

1155. CJEU C-445/02 P of 28.6.2004 – Glaverbel/OHIM, para. 22-24; C-26/17 P of 13.9.2018 – Birkenstock Sales/EUIPO, para. 34.

1156. CJEU C-26/17 P of 13.9.2018 – Birkenstock Sales/EUIPO, para. 35, with reference to CJEU C-97/12 P of 15.5.2014 – Louis Vuitton Malletier/OHIM, para. 54.

1157. CJEU C-417/16 P of 4.5.2017 – August Storck/EUIPO, para. 37.

1158. CJEU C-417/16 P of 4.5.2017 – August Storck/EUIPO, para. 40, with reference to CJEU C-96/11 P of 6.9.2012 – Storck/OHIM, para. 38.

1159. CJEU C-337/12 P to C-340/12 P of 6.3.2014 – Pi-Design/OHIM, para. 55.

1160. CJEU C-546/10 P of 13.9.2011 – Wilfer/OHIM, para. 59; C-97/12 P of 15.5.2014 – Louis Vuitton Malletier/OHIM, para. 54, *see also* CJEU C-26/17 P of 13.9.2018 – Birkenstock Sales/EUIPO, para. 35.

that product which will be recognized by the relevant public, such a mark need not be perceived as an essential part of the product concerned.[1161]

[14] In particular: designs

Articles 2 and 3 TMD2008 must be interpreted as meaning that the representation, by a design alone, without indicating the size or the proportions, of the layout of a retail store, may be registered as a trade mark for services consisting in services relating to those goods but which do not form an integral part of the offer for sale thereof, provided that the sign is capable of distinguishing the services of the applicant for registration from those of other undertakings and that registration is not precluded by any of the grounds for refusal set out in that directive.[1162]

[D] Indications designating characteristics

[1] Principles

As the grounds for refusal or invalidity set out in Article 3(1)(b) and (c) **TMD2008** are **identical** to the grounds for refusal referred to in Article 7(1)(b) and (c) **CTMR**, the case law of the Court relating to those regulations is applicable to the provisions of the directive which are at issue in the disputes in the main proceedings.[1163]

The signs and indications referred to in Article 7(1)(c) CTMR are only those which may serve in normal usage from a consumer's point of view to **designate**, either directly or by reference to one of their essential characteristics, goods or services such as those in respect of which registration is sought.[1164]

In addition, Article 6(1)(b) TMD2008 does not run counter to what has been stated as to the objective of Article 3(1)(c) TMD2008, nor does it have a decisive bearing on the interpretation of that provision.[1165]

Article 12 CTMR concerns the limits on the effects of a Community trade mark, whereas Article 7 CTMR relates to the grounds for refusal to register signs as marks.[1166]

The fact that Article 12(b) CTMR ensures that every trader may freely use indications relating to the characteristics of goods and services in no way limits the scope of Article 7(1)(c) CTMR. On the contrary, that fact clearly discloses the need for

1161. CJEU C-97/12 P of 15.5.2014 – Louis Vuitton Malletier/OHIM, para. 55.
1162. CJEU C-421/13 of 10.7.2014 – Apple, para. 27.
1163. CJEU C-90/11 and C-91/11 of 15.3.2012 – Strigl and Securvita, para. 19.
1164. CJEU C-383/99 P of 20.9.2001 – Procter & Gamble/OHIM (baby-dry), para. 39; C-494/08 P of 9.12.2009 – Prana Haus/HABM, para. 28; C-306/11 P of 28.6.2012 – XXXLutz Marken/OHIM, para. 77; C-629/17 of 6.12.2018 J. Portugal Ramos Vinhos/Adega Cooperativa de Borba, para. 17.
1165. CJEU C-108/97 and C-109/97 of 4.5.1999 – Windsurfing Chiemsee, para. 28; C-404/02 of 16.9.2004 – Nichols, para. 32 f.; C-51/10 P of 10.3.2011 – Agencja Wydawnicza Technopol/HABM, para. 59; C-54/10 P and C-55/10 P of 22.6.2011 – Agencja Wydawnicza Technopol/HABM, para. 33.
1166. CJEU C-51/10 P of 10.3.2011 – Agencja Wydawnicza Technopol/HABM, para. 60.

the ground of refusal set out in Article 7(1)(c) CTMR – which, moreover, is an absolute ground for refusal – to be actually applied to any sign which may designate a characteristic of the goods or the services in respect of which its registration as a mark is sought.[1167]

If, for holding that the word at issue could not be refused registration under Article 7(1)(c), the reason given is that signs or indications whose meaning goes beyond the merely descriptive are capable of being registered as Community trade marks and that that term cannot be characterized as exclusively descriptive, a test is applied based on whether the mark is exclusively descriptive, which is not the test laid down by Article 7(1)(c) CTMR.[1168]

It is not necessary that the signs and indications composing the mark that are referred to in Article 3(1)(c) TMD2008 actually be in use at the time of the application for registration in a way that is descriptive of goods or services such as those in relation to which the application is filed, or of characteristics of those goods or services. It is sufficient, as the wording of those provisions itself indicates, that those signs and indications **could be used** for such purposes. A word must therefore be refused registration under that provision if **at least one of its possible meanings** designates a characteristic of the goods or services concerned.[1169]

Once it has been established that the trade mark applied for is descriptive of the characteristics of the services it designates, no further examination is necessary as to whether the trade mark could become descriptive in the future.[1170]

The **situations specifically covered** by Article 7(1)(c) CTMR are those in which the sign in respect of which registration as a mark is sought is capable of designating a 'characteristic' of the goods or services referred to in the application. By using, in Article 7(1)(c) CTMR, the terms 'the kind, quality, quantity, intended purpose, value, geographical origin or the time of production of the goods or of rendering of the service, or other characteristics of the goods or service', the legislature made it clear, first, that the kind, quality, quantity, intended purpose, value, geographical origin or the time of production of the goods or of rendering of the service must all be regarded as characteristics of goods or services and, secondly, that that list is not exhaustive, since any other characteristics of goods or services may also be taken into account.[1171]

The fact that the legislature chose to use the word 'characteristic' highlights the fact that the signs referred to in Article 7(1)(c) CTMR are merely those which serve to

1167. CJEU C-51/10 P of 10.3.2011 – Agencja Wydawnicza Technopol/HABM, para. 61.
1168. CJEU C-191/01 P of 23.10.2003 – OHIM/Wrigley, para. 33 f.
1169. CJEU C-191/01 P of 23.10.2003 – OHIM/Wrigley, para. 32; C-363/99 of 12.2.2004 – Koninklijke KPN Nederland, para. 97; C-212/07 P of 13.2.2008 – Indorata-Serviços e Gestão, para. 35; C-494/08 P of 9.12.2009 – Prana Haus/HABM, para. 52; C-80/09 P of 5.2.2010 – Mergel a. o./OHIM, para. 37; C-51/10 P of 10.3.2011 – Agencja Wydawnicza Technopol/HABM, para. 38; C-214/19 P of 3.9.2020 – achtung!/EUIPO, para. 34; *see also* CJEU C-54/10 P and C-55/10 P of 22.6.2011 – Agencja Wydawnicza Technopol/HABM, para. 28.
1170. CJEU C-655/17 P of 31.5.2018 – Berliner Stadtwerke/EUIPO, paras 3/7 and 6, unofficial translation; C-656/17 P of 31.5.2018 – Berliner Stadtwerke/EUIPO, paras 3/11 and 6, unofficial translation.
1171. CJEU C-51/10 P of 10.3.2011 – Agencja Wydawnicza Technopol/HABM, para. 49; C-126/13 P of 10.7.2014 – BSH Bosch und Siemens Hausgeräte/OHIM, para. 20; C-629/17 of 6.12.2018 J. Portugal Ramos Vinhos/Adega Cooperativa de Borba, para. 18.

designate a property, easily recognizable by the relevant class of persons, of the goods or the services in respect of which registration is sought. As the Court has pointed out,[1172] a sign can be refused registration on the basis of Article 7(1)(c) CTMR only if it is reasonable to believe that it will actually be recognized by the relevant class of persons as a description of one of those characteristics.[1173]

[2] Public interest

The **purpose** of the prohibition of registration of purely descriptive signs or indications as trade marks is to prevent registration as trade marks of signs or indications which, because they are no different from the usual way of designating the relevant goods or services or their characteristics, could not fulfil the function of identifying the undertaking that markets them and are thus devoid of the distinctive character needed for that function.[1174]

Article 3(1)(c) TMD2008 pursues an aim which is in the public interest, namely that descriptive signs or indications relating to the categories of goods or services in respect of which registration is applied for may be freely used by all, including as collective marks or as part of complex or graphic marks. Article 3(1)(c) therefore prevents such signs and indications from being reserved to one undertaking alone because they have been registered as trade marks.[1175]

1172. *See*, by analogy, as regards the identical provision laid down in Art. 3 TMD, CJEU C-108/97 and C-109/97 of 4.5.1999 – Windsurfing Chiemsee, para. 31; C-363/99 of 12.2.2004 – Koninklijke KPN Nederland, para. 56.

1173. CJEU C-51/10 P of 10.3.2011 – Agencja Wydawnicza Technopol/HABM, para. 50; C-369/10 P of 14.3.2011 – Ravensburger/OHIM, para. 53; C-126/13 P of 10.7.2014 – BSH Bosch und Siemens Hausgeräte/OHIM, paras 21 and 22; C-411/18 P of 3.10.2018 – Romantik Hotels & Restaurants/EUIPO, paras 4/9 and 5; C-629/17 of 6.12.2018 J. Portugal Ramos Vinhos/Adega Cooperativa de Borba, para. 19; C-629/17 of 6.12.2018 J. Portugal Ramos Vinhos/Adega Cooperativa de Borba, para. 20.

1174. CJEU C-383/99 P of 20.9.2001 – Procter & Gamble/OHIM (baby-dry), para. 37; C-191/01 P of 23.10.2003 – OHIM/Wrigley, para. 30; C-326/01 P of 5.2.2004 – Telefon & Buch/OHIM, para. 26; C-150/02 P of 5.2.2004 – Streamserve/OHIM, para. 24; *see also* CJEU C-51/10 P of 10.3.2011 – Agencja Wydawnicza Technopol/HABM, paras 33 and 46; C-56/10 P of 22.6.2011 – Agencja Wydawnicza Technopol/HABM, para. 29.

1175. CJEU C-108/97 and C-109/97 of 4.5.1999 – Windsurfing Chiemsee, para. 25; C-53/01 to C-55/01 of 8.4.2003 – Linde and Others, paras 73 and 77; C-104/01 of 6.5.2003 – Libertel, para. 52; C-191/01 P of 23.10.2003 – OHIM/Wrigley, para. 31; C-326/01 P of 5.2.2004 – Telefon & Buch/OHIM, paras 27 and 32; C-150/02 P of 5.2.2004 – Streamserve/OHIM, para. 25; C-363/99 of 12.2.2004 – Koninklijke KPN Nederland, para. 54 f. and 95; C-265/00 of 12.2.2004 – Campina Melkunie, para. 35 f.; C-173/04 P of 12.1.2006 – Deutsche SiSi-Werke/OHIM, para. 62; C-273/05 P of 19.4.2007 – OHIM/Celltech, para. 75; C-80/09 P of 5.2.2010 – Mergel a. o./OHIM, para. 34; C-51/10 P of 10.3.2011 – Agencja Wydawnicza Technopol/HABM, para. 37; C-369/10 P of 14.3.2011 – Ravensburger/OHIM, para. 52; C-90/11 and C-91/11 of 15.3.2012 – Strigl and Securvita, para. 31; C-126/13 P of 10.7.2014 – BSH Bosch und Siemens Hausgeräte/OHIM, para. 19; C-20/14 of 22.10.2015 – BGW Beratungs-Gesellschaft Wirtschaft, para. 24; C-139/16 of 6.7.2017 – Marín a.o./Abadía, para. 23; C-488/16 P of 6.9.2018 – Bundesverband – Souvenir – Geschenke – Ehrenpreise/EUIPO, para. 36; C-411/18 P of 3.10.2018 – Romantik Hotels & Restaurants/EUIPO, paras 4/9 and 5; *see also* CJEU C-218/01 of 12.2.2004 – Henkel, para. 41; C-673/15 P to C-676/15 P of 20.9.2017 – The Tea Board/EUIPO, para. 59.

[3] Irrelevant criteria

For the purposes of determining whether the ground for refusal set out in Article 3(1)(c) TMD2008 applies to such a mark, it is irrelevant whether or not there are synonyms capable of designating the same characteristics of the goods or services referred to in the application for registration. Although Article 3(1)(c) TMD2008 provides that, if the ground for refusal set out there is to apply, the mark must consist exclusively of signs or indications which may serve to designate characteristics of the goods or services concerned, it does not require that those signs or indications should be the **only way of designating** such characteristics.[1176]

As regards the argument that, in order for registration of an indication to be refused on the basis of that provision, it is necessary that the characteristics of the goods may not be described otherwise than by using that indication, such an argument must be rejected as without legal foundation. As is apparent from the precise wording of Article 7(1)(c) CTMR, where the signs or indications at issue may serve to designate the goods or services concerned or the characteristics of those goods, the registration of those signs or indications must be refused.[1177]

Article 3(1)(c) TMD2008 precludes registration of a trade mark which consists exclusively of signs or indications which may serve, in trade, to designate characteristics of the goods or services in respect of which registration is sought, and that is the case even when there are **more usual signs or indications** for designating the same characteristics and regardless of the number of competitors who may have an interest in using the signs or indications of which the mark consists.[1178]

It is also irrelevant whether the characteristics of the goods or services which may be the subject of the description are **commercially essential or merely ancillary**. The wording of Article 3(1)(c) TMD2008 does not draw any distinction by reference to the characteristics which may be designated by the signs or indications of which the mark consists. In fact, in the light of the public interest underlying the provision, any undertaking must be able freely to use such signs and indications to describe any characteristic whatsoever of its own goods, irrespective of how significant the characteristic may be commercially.[1179]

Article 7(1)(c) CTMR precludes registration of a trade mark when the target public could immediately and without further reflection establish a specific and direct association between those words and the goods and services covered by the applications.[1180]

1176. CJEU C-265/00 of 12.2.2004 – Campina Melkunie, para. 42; C-51/10 P of 10.3.2011 – Agencja Wydawnicza Technopol/HABM, para. 39; C-54/10 P and C-55/10 P of 22.6.2011 – Agencja Wydawnicza Technopol/HABM, para. 35; C-56/10 P of 22.6.2011 – Agencja Wydawnicza Technopol/HABM, para. 60.
1177. CJEU C-728/18 P of 25.9.2019 – EM Research Organization/EUIPO, paras 4/42 and 5.
1178. CJEU C-363/99 of 12.2.2004 – Koninklijke KPN Nederland, para. 61; C-265/00 of 12.2.2004 – Campina Melkunie, para. 42.
1179. CJEU C-363/99 of 12.2.2004 – Koninklijke KPN Nederland, para. 102.
1180. CJEU C-494/08 P of 9.12.2009 – Prana Haus/HABM, para. 29; unofficial translation; *see also* CJEU C-326/01 P of 5.2.2004 – Telefon & Buch/OHIM, para. 33.

The fact that an undertaking wishes to give its goods a certain image, without directly and immediately informing the consumer of one of the qualities or specific characteristics of the goods, is a case of **evocation** and not designation for the purposes of Article 7(1)(c) CTMR.[1181]

[4] In particular: abbreviations

Article 3(1)(b) and (c) TMD2008 must be interpreted as meaning that it is applicable to a word mark which consists of the juxtaposition of a descriptive word combination and a letter sequence which is non-descriptive in itself, if the relevant public perceives that sequence as being an abbreviation of that word combination by reason of the fact that it reproduces the first letter of each word of that combination, and that the mark in question, considered as a whole, can thus be understood as a combination of descriptive indications or abbreviations which is therefore devoid of distinctive character.[1182]

With regard to the **letter sequences at issue in the main proceedings**, the referring court finds that, taken in isolation, the signs 'MMF' and 'NAI' are not descriptive within the meaning of Article 3(1)(c) TMD2008.[1183]

Those sequences are not, as such, capable of designating any characteristic of the services concerned within the meaning of Article 3(1)(c) TMD2008.[1184]

In the main proceedings, it must be noted that, in each of the two cases, the three capital letters at issue, that is to say, 'MMF' and 'NAI' respectively, represent the initial letters of the word combinations to which they are attached. Thus, the word combination and the letter sequence, in each case, are intended to clarify each other and to draw attention to the fact that they are linked. Each letter sequence is therefore designed to support the relevant public's perception of the word combination, by simplifying its use and by making it easier to remember.[1185]

In that regard, the fact that the letter sequence precedes or follows the word combination is of no importance.[1186]

As regards the composition 'NAI – Der Natur-Aktien-Index', it must also be noted that the letter sequence 'NAI' is followed by a hyphen which links it to the word combination. That hyphen is liable, as is apparent from the order for reference, to reinforce the overall impression that the letter sequence is merely an abbreviation of the word combination that follows it. In addition, and as the referring court points out, that conclusion is not affected by the fact that the letter sequence 'NAI' does not

1181. CJEU C-306/11 P of 28.6.2012 – XXXLutz Marken/OHIM, para. 79; unofficial translation, based on CFI T-67/07 of 2.12.2008 – Ford Motor/HABM, para. 33; *see also* CJEU C-343/14 P of 7.5.2015 – Adler Modemärkte/OHIM, paras 36–38.
1182. CJEU C-90/11 and C-91/11 of 15.3.2012 – Strigl and Securvita, para. 40.
1183. CJEU C-90/11 and C-91/11 of 15.3.2012 – Strigl and Securvita, para. 27.
1184. CJEU C-90/11 and C-91/11 of 15.3.2012 – Strigl and Securvita, para. 28.
1185. CJEU C-90/11 and C-91/11 of 15.3.2012 – Strigl and Securvita, para. 32.
1186. CJEU C-90/11 and C-91/11 of 15.3.2012 – Strigl and Securvita, para. 33.

encompass the initial letter of the definite article 'Der' contained in the word combination that follows it, in so far as the article 'Der' is merely an accessory to the nouns the initial letters of which are repeated in the letter sequence at issue.[1187]

Furthermore, there is no additional element which would allow the view to be taken that the juxtaposition of the word combination and the letter sequence is unusual or might have its own meaning which, in the perception of the relevant public, distinguishes the services offered from those of a different commercial origin.[1188]

By contrast, the mere fact of bringing a letter sequence, as an abbreviation, and a word combination together, without introducing any unusual variations, is liable to result in a verbal expression consisting exclusively of signs or indications which may serve, in trade, to designate characteristics of the services concerned.[1189]

Moreover, if the letter sequences at issue in the main proceedings are perceived by the relevant public to be abbreviations of the word combinations to which they are juxtaposed, those sequences cannot be more than the sum of all the elements of the mark, taken as a whole, even though they may be considered to have distinctive character in themselves.[1190]

On the contrary, the letter sequence which reproduces the initial letters of the words comprising that word combination occupies only an ancillary position in relation to the word combination. Each of the letter sequences at issue, although not descriptive when considered in isolation, may be descriptive when combined, within the mark at issue, with a principal expression, which itself is descriptive as such, of which it is perceived to be an abbreviation.[1191]

It follows that if the relevant public perceive the marks at issue in the main proceedings, considered overall, as providing information on the characteristics of the financial services which they designate, those marks should then be considered to be descriptive, within the meaning of Article 3(1)(c) TMD2008, and, therefore, as being necessarily devoid of any distinctive character with regard to those services within the meaning of Article 3(1)(b) TMD2008.[1192]

It is apparent from the grounds of the judgment in *Strigl* and *Securvita*[1193] that whether a sign consisting of a letter sequence juxtaposed with a word combination is to be refused registration under Article 3(1)(b) and (c) TMD2008 must be assessed on a case-by-case basis, according to the perception which the relevant public has of the interdependence between the various elements of the sign and of the sign as a whole.[1194]

1187. CJEU C-90/11 and C-91/11 of 15.3.2012 – Strigl and Securvita, para. 34.
1188. CJEU C-90/11 and C-91/11 of 15.3.2012 – Strigl and Securvita, para. 35; *see* CJEU C-304/06 P of 8.5.2008 – Eurohypo/OHIM, para. 69.
1189. CJEU C-90/11 and C-91/11 of 15.3.2012 – Strigl and Securvita, para. 36; *see also* CJEU C-363/99 of 12.2.2004 – Koninklijke KPN Nederland, para. 98.
1190. CJEU C-90/11 and C-91/11 of 15.3.2012 – Strigl and Securvita, para. 37.
1191. CJEU C-90/11 and C-91/11 of 15.3.2012 – Strigl and Securvita, para. 38.
1192. CJEU C-90/11 and C-91/11 of 15.3.2012 – Strigl and Securvita, para. 39; C-363/99 of 12.2.2004 – Koninklijke KPN Nederland, para. 86.
1193. CJEU C-90/11 and C-91/11 of 15.3.2012 – Strigl and Securvita.
1194. CJEU C-20/14 of 22.10.2015 – BGW Beratungs-Gesellschaft Wirtschaft, para. 31.

Consequently, the statement in paragraph 38 of that judgment[1195] that the letter sequence which reproduces the initial letters of the words comprising that word combination occupies only an ancillary position in relation to the word combination must be read in that way and cannot be interpreted as being the expression of a general rule for assessing the ancillary nature of a sequence of letters which reproduces the first letter of each of the words in the word combination with which it is juxtaposed.[1196]

That statement simply makes clear, for the purposes of the application of the grounds for refusal set out in Article 3(1)(b) and (c) TMD2008, that a letter sequence, even if it is distinctive in itself, may be descriptive when it is reproduced in a composite mark in which it is combined with a descriptive principal expression of which it is perceived to be the abbreviation, which must be determined on a case-by-case basis.[1197]

[5] In particular: numerals

Given that signs which are composed exclusively of numerals are generally equated with numbers, one of the things that they can do, in trade, is to designate a quantity. Nevertheless, in order for a sign which is composed exclusively of numerals to be refused registration on the basis of Article 7(1)(c) CTMR on the ground that it designates a quantity, it must be reasonable to believe that, in the mind of the relevant class of persons, the quantity indicated by those numerals characterizes the goods or services in respect of which registration is sought.[1198]

The General Court based its decision on the fact that the sign '1000' can indicate the number of pages in the goods covered by the application for registration and on the fact that ranking lists and collections of data and puzzles – in respect of which there is a preference for the content to be indicated by one or more words coupled with round numbers – are frequently published in those goods.[1199]

Without it being necessary to determine whether each of those factors supported the inference that the number 1000 characterizes the goods referred to in the application for registration, the fact remains that, at the very least, the finding made by the General Court, to the effect that the sign '1000' is descriptive in relation to the collections of puzzles contained in those goods, is not incompatible with the specific points made above regarding the scope of Article 7(1)(c) CTMR.[1200]

Where an application for registration refers, in particular, to a category of goods the content of which is easily and typically designated by the numeral indicating the number of units they contain, it is reasonable to believe that a sign composed of numerals – such as that at issue – will actually be recognized by the relevant class of

1195. CJEU C-90/11 and C-91/11 of 15.3.2012 – Strigl and Securvita.
1196. CJEU C-20/14 of 22.10.2015 – BGW Beratungs-Gesellschaft Wirtschaft, para. 32.
1197. CJEU C-20/14 of 22.10.2015 – BGW Beratungs-Gesellschaft Wirtschaft, para. 33.
1198. CJEU C-51/10 P of 10.3.2011 – Agencja Wydawnicza Technopol/HABM, para. 52.
1199. CJEU C-51/10 P of 10.3.2011 – Agencja Wydawnicza Technopol/HABM, para. 53.
1200. CJEU C-51/10 P of 10.3.2011 – Agencja Wydawnicza Technopol/HABM, para. 54.

persons as a description of that quantity and therefore as a characteristic of those goods.[1201]

It was therefore open to the General Court to find, without erring in law, that registration of the sign '1000' had to be refused, on the basis of Article 7(1)(c) CTMR, in respect of the goods covered by the application [periodicals, including periodicals containing crossword puzzles].[1202]

[6] In particular: geographical names

Indeed, it is clear from the actual wording of Article 3(1)(c) TMD2008, which refers to '... indications which may serve ... to designate ... geographical origin', that geographical names which are liable to be used by undertakings must remain available to such undertakings as indications of the geographical origin of the category of goods concerned.[1203]

Thus, under Article 3(1)(c) TMD2008, the competent authority must assess whether a geographical name in respect of which application for registration as a trade mark is made **designates a place** which is currently associated in the mind of the relevant class of persons with the category of goods concerned, or whether it is reasonable to assume that such an association may be established in the future.[1204]

As regards signs or indications which may serve to designate the geographical origin of the categories of goods in respect of which registration of the mark is sought, especially geographical names, the Court has held that it is in the public interest that they remain available, not least because they may be an indication of the quality and other characteristics of the categories of goods concerned, and may also, in various ways, influence consumer tastes by, for instance, associating the goods with a place that may give rise to a favourable response.[1205]

The sign must be accompanied by a name designating **a given geographical place** so that the geographical origin of the goods or services concerned may be identified, the latter being characterized by the possibility of finding in abundance, in that determined physical space, such goods or services of a high degree of value or quality.[1206]

It follows that there is no connection between the product concerned in the present case, namely wine, and the geographical origin attributed to the sign 'la Milla de Oro', since it is precisely on the basis of the name of the given geographical place

1201. CJEU C-51/10 P of 10.3.2011 – Agencja Wydawnicza Technopol/HABM, para. 56.
1202. CJEU C-51/10 P of 10.3.2011 – Agencja Wydawnicza Technopol/HABM, para. 57.
1203. CJEU C-108/97 and C-109/97 of 4.5.1999 – Windsurfing Chiemsee, para. 30.
1204. CJEU C-108/97 and C-109/97 of 4.5.1999 – Windsurfing Chiemsee, paras 31 and 37; C-363/99 of 12.2.2004 – Koninklijke KPN Nederland, para. 56; C-494/08 P of 9.12.2009 – Prana Haus/HABM, para. 53; *see also* CJEU C-326/01 P of 5.2.2004 – Telefon & Buch/OHIM, para. 31; C-51/10 P of 10.3.2011 – Agencja Wydawnicza Technopol/HABM, para. 50; C-139/16 of 6.7.2017 – Marín a.o./Abadía, para. 16; C-488/16 P of 6.9.2018 – Bundesverband – Souvenir – Geschenke – Ehrenpreise/EUIPO, para. 38.
1205. CJEU C-108/97 and C-109/97 of 4.5.1999 – Windsurfing Chiemsee, paras 26; C-488/16 P of 6.9.2018 – Bundesverband – Souvenir – Geschenke – Ehrenpreise/EUIPO, para. 37.
1206. CJEU C-139/16 of 6.7.2017 – Marín a.o./Abadía, para. 19.

with which they are associated that the geographical origin of the goods or services in question can be determined.[1207]

In light of the foregoing considerations, the answer to the second question is that a sign such as 'la Milla de Oro', referring to the characteristic of a product or service which is that it can be found in abundance in a single place with a high degree of value and quality, cannot constitute an indication of geographical origin, since that sign must be accompanied by a name designating a geographical place so that the actual physical space with which a strong concentration of a product or service of a high degree of value or quality is associated may be identified.[1208]

Article 3(1)(c) TMD2008 is not confined to prohibiting the registration of geographical names as trade marks solely where they designate specified geographical locations which are already famous, or are known for the category of goods concerned, and which are therefore **associated with those goods** in the mind of the relevant class of persons, that is to say in the trade and amongst average consumers of that category of goods in the territory in respect of which registration is applied for.[1209]

In the latter case, when assessing whether the geographical name is capable, in the mind of the relevant class of persons, of designating the origin of the category of goods in question, regard must be had more particularly to the **degree of familiarity** amongst such persons with that name, with the characteristics of the place designated by the name, and with the category of goods concerned.[1210]

In that connection, Article 3(1)(c) TMD2008 does not in principle preclude the registration of geographical names which are unknown to the relevant class of persons - or at least unknown as the designation of a geographical location - or of names in respect of which, because of the type of place they designate (say, a **mountain or lake**), such persons are unlikely to believe that the category of goods concerned originates there.[1211]

However, it cannot be ruled out that the name of a lake may serve to designate geographical origin within the meaning of Article 3(1)(c) TMD2008, provided that the name could be understood by the relevant class of persons to include the shores of the lake or the surrounding area.[1212]

It follows from the foregoing that the application of Article 3(1)(c) TMD2008 does not depend on there being a real, current or serious need to leave a sign or indication free ('**Freihaltebedürfnis**') under German case law.[1213]

1207. CJEU C-139/16 of 6.7.2017 - Marín a.o./Abadía, para. 20.
1208. CJEU C-139/16 of 6.7.2017 - Marín a.o./Abadía, para. 21.
1209. CJEU C-108/97 and C-109/97 of 4.5.1999 - Windsurfing Chiemsee, para. 29.
1210. CJEU C-108/97 and C-109/97 of 4.5.1999 - Windsurfing Chiemsee, para. 32.
1211. CJEU C-108/97 and C-109/97 of 4.5.1999 - Windsurfing Chiemsee, para. 33; *see also* CJEU C-488/16 P of 6.9.2018 - Bundesverband - Souvenir - Geschenke - Ehrenpreise/EUIPO, para. 39.
1212. CJEU C-108/97 and C-109/97 of 4.5.1999 - Windsurfing Chiemsee, para. 34.
1213. CJEU C-108/97 and C-109/97 of 4.5.1999 - Windsurfing Chiemsee, para. 35; C-51/10 P of 10.3.2011 - Agencja Wydawnicza Technopol/HABM, para. 39; C-285/19 P of 6.11.2019 - Geske/EUIPO, paras 5/19 and 6; *see also* CJEU C-80/09 P of 5.2.2010 - Mergel a. o./OHIM, para. 35.

Finally, it is important to note that whilst an indication of the geographical origin of goods to which Article 3(1)(c) TMD2008 applies usually indicates the place where the goods were or could be manufactured, the connection between a category of goods and a geographical location might depend on other ties, such as the fact that the goods were conceived and designed in the geographical location concerned.[1214]

The General Court did not err in law in finding that, as **Neuschwanstein** Castle is not, as such, a place where goods are produced or services are rendered, the contested trade mark could not be indicative of the geographical origin of the goods and services it covers.[1215]

[7] In particular: forms of the packaging

For three-dimensional trade marks consisting of the packaging of goods which are packaged in trade for reasons linked to the very nature of the goods, the packaging thereof may serve to designate characteristics of the packaged goods, including their quality, within the meaning of Article 3(1)(c) TMD2008.[1216]

Article 3(1)(c) TMD2008 does not exclude the possibility that a trade mark which consists of a packaging of a three-dimensional shape assimilated to the shape of the goods may serve to designate certain characteristics of the goods thus packaged. Whilst it might be difficult to identify such characteristics, the possibility that the packaging might describe the characteristics of the product, including its quality, cannot be ruled out.[1217]

In that connection, the competent authority called on to apply that provision must examine the relationship between the packaging and the nature of the goods for which registration of the mark is sought and must determine, in relation to those goods and in the light of a specific examination of all the relevant elements characterizing that trade mark, and, in particular in the light of the above-mentioned public interest, whether the ground for refusal of registration provided for by that provision applies in the case before it.[1218]

[8] Further examples

In concluding from all the findings made that the word '**Streamserve**' could serve, in trade, to designate a characteristic of most of the goods referred to in the application for registration, the Court of First Instance applied Article 7(1)(c) CTMR correctly.[1219]

The reasons that, in German, the combinations of the words '**Telefonbuch**' and '**Kommunikationsverzeichnis**' designated the kind of goods and the intended use of

1214. CJEU C-108/97 and C-109/97 of 4.5.1999 – Windsurfing Chiemsee, para. 36.
1215. CJEU C-488/16 P of 6.9.2018 – Bundesverband – Souvenir – Geschenke – Ehrenpreise/EUIPO, para. 54.
1216. CJEU C-218/01 of 12.2.2004 – Henkel, para. 44.
1217. CJEU C-218/01 of 12.2.2004 – Henkel, para. 42.
1218. CJEU C-218/01 of 12.2.2004 – Henkel, para. 43.
1219. CJEU C-150/02 P of 5.2.2004 – Streamserve/OHIM, para. 31.

the services described words and could therefore be regarded as descriptive of those goods and services follow the interpretation of Article 7(1)(c) CTMR set out.[1220]

As it is, the word combination '**Baby-dry**', whilst it does unquestionably allude to the function which the goods are supposed to fulfil, still does not satisfy the disqualifying criteria. Whilst each of the two words in the combination may form part of expressions used in everyday speech to designate the function of babies' nappies, their syntactically unusual juxtaposition is not a familiar expression in the English language, either for designating babies' nappies or for describing their essential characteristics.[1221]

A trade mark [here '**adegaborba.pt**'] consisting of a word sign, such as that at issue in the main proceedings, designating wine products and including a geographical name, must be refused registration, where that sign contains, in particular, a term which is commonly used to designate facilities or sites in which such products are produced and is also one of the word elements of the business name of the legal person seeking to register that trade mark.[1222]

The relevant term in the main proceedings, 'adega', has two meanings in Portuguese. The first corresponds to underground premises in which wine in particular is kept. The second refers to premises or facilities in which wine products, such as wine itself, are produced.[1223]

Where a term refers to the place of production of a product, such as wine, or to a facility in which it is produced, it is, in principle, an indication which may serve to designate a property of those goods, easily recognizable by the relevant class of people.[1224]

Since, as a general rule, the relevant class of people will perceive the term 'adega' to be a reference to a facility in which wine is produced and stored, and, therefore, as a reference to properties of those goods, just as they do in regard to the geographical origin or the time of production of goods, mentioned by way of example in Article 3(1)(c) TMD2008.[1225]

Therefore, a term designating such a facility constitutes a characteristic of those goods and falls within the scope of application of that provision. It must therefore be regarded as descriptive of the goods which it designates.[1226]

It follows that where a sign serving to designate goods associates two word elements, namely a descriptive term and a geographical name, such as 'Borba' in this case, relating to the geographical origin of those goods, which is also descriptive of them, the sign composed of those two word elements must be considered to be of a descriptive character and, as such, devoid of any distinctive character.[1227]

1220. CJEU C-326/01 P of 5.2.2004 - Telefon & Buch/OHIM, para. 30.
1221. CJEU C-383/99 P of 20.9.2001 - Procter & Gamble/OHIM (baby-dry), para. 43.
1222. CJEU C-629/17 of 6.12.2018 J. Portugal Ramos Vinhos/Adega Cooperativa de Borba, para. 28.
1223. CJEU C-629/17 of 6.12.2018 J. Portugal Ramos Vinhos/Adega Cooperativa de Borba, para. 21.
1224. CJEU C-629/17 of 6.12.2018 J. Portugal Ramos Vinhos/Adega Cooperativa de Borba, para. 22.
1225. CJEU C-629/17 of 6.12.2018 J. Portugal Ramos Vinhos/Adega Cooperativa de Borba, para. 23.
1226. CJEU C-629/17 of 6.12.2018 J. Portugal Ramos Vinhos/Adega Cooperativa de Borba, para. 24.
1227. CJEU C-629/17 of 6.12.2018 J. Portugal Ramos Vinhos/Adega Cooperativa de Borba, para. 25.

The fact, even if proven, that such a geographical name constitutes a protected designation of origin by virtue of Regulation No. 1308/2013[1228] is in no way capable of calling such an interpretation into question since it is evident from Article 102 of this regulation that, in essence, such a designation may not be registered as a commercial trade mark.[1229]

Furthermore, the fact that a term used to designate a place of production of goods, or a facility in which the goods are produced, is part of various word elements of the corporate name of a legal person is irrelevant for the purposes of examining the descriptive character of that term, having regard to the fact that such an examination is carried out by reference to the goods for which registration of the trade mark is sought and by reference to its perception by the relevant public.[1230]

[E] Customary indications

Article 3(1)(d) TMD2008 must be interpreted as meaning that it subjects refusal to register a trade mark to the sole condition that the signs or indications of which the trade mark is exclusively composed have become customary in the current language or in the bona fide and established practices of the trade to designate the goods or services in respect of which registration of that mark is sought. It is immaterial, when that provision is applied, whether the signs or indications in question describe the properties or characteristics of those goods or services.[1231]

Under Article 3(1)(d) TMD2008, trade marks which consist exclusively of signs or indications which have become customary in the current language or trade practices are to be refused registration.[1232]

Unlike paragraph 8(2)(3) of the Markengesetz,[1233] which refers to trade marks that consist exclusively of signs or indications which have become **customary** in the current language or trade practices **to designate the goods or services**, Article 3(1)(d) TMD2008 contains no such qualification. It cannot, however, be concluded from that that, in order to assess the merits of an application for registration of a trade mark, account should not be taken of the connection between the signs or indications constituting the trade mark and the goods or services covered by that mark.[1234]

The purpose of Article 3(1)(d) TMD2008 is to prevent the registration of signs or indications that are not capable of distinguishing the goods or services of one

1228. Regulation (EU) No 1308/2013 of the European Parliament and of the Council of 17 December 2013 establishing a common organization of the markets in agricultural products and repealing Council Regulations (EEC) No 922/72, (EEC) No 234/79, (EC) No 1037/2001 and (EC) No 1234/2007 (OJ 2013, L 347, p. 671).
1229. CJEU C-629/17 of 6.12.2018 J. Portugal Ramos Vinhos/Adega Cooperativa de Borba, para. 26.
1230. CJEU C-629/17 of 6.12.2018 J. Portugal Ramos Vinhos/Adega Cooperativa de Borba, para. 27, with further reference.
1231. CJEU C-517/99 of 4.10.2001 – Merz & Krell, para. 41.
1232. CJEU C-517/99 of 4.10.2001 – Merz & Krell, para. 26.
1233. German trade mark act.
1234. CJEU C-517/99 of 4.10.2001 – Merz & Krell, para. 27.

undertaking from those of other undertakings and so do not satisfy the criterion laid down in Article 2 TMD2008.[1235]

The question of whether particular signs or indications possess distinctive character cannot, however, be considered in the abstract and separately from the goods or services those signs or indications are intended to distinguish.[1236]

That finding is corroborated by Article 3(3) TMD2008. It is through the use made of it that such a sign acquires the distinctive character which is a prerequisite for its registration under that provision. However, whether a sign does have the capacity to distinguish as a result of the use made of it can only be assessed in relation to the goods or services covered by it.[1237]

It follows that Article 3(1)(d) TMD2008 must be interpreted as only precluding registration of a trade mark where the signs or indications of which the mark is exclusively composed have become customary in the current language or in the bona fide and established practices of the trade to designate the goods or services in respect of which registration of that mark is sought.[1238]

In order for Article 3(1)(d) TMD2008 to be effective, the scope of the provision in respect of which the Court's interpretation is sought should not be limited solely to trade marks which describe the properties or characteristics of the goods or services covered by them.[1239]

However, registration of a trade mark which consists of signs or indications that are also used as **advertising slogans, indications of quality or incitements to purchase the goods or services** covered by that mark is not excluded as such by virtue of such use. It is for the national court to determine in each case whether the signs or indications have become customary in the current language or in the bona fide and established practices of the trade to designate the goods or services covered by that mark.[1240]

It also follows that where the signs or indications concerned have become customary in the current language or in the bona fide and established practices of the trade to designate the goods or services covered by the mark, it is of little consequence that they are used as advertising slogans, indications of quality or incitements to purchase those goods or services.[1241]

The fact that it has been shown that the trade mark applied for is commonly used by the public or by competitors is a relevant factor under Article 7(1)(d) CTMR, but not under Article 7(1)(b).[1242]

1235. CJEU C-517/99 of 4.10.2001 – Merz & Krell, para. 28.
1236. CJEU C-517/99 of 4.10.2001 – Merz & Krell, para. 29.
1237. CJEU C-517/99 of 4.10.2001 – Merz & Krell, para. 30.
1238. CJEU C-517/99 of 4.10.2001 – Merz & Krell, para. 31.
1239. CJEU C-517/99 of 4.10.2001 – Merz & Krell, para. 36; similar CJEU C-64/02 P of 21.10.2004 – OHIM/ERPO MÖBELWERK, para. 38.
1240. CJEU C-517/99 of 4.10.2001 – Merz & Krell, para. 40.
1241. CJEU C-517/99 of 4.10.2001 – Merz & Krell, para. 39; C-64/02 P of 21.10.2004 – OHIM/ERPO MÖBELWERK, para. 41.
1242. CJEU C-37/03 P of 15.9.2005 – BioID/OHIM, para. 41.

[F] Shape of goods, or another characteristic

Take care: There was a major change in the wording of TMD2008 from 'the shape' to 'the shape, or another characteristic'.

Principles

Basically still applicable: Article 3(1)(e) TMD2008 explicitly **singles out certain signs consisting of the shape of the goods** by listing the specific grounds for refusing their registration, namely where those signs consist exclusively of the shape which results from the nature of the goods themselves, of the shape of goods which is necessary to obtain a technical result, or of the shape which gives substantial value to the goods.[1243]

Basically still applicable: In the context of an application for registration of a sign consisting exclusively of the shape of goods, it must **first** be ascertained that there is no obstacle under Article 3(1)(e) TMD2008 which may preclude registration, **before** going on to analyse, as appropriate, whether the sign at issue might have acquired a **distinctive character** within the meaning of Article 3(3) TMD2008.[1244]

Basically still applicable: Article 3(1)(e), second indent, TMD2008 must be interpreted to mean that a sign consisting exclusively of the shape of a product is unregistrable by virtue thereof if it is established that the **essential functional features** of that shape are attributable only to the technical result. Moreover, the ground for refusal or invalidity of registration imposed by that provision cannot be overcome by establishing that there are other shapes which allow the same technical result to be obtained.[1245]

Basically still applicable: The grounds for refusal to register signs consisting of the shape of a product are **expressly listed** in Article 3(1)(e) TMD2008. Under that provision, signs which consist exclusively of the shape which results from the nature of the goods themselves, or the shape of the goods which is necessary to obtain a technical result, or the shape which gives substantial value to the goods cannot be registered or if registered are liable to be declared invalid.[1246]

Still applicable: It must be observed that, unlike in the situation covered by Article 3(1)(b) TMD2008 and Article 7(1)(b) CTMR, where the perception of the **target public** must be taken into account since it is essential in order to determine whether the sign filed for registration as a trade mark enables the goods or services concerned to be recognized as originating from a particular undertaking, such an obligation cannot be imposed in the context of paragraph 1(e) of those articles.[1247]

Still applicable: The presumed perception of the sign by the average consumer is not a decisive element when applying the ground for refusal under Article 7(1)(e)(ii)

1243. CJEU C-215/14 of 16.9.2015 – Société des Produits Nestlé, para. 37.
1244. CJEU C-215/14 of 16.9.2015 – Société des Produits Nestlé, para. 40.
1245. CJEU C-299/99 of 18.6.2002 – Philips, para. 84.
1246. CJEU C-299/99 of 18.6.2002 – Philips, para. 74.
1247. CJEU C-48/09 P of 14.9.2010 – Lego Juris/OHIM, para. 75; C-205/13 of 18.9.2014 – Hauck, paras 33 and 36.

CTMR, but, at most, may be a relevant criterion of assessment for the competent authority when it identifies the essential characteristics of the sign.[1248]

Still applicable: The marks which may be refused registration on the grounds listed in Article 3(1)(b), (c) or (d) TMD2008 may under Article 3(3) acquire a distinctive character through the use made of them. However, a sign which is refused registration under Article 3(1)(e) TMD2008 can **never acquire a distinctive character** for the purposes of Article 3(3) by the use made of it.[1249]

Still applicable: Article 7(1)(e)(ii) of Regulation No. 40/94 constitutes an obstacle that may prevent a sign consisting exclusively of the shape of goods which is necessary to obtain a technical result from being registered as a trade mark, even though that sign is capable of performing the essential function of a trade mark, that of guaranteeing the identity of the origin of the goods or services in question to the consumer by enabling him, without any possibility of confusion, to distinguish those goods or services from others which have another origin.[1250]

Still applicable: Article 3(3) TMD2008 does not refer, for the purposes of establishing the extent of the exception laid down therein, to the signs referred to in Article 3(1)(e).[1251]

Basically still applicable: Article 3(1)(e) TMD2008 thus concerns certain signs which are not such as to constitute trade marks and is a preliminary obstacle liable to prevent a sign consisting exclusively of the shape of a product from being registrable. If **any one of the criteria listed** in Article 3(1)(e) is satisfied, a sign consisting exclusively of the shape of the product or of a graphic representation of that shape cannot be registered as a trade mark.[1252]

Basically still applicable: The third indent of Article 3(1)(e) TMD2008 is to be interpreted as meaning that the shape of a product which gives substantial value to that product cannot constitute a trade mark under Article 3(3) TMD2008 where, prior to the application for registration, it acquired attractiveness as a result of its recognition as a distinctive sign following **advertising campaigns** presenting the specific characteristics of the product in question.[1253]

Still applicable: Article 3(1)(e) TMD2008 must be interpreted as meaning that the grounds for refusal of registration set out in the first and third **indents of that provision may not be applied in combination.**[1254]

1248. CJEU C-48/09 P of 14.9.2010 – Lego Juris/OHIM, para. 76; C-205/13 of 18.9.2014 – Hauck, para. 34; C-237/19 of 23.4.2020 – Gömböc Kutató, Szolgáltató és Kereskedelmi/Tulajdon Nemzeti Hivatala, para. 31 and 44.
1249. CJEU C-299/99 of 18.6.2002 – Philips, paras 57 and 75; C-53/01 to C-55/01 of 8.4.2003 – Linde and Others, paras 44 and 65; C-218/01 of 12.2.2004 – Henkel, para. 36; C-371/06 of 20.9.2007 – Benetton Group, para. 26; C-48/09 P of 14.9.2010 – Lego Juris/OHIM, para. 47; C-215/14 of 16.9.2015 – Société des Produits Nestlé, para. 39.
1250. CJEU C-421/15 P of 11.5.2017 – Yoshida Metal Industry/EUIPO, para. 33, with further reference.
1251. CJEU C-371/06 of 20.9.2007 – Benetton Group, para. 25.
1252. CJEU C-299/99 of 18.6.2002 – Philips, para. 76; C-371/06 of 20.9.2007 – Benetton Group, para. 26; C-205/13 of 18.9.2014 – Hauck, para. 40; C-215/14 of 16.9.2015 – Société des Produits Nestlé, paras 38 and 47.
1253. CJEU C-371/06 of 20.9.2007 – Benetton Group, para. 28.
1254. CJEU C-205/13 of 18.9.2014 – Hauck, para. 43.

Still applicable: It is clear from this wording that the three grounds for refusal of registration set out in that provision operate independently of one another: the fact that they are set out as successive points, coupled with the use of the word 'exclusively', shows that each of those grounds must be applied independently of the others.[1255]

Still applicable: In that regard, the fact that the sign in question could be denied registration on the basis of a number of grounds for refusal is irrelevant so long as any one of those grounds fully applies to that sign.[1256]

Still applicable: Accordingly, it is possible that the essential features of a sign may be covered by one or more grounds of refusal set out under Article 3(1)(e) TMD2008. However, in such a case, registration may be refused only where at least one of those grounds is fully applicable to the sign at issue.[1257]

Still applicable: In addition, it must be pointed out that the public interest objective underlying the application of the three grounds for refusal of registration set out in Article 3(1)(e) TMD2008 precludes refusal of registration where none of those three grounds is fully applicable.[1258]

Still applicable: An interpretation of Article 3(1)(e) TMD2008 under which registration of a mark could not be refused where, following analysis, more than one of the three grounds for refusal were found to be applicable, or vice versa, which allowed the application of that provision where each of the three grounds for refusal set out was only partially established, would clearly run counter to the public interest objective underlying the application of the three grounds for refusal of registration set out in Article 3(1)(e) TMD2008.[1259]

[1] Public interest

Still applicable: The **rationale** of the grounds for refusal of registration laid down in Article 3(1)(e) TMD2008 is to prevent trade mark protection from granting its proprietor a monopoly on technical solutions or functional characteristics of a product which a user is likely to seek in the products of competitors. Article 3(1)(e) is thus intended to prevent the protection conferred by the trade mark right from being extended, beyond signs which serve to distinguish a product or service from those offered by competitors, so as to form an obstacle preventing competitors from freely offering for sale products incorporating such technical solutions or functional characteristics in competition with the proprietor of the trade mark.[1260]

1255. CJEU C-205/13 of 18.9.2014 – Hauck, para. 39; C-215/14 of 16.9.2015 – Société des Produits Nestlé, para. 46.
1256. CJEU C-205/13 of 18.9.2014 – Hauck, para. 41; C-215/14 of 16.9.2015 – Société des Produits Nestlé, para. 47.
1257. CJEU C-215/14 of 16.9.2015 – Société des Produits Nestlé, para. 48.
1258. CJEU C-205/13 of 18.9.2014 – Hauck, para. 42; C-215/14 of 16.9.2015 – Société des Produits Nestlé, paras 49 and 51.
1259. CJEU C-215/14 of 16.9.2015 – Société des Produits Nestlé, para. 50.
1260. CJEU C-299/99 of 18.6.2002 – Philips, para. 78; C-48/09 P of 14.9.2010 – Lego Juris/OHIM, para. 43; C-337/12 P to C-340/12 P of 6.3.2014 – Pi-Design/OHIM, para. 45; C-205/13 of 18.9.2014 – Hauck, para. 18; C-215/14 of 16.9.2015 – Société des Produits Nestlé, para. 44;

Still applicable: The ground for refusal of registration set out in the first indent of Article 3(1)(e) TMD2008 pursues the same objective as the grounds set out in the second and third indents of that provision. Accordingly, the first indent must be interpreted in a way that is consistent with the aims of the other two indents.[1261]

Still applicable: The requirements which must be satisfied by the graphic representation in order to fulfil its function, which concern a sign's general aptness to constitute a trade mark within the meaning of Article 4 CTMR, cannot restrict the competent authority's examination under Article 7(1)(e)(ii) CTMR in such a way as might undermine the public interest underlying the latter provision.[1262]

Basically still applicable: As regards signs consisting exclusively of the shape of the product necessary to obtain a technical result, listed in Article 3(1)(e), second indent, TMD2008, that provision is intended to preclude the registration of shapes whose essential characteristics perform a technical function, with the result that the exclusivity inherent in the trade mark right would limit the possibility of competitors supplying a product incorporating such a function or at least limit their freedom of choice in regard to the technical solution they wish to adopt in order to incorporate such a function in their product.[1263]

Basically still applicable: As Article 3(1)(e) TMD2008 pursues an aim which is in the public interest, namely that a shape whose essential characteristics perform a technical function and were chosen to fulfil that function may be freely used by all, that provision prevents such signs and indications from being reserved to one undertaking alone because they have been registered as trade marks.[1264]

Basically still applicable: In that connection, the rules laid down by the legislature reflect the **balancing of two considerations**, both of which are likely to help establish a healthy and fair system of competition.[1265]

Basically still applicable: First, the inclusion in Article 7(1) CTMR of the prohibition on registration as a trade mark of any sign consisting of the shape of goods which is necessary to obtain a technical result ensures that undertakings may not use trade mark law in order to perpetuate, indefinitely, exclusive rights relating to technical solutions.[1266]

Basically still applicable: When the shape of a product merely incorporates the technical solution developed by the manufacturer of that product and patented by it, protection of that shape as a trade mark once the patent has expired would considerably and permanently reduce the opportunity for other undertakings to use that

C-237/19 of 23.4.2020 – Gömböc Kutató, Szolgáltató és Kereskedelmi/Tulajdon Nemzeti Hivatala, para. 25; *see also* CJEU C-30/15 P of 10.11.2016 – Simba Toys/EUIPO, para. 39.

1261. CJEU C-205/13 of 18.9.2014 – Hauck, para. 20.

1262. CJEU C-337/12 P to C-340/12 P of 6.3.2014 – Pi-Design/OHIM, para. 58.

1263. CJEU C-299/99 of 18.6.2002 – Philips, para. 79; *see also* CJEU C-237/19 of 23.4.2020 – Gömböc Kutató, Szolgáltató és Kereskedelmi/Tulajdon Nemzeti Hivatala, para. 26.

1264. CJEU C-299/99 of 18.6.2002 – Philips, para. 80; C-104/01 of 6.5.2003 – Libertel, para. 53.

1265. CJEU C-48/09 P of 14.9.2010 – Lego Juris/OHIM, para. 44.

1266. CJEU C-48/09 P of 14.9.2010 – Lego Juris/OHIM, para. 45; C-205/13 of 18.9.2014 – Hauck, para. 19; C-215/14 of 16.9.2015 – Société des Produits Nestlé, para. 45; C-421/15 P of 11.5.2017 – Yoshida Metal Industry/EUIPO, para. 33; C-237/19 of 23.4.2020 – Gömböc Kutató, Szolgáltató és Kereskedelmi/Tulajdon Nemzeti Hivatala, para. 27 and 50.

technical solution. In the system of intellectual property rights developed in the EU, technical solutions are capable of protection only for a limited period, so that subsequently they may be freely used by all economic operators. That consideration underlies not only Directive 89/104 and Regulation No. 40/94, with regard to trade mark law, but also Regulation No. 6/2002, in relation to designs.[1267]

Probably no longer applicable: Furthermore, the legislature has laid down with particular strictness that shapes necessary to obtain a technical result are unsuitable for registration as trade marks since it has excluded the grounds for refusal listed in Article 7(1)(e) CTMR from the scope of the exception under Article 7(3).[1268]

Probably no longer applicable: Second, by restricting the ground for refusal set out in Article 7(1)(e)(ii) CTMR to signs which consist 'exclusively' of the shape of goods which is 'necessary' to obtain a technical result, the legislature duly took into account that any shape of goods is, to a certain extent, functional and that it would therefore be inappropriate to refuse to register a shape of goods as a trade mark solely on the ground that it has functional characteristics. By the **terms 'exclusively' and 'necessary'**, that provision ensures that solely shapes of goods which only incorporate a technical solution, and whose registration as a trade mark would therefore actually impede the use of that technical solution by other undertakings, are not to be registered.[1269]

[2] Shape of the goods or other characteristics

Probably only modified applicable: Article 3(1)(e)(iii) TMD2008 must be interpreted as meaning that a sign consisting of a colour applied to the **sole of a high-heeled shoe**, such as that at issue in the main proceedings, does not consist exclusively of a 'shape', within the meaning of that provision.[1270]

Probably only modified applicable: Given that TMD2008 provides no definition of the concept of 'shape', the meaning and scope of that concept must, as the Court has consistently held, be determined by considering its usual meaning in everyday language, while also taking into account the context in which it occurs and the purposes of the rules of which it is part.[1271]

Probably only modified applicable: As noted by the European Commission, in the context of trade mark law, the concept of 'shape' is usually understood as a set of lines or contours that outline the product concerned.[1272]

1267. CJEU C-48/09 P of 14.9.2010 – Lego Juris/OHIM, para. 46.
1268. CJEU C-48/09 P of 14.9.2010 – Lego Juris/OHIM, para. 47; C-421/15 P of 11.5.2017 – Yoshida Metal Industry/EUIPO, para. 34.
1269. CJEU C-48/09 P of 14.9.2010 – Lego Juris/OHIM, para. 48; *see also* CJEU C-337/12 P to C-340/12 P of 6.3.2014 – Pi-Design/OHIM, para. 56; C-421/15 P of 11.5.2017 – Yoshida Metal Industry/EUIPO, para. 26.
1270. CJEU C-163/16 of 12.6.2018 – Louboutin a.o./Van Haren Schoenen, para. 27.
1271. CJEU C-163/16 of 12.6.2018 – Louboutin a.o./Van Haren Schoenen, para. 20, with further proof; C-21/18 of 14.3.2019 – Textilis a.o./Svenskt Tenn, para. 35.
1272. CJEU C-163/16 of 12.6.2018 – Louboutin a.o./Van Haren Schoenen, para. 21; C-21/18 of 14.3.2019 – Textilis a.o./Svenskt Tenn, para. 36.

Probably only modified applicable: It does not follow from the TMD2008, the case law of the Court, or the usual meaning of that concept, that a colour per se, without an outline, may constitute a 'shape'.[1273]

Probably only modified applicable: Nevertheless, the question arises as to whether the fact that a particular colour is applied to a specific part of the product concerned results in the sign at issue consisting of a shape within the meaning of Article 3(1)(e)(iii) TMD2008.[1274]

Probably only modified applicable: In that regard, it must be noted that, while it is true that the shape of the product or of a part of the product plays a role in creating an outline for the colour, it cannot, however, be held that a sign consists of that shape in the case where the registration of the mark did not seek to protect that shape but sought solely to protect the application of a colour to a specific part of that product.[1275]

Probably only modified applicable: As has been observed by the German, French and United Kingdom Governments, as well as by the Commission, the mark at issue does not relate to a specific shape of sole for high-heeled shoes since the description of that mark explicitly states that the contour of the shoe does not form part of the mark and is intended purely to show the positioning of the red colour covered by the registration.[1276]

Probably only modified applicable: In any event, a sign, such as that at issue in the main proceedings, cannot be regarded as consisting 'exclusively' of a shape, where, as in the present instance, the main element of that sign is a specific colour designated by an internationally recognized identification code.[1277]

Article 7(1)(e)(iii) CTMR must be interpreted as meaning that a sign, consisting of **two-dimensional decorative motifs**, which are affixed to goods, such as fabric or paper, does **not** 'consist exclusively of the shape', within the meaning of that provision.[1278]

It is common ground that, unlike a sign relating to a colour per se, the sign at issue in the main proceedings, which is made up of two-dimensional and decorative motifs and which is affixed to goods such as fabric or paper, contains lines and contours.[1279]

However, that sign cannot be regarded as consisting 'exclusively of the shape', within the meaning of Article 7(1)(e)(iii) CTMR.[1280]

Although it is true that, in the main proceedings, the sign under consideration represents shapes which are formed by the external outline of drawings representing, in a stylized manner, parts of geographical maps, the fact remains that, apart from those shapes, that sign contains decorative elements which are situated both inside and outside those outlines.[1281]

1273. CJEU C-163/16 of 12.6.2018 – Louboutin a.o./Van Haren Schoenen, para. 22.
1274. CJEU C-163/16 of 12.6.2018 – Louboutin a.o./Van Haren Schoenen, para. 23.
1275. CJEU C-163/16 of 12.6.2018 – Louboutin a.o./Van Haren Schoenen, para. 24; C-21/18 of 14.3.2019 – Textilis a.o./Svenskt Tenn, para. 37.
1276. CJEU C-163/16 of 12.6.2018 – Louboutin a.o./Van Haren Schoenen, para. 25.
1277. CJEU C-163/16 of 12.6.2018 – Louboutin a.o./Van Haren Schoenen, para. 26.
1278. CJEU C-21/18 of 14.3.2019 – Textilis a.o./Svenskt Tenn, para. 46.
1279. CJEU C-21/18 of 14.3.2019 – Textilis a.o./Svenskt Tenn, para. 38.
1280. CJEU C-21/18 of 14.3.2019 – Textilis a.o./Svenskt Tenn, para. 39.
1281. CJEU C-21/18 of 14.3.2019 – Textilis a.o./Svenskt Tenn, para. 40.

Furthermore, that sign highlights words, in particular the word 'Manhattan'.[1282]

In any event, it cannot be held that a sign consisting of two-dimensional decorative motifs is indissociable from the shape of the goods where that sign is affixed to goods, such as fabric or paper, the form of which differs from those decorative motifs.[1283]

For those reasons, the view cannot be taken that a sign such as that at issue in the main proceedings consists exclusively of the shape, within the meaning of Article 7(1)(e)(iii) CTMR.[1284]

Accordingly, the exclusion laid down in Article 7(1)(e)(iii) CTMR cannot apply to such a sign.[1285]

In that regard, it must be pointed out that the fact that the sign at issue in the main proceedings is also **protected by copyright has no bearing** on whether or not it consists exclusively of a 'shape', within the meaning of Article 7(1)(e)(iii) CTMR.[1286]

[3] Nature of the goods themselves

Probably basically still applicable: The first indent of Article 3(1)(e) TMD2008 directive must be interpreted as meaning that the ground for refusal of registration set out in that provision may apply to a sign which consists exclusively of the shape of a product **with one or more essential characteristics** which are inherent to the generic function or functions of that product and which consumers may be looking for in the products of competitors.[1287]

Still applicable: In order to apply the first indent of Article 3(1)(e) TMD2008 directive correctly, it is necessary to identify the essential characteristics – that is, the most important elements – of the sign concerned on a case-by-case basis, that assessment being based either on the overall impression produced by the sign or on an examination of each the components of that sign in turn.[1288]

Probably basically still applicable: In that regard, it must be emphasized that the ground for refusal of registration set out in the first indent of Article 3(1)(e) TMD2008 cannot be applicable where the trade mark application relates to a shape of goods in which another element, such as a decorative or imaginative element, which is not inherent to the generic function of the goods, plays an important or essential role.[1289]

Probably basically still applicable: Thus, an interpretation of the first indent of that provision whereby that indent is to apply only to signs which consist exclusively of shapes which are indispensable to the function of the goods in question, leaving the

1282. CJEU C-21/18 of 14.3.2019 – Textilis a.o./Svenskt Tenn, para. 41.
1283. CJEU C-21/18 of 14.3.2019 – Textilis a.o./Svenskt Tenn, para. 42.
1284. CJEU C-21/18 of 14.3.2019 – Textilis a.o./Svenskt Tenn, para. 43.
1285. CJEU C-21/18 of 14.3.2019 – Textilis a.o./Svenskt Tenn, para. 44.
1286. CJEU C-21/18 of 14.3.2019 – Textilis a.o./Svenskt Tenn, para. 45.
1287. CJEU C-205/13 of 18.9.2014 – Hauck, para. 27.
1288. CJEU C-205/13 of 18.9.2014 – Hauck, para. 21; *see also* CJEU C-48/09 P of 14.9.2010 – Lego Juris/OHIM, paras 68–70; C-30/15 P of 10.11.2016 – Simba Toys/EUIPO, para. 40.
1289. CJEU C-205/13 of 18.9.2014 – Hauck, para. 22; *see also* CJEU C-48/09 P of 14.9.2010 – Lego Juris/OHIM, paras 52 and 72.

producer of those goods no leeway to make a personal essential contribution, would not allow the objective of the ground for refusal set out therein to be fully realized.[1290]

Probably basically still applicable: Indeed, an interpretation to that effect would result in limiting the products to which that ground for refusal could apply to: (i) 'natural' products (which have no substitute) and (ii) 'regulated' products (the shape of which is prescribed by legal standards), even though signs consisting of the shapes formed by such products could not be registered in any event because of their lack of distinctive character.[1291]

Probably basically still applicable: Instead, when applying the ground for refusal set out in the first indent of Article 3(1)(e) TMD2008, account should be taken of the fact that the concept of a 'shape which results from the nature of the goods themselves' means that shapes with essential characteristics which are inherent to the generic function or functions of such goods must, in principle, also be denied registration.[1292]

Probably basically still applicable: Reserving such characteristics to a single economic operator would make it difficult for competing undertakings to give their goods a shape which would be suited to the use for which those goods are intended. Moreover, it is clear that those are essential characteristics which consumers will be looking for in the products of competitors, given that they are intended to perform an identical or similar function.[1293]

[4] Technical result

Probably basically still applicable: The presence of one or more **minor arbitrary elements** in a three-dimensional sign, all of whose essential characteristics are dictated by the technical solution to which that sign gives effect, does not alter the conclusion that the sign consists exclusively of the shape of goods which is necessary to obtain a technical result. In addition, since that interpretation implies that the ground for refusal under Article 7(1)(e)(ii) CTMR is applicable only where all the essential characteristics of the sign are functional, it ensures that such a sign cannot be refused registration as a trade mark under that provision if the shape of the goods at issue incorporates a major non-functional element, such as a decorative or imaginative element which plays an important role in the shape.[1294]

Still applicable: The correct application of Article 7(1)(e)(ii) CTMR requires that the **essential characteristics** of the three-dimensional sign at issue be properly identified by the authority deciding on the application for registration of the sign as a trade mark.[1295]

1290. CJEU C-205/13 of 18.9.2014 – Hauck, para. 23.
1291. CJEU C-205/13 of 18.9.2014 – Hauck, para. 24.
1292. CJEU C-205/13 of 18.9.2014 – Hauck, para. 25.
1293. CJEU C-205/13 of 18.9.2014 – Hauck, para. 26.
1294. CJEU C-48/09 P of 14.9.2010 – Lego Juris/OHIM, para. 52; C-421/15 P of 11.5.2017 – Yoshida Metal Industry/EUIPO, para. 27; C-237/19 of 23.4.2020 – Gömböc Kutató, Szolgáltató és Kereskedelmi/Tulajdon Nemzeti Hivatala, para. 26.
1295. CJEU C-48/09 P of 14.9.2010 – Lego Juris/OHIM, para. 68; C-337/12 P to C-340/12 P of 6.3.2014 – Pi-Design/OHIM, para. 46; C-421/15 P of 11.5.2017 – Yoshida Metal Industry/

Still applicable: The expression 'essential characteristics' must be understood as referring to the most important elements of the sign.[1296]

Probably basically still applicable: Once the sign's essential characteristics have been identified, the competent authority still has to ascertain whether they all perform the technical function of the goods at issue. Article 7(1)(e)(ii) CTMR cannot be applicable where the application for registration as a trade mark relates to a shape of goods in which a non-functional element, such as a decorative or imaginative element, plays an important role. In that case, competitor undertakings easily have access to alternative shapes with equivalent functionality, so that there is no risk that the availability of the technical solution will be impaired. That solution may, in that case, be incorporated without difficulty by the competitors of the mark's proprietor in shapes which do not have the same non-functional element as that contained in the proprietor's shape and which are therefore neither identical nor similar to that shape.[1297]

Probably basically still applicable: In order to analyse the functionality of a sign for the purposes of Article 7(1)(e)(ii) CTMR, which concerns only signs which consist of the shape of the actual goods, the essential characteristics of a shape must be assessed in the light of the technical function of the actual goods concerned.[1298]

Probably basically still applicable: In **examining the functionality** of a sign consisting of the shape of goods, once the essential characteristics of the sign have been identified, it is only necessary to assess whether those characteristics perform the technical function of the product concerned. Clearly, that examination must be carried out by analysing the sign filed with a view to its registration as a trade mark, and not signs consisting of other shapes of goods.[1299]

Still applicable: The identification of the essential characteristics must be carried out on a case-by-case basis. There is no hierarchy that applies systematically between the various types of elements of which a sign may consist. Moreover, in determining the essential characteristics of a sign, the competent authority may either base its assessment directly on the overall impression produced by the sign or first examine in turn each of the components of the sign concerned.[1300]

Still applicable: Consequently, the identification of the essential characteristics of a three-dimensional sign with a view to a possible application of the ground for refusal under Article 7(1)(e)(ii) CTMR may, depending on the case, and in particular in view of its degree of difficulty, be carried out by means of a simple visual analysis of the sign

---

EUIPO, para. 31; C-237/19 of 23.4.2020 – Gömböc Kutató, Szolgáltató és Kereskedelmi/ Tulajdon Nemzeti Hivatala, para. 28; C-818/18 P and C-6/19 P of 3.6.2021 – The Yokohama Rubber/EUIPO, para. 60.

1296. CJEU C-48/09 P of 14.9.2010 – Lego Juris/OHIM, para. 69.

1297. CJEU C-48/09 P of 14.9.2010 – Lego Juris/OHIM, para. 72; *see also* CJEU C-205/13 of 18.9.2014 – Hauck, para. 22; C-421/15 P of 11.5.2017 – Yoshida Metal Industry/EUIPO, para. 29; C-237/19 of 23.4.2020 – Gömböc Kutató, Szolgáltató és Kereskedelmi/Tulajdon Nemzeti Hivatala, para. 28.

1298. CJEU C-30/15 P of 10.11.2016 – Simba Toys/EUIPO, para. 46, with reference to CJEU C-48/09 P of 14.9.2010 – Lego Juris/OHIM, para. 72.

1299. CJEU C-48/09 P of 14.9.2010 – Lego Juris/OHIM, para. 84.

1300. CJEU C-48/09 P of 14.9.2010 – Lego Juris/OHIM, para. 70; C-337/12 P to C-340/12 P of 6.3.2014 – Pi-Design/OHIM, para. 47; *see also* CJEU C-237/19 of 23.4.2020 – Gömböc Kutató, Szolgáltató és Kereskedelmi/Tulajdon Nemzeti Hivatala, para. 29.

or, on the other hand, be based on a detailed examination in which relevant criteria of assessment are taken into account, such as surveys or expert opinions, or data relating to intellectual property rights conferred previously in respect of the goods concerned.[1301]

Basically still applicable: Article 3(1)(e)(ii) CTMR must be interpreted as meaning that, in order to establish whether a sign consists exclusively of the shape of goods which is necessary to obtain a technical result, **assessment** does not have to be limited to the graphic representation of that sign. Information other than that relating to the graphic representation alone, such as the perception of the relevant public, may be used in order to identify the essential characteristics of the sign at issue. However, while information which is not apparent from the graphic representation of the sign may be taken into consideration in order to establish whether those characteristics perform a technical function of the goods in question, such information must originate from objective and reliable sources and may not include the perception of the relevant public.[1302]

Basically still applicable: Under that provision, signs which consist exclusively of the shape of goods which is necessary to obtain a technical result are not to be registered or are to be declared invalid.[1303]

Basically still applicable: While the identification of the essential characteristics of the sign at issue, in connection with the application of the ground for refusal of registration provided for in Article 3(1)(e)(ii) CTMR, must in principle begin with the assessment of the graphic representation of that sign, the competent authority may also refer to other useful information that allows it to correctly identify those characteristics.[1304]

Basically still applicable: In that regard, the Court has held that the presumed perception by the relevant public is not a decisive factor when applying that ground for refusal, and may, at most, be a relevant criterion of assessment for the competent authority when identifying the essential characteristics of the sign.[1305]

Basically still applicable: As regards the second step of the analysis referred to above [whether the identified elements perform a technical function], it should be noted, first, that the ground for refusal of registration provided for in Article 3(1)(e)(ii) CTMR may be applied when the graphic representation of the shape of the product allows only part of the shape to be seen, provided that the visible part of the shape is necessary to obtain the technical result sought by that product, even if it is not

1301. CJEU C-48/09 P of 14.9.2010 – Lego Juris/OHIM, para. 71; C-337/12 P to C-340/12 P of 6.3.2014 – Pi-Design/OHIM, para. 48; *see also* CJEU C-237/19 of 23.4.2020 – Gömböc Kutató, Szolgáltató és Kereskedelmi/Tulajdon Nemzeti Hivatala, para. 29.
1302. CJEU C-237/19 of 23.4.2020 – Gömböc Kutató, Szolgáltató és Kereskedelmi/Tulajdon Nemzeti Hivatala, para. 37.
1303. CJEU C-237/19 of 23.4.2020 – Gömböc Kutató, Szolgáltató és Kereskedelmi/Tulajdon Nemzeti Hivatala, para. 24.
1304. CJEU C-237/19 of 23.4.2020 – Gömböc Kutató, Szolgáltató és Kereskedelmi/Tulajdon Nemzeti Hivatala, para. 30.
1305. CJEU C-237/19 of 23.4.2020 – Gömböc Kutató, Szolgáltató és Kereskedelmi/Tulajdon Nemzeti Hivatala, para. 31, with reference to CJEU C-48/09 P of 14.9.2010 – Lego Juris/OHIM, para. 76.

sufficient, on its own, to obtain that result. Such an interpretation ensures that the objective of that ground for refusal of registration is achieved since it prevents any monopoly on technical solutions or functional features of the product in question being acquired. Therefore, as the Commission stated in its written observations, that ground for refusal is applicable to a sign consisting of the shape of the product concerned which does not show all the essential characteristics required to obtain the technical result sought, provided that at least one of the essential characteristics required to obtain that technical result is visible in the graphic representation of the shape of that product.[1306]

Basically still applicable: Second, the Court has stated that, although it is necessary to take as a starting point the shape as represented graphically in the sign at issue, that second step of analysis cannot be carried out without taking into consideration, where appropriate, the additional features relating to the function of the goods in question.[1307]

Basically still applicable: In that regard, it is important to point out that the determination by the competent authority of the technical functions of the product in question must be based on objective and reliable information. That authority may look for such features, *inter alia*, in any description of the product submitted at the time of filing of the application for registration of the mark, in data relating to intellectual property rights conferred previously in respect of that product, by looking at surveys or expert opinions on the functions of the product, or in any relevant documentation, such as scientific publications, catalogues and websites, which describes the technical features of the product.[1308]

Basically still applicable: On the other hand, information concerning any knowledge the relevant public may have of the technical functions of the product in question and the way in which they are achieved forms part of an assessment necessarily involving subjective factors, potentially giving rise to uncertainty as to the extent and accuracy of that public's knowledge, which risks undermining the objective pursued by the ground for refusal of registration provided for in Article 3(1)(e)(ii) CTMR, that being to prevent trade mark law from granting an undertaking a monopoly on technical solutions or functional features of a product.[1309]

Basically still applicable: That is all the more so since the relevant public does not necessarily have the required expertise to enable it to determine with accuracy what the technical features of the product in question are and the extent to which the shape of that product forming the sign contributes to the technical result sought.[1310]

1306. CJEU C-237/19 of 23.4.2020 – Gömböc Kutató, Szolgáltató és Kereskedelmi/Tulajdon Nemzeti Hivatala, para. 32.
1307. CJEU C-237/19 of 23.4.2020 – Gömböc Kutató, Szolgáltató és Kereskedelmi/Tulajdon Nemzeti Hivatala, para. 33, with reference to CJEU C-30/15 P of 10.11.2016 – Simba Toys/EUIPO, para. 48.
1308. CJEU C-237/19 of 23.4.2020 – Gömböc Kutató, Szolgáltató és Kereskedelmi/Tulajdon Nemzeti Hivatala, para. 34.
1309. CJEU C-237/19 of 23.4.2020 – Gömböc Kutató, Szolgáltató és Kereskedelmi/Tulajdon Nemzeti Hivatala, para. 35.
1310. CJEU C-237/19 of 23.4.2020 – Gömböc Kutató, Szolgáltató és Kereskedelmi/Tulajdon Nemzeti Hivatala, para. 36.

Basically still applicable: The technical functionality of the characteristics of a shape may be assessed, *inter alia*, by taking account of the documents relating to previous **patents** describing the functional elements of the shape concerned.[1311]

Probably basically still applicable: Article 3(1)(e)(ii) TMD2008, under which registration may be refused of signs consisting exclusively of the shape of goods which is necessary to obtain a technical result, must be interpreted as referring only to the manner in which the goods at issue function and it does **not** apply to **the manner in which the goods are manufactured**.[1312]

Probably basically still applicable: The wording of that provision refers expressly to the shape of goods which is necessary to obtain a 'technical result', without mentioning the process for manufacturing those goods.[1313]

Probably basically still applicable: If that provision is to be interpreted literally, the ground for refusal provided for therein is restricted to the manner in which the goods function since the technical result constitutes the outcome of a particular method of manufacturing the shape in question.[1314]

Still applicable: That interpretation is confirmed by the objective of Article 3(1)(e)(ii) TMD2008, which consists in preventing a monopoly from being granted on technical solutions which a user is likely to seek in the goods of competitors. From the consumer's perspective, the manner in which the goods function is decisive, and their method of manufacture is not important.[1315]

Probably basically still applicable: Moreover, it follows from the case law[1316] that the manufacturing method is not decisive in the context of the assessment of the essential functional characteristics of the shape of goods either. The registration of a sign consisting of a shape attributable solely to the technical result must be refused even if that technical result can be achieved by other shapes, and consequently by other manufacturing methods.[1317]

Probably basically still applicable: As regards the condition that registration of a shape of goods as a trade mark may be refused under Article 7(1)(e)(ii) CTMR only if the shape is '**necessary**' to obtain the technical result intended, the General Court rightly found that that condition does not mean that the shape at issue must be the only one capable of obtaining that result.[1318]

Probably basically still applicable: In some cases, the same technical result may be achieved by various solutions. Thus, there may be alternative shapes, with other dimensions or another design, capable of achieving the same technical result.[1319]

1311. CJEU C-48/09 P of 14.9.2010 – Lego Juris/OHIM, para. 85; C-893/19 P of 12.3.2020 – Roxtec/EUIPO, para. 16.
1312. CJEU C-215/14 of 16.9.2015 – Société des Produits Nestlé, para. 57.
1313. CJEU C-215/14 of 16.9.2015 – Société des Produits Nestlé, para. 53.
1314. CJEU C-215/14 of 16.9.2015 – Société des Produits Nestlé, para. 54.
1315. CJEU C-215/14 of 16.9.2015 – Société des Produits Nestlé, para. 55.
1316. CJEU C-299/99 of 18.6.2002 – Philips, para. 83.
1317. CJEU C-215/14 of 16.9.2015 – Société des Produits Nestlé, para. 56.
1318. CJEU C-48/09 P of 14.9.2010 – Lego Juris/OHIM, para. 53; C-421/15 P of 11.5.2017 – Yoshida Metal Industry/EUIPO, para. 28.
1319. CJEU C-48/09 P of 14.9.2010 – Lego Juris/OHIM, para. 54.

Probably basically still applicable: However, that fact does not in itself mean that registering the shape at issue as a trade mark would have no effect on the availability, to other economic operators, of the technical solution which it incorporates.[1320]

Probably basically still applicable: In that connection, it should be observed that under Article 9(1) CTMR, registration as a trade mark of a purely functional product shape is likely to allow the proprietor of that trade mark to prevent other undertakings not only from using the same shape but also from using similar shapes. A significant number of alternative shapes might therefore become unusable for the proprietor's competitors.[1321]

Probably basically still applicable: That would be particularly so if various purely functional shapes of goods were registered at the same time, which might completely prevent other undertakings from manufacturing and marketing certain goods having a particular technical function.[1322]

Probably basically still applicable: That applies, *a fortiori* in a case, where it has been found by the competent authority that the solution incorporated in the shape of goods examined is the technically preferable solution for the category of goods concerned. If the three-dimensional sign consisting of such a shape were registered as a trade mark, it would be difficult for the competitors of the proprietor of that mark to place on the market shapes of goods constituting a real alternative, that is to say, shapes which are not similar and which are nevertheless attractive to the consumer from a functional perspective.[1323]

Probably basically still applicable: In those circumstances, the position of an undertaking which has developed a technical solution cannot be protected – with regard to competitors placing on the market slavish copies of the product shape incorporating exactly the same solution – by conferring a monopoly on that undertaking through registering as a trade mark the three-dimensional sign consisting of that shape, but can, where appropriate, be examined in the light of rules on unfair competition. Such an examination is, however, outside the scope of these proceedings.[1324]

Probably basically still applicable: As to the question of whether the establishment that there are **other shapes** which could achieve the same technical result can overcome the ground for refusal or invalidity contained in Article 3(1)(e), second indent, TMD2008, there is nothing in the wording of that provision to allow such a conclusion.[1325]

Probably basically still applicable: In refusing registration of such signs, Article 3(1)(e), second indent, TMD2008 reflects the legitimate aim of not allowing individuals

1320. CJEU C-48/09 P of 14.9.2010 – Lego Juris/OHIM, para. 55.
1321. CJEU C-48/09 P of 14.9.2010 – Lego Juris/OHIM, para. 56.
1322. CJEU C-48/09 P of 14.9.2010 – Lego Juris/OHIM, para. 57.
1323. CJEU C-48/09 P of 14.9.2010 – Lego Juris/OHIM, para. 60.
1324. CJEU C-48/09 P of 14.9.2010 – Lego Juris/OHIM, para. 61.
1325. CJEU C-299/99 of 18.6.2002 – Philips, para. 81; C-48/09 P of 14.9.2010 – Lego Juris/OHIM, paras 58 and 83.

to use registration of a mark in order to acquire or perpetuate exclusive rights relating to technical solutions.[1326]

Probably basically still applicable: Where the essential functional characteristics of the shape of a product are attributable solely to the technical result, Article 3(1)(e), second indent, TMD2008 precludes registration of a sign consisting of that shape, even if that technical result can be achieved by other shapes.[1327]

Probably still applicable: Thus, and since it is not disputed that the sign at issue consists of the **shape of actual goods** [Rubik's Cube] and not of an abstract shape, the General Court should have defined the technical function of the actual goods at issue, namely a three-dimensional puzzle, and it should have taken this into account when assessing the functionality of the essential characteristics of that sign.[1328]

Probably still applicable: While it was necessary for the purpose of that analysis, to proceed on the basis of the shape at issue, as represented graphically, that analysis could not be made without taking into consideration, where appropriate, the additional elements relating to the function of the actual goods at issue.[1329]

Probably still applicable: First, it follows from the case law of the Court that, when examining the functional characteristics of a sign, the competent authority may carry out a detailed examination that takes into account material relevant to identifying appropriately the essential characteristics of a sign, in addition to the graphic representation and any descriptions filed at the time of application for registration.[1330]

Probably still applicable: Secondly, in each of the cases which gave rise to the Court's judgments *Philips* (C-299/99), *Lego Juris v OHIM* (C-48/09 P), and *Pi-Design and Others v Yoshida Metal Industry* (C-337/12 P to C-340/12 P), the competent authority would not have been able to analyse the shape concerned solely on the basis of its graphic representation without using additional information on the actual goods.[1331]

Probably still applicable: It follows that the General Court interpreted the criteria for assessing Article 7(1)(e)(ii) CTMR too narrowly, in that it took the view that for the purpose of examining the functionality of the essential characteristics of the sign concerned, in particular the grid structure on each surface of the cube, the shape at issue, as represented graphically, should have been taken as a basis, without necessarily having to take into consideration any additional circumstances which an objective observer would not have been able to 'fathom precisely' on the basis of the graphic representations of the contested mark, such as the rotating capability of individual elements in a three-dimensional 'Rubik's Cube'-type puzzle.[1332]

1326. CJEU C-299/99 of 18.6.2002 – Philips, para. 82.
1327. CJEU C-299/99 of 18.6.2002 – Philips, para. 83.
1328. CJEU C-30/15 P of 10.11.2016 – Simba Toys/EUIPO, para. 47.
1329. CJEU C-30/15 P of 10.11.2016 – Simba Toys/EUIPO, para. 48; C-237/19 of 23.4.2020 – Gömböc Kutató, Szolgáltató és Kereskedelmi/Tulajdon Nemzeti Hivatala, para. 33.
1330. CJEU C-30/15 P of 10.11.2016 – Simba Toys/EUIPO, para. 49, with reference to CJEU C-337/12 P to C-340/12 P of 6.3.2014 – Pi-Design/OHIM, para. 54.
1331. CJEU C-30/15 P of 10.11.2016 – Simba Toys/EUIPO, para. 50.
1332. CJEU C-30/15 P of 10.11.2016 – Simba Toys/EUIPO, para. 51.

Probably still applicable: Furthermore, the fact that the contested mark was registered for 'three-dimensional puzzles' in general, that is to say, without being restricted to those that have a rotating capability, and that the proprietor of that mark did not append to its application for registration a description specifying that the shape at issue had such a rotating capability, cannot preclude account from being taken of the technical function of the actual goods represented by the sign at issue for the purpose of examining the functionality of the essential characteristics of that sign, as the proprietor of that mark would otherwise be allowed to broaden the scope of the protection arising from the registration thereof to cover every type of puzzle with a similar shape, namely any three-dimensional puzzle with cube-shaped elements, regardless of the principles by which it functions.[1333]

Probably still applicable: However, that last option would be contrary to the objective pursued by Article 7(1)(e)(ii) CTMR, which is to prevent an undertaking from being granted a monopoly on technical solutions or functional characteristics of a product.[1334]

[5] Substantial value

Probably basically still applicable: The third indent of Article 3(1)(e) TMD2008 must be interpreted as meaning that the ground for refusal of registration set out in that provision may apply to a sign which consists exclusively of the shape of a product with **several characteristics each of which may give that product substantial value**. The target public's perception of the shape of that product is only one of the assessment criteria which may be used to determine whether that ground for refusal is applicable.[1335]

Probably basically still applicable: In that regard, the fact that the shape of a product is regarded as giving substantial value to that product does not mean that other characteristics may not also give the product significant value.[1336]

Probably basically still applicable: Thus, the aim of preventing the exclusive and permanent right which a trade mark confers from serving to extend indefinitely the life of other rights which the EU legislature has sought to make subject to limited periods requires that the possibility of **applying** the third indent of Article 3(1)(e) TMD2008 not be automatically ruled out **when**, in addition to its aesthetic function, the product concerned **also performs other essential functions**.[1337]

Probably basically still applicable: Indeed, the concept of a 'shape which gives substantial value to the goods' cannot be limited purely to the shape of products having only artistic or ornamental value, as there is otherwise a risk that products which have essential functional characteristics as well as a significant aesthetic element will not be covered. In that case, the right conferred by the trade mark on its proprietor would

1333. CJEU C-30/15 P of 10.11.2016 – Simba Toys/EUIPO, para. 52.
1334. CJEU C-30/15 P of 10.11.2016 – Simba Toys/EUIPO, para. 53.
1335. CJEU C-205/13 of 18.9.2014 – Hauck, para. 36.
1336. CJEU C-205/13 of 18.9.2014 – Hauck, para. 30.
1337. CJEU C-205/13 of 18.9.2014 – Hauck, para. 31.

grant that proprietor a monopoly on the essential characteristics of such products, which would not allow the objective of that ground for refusal to be fully realized.[1338]

Probably basically still applicable: Article 3(1)(e)(iii) CTMR must be interpreted as meaning that the ground for refusal of registration provided for in that provision must not be applied systematically to a sign which consists exclusively of the shape of the product where that sign enjoys protection under the law relating to **designs** or where the sign consists exclusively of the **shape of a decorative item**.[1339]

Probably basically still applicable: In this regard, it should be borne in mind that the objective of the ground for refusal of registration provided for in Article 3(1)(e)(iii) CTMR, like that of the ground for refusal of registration provided for in Article 3(1)(e)(ii) CTMR is, indeed, to prevent the exclusive and permanent right that a trade mark confers from serving to extend indefinitely the life of other rights in respect of which the EU legislature has sought to impose time limits.[1340]

Probably basically still applicable: However, such an objective does not mean that EU intellectual property law prevents the coexistence of several forms of legal protection.[1341]

Probably basically still applicable: As regards the protection of designs, Article 16 of Directive 98/71[1342] provides that that directive 'shall be without prejudice to any provisions of [European Union] law or of the law of the Member State concerned relating to unregistered design rights, trade marks or other distinctive signs, patents and utility models'.[1343]

Probably basically still applicable: It is apparent from the above that the fact that the appearance of a product is protected as a design does not prevent a sign consisting of the shape of that product from benefiting from protection under trade mark law, provided that the conditions for registration of that sign as a trade mark are satisfied.[1344]

Probably basically still applicable: It also follows that the rules of EU law concerning the registration of designs and those applicable to the registration of trade marks are independent, without any hierarchy existing as between those rules.[1345]

Probably basically still applicable: Accordingly, the fact that the appearance of a product is protected as a design as a result, *inter alia*, of that design's individual character does not mean that a sign which consists of the shape of that product may not

1338. CJEU C-205/13 of 18.9.2014 – Hauck, para. 32.
1339. CJEU C-237/19 of 23.4.2020 – Gömböc Kutató, Szolgáltató és Kereskedelmi/Tulajdon Nemzeti Hivatala, para. 62.
1340. CJEU C-237/19 of 23.4.2020 – Gömböc Kutató, Szolgáltató és Kereskedelmi/Tulajdon Nemzeti Hivatala, para. 50, with reference to CJEU C-205/13 of 18.9.2014 – Hauck, para. 19.
1341. CJEU C-237/19 of 23.4.2020 – Gömböc Kutató, Szolgáltató és Kereskedelmi/Tulajdon Nemzeti Hivatala, para. 51.
1342. Directive 98/71/EC of the European Parliament and of the Council of 13 October 1998 on the legal protection of designs (OJ 1998 L 289, p. 28).
1343. CJEU C-237/19 of 23.4.2020 – Gömböc Kutató, Szolgáltató és Kereskedelmi/Tulajdon Nemzeti Hivatala, para. 52.
1344. CJEU C-237/19 of 23.4.2020 – Gömböc Kutató, Szolgáltató és Kereskedelmi/Tulajdon Nemzeti Hivatala, para. 53.
1345. CJEU C-237/19 of 23.4.2020 – Gömböc Kutató, Szolgáltató és Kereskedelmi/Tulajdon Nemzeti Hivatala, para. 54.

be registered as a trade mark because the ground for refusal provided for in Article 3(1)(e)(iii) CTMR is applicable.[1346]

Probably basically still applicable: As is apparent from Article 3(2) of Directive 98/71, a design is to be protected by a design right to the extent that it is new and has individual character. It should be noted that, as is apparent from Article 5(1) of Directive 98/71, a design is to be considered to have individual character if the overall impression it produces on the informed user differs from the overall impression produced on such a user by any design which has been made available to the public before the date of filing of the application for registration or, if priority is claimed, the date of priority.[1347]

Probably basically still applicable: As a result, the analysis which allows the individual character of a design to be established differs from the analysis referred to in the second question referred for a preliminary ruling which the competent authority must carry out in order to establish whether a sign consists exclusively of the shape which gives substantial value to the goods, within the meaning of Article 3(1)(e)(iii) CTMR.[1348]

Probably basically still applicable: As regards the second situation referred to by the referring court in its third question, it must be acknowledged that, by referring to 'the shape which gives substantial value to the goods', Article 3(1)(e)(iii) CTMR may, *inter alia*, apply to a sign consisting exclusively of the shape of a product with an artistic or ornamental value.[1349]

Probably basically still applicable: Nevertheless, that does not mean that an application for registration as a trade mark of signs consisting of the shape of a product such as, as in the case in the main proceedings, 'decorative items' or 'decorative crystalware and chinaware' in Classes 14 and 21 of the Nice Agreement, respectively, must be rejected automatically on the basis of that ground for refusal. In order for this ground to apply, it must be apparent from objective and reliable evidence that the consumer's decision to purchase the product in question is based to a very large extent on one or more characteristics of that shape.[1350]

Probably basically still applicable: In that regard, it should be noted that it is in no way inconceivable that the substantial value of this type of item may result from factors other than its shape, such as, *inter alia*, the story of its creation, its method of production, whether industrial or artisanal, the materials that it contains, which may be rare or precious, or even the identity of its designer.[1351]

1346. CJEU C-237/19 of 23.4.2020 – Gömböc Kutató, Szolgáltató és Kereskedelmi/Tulajdon Nemzeti Hivatala, para. 55.
1347. CJEU C-237/19 of 23.4.2020 – Gömböc Kutató, Szolgáltató és Kereskedelmi/Tulajdon Nemzeti Hivatala, para. 56.
1348. CJEU C-237/19 of 23.4.2020 – Gömböc Kutató, Szolgáltató és Kereskedelmi/Tulajdon Nemzeti Hivatala, para. 57.
1349. CJEU C-237/19 of 23.4.2020 – Gömböc Kutató, Szolgáltató és Kereskedelmi/Tulajdon Nemzeti Hivatala, para. 58.
1350. CJEU C-237/19 of 23.4.2020 – Gömböc Kutató, Szolgáltató és Kereskedelmi/Tulajdon Nemzeti Hivatala, para. 59.
1351. CJEU C-237/19 of 23.4.2020 – Gömböc Kutató, Szolgáltató és Kereskedelmi/Tulajdon Nemzeti Hivatala, para. 60.

Probably basically still applicable: It is therefore for the competent authority to assess whether the conditions for the application of the ground for refusal of registration provided for in Article 3(1)(e)(iii) CTMR are in fact satisfied, in order to establish whether the sign at issue consists exclusively of the shape which gives substantial value to the goods.[1352]

Probably basically still applicable: **Other assessment criteria** may also be taken into account, such as the nature of the category of goods concerned, the artistic value of the shape in question, its dissimilarity from other shapes in common use on the market concerned, a substantial price difference in relation to similar products, and the development of a promotion strategy which focuses on accentuating the aesthetic characteristics of the product in question.[1353]

Probably basically still applicable: Article 3(1)(e)(iii) CTMR must be interpreted as meaning that the **perception or knowledge of the relevant public** as regards the product represented graphically by a sign that consists exclusively of the shape of that product may be taken into consideration in order to **identify an essential characteristic** of that shape. The ground for refusal set out in that provision may be applied if it is apparent from objective and reliable evidence that the consumer's decision to purchase the product in question is to a large extent determined by that characteristic.[1354]

Probably basically still applicable: Pursuant to Article 3(1)(e)(iii) CTMR, signs which consist exclusively of the shape which gives substantial value to the goods are not to be registered or, if registered, are liable to be declared invalid.[1355]

Probably basically still applicable: The application of this ground for refusal is based therefore on an objective analysis, intended to demonstrate that the shape in question, on account of its characteristics, has such a great influence on the attractiveness of the product that restricting the benefit of the shape to a single undertaking would distort the conditions of competition on the market concerned.[1356]

Probably basically still applicable: As a result, in order for the ground for refusal provided for in Article 3(1)(e)(iii) CTMR to apply, it must be apparent from objective and reliable evidence that a consumer's decision to purchase the goods in question is, to a very great extent, determined by one or more features of the shape which alone forms the sign.[1357]

1352. CJEU C-237/19 of 23.4.2020 – Gömböc Kutató, Szolgáltató és Kereskedelmi/Tulajdon Nemzeti Hivatala, para. 61.
1353. CJEU C-205/13 of 18.9.2014 – Hauck, para. 35.
1354. CJEU C-237/19 of 23.4.2020 – Gömböc Kutató, Szolgáltató és Kereskedelmi/Tulajdon Nemzeti Hivatala, para. 47.
1355. CJEU C-237/19 of 23.4.2020 – Gömböc Kutató, Szolgáltató és Kereskedelmi/Tulajdon Nemzeti Hivatala, para. 39.
1356. CJEU C-237/19 of 23.4.2020 – Gömböc Kutató, Szolgáltató és Kereskedelmi/Tulajdon Nemzeti Hivatala, para. 40.
1357. CJEU C-237/19 of 23.4.2020 – Gömböc Kutató, Szolgáltató és Kereskedelmi/Tulajdon Nemzeti Hivatala, para. 41.

Probably basically still applicable: Characteristics of the product not connected to its shape, such as technical qualities or the reputation of the product, are, on the other hand, irrelevant.[1358]

Probably basically still applicable: Although the presumed perception of the sign at issue by the average consumer is not, in itself, a decisive element when applying the ground for refusal set out in Article 3(1)(e)(iii) CTMR, it may, nevertheless, be a useful criterion of assessment for the competent authority in identifying the essential characteristics of that sign.[1359]

Probably basically still applicable: It follows that, in a situation such as that at issue in the main proceedings, Article 3(1)(e)(iii) CTMR allows the competent authority to find, in the light of the perception of the sign at issue by the relevant public and the knowledge of that public, that the shape which alone forms the sign is the tangible symbol of a mathematic discovery. Since it took the view that that fact makes that shape special and striking, the competent authority was entitled to conclude that it is an essential characteristic and that it was necessary to assess whether, as a result of that fact, the shape which alone forms the sign at issue gives substantial value to the goods.[1360]

Probably basically still applicable: The fact that such a characteristic does not, in itself, concern the aesthetic merits of the shape does not exclude the application of Article 3(1)(e)(iii) CTMR. It should be borne in mind, in this regard, that the concept of a 'shape which gives substantial value to the goods' is not limited to the shape of goods having an exclusively artistic or ornamental value. The question as to whether the shape gives substantial value to the goods may be examined on the basis of other relevant factors, including, *inter alia*, whether the shape is dissimilar from other shapes in common use on the market concerned.[1361]

[G] Public policy or accepted principles of morality

Pursuant to Article 7(1)(f) CTMR, trade marks which are contrary to public policy or to accepted principles of morality are not to be registered. Furthermore, it follows from Article 7(2) CTMR that the absolute grounds for refusal set out in Article 7(1) CTMR are applicable even if they obtain in only part of the European Union.[1362]

As regards that ground for refusal, it should be noted that since the concept of 'accepted principles of morality' is not defined by the CTMR, it must be interpreted in the light of its usual meaning and the context in which it is generally used. However,

1358. CJEU C-237/19 of 23.4.2020 – Gömböc Kutató, Szolgáltató és Kereskedelmi/Tulajdon Nemzeti Hivatala, para. 42.
1359. CJEU C-237/19 of 23.4.2020 – Gömböc Kutató, Szolgáltató és Kereskedelmi/Tulajdon Nemzeti Hivatala, para. 44, with reference to CJEU C-205/13 of 18.9.2014 – Hauck, para. 34.
1360. CJEU C-237/19 of 23.4.2020 – Gömböc Kutató, Szolgáltató és Kereskedelmi/Tulajdon Nemzeti Hivatala, para. 45.
1361. CJEU C-237/19 of 23.4.2020 – Gömböc Kutató, Szolgáltató és Kereskedelmi/Tulajdon Nemzeti Hivatala, para. 46, with reference to CJEU C-205/13 of 18.9.2014 – Hauck, para. 32 and 35.
1362. CJEU C-240/18 P of 27.2.2020 – Constantin Film Produktion/EUIPO, para. 37.

that concept refers, in its usual sense, to the fundamental moral values and standards to which a society adheres at a given time. Those values and norms, which are likely to change over time and vary in space, should be determined according to the social consensus prevailing in that society at the time of the assessment. In making that determination, due account is to be taken of the social context, including, where appropriate, the cultural, religious or philosophical diversities that characterize it, in order to assess objectively what that society considers to be morally acceptable at that time.[1363]

Moreover, in the context of the application of Article 7(1)(f) CTMR, the examination as to whether a sign, in respect of which registration as an EU trade mark is sought, is contrary to accepted principles of morality requires an examination of all the elements specific to the case in order to determine how the relevant public would perceive such a sign if it were used as a trade mark for the goods or services claimed.[1364]

In that connection, in order to come within the scope of Article 7(1)(f) CTMR, it is not sufficient for the sign concerned to be regarded as being in bad taste. It must, at the time of the examination, be perceived by the relevant public as contrary to the fundamental moral values and standards of society as they exist at that time.[1365]

In order to establish whether that is the case, the examination is to be based on the perception of a reasonable person with average thresholds of sensitivity and tolerance, taking into account the context in which the mark may be encountered and, where appropriate, the particular circumstances of the part of the Union concerned. To that end, elements such as legislation and administrative practices, public opinion and, where appropriate, the way in which the relevant public has reacted in the past to that sign or similar signs, as well as any other factor which may make it possible to assess the perception of that public, are relevant.[1366]

The examination to be carried out cannot be confined to an abstract assessment of the mark applied for, or even of certain components of it, but it must be established, in particular where an applicant has relied on factors that are liable to cast doubt on the fact that that mark is perceived by the relevant public as contrary to accepted principles of morality, that the use of that mark in the concrete and current social context would indeed be perceived by that public as being contrary to the fundamental moral values and standards of society.[1367]

In the present case, it is not disputed that the relevant public consists of the German-speaking general public of the Union, namely that of Germany and Austria in particular.[1368]

As regards the perception of the mark applied for by that public, the General Court noted that that public will assimilate that mark to the English phrase 'Fuck you' along with the surname Goethe, the whole written with a different spelling resulting from a phonetic transcription in German of those terms. Although, in its original

1363. CJEU C-240/18 P of 27.2.2020 – Constantin Film Produktion/EUIPO, para. 39.
1364. CJEU C-240/18 P of 27.2.2020 – Constantin Film Produktion/EUIPO, para. 40.
1365. CJEU C-240/18 P of 27.2.2020 – Constantin Film Produktion/EUIPO, para. 41.
1366. CJEU C-240/18 P of 27.2.2020 – Constantin Film Produktion/EUIPO, para. 42.
1367. CJEU C-240/18 P of 27.2.2020 – Constantin Film Produktion/EUIPO, para. 43.
1368. CJEU C-240/18 P of 27.2.2020 – Constantin Film Produktion/EUIPO, para. 45.

meaning, the English phrase 'Fuck you' had a sexual connotation and was vulgar, it could also be used in a different context to express anger, mistrust or contempt for a person. However, even in such a situation, that phrase would still be intrinsically vulgar, and the addition of the element 'Göhte' at the end of the sign at issue – while it would make it possible to identify to whom the terms making up the beginning of the sign are 'addressed' – could not attenuate its vulgarity.[1369]

The General Court added that, contrary to the appellant's suggestion, the fact that the film *Fack Ju Göhte* was seen by several million people at the time of its cinema release does not mean that the relevant public would not be shocked by the mark applied for.[1370]

It concluded that, in those circumstances, the Board of Appeal had rightly found that the English expression 'Fuck you' – and, therefore, the mark applied for as a whole – were inherently vulgar and liable to offend the relevant public. Consequently, the Board had been right to infer that the mark applied for had to be refused registration on the basis of Article 7(1)(f) CTMR.[1371]

In that connection, it must be held that the examination carried out by the General Court does not meet the standards required by Article 7(1)(f) CTMR, as set out above.[1372]

In fact, having regard to the social context and the factors relied on in that regard by the appellant – and in particular the fact that the word sign 'Fack Ju Göhte' corresponds to a German cinematic comedy produced by the appellant, having been one of the greatest film successes of 2013 in Germany and having been seen by several million people when it was released in cinemas – the General Court, in order to establish to the requisite legal standard that the mark applied for is perceived by the German-speaking public at large as contrary to accepted principles of morality, could not confine itself to an abstract assessment of that mark and of the English expression to which the first part of it is assimilated by that public.[1373]

Thus, the fact that it is that mark itself which is to be examined does not mean that, in the course of that examination, contextual elements capable of shedding light on how the relevant public perceives that mark could be disregarded.[1374]

It should also be added that the relevance of the success of the eponymous comedies as one of the contextual factors is in no way invalidated by the fact that the absolute ground for refusal in Article 7(1)(f) CTMR cannot be overcome by proof of the distinctive character acquired through use, within the meaning of Article 7(3) CTMR, of the mark applied for. Indeed, the success of the eponymous comedies with the relevant public and, in particular, the absence of controversy as regards their title must be taken into account in order to determine whether the relevant public perceives the mark applied for as contrary to accepted principles of morality and, therefore, to establish whether that absolute ground for refusal precludes its registration, and not

1369. CJEU C-240/18 P of 27.2.2020 – Constantin Film Produktion/EUIPO, para. 46.
1370. CJEU C-240/18 P of 27.2.2020 – Constantin Film Produktion/EUIPO, para. 47.
1371. CJEU C-240/18 P of 27.2.2020 – Constantin Film Produktion/EUIPO, para. 48.
1372. CJEU C-240/18 P of 27.2.2020 – Constantin Film Produktion/EUIPO, para. 49.
1373. CJEU C-240/18 P of 27.2.2020 – Constantin Film Produktion/EUIPO, para. 50.
1374. CJEU C-240/18 P of 27.2.2020 – Constantin Film Produktion/EUIPO, para. 51.

with a view to disregarding that ground once its applicability to the case in point has been established.[1375]

Those factors include the great success of the comedy of the same name amongst the German-speaking public at large and the fact that its title does not appear to have caused controversy, as well as the fact that access to it by young people had been authorized and that the Goethe Institute – which is the cultural institute of the Federal Republic of Germany, active worldwide and tasked, *inter alia*, with promoting knowledge of the German language – uses it for educational purposes.[1376]

In so far as those factors are, a priori, capable of constituting an indication that, notwithstanding the assimilation of the first part of the mark applied for to the English phrase 'Fuck you', the German-speaking public at large does not perceive the word sign 'Fack Ju Göhte' as morally unacceptable, the General Court, in concluding that that sign is incompatible with accepted principles of morality, could not rely solely on the intrinsically vulgar character of that English phrase without examining those factors or setting out conclusively the reasons why it considered, despite those factors, that the German-speaking public at large perceives that sign as running counter to the fundamental moral values and standards of society when it is used as a trade mark.[1377]

In particular, mere statements – according to which it has not been established that, in the course of activities in which the relevant public is likely to be confronted with the trade mark applied for, that public recognizes in that mark the title of a successful film and perceives that mark as a 'joke' – are not sufficient to satisfy those requirements of examination and reasoning.[1378]

As regards the latter claim in particular, it is important to note, first, that the General Court was required, in the judgment under appeal, to ascertain that EUIPO had not infringed Article 76(1) CTMR which, in proceedings concerning absolute grounds for refusal, requires the latter to carry out an ex officio examination of the facts and establish to the requisite legal standard the presence of such grounds. Secondly, the need to examine contextual factors for the purposes of a concrete assessment of how the relevant public perceives the mark applied for is in no way subject to the condition that it must be established that that public recognizes in that mark the title of the eponymous comedy or that it perceives that mark as a 'joke', since the absence of those two circumstances does not, in fact, serve to establish an affront to accepted principles of morality.[1379]

Lastly, it should also be added that contrary to the approach that 'there is, in the field of art, culture and literature, a constant concern to preserve freedom of expression which does not exist in the field of trade marks', freedom of expression, enshrined in Article 11 of the Charter of Fundamental Rights of the European Union, must be taken into account when applying Article 7(1)(f) CTMR. Such a finding is corroborated, moreover, by recital 21 of Regulation No. 2015/2424, which amended CTMR and

1375. CJEU C-240/18 P of 27.2.2020 – Constantin Film Produktion/EUIPO, para. 70.
1376. CJEU C-240/18 P of 27.2.2020 – Constantin Film Produktion/EUIPO, para. 52.
1377. CJEU C-240/18 P of 27.2.2020 – Constantin Film Produktion/EUIPO, para. 53.
1378. CJEU C-240/18 P of 27.2.2020 – Constantin Film Produktion/EUIPO, para. 54.
1379. CJEU C-240/18 P of 27.2.2020 – Constantin Film Produktion/EUIPO, para. 55.

recital 21 of the EUTMR, both of which expressly emphasize the need to apply those regulations in such a way as to ensure full respect for fundamental rights and freedoms, in particular freedom of expression.[1380]

It follows from all of the foregoing considerations that the interpretation and application of Article 7(1)(f) CTMR, as carried out by the General Court in the judgment under appeal, are vitiated by errors of law.[1381]

[H] Deceptive trade marks

In the case of a trade mark corresponding to the **name of a person**, the public interest ground which justifies the prohibition laid down by Article 3(1)(g) TMD2008 to register a trade mark which is liable to deceive the public, namely consumer protection, must raise the question of the risk of confusion which such a trade mark may engender in the mind of the average consumer, especially where the person to whose name the mark corresponds originally personified the goods bearing that mark.[1382]

Nevertheless, the circumstances for refusing registration referred to in Article 3(1)(g) TMD2008 presuppose the existence of actual deceit or a sufficiently serious risk that the consumer will be deceived.[1383]

Even if the average consumer might be influenced in his act of purchasing a garment bearing the trade mark 'ELIZABETH EMANUEL' by imagining that Ms Elizabeth Emanuel was involved in the design of that garment, the characteristics and the qualities of that garment remain guaranteed by the undertaking which owns the trade mark.[1384]

Consequently, the name Elizabeth Emanuel cannot be regarded in itself as being of such a nature as to deceive the public as to the nature, quality or geographical origin of the product it designates.[1385]

On the other hand, it would be for the national court to determine whether or not, in the presentation of the trade mark 'ELIZABETH EMANUEL', there is an intention on the part of the undertaking which lodged the application to register that mark to make the consumer believe that Ms Emanuel is still the designer of the goods bearing the mark or that she is involved in their design. In that case, there would be conduct which might be held to be fraudulent but which could not be analysed as deception for the purposes of Article 3 TMD2008 and which, for that reason, would not affect the trade mark itself and, consequently, its prospects of being registered.[1386]

A trade mark corresponding to the name of the designer and first manufacturer of the goods bearing that mark may not, by reason of that particular feature alone, be refused registration on the ground that it would deceive the public, within the meaning

1380. CJEU C-240/18 P of 27.2.2020 – Constantin Film Produktion/EUIPO, para. 56.
1381. CJEU C-240/18 P of 27.2.2020 – Constantin Film Produktion/EUIPO, para. 57.
1382. CJEU C-259/04 of 30.3.2006 – Emanuel, para. 46.
1383. CJEU C-259/04 of 30.3.2006 – Emanuel, para. 47; C-689/15 of 8.6.2017 – W.F. Gözze Frottierweberei a.o./Verein Bremer Baumwollbörse, para. 54.
1384. CJEU C-259/04 of 30.3.2006 – Emanuel, para. 48.
1385. CJEU C-259/04 of 30.3.2006 – Emanuel, para. 49.
1386. CJEU C-259/04 of 30.3.2006 – Emanuel, para. 50.

of Article 3(1)(g) TMD2008, in particular where the goodwill associated with that trade mark, previously registered in a different graphic form, has been assigned together with the business making the goods to which the mark relates.[1387]

The registration of a **mark containing a geographical indication**, or the generic term corresponding to that indication and its translation, with respect to spirit drinks which do not meet the specifications set for that indication, falls, at the very least, within the situations referred to in Article 16(a) and (b) of Regulation No. 110/2008[1388] and that the competent national authorities must, on the basis of Article 23(1) of Regulation No. 110/2008, refuse or invalidate the registration of such a mark.[1389]

In that connection, it should be recalled that the direct application of a regulation means that its entry into force and its application in favour of or against those subject to it are independent of any measure of reception into national law, strict compliance with that obligation being an indispensable condition for the simultaneous and uniform application of regulations throughout the EU. Accordingly, Regulation No. 110/2008 must apply independently of the rules transposing the TMD into the national legal order.[1390]

Article 52(1)(a) and Article 7(1)(g) CTMR must be interpreted as meaning that an individual mark cannot be declared invalid, on the basis of a joint application of those provisions, because the proprietor of the mark fails to ensure, by carrying out periodic quality controls at its licensees, that **expectations relating to the quality** which the public associates with the mark are being met.[1391]

In this respect, it should be noted first of all that Article 52(1)(a) CTMR provides that the mark is invalid not only if it is of such a nature as to deceive the public within the meaning of Article 7(1)(g) CTMR but also, generally, where the mark has been registered in breach of Article 7 CTMR. Consequently, if there is no risk of deception within the meaning of Article 7(1)(g), the invalidity of the mark must, in principle, nevertheless be declared if it is clear that the registration of the mark took place in breach of one of the other grounds for refusal laid down in Article 7.[1392]

In order to find that a mark had been registered in breach of the ground for refusal relating to the risk of deception, it must be established that the sign filed for the purposes of registration as a trade mark creates per se such a risk.[1393]

1387. CJEU C-259/04 of 30.3.2006 – Emanuel, para. 51.
1388. Regulation (EC) No. 110/2008 of the European Parliament and of the Council of 15 Jan. 2008 on the definition, description, presentation, labelling and the protection of geographical indications of spirit drinks and repealing Council Regulation (EEC) No. 1576/89 (OJ 2008 L 39, p. 16).
1389. CJEU C-4/10 and C-27/10 of 14.7.2011 – Bureau national interprofessionnel du Cognac, para. 65.
1390. CJEU C-4/10 and C-27/10 of 14.7.2011 – Bureau national interprofessionnel du Cognac, para. 66.
1391. CJEU C-689/15 of 8.6.2017 – W.F. Gözze Frottierweberei a.o./Verein Bremer Baumwollbörse, para. 57.
1392. CJEU C-689/15 of 8.6.2017 – W.F. Gözze Frottierweberei a.o./Verein Bremer Baumwollbörse, para. 53.
1393. CJEU C-689/15 of 8.6.2017 – W.F. Gözze Frottierweberei a.o./Verein Bremer Baumwollbörse, para. 55, with reference to CJEU C-87/97 of 4.3.1999 – Consorzio per la tutela del formaggio Gorgonzola, paras 42 and 43.

It is for the referring court to examine whether the [...] sign [...] was capable per se of deceiving the consumer.[1394]

The CTMR must be interpreted as meaning that its provisions on collective EU trade marks may not be applied *mutatis mutandis* to individual EU trade marks.[1395]

In that regard, it is important to note that the scope of Articles 66 to 74 CTMR, relating to collective EU trade marks, is expressly confined, according to the wording of Article 66(1) CTMR, to marks described as such when applied for.[1396]

The demarcation of the applicability of those articles must be strictly adhered to, especially as the rules they introduce, such as those set out in Article 67 CTMR concerning regulations governing use of the mark, go hand in hand with the requirement when making the application for registration, to expressly describe the mark applied for as a collective mark. Therefore, it is not possible to apply those rules by analogy to individual EU trade marks.[1397]

[I] Trade marks which have not been authorized by the competent authorities

Some of the essential functions which may be attributed to a State emblem include that of identifying a State and that of representing its sovereignty and unity. The essential function of the trade mark, for its part, is to guarantee the identity of the origin of the marked product or service to the consumer or end user by enabling him, without any possibility of confusion, to distinguish the product or service from others which have another origin.[1398]

That discrepancy between the essential functions of trade marks and those of State emblems is also reflected in the difference in their treatment under both Community and international law.[1399]

Thus, Article 6 CTMR sets out the **principle** that a trade mark is to be obtained by registration, whereas, under Article 6*ter*(3)(a) of the Paris Convention, the States are merely to communicate the list of emblems to be protected to the International Bureau of the WIPO, such a communication not being obligatory in respect of flags of States. In respect of trade marks, the principle is that protection is provided in respect of certain determined classes of goods and services, whereas emblems, on the other hand, are entitled to general protection whatever the use one wishes to make of them. In addition, unlike trade marks, emblems cannot be declared invalid, and their proprietor cannot be deprived of his rights. Moreover, the duration of their protection is not

1394. CJEU C-689/15 of 8.6.2017 – W.F. Gözze Frottierweberei a.o./Verein Bremer Baumwollbörse, para. 56.
1395. CJEU C-689/15 of 8.6.2017 – W.F. Gözze Frottierweberei a.o./Verein Bremer Baumwollbörse, para. 61.
1396. CJEU C-689/15 of 8.6.2017 – W.F. Gözze Frottierweberei a.o./Verein Bremer Baumwollbörse, para. 59.
1397. CJEU C-689/15 of 8.6.2017 – W.F. Gözze Frottierweberei a.o./Verein Bremer Baumwollbörse, para. 60.
1398. CJEU C-202/08 and C-208/08 of 16.7.2009 – American Clothing Associates/OHIM, para. 40.
1399. CJEU C-202/08 and C-208/08 of 16.7.2009 – American Clothing Associates/OHIM, para. 42.

limited. Many aspects governing the protection of trade marks are therefore not capable of being transposed to the protection of State emblems.[1400]

The same is true of the existence of a **likelihood of confusion** which, although it is the specific condition for the protection of the trade mark in the case of similarity between the trade mark and the sign and between the goods or services, is **not required** for the protection of an emblem, since Article 6*ter*(1)(a) of the Paris Convention makes no reference to it.[1401]

It is apparent from the second sentence of Article 6*ter*(1)(c) of the Paris Convention that the protection of State emblems is **not subject to there being a connection, in the mind of the public**, between the trade mark for which registration is sought and the emblem. In the case of emblems of international organizations, that provision authorizes the registration and use of a trade mark if that mark is not of a nature such as to mislead the public regarding the existence of a connection between the user of the trade mark and the organization. It follows that, in other cases, namely those involving State emblems, that possibility does not exist, and there is therefore no need to ascertain whether there is such a connection.[1402]

Therefore, the argument as regards the effect of the essential function of a State emblem on its scope of protection and the application, by analogy, of the same criteria for protection as those applicable to trade marks must be rejected.[1403]

As regards the arguments on the interpretation of the expression 'any imitation from a heraldic point of view' in Article 6*ter*(1)(a) of the Paris Convention, let me start by observing that that provision prohibits the registration and use of a State emblem not only as a trade mark but also as an element of a trade mark. The protection granted to emblems is therefore, in this regard, also very broad. Furthermore, the last part of that provision also contributes to guaranteeing broad protection to State emblems, in so far as it prohibits the imitation of the emblem in addition to prohibiting its exact replication.[1404]

However, the prohibition of the imitation of an emblem applies only to imitations of it from a heraldic perspective, that is to say, those which contain heraldic connotations which distinguish the emblem from other signs. Thus, the protection against any imitation from a heraldic point of view refers not to the image as such but to its heraldic expression. It is therefore necessary, in order to determine whether the trade mark contains an imitation from a heraldic point of view, to consider the heraldic description of the emblem at issue.[1405]

Thus, a **trade mark which does not exactly reproduce a State emblem can nevertheless be covered** by Article 6*ter*(1)(a) of the Paris Convention, where it is

1400. CJEU C-202/08 and C-208/08 of 16.7.2009 – American Clothing Associates/OHIM, para. 43.
1401. CJEU C-202/08 and C-208/08 of 16.7.2009 – American Clothing Associates/OHIM, para. 44.
1402. CJEU C-202/08 and C-208/08 of 16.7.2009 – American Clothing Associates/OHIM, para. 45.
1403. CJEU C-202/08 and C-208/08 of 16.7.2009 – American Clothing Associates/OHIM, para. 46.
1404. CJEU C-202/08 and C-208/08 of 16.7.2009 – American Clothing Associates/OHIM, paras 47 and 59.
1405. CJEU C-202/08 and C-208/08 of 16.7.2009 – American Clothing Associates/OHIM, para. 48.

perceived by the relevant public, in the present case the average consumer, as imitating such an emblem.[1406]

So far as the expression 'imitation from a heraldic point of view' in that provision is concerned, a difference detected by a specialist in heraldic art between the trade mark applied for and the State emblem will not necessarily be perceived by the average consumer who, in spite of differences at the level of certain heraldic details, can see in the trade mark an imitation of the emblem in question.[1407]

Furthermore, the **heraldic description** of the emblem, which must be referred to in order to determine whether there is an imitation from a heraldic point of view within the meaning of Article *6ter*(1)(a) of the Paris Convention, normally contains only certain descriptive elements, and does not necessarily concern itself with particular features of the artistic interpretation. The Court of First Instance therefore did not err in law by holding that a number of artistic interpretations of one and the same emblem on the basis of the same heraldic description were possible.[1408]

Article *6ter* leaves the **extension** of the protection guaranteed to trade marks for goods to **service marks** to the discretion of the States party to the Convention. In doing so, the Paris Convention does not require those States to distinguish between the two types of marks.[1409]

The Paris Convention provides for a minimum level of protection for elements falling within its scope while leaving the Member States party to the Convention free to extend the scope of the protection. Consequently, although the Paris Convention did not oblige the States party to it to register service marks and the provisions of the Convention did not apply to those service marks, those States are nevertheless free to provide for such an application unilaterally. As is apparent from a WIPO document,[1410] Article *6ter* 'does not oblige States party to the Paris Convention to refuse or to invalidate the registration, and to prohibit the use of State emblems or other official signs as a service mark or as an element of a service mark. States are nevertheless free to do so ...'.[1411]

It is therefore necessary to consider whether the Community legislature intended to exercise that power of discretion and to extend to service marks the protection granted to trade marks for goods under the Paris Convention.[1412]

The mere fact that some provisions of the CTMR, such as Article 7(1)(e), (j) and (k), restrict their scope, so far as absolute grounds for refusal of registration are concerned, since the restriction laid down in those provisions is limited to certain types of goods, cannot call into question the finding that the provisions of that regulation as a whole apply without distinction to trade marks for goods and service marks.[1413]

1406. CJEU C-202/08 and C-208/08 of 16.7.2009 – American Clothing Associates/OHIM, para. 50.
1407. CJEU C-202/08 and C-208/08 of 16.7.2009 – American Clothing Associates/OHIM, para. 51.
1408. CJEU C-202/08 and C-208/08 of 16.7.2009 – American Clothing Associates/OHIM, para. 52.
1409. CJEU C-202/08 and C-208/08 of 16.7.2009 – American Clothing Associates/OHIM, para. 73.
1410. 'General Information on Article 6ter', available on the WIPO internet site.
1411. CJEU C-202/08 and C-208/08 of 16.7.2009 – American Clothing Associates/OHIM, para. 72.
1412. CJEU C-202/08 and C-208/08 of 16.7.2009 – American Clothing Associates/OHIM, para. 74.
1413. CJEU C-202/08 and C-208/08 of 16.7.2009 – American Clothing Associates/OHIM, para. 76.

Such a finding must apply to Article 7(1)(h) CTMR, which does not contain any express restriction of the marks covered by it. That interpretation is not affected by the mere fact that that provision in question refers to the Paris Convention. That reference is intended solely to determine the type of signs which must be refused registration and not to restrict the scope of the provision.[1414]

Consequently, as in the case of the majority of absolute grounds for refusal set out in Article 7(1) CTMR, registration of a trade mark must be refused, whether the application concerns goods or services, where one of the grounds for refusal listed in Article 6*ter* of the Paris Convention applies to it.[1415]

That interpretation of Article 7(1)(h) CTMR is, furthermore, supported by Article 7(1)(i), the scope of application of which is analogous to that of subparagraph (h), namely trade marks which include badges, emblems or escutcheons other than those covered by Article 6*ter* of the Paris Convention.[1416]

Article 7(1)(i) CTMR applies without distinction to trade marks for goods and service marks, so that registration could be refused, for example, to a service mark containing a badge. There is no reason why registration should be refused to a service mark containing a badge and not a service mark containing a State flag. If the Community legislature wished to grant such protection to badges and escutcheons, it should be assumed that, *a fortiori*, it also intended to grant at least an equivalent level of protection to armorial bearings, flags and other emblems of States or international organizations. Thus, it seems unlikely that the Community legislature would have allowed a service provider to use a mark containing a national flag when, at the same time, it would have prohibited that use in respect of badges such as those of a sports association, for example.[1417]

[J] Bad faith

[1] Principles

Article 4(4)(g) TMD2008 must be interpreted as meaning that the concept of 'bad faith', within the meaning of that provision, is an **autonomous concept of European Union law** which must be given a **uniform interpretation** in the EU.[1418]

It should be recalled at the outset that if a concept set out in the CTMR is not defined by that regulation, its meaning and scope must be determined by considering its usual meaning in everyday language whilst also taking into account the context in which it occurs and the objectives pursued by that regulation.[1419]

That applies to the **concept of 'bad faith'** referred to in Article 52(1)(b) CTMR, in the absence of any definition of that concept by the EU legislature.[1420]

1414. CJEU C-202/08 and C-208/08 of 16.7.2009 – American Clothing Associates/OHIM, para. 77.
1415. CJEU C-202/08 and C-208/08 of 16.7.2009 – American Clothing Associates/OHIM, para. 78.
1416. CJEU C-202/08 and C-208/08 of 16.7.2009 – American Clothing Associates/OHIM, para. 79.
1417. CJEU C-202/08 and C-208/08 of 16.7.2009 – American Clothing Associates/OHIM, para. 80.
1418. CJEU C-320/12 of 27.6.2013 – Malaysia Dairy Industries, para. 29.
1419. CJEU C-104/18 P of 12.9.2019 – Koton Mağazacilik Tekstil Sanayi ve Ticaret/EUIPO, para. 43, with further proof.
1420. CJEU C-104/18 P of 12.9.2019 – Koton Mağazacilik Tekstil Sanayi ve Ticaret/EUIPO, para. 44.

It should first of all be recalled that Articles 3 and 4 TMD2008 list the absolute or relative grounds on the basis of which a mark may be refused registration or, if registered, may be declared invalid. Some of those grounds are listed as an option for the Member States which, as is noted in recital 8 in the preamble to the TMD, 'should therefore be able to maintain or introduce those grounds in their legislation'.[1421]

Article 4(4)(g) TMD2008 contains such an optional ground of refusal or invalidity.[1422]

In accordance with settled case law, the need for a uniform application of EU law and the principle of equality require that the terms of a provision of EU law which makes no express reference to the law of the Member States for the purpose of determining its meaning and scope must normally be given an independent and uniform interpretation throughout the EU; that interpretation must take into account the context of the provision and the objective of the relevant legislation.[1423]

It is common ground that the wording of Article 4(4)(g) TMD2008 contains no definition of the concept of 'bad faith', nor is that concept defined in the other articles of that directive. Further, that provision makes no express reference to the law of the Member States in respect of that concept. Accordingly, the meaning and scope of that concept must be determined in the light of the context of the provision concerned of the TMD2008 and the objective of that directive.[1424]

As regards the subject matter and purpose of the TMD2008, whilst it is true that, according to recital 4 in the preamble to that directive, it does not appear to be necessary to undertake full-scale approximation of the trade mark laws of the Member States, the directive none the less provides for harmonization in relation to substantive rules of central importance in this sphere, that is to say, according to the same recital, the rules concerning the provisions of national law which most directly affect the functioning of the internal market, and that recital does not preclude the harmonization relating to those rules from being complete.[1425]

It should be added that the optional nature of a provision of the TMD has no effect on whether a uniform interpretation must be given to the wording of that provision.[1426]

Article 4(4)(g) TMD2008 must be interpreted as meaning that it **does not allow** Member States to introduce a system of specific **protection of foreign marks which differs** from the system established by that provision and which is based on the fact that the applicant knew or should have known of a foreign mark.[1427]

It should be noted that although the grounds set out in Article 4(4) TMD2008 are listed as an option by the EU legislature, the fact remains that a Member State's latitude

1421. CJEU C-320/12 of 27.6.2013 – Malaysia Dairy Industries, para. 23.
1422. CJEU C-320/12 of 27.6.2013 – Malaysia Dairy Industries, para. 24.
1423. CJEU C-320/12 of 27.6.2013 – Malaysia Dairy Industries, para. 25; *see also* CJEU C-482/09 of 22.9.2011 – Budějovický Budvar, para. 29.
1424. CJEU C-320/12 of 27.6.2013 – Malaysia Dairy Industries, para. 26.
1425. CJEU C-320/12 of 27.6.2013 – Malaysia Dairy Industries, para. 27; *see also* CJEU C-355/96 of 16.7.1998 – Silhouette International Schmied/Hartlauer Handelsgesellschaft, para. 23; C-482/09 of 22.9.2011 – Budějovický Budvar, para. 30.
1426. CJEU C-320/12 of 27.6.2013 – Malaysia Dairy Industries, para. 28; *see also* CJEU C-408/01 of 23.10.2003 – Adidas-Salomon and Adidas Benelux, paras 18–21.
1427. CJEU C-320/12 of 27.6.2013 – Malaysia Dairy Industries, para. 43.

is limited to providing or not providing for that ground, as specifically delimited by the legislature, in its national law.[1428]

The TMD prohibits Member States from introducing grounds of refusal or invalidity other than those set out in that directive; this is confirmed by recital 8 in the preamble thereto, according to which the grounds for refusal or invalidity concerning the trade mark itself, for example, concerning conflicts between the trade mark and earlier rights, should be listed in an exhaustive manner, even if some of these grounds are listed as an option for the Member States which should therefore be able to maintain or introduce those grounds in their legislation.[1429]

It is clear from the wording of Article 51(1)(b) CTMR that bad faith is one of the absolute grounds for the invalidity of a **Community trade mark** to be relied on either before OHIM or by means of a counterclaim in infringement proceedings.[1430]

The TMD, which supplements EU trade mark legislation by creating a Community regime for trade marks, pursues the same objective as the CMTR, namely the establishment and functioning of the internal market. In the light of the need for harmonious interaction between the two systems of Community and national marks, it is necessary to interpret the concept of 'bad faith' within the meaning of Article 4(4)(g) TMD2008 in the same manner as in the context of the CTMR. Such an approach ensures a coherent application of the various trade mark rules in the legal order of the EU.[1431]

[2] Overall assessment

The absolute ground for invalidity referred to in Article 52(1)(b) of Regulation No. 207/2009 applies where it is apparent from relevant and consistent indicia that the proprietor of an EU trade mark has filed the application for registration of that mark **not with the aim of engaging fairly in competition** but with the intention of undermining, in a manner inconsistent with honest practices, the interests of third parties, or with the intention of obtaining, without even targeting a specific third party, an exclusive right for purposes other than those falling within the functions of a trade mark, in particular the essential function of indicating origin recalled in the previous paragraph of this judgment.[1432]

The **intention of an applicant** for a trade mark is a subjective factor which must, however, be determined objectively by the competent administrative or judicial authorities. Consequently, any claim of bad faith must be the subject of an overall

1428. CJEU C-320/12 of 27.6.2013 – Malaysia Dairy Industries, para. 41; *see also* CJEU C-408/01 of 23.10.2003 – Adidas-Salomon and Adidas Benelux, paras 18–20.
1429. CJEU C-320/12 of 27.6.2013 – Malaysia Dairy Industries, para. 42; *see also* CJEU C-371/18 of 29.1.2020 – Sky a.o./SkyKick UK a.o., para. 56.
1430. CJEU C-529/07 of 11.6.2009 – Chocoladefabriken Lindt & Sprüngli, para. 34.
1431. CJEU C-320/12 of 27.6.2013 – Malaysia Dairy Industries, para. 35, *see also* CJEU C-104/18 P of 12.9.2019 – Koton Mağazacilik Tekstil Sanayi ve Ticaret/EUIPO, para. 45; C-371/18 of 29.1.2020 – Sky a.o./SkyKick UK a.o., paras 73 et seq.
1432. CJEU C-104/18 P of 12.9.2019 – Koton Mağazacilik Tekstil Sanayi ve Ticaret/EUIPO, para. 46; C-371/18 of 29.1.2020 – Sky a.o./SkyKick UK a.o., para. 75.

assessment, taking into account all the factual circumstances relevant to the particular case.[1433]

Whether the applicant is acting in bad faith, within the meaning of Article 51(1)(b) CTMR, must be the subject of an **overall assessment**, taking into account all the factors relevant to the particular case.[1434]

In order to determine whether the applicant is acting in bad faith within the meaning of Article 51(1)(b) CTMR, the national court must take into consideration all the relevant factors specific to the particular case which pertained at the time of filing the application for registration of the sign as a Community trade mark, in particular:

- the fact that **the applicant knows or must know that a third party is using**, in at least one Member State, an identical or similar sign for an identical or similar product capable of being confused with the sign for which registration is sought;
- the **applicant's intention to prevent** that third party from continuing to use such a sign; and
- the **degree of legal protection** enjoyed by the third party's sign and by the sign for which registration is sought.[1435]

It does **not** follow from that judgment that the existence of bad faith, within the meaning of Article 52(1)(b) CTMR, may **only** be established in the situation where there is use on the internal market of an **identical or similar sign for identical or similar goods** capable of being confused with the sign for which registration is sought.[1436]

There may be situations, which are unrelated to the situation which led to the judgment *Chocoladefabriken Lindt & Sprüngli*, where the application for registration of a trade mark is liable to be regarded as having been filed in bad faith, notwithstanding the fact that, at the time of that application, there was no use by a third party on the internal market of an identical or similar sign for identical or similar goods.[1437]

In that regard, the absolute ground for invalidity referred to in Article 52(1)(b) CTMR is fundamentally different from the relative ground for invalidity referred to in Article 53(1)(a) CTMR since the latter provision presupposes the existence of an earlier trade mark referred to in Article 8(2) CTMR as well as the existence of a likelihood of confusion, within the meaning of Article 8(1)(b) CTMR, unless that earlier mark has a reputation within the meaning of Article 8(5) CTMR or unless Article 8(1)(a) CTMR

1433. CJEU C-104/18 P of 12.9.2019 – Koton Mağazacilik Tekstil Sanayi ve Ticaret/EUIPO, para. 47; C-528/18 P of 13.11.2019 – Outsource Professional Services/EUIPO, para. 63.
1434. CJEU C-529/07 of 11.6.2009 – Chocoladefabriken Lindt & Sprüngli, para. 37; C-104/18 P of 12.9.2019 – Koton Mağazacilik Tekstil Sanayi ve Ticaret/EUIPO, para. 47; *see also* CJEU C-569/08 of 3.6.2010 – Internetportal und Marketing, para. 42.
1435. CJEU C-529/07 of 11.6.2009 – Chocoladefabriken Lindt & Sprüngli, para. 53; *see also* CJEU C-266/12 P of 7.2.2013 – Majczak/OHIM, para. 38; C-320/12 of 27.6.2013 – Malaysia Dairy Industries, paras 36 and 37; C-104/18 P of 12.9.2019 – Koton Mağazacilik Tekstil Sanayi ve Ticaret/EUIPO, para. 50.
1436. CJEU C-104/18 P of 12.9.2019 – Koton Mağazacilik Tekstil Sanayi ve Ticaret/EUIPO, para. 51.
1437. CJEU C-104/18 P of 12.9.2019 – Koton Mağazacilik Tekstil Sanayi ve Ticaret/EUIPO, para. 52.

applies. In the case of an application for a declaration of invalidity based on Article 52(1)(b) CTMR, there is no requirement whatsoever that the applicant for that declaration be the proprietor of an earlier mark for identical or similar goods or services.[1438]

It should be added that, in cases where it transpires that, at the time of the application for the contested mark, a third party was using, in at least one Member State, a sign identical with, or similar to, that mark, the existence of a likelihood of confusion on the part of the public need not necessarily be established in order for Article 52(1)(b) CTMR to apply.[1439]

It is to be inferred from the interpretation provided by the Court in the judgment *Chocoladefabriken Lindt & Sprüngli*[1440] merely that, where it is established that use by a third party of an identical or similar sign for identical or similar goods or services existed and was capable of causing confusion, it is necessary to examine, in the context of the overall assessment of the relevant circumstances of the particular case, whether the applicant for the contested mark had knowledge of this. That factor is, however, only one relevant factor among others to be taken into consideration.[1441]

In the absence of any likelihood of confusion between the sign used by a third party and the contested mark, or if there has been no use, by a third party, of a sign identical with, or similar to, the contested mark, other factual circumstances may, depending on the circumstances, constitute relevant and consistent indicia establishing the bad faith of the applicant.[1442]

Where it is apparent from those other circumstances that the holder of the contested mark filed the application for registration of that mark with the intention of undermining, in a manner inconsistent with honest practice, the interests of third parties, or with the intention of obtaining, without even targeting a specific third party, an exclusive right for purposes other than those falling within the functions of a trade mark, such an intention must result in the application of the absolute ground for invalidity referred to in Article 52(1)(b) CTMR, whether or not there was a likelihood of confusion on the part of the public.[1443]

It is also apparent from that provision that the **relevant time** for determining whether there was bad faith on the part of the applicant is the time of filing the **application** for registration.[1444]

First, with regard to the **expression 'must know'** in the second question, a presumption of knowledge, by the applicant, of the use by a third party of an identical or similar sign for an identical or similar product capable of being confused with the

1438. CJEU C-104/18 P of 12.9.2019 – Koton Mağazacilik Tekstil Sanayi ve Ticaret/EUIPO, para. 53; C-528/18 P of 13.11.2019 – Outsource Professional Services/EUIPO, para. 72.
1439. CJEU C-104/18 P of 12.9.2019 – Koton Mağazacilik Tekstil Sanayi ve Ticaret/EUIPO, para. 54; C-528/18 P of 13.11.2019 – Outsource Professional Services/EUIPO, para. 61.
1440. CJEU C-529/07 of 11.6.2009 – Chocoladefabriken Lindt & Sprüngli, para. 53.
1441. CJEU C-104/18 P of 12.9.2019 – Koton Mağazacilik Tekstil Sanayi ve Ticaret/EUIPO, para. 55; C-528/18 P of 13.11.2019 – Outsource Professional Services/EUIPO, para. 62.
1442. CJEU C-104/18 P of 12.9.2019 – Koton Mağazacilik Tekstil Sanayi ve Ticaret/EUIPO, para. 56; C-528/18 P of 13.11.2019 – Outsource Professional Services/EUIPO, para. 61.
1443. CJEU C-528/18 P of 13.11.2019 – Outsource Professional Services/EUIPO, para. 61.
1444. CJEU C-529/07 of 11.6.2009 – Chocoladefabriken Lindt & Sprüngli, para. 35.

sign for which registration is sought may arise, *inter alia*, from general knowledge in the economic sector concerned of such use, and that knowledge can be inferred, *inter alia*, from the duration of such use. The more that use is longstanding, the more probable it is that the applicant will, when filing the application for registration, have knowledge of it.[1445]

However, the fact that the applicant knows or must know that a third party has long been using, in at least one Member State, an identical or similar sign for an identical or similar product capable of being confused with the sign for which registration is sought is not sufficient, in itself, to permit the conclusion that the applicant was acting in bad faith.[1446]

Consequently, in order to determine whether there was bad faith, consideration must also be given to the applicant's intention at the time when he files the application for registration.[1447]

It must be observed in that regard that the applicant's intention at the relevant time is a subjective factor which must be determined by reference to the objective circumstances of the particular case.[1448]

Accordingly, the **intention to prevent a third party** from marketing a product may, in certain circumstances, be an element of bad faith on the part of the applicant.[1449]

That is in particular the case when it becomes apparent, subsequently, that the applicant applied for registration of a sign as a Community trade mark without intending to use it, his sole objective being to prevent a third party from entering the market.[1450]

In such a case, the mark does not fulfil its essential function, namely that of ensuring that the consumer or end user can identify the origin of the product or service concerned by allowing him to distinguish that product or service from those of different origin, without any confusion.[1451]

Equally, the fact that a **third party has long used a sign** for an identical or similar product capable of being confused with the mark applied for and that that sign enjoys some degree of **legal protection** is one of the factors relevant to the determination of whether the applicant was acting in bad faith.[1452]

In such a case, the applicant's sole aim in taking advantage of the rights conferred by the Community trade mark might be to compete unfairly with a competitor who is

1445. CJEU C-529/07 of 11.6.2009 – Chocoladefabriken Lindt & Sprüngli, para. 39; *see also* CJEU C-104/18 P of 12.9.2019 – Koton Mağazacilik Tekstil Sanayi ve Ticaret/EUIPO, para. 50.
1446. CJEU C-529/07 of 11.6.2009 – Chocoladefabriken Lindt & Sprüngli, para. 40; C-320/12 of 27.6.2013 – Malaysia Dairy Industries, paras 36 and 37.
1447. CJEU C-529/07 of 11.6.2009 – Chocoladefabriken Lindt & Sprüngli, para. 41; C-320/12 of 27.6.2013 – Malaysia Dairy Industries, para. 36; *see also* CJEU C-569/08 of 3.6.2010 – Internetportal und Marketing, para. 45.
1448. CJEU C-529/07 of 11.6.2009 – Chocoladefabriken Lindt & Sprüngli, para. 42; C-320/12 of 27.6.2013 – Malaysia Dairy Industries, para. 36; *see also* CJEU C-569/08 of 3.6.2010 – Internetportal und Marketing, para. 45.
1449. CJEU C-529/07 of 11.6.2009 – Chocoladefabriken Lindt & Sprüngli, para. 43.
1450. CJEU C-529/07 of 11.6.2009 – Chocoladefabriken Lindt & Sprüngli, para. 44.
1451. CJEU C-529/07 of 11.6.2009 – Chocoladefabriken Lindt & Sprüngli, para. 45.
1452. CJEU C-529/07 of 11.6.2009 – Chocoladefabriken Lindt & Sprüngli, para. 46.

using a sign which, because of characteristics of its own, has by that time obtained some degree of legal protection.[1453]

That said, it cannot however be excluded that even in such circumstances, and in particular when several producers were using, on the market, identical or similar signs for identical or similar products capable of being confused with the sign for which registration is sought, the applicant's registration of the sign may be in pursuit of a legitimate objective.[1454]

That may in particular be the case when filing the application for registration that a third party, who is a newcomer in the market, is trying to take advantage of that sign by copying its presentation, and the applicant seeks to register the sign with a view to preventing use of that presentation.[1455]

Moreover, the nature of the mark applied for may also be relevant to determining whether the applicant is acting in bad faith. In a case where the sign for which registration is sought consists of the entire shape and presentation of a product, the fact that the applicant is acting in bad faith might more readily be established where the competitors' freedom to choose the shape of a product and its presentation is restricted by technical or commercial factors so that the trade mark proprietor is able to prevent his competitors not merely from using an identical or similar sign but also from marketing comparable products.[1456]

Furthermore, in order to determine whether the applicant is acting in bad faith, consideration may be given to the extent of the **reputation** enjoyed by a sign at the time when the application for its registration as a Community trade mark is filed.[1457]

The extent of that reputation might justify the applicant's interest in ensuring a wider legal protection for his sign.[1458]

[3] No intention to use

Article 51(1)(b) of Regulation No. 40/94 and Article 3(2)(d) of First Directive 89/104 must be interpreted as meaning that a trade mark application made without any intention to use the trade mark in relation to the goods and services covered by the registration constitutes bad faith, within the meaning of those provisions, if the applicant for registration of that mark had the intention either of undermining, in a manner inconsistent with honest practices, the interests of third parties or of obtaining, without even targeting a specific third party, an exclusive right for purposes other than those falling within the functions of a trade mark. When the absence of the intention to use the trade mark in accordance with the essential functions of a trade mark concerns

1453. CJEU C-529/07 of 11.6.2009 – Chocoladefabriken Lindt & Sprüngli, para. 47.
1454. CJEU C-529/07 of 11.6.2009 – Chocoladefabriken Lindt & Sprüngli, para. 48.
1455. CJEU C-529/07 of 11.6.2009 – Chocoladefabriken Lindt & Sprüngli, para. 49; *see also* CJEU C-569/08 of 3.6.2010 – Internetportal und Marketing, para. 49; C-488/16 P of 6.9.2018 – Bundesverband – Souvenir – Geschenke – Ehrenpreise/EUIPO, para. 83.
1456. CJEU C-529/07 of 11.6.2009 – Chocoladefabriken Lindt & Sprüngli, para. 50.
1457. CJEU C-529/07 of 11.6.2009 – Chocoladefabriken Lindt & Sprüngli, para. 51.
1458. CJEU C-529/07 of 11.6.2009 – Chocoladefabriken Lindt & Sprüngli, para. 52.

only certain goods or services referred to in the application for registration, that application constitutes bad faith only in so far as it relates to those goods or services.[1459]

As regards, in the first place, the question of whether Article 51(1)(b) of Regulation No. 40/94 and Article 3(2)(d) of First Directive 89/104 must be interpreted as meaning that a trade mark application made without any intention to use the trade mark in relation to the goods and services covered by the registration constitutes bad faith within the meaning of those provisions, it must be borne in mind that those provisions state, in essence, that a trade mark may be declared invalid where the applicant was acting in bad faith when he or she filed the application for the trade mark. Neither that regulation nor that directive provides a definition of the concept of 'bad faith'. It must, however, be pointed out that that concept is an autonomous concept of EU law and that, in the light of the need for a coherent application of the national systems and the EU system of marks, the concept of 'bad faith' must be interpreted in the context of First Directive 89/104 in the same manner as in the context of Regulation No. 40/94.[1460]

Admittedly, the applicant for a trade mark is not required to indicate or even to know precisely, on the date on which his or her application for registration of a mark is filed or of the examination of that application, the use he or she will make of the mark applied for and he or she has a period of five years for beginning actual use consistent with the essential function of that trade mark.[1461]

However, the registration of a trade mark by an applicant without any intention to use it in relation to the goods and services covered by that registration may constitute bad faith, where there is no rationale for the application for registration in the light of the aims referred to in Regulation No. 40/94 and First Directive 89/104. Such bad faith may, however, be established only if there is objective, relevant and consistent indicia tending to show that, when the application for a trade mark was filed, the trade mark applicant had the intention either of undermining, in a manner inconsistent with honest practices, the interests of third parties, or of obtaining, without even targeting a specific third party, an exclusive right for purposes other than those falling within the functions of a trade mark.[1462]

The bad faith of the trade mark applicant cannot, therefore, be presumed on the basis of the mere finding that, at the time of filing his or her application, that applicant had no economic activity corresponding to the goods and services referred to in that application.[1463]

In the second place, it must be determined whether Article 51(3) of Regulation No. 40/94 and Article 13 of First Directive 89/104 must be interpreted as meaning that when the absence of the intention to use a trade mark in accordance with its essential

1459. CJEU C-371/18 of 29.1.2020 – Sky a.o./SkyKick UK a.o., para. 81.
1460. CJEU C-371/18 of 29.1.2020 – Sky a.o./SkyKick UK a.o., para. 73, with reference to CJEU C-320/12 of 27.6.2013 – Malaysia Dairy Industries, paras 34 et seq.
1461. CJEU C-371/18 of 29.1.2020 – Sky a.o./SkyKick UK a.o., para. 76, with reference to CJEU C-541/18 of 12.9.2019 – AS/Deutsches Patent- und Markenamt, para. 22.
1462. CJEU C-371/18 of 29.1.2020 – Sky a.o./SkyKick UK a.o., para. 77.
1463. CJEU C-371/18 of 29.1.2020 – Sky a.o./SkyKick UK a.o., para. 78.

functions concerns only certain goods or services covered by the registration, the invalidity of that trade mark covers those goods or services only.[1464]

In that regard, it is sufficient to note that it follows clearly from those provisions that, where the ground for invalidity exists in respect of only some of the goods or services for which the trade mark is sought to be registered, the trade mark is to be declared invalid as regards those goods or services only.[1465]

First Directive 89/104 must be interpreted as not precluding a **provision of national law under which an applicant for registration of a trade mark must state that the trade mark is being used** in relation to the goods and services in relation to which it is sought to register the trade mark, or that he or she has a bona fide intention that it should be so used, in so far as the infringement of such an obligation does not constitute, in itself, a ground for invalidity of a trade mark already registered.[1466]

In that regard, it must be pointed out that the seventh recital of that directive states that the absolute grounds for invalidity provided for by that directive are listed in an exhaustive manner, even if some of those grounds were listed as an option for the Member States. Accordingly, the directive prohibits the Member States from introducing, in the national legislation transposing it, grounds for refusal or invalidity other than those appearing in that directive.[1467]

On the other hand, Member States remain free, as is apparent from the fifth recital of First Directive 89/104, to fix the provisions of procedure concerning the registration, the revocation and the invalidity of trade marks acquired by registration.[1468]

It follows that while Member States may fix the provisions of procedure which appear to them to be appropriate, such provisions cannot, in practice, have the effect of introducing grounds of refusal of registration or invalidity not provided for by First Directive 89/104.[1469]

Consequently, a provision of national law under which an applicant for registration of a national trade mark must, pursuant to a mere procedural requirement relating to the registration of that mark, state that the trade mark is being used in relation to the goods and services in relation to which it is sought to register the trade mark, or that he or she has a bona fide intention that it should be so used, cannot be considered incompatible with the provisions of First Directive 89/104. While the infringement of such an obligation to make such a statement may constitute evidence for the purposes of establishing possible bad faith on the part of the trade mark applicant when he or she filed the trade mark application, such an infringement cannot, however, constitute a ground for invalidity of the trade mark concerned.[1470]

1464. CJEU C-371/18 of 29.1.2020 – Sky a.o./SkyKick UK a.o., para. 79.
1465. CJEU C-371/18 of 29.1.2020 – Sky a.o./SkyKick UK a.o., para. 80.
1466. CJEU C-371/18 of 29.1.2020 – Sky a.o./SkyKick UK a.o., para. 87.
1467. CJEU C-371/18 of 29.1.2020 – Sky a.o./SkyKick UK a.o., para. 83, corrected wording.
1468. CJEU C-371/18 of 29.1.2020 – Sky a.o./SkyKick UK a.o., para. 84.
1469. CJEU C-371/18 of 29.1.2020 – Sky a.o./SkyKick UK a.o., para. 85.
1470. CJEU C-371/18 of 29.1.2020 – Sky a.o./SkyKick UK a.o., para. 86.

[K] Interference with the protection of geographical indications and designations of origin

In particular, the fact that there is no likelihood of confusion on the part of the consumer, for the purposes of Article 14(3) of Regulation No. 2081/92,[1471] between a name at issue and a pre-existing mark does not preclude the use of the mark from being covered by a situation referred to in Article 13(1) of that regulation or the possibility that the mark may be subject to one of the grounds for invalidity or revocation as provided for by Article 3(1)(c) and (g) TMD2008 and Article 12(2)(b) TMD2008, respectively. Furthermore, the fact that there is no likelihood of confusion does not mean that it is not necessary to ascertain that the trade mark in question was registered in good faith before the date on which the application for registration of the PDO[1472] or PGI[1473] was lodged.[1474]

Regulation No. 1347/2001[1475] must be interpreted as having no adverse effects on the validity and the possibility of using, in one of the situations referred to in Article 13 of Regulation No. 2081/92, pre-existing trade marks of third parties in which the word 'Bavaria' appears and which were registered in good faith before the date on which the application for registration of the PGI 'Bayerisches Bier' was lodged, provided that those marks are not affected by the grounds for invalidity or revocation as provided for by Article 3(1)(c) and (g) TMD2008 and Article 12(2)(b) TMD2008.[1476]

[L] Acquisition of distinctive character following the use

[1] Principles

The provision of Article 7(3) CTMR and Article 3(3) TMD2008 are essentially identical.[1477]

Article 3(3) TMD2008 is linked to the concept of '**distinctive character of a sign**' for the purposes of Article 2 TMD2008. According to the wording of Article 3(3) TMD2008, the registration or validity of marks referred to in Article 3(1)(b), (c) or (d) TMD2008 is to be allowed by virtue of the use which has been made of them where, on account of that use, the marks have 'acquired a distinctive character'.[1478]

1471. Council Regulation (EEC) No. 2081/92 of 14 Jul. 1992 on the protection of geographical indications and designations of origin for agricultural products and foodstuffs (OJ 1992 L 208, p. 1).
1472. Protected designation of origin.
1473. Protected geographical indication.
1474. CJEU C-343/07 of 2.7.2009 – Bavaria, para. 124.
1475. Council Regulation (EC) No. 1347/2001 of 28 Jun. 2001 supplementing the Annex to Commission Regulation (EC) No. 1107/96 on the registration of geographical indications and designations of origin.
1476. CJEU C-343/07 of 2.7.2009 – Bavaria, para. 125.
1477. CJEU C-24/05 P of 22.6.2006 – Storck/OHIM (light-brown sweet), para. 58; C-542/07 P of 11.6.2009 – Imagination Technologies/OHIM, para. 45.
1478. CJEU C-371/06 of 20.9.2007 – Benetton Group, para. 24.

A sign's **distinctive character**, which thus constitutes one of the general conditions to be met before that sign can be registered as a trade mark, may be **intrinsic**, as provided for in Article 3(1)(b) TMD2008, **or** may have been **acquired by the use** made of that sign, as provided for in Article 3(3) TMD2008.[1479]

Furthermore, it must be stated that Article 3(3) of the Directive does not refer, for the purposes of establishing the extent of the exception laid down therein, to the signs referred to in Article 3(1)(e) TMD2008.[1480]

The first point to note is that Article 3(3) TMD2008 provides that a sign may, through use, acquire a distinctive character which it initially lacked and thus be registered as a trade mark. It is therefore through the use made of it that the sign acquires the distinctive character which is a prerequisite for its registration.[1481]

Article 3(3) TMD2008 therefore constitutes a major exception to the rule laid down in Article 3(1)(b), (c) and (d) TMD2008, whereby registration is to be refused in relation to trade marks which are devoid of any distinctive character, descriptive marks, and marks which consist exclusively of indications which have become customary in the current language or in the bona fide and established practices of the trade.[1482]

Second, just as distinctive character is one of the general conditions for registering a trade mark under Article 3(1)(b) TMD2008, distinctive character acquired through use means that the mark must serve to identify the product in respect of which registration is applied for as originating from a particular undertaking, and thus to distinguish that product from goods of other undertakings.[1483]

If the appellant had not invoked it at any point in the proceedings, it is not necessary to determine whether the mark in question had succeeded in becoming distinctive within the meaning of that provision.[1484]

[2] Conditions

As regards the question of how to **determine** whether a mark has acquired a distinctive character through use, it is settled case law that the competent authority for registering trade marks must carry out an examination by reference to the actual situation.[1485]

1479. CJEU C-215/14 of 16.9.2015 – Société des Produits Nestlé, para. 62; C-541/18 of 12.9.2019 – AS/Deutsches Patent- und Markenamt, para. 19.
1480. CJEU C-371/06 of 20.9.2007 – Benetton Group, para. 25.
1481. CJEU C-108/97 and C-109/97 of 4.5.1999 – Windsurfing Chiemsee, para. 44; C-517/99 of 4.10.2001 – Merz & Krell, para. 30; C-299/99 of 18.6.2002 – Philips, paras 34 and 58; C-104/01 of 6.5.2003 – Libertel, para. 67; *see also* CJEU C-24/05 P of 22.6.2006 – Storck/OHIM (light-brown sweet), para. 70; C-578/17 of 27.3.2019 – Oy Hartwall/Patentti- ja rekisterihallitus, para. 30.
1482. CJEU C-108/97 and C-109/97 of 4.5.1999 – Windsurfing Chiemsee, para. 45.
1483. CJEU C-108/97 and C-109/97 of 4.5.1999 – Windsurfing Chiemsee, paras 46 and 54; C-299/99 of 18.6.2002 – Philips, para. 35; C-217/13 and 218/13 of 19.6.2014 – Oberbank, para. 38; C-215/14 of 16.9.2015 – Société des Produits Nestlé, para. 60.
1484. CJEU C-136/02 P of 7.10.2004 – Mag Instrument/OHIM, para. 53, no original wording.
1485. CJEU C-217/13 and 218/13 of 19.6.2014 – Oberbank, para. 40; *see also* CJEU C-104/01 of 6.5.2003 – Libertel, para. 77; C-404/02 of 16.9.2004 – Nichols, para. 27.

In determining whether a mark has acquired distinctive character following the use made of it, the competent authority must make an overall assessment of the evidence that the mark has come to identify the product concerned as originating from a particular undertaking, and thus to distinguish that product from goods of other undertakings.[1486]

Moreover, that evidence must relate to use of the mark as a trade mark, that is to say, for the purposes of such identification by the relevant class of persons.[1487]

It follows that a geographical name may be registered as a trade mark if, following the use which has been made of it, it has come to identify the product in respect of which registration is applied for as originating from a particular undertaking and thus to distinguish that product from goods of other undertakings. Where that is the case, the geographical designation has gained a new significance and its connotation, no longer purely descriptive, justifies its registration as a trade mark.[1488]

In that connection, regard must be had in particular to the **specific nature** of the geographical name in question. Indeed, where a geographical name is very well known, it can acquire distinctive character under Article 3(3) TMD2008 only if there has been longstanding and intensive use of the mark by the undertaking applying for registration. *A fortiori*, where a name is already familiar as an indication of geographical origin in relation to a certain category of goods, an undertaking applying for registration of the name in respect of goods in that category must show that the use of the mark - both longstanding and intensive - is particularly well established.[1489]

Article 3(3) TMD2008 does not permit any differentiation as regards distinctiveness by reference to the perceived **importance of keeping** the geographical name **available** for use by other undertakings.[1490]

Whether a sign does have the capacity to distinguish as a result of the use made of it can only be assessed **in relation to the goods or services** covered by it.[1491]

The distinctive character of a mark must be assessed in relation to the presumed expectations within the trade circles concerned, that is to say, an **average consumer** of the category of goods or services in question, who is reasonably well informed and reasonably observant and circumspect.[1492]

1486. CJEU C-108/97 and C-109/97 of 4.5.1999 - Windsurfing Chiemsee, paras 49 and 54; C-104/01 of 6.5.2003 - Libertel, para. 67; C-136/02 P of 7.10.2004 - Mag Instrument/OHIM, para. 47; C-217/13 and 218/13 of 19.6.2014 - Oberbank, para. 40; *see also* CJEU C-108/05 of 7.9.2006 - Bovemij Verzekeringen, paras 27 et seq.
1487. CJEU C-217/13 and 218/13 of 19.6.2014 - Oberbank, para. 40; *see also* CJEU C-299/99 of 18.6.2002 - Philips, para. 64; C-353/03 of 7.7.2005 - Nestlé, paras 26 and 29; C-215/14 of 16.9.2015 - Société des Produits Nestlé, para. 63.
1488. CJEU C-108/97 and C-109/97 of 4.5.1999 - Windsurfing Chiemsee, para. 47.
1489. CJEU C-108/97 and C-109/97 of 4.5.1999 - Windsurfing Chiemsee, para. 50.
1490. CJEU C-108/97 and C-109/97 of 4.5.1999 - Windsurfing Chiemsee, para. 48.
1491. CJEU C-517/99 of 4.10.2001 - Merz & Krell, para. 30; C-299/99 of 18.6.2002 - Philips, para. 59; C-353/03 of 7.7.2005 - Nestlé, para. 25; C-217/13 and 218/13 of 19.6.2014 - Oberbank, para. 39; C-215/14 of 16.9.2015 - Société des Produits Nestlé, para. 61.
1492. CJEU C-217/13 and 218/13 of 19.6.2014 - Oberbank, para. 39; C-215/14 of 16.9.2015 - Société des Produits Nestlé, para. 61; *see also* CJEU C-363/99 of 12.2.2004 - Koninklijke KPN Nederland, para. 34; C-353/03 of 7.7.2005 - Nestlé, para. 25.

In assessing the distinctive character of a mark in respect of which registration has been applied for, the **following may also be taken into account**: the market share held by the mark; how intensive, geographically widespread and longstanding use of the mark has been; the amount invested by the undertaking in promoting the mark; the proportion of the relevant class of persons who, because of the mark, identify goods as originating from a particular undertaking; and statements from chambers of commerce and industry or other trade and professional associations.[1493]

The **market share** held by the mark is therefore an indication which may be relevant for the purposes of assessing whether that mark has acquired distinctive character through use. Such is the case, in particular, where, as in the present case, a mark consisting of the appearance of the product in respect of which registration is sought appears to be devoid of any distinctive character because it does not depart significantly from the norm or customs of the sector. It is probable, in such a case, that such a mark is likely to acquire distinctive character only if, following the use which is made of it, the products which bear it have more than a negligible share of the market in the products at issue.[1494]

For the same reasons, the share of the amount of publicity for the market in the products in dispute represented by **advertising investment** in promoting a mark may also be relevant for assessing whether the mark has acquired distinctive character through use.[1495]

The **sales figures** for the appellant's products and the publicity costs which it incurred are not sufficient, in the absence of information relating to the market share which they represent in respect of both the global confectionery market and the global amount of advertising costs in that market, to show that the mark applied for has acquired distinctive character as a result of the use which has been made of it.[1496]

Moreover, the question of whether or not such information is necessary for assessing whether a given mark has acquired distinctive character through use for the purposes of Article 7(3) CTMR comes within the scope of the assessment of the facts by OHIM and, on appeal, by the Court of First Instance.[1497]

If, on the basis of those factors, the competent authority finds that the **relevant class of persons** or at least a significant proportion thereof, identify goods as originating from a particular undertaking because of the trade mark, it must hold that the requirement for registering the mark laid down in Article 3(3) TMD2008 is satisfied.[1498]

1493. CJEU C-108/97 and C-109/97 of 4.5.1999 – Windsurfing Chiemsee, para. 51; C-299/99 of 18.6.2002 – Philips, para. 60; C-104/01 of 6.5.2003 – Libertel, para. 67; C-353/03 of 7.7.2005 – Nestlé, para. 31; C-25/05 P of 22.6.2006 – Storck/OHIM (gold-coloured sweet wrapper), para. 75; C-217/13 and 218/13 of 19.6.2014 – Oberbank, para. 41.
1494. CJEU C-25/05 P of 22.6.2006 – Storck/OHIM (gold-coloured sweet wrapper), para. 76.
1495. CJEU C-25/05 P of 22.6.2006 – Storck/OHIM (gold-coloured sweet wrapper), para. 77.
1496. CJEU C-25/05 P of 22.6.2006 – Storck/OHIM (gold-coloured sweet wrapper), para. 79.
1497. CJEU C-25/05 P of 22.6.2006 – Storck/OHIM (gold-coloured sweet wrapper), para. 78.
1498. CJEU C-108/97 and C-109/97 of 4.5.1999 – Windsurfing Chiemsee, para. 52; C-299/99 of 18.6.2002 – Philips, para. 61; C-217/13 and 218/13 of 19.6.2014 – Oberbank, para. 42.

However, the circumstances in which that requirement may be regarded as satisfied cannot be shown to exist solely by reference to general, abstract data such as predetermined **percentages**.[1499]

As regards the method to be used to assess the distinctive character of a mark in respect of which registration is applied for, Community law does not preclude the competent authority, where it has particular difficulty in that connection, from having recourse, under the conditions laid down by its own national law, to an **opinion poll** as guidance for its judgment.[1500]

If the competent authority finds it necessary to resort to such a survey, it must determine the **percentage** of consumers that would be sufficiently significant.[1501]

In the context of that assessment, it may indeed appear that the **perception of the relevant public** is not necessarily the same for each of the categories and that, accordingly, it could prove more difficult to establish the distinctive character of trade marks in certain categories than that of those in other categories.[1502]

However, Article 2 and Article 3(1)(b) and (3) TMD2008 make no distinction between different categories of trade marks. The criteria for assessing the distinctive character of contourless colour marks, such as the mark at issue in the main proceedings, including whether that mark has acquired a distinctive character following the use which has been made of it, are thus no different from those to be applied to other categories of trade mark.[1503]

The difficulties in establishing distinctive character which may be associated with certain categories of marks because of their nature – difficulties which it is legitimate to take into account – do not therefore justify laying down stricter criteria supplementing or derogating from application of the criterion of distinctiveness as interpreted in the case law on other categories of marks.[1504]

1499. CJEU C-108/97 and C-109/97 of 4.5.1999 – Windsurfing Chiemsee, para. 52; C-299/99 of 18.6.2002 – Philips, para. 62; C-217/13 and 218/13 of 19.6.2014 – Oberbank, para. 44.
1500. CJEU C-108/97 and C-109/97 of 4.5.1999 – Windsurfing Chiemsee, para. 53; C-217/13 and 218/13 of 19.6.2014 – Oberbank, para. 43.
1501. CJEU C-217/13 and 218/13 of 19.6.2014 – Oberbank, para. 43; *see also* CJEU C-478/07 of 5.2.2009 – Budějovický Budvar, para. 79.
1502. CJEU C-217/13 and 218/13 of 19.6.2014 – Oberbank, para. 45; *see also* CJEU C-53/01 to C-55/01 of 8.4.2003 – Linde and Others, para. 48; C-218/01 of 12.2.2004 – Henkel, para. 52; C-456/01 P and C-457/01 P of 29.4.2004 – Henkel/OHIM, para. 38; C-468/01 P to C-472/01 P of 29.4.2004 – Procter & Gamble/OHIM (three-dimensional form of tablet I), para. 36; C-473/01 P and C-474/01 P of 29.4.2004 – Procter & Gamble/OHIM (three-dimensional form of tablet II), para. 36; C-445/02 P of 28.6.2004 – Glaverbel/OHIM, para. 23; C-404/02 of 16.9.2004 – Nichols, para. 28; C-107/03 P of 23.9.2004 – Procter & Gamble/OHIM (form of a soap), para. 49 f.; C-136/02 P of 7.10.2004 – Mag Instrument/OHIM, para. 30; C-398/08 P of 21.1.2010 – Audi/OHIM, para. 37; C-265/09 P of 9.9.2010 – OHIM/BORCO-Marken-Import Matthiesen, para. 33; C-344/10 P and C-345/10 P of 20.10.2011 – Freixenet/OHIM, para. 46; C-311/11 P of 12.7.2012 – Smart Technologies/OHIM, para. 26; C-96/11 P of 6.9.2012 – Storck/OHIM, para. 34; C-417/16 P of 4.5.2017 – August Storck/EUIPO, para. 34.
1503. CJEU C-217/13 and 218/13 of 19.6.2014 – Oberbank, para. 46; C-578/17 of 27.3.2019 – Oy Hartwall/Patentti- ja rekisterihallitus, para. 28; *see also* CJEU C-299/99 of 18.6.2002 – Philips, para. 48; C-404/02 of 16.9.2004 – Nichols, paras 24 and 25.
1504. CJEU C-217/13 and 218/13 of 19.6.2014 – Oberbank, para. 47; C-578/17 of 27.3.2019 – Oy Hartwall/Patentti- ja rekisterihallitus, para. 28; *see also* CJEU C-404/02 of 16.9.2004 – Nichols, para. 26; C-265/09 P of 9.9.2010 – OHIM/BORCO-Marken-Import Matthiesen, para. 34.

It follows from the foregoing that it is not possible to state in general terms, for example, by referring to predetermined percentages relating to the degree of recognition attained by the mark within the relevant section of the public, when a mark has acquired a distinctive character through use and that, even with regard to contourless colour marks, such as the mark at issue in the main proceedings, and even if a consumer survey may be one of the factors to be taken into account when assessing whether such a mark has acquired a distinctive character through use, the results of a consumer survey cannot be the only decisive criterion to support the conclusion that a distinctive character has been acquired through use.[1505]

In the light of those considerations, Article 3(1) and (3) TMD2008 must be interpreted as precluding an interpretation of national law according to which, in the context of proceedings raising the question of whether a contourless colour mark has acquired a distinctive character through use, it is necessary in every case that a consumer survey indicates a degree of recognition of at least 70%.[1506]

[3] Use as a trade mark

The identification, by the **relevant class of persons**, of the product as originating from a given undertaking must be as a result of the use of the mark as a trade mark and thus as a result of the nature and effect of it, which make it capable of distinguishing the product concerned from those of other undertakings.[1507]

In order for the latter condition to be satisfied, the mark in respect of which registration is sought need **not necessarily** have been **used independently**.[1508]

In fact, Article 3(3) TMD2008 contains no restriction in that regard, referring solely to the 'use which has been made' of the mark.[1509]

The expression 'use of the mark as a trade mark' must therefore be understood as referring solely to use of the mark for the purposes of the identification, by the relevant class of persons, of the product or service as originating from a given undertaking.[1510]

Yet, such identification, and thus acquisition of distinctive character, may be as a result both of the use, as part of a registered trade mark, of a component thereof and of the use of a separate mark in conjunction with a registered trade mark. In both cases, it is sufficient that, in consequence of such use, the relevant class of persons actually perceive the product or service, designated exclusively by the mark applied for, as originating from a given undertaking.[1511]

1505. CJEU C-217/13 and 218/13 of 19.6.2014 – Oberbank, para. 48.
1506. CJEU C-217/13 and 218/13 of 19.6.2014 – Oberbank, para. 49.
1507. CJEU C-299/99 of 18.6.2002 – Philips, para. 64; C-353/03 of 7.7.2005 – Nestlé, para. 26; C-24/05 P of 22.6.2006 – Storck/OHIM (light-brown sweet), para. 61.
1508. CJEU C-353/03 of 7.7.2005 – Nestlé, para. 27.
1509. CJEU C-353/03 of 7.7.2005 – Nestlé, para. 28.
1510. CJEU C-353/03 of 7.7.2005 – Nestlé, para. 29; C-24/05 P of 22.6.2006 – Storck/OHIM (light-brown sweet), para. 61.
1511. CJEU C-353/03 of 7.7.2005 – Nestlé, para. 30, 32; C-245/06 P of 9.3.2007 – Saiwa/OHIM, para. 43; C-12/12 of 18.4.2013 – Colloseum Holding, para. 27; C-252/12 of 18.7.2013 – Specsavers International Healthcare, para. 23; C-215/14 of 16.9.2015 – Société des Produits Nestlé, para. 64; *see also* CJEU C-24/05 P of 22.6.2006 – Storck/OHIM (light-brown sweet), para. 57.

This finding is of general application and applies also where the issue is establishing whether an earlier mark has a particularly distinctive character in order to ascertain whether there is a likelihood of confusion within the meaning of Article 8(1)(b) CTMR.[1512]

Therefore, regardless of whether the sign is used as part of a registered trade mark or in conjunction with the registered trade mark, the fundamental condition is that, as a consequence of that use, the sign for which registration as a trade mark is sought may serve to identify, in the minds of the relevant class of persons, the goods to which it relates as originating from a particular undertaking.[1513]

Therefore, a three-dimensional mark may in certain circumstances acquire distinctive character through use even if it is used in conjunction with a word mark or a figurative mark. Such is the case where the mark consists of the shape of the product or its packaging and where they systematically bear a word mark under which they are marketed.[1514]

Regardless of whether that use is as **part of another registered trade mark or in conjunction with such a mark**, the trade mark applicant must prove that the relevant class of persons perceive the goods or services designated exclusively by the mark applied for, as opposed to any other mark which might also be present, as originating from a particular company.[1515]

Although the trade mark for which registration is sought may have been used as part of a registered trade mark or in conjunction with such a mark, the fact remains that, for the purposes of the registration of the mark itself, the trade mark applicant must prove that that mark alone, as opposed to any other trade mark which may also be present, identifies the particular undertaking from which the goods originate.[1516]

However, it must be stressed that a **three-dimensional mark** is essentially **different from its two-dimensional graphic representation**. It follows that where, as in the present case, a picture of the product features on the packaging, consumers do not actually see the mark itself, being the mark consisting of the three-dimensional form of the product. It is possible, however, that the two-dimensional representation of such a mark may in certain circumstances facilitate awareness of the mark by the relevant public where it enables the essential elements of the three-dimensional shape of the product to be perceived.[1517]

Therefore, not every use of the mark, *a fortiori* use of a two-dimensional representation of a three-dimensional mark, amounts necessarily to use as a mark.[1518]

Where a **trader** has been the **only supplier** of particular goods to the market, extensive use of a sign which consists of the shape of those goods may be sufficient to

1512. CJEU C-12/12 of 18.4.2013 – Colloseum Holding, para. 29; *see also* CJEU C-488/06 P of 17.7.2008 – L & D/OHIM, paras 50 et seq.
1513. CJEU C-12/12 of 18.4.2013 – Colloseum Holding, para. 28; C-215/14 of 16.9.2015 – Société des Produits Nestlé, para. 65, *see also* CJEU C-340/17 P of 29.11.2018 – Alcohol Countermeasure Systems/EUIPO, para. 59.
1514. CJEU C-24/05 P of 22.6.2006 – Storck/OHIM (light-brown sweet), para. 59.
1515. CJEU C-215/14 of 16.9.2015 – Société des Produits Nestlé, para. 67.
1516. CJEU C-215/14 of 16.9.2015 – Société des Produits Nestlé, para. 66.
1517. CJEU C-24/05 P of 22.6.2006 – Storck/OHIM (light-brown sweet), para. 60.
1518. CJEU C-24/05 P of 22.6.2006 – Storck/OHIM (light-brown sweet), para. 62.

give the sign a distinctive character for the purposes of Article 3(3) TMD2008 in circumstances where, as a result of that use, a substantial proportion of the relevant class of persons associates that shape with that trader and no other undertaking or believes that goods of that shape come from that trader. However, it is for the national court to verify that the circumstances in which the requirement under that provision is satisfied are shown to exist on the basis of specific and reliable data, that the presumed expectations of an average consumer of the category of goods or services in question, who is reasonably well informed and reasonably observant and circumspect, are taken into account and that the identification, by the relevant class of persons, of the product as originating from a given undertaking is as a result of the use of the mark as a trade mark.[1519]

[4] Relevant time

It is apparent from the very wording of that provision and more particularly from the use of the verbs in the past tense in the phrases 'the mark has become' and 'in consequence of the use which has been made of it' that the mark must, **at the time of filing of the application** for registration, already have acquired distinctive character through prior use.[1520]

That interpretation concerning the relevant date for the purpose of assessing whether there are absolute grounds for refusal is, according to the Court, **also applicable in invalidity proceedings**, as provided for in Article 52 CTMR, when a mark has been registered contrary to the provisions of Article 7 CTMR.[1521]

By using the wording 'shall not be registered' in Article 7(1) CTMR, and the trade mark 'has been registered' in Article 52(1)(a) CTMR, the EU legislature sets out the circumstances in which a mark must be refused registration or declared invalid and not the material date for the examination of absolute grounds for refusal or absolute grounds for invalidity.[1522]

It must be pointed out that that finding, which relates to the French version of Regulation No. 40/94, is borne out by examination of the various other language versions such as, *inter alia*, the English, German, Italian and Dutch versions.[1523]

Furthermore, the development of the relevant legislation clearly indicates that it was the intention of the Community legislature to grant protection as a Community trade mark only to those marks whose distinctive character had been acquired through use prior to the date of application for registration.[1524]

1519. CJEU C-299/99 of 18.6.2002 – Philips, para. 65.
1520. CJEU C-542/07 P of 11.6.2009 – Imagination Technologies/OHIM, para. 42; C-332/09 P of 23.4.2010 – OHIM/Frosch Touristik, para. 52; C-217/13 and 218/13 of 19.6.2014 – Oberbank, para. 73; C-326/18 P of 4.10.2018 – Safe Skies/EUIPO, paras 5/6 and 6.
1521. CJEU C-332/09 P of 23.4.2010 – OHIM/Frosch Touristik, para. 54; C-326/18 P of 4.10.2018 – Safe Skies/EUIPO, paras 5/6 and 6.
1522. CJEU C-332/09 P of 23.4.2010 – OHIM/Frosch Touristik, para. 57; C-326/18 P of 4.10.2018 – Safe Skies/EUIPO, paras 5/11 and 6.
1523. CJEU C-542/07 P of 11.6.2009 – Imagination Technologies/OHIM, para. 43.
1524. CJEU C-542/07 P of 11.6.2009 – Imagination Technologies/OHIM, para. 44.

In that regard, the fourth recital in the preamble to Directive 89/104 states that that directive does not deprive the Member States of the right to continue to protect trade marks acquired through use, but takes them into account only in regard to the relationship between them and trade marks acquired by registration.[1525]

However, in so far as Community law, since the entry into force of the CTMR, the objective of which is to establish Community arrangements for trade marks, no longer provides for the option for Member States to apply Article 7(3) CTMR to trade marks which acquired distinctive character after the date of application for registration or after the date of registration, it must be concluded that the Community legislature intended to restrict the protection of marks under Article 7(3) CTMR only to marks whose distinctive character had been acquired through use prior to the date of application for registration.[1526]

A literal interpretation of both Article 7(3) CTMR and the first sentence of Article 3(3) TMD2008 thus supports the conclusion that distinctive character must have been acquired through use of the trade mark prior to the date of application for registration.[1527]

Regarding the argument that that interpretation does not make it possible for events which might occur after the application for registration has been filed to be taken into consideration, it is sufficient to point out that that argument does not state in what respect an amendment to the specification or withdrawal of the application for registration might affect the date to be taken into account in assessing the distinctive character of a trade mark. That argument must therefore be rejected.[1528]

Furthermore, such a literal interpretation of Article 7(3) CTMR is the only one compatible with the logic of the system of absolute and relative grounds for refusal in regard to the registration of Community trade marks, according to which the date of filing of the application for registration determines the priority of one mark over another.[1529]

Moreover, a trade mark which is devoid of any distinctive character at the time when the application for registration is filed might serve as a basis for the application, in the context of opposition proceedings or an application for a declaration of invalidity, of a relative ground for refusal against a second mark whose filing date is after that of the first mark. Such a situation is particularly unacceptable when the second mark already has distinctive character at the time of filing, whereas the first has not yet acquired it through use.[1530]

In that regard, the argument to the effect that Article 51(2) CTMR allows evidence of use of the trade mark after the application for registration has been filed cannot be accepted.[1531]

1525. CJEU C-542/07 P of 11.6.2009 – Imagination Technologies/OHIM, para. 47.
1526. CJEU C-542/07 P of 11.6.2009 – Imagination Technologies/OHIM, para. 48.
1527. CJEU C-542/07 P of 11.6.2009 – Imagination Technologies/OHIM, para. 49.
1528. CJEU C-542/07 P of 11.6.2009 – Imagination Technologies/OHIM, para. 50.
1529. CJEU C-542/07 P of 11.6.2009 – Imagination Technologies/OHIM, para. 51.
1530. CJEU C-542/07 P of 11.6.2009 – Imagination Technologies/OHIM, para. 52; *see also* CJEU C-332/09 P of 23.4.2010 – OHIM/Frosch Touristik, para. 52.
1531. CJEU C-542/07 P of 11.6.2009 – Imagination Technologies/OHIM, para. 53.

First, Article 51(2) CTMR must be interpreted restrictively in so far as it establishes an exception to the absolute grounds for invalidity governed by Article 51(1) and cannot therefore serve as a basis for reasoning by analogy in the interpretation of Article 7(3) of that regulation.[1532]

Second, Article 51(2) CTMR is justified by reason of the legitimate expectations of the proprietor of the mark in respect of the registration of that mark, and it is on the basis of those expectations that the proprietor of the mark may have made investments in the period which has elapsed since registration. Clearly, it cannot be claimed that such legitimate expectations in respect of the registration of the mark exist at the time when the application for registration is filed.[1533]

In that context, it cannot be convincingly argued that the legitimate expectations which may be relied on by the proprietor of a trade mark registered erroneously must be tempered on account of his awareness of the fragility of the registration of the mark. If each proprietor of a trade mark registered erroneously were to be regarded as having acted in bad faith, Article 51(1)(b) CTMR, which establishes bad faith on the part of the applicant as an absolute ground for invalidity, would have to be applied in all cases where trade marks were registered erroneously with the result that Article 51(2) would be rendered meaningless.[1534]

Concerning Article 9(3) CTMR, it is sufficient to point out that that article, besides the fact that it is also consistent with the interpretation that distinctive character must have been acquired before the date of application for registration, relates to the compensation which may be imposed on third parties in respect of matters arising after the date of publication of the Community trade mark application but prior to registration of that trade mark.[1535]

Where a Member State has **not exercised the power laid down in the second sentence of Article 3(3) TMD2008**, the first sentence of Article 3(3) TMD2008 must be interpreted as meaning that, in the context of invalidity proceedings in respect of a mark which is intrinsically devoid of distinctive character, in order to assess whether that mark has acquired a distinctive character through use, it is necessary to examine whether such character was acquired before the date of filing of the application for registration of that mark. It is irrelevant in that regard that the proprietor of the mark at issue maintains that the mark has, in any event, acquired a distinctive character through use after the date of filing of the application for registration, but before the date of registration of that mark.[1536]

It is clear from the unequivocal terms of the first sentence of Article 3(3) TMD2008 that in the context of invalidity proceedings relating to a mark in respect of which one or more of the grounds for invalidity set out in Article 3(1)(b), (c) or (d) TMD2008 have been invoked, and where the applicability of at least one of those grounds has been established, it is only if the mark at issue has acquired a distinctive

1532. CJEU C-542/07 P of 11.6.2009 – Imagination Technologies/OHIM, para. 54.
1533. CJEU C-542/07 P of 11.6.2009 – Imagination Technologies/OHIM, para. 55.
1534. CJEU C-542/07 P of 11.6.2009 – Imagination Technologies/OHIM, para. 56.
1535. CJEU C-542/07 P of 11.6.2009 – Imagination Technologies/OHIM, para. 57.
1536. CJEU C-217/13 and 218/13 of 19.6.2014 – Oberbank, para. 61.

character following the use which has been made of it before the date of filing of the application for registration of that mark that it may escape the application of one or more of the grounds of invalidity invoked.[1537]

That literal interpretation is confirmed by the purpose of the provision of which that first sentence forms part. The second sentence of Article 3(3) TMD2008 expressly provides for Member States to extend the possibility set out in the first sentence thereof, in a situation where the mark has acquired a distinctive character following the use which has been made of it after the date of filing of the application for registration or, even, after the date of registration of that mark.[1538]

If the first sentence of Article 3(3) TMD2008 were to be interpreted as also concerning distinctive character acquired following use which has been made of the mark at issue after the filing of the application for registration, the power offered to Member States by the second sentence of that article would be illusory, and that provision would be rendered ineffective.[1539]

It should nevertheless be borne in mind that the interpretation set out in paragraph 57 above does not exclude the possibility that account may be taken, by the competent authority, of evidence which, although subsequent to the date of filing the application for registration, enables the drawing of conclusions on the situation as it was on that date.[1540]

In order to assess whether a mark has acquired distinctive character through use, **all the circumstances** in which the relevant public may see that mark must be borne in mind. That means not only when the **decision to purchase is made but also before that point**, for example, as a result of advertising, and when the product is consumed.[1541]

None the less, it is when making his choice between different products in the category concerned that the average consumer exhibits the highest level of attention, so that the question of whether or not the average consumer sees the mark at the time of purchase is of particular importance for determining whether the mark has acquired distinctive character through use.[1542]

[5] Territory

Article 3(3) TMD2008 must be interpreted as meaning that the registration of a **national trade mark** can be allowed on the basis of that provision only if it is proven that that trade mark has acquired distinctive character through use throughout the **territory** of the Member State or, in the case of Benelux, throughout the part of the territory of Benelux **in which there exists a ground for refusal.**[1543]

1537. CJEU C-217/13 and 218/13 of 19.6.2014 – Oberbank, para. 57.
1538. CJEU C-217/13 and 218/13 of 19.6.2014 – Oberbank, para. 58.
1539. CJEU C-217/13 and 218/13 of 19.6.2014 – Oberbank, para. 59.
1540. CJEU C-217/13 and 218/13 of 19.6.2014 – Oberbank, para. 60; *see also* CJEU C-488/06 P of 17.7.2008 – L & D/OHIM, para. 71.
1541. CJEU C-24/05 P of 22.6.2006 – Storck/OHIM (light-brown sweet), para. 71.
1542. CJEU C-24/05 P of 22.6.2006 – Storck/OHIM (light-brown sweet), para. 72.
1543. CJEU C-108/05 of 7.9.2006 – Bovemij Verzekeringen, para. 23.

It must first of all be recalled that, as regards the trade marks registered at BMB, the Benelux territory must be treated like the territory of a Member State since Article 1 TMD2008 regards Benelux trade marks as trade marks registered in a Member State.[1544]

Article 3(3) TMD2008 does not provide an independent right to have a trade mark registered. It is an exception to the grounds for refusal listed in Article 3(1)(b)-(d) TMD2008. Its scope must therefore be interpreted in light of those grounds for refusal.[1545]

In order to assess whether those grounds for refusal must be disregarded because of the acquisition of distinctive character through use under Article 3(3) TMD2008, only the situation prevailing in the part of the territory of the Member State concerned (or, as the case may be, in the part of the Benelux territory) where the grounds for refusal have been noted is relevant.[1546]

As regards a mark consisting of one or more words of an official language of a Member State or of Benelux, if the ground for refusal exists only in one of the linguistic areas of the Member State or, in the case of Benelux, in one of its linguistic areas, it must be established that the mark has acquired distinctive character through use throughout that linguistic area. In the linguistic area thus defined, it must be assessed whether the relevant class of persons, or at least a significant proportion thereof, identifies the product or service in question as originating from a particular undertaking because of the trade mark.[1547]

A **EU trade mark** can be registered under Article 7(3) CTMR only if evidence is provided that it has acquired, through the use which has been made of it, distinctive character in the **part of the Community** in which it did not, *ab initio*, have such character for the purposes of Article 7(1)(b). The part of the Community referred to in Article 7(2) may be comprised of a single Member State.[1548]

Under Article 7(1)(b) CTMR, read in conjunction with Article 7(2) thereof, a mark must be refused registration if it is devoid of any distinctive character in part of the Community.[1549]

In addition, under Article 7(3) CTMR, Article 7(1)(b) thereof does not apply if the trade mark has become distinctive in relation to the goods or services for which registration is requested in consequence of the use which has been made of it.[1550]

1544. CJEU C-108/05 of 7.9.2006 – Bovemij Verzekeringen, para. 20.
1545. CJEU C-108/05 of 7.9.2006 – Bovemij Verzekeringen, para. 21.
1546. CJEU C-108/05 of 7.9.2006 – Bovemij Verzekeringen, para. 22.
1547. CJEU C-108/05 of 7.9.2006 – Bovemij Verzekeringen, paras 27 et seq.
1548. CJEU C-25/05 P of 22.6.2006 – Storck/OHIM (gold-coloured sweet wrapper), para. 83; C-98/11 P of 24.5.2012 – Chocoladefabriken Lindt & Sprüngli/OHIM, para. 60, *see also* CJEU C-84/17 P, C-85/17 P and C-95/17 P of. 25.7.2018 – Société des produits Nestlé/EUIPO, para. 68.
1549. CJEU C-25/05 P of 22.6.2006 – Storck/OHIM (gold-coloured sweet wrapper), para. 81; C-84/17 P, C-85/17 P and C-95/17 P of. 25.7.2018 – Société des produits Nestlé/EUIPO, para. 67.
1550. CJEU C-25/05 P of 22.6.2006 – Storck/OHIM (gold-coloured sweet wrapper), para. 82.

Article 142a CTMR, in the version resulting from the Act of Accession, supports the latter interpretation.[1551]

As they found it necessary to introduce an express provision to the effect that registration of a Community trade mark which is under application at the date of accession may not be refused on the basis of any of the absolute grounds for refusal listed in Article 7(1) CTMR, if these grounds became applicable merely because of the accession of a new Member State, the authors of the Act of Accession considered that, if that provision did not exist, such an application would have had to have been refused if the mark was devoid of any distinctive character in one of the new Member States.[1552]

In that regard, at the outset, it is necessary to point out that the judgment *Leno Merken*[1553] is not relevant as it relates to the interpretation of Article 15(1) CTMR, which concerns the genuine use of EU trade marks that have already been registered.[1554]

It is true that the Court held that the requirements that apply to verification of the genuine use of a mark, within the meaning of Article 15(1) CTMR, are analogous to those concerning the acquisition by a sign of distinctive character through use for the purpose of its registration, within the meaning of Article 7(3) CTMR.[1555]

However, it must be pointed out that, unlike the case that gave rise to the judgment *Leno Merken*, in which the Court noted that, in order to assess the existence of 'genuine use in the Community' within the meaning of Article 15(1) CTMR, it is necessary to disregard the territorial borders of the Member States, the judgment *Colloseum Holding* does not relate to the geographic scope that is relevant for the purposes of assessing the existence of genuine use within the meaning of that provision, but to the possibility of concluding that the requirement for genuine use of a trade mark within the meaning of that provision is satisfied when a registered mark that has acquired its distinctive character as a result of the use of another composite mark, of which it is one of the elements, is used only as part of that composite mark, or when it is used only in combination with another mark, the combination of the two marks being, in addition, itself registered as a mark.[1556]

Therefore, the judgment *Colloseum Holding* cannot be read as meaning that the requirements for assessing the territorial scope that permits the registration of a mark in consequence of its use are analogous to the requirements permitting the preservation of the rights of the proprietor of a registered mark.[1557]

1551. CJEU C-25/05 P of 22.6.2006 – Storck/OHIM (gold-coloured sweet wrapper), para. 84.
1552. CJEU C-25/05 P of 22.6.2006 – Storck/OHIM (gold-coloured sweet wrapper), para. 85.
1553. CJEU C-149/11 of 19.12.2012 – Leno Merken.
1554. CJEU C-84/17 P, C-85/17 P and C-95/17 P of. 25.7.2018 – Société des produits Nestlé/EUIPO, para. 69.
1555. CJEU C-84/17 P, C-85/17 P and C-95/17 P of. 25.7.2018 – Société des produits Nestlé/EUIPO, para. 70, with reference to CJEU C-12/12 of 18.4.2013 – Colloseum Holding, para. 34; *see also* CJEU C-223/18 P of 6.6.2019 – Deichmann/EUIPO, para. 43.
1556. CJEU C-84/17 P, C-85/17 P and C-95/17 P of. 25.7.2018 – Société des produits Nestlé/EUIPO, para. 71.
1557. CJEU C-84/17 P, C-85/17 P and C-95/17 P of. 25.7.2018 – Société des produits Nestlé/EUIPO, para. 72.

In addition, it must be noted that, with regard to the genuine use of an EU mark that is already registered, there is no analogous provision to that in Article 7(2) CTMR, with the result that it cannot automatically be assumed that there is no such use simply because that the mark concerned has not been used in part of the European Union.[1558]

The part of the European Union referred to in Article 7(2) may be comprised, where necessary, of a single Member State.[1559]

It follows that, with regard to a mark that is, *ab initio*, devoid of distinctive character across all Member States, such a mark can be registered pursuant to that provision only if it is proved that it has acquired distinctive character through use throughout the territory of the European Union.[1560]

Admittedly, in paragraph 62 of the judgment *Chocoladefabriken Lindt & Sprüngli v OHIM*, the Court did find that even if it is true that the acquisition by a mark of distinctive character through use must be proved for the part of the European Union in which that mark did not, *ab initio*, have such character, it would be unreasonable to require proof of such acquisition for each individual Member State.[1561]

However, it does not follow from that finding that where a mark is devoid of inherent distinctive character throughout the European Union, it is sufficient, in order for it to be registered as an EU trade mark pursuant to Article 7(3) CTMR, to prove that it has acquired distinctive character through use in a significant part of the European Union, even though such evidence has not been provided in respect of every Member State.[1562]

In that regard, it must be pointed out that there is a distinction between, first, the facts to be proved, namely the acquisition of distinctive character through use by a sign that is devoid of inherent distinctive character, and, second, the means of proving such facts.[1563]

No provision of the CTMR requires that the acquisition of distinctive character through use be established by separate evidence in each individual Member State. Therefore, it is not inconceivable that the evidence provided to establish that a particular sign has acquired distinctive character through use is relevant with regard to several Member States, or even to the whole of the European Union.[1564]

In particular, it is possible that, for certain goods or services, the economic operators have grouped several Member States together in the same distribution

1558. CJEU C-84/17 P, C-85/17 P and C-95/17 P of. 25.7.2018 – Société des produits Nestlé/EUIPO, para. 73.
1559. CJEU C-84/17 P, C-85/17 P and C-95/17 P of. 25.7.2018 – Société des produits Nestlé/EUIPO, para. 75; C-547/17 P of 6.9.2018 – Basic Net/EUIPO, para. 24.
1560. CJEU C-84/17 P, C-85/17 P and C-95/17 P of. 25.7.2018 – Société des produits Nestlé/EUIPO, para. 76, with reference to CJEU C-98/11 P of 24.5.2012 – Chocoladefabriken Lindt & Sprüngli/OHIM, paras 61 and 63; C-547/17 P of 6.9.2018 – Basic Net/EUIPO, para. 25.
1561. CJEU C-84/17 P, C-85/17 P and C-95/17 P of. 25.7.2018 – Société des produits Nestlé/EUIPO, para. 77; C-547/17 P of 6.9.2018 – Basic Net/EUIPO, para. 26.
1562. CJEU C-84/17 P, C-85/17 P and C-95/17 P of. 25.7.2018 – Société des produits Nestlé/EUIPO, para. 78; C-547/17 P of 6.9.2018 – Basic Net/EUIPO, para. 27.
1563. CJEU C-84/17 P, C-85/17 P and C-95/17 P of. 25.7.2018 – Société des produits Nestlé/EUIPO, para. 79.
1564. CJEU C-84/17 P, C-85/17 P and C-95/17 P of. 25.7.2018 – Société des produits Nestlé/EUIPO, para. 80.

network and have treated those Member States, especially for marketing strategy purposes, as if they were one and the same national market. In such circumstances, the evidence for the use of a sign within such a cross-border market is likely to be relevant for all Member States concerned.[1565]

The same is true when, due to a geographic, cultural or linguistic proximity between two Member States, the relevant public of the first has a sufficient knowledge of the products and services that are present on the national market of the second.[1566]

It follows from those findings that, although it is not necessary, for the purposes of registering, on the basis of Article 7(3) CTMR, a mark that is, *ab initio*, devoid of distinctive character throughout all the Member States of the European Union, that evidence be submitted, in respect of each individual Member State, of the acquisition by that mark of distinctive character through use, the evidence submitted must be capable of establishing such acquisition throughout the Member States of the European Union.[1567]

That said, the question of whether the evidence submitted is sufficient to prove a particular sign's acquisition through use of distinctive character in the part of the territory of the European Union in which that sign did not, *ab initio*, have distinctive character is a matter of the assessment of evidence, for which the bodies of EUIPO are primarily responsible.[1568]

Nevertheless, if the bodies of EUIPO or the General Court, after having assessed all of the evidence that has been submitted to them, find that some of that evidence is sufficient to prove the acquisition by a particular sign of distinctive character through use in the part of the European Union in which it is, *ab initio*, devoid of distinctive character and therefore to justify its registration as an EU trade mark, they must clearly state that that is the case in their respective decisions.[1569]

[6] Invalidation

Where a Member State does not exercise the power laid down in the second sentence of Article 3(3) TMD2008, the first sentence of Article 3(3) TMD2008 must be interpreted to the effect that it does not preclude, in the context of invalidity proceedings, the mark at issue from being declared invalid where it is intrinsically devoid of distinctive character and the proprietor of that mark has failed to show that it has

1565. CJEU C-84/17 P, C-85/17 P and C-95/17 P of. 25.7.2018 – Société des produits Nestlé/EUIPO, para. 81.
1566. CJEU C-84/17 P, C-85/17 P and C-95/17 P of. 25.7.2018 – Société des produits Nestlé/EUIPO, para. 82.
1567. CJEU C-84/17 P, C-85/17 P and C-95/17 P of. 25.7.2018 – Société des produits Nestlé/EUIPO, para. 83; C-547/17 P of 6.9.2018 – Basic Net/EUIPO, para. 28.
1568. CJEU C-84/17 P, C-85/17 P and C-95/17 P of. 25.7.2018 – Société des produits Nestlé/EUIPO, para. 84.
1569. CJEU C-84/17 P, C-85/17 P and C-95/17 P of. 25.7.2018 – Société des produits Nestlé/EUIPO, para. 86.

acquired a distinctive character following the use which has been made of it before the date of filing of the application for registration.[1570]

Recital 6 in the preamble to the TMD states, *inter alia*, that Member States should remain free to fix the procedural provisions concerning the invalidity of trade marks acquired by registration and determine, for example, the form of invalidity procedures. However, it cannot be inferred that the question of the **burden of proof** concerning distinctive character acquired through use in the context of invalidity proceedings pursuant to Article 3(1)(b), (c) or (d) TMD2008 constitutes such a procedural provision falling within the competence of Member States.[1571]

If the question of the burden of proof concerning distinctive character acquired by use which has been made of a mark in the context of invalidity proceedings were a matter for the national law of the Member States, the consequence for proprietors of trade marks could be that protection would vary according to the legal system concerned, with the result that the objective of 'the same protection under the legal systems of all the Member States' set out in recital 10 in the preamble to the TMD2008, where it is described as 'fundamental', would not be attained.[1572]

In view of that objective and the structure and purpose of Article 3(3) TMD2008, the Court finds that, in the context of invalidity proceedings, the burden of proof concerning distinctive character acquired following the use which has been made of the mark at issue must be borne by the proprietor of that mark which invokes that distinctive character.[1573]

First, in the same way that distinctive character acquired following the use which is made of a mark is, in proceedings for registration, an exception to the grounds for refusal listed in Article 3(1)(b), (c) or (d) TMD2008,[1574] distinctive character acquired following the use which is made of a mark is, in the context of invalidity proceedings, an exception to the grounds for invalidity listed in Article 3(1)(b), (c) or (d). Since it is an exception, the onus is on the party seeking to rely on it to justify its application.[1575]

Second, the Court finds that it is the proprietor of the mark at issue which is best placed to adduce evidence in support of the assertion that its mark has acquired a distinctive character following the use which has been made of it. The same applies, in particular, to evidence capable of establishing such use, in respect of which the case law[1576] contains a list of examples, such as evidence relating to how intensive, widespread and longstanding use of the mark has been and the amount invested in promoting it.[1577]

1570. CJEU C-217/13 and 218/13 of 19.6.2014 – Oberbank, para. 74.
1571. CJEU C-217/13 and 218/13 of 19.6.2014 – Oberbank, para. 66.
1572. CJEU C-217/13 and 218/13 of 19.6.2014 – Oberbank, para. 67; *see also* CJEU C-405/03 of 18.10.2005 – Class International, para. 73; C-479/12 of 13.2.2014 – H. Gautzsch Großhandel, para. 40; C-705/17 of 12.6.2019 – Patent- och registreringsverket/Hansson, para. 38.
1573. CJEU C-217/13 and 218/13 of 19.6.2014 – Oberbank, para. 68.
1574. *See*, to that effect: CJEU C-108/05 of 7.9.2006 – Bovemij Verzekeringen, para. 21.
1575. CJEU C-217/13 and 218/13 of 19.6.2014 – Oberbank, para. 69.
1576. *See* above Art. 4 'Acquisition of distinctive character/Conditions'.
1577. CJEU C-217/13 and 218/13 of 19.6.2014 – Oberbank, para. 70.

Consequently, where the proprietor of the mark at issue is requested by the competent authority to adduce proof of distinctive character acquired following the use which has been made of a mark which is intrinsically devoid of distinctive character but fails to do so, that mark must be declared invalid.[1578]

The reasons why the proprietor of the mark fails to adduce that evidence are irrelevant in that regard. Otherwise, it would be possible for a mark to continue to be protected under Directive 2008/95 even though, since it falls within the scope of one of the grounds for invalidity set out in Article 3(1)(b), (c) or (d) TMD2008, it is incapable of fulfilling the essential function of the mark and ought not, consequently, to be protected under that directive. For that very reason, imposing the burden of proof in that way does not breach the principle of the protection of the legitimate expectations of the proprietor of the mark.[1579]

Article 5 Relative grounds for refusal or invalidity

1. *A trade mark shall not be registered or, if registered, shall be liable to be declared invalid where:*
   (a) *it is identical with an earlier trade mark, and the goods or services for which the trade mark is applied for or is registered are identical with the goods or services for which the earlier trade mark is protected;*
   (b) *because of its identity with, or similarity to, the earlier trade mark and the identity or similarity of the goods or services covered by the trade marks, there exists a likelihood of confusion on the part of the public; the likelihood of confusion includes the likelihood of association with the earlier trade mark.*
2. *'Earlier trade marks' within the meaning of paragraph 1 means:*
   (a) *trade marks of the following kinds with a date of application for registration which is earlier than the date of application for registration of the trade mark, taking account, where appropriate, of the priorities claimed in respect of those trade marks;*
      (i) *EU trade marks;*
      (ii) *trade marks registered in the Member State concerned or, in the case of Belgium, Luxembourg or the Netherlands, at the Benelux Office for Intellectual Property;*
      (iii) *trade marks registered under international arrangements which have effect in the Member State concerned;*
   (b) *EU trade marks which validly claim seniority, in accordance with Regulation (EC) No 207/2009, of a trade mark referred to in points (a)(ii) and (iii), even when the latter trade mark has been surrendered or allowed to lapse;*
   (c) *applications for the trade marks referred to in points (a) and (b), subject to their registration;*
   (d) *trade marks which, on the date of application for registration of the trade mark, or, where appropriate, of the priority claimed in respect of the application for registration of the trade mark, are well known in the Member State concerned, in the sense in which the words 'well known' are used in Article 6bis of the Paris Convention.*

1578. CJEU C-217/13 and 218/13 of 19.6.2014 – Oberbank, para. 71.
1579. CJEU C-217/13 and 218/13 of 19.6.2014 – Oberbank, para. 72.

3. *Furthermore, a trade mark shall not be registered or, if registered, shall be liable to be declared invalid where:*
   (a) *it is identical with, or similar to, an earlier trade mark irrespective of whether the goods or services for which it is applied or registered are identical with, similar to or not similar to those for which the earlier trade mark is registered, where the earlier trade mark has a reputation in the Member State in respect of which registration is applied for or in which the trade mark is registered or, in the case of a EU trade mark, has a reputation in the Union and the use of the later trade mark without due cause would take unfair advantage of, or be detrimental to, the distinctive character or the repute of the earlier trade mark;*
   (b) *an agent or representative of the proprietor of the trade mark applies for registration thereof in his own name without the proprietor's authorisation, unless the agent or representative justifies his action;*
   (c) *and to the extent that, pursuant to Union legislation or the law of the Member State concerned providing for protection of designations of origin and geographical indications:*
      (i) *an application for a designation of origin or a geographical indication had already been submitted in accordance with Union legislation or the law of the Member State concerned prior to the date of application for registration of the trade mark or the date of the priority claimed for the application, subject to its subsequent registration;*
      (ii) *that designation of origin or geographical indication confers on the person authorised under the relevant law to exercise the rights arising therefrom the right to prohibit the use of a subsequent trade mark.*
4. *Any Member State may provide that a trade mark is not to be registered or, if registered, is liable to be declared invalid where, and to the extent that:*
   (a) *rights to a non-registered trade mark or to another sign used in the course of trade were acquired prior to the date of application for registration of the subsequent trade mark, or the date of the priority claimed for the application for registration of the subsequent trade mark, and that non-registered trade mark or other sign confers on its proprietor the right to prohibit the use of a subsequent trade mark;*
   (b) *the use of the trade mark may be prohibited by virtue of an earlier right, other than the rights referred to in paragraph 2 and point (a) of this paragraph and in particular:*
      (i) *a right to a name,*
      (ii) *a right of personal portrayal,*
      (iii) *a copyright,*
      (iv) *an industrial property right;*
   (c) *the trade mark is liable to be confused with an earlier trade mark protected abroad, provided that, at the date of the application, the applicant was acting in bad faith.*
5. *The Member States shall ensure that in appropriate circumstances there is no obligation to refuse registration or to declare a trade mark invalid where the proprietor of the earlier trade mark or other earlier right consents to the registration of the later trade mark.*
6. *Member States may provide that, by derogation from paragraphs 1 to 5, the grounds for refusal of registration or invalidity in force in that Member State prior to the date of the entry into force of the provisions necessary to comply*

with Council Directive 89/104/EEC[1580]*, are to apply to trade marks for which application has been made prior to that date.*

[A] Principles

The conditions of application of Article 4(1)(a) TMD2008 correspond essentially to those of Article 5(1)(a) TMD2008, which determines the circumstances in which the proprietor of a trade mark is entitled to prevent third parties from using signs which are identical with his trade mark. There is a similar correspondence between Articles 8(1)(a) and 9(1)(a) CTMR.[1581]

Article 4(1)(b) TMD2008 is essentially identical to Article 8(1)(b) CTMR.[1582]

Article 4(1)(b) TMD2008, however, concerns the application for registration of a mark. Once a mark has been registered, its proprietor has the right to use it as he sees fit so that, for the purposes of assessing whether the application for registration falls within the ground for refusal laid down in that provision, it is necessary to ascertain whether there is a likelihood of confusion with the opponent's earlier mark in all the circumstances in which the mark applied for might be used if it were to be registered.[1583]

According to Article 8(1)(b) and (2) CTMR, where an earlier trade mark upon which its proprietor relies in support of his opposition is a national mark, the trade mark applied for is not to be registered if because of its identity with or similarity to the earlier trade mark and the identity or similarity of the goods or services covered by the trade marks there exists a likelihood of confusion on the part of the public in the territory of the Member State in which the earlier trade mark is protected or registered.[1584]

By contrast, in the case provided for in Article 5(1)(b) TMD2008, the third-party user of a sign identical with, or similar to, a registered mark does not assert any trade mark rights over that sign but is using it on an ad hoc basis. In those circumstances, in order to assess whether the proprietor of the registered mark is entitled to oppose that specific use, the assessment must be limited to the circumstances characterizing that use, without there being any need to investigate whether another use of the same sign in different circumstances would also be likely to give rise to a likelihood of confusion.[1585]

In this context, it is important to note that even if the suggested interpretation makes the registration procedure much lengthier, that cannot be decisive for the interpretation of Article 4(1)(b) TMD2008. In any event, for reasons of legal certainty

1580. First Council Directive 89/104/EEC of 21 Dec. 1988 to approximate the laws of the Member States relating to trade marks (OJ L 40, 11.2.1989, p. 1).
1581. CJEU C-291/00 of 20.3.2003 - LTJ Diffusion, para. 41; C-533/06 of 12.6.2008 - O2 Holdings/Hutchison 3G UK, para. 65.
1582. CJEU C-16/06 P of 18.12.2008 - Les Éditions Albert René/OHIM, para. 64.
1583. CJEU C-533/06 of 12.6.2008 - O2 Holdings/Hutchison 3G UK, para. 66.
1584. CJEU C-394/08 P of 3.6.2009 - Zipcar/OHIM, para. 48.
1585. CJEU C-533/06 of 12.6.2008 - O2 Holdings/Hutchison 3G UK, para. 67.

and proper administration, it is necessary to ensure that trade marks whose use could successfully be challenged before the courts are not registered.[1586]

For an EU trade mark to be refused registration under that provision, the likelihood of confusion must exist in all Member States and in all language areas of the [European] Union. The unitary character of the EU trade mark, as laid down in Article 1(2) CTMR, means that an earlier EU trade mark can be relied on in opposition proceedings against any application for registration of an EU trade mark which would adversely affect the protection of the first mark, even if only in relation to the perception of consumers in part of the European Union.[1587]

If the two marks are not identical or if in spite of their similarity there is no likelihood of confusion, however, the proprietor of the older mark may not object to the registration of the application mark.[1588]

The **absolute grounds** for refusal of registration set out in Article 3(1)(b) and (c) TMD2008 **and** the **relative grounds** for refusal of registration set out in Article 4(1)(b) pursue **different aims** and are intended to protect distinct interests.[1589]

Article 4(1)(b) TMD2008 is intended to protect the individual interests of proprietors of earlier marks that come into conflict with the sign applied for and thus guarantees the trade mark as an indication of origin if there is a likelihood of confusion.[1590]

Although the relevant public's perception of a sign cannot be dependent on the ground for refusal of registration in question, the angle from which that perception is viewed, however, varies according to whether what is being assessed is the descriptiveness of a sign or the existence of a likelihood of confusion.[1591]

Whereas, in assessing the descriptiveness of a sign, attention is focused on the mental processes which may lead to relationships being established between the sign or its various components and the goods/and/or services concerned, in assessing the likelihood of confusion, the examination relates to the processes by means of which the sign is remembered, recognized and recalled and to associative mechanisms.[1592]

Although the principles that the examination of trade mark applications must be **stringent and full**, and must be undertaken in each individual case, were established by the Court of Justice in a case concerning an absolute ground for refusal, that is to say, the ground referred to in Article 7(1)(c) CTMR, the Court of Justice then expressly

1586. CJEU C-39/97 of 29.9.1998 – Canon Kabushiki Kaisha/Metro-Goldwyn-Mayer, para. 21; C-104/01 of 6.5.2003 – Libertel, para. 59; C-29/05 P of 13.3.2007 – OHIM/Kaul, para. 48.
1587. CJEU C-401/16 P 1.12.2016 – Market Watch Franchise & Consulting/EUIPO, paras 5/7 and 6; C-402/16 P 1.12.2016 – Market Watch Franchise & Consulting/EUIPO, paras 5/7 and 6.
1588. CJEU C-324/05 P of 1.6.2006 – Plus Warenhandelsgesellschaft/OHIM, para. 34; unofficial translation.
1589. CJEU C-20/14 of 22.10.2015 – BGW Beratungs-Gesellschaft Wirtschaft, para. 23.
1590. CJEU C-20/14 of 22.10.2015 – BGW Beratungs-Gesellschaft Wirtschaft, para. 26; C-705/17 of 12.6.2019 – Patent- och registreringsverket/Hansson, para. 35; *see also* CJEU C-120/04 of 6.10.2005 – Medion, paras 24 and 26.
1591. CJEU C-20/14 of 22.10.2015 – BGW Beratungs-Gesellschaft Wirtschaft, para. 27.
1592. CJEU C-20/14 of 22.10.2015 – BGW Beratungs-Gesellschaft Wirtschaft, para. 28.

ruled that they also applied to opposition proceedings based on a relative ground for refusal.[1593]

[B] Affection of functions in the context of a trade mark application

Article 4(1)(a) TMD2008 must be interpreted as meaning that the proprietor of an earlier trade mark cannot obtain the cancellation of an identical later trade mark designating identical goods where there has been a long period of honest concurrent use of those two trade marks where that use neither has nor is liable to have an adverse effect on the essential function of the trade mark which is to guarantee to consumers the origin of the goods or services.[1594]

It should be recalled that Article 4 TMD2008 defines further grounds for refusal or invalidity in cases of conflict concerning earlier rights. Article 4(1)(a) thus provides that a registered trade mark is liable to be declared invalid where it is identical with an earlier trade mark and the goods or services for which the trade mark was registered are identical with those for which the earlier trade mark is protected.[1595]

In that regard, the tenth recital in the preamble to TMD2008 states that the protection conferred by the registered trade mark, the function of which is in particular to guarantee the trade mark as an indication of origin, is absolute in the case of identity between the mark and the sign and between the goods or services.[1596]

According to the Court's case law, the conditions of application of Article 4(1)(a) TMD2008 correspond essentially to those of Article 5(1)(a) TMD2008, which determines the circumstances in which the proprietor of a trade mark is entitled to prevent third parties from using signs which are identical with his trade mark for goods or services identical with those for which that trade mark is registered.[1597]

Consequently, the Court's interpretation of Article 5(1)(a) TMD2008 is also applicable to Article 4(1)(a) TMD2008 since that interpretation is transposable, *mutatis mutandis*, to the latter provision.[1598]

It follows from the Court's case law that the exclusive right under Article 5(1)(a) TMD2008 was conferred in order to enable the trade mark proprietor to protect his specific interests as proprietor, that is, to ensure that the trade mark can fulfil its functions and that, therefore, the exercise of that right must be reserved to cases in which another party's use of the sign affects or is liable to affect the functions of the trade mark. Those functions include not only the essential function of the trade mark, which is to guarantee to consumers the origin of the goods or services, but also its other

1593. CJEU C-141/13 P of 17.7.2014 – Reber Holding/OHIM, para. 46; C-354/12 P of 11.4.2013 – ASA/OHIM, para. 42; C-33/15 P of 15.10.2015 – Cantina Broglie 1, para. 49; C-34/15 P of 15.10.2015 – Cantina Broglie 1, para. 49; C-480/15 P of 14.4.2016 – KS Sports IPCo/EUIPO, para. 37; C-564/16 P of 28.6.2018 – EUIPO/Puma, para. 63.
1594. CJEU C-482/09 of 22.9.2011 – Budějovický Budvar, para. 84.
1595. CJEU C-482/09 of 22.9.2011 – Budějovický Budvar, para. 67.
1596. CJEU C-482/09 of 22.9.2011 – Budějovický Budvar, para. 68.
1597. CJEU C-482/09 of 22.9.2011 – Budějovický Budvar, para. 69; *see also* CJEU C-291/00 of 20.3.2003 – LTJ Diffusion, para. 41.
1598. CJEU C-482/09 of 22.9.2011 – Budějovický Budvar, para. 70; *see also* CJEU C-291/00 of 20.3.2003 – LTJ Diffusion, para. 43.

functions, in particular that of guaranteeing the quality of the goods or services in question and those of communication, investment or advertising.[1599]

It should be added that Article 5(1)(a) TMD2008 does not require evidence that there exists a likelihood of confusion on the part of the public in order to afford absolute protection in the case of identity of the sign and the trade mark and of the goods or services.[1600]

It follows from the foregoing that Article 4(1)(a) TMD2008 must be interpreted as meaning that a later registered trade mark is liable to be declared invalid where it is identical with an earlier trade mark, where the goods for which the trade mark was registered are identical with those for which the earlier trade mark is protected and where the use of the later trade mark has or is liable to have an adverse effect on the essential function of the trade mark which is to guarantee to consumers the origin of the goods.[1601]

In **the present case**, it is to be noted that the use by Budvar of the Budweiser trade mark in the United Kingdom neither has nor is liable to have an adverse effect on the essential function of the Budweiser trade mark owned by Anheuser-Busch.[1602]

In that regard, it should be stressed that the circumstances which gave rise to the dispute in the main proceedings are **exceptional**.[1603]

First, the referring court states that Anheuser-Busch and Budvar have each been marketing their beers in the United Kingdom under the word sign 'Budweiser' or under a trade mark including that sign for almost thirty years prior to the registration of the marks concerned.[1604]

Second, Anheuser-Busch and Budvar were authorized to register jointly and concurrently their Budweiser trade marks following a judgment delivered by the Court of Appeal (England & Wales) (Civil Division) in February 2000.[1605]

Third, the order for reference also states that, while Anheuser-Busch submitted an application for registration of the word 'Budweiser' as a trade mark in the United Kingdom earlier than Budvar, both of those companies have from the beginning used their Budweiser trade marks in good faith.[1606]

1599. CJEU C-482/09 of 22.9.2011 – Budějovický Budvar, para. 71; *see also* C-487/07 of 18.6.2009 – L'Oréal, para. 58; C-236/08 to C-238/08 of 23.3.2010 – Google France, para. 77; C-376/11 of 19.7.2012 – Pie Optiek, para. 46; C-661/11 of 19.9.2013 – Martin Y Paz Diffusion, para. 58; C-65/12 of 6.2.2014 – Leidseplein Beheer, para. 30; C-179/15 of 3.3.2016 – Daimler/Együd Garage Gépjárműjavító és Értékesítő, para. 26; C-673/15 P to C-676/15 P of 20.9.2017 – The Tea Board/EUIPO, para. 53; C-129/17 of 25.7.2018 – Mitsubishi Shoji Kaisha a.o./Duma Forklifts a.o., para. 34; C-147/20 of 17.11.2022 – Novartis Pharma/Abacus Medicine, para. 44; C-204/20 of 17.11.2022 – Bayer Intellectual Property/kohlpharma, para. 55; C-224/20 of 17.11.2022 – Merck Sharp & Dohme a.o./Abacus a.o., para. 45; C-253/20 and C-254/20 of 17.11.2022 – Impexeco/Novartis a.o., para. 46; C-148/21 and C-184/21 of 22.12.2022 – Louboutin/Amazon Europe Core a.o., para. 26.
1600. CJEU C-482/09 of 22.9.2011 – Budějovický Budvar, para. 72; *see also* CJEU C-291/00 of 20.3.2003 – LTJ Diffusion, para. 49.
1601. CJEU C-482/09 of 22.9.2011 – Budějovický Budvar, para. 74.
1602. CJEU C-482/09 of 22.9.2011 – Budějovický Budvar, para. 75.
1603. CJEU C-482/09 of 22.9.2011 – Budějovický Budvar, para. 76.
1604. CJEU C-482/09 of 22.9.2011 – Budějovický Budvar, para. 77.
1605. CJEU C-482/09 of 22.9.2011 – Budějovický Budvar, para. 78.
1606. CJEU C-482/09 of 22.9.2011 – Budějovický Budvar, para. 79.

Fourth, the referring court found that, although the names are identical, United Kingdom consumers are well aware of the difference between the beers of Budvar and those of Anheuser-Busch since their tastes, prices and get-ups have always been different.[1607]

Fifth, it follows from the coexistence of those two trade marks on the United Kingdom market that, even though the trade marks were identical, the beers of Anheuser-Busch and Budvar were clearly identifiable as being produced by different companies.[1608]

Consequently, as correctly stated by the Commission in its written observations, Article 4(1)(a) TMD2008 must be interpreted as meaning that, in circumstances such as those of the main proceedings, a long period of honest concurrent use of two identical trade marks designating identical products neither has nor is liable to have an adverse effect on the essential function of the trade mark which is to guarantee to consumers the origin of the goods or services.[1609]

It should be added that in the event that, in the future, there is any **dishonesty** associated with the use of the Budweiser trade marks, such a situation could, where necessary, be examined in the light of the rules relating to unfair competition.[1610]

Although the possibility cannot be ruled out that the **coexistence** of two marks on a particular market might, together with other elements, contribute to diminishing the likelihood of confusion between those marks on the part of the relevant public, certain conditions must be met. Thus, the absence of a likelihood of confusion may, in particular, be inferred from the 'peaceful' nature of the coexistence of the marks at issue on the market concerned.[1611]

[C] Non-registered trade marks – especially well-known trade marks

Article 4(2)(d) TMD2008 is to be interpreted as meaning that the earlier trade mark must be well known throughout the territory of the Member State of registration or in a substantial part of it.[1612]

As regards the geographical area in which the mark is well known, it should be noted that, under Article 4(2)(d) TMD2008, the existence of 'well-known marks' within the meaning of Article *6bis* of the Paris Convention is to be assessed 'in a Member State'.[1613]

Since the Community provision being interpreted lacks a definition to that effect, a trade mark certainly cannot be required to be well known 'throughout' the territory

1607. CJEU C-482/09 of 22.9.2011 – Budějovický Budvar, para. 80.
1608. CJEU C-482/09 of 22.9.2011 – Budějovický Budvar, para. 81.
1609. CJEU C-482/09 of 22.9.2011 – Budějovický Budvar, para. 82; *see also* CJEU C-112/21 of 2.6.2022 – X/Classic Coach Company a.o., para. 54.
1610. CJEU C-482/09 of 22.9.2011 – Budějovický Budvar, para. 83; *see also* CJEU C-112/21 of 2.6.2022 – X/Classic Coach Company a.o., para. 54.
1611. CJEU C-498/07 P of 3.9.2009 – Aceites del Sur-Coosur/OHIM, para. 82.
1612. CJEU C-328/06 of 22.11.2007 – Nuño, para. 20.
1613. CJEU C-328/06 of 22.11.2007 – Nuño, para. 14.

of the Member State, and it is sufficient for it to be well known in a substantial part of it.[1614]

However, the customary meaning of the words used in the expression 'in a Member State' precludes the application of that expression to a situation where the fact of being well known is limited to a city and to its surrounding area which, together, do not constitute a substantial part of the Member State.[1615]

In any event, it should be noted that an earlier non-registered mark may, where appropriate, be covered in particular by:

- Article 4(4)(b) TMD2008, which allows a Member State to provide that a trade mark is not to be registered or, if registered, is not to be liable to be declared invalid where and to the extent that the rights of a non-registered trade mark were acquired earlier and that that non-registered mark confers on its proprietor the right to prohibit the use of a subsequent trade mark.
- Article 6(2) TMD2008, which entitles a Member State to authorize the using of an earlier right which only applies in a particular locality, within the limits of the territory in which it is recognized.[1616]

[D] Identity of trade marks and goods or services

As regards Article 9(1)(a) CTMR and Article 5(1)(a) TMD2008, it should be noted that those provisions refer to the so-called double identity situation, in which use by a third party of a sign identical with the trade mark is made in relation to goods or services that are identical with those for which the trade mark is registered.[1617]

Article 5(1)(a) TMD2008 does **not** require **evidence of a likelihood of confusion** in order to afford absolute protection in the case of identity of the sign and the trade mark and of the goods or services.[1618]

Article 5(1)(a) TMD2008 must be interpreted as meaning that a sign is identical with the trade mark where it reproduces, without any modification or addition, all the elements constituting the trade mark or where, viewed as a whole, it contains **differences** so **insignificant** that they may go unnoticed by an average consumer.[1619]

It is for the **national court** to assess, in the light of all of the information available to it, whether that sign must be so classified.[1620]

1614. CJEU C-328/06 of 22.11.2007 – Nuño, para. 17.
1615. CJEU C-328/06 of 22.11.2007 – Nuño, para. 18.
1616. CJEU C-328/06 of 22.11.2007 – Nuño, para. 19.
1617. CJEU C-323/09 of 22.9.2011 – Interflora, para. 33; C-690/17 of 11.4.2019 – Oko-Text Verlag/Dr. Rudolf Liebe Nachf., para. 28.
1618. CJEU C-291/00 of 20.3.2003 – LTJ Diffusion, para. 49; C-245/02 of 16.11.2004 – Anheuser-Busch, para. 63; C-323/09 of 22.9.2011 – Interflora, para. 36; C-65/12 of 6.2.2014 – Leidseplein Beheer, para. 31.
1619. CJEU C-291/00 of 20.3.2003 – LTJ Diffusion, para. 54; C-278/08 of 25.3.2010 – BergSpechte, para. 25; C-558/08 of 8.7.2010 – Portakabin, para. 47.
1620. CJEU C-278/08 of 25.3.2010 – BergSpechte, para. 27; C-558/08 of 8.7.2010 – Portakabin, para. 48.

For that guarantee of origin to be ensured, the proprietor must be protected against competitors wishing to take unfair advantage of the status and reputation of the trade mark by selling products illegally bearing it.[1621]

Protection for the proprietor of a trade mark is guaranteed by Article 5 TMD2008, which determines the rights conferred by a registered trade mark and provides, in paragraph (1), that that mark is to confer on the proprietor exclusive rights therein and that the proprietor is to be entitled, within certain limits, to prevent all third parties from using his trade mark in the course of trade.[1622]

As regards Article 5(1)(b) TMD2008, the Court has already held that that provision is designed to apply only if, because of the identity or similarity between the signs and marks and between the goods or services which they designate, there exists a likelihood of confusion on the part of the public.[1623]

The criterion of identity of the sign and the trade mark must be interpreted strictly. The very definition of identity implies that the two elements compared should be the same in all respects. Indeed, the absolute protection in the case of a sign which is identical with the trade mark in relation to goods or services which are identical with those for which the trade mark is registered, which is guaranteed by Article 5(1)(a) TMD2008, cannot be extended beyond the situations for which it was envisaged, in particular, to those situations which are more specifically protected by Article 5(1)(b) TMD2008.[1624]

There is therefore identity between the sign and the trade mark where the former reproduces, without any modification or addition, all the elements constituting the latter.[1625]

However, the perception of identity between the sign and the trade mark must be assessed globally with respect to an **average consumer** who is deemed to be reasonably well informed, reasonably observant and circumspect. The sign produces an overall impression on such a consumer. That consumer only rarely has the chance to make a direct comparison between signs and trade marks and must place his trust in the imperfect picture of them that he has kept in his mind. Moreover, his level of attention is likely to vary according to the category of goods or services in question.[1626]

Since the perception of identity between the sign and the trade mark is not the result of a direct comparison of all the characteristics of the elements compared, insignificant differences between the sign and the trade mark may go unnoticed by an average consumer.[1627]

With regard to keywords reproducing a trade mark with **minor spelling mistakes**, it is not in dispute that they do not reproduce all the elements constituting the

1621. CJEU C-291/00 of 20.3.2003 – LTJ Diffusion, para. 46.
1622. CJEU C-291/00 of 20.3.2003 – LTJ Diffusion, para. 47; C-16/03 of 30.11.2004 – Peak Holding, para. 34; C-48/05 of 25.1.2007 – Adam Opel, para. 16; C-449/09 of 28.10.2010 – Canon Kabushiki Kaisha, para. 24.
1623. CJEU C-291/00 of 20.3.2003 – LTJ Diffusion, para. 48.
1624. CJEU C-291/00 of 20.3.2003 – LTJ Diffusion, para. 50.
1625. CJEU C-291/00 of 20.3.2003 – LTJ Diffusion, para. 51.
1626. CJEU C-291/00 of 20.3.2003 – LTJ Diffusion, para. 52.
1627. CJEU C-291/00 of 20.3.2003 – LTJ Diffusion, para. 53.

trade mark. They may, however, be regarded as containing differences which are so insignificant that they may go unnoticed by the average consumer.[1628]

In so far as eBay used keywords corresponding to L'Oréal trade marks to promote its own service of making an online marketplace available to sellers and buyers of products, that use was not made in relation to either: (i) goods or services 'identical with those for which the trade mark is registered' within the meaning of Article 5(1)(a) TMD and Article 9(1)(a) CTMR or (ii) goods or services similar to those for which the trade mark is registered within the meaning of paragraph 1(b) of those articles.[1629]

A use of identical marks in respect of products which are identical falls within the scope of application of Article 5(1)(a) TMD2008 and not that of Article 5(1)(b) TMD2008.[1630]

[E] Likelihood of confusion

Article 5(1)(b) TMD2008 is designed to apply only if, by reason of the identity or similarity, both of the marks and of the goods or services which they designate, there exists a likelihood of confusion on the part of the public.[1631]

The likelihood of confusion must be appreciated **globally**, taking into account all factors relevant to the circumstances of the case.[1632]

1628. CJEU C-558/08 of 8.7.2010 – Portakabin, para. 48.
1629. CJEU C-324/09 of 12.7.2011 – L'Oréal, para. 89.
1630. CJEU C-487/07 of 18.6.2009 – L'Oréal, para. 56.
1631. CJEU C-120/04 of 6.10.2005 – Medion, para. 25; C-533/06 of 12.6.2008 – O2 Holdings/Hutchison 3G UK, para. 47; C-278/08 of 25.3.2010 – BergSpechte, para. 22; C-558/08 of 8.7.2010 – Portakabin, para. 50.
1632. CJEU C-251/95 of 11.11.1997 – SABEL/Puma, Rudolf Dassler Sport, para. 22; C-39/97 of 29.9.1998 – Canon Kabushiki Kaisha/Metro-Goldwyn-Mayer, para. 15, 16, 24; C-342/97 of 22.6.1999 – Lloyd Schuhfabrik Meyer, para. 18; C-425/98 of 22.6.2000 – Marca Mode, para. 40; C-3/03 P of 28.4.2004 – Matratzen Concord/OHIM, para. 28; C-418/02 of 7.7.2005 – Praktiker Bau- und Heimwerkermärkte, para. 48; C-120/04 of 6.10.2005 – Medion, para. 27; C-512/04 P of 1.12.2005 – Vitakraft-Werke Wührmann/OHIM, para. 22; C-361/04 P of 12.1.2006 – Ruiz-Picasso and Others/OHIM, para. 18; C-206/04 P of 23.3.2006 – Mülhens/OHIM, para. 18; C-235/05 P of 27.4.2006 – L'Oréal/OHIM, para. 34; C-324/05 P of 1.6.2006 – Plus Warenhandelsgesellschaft/OHIM, para. 25, 43; C-314/05 P of 29.6.2006 – Creative Technology/OHIM, para. 32; C-196/06 P of 9.3.2007 – Alecansan/OHIM, para. 22; C-245/06 P of 9.3.2007 – Saiwa/OHIM, para. 46; C-171/06 P of 15.3.2007 – T.I.M.E. ART/OHIM, para. 33; C-131/06 P of 24.4.2007 – Castellblanch/OHIM, para. 55; C-334/05 P of 12.6.2007 – OHIM/Shaker, para. 34; C-193/06 P of 20.9.2007 – Nestlé/OHIM, para. 33; C-108/07 P of 17.4.2008 – Ferrero Deutschland/OHIM, para. 44; C-57/08 P of 11.12.2008 – Gateway/OHIM, para. 46; C-16/06 P of 18.12.2008 – Les Éditions Albert René/OHIM, para. 45; C-398/07 P of 7.5.2009 – Waterford Wedgwood/OHIM, para. 30; C-394/08 P of 3.6.2009 – Zipcar/OHIM, para. 58; C-300/08 P of 11.6.2009 – Leche Celta/OHIM, para. 32; C-498/07 P of 3.9.2009 – Aceites del Sur-Coosur/OHIM, para. 59; C-579/08 P of 15.1.2010 – Messer Group/OHIM, para. 69; C-51/09 P of 24.6.2010 – Barbara Becker/OHIM, para. 32; C-254/09 P of 2.9.2010 – Calvin Klein/OHIM, para. 44; C-353/09 P of 15.2.2011 – Perfetti Van Melle/OHIM, para. 30; C-418/10 P of 28.3.2011 – Herhof-Verwaltungsgesellschaft/OHIM, para. 61; C-317/10 P of 16.6.2011 – Union Investment Privatfonds/OHIM, paras 45 and 55; C-532/10 P of 29.6.2011 – adp Gauselmann/OHIM, paras 23 and 43; C-67/11 P of 20.10.2011 – DTL Corporación/OHIM, para. 39; C-354/11 P of 22.3.2012 – Emram/OHIM, para. 39; C-327/11 P of 6.9.2012 – United States Polo/OHIM, para. 44; C-42/12 P of 29.11.2012 – Hrbek/OHIM, para. 58; C-261/12 P of 17.1.2013 – Annunziata Del Prete/OHIM, para. 36; C-655/11 P of 21.2.2013 – Seven for all

In that respect, it is clear from the tenth recital in the preamble to the Directive that the appreciation of the likelihood of confusion 'depends on numerous elements and, in particular, on the recognition of the trade mark on the market, of the association which can be made with the used or registered sign, of the degree of similarity between the trade mark and the sign and between the goods or services identified'.[1633]

For the purposes of applying Article 8(1)(b) CTMR, the likelihood of confusion presupposes both that the mark applied for and the earlier mark are identical or similar and that the goods or services covered in the application for registration are identical or similar to those in respect of which the earlier mark is registered. Those **conditions are cumulative.**[1634]

mankind/OHIM, para. 70; C-393/12 P of 21.3.2013 – Foundation for the Protection of the Traditional Cheese of Cyprus named Halloumi/OHIM, para. 32; C-14/12 P of 30.5.2013 – Shah/OHIM, para. 37; C-252/12 of 18.7.2013 – Specsavers International Healthcare, para. 34; C-597/12 P of 17.10.2013 – Isdin/OHIM, para. 18; C-193/13 P of 16.1.2014 – nfon/OHIM, paras 36 and 51; C-177/13 P of 13.2.2014 – Marszałkowski/OHIM, para. 51; C-374/13 P of 10.4.2014 – Metropolis Inmobiliarias y Restauraciones/OHIM, para. 34; C-591/12 P of 8.5.2014 – Bimbo/OHIM, para. 20; C-509/13 P of 4.92014 – Metropolis Inmobiliarias y Restauraciones, paras 37 and 49; C-669/13 P of 21.10.2014 – Mundipharma/OHIM, para. 44; C-466/13 P of 22.10.2014 – Repsol YPF/OHIM, para. 48; C-311/14 P of 20.1.2015 – Longevity Health Products/OHIM, para. 38; C-414/14 P of 26.2.2015 – Fundação Calouste Gulbenkian, para. 49; C-343/14 P of 7.5.2015 – Adler Modemärkte/OHIM, para. 31; C-147/14 of 25.6.2015 – Loutfi Management Propriété intellectuelle, para. 23; C-548/14 P of 17.9.2015 – Arnoldo Mondadori Editore/OHIM, para. 45; C-270/14 P of 15.10.2015 – Debonair Trading Internacional/OHIM, para. 33; C-190/15 P of 19.11.2015 – Fetim/OHIM, para. 37; C-374/15 P of 28.1.2016 – Harper Hygienics/OHIM, para. 70; C-396/15 P of 17.2.2016 – Shoe Branding Europe/OHIM, para. 26; C-474/15 P of 7.4.2016 – Harper Hygienics/EUIPO, para. 70; C-475/15 P of 7.4.2016 – Harper Hygienics/EUIPO, para. 72; C-223/15 of 22.9.2016 – combit Software/Commit Business Solutions, para. 33; C-23/17 P of 15.6.2017 – For Tune/EUIPO, paras 5/2 and 6; C-93/16 of 20.7.2017 – Ornua Co-operative/Tindale & Stanton, para. 36 and 58; C-84/16 P of 26.7.2017 – Continental Reifen Deutschland/EUIPO, para. 97; C-182/16 P of 26.7.2017 – Meica Ammerländische Fleischwarenfabrik Fritz Meinen/EUIPO, para. 24; C-158/17 P of 20.9.2017 – Anton Riemerschmid Weinbrennerei und Likörfabrik/EUIPO, paras 6/13 and 7; C-780/18 P of 22.5.2019 – Cuervo y Sobrinos 1882/EUIPO, paras 5/8 and 7; C-705/17 of 12.6.2019 – Patent- och registreringsverket/Hansson, para. 41; C-99/18 P of 4.7.2019 – FTI Touristik/EUIPO, para. 13; C-328/18 P of 4.3.2020 – EUIPO/Equivalenza Manufactory, para. 57; C-766/18 P of 5.3.2020 – Foundation for the Protection of the Traditional Cheese of Cyprus named Halloumi/EUIPO, para. 67; C-115/19 P of 11.6.2020 – China Construction Bank/EUIPO, para. 54; C-702/18 P of 18.6.2020 – Przedsiębiorstwo Produkcyjno-Handlowe 'Primart' Marek Łukasiewicz/EUIPO, para. 51; C-449/18 P and C-474/18 P of 17.9.2020 – EUIPO/Messi Cuccittini, para. 44.

1633. CJEU C-251/95 of 11.11.1997 – SABEL/Puma, Rudolf Dassler Sport, para. 22; C-39/97 of 29.9.1998 – Canon Kabushiki Kaisha/Metro-Goldwyn-Mayer, para. 15, 16, 24; C-361/04 P of 12.1.2006 – Ruiz-Picasso and Others/OHIM, para. 18; C-206/04 P of 23.3.2006 – Mülhens/OHIM, para. 17; C-171/06 P of 15.3.2007 – T.I.M.E. ART/OHIM, para. 31; C-334/05 P of 12.6.2007 – OHIM/Shaker, para. 32; C-108/07 P of 17.4.2008 – Ferrero Deutschland/OHIM, para. 31; C-16/06 P of 18.12.2008 – Les Éditions Albert René/OHIM, para. 62; C-84/16 P of 26.7.2017 – Continental Reifen Deutschland/EUIPO, para. 95.

1634. CJEU C-106/03 P of 12.10.2004 – VEDIAL/OHIM, para. 51; C-234/06 P of 13.9.2007 – Il Ponte Finanziaria/HABM, Rn. 48; C-57/08 P of 11.12.2008 – Gateway/OHIM, para. 45; C-16/06 P of 18.12.2008 – Les Éditions Albert René/OHIM, para. 44; C-193/09 P of 4.3.2010 – Kaul/OHIM, para. 43; C-216/10 P of 25.11.2010 – Lufthansa AirPlus Servicekarten/OHIM, para. 26; C-558/12 P of 23.1.2014 – OHIM/riha WeserGold Getränke, para. 41; C-509/13 P of 4.9.2014 – Metropolis Inmobiliarias y Restauraciones/OHIM, para. 42; C-414/14 P of 26.2.2015 – Fundação Calouste Gulbenkian, para. 48; C-224/17 P of 19.10.2017 – Hernández Zamora/

When two opposing marks do not display the minimum degree of similarity required for it to be possible to establish a likelihood of confusion solely on the basis of the highly distinctive character of the earlier mark or solely because the goods covered by the earlier mark and those covered by the trade mark applied for are identical, an opposition must be rejected, and this is not precluded by the principle of interdependence.[1635]

There is a likelihood of confusion within the meaning of Article 4(1)(b) TMD2008 where the public can be mistaken as to the origin of the goods or services in question.[1636]

Indeed, Article 2 TMD2008 provides that a trade mark must be capable of distinguishing the goods or services of one undertaking from those of other undertakings, while the tenth recital in the preamble to the Directive states that the function of the protection conferred by the mark is primarily to **guarantee the indication of origin**.[1637]

Moreover, according to the settled case law of the Court, the essential function of the trade mark is to guarantee the identity of the origin of the marked product to the consumer or end user by enabling him, without any possibility of confusion, to distinguish the product or service from others which have another origin. For the trade mark to be able to fulfil its essential role in the system of undistorted competition which the Treaty seeks to establish, it must offer a guarantee that all the goods or services bearing it have originated under the control of a single undertaking which is responsible for their quality.[1638]

That must also be the case where, on the basis of a similarity between the signs and the mark in question, there is a likelihood of confusion between them.[1639]

Accordingly, the risk that the **public** might believe that the goods or services in question come from the **same undertaking or**, as the case may be, from **economically linked undertakings** constitutes a likelihood of confusion within the meaning of Article 4(1)(b) TMD2008. Consequently, in order to demonstrate that there is no likelihood of confusion, it is not sufficient to show simply that there is no likelihood of the public being confused as to the place of production of the goods or services.[1640]

EUIPO, paras 5/8 and 6; *see* CJEU C-150/14 P of 4.9.2014 – Goldsteig Käsereien Bayerwald/OHIM, para. 33; C-673/15 P to C-676/15 P of 20.9.2017 – The Tea Board/EUIPO, para. 47.

1635. CJEU C-234/06 P of 13.9.2007 – Il Ponte Finanziaria/HABM, Rn. 50; C-193/09 P of 4.3.2010 – Kaul/OHIM, para. 44.
1636. CJEU C-39/97 of 29.9.1998 – Canon Kabushiki Kaisha/Metro-Goldwyn-Mayer, para. 26.
1637. CJEU C-39/97 of 29.9.1998 – Canon Kabushiki Kaisha/Metro-Goldwyn-Mayer, para. 27.
1638. CJEU C-39/97 of 29.9.1998 – Canon Kabushiki Kaisha/Metro-Goldwyn-Mayer, para. 28; C-145/05 of 27.4.2006 – Levi Strauss, para. 15; C-412/05 P of 26.4.2007 – Alcon/OHIM (II), paras 53 et seq.; C-307/10 of 19.6.2012 – Chartered Institute of Patent Attorneys, para. 36; C-689/15 of 8.6.2017 – W.F. Gözze Frottierweberei a.o./Verein Bremer Baumwollbörse, para. 41; C-194/17 P of 31.1.2019 – Pandalis/EUIPO, para. 84; C-705/17 of 12.6.2019 – Patent- och registreringsverket/Hansson, para. 31; C-456/19 of 8.10.2020 – Aktiebolaget Östgötatrafiken/Patent- och registreringsverket, para. 32.
1639. CJEU C-145/05 of 27.4.2006 – Levi Strauss, para. 15.
1640. CJEU C-39/97 of 29.9.1998 – Canon Kabushiki Kaisha/Metro-Goldwyn-Mayer, para. 29, 30; C-342/97 of 22.6.1999 – Lloyd Schuhfabrik Meyer, para. 16, 17, 18; C-120/04 of 6.10.2005 – Medion, para. 26; C-334/05 P of 12.6.2007 – OHIM/Shaker, para. 33; C-412/05 P of 26.4.2007 – Alcon/OHIM (II), para. 55; C-193/06 P of 20.9.2007 – Nestlé/OHIM, para. 32; C-533/06 of

By contrast, there can be no such likelihood where it does not appear that the public could believe that the goods or services come from the same undertaking or, as the case may be, from economically linked undertakings.[1641]

The General Court simply found that the **economic link that existed** between Gugler France and Gugler GmbH on the date on which the application for registration of the contested mark was filed **precluded any finding of a likelihood of confusion.**[1642]

Moreover, the case law to which the appellant refers does not cast any doubt on that approach. It is not apparent from the judgment *Schweppes*,[1643] which relates to the concept of 'economic links' in the context of exhaustion of the rights conferred by a trade mark in accordance with Article 7 TMD2008, that, in order to establish the existence of a likelihood of confusion, within the meaning of Article 8(4) CTMR and, consequently, of Article L. 711-4 of the French Intellectual Property Code, the economic link should be assessed on the basis of the link of the proprietor of the earlier rights to the applicant for the trade mark in question.[1644]

It suffices to note, in that regard, that the Court held, in paragraph 46 of the judgment *Schweppes*, that the concept of 'economic links', for the purposes of the TMD2008, refers to a substantive, rather than formal, criterion, which is in no way confined to situations in which the goods in question have been put into circulation by a licensee, by a parent company, by a subsidiary of the same group, or by an exclusive distributor and which, in particular, is also fulfilled where, following the division of national parallel trade marks resulting from a territorially limited assignment, the proprietors of those marks coordinate their commercial policies or reach an agreement in order to exercise joint control over the use of those marks, so that it is possible for them to determine, directly or indirectly, the goods to which those marks are affixed and to control the quality of those goods.[1645]

It has not therefore been held that the existence of an economic link presupposes a particular order between the undertakings concerned. On the contrary, it may be sufficient in that regard that there is a single point of control within a group of operators

---

12.6.2008 – O2 Holdings/Hutchison 3G UK, para. 59; C-278/08 of 25.3.2010 – BergSpechte, para. 38; C-51/09 P of 24.6.2010 – Barbara Becker/OHIM, para. 31; C-558/08 of 8.7.2010 – Portakabin, para. 51; C-559/08 P of 16.9.2010 – Deepak Rajani/OHIM, para. 74; C-353/09 P of 15.2.2011 – Perfetti Van Melle/OHIM, para. 29; C-418/10 P of 28.3.2011 – Herhof-Verwaltungsgesellschaft/OHIM, para. 60; C-317/10 P of 16.6.2011 – Union Investment Privatfonds/OHIM, para. 53; C-354/11 P of 22.3.2012 – Emram/OHIM, para. 78; C-597/12 P of 17.10.2013 – Isdin/OHIM, para. 17; C-591/12 P of 8.5.2014 – Bimbo/OHIM, para. 19; C-343/14 P of 7.5.2015 – Adler Modemärkte/OHIM, para. 31; C-190/15 P of 19.11.2015 – Fetim/OHIM, para. 38; C-251/15 P of 4.2.2016 – Emsibeth/OHIM, para. 45; C-689/15 of 8.6.2017 – W.F. Gözze Frottierweberei a.o./Verein Bremer Baumwollbörse, para. 35; C-705/17 of 12.6.2019 – Patent- och registreringsverket/Hansson, para. 40; C-766/18 P of 5.3.2020 – Foundation for the Protection of the Traditional Cheese of Cyprus named Halloumi/EUIPO, para. 63; C-115/19 P of 11.6.2020 – China Construction Bank/EUIPO, para. 54.

1641. CJEU C-39/97 of 29.9.1998 – Canon Kabushiki Kaisha/Metro-Goldwyn-Mayer, para. 30.
1642. CJEU C-736/18 P of 23.4.2020 – Gugler France/EUIPO, para. 33.
1643. CJEU C-291/16 of 20.12.2017 – Schweppes/Red Paralela.
1644. CJEU C-736/18 P of 23.4.2020 – Gugler France/EUIPO, para. 34.
1645. CJEU C-736/18 P of 23.4.2020 – Gugler France/EUIPO, para. 35.

in respect of the goods manufactured by one of them and distributed by another, thus ruling out any likelihood of confusion as to the commercial origin of those goods.[1646]

Furthermore, the methodological approach adopted by the General Court complies with the requirement that the examination of whether an economic link exists must be conducted globally, taking into account all the relevant circumstances, as observed, moreover, without there being any need to give priority in that connection to methodological principles such as those advocated by the appellant.[1647]

There is **no requirement** that evidence of a likelihood of confusion on the part of a significant number of consumers be adduced in order for a mark or other forms of advertising to be held **to be 'misleading'**.[1648]

Article 9(1)(b) and (c) CTMR must be interpreted as meaning that where a Community trade mark is **not registered in colour**, but the proprietor has used it extensively in a particular colour or combination of colours with the result that it has become associated in the mind of a significant portion of the public with that colour or combination of colours, the colour or colours which a third party uses in order to represent a sign alleged to infringe that trade mark are relevant in the global assessment of the likelihood of confusion or unfair advantage under that provision.[1649]

Where there is a trade mark which is registered not in a particular colour or characteristic, but in black and white, the colour or combination of colours in which the trade mark is later used affects how the average consumer of the goods at issue perceives that trade mark, and it is, therefore, liable to increase the likelihood of confusion or association between the earlier trade mark and the sign alleged to infringe it.[1650]

In those circumstances, it would not be logical to consider that the fact that a third party, for the representation of a sign which is alleged to infringe an earlier Community trade mark, uses a colour or combination of colours which has become associated, in the mind of a significant portion of the public, with that earlier trade mark by the use which has been made of it by its proprietor in that colour or combination of colours cannot be taken into consideration in the global assessment for the sole reason that that earlier trade mark was registered in black and white.[1651]

Article 9(1)(b) and (c) CTMR must be interpreted as meaning that the fact that the third party making use of a sign which allegedly infringes the registered trade mark is itself associated, in the mind of a significant portion of the public, with the **colour** or particular combination of colours which it **uses for the representation** of that sign is relevant to the global assessment of the likelihood of confusion and unfair advantage for the purposes of that provision.[1652]

1646. CJEU C-736/18 P of 23.4.2020 – Gugler France/EUIPO, para. 36.
1647. CJEU C-736/18 P of 23.4.2020 – Gugler France/EUIPO, para. 37, with reference to CJEU C-291/16 of 20.12.2017 – Schweppes/Red Paralela, para. 51.
1648. CJEU C-396/15 P of 17.2.2016 – Shoe Branding Europe/OHIM, para. 30.
1649. CJEU C-252/12 of 18.7.2013 – Specsavers International Healthcare, para. 41.
1650. CJEU C-252/12 of 18.7.2013 – Specsavers International Healthcare, para. 37.
1651. CJEU C-252/12 of 18.7.2013 – Specsavers International Healthcare, para. 38.
1652. CJEU C-252/12 of 18.7.2013 – Specsavers International Healthcare, para. 50.

In that regard, it should be noted that both the likelihood of confusion under Article 9(1)(b) CTMR and unfair advantage under Article 9(1)(c) CTMR must be assessed globally, taking into account all the relevant factors of the present case.[1653]

Moreover, it is apparent from the case law of the Court that those assessments must take account of the precise context in which the sign which is allegedly similar to the registered trade mark was used.[1654]

In those circumstances, it should be noted that the fact that the third party making use of a sign which allegedly infringed the registered trade mark is itself associated, in the mind of a significant portion of the public, with the colour or particular combination of colours which it uses for the representation of that sign is a factor which, amongst others, may have a certain importance while determining the existence of a likelihood of confusion or unfair advantage under Article 9(1)(b) or (c) CTMR.[1655]

It is not inconceivable that such a fact could influence the public's perception of the signs at issue, and, therefore, have an effect on the existence of a likelihood of confusion between those signs for the purposes of Article 9(1) of that regulation.[1656]

Therefore, in the main proceedings, the fact that Asda is itself associated with the colour green, which it uses for the signs alleged to infringe the trade marks of the Specsavers group, could, *inter alia*, result in a reduction of the likelihood of confusion or association between those signs and the trade marks of the Specsavers group, to the extent that the relevant public could perceive that the colour green of those signs is that of Asda, a matter which is to be determined by the referring court.[1657]

The question of the reputation of the later mark is not legally relevant for assessing the likelihood of confusion.[1658]

The determination of the relevant public and the finding of the identity or similarity of the goods and services covered by the Community trade marks and the sign considered stem from the factual assessment that the **national court** must undertake.[1659]

It will be for the national court to ascertain the overall impression made on the relevant public by the later mark, by means of, *inter alia*, an analysis of the components of that mark and of their relative weight in the perception of that public, and then, in the light of that overall impression and all factors relevant to the circumstances of the case, to assess the likelihood of confusion.[1660]

Under Article 8(1)(b) CTMR, which is, in the absence of any provision to the contrary in Articles 67 to 74 CTMR, applicable to **EU collective marks** pursuant to Article 66(3) CTMR, the trade mark applied for is not to be registered if, because of its

1653. CJEU C-252/12 of 18.7.2013 – Specsavers International Healthcare, para. 44.
1654. CJEU C-252/12 of 18.7.2013 – Specsavers International Healthcare, para. 45; *see also* CJEU C-533/06 of 12.6.2008 – O2 Holdings/Hutchison 3G UK, para. 65.
1655. CJEU C-252/12 of 18.7.2013 – Specsavers International Healthcare, para. 46.
1656. CJEU C-252/12 of 18.7.2013 – Specsavers International Healthcare, para. 47.
1657. CJEU C-252/12 of 18.7.2013 – Specsavers International Healthcare, para. 48.
1658. CJEU C-381/12 P of 6.6.2013 – I Marchi Italiani/OHIM, para. 40; unofficial translation.
1659. CJEU C-147/14 of 25.6.2015 – Loutfi Management Propriété intellectuelle, para. 22.
1660. CJEU C-20/14 of 22.10.2015 – BGW Beratungs-Gesellschaft Wirtschaft, para. 41; *see also* CJEU C-591/12 P of 8.5.2014 – Bimbo/OHIM, para. 34.

identity with, or similarity to, the earlier trade mark and the identity or similarity of the goods or services covered by the mark applied for and the earlier mark, there exists a likelihood of confusion on the part of the public in the territory in which the earlier trade mark is protected.[1661]

Where the earlier mark is a collective mark, the essential function of which is, pursuant to Article 66(1) CTMR, to distinguish the goods or services of the members of the association which is the proprietor from those of other undertakings, the likelihood of confusion, within the meaning of Article 8(1)(b) CTMR, must be understood as being the risk that the public might believe that the goods or services covered by the earlier trade mark and those covered by the trade mark applied for all originate from members of the association which is the proprietor of the earlier trade mark or, where appropriate, from undertakings economically linked to those members or to that association.[1662]

Although, as a result, in the event of opposition by the proprietor of a collective mark, the essential function of that type of mark, as set out in Article 66(1) CTMR, must be taken into account in order to understand what is meant by likelihood of confusion, within the meaning of Article 8(1)(b) CTMR, the fact remains that the case law establishing the criteria with regard to which the existence of such a likelihood must be assessed in practice is applicable to cases concerning an earlier collective mark.[1663]

None of the characteristics of EU collective marks justifies derogation, in the event of opposition based on such a mark, from the assessment criteria of the likelihood of confusion which emerge from that case law.[1664]

[1] Interdependence

A global assessment of the likelihood of confusion implies some interdependence between the relevant factors, and in particular a similarity between the trade marks and between these goods or services. Accordingly, a lesser degree of similarity between these goods or services **may be offset** by a greater degree of similarity between the marks, and vice versa.[1665]

1661. CJEU C-766/18 P of 5.3.2020 – Foundation for the Protection of the Traditional Cheese of Cyprus named Halloumi/EUIPO, para. 59, with reference to CJEU C-673/15 P to C-676/15 P of 20.9.2017 – The Tea Board/EUIPO, para. 46.
1662. CJEU C-766/18 P of 5.3.2020 – Foundation for the Protection of the Traditional Cheese of Cyprus named Halloumi/EUIPO, para. 64, with reference to CJEU C-673/15 P to C-676/15 P of 20.9.2017 – The Tea Board/EUIPO, para. 63; C-143/19 P of 12.12.2019 – Der Grüne Punkt – Duales System Deutschland /EUIPO, para. 52.
1663. CJEU C-766/18 P of 5.3.2020 – Foundation for the Protection of the Traditional Cheese of Cyprus named Halloumi/EUIPO, para. 65.
1664. CJEU C-766/18 P of 5.3.2020 – Foundation for the Protection of the Traditional Cheese of Cyprus named Halloumi/EUIPO, para. 66.
1665. CJEU C-39/97 of 29.9.1998 – Canon Kabushiki Kaisha/Metro-Goldwyn-Mayer, para. 17; C-342/97 of 22.6.1999 – Lloyd Schuhfabrik Meyer, para. 19; C-425/98 of 22.6.2000 – Marca Mode, para. 40; C-235/05 P of 27.4.2006 – L'Oréal/OHIM, para. 35; C-171/06 P of 15.3.2007 – T.I.M.E. ART/OHIM, para. 35; C-234/06 P of 13.9.2007 – Il Ponte Finanziaria/OHIM, para. 48; C-108/07 P of 17.4.2008 – Ferrero Deutschland/OHIM, para. 45; C-57/08 P of 11.12.2008 – Gateway/OHIM, para. 47; C-16/06 P of 18.12.2008 – Les Éditions Albert René/OHIM, paras

The occurrence in combination of certain factors [like average distinctiveness of the earlier trade mark, an average level of attention on the part of the relevant public, the fact that the goods concerned are identical and a low degree of similarity between the signs at issue] – which are present to a certain level and degree – in no way entails a presumption that there is a likelihood of confusion.[1666]

The interdependence of these factors is expressly mentioned in the tenth recital of the preamble to the Directive, which states that it is indispensable to give an interpretation of the concept of similarity in relation to the likelihood of confusion, the appreciation of which depends, in particular, on the recognition of the trade mark on the market and the degree of similarity between the mark and the sign and between the goods or services identified.[1667]

The more distinctive the earlier mark, the greater will be the likelihood of confusion.[1668]

The distinctive character of the earlier trade mark and, in particular, its reputation must therefore be taken into account in the assessment of whether there exists a likelihood of confusion.[1669]

---

46 and 63; C-655/11 P of 21.2.2013 – Seven for all mankind/OHIM, para. 86; C-193/13 P of 16.1.2014 – nfon/OHIM, para. 37; C-669/13 P of 21.10.2014 – Mundipharma/OHIM, para. 45; C-398/07 P of 7.5.2009 – Waterford Wedgwood/OHIM, para. 31; C-14/12 P of 30.5.2013 – Shah/OHIM, para. 38; *see also* CJEU C-306/11 P of 28.6.2012 – XXXLutz Marken/OHIM, para. 63; C-42/12 P of 29.11.2012 – Hrbek/OHIM, para. 59; C-509/13 P of 4.9.2014 – Metropolis Inmobiliarias y Restauraciones/OHIM, para. 37; C-414/14 P of 26.2.2015 – Fundação Calouste Gulbenkian, para. 49; C-343/14 P of 7.5.2015 – Adler Modemärkte/OHIM, para. 59; C-548/14 P of 17.9.2015 – Arnoldo Mondadori Editore/OHIM, para. 45; C-224/17 P of 19.10.2017 – Hernández Zamora/EUIPO, paras 5/7 and 6; C-182/16 P of 26.7.2017 – Meica Ammerländische Fleischwarenfabrik Fritz Meinen/EUIPO, para. 24; C-158/17 P of 20.9.2017 – Anton Riemerschmid Weinbrennerei und Likörfabrik/EUIPO, paras 6/13 and 7; C-651/17 of 12.4.2018 – Grupo Osborne/EUIPO, paras 6/25 and 7, unofficial transcription; C-652/17 of 12.4.2018 – Grupo Osborne/EUIPO, paras 6/25 and 7, unofficial transcription; C-705/17 of 12.6.2019 – Patent- och registreringsverket/Hansson, para. 43; C-766/18 P of 5.3.2020 – Foundation for the Protection of the Traditional Cheese of Cyprus named Halloumi/EUIPO, para. 69; C-328/18 P of 4.3.2020 – EUIPO/Equivalenza Manufactory, para. 59.

1666. CJEU C-182/16 P of 26.7.2017 – Meica Ammerländische Fleischwarenfabrik Fritz Meinen/EUIPO, para. 25.

1667. CJEU C-39/97 of 29.9.1998 – Canon Kabushiki Kaisha/Metro-Goldwyn-Mayer, para. 17; C-342/97 of 22.6.1999 – Lloyd Schuhfabrik Meyer, para. 19; C-235/05 P of 27.4.2006 – L'Oréal/OHIM, para. 35; C-42/12 P of 29.11.2012 – Hrbek/OHIM, para. 59.

1668. CJEU C-251/95 of 11.11.1997 – SABEL/Puma, Rudolf Dassler Sport, para. 24; C-39/97 of 29.9.1998 – Canon Kabushiki Kaisha/Metro-Goldwyn-Mayer, para. 18; C-235/05 P of 27.4.2006 – L'Oréal/OHIM, para. 36; C-108/07 P of 17.4.2008 – Ferrero Deutschland/OHIM, para. 32; C-398/07 P of 7.5.2009 – Waterford Wedgwood/OHIM, para. 32; C-579/08 P of 15.1.2010 – Messer Group/OHIM, para. 70; C-23/09 P of 22.1.2010 – ecoblue/OHIM, para. 39; C-42/12 P of 29.11.2012 – Hrbek/OHIM, para. 60; C-14/12 P of 30.5.2013 – Shah/OHIM, para. 39; C-190/15 P of 19.11.2015 – Fetim/OHIM, para. 40; C-73/18 P of 7.6.2018 – Cotécnica/EUIPO, paras 5/9 and 6; *see also* CJEU C-381/12 P of 6.6.2013 – I Marchi Italiani/OHIM, para. 40; C-50/17 P of 1.6.2017 – Universidad Internacional de la Rioja/EUIPO, paras 5/4 and 6; C-705/17 of 12.6.2019 – Patent- och registreringsverket/Hansson, para. 42.

1669. CJEU C-108/07 P of 17.4.2008 – Ferrero Deutschland/OHIM, para. 33; C-396/15 P of 17.2.2016 – Shoe Branding Europe/OHIM, para. 74; *see also* CJEU C-498/07 P of 3.9.2009 – Aceites del Sur-Coosur/OHIM, para. 84; C-449/18 P and C-474/18 P of 17.9.2020 – EUIPO/Messi Cuccittini, para. 46.

Since protection of a trade mark depends, in accordance with Article 4(1)(b) TMD2008, on there being a likelihood of confusion, marks with a highly distinctive character, either per se or because of the reputation they possess on the market, enjoy **broader protection** than marks with a less distinctive character.[1670]

Once proof of the reputation of a mark has been made out, it is irrelevant to prove the inherent distinctive character of that mark in order to obtain a finding that it has distinctive character.[1671]

It is therefore not impossible that the conceptual similarity resulting from the fact that two marks use images with analogous semantic content may give rise to a likelihood of confusion where the earlier mark has a particularly distinctive character, either per se or because of the reputation it enjoys with the public.[1672]

It follows that, for the purposes of Article 4(1)(b) TMD2008, registration of a trade mark may have to be refused, despite a lesser degree of similarity between the goods or services covered, where the marks are very similar and the earlier mark, in particular its reputation, is highly distinctive.[1673]

There may be a likelihood of confusion, notwithstanding a low degree of similarity between the marks, where the similarity of the goods or services covered is high and the earlier mark possesses a strong distinctive character.[1674]

Where the earlier mark is not especially well known to the public and consists of an image with little imaginative content, the mere fact that the two marks are conceptually similar is not sufficient to give rise to a likelihood of confusion.[1675]

The Court of First Instance cannot be criticized for not having disregarded, in its examination of the similarity of the signs in question, the element 'FLEX', which is common to the marks, on the ground that the earlier mark is only of weak distinctive character.[1676]

However, the interdependence of those different factors does not mean that the complete lack of similarity can be fully offset by the strong distinctive character of the

1670. CJEU C-39/97 of 29.9.1998 - Canon Kabushiki Kaisha/Metro-Goldwyn-Mayer, para. 18; C-342/97 of 22.6.1999 - Lloyd Schuhfabrik Meyer, para. 20; C-235/05 P of 27.4.2006 - L'Oréal/OHIM, para. 36; C-108/07 P of 17.4.2008 - Ferrero Deutschland/OHIM, para. 32; C-42/12 P of 29.11.2012 - Hrbek/OHIM, para. 60; C-261/12 P of 17.1.2013 - Annunziata Del Prete/OHIM, para. 36; C-379/12 P of 16.5.2013 - Arav Holding/OHIM, para. 71; C-14/12 P of 30.5.2013 - Shah/OHIM, para. 39; C-252/12 of 18.7.2013 - Specsavers International Healthcare, para. 36; C-466/13 P of 22.10.2014 - Repsol YPF/OHIM, para. 66; C-396/15 P of 17.2.2016 - Shoe Branding Europe/OHIM, para. 74; *see also* CJEU C-16/06 P of 18.12.2008 - Les Éditions Albert René/OHIM, para. 64; C-398/07 P of 7.5.2009 - Waterford Wedgwood/OHIM, para. 32; C-354/11 P of 22.3.2012 - Emram/OHIM, para. 44.
1671. CJEU C-396/15 P of 17.2.2016 - Shoe Branding Europe/OHIM, para. 75; *see also* CJEU C-488/06 P of 17.7.2008 - L & D/OHIM, paras 65 and 67.
1672. CJEU C-251/95 of 11.11.1997 - SABEL/Puma, Rudolf Dassler Sport, para. 24; *see also* CJEU C-488/06 P of 17.7.2008 - L & D/OHIM, para. 65.
1673. CJEU C-39/97 of 29.9.1998 - Canon Kabushiki Kaisha/Metro-Goldwyn-Mayer, para. 19; C-342/97 of 22.6.1999 - Lloyd Schuhfabrik Meyer, para. 21; C-425/98 of 22.6.2000 - Marca Mode, para. 40; C-42/12 P of 29.11.2012 - Hrbek/OHIM, para. 60; C-14/12 P of 30.5.2013 - Shah/OHIM, para. 39.
1674. CJEU C-235/05 P of 27.4.2006 - L'Oréal/OHIM, para. 37; C-398/07 P of 7.5.2009 - Waterford Wedgwood/OHIM, para. 33; C-579/08 P of 15.1.2010 - Messer Group/OHIM, para. 70.
1675. CJEU C-251/95 of 11.11.1997 - SABEL/Puma, Rudolf Dassler Sport, para. 25.
1676. CJEU C-235/05 P of 27.4.2006 - L'Oréal/OHIM, para. 39.

earlier trade mark. For the purposes of applying Article 8(1)(b) CTMR, even where one trade mark is identical to another with a particularly high distinctive character, it is still necessary to adduce evidence of similarity between the goods or services covered. In contrast to Article 8(5) CTMR, which expressly refers to the situation in which the goods or services are not similar, Article 8(1)(b) CTMR provides that the likelihood of confusion presupposes that the goods or services covered are identical or similar.[1677]

Where there is no similarity between the earlier mark and the mark applied for, the reputation of the earlier mark and the fact that the goods or services concerned are identical or similar are not sufficient for it to be found that there is a likelihood of confusion between the marks at issue.[1678]

According to the principle of interdependence, one of the cumulative conditions which must be satisfied in order to prove that there is a likelihood of confusion within the meaning of Article 8(1)(b) CTMR is the **similarity or identity of the signs.**[1679]

Although it is true that the finding that there is a likelihood of confusion should not be subject to the condition that the overall impression produced by the composite sign be dominated by the part of it which is represented by the earlier mark, it must, on the other hand, be pointed out that the signs in the present case are not similar or identical.[1680]

Similarity of the marks in question is thus a **necessary condition** for it to be found that there is a likelihood of confusion for the purposes of Article 8(1)(b) CTMR. Accordingly, the lack of similarity between the marks at issue renders Article 8 CTMR inapplicable.[1681]

The distinctive character of the earlier mark **is not a factor that influences the perception** which the consumer has **of the similarity** of the signs.[1682]

Unlike the factor of the similarity of the signs at issue, the factor of the reputation and distinctive character of the earlier mark does not involve a comparison between a number of signs, but concerns only one sign, namely the sign which the opponent has registered as a mark. Since those two factors are thus fundamentally different in scope, examination of one of them does not allow conclusions to be drawn concerning the other. Even where the earlier mark has a high degree of distinctive character by reason

1677. CJEU C-398/07 P of 7.5.2009 – Waterford Wedgwood/OHIM, para. 34; *see also* CJEU C-193/09 P of 4.3.2010 – Kaul/OHIM, para. 45; C-294/12 P of 14.5.2013 – You-Q/OHIM, para. 67; C-558/12 P of 23.1.2014 – OHIM/riha WeserGold Getränke, para. 43; C-301/13 P of 6.2.2014 – El Corte Inglés, para. 65; C-509/13 P of 4.9.2014 – Metropolis Inmobiliarias y Restauraciones/OHIM, para. 42; C-548/14 P of 17.9.2015 – Arnoldo Mondadori Editore/ OHIM, para. 46.

1678. CJEU C-254/09 P of 2.9.2010 – Calvin Klein/OHIM, para. 53; C-216/10 P of 25.11.2010 – Lufthansa AirPlus Servicekarten/OHIM, para. 26; C-370/10 P of 14.3.2011 – Ravensburger/ OHIM, para. 51; C-552/09 P of 24.3.2011 – Ferrero/OHIM, para. 65; C-261/12 P of 17.1.2013 – Annunziata Del Prete/OHIM, para. 38; C-558/12 P of 23.1.2014 – OHIM/riha WeserGold Getränke, para. 42; C-509/13 P of 4.9.2014 – Metropolis Inmobiliarias y Restauraciones/ OHIM, para. 42; C-328/18 P of 4.3.2020 – EUIPO/Equivalenza Manufactory, para. 60.

1679. CJEU C-57/08 P of 11.12.2008 – Gateway/OHIM, para. 52.

1680. CJEU C-57/08 P of 11.12.2008 – Gateway/OHIM, para. 53.

1681. CJEU C-558/12 P of 23.1.2014 – OHIM/riha WeserGold Getränke, para. 44.

1682. CJEU C-235/05 P of 27.4.2006 – L'Oréal/OHIM, para. 42; C-42/12 P of 29.11.2012 – Hrbek/OHIM, para. 57; *see also* CJEU C-370/10 P of 14.3.2011 – Ravensburger/OHIM, para. 50; *see also* CJEU C-115/19 P of 11.6.2020 – China Construction Bank/EUIPO, paras 58 et seq.

of its reputation, that fact does not make it possible to determine whether and, if so, to what extent that mark is visually, phonetically and conceptually similar to the mark in respect of which registration is sought.[1683]

The conceptual similarity between the signs at issue must be assessed independently of their degree of distinctiveness.[1684]

The enhanced distinctiveness of a mark, acquired through use, must be taken into account when determining whether the similarity between the signs or between the goods or services covered is sufficient to give rise to a likelihood of confusion.[1685]

Although the distinctive character of the earlier mark must thus be taken into account when assessing the likelihood of confusion, it is **only one factor among others** involved in that assessment.[1686]

The applicant has misconstrued the concepts which govern the determination of whether a likelihood of confusion between two marks exists, by failing to distinguish between the notion of the distinctive character of the earlier mark, which determines the protection afforded to that mark, and the notion of the distinctive character which an element of a complex mark possesses, which is concerned with its ability to dominate the overall impression created by the mark.[1687]

The applicant's approach would have the effect of disregarding the notion of the similarity of the marks in favour of one based on the distinctive character of the earlier mark, which would then be given undue importance. The result would be that where the earlier mark is only of weak distinctive character, a likelihood of confusion would exist only where there was a complete reproduction of that mark by the mark applied for, whatever the degree of similarity between the marks in question. If that were the case, it would be possible to register a complex mark, one of the elements of which was identical with or similar to those of an earlier mark with a weak distinctive character, even where the other elements of that complex mark were still less distinctive than the common element and notwithstanding a likelihood that consumers would believe that the slight difference between the signs reflected a variation in the nature of the products or stemmed from marketing considerations and not that that difference denoted goods from different traders.[1688]

It cannot be deduced from the Court's case law that the **weak distinctive character** of the earlier mark precludes, in principle, all likelihood of confusion, even

1683. CJEU C-115/19 P of 11.6.2020 - China Construction Bank/EUIPO, para. 58.
1684. CJEU C-42/12 P of 29.11.2012 - Hrbek/OHIM, para. 66; C-343/14 P of 7.5.2015 - Adler Modemärkte/OHIM, para. 39.
1685. CJEU C-558/12 P of 23.1.2014 - OHIM/riha WeserGold Getränke, para. 45.
1686. CJEU C-42/12 P of 29.11.2012 - Hrbek/OHIM, para. 61; C-14/12 P of 30.5.2013 - Shah/OHIM, para. 40; C-43/15 P of 8.11.2016 - BSH Bosch und Siemens Hausgeräte/EUIPO, para. 61; C-84/16 P of 26.7.2017 - Continental Reifen Deutschland/EUIPO, para. 98.
1687. CJEU C-235/05 P of 27.4.2006 - L'Oréal/OHIM, para. 43; C-343/14 P of 7.5.2015 - Adler Modemärkte/OHIM, para. 39.
1688. CJEU C-235/05 P of 27.4.2006 - L'Oréal/OHIM, para. 45; C-171/06 P of 15.3.2007 - T.I.M.E. ART/OHIM, para. 41; C-42/12 P of 29.11.2012 - Hrbek/OHIM, para. 62; C-14/12 P of 30.5.2013 - Shah/OHIM, para. 41; C-343/14 P of 7.5.2015 - Adler Modemärkte/OHIM, para. 61; *see also* CJEU C-190/15 P of 19.11.2015 - Fetim/OHIM, para. 46; C-43/15 P of 8.11.2016 - BSH Bosch und Siemens Hausgeräte/EUIPO, para. 64 and 70.

if the marks at issue, assessed as a whole, are similar and the goods concerned are identical.[1689]

The interdependence cannot preclude a likelihood of confusion where the distinctive character of the earlier mark is weak.[1690]

Where the earlier trade mark and the sign whose registration is sought coincide in an element that is weakly distinctive or descriptive with regard to the goods or services at issue, the global assessment of the likelihood of confusion within the meaning of Article 4(1)(b) TMD2008 will admittedly not often lead to a finding that that likelihood exists. However, it follows from the Court's case law that a finding that a likelihood of confusion exists cannot, because of the interdependence of the relevant factors, be ruled out in advance and in any event.[1691]

[2] Average consumer

The perception of the marks by the average consumer of the goods or services in question plays a **decisive role** in the global appreciation of that likelihood of confusion.[1692]

The similarity of the marks at issue must be assessed from the point of view of the average consumer by referring to the intrinsic qualities of the marks and **not to**

1689. CJEU C-579/08 P of 15.1.2010 – Messer Group/OHIM, para. 68; C-343/14 P of 7.5.2015 – Adler Modemärkte/OHIM, para. 59; *see also* C-193/13 P of 16.1.2014 – nfon/OHIM, para. 30; *see also* CJEU C-43/15 P of 8.11.2016 – BSH Bosch und Siemens Hausgeräte/EUIPO, para. 63; C-84/16 P of 26.7.2017 – Continental Reifen Deutschland/EUIPO, para. 100; C-705/17 of 12.6.2019 – Patent- och registreringsverket/Hansson, para. 44.
1690. CJEU C-579/08 P of 15.1.2010 – Messer Group/OHIM, para. 70; C-23/09 P of 22.1.2010 – ecoblue/OHIM, para. 39; C-466/13 P of 22.10.2014 – Repsol YPF/OHIM, para. 66; C-190/15 P of 19.11.2015 – Fetim/OHIM, para. 40; C-43/15 P of 8.11.2016 – BSH Bosch und Siemens Hausgeräte/EUIPO, para. 62; C-50/17 P of 1.6.2017 – Universidad Internacional de la Rioja/EUIPO, paras 5/8 and 6; C-84/16 P of 26.7.2017 – Continental Reifen Deutschland/EUIPO, para. 99; C-73/18 P of 7.6.2018 – Cotécnica/EUIPO, paras 5/9 and 6; C-702/18 P of 18.6.2020 – Przedsiębiorstwo Produkcyjno-Handlowe 'Primart' Marek Łukasiewicz/EUIPO, para. 49.
1691. CJEU C-705/17 of 12.6.2019 – Patent- och registreringsverket/Hansson, para. 55, with further proof; C-702/18 P of 18.6.2020 – Przedsiębiorstwo Produkcyjno-Handlowe 'Primart' Marek Łukasiewicz/EUIPO, para. 53.
1692. CJEU C-251/95 of 11.11.1997 – SABEL/Puma, Rudolf Dassler Sport, para. 23; C-342/97 of 22.6.1999 – Lloyd Schuhfabrik Meyer, para. 25; C-498/07 P of 3.9.2009 – Aceites del Sur-Coosur/OHIM, para. 74; C-51/09 P of 24.6.2010 – Barbara Becker/OHIM, para. 33; C-254/09 P of 2.9.2010 – Calvin Klein/OHIM, para. 45; C-353/09 P of 15.2.2011 – Perfetti Van Melle/OHIM, para. 31; C-532/10 P of 29.6.2011 – adp Gauselmann/OHIM, para. 24; C-67/11 P of 20.10.2011 – DTL Corporación/OHIM, para. 40; C-327/11 P of 6.9.2012 – United States Polo/OHIM, para. 45; C-42/12 P of 29.11.2012 – Hrbek/OHIM, para. 40; C-597/12 P of 17.10.2013 – Isdin/OHIM, para. 19; C-591/12 P of 8.5.2014 – Bimbo/OHIM, para. 21; C-343/14 P of 7.5.2015 – Adler Modemärkte/OHIM, para. 31; C-147/14 of 25.6.2015 – Loutfi Management Propriété intellectuelle, para. 21; C-20/14 of 22.10.2015 – BGW Beratungs-Gesellschaft Wirtschaft, para. 35; C-23/17 P of 15.6.2017 – For Tune/EUIPO, paras 5/2 and 6; C-705/17 of 12.6.2019 – Patent- och registreringsverket/Hansson, para. 45; C-328/18 P of 4.3.2020 – EUIPO/Equivalenza Manufactory, para. 58.

circumstances relating to the conduct of the person applying for a Community trade mark.[1693]

For the purposes of that global appreciation, the average consumer[1694] of the category of products concerned is deemed to be **reasonably well informed and reasonably observant and circumspect.**[1695]

Under Article 8(1)(b) CTMR, the existence of a likelihood of confusion resulting from the similarity, on the one hand, between the trade mark in the application for registration and an earlier trade mark and, on the other hand, between the goods or services covered by the trade marks must be assessed on the part of the public in the territory in which the earlier trade mark is protected.[1696]

However, account should be taken of the fact that the average consumer only rarely has the chance to make a direct comparison between the different marks but must place his trust in the imperfect picture of them that he has kept in his mind.[1697]

It should also be borne in mind that the average consumer's level of attention is likely to vary according to the category of goods or services in question.[1698]

Where it is established in fact that the objective characteristics of a given product mean that the average consumer purchases it only after a particularly careful examination, it is important in law to take into account that such a fact may reduce the likelihood of confusion between marks relating to such goods at the crucial moment when the choice between those goods and marks is made.[1699]

The average consumer normally perceives a mark **as a whole** and does not proceed to analyse its various details.[1700]

1693. CJEU C-254/09 P of 2.9.2010 – Calvin Klein/OHIM, para. 46; C-354/11 P of 22.3.2012 – Emram/OHIM, para. 44; C-328/18 P of 4.3.2020 – EUIPO/Equivalenza Manufactory, para. 71; C-115/19 P of 11.6.2020 – China Construction Bank/EUIPO, para. 56.
1694. *See* above Preamble 'Relevant classes of persons'.
1695. CJEU C-251/95 of 11.11.1997 – SABEL/Puma, Rudolf Dassler Sport, para. 23; C-342/97 of 22.6.1999 – Lloyd Schuhfabrik Meyer, para. 25, 26; C-3/03 P of 28.4.2004 – Matratzen Concord/OHIM, para. 29; C-361/04 P of 12.1.2006 – Ruiz-Picasso and Others/OHIM, para. 36; C-235/05 P of 27.4.2006 – L'Oréal/OHIM, para. 41; C-334/05 P of 12.6.2007 – OHIM/Shaker, para. 35; C-412/05 P of 26.4.2007 – Alcon/OHIM (II), para. 59, 62; C-193/06 P of 20.9.2007 – Nestlé/OHIM, para. 34; C-108/07 P of 17.4.2008 – Ferrero Deutschland/OHIM, para. 46; C-498/07 P of 3.9.2009 – Aceites del Sur-Coosur/OHIM, para. 74; C-353/09 P of 15.2.2011 – Perfetti Van Melle/OHIM, para. 48; C-308/13 P and C-309/13 P of 18.9.2014 – Società Italiana Calzature/OHIM, para. 41; C-147/14 of 25.6.2015 – Loutfi Management Propriété intellectuelle, para. 21; C-440/16 P of 12.1.2017 – Staywell Hospitality Group/EUIPO, paras 5/5 and 6; C-93/16 of 20.7.2017 – Ornua Co-operative/Tindale & Stanton, para. 41; C-328/18 P of 4.3.2020 – EUIPO/Equivalenza Manufactory, para. 58.
1696. CJEU C-412/05 P of 26.4.2007 – Alcon/OHIM (II), para. 51; C-234/06 P of 13.9.2007 – Il Ponte Finanziaria/OHIM, para. 60.
1697. CJEU C-342/97 of 22.6.1999 – Lloyd Schuhfabrik Meyer, para. 26; C-412/05 P of 26.4.2007 – Alcon/OHIM (II), para. 60; *see also* CJEU C-498/07 P of 3.9.2009 – Aceites del Sur-Coosur/OHIM, para. 74.
1698. CJEU C-342/97 of 22.6.1999 – Lloyd Schuhfabrik Meyer, para. 26; C-361/04 P of 12.1.2006 – Ruiz-Picasso and Others/OHIM, para. 38; C-498/07 P of 3.9.2009 – Aceites del Sur-Coosur/OHIM, para. 74; C-579/08 P of 15.1.2010 – Messer Group/OHIM, para. 51; C-354/11 P of 22.3.2012 – Emram/OHIM, para. 68.
1699. CJEU C-361/04 P of 12.1.2006 – Ruiz-Picasso and Others/OHIM, para. 40.
1700. CJEU C-251/95 of 11.11.1997 – SABEL/Puma, Rudolf Dassler Sport, para. 23; C-342/97 of 22.6.1999 – Lloyd Schuhfabrik Meyer, para. 25; C-3/03 P of 28.4.2004 – Matratzen Concord/

Indeed, it is necessary to ascertain, in each individual case, the overall impression made on the target public by the sign for which registration is sought, by means of, *inter alia*, an analysis of the components of a sign and of their relative weight in the perception of the target public, and then, in the light of that overall impression and all factors relevant to the circumstances of the case, to assess the likelihood of confusion.[1701]

The fact that a **mark has been registered as a figurative mark** is not relevant here for the purpose of determining the scope of the application for protection. When assessing the characteristics of a sign, in addition to the graphic representation and any descriptions filed at the time of the application for registration, other material relevant to identifying appropriately the essential characteristics of a sign may be taken into consideration.[1702]

[3] Visual, aural or conceptual similarity and distinctive and dominant components

That global appreciation of the visual, aural or conceptual similarity of the marks in question must be based on the **overall impression** given by the marks, bearing in mind, **in particular, their distinctive and dominant components.**[1703]

OHIM, para. 29; C-334/05 P of 12.6.2007 – OHIM/Shaker, para. 35; C-193/06 P of 20.9.2007 – Nestlé/OHIM, para. 34; C-254/09 P of 2.9.2010 – Calvin Klein/OHIM, para. 45; C-204/10 P of 23.11.2010 – Enercon/OHIM, para. 23; C-353/09 P of 15.2.2011 – Perfetti Van Melle/OHIM, para. 31; C-532/10 P of 29.6.2011 – adp Gauselmann/OHIM, para. 24; C-67/11 P of 20.10.2011 – DTL Corporación/OHIM, para. 40; C-327/11 P of 6.9.2012 – United States Polo/OHIM, para. 45; C-42/12 P of 29.11.2012 – Hrbek/OHIM, para. 40; C-252/12 of 18.7.2013 – Specsavers International Healthcare, para. 35; C-597/12 P of 17.10.2013 – Isdin/OHIM, para. 19; C-591/12 P of 8.5.2014 – Bimbo/OHIM, paras 21 and 35; C-308/13 P and C-309/13 P of 18.9.2014 – Società Italiana Calzature/OHIM, para. 41; C-343/14 P of 7.5.2015 – Adler Modemärkte/OHIM, para. 31; C-23/17 P of 15.6.2017 – For Tune/EUIPO, paras 5/2 and 6; *see also* CJEU C-739/18 P of 2.5.2019 – Chefaro Ireland/EUIPO, paras 5/7 and 6; C-328/18 P of 4.3.2020 – EUIPO/Equivalenza Manufactory, para. 58.

1701. CJEU C-591/12 P of 8.5.2014 – Bimbo/OHIM, para. 34; C-20/14 of 22.10.2015 – BGW Beratungs-Gesellschaft Wirtschaft, para. 41; C-182/16 P of 26.7.2017 – Meica Ammerländische Fleischwarenfabrik Fritz Meinen/EUIPO, para. 58.

1702. CJEU C-223/18 P of 6.6.2019 – Deichmann/EUIPO, para. 47, unofficial transcription, with reference to CJEU C-337/12 P to C-340/12 P of 6.3.2014 – Pi-Design/OHIM, para. 54.

1703. CJEU C-251/95 of 11.11.1997 – SABEL/Puma, Rudolf Dassler Sport, para. 23; C-342/97 of 22.6.1999 – Lloyd Schuhfabrik Meyer, para. 25; C-3/03 P of 28.4.2004 – Matratzen Concord/ OHIM, para. 29; C-120/04 of 6.10.2005 – Medion, para. 28; C-512/04 P of 1.12.2005 – Vitakraft-Werke Wührmann/OHIM, para. 22; C-361/04 P of 12.1.2006 – Ruiz-Picasso and Others/OHIM, para. 19; C-206/04 P of 23.3.2006 – Mülhens/OHIM, para. 19; C-235/05 P of 27.4.2006 – L'Oréal/OHIM, para. 41; C-324/05 P of 1.6.2006 – Plus Warenhandelsgesellschaft/OHIM, para. 25, 43; C-314/05 P of 29.6.2006 – Creative Technology/OHIM, para. 32, 37; C-196/06 P of 9.3.2007 – Alecansan/OHIM, para. 22; C-245/06 P of 9.3.2007 – Saiwa/OHIM, para. 46; C-171/06 P of 15.3.2007 – T.I.M.E. ART/OHIM, para. 34; C-131/06 P of 24.4.2007 – Castellblanch/OHIM, para. 55; C-334/05 P of 12.6.2007 – OHIM/Shaker, para. 35; C-234/06 P of 13.9.2007 – Il Ponte Finanziaria/OHIM, para. 33; C-193/06 P of 20.9.2007 – Nestlé/OHIM, para. 34; C-57/08 P of 11.12.2008 – Gateway/OHIM, para. 48; C-300/08 P of 11.6.2009 – Leche Celta/OHIM, para. 32; C-498/07 P of 3.9.2009 – Aceites del Sur-Coosur/OHIM, para. 60; C-579/08 P of 15.1.2010 – Messer Group/OHIM, para. 47; C-23/09 P of 22.1.2010 – ecoblue/OHIM, para. 47; C-51/09 P of

The wording of Article 4(1)(b) TMD2008 – '... there exists a likelihood of confusion on the part of the public ...' – shows that the perception of marks in the mind of the average consumer of the type of goods or services in question plays a decisive role in the global appreciation of the likelihood of confusion. The average consumer normally perceives a mark as a whole and does not proceed to analyse its various details.[1704]

In order to assess the degree of similarity between the marks concerned, the national court must determine the **degree of visual, aural or conceptual similarity** between them and, where appropriate, evaluate the importance to be attached to those different elements, taking account of the **category of goods or services** in question and the **circumstances in which they are marketed**.[1705]

24.6.2010 – Barbara Becker/OHIM, para. 33; C-254/09 P of 2.9.2010 – Calvin Klein/OHIM, para. 45; C-204/10 P of 23.11.2010 – Enercon/OHIM, para. 23; C-216/10 P of 25.11.2010 – Lufthansa AirPlus Servicekarten/OHIM, para. 30; C-353/09 P of 15.2.2011 – Perfetti Van Melle/OHIM, para. 31; C-532/10 P of 29.6.2011 – adp Gauselmann/OHIM, para. 24; C-67/11 P of 20.10.2011 – DTL Corporación/OHIM, para. 40; C-306/11 P of 28.6.2012 – XXXLutz Marken/OHIM, paras 39 and 63; C-599/11 P of 28.6.2012 – TofuTown.com/OHIM, paras 24 and 30; C-327/11 P of 6.9.2012 – United States Polo/OHIM, para. 45; C-42/12 P of 29.11.2012 – Hrbek/OHIM, para. 40; C-655/11 P of 21.2.2013 – Seven for all mankind/OHIM, para. 71; C-252/12 of 18.7.2013 – Specsavers International Healthcare, para. 35; C-597/12 P of 17.10.2013 – Isdin/OHIM, para. 19; C-524/12 P of 14.11.2013 – TeamBank/OHIM, para. 48; C-193/13 P of 16.1.2014 – nfon/OHIM, para. 36; C-422/12 P of 30.1.2014 – Industrias Alen/OHIM, para. 42; C-177/13 P of 13.2.2014 – Marszałkowski/OHIM, para. 54; C-374/13 P of 10.4.2014 – Metropolis Inmobiliarias y Restauraciones/OHIM, para. 34; C-591/12 P of 8.5.2014 – Bimbo/OHIM, para. 21; C-308/13 P and C-309/13 P of 18.9.2014 – Società Italiana Calzature/OHIM, para. 40; C-669/13 P of 21.10.2014 – Mundipharma/OHIM, para. 44; C-466/13 P of 22.10.2014 – Repsol YPF/OHIM, para. 82; C-311/14 P of 20.1.2015 – Longevity Health Products/OHIM, para. 41; C-420/14 P of 5.2.2015 – Jyoti Ceramic Industries/OHIM, para. 25; C-182/14 P of 19.3.2015 – MEGA Brands International/OHIM, para. 31; C-343/14 P of 7.5.2015 – Adler Modemärkte/OHIM, para. 31; C-147/14 of 25.6.2015 – Loutfi Management Propriété intellectuelle, para. 23; C-190/15 P of 19.11.2015 – Fetim/OHIM, para. 39; C-251/15 P of 4.2.2016 – Emsibeth/OHIM, para. 46; C-396/15 P of 17.2.2016 – Shoe Branding Europe/OHIM, paras 26 and 43; C-50/17 P of 1.6.2017 – Universidad Internacional de la Rioja/EUIPO, paras 5/8 and 6; C-93/16 of 20.7.2017 – Ornua Co-operative/Tindale & Stanton, para. 41; C-162/17 P of 16.1.2019 – Republic of Poland/EUIPO, para. 41; C-505/17 P of 28.2.2019 – Groupe Léa Nature/EUIPO, para. 36; C-739/18 P of 2.5.2019 – Chefaro Ireland/EUIPO, paras 5/4 and 6; C-705/17 of 12.6.2019 – Patent- och registreringsverket/Hansson, para. 45 and 48; *see also* CJEU C-678/19 P of 20.11.2019 – Retail Royalty/EUIPO, para. 18; C-766/18 P of 5.3.2020 – Foundation for the Protection of the Traditional Cheese of Cyprus named Halloumi/EUIPO, para. 68; C-449/18 P and C-474/18 P of 17.9.2020 – EUIPO/Messi Cuccittini, para. 45.

1704. CJEU C-251/95 of 11.11.1997 – SABEL/Puma, Rudolf Dassler Sport, para. 23; C-342/97 of 22.6.1999 – Lloyd Schuhfabrik Meyer, para. 25; C-120/04 of 6.10.2005 – Medion, para. 28.

1705. CJEU C-342/97 of 22.6.1999 – Lloyd Schuhfabrik Meyer, para. 27; C-361/04 P of 12.1.2006 – Ruiz-Picasso and Others/OHIM, para. 37; C-235/05 P of 27.4.2006 – L'Oréal/OHIM, para. 40; C-334/05 P of 12.6.2007 – OHIM/Shaker, para. 36; C-394/08 P of 3.6.2009 – Zipcar/OHIM, para. 59; C-579/08 P of 15.1.2010 – Messer Group/OHIM, para. 48; C-552/09 P of 24.3.2011 – Ferrero/OHIM, para. 85; C-597/12 P of 17.10.2013 – Isdin/OHIM, para. 20; C-374/15 P of 28.1.2016 – Harper Hygienics/OHIM, paras 52 and 70; C-396/15 P of 17.2.2016 – Shoe Branding Europe/OHIM, para. 41; C-474/15 P of 7.4.2016 – Harper Hygienics/EUIPO, para. 70; C-475/15 P of 7.4.2016 – Harper Hygienics/EUIPO, para. 72; C-328/18 P of 4.3.2020 – EUIPO/Equivalenza Manufactory, para. 68; *see also* CJEU C-354/11 P of 22.3.2012 – Emram/OHIM, para. 83; C-524/12 P of 14.11.2013 – TeamBank/OHIM, para. 72; C-182/16 P of 26.7.2017 – Meica Ammerländische Fleischwarenfabrik Fritz Meinen/EUIPO, para. 31.

Pursuant to this, the aural similarity between two opposing figurative marks on the basis of the marketing method of the products in question is not neutralized but only limited.[1706]

Moreover, the legal matter in which that judgment[1707] was passed was concerned with everyday, over-the-counter goods made of leather and leather imitations as well as clothing items, shoes and headgear, whereas the case at hand deals with financial services which could have significant financial consequences for the consumer and which are not freely available on the market.[1708]

However, it does not follow from that case law that determination of the degree of similarity must be carried out on the basis of figures or specified percentages.[1709]

Mere aural similarity between trade marks may create a likelihood of confusion within the meaning of Article 5(1)(b) TMD2008.[1710]

However, it must be noted that the existence of such a likelihood must be established as part of a global assessment as regards the conceptual, visual and aural similarities between the signs at issue. In that regard, the assessment of any aural similarity is but one of the relevant factors for the purpose of that global assessment.[1711]

Therefore, one cannot deduce from paragraph 28 of the judgment in *Lloyd Schuhfabrik Meyer* that there is necessarily a likelihood of confusion each time that mere phonetic similarity between two signs is established.[1712]

In order to assess the likelihood of confusion that may exist between a Community trade mark and a sign which covers the same or similar goods and which both contain a dominant **Arabic word in Latin and Arabic script**, those words being visually similar, in circumstances where the relevant public for the Community mark and for the sign at issue has a basic knowledge of written Arabic, the meaning and pronunciation of those words must be taken into account.[1713]

Certain phonetic and conceptual differences should be taken into account because, if they are not, the assessment of the likelihood of confusion could be made only partially and, as a result, without taking into account the overall impression made by the Community trade marks and the sign considered on the relevant public.[1714]

In the present case, the pleas raised by OHIM concern a question of law, in that it seeks to demonstrate that the Court of First Instance misinterpreted the scope of Article 8(1)(b) CTMR, in so far as it limited itself to a visual analysis of the marks at issue and did not proceed to a phonetic and conceptual assessment of those marks.[1715]

1706. CJEU C-524/12 P of 14.11.2013 – TeamBank/OHIM, para. 61.
1707. CJEU C-234/06 P of 13.9.2007 – Il Ponte Finanziaria/OHIM.
1708. CJEU C-524/12 P of 14.11.2013 – TeamBank/OHIM, para. 61.
1709. CJEU C-579/08 P of 15.1.2010 – Messer Group/OHIM, para. 49; C-354/11 P of 22.3.2012 – Emram/OHIM, para. 84.
1710. CJEU C-342/97 of 22.6.1999 – Lloyd Schuhfabrik Meyer, para. 28; C-206/04 P of 23.3.2006 – Mülhens/OHIM, para. 21; C-234/06 P of 13.9.2007 – Il Ponte Finanziaria/OHIM, para. 32.
1711. CJEU C-206/04 P of 23.3.2006 – Mülhens/OHIM, para. 21; C-234/06 P of 13.9.2007 – Il Ponte Finanziaria/OHIM, para. 35; C-552/09 P of 24.3.2011 – Ferrero/OHIM, para. 86.
1712. CJEU C-206/04 P of 23.3.2006 – Mülhens/OHIM, para. 22.
1713. CJEU C-147/14 of 25.6.2015 – Loutfi Management Propriété intellectuelle, para. 26.
1714. CJEU C-147/14 of 25.6.2015 – Loutfi Management Propriété intellectuelle, para. 25.
1715. CJEU C-334/05 P of 12.6.2007 – OHIM/Shaker, para. 29.

Although the possibility cannot be ruled out that the **coexistence** of two marks on a particular market might, together with other elements, contribute to diminishing the likelihood of confusion between those marks on the part of the relevant public, certain conditions must be met. Thus, the absence of a likelihood of confusion may, in particular, be inferred from the 'peaceful' nature of the coexistence of the marks at issue on the market concerned.[1716]

[4] Counteraction of similarities

By stating that where the meaning of at least one of the two signs at issue is clear and specific so that it can be grasped immediately by the relevant public, the conceptual differences observed between those signs may counteract the visual and phonetic similarities between them the Court of First Instance did not in any way err in law.[1717]

Therefore, the Court of First Instance cannot be criticized for having applied the 'counteraction' theory.[1718]

The global assessment must, as regards the visual, aural or conceptual similarity of the marks in question, be based on the overall impression created by those marks, bearing in mind, in particular, their distinctive and dominant components.[1719]

That global assessment means that conceptual and visual differences between two signs may counteract aural similarities between them, provided that at least one of those signs has, from the point of view of the relevant public, **a clear and specific meaning**, so that the public is capable of grasping it immediately.[1720]

Since that case law relates to the signs at issue and the scope to be given to their conceptual differences in the context of the overall assessment of the likelihood of confusion, it cannot be maintained that the existence of an earlier well-known trade mark relied on in opposition constitutes a condition for the application of that case law. In that regard, the assessment of whether a sign has, from the point of view of the public, a clear and specific meaning may, therefore, **relate both to the sign relating to the earlier trade mark and to the sign corresponding to the trade mark applied for**.[1721]

1716. CJEU C-498/07 P of 3.9.2009 – Aceites del Sur-Coosur/OHIM, para. 82.

1717. CJEU C-361/04 P of 12.1.2006 – Ruiz-Picasso and Others/OHIM, para. 20; C-16/06 P of 18.12.2008 – Les Éditions Albert René/OHIM, para. 98; C-579/08 P of 15.1.2010 – Messer Group/OHIM, para. 57; *see also* CJEU C-206/04 P of 23.3.2006 – Mülhens/OHIM, para. 36; C-437/16 P of 5.10.2017 – Wolf Oil/EUIPO, paras 43 et seq.; C-449/18 P and C-474/18 P of 17.9.2020 – EUIPO/Messi Cuccittini, para. 85.

1718. CJEU C-16/06 P of 18.12.2008 – Les Éditions Albert René/OHIM, para. 99.

1719. CJEU C-206/04 P of 23.3.2006 – Mülhens/OHIM, para. 34; C-234/06 P of 13.9.2007 – Il Ponte Finanziaria/OHIM, para. 33.

1720. CJEU C-206/04 P of 23.3.2006 – Mülhens/OHIM, para. 35; C-171/06 P of 15.3.2007 – T.I.M.E. ART/OHIM, para. 49; C-234/06 P of 13.9.2007 – Il Ponte Finanziaria/OHIM, para. 34; C-249/14 P of 9.7.2015 – Pêra-Grave/OHIM, para. 39; *see also* CJEU C-437/16 P of 5.10.2017 – Wolf Oil/EUIPO, para. 44; C-328/18 P of 4.3.2020 – EUIPO/Equivalenza Manufactory, para. 74; C-449/18 P and C-474/18 P of 17.9.2020 – EUIPO/Messi Cuccittini, para. 85.

1721. CJEU C-449/18 P and C-474/18 P of 17.9.2020 – EUIPO/Messi Cuccittini, para. 86, with further proof.

The Court of First Instance's decision, according to which the visual and conceptual differences between the signs at issue counteract their phonetic similarity, constitutes a finding of fact which is outside the jurisdiction of the Court of Justice to review on appeal.[1722]

In terms of that global appreciation, the Court of First Instance was entitled to consider that, in order for the conceptual difference between the QUANTUM and Quantième marks to be able to counteract to a large extent the similarities existing between them, it was necessary that at least one of the marks in question had, from the point of view of the relevant public, a clear and specific meaning, so that the public is capable of grasping it immediately.[1723]

By holding in this case that, as a general rule, the relevant public would not immediately attribute a precise meaning to the verbal elements of the opposing marks, the Court of First Instance was carrying out an appraisal of a factual nature.[1724]

By contrast, in the **absence**, in the case of either of the signs at issue, **of such a clear and specific meaning** which can be grasped immediately by the relevant public, the General Court cannot counteract it by dispensing with a global assessment of the likelihood of confusion. In such a case, rather, it falls to the General Court to carry out a global assessment of that likelihood, taking into account all the similarities and differences noted in the same way as the other relevant elements, such as the level of attention of the relevant public or the degree of distinctive character of the earlier mark.[1725]

[5] Trade marks as a whole and independent distinctive role

In the context of consideration of the likelihood of confusion, assessment of the similarity between two marks means more than taking just one component of a composite trade mark and comparing it with another mark. On the contrary, the comparison must be made by examining each of the **marks in question as a whole**.[1726]

1722. CJEU C-206/04 P of 23.3.2006 – Mülhens/OHIM, para. 41.
1723. CJEU C-171/06 P of 15.3.2007 – T.I.M.E. ART/OHIM, para. 49.
1724. CJEU C-171/06 P of 15.3.2007 – T.I.M.E. ART/OHIM, para. 50.
1725. CJEU C-328/18 P of 4.3.2020 – EUIPO/Equivalenza Manufactory, para. 76, with reference to CJEU C-361/04 P of 12.1.2006 – Ruiz-Picasso and Others/OHIM, para. 21 and 23.
1726. CJEU C-3/03 P of 28.4.2004 – Matratzen Concord/OHIM, para. 32; C-120/04 of 6.10.2005 – Medion, para. 29; C-334/05 P of 12.6.2007 – OHIM/Shaker, para. 41; C-193/06 P of 20.9.2007 – Nestlé/OHIM, para. 35; C-498/07 P of 3.9.2009 – Aceites del Sur-Coosur/OHIM, para. 61; C-532/10 P of 29.6.2011 – adp Gauselmann/OHIM, para. 25; C-67/11 P of 20.10.2011 – DTL Corporación/OHIM, para. 41; C-422/12 P of 30.1.2014 – Industrias Alen/OHIM, para. 43; C-591/12 P of 8.5.2014 – Bimbo/OHIM, para. 22; *see also* CJEU C-235/05 P of 27.4.2006 – L'Oréal/OHIM, para. 46; C-579/08 P of 15.1.2010 – Messer Group/OHIM, para. 71; C-51/09 P of 24.6.2010 – Barbara Becker/OHIM, para. 33; C-177/13 P of 13.2.2014 – Marszałkowski/OHIM, para. 55; C-308/13 P and C-309/13 P of 18.9.2014 – Società Italiana Calzature/OHIM, para. 42; C-466/13 P of 22.10.2014 – Repsol YPF/OHIM, para. 82; C-420/14 P of 5.2.2015 – Jyoti Ceramic Industries/OHIM, para. 26; C-182/14 P of 19.3.2015 – MEGA Brands International/OHIM, para. 32; C-343/14 P of 7.5.2015 – Adler Modemärkte/OHIM, para. 38; C-20/14 of 22.10.2015 – BGW Beratungs-Gesellschaft Wirtschaft, para. 36; C-73/18 P of 7.6.2018 – Cotécnica/EUIPO, paras 5/3 and 6; C-162/17 P of 16.1.2019 – Republic of Poland/EUIPO, para. 42; C-505/17 P of 28.2.2019 – Groupe Léa Nature/EUIPO, para. 36.

Contrary to the submission of the claimant, trade mark law **does not grant** the proprietor of a registered trade mark a **monopoly on the entirety of combinations of his mark** and other verbal or figurative elements.[1727]

On the contrary, the comparison must be made by examining each of the marks in question as a whole, which does not mean that the overall impression conveyed to the relevant public by a composite trade mark may not, in certain circumstances, be **dominated** by one or more of its components.[1728]

That overall assessment of the marks at issue taking into account all of the factors relevant to the case is required even if one of the components of the mark applied for is the **name of the company** seeking registration of the mark.[1729]

The fact that a word mark consists of a **single word** does not preclude one component of the trade mark dominating the overall impression conveyed to the relevant public by the trade mark.[1730]

However, it cannot be deduced from that case law **concerning exceptional situations** that only the distinctive element of a mark composed of a descriptive element and a distinctive element is decisive when assessing the likelihood of confusion.[1731]

It is **only if all the other components of the mark are negligible** that the assessment of the similarity can be carried out solely on the basis of the dominant element.[1732]

1727. CJEU C-324/05 P of 1.6.2006 – Plus Warenhandelsgesellschaft/OHIM, para. 35; unofficial translation.
1728. CJEU C-3/03 P of 28.4.2004 – Matratzen Concord/OHIM, para. 32; C-120/04 of 6.10.2005 – Medion, para. 29; C-498/07 P of 3.9.2009 – Aceites del Sur-Coosur/OHIM, para. 62; C-254/09 P of 2.9.2010 – Calvin Klein/OHIM, para. 56; C-388/10 P of 24.3.2011 – Muñoz Arraiza/OHIM, para. 53; C-67/11 P of 20.10.2011 – DTL Corporación/OHIM, para. 41; C-327/11 P of 6.9.2012 – United States Polo/OHIM, para. 57; C-655/11 P of 21.2.2013 – Seven for all mankind/OHIM, para. 72; C-341/12 P of 21.3.2013 – Mizuno/OHIM, para. 35; C-177/13 P of 13.2.2014 – Marszałkowski/OHIM, para. 55; C-420/14 P of 5.2.2015 – Jyoti Ceramic Industries/OHIM, para. 27; *see also* CJEU C-235/05 P of 27.4.2006 – L'Oréal/OHIM, para. 46; C-204/10 P of 23.11.2010 – Enercon/OHIM, para. 23; C-591/12 P of 8.5.2014 – Bimbo/OHIM, para. 23; C-182/14 P of 19.3.2015 – MEGA Brands International/OHIM, paras 32 and 38; C-33/15 P of 15.10.2015 – Cantina Broglie 1, para. 58; C-34/15 P of 15.10.2015 – Cantina Broglie 1, para. 58.
1729. CJEU C-532/10 P of 29.6.2011 – adp Gauselmann/OHIM, para. 43; *see also* CJEU C-204/10 P of 23.11.2010 – Enercon/OHIM, paras 23 et seqq.
1730. CJEU C-512/04 P of 1.12.2005 – Vitakraft-Werke Wührmann/OHIM, para. 23; unofficial translation; *see also* CJEU C-374/13 P of 10.4.2014 – Metropolis Inmobiliarias y Restauraciones/OHIM, para. 35; C-669/13 P of 21.10.2014 – Mundipharma/OHIM, para. 51.
1731. CJEU C-579/08 P of 15.1.2010 – Messer Group/OHIM, para. 72; C-466/13 P of 22.10.2014 – Repsol YPF/OHIM, para. 83; C-182/14 P of 19.3.2015 – MEGA Brands International/OHIM, para. 38.
1732. CJEU C-334/05 P of 12.6.2007 – OHIM/Shaker, para. 42; C-193/06 P of 20.9.2007 – Nestlé/OHIM, para. 43; C-405/06 P of 24.9.2007 – Torres/OHIM, para. 32; C-498/07 P of 3.9.2009 – Aceites del Sur-Coosur/OHIM, para. 62; C-579/08 P of 15.1.2010 – Messer Group/OHIM, para. 72; C-254/09 P of 2.9.2010 – Calvin Klein/OHIM, para. 56; C-388/10 P of 24.3.2011 – Muñoz Arraiza/OHIM, para. 53; C-532/10 P of 29.6.2011 – adp Gauselmann/OHIM, para. 25; C-306/11 P of 28.6.2012 – XXXLutz Marken/OHIM, para. 40; C-327/11 P of 6.9.2012 – United States Polo/OHIM, para. 57; C-655/11 P of 21.2.2013 – Seven for all mankind/OHIM, para. 72; C-422/12 P of 30.1.2014 – Industrias Alen/OHIM, para. 44; C-591/12 P of 8.5.2014 – Bimbo/OHIM, para. 23; C-308/13 P and C-309/13 P of 18.9.2014 – Società Italiana Calzature/OHIM, para. 43; C-466/13 P of 22.10.2014 – Repsol YPF/OHIM,

The Court did not state that the word element was dominant and that the figurative element was negligible for the overall impression evoked by the mark. Quite to the contrary, the court confined itself to establishing that the word element was not negligible and that the figurative element was not dominant. Now, the fact that an element is not negligible does not mean that it is dominant. Nor may the fact that an element is not dominant lead to the conclusion that it is negligible.[1733]

There is **no rule** that the **word element** of a complex mark is systematically **more distinctive** and dominant **than the figurative element.**[1734]

The presence of the colour red in both trade marks is not sufficient to establish a similarity of the signs.[1735]

It must also be pointed out that, in principle, **even an element which has only a weak distinctive character** may dominate the overall impression of a composite mark or have an independent distinctive role in that mark within the meaning of the case law resulting from the judgment in *Medion*,[1736] since, it may, because of, *inter alia*, its position in the sign or its size, make an impression on consumers and be remembered by them.[1737]

Even if a verbal element should be considered to have a **purely descriptive character**, that character does not preclude that element from being acknowledged as dominant for the purposes of assessing the similarity of the signs at issue.[1738]

On the one hand, the court makes a finding of facts according to which the use of animals for the group of products in question tends to diminish the distinctive quality of the figurative element. On the other hand, it follows from the finding of facts that notwithstanding its lack of dominance, the figurative element does possess an intensity that is far from being negligible when compared with the word element. The court held that the width of the graphic representation of the word element corresponds to that of the figurative element and that the word element occupies quite as important a position as the figurative element.[1739]

The assessment of the Court would amount to the assumption that the visual similarity of a complex mark that is made up of a word element and a figurative element, and whose figurative element possesses the same intensity as or an inferior

---

para. 83; C-420/14 P of 5.2.2015 – Jyoti Ceramic Industries/OHIM, para. 27; C-182/14 P of 19.3.2015 – MEGA Brands International/OHIM, para. 38; C-33/15 P of 15.10.2015 – Cantina Broglie 1, para. 58; C-34/15 P of 15.10.2015 – Cantina Broglie 1, para. 58; C-20/14 of 22.10.2015 – BGW Beratungs-Gesellschaft Wirtschaft, para. 37; C-374/15 P of 28.1.2016 – Harper Hygienics/OHIM, para. 41; C-396/15 P of 17.2.2016 – Shoe Branding Europe/OHIM, para. 40; *see also* CJEU C-341/12 P of 21.3.2013 – Mizuno/OHIM, para. 33; C-515/15 P of 14.4.2016 – Roland/EUIPO, para. 32; C-505/17 P of 28.2.2019 – Groupe Léa Nature/EUIPO, para. 38.

1733. CJEU C-193/06 P of 20.9.2007 – Nestlé/OHIM, para. 44; unofficial translation.

1734. CJEU C-308/13 P and C-309/13 P of 18.9.2014 – Società Italiana Calzature/OHIM, para. 47, with reference to CJEU C-488/06 P of 17.7.2008 – L & D/OHIM, paras 55 and 84.

1735. CJEU C-515/15 P of 14.4.2016 – Roland/EUIPO, para. 45, unofficial translation.

1736. CJEU C-120/04 of 6.10.2005 – Medion.

1737. CJEU C-20/14 of 22.10.2015 – BGW Beratungs-Gesellschaft Wirtschaft, para. 40.

1738. CJEU C-182/14 P of 19.3.2015 – MEGA Brands International/OHIM, para. 34; *see also* CJEU C-388/10 P of 24.3.2011 – Muñoz Arraiza/OHIM, para. 65; C-343/14 P of 7.5.2015 – Adler Modemärkte/OHIM, paras 36–39.

1739. CJEU C-193/06 P of 20.9.2007 – Nestlé/OHIM, para. 45; unofficial translation.

intensity than the word element, could be assessed exclusively on the basis of the similarity of the word elements. Thus, even if both elements were of equal strength, only the word elements would be decisive for determining the visual similarity of the signs.[1740]

It follows that by failing to compare the visual similarity of the signs in question according to the overall impression they evoke, the court has misinterpreted Article 8(1)(b) CTMR and thus erred in law.[1741]

The Court of First Instance, in the context of the analysis of the signs at issue, firstly held that the mark for which registration was sought contained a dominant element comprising the representation of a round dish decorated with lemons. It then inferred that it was not necessary to examine the phonetic or conceptual features of the other elements of that mark. It finally concluded that the dominance of the figurative representation of a round dish decorated with lemons in comparison with the other components of the mark prevented any likelihood of confusion arising from the visual, phonetic or conceptual similarities between the words 'limonchelo' and 'limoncello' which appear in the marks at issue.[1742]

However, in so doing, the Court of First Instance did not carry out a global assessment of the likelihood of confusion of the marks at issue.[1743]

Article 4(1)(b) TMD2008 must be interpreted as meaning that, in the case of identical or similar goods and services, there may be a likelihood of confusion on the part of the relevant public between an earlier mark consisting of a **letter sequence**, which is distinctive and is the dominant element in that mark of average distinctiveness, and a later mark which reproduces that letter sequence and to which is added a descriptive combination of words, the initial letters of which correspond to the letters of that sequence, with the result that that sequence is perceived by that public as the acronym of that combination of words.[1744]

In paragraph 32 of the judgment in *Strigl* and *Securvita*,[1745] the Court pointed out that the three capital letters in each of the signs, namely, 'MMF' and 'NAI', represented the initial letters of the word combinations to which they were attached and that the word combination and the letter sequence, in each case, were intended to clarify each other and to draw attention to the fact that they were linked, each letter sequence being designed to support the public's perception of the word combination, by simplifying its use and by making it easier to remember.[1746]

In that regard, the Court stated, in paragraphs 37 and 38 of that judgment, that if the letter sequences at issue were perceived by the relevant public to be abbreviations of the word combinations with which they were juxtaposed, those sequences could not be more than the sum of all the elements of the mark, taken as a whole, even though

1740. CJEU C-193/06 P of 20.9.2007 – Nestlé/OHIM, para. 46; unofficial translation.
1741. CJEU C-193/06 P of 20.9.2007 – Nestlé/OHIM, para. 47; unofficial translation.
1742. CJEU C-334/05 P of 12.6.2007 – OHIM/Shaker, para. 39; *see also* CJEU C-193/06 P of 20.9.2007 – Nestlé/OHIM, para. 41.
1743. CJEU C-334/05 P of 12.6.2007 – OHIM/Shaker, para. 40.
1744. CJEU C-20/14 of 22.10.2015 – BGW Beratungs-Gesellschaft Wirtschaft, para. 44.
1745. CJEU C-90/11 and C-91/11 of 15.3.2012 – Strigl and Securvita.
1746. CJEU C-20/14 of 22.10.2015 – BGW Beratungs-Gesellschaft Wirtschaft, para. 29.

they might be considered to have distinctive character in themselves. On the contrary, according to the Court, such letter sequences occupied only an 'ancillary position' in relation to the word combination to which they were attached.[1747]

It is apparent from the grounds of the judgment in *Strigl* and *Securvita*[1748] that whether a sign consisting of a letter sequence juxtaposed with a word combination is to be refused registration under Article 3(1)(b) and (c) TMD2008 must be assessed on a case-by-case basis, according to the perception which the relevant public has of the interdependence between the various elements of the sign and of the sign as a whole.[1749]

It follows from the foregoing that, in the light of the different legal context of the cases which gave rise to the judgment in *Strigl* and *Securvita*[1750] and the scope which must be attributed to that judgment, the findings in it are not capable of being applied to proceedings for the purposes of assessing whether there is a similarity between the two marks at issue.[1751]

In the second place, it is necessary to bear in mind the case law according to which the global assessment of the likelihood of confusion must, so far as concerns the visual, phonetic or conceptual similarity of the marks at issue, be based on the overall impression given by the marks, bearing in mind, in particular, their distinctive and dominant elements.[1752]

It is, however, important to point out that the mere fact that the later mark consists of a sign reproducing the letter sequence that constitutes the only word element of the earlier mark and of a combination of words the initial letters of which correspond to that sequence cannot, on its own, preclude a likelihood of confusion with that earlier mark.[1753]

Accordingly, the national court will have to examine, among other factors, whether the links which the relevant public may establish between the letter sequence and the word combination, in particular the possibility that the former may be perceived as an acronym of the latter, are such that that sequence may be perceived and remembered separately by the relevant public in the later mark. Likewise, it will, if necessary, have to assess whether the elements of which the later mark consists, taken as a whole, form a separate logical unit which has a different meaning from that of those elements taken separately.[1754]

In order to establish the likelihood of confusion, it suffices that because the earlier mark still has an **independent distinctive role**, the origin of the goods or services covered by the composite sign is attributed by the public also to the owner of that mark.[1755]

1747. CJEU C-20/14 of 22.10.2015 – BGW Beratungs-Gesellschaft Wirtschaft, para. 30.
1748. CJEU C-90/11 and C-91/11 of 15.3.2012 – Strigl and Securvita.
1749. CJEU C-20/14 of 22.10.2015 – BGW Beratungs-Gesellschaft Wirtschaft, para. 31.
1750. CJEU C-90/11 and C-91/11 of 15.3.2012 – Strigl and Securvita.
1751. CJEU C-20/14 of 22.10.2015 – BGW Beratungs-Gesellschaft Wirtschaft, para. 34.
1752. CJEU C-20/14 of 22.10.2015 – BGW Beratungs-Gesellschaft Wirtschaft, para. 35.
1753. CJEU C-20/14 of 22.10.2015 – BGW Beratungs-Gesellschaft Wirtschaft, para. 42.
1754. CJEU C-20/14 of 22.10.2015 – BGW Beratungs-Gesellschaft Wirtschaft, para. 43.
1755. CJEU C-120/04 of 6.10.2005 – Medion, para. 36; C-591/12 P of 8.5.2014 – Bimbo/OHIM, para. 24.

However, beyond the usual case where the average consumer perceives a mark as a whole, and notwithstanding that the overall impression may be dominated by one or more components of a composite mark, it is quite possible that in a particular case an earlier mark used by a third party in a composite sign including the name of the company of the third party still has an independent distinctive role in the composite sign, without necessarily constituting the dominant element.[1756]

In such a case, the overall impression produced by the composite sign may lead the public to believe that the goods or services at issue derive, at the very least, from companies which are linked economically, in which case the likelihood of confusion must be held to be established.[1757]

The finding that there is a likelihood of confusion should not be subject to the condition that the overall impression produced by the composite sign be dominated by the part of it which is represented by the earlier mark.[1758]

If such a condition were imposed, the owner of the earlier mark would be deprived of the exclusive right conferred by Article 5(1) TMD2008 even where the mark retained an independent distinctive role in the composite sign, but that role was not dominant.[1759]

This would be the case where, for example, the owner of a widely known mark makes use of a composite sign juxtaposing this mark and an earlier mark which is not itself widely known. It would also be the case if the composite sign was made up of the earlier mark and a widely known commercial name. In fact, the overall impression would be, most often, dominated by the widely known mark or commercial name included in the composite sign.[1760]

Thus, contrary to the intention of the Community legislator expressed in the tenth recital in the preamble to the directive, the guarantee of the earlier mark as an indication of origin would not be assured, even though it still had an independent distinctive role in the composite sign.[1761]

Where the goods or services are identical, there may be a likelihood of confusion on the part of the public where the contested sign is composed by juxtaposing the company name of another party and a registered mark which has normal distinctiveness and which, without alone determining the overall impression conveyed by the composite sign, still has an independent distinctive role therein.[1762]

1756. CJEU C-120/04 of 6.10.2005 – Medion, para. 30; C-51/09 P of 24.6.2010 – Barbara Becker/OHIM, para. 34; C-353/09 P of 15.2.2011 – Perfetti Van Melle/OHIM, para. 36; C-327/11 P of 6.9.2012 – United States Polo/OHIM, para. 46; *see also* CJEU C-591/12 P of 8.5.2014 – Bimbo/OHIM, para. 24; C-20/14 of 22.10.2015 – BGW Beratungs-Gesellschaft Wirtschaft, para. 38.
1757. CJEU C-120/04 of 6.10.2005 – Medion, para. 31; C-23/09 P of 22.1.2010 – ecoblue/OHIM, para. 45; C-51/09 P of 24.6.2010 – Barbara Becker/OHIM, para. 34; C-327/11 P of 6.9.2012 – United States Polo/OHIM, para. 46; C-20/14 of 22.10.2015 – BGW Beratungs-Gesellschaft Wirtschaft, para. 38.
1758. CJEU C-120/04 of 6.10.2005 – Medion, para. 32; C-505/17 P of 28.2.2019 – Groupe Léa Nature/EUIPO, para. 47.
1759. CJEU C-120/04 of 6.10.2005 – Medion, para. 33.
1760. CJEU C-120/04 of 6.10.2005 – Medion, para. 34.
1761. CJEU C-120/04 of 6.10.2005 – Medion, para. 35.
1762. CJEU C-120/04 of 6.10.2005 – Medion, para. 37.

None the less, a component of a composite sign does **not retain such an independent distinctive role if**, together with the other component or components of the sign, that component **forms a unit** having a different meaning as compared with the meaning of those components taken separately.[1763]

It is clear, in particular, from the case law subsequent to *Medion*[1764] that the Court of Justice did **not** introduce, in that judgment, **a derogation from the principles governing the assessment of the likelihood of confusion**.[1765]

Although it is possible that, in a part of the EU, **surnames** have, as a general rule, a more distinctive character than forenames, it is appropriate, however, to take account of factors specific to the case and, in particular, the fact that the surname concerned is unusual or, on the contrary, very common, which is likely to have an effect on that distinctive character. That is true of the surname 'Becker' which is common.[1766]

Furthermore, in a composite mark, a surname does not always retain an independent distinctive role merely because it is perceived as a surname. The finding of such a role can only be based on an examination of all the relevant factors of the case.[1767]

Account must also be taken of whether the person who requests that his first name and surname, taken together, be registered as a trade mark is well known since that factor may obviously influence the perception of the mark by the relevant public.[1768]

Furthermore, it must be held that, in a composite mark, a surname does not retain an independent distinctive role in every case solely because it will be perceived as a surname. The finding with respect to such a role may be based only on an examination of all the relevant factors of each case.[1769]

Moreover, the grounds in order to conclude that the marks at issue are conceptually similar, if they were held to be consistent with Article 8(1)(b) CTMR, would result in acknowledging that any surname which constitutes an earlier mark could be effectively relied on to oppose registration of a mark composed of a first name and that surname, even though, for example, the surname was common or the addition of the first name would have an effect, from a conceptual point of view, on the perception by the relevant public of the composite mark.[1770]

In this regard, it has been taken into account that the trade mark ORO is of little distinctive character. Furthermore, it could not be established that the relevant public

1763. CJEU C-591/12 P of 8.5.2014 – Bimbo/OHIM, para. 25; C-20/14 of 22.10.2015 – BGW Beratungs-Gesellschaft Wirtschaft, para. 39; *see also* CJEU C-23/09 P of 22.1.2010 – ecoblue/ OHIM, para. 47; C-51/09 P of 24.6.2010 – Barbara Becker/OHIM, paras 37 and 38; C-353/09 P of 15.2.2011 – Perfetti Van Melle/OHIM, paras 36 and 37.
1764. CJEU C-120/04 of 6.10.2005 – Medion.
1765. CJEU C-591/12 P of 8.5.2014 – Bimbo/OHIM, para. 36.
1766. CJEU C-51/09 P of 24.6.2010 – Barbara Becker/OHIM, para. 36; C-379/12 P of 16.5.2013 – Arav Holding/OHIM, para. 44.
1767. CJEU C-308/13 P and C-309/13 P of 18.9.2014 – Società Italiana Calzature/OHIM, para. 64.
1768. CJEU C-51/09 P of 24.6.2010 – Barbara Becker/OHIM, para. 37; C-449/18 P and C-474/18 P of 17.9.2020 – EUIPO/Messi Cuccittini, para. 47.
1769. CJEU C-51/09 P of 24.6.2010 – Barbara Becker/OHIM, para. 38; C-381/12 P of 6.6.2013 – I Marchi Italiani/OHIM, para. 69.
1770. CJEU C-51/09 P of 24.6.2010 – Barbara Becker/OHIM, para. 39.

assumes that there is a connection between the proprietor of the marks ORO and ORO SAIWA with the origin of the mark 'SELEZIONE ORO Barilla'.[1771]

[6] *Mere association*

The mere association which the public might make between two trade marks as a result of their analogous semantic content is not in itself a sufficient ground for concluding that there is a likelihood of confusion within the meaning of Article 4(1)(b) TMD2008.[1772]

It follows from that wording that the concept of likelihood of association is not an alternative to that of likelihood of confusion, but serves to define its scope. The terms of the provision itself exclude its application where there is no likelihood of confusion on the part of the public.[1773]

[7] *Family or series of marks*

While it is true that, in the case of opposition to an application for registration of a Community trade mark based on the existence of only one earlier trade mark that is not yet subject to an obligation of use, the assessment of the likelihood of confusion is to be carried by comparing the two marks as they were registered, the same does not apply where the opposition is based on the existence of several trade marks possessing common characteristics which make it possible for them to be regarded as part of a 'family' or 'series' of marks.[1774]

The risk that the public might believe that the goods or services in question come from the same undertaking or, as the case may be, from economically linked undertakings constitutes a likelihood of confusion within the meaning of Article 8(1)(b) CTMR. Where there is a 'family' or 'series' of trade marks, the likelihood of confusion results more specifically from the possibility that the consumer may be mistaken as to the provenance or origin of goods or services covered by the trade mark applied for or considers erroneously that that trade mark is part of that family or series of marks.[1775]

No consumer can be expected, in the absence of use of a sufficient number of trade marks capable of constituting a family or a series, to detect a common element in such a family or series and/or to associate with that family or series another trade mark

1771. CJEU C-245/06 P of 9.3.2007 – Saiwa/OHIM, para. 51; unofficial translation.
1772. CJEU C-251/95 of 11.11.1997 – SABEL/Puma, Rudolf Dassler Sport, para. 26.
1773. CJEU C-251/95 of 11.11.1997 – SABEL/Puma, Rudolf Dassler Sport, para. 18; C-3/03 P of 28.4.2004 – Matratzen Concord/OHIM, para. 27; C-354/11 P of 22.3.2012 – Emram/OHIM, para. 79; C-248/18 P of 11.9.2018 – Moscow Confectionery Factory 'Krasnyiy oktyabr'/ EUIPO, paras 6/20 and 7.
1774. CJEU C-234/06 P of 13.9.2007 – Il Ponte Finanziaria/OHIM, para. 62.
1775. CJEU C-234/06 P of 13.9.2007 – Il Ponte Finanziaria/OHIM, para. 63; C-16/06 P of 18.12.2008 – Les Éditions Albert René/OHIM, para. 101; C-552/09 P of 24.3.2011 – Ferrero/OHIM, para. 97; C-317/10 P of 16.6.2011 – Union Investment Privatfonds/OHIM, para. 54; C-553/11 of 25.10.2012 – Rintisch, para. 27; C-270/14 P of 15.10.2015 – Debonair Trading Internacional/ OHIM, para. 32.

containing the same common element. Accordingly, in order for there to be a likelihood that the public may be mistaken as to whether the trade mark applied for belongs to a 'family' or 'series', the earlier trade marks which are part of that 'family' or 'series' must be present on the market.[1776]

The General Court justified that approach by the consideration that if the likelihood of confusion with regard to a family of marks results from the possibility that the relevant public may believe that a mark in respect of which registration is sought is part of the same family as that formed by earlier trade marks, it is then necessary, in order for that likelihood of confusion to exist, that **the mark concerned should have characteristics which might suggest that it belongs to the family** of marks in question.[1777]

Such an approach cannot be regarded as incorrect in itself in so far as, in the present case, it initially consisted of ascertaining whether there was an element enabling the mark applied for to be associated with the family of marks relied on in order subsequently to examine, in the context of a global assessment, whether consumers were likely to establish a connection between that mark and that family of marks, and whether there was a possibility that consumers might perceive the former as a new member of the latter.[1778]

[8] Similarity of the goods or services

It is important to stress that, for the purposes of applying Article 4(1)(b) TMD2008, even where a mark is identical to another with a highly distinctive character, it is still necessary to adduce evidence of similarity between the goods or services covered. In contrast to Article 4(4)(a) TMD2008, which expressly refers to the situation in which the goods or services are not similar, Article 4(1)(b) provides that the likelihood of confusion presupposes that the goods or services covered are identical or similar.[1779]

In assessing the similarity of the goods or services concerned, all the relevant factors relating to those goods or services themselves should be taken into account. Those **factors** include, *inter alia*, their nature, their end users and their method of use and whether they are in competition with each other or are complementary.[1780]

1776. CJEU C-234/06 P of 13.9.2007 – Il Ponte Finanziaria/OHIM, para. 64; C-553/11 of 25.10.2012 – Rintisch, para. 28.
1777. CJEU C-270/14 P of 15.10.2015 – Debonair Trading Internacional/OHIM, para. 34.
1778. CJEU C-270/14 P of 15.10.2015 – Debonair Trading Internacional/OHIM, para. 35.
1779. CJEU C-39/97 of 29.9.1998 – Canon Kabushiki Kaisha/Metro-Goldwyn-Mayer, para. 22; C-196/06 P of 9.3.2007 – Alecansan/OHIM, para. 24, 37, 44.
1780. CJEU C-39/97 of 29.9.1998 – Canon Kabushiki Kaisha/Metro-Goldwyn-Mayer, para. 23; C-416/04 P of 11.5.2006 – Sunrider/OHIM, para. 85; C-196/06 P of 9.3.2007 – Alecansan/OHIM, para. 28; C-412/05 P of 26.4.2007 – Alcon/OHIM (II), para. 72; C-16/06 P of 18.12.2008 – Les Éditions Albert René/OHIM, para. 65; C-394/08 P of 3.6.2009 – Zipcar/OHIM, para. 60; C-418/10 P of 28.3.2011 – Herhof-Verwaltungsgesellschaft/OHIM, para. 41; C-411/13 P of 8.5.2014 – OHIM/Sanco, paras 39 and 73; C-50/15 P of 21.1.2016 – Hesse/OHIM, para. 21; C-480/15 P of 14.4.2016 – KS Sports IPCo/EUIPO, para. 69; C-673/15 P to C-676/15 P of 20.9.2017 – The Tea Board/EUIPO, para. 48; C-533/18 P of 8.1.2019 – Emcur Gesundheitsmittel aus Bad Ems/EUIPO, paras 5/13 and 6; C-809/18 P of 11.11.2020 – EUIPO/John Mills, para. 100.

The destination, the distribution channels of the goods, and whether they are in competition with each other are factors that must be taken into account by the court in assessing the similarity of goods.[1781]

Although the **complementary nature of the goods** at issue represents only one factor amongst several others – such as the nature, the method of use or the distribution channels of those goods – in the light of which the similarity of the goods can be assessed, the fact remains that it is an autonomous criterion capable of being the sole basis for the existence of such a similarity.[1782]

The goods or services which are complementary are those between which there is a close connection, in the sense that one is indispensable or important for the use of the other, in such a way that consumers may think that the responsibility for the production of those goods or supply of those services lies with the same undertaking.[1783]

The assessment of whether the goods and services are complementary therefore requires the nature of the relationship or link between them to be specified, by examining whether the use of those goods is indispensable or important for the purposes of supplying those services and, vice-versa, whether the supply of those services is indispensable or important for the purpose of using those goods.[1784]

The question of whether the relevant public is likely to think that one and the same undertaking is alone responsible for supplying the services at issue and producing the goods concerned does not, according to that case law, constitute a relevant factor that is capable of determining the relationship between those goods and those services, and which it would therefore be necessary to take into account for the purposes of assessing whether they are complementary. As is clear from the wording of that case law and, in particular, from the use of the expression 'in such a way that', the likelihood of confusion in the mind of the consumers arises as a result of the goods and services being complementary and thus comes under the very definition of the concept of 'complementary goods or services'.[1785]

In accordance with that case law, the Court of First Instance found that the goods 'herbal and vitamin beverages', for which registration is sought, and the goods 'concentrated fruit juices', for which genuine use of the earlier trade mark has been established, are intended for end-consumers. Likewise, it held that those goods share the same purpose, that of quenching thirst, are to a large extent in competition, have the same nature and method of use – both are non-alcoholic beverages normally drunk cold – and that the fact that their ingredients differ does not affect the finding that they are interchangeable because they are intended to meet an identical need.[1786]

1781. CJEU C-374/15 P of 28.1.2016 – Harper Hygienics/OHIM, para. 30; unofficial translation.
1782. CJEU C-50/15 P of 21.1.2016 – Hesse/OHIM, para. 23.
1783. CJEU C-533/18 P of 8.1.2019 – Emcur Gesundheitsmittel aus Bad Ems/EUIPO, paras 5/14 and 6.
1784. CJEU C-533/18 P of 8.1.2019 – Emcur Gesundheitsmittel aus Bad Ems/EUIPO, paras 5/15 and 6.
1785. CJEU C-533/18 P of 8.1.2019 – Emcur Gesundheitsmittel aus Bad Ems/EUIPO, paras 5/16 and 6.
1786. CJEU C-416/04 P of 11.5.2006 – Sunrider/OHIM, para. 86.

In complaining that the Court of First Instance did not take into account the nature of the goods in question in order to assess the similarities between them, the appellant relies on an incorrect interpretation of the judgment under appeal. The Court of First Instance indeed considered whether or not the goods were similar, examining, *inter alia*, their respective natures.[1787]

As regards the fact that the particular circumstances in which the goods in question were marketed were not taken into account, the Court of First Instance was fully entitled to hold that since these may vary in time and depending on the wishes of the proprietors of the opposing marks, it is inappropriate to take those circumstances into account in the prospective analysis of the likelihood of confusion between those marks.[1788]

It follows that, for the purposes of the examination of the similarity of the goods or services at issue, it is neither for the General Court nor the Board of Appeal to first identify, from each of the categories or each of the types of goods or services in respect of which registration of a trade mark is applied for, the specific goods or services within those categories or types which could be marketed by the applicant. That examination must therefore, as to the goods or services for which registration of a trade mark is applied for, be performed in the light of the wording of the list of goods or services for which registration is applied for as it appears in the registration application or, where appropriate, as delimited in the course of the proceedings.[1789]

A motor vehicle and a scale model of that vehicle are not similar products.[1790]

In so far as eBay used keywords corresponding to L'Oréal trade marks to promote its own service of making an online marketplace available to sellers and buyers of products, that use was not made in relation to goods or services similar to those for which the trade mark is registered within the meaning of paragraph 1(b) of those articles.[1791]

[9] Distinctive character

In determining the distinctive character of a mark and, accordingly, in assessing whether it is highly distinctive, the national court must make an overall assessment of the greater or lesser capacity of the mark to identify the goods or services for which it has been registered as coming from a particular undertaking, and thus to distinguish those goods or services from those of other undertakings.[1792]

In making that **assessment**, account should be taken, in particular, of the inherent characteristics of the mark, including the fact that it does or does not contain an element descriptive of the goods or services for which it has been registered; the

1787. CJEU C-416/04 P of 11.5.2006 – Sunrider/OHIM, para. 87.
1788. CJEU C-171/06 P of 15.3.2007 – T.I.M.E. ART/OHIM, para. 59; C-354/11 P of 22.3.2012 – Emram/OHIM, para. 73; C-480/15 P of 14.4.2016 – KS Sports IPCo/EUIPO, para. 57; C-437/16 P of 5.10.2017 – Wolf Oil/EUIPO, para. 56.
1789. CJEU C-480/15 P of 14.4.2016 – KS Sports IPCo/EUIPO, para. 57.
1790. CJEU C-48/05 of 25.1.2007 – Adam Opel, para. 34.
1791. CJEU C-324/09 of 12.7.2011 – L'Oréal, para. 89.
1792. CJEU C-342/97 of 22.6.1999 – Lloyd Schuhfabrik Meyer, para. 22, 28.

market share held by the mark; how intensive, geographically widespread and longstanding use of the mark has been; the amount invested by the undertaking in promoting the mark; the proportion of the relevant section of the public which, because of the mark, identifies the goods or services as originating from a particular undertaking; and statements from chambers of commerce and industry or other trade and professional associations.[1793]

The determination of distinctiveness depends on the inherent characteristics of the trade mark, including the presence or absence of elements that are descriptive of the goods or services for which it has been registered as a mark.[1794]

The descriptive, non-distinctive or weakly distinctive elements of a complex trade mark, whether or not mentioned in a disclaimer such as that at issue in the main proceedings, generally have less weight in the analysis of the similarity between the signs than the elements of greater distinctiveness, which are also more able to dominate the overall impression created by the mark.[1795]

It follows that it is not possible to state in general terms, for example, by referring to given **percentages** relating to the degree of recognition attained by the mark within the relevant section of the public, when a mark has a strong distinctive character.[1796]

In order to determine the scope of protection of a trade mark which has been lawfully acquired on the basis of its distinctive character, the national court must take into account the perception of the public concerned at the **time** when the sign, the use of which infringes that trade mark, began to be used.[1797]

The case law of the Court of Justice[1798] shows that account may be taken of evidence which, although subsequent to the date of filing the application, enables the drawing of conclusions on the situation as it was on that date.[1799]

The proprietor's right to protection of his mark from infringement is neither genuine nor effective if account may not be taken of the perception of the public concerned at the time when the sign, the use of which infringes the mark in question, began to be used.[1800]

If the likelihood of confusion were assessed at a time after the sign in question began to be used, the user of that sign might take undue advantage of his own unlawful behaviour by alleging that the product had become less renowned, a matter for which he himself was responsible or to which he himself contributed.[1801]

1793. CJEU C-342/97 of 22.6.1999 – Lloyd Schuhfabrik Meyer, para. 23, 28; *see also* CJEU C-115/19 P of 11.6.2020 – China Construction Bank/EUIPO, para. 72.
1794. CJEU C-705/17 of 12.6.2019 – Patent- och registreringsverket/Hansson, para. 50, with reference to CJEU C-342/97 of 22.6.1999 – Lloyd Schuhfabrik Meyer, para. 20, 22 and 23.
1795. CJEU C-705/17 of 12.6.2019 – Patent- och registreringsverket/Hansson, para. 53, with reference to CJEU C-251/95 of 11.11.1997 – SABEL/Puma, Rudolf Dassler Sport, para. 23; C-235/05 P of 27.4.2006 – L'Oréal/OHIM, para. 43.
1796. CJEU C-342/97 of 22.6.1999 – Lloyd Schuhfabrik Meyer, para. 24, 28.
1797. CJEU C-145/05 of 27.4.2006 – Levi Strauss, para. 20.
1798. CJEU C-192/03 P of 5.10.2004 – ALCON/OHIM (I), para. 41.
1799. CJEU C-488/06 P of 17.7.2008 – L & D/OHIM, para. 71; *see also* CJEU C-217/13 and 218/13 of 19.6.2014 – Oberbank, para. 60.
1800. CJEU C-145/05 of 27.4.2006 – Levi Strauss, para. 17.
1801. CJEU C-145/05 of 27.4.2006 – Levi Strauss, para. 18.

Article 12(2)(a) TMD2008 provides that a trade mark is liable to revocation if, after the date on which it was registered, in consequence of acts or inactivity of the proprietor, it has become the common name in the trade for a product or service in respect of which it is registered. Thus, by balancing the interests of the proprietor against those of his competitors in the availability of signs, the legislator considered, in adopting this provision, that the loss of that mark's distinctive character can be relied on against the proprietor thereof only where that loss is due to his action or inaction. Therefore, as long as this is not the case, and particularly when the loss of the distinctive character is linked to the activity of a third party using a sign which infringes the mark, the proprietor must continue to enjoy protection.[1802]

A high level of distinctiveness allegedly acquired by earlier mark and, accordingly, the reputation allegedly enjoyed by the marks have to be established sufficiently by the material submitted during the administrative procedure.[1803]

There is no rule according to which the **absence of a conceptual link between the mark and the goods or services** covered by it automatically confers to this mark an intrinsic distinctive character by nature in order to protect it in a more extensive way.[1804]

Correctly, the Court of First Instance did consider, after a **factual assessment** which may not be reviewed by the Court in the context of an appeal, that the sign PICASSO is devoid of any highly distinctive character per se with respect to motor vehicles.[1805]

The argument that the distinctiveness of the earlier mark should, having regard, in particular, to Article 66(2) CTMR, be assessed differently where the earlier mark is an **EU collective mark** cannot be accepted.[1806]

[10] Principle of the free movement of goods

Articles 30 and 36 of the EEC Treaty[1807] do not lay down any strict interpretative criterion for the concept of risk of confusion.[1808]

Under the case law of the Court of Justice, the Treaty does not affect the existence of rights recognized by the legislation of a Member State in matters of intellectual property, although the exercise of those rights may none the less, depending on the circumstances, be restricted.[1809]

1802. CJEU C-145/05 of 27.4.2006 – Levi Strauss, para. 19; *see also* CJEU C-102/07 of 10.4.2008 – adidas/Marca Mode, para. 24; C-409/12 of 6.3.2014 – Backaldrin Österreich The Kornspitz Company, para. 32.
1803. CJEU C-388/10 P of 24.3.2011 – Muñoz Arraiza/OHIM, para. 47; unofficial translation based on CFI T-8/03 of 13.12.2004 – El Corte Inglés, para. 73.
1804. CJEU C-379/12 P of 16.5.2013 – Arav Holding/OHIM, para. 71; unofficial translation.
1805. CJEU C-361/04 P of 12.1.2006 – Ruiz-Picasso and Others/OHIM, para. 32.
1806. CJEU C-766/18 P of 5.3.2018 – Foundation for the Protection of the Traditional Cheese of Cyprus named Halloumi, para. 71.
1807. Articles 28, 30 EC.
1808. CJEU C-317/91 of 30.11.1993 – Deutsche Renault/AUDI, para. 32.
1809. CJEU C-3/03 P of 28.4.2004 – Matratzen Concord/OHIM, para. 40; translation according to EuG T-6/01, 23.10.2002 – MATRATZEN Markt CONCORD, para. 54.

The principle of the free movement of goods does not prohibit a Member State from registering, as a national trade mark, a sign which, in the **language of another Member State**, is descriptive of the goods or services concerned, nor, in the case of likelihood of confusion between the national trade mark and the Community trade mark applied for, prohibit the owner of such trade mark from filing a notice of opposition against the registration of the Community trade mark.[1810]

[11] Proof

The individual assessment of each sign, as required by the settled case law of the Court of Justice, must be made in the light of the particular circumstances of the case and **cannot** therefore be regarded as being **subject to general presumptions**. It is clear, in particular, from the case law subsequent to *Medion*[1811] that the Court of Justice did not introduce, in that judgment, a derogation from the principles governing the assessment of the likelihood of confusion.[1812]

The reputation of a mark does not give grounds for presuming the existence of a likelihood of confusion simply because of the existence of a likelihood of association in the strict sense.[1813]

Article 5(1)(b) TMD2008 cannot be interpreted as meaning that where a trade mark has a particularly distinctive character, either per se or because of the reputation it enjoys with the public, and a third party, without the consent of the proprietor of the mark, uses, in the course of trade in goods or services which are identical with, or similar to, those for which the trade mark is registered, a sign which so closely corresponds to the mark as to give rise to the possibility of its being associated with that mark, the exclusive right enjoyed by the proprietor entitles him to prevent the use of the sign by that third party if the distinctive character of the mark is such that the possibility of such association giving rise to confusion cannot be ruled out.[1814]

[12] Relevance of a notice excluding a likelihood of confusion

That conclusion is not affected by the presence on Mr Reed's stall of the notice stating that the goods at issue in the main proceedings are not official Arsenal FC products. Even on the assumption that such a notice may be relied on by a third party as a defence to an action for trade mark infringement, there is a clear possibility in the present case that some consumers, in particular if they come across the goods after they have been sold by Mr Reed and taken away from the stall where the notice appears,

1810. CJEU C-3/03 P of 28.4.2004 – Matratzen Concord/OHIM, para. 42; unofficial translation.
1811. CJEU C-120/04 of 6.10.2005 – Medion.
1812. CJEU C-591/12 P of 8.5.2014 – Bimbo/OHIM, para. 36; C-182/16 P of 26.7.2017 – Meica Ammerländische Fleischwarenfabrik Fritz Meinen/EUIPO, para. 59; C-705/17 of 12.6.2019 – Patent- och registreringsverket/Hansson, para. 54.
1813. CJEU C-425/98 of 22.6.2000 – Marca Mode, para. 41.
1814. CJEU C-425/98 of 22.6.2000 – Marca Mode, para. 42.

may interpret the sign as designating Arsenal FC as the undertaking of origin of the goods.[1815]

[13] *Irrelevance of a disclaimer*

It follows from all the above considerations that Article 4(1)(b) TMD2008 must be interpreted as precluding national legislation making provision for a disclaimer whose effect would be to exclude an element of a complex trade mark, referred to in that disclaimer, from the global analysis of the relevant factors for showing the existence of a likelihood of confusion within the meaning of that provision, or to attribute to such an element, in advance and permanently, limited importance in that analysis.[1816]

Neither Article 5(1)(b) TMD2008, Article 4(1)(b) TMD2008 nor any other provisions of the TMD2008 contain an obligation for Member States to introduce, or a prohibition on their introducing, provisions in their national law under which the registration of a sign as a trade mark may be accompanied by a disclaimer. Nor do those provisions specify the effects of such a disclaimer on the examination of the likelihood of confusion within the meaning of that directive.[1817]

In those circumstances, it must be stated that the Member States in principle remain free to lay down provisions in their national law allowing disclaimers to be recorded at the time of registration of signs as trade marks, whether those disclaimers are entered voluntarily by the applicant or at the request of the national authority with competence for registration, provided that the disclaimers do not impair the effectiveness of the provisions of TMD2008, in particular the protection given to proprietors of earlier trade marks against the registration of trade marks liable to create a likelihood of confusion on the part of consumers or end users.[1818]

In addition, such disclaimers must not have the effect of calling in question the objectives pursued by TMD2008, referred to in recitals 8 and 10 of the directive, namely to ensure that the conditions for obtaining a registered trade mark are, in general, identical in all Member States, and to guarantee equal protection of trade marks under the legal systems of all the Member States.[1819]

In the present case, the referring court sets out three possible effects of a disclaimer, as provided for by national law, on the analysis of the likelihood of confusion within the meaning of Article 4(1)(b) TMD2008. According to that court, a first interpretation of national law would be that the element of a complex mark that is the subject of such a disclaimer is excluded from the analysis of the likelihood of confusion. A second interpretation of that law would be that such an element is indeed

1815. CJEU C-206/01 of 12.11.2002 – Arsenal Football Club, para. 57; *see also* CJEU C-245/02 of 16.11.2004 – Anheuser-Busch, para. 60.
1816. CJEU C-705/17 of 12.6.2019 – Patent- och registreringsverket/Hansson, para. 62.
1817. CJEU C-705/17 of 12.6.2019 – Patent- och registreringsverket/Hansson, para. 36.
1818. CJEU C-705/17 of 12.6.2019 – Patent- och registreringsverket/Hansson, para. 37.
1819. CJEU C-705/17 of 12.6.2019 – Patent- och registreringsverket/Hansson, para. 38, with reference to CJEU C-348/04 of 26.4.2007 – Boehringer Ingelheim and Others (II), para. 58 seq.; C-217/13 and 218/13 of 19.6.2014 – Oberbank, para. 66 seq.; C-482/09 of 22.9.2011 – Budějovický Budvar, para. 30 and 32.

taken into account in that analysis, but its importance for that purpose must be limited, even if it is in reality the distinctive and dominant element of the trade mark. A third interpretation would, in substance, be that in the analysis of the likelihood of confusion account must be taken of such an element in a manner consistent with the principles applicable to that analysis identified in the settled case law of the Court.[1820]

On this point, it must be recalled that the risk that the public might believe that the goods or services in question come from the same undertaking or, as the case may be, from economically linked undertakings, constitutes a likelihood of confusion within the meaning of Article 4(1)(b) TMD2008.[1821]

According to settled case law of the Court, the existence of a likelihood of confusion depends on numerous elements, in particular the recognition of the trade mark on the market, the association which can be made with the used or registered sign, and the degree of similarity between the trade mark and the sign and between the goods or services identified. The likelihood of confusion must therefore be appreciated globally, taking into account all the relevant factors of the particular case.[1822]

In the light of those principles and of all the case law, it must be concluded, in the first place, that a disclaimer provided for by national law whose effect was to exclude an element of a complex trade mark, mentioned in the disclaimer, from the analysis of the relevant factors for establishing the existence of a likelihood of confusion within the meaning of Article 4(1)(b) TMD2008 because that element is descriptive or not distinctive would not be compatible with the requirements of that provision.[1823]

Such an exclusion could lead to an incorrect assessment both of the similarity between the signs at issue and of the distinctiveness of the earlier trade mark, which would lead to a distorted global assessment of the likelihood of confusion within the meaning of Article 4(1)(b) TMD2008, all the more so as those factors are interdependent, that interdependence being directed to bringing the assessment of the likelihood of confusion into line as far as possible with the actual perception of the relevant public.[1824]

As regards, first, the assessment of the similarity between the signs at issue, it should be recalled that it cannot be confined to taking one sole component of a complex trade mark and comparing it with another mark. On the contrary, the comparison must be made by examining each of the marks in question as a whole, taking account in particular of their distinctive and dominant elements.[1825]

It is therefore necessary in each individual case to analyse the components of a sign and their relative weight in the perception of the public, in order to determine in the light of the particular circumstances of the case the overall impression made on the public by the signs at issue. It cannot therefore be considered in advance and in general

1820. CJEU C-705/17 of 12.6.2019 – Patent- och registreringsverket/Hansson, para. 39.
1821. CJEU C-705/17 of 12.6.2019 – Patent- och registreringsverket/Hansson, para. 40, with further proof.
1822. CJEU C-705/17 of 12.6.2019 – Patent- och registreringsverket/Hansson, para. 41, with further proof.
1823. CJEU C-705/17 of 12.6.2019 – Patent- och registreringsverket/Hansson, para. 46.
1824. CJEU C-705/17 of 12.6.2019 – Patent- och registreringsverket/Hansson, para. 47.
1825. CJEU C-705/17 of 12.6.2019 – Patent- och registreringsverket/Hansson, para. 48.

that the descriptive elements of signs at issue must be excluded from the assessment of their similarity.[1826]

As regards, second, the distinctiveness of the earlier trade mark, it follows from the Court's case law that the determination of distinctiveness depends on the inherent characteristics of the trade mark, including the presence or absence of elements that are descriptive of the goods or services for which it has been registered as a mark.[1827]

The power of a trade mark to identify the goods or services for which it has been registered as a mark as coming from a particular undertaking must be assessed in relation to the sign as a whole, and hence in the light of all its components, so that the exclusion of one of the elements of the earlier trade mark from the analysis of the distinctiveness of that mark may have an effect on the extent of protection of that mark.[1828]

It must be stated, in the second place, that a disclaimer provided for in national law whose effect were to attribute, in advance and permanently, a lack of distinctiveness to the element of a complex trade mark mentioned by it, so that the element has only limited importance in the analysis of the likelihood of confusion within the meaning of Article 4(1)(b) TMD2008, would also be incompatible with the requirements of that provision.[1829]

In this respect, it must be observed, first, that the descriptive, non-distinctive or weakly distinctive elements of a complex trade mark, whether or not mentioned in a disclaimer such as that at issue in the main proceedings, generally have less weight in the analysis of the similarity between the signs than the elements of greater distinctiveness, which are also more able to dominate the overall impression created by the mark.[1830]

However, the Court has held that the individual assessment of each sign for the purpose of determining the overall impression produced by it, as required by the Court's settled case law, must be made in the light of the particular circumstances of the case and cannot be regarded as being subject to general presumptions.[1831]

Second, where the earlier trade mark and the sign whose registration is sought coincide in an element that is weakly distinctive or descriptive with regard to the goods or services at issue, the global assessment of the likelihood of confusion within the meaning of Article 4(1)(b) TMD2008 will admittedly not often lead to a finding that that likelihood exists. However, it follows from the Court's case law that a finding that a

1826. CJEU C-705/17 of 12.6.2019 – Patent- och registreringsverket/Hansson, para. 49, with further proof.
1827. CJEU C-705/17 of 12.6.2019 – Patent- och registreringsverket/Hansson, para. 50, with reference to CJEU C-342/97 of 22.6.1999 – Lloyd Schuhfabrik Meyer, para. 20, 22 and 23.
1828. CJEU C-705/17 of 12.6.2019 – Patent- och registreringsverket/Hansson, para. 51.
1829. CJEU C-705/17 of 12.6.2019 – Patent- och registreringsverket/Hansson, para. 52.
1830. CJEU C-705/17 of 12.6.2019 – Patent- och registreringsverket/Hansson, para. 53, with reference to CJEU C-251/95 of 11.11.1997 – SABEL/Puma, Rudolf Dassler Sport, para. 23; C-235/05 P of 27.4.2006 – L'Oréal/OHIM, para. 43.
1831. CJEU C-705/17 of 12.6.2019 – Patent- och registreringsverket/Hansson, para. 54, with reference to CJEU C-591/12 P of 8.5.2014 – Bimbo/OHIM, para. 36.

likelihood of confusion exists cannot, because of the interdependence of the relevant factors, be ruled out in advance and in any event.[1832]

It follows from the above that the attribution to an element of a complex trade mark, mentioned in a disclaimer, of non-distinctiveness and hence of limited weight in the global assessment of the likelihood of confusion within the meaning of Article 4(1)(b) TMD2008 could indeed correspond in some situations to the relevant public's perception of the signs at issue. However, it cannot be considered that that will necessarily be so in every case, so that a disclaimer having that effect could lead to the registration of signs liable to produce a likelihood of confusion on the part of the public within the meaning of that provision.[1833]

In the third place, the interpretation set out above cannot be called into question by the fact that the element mentioned in the disclaimer at issue in the main proceedings is, under national law and because of its descriptive character, excluded from the protection granted to a registered trade mark, so that taking it into account in the analysis of the relevant factors for finding a likelihood of confusion within the meaning of Article 4(1)(b) TMD2008 would allow it to enjoy a protection which it cannot have in the system of that directive.[1834]

A finding of a likelihood of confusion leads solely to the protection of a certain combination of elements without, however, a descriptive element which forms part of that combination being protected as such. Consequently, the proprietor of a complex trade mark cannot in any event claim an exclusive right solely in one element of the trade mark, whether or not it is referred to in a disclaimer provided for by national law.[1835]

Moreover, TMD2008 provides sufficient guarantees to ensure that signs consisting exclusively of signs or indications that are descriptive of categories of goods or services for which registration is sought are, pursuant to Article 3(1)(c), not registered or are declared invalid, and may thus be freely used by other economic operators.[1836]

In addition, it follows from Article 6(1)(b) TMD2008 that, where a sign is validly registered as a trade mark, the exclusive right conferred by the mark does not allow its proprietor to prohibit a third party from using in the course of trade descriptive indications for the goods and services concerned, subject to compliance with certain conditions.[1837]

Furthermore, it must be observed that that interpretation is in line with the objectives of the TMD2008 referred to above, in so far as it aims to ensure that a registered national trade mark is protected against a likelihood of confusion in

1832. CJEU C-705/17 of 12.6.2019 – Patent- och registreringsverket/Hansson, para. 55, with further proof; C-702/18 P of 18.6.2020 – Przedsiębiorstwo Produkcyjno-Handlowe 'Primart' Marek Łukasiewicz/EUIPO, para. 53.
1833. CJEU C-705/17 of 12.6.2019 – Patent- och registreringsverket/Hansson, para. 56.
1834. CJEU C-705/17 of 12.6.2019 – Patent- och registreringsverket/Hansson, para. 57.
1835. CJEU C-705/17 of 12.6.2019 – Patent- och registreringsverket/Hansson, para. 58, with reference to CJEU C-579/08 P of 15.1.2010 – Messer Group/OHIM, para. 73; C-422/12 P of 30.1.2014 – Industrias Alen/OHIM, para. 45.
1836. CJEU C-705/17 of 12.6.2019 – Patent- och registreringsverket/Hansson, para. 59.
1837. CJEU C-705/17 of 12.6.2019 – Patent- och registreringsverket/Hansson, para. 60, with further proof.

accordance with the same criteria and thus in a uniform manner in all the Member States, having regard in particular to the fact that numerous Member States do not provide for the possibility of registering signs as trade marks with such disclaimers and that the conditions of recording those disclaimers and the effects of the disclaimers may vary between the legal systems of the Member States.[1838]

[F] Trade mark with reputation

The wording of Articles 4(4)(a) and 5(2) TMD2008 is essentially identical and is designed to give trade marks with a reputation the same protection.[1839]

The Court points out in limine that the question will be examined below solely in the light of Article 5(2) TMD2008, but that the interpretation reached at the end of that examination will apply *mutatis mutandis* to Article 4(4)(a) TMD2008.[1840]

It should be recalled that, unlike Article 5(1) TMD2008, Article 5(2) TMD2008 does not require Member States to provide in their national law for the protection to which it refers. It merely permits them to provide such protection. When that power has been used, marks with a reputation thus benefit from the protection under both Article 5(1) TMD2008 and Article 5(2) TMD2008.[1841]

Article 5(2) TMD2008 allows **wider form of protection** to be given to marks with a reputation than that conferred under Article 5(1).[1842]

It is apparent from the wording of Article 8(5) CTMR that the application of that provision is subject to **three cumulative conditions** that, first, the marks at issue must be identical or similar; second, the earlier mark cited in opposition must have a reputation; and, third, there must be a risk that the use without due cause of the trade mark applied for would take unfair advantage of, or be detrimental to, the distinctive character or the repute of the earlier mark.[1843]

The condition that the signs at issue must be identical or similar is common to Article 8(1)(b) and Article 8(5) CTMR.[1844]

The provision covers, *inter alia*, the situation in which a third party uses signs corresponding to such trade marks in relation to goods or services which are not similar to the goods or services for which those marks are registered.[1845]

1838. CJEU C-705/17 of 12.6.2019 – Patent- och registreringsverket/Hansson, para. 61.
1839. CJEU C-252/07 of 27.11.2008 – Intel Corporation, para. 24.
1840. CJEU C-292/00 of 9.1.2003 – Davidoff, para. 17; *see also* CJEU C-252/07 of 27.11.2008 – Intel Corporation, para. 25.
1841. CJEU C-292/00 of 9.1.2003 – Davidoff, para. 18.
1842. CJEU C-292/00 of 9.1.2003 – Davidoff, para. 19; C-252/07 of 27.11.2008 – Intel Corporation, para. 26; C-487/07 of 18.6.2009 – L'Oréal, para. 34; C-324/09 of 12.7.2011 – L'Oréal, para. 90; C-65/12 of 6.2.2014 – Leidseplein Beheer, para. 33; C-85/16 P and C-86/16 P of 30.5.2018 – Kenzo Tsujimoto/EUIPO, para. 89.
1843. CJEU C-548/14 P of 17.9.2015 – Arnoldo Mondadori Editore/OHIM, para. 54; C-603/14 P of 10.12.2015 – El Corte Inglés/OHIM, para. 38; C-564/16 P of 28.6.2018 – EUIPO/Puma, para. 54; C-155/18 P to C-158/18 P of 4.3.2020 – Tulliallan Burlington/EUIPO, para. 66.
1844. CJEU C-603/14 P of 10.12.2015 – El Corte Inglés/OHIM, para. 38.
1845. CJEU C-324/09 of 12.7.2011 – L'Oréal, para. 90.

Protection is stronger for the goods and services to which it applies in that the proprietor may prevent the use of a sign which is identical with or similar to his mark for goods and services which are not similar to those in respect of which the mark is registered, that is, in situations where there is no protection under Article 5(1) TMD2008 since that provision applies only where goods or services are identical or similar.[1846]

This stronger protection is given when the use of the sign without due cause takes unfair advantage of, or is detrimental to, the distinctive character or the repute of the mark. This is thus specific **protection against impairment of the distinctive character or repute of the ma**rks in question.[1847]

In that regard, it must be noted at the outset that, unlike Article 5(1)(b) TMD2008, which is designed to apply only if there exists a likelihood of confusion on the part of the public, Article 5(2) TMD2008 establishes, for the benefit of trade marks with a reputation, a form of protection whose implementation does not require the existence of such a likelihood. Article 5(2) applies to situations in which the specific condition of the protection consists of a use of the sign in question without due cause which takes unfair advantage of, or is detrimental to, the distinctive character or the repute of the trade mark.[1848]

Where a trade mark is registered for motor vehicles – in respect of which it is well known – the affixing by a third party, without authorization from the trade mark proprietor, of a sign identical to that trade mark on scale models of vehicles bearing that trade mark, in order faithfully to reproduce those vehicles, and the marketing of those scale models constitute, within the meaning of Article 5(2) TMD2008, a use which the proprietor of the trade mark is entitled to prevent – where the protection defined in that provision has been introduced into national law – if, without due cause, use of that sign takes unfair advantage of, or is detrimental to, the distinctive character or the repute of the trade mark as a trade mark registered for motor vehicles.[1849]

[1] Trade mark with reputation

Article 5(2) TMD2008 is to be interpreted as meaning that, in order to enjoy protection extending to non-similar products or services, a registered trade mark must be known by a significant part of the public concerned by the products or services which it covers. In the Benelux territory, it is sufficient for the registered trade mark to be known by a **significant part of the public** concerned in a substantial part of that territory, which part may consist of a part of one of the countries composing that territory.[1850]

1846. CJEU C-292/00 of 9.1.2003 – Davidoff, para. 20.
1847. CJEU C-292/00 of 9.1.2003 – Davidoff, para. 21.
1848. CJEU C-408/01 of 23.10.2003 – Adidas-Salomon and Adidas Benelux, para. 27; C-102/07 of 10.4.2008 – adidas/Marca Mode, para. 40; C-252/07 of 27.11.2008 – Intel Corporation, para. 26; *see also* CJEU C-487/07 of 18.6.2009 – L'Oréal, para. 36.
1849. CJEU C-48/05 of 25.1.2007 – Adam Opel, para. 37.
1850. CJEU C-375/97 of 14.9.1999 – General Motors, para. 31; C-115/19 P of 11.6.2020 – China Construction Bank/EUIPO, para. 57.

As regards the provisions concerning the requirement for **genuine use** of the Community mark in the EU, such as Articles 15(1) and 51 CTMR, those provisions pursue a **different** objective from that pursued by the provisions relating to the extended protection conferred on trade marks that have a reputation in the EU, such as Article 9(1)(c) thereof. While the latter provision concerns conditions governing protection extended beyond the categories of goods and services for which a Community trade mark has been registered, the notion of 'genuine use' in Articles 15(1) and 51 CTMR expresses the minimum condition for use that all the marks must satisfy in order to be protected.[1851]

It follows that the provisions concerning the requirement of genuine use of the Community mark and, in particular, the criteria laid down by the case law, in order to prove genuine use, are to be distinguished from the provisions and criteria relating to the reputation of such a mark in the EU.[1852]

Consequently, the criteria laid down by the case law concerning genuine use of a Community mark are not relevant as such for the purpose of establishing a 'reputation' within the meaning of Article 4(3) TMD2008.[1853]

The German, Dutch and Swedish versions use words signifying that the trade mark must be **'known'** without indicating the extent of knowledge required, whereas the other language versions use the term 'reputation' or expressions implying, like that term, at a quantitative level a certain degree of knowledge amongst the public.[1854]

That nuance, which does not entail any real contradiction, is due to the greater neutrality of the terms used in the German, Dutch and Swedish versions. Despite that nuance, it cannot be denied that, in the context of a uniform interpretation of Community law, a **knowledge threshold requirement** emerges from a comparison of all the language versions of the Directive.[1855]

Such a requirement is also indicated by the general scheme and purpose of the Directive. In so far as Article 5(2) TMD2008, unlike Article 5(1), protects trade marks registered for non-similar products or services, its first condition implies a certain degree of knowledge of the earlier trade mark among the public. It is only where there is a sufficient degree of knowledge of that mark that the public, when confronted by the later trade mark, may possibly make an association between the two trade marks, even when used for non-similar products or services, and that the earlier trade mark may consequently be damaged.[1856]

The **public** amongst which the earlier trade mark must have acquired a reputation is that concerned by that trade mark, that is to say, depending on the product or

1851. CJEU C-125/14 of 3.9.2015 – Iron & Smith, para. 21; *see also* CJEU C-149/11 of 19.12.2012 – Leno Merken, para. 53; C-564/16 P of 28.6.2018 – EUIPO/Puma, para. 55; C-115/19 P of 11.6.2020 – China Construction Bank/EUIPO, para. 57.
1852. CJEU C-125/14 of 3.9.2015 – Iron & Smith, para. 23.
1853. CJEU C-125/14 of 3.9.2015 – Iron & Smith, paras 24 and 25.
1854. CJEU C-375/97 of 14.9.1999 – General Motors, para. 21.
1855. CJEU C-375/97 of 14.9.1999 – General Motors, para. 22.
1856. CJEU C-375/97 of 14.9.1999 – General Motors, para. 23.

service marketed, either the public at large or a more specialized public, for example, traders in a specific sector.[1857]

It cannot be inferred from either the letter or the spirit of Article 5(2) TMD2008 that the trade mark must be known by a given percentage of the public so defined.[1858]

The degree of knowledge required must be considered to be reached when the earlier mark is known by a significant part of the public concerned by the products or services covered by that trade mark.[1859]

In examining whether this condition is fulfilled, the national court must take into consideration **all the relevant facts** of the case, in particular the market share held by the trade mark, the intensity, geographical extent and duration of its use, and the size of the investment made by the undertaking in promoting it.[1860]

Territorially, the condition is fulfilled when, in the terms of Article 5(2) TMD2008, the trade mark has a reputation 'in the Member State'. In the absence of any definition of the Community provision in this respect, a trade mark cannot be required to have a reputation 'throughout' the territory of the Member State. It is sufficient for it to exist in a substantial part of it.[1861]

As far as trade marks registered at the Benelux Trade mark Office are concerned, the **Benelux territory** must be treated like the territory of a Member State since Article 1 TMD2008 regards Benelux trade marks as trade marks registered in a Member State. Article 5(2) TMD2008 must therefore be understood as meaning a reputation acquired 'in' the Benelux territory. For the same reasons as those relating to the condition as to the existence of a reputation in a Member State, a Benelux trade mark cannot therefore be required to have a reputation throughout the Benelux territory. It is sufficient for a Benelux trade mark to have a reputation in a substantial part of the Benelux territory, which part may consist of a part of one of the Benelux countries.[1862]

Article 9(1)(c) CTMR must be interpreted as meaning that, in order to benefit from the protection afforded in that provision, a **Community trade mark** must be known by a significant part of the public concerned by the products or services covered by that trade mark, in a substantial part of the territory of the Community, and that, in view of the facts of the main proceedings, the territory of the Member State in question may be considered to constitute a substantial part of the territory of the Community.[1863]

The expression 'has a reputation in the Community', in Article 4(3) **TMD2008**, has the **same** meaning as the identical expression in Article 9(1)(c) **CTMR**.[1864]

The concept of 'reputation' assumes a certain degree of knowledge amongst the relevant public.[1865]

1857. CJEU C-375/97 of 14.9.1999 – General Motors, para. 24.
1858. CJEU C-375/97 of 14.9.1999 – General Motors, para. 25.
1859. CJEU C-375/97 of 14.9.1999 – General Motors, para. 26.
1860. CJEU C-375/97 of 14.9.1999 – General Motors, para. 27; C-564/16 P of 28.6.2018 – EUIPO/Puma, para. 56; C-115/19 P of 11.6.2020 – China Construction Bank/EUIPO, para. 57.
1861. CJEU C-375/97 of 14.9.1999 – General Motors, para. 28.
1862. CJEU C-375/97 of 14.9.1999 – General Motors, para. 29; *see also* CJEU C-108/05 of 7.9.2006 – Bovemij Verzekeringen, para. 20.
1863. CJEU C-301/07 of 6.10.2009 – PAGO International, para. 30.
1864. CJEU C-125/14 of 3.9.2015 – Iron & Smith, para. 16.
1865. CJEU C-301/07 of 6.10.2009 – PAGO International, para. 21.

The relevant public is that concerned by the Community trade mark, that is to say, depending on the product or service marketed, either the public at large or a more specialized public, for example, traders in a specific sector.[1866]

It cannot be required that the Community trade mark be known by a given percentage of the public so defined.[1867]

The degree of knowledge required must be considered to be reached when the Community trade mark is known by a significant part of the public concerned by the products or services covered by that trade mark.[1868]

In examining this condition, the national court must take into consideration all the relevant facts of the case, in particular the market share held by the trade mark, the intensity, geographical extent and duration of its use, and the size of the investment made by the undertaking in promoting it.[1869]

Territorially, the condition as to reputation must be considered to be fulfilled when the Community trade mark has a reputation in a substantial part of the territory of the Community.[1870]

It should be noted that the Court has already ruled that, with regard to a Benelux trade mark, it is sufficient, for the purposes of Article 5(2) TMD2008, that it has a reputation in a substantial part of the Benelux territory, which part may consist of a part of one of the Benelux countries.[1871]

As the present case concerns a Community trade mark with a reputation throughout the territory of a Member State, namely Austria, the view may be taken, regard being had to the circumstances of the main proceedings, that the territorial requirement imposed by Article 9(1)(c) CTMR is satisfied.[1872]

Thus, if the reputation of an earlier Community trade mark is established in a substantial part of the territory of the EU which may, in some circumstances, coincide with the territory of a single Member State, it must be held that that mark has a 'reputation in the [European Union]', within the meaning of Article 4(3) TMD2008, and the proprietor of that mark is not required to produce evidence of that reputation in the Member State in which the application for registration of the later national mark, which is the subject of an opposition, has been filed.[1873]

1866. CJEU C-301/07 of 6.10.2009 – PAGO International, para. 22.
1867. CJEU C-301/07 of 6.10.2009 – PAGO International, para. 23.
1868. CJEU C-301/07 of 6.10.2009 – PAGO International, para. 24; C-125/14 of 3.9.2015 – Iron & Smith, para. 17; C-690/17 of 11.4.2019 – Oko-Text Verlag/Dr. Rudolf Liebe Nachf., para. 47.
1869. CJEU C-301/07 of 6.10.2009 – PAGO International, para. 25; C-125/14 of 3.9.2015 – Iron & Smith, para. 18.
1870. CJEU C-301/07 of 6.10.2009 – PAGO International, para. 27; C-125/14 of 3.9.2015 – Iron & Smith, para. 19.
1871. CJEU C-301/07 of 6.10.2009 – PAGO International, para. 28.
1872. CJEU C-301/07 of 6.10.2009 – PAGO International, para. 29; *see also* CJEU C-125/14 of 3.9.2015 – Iron & Smith, paras 19 and 25; C-93/16 of 20.7.2017 – Ornua Co-operative/Tindale & Stanton, para. 51.
1873. CJEU C-125/14 of 3.9.2015 – Iron & Smith, para. 20, *see also* CJEU C-93/16 of 20.7.2017 – Ornua Co-operative/Tindale & Stanton, para. 51.

[2] *Similarity between the mark and the sign*

Given that it is **not** apparent either from the wording of paragraphs 1(b) and 5 of Article 8 CTMR or from the case law of the Court of Justice that the **concept of similarity** has a **different meaning in each of those paragraphs**, it follows, *inter alia*, that, if, in examining the conditions for the application of Article 8(1)(b) CTMR, the General Court concludes that there is no similarity between the signs at issue, paragraph 5 of Article 8 also necessarily does not apply to the case in point. Conversely, if the General Court takes the view, in the context of that same examination, that there is some similarity between the signs at issue, such a finding is equally valid with regard to the application of both Article 8(1)(b) and Article 8(5) CTMR.[1874]

The protection conferred by Article 5(2) TMD2008 is not conditional on a finding of a degree of similarity between the mark with a reputation and the sign such that there exists a likelihood of confusion between them on the part of the relevant section of the public. It is sufficient for the degree of similarity between the mark with a reputation and the sign to have the effect that the relevant section of the **public establishes a link** between the sign and the mark.[1875]

The types of injury referred to in Article 8(5) of that regulation do not require the connection which consumers are capable of making between the signs at issue to be immediate.[1876]

The condition of similarity between the mark and the sign, referred to in Article 5(2) TMD2008, requires the existence, in particular, of elements of visual, aural or conceptual similarity.[1877]

However, in a situation in which the **degree of similarity** in question does not prove to be sufficient to result in the application of Article 8(1)(b) CTMR, it cannot be deduced from that that the application of paragraph 5 of that article is necessarily precluded.[1878]

It is true that Article 8(1)(b) CTMR and Article 8(5) CTMR **differ** in terms of the degree of similarity required. Whereas the implementation of the protection provided for under Article 8(1)(b) CTMR is conditional upon a finding of a degree of similarity between the marks at issue such that there exists a likelihood of confusion between them on the part of the relevant section of the public, the existence of such a likelihood is not necessary for the protection conferred by Article 8(5) CTMR. Accordingly, the types of injury referred to in Article 8(5) may be the consequence of a lesser degree of similarity between the earlier and later marks, provided that it is sufficient for the

1874. CJEU C-603/14 P of 10.12.2015 – El Corte Inglés/OHIM, para. 39; C-505/17 P of 28.2.2019 – Groupe Léa Nature/EUIPO, para. 79.
1875. CJEU C-408/01 of 23.10.2003 – Adidas-Salomon and Adidas Benelux, para. 31; C-102/07 of 10.4.2008 – adidas/Marca Mode, para. 41; *see also* CJEU C-252/07 of 27.11.2008 – Intel Corporation, para. 58; C-323/09 of 22.9.2011 – Interflora, para. 71.
1876. CJEU C-603/14 P of 10.12.2015 – El Corte Inglés/OHIM, para. 50.
1877. CJEU C-408/01 of 23.10.2003 – Adidas-Salomon and Adidas Benelux, para. 28; C-552/09 P of 24.3.2011 – Ferrero/OHIM, para. 52; *see also* CJEU C-85/16 P and C-86/16 P of 30.5.2018 – Kenzo Tsujimoto/EUIPO, para. 56.
1878. CJEU C-603/14 P of 10.12.2015 – El Corte Inglés/OHIM, para. 40.

relevant section of the public to make a connection between those marks, that is to say, to establish a link between them.[1879]

On the other hand, it is not apparent either from the wording of those provisions or from the case law that the similarity between the marks at issue must be assessed in a different way, according to whether the assessment is carried out under Article 8(1)(b) CTMR or under Article 8(5).[1880]

Under Article 8(1)(b) and (5) CTMR, the factual assessment of similarity is carried out according to the same criteria. When the condition of similarity is not met under Article 8(1)(b) CTMR, it must also be held, on the basis of the **same analysis**, that nor is that condition met under Article 8(5) CTMR.[1881]

The infringements referred to in Article 5(2) TMD2008, where they occur, are the consequence of a certain degree of similarity between the mark and the sign, by virtue of which the relevant section of the public makes a connection between the sign and the mark, that is to say, establishes a link between them even though it does not confuse them.[1882]

One of the conditions of the protection conferred by Article 5(2) TMD2008 is that the degree of similarity between the mark with a reputation and the sign must have the effect that the relevant section of the public establishes a link between the sign and the mark.[1883]

The existence of such a link must, just like a likelihood of confusion in the context of Article 5(1)(b) TMD2008, be appreciated globally, taking into account **all factors relevant** to the circumstances of the case.[1884]

Those factors include:

- the degree of similarity between the conflicting marks;
- the nature of the goods or services for which the conflicting marks were registered, including the degree of closeness or dissimilarity between those goods or services, and the relevant section of the public;
- the strength of the earlier mark's reputation;

1879. CJEU C-552/09 P of 24.3.2011 – Ferrero/OHIM, para. 53; C-581/13 P and C-582/13 P of 20.11.2014 – Intra-Presse/OHIM, para. 72; C-603/14 P of 10.12.2015 – El Corte Inglés/OHIM, paras 41 et seq.; *see also* CJEU C-690/17 of 11.4.2019 – Oko-Text Verlag/Dr. Rudolf Liebe Nachf., para. 45.
1880. CJEU C-552/09 P of 24.3.2011 – Ferrero/OHIM, para. 54.
1881. CJEU C-370/10 P of 14.3.2011 – Ravensburger/OHIM, para. 63.
1882. CJEU C-408/01 of 23.10.2003 – Adidas-Salomon and Adidas Benelux, para. 29; C-102/07 of 10.4.2008 – adidas/Marca Mode, para. 41.
1883. CJEU C-408/01 of 23.10.2003 – Adidas-Salomon and Adidas Benelux, para. 38.
1884. CJEU C-408/01 of 23.10.2003 – Adidas-Salomon and Adidas Benelux, para. 30; C-102/07 of 10.4.2008 – adidas/Marca Mode, para. 42; C-252/07 of 27.11.2008 – Intel Corporation, paras 41 and 62; C-320/07 P of 12.3.2009 – Antartica/OHIM, para. 45; C-136/08 P of 30.4.2009 – Japan Tobacco/OHIM, para. 26; C-552/09 P of 24.3.2011 – Ferrero/OHIM, paras 56 and 64; C-125/14 of 3.9.2015 – Iron & Smith, para. 31; C-548/14 P of 17.9.2015 – Arnoldo Mondadori Editore/OHIM, para. 63; C-471/16 P of 26.7.2017 – Staatliche Porzellan-Manufaktur Meissen/EUIPO, para. 52; C-85/16 P and C-86/16 P of 30.5.2018 – Kenzo Tsujimoto/EUIPO, para. 56; C-505/17 P of 28.2.2019 – Groupe Léa Nature/EUIPO, para. 83; C-328/18 P of 4.3.2020 – EUIPO/Equivalenza Manufactory, para. 57.

- the degree of the earlier mark's distinctive character, whether inherent or acquired through use;
- the existence of the likelihood of confusion on the part of the public.[1885]

As regards the degree of similarity between the conflicting marks, the more similar they are, the more likely it is that the later mark will bring the earlier mark with a reputation to the mind of the relevant public. That is particularly the case where those **marks** are **identical.**[1886]

However, the fact that the conflicting marks are identical, and even more so if they are merely similar, is not sufficient for it to be concluded that there is a link between those marks.[1887]

The **nature of the goods or services** for which the conflicting marks are registered must be taken into consideration for the purposes of assessing whether there is a link between those marks.[1888]

Even if the relevant section of the public as regards the goods or services for which the conflicting marks are registered is the same or overlaps to some extent, those goods or services may be so dissimilar that the later mark is unlikely to bring the earlier mark to the mind of the relevant public.[1889]

For the purposes of assessing where there is a link between the conflicting marks, it may therefore be necessary to take into account **the strength of the earlier mark's reputation** in order to determine whether that reputation extends beyond the public targeted by that mark.[1890]

Likewise, the stronger the distinctive character of the earlier mark, whether inherent or acquired through the use which has been made of it, the more likely it is that, confronted with a later identical or similar mark, the relevant public will call that earlier mark to mind.[1891]

Accordingly, for the purposes of assessing whether there is a link between the conflicting marks, the degree of the earlier mark's distinctive character must be taken into consideration.[1892]

1885. CJEU C-252/07 of 27.11.2008 – Intel Corporation, para. 42; C-320/07 P of 12.3.2009 – Antartica/OHIM, para. 45; C-136/08 P of 30.4.2009 – Japan Tobacco/OHIM, para. 26; C-552/09 P of 24.3.2011 – Ferrero/OHIM, paras 56 and 64; C-548/14 P of 17.9.2015 – Arnoldo Mondadori Editore/OHIM, para. 63; C-471/16 P of 26.7.2017 – Staatliche Porzellan-Manufaktur Meissen/EUIPO, para. 52; C-505/17 P of 28.2.2019 – Groupe Léa Nature/EUIPO, para. 83; *see also* CJEU C-499/17 P of 14.12.2017 – Miguel Torres/EUIPO, paras 7/8 and 8, unofficial transcription; C-328/18 P of 4.3.2020 – EUIPO/Equivalenza Manufactory, para. 57; C-115/19 P of 11.6.2020 – China Construction Bank/EUIPO, para. 55.
1886. CJEU C-252/07 of 27.11.2008 – Intel Corporation, para. 44.
1887. CJEU C-252/07 of 27.11.2008 – Intel Corporation, para. 45; C-471/16 P of 26.7.2017 – Staatliche Porzellan-Manufaktur Meissen/EUIPO, para. 51.
1888. CJEU C-252/07 of 27.11.2008 – Intel Corporation, para. 50; C-471/16 P of 26.7.2017 – Staatliche Porzellan-Manufaktur Meissen/EUIPO, para. 53.
1889. CJEU C-252/07 of 27.11.2008 – Intel Corporation, para. 49; C-471/16 P of 26.7.2017 – Staatliche Porzellan-Manufaktur Meissen/EUIPO, para. 53.
1890. CJEU C-252/07 of 27.11.2008 – Intel Corporation, para. 53; C-552/09 P of 24.3.2011 – Ferrero/OHIM, para. 57.
1891. CJEU C-252/07 of 27.11.2008 – Intel Corporation, para. 54.
1892. CJEU C-252/07 of 27.11.2008 – Intel Corporation, para. 55.

In that regard, in so far as the ability of a trade mark to identify the goods or services for which it is registered and used as coming from the proprietor of that mark and, therefore, its distinctive character are all the stronger if that mark is unique – that is to say, as regards a word mark such as INTEL if the word of which it consists has not been used by anyone for any goods or services other than by the proprietor of the mark for the goods and services it markets – it must be ascertained whether the earlier mark is unique or essentially unique.[1893]

Finally, a link between the conflicting marks is necessarily established when there is a **likelihood of confusion**, that is to say, when the relevant public believes or might believe that the goods or services marketed under the earlier mark and those marketed under the later mark come from the same undertaking or from economically linked undertakings.[1894]

By contrast, where, according to a finding of fact by the national court, the relevant section of the public views the sign purely as an embellishment, it necessarily does not establish any link with a registered mark. That therefore means that the degree of similarity between the sign and the mark is not sufficient for such a link to be established.[1895]

As regards the fact that, for the average consumer, who is reasonably well informed and reasonably observant and circumspect, the later mark would call the earlier mark to mind is tantamount to the existence of such a link.[1896]

The fact that a sign is viewed as an **embellishment** by the relevant section of the public is not, in itself, an obstacle to the protection conferred by Article 5(2) TMD2008 where the degree of similarity is none the less such that the relevant section of the public establishes a link between the sign and the mark.[1897]

The fact that:

- the earlier mark has a huge reputation for certain specific types of goods or services; and
- those goods or services and the goods or services for which the later mark is registered are dissimilar or dissimilar to a substantial degree; and
- the earlier mark is unique in respect of any goods or services, does **not** necessarily **imply** that there is a **link**, within the meaning of *Adidas-Salomon and Adidas Benelux,*[1898] between the conflicting marks.[1899]

The fact that for the average consumer, who is reasonably well informed and reasonably observant and circumspect, the later mark calls the earlier mark with a reputation to mind is tantamount to the existence of such a link, within the meaning of *Adidas-Salomon and Adidas Benelux*, between the conflicting marks.[1900]

1893. CJEU C-252/07 of 27.11.2008 – Intel Corporation, para. 56.
1894. CJEU C-252/07 of 27.11.2008 – Intel Corporation, para. 57.
1895. CJEU C-408/01 of 23.10.2003 – Adidas-Salomon and Adidas Benelux, para. 40, 41.
1896. CJEU C-252/07 of 27.11.2008 – Intel Corporation, para. 60.
1897. CJEU C-408/01 of 23.10.2003 – Adidas-Salomon and Adidas Benelux, para. 39, 41.
1898. CJEU C-408/01 of 23.10.2003 – Adidas-Salomon and Adidas Benelux.
1899. CJEU C-252/07 of 27.11.2008 – Intel Corporation, para. 64.
1900. CJEU C-252/07 of 27.11.2008 – Intel Corporation, para. 63.

It is clear that the **requirement of availability is extraneous** both to the assessment of the degree of similarity between the mark with a reputation and the sign used by the third party and to the link which may be made by the relevant public between that mark and the sign. It cannot therefore constitute a relevant factor for determining whether the use of the sign takes unfair advantage of, or is detrimental to, the distinctive character or the repute of the trade mark.[1901]

It is for the national court to base its analysis on all the facts of the case in the main proceedings.[1902]

In order for Article 8(5) CTMR to be applicable, the marks at issue must be identical or similar. Consequently, that provision is manifestly **inapplicable** where, as in the present case, the **General Court rules out any similarity** between the marks at issue.[1903]

It is only **if there is some similarity, even faint**, between the marks at issue that the General Court must carry out a global assessment in order to ascertain whether, notwithstanding the low degree of similarity between them, there is, on account of the presence of other relevant factors such as the reputation or recognition enjoyed by the earlier mark, a likelihood of confusion or a link made between those marks by the relevant public.[1904]

That finding is not called into question by the case law of the Court of Justice resulting from the judgments in *Calvin Klein Trademark Trust v. OHIM*[1905] and *Ferrero v. OHIM*[1906] relied on by OHIM, since those judgments relate to different situations. In particular, although, in those cases, there was a word or element which was common to the signs at issue, the General Court had formally held, contrary to what is the case in the judgment under appeal, that there was no similarity between the signs at issue.[1907]

The reputation of the earlier mark and the similarity between the goods respectively covered by the marks at issue - even if those factors may be taken into consideration in order to assess likelihood of confusion - do not affect the assessment of the similarity of the signs at issue, with the result that they are incapable of calling into question the lack of similarity that was found to exist.[1908]

1901. CJEU C-102/07 of 10.4.2008 - adidas/Marca Mode, para. 43.
1902. CJEU C-252/07 of 27.11.2008 - Intel Corporation, para. 61.
1903. CJEU C-342/09 P of 27.10.2010 - Victor Guedes/OHIM, para. 25; C-552/09 P of 24.3.2011 - Ferrero/OHIM, para. 66; C-581/13 P and C-582/13 P of 20.11.2014 - Intra-Presse/OHIM, para. 73; C-603/14 P of 10.12.2015 - El Corte Inglés/OHIM, para. 39; *see also* CJEU C-254/09 P of 2.9.2010 - Calvin Klein/OHIM, para. 65; C-216/10 P of 25.11.2010 - Lufthansa AirPlus Servicekarten/OHIM, para. 36; C-374/15 P of 28.1.2016 - Harper Hygienics/OHIM, para. 74; C-328/18 P of 4.3.2020 - EUIPO/Equivalenza Manufactory, para. 60.
1904. CJEU C-552/09 P of 24.3.2011 - Ferrero/OHIM, para. 66; C-581/13 P and C-582/13 P of 20.11.2014 - Intra-Presse/OHIM, para. 73; C-603/14 P of 10.12.2015 - El Corte Inglés/OHIM, para. 43.
1905. CJEU C-254/09 P of 2.9.2010 - Calvin Klein/OHIM.
1906. CJEU C-552/09 P of 24.3.2011 - Ferrero/OHIM.
1907. CJEU C-603/14 P of 10.12.2015 - El Corte Inglés/OHIM, para. 49.
1908. CJEU C-552/09 P of 24.3.2011 - Ferrero/OHIM, para. 68; *see also* CJEU C-57/08 P of 11.12.2008 - Gateway/OHIM, paras 55 et seqq.; C-370/10 P of 14.3.2011 - Ravensburger/OHIM, para. 49.

Although that global assessment implies some interdependence between the relevant factors, and a low degree of similarity between the marks may therefore be offset by the strong distinctive character of the earlier mark, the fact remains that where there is no similarity between the earlier mark and the challenged mark, the reputation or recognition enjoyed by the earlier mark and the fact that the goods or services respectively covered are identical or similar are not sufficient for it to be found that there is a likelihood of confusion between the marks at issue or that the relevant public makes a link between them.[1909]

[3] No requirement of non-similar goods or services

Take care: There was a major change in the wording of TMD2008 from 'registered for goods or services which are not similar to those for which the earlier trade mark is registered' to 'irrespective of whether the goods or services for which it is applied or registered are identical with, similar to or not similar to those for which the earlier trade mark is registered'.

Now expressly applicable: Articles 4(4)(a) and 5(2) TMD2008 are to be interpreted as entitling the Member States to provide specific protection for registered trade marks with a reputation in cases where a later mark or sign, which is identical with or similar to the registered mark, is intended to be used or is used for **goods or services identical with or similar** to those covered by the registered mark.[1910]

[4] Without due cause

It must be stated at the outset that the **concept of 'due cause'** is not defined in the TMD2008.[1911]

That concept must therefore be interpreted in the light of the overall scheme and objectives of the system of which it forms part,[1912] and, in particular, must take into account the context of the provision which contains it.[1913]

As a preliminary point, it should be borne in mind that while Article 5 TMD2008 provides that the registered trade mark confers on its proprietor an exclusive right, restrictions on the exercise of that right also arise from that provision.[1914]

1909. CJEU C-552/09 P of 24.3.2011 – Ferrero/OHIM, para. 65.
1910. CJEU C-292/00 of 9.1.2003 – Davidoff, para. 30; C-487/07 of 18.6.2009 – L'Oréal, para. 35; *see also* CJEU C-408/01 of 23.10.2003 – Adidas-Salomon and Adidas Benelux, para. 22; C-102/07 of 10.4.2008 – adidas/Marca Mode, para. 37; C-236/08 to C-238/08 of 23.3.2010 – Google France, para. 48; C-323/09 of 22.9.2011 – Interflora, para. 68; C-294/12 P of 14.5.2013 – You-Q/OHIM, para. 67; C-65/12 of 6.2.2014 – Leidseplein Beheer, para. 21; C-93/16 of 20.7.2017 – Ornua Co-operative/Tindale & Stanton, para. 50; C-690/17 of 11.4.2019 – Oko-Text Verlag/Dr. Rudolf Liebe Nachf., para. 45.
1911. CJEU C-65/12 of 6.2.2014 – Leidseplein Beheer, para. 27.
1912. *See* CJEU C-292/00 of 9.1.2003 – Davidoff, para. 24.
1913. CJEU C-65/12 of 6.2.2014 – Leidseplein Beheer, para. 28; *see also* CJEU C-320/12 of 27.6.2013 – Malaysia Dairy Industries, para. 25.
1914. CJEU C-65/12 of 6.2.2014 – Leidseplein Beheer, para. 29.

Such a finding, however, cannot mean that the concept of 'due cause' should be interpreted by having regard to the scope of Article 5(1) TMD2008.[1915]

The purpose of Article 5(1) and (2) TMD2008 is not the same, and, accordingly, the rules for the protection of simple marks may apply in cases which are not governed by the provisions relating to the protection of marks with a reputation. Conversely, the rules for the protection of marks with a reputation may apply in cases which are not governed by the rules for the protection of simple marks.[1916]

It is only in certain circumstances that Article 5(2) TMD2008 entitles proprietors of trade marks with a reputation to prohibit third parties from using signs identical or similar to their trade marks in relation to goods or services which are not similar to those in respect of which those marks are registered.[1917]

The protection of trade marks with a reputation is more extensive than that for simple marks, in that the prohibition of the use of a sign by a third party is not dependent on either the identity of the sign and mark in question, as referred to in Article 5(1)(a) TMD2008, or the likelihood of confusion referred to in Article 5(1)(b) TMD2008.[1918]

In particular, the proprietor of a mark with a reputation is not required, in order to claim the protection provided for in Article 5(2) TMD2008, to prove detriment to the distinctive character or repute of that mark, where a third party, by using a sign identical or similar to that mark, takes unfair advantage of its reputation.[1919]

In a system for the protection of marks such as that adopted, on the basis of the TMD2008, however, the interests of a third party in using, in the course of trade, a sign similar to a mark with a reputation must be considered, in the context of Article 5(2) TMD2008, in the light of the possibility for the user of that sign to claim 'due cause'.[1920]

Where the proprietor of the mark with a reputation has demonstrated the existence of one of the forms of injury referred to in Article 5(2) TMD2008 and, in particular, has shown that unfair advantage has been taken of the distinctive character or the repute of that mark, the onus is on the third party using a sign similar to the mark with a reputation to establish that he has due cause for using such a sign.[1921]

It follows that the concept of 'due cause' may not only include objectively overriding reasons but may **also relate to the subjective interests of a third party** using a sign which is identical or similar to the mark with a reputation.[1922]

Thus, the concept of 'due cause' is intended, not to resolve a conflict between a mark with a reputation and a similar sign which was being used before that trade mark was filed or to restrict the rights which the proprietor of that mark is recognized as

1915. CJEU C-65/12 of 6.2.2014 – Leidseplein Beheer, para. 35.
1916. CJEU C-65/12 of 6.2.2014 – Leidseplein Beheer, para. 36.
1917. CJEU C-65/12 of 6.2.2014 – Leidseplein Beheer, para. 38.
1918. CJEU C-65/12 of 6.2.2014 – Leidseplein Beheer, para. 39.
1919. CJEU C-65/12 of 6.2.2014 – Leidseplein Beheer, para. 40.
1920. CJEU C-65/12 of 6.2.2014 – Leidseplein Beheer, para. 43; *see also* CJEU C-85/16 P and C-86/16 P of 30.5.2018 – Kenzo Tsujimoto/EUIPO, para. 90; C-690/17 of 11.4.2019 – Oko-Text Verlag/Dr. Rudolf Liebe Nachf., para. 52.
1921. CJEU C-65/12 of 6.2.2014 – Leidseplein Beheer, para. 44; *see also* CJEU C-252/07 of 27.11.2008 – Intel Corporation, para. 39.
1922. CJEU C-65/12 of 6.2.2014 – Leidseplein Beheer, para. 45.

having, but to strike a balance between the interests in question by taking account, in the specific context of Article 5(2) TMD2008 and in the light of the enhanced protection enjoyed by that mark, of the interests of the third party using that sign. In so doing, the claim by a third party that there is due cause for using a sign which is similar to a mark with a reputation cannot lead to the recognition, for the benefit of that third party, of the rights connected with a registered mark, but rather obliges the proprietor of the mark with a reputation to tolerate the use of the similar sign.[1923]

Consequently, the concept of 'due cause' cannot be interpreted as being restricted to objectively overriding reasons.[1924]

It is thus necessary to examine under what **conditions** the use by a third party of a sign which is similar to a trade mark with a reputation in relation to goods which are identical to those for which that mark is registered, where that sign was already being used before that mark was filed, may be covered by that concept.[1925]

In order to determine whether the use by a third party, before a trade mark with a reputation was filed, of a sign similar to that mark may constitute 'due cause', within the meaning of Article 5(2) TMD2008, and justify the fact that that third party takes advantage of the repute of that mark, the referring court must carry out an assessment, taking into account, **in particular, two factors**.[1926]

In the first place, such an assessment requires a determination as to how that sign has been accepted by, and what its reputation is with the relevant public.[1927]

In the second place, it is necessary to examine the intention of the person using that sign.[1928]

In this regard, in order to determine whether the use of the sign similar to the mark with a reputation was in good faith, it is necessary to take account of the degree of proximity between the goods and services for which that sign has been used and the product for which that mark was registered, as well as to have regard for when that sign was first used for a product identical to that for which that mark was registered, and when that mark acquired its reputation.[1929]

Article 5(2) TMD2008 must be interpreted as meaning that the proprietor of a trade mark with a reputation may be obliged, pursuant to the concept of 'due cause' within the meaning of that provision, to tolerate the use by a third party of a sign similar to that mark in relation to a product which is identical to that for which that mark was registered, if it is demonstrated that that sign was **being used before that mark was filed** and that the use of that sign in relation to the identical product is in good faith. In order to determine whether that is so, the national court must take account, in particular, of:

1923. CJEU C-65/12 of 6.2.2014 – Leidseplein Beheer, para. 46; *see also* CJEU C-85/16 P and C-86/16 P of 30.5.2018 – Kenzo Tsujimoto/EUIPO, para. 91.
1924. CJEU C-65/12 of 6.2.2014 – Leidseplein Beheer, para. 48.
1925. CJEU C-65/12 of 6.2.2014 – Leidseplein Beheer, para. 49.
1926. CJEU C-65/12 of 6.2.2014 – Leidseplein Beheer, para. 53.
1927. CJEU C-65/12 of 6.2.2014 – Leidseplein Beheer, para. 54.
1928. CJEU C-65/12 of 6.2.2014 – Leidseplein Beheer, para. 55.
1929. CJEU C-65/12 of 6.2.2014 – Leidseplein Beheer, para. 56.

- how that sign has been accepted by, and what its reputation is with, the relevant public;
- the degree of proximity between the goods and services for which that sign was originally used and the product for which the mark with a reputation was registered; and
- the economic and commercial significance of the use for that product of the sign which is similar to that mark.[1930]

First, where a sign has been used prior to the registration of a mark with a reputation in relation to services and goods which may be linked to the product for which that mark has been registered, the use of that sign in relation to that latter product may appear to be a natural extension of the range of services and goods for which that sign already enjoys a certain reputation with the relevant public.[1931]

Second, the greater the repute of the sign used, prior to the registration of a similar mark with a reputation, for a certain range of goods and services, the more its use will be necessary for the marketing of a product identical to that for which the mark was registered, *a fortiori* as that product is close, by its nature, to the range of goods and services for which that sign was previously used.[1932]

Where the advertisement displayed on the internet on the basis of a **keyword** corresponding to a trade mark with a reputation puts forward – without offering a mere imitation of the goods or services of the proprietor of that trade mark, without causing dilution or tarnishment and without, moreover, adversely affecting the functions of the trade mark concerned – an alternative to the goods or services of the proprietor of the trade mark with a reputation, it must be concluded that such use falls, as a rule, within the ambit of **fair competition** in the sector for the goods or services concerned and is thus not without 'due cause' for the purposes of Article 5(2) TMD2008 and Article 9(1)(c) CTMR.[1933]

[5] Further conditions of protection

If, at the end of its examination, the national court decides that the condition as to the existence of a reputation is fulfilled, as regards both the public concerned and the territory in question, it must then go on to examine the second condition laid down in Article 5(2) TMD2008, which is that the earlier trade mark must be detrimentally affected **without due cause**. Here, it should be observed that the stronger the earlier mark's distinctive character and reputation, the easier it will be to accept that detriment has been caused to it.[1934]

1930. CJEU C-65/12 of 6.2.2014 – Leidseplein Beheer, para. 60.
1931. CJEU C-65/12 of 6.2.2014 – Leidseplein Beheer, para. 57.
1932. CJEU C-65/12 of 6.2.2014 – Leidseplein Beheer, para. 59.
1933. CJEU C-323/09 of 22.9.2011 – Interflora, para. 91; *see also* CJEU C-65/12 of 6.2.2014 – Leidseplein Beheer, para. 47.
1934. CJEU C-375/97 of 14.9.1999 – General Motors, para. 30.

The types of injury against which Article 4(4)(a) TMD2008 ensures such protection for the benefit of trade marks with a reputation are, **first, detriment to the distinctive character of the earlier mark, secondly, detriment to the repute of that mark and, thirdly, unfair advantage taken of the distinctive character or the repute of that mark.**[1935]

Just **one of those three types** of injury **suffices** for that provision to apply.[1936]

The types of injury referred to in Article 4(4)(a) TMD2008, where they occur, are the consequence of a certain degree of similarity between the earlier and later marks, by virtue of which the relevant section of the public makes a connection between those two marks, that is to say, establishes a link between them even though it does not confuse them.[1937]

In the absence of such a link in the mind of the public, the use of the later mark is not likely to take unfair advantage of, or be detrimental to, the distinctive character or the repute of the earlier mark.[1938]

However, the **existence of** such a **link is not sufficient**, in itself, to establish that there is one of the types of injury referred to in Article 4(4)(a) TMD2008, which constitute the specific condition of the protection of trade marks with a reputation laid down by that provision.[1939]

Article 4(4)(a) TMD2008 is to be interpreted as meaning that whether a use of the later mark takes or would take unfair advantage of, or is or would be detrimental to, the distinctive character or the repute of the earlier mark must be **assessed globally**, taking into account all factors relevant to the circumstances of the case.[1940]

The fact that:

- the earlier mark has a huge reputation for certain specific types of goods or services; and
- those goods or services and the goods or services for which the later mark is registered are dissimilar or dissimilar to a substantial degree; and

1935. CJEU C-252/07 of 27.11.2008 – Intel Corporation, para. 27; C-487/07 of 18.6.2009 – L'Oréal, para. 38; C-323/09 of 22.9.2011 – Interflora, para. 72; C-155/18 P to C-158/18 P of 4.3.2020 – Tulliallan Burlington/EUIPO, para. 73.
1936. CJEU C-252/07 of 27.11.2008 – Intel Corporation, para. 28; C-487/07 of 18.6.2009 – L'Oréal, para. 42; C-155/18 P to C-158/18 P of 4.3.2020 – Tulliallan Burlington/EUIPO, para. 74.
1937. CJEU C-252/07 of 27.11.2008 – Intel Corporation, paras 30 and 66; C-320/07 P of 12.3.2009 – Antartica/OHIM, para. 43; C-136/08 P of 30.4.2009 – Japan Tobacco/OHIM, para. 25; C-487/07 of 18.6.2009 – L'Oréal, para. 36; C-548/14 P of 17.9.2015 – Arnoldo Mondadori Editore/OHIM, paras 62 and 74; C-471/16 P of 26.7.2017 – Staatliche Porzellan-Manufaktur Meissen/EUIPO, para. 50; C-155/18 P to C-158/18 P of 4.3.2020 – Tulliallan Burlington/EUIPO, para. 63.
1938. CJEU C-252/07 of 27.11.2008 – Intel Corporation, para. 31; C-320/07 P of 12.3.2009 – Antartica/OHIM, para. 44; C-136/08 P of 30.4.2009 – Japan Tobacco/OHIM, para. 27; C-125/14 of 3.9.2015 – Iron & Smith, para. 28; C-548/14 P of 17.9.2015 – Arnoldo Mondadori Editore/OHIM, paras 64 and 75; C-510/18 P of 14.2.2019 – Prada/EUIPO, para. 9; C-155/18 P to C-158/18 P of 4.3.2020 – Tulliallan Burlington/EUIPO, para. 64.
1939. CJEU C-252/07 of 27.11.2008 – Intel Corporation, para. 32; C-136/08 P of 30.4.2009 – Japan Tobacco/OHIM, paras 27 and 37; C-487/07 of 18.6.2009 – L'Oréal, para. 37; C-125/14 of 3.9.2015 – Iron & Smith, para. 31; C-155/18 P to C-158/18 P of 4.3.2020 – Tulliallan Burlington/EUIPO, para. 65.
1940. CJEU C-252/07 of 27.11.2008 – Intel Corporation, para. 79.

- the earlier mark is unique in respect of any goods or services; and
- for the average consumer, who is reasonably well informed and reasonably observant and circumspect, the later mark calls the earlier mark to mind, is **not sufficient** to establish that the use of the later mark takes or would take unfair advantage of, or is or would be detrimental to, the distinctive character or the repute of the earlier mark, within the meaning of Article 4(4)(a) TMD2008.[1941]

The more immediately and strongly the earlier mark is brought to mind by the later mark, the greater the likelihood that the current or future use of the later mark is taking unfair advantage of, or is detrimental to, the distinctive character or the repute of the earlier mark.[1942]

It follows that, like the existence of a link between the conflicting marks, the existence of one of the types of injury referred to in Article 4(4)(a) TMD2008, or a serious likelihood that such an injury will occur in the future, must be assessed globally, taking into account all factors relevant to the circumstances of the case.[1943]

As regards, in particular, **detriment to the distinctive character** of the earlier mark, also referred to as 'dilution', 'whittling away' or 'blurring', such detriment is caused when that mark's ability to identify the goods or services for which it is registered and used as coming from the proprietor of that mark is weakened since use of the later mark leads to dispersion of the identity and hold upon the public mind of the earlier mark. That is notably the case when the earlier mark, which used to arouse immediate association with the goods and services for which it is registered, is no longer capable of doing so.[1944]

Detriment is caused to the distinctive character of a trade mark with a reputation when the use of a sign identical with or similar to that mark reduces the ability of the mark to distinguish the goods or services of its proprietor from those which have a different origin. At the end of the process of dilution, the trade mark is no longer capable of creating an immediate association, in the minds of consumers, with a specific commercial origin.[1945]

For the proprietor of a trade mark with a reputation to be effectively protected against that type of injury, Article 5(2) TMD2008 and Article 9(1)(c) CTMR must be interpreted as entitling the proprietor to prevent all use of a sign identical with or similar to that trade mark which reduces the distinctiveness of the mark, without it being required to wait for the end of the process of dilution, that is to say, the total loss of the trade mark's distinctive character.[1946]

1941. CJEU C-252/07 of 27.11.2008 – Intel Corporation, para. 80.
1942. CJEU C-252/07 of 27.11.2008 – Intel Corporation, para. 67; C-125/14 of 3.9.2015 – Iron & Smith, para. 33.
1943. CJEU C-252/07 of 27.11.2008 – Intel Corporation, para. 68; C-125/14 of 3.9.2015 – Iron & Smith, para. 32; C-155/18 P to C-158/18 P of 4.3.2020 – Tulliallan Burlington/EUIPO, para. 76.
1944. CJEU C-252/07 of 27.11.2008 – Intel Corporation, para. 29; C-487/07 of 18.6.2009 – L'Oréal, para. 39; C-323/09 of 22.9.2011 – Interflora, para. 73; C-155/18 P to C-158/18 P of 4.3.2020 – Tulliallan Burlington/EUIPO, para. 77.
1945. CJEU C-323/09 of 22.9.2011 – Interflora, para. 76.
1946. CJEU C-323/09 of 22.9.2011 – Interflora, para. 77.

It is true that the use, by a third party in the course of trade, of a sign identical with or similar to a trade mark with a reputation reduces the latter's distinctiveness and is thus detrimental to the distinctive character of that trade mark for the purposes of Article 5(2)4 TMD2008 or, in the case of a Community trade mark, of Article 9(1)(c) CTMR, when it contributes to turning the trade mark into a generic term.[1947]

Article 9(1)(b) and (c) CTMR must be interpreted as meaning that where a Community trade mark is **not registered in colour**, but the proprietor has used it extensively in a particular colour or combination of colours with the result that it has become associated in the mind of a significant portion of the public with that colour or combination of colours, the colour or colours which a third party uses in order to represent a sign alleged to infringe that trade mark are relevant in the global assessment of the likelihood of confusion or unfair advantage under that provision.[1948]

In that regard, it is clear from the order for reference that the similarity between the trade marks of the Specsavers group and the signs used by Asda was created intentionally in order to create an association in the mind of the public between the two trade signs. The fact that Asda used a similar colour to that used by the Specsavers group with the intention of taking advantage of the distinctive character and reputation of the latter's trade marks is a factor which must be taken into account in order to ascertain whether it can be held that unfair advantage is being taken of the distinctive character or reputation of the trade mark.[1949]

Article 9(1)(b) and (c) CTMR must be interpreted as meaning that the fact that the third party making use of a sign which allegedly infringes the registered trade mark is itself associated, in the mind of a significant portion of the public, with the **colour** or particular combination of colours which it **uses for the representation** of that sign is relevant to the global assessment of the likelihood of confusion and unfair advantage for the purposes of that provision.[1950]

In that regard, it should be noted that both the likelihood of confusion under Article 9(1)(b) CTMR and unfair advantage under Article 9(1)(c) CTMR must be assessed globally, taking into account all the relevant factors of the present case.[1951]

Moreover, it is apparent from the case law of the Court that those assessments must take account of the precise context in which the sign which is allegedly similar to the registered trade mark was used.[1952]

In those circumstances, it should be noted that the fact that the third party making use of a sign which allegedly infringed the registered trade mark is itself associated, in the mind of a significant portion of the public, with the colour or particular combination of colours which it uses for the representation of that sign is a factor which, amongst others, may have a certain importance while determining the

1947. CJEU C-323/09 of 22.9.2011 – Interflora, para. 79.
1948. CJEU C-252/12 of 18.7.2013 – Specsavers International Healthcare, para. 41.
1949. CJEU C-252/12 of 18.7.2013 – Specsavers International Healthcare, para. 40; *see also* CJEU C-487/07 of 18.6.2009 – L'Oréal, para. 48.
1950. CJEU C-252/12 of 18.7.2013 – Specsavers International Healthcare, para. 50.
1951. CJEU C-252/12 of 18.7.2013 – Specsavers International Healthcare, para. 44.
1952. CJEU C-252/12 of 18.7.2013 – Specsavers International Healthcare, para. 45; *see also* CJEU C-533/06 of 12.6.2008 – O2 Holdings/Hutchison 3G UK, para. 65.

existence of a likelihood of confusion or unfair advantage under Article 9(1)(b) or (c) CTMR.[1953]

Therefore, in the main proceedings, the fact that Asda is itself associated with the colour green, which it uses for the signs alleged to infringe the trade marks of the Specsavers group, could, *inter alia*, result in a reduction of the likelihood of confusion or association between those signs and the trade marks of the Specsavers group, to the extent that the relevant public could perceive that the colour green of those signs is that of Asda, a matter which is to be determined by the referring court.[1954]

Second, the fact that the third party making use of a sign which is alleged to infringe the registered trade mark is itself associated, in the mind of a significant portion of the public, with the colour or particular combination of colours which it uses for the representation of that sign can be relevant to determining whether the use of that sign has a 'due cause' within the meaning of Article 9(1)(c) CTMR.[1955]

However, the selection of a sign which is identical with or similar to a trade mark with a reputation as a **keyword within an internet referencing service** does not necessarily contribute to such a development.[1956]

Thus, when the use, as a keyword, of a sign corresponding to a trade mark with a reputation triggers the display of an advertisement which enables the reasonably well informed and reasonably observant internet user to tell that the goods or services offered originate not from the proprietor of the trade mark but, on the contrary, from a competitor of that proprietor, the conclusion will have to be that the trade mark's distinctiveness has not been reduced by that use, the latter having merely served to draw the internet user's attention to the existence of an alternative product or service to that of the proprietor of the trade mark.[1957]

Article 4(4)(a) TMD2008 must be interpreted as meaning that:

- the use of the later mark may be detrimental to the distinctive character of the earlier mark with a reputation even if that mark is not unique;
- a first use of the later mark may suffice to be detrimental to the distinctive character of the earlier mark;
- proof that the use of the later mark is or would be detrimental to the distinctive character of the earlier mark requires **evidence** of a change in the economic behaviour of the average consumer of the goods or services for which the earlier mark was registered consequent on the use of the later mark, or a serious likelihood that such a change will occur in the future.[1958]

As regards the strength of the reputation and the degree of distinctive character of the earlier mark, the Court has already held that the stronger the earlier mark's

1953. CJEU C-252/12 of 18.7.2013 – Specsavers International Healthcare, para. 46.
1954. CJEU C-252/12 of 18.7.2013 – Specsavers International Healthcare, para. 48.
1955. CJEU C-252/12 of 18.7.2013 – Specsavers International Healthcare, para. 49.
1956. CJEU C-323/09 of 22.9.2011 – Interflora, para. 80.
1957. CJEU C-323/09 of 22.9.2011 – Interflora, para. 81.
1958. CJEU C-252/07 of 27.11.2008 – Intel Corporation, para. 81.

distinctive character and reputation, the easier it will be to accept that detriment has been caused to it.[1959]

The existence of a link between the conflicting marks does not dispense the proprietor of the earlier trade mark from having to prove actual and present injury to its mark, for the purposes of Article 4(4)(a) TMD2008, or a serious likelihood that such an injury will occur in the future.[1960]

First, it is not necessary for the earlier mark to be unique in order to establish such injury or a serious likelihood that it will occur in the future.[1961]

A trade mark with a reputation necessarily has distinctive character, at the very least acquired through use. Therefore, even if an earlier mark with a reputation is not unique, the use of a later identical or similar mark may be such as to weaken the distinctive character of that earlier mark.[1962]

However, the more 'unique' the earlier mark appears, the greater the likelihood that the use of a later identical or similar mark will be detrimental to its distinctive character.[1963]

Second, a first use of an identical or similar mark may suffice, in some circumstances, to cause actual and present detriment to the distinctive character of the earlier mark or to give rise to a serious likelihood that such detriment will occur in the future.[1964]

Third, detriment to the distinctive character of the earlier mark is caused when that mark's ability to identify the goods or services for which it is registered and used as coming from the proprietor of that mark is weakened since use of the later mark leads to dispersion of the identity and hold upon the public mind of the earlier mark.[1965]

It follows that proof that the use of the later mark is or would be detrimental to the distinctive character of the earlier mark requires evidence of a change in the **economic behaviour of the average consumer** of the goods or services for which the earlier mark was registered consequent on the use of the later mark, or a serious likelihood that such a change will occur in the future.[1966]

Admittedly, paragraph 77 of the *Intel Corporation* judgment, which begins with the words '[i]t follows that', immediately follows the assessment of the weakening of the ability to identify and the dispersion of the identity of the earlier mark; it could thus be considered to be merely an explanation of the previous paragraph. However, the same wording, reproduced in paragraph 81 and in the operative part of that judgment, is autonomous. The fact that it appears in the operative part of the judgment makes its importance clear.[1967]

1959. CJEU C-252/07 of 27.11.2008 – Intel Corporation, para. 69.
1960. CJEU C-252/07 of 27.11.2008 – Intel Corporation, para. 71.
1961. CJEU C-252/07 of 27.11.2008 – Intel Corporation, para. 72.
1962. CJEU C-252/07 of 27.11.2008 – Intel Corporation, para. 73.
1963. CJEU C-252/07 of 27.11.2008 – Intel Corporation, para. 74.
1964. CJEU C-252/07 of 27.11.2008 – Intel Corporation, para. 75.
1965. CJEU C-252/07 of 27.11.2008 – Intel Corporation, para. 76.
1966. CJEU C-252/07 of 27.11.2008 – Intel Corporation, paras 77 and 81; C-383/12 P of 14.11.2013 – Environmental Manufacturing/OHIM, para. 34; C-155/18 P to C-158/18 P of 4.3.2020 – Tulliallan Burlington/EUIPO, para. 78.
1967. CJEU C-383/12 P of 14.11.2013 – Environmental Manufacturing/OHIM, para. 35.

The wording of the above case law is explicit. It follows that, without adducing evidence that that condition is met, the detriment or the risk of detriment to the distinctive character of the earlier mark provided for in Article 8(5) CTMR cannot be established.[1968]

The concept of 'change in the economic behaviour of the average consumer' lays down an objective condition. That change cannot be deduced solely from subjective elements such as consumers' perceptions. The mere fact that consumers note the presence of a new sign similar to an earlier sign is not sufficient of itself to establish the existence of a detriment or a risk of detriment to the distinctive character of the earlier mark within the meaning of Article 8(5) CTMR, in as much as that similarity does not cause any confusion in their minds.[1969]

The CTMR and the Court's case law not only do not require evidence to be adduced of actual detriment but also **admit the serious risk** of such detriment, allowing the use of logical deductions.[1970]

None the less, such deductions must not be the result of mere suppositions but must be founded on 'an analysis of the probabilities and by taking account of the normal practice in the relevant commercial sector as well as all the other circumstances of the case'.[1971]

It is immaterial, however, for the purposes of assessing whether the use of the later mark is or would be detrimental to the distinctive character of the earlier mark, whether or not the proprietor of the later mark draws **real commercial benefit** from the distinctive character of the earlier mark.[1972]

As regards **detriment to the repute of the mark**, also referred to as 'tarnishment' or 'degradation', such detriment is caused when the goods or services for which the identical or similar sign is used by the third party may be perceived by the public in such a way that the trade mark's power of attraction is reduced. The likelihood of such detriment may arise in particular from the fact that the goods or services offered by the third party possess a characteristic or a quality which is liable to have a negative impact on the image of the mark.[1973]

As regards the concept of '**taking unfair advantage of the distinctive character or the repute of the trade mark**', also referred to as 'parasitism' or 'free-riding', that concept relates not to the detriment caused to the mark but to the advantage taken by the third party as a result of the use of the identical or similar sign. It covers, in particular, cases where, by reason of a transfer of the image of the mark or of the characteristics which it projects to the goods identified by the identical or similar sign, there is clear exploitation on the coat-tails of the mark with a reputation.[1974]

Article 5(2) TMD2008 must be interpreted as meaning that the taking of unfair advantage of the distinctive character or the repute of a mark, within the meaning of

1968. CJEU C-383/12 P of 14.11.2013 - Environmental Manufacturing/OHIM, para. 36.
1969. CJEU C-383/12 P of 14.11.2013 - Environmental Manufacturing/OHIM, para. 37.
1970. CJEU C-383/12 P of 14.11.2013 - Environmental Manufacturing/OHIM, para. 42.
1971. CJEU C-383/12 P of 14.11.2013 - Environmental Manufacturing/OHIM, para. 43.
1972. CJEU C-252/07 of 27.11.2008 - Intel Corporation, para. 78.
1973. CJEU C-487/07 of 18.6.2009 - L'Oréal, para. 40; C-323/09 of 22.9.2011 - Interflora, para. 73.
1974. CJEU C-487/07 of 18.6.2009 - L'Oréal, para. 41; C-323/09 of 22.9.2011 - Interflora, para. 74.

that provision, does **not require** that there be a likelihood of confusion or **a likelihood of detriment to the distinctive character or the repute of the mark** or, more generally, to its proprietor.[1975]

It follows that an advantage taken by a third party of the distinctive character or the repute of the mark may be unfair, even if the use of the identical or similar sign is not detrimental either to the distinctive character or to the repute of the mark or, more generally, to its proprietor.[1976]

In order to **determine** whether the use of a sign takes unfair advantage of the distinctive character or the repute of the mark, it is necessary to undertake a global assessment, taking into account all factors relevant to the circumstances of the case, which include the strength of the mark's reputation and the degree of distinctive character of the mark, the degree of similarity between the marks at issue and the nature and degree of proximity of the goods or services concerned. As regards the strength of the reputation and the degree of distinctive character of the mark, the Court has already held that the stronger that mark's distinctive character and reputation are, the easier it will be to accept that detriment has been caused to it. It is also clear from the case law that the more immediately and strongly the mark is brought to mind by the sign, the greater the likelihood that the current or future use of the sign is taking, or will take, unfair advantage of the distinctive character or the repute of the mark or is, or will be, detrimental to them.[1977]

In addition, it must be stated that any such global assessment may also take into account, where necessary, the fact that there is a likelihood of dilution or tarnishment of the mark.[1978]

In the present case, it is a matter of agreement that the infringers use packaging and bottles similar to the marks with a reputation in order to market perfumes which constitute 'downmarket' imitations of the luxury fragrances for which those marks are registered and used.[1979]

In addition, it is apparent from the order for reference that that link confers a commercial advantage on the defendants in the main proceedings. It is also apparent from the order for reference that the similarity between those marks and the products marketed by Malaika and Starion was created intentionally in order to create an association in the mind of the public between fine fragrances and their imitations, with the aim of facilitating the marketing of those imitations.[1980]

In the general assessment which the referring court will have to undertake in order to determine whether, in those circumstances, it can be held that unfair advantage is being taken of the distinctive character or the repute of the mark, that court will, in particular, have to take account of the fact that the use of packaging and

1975. CJEU C-487/07 of 18.6.2009 – L'Oréal, para. 50.
1976. CJEU C-487/07 of 18.6.2009 – L'Oréal, paras 43 and 50.
1977. CJEU C-487/07 of 18.6.2009 – L'Oréal, para. 44; C-100/11 P of 10.5.2012 – Helena Rubinstein and L'Oréal/OHIM, para. 94; C-252/12 of 18.7.2013 – Specsavers International Healthcare, para. 39.
1978. CJEU C-487/07 of 18.6.2009 – L'Oréal, para. 45.
1979. CJEU C-487/07 of 18.6.2009 – L'Oréal, para. 46.
1980. CJEU C-487/07 of 18.6.2009 – L'Oréal, para. 47.

bottles similar to those of the fragrances that are being imitated is intended to take advantage, for promotional purposes, of the distinctive character and the repute of the marks under which those fragrances are marketed.[1981]

In that regard, where a third party attempts, through the use of a sign similar to a mark with a reputation, to ride on the coat-tails of that mark in order to benefit from its power of attraction, its reputation and its prestige, and to exploit, **without paying any financial compensation and without being required to make efforts of his own** in that regard, the marketing effort expended by the proprietor of that mark in order to create and maintain the image of that mark, the advantage resulting from such use must be considered to be an advantage that has been unfairly taken of the distinctive character or the repute of that mark.[1982]

It is also apparent that the fact that a trade mark enjoys a reputation makes it likely that a large number of internet users will use the name of that mark as a **keyword** when carrying out an internet search to find information or offers relating to the goods or services covered by that trade mark.[1983]

Where a competitor of the proprietor of a trade mark with a reputation selects that trade mark as a keyword in an internet referencing service, the purpose of that use is to take advantage of the distinctive character and repute of the trade mark. In fact, that selection is liable to create a situation in which the probably large number of consumers using that keyword to carry out an internet search for goods or services covered by the trade mark with a reputation will see that competitor's advertisement displayed on their screens.[1984]

Nor can it be denied that when internet users, having studied the competitor's advertisement, purchase the product or service offered by the competitor instead of that of the proprietor of the trade mark to which their search originally related, that competitor derives a real advantage from the distinctive character and repute of the trade mark.[1985]

Furthermore, it is not disputed that, in the context of a referencing service, an advertiser which selects signs identical with or similar to the trade marks of other persons does not, as a general rule, pay the proprietors of the trade marks any compensation in respect of that use.[1986]

It is clear from those particular aspects of the selection as internet keywords of signs corresponding to trade marks with a reputation which belong to other persons that such a selection can, in the absence of any 'due cause' as referred to in Article 5(2) TMD2008 and Article 9(1)(c) CTMR, be construed as a use whereby the advertiser rides on the coat-tails of a trade mark with a reputation in order to benefit from its power of attraction, its reputation and its prestige, and to exploit, without paying any financial

1981. CJEU C-487/07 of 18.6.2009 – L'Oréal, para. 48; *see also* CJEU C-252/12 of 18.7.2013 – Specsavers International Healthcare, para. 40.
1982. CJEU C-487/07 of 18.6.2009 – L'Oréal, paras 49 et seq.; C-236/08 to C-238/08 of 23.3.2010 – Google France, para. 102; C-65/12 of 6.2.2014 – Leidseplein Beheer, para. 52.
1983. CJEU C-323/09 of 22.9.2011 – Interflora, para. 85.
1984. CJEU C-323/09 of 22.9.2011 – Interflora, para. 86.
1985. CJEU C-323/09 of 22.9.2011 – Interflora, para. 87.
1986. CJEU C-323/09 of 22.9.2011 – Interflora, para. 88.

compensation and without being required to make efforts of its own in that regard, the marketing effort expended by the proprietor of that mark in order to create and maintain the image of that mark. If that is the case, the advantage thus obtained by the third party must be considered to be **unfair**.[1987]

As the Court has already stated, that is particularly **likely to be** the conclusion in cases in which internet advertisers offer for sale, by means of the selection of keywords corresponding to trade marks with a reputation, goods which are **imitations** of the goods of the proprietor of those marks.[1988]

By contrast, where the advertisement displayed on the internet on the basis of a keyword corresponding to a trade mark with a reputation puts forward – without offering a mere imitation of the goods or services of the proprietor of that trade mark, without causing dilution or tarnishment and without, moreover, adversely affecting the functions of the trade mark concerned – an alternative to the goods or services of the proprietor of the trade mark with a reputation, it must be concluded that such use falls, as a rule, within the ambit of **fair competition** in the sector for the goods or services concerned and is thus not without 'due cause' for the purposes of Article 5(2) TMD2008 and Article 9(1)(c) CTMR.[1989]

[6] Further conditions in relation to Community trade marks

An earlier Community trade mark has already acquired a reputation in a substantial part of the territory of the European Union, but not with the relevant public in the Member State in which registration of the later national mark concerned by the opposition has been applied for; the proprietor of the Community trade mark may benefit from the protection introduced by Article 4(3) TMD2008 where it is shown that a commercially significant part of that public is familiar with that mark, makes a connection between it and the later national mark, and that there is, taking account of all the relevant factors in the case, either actual and present injury to its mark, for the purposes of that provision or, failing that, a serious risk that such injury may occur in the future.[1990]

Also, even assuming that the earlier Community trade mark is unknown to the relevant public in the Member State in which the registration of the later national mark is applied for, which it is for the referring court to ascertain, the use of the national mark does not, in principle, enable unfair advantage to be taken of it or of the distinctive character or reputation of the earlier mark and is not detrimental to them.[1991]

However, even if the earlier Community trade mark is not known to a significant part of the relevant public in the Member State in which registration of the later

1987. CJEU C-323/09 of 22.9.2011 – Interflora, para. 89.
1988. CJEU C-323/09 of 22.9.2011 – Interflora, para. 90.
1989. CJEU C-323/09 of 22.9.2011 – Interflora, para. 91; *see also* CJEU C-65/12 of 6.2.2014 – Leidseplein Beheer, para. 47.
1990. CJEU C-125/14 of 3.9.2015 – Iron & Smith, para. 34.
1991. CJEU C-125/14 of 3.9.2015 – Iron & Smith, para. 29.

national mark has been applied for, it is conceivable that a commercially significant part of the latter may be familiar with it and make a connection between that mark and the later national mark.[1992]

[7] Relevant public

It is possible that the conflicting marks are registered for goods or services in respect of which the relevant sections of the public do not overlap.[1993]

The public to be taken into account in order to determine whether registration of the later mark may be declared invalid pursuant to Article 4(4)(a) TMD2008 varies **depending on the type of injury** alleged by the proprietor of the earlier trade mark.[1994]

First, both a **trade mark's distinctiveness and its reputation** must be assessed, first, by reference to the perception of the relevant public, which consists of average consumers of the goods or services for which that mark is registered, who are reasonably well informed and reasonably observant and circumspect.[1995]

The **reputation of a trade mark** must be assessed in relation to the relevant section of the public as regards the goods or services for which that mark was registered. That may be either the public at large or a more specialized public.[1996]

It is therefore conceivable that the relevant section of the public as regards the goods or services for which the earlier mark was registered is completely distinct from the relevant section of the public as regards the goods or services for which the later mark was registered and that the earlier mark, although it has a reputation, is not known to the public targeted by the later mark. In such a case, the public targeted by each of the two marks may never be confronted with the other mark, so that it will not establish any **link between those marks**.[1997]

It must also be pointed out that certain marks may have acquired such a reputation that it goes beyond the relevant public as regards the goods or services for which those marks were registered.[1998]

In such a case, it is possible that the relevant section of the public as regards the goods or services for which the later mark is registered will make a connection between the conflicting marks, even though that public is wholly distinct from the relevant section of the public as regards goods or services for which the earlier mark was registered.[1999]

1992. CJEU C-125/14 of 3.9.2015 – Iron & Smith, para. 30.
1993. CJEU C-252/07 of 27.11.2008 – Intel Corporation, para. 46.
1994. CJEU C-252/07 of 27.11.2008 – Intel Corporation, para. 33; C-320/07 P of 12.3.2009 – Antartica/OHIM, para. 46; C-673/15 P to C-676/15 P of 20.9.2017 – The Tea Board/EUIPO, para. 92.
1995. CJEU C-252/07 of 27.11.2008 – Intel Corporation, para. 34.
1996. CJEU C-252/07 of 27.11.2008 – Intel Corporation, para. 47.
1997. CJEU C-252/07 of 27.11.2008 – Intel Corporation, para. 48.
1998. CJEU C-252/07 of 27.11.2008 – Intel Corporation, para. 51; C-294/12 P of 14.5.2013 – You-Q/OHIM, para. 68.
1999. CJEU C-252/07 of 27.11.2008 – Intel Corporation, para. 52; C-552/09 P of 24.3.2011 – Ferrero/OHIM, para. 57; C-294/12 P of 14.5.2013 – You-Q/OHIM, para. 68.

Accordingly, the existence of **injury consisting of detriment to the distinctive character or the repute** of the earlier mark must be assessed by reference to average consumers of the goods and services for which that mark is registered, who are reasonably well informed and reasonably observant and circumspect.[2000]

Second, as regards injury consisting of **unfair advantage** taken of the distinctive character or the repute of the earlier mark, in so far as what is prohibited is the drawing of benefit from that mark by the proprietor of the later mark, the existence of such injury must be assessed by reference to average consumers of the goods or services for which the later mark is registered, who are reasonably well informed and reasonably observant and circumspect.[2001]

[8] Proof

In order to benefit from the protection introduced by Article 4(4)(a) TMD2008, the proprietor of the earlier mark must adduce proof that the use of the later mark 'would take unfair advantage of, or be detrimental to, the distinctive character or the repute of the earlier trade mark'.[2002]

The proprietor of the earlier trade mark is not required, for that purpose, to demonstrate actual and present injury to its mark for the purposes of Article 4(4)(a) TMD2008. When it is foreseeable that such injury will ensue from the use which the proprietor of the later mark may be led to make of its mark, the proprietor of the earlier mark cannot be required to wait for it actually to occur in order to be able to prohibit that use. The proprietor of the earlier mark must, however, **prove that there is a serious risk**[2003] that such an **injury will occur in the future**.[2004]

When the proprietor of the earlier mark has shown that there is either actual and present injury to its mark for the purposes of Article 4(4)(a) TMD2008 or, failing that, a serious risk that such injury will occur in the future, it is for the proprietor of the later mark to establish that there is **due cause** for the use of that mark.[2005]

Accordingly, the General Court was correct in holding that the proprietor of the earlier mark is not required to demonstrate actual and present harm to its mark but must, however, adduce prima facie evidence of a future risk, which is not hypothetical,

2000. CJEU C-252/07 of 27.11.2008 – Intel Corporation, para. 35; C-673/15 P to C-676/15 P of 20.9.2017 – The Tea Board/EUIPO, para. 92.
2001. CJEU C-252/07 of 27.11.2008 – Intel Corporation, para. 36; C-320/07 P of 12.3.2009 – Antartica/OHIM, paras 47 et seq.; C-673/15 P to C-676/15 P of 20.9.2017 – The Tea Board/EUIPO, para. 92.
2002. CJEU C-252/07 of 27.11.2008 – Intel Corporation, para. 37; C-136/08 P of 30.4.2009 – Japan Tobacco/OHIM, para. 42; C-100/11 P of 10.5.2012 – Helena Rubinstein and L'Oréal/OHIM, para. 93; C-125/14 of 3.9.2015 – Iron & Smith, para. 31.
2003. CJEU C-197/07 P of 12.12.2008 – Aktieselskabet af 21. Nov. 2001/OHIM, para. 22: 'risk, which is not hypothetical'.
2004. CJEU C-252/07 of 27.11.2008 – Intel Corporation, para. 38; C-197/07 P of 12.12.2008 – Aktieselskabet af 21. Nov. 2001/OHIM, para. 22; C-136/08 P of 30.4.2009 – Japan Tobacco/OHIM, para. 42; C-100/11 P of 10.5.2012 – Helena Rubinstein and L'Oréal/OHIM, para. 93; C-155/18 P to C-158/18 P of 4.3.2020 – Tulliallan Burlington/EUIPO, para. 75.
2005. CJEU C-252/07 of 27.11.2008 – Intel Corporation, para. 39; C-65/12 of 6.2.2014 – Leidseplein Beheer, para. 44; C-125/14 of 3.9.2015 – Iron & Smith, para. 31.

of unfair advantage or detriment, and such a conclusion may be established, in particular, on the basis of logical deductions made from an analysis of the probabilities and by taking account of the normal practice in the relevant commercial sector as well as all the other circumstances of the case.[2006]

[G] Trade mark application by an agent or representative of the proprietor

The attainment of that objective requires a broad interpretation of the **concepts of 'agent' and 'representative'** within the meaning of that provision. That finding as to the meaning of the condition relating to the status of the applicant for registration of the mark vis-à-vis the proprietor of the earlier mark is, moreover, corroborated by the fact that, under that provision, those two concepts are linked by the coordinating conjunction 'or', which testifies to the application of Article 8(3) CTMR in the various cases of representation of the interests of one party by another.[2007]

Those concepts must be interpreted in such a way as to cover all forms of relationship based on a contractual agreement under which one of the parties represents the interests of the other, with the result that it is sufficient, for the purposes of the application of that provision, that there is some agreement or commercial cooperation between the parties of a kind that gives rise to a fiduciary relationship by imposing on the applicant, whether expressly or implicitly, a general duty of trust and loyalty as regards the interests of the proprietor of the earlier mark.[2008]

The objective of Article 8(3) CTMR is to prevent the misuse of the earlier mark by the agent or representative of the proprietor of that mark, as those persons may exploit the knowledge and experience acquired during their business relationship with the proprietor and may therefore improperly benefit from the effort and investment which the proprietor himself has made.[2009]

In that regard, it should be noted that there was a distribution agreement between John Mills and the proprietor of the earlier mark by which they had agreed that the proprietor would supply the goods under the designation 'Magic Minerals by Jerome Alexander' to John Mills and that the latter would be responsible for distributing the goods of that proprietor within the European Union and worldwide. Furthermore, that agreement contained – a fact not disputed by John Mills – provisions under which John Mills was, at the very least, a preferred distributor of those goods, as well as a non-competition clause and provisions relating to the intellectual property rights of the proprietor of the earlier mark with respect to those goods. Moreover, the last purchase order by which John Mills ordered 'Magic Minerals' goods from the proprietor of that mark was dated only approximately two months before John Mills filed its application for registration of the contested mark.[2010]

2006. CJEU C-100/11 P of 10.5.2012 – Helena Rubinstein and L'Oréal/OHIM, para. 95.
2007. CJEU C-809/18 P of 11.11.2020 – EUIPO/John Mills, para. 84.
2008. CJEU C-809/18 P of 11.11.2020 – EUIPO/John Mills, para. 85.
2009. CJEU C-809/18 P of 11.11.2020 – EUIPO/John Mills, para. 83.
2010. CJEU C-809/18 P of 11.11.2020 – EUIPO/John Mills, para. 86.

It follows from those factors that, having regard to the considerations set out in paragraph 85 of the present judgment, the Board of Appeal acted correctly in concluding, in paragraph 25 of the decision at issue, that John Mills had to be regarded as an 'agent' of the proprietor of the earlier mark within the meaning of Article 8(3) CTMR.[2011]

By limiting the application of Article 8(3) CTMR solely to the situation in which the earlier mark and the mark applied for by the agent or representative of the proprietor of the earlier mark are **identical**, to the exclusion of any similarity between them, the General Court **erred in law**.[2012]

It must be recalled that, according to settled case law of the Court, the interpretation of a provision of EU law requires account to be taken not only of its wording but also of its context and the objectives and purpose pursued by the act of which it forms part. The legislative history of a provision of EU law may also reveal elements that are relevant to its interpretation.[2013]

As regards, first, the wording of Article 8(3) CTMR, it should be noted that that provision merely provides that, upon opposition by the proprietor of the trade mark, a trade mark is not to be registered where an agent or representative of the proprietor of the trade mark applies for registration thereof in his own name without the proprietor's consent, unless that agent or representative justifies his action.[2014]

Thus, although the wording of that provision suggests a close relationship between 'the' earlier mark and the mark applied for by the agent or representative of the proprietor of the earlier mark, that provision does not, however, explicitly state whether it applies only in the case where the mark applied for by that agent or representative is identical to the earlier mark or whether cases in which the marks at issue are similar may also come within the scope of that provision.[2015]

Secondly, as regards the background to Article 8(3) CTMR, it is apparent from the *travaux préparatoires* relating to that provision that the EU legislature, it is true, expressly refused to state therein that it applies in cases where there is similarity between the earlier mark and the mark applied for by the agent or representative of the proprietor of the earlier mark.[2016]

However, it was, first, to take account of the fact that the EU legislature also did not intend to retain, in that provision, the explicit reference to the identity between the earlier trade mark and that applied for by the agent or representative of the proprietor of the earlier trade mark provided for by the pre-draft version of the regulation relating to the EU trade mark.[2017]

Secondly, the General Court could not find that the fact that the EU legislature had twice refrained from making express mention of the fact that the provision concerned should apply in the case of similar marks is sufficient proof of its intention

2011. CJEU C-809/18 P of 11.11.2020 – EUIPO/John Mills, para. 87.
2012. CJEU C-809/18 P of 11.11.2020 – EUIPO/John Mills, para. 74.
2013. CJEU C-809/18 P of 11.11.2020 – EUIPO/John Mills, para. 55, with further proof.
2014. CJEU C-809/18 P of 11.11.2020 – EUIPO/John Mills, para. 56.
2015. CJEU C-809/18 P of 11.11.2020 – EUIPO/John Mills, para. 57.
2016. CJEU C-809/18 P of 11.11.2020 – EUIPO/John Mills, para. 58.
2017. CJEU C-809/18 P of 11.11.2020 – EUIPO/John Mills, para. 59.

in that regard since the *travaux préparatoires* do not indicate the reasons which justified the refusal to include such a reference to the similarity of the marks at issue.[2018]

It follows that it cannot be inferred from the *travaux préparatoires* relating to Article 8(3) CTMR that, by reason of the fact that that provision does not mention similarity between the earlier mark and the mark applied for by the agent or representative of the proprietor of the earlier mark, the scope of that provision is limited solely to cases in which the marks at issue are identical.[2019]

By contrast, it is apparent from the *travaux préparatoires* that Article 8(3) CTMR reflects the choice of the EU legislature to reproduce, in essence, Article 6 *septies*(1) of the Paris Convention.[2020]

In that regard, it should be noted that Council Document No 11035/82 of 1 December 1982 relating to, *inter alia*, the conclusions of the Working Group on the regulation on the Community trade mark states that that group agreed that the provision in Article 8(3) CTMR should be interpreted as applying within the meaning of Article 6 *septies* of the Paris Convention.[2021]

Furthermore, since the European Union is a party to the TRIPS Agreement, it is under an obligation to interpret its trade mark legislation, so far as possible, in the light of the wording and purpose of that agreement. In particular, Article 2(1) of the TRIPS Agreement provides that, with respect to Parts II, III and IV of that agreement, the States which are parties thereto must comply with Articles 1 to 12 and 19 of the Paris Convention.[2022]

It follows that, so far as the interpretation of Article 8(3) CTMR is concerned, account should be taken of Article 6 *septies* of that convention.[2023]

In that regard, in the French-language version of the Paris Convention, which is the authentic version, in accordance with its Article 29, Article 6 *septies* thereof admittedly uses, for the purposes of designating the earlier mark when registration is applied for by the agent or representative of the proprietor of the earlier mark in his own name, the expression 'cette marque' ('the mark').[2024]

However, the General Court could not, on the basis of that finding alone and in the absence of further justification, affirm that that provision of the Paris Convention, as it is worded, cannot be interpreted otherwise than as meaning that the earlier mark and the mark applied for by the agent or representative of the proprietor of the earlier mark are the same, and consequently find that, in view of the absence of ambiguity in the wording of Article 6 *septies* of the Paris Convention, there was no need to take account of the *travaux préparatoires* relating to that provision.[2025]

2018. CJEU C-809/18 P of 11.11.2020 – EUIPO/John Mills, para. 60.
2019. CJEU C-809/18 P of 11.11.2020 – EUIPO/John Mills, para. 61.
2020. CJEU C-809/18 P of 11.11.2020 – EUIPO/John Mills, para. 62.
2021. CJEU C-809/18 P of 11.11.2020 – EUIPO/John Mills, para. 63.
2022. CJEU C-809/18 P of 11.11.2020 – EUIPO/John Mills, para. 64, with reference to CJEU C-245/02 of 16.11.2004 – Anheuser-Busch, paras 42.
2023. CJEU C-809/18 P of 11.11.2020 – EUIPO/John Mills, para. 65.
2024. CJEU C-809/18 P of 11.11.2020 – EUIPO/John Mills, para. 66.
2025. CJEU C-809/18 P of 11.11.2020 – EUIPO/John Mills, para. 67.

It is apparent from the Acts of the Conference of Lisbon, held from 6 to 31 October 1958 for the purpose of revising the Paris Convention, during which Article 6 *septies* was introduced, that a trade mark applied for by the agent or representative of the proprietor of the earlier mark may also be covered by that provision in the case where the mark applied for is similar to that earlier mark.[2026]

It follows that it is not possible to uphold an interpretation according to which, in so far as Article 8(3) CTMR does not refer to the identity or similarity of the earlier mark and the mark applied for by the agent or representative of the proprietor of the earlier mark, the application of that provision is limited solely to the situation in which the marks at issue are identical, to the exclusion of any other factor.[2027]

Thirdly, such an interpretation would have the effect of calling into question the general scheme of the CTMR in that it would result in the proprietor of the earlier mark being deprived of the possibility of opposing, on the basis of Article 8(3) CTMR, the registration of a similar mark by his agent or representative even though, following such registration, the latter would be entitled to file a notice of opposition, pursuant, in particular, to Article 8(1)(b) CTMR, to the application for subsequent registration of the initial mark by that proprietor on the ground of its similarity to the mark registered by the agent or representative of that proprietor.[2028]

Fourthly, an interpretation according to which Article 8(3) CTMR also allows the proprietor of the earlier mark to oppose the registration of a similar mark applied for by his agent or representative is supported by the objective pursued by that provision.[2029]

The objective pursued by that provision is to prevent the misuse of the earlier mark by the agent or representative of the proprietor of that mark, as those persons may exploit the knowledge and experience acquired during their business relationship with that proprietor and may therefore improperly benefit from the effort and investment which the proprietor himself has made.[2030]

However, the view cannot be taken that such misuse may be considered liable to occur only in cases where the earlier mark and the mark applied for by the agent or representative of the proprietor of the earlier mark are identical, and not in cases where the marks at issue are similar.[2031]

While the application of Article 8(3) CTMR stems from, *inter alia*, the **similarity between the marks** at issue, the specific condition for the protection guaranteed by that provision is that the application for registration must have been made by the agent or representative of the proprietor of the earlier mark, in his own name and without the proprietor's consent, and without that agent or representative justifying his actions. Consequently, the similarity between the marks at issue for the purposes of the

2026. CJEU C-809/18 P of 11.11.2020 – EUIPO/John Mills, para. 68, with reference to Proceedings of the Lisbon Conference, p. 681.
2027. CJEU C-809/18 P of 11.11.2020 – EUIPO/John Mills, para. 69.
2028. CJEU C-809/18 P of 11.11.2020 – EUIPO/John Mills, para. 70.
2029. CJEU C-809/18 P of 11.11.2020 – EUIPO/John Mills, para. 71.
2030. CJEU C-809/18 P of 11.11.2020 – EUIPO/John Mills, para. 72.
2031. CJEU C-809/18 P of 11.11.2020 – EUIPO/John Mills, para. 73.

application of Article 8(3) CTMR is **not** to be assessed on the basis of the existence of a **likelihood of confusion**, that condition being specific to Article 8(1)(b) CTMR.[2032]

In so far as John Mills criticizes the Board of Appeal on the ground that it found that Article 8(3) CTMR was applicable in the present case, even though not all of the **goods** to which the application for registration of the contested mark refers were identical to those covered by the earlier mark, it should be borne in mind that, even though that provision does not mention the goods or services for which the mark is sought, the essential function of a mark is to indicate the commercial origin of the goods or services covered.[2033]

Consequently, for reasons similar to those set out [above concerning the similarity of the signs], having regard to the general scheme of Article 8(3) CTMR and the objective pursued by it, the application of that provision cannot be precluded by the fact that the goods or services covered by the application for registration and those covered by the earlier mark are similar, and not identical.[2034]

Furthermore, in the present case, it should be noted, first, that John Mills does not dispute the fact that the 'face powder featuring mineral enhancements' covered by the earlier mark is identical to the 'cosmetics' and 'preparations for … care of the skin' covered by the application for registration of the contested mark. Secondly, in paragraph 31 of the decision at issue, the Board of Appeal observed, *inter alia*, that, as regards the remaining goods covered by the marks at issue, they might be made of the same ingredients, they were often produced by the same companies and they were often offered together in drugstores and the same retail store aisles. According to the Court's settled case law, in assessing the similarity of the goods or services at issue, all the relevant factors relating to those goods or services should be taken into account. Those factors include, in particular, their nature, their intended purpose, their method of use and whether they are in competition with each other or are complementary.[2035]

Accordingly, the Board of Appeal acted correctly in finding that those remaining goods were similar.[2036]

Article 6 Establishment a posteriori of invalidity or revocation of a trade mark

Where the seniority of a national trade mark or of a trade mark registered under international arrangements having effect in the Member State, which has been surrendered or allowed to lapse, is claimed for an EU trade mark, the invalidity or revocation of the trade mark providing the basis for the seniority claim may be established a posteriori, provided that the invalidity or revocation could have been

2032. CJEU C-809/18 P of 11.11.2020 – EUIPO/John Mills, para. 92, with reference to CJEU C-487/07 of 18.6.2009 – L'Oréal, para. 34 to 36.
2033. CJEU C-809/18 P of 11.11.2020 – EUIPO/John Mills, para. 98, with reference to CJEU C-541/18 of 12.9.2019 – AS/Deutsches Patent- und Markenamt, para. 18.
2034. CJEU C-809/18 P of 11.11.2020 – EUIPO/John Mills, para. 99.
2035. CJEU C-809/18 P of 11.11.2020 – EUIPO/John Mills, para. 100, with reference to CJEU C-673/15 P to C-676/15 P of 20.9.2017 – The Tea Board/EUIPO, para. 48.
2036. CJEU C-809/18 P of 11.11.2020 – EUIPO/John Mills, para. 101.

declared at the time the mark was surrendered or allowed to lapse. In such a case, the seniority shall cease to produce its effects.

Article 7 Grounds for refusal or invalidity relating to only some of the goods or services

Where grounds for refusal of registration or for invalidity of a trade mark exist in respect of only some of the goods or services for which that trade mark has been applied or registered, refusal of registration or invalidity shall cover those goods or services only.

[A] Principles

Where registration of a mark is sought in respect of various goods or services, the competent authority must check, in relation to each of the goods or services claimed, that none of the grounds for refusal listed in Article 3(1) TMD2008 applies to the mark and may reach different conclusions depending upon the goods or services in question.[2037]

It does not follow from either Article 3 TMD2008 or from any other provisions thereof that the fact that a mark is descriptive of certain goods or services is a ground for refusing to register that mark for other goods or services.[2038]

Therefore, the fact that a mark has been registered in one Member State in respect of certain goods and services cannot have any bearing on whether or not any of the grounds for refusal set out in Article 3 TMD2008 apply to a similar mark, registration of which is applied for in a second Member State in respect of **similar goods or services.**[2039]

The Directive prevents a trade mark registration authority from registering a mark for certain goods or services on condition that they do **not possess** a particular **characteristic.**[2040]

Such a practice would lead to legal uncertainty as to the extent of the protection afforded by the mark. Third parties – particularly competitors – would not, as a general rule, be aware that for given goods or services the protection conferred by the mark did not extend to those products or services having a particular characteristic, and they might thus be led to refrain from using the signs or indications of which the mark consists and which are descriptive of that characteristic for the purpose of describing their own goods.[2041]

2037. CJEU C-363/99 of 12.2.2004 – Koninklijke KPN Nederland, para. 73; C-239/05 of 15.2.2007 – BVBA Management, Training en Consultancy, para. 32; C-17/08 P of 6.2.2009 – MPDV Mikrolab, para. 34; C-282/09 P of 18.3.2010 – CFCMCEE/OHIM, para. 37; C-278/15 P of 14.1.2016 – Royal County of Berkshire Polo Club/OHIM, para. 44; C-480/15 P of 14.4.2016 – KS Sports IPCo/EUIPO, para. 56.
2038. CJEU C-363/99 of 12.2.2004 – Koninklijke KPN Nederland, para. 78.
2039. CJEU C-363/99 of 12.2.2004 – Koninklijke KPN Nederland, para. 43; C-39/08 und C-43/08 of 12.2.2009 – bild digital, para. 14.
2040. CJEU C-363/99 of 12.2.2004 – Koninklijke KPN Nederland, para. 117.
2041. CJEU C-363/99 of 12.2.2004 – Koninklijke KPN Nederland, para. 115.

Article 13 TMD2008 provides that, where **grounds for refusal of registration** of a trade mark exist **in respect of only some of the goods or services** for which that trade mark has been applied for, refusal of registration is to cover those goods or services only.[2042]

It follows, firstly, that an examination of the grounds for refusal listed in Article 3 TMD2008 must be carried out in relation to each of the goods and services for which trade mark registration is sought and, secondly, that the decision of the competent authority refusing registration of a trade mark must, in principle, state reasons in respect of each of those goods or services.[2043]

[B] Requirement to state reasons

When refusing registration of a trade mark, the competent **authority is required to state** in its decision its conclusion **for each of the individual goods and services** specified in the application for registration, regardless of the manner in which that application was formulated.[2044]

Indeed, the fact that the demand for a Community mark could be limited, a posteriori, in regard to the list of products or services by virtue of Article 44 CTMR or that a mark could be transferred for a part of the products or services by virtue of Article 17 CTMR confirms that each product must be analysed on its own merits.[2045]

That conclusion cannot be any different where an application to the competent authority for a range of goods or services does not contain a subsidiary application for registration of the mark concerned for specific classes of goods or services or for goods and services considered separately.[2046]

The duty upon the competent authority to state reasons for refusing to register a trade mark in relation to each of the goods or services for which such registration is sought also arises from the essential requirement for any decision of a national authority refusing the benefit of a right conferred by Community law to be subject to judicial review which is designed to secure effective protection for that right and which, accordingly, must cover the legality of the reasons for the decision.[2047]

2042. CJEU C-239/05 of 15.2.2007 – BVBA Management, Training en Consultancy, para. 33.
2043. CJEU C-239/05 of 15.2.2007 – BVBA Management, Training en Consultancy, para. 34; C-282/09 P of 18.3.2010 – CFCMCEE/OHIM, para. 37; C-597/12 P of 17.10.2013 – Isdin/OHIM, para. 25; C-437/15 P of 17.5.2017 – EUIPO/Deluxe Entertainment Services Group, para. 29.
2044. CJEU C-239/05 of 15.2.2007 – BVBA Management, Training en Consultancy, para. 38; C-238/06 P of 25.10.2007 – Develey Holding/OHIM, para. 91; C-87/11 P of 21.3.2012 – Fidelio/OHIM, para. 43.
2045. CJEU C-170/14 P of 6.11.2014 – Big Line Sas di Graziani Lorenzo/OHIM, para. 36; unofficial translation.
2046. CJEU C-239/05 of 15.2.2007 – BVBA Management, Training en Consultancy, para. 35.
2047. CJEU C-239/05 of 15.2.2007 – BVBA Management, Training en Consultancy, para. 36; C-282/09 P of 18.3.2010 – CFCMCEE/OHIM, para. 39.

However, where the same ground of refusal is given for a category or **group of goods or services**, the competent authority may use only general reasoning for all of the goods or services concerned.[2048]

Article 8 Lack of distinctive character or of reputation of an earlier trade mark precluding a declaration of invalidity of a registered trade mark

An application for a declaration of invalidity on the basis of an earlier mark shall not succeed at the date of application for invalidation if it would not have been successful at the filing date or the priority date of the later trade mark for any of the following reasons:

(a) the earlier trade mark, liable to be declared invalid pursuant to Article 4(1)(b), (c) or (d), had not yet acquired a distinctive character in accordance with Article 4(4);
(b) the application for a declaration of invalidity is based on Article 5(1)(b) and the earlier trade mark had not yet become sufficiently distinctive to support a finding of likelihood of confusion within the meaning of Article 5(1)(b);
(c) the application for a declaration of invalidity is based on Article 5(3)(a) and the earlier trade mark had not yet acquired a reputation within the meaning of Article 5(3)(a).

Article 9 Preclusion of a declaration of invalidity due to acquiescence

1. *Where, in a Member State, the proprietor of an earlier trade mark as referred to in Article 5(2) or Article 5(3)(a) has acquiesced, for a period of five successive years, in the use of a later trade mark registered in that Member State while being aware of such use, that proprietor shall no longer be entitled on the basis of the earlier trade mark to apply for a declaration that the later trade mark is invalid in respect of the goods or services for which the later trade mark has been used, unless registration of the later trade mark was applied for in bad faith.*
2. *Member States may provide that paragraph 1 of this Article is to apply to the proprietor of any other earlier right referred to in Article 5(4)(a) or (b).*
3. *In the cases referred to in paragraphs 1 and 2, the proprietor of a later registered trade mark shall not be entitled to oppose the use of the earlier right, even though that right may no longer be invoked against the later trade mark.*

2048. CJEU C-239/05 of 15.2.2007 – BVBA Management, Training en Consultancy, para. 37, 38; C-238/06 P of 25.10.2007 – Develey Holding/OHIM, para. 91; C-494/08 P of 9.12.2009 – Prana Haus/HABM, para. 46; C-282/09 P of 18.3.2010 – CFCMCEE/OHIM, para. 38; C-87/11 P of 21.3.2012 – Fidelio/OHIM, para. 43; C-597/12 P of 17.10.2013 – Isdin/OHIM, para. 26; C-278/15 P of 14.1.2016 – Royal County of Berkshire Polo Club/OHIM, para. 44; C-437/15 P of 17.5.2017 – EUIPO/Deluxe Entertainment Services Group, para. 30; C-214/19 P of 3.9.2020 – achtung!/EUIPO, para. 40.

[A] Principles

It must be noted at the outset that Article 9(1) TMD2008 contains no definition of the concept of 'acquiescence', nor is that concept defined in the other articles of that directive. Further, the directive contains no express reference to the law of the Member States in respect of that concept.[2049]

In accordance with settled case law, the need for a uniform application of EU law and the principle of equality require that the terms of a provision of EU law which makes no express reference to the law of the Member States for the purpose of determining its meaning and scope must normally be given an **independent and uniform interpretation throughout the European Union**; that interpretation must take into account the context of the provision and the objective of the relevant legislation.[2050]

Although the third recital in the preamble to TMD states that 'it does not appear to be necessary at present to undertake full-scale approximation of the trade mark laws of the Member States', the directive none the less provides for harmonization in relation to substantive rules of central importance in this sphere, that is to say, according to the same recital, the rules concerning the provisions of national law which most directly affect the functioning of the internal market, and that recital does not preclude the harmonization relating to those rules from being complete.[2051]

Further, it is stated, in the seventh recital in the preamble to TMD, that the 'attainment of the objectives at which this approximation [of the legislation of Member States] is aiming requires that the conditions for obtaining and continuing to hold a registered trade mark are, in general, identical in all Member States'. The ninth recital of the same directive states that 'it is fundamental, in order to facilitate the free circulation of goods and services, to ensure that henceforth registered trade marks enjoy the same protection under the legal systems of all the Member States'. Lastly, the eleventh recital of that directive further states that:

> *it is important, for reasons of legal certainty and without inequitably prejudicing the interests of a proprietor of an earlier trade mark, to provide that the latter may no longer request a declaration of invalidity nor may he oppose the use of a trade mark subsequent to his own of which he has knowingly tolerated the use for a substantial length of time, unless the application for the subsequent trade mark was made in bad faith.*[2052]

In the light of the recitals in the preamble to TMD, the Court has held that Articles 5-7 TMD2008 effect a complete harmonization of the rules relating to the rights

2049. CJEU C-482/09 of 22.9.2011 - Budějovický Budvar, para. 28.
2050. CJEU C-482/09 of 22.9.2011 - Budějovický Budvar, para. 29; *see also* CJEU C-320/12 of 27.6.2013 - Malaysia Dairy Industries, para. 25.
2051. CJEU C-482/09 of 22.9.2011 - Budějovický Budvar, para. 30; C-190/10 of 22.3.2012 - Génesis, para. 32.
2052. CJEU C-482/09 of 22.9.2011 - Budějovický Budvar, para. 31; *see also* CJEU C-307/10 of 19.6.2012 - Chartered Institute of Patent Attorneys, para. 41.

conferred by a trade mark and accordingly define the rights of proprietors of trade marks in the EU.[2053]

Similarly, it must be inferred from those recitals that Article 9 TMD2008 effects a complete harmonization of the conditions under which the proprietor of a later registered trade mark may, through the limitation in consequence of acquiescence, maintain his rights to that mark where the proprietor of an identical earlier trade mark seeks a declaration that the later trade mark is invalid or opposes its use.[2054]

In that regard, it should be borne in mind that, according to the Court's case law, the provisions of TMD, and in particular Article 9 TMD2008 thereof, indicate that the purpose of the directive is generally to strike a balance between the interest of the proprietor of a trade mark to safeguard its essential function, on the one hand, and the interests of other economic operators in having signs capable of denoting their goods and services, on the other.[2055]

Moreover, it must be observed that the same concept of 'acquiescence' is used in Article 54(1) CTMR with the same meaning as in Article 9(1) TMD2008.[2056]

The Community trade mark regime is an autonomous system with its own set of objectives and rules peculiar to it, and it applies independently of any national system.[2057]

Consequently, 'acquiescence', within the meaning of Article 9(1) TMD2008, constitutes a concept of EU law, the meaning and scope of which must be identical in all Member States. Accordingly, it is for the Court to provide an autonomous and uniform interpretation of that concept within the EU legal order.[2058]

[B] Acquiescence

Acquiescence, within the meaning of Article 9(1) TMD2008, is a **concept of EU law** and that the proprietor of an earlier trade mark cannot be held to have acquiesced in the long and well-established honest use, of which he has long been aware, by a third party of a later trade mark identical with that of the proprietor if that proprietor was not in any position to oppose that use.[2059]

2053. CJEU C-482/09 of 22.9.2011 – Budějovický Budvar, para. 32; C-197/21 of 27.10.2022 – Soda-Club (CO2) a.o./MySoda, para. 33; *see also* CJEU C-59/08 of 23.4.2009 – Copad, para. 40; C-324/08 of 15.10.2009 – Makro Zelfbedieningsgroothandel, para. 20; C-127/09 of 3.6.2010 – Coty Prestige Lancaster Group, para. 27; C-661/11 of 19.9.2013 – Martin Y Paz Diffusion, para. 54; C-500/14 of 6.10.2015 – Ford Motor Company, para. 44; C-705/17 of 12.6.2019 – Patent- och registreringsverket/Hansson, para. 38; C-112/21 of 2.6.2022 – X/Classic Coach Company a.o., para. 53.
2054. CJEU C-482/09 of 22.9.2011 – Budějovický Budvar, para. 33.
2055. CJEU C-482/09 of 22.9.2011 – Budějovický Budvar, para. 34; C-466/20 of 19.5.2022 – HEITEC/HEITECH Promotion, para. 46; *see also* CJEU C-145/05 of 27.4.2006 – Levi Strauss, paras 28 et seq.; C-65/12 of 6.2.2014 – Leidseplein Beheer, para. 41; C-112/21 of 2.6.2022 – X/Classic Coach Company a.o., para. 49.
2056. CJEU C-482/09 of 22.9.2011 – Budějovický Budvar, para. 35; C-466/20 of 19.5.2022 – HEITEC/HEITECH Promotion, para. 49.
2057. CJEU C-482/09 of 22.9.2011 – Budějovický Budvar, para. 36.
2058. CJEU C-482/09 of 22.9.2011 – Budějovický Budvar, para. 37.
2059. CJEU C-482/09 of 22.9.2011 – Budějovický Budvar, para. 50; C-381/12 P of 6.6.2013 – I Marchi Italiani/OHIM, para. 54.

In accordance with the Court's settled case law, the meaning and scope of terms for which EU law provides no definition must be determined by considering their usual meaning in everyday language while also taking into account the context in which they occur and the purposes of the rules of which they form part.[2060]

Further, the preamble of an EU measure may explain its content.[2061]

First, it is clear that, in the majority of language versions of TMD, the same word is used both in the eleventh recital and in Article 9(1) TMD2008 to designate 'acquiescence'. The fact that the English language version uses the words 'tolerated' in the eleventh recital and 'acquiesced in' in Article 9(1) is immaterial since the use of the word 'tolerated' does not imply that a less restrictive interpretation of Article 9(1) should be adopted.[2062]

Next, it must be observed that the **verb 'acquiesce'** has several usual meanings in everyday language, one of those signifying 'allow to continue' or 'not prevent'.[2063]

'Acquiescence' is therefore **not the same as 'consent'**, as referred to in Article 7(1) TMD2008, which must be so expressed[2064] that an intention to renounce a right is unequivocally demonstrated.[2065]

Referring in particular to the Danish and Swedish language versions of Article 9 TMD2008, the characteristic of a person who acquiesces is that he is passive and declines to take measures open to him to remedy a situation of which he is aware and which is not necessarily as he wishes. To put that another way, the concept of 'acquiescence' implies that the person who acquiesces remains inactive when faced with a situation which he would be in a position to oppose.[2066]

For the purposes of Article 9(1) TMD2008, that concept of **'acquiescence'** must therefore be interpreted as **meaning** that the proprietor of an earlier trade mark cannot be held to have acquiesced in the long and well-established honest use, of which he has long been aware, by a third party of a later trade mark which is identical with that of the proprietor if that proprietor was not in any position to oppose that use.[2067]

That interpretation is supported by the context of Article 9(1) TMD2008 and by the objectives of the TMD2008.[2068]

First, the eleventh recital of the TMD2008 states that the proprietor of the earlier trade mark must have 'knowingly tolerated' the use of a trade mark subsequent to his own for a substantial length of time, in other words 'intentionally', 'in full knowledge of the facts'. The eleventh recital also states that the interests of the proprietor of an earlier trade mark must not be 'inequitably' prejudiced. It would be inequitable if the proprietor of the earlier trade mark were to be excluded by limitation from seeking a

2060. CJEU C-482/09 of 22.9.2011 – Budějovický Budvar, para. 39.
2061. CJEU C-482/09 of 22.9.2011 – Budějovický Budvar, para. 40.
2062. CJEU C-482/09 of 22.9.2011 – Budějovický Budvar, para. 41.
2063. CJEU C-482/09 of 22.9.2011 – Budějovický Budvar, para. 42.
2064. *See* CJEU C-145/05 of 27.4.2006 – Levi Strauss, para. 45.
2065. CJEU C-482/09 of 22.9.2011 – Budějovický Budvar, para. 43.
2066. CJEU C-482/09 of 22.9.2011 – Budějovický Budvar, para. 44; *see also* CJEU C-466/20 of 19.5.2022 – HEITEC/HEITECH Promotion, para. 49.
2067. CJEU C-482/09 of 22.9.2011 – Budějovický Budvar, para. 45.
2068. CJEU C-482/09 of 22.9.2011 – Budějovický Budvar, para. 46.

declaration of invalidity or opposing the use of an identical later trade mark, in circumstances even where he was not in a position to do so.[2069]

Second, the objective of the TMD2008 is to strike a balance between the interest of the proprietor of a trade mark to safeguard its essential function and the interests of other economic operators in having signs capable of denoting their goods and services. That objective implies that, in order to safeguard that essential function, the proprietor of an earlier trade mark must be capable, in the context of the application of Article 9(1) TMD2008, of opposing the use of a later trade mark identical with his own.[2070]

It must be added that the effect of **any administrative action or court action** initiated by the proprietor of the earlier trade mark within the period prescribed in Article 9(1) TMD2008 is to **interrupt the period of limitation** in consequence of acquiescence.[2071]

By bringing such an action, the proprietor of the earlier mark or other earlier right unequivocally expresses its wish to oppose the use of the later mark and to remedy the alleged infringement of its rights.[2072]

Article 9 TMD2008 and Articles 54, 110 and 111 CTMR must be interpreted as meaning that an act, such as a **warning letter**, by which the proprietor of an earlier mark or other earlier right opposes the use of a later mark without taking the necessary steps to obtain a legally binding solution, **does not stop acquiescence** and, consequently, does not interrupt the period of limitation.[2073]

By setting a period of limitation in consequence of acquiescence of five consecutive years with knowledge of the use of the later trade mark, the EU legislature sought to ensure that the protection conferred by an earlier trade mark on its proprietor remains limited to cases where the proprietor shows itself to be sufficiently vigilant by opposing the use of signs by other operators likely to infringe its mark.[2074]

More specifically, as noted in recital 12 of TMD2008, the rule on limitation in consequence of acquiescence is intended to safeguard legal certainty. Where the proprietor of an earlier mark or other earlier right, within the meaning of the TMD2008 or the CTMR, has knowingly 'acquiesced' in the use of a later mark applied for in good faith for a continuous period of five years, the proprietor of the latter mark must be certain in law that such use can no longer be challenged by the proprietor of that earlier mark or other earlier right.[2075]

For the purposes of applying that rule, the concept of 'acquiescence' means that the proprietor of that earlier mark or other earlier right remains inactive even though it

2069. CJEU C-482/09 of 22.9.2011 – Budějovický Budvar, para. 47.
2070. CJEU C-482/09 of 22.9.2011 – Budějovický Budvar, para. 48.
2071. CJEU C-482/09 of 22.9.2011 – Budějovický Budvar, para. 49; C-466/20 of 19.5.2022 – HEITEC/HEITECH Promotion, para. 52.
2072. CJEU C-466/20 of 19.5.2022 – HEITEC/HEITECH Promotion, para. 53.
2073. CJEU C-466/20 of 19.5.2022 – HEITEC/HEITECH Promotion, para. 57.
2074. CJEU C-466/20 of 19.5.2022 – HEITEC/HEITECH Promotion, para. 47, with reference to CJEU C-145/05 of 27.4.2006 – Levi Strauss, para. 30.
2075. CJEU C-466/20 of 19.5.2022 – HEITEC/HEITECH Promotion, para. 48.

is aware of the use of a later mark which it would be in a position to oppose. It 'acquiesced' by failing to take measures open to it to remedy that situation.[2076]

It follows from the foregoing that the proprietor of an earlier mark or other earlier right is time-barred from seeking a declaration of invalidity or opposing the use of a later mark applied for in good faith, where, for a period of five consecutive years, while being aware of such use, it failed to carry out an act that clearly expressed its wish to oppose that use and to remedy the alleged infringement of its rights.[2077]

Such an interpretation of Article 9 TMD2008 and Articles 54 and 111 CTMR also applies to Article 110 of that regulation which may be relevant in a situation such as that at issue in the main proceedings, even though it was not mentioned in the questions referred. It must be observed, in that regard, that the rule regarding limitation in consequence of acquiescence as from the date of expiry of a period of five consecutive years with knowledge of the use of the later mark, laid down in Article 9 TMD2008, is referenced, as regards the EU trade mark, in Articles 54, 110 and 111 CTMR.[2078]

Where the bringing of that action was preceded by the sending of a warning letter, with which the proprietor of the later mark did not comply, that warning letter may interrupt the period of limitation in consequence of acquiescence provided that, **following the unsatisfactory response** to that warning letter, the proprietor of the earlier mark or other earlier right continues to express its opposition to the use of the later mark and **takes the measures** available to it to enforce its rights.[2079]

In contrast, if the proprietor of the earlier mark or other earlier right, having expressed its opposition to the use of the later mark by a warning letter, did not, after noting the refusal of the addressee of that letter to comply with it or to enter into negotiations, pursue its efforts within a reasonable period in order to remedy that situation, where appropriate by bringing an administrative or court action, it must be inferred that that proprietor failed to take the measures available to it to put an end to the alleged infringement of its rights.[2080]

Any interpretation of Article 9 TMD2008 and Articles 54, 110 and 111 CTMR to the effect that sending a warning letter is sufficient, in itself, to interrupt the period of limitation would allow the proprietor of the earlier mark or other earlier right to circumvent the regime for limitation in consequence of acquiescence by repeatedly sending a warning letter approximately every five years. Such a situation would undermine the objectives of the regime for limitation in consequence of acquiescence and would deprive that regime of its effectiveness.[2081]

Article 9 TMD2008 and Articles 54, 110 and 111 CTMR must be interpreted to mean that the limitation in consequence of acquiescence referred to in those provisions may **not be prevented by the bringing of a court action** in which the proprietor of an

2076. CJEU C-466/20 of 19.5.2022 – HEITEC/HEITECH Promotion, para. 49, with reference to CJEU C-482/09 of 22.9.2011 – Budějovický Budvar, paras 35 and 44.
2077. CJEU C-466/20 of 19.5.2022 – HEITEC/HEITECH Promotion, para. 50.
2078. CJEU C-466/20 of 19.5.2022 – HEITEC/HEITECH Promotion, para. 51.
2079. CJEU C-466/20 of 19.5.2022 – HEITEC/HEITECH Promotion, para. 54.
2080. CJEU C-466/20 of 19.5.2022 – HEITEC/HEITECH Promotion, para. 55.
2081. CJEU C-466/20 of 19.5.2022 – HEITEC/HEITECH Promotion, para. 56.

earlier mark or other earlier right sought a declaration of invalidity of a later mark or opposed the use of that mark, where the application initiating proceedings, although filed before the date of expiry of the period of limitation, did not, **owing to a lack of diligence on the part of the applicant**, satisfy the requirements of the applicable national law for service and was rectified only after that date for reasons attributable to the applicant.[2082]

As noted above, the bringing of an administrative or court action before the expiry of that period ends acquiescence and consequently prevents limitation.[2083]

As regards the date on which a court action must be deemed to have been brought, the Court has held, in the context of its interpretation of rules adopted in the field of judicial cooperation in civil matters, that that date may be the date on which the application initiating proceedings was lodged, although the court concerned can be deemed to be seised at that time only if the applicant has not subsequently failed to take the steps it was required to take to have service effected on the defendant.[2084]

Although those rules, adopted in the field of judicial cooperation in civil matters, are not formally applicable in the present case, they are nevertheless relevant for the purposes of answering the third question. The time limit directly and immediately affects the possibility for the proprietor of the earlier mark or other earlier right to rely on that mark or right in court against the proprietor of the later mark. The applicant is therefore not time-barred as long as the action is brought within that five-year period.[2085]

In that regard, it must be held that the lodging of the application initiating proceedings normally reflects the genuine and unambiguous wish of the applicant to assert its rights, which is sufficient, in principle, to end acquiescence and, consequently, to interrupt the period of limitation.[2086]

The conduct of that party may nevertheless, in certain cases, raise doubts as to that wish and the serious nature of the action brought before the court seised. That is the case, in particular, where, owing to a lack of diligence on the part of the applicant, the application initiating proceedings is not rectified in good time when it fails to meet the formal requirements of national law for service on the defendant.[2087]

In such circumstances, which are attributable to the applicant, the latter cannot claim to have put an end to the acquiescence of the use of the later mark by lodging the application initiating proceedings. It is only by rectifying that application, in accordance with the requirements of the applicable national law, that the applicant is to be regarded as having unequivocally expressed a clear and serious intention to assert its rights and that, consequently, the action may be deemed to have been effectively initiated.[2088]

2082. CJEU C-466/20 of 19.5.2022 – HEITEC/HEITECH Promotion, para. 68.
2083. CJEU C-466/20 of 19.5.2022 – HEITEC/HEITECH Promotion, para. 59.
2084. CJEU C-466/20 of 19.5.2022 – HEITEC/HEITECH Promotion, para. 60, with further proof.
2085. CJEU C-466/20 of 19.5.2022 – HEITEC/HEITECH Promotion, para. 61.
2086. CJEU C-466/20 of 19.5.2022 – HEITEC/HEITECH Promotion, para. 62.
2087. CJEU C-466/20 of 19.5.2022 – HEITEC/HEITECH Promotion, para. 63.
2088. CJEU C-466/20 of 19.5.2022 – HEITEC/HEITECH Promotion, para. 64.

It is for the referring court to ascertain the date on which the application initiating proceedings was rectified in such a way as to enable the court seised to commence the proceedings and to serve that document on the defendants in the main proceedings. If the rectification did not take place until after the expiry of the period of limitation in consequence of acquiescence, it is for the referring court to assess whether that fact is mainly due to conduct on the part of the applicant in the main proceedings which may be characterized as a lack of diligence. If that court were to take the view that that was the case, it would have to conclude that, due to the plaintiff's lack of diligence, its action must be regarded as time-barred.[2089]

[C] Period of limitation

The registration of the earlier trade mark in the Member State concerned does not constitute a prerequisite for the running of the period of limitation in consequence of acquiescence prescribed in Article 9(1) TMD2008. The prerequisites for the running of that period of limitation, which it is for the national court to determine, are, first, registration of the later trade mark in the Member State concerned, second, the application for registration of that mark being made in good faith, third, use of the later trade mark by its proprietor in the Member State where it has been registered and, fourth, knowledge by the proprietor of the earlier trade mark that the later trade mark has been registered and used after its registration.[2090]

As a preliminary point, it should be borne in mind that, as follows from the eleventh recital of the TMD2008, the rule governing limitation in consequence of acquiescence provided for in Article 9 TMD2008 was established for reasons of legal certainty.[2091]

It is apparent from the wording of Article 9(1) TMD2008 that **four conditions** must be satisfied before the period of limitation in consequence of acquiescence starts running if there is use of a later trade mark which is identical with the earlier trade mark or confusingly similar.[2092]

First, since Article 9(1) TMD2008 refers to a 'later registered trade mark', registration of that mark in the Member State concerned constitutes a necessary condition. The period of limitation in consequence of acquiescence cannot therefore start to run from the date of mere use of a later trade mark, even if the proprietor of that mark subsequently has it registered.[2093]

As regards the registration of the later trade mark in the Member State concerned, it must be observed that the fifth recital of the TMD2008 states that:

2089. CJEU C-466/20 of 19.5.2022 – HEITEC/HEITECH Promotion, para. 67.
2090. CJEU C-482/09 of 22.9.2011 – Budějovický Budvar, para. 62; *see also* CJEU C-381/12 P of 6.6.2013 – I Marchi Italiani/OHIM, para. 53.
2091. CJEU C-482/09 of 22.9.2011 – Budějovický Budvar, para. 52.
2092. CJEU C-482/09 of 22.9.2011 – Budějovický Budvar, para. 53.
2093. CJEU C-482/09 of 22.9.2011 – Budějovický Budvar, para. 54; *see also* CJEU C-381/12 P of 6.6.2013 – I Marchi Italiani/OHIM, para. 53.

> *Member States ... remain free to fix the provisions of procedure concerning the registration, the revocation and the invalidity of trade marks acquired by registration; ... they can, for example, determine the form of trade mark registration and invalidity procedures, decide whether earlier rights should be invoked either in the registration procedure or in the invalidity procedure or in both and, if they allow earlier rights to be invoked in the registration procedure, have an opposition procedure or an ex officio examination procedure or both; ... Member States remain free to determine the effects of revocation or invalidity of trade marks.*[2094]

Second, the application for registration of the later trade mark must have been made by its proprietor in good faith.[2095]

Third, the proprietor of the later trade mark must use his trade mark in the Member State where it is registered.[2096]

Fourth, the proprietor of the earlier trade mark must be aware of the registration of the later trade mark and of the use of that trade mark after its registration.[2097]

It is for the referring court to determine whether those four prerequisites for the running of the period of limitation in consequence of acquiescence are satisfied in the main proceedings.[2098]

That said, it should be added that registration of the earlier trade mark in the Member State concerned does not constitute a prerequisite for the period of limitation in consequence of acquiescence to commence.[2099]

Article 9(1) TMD2008 states that the 'earlier trade mark' is 'as referred to in Article 4(2)' TMD2008. Within the meaning of Article 4(2) a trade mark can be considered to be earlier without having been registered, as in the case of 'applications for trade marks ... subject to their registration' and trade marks which are 'well known', referred to in Article 4(2)(c) and (d), respectively.[2100]

[D] Legal consequences

Article 9 TMD2008 and Articles 54, 110 and 111 CTMR must be interpreted as meaning that, where the proprietor of an earlier mark or other earlier right, within the meaning of those provisions, is time-barred from seeking a declaration of invalidity of a later mark and from opposing the use of that mark, that proprietor is also time-barred from bringing **ancillary or related claims**, such as claims for damages, the provision of information or the destruction of goods.[2101]

As explained in the context of the examination of the first and second questions, the proprietor of an earlier mark or other earlier right that, while being aware of the use of a later mark applied for in good faith, fails, for a continuous period of five years, to

2094. CJEU C-482/09 of 22.9.2011 – Budějovický Budvar, para. 55.
2095. CJEU C-482/09 of 22.9.2011 – Budějovický Budvar, para. 56.
2096. CJEU C-482/09 of 22.9.2011 – Budějovický Budvar, para. 57.
2097. CJEU C-482/09 of 22.9.2011 – Budějovický Budvar, para. 58; *see also* CJEU C-381/12 P of 6.6.2013 – I Marchi Italiani/OHIM, para. 53.
2098. CJEU C-482/09 of 22.9.2011 – Budějovický Budvar, para. 59.
2099. CJEU C-482/09 of 22.9.2011 – Budějovický Budvar, para. 60.
2100. CJEU C-482/09 of 22.9.2011 – Budějovický Budvar, para. 61.
2101. CJEU C-466/20 of 19.5.2022 – HEITEC/HEITECH Promotion, para. 73.

act in a manner that unequivocally expresses its wish to oppose that use and to remedy the alleged infringement of its rights is time-barred from challenging the use of that later mark.[2102]

It would be contrary to the objectives of the regime for limitation in consequence of acquiescence, most notably the safeguarding of legal certainty, to allow, in such a situation, that proprietor to bring an action against the proprietor of that later mark after the end of that period of five consecutive years seeking that the latter be ordered to pay damages or seeking injunctions against the latter.[2103]

If such an action or such claims were to succeed after the expiry of the period of limitation, it would amount to leaving intact, beyond that date, the possibility of a finding that the use of the later mark infringes the earlier mark or the earlier right and of attributing, on that basis, non-contractual liability to the proprietor of the later mark. Such an interpretation of the regime of limitation in consequence of acquiescence would undermine the objective pursued by that regime, which is to give the proprietor of the later trade mark the certainty, at the end of that period, that the use of that mark can no longer be challenged, by whatever legal means, by the person that has knowingly acquiesced in its use for an uninterrupted period of five years.[2104]

[E] Coexistence

According to settled case law, the **two criteria** which must be satisfied in order for the existence of coexistence of trade marks to be taken into consideration are, first, the absence of a likelihood of confusion, in the mind of the relevant public, between the earlier trade marks relied on and the earlier trade mark and, second, the identity of the earlier trade marks at issue and the conflicting trade marks.[2105]

Article 9(1)(b) CTMR must be interpreted as meaning that the fact that, in part of the European Union, an EU trade mark and a national mark peacefully coexist does not allow the conclusion that **in another part of the European Union**, where peaceful coexistence between that EU trade mark and the sign identical to that national mark is absent, there is no likelihood of confusion between that EU trade mark and that sign.[2106]

Pursuant to that principle, expressed in recital 3 of the CTMR and specified in Article 1(2) thereof, EU trade marks are given uniform protection and produce their effects throughout the entire area of the European Union. Under Article 1(2), the EU trade mark may not, save as otherwise provided in that regulation, be registered, transferred or surrendered or be the subject of a decision revoking the rights of the proprietor or declaring it invalid, nor shall its use be prohibited, save in respect of the whole [of the European Union].[2107]

2102. CJEU C-466/20 of 19.5.2022 – HEITEC/HEITECH Promotion, para. 70.
2103. CJEU C-466/20 of 19.5.2022 – HEITEC/HEITECH Promotion, para. 71.
2104. CJEU C-466/20 of 19.5.2022 – HEITEC/HEITECH Promotion, para. 72.
2105. CJEU C-412/16 P and 413/16 P of 1.3.2018 – Ice Mountain Ibiza/EUIPO, para. 103, with further proof; *see also* CJEU C-73/18 P of 7.6.2018 – Cotécnica/EUIPO, paras 5/11 and 6.
2106. CJEU C-93/16 of 20.7.2017 – Ornua Co-operative/Tindale & Stanton, para. 38.
2107. CJEU C-93/16 of 20.7.2017 – Ornua Co-operative/Tindale & Stanton, para. 26.

Although Article 1(2) CTMR refers only to the registration of the trade mark, the transfer thereof, the loss of the rights conferred by the trade mark and the prohibition on making use of the latter, it is, however, clear from a combined reading of that article and recital 3 of that regulation that the effects of the EU trade mark listed under section 2 of Title II of that regulation apply, as well, in a uniform manner throughout the entire territory of the European Union.[2108]

Accordingly, the Court has already held that the exclusive right conferred by an EU trade mark on its proprietor, under Article 9(1) CTMR, extends, as a rule, to the entire area of the European Union.[2109]

As regards Article 9(1)(b) CTMR, it is clear from the settled case law of the Court that that article protects the proprietor of an EU trade mark against any use which adversely affects that trade mark's function of indicating origin or is liable to do so.[2110]

The uniform protection thus conferred on the proprietor of the EU trade mark by that article is to entitle that proprietor, throughout the European Union, to prohibit a third party from using, in the course of trade and without the consent of that proprietor, an identical or similar sign for identical or similar goods or services which adversely affects that trade mark's function of indicating origin or is liable to do so and thus gives rise to a likelihood of confusion.[2111]

In order for the proprietor of the EU trade mark to avail himself of that right, there is no need for the use of the identical or similar sign creating a likelihood of confusion to take place throughout the entire territory of the European Union.[2112]

If the proprietor of the EU trade mark was only protected against infringements committed throughout the entire territory of the European Union, he would not be able to contest the use of identical or similar signs which give rise to a likelihood of confusion in only part of that territory, even though Article 9(1)(b) CTMR is intended to protect that proprietor, throughout the European Union, against any use which adversely affects his trade mark's function of indicating origin.[2113]

Consequently, when the use of a sign gives rise, in one part of the European Union, to a likelihood of confusion with an EU trade mark, whilst, in another part of the European Union, that same use does not give rise to such a likelihood of confusion, there is an infringement of the exclusive right conferred by that trade mark. In that case, the European Union trade marks court hearing the case must prevent the marketing of the goods concerned under the sign at issue throughout the entire territory of the European Union, with the exception of the part in respect of which there has been found to be no likelihood of confusion.[2114]

2108. CJEU C-93/16 of 20.7.2017 – Ornua Co-operative/Tindale & Stanton, para. 27.
2109. CJEU C-93/16 of 20.7.2017 – Ornua Co-operative/Tindale & Stanton, para. 28, with reference to CJEU C-235/09 of 12.4.2011 – DHL Express France, para. 39.
2110. CJEU C-93/16 of 20.7.2017 – Ornua Co-operative/Tindale & Stanton, para. 29, with reference to CJEU C-223/15 of 22.9.2016 – combit Software/Commit Business Solutions, para. 27.
2111. CJEU C-93/16 of 20.7.2017 – Ornua Co-operative/Tindale & Stanton, para. 30.
2112. CJEU C-93/16 of 20.7.2017 – Ornua Co-operative/Tindale & Stanton, para. 31.
2113. CJEU C-93/16 of 20.7.2017 – Ornua Co-operative/Tindale & Stanton, para. 32.
2114. CJEU C-93/16 of 20.7.2017 – Ornua Co-operative/Tindale & Stanton, para. 33, with reference to CJEU C-223/15 of 22.9.2016 – combit Software/Commit Business Solutions, para. 25 and 36.

It is clear, moreover, from the case law of the Court that the examination of the likelihood of confusion in part of the European Union must be based on a global assessment of all the relevant factors in the case concerned and that that assessment must include a visual, phonetic or conceptual comparison of the mark and the sign used by the third party, which may lead, in particular for linguistic reasons, to **different conclusions for one part of the European Union and for another**.[2115]

In a situation, in which peaceful coexistence between EU trade marks and a sign has been found in Ireland and the United Kingdom, the European Union trade marks court hearing infringement proceedings on the use of that sign in another Member State, here the Kingdom of Spain, cannot merely base its assessment on the peaceful coexistence prevailing in Ireland and the United Kingdom. That court must, on the contrary, make a global assessment of all the relevant factors.[2116]

Article 9(1)(b) CTMR must be interpreted as meaning that the elements which, according to the European Union trade marks court hearing an infringement action, are relevant for assessing whether the proprietor of an EU trade mark is entitled to prohibit the use of a sign in part of the European Union not covered by that action may be taken into account by that court to assess whether that proprietor is entitled to prohibit the use of that sign in the part of the European Union which is the subject of the infringement action, provided that the market conditions and the sociocultural circumstances are not significantly different in one of those parts of the European Union and in the other.[2117]

As has been stated before, the examination to be carried out by the competent European Union trade marks court must be based on a global assessment of all of the relevant factors of the case before it.[2118]

That global assessment must, as regards the visual, auditory or conceptual comparison between the EU trade mark at issue and the sign used by the third party, be based on the overall impression produced by that mark and that sign on the relevant public, which comprises the average consumer of the goods or services concerned, who is reasonably well informed and reasonably observant and circumspect.[2119]

Where the market conditions and the sociocultural or other circumstances contributing to the overall impression produced by the EU trade mark and the sign at issue on the average consumer do not vary significantly from one part of the European Union to another, there is nothing to prevent the relevant factors, the presence of which in part of the European Union has been established, being taken into account in assessing whether the proprietor of that trade mark is entitled to prohibit the use of that sign in another part of the European Union or throughout the entire territory of the European Union.[2120]

2115. CJEU C-93/16 of 20.7.2017 – Ornua Co-operative/Tindale & Stanton, para. 36, with reference to CJEU C-223/15 of 22.9.2016 – combit Software/Commit Business Solutions, para. 31 and 33.
2116. CJEU C-93/16 of 20.7.2017 – Ornua Co-operative/Tindale & Stanton, para. 37.
2117. CJEU C-93/16 of 20.7.2017 – Ornua Co-operative/Tindale & Stanton, para. 47.
2118. CJEU C-93/16 of 20.7.2017 – Ornua Co-operative/Tindale & Stanton, para. 40.
2119. CJEU C-93/16 of 20.7.2017 – Ornua Co-operative/Tindale & Stanton, para. 41, with further reference.
2120. CJEU C-93/16 of 20.7.2017 – Ornua Co-operative/Tindale & Stanton, para. 42.

The restriction of the exclusive right conferred by Article 9 CTMR is subject to the condition that the use of the sign with the indication of geographical origin complies with **honest practices** in industrial or commercial matters. In order to examine whether that condition, which is an expression of an obligation of loyalty to the legitimate interests of the proprietor of the mark, is satisfied, the court hearing the case must make a global assessment of all the relevant circumstances.[2121]

In that regard, account should be taken, in particular, of the overall presentation of the product marketed by the third party, the circumstances in which a distinction is made between that mark and the sign used by that the third party, and the effort made by that third party to ensure that consumers distinguish its products from those of which it is not the trade mark owner.[2122]

Although, for the purpose of assessing whether Ornua is entitled to prohibit the use of the sign KERRYMAID in Spain, the referring court should consider taking into account elements present in Ireland and the United Kingdom, it should first of all ensure that there is no significant difference between the market conditions or the sociocultural circumstances which may be observed, respectively, in the part of the European Union covered by the infringement action and in that in which the geographical area corresponding to the geographical word contained in the sign at issue is located. It cannot be excluded that the conduct which can be expected of the third party so that its use of the sign follows honest practices in industrial or commercial matters must be analysed differently in a part of the European Union where consumers have a particular affinity with the geographical word contained in the mark and the sign at issue than in a part of the European Union where that affinity is weaker.[2123]

Article 9(1)(c) CTMR must be interpreted as meaning that the fact that, in part of the European Union, an EU trade mark with a reputation and a sign peacefully coexist does not allow the conclusion that in another part of the European Union, where that peaceful coexistence is absent, there is due cause legitimizing the use of that sign.[2124]

The exclusive right conferred by the EU trade mark on its proprietor pursuant to Article 9(1) CTMR extends, as a rule, to the entire territory of the European Union.[2125]

The extended protection conferred by Article 9(1)(c) CTMR on proprietors of EU trade marks with a reputation consists in empowering those holders to prohibit any third party from making, in the course of trade and without the consent of the proprietor, use without due cause of an identical or similar sign – whether for similar goods or services or for goods or services not similar to those for which those marks are registered – which takes unfair advantage of the distinctive character or the repute of those marks or is detrimental to that distinctive character or repute.[2126]

2121. CJEU C-93/16 of 20.7.2017 – Ornua Co-operative/Tindale & Stanton, para. 44, with further reference.
2122. CJEU C-93/16 of 20.7.2017 – Ornua Co-operative/Tindale & Stanton, para. 45, with reference to CJEU C-228/03 of 17.3.2005 – Gillette Company and Gillette Group Finland, para. 46.
2123. CJEU C-93/16 of 20.7.2017 – Ornua Co-operative/Tindale & Stanton, para. 46.
2124. CJEU C-93/16 of 20.7.2017 – Ornua Co-operative/Tindale & Stanton, para. 60; *see also* CJEU C-690/17 of 11.4.2019 – Oko-Text Verlag/Dr. Rudolf Liebe Nachf., para. 45.
2125. CJEU C-93/16 of 20.7.2017 – Ornua Co-operative/Tindale & Stanton, para. 49.
2126. CJEU C-93/16 of 20.7.2017 – Ornua Co-operative/Tindale & Stanton, para. 50, with reference to CJEU C-323/09 of 22.9.2011 – Interflora, para. 68 and 70.

So that the proprietor of an EU trade mark has that extended protection, it must be established, within the meaning of Article 9(1)(c) CTMR, that that mark has a 'reputation in the [European Union]'. To that end, it is sufficient that it be established that the mark has such a reputation in a substantial part of the territory of the European Union, and that part may, in some circumstances, correspond to the territory of a single Member State. If that condition is satisfied, the EU trade mark at issue must be held to have a reputation in the whole of the European Union.[2127]

That case law ensures that the proprietor of an EU trade mark can either be entitled to the extended protection conferred by Article 9(1)(c) CTMR throughout the European Union, or cannot rely on it at all. Accordingly, the scope of the protection conferred by any EU trade mark has a uniform character on the entire territory of the European Union.[2128]

In contrast, in order for the proprietor of an EU trade mark having that extended protection to be able to rely on his right conferred by Article 9(1)(c), it is not at all necessary that the use of the sign infringing that right takes place on the entire territory of the European Union.[2129]

If that proprietor were only protected against infringements committed on the entire territory of the European Union, it would be impossible to contest infringements committed in only part of that territory, even though the purpose of Article 9(1)(c) CTMR is to protect that proprietor, throughout the European Union, from any use without due cause of an identical or similar sign which takes unfair advantage of the distinctive character or the repute of those marks or is detrimental to that distinctive character or repute.[2130]

SECTION 3 RIGHTS CONFERRED AND LIMITATIONS

Article 10 Rights conferred by a trade mark

1. *The registration of a trade mark shall confer on the proprietor exclusive rights therein.*
2. *Without prejudice to the rights of proprietors acquired before the filing date or the priority date of the registered trade mark, the proprietor of that registered trade mark shall be entitled to prevent all third parties not having his consent from using in the course of trade, in relation to goods or services, any sign where:*
   (a) *the sign is identical with the trade mark and is used in relation to goods or services which are identical with those for which the trade mark is registered;*
   (b) *the sign is identical with, or similar to, the trade mark and is used in relation to goods or services which are identical with or similar to the goods*

2127. CJEU C-93/16 of 20.7.2017 – Ornua Co-operative/Tindale & Stanton, para. 51, with reference to CJEU C-301/07 of 6.10.2009 – PAGO International, para. 27, 29 and 30; C-125/14 of 3.9.2015 – Iron & Smith, paras 19 and 20.
2128. CJEU C-93/16 of 20.7.2017 – Ornua Co-operative/Tindale & Stanton, para. 52.
2129. CJEU C-93/16 of 20.7.2017 – Ornua Co-operative/Tindale & Stanton, para. 53.
2130. CJEU C-93/16 of 20.7.2017 – Ornua Co-operative/Tindale & Stanton, para. 54.

or services for which the trade mark is registered, if there exists a likelihood of confusion on the part of the public; the likelihood of confusion includes the likelihood of association between the sign and the trade mark;

(c) the sign is identical with, or similar to, the trade mark irrespective of whether it is used in relation to goods or services which are identical with, similar to, or not similar to those for which the trade mark is registered, where the latter has a reputation in the Member State and where use of that sign without due cause takes unfair advantage of, or is detrimental to, the distinctive character or the repute of the trade mark.

3. The following, in particular, may be prohibited under paragraph 2:

(a) affixing the sign to the goods or to the packaging thereof;

(b) offering the goods or putting them on the market, or stocking them for those purposes, under the sign, or offering or supplying services thereunder;

(c) importing or exporting the goods under the sign;

(d) using the sign as a trade or company name or part of a trade or company name;

(e) using the sign on business papers and in advertising;

(f) using the sign in comparative advertising in a manner that is contrary to Directive 2006/114/EC.

4. Without prejudice to the rights of proprietors acquired before the filing date or the priority date of the registered trade mark, the proprietor of that registered trade mark shall also be entitled to prevent all third parties from bringing goods, in the course of trade, into the Member State where the trade mark is registered, without being released for free circulation there, where such goods, including packaging, come from third countries and bear without authorisation a trade mark which is identical with the trade mark registered in respect of such goods, or which cannot be distinguished in its essential aspects from that trade mark.

The entitlement of the trade mark proprietor pursuant to the first subparagraph shall lapse if, during the proceedings to determine whether the registered trade mark has been infringed, initiated in accordance with Regulation (EU) No 608/2013, evidence is provided by the declarant or the holder of the goods that the proprietor of the registered trade mark is not entitled to prohibit the placing of the goods on the market in the country of final destination.

5. Where, under the law of a Member State, the use of a sign under the conditions referred to in paragraph 2 (b) or (c) could not be prohibited before the date of entry into force of the provisions necessary to comply with Directive 89/104/EEC in the Member State concerned, the rights conferred by the trade mark may not be relied on to prevent the continued use of the sign.

6. Paragraphs 1, 2, 3 and 5 shall not affect provisions in any Member State relating to the protection against the use of a sign other than use for the purposes of distinguishing goods or services, where use of that sign without due cause takes unfair advantage of, or is detrimental to, the distinctive character or the repute of the trade mark.

[A] Principles

Article 5(1) TMD2008 is a provision which is identical to Article 9(1) CTMR and must be interpreted in the same way.[2131]

2131. CJEU C-62/08 of 19.2.2009 – UDV North America, para. 42; C-129/17 of 25.7.2018 – Mitsubishi Shoji Kaisha a.o./Duma Forklifts a.o., para. 29.

It is clear from the wording of Article 5 TMD2008 that the purpose of that provision is to harmonize the **scope of the protection** to be afforded to trade marks within the Community.[2132]

Articles 5–7 TMD2008 embody a complete harmonization of the rules relating to the rights conferred by a trade mark and accordingly define the rights of proprietors of trade marks in the Community.[2133]

Consequently, save for the specific cases governed by Articles 8 et seq. TMD2008, a national court may not, in a dispute relating to the exercise of the exclusive right conferred by a trade mark, limit that exclusive right in a manner which exceeds the limitations arising from Articles 5–7 TMD2008.[2134]

Article 5 TMD2008 precludes a proprietor of trade marks which, in a situation where there has been use shared with a third party, had consented to the use by that third party of signs which are identical to its marks in respect of certain goods in classes for which those marks are registered and which no longer consents to that use, from being deprived of any possibility of asserting the exclusive right conferred upon it by those marks against that third party and of itself exercising that exclusive right in respect of goods which are identical to those of that third party.[2135]

The conditions of application of Article 4(1)(a) TMD2008 correspond essentially to those of Article 5(1)(a) TMD2008, which determines the circumstances in which the proprietor of a trade mark is entitled to prevent third parties from using signs which are identical with his trade mark. There is a similar correspondence between Articles 8(1)(a) and 9(1)(a) CTMR.[2136]

Article 16 of the **TRIPS Agreement** confers on the proprietor of a registered trade mark a minimum standard of exclusive rights agreed at international level which all the members of the WTO must guarantee in their domestic legislation. Those exclusive rights protect the proprietor against any infringements of the registered trade mark that may be committed by non-authorized third parties.[2137]

It follows from those factors that the interpretation of the relevant provisions of the national trade mark law so far as possible in the light of the wording and purpose of the relevant provisions of Community law, in the present case those of Directive 89/104, is not prejudiced by an interpretation in keeping with the wording and purpose of the relevant provisions of the TRIPS Agreement.[2138]

The relevant provisions of national trade mark law must therefore be applied and interpreted to the effect that the exercise of the exclusive right conferred on the proprietor of the trade mark to prevent the use of the sign of which that mark consists

2132. CJEU C-23/01 of 21.11.2002 – Robelco, para. 27.
2133. CJEU C-59/08 of 23.4.2009 – Copad, para. 40; C-324/08 of 15.10.2009 – Makro Zelfbedieningsgroothandel, para. 20; C-127/09 of 3.6.2010 – Coty Prestige Lancaster Group, para. 27; C-46/10 of 14.7.2011 – Viking Gas, para. 25; C-482/09 of 22.9.2011 – Budějovický Budvar, para. 32; C-661/11 of 19.9.2013 – Martin Y Paz Diffusion, para. 54; C-500/14 of 6.10.2015 – Ford Motor Company, para. 44.
2134. CJEU C-661/11 of 19.9.2013 – Martin Y Paz Diffusion, para. 55.
2135. CJEU C-661/11 of 19.9.2013 – Martin Y Paz Diffusion, para. 62.
2136. CJEU C-291/00 of 20.3.2003 – LTJ Diffusion, para. 41.
2137. CJEU C-245/02 of 16.11.2004 – Anheuser-Busch, para. 67.
2138. CJEU C-245/02 of 16.11.2004 – Anheuser-Busch, para. 70.

or of a sign similar to that mark must be reserved to cases in which a third party's use of the sign prejudices or is liable to prejudice the functions of the trade mark, in particular its essential function of guaranteeing to consumers the origin of the goods.[2139]

Such an interpretation is, moreover, supported by the general purpose of the TRIPS Agreement, which is to ensure that a balance is maintained between the aim of reducing distortions and impediments to international trade and that of promoting effective and adequate protection of intellectual property rights so as to ensure that the measures and procedures to enforce intellectual property rights do not themselves become barriers to legitimate trade. That distinction also appears to be appropriate in the light of the specific object of Article 16 of the TRIPS Agreement, which is to guarantee a minimum standard of exclusive rights agreed at international level.[2140]

Moreover, the conditions laid down in Article 16 of the TRIPS Agreement, in the authentic French, English and Spanish versions, that the use must be made 'in the course of trade' ('au cours d'opérations commerciales', 'en el curso de operaciones comerciales') and 'for goods' ('pour des produits', 'para bienes') appear to correspond to those laid down in Article 5(1) TMD2008, which require that the use be made 'in the course of trade' (in the French and Spanish versions, 'dans la vie des affaires' and 'en el tráfico económico') and 'for goods' (in those other versions, 'pour des produits' and 'para productos').[2141]

In conferring on the proprietor of a trade mark the right to prevent all third parties from using an identical or similar sign, where there is a likelihood of confusion, and in setting out the uses of such a sign which may be prohibited, Article 5 TMD2008 seeks to protect that proprietor from uses of signs likely to infringe that trade mark.[2142]

Article 5 TMD2008 **defines** the 'rights conferred by a trade mark'.[2143]

Article 5 TMD2008 defines the '[r]ights conferred by a trade mark', and Article 6 contains provisions on the '[l]imitation of the effects of a trade mark'.[2144]

Under the first sentence of Article 5(1) TMD2008, the registered trade mark confers exclusive rights on its proprietor. Under Article 5(1)(a), that exclusive right entitles the proprietor to prevent all third parties, acting without his consent, from using in the course of trade any sign which is identical to the trade mark in relation to goods or services which are identical to those for which the trade mark is registered. Article 5(3) gives a non-exhaustive list of the kinds of use which the proprietor may prohibit under Article 5(1). Other provisions of the Directive, such as Article 6, define certain limitations on the effects of a trade mark.[2145]

2139. CJEU C-245/02 of 16.11.2004 – Anheuser-Busch, para. 71.
2140. CJEU C-245/02 of 16.11.2004 – Anheuser-Busch, para. 72.
2141. CJEU C-245/02 of 16.11.2004 – Anheuser-Busch, para. 73.
2142. CJEU C-145/05 of 27.4.2006 – Levi Strauss, para. 14.
2143. CJEU C-355/96 of 16.7.1998 – Silhouette International Schmied/Hartlauer Handelsgesellschaft, para. 16.
2144. CJEU C-206/01 of 12.11.2002 – Arsenal Football Club, para. 37; C-228/03 of 17.3.2005 – Gillette Company and Gillette Group Finland, para. 27; C-48/05 of 25.1.2007 – Adam Opel, para. 15.
2145. CJEU C-206/01 of 12.11.2002 – Arsenal Football Club, para. 38; C-228/03 of 17.3.2005 – Gillette Company and Gillette Group Finland, para. 28; C-48/05 of 25.1.2007 – Adam Opel,

As is clear from the Court's case law, the proprietor of a registered mark may prevent the use of a sign by a third party which is identical to his mark under Article 5(1)(a) TMD2008 only if the following **four conditions** are satisfied:

(i) that use must be in the course of trade;
(ii) it must be without the consent of the proprietor of the mark;
(iii) it must be in respect of goods or services which are identical to those for which the mark is registered; and
(iv) it must affect or be liable to affect the functions of the trade mark, in particular its essential function of guaranteeing to consumers the origin of the goods or services.[2146]

Where there was a likelihood of confusion between the registered trade mark and a similar sign at the **time** when the sign in question began to be used, the proprietor is to be entitled to prevent all third parties not having his consent from using that sign in the course of trade.[2147]

[B] Use in the course of trade

The use of a sign identical with a trade mark constitutes use in the course of trade where it occurs in the context of commercial activity with a view to **economic advantage and not as a private matter**.[2148]

The exclusive rights conferred by trade marks may, as a rule, be relied on only as against economic operators.[2149]

When an individual sells a product bearing a trade mark through an **online marketplace** and the transaction does not take place in the context of a commercial activity, the proprietor of the trade mark cannot rely on his exclusive right as expressed in Article 5 TMD2008 and Article 9 CTMR. If, however, owing to their volume, their frequency or other characteristics, the sales made on such a marketplace go beyond the realms of a private activity, the seller will be acting 'in the course of trade' within the meaning of those provisions.[2150]

The use involved in the case in the main proceedings is in point of fact use 'in the course of trade' within the meaning of Article 5(1) and (2). Article 5(3) TMD2008

para. 16; C-17/06 of 11.9.2007 – Céline, para. 14; *see also* CJEU C-145/05 of 27.4.2006 – Levi Strauss, para. 27; C-533/06 of 12.6.2008 – O2 Holdings/Hutchison 3G UK, para. 32.

2146. CJEU C-17/06 of 11.9.2007 – Céline, para. 16; C-62/08 of 19.2.2009 – UDV North America, para. 42.

2147. CJEU C-145/05 of 27.4.2006 – Levi Strauss, para. 22.

2148. CJEU C-206/01 of 12.11.2002 – Arsenal Football Club, para. 40; C-48/05 of 25.1.2007 – Adam Opel, para. 18; C-325/06 P of 20.3.2007 – Galileo International Technology and Others/ Commission, para. 32; C-17/06 of 11.9.2007 – Céline, para. 17; C-62/08 of 19.2.2009 – UDV North America, para. 44; C-236/08 to C-238/08 of 23.3.2010 – Google France, para. 50; C-379/14 of 16.7.2015 – TOP Logistics, para. 43; C-129/17 of 25.7.2018 – Mitsubishi Shoji Kaisha a.o./Duma Forklifts a.o., para. 39.

2149. CJEU C-324/09 of 12.7.2011 – L'Oréal, para. 54; C-772/18 of 30.4.2020 – A/B, para. 23.

2150. CJEU C-324/09 of 12.7.2011 – L'Oréal, para. 55; C-772/18 of 30.4.2020 – A/B, para. 23.

expressly mentions use of the **sign in advertising** as an example of those uses of a trade mark which may be prohibited under paragraphs (1) and (2).[2151]

With respect to the situation in point in the main proceedings, it should be observed that the word 'Arsenal' appears in large letters on the scarves offered for sale by Mr Reed, together with other much less prominent markings including the words 'The Gunners', all referring to the trade mark proprietor, namely Arsenal FC. Those scarves are intended, *inter alia*, for supporters of Arsenal FC who wear them in particular at matches in which the club plays.[2152]

An advertiser purchasing the referencing service and choosing as a **keyword** a sign identical with another's trade mark is using that sign in the course of trade.[2153]

From the advertiser's point of view, the selection of a keyword identical with a trade mark has the object and effect of displaying an advertising link to the site on which he offers his goods or services for sale. Since the sign selected as a keyword is the means used to trigger that ad display, it cannot be disputed that the advertiser indeed uses it in the context of commercial activity and not as a private matter.[2154]

In addition, it is settled case law that such use of a sign that is identical with or similar to another person's trade mark exists where that sign, selected by an advertiser as a keyword in an online referencing service, is the means used by the advertiser to trigger the display of its advertisement, **even where that sign does not appear in the advertisement itself.**[2155]

A **referencing service provider** is not involved in use in the course of trade.[2156]

With regard to the referencing service provider, it is common ground that it is carrying out a commercial activity with a view to economic advantage when it stores as keywords, for certain of its clients, signs which are identical with trade marks and arranges for the display of ads on the basis of those keywords.[2157]

It is also common ground that that service is not supplied only to the proprietors of those trade marks or to operators entitled to market their goods or services, but, at least in the proceedings in question, is provided without the consent of the proprietors and is supplied to their competitors or to imitators.[2158]

Although it is clear from those factors that the referencing service provider operates 'in the course of trade' when it permits advertisers to select, as keywords, signs identical with trade marks, stores those signs and displays its clients' ads on the

2151. CJEU C-63/97 of 23.2.1999 – BMW, para. 41.
2152. CJEU C-206/01 of 12.11.2002 – Arsenal Football Club, para. 39.
2153. CJEU C-236/08 to C-238/08 of 23.3.2010 – Google France, para. 51; C-278/08 of 25.3.2010 – BergSpechte, para. 18; C-91/09 of 26.3.2010 – Eis.de, para. 17; C-558/08 of 8.7.2010 – Portakabin, para. 27; C-324/09 of 12.7.2011 – L'Oréal, para. 87; C-323/09 of 22.9.2011 – Interflora, para. 30; C-684/19 of 2.7.2020 – mk advokaten/MBK Rechtsanwälte, para. 20.
2154. CJEU C-236/08 to C-238/08 of 23.3.2010 – Google France, para. 52; *see also* CJEU C-278/08 of 25.3.2010 – BergSpechte, para. 18; C-324/09 of 12.7.2011 – L'Oréal, para. 87.
2155. CJEU C-684/19 of 2.7.2020 – mk advokaten/MBK Rechtsanwälte, para. 20, with reference to CJEU C-323/09 of 22.9.2011 – Interflora, paras 30 et seq.
2156. CJEU C-236/08 to C-238/08 of 23.3.2010 – Google France, paras 58, 99 and 104.
2157. CJEU C-236/08 to C-238/08 of 23.3.2010 – Google France, para. 53.
2158. CJEU C-236/08 to C-238/08 of 23.3.2010 – Google France, para. 54.

basis thereof, it does not follow, however, from those factors that that service provider itself 'uses' those signs within the terms of Article 9 CTMR and Article 5 TMD2008.[2159]

In that regard, suffice it to note that the use, by a third party, of a sign identical with, or similar to, the proprietor's trade mark implies, at the very least, that that third party uses the sign in its own commercial communication. A referencing service provider allows its clients to use signs which are identical with, or similar to, trade marks, without itself using those signs.[2160]

That conclusion is not called into question by the fact that that service provider is paid by its clients for the use of those signs. The fact of creating the technical conditions necessary for the use of a sign and being paid for that service does not mean that the party offering the service itself uses the sign. To the extent to which it has permitted its client to make such a use of the sign, its role must, as necessary, be examined from the angle of rules of law other than Article 5 TMD2008 and Article 9 CTMR.[2161]

Article 5(1)(b) TMD2008 must be interpreted as meaning that a **service provider who**, under an order from and on the instructions of another person, **fills packaging** which was supplied to it by the other person who, in advance, affixed to it a sign which is identical with, or similar to, a sign protected as a trade mark does not itself make use of the sign that is liable to be prohibited under that provision.[2162]

Although it is clear from those factors that a service provider such as Winters operates in the course of trade when it fills such cans under an order from another person, it does not follow, however, therefrom that the service provider itself 'uses' those signs within the meaning of Article 5 TMD2008.[2163]

It must be stated that a service provider who, in circumstances such as those in the main action, merely fills, under an order from and on the instructions of another person, cans already bearing signs similar to trade marks and therefore merely executes a technical part of the production process of the final product without having any interest in the external presentation of those cans and in particular in the signs thereon does not itself 'use' those signs within the meaning of Article 5 TMD2008, but only creates the technical conditions necessary for the other person to use them.[2164]

Moreover, such a service provider does not, on any view, use those signs 'for goods or services' which are identical with, or similar to, those for which the trade mark was registered, within the meaning of that article. Indeed, the Court has already

2159. CJEU C-236/08 to C-238/08 of 23.3.2010 – Google France, para. 55; *see also* CJEU C-119/10 of 15.12.2011 – Frisdranken Industrie Winters, para. 28.
2160. CJEU C-236/08 to C-238/08 of 23.3.2010 – Google France, para. 56; C-324/09 of 12.7.2011 – L'Oréal, para. 102; C-379/14 of 16.7.2015 – TOP Logistics, para. 41; *see also* CJEU C-129/17 of 25.7.2018 – Mitsubishi Shoji Kaisha a.o./Duma Forklifts a.o., para. 39; C-567/18 of 2.4.2020 – Coty Germany/Amazon Services Europe a.o., para. 39; C-684/19 of 2.7.2020 – mk advokaten/MBK Rechtsanwälte, para. 27.
2161. CJEU C-236/08 to C-238/08 of 23.3.2010 – Google France, para. 57; *see also* CJEU C-567/18 of 2.4.2020 – Coty Germany/Amazon Services Europe a.o., para. 43.
2162. CJEU C-119/10 of 15.12.2011 – Frisdranken Industrie Winters, para. 37.
2163. CJEU C-119/10 of 15.12.2011 – Frisdranken Industrie Winters, para. 28.
2164. CJEU C-119/10 of 15.12.2011 – Frisdranken Industrie Winters, para. 30; *see also* CJEU C-567/18 of 2.4.2020 – Coty Germany/Amazon Services Europe a.o., para. 41.

stated[2165] that that expression generally applies to goods or services of third parties who use the sign.[2166]

It is true that the Court has also held[2167] that that expression may, under certain conditions, include goods and services of another person on whose behalf the third party acts. Thus, the Court considered that a situation in which the service provider uses a sign corresponding to the trade mark of another person in order to promote goods which one of its customers is marketing with the assistance of that service is covered by that same expression when that use is carried out in such a way that it establishes a link between that sign and that service.[2168]

However, the filling of cans bearing signs similar to trade marks is not, by its very nature, comparable to a service aimed at promoting the marketing of goods bearing those signs and does not imply, *inter alia*, the creation of a link between the signs and the filling service. The undertaking which carries out the filling is not apparent to the consumer, which excludes any association between its services and those signs.[2169]

Since it follows from the foregoing that the conditions set out in Article 5(1)(b) TMD2008 are not fulfilled in a situation such as that at issue in the main action and, therefore the proprietor cannot, on that basis, prohibit the service provider from filling cans bearing signs similar to its trade marks, the question of whether the filling constitutes affixing signs to the goods or to their packaging within the meaning of Article 5(3)(a) TMD2008 is irrelevant.[2170]

Inasmuch as such a service provider enables its customers to make use of signs similar to trade marks, its role cannot be assessed under the TMD but must be examined, if necessary, from the point of view of other rules of law.[2171]

Furthermore, the finding that a trade mark proprietor cannot act, solely on the basis of the TMD, against a service provider does not have the consequence of allowing the customer of that service provider to circumvent the protection given to the proprietor by that directive, by dividing the production process and by awarding different elements of the process to service providers. In that regard, suffice it to state that those services may be attributed to the customer who therefore remains liable under that directive.[2172]

2165. *See* CJEU C-48/05 of 25.1.2007 – Adam Opel, paras 28 et seq.; C-533/06 of 12.6.2008 – O2 Holdings/Hutchison 3G UK, para. 34; C-236/08 to C-238/08 of 23.3.2010 – Google France, para. 60.
2166. CJEU C-119/10 of 15.12.2011 – Frisdranken Industrie Winters, para. 31.
2167. CJEU C-62/08 of 19.2.2009 – UDV North America, paras 43–51; C-236/08 to C-238/08 of 23.3.2010 – Google France, para. 60; C-324/09 of 12.7.2011 – L'Oréal, paras 91 et seq.
2168. CJEU C-119/10 of 15.12.2011 – Frisdranken Industrie Winters, para. 32; *see also* CJEU C-148/21 and C-184/21 of 22.12.2022 – Louboutin/Amazon Europe Core a.o., para. 40.
2169. CJEU C-119/10 of 15.12.2011 – Frisdranken Industrie Winters, para. 33; *see also* CJEU C-148/21 and C-184/21 of 22.12.2022 – Louboutin/Amazon Europe Core a.o., para. 40.
2170. CJEU C-119/10 of 15.12.2011 – Frisdranken Industrie Winters, para. 34.
2171. CJEU C-119/10 of 15.12.2011 – Frisdranken Industrie Winters, para. 35; C-379/14 of 16.7.2015 – TOP Logistics, para. 45; *see also* CJEU C-236/08 to C-238/08 of 23.3.2010 – Google France, para. 57; C-324/09 of 12.7.2011 – L'Oréal, para. 104; C-567/18 of 2.4.2020 – Coty Germany/Amazon Services Europe a.o., para. 42.
2172. CJEU C-119/10 of 15.12.2011 – Frisdranken Industrie Winters, para. 36; *see also* CJEU C-179/15 of 3.3.2016 – Daimler/Együd Garage Gépjárműjavító és Értékesítő, para. 34.

Article 5(1) TMD2008, read in conjunction with Article 5(3)(b) and (c) TMD2008, must be interpreted as meaning that a **person who does not engage in trade as an occupation**, who takes delivery of, releases for free circulation in a Member State and retains **goods that are manifestly not intended for private use**, where those goods were sent to his or her address from a third country and where a trade mark, without the consent of the proprietor of that trade mark, is affixed to those goods, must be regarded as using that trade mark in the course of trade, within the meaning of Article 5(1) TMD2008.[2173]

First, it must be observed that the question of whether the conditions laid down in Article 5(1) TMD2008 are satisfied must be determined solely on the basis of objective factors.[2174]

In that regard, the expression 'use in the course of trade', to be found in that provision, entails that the exclusive rights conferred by a trade mark may, as a rule, be relied on by the proprietor of that trade mark only as against economic operators and, consequently, only in the context of a trading business. Further, if the transactions carried out, by reason of their volume, their frequency or other characteristics, go beyond the scope of a private activity, whoever carries out those transactions will be acting in the course of trade.[2175]

In this case, it is clear from the information available to the Court that the goods at issue in the main proceedings are ball bearings weighing, in total, 710 kg, generally used in heavy industry.[2176]

Accordingly, since those goods, having regard to their nature and their volume, are manifestly not intended for private use, the relevant transactions must be considered to fall within the scope of a trading business, though that is a matter to be determined by the referring court.[2177]

Further, a person who makes known his or her address as the place to which the goods concerned are to be shipped, who completes or has completed by an agent the customs clearance of those goods and who releases them for free circulation is importing those goods within the meaning of Article 5(3)(c) TMD2008.[2178]

As regards whether the person concerned can be considered to have himself used a sign identical to a trade mark, although that person was acting in the economic interests of a third party, it must be observed that, in order to identify use in the course of trade, ownership of the goods on which the trade mark is affixed is of no relevance. The Court has held that the fact that an economic operator uses a sign corresponding to a trade mark in relation to goods which are not his own goods – in the sense that he does not have title to them – does not in itself prevent that use from falling within the

2173. CJEU C-772/18 of 30.4.2020 – A/B, para. 30.
2174. CJEU C-772/18 of 30.4.2020 – A/B, para. 22.
2175. CJEU C-772/18 of 30.4.2020 – A/B, para. 23, with reference to CJEU C-324/09 of 12.7.2011 – L'Oréal, paras 54 et seq.
2176. CJEU C-772/18 of 30.4.2020 – A/B, para. 24.
2177. CJEU C-772/18 of 30.4.2020 – A/B, para. 25.
2178. CJEU C-772/18 of 30.4.2020 – A/B, para. 26.

scope of Article 5(1) TMD2008 (*see*, to that effect, judgment of 12 July 2011, L'Oréal and Others, C-324/09, EU:C:2011:474, paragraph 91).[2179]

The fact that a person has imported and released for free circulation such goods justifies in itself a finding that that person has acted in the course of trade, there being no need to examine subsequent dealings with those goods, whether, for example, they have been stored by the importer or put on the market within the European Union or exported to non-Member countries.[2180]

Last, the significance of the remuneration that the importer has received by way of consideration for his so acting is also of no relevance.[2181]

[C] Use in relation to goods or services

Take care: The new wording of the TMD expressly mentions 'using the sign as a trade or company name or part of a trade or company name'.

The types of conduct listed in Article 5(3) TMD2008 and Article 9(2) CTMR, namely, the affixing of a sign identical to the trade mark onto goods and the **offering** of the goods, the **importing or exporting** of the goods under the sign and the use of the sign on **business papers** and in **advertising**, constitute use in relation to the goods or services.[2182]

It should be borne in mind that Article 5(3) TMD2008 and Article 9(2) CTMR provide only a **non-exhaustive list** of the kinds of use which the proprietor may prohibit. Accordingly, the fact that the sign used by the third party for advertising purposes does not appear in the ad itself cannot of itself mean that that use falls outside the concept of '[use] ... in relation to goods or services' within the terms of Article 5 TMD2008.[2183]

Furthermore, an interpretation according to which only the uses mentioned in that list are relevant would fail to have regard for the fact that that list was drawn up before the full emergence of electronic commerce and the advertising produced in that context. It is those electronic forms of commerce and advertising which can, by means of computer technology, typically give rise to uses which differ from those listed in Article 5(3) TMD2008 and Article 9(2) CTMR.[2184]

2179. CJEU C-772/18 of 30.4.2020 – A/B, para. 27, with reference to CJEU C-324/09 of 12.7.2011 – L'Oréal, para. 91.
2180. CJEU C-772/18 of 30.4.2020 – A/B, para. 28.
2181. CJEU C-772/18 of 30.4.2020 – A/B, para. 29.
2182. CJEU C-236/08 to C-238/08 of 23.3.2010 – Google France, para. 61; *see also* CJEU C-684/19 of 2.7.2020 – mk advokaten/MBK Rechtsanwälte, para. 19.
2183. CJEU C-236/08 to C-238/08 of 23.3.2010 – Google France, para. 65; C-129/17 of 25.7.2018 – Mitsubishi Shoji Kaisha a.o./Duma Forklifts a.o., para. 38, with further proof; C-567/18 of 2.4.2020 – Coty Germany/Amazon Services Europe a.o., para. 32 and 37; C-224/20 of 17.11.2022 – Merck Sharp & Dohme a.o./Abacus a.o., para. 112; *see also* CJEU C-148/21 and C-184/21 of 22.12.2022 – Louboutin/Amazon Europe Core a.o., para. 27.
2184. CJEU C-236/08 to C-238/08 of 23.3.2010 – Google France, para. 66.

Use by an advertiser of a sign identical with a trade mark as a **keyword** in the context of an **internet referencing service** falls within the concept of use 'in relation to goods or services' within the meaning of Article 5(1)(a) TMD2008.[2185]

Likewise, there is use 'in relation to goods or services' within the meaning of Article 9(1)(a) CTMR where the sign so used is identical with a Community trade mark.[2186]

In the case of the referencing service, it is common ground that the advertiser, having chosen as a keyword a sign identical with another person's trade mark, intends that internet users who enter that word as a search term should click not only on the links displayed which come from the proprietor of the trade mark but also on the advertising link of that advertiser.[2187]

It is also clear that in most cases an internet user entering the name of a trade mark as a search term is looking for information or offers on the goods or services covered by that trade mark. Accordingly, when advertising links to sites offering goods or services of competitors of the proprietor of that mark are displayed beside or above the natural results of the search, the internet user may, if he does not immediately disregard those links as being irrelevant and does not confuse them with those of the proprietor of the mark, perceive those advertising links as offering an alternative to the goods or services of the trade mark proprietor.[2188]

In that situation, characterized by the fact that a sign identical with a trade mark is selected as a keyword by a competitor of the proprietor of the mark with the aim of offering internet users an alternative to the goods or services of that proprietor, there is a use of that sign in relation to the goods or services of that competitor.[2189]

Without it being necessary to examine whether or not advertising on the internet on the basis of keywords which are identical with competitors' trade marks constitutes a form of comparative advertising, it is clear in any event that, as has been held in the case law cited in the preceding paragraph, the use made by the advertiser of a sign identical with the trade mark of a competitor in order that internet users become aware not only of the goods or services offered by that competitor but also of those of the advertiser constitutes a use in relation to the goods or services of that advertiser.[2190]

In addition, even in cases in which the advertiser does not seek, by its use, as a keyword, of a sign identical with the trade mark, to present its goods or services to internet users as an alternative to the goods or services of the proprietor of the trade mark but, on the contrary, seeks to mislead internet users as to the origin of its goods or services by making them believe that they originate from the proprietor of the trade

2185. CJEU C-236/08 to C-238/08 of 23.3.2010 - Google France, para. 73; C-278/08 of 25.3.2010 - BergSpechte, para. 19; C-91/09 of 26.3.2010 - Eis.de, para. 18; C-558/08 of 8.7.2010 - Portakabin, para. 28; C-323/09 of 22.9.2011 - Interflora, para. 31; C-684/19 of 2.7.2020 - mk advokaten/MBK Rechtsanwälte, para. 20.
2186. CJEU C-236/08 to C-238/08 of 23.3.2010 - Google France, para. 74.
2187. CJEU C-236/08 to C-238/08 of 23.3.2010 - Google France, para. 67; C-323/09 of 22.9.2011 - Interflora, para. 84.
2188. CJEU C-236/08 to C-238/08 of 23.3.2010 - Google France, para. 68.
2189. CJEU C-236/08 to C-238/08 of 23.3.2010 - Google France, para. 69; C-558/08 of 8.7.2010 - Portakabin, para. 28; *see also* CJEU C-323/09 of 22.9.2011 - Interflora, para. 58.
2190. CJEU C-236/08 to C-238/08 of 23.3.2010 - Google France, para. 71.

mark or from an undertaking economically connected to it, there is use 'in relation to goods or services'. As the Court has previously held, such use exists in any event where the third party uses the sign identical with the trade mark in such a way that a link is established between that sign and the goods marketed or the services provided by the third party.[2191]

No purpose is served by examining whether the goods or services referred to by the ad are **actually offered for sale** in the wording of that ad, as set out by the reference service provider, or whether they are offered for sale only on the advertiser's website to which the internet user is referred if he clicks on the advertising link.[2192]

It is, in principle, also unnecessary to carry out such an examination when considering the question of whether the use of the sign - identical with the mark - as a keyword is likely to have an adverse effect on the functions of the mark and, in particular, on the function of indicating its origin. It is for the national court to assess, in the light of how the ad is presented as a whole, whether it enables normally informed and reasonably attentive internet users to determine if the advertiser is a third party vis-à-vis the trade mark proprietor or, on the contrary, economically linked to that proprietor. The presence or absence, in the ad, of actual offers for the sale of the goods or services in question is not, in general, a decisive factor for purposes of that assessment.[2193]

The use by an advertiser, in a **comparative advertisement**, of a sign identical with, or similar to, the mark of a competitor for the purposes of identifying the goods and services offered by the latter can be regarded as use for the advertiser's own goods and services for the purposes of Article 5(1) and (2).[2194]

Probably still applicable: However, where the examinations to be carried out by the national court show that the sign in question in the main case is used for purposes other than to distinguish the goods concerned - for example, as a **trade or company name** - reference must, pursuant to Article 5(5) TMD2008, be made to the legal order of the Member State concerned to determine the extent and nature, if any, of the protection afforded to the trade mark proprietor who claims to be suffering damage as a result of use of that sign as a trade name or company name.[2195]

Probably still applicable: The purpose of a company, trade or shop name is not, of itself, to distinguish goods or services. The purpose of a company name is to identify a company, whereas the purpose of a trade name or a shop name is to designate a business which is being carried on. Accordingly, where the use of a company name, trade name or shop name is limited to identifying a company or designating a business which is being carried on, such use cannot be considered as being 'in relation to goods or services' within the meaning of Article 5(1) TMD2008.[2196]

2191. CJEU C-236/08 to C-238/08 of 23.3.2010 - Google France, para. 72.
2192. CJEU C-558/08 of 8.7.2010 - Portakabin, para. 43.
2193. CJEU C-558/08 of 8.7.2010 - Portakabin, para. 44.
2194. CJEU C-533/06 of 12.6.2008 - O2 Holdings/Hutchison 3G UK, para. 36; C-487/07 of 18.6.2009 - L'Oréal, para. 53; C-236/08 to C-238/08 of 23.3.2010 - Google France, para. 70.
2195. CJEU C-23/01 of 21.11.2002 - Robelco, para. 34; C-245/02 of 16.11.2004 - Anheuser-Busch, para. 64.
2196. CJEU C-17/06 of 11.9.2007 - Céline, para. 21.

Probably still applicable: Conversely, there is use 'in relation to goods' within the meaning of Article 5(1) TMD2008 where a third party affixes the sign constituting his company name, trade name or shop name to the goods which he markets.[2197]

Probably still applicable: In addition, even where the sign is not affixed, there is use 'in relation to goods or services' within the meaning of that provision where the third party uses that sign in such a way that a link is established between the sign which constitutes the company, trade or shop name of the third party and the goods marketed or the services provided by the third party.[2198]

Probably still applicable: It is for the **national court** to determine whether the use of the sign constitutes use in relation to those goods for the purposes of Article 5(1) TMD2008.[2199]

The concept of 'use' for the purpose of Article 9(1)(a) and (2)(d) CTMR covers a situation, in which a **trade intermediary**, which is acting in its own name but on behalf of the vendor and is thus not an interested party in relation to trade in goods in which it is itself a contractual party, uses, in its business papers, a sign which is identical with a Community trade mark in relation to goods or services which are identical with those for which the mark is registered.[2200]

The use by a third party of a sign which is identical to a registered mark, in circumstances such as those in the main proceedings, falls under the concept of 'use' for the purpose of Article 9(1) CTMR since all the conditions of application laid down in that provision with regard to that concept are clearly fulfilled.[2201]

The fact that the third party at issue uses a sign which is identical with a registered mark in relation to goods which are not its own goods, in that it does not have title to them, is not relevant and can therefore not mean by itself that that use does not fall under the concept of 'use' for the purpose of Article 9(1) CTMR.[2202]

The fact that the **broker** acted on behalf of the vendor is in that regard irrelevant.[2203]

It is irrelevant that the third party uses a sign which is identical with a registered mark for the marketing of goods which are not its own goods in the sense that it does not acquire title to those goods in the course of the transaction in which it acts.[2204]

Indeed, by such use, the third party assumes de facto the essential prerogative that is granted to the proprietor of a mark, namely the exclusive power to use the sign at issue so as to distinguish goods.[2205]

2197. CJEU C-17/06 of 11.9.2007 – Céline, para. 22.
2198. CJEU C-17/06 of 11.9.2007 – Céline, para. 23; C-62/08 of 19.2.2009 – UDV North America, para. 47; C-236/08 to C-238/08 of 23.3.2010 – Google France, para. 72; *see also* CJEU C-324/09 of 12.7.2011 – L'Oréal, para. 92; C-119/10 of 15.12.2011 – Frisdranken Industrie Winters, para. 32.
2199. CJEU C-17/06 of 11.9.2007 – Céline, para. 24.
2200. CJEU C-62/08 of 19.2.2009 – UDV North America, para. 54.
2201. CJEU C-62/08 of 19.2.2009 – UDV North America, para. 53.
2202. CJEU C-62/08 of 19.2.2009 – UDV North America, para. 43; C-324/09 of 12.7.2011 – L'Oréal, para. 91; C-772/18 of 30.4.2020 – A/B, para. 27.
2203. CJEU C-62/08 of 19.2.2009 – UDV North America, para. 46.
2204. CJEU C-62/08 of 19.2.2009 – UDV North America, para. 48.
2205. CJEU C-62/08 of 19.2.2009 – UDV North America, para. 50.

In such a case, this is clearly a question of use of the mark as a mark. In that regard, it is, moreover, irrelevant that the use is by the third party in the context of the marketing of goods on behalf of another operator having sole title to those goods.[2206]

Article 5(5) TMD2008 must be interpreted as meaning that a Member State may, if it sees fit, and subject to such conditions as it may determine, protect a trade mark against use of a sign **other than for the purposes of distinguishing goods or services,** where use of that sign without due cause takes unfair advantage of, or is detrimental to, the distinctive character or the repute of the trade mark.[2207]

It follows from the structure of Article 5(1), (2) and (5) TMD2008 that reinforced **protection of a trade mark's distinctive character or reputation** against certain uses of a sign other than for the purpose of distinguishing goods or services is not covered by Community harmonization.[2208]

That conclusion is confirmed first of all by the third recital in the preamble to the Directive which states that 'it does not appear to be necessary at present to undertake full-scale approximation of the trade mark laws of the Member States and it will be sufficient if approximation is limited to those national provisions of law which most directly affect the functioning of the internal market' and, secondly, by the sixth recital in the preamble which states that 'this Directive does not exclude the application to trade marks of provisions of law of the Member States other than trade mark law, such as the provisions relating to unfair competition, civil liability or consumer protection'.[2209]

The purpose of the Directive, which is the first harmonizing directive in the area of trade mark law, is, according to the first recital in the preamble thereto, to approximate the laws of Member States on trade marks in order to abolish existing disparities which may impede the free movement of goods and freedom to provide services. The Directive does not, however, as the third recital of the preamble makes clear, seek a full-scale approximation of those laws.[2210]

Accordingly, where the sign is not used for the purposes of distinguishing goods or services, it is necessary to refer to the legal orders of the Member States to determine the extent and nature, if any, of the protection afforded to owners of trade marks who claim to be suffering damage as a result of use of that sign as a trade name or company name.[2211]

The Member States may adopt no legislation in this area, or they may, subject to such conditions as they may determine, require that the sign and the trade mark be either identical or similar, or that there be some other connection between them.[2212]

2206. CJEU C-62/08 of 19.2.2009 – UDV North America, para. 51.
2207. CJEU C-23/01 of 21.11.2002 – Robelco, para. 36.
2208. CJEU C-23/01 of 21.11.2002 – Robelco, para. 31.
2209. CJEU C-23/01 of 21.11.2002 – Robelco, para. 32.
2210. CJEU C-23/01 of 21.11.2002 – Robelco, para. 33; *see also* CJEU C-686/21 of 27.4.2023 – VW/SW a.o., para. 35.
2211. CJEU C-23/01 of 21.11.2002 – Robelco, para. 34.
2212. CJEU C-23/01 of 21.11.2002 – Robelco, para. 35.

[D] Use in the own name

Article 9(2)(b) CTMR and Article 9(3)(b) EUTMR must be interpreted as meaning that a person who, on **behalf of a third party**, stores goods which infringe trade mark rights, without being aware of that infringement, must be regarded as not stocking those goods in order to offer them or put them on the market for the purposes of those provisions, if that person does not itself pursue those aims.[2213]

It should be borne in mind, as a preliminary point, that, according to Article 9(1) CTMR, the substance of which is reproduced in Article 9(1) and (2) EUTMR, an EU trade mark confers on the proprietor the exclusive right to prevent all third parties from using in the course of trade any sign which is identical to that mark in relation to goods or services which are identical to those for which the mark is registered, or any sign where, because of its identity with, or similarity to, the EU trade mark and the identity or similarity of the goods or services covered by that mark and the sign, there exists a likelihood of confusion on the part of the public, or any sign which is identical or similar to the EU trade mark in relation to goods or services which are not similar to those for which that mark is registered, where the latter has a reputation in the European Union and where use of that sign without due cause takes unfair advantage of, or is detrimental to, the distinctive character or the repute of that mark.[2214]

Article 9(2) CTMR, the substance of which is reproduced in Article 9(3) EUTMR, sets out a non-exhaustive list of the types of use which may be prohibited by a trade mark proprietor under Article 9(1) CTMR and Article 9(1) EUTMR.[2215]

Those types of use include, in Article 9(2)(b) CTMR, the substance of which is reproduced in Article 9(3)(b) EUTMR, offering the goods, putting them on the market or stocking them for those purposes.[2216]

In the present case, it is apparent from the order for reference, first, that the respondents in the main proceedings merely stored the goods concerned, without themselves offering them for sale or putting them on the market and, secondly, that they did not intend to offer those goods for sale or put them on the market either.[2217]

It must therefore be determined whether such a storage operation may be regarded as 'using' the trade mark for the purposes of Article 9(1) CTMR and Article 9(1) and (2) EUTMR and, in particular, as 'stocking' those goods in order to offer them or put them on the market for the purposes of Article 9(2)(b) CTMR, the substance of which is reproduced in Article 9(3)(b) EUTMR.[2218]

2213. CJEU C-567/18 of 2.4.2020 – Coty Germany/Amazon Services Europe a.o., para. 53, *see also* CJEU C-148/21 and C-184/21 of 22.12.2022 – Louboutin/Amazon Europe Core a.o., para. 32.
2214. CJEU C-567/18 of 2.4.2020 – Coty Germany/Amazon Services Europe a.o., para. 31.
2215. CJEU C-567/18 of 2.4.2020 – Coty Germany/Amazon Services Europe a.o., para. 32, with reference to CJEU C-236/08 to C-238/08 of 23.3.2010 – Google France, para. 65.
2216. CJEU C-567/18 of 2.4.2020 – Coty Germany/Amazon Services Europe a.o., para. 33.
2217. CJEU C-567/18 of 2.4.2020 – Coty Germany/Amazon Services Europe a.o., para. 34.
2218. CJEU C-567/18 of 2.4.2020 – Coty Germany/Amazon Services Europe a.o., para. 35.

In that regard, it should be borne in mind, in the first place, that neither the CTMR nor the EUTMR defines the concept of 'using' referred to in Article 9 of those regulations.[2219]

The Court has, however, already had occasion to point out that, according to its ordinary meaning, the expression 'using' involves active behaviour and direct or indirect control of the act constituting the use. In that regard, it has noted that Article 9(2) of Regulation No. 207/2009, the substance of which is reproduced in Article 9(3) of Regulation 2017/1001, which lists in a non-exhaustive manner the types of use which the trade mark proprietor may prohibit, refers exclusively to active behaviour on the part of the third party.[2220]

The Court has also noted that those provisions are intended to provide a trade mark proprietor with a legal instrument allowing him to prohibit, and thus to prevent, any use of his trade mark by a third party without his consent. However, only a third party who has direct or indirect control of the act constituting the use is effectively able to stop that use and therefore comply with that prohibition.[2221]

The Court has also repeatedly held that the use, by a third party, of a sign identical or similar to the proprietor's trade mark implies, at the very least, that that third party uses the sign in its own commercial communication. A person may thus allow its clients to use signs which are identical or similar to trade marks without itself using those signs.[2222]

Thus, the Court has held, as regards the operation of an e-commerce platform, that the use of signs identical or similar to trade marks in offers for sale displayed in an online marketplace is made by the sellers who are customers of the operator of that marketplace and not by that operator itself.[2223]

It has also noted, as regards an undertaking whose main activity is filling cans with drinks produced by it or by third parties, that a service provider who merely fills, under an order from and on the instructions of a third party, cans already bearing signs similar to trade marks and therefore merely executes a technical part of the production process of the final product without having any interest in the external presentation of

2219. CJEU C-567/18 of 2.4.2020 – Coty Germany/Amazon Services Europe a.o., para. 36.
2220. CJEU C-567/18 of 2.4.2020 – Coty Germany/Amazon Services Europe a.o., para. 37, with reference to CJEU C-129/17 of 25.7.2018 – Mitsubishi Shoji Kaisha a.o./Duma Forklifts a.o., para. 38; also CJEU C-148/21 and C-184/21 of 22.12.2022 – Louboutin/Amazon Europe Core a.o., para. 27.
2221. CJEU C-567/18 of 2.4.2020 – Coty Germany/Amazon Services Europe a.o., para. 38, with reference to CJEU C-179/15 of 3.3.2016 – Daimler/Együd Garage Gépjárműjavító és Értékesítő, para. 41; also CJEU C-148/21 and C-184/21 of 22.12.2022 – Louboutin/Amazon Europe Core a.o., para. 28; *see also* CJEU C-684/19 of 2.7.2020 – mk advokaten/MBK Rechtsanwälte, para. 29.
2222. CJEU C-567/18 of 2.4.2020 – Coty Germany/Amazon Services Europe a.o., para. 39, with reference to CJEU C-236/08 to C-238/08 of 23.3.2010 – Google France, para. 56; also CJEU C-148/21 and C-184/21 of 22.12.2022 – Louboutin/Amazon Europe Core a.o., para. 29; *see also* CJEU C-684/19 of 2.7.2020 – mk advokaten/MBK Rechtsanwälte, para. 27.
2223. CJEU C-567/18 of 2.4.2020 – Coty Germany/Amazon Services Europe a.o., para. 40, with reference to CJEU C-324/09 of 12.7.2011 – L'Oréal, para. 103; also CJEU C-148/21 and C-184/21 of 22.12.2022 – Louboutin/Amazon Europe Core a.o., para. 30; *see also* CJEU C-684/19 of 2.7.2020 – mk advokaten/MBK Rechtsanwälte, para. 27.

those cans and in particular in the signs thereon is not itself 'using' those signs, but is only creating the technical conditions necessary for the third party to use them.[2224]

Similarly, the Court has held that, although an economic operator who imports or sends to a warehouse keeper, for the purposes of their being put on the market, goods bearing a trade mark of which it is not the proprietor may be regarded as 'using' a sign identical to that trade mark, that is not necessarily true of the warehouse keeper who provides a storage service in relation to goods bearing another person's trade mark.[2225]

The fact of creating the technical conditions necessary for the use of a sign and being paid for that service does not mean that the party offering the service itself uses the sign.[2226]

In the second place, it is apparent from the wording of Article 9(2)(b) CTMR, the substance of which is reproduced in Article 9(3)(b) EUTMR, that that provision relates specifically to the offering of goods, their being put on the market, their being stocked 'for those purposes' or the supply of services under the sign concerned.[2227]

It follows that, in order for the storage of goods bearing signs identical, or similar to trade marks to be classified as 'using' those signs, it is also necessary for the economic operator providing the storage itself to pursue the aim referred to by those provisions, which is offering the goods or putting them on the market.[2228]

Failing that, it cannot be concluded that the act constituting the use of the trade mark is carried out by that person, or that the sign is used in that person's own commercial communication.[2229]

In the present case, as regards the respondents in the main proceedings, as noted in paragraph 34 above, the referring court states unequivocally that they have not themselves offered the goods concerned for sale or put them on the market, that court stating, moreover, in the wording of its question, that it is the third party alone who intends to offer the goods or put them on the market. It follows that the respondents do not themselves use the sign in their own commercial communication.[2230]

That conclusion is, however, without prejudice to the possibility of considering that those parties themselves use the sign in connection with bottles of perfume which they stock not on behalf of third-party sellers but on their own behalf or which, if they were unable to identify the third-party seller, would be offered or put on the market by those parties themselves.[2231]

2224. CJEU C-567/18 of 2.4.2020 – Coty Germany/Amazon Services Europe a.o., para. 41, with reference to CJEU C-119/10 of 15.12.2011 – Frisdranken Industrie Winters, para. 30.
2225. CJEU C-567/18 of 2.4.2020 – Coty Germany/Amazon Services Europe a.o., para. 42, with reference to CJEU C-379/14 of 16.7.2015 – TOP Logistics, para. 42 and 45.
2226. CJEU C-567/18 of 2.4.2020 – Coty Germany/Amazon Services Europe a.o., para. 43, with reference to CJEU C-236/08 to C-238/08 of 23.3.2010 – Google France, para. 57; C-119/10 of 15.12.2011 – Frisdranken Industrie Winters, para. 29; also CJEU C-148/21 and C-184/21 of 22.12.2022 – Louboutin/Amazon Europe Core a.o., para. 31.
2227. CJEU C-567/18 of 2.4.2020 – Coty Germany/Amazon Services Europe a.o., para. 44.
2228. CJEU C-567/18 of 2.4.2020 – Coty Germany/Amazon Services Europe a.o., para. 45, *see also* CJEU C-148/21 and C-184/21 of 22.12.2022 – Louboutin/Amazon Europe Core a.o., para. 32.
2229. CJEU C-567/18 of 2.4.2020 – Coty Germany/Amazon Services Europe a.o., para. 46.
2230. CJEU C-567/18 of 2.4.2020 – Coty Germany/Amazon Services Europe a.o., para. 47, *see also* CJEU C-148/21 and C-184/21 of 22.12.2022 – Louboutin/Amazon Europe Core a.o., para. 33.
2231. CJEU C-567/18 of 2.4.2020 – Coty Germany/Amazon Services Europe a.o., para. 48.

Lastly, it should be borne in mind that it is apparent from settled case law that where an economic operator has enabled another operator to make use of the trade mark, its role must, as necessary, be examined from the point of view of rules of law other than Article 9 CTMR or Article 9 EUTMR, such as Article 14(1) of Directive 2000/31[2232] or the first sentence of Article 11 of Directive[2233] 2004/48.[2234]

In the light of the foregoing, the answer to the question referred to is that Article 5(1) TMD2008 must be interpreted as meaning that a person operating in the course of trade that has arranged for an advertisement which infringes another person's trade mark to be placed on a website is not using a sign which is identical with that trade mark where the **operators** of other websites reproduce that advertisement by placing it online, **on their own initiative and in their own name**, on other websites.[2235]

In that regard, it must first of all be noted that the offering of goods or services under a sign which is identical with or similar to another person's trade mark and advertising those goods or services under that sign constitutes 'use' in relation to that sign.[2236]

In addition, it is settled case law that such use of a sign that is identical with or similar to another person's trade mark exists where that sign, selected by an advertiser as a keyword in an online referencing service, is the means used by the advertiser to trigger the display of its advertisement, even where that sign does not appear in the advertisement itself.[2237]

Thus, where a person operating in the course of trade orders, from the operator of a referencing website, the publication of an advertisement, the display of which contains or is triggered by a sign which is identical with or similar to another person's trade mark, that person must be considered to be using that sign, within the meaning of Article 5(1) TMD2008.[2238]

By contrast, that person cannot be held liable, under Article 5(1) TMD2008, for the independent actions of other economic operators, such as those of referencing website operators with whom that person has no direct or indirect dealings and who do

2232. Directive 2000/31/EC of the European Parliament and of the Council of 8 June 2000 on certain legal aspects of information society services, in particular electronic commerce, in the Internal Market ('Directive on electronic commerce') (OJ 2000 L 178, p. 1).
2233. Directive 2004/48/EC of the European Parliament and of the Council of 29 April 2004 on the enforcement of intellectual property rights (OJ 2004 L 157, p. 45, corrigendum OJ 2004 L 195, p. 16).
2234. CJEU C-567/18 of 2.4.2020 – Coty Germany/Amazon Services Europe a.o., para. 49, with further proof; C-148/21 and C-184/21 of 22.12.2022 – Louboutin/Amazon Europe Core a.o., para. 37.
2235. CJEU C-684/19 of 2.7.2020 – mk advokaten/MBK Rechtsanwälte, para. 31.
2236. CJEU C-684/19 of 2.7.2020 – mk advokaten/MBK Rechtsanwälte, para. 19, with reference to CJEU C-236/08 to C-238/08 of 23.3.2010 – Google France, para. 45 and 61.
2237. CJEU C-684/19 of 2.7.2020 – mk advokaten/MBK Rechtsanwälte, para. 20, with reference to CJEU C-323/09 of 22.9.2011 – Interflora, paras 30 et seq.
2238. CJEU C-684/19 of 2.7.2020 – mk advokaten/MBK Rechtsanwälte, para. 21, with reference to CJEU C-179/15 of 3.3.2016 – Daimler/Együd Garage Gépjárműjavító és Értékesítő, paras 29 et seq.

not act by order and on behalf of that person, but on their own initiative and in their own name.[2239]

The term 'using' in Article 5(1) TMD2008 involves active conduct and direct or indirect control of the act constituting the use. However, that is not the case if that act is carried out by an independent operator without the consent of the advertiser.[2240]

That provision cannot therefore be interpreted as meaning that a person may, irrespective of its conduct, be considered to be a user of a sign that is identical with or similar to another person's trade mark on the sole ground that such use is capable of providing a financial benefit to the former.[2241]

According to that line of case law of the Court, in the present case, it is for the referring court to examine whether it follows from the conduct of mk advokaten, in the context of either a direct or indirect relationship between mk advokaten and the operators of the websites in question, that those operators had placed the advertisement online by order and on behalf of mk advokaten. In the absence of such conduct, it must be concluded that MBK Rechtsanwälte is not justified, under the exclusive rights provided for in Article 5(1) of Directive 2008/95, in bringing an action against mk advokaten on the ground that the advertisement was published online on websites other than the Das Örtliche directory.[2242]

This would not alter the fact that it would remain open to MBK Rechtsanwälte to claim from mk advokaten, where appropriate, restitution for financial benefits on the basis of national law, and to bring an action against the operators of the websites in question.[2243]

In that regard, it must be noted that, in a situation where the website operators reproduce an advertisement on their own initiative and in their own name, the economic operator whose goods or services are thus promoted cannot be regarded as their customer. Accordingly, the Court's case law, according to which the operator of a referencing website does not itself use signs that are identical or similar to another person's trade marks where those signs are contained in its customer's advertisements or trigger the display of those advertisements, does not apply in such a situation.[2244]

In such a case, those website operators are using, within the meaning of Article 5(1) TMD2008, signs identical with or similar to another person's trade mark which are contained in offers for sale or advertisements that those operators display or which trigger the display of those advertisements. The proprietors of those marks may

2239. CJEU C-684/19 of 2.7.2020 – mk advokaten/MBK Rechtsanwälte, para. 22, with reference to CJEU C-179/15 of 3.3.2016 – Daimler/Együd Garage Gépjárműjavító és Értékesítő, paras 36 et seq.
2240. CJEU C-684/19 of 2.7.2020 – mk advokaten/MBK Rechtsanwälte, para. 23, with reference to CJEU C-179/15 of 3.3.2016 – Daimler/Együd Garage Gépjárműjavító és Értékesítő, para. 39.
2241. CJEU C-684/19 of 2.7.2020 – mk advokaten/MBK Rechtsanwälte, para. 24, with reference to CJEU C-179/15 of 3.3.2016 – Daimler/Együd Garage Gépjárműjavító és Értékesítő, para. 42.
2242. CJEU C-684/19 of 2.7.2020 – mk advokaten/MBK Rechtsanwälte, para. 25.
2243. CJEU C-684/19 of 2.7.2020 – mk advokaten/MBK Rechtsanwälte, para. 26, with reference to CJEU C-179/15 of 3.3.2016 – Daimler/Együd Garage Gépjárműjavító és Értékesítő, para. 43.
2244. CJEU C-684/19 of 2.7.2020 – mk advokaten/MBK Rechtsanwälte, para. 27, with reference CJEU C-236/08 to C-238/08 of 23.3.2010 – Google France, para. 56; C-567/18 of 2.4.2020 – Coty Germany/Amazon Services Europe a.o., para. 39 and 40.

therefore bring an action against those operators under the exclusive rights provided for in Article 5(1), where those offers or advertisements promote goods or services that are identical with or similar to those for which those marks are registered.[2245]

Such an interpretation of that provision is compatible with its objective which is to provide a trade mark proprietor with a legal means whereby it may prohibit, and thus prevent, any use of its trade mark by a third party without its consent.[2246]

Finally, as regards the fact, referred to in the order for reference, that, in the case of *Daimler*,[2247] the advertisement which infringed another person's trade mark was initially lawful, whereas the advertisement at issue in the dispute in the main proceedings infringed another person's trade mark from the outset, it is sufficient to note that that circumstance is irrelevant as regards the only question under consideration in the present reference for a preliminary ruling, which is, where an advertisement infringing another person's trade mark is reproduced, who is using the sign which is identical with or similar to that mark.[2248]

[E] Use liable to have an adverse effect on the functions of the trade mark

[1] Affecting the functions with regard to double identity

For the guarantee of origin, which constitutes the essential function of a trade mark, to be ensured, the proprietor must be protected against competitors wishing to take unfair advantage of the status and reputation of the trade mark by selling products illegally bearing it. In this respect, the tenth recital of the preamble to the Directive points out the absolute nature of the protection afforded by the trade mark in the case of identity between the mark and the sign and between the goods or services concerned and those for which the mark is registered. It states that the aim of that protection is in particular to guarantee the trade mark as an indication of origin.[2249]

The exclusive nature of the right conferred by a registered trade mark on its proprietor under Article 5(1)(a) TMD2008 can be justified only within the limits of the application of that article.[2250]

It is apparent from the case law of this judgment that the proprietor of the mark cannot oppose the use of a sign identical with the mark on the basis of Article 5(1)(a) TMD2008 if that use is not liable to cause detriment to any of the functions of that mark.[2251]

2245. CJEU C-684/19 of 2.7.2020 – mk advokaten/MBK Rechtsanwälte, para. 28, with reference CJEU C-567/18 of 2.4.2020 – Coty Germany/Amazon Services Europe a.o., para. 48.
2246. CJEU C-684/19 of 2.7.2020 – mk advokaten/MBK Rechtsanwälte, para. 29, with reference CJEU C-567/18 of 2.4.2020 – Coty Germany/Amazon Services Europe a.o., para. 38.
2247. CJEU C-179/15 of 3.3.2016 – Daimler/Együd Garage Gépjárműjavító és Értékesítő.
2248. CJEU C-684/19 of 2.7.2020 – mk advokaten/MBK Rechtsanwälte, para. 30.
2249. CJEU C-206/01 of 12.11.2002 – Arsenal Football Club, para. 50.
2250. CJEU C-206/01 of 12.11.2002 – Arsenal Football Club, para. 52.
2251. CJEU C-487/07 of 18.6.2009 – L'Oréal, para. 60; C-236/08 to C-238/08 of 23.3.2010 – Google France, para. 76; C-278/08 of 25.3.2010 – BergSpechte, para. 30; C-558/08 of 8.7.2010 – Portakabin, para. 29.

It follows that the exclusive right under Article 5(1)(a) TMD2008 was conferred in order to enable the trade mark proprietor to protect his specific interests as proprietor, that is, to ensure that the trade mark can fulfil its functions. The exercise of that right must therefore be reserved to cases in which a third party's use of the sign affects or is liable to affect the **functions of the trade mark, in particular its essential function** of guaranteeing to consumers the origin of the goods.[2252]

The Court has already held that the exclusive right under Article 5(1)(a) TMD2008 was conferred in order to enable the trade mark proprietor to protect his specific interests as proprietor, that is, to ensure that the trade mark can fulfil its functions and that, therefore, the exercise of that right must be reserved to cases in which a third party's use of the sign affects or is liable to affect the functions of the trade mark.[2253]

These functions include not only the essential function of the trade mark, which is to guarantee to consumers the origin of the goods or services, **but also its other functions**, in particular that of guaranteeing the quality of the goods or services in question and those of communication, investment or advertising.[2254]

With regard to the functions of the trade mark other than that of indicating origin, it should be noted that both the European Union legislature – by using the words 'in particular' in the tenth recital to TMD and in the seventh recital to CTMR – and the Court – by using since its judgment in Arsenal Football Club the words 'functions of the trade mark' – have indicated that a trade mark's function of indicating origin is not the only function of the mark that is worthy of protection against injury by third parties. They have thus taken into account the fact that a trade mark is often, in addition to an indication of the origin of the goods or services, an instrument of commercial strategy used, *inter alia*, for advertising purposes or to acquire a reputation in order to develop consumer loyalty.[2255]

Admittedly, a trade mark is always supposed to fulfil its function of indicating origin, whereas it performs its other functions only in so far as its proprietor uses it to that end, in particular for the purposes of advertising or investment. However, that difference between the essential function of the trade mark and its other functions can in no way justify – when a trade mark fulfils one or more of those other functions – excluding from the scope of Article 5(1)(a) TMD2008 and Article 9(1)(a) CTMR acts adversely affecting those functions. Likewise, there are no grounds for holding that

2252. CJEU C-206/01 of 12.11.2002 – Arsenal Football Club, para. 51; C-245/02 of 16.11.2004 – Anheuser-Busch, para. 59; C-48/05 of 25.1.2007 – Adam Opel, para. 21; C-17/06 of 11.9.2007 – Céline, para. 16, 26; C-323/09 of 22.9.2011 – Interflora, para. 37; C-65/12 of 6.2.2014 – Leidseplein Beheer, para. 32.

2253. CJEU C-487/07 of 18.6.2009 – L'Oréal, para. 58; C-236/08 to C-238/08 of 23.3.2010 – Google France, para. 75; C-278/08 of 25.3.2010 – BergSpechte, para. 29; C-558/08 of 8.7.2010 – Portakabin, para. 26; C-235/09 of 12.4.2011 – DHL Express France, para. 46; C-561/11 of 21.2.2013 – Fédération Cynologique Internationale, para. 50; C-179/15 of 3.3.2016 – Daimler/Együd Garage Gépjárműjavító és Értékesítő, para. 26; *see also* CJEU C-98/13 of 6.2.2014 – Blomqvist, para. 27.

2254. CJEU C-487/07 of 18.6.2009 – L'Oréal, para. 58; C-236/08 to C-238/08 of 23.3.2010 – Google France, para. 77; C-278/08 of 25.3.2010 – BergSpechte, para. 31; C-558/08 of 8.7.2010 – Portakabin, paras 30 and 38.

2255. CJEU C-323/09 of 22.9.2011 – Interflora, para. 39.

only trade marks with a reputation are capable of having functions other than that of indicating origin.[2256]

The protection conferred by Article 5(1)(a) TMD2008 is thus broader than that provided by Article 5(1)(b) TMD2008, the application of which requires that there be a likelihood of confusion and accordingly the possibility that the essential function of the mark may be affected. By virtue of the tenth recital in the preamble to Directive 89/104, the protection afforded by the registered trade mark is absolute in the case of identity between the mark and the sign and also between the goods or services, whereas, in case of similarity between the mark and the sign and between the goods or services, the likelihood of confusion constitutes the specific condition for such protection.[2257]

It is apparent from the case law that in the situation envisaged in Article 5(1)(a) TMD2008 and Article 9(1)(a) CTMR, in which a third party uses a sign identical with a trade mark in relation to goods or services which are identical with those for which that mark is registered, the proprietor of the mark is entitled to prohibit that use if it is liable to have an adverse **effect on one of the functions of the mark**, whether that be the function of indicating origin or one of the other functions.[2258]

The use of a sign identical with another person's trade mark in a **referencing service** such as that at issue in the cases in the main proceedings is not liable to have an adverse effect on the **advertising function** of the trade mark.[2259]

Since the course of trade provides a varied offer of goods and services, the proprietor of a trade mark may have not only the objective of indicating, by means of that mark, the origin of its goods or services, but also that of using its mark for advertising purposes designed to inform and persuade consumers.[2260]

Accordingly, the proprietor of a trade mark is entitled to prohibit a third party from using, without the proprietor's consent, a sign identical with its trade mark in relation to goods or services which are identical with those for which that trade mark is registered, in the case where that use adversely affects the proprietor's use of its mark as a factor in sales promotion or as an instrument of commercial strategy.[2261]

With regard to the use by internet advertisers of a sign identical with another person's trade mark as a **keyword** for the purposes of displaying advertising messages,

2256. CJEU C-323/09 of 22.9.2011 – Interflora, para. 40.
2257. CJEU C-487/07 of 18.6.2009 – L'Oréal, para. 59; C-236/08 to C-238/08 of 23.3.2010 – Google France, para. 78; *see also* CJEU C-278/08 of 25.3.2010 – BergSpechte, para. 22.
2258. CJEU C-236/08 to C-238/08 of 23.3.2010 – Google France, para. 79; C-278/08 of 25.3.2010 – BergSpechte, para. 21; C-91/09 of 26.3.2010 – Eis.de, para. 20; C-324/09 of 12.7.2011 – L'Oréal, para. 88; C-323/09 of 22.9.2011 – Interflora, para. 34.
2259. CJEU C-236/08 to C-238/08 of 23.3.2010 – Google France, para. 98; C-278/08 of 25.3.2010 – BergSpechte, para. 33; C-91/09 of 26.3.2010 – Eis.de, para. 22; C-558/08 of 8.7.2010 – Portakabin, para. 32; C-323/09 of 22.9.2011 – Interflora, para. 54.
2260. CJEU C-236/08 to C-238/08 of 23.3.2010 – Google France, para. 91; C-129/17 of 25.7.2018 – Mitsubishi Shoji Kaisha a.o./Duma Forklifts a.o., para. 37.
2261. CJEU C-236/08 to C-238/08 of 23.3.2010 – Google France, para. 92; C-129/17 of 25.7.2018 – Mitsubishi Shoji Kaisha a.o./Duma Forklifts a.o., para. 37.

it is clear that that use is liable to have certain repercussions on the advertising use of that mark by its proprietor and on the latter's commercial strategy.[2262]

Having regard to the important position which internet advertising occupies in trade and commerce, it is plausible that the proprietor of a trade mark may register its own trade mark as a keyword with a referencing service provider in order to have an ad appear under the heading 'sponsored links'. Where that is the case, the proprietor of the mark must, as necessary, agree to pay a higher price per click than certain other economic operators if it wishes to ensure that its ad appears before those of those operators which have also selected its mark as a keyword. Furthermore, even if the proprietor of the mark is prepared to pay a higher price per click than that offered by third parties which have also selected that trade mark, the proprietor cannot be certain that its ad will appear before those of those third parties, given that other factors are also taken into account in determining the order in which the ads are displayed.[2263]

Nevertheless, those repercussions of use by third parties of a sign identical with the trade mark do not of themselves constitute an adverse effect on the advertising function of the trade mark.[2264]

The situation covered is that of the display of advertising links following the entry by internet users of a search term corresponding to the trade mark selected as a keyword. It is also common ground, in these cases, that those advertising links are displayed beside or above the list of the natural results of the search. Finally, it is not in dispute that the order in which the natural results are set out results from the relevance of the respective sites to the search term entered by the internet user and that the search engine operator does not claim any remuneration for displaying those results.[2265]

It follows from those factors that, when internet users enter the name of a trade mark as a search term, the home and advertising page of the proprietor of that mark will appear in the list of the natural results, usually in one of the highest positions on that list. That display, which is, moreover, free of charge, means that the visibility to internet users of the goods or services of the proprietor of the trade mark is guaranteed, irrespective of whether or not that proprietor is successful in also securing the display, in one of the highest positions, of an ad under the heading 'sponsored links'.[2266]

Therefore, the selection of a sign identical with another person's trade mark, in a referencing service with the characteristics of 'AdWords', does not, moreover, have the effect of denying the proprietor of that trade mark the opportunity of using its mark effectively to inform and win over consumers.[2267]

The mere fact that the use, by a third party, of a sign identical with a trade mark in relation to goods or services identical with those for which that mark is registered

2262. CJEU C-236/08 to C-238/08 of 23.3.2010 – Google France, para. 93; C-323/09 of 22.9.2011 – Interflora, para. 55.
2263. CJEU C-236/08 to C-238/08 of 23.3.2010 – Google France, para. 94; C-323/09 of 22.9.2011 – Interflora, para. 56.
2264. CJEU C-236/08 to C-238/08 of 23.3.2010 – Google France, para. 95.
2265. CJEU C-236/08 to C-238/08 of 23.3.2010 – Google France, para. 96.
2266. CJEU C-236/08 to C-238/08 of 23.3.2010 – Google France, para. 97.
2267. CJEU C-323/09 of 22.9.2011 – Interflora, para. 59.

obliges the proprietor of that mark to intensify its advertising in order to maintain or enhance its profile with consumers is not a sufficient basis, in every case, for concluding that the trade mark's advertising function is adversely affected. In that regard, although the trade mark is an essential element in the system of undistorted competition which European law seeks to establish, its purpose is not, however, to protect its proprietor against practices inherent in competition.[2268]

In addition to its function of indicating origin and, as the case may be, its advertising function, a trade mark may also be used by its proprietor to acquire or preserve a reputation capable of attracting consumers and retaining their loyalty.[2269]

Although that function of a trade mark – called the '**investment function**' – may overlap with the advertising function, it is none the less distinct from the latter. Indeed, when the trade mark is used to acquire or preserve a reputation, not only advertising is employed but also various commercial techniques.[2270]

When the use by a third party, such as a competitor of the trade mark proprietor, of a sign identical with the trade mark in relation to goods or services identical with those for which the mark is registered substantially interferes with the proprietor's use of its trade mark to acquire or preserve a reputation capable of attracting consumers and retaining their loyalty, the third party's use must be regarded as adversely affecting the trade mark's investment function. The proprietor is, as a consequence, entitled to prevent such use under Article 5(1)(a) TMD2008 or, in the case of a Community trade mark, under Article 9(1)(a) CTMR.[2271]

However, it cannot be accepted that the proprietor of a trade mark may – in conditions of fair competition that respect the trade mark's function as an indication of origin – prevent a competitor from using a sign identical with that trade mark in relation to goods or services identical with those for which the mark is registered, if the only consequence of that use is to oblige the proprietor of that trade mark to adapt its efforts to acquire or preserve a reputation capable of attracting consumers and retaining their loyalty. Likewise, the fact that that use may prompt some consumers to switch from goods or services bearing that trade mark cannot be successfully relied on by the proprietor of the mark.[2272]

Article 5(3) of Regulation No. 44/2001[2273] must be interpreted as meaning that an action relating to infringement of a trade mark registered in a Member State because of the use, by an advertiser, of a keyword identical to that trade mark on a search engine website operating under a country-specific top-level domain of another Member State may be brought before either the **courts of the Member State** in which the trade mark

2268. CJEU C-323/09 of 22.9.2011 – Interflora, para. 57.
2269. CJEU C-323/09 of 22.9.2011 – Interflora, para. 60.
2270. CJEU C-323/09 of 22.9.2011 – Interflora, para. 61.
2271. CJEU C-323/09 of 22.9.2011 – Interflora, para. 62; C-129/17 of 25.7.2018 – Mitsubishi Shoji Kaisha a.o./Duma Forklifts a.o., para. 36.
2272. CJEU C-323/09 of 22.9.2011 – Interflora, para. 64.
2273. Council Regulation (EC) No. 44/2001 of 22 Dec. 2000 on jurisdiction and the recognition and enforcement of judgments in civil and commercial matters (OJ 2001 L 12, p. 1).

is registered or the courts of the Member State of the place of establishment of the advertiser.[2274]

Certain uses for **purely descriptive purposes** are excluded from the scope of application of Article 5(1) TMD2008 because they do not affect any of the interests which that provision is intended to protect and accordingly do not constitute 'use' within the meaning of that provision.[2275]

The situation, in that the word marks belonging to others are used in the **comparison lists** not for purely descriptive purposes but for the purpose of **advertising** is fundamentally different from that which gave rise to the judgment in *Hölterhoff*.[2276]

According to Article 5(1) TMD2008, the registered trade mark confers on the proprietor exclusive rights therein. In addition, Article 5(1)(a) TMD2008 provides that those exclusive rights entitle the proprietor to prevent all third parties not having his consent from use in the course of trade of, *inter alia*, any sign identical with the trade mark in relation to goods or services which are identical to those for which the trade mark is registered. Article 5(3) sets out a non-exhaustive list of the kinds of practice which the proprietor is entitled to prohibit under paragraph 1, including, in particular, **importing** or **exporting** goods under the trade mark concerned.[2277]

The use of a trade mark, without the proprietor's authorization, for the purpose of informing the public that another undertaking carries out the **repair and maintenance of goods** covered by that mark or that it has specialized or is a **specialist in such goods** constitutes, is in certain circumstances use of the mark within the meaning of Article 5(1)(a) TMD2008.[2278]

The advertiser uses the BMW mark to identify the source of the goods in respect of which the services are supplied, and thus to distinguish those goods from any others in respect of which the same services might have been provided. If the use of the trade mark in advertisements for the service which consists of selling second-hand BMW cars is undoubtedly intended to distinguish the subject of the services provided, it is not necessary to treat any differently the advertisements for the service consisting of repair and maintenance of BMW cars. In that case, too, the mark is used to identify the source of the goods which are the subject of the service.[2279]

In that respect, it is true that BMW concerned the use of a sign identical to the trade mark for services which were not identical to those for which that trade mark was registered, since the BMW trade mark, at issue in the main proceedings, was registered for vehicles but not for vehicle repair services. However, the vehicles marketed under the BMW trade mark by the proprietor of that mark constituted the subject matter of the services – the repairing of vehicles – supplied by the third party, so that it was essential

2274. CJEU C-523/10 of 19.4.2012 – Wintersteiger, para. 39.
2275. CJEU C-487/07 of 18.6.2009 – L'Oréal, para. 61.
2276. CJEU C-487/07 of 18.6.2009 – L'Oréal, para. 62.
2277. CJEU C-355/96 of 16.7.1998 – Silhouette International Schmied/Hartlauer Handelsgesellschaft, para. 17.
2278. CJEU C-63/97 of 23.2.1999 – BMW, para. 42; C-179/15 of 3.3.2016 – Daimler/Együd Garage Gépjárműjavító és Értékesítő, para. 28.
2279. CJEU C-63/97 of 23.2.1999 – BMW, para. 39; *see also* CJEU C-179/15 of 3.3.2016 – Daimler/Együd Garage Gépjárműjavító és Értékesítő, para. 22.

to identify the origin of the BMW cars, the subject matter of those services. It was having regard to that specific and indissociable link between the products bearing the trade mark and the services provided by the third party that the Court of Justice held that, in the specific circumstances of the *BMW* case, use by the third party of the sign identical to the trade mark in respect of goods marketed not by the third party but by the holder of the trade mark fell within Article 5(1)(a) TMD2008.[2280]

Apart from that specific case of use of a trade mark by a third-party provider of services having as subject matter the products bearing that trade mark, Article 5(1)(a) TMD2008 must be interpreted as covering the use of a sign identical to the trade mark in respect of goods marketed or services supplied by the third party which are identical to those in respect of which the trade mark is registered.[2281]

First of all, the interpretation whereby the goods or services referred to in Article 5(1)(a) TMD2008 are those marketed or supplied by the third party follows from the wording of that provision itself, particularly the words 'using ... in relation to goods or services'. Second, the contrary interpretation could lead to the words 'goods' and 'services' used in Article 5(1)(a) of the directive designating goods or services of the trade mark proprietor, whereas the words 'goods' and 'service' appearing in Article 6(1)(b) and (c) TMD2008 necessarily refer to those marketed or supplied by the third party, thereby leading, contrary to the scheme of the directive, to interpreting the same words in a different way according to whether they appear in Article 5 or in Article 6.[2282]

Therefore, the affixing by a third party of a sign identical to a trade mark registered for toys to scale **models of vehicles** cannot be prohibited under Article 5(1)(a) TMD2008 unless it affects or is liable to affect the functions of that trade mark.[2283]

In the case in the main proceedings, which is characterized by the fact that the trade mark in question is registered both for motor vehicles and for toys, the referring court has explained that, in Germany, the average consumer of the products of the toy industry, normally informed and reasonably attentive and circumspect, is used to scale models being based on real examples and even accords great importance to absolute fidelity to the original, so that that consumer will understand that the Opel logo appearing on Autec's products indicates that this is a reduced-scale reproduction of an Opel car.[2284]

If, by those explanations, the referring court intended to emphasize that the relevant public does not perceive the sign identical to the Opel logo appearing on the scale models marketed by Autec as an indication that those products come from Adam Opel or an undertaking economically linked to it, it would have to conclude that the use

2280. CJEU C-48/05 of 25.1.2007 – Adam Opel, para. 27.
2281. CJEU C-48/05 of 25.1.2007 – Adam Opel, para. 28; *see also* CJEU C-690/17 of 11.4.2019 – Oko-Text Verlag/Dr. Rudolf Liebe Nachf., para. 31.
2282. CJEU C-48/05 of 25.1.2007 – Adam Opel, para. 29.
2283. CJEU C-48/05 of 25.1.2007 – Adam Opel, para. 22, 37.
2284. CJEU C-48/05 of 25.1.2007 – Adam Opel, para. 23.

at issue in the main proceedings does not affect the essential function of the Opel logo as a trade mark registered for toys.[2285]

It is for the referring court to determine, by reference to the average consumer of toys in Germany, whether the use at issue in the main proceedings affects the functions of the Opel logo as a trade mark registered for toys.[2286]

It is for the **referring court** to determine whether the use which is made of the marks is liable to affect one of the functions of those marks, such as, in particular, their functions of communication, investment or advertising.[2287]

[2] Affecting the functions with regard to the likelihood of confusion

When a third party relies on the requirement of availability to argue its right to use a sign other than that registered by the trade mark proprietor, the relevance of such an argument cannot be assessed under Articles 3 and 12 TMD2008, but must be examined in the light of Article 5 TMD2008, which concerns the protection of the registered mark against use by third parties, as well as of Article 6(1)(b) TMD2008, if the sign in question comes within the scope of that provision.[2288]

The scope of application of Article 5(1) and (2) TMD2008, on the one hand, and Article 5(5) TMD2008, on the other, depends on whether the trade mark is used for the purpose of distinguishing the goods or services in question as originating from a particular undertaking, that is to say, as a trade mark as such, or whether it is used for other purposes. In a situation such as that in the main proceedings, the issue is the **use** of the same trade mark **intended to distinguish the goods** in question as the subject of the services provided by the advertiser.[2289]

Article 5(1) TMD2008 carries out a **complete harmonization** and defines the exclusive rights of trade mark proprietors in the Community.[2290]

The ninth recital of the preamble to the TMD2008 sets out its objective of ensuring that the trade mark proprietor enjoys 'the same protection under the legal systems of all the Member States' and describes that objective as 'fundamental'.[2291]

In order to prevent the protection afforded to the proprietor varying from one State to another, the Court must therefore give a **uniform interpretation** to Article 5(1) TMD2008, in particular the term 'use' which is the subject of the questions referred for a preliminary ruling in the present case.[2292]

As is apparent from the Court's case law (*Arsenal Football Club*; *Anheuser-Busch*; *Medion*; *Adam Opel*; and *Céline*), the proprietor of a registered mark may prevent the

2285. CJEU C-48/05 of 25.1.2007 – Adam Opel, para. 24.
2286. CJEU C-48/05 of 25.1.2007 – Adam Opel, para. 25; *see also* CJEU C-17/06 of 11.9.2007 – Céline, para. 28.
2287. CJEU C-487/07 of 18.6.2009 – L'Oréal, para. 63; C-323/09 of 22.9.2011 – Interflora, para. 41.
2288. CJEU C-102/07 of 10.4.2008 – adidas/Marca Mode, para. 26.
2289. CJEU C-63/97 of 23.2.1999 – BMW, para. 38; C-17/06 of 11.9.2007 – Céline, para. 20.
2290. CJEU C-206/01 of 12.11.2002 – Arsenal Football Club, para. 43.
2291. CJEU C-206/01 of 12.11.2002 – Arsenal Football Club, para. 44.
2292. CJEU C-206/01 of 12.11.2002 – Arsenal Football Club, para. 45; C-48/05 of 25.1.2007 – Adam Opel, para. 17; C-17/06 of 11.9.2007 – Céline, para. 15; C-533/06 of 12.6.2008 – O2 Holdings/Hutchison 3G UK, para. 56.

use of a sign by a third party which is identical with, or similar to, his mark under Article 5(1)(b) TMD2008 only if the following four conditions are satisfied:

- that use must be in the course of trade;
- it must be without the consent of the proprietor of the mark;
- it must be in respect of goods or services which are identical with, or similar to, those for which the mark is registered; and
- it must affect or be liable to affect the essential function of the trade mark, which is to guarantee to consumers the origin of the goods or services, by reason of a likelihood of confusion on the part of the public.[2293]

The Directive is intended, as the first recital of the preamble shows, to eliminate disparities between the trade mark laws of the Member States which may impede the free movement of goods and the freedom to provide services and distort competition within the common market.[2294]

Trade mark rights constitute an essential element in the system of undistorted competition which the Treaty is intended to establish and maintain. In such a system, undertakings must be able to attract and retain customers by the quality of their goods or services, which is made possible only by distinctive signs allowing them to be identified.[2295]

Use of a sign which is identical with, or similar to, the trade mark which gives rise to a likelihood of confusion on the part of the public affects or is liable to affect the essential function of the mark.[2296]

That is the situation where the sign is used by the third party in relation to his goods or services in such a way that consumers are liable to interpret it as designating the origin of the goods or services in question. In such a case, the use of the sign is liable to imperil the essential function of the mark, since, for the trade mark to be able to fulfil its essential role in the system of undistorted competition which the EC Treaty seeks to establish and maintain, it must offer a guarantee that all the goods or services bearing it have been manufactured or supplied under the control of a single undertaking which is responsible for their quality.[2297]

It should be noted that Article 5(5) TMD2008 provides that Article 5(1)-(4) TMD2008 does not affect provisions in a Member State relating to protection against the use of a sign for purposes other than that of distinguishing goods or services.[2298]

Where the signs in question and/or the goods or services for which those signs are used are only similar, the proprietor of the trade mark is entitled, under Article 5(1)(b) TMD2008, to prevent such use of the sign only if, due to a likelihood of

2293. CJEU C-533/06 of 12.6.2008 - O2 Holdings/Hutchison 3G UK, para. 57; *see also* CJEU C-119/10 of 15.12.2011 - Frisdranken Industrie Winters, para. 25.
2294. CJEU C-206/01 of 12.11.2002 - Arsenal Football Club, para. 46.
2295. CJEU C-206/01 of 12.11.2002 - Arsenal Football Club, para. 47.
2296. CJEU C-533/06 of 12.6.2008 - O2 Holdings/Hutchison 3G UK, para. 59.
2297. CJEU C-17/06 of 11.9.2007 - Céline, para. 27.
2298. CJEU C-206/01 of 12.11.2002 - Arsenal Football Club, para. 53.

confusion on the part of the public, that use affects, or is liable to affect, the origin function.[2299]

The proprietor may not prohibit the use of a sign identical to the trade mark for goods identical to those for which the mark is registered if that use cannot affect his own interests as proprietor of the mark, having regard to its functions. Thus certain uses for purely descriptive purposes are excluded from the scope of Article 5(1) TMD2008 because they do not affect any of the interests which that provision aims to protect, and do not therefore fall within the concept of use within the meaning of that provision.[2300]

The **interests** which Article 5(1) TMD2008 is intended to protect are not affected by a situation in which:

- the third party refers to the trade mark in the course of **commercial negotiations** with a potential customer, who is a professional jeweller;
- the reference is made for purely descriptive purposes, namely in order to reveal the characteristics of the product offered for sale to the potential customer, who is familiar with the characteristics of the products covered by the trade mark concerned;
- the reference to the trade mark cannot be interpreted by the potential customer as indicating the origin of the product.[2301]

Article 5(1) TMD2008 is to be interpreted as meaning that the proprietor of a trade mark cannot rely on his exclusive right where a third party, in the course of commercial negotiations, reveals the origin of goods which he has produced himself and uses the sign in question solely to denote the particular characteristics of the goods he is offering for sale so that there can be no question of the trade mark used being perceived as a sign indicative of the undertaking of origin.[2302]

If the use of the sign takes place in the **context of sales** to consumers and is obviously not intended for purely descriptive purposes, the situation in question in the main proceedings is fundamentally different from that in Hölterhoff.[2303]

Having regard to the presentation of the word 'Arsenal' on the goods at issue in the main proceedings and the other secondary markings on them, the use of that sign is such as to create the impression that there is a material link in the course of trade between the goods concerned and the trade mark proprietor.[2304]

In those circumstances, the use of a sign which is identical to the trade mark at issue in the main proceedings is liable to jeopardize the guarantee of origin which

2299. CJEU C-119/10 of 15.12.2011 – Frisdranken Industrie Winters, paras 25; C-179/15 of 3.3.2016 – Daimler/Együd Garage Gépjárműjavító és Értékesítő, para. 27.
2300. CJEU C-206/01 of 12.11.2002 – Arsenal Football Club, para. 54.
2301. CJEU C-2/00 of 14.5.2002 – Hölterhoff, para. 16.
2302. CJEU C-2/00 of 14.5.2002 – Hölterhoff, para. 17.
2303. CJEU C-206/01 of 12.11.2002 – Arsenal Football Club, para. 55.
2304. CJEU C-206/01 of 12.11.2002 – Arsenal Football Club, para. 56; *see also* CJEU C-245/02 of 16.11.2004 – Anheuser-Busch, para. 60.

constitutes the essential function of the mark. It is consequently a use which the trade mark proprietor may prevent in accordance with Article 5(1) TMD2008.[2305]

Once it has been found that, in the present case, the use of the sign in question by the third party is liable to affect the **guarantee of origin** of the goods and that the trade mark proprietor must be able to prevent this, it is immaterial that in the context of that use the sign is perceived as a **badge of support for or loyalty or affiliation** to the proprietor of the mark.[2306]

Article 5(1)(a) TMD2008 and Article 9(1)(a) CTMR must be interpreted as meaning that the proprietor of a trade mark is entitled to prohibit an advertiser from advertising, on the basis of a **keyword** identical with that trade mark which that advertiser has, without the consent of the proprietor, selected in connection with an **internet referencing service**, goods or services identical with those for which that mark is registered, in the case where that ad does not enable an average internet user, or enables that user only with difficulty, to ascertain whether the goods or services referred to therein originate from the proprietor of the trade mark or an undertaking economically connected to it or, on the contrary, originate from a third party.[2307]

The question whether that function of the trade mark is adversely affected when internet users are shown, on the basis of a keyword identical with a mark, a third party's ad, such as that of a competitor of the proprietor of that mark, depends in particular on the manner in which that ad is presented.[2308]

The function of indicating the origin of the mark is adversely affected if the ad does not enable normally informed and reasonably attentive internet users, or enables them only with difficulty, to ascertain whether the goods or services referred to by the ad originate from the proprietor of the trade mark or an undertaking economically connected to it or, on the contrary, originate from a third party.[2309]

In such a situation, which is, moreover, characterized by the fact that the ad in question appears immediately after entry of the trade mark as a search term by the internet user concerned and is displayed at a point when the trade mark is, in its capacity as a search term, also displayed on the screen, the internet user may err as to the origin of the goods or services in question. In those circumstances, the use by the third party of the sign identical with the mark as a keyword triggering the display of that

2305. CJEU C-206/01 of 12.11.2002 – Arsenal Football Club, para. 60.
2306. CJEU C-206/01 of 12.11.2002 – Arsenal Football Club, para. 61.
2307. CJEU C-236/08 to C-238/08 of 23.3.2010 – Google France, para. 99; C-324/09 of 12.7.2011 – L'Oréal, para. 94; *see also* CJEU C-148/21 and C-184/21 of 22.12.2022 – Louboutin/Amazon Europe Core a.o., para. 50.
2308. CJEU C-236/08 to C-238/08 of 23.3.2010 – Google France, para. 83; C-278/08 of 25.3.2010 – BergSpechte, para. 35; C-91/09 of 26.3.2010 – Eis.de, para. 24; C-558/08 of 8.7.2010 – Portakabin, para. 34; *see also* CJEU C-323/09 of 22.9.2011 – Interflora, para. 44; C-224/20 of 17.11.2022 – Merck Sharp & Dohme a.o./Abacus a.o., para. 127.
2309. CJEU C-236/08 to C-238/08 of 23.3.2010 – Google France, para. 84; C-278/08 of 25.3.2010 – BergSpechte, para. 35; C-91/09 of 26.3.2010 – Eis.de, para. 24; C-558/08 of 8.7.2010 – Portakabin, para. 34; C-323/09 of 22.9.2011 – Interflora, para. 44; C-224/20 of 17.11.2022 – Merck Sharp & Dohme a.o./Abacus a.o., para. 127.

ad is liable to create the impression that there is a material link in the course of trade between the goods or services in question and the proprietor of the trade mark.[2310]

Still with regard to adverse effect on the function of indicating origin, it is worthwhile noting that the need for transparency in the display of advertisements on the internet is emphasized in the EU legislation on electronic commerce. Having regard to the interests of fair trading and consumer protection, referred to in recital 29 in the preamble to Directive 2000/31, Article 6 TMD2008 lays down the rule that the natural or legal person on whose behalf a commercial communication which is part of an information society service is made must be clearly identifiable.[2311]

Advertising originating from the operator of an online marketplace and displayed by a search engine operator must thus, in any event, disclose both the identity of the online marketplace operator and the fact that the trade marked goods advertised are being sold through the marketplace that it operates.[2312]

Although it thus proves to be the case that advertisers on the internet can, as appropriate, be made liable under rules governing other areas of law, such as the rules on unfair competition, the fact none the less remains that the allegedly unlawful use on the internet of signs identical with, or similar to, trade marks lends itself to examination from the perspective of trade mark law. Having regard to the essential function of a trade mark, which, in the area of electronic commerce, consists in particular in enabling internet users browsing the ads displayed in response to a search relating to a specific trade mark to distinguish the goods or services of the proprietor of that mark from those which have a different origin, that proprietor must be entitled to prohibit the display of third party ads which internet users may erroneously perceive as emanating from that proprietor.[2313]

It is **for the national court** to assess, on a case-by-case basis, whether the facts of the dispute before it indicate adverse effects, or a risk thereof, on the function of indicating origin.[2314]

In the case where a third party's ad **suggests that there is an economic link** between that third party and the proprietor of the trade mark, the conclusion must be that there is an adverse effect on the function of indicating origin.[2315]

In the case where the ad, while not suggesting the existence of an economic link, is vague to such an extent on the origin of the goods or services at issue that normally informed and reasonably attentive **internet users are unable to determine**, on the

2310. CJEU C-236/08 to C-238/08 of 23.3.2010 – Google France, para. 85; C-323/09 of 22.9.2011 – Interflora, para. 44.
2311. CJEU C-236/08 to C-238/08 of 23.3.2010 – Google France, para. 86; C-324/09 of 12.7.2011 – L'Oréal, para. 95; *see also* CJEU C-148/21 and C-184/21 of 22.12.2022 – Louboutin/Amazon Europe Core a.o., para. 50.
2312. CJEU C-324/09 of 12.7.2011 – L'Oréal, para. 96.
2313. CJEU C-236/08 to C-238/08 of 23.3.2010 – Google France, para. 87.
2314. CJEU C-236/08 to C-238/08 of 23.3.2010 – Google France, para. 88; C-91/09 of 26.3.2010 – Eis.de, para. 25; C-323/09 of 22.9.2011 – Interflora, para. 46.
2315. CJEU C-236/08 to C-238/08 of 23.3.2010 – Google France, para. 89; C-278/08 of 25.3.2010 – BergSpechte, para. 36; C-91/09 of 26.3.2010 – Eis.de, para. 26; C-558/08 of 8.7.2010 – Portakabin, para. 35; C-323/09 of 22.9.2011 – Interflora, para. 45; C-179/15 of 3.3.2016 – Daimler/Együd Garage Gépjárműjavító és Értékesítő, para. 30.

basis of the advertising link and the commercial message attached thereto, whether the advertiser is a third party vis-à-vis the proprietor of the trade mark or, on the contrary, economically linked to that proprietor, the conclusion must also be that there is an adverse effect on that function of the trade mark.[2316]

For the purposes of that assessment, the fact that the referencing service provider has not permitted trade mark proprietors to prevent the selection of a sign identical with that trade mark as a keyword is irrelevant. Only the opposite case - in which the referencing service provider gives trade mark proprietors such an option - could have legal consequences inasmuch as, in that case and under certain conditions, a failure on the part of those proprietors, when signs identical with their trade marks are selected as keywords, to object to such selection could be regarded as tacit consent on their part. However, the fact that the trade mark proprietor has neither been asked for its consent nor given it merely confirms that a sign identical with its trade mark has been used without its consent.[2317]

[3] Affecting the functions with regard to well-known marks

It is settled case law that the exclusive right under that provision was conferred in order to enable the trade mark proprietor to protect his specific interests as proprietor of that mark, that is, to ensure that the trade mark can fulfil its functions. Therefore, the exercise of that right must be reserved to cases in which another party's use of the sign adversely affects or is liable adversely to affect one of the functions of the trade mark. Those functions include **not only the essential function of the trade mark**, which is to guarantee to consumers the origin of the goods or services in question, but also its other functions, such as that of guaranteeing the quality of those goods or services or those of communication, investment or advertising.[2318]

Where a trade mark is registered for motor vehicles - in respect of which it is well known - the affixing by a third party, without authorization from the trade mark proprietor, of a sign identical to that trade mark on scale models of vehicles bearing that trade mark, in order faithfully to reproduce those vehicles, and the marketing of those scale models constitute, within the meaning of Article 5(2) TMD2008, a use which the proprietor of the trade mark is entitled to prevent - where the protection defined in that provision has been introduced into national law - if, without due cause, **use of that sign takes unfair advantage of, or is detrimental to, the distinctive character or the repute of the trade mark** as a trade mark registered for motor vehicles.[2319]

In a situation in which the trade mark already enjoys such a reputation, the investment function is adversely affected where use by a third party of a sign identical

2316. CJEU C-236/08 to C-238/08 of 23.3.2010 - Google France, para. 90; C-278/08 of 25.3.2010 - BergSpechte, para. 36; C-91/09 of 26.3.2010 - Eis.de, paras 27 et seq.; C-558/08 of 8.7.2010 - Portakabin, para. 35; C-323/09 of 22.9.2011 - Interflora, para. 45.
2317. CJEU C-323/09 of 22.9.2011 - Interflora, para. 47.
2318. CJEU C-487/07 of 18.6.2009 - L'Oréal, para. 58; C-376/11 of 19.7.2012 - Pie Optiek, para. 46; C-661/11 of 19.9.2013 - Martin Y Paz Diffusion, para. 58; C-65/12 of 6.2.2014 - Leidseplein Beheer, para. 30.
2319. CJEU C-48/05 of 25.1.2007 - Adam Opel, para. 37.

with that mark in relation to identical goods or services affects that reputation and thereby jeopardizes its maintenance. As the Court has already held,[2320] the proprietor of a trade mark must be able, by virtue of the exclusive right conferred upon it by the mark, to prevent such use.[2321]

In this case, first, the Opel logo is also registered for motor vehicles; secondly, subject to verification by the referring court, it is a trade mark well known in Germany for that kind of products, and, finally, a motor vehicle and a scale model of that vehicle are not similar products. Therefore, the use at issue in the main proceedings is also capable of being prohibited, in accordance with Article 5(2) TMD2008, if such use without due cause takes unfair advantage of, or is detrimental to, the distinctive character or the repute of that trade mark registered for motor vehicles.[2322]

Adam Opel has argued at the hearing before the Court that it has an interest in the quality of scale models of vehicles bearing the Opel trade mark being good, and in those models being absolutely up-to-date, as otherwise the reputation of that trade mark, as a trade mark registered for motor vehicles, would be affected.[2323]

This is, in any event, an assessment of a factual nature. It is for the referring court, where necessary, to determine whether the use at issue in the main proceedings constitutes use without due cause which takes unfair advantage of, or is detrimental to, the distinctive character or the repute of the registered trade mark.[2324]

The presence or absence, in the ad, of actual offers for the sale of the goods or services in question is not, in general, a decisive factor for purposes of that assessment.[2325]

In that context, it is only in the situations covered by Article 5(2) or (5) TMD2008 that the question arises whether use of the mark takes unfair advantage of, or is detrimental to, the distinctive character or the repute of the trade mark by, for example, giving the public a false impression of the relationship between the advertiser and the trade mark owner. Those matters are accordingly to be taken into account, not when classifying use under Article 5, but when assessing the legality of that use in the situations covered by Article 5(2) or (5).[2326]

In so far as marks have a reputation, their use in the **comparison lists** may also be prevented under Article 5(2) TMD2008, the applicability of which does not necessarily require that there be a likelihood of detriment to the mark or its proprietor, provided that the third party takes unfair advantage of the use of that mark.[2327]

2320. CJEU C-487/07 of 18.6.2009 – L'Oréal, para. 83.
2321. CJEU C-323/09 of 22.9.2011 – Interflora, para. 63.
2322. CJEU C-48/05 of 25.1.2007 – Adam Opel, para. 34.
2323. CJEU C-48/05 of 25.1.2007 – Adam Opel, para. 35.
2324. CJEU C-48/05 of 25.1.2007 – Adam Opel, para. 36.
2325. CJEU C-558/08 of 8.7.2010 – Portakabin, para. 44.
2326. CJEU C-63/97 of 23.2.1999 – BMW, para. 40.
2327. CJEU C-487/07 of 18.6.2009 – L'Oréal, para. 64.

[F] Online market places

The **operator of an online marketplace** does not 'use' – for the purposes of Article 5 TMD2008 or Article 9 CTMR – signs identical with or similar to trade marks which appear in offers for sale displayed on its site.[2328]

In that regard, it is first necessary to point out that, where sales are made through online marketplaces, the service provided by the operator of the marketplace includes the display, for its customer-sellers, of offers for sale originating from the latter.[2329]

Next, when such offers relate to trade marked goods, signs identical with or similar to trade marks will inevitably be displayed on the website of the operator of the online marketplace.[2330]

Although it is true that, in those circumstances, those signs are 'used' on that site, it is none the less not evident that it is the operator of the online marketplace that is 'using' them, within the meaning of TMD and CTMR.[2331]

If a sign identical with, or similar to, the proprietor's trade mark is to be 'used', within the meaning of Article 5 TMD2008 and Article 9 CTMR, by a third party, that implies, at the very least, that that third party uses the sign in its own commercial communication. In so far as that third party provides a service consisting in enabling its customers to display on its website, in the course of their commercial activities such as their offers for sale, signs corresponding to trade marks, it does not itself use those signs within the meaning of that EU legislation.[2332]

It follows that the use of signs identical with or similar to trade marks in offers for sale displayed on an online marketplace is made by the sellers who are customers of the operator of that marketplace and not by that operator itself.[2333]

Inasmuch as it enables that use to be made by its customers, the role of the online marketplace operator cannot be assessed under TMD or CTMR, but must be examined[2334] from the point of view of other rules of law, such as those set out in Directive 2000/31, in particular in section 4 of Chapter II, which concerns the 'liability of intermediary service providers' in electronic commerce and comprises Articles 12–15 of that directive.[2335]

Article 9(2)(a) EUTMR must be interpreted as meaning that the **operator** of an online sales website incorporating, as well as that operator's own sales offerings, an online marketplace may be regarded as **itself using a sign** which is identical with an EU trade mark of another person for goods which are identical with those for which that trade mark is registered, **where** third-party sellers offer for sale, on that marketplace, without the consent of the proprietor of that trade mark, such goods bearing that sign

2328. CJEU C-324/09 of 12.7.2011 – L'Oréal, para. 105.
2329. CJEU C-324/09 of 12.7.2011 – L'Oréal, para. 99.
2330. CJEU C-324/09 of 12.7.2011 – L'Oréal, para. 100.
2331. CJEU C-324/09 of 12.7.2011 – L'Oréal, para. 101.
2332. CJEU C-324/09 of 12.7.2011 – L'Oréal, para. 102.
2333. CJEU C-324/09 of 12.7.2011 – L'Oréal, para. 103; C-567/18 of 2.4.2020 – Coty Germany/Amazon Services Europe a.o., para. 40.
2334. *See* CJEU C-324/09 of 12.7.2011 – L'Oréal, paras 106 et seqq.
2335. CJEU C-324/09 of 12.7.2011 – L'Oréal, para. 104.

if a well-informed and reasonably observant user of that site establishes a link between the services of that operator and the sign at issue, which is in particular the case where, in view of all the circumstances of the situation in question, such a user may have the impression that that operator itself is marketing, in its own name and on its own account, the goods bearing that sign. In that regard, the following are relevant: the fact that that operator uses a uniform method of presenting the offers published on its website, displaying both the advertisements relating to the goods which it sells in its own name and on its own behalf and those relating to goods offered by third-party sellers on that marketplace; the fact that it places its own logo as a renowned distributor on all those advertisements; and the fact that it offers third-party sellers, in connection with the marketing of goods bearing the sign at issue, additional services consisting *inter alia* in the storing and shipping of those goods.[2336]

In that regard, it should be noted at the outset that the **concept of 'using'** within the meaning of Article 9(2) EUTMR is not defined by that regulation.[2337]

The Court held that where the operator of an online marketplace offers storage services to the third-party sellers active on that marketplace, so that it stores for those third-party sellers goods which infringe a trade mark right, without however being aware of the infringing nature of the goods at issue and without having the aim of itself offering the goods which it stores or of itself putting them on the market, it is not the operator, but those sellers alone which make use of the signs affixed to the stored goods.[2338]

However, it is important to point out that, although the case which gave rise to that judgment concerned the operator of the same online sales website incorporating the online marketplace, namely Amazon, the referring court in that case, which alone had jurisdiction to make the necessary factual findings, had made it clear that that operator was unaware of the fact that the goods at issue infringed a trade mark right, that it had not itself offered the goods concerned for sale or put them on the market and that it also did not intend to do it itself. That court had also pointed out that those goods were dispatched by external service providers.[2339]

Moreover, the Court was not asked in the case *Coty Germany* and the case *L'Oréal*[2340] about the impact of the fact that the online sales website in question incorporates, as well as the online marketplace, sales offers of the operator of that site itself.[2341]

However, in the present cases, the referring courts specifically raise the issue of that impact and the significance, in that context, of the perception of the users of the website in question and of other circumstances, such as the fact that the operator

2336. CJEU C-148/21 and C-184/21 of 22.12.2022 – Louboutin/Amazon Europe Core a.o., para. 54.
2337. CJEU C-148/21 and C-184/21 of 22.12.2022 – Louboutin/Amazon Europe Core a.o., para. 25.
2338. CJEU C-148/21 and C-184/21 of 22.12.2022 – Louboutin/Amazon Europe Core a.o., para. 32, with reference to CJEU C-567/18 of 2.4.2020 – Coty Germany/Amazon Services Europe a.o., para. 45 and 53.
2339. CJEU C-148/21 and C-184/21 of 22.12.2022 – Louboutin/Amazon Europe Core a.o., para. 33, with reference to CJEU C-567/18 of 2.4.2020 – Coty Germany/Amazon Services Europe a.o., paras 9, 30 and 47.
2340. CJEU C-324/09 of 12.7.2011 – L'Oréal.
2341. CJEU C-148/21 and C-184/21 of 22.12.2022 – Louboutin/Amazon Europe Core a.o., para. 34.

presents the sales offers published on its website in a uniform manner, displaying at the same time its own advertisements and those of third-party sellers and attaching its own logo as a renowned distributor to all those advertisements, and also the fact that it offers additional services to those third-party sellers in connection with the marketing of their goods, such as support in the presentation of their advertisements and the storing and shipping of their goods.[2342]

In that connection, the referring courts are uncertain, in particular, whether, in such circumstances, as well as the third-party seller, the operator of the online sales website incorporating an online marketplace may be regarded as using, in some cases, in its own commercial communication, a sign which is identical with a trade mark of another person for goods which are identical with those for which that trade mark is registered, and may thus be held liable for the infringement of the rights of the proprietor of that trade mark, within the meaning of Article 9(2)(a) EUTMR, where that third-party seller offers goods bearing that sign for sale on that marketplace.[2343]

It must be stated, in that regard, that that issue arises irrespective of the fact that the role of that operator, in so far as it enables another economic operator to make use of the trade mark, may, if necessary, be examined from the point of view of other rules of law such as Article 14(1) of Directive 2000/31 or the first sentence of Article 11 of Directive 2004/48.[2344]

Although, in the end, it is for the referring courts to assess whether, in each of the cases in the main proceedings, Amazon, in its capacity as operator of an online sales website incorporating an online marketplace, makes use of a sign which is identical with the trade mark at issue for goods which are identical with those for which that trade mark is registered, within the meaning of Article 9(2)(a) EUTMR, the Court may nevertheless provide those courts with the elements of interpretation under EU law which may be useful to them in that regard.[2345]

In that regard, it should be pointed out that the 'commercial communication' of an undertaking, within the meaning of the case law cited above, generally designates any form of communication to third parties designed to promote its activity, goods or services or to indicate the exercise of such an activity. The use of a sign in that undertaking's own commercial communication thus presupposes that that sign appears, in the eyes of third parties, to be an integral part of the communication and, consequently, a part of that undertaking's activity.[2346]

In that context, the Court has already found that, in a situation in which the supplier of the service uses a sign which is identical or similar to the trade mark of another person in order to promote goods which one of its customers is marketing with the assistance of that service, that operator does itself make use of that sign if it uses it

2342. CJEU C-148/21 and C-184/21 of 22.12.2022 – Louboutin/Amazon Europe Core a.o., para. 35.
2343. CJEU C-148/21 and C-184/21 of 22.12.2022 – Louboutin/Amazon Europe Core a.o., para. 36.
2344. CJEU C-148/21 and C-184/21 of 22.12.2022 – Louboutin/Amazon Europe Core a.o., para. 37, with reference to CJEU C-567/18 of 2.4.2020 – Coty Germany/Amazon Services Europe a.o., para. 49.
2345. CJEU C-148/21 and C-184/21 of 22.12.2022 – Louboutin/Amazon Europe Core a.o., para. 38, with further proof.
2346. CJEU C-148/21 and C-184/21 of 22.12.2022 – Louboutin/Amazon Europe Core a.o., para. 39.

in such a way that it establishes a link between the sign and the services provided by that operator.[2347]

Accordingly, the Court has held that such a service provider does not itself make use of a sign which is identical with or similar to a trade mark of another person when the service it provides is not, by its very nature, comparable to a service aimed at promoting the marketing of goods bearing that sign and does not imply the creation of a link between the sign and that service, since the service provider in question is not apparent to the consumer, which excludes any association between its services and the sign at issue.[2348]

On the other hand, the Court has held that such a link does exist where the operator of an online marketplace, by means of an internet referencing service and on the basis of a keyword which is identical with a trade mark of another person, advertises goods bearing that trade mark which are offered for sale by its customers on the online marketplace. For internet users carrying out a search on the basis of a keyword, such advertising creates an obvious association between those trade marked goods and the possibility of buying them through that marketplace. That is why the proprietor of that trade mark is entitled to prohibit that operator from such use, where that advertising infringes the trade mark right owing to the fact that it does not enable well-informed and reasonably observant internet users, or enables them only with difficulty, to ascertain whether the goods concerned originate from the proprietor of the trade mark or from an undertaking economically linked to that proprietor or, on the contrary, originate from a third party.[2349]

It is apparent from that case law that in order to determine whether the operator of an online sales website incorporating an online marketplace does itself make use of a sign which is identical with a trade mark of another person, which appears in advertisements relating to goods offered by third-party sellers on that marketplace, it is necessary to assess whether a well-informed and reasonably observant user of that website establishes a link between that operator's services and the sign in question.[2350]

The relevance of such an analysis is by no means called into question by the argument put forward by Amazon and the European Commission in their written observations that the Court's existing case law has not taken the perception of users into consideration.[2351]

It is true that, in the judgment *L'Oréal and Others*,[2352] the Court did not expressly mention the perception of the user of the online marketplace, to whom the commercial communication at issue is addressed.[2353]

2347. CJEU C-148/21 and C-184/21 of 22.12.2022 – Louboutin/Amazon Europe Core a.o., para. 40, with reference to CJEU C-324/09 of 12.7.2011 – L'Oréal, para. 92; C-119/10 of 15.12.2011 – Frisdranken Industrie Winters, para. 32.
2348. CJEU C-148/21 and C-184/21 of 22.12.2022 – Louboutin/Amazon Europe Core a.o., para. 41, with reference to CJEU C-119/10 of 15.12.2011 – Frisdranken Industrie Winters, para. 33.
2349. CJEU C-148/21 and C-184/21 of 22.12.2022 – Louboutin/Amazon Europe Core a.o., para. 42, with reference to CJEU C-324/09 of 12.7.2011 – L'Oréal, paras 93 and 97.
2350. CJEU C-148/21 and C-184/21 of 22.12.2022 – Louboutin/Amazon Europe Core a.o., para. 43.
2351. CJEU C-148/21 and C-184/21 of 22.12.2022 – Louboutin/Amazon Europe Core a.o., para. 44.
2352. CJEU C-324/09 of 12.7.2011 – L'Oréal, paras 102 et seq.
2353. CJEU C-148/21 and C-184/21 of 22.12.2022 – Louboutin/Amazon Europe Core a.o., para. 45.

However, that does not mean that the Court precluded consideration of the perception of the users of the online marketplace as a relevant factor for determining whether the sign in question is used in the market place operator's own commercial communication.[2354]

In the case which gave rise to that judgment, the website in question comprised only an online marketplace and did not also include sales offers of the operator of that site.[2355]

Therefore, in order to determine whether an advertisement, published on an online sales website incorporating an online marketplace by a third-party seller active on that marketplace, using a sign which is identical with a trade mark of another person may be regarded as forming an integral part of the commercial communication of the operator of that website, it is necessary to ascertain whether that advertisement may establish a link between the services offered by that operator and the sign in question, on the ground that a well-informed and reasonably observant user might believe that the operator is marketing, in its own name and on its own account, the goods for which the sign in question is being used.[2356]

In the overall assessment of the circumstances of the present case, the method of presenting the advertisements, both individually and as a whole, on the website in question and the nature and scope of the services provided by the operator of the website are particularly important.[2357]

As regards, first, the method of presenting those advertisements, it should be pointed out that the need for transparency in the display of those advertisements is provided for in EU legislation on electronic commerce. Advertisements displayed on an online sales website incorporating an online marketplace must, therefore, be presented in a way which enables a well-informed and reasonably observant user to distinguish easily between offers originating, on the one hand, from the operator of that website and, on the other, from third-party sellers active on the online marketplace which is incorporated therein.[2358]

However, the fact that the operator of an online sales website incorporating an online marketplace uses a uniform method of presenting the offerings published on its website, displaying both its own advertisements and those of third-party sellers and placing its own logo as a renowned distributor on its own website and on all those advertisements, including those relating to goods offered by third-party sellers, may make it difficult to draw such a clear distinction and thus to give the well-informed and reasonably observant user the impression that that operator is marketing, in its own name and on its own behalf, the goods offered for sale by those third-party sellers. Consequently, when those goods bear a sign which is identical with a trade mark of

2354. CJEU C-148/21 and C-184/21 of 22.12.2022 – Louboutin/Amazon Europe Core a.o., para. 46.
2355. CJEU C-148/21 and C-184/21 of 22.12.2022 – Louboutin/Amazon Europe Core a.o., para. 47.
2356. CJEU C-148/21 and C-184/21 of 22.12.2022 – Louboutin/Amazon Europe Core a.o., para. 48.
2357. CJEU C-148/21 and C-184/21 of 22.12.2022 – Louboutin/Amazon Europe Core a.o., para. 49.
2358. CJEU C-148/21 and C-184/21 of 22.12.2022 – Louboutin/Amazon Europe Core a.o., para. 50, with reference to CJEU C-324/09 of 12.7.2011 – L'Oréal, paras 94 et seq.

another person, that uniform presentation may establish a link, in the eyes of those users, between that sign and the services provided by that same operator.[2359]

In particular, where the operator of an online sales website describes the various offerings, from itself or a third party, without distinguishing them as to their origin, as 'bestsellers' or 'most sought after' or 'most popular' for the purpose *inter alia* of promoting some of those offerings, that presentation is likely to strengthen the impression of the well-informed and reasonably observant user that those goods thus promoted are being marketed by that operator, in its own name and on its own behalf.[2360]

Second, the nature and scope of the services provided by the operator of an online sales website incorporating an online marketplace to the third-party sellers who offer goods bearing the sign at issue on that marketplace, such as the services consisting *inter alia* in dealing with the questions of the users relating to those goods or to the storage, shipping and management of returns of those goods, are also likely to give the impression, to a well-informed and reasonably observant user, that those same goods are being marketed by that operator, in its own name and on its own behalf, and may thus establish a link, in the eyes of those users, between its services and the signs placed on those goods and in the advertisements of those third-party sellers.[2361]

[G] Import and transit

Article 28 EC is to be interpreted as precluding the implementation, pursuant to a legislative measure of a Member State concerning intellectual property, of procedures for detention by the customs authorities of goods lawfully manufactured in another Member State and intended, following their transit through the territory of the first Member State, to be placed on the market in a non-member country.[2362]

'Offering' and 'putting on the market', within the meaning of Article 5(3)(b) TMD2008 and Article 9(2)(b) CTMR, may include, respectively, the offering and sale of original goods bearing a trade mark and having the customs status of non-Community goods, when the offering is done and/or the sale is effected while the goods are placed under the external transit procedure or the customs warehousing procedure. The trade mark proprietor may oppose the offering or the sale of such goods **when it necessarily entails the putting of those goods** on the market in the Community.[2363]

Non-Community goods placed under the external transit procedure or the customs warehousing procedure are not regarded as 'imported' for the purposes of Article 5(3)(c) TMD2008 and Article 9(2)(c) CTMR.[2364]

2359. CJEU C-148/21 and C-184/21 of 22.12.2022 – Louboutin/Amazon Europe Core a.o., para. 51.
2360. CJEU C-148/21 and C-184/21 of 22.12.2022 – Louboutin/Amazon Europe Core a.o., para. 52.
2361. CJEU C-148/21 and C-184/21 of 22.12.2022 – Louboutin/Amazon Europe Core a.o., para. 53.
2362. CJEU C-115/02 of 23.10.2003 – Rioglass and Transremar, para. 30.
2363. CJEU C-405/03 of 18.10.2005 – Class International, para. 61.
2364. CJEU C-405/03 of 18.10.2005 – Class International, para. 55.

Regulations No. 3295/94[2365] **and No. 1383/2003**[2366] must be interpreted as meaning that:

- goods coming from a non-Member State which are imitations of goods protected in the European Union by a trade mark right or copies of goods protected in the European Union by copyright, a related right or a design cannot be classified as 'counterfeit goods' or 'pirated goods' within the meaning of those regulations merely on the basis of the fact that they are brought into the customs territory of the European Union under a suspensive procedure;
- those goods may, on the other hand, infringe the right in question and therefore be classified as 'counterfeit goods' or 'pirated goods' where it is proven that they are intended to be put on sale in the European Union, such proof being provided, *inter alia,* where it turns out that the goods have been sold to a customer in the European Union or offered for sale or advertised to consumers in the European Union, or where it is apparent from documents or correspondence concerning the goods that their diversion to European Union consumers is envisaged;
- in order that the authority competent to take a substantive decision may profitably examine whether such proof and the other elements constituting an infringement of the intellectual property right relied upon exist, the customs authority to which an application for action is made must, as soon as there are indications before it giving grounds for suspecting that such an infringement exists, suspend the release of or detain those goods; and
- those indications may include, *inter alia,* the fact that the destination of the goods is not declared, whereas the suspensive procedure requested requires such a declaration, the lack of precise or reliable information as to the identity or address of the manufacturer or consignor of the goods, a lack of cooperation with the customs authorities or the discovery of documents or correspondence concerning the goods in question suggesting that there is liable to be a diversion of those goods to European Union consumers.[2367]

Thus, goods coming from a non-Member State which are imitations of goods protected in the EU by a trade mark right or copies of goods protected in the EU by copyright, a related right or a design can be classified as 'counterfeit goods' or 'pirated goods' where it is proven that they are intended to be put on sale in the EU, such proof

2365. Council Regulation (EC) No. 3295/94 of 22 Dec. 1994 laying down measures concerning the entry into the Community and the export and re-export from the Community of goods infringing certain intellectual property rights (OJ 1994 L 341, p. 8), as amended by Council Regulation (EC) No. 241/1999 of 25 Jan. 1999 (OJ 1999 L 27, p. 1).
2366. Council Regulation (EC) No. 1383/2003 of 22 Jul. 2003 concerning customs action against goods suspected of infringing certain intellectual property rights and the measures to be taken against goods found to have infringed such rights (OJ 2003 L 196, p. 7).
2367. CJEU C-446/09 and C-495/09 of 1.12.2011 – Koninklijke Philips Electronics, para. 78.

being provided, *inter alia*, where it turns out that the goods have been sold to a customer in the EU or offered for sale or advertised to consumers in the EU.[2368]

The Court has held, on the one hand, that the external transit of non-Community goods is based on a legal fiction. Goods placed under this procedure are subject neither to the corresponding import duties nor to the other measures of commercial policy; it is as if they had not entered Community territory.[2369]

Everything happens as if, before the goods entered into free circulation, which was to happen in Ireland, they had not entered Community territory.[2370]

Such goods may be the subject of offering for sale or sales to a third country.[2371]

In those situations, when the goods are original goods bearing a trade mark, the trade mark proprietor's right to control the initial marketing in the Community is not adversely affected.[2372]

On the other hand, the Court has also held that transit, which consists in transporting goods lawfully manufactured in a Member State to a non-member country by passing through one or more Member States, does not involve any marketing of the goods in question and is therefore not liable to infringe the specific subject matter of the trade mark.[2373]

It is in that regard, in principle, irrelevant whether goods whose destination is a Member State come from an **associated State** or a **third country**, or whether those goods have been manufactured in the country of origin lawfully or in infringement of the existing trade mark rights of the proprietor in that country.[2374]

As non-Community goods, the goods originating in Poland could be placed under the external transit procedure, and it was thus irrelevant that the goods came from an associated State, such as was the Republic of Poland prior to its accession to the Union, rather than from another non-associated third country.[2375]

It follows that it is irrelevant for the purposes of answering the first question that, at the time material to the facts in the main proceedings, the goods in question originated in an associated State, namely the Republic of Poland prior to its accession to the Union, rather than a non-associated third country.[2376]

The proprietor of a trade mark can prohibit the transit through a Member State in which that mark is protected of goods bearing the trade mark and placed under the external transit procedure with another Member State as their destination where the mark is not so protected, only if those goods are subject to the act of a third party while they are placed under the external transit procedure which necessarily entails their being put on the market in that transit Member State. Whether the manufacture of the goods in issue was lawful or unlawful is in that respect irrelevant.[2377]

2368. CJEU C-98/13 of 6.2.2014 – Blomqvist, para. 33.
2369. CJEU C-281/05 of 9.11.2006 – Montex Holdings, para. 17.
2370. CJEU C-281/05 of 9.11.2006 – Montex Holdings, para. 18.
2371. CJEU C-405/03 of 18.10.2005 – Class International, para. 56.
2372. CJEU C-405/03 of 18.10.2005 – Class International, para. 57.
2373. CJEU C-281/05 of 9.11.2006 – Montex Holdings, para. 19.
2374. CJEU C-281/05 of 9.11.2006 – Montex Holdings, para. 41.
2375. CJEU C-281/05 of 9.11.2006 – Montex Holdings, para. 31.
2376. CJEU C-281/05 of 9.11.2006 – Montex Holdings, para. 32.
2377. CJEU C-281/05 of 9.11.2006 – Montex Holdings, para. 34.

Such an interpretation of Article 5 TMD2008 is not affected by the judgment in Case C-60/02 X [2004] ECR I-651, regarding, in particular, the interpretation of Articles 2 and 11 of Regulation No. 3295/94.[2378]

In that judgment, the Court pointed out that Article 1 of Regulation No. 3295/94 is to be interpreted as being applicable where goods imported from a non-Member State are, in the course of their transit to another non-Member State, temporarily detained in a Member State by the customs authorities of this latter State on the basis of that regulation and at the request of the company which holds the rights claimed to have been infringed.[2379]

In that regard, the Court notes that Article 1 of Regulation No. 3295/94 lays down, first, the conditions under which the customs authorities are to take action where goods suspected of being counterfeit goods are, in particular, found in the course of checks on goods under customs supervision within the meaning of Article 37 of the Customs Code, placed under a suspensive procedure within the meaning of Article 84(1)(a) of that Code, re-exported subject to notification or placed in a free zone or free warehouse under Article 166 thereof.[2380]

Second, Article 1 of Regulation No. 3295/94 lays down the measures which can be taken by the competent customs authorities with regard to those goods.[2381]

Third, the second and third recitals of that regulation, reproduced in paragraph 4 above, refer expressly to the marketing of counterfeit goods or the placing of such goods on the market, and to the need to prohibit the release of such goods for free circulation in the Community.[2382]

It follows that none of the provisions of Regulation No. 3295/94 introduces a new criterion for the purposes of ascertaining the existence of an infringement of trade mark law or to determine whether there is a use of the mark liable to be prohibited because it infringes that law.[2383]

On the other hand, if the offering or the sale necessarily entails putting goods bearing the mark on the market in the Community, the exclusive rights conferred on the proprietor of that mark by Article 5(1) TMD2008 and Article 9(1) CTMR have been adversely affected, regardless of the place in which the addressee of the offer or the purchaser is established and irrespective of the provisions of the contract ultimately concluded regarding any restrictions on resale or the customs status of the goods. The offering or the sale is then 'using [the mark] in the course of trade' within the meaning of Article 5(1) TMD2008 and Article 9(1) CTMR. It follows that the trade mark proprietor may oppose it pursuant to Article 5(3)(b) TMD2008 and Article 9(2)(b) CTMR.[2384]

2378. CJEU C-281/05 of 9.11.2006 – Montex Holdings, para. 35.
2379. CJEU C-281/05 of 9.11.2006 – Montex Holdings, para. 36.
2380. CJEU C-281/05 of 9.11.2006 – Montex Holdings, para. 37.
2381. CJEU C-281/05 of 9.11.2006 – Montex Holdings, para. 38.
2382. CJEU C-281/05 of 9.11.2006 – Montex Holdings, para. 39.
2383. CJEU C-281/05 of 9.11.2006 – Montex Holdings, para. 40.
2384. CJEU C-405/03 of 18.10.2005 – Class International, para. 58; C-449/09 of 28.10.2010 – Canon Kabushiki Kaisha, para. 19.

The **likelihood that the goods will be put on the market** in the Community **cannot**, however, **be assumed** on the sole basis of the fact that the owner of the goods, the addressee of the offer or the purchaser engage in parallel trade. Other evidence must prove that the offering or the sale necessarily entails putting on the market in the Community the specific goods at issue.[2385]

In that regard, the argument that the mere risk that the goods could fail to reach their destination, namely Ireland, a Member State in which the mark is not protected, and that they could theoretically be marketed fraudulently in Germany is sufficient to allow the conclusion that the transit infringes the essential functions of the trade mark in Germany cannot be accepted.[2386]

According to that argument, every external transit of goods bearing the sign would have to be regarded as use of the mark in the course of trade within the meaning of Article 5(1) TMD2008. However, under the Court's case law, by contrast, such external transit does not constitute use of the mark liable to infringe the right of the mark's proprietor to control the putting of the goods in question on the Community market because it does not imply any marketing of those goods.[2387]

In addition, the trade mark proprietor can assert its right of prohibition only against the trader who puts or is preparing to put non-Community goods bearing that mark on the market in the Community, or else offers or sells those goods to another trader who is bound to put them on the market in the Community. He cannot rely on his right against a trader who offers or sells those goods to another trader on the sole ground that that trader is likely then to put them on the market in the Community.[2388]

It is for the trade mark proprietor to **prove the facts** which would give grounds for exercising the right of prohibition provided for in Article 5(3)(b) and (c) TMD2008 and Article 9(2)(b) and (c) CTMR, by proving either release for free circulation of the non-Community goods bearing his mark or an offering or sale of the goods which necessarily entails their being put on the market in the Community.[2389]

In respect of the issue of the onus of proving that interference, it must be pointed out, first, that if it were a matter for the national laws of the Member States, the consequence for trade mark proprietors could be that protection would vary according to the legal system concerned. The objective of 'the same protection under the legal systems of all the Member States' set out in the ninth recital in the preamble to the Directive, where it is described as fundamental, would not be attained.[2390]

The onus of proving interference must lie with the trade mark proprietor who alleges it. If that is proven, it is then for the trader sued to prove the existence of the consent of the proprietor to the marketing of the goods in the Community.[2391]

2385. CJEU C-405/03 of 18.10.2005 – Class International, para. 59; C-281/05 of 9.11.2006 – Montex Holdings, paras 23 and 27.
2386. CJEU C-281/05 of 9.11.2006 – Montex Holdings, para. 24.
2387. CJEU C-281/05 of 9.11.2006 – Montex Holdings, para. 25.
2388. CJEU C-405/03 of 18.10.2005 – Class International, para. 60; *see also* CJEU C-449/09 of 28.10.2010 – Canon Kabushiki Kaisha, para. 20.
2389. CJEU C-405/03 of 18.10.2005 – Class International, para. 75; C-281/05 of 9.11.2006 – Montex Holdings, para. 26.
2390. CJEU C-405/03 of 18.10.2005 – Class International, para. 73.
2391. CJEU C-405/03 of 18.10.2005 – Class International, para. 74.

[H] Advertisements by third parties

A third party, who is named in an advertisement on a website, which contains a sign identical or similar to a trade mark in such a way as to give the impression that there is a commercial relationship between him and the proprietor of the trade mark, does not make use of that sign that may be prohibited by that proprietor under that provision, where that advertisement has not been placed by that third party or on his behalf or, if that advertisement has been placed by that third party or on his behalf with the consent of the proprietor, where that third party has expressly requested the operator of that website, from whom the third party ordered the advertisement, to remove the advertisement or the reference to the mark contained therein.[2392]

In that regard, it must be pointed out that an advertiser cannot be held liable for the independent actions of other economic operators, such as those of referencing website operators with whom the advertiser has no direct or indirect dealings and who do not act by order and on behalf of that advertiser, but on their own initiative and in their own name.[2393]

The proprietor of the mark is not entitled, under Article 5(1)(a) or (b) TMD2008, to take action against the advertiser in order to prevent him from publishing online the advertisement containing the reference to its trade mark.[2394]

That conclusion is supported by the wording, scheme and purpose of Article 5 TMD2008.[2395]

With regard, first, to the wording of Article 5(1), it must be noted, by way of example, that, according to its ordinary meaning, the expression 'zu benutzen', 'using', 'faire usage', 'usare', 'het gebruik', 'használ', used respectively in the German, English, French, Italian, Dutch and Hungarian versions of that provision, involves active behaviour and direct or indirect control of the act constituting the use. However, that is not the case if that act is carried out by an independent operator without the consent of the advertiser, or even against his express will.[2396]

Secondly, as regards the scheme of Article 5 of Directive 2008/95, it should be noted that Article 5(3), which lists in a non-exhaustive manner the types of use which the trade mark proprietor may prohibit, refers exclusively to active behaviour on the part of the third party, such as that of 'affixing' the sign on the goods and their packaging or 'using' it in business papers and advertising, 'offering' the goods, 'putting them on the market' or 'stocking' them for those purposes, 'importing' or 'exporting' them or 'offering' or 'supplying' services under that sign.[2397]

2392. CJEU C-179/15 of 3.3.2016 – Daimler/Együd Garage Gépjárműjavító és Értékesítő, para. 44.
2393. CJEU C-179/15 of 3.3.2016 – Daimler/Együd Garage Gépjárműjavító és Értékesítő, para. 36, *see also* CJEU C-684/19 of 2.7.2020 – mk advokaten/MBK Rechtsanwälte, para. 22.
2394. CJEU C-179/15 of 3.3.2016 – Daimler/Együd Garage Gépjárműjavító és Értékesítő, para. 37.
2395. CJEU C-179/15 of 3.3.2016 – Daimler/Együd Garage Gépjárműjavító és Értékesítő, para. 38.
2396. CJEU C-179/15 of 3.3.2016 – Daimler/Együd Garage Gépjárműjavító és Értékesítő, para. 39; *see also* CJEU C-684/19 of 2.7.2020 – mk advokaten/MBK Rechtsanwälte, para. 23.
2397. CJEU C-179/15 of 3.3.2016 – Daimler/Együd Garage Gépjárműjavító és Értékesítő, para. 40, with further proof; *see also* CJEU C-129/17 of 25.7.2018 – Mitsubishi Shoji Kaisha a.o./Duma Forklifts a.o., para. 38.

Finally, with regard to the purpose of Article 5(1) TMD2008, it is clear from that provision that it is intended to provide the proprietor with a legal instrument allowing him to prohibit, and to prevent, any use of his trade mark by a third party without his consent. However, only a third party who has direct or indirect control of the act constituting the use is effectively able to stop that use and therefore comply with that prohibition.[2398]

In those circumstances, it must be observed that an interpretation of Article 5(1) TMD2008, allowing, in a situation such as that at issue in the main proceedings, the proprietor of the mark to prohibit the advertiser from making the use complained of, on the sole ground that such use could possibly provide a financial benefit to the advertiser, would misconstrue the purpose of that provision and conflict with the principle that no one can be legally obliged to do the impossible (impossibilium nulla obligatio est).[2399]

That finding does not affect the possibility for the proprietor to claim from the advertiser, where appropriate, reimbursement of any such financial advantage on the basis of national law, nor that of taking action against the operators of the referencing websites at issue.[2400]

[I] Offer for sale

The rules of TMD and CTMR apply as soon as it is clear that the offer for sale of a trade marked product located in a third State is **targeted at consumers in the territory** covered by the trade mark.[2401]

The rights thus protected may be **infringed** where, even **before their arrival in the territory** covered by that protection, goods coming from non-Member States are the subject of a commercial act directed at consumers in that territory, such as a sale, offer for sale or advertising.[2402]

If it were otherwise, operators which use electronic commerce by offering for sale, on an online market place targeted at consumers within the EU, trade marked goods located in a third State, which it is possible to view on the screen and to order via that marketplace, would, so far as offers for sale of that type are concerned, have no obligation to comply with the EU intellectual property rules. Such a situation would have an impact on the effectiveness (*effet utile*) of those rules.[2403]

2398. CJEU C-179/15 of 3.3.2016 – Daimler/Együd Garage Gépjárműjavító és Értékesítő, para. 41; C-567/18 of 2.4.2020 – Coty Germany/Amazon Services Europe a.o., para. 38.
2399. CJEU C-179/15 of 3.3.2016 – Daimler/Együd Garage Gépjárműjavító és Értékesítő, para. 42; *see also* CJEU C-684/19 of 2.7.2020 – mk advokaten/MBK Rechtsanwälte, para. 24.
2400. CJEU C-179/15 of 3.3.2016 – Daimler/Együd Garage Gépjárműjavító és Értékesítő, para. 43; *see also* CJEU C-684/19 of 2.7.2020 – mk advokaten/MBK Rechtsanwälte, para. 26.
2401. CJEU C-324/09 of 12.7.2011 – L'Oréal, paras 61 and 67; *see also* CJEU C-446/09 and C-495/09 of 1.12.2011 – Koninklijke Philips Electronics, para. 57; C-104/22 of 27.4.2023 – Lännen MCE/Berky a.o., para. 53.
2402. CJEU C-446/09 and C-495/09 of 1.12.2011 – Koninklijke Philips Electronics, para. 57; C-98/13 of 6.2.2014 – Blomqvist, para. 32.
2403. CJEU C-324/09 of 12.7.2011 – L'Oréal, para. 62.

It is sufficient to state in that regard that, under Article 5(3)(b) and (d) TMD2008 and Article 9(2)(b) and (d) CTMR, the use by third parties of signs identical with or similar to trade marks which proprietors of those marks may prevent includes the use of such signs in offers for sale and advertising. The effectiveness of those rules would be undermined if they were not to apply to the use, in an internet offer for sale or advertisement targeted at consumers within the EU, of a sign identical with or similar to a trade mark registered in the EU merely because the third party behind that offer or advertisement is established in a third State, because the server of the internet site used by the third party is located in such a State or because the product that is the subject of the offer or the advertisement is located in a third State.[2404]

It must, however, be made clear that the mere fact that a website is accessible from the territory covered by the trade mark is not a sufficient basis for concluding that the offers for sale displayed there are targeted at consumers in that territory.[2405] Indeed, if the fact that an online marketplace is accessible from that territory were sufficient for the advertisements displayed there to be within the scope of TDM and CTMR, websites and advertisements which, although obviously targeted solely at consumers in third States, are nevertheless technically accessible from EU territory would wrongly be subject to EU law.[2406]

It therefore falls to the national courts to assess on a case-by-case basis whether there are any relevant factors on the basis of which it may be concluded that an offer for sale, displayed on an online marketplace accessible from the territory covered by the trade mark, is targeted at consumers in that territory. When the offer for sale is accompanied by details of the geographic areas to which the seller is willing to dispatch the product, that type of detail is of particular importance in the said assessment.[2407]

A website with the address 'www.ebay.co.uk' appears, in the absence of any evidence to the contrary, to be targeted at consumers in the territory covered by the national [UK] and Community trade marks relied on; the offers for sale on that website which form the subject matter of the main proceedings therefore fall within the scope of the EU rules on intellectual property.[2408]

[J] Existing prior rights

However, the third sentence of Article 16(1) of the TRIPS Agreement provides that that exclusive right must not prejudice any 'existing prior right'.[2409]

2404. CJEU C-324/09 of 12.7.2011 – L'Oréal, para. 63; *see also* CJEU C-172/18 of 5.9.2019 – AMS Neve a.o./Heritage Audio a.o., para. 47.
2405. *See*, by analogy, CJEU C-585/08 and C-144/09 of 7.12.2010 – Pammer and Hotel Alpenhof, para. 69.
2406. CJEU C-324/09 of 12.7.2011 – L'Oréal, para. 64; C-98/13 of 6.2.2014 – Blomqvist, para. 31; *see also* CJEU C-104/22 of 27.4.2023 – Lännen MCE/Berky a.o., para. 48.
2407. CJEU C-324/09 of 12.7.2011 – L'Oréal, paras 65 and 67; *see also* CJEU C-104/22 of 27.4.2023 – Lännen MCE/Berky a.o., para. 42.
2408. CJEU C-324/09 of 12.7.2011 – L'Oréal, para. 66.
2409. CJEU C-245/02 of 16.11.2004 – Anheuser-Busch, para. 88.

That provision must be understood as meaning that where the proprietor of a trade name has a right falling within the scope of the TRIPS Agreement which arose prior to that conferred by the trade mark with which it is alleged to conflict and which entitles him to use a sign identical or similar to that trade mark, such use cannot be prohibited by virtue of the exclusive right conferred by the trade mark on its proprietor under the first sentence of Article 16(1) of the TRIPS Agreement.[2410]

For that provision, thus understood, to be applicable, the third party must first of all be able to rely on a right falling within the substantive scope of the TRIPS Agreement.[2411]

It should be observed that a **trade name** is a right falling within the scope of the term 'intellectual property' within the meaning of Article 1(2) of the TRIPS Agreement. Moreover, it follows from Article 2(1) of the TRIPS Agreement that the protection of trade names, for which specific provision is made in Article 8 of the Paris Convention, is expressly incorporated into that agreement. Therefore, by virtue of the TRIPS Agreement, the members of the WTO are under an obligation to protect trade names.[2412]

Accordingly, in so far as it is existing subject matter within the meaning of Article 70(2) of the TRIPS Agreement, as was explained in paragraph 49 of this judgment, the trade name in question must be protected under the TRIPS Agreement.[2413]

The trade name is therefore a right falling within the substantive scope of the TRIPS Agreement, so that the first condition laid down by the third sentence of Article 16(1) of that agreement is satisfied.[2414]

It must, moreover, be an existing right. The term 'existing' means that the right concerned must fall within the temporal scope of the TRIPS Agreement and still be protected at the time when it is relied on by its proprietor in order to counter the claims of the proprietor of the trade mark with which it is alleged to conflict.[2415]

It must therefore be ascertained whether the trade name in question, which is neither registered nor established by use in the Member State in which the trade mark is registered and in which the protection afforded by that mark against the trade name in question is sought, satisfies the conditions set out in the preceding paragraph of this judgment.[2416]

Finally, '**priority**' of the right in question for the purposes of the third sentence of Article 16(1) of the TRIPS Agreement means that the basis for the right concerned must have arisen at a time prior to the grant of the trade mark with which it is alleged to conflict. That requirement is an expression of the principle of the primacy of the prior

2410. CJEU C-245/02 of 16.11.2004 – Anheuser-Busch, para. 89.
2411. CJEU C-245/02 of 16.11.2004 – Anheuser-Busch, para. 90.
2412. CJEU C-245/02 of 16.11.2004 – Anheuser-Busch, para. 91; C-112/21 of 2.6.2022 – X/Classic Coach Company a.o., para. 37, with further reference.
2413. CJEU C-245/02 of 16.11.2004 – Anheuser-Busch, para. 92.
2414. CJEU C-245/02 of 16.11.2004 – Anheuser-Busch, para. 93.
2415. CJEU C-245/02 of 16.11.2004 – Anheuser-Busch, para. 94; CJEU C-112/21 of 2.6.2022 – X/Classic Coach Company a.o., para. 38.
2416. CJEU C-245/02 of 16.11.2004 – Anheuser-Busch, para. 95.

exclusive right, which is one of the basic principles of trade mark law and, more generally, of all industrial property law.[2417]

It should be added that the principle of priority is likewise enshrined in Directive 89/104 and, more specifically, in Articles 4(2) and 6(2) thereof.[2418]

A trade name which is not registered or established by use in the Member State in which the trade mark is registered and in which protection against the trade name in question is sought may be regarded as an existing prior right within the meaning of the third sentence of Article 16(1) of the TRIPS Agreement if the proprietor of the trade name has a right falling within the substantive and temporal scope of the TRIPS Agreement which arose prior to the trade mark with which it is alleged to conflict and which entitles him to use a sign identical or similar to that trade mark.[2419]

Article 6(2) TMD2008 must be interpreted as meaning that, **for the purposes of establishing the existence of an 'earlier right'** within the meaning of that provision, there is **no requirement that the proprietor of that right must be able to prohibit the use of the later mark** by the proprietor of that mark.[2420]

It should be recalled that the concept of an 'earlier right', within the meaning of Article 6(2) TMD2008, must be interpreted in the light of the equivalent concepts contained in the texts of international law and in such a way that it is consistent with them, also taking account of the context in which those concepts are found and the purpose of the relevant provisions of the agreements as regards intellectual property.[2421]

Furthermore, under Article 4(4)(c) TMD2008, the concept of an 'earlier right' means, *inter alia*, an industrial property right, which is merely one type of intellectual property. It is apparent from Article 1(2) of the Paris Convention that a trade name constitutes an industrial property right.[2422]

In that context, although Article 4(4)(c) TMD2008 primarily serves purposes other than those referred to in Article 6(2) TMD2008, namely to enable the proprietor of an earlier right to oppose the registration of a mark or to request that a registered trade mark be declared invalid, the fact remains that the concept of 'earlier right' used in those two provisions must have the same meaning, since, in this instance, the European Union legislature has not expressed a different intention.[2423]

Consequently, a **trade name may constitute an earlier right** for the purposes of the application of Article 6(2) TMD2008.[2424]

As regards the conditions for the application of Article 6(2) TMD2008, it should be noted, as a preliminary point, that the terms of a provision of EU law which makes no express reference to the law of the Member States for the purpose of determining its

2417. CJEU C-245/02 of 16.11.2004 – Anheuser-Busch, para. 98; C-112/21 of 2.6.2022 – X/Classic Coach Company a.o., para. 40.
2418. CJEU C-245/02 of 16.11.2004 – Anheuser-Busch, para. 99.
2419. CJEU C-245/02 of 16.11.2004 – Anheuser-Busch, para. 100.
2420. CJEU C-112/21 of 2.6.2022 – X/Classic Coach Company a.o., para. 55.
2421. CJEU C-112/21 of 2.6.2022 – X/Classic Coach Company a.o., para. 36, with further proof.
2422. CJEU C-112/21 of 2.6.2022 – X/Classic Coach Company a.o., para. 41.
2423. CJEU C-112/21 of 2.6.2022 – X/Classic Coach Company a.o., para. 42, with further proof.
2424. CJEU C-112/21 of 2.6.2022 – X/Classic Coach Company a.o., para. 43.

meaning and scope must normally be given an autonomous and uniform interpretation throughout the European Union, irrespective of its treatment in the Member States, having regard to its wording, its context and the objectives pursued by the legislation of which it forms part.[2425]

In this respect, as regards the wording of Article 6(2) TMD2008, it must be observed that, in addition to the conditions relating, first, to the use of such a right in the course of trade, second, to the priority of that right, third, to its applicability in a particular locality and, fourth, to the recognition of that right by the laws of the Member State in question, that provision does not in any way provide that, in order to be able to assert the same right against the proprietor of a later mark, the third party must be able to prohibit the use of that mark.[2426]

That interpretation is borne out both by the context of that provision and by the general scheme of the TMD2008. Under Article 4(4)(b) and (c) TMD2008, a Member State may provide that a trade mark is not to be registered or, if registered, is liable to be declared invalid, in particular, first, where and to the extent that the rights to a sign used in the course of trade were acquired prior to the date of application for registration of the subsequent trade mark, or the date of the priority claimed for the application for registration of the subsequent trade mark, and that sign confers on its proprietor the right to prohibit the use of a subsequent trade mark and, second, where and to the extent that the use of the trade mark may be prohibited by virtue of an earlier right, such as an industrial property right.[2427]

Unlike the grounds for refusal or invalidity concerning conflicts with earlier rights laid down, *inter alia*, in Article 4(4)(b) and (c) TMD2008 which are intended either to prevent the registration of a mark or to have it cancelled, Article 6(2) TMD2008 provides only for a limitation of the rights conferred by a registered trade mark, as provided for in Article 5 TMD2008.[2428]

Furthermore, 'earlier rights', within the meaning of Article 6(2) TMD2008, must only apply in a particular locality, which means that, from a geographical point of view, they cannot cover a territory as large as that covered by a registered trade mark, since that mark normally covers the whole of the territory for which it was registered.[2429]

Such an approach, according to which the limitation of the rights conferred by a registered trade mark is subject to more flexible conditions than those required in order to prevent registration of a mark or to declare it invalid, is also consistent with the objectives pursued by the TMD2008, which seeks generally to strike a balance between the interest of the proprietor of a trade mark to safeguard its essential function, on the one hand, and the interests of other economic operators in having signs capable of denoting their goods and services, on the other.[2430]

2425. CJEU C-112/21 of 2.6.2022 – X/Classic Coach Company a.o., para. 44, with further proof.
2426. CJEU C-112/21 of 2.6.2022 – X/Classic Coach Company a.o., para. 45.
2427. CJEU C-112/21 of 2.6.2022 – X/Classic Coach Company a.o., para. 46.
2428. CJEU C-112/21 of 2.6.2022 – X/Classic Coach Company a.o., para. 47.
2429. CJEU C-112/21 of 2.6.2022 – X/Classic Coach Company a.o., para. 48.
2430. CJEU C-112/21 of 2.6.2022 – X/Classic Coach Company a.o., para. 49, with reference to CJEU C-482/09 of 22.9.2011 – Budějovický Budvar, para. 34.

That interpretation cannot be called into question by the legislative history of that provision, even if the legislative history of an EU act may provide information relevant to its interpretation. In the present case, it should be noted that, at the time of the adoption of Directive 89/104, which was subsequently codified by TMD2008, the text of the current Article 6(2) TMD2008, as proposed by the Italian delegation to the Council of the European Union, was not adopted in its entirety. According to the proposal of that delegation, the limitation of the effects of the mark would apply 'even though that [earlier] right may no longer be invoked against the later registered trade mark'.[2431]

Nevertheless, it cannot be inferred from this that the EU legislature intended to limit the scope of Article 6(2) TMD2008 solely to earlier rights which entitle their proprietor to prohibit the use of the subsequent mark. Such a condition would deprive that provision of all practical effect, in so far as it would treat the conditions for the application of that provision in the same way as the conditions for the application of the further grounds for refusal or invalidity laid down in Article 4(4)(b) and (c) of that directive.[2432]

Consequently, under Article 6(2) TMD2008, in order to be enforceable against the proprietor of a subsequent trade mark, it is sufficient, in principle, that the earlier right which only applies in a particular locality, such as a trade name, is recognized by the laws of the Member State in question and that it is used in the course of trade.[2433]

National legislation under which the earlier right is required to confer on its proprietor the right to prohibit local use of a trade mark registered subsequently would go beyond the requirements laid down in Article 6 TMD2008, given that that provision, together with Articles 5 and 7 TMD2008, effect a complete harmonization of the rules relating to the rights conferred by a trade mark and accordingly define the rights of proprietors of trade marks in the European Union.[2434]

It should also be borne in mind that a long period of honest concurrent use of two identical signs designating identical products neither has nor is liable to have an adverse effect on the essential function of the trade mark which is to guarantee to consumers the origin of the goods or services. However, in the event that, in the future, there is any dishonesty associated with the use of those signs, such a situation could, where necessary, be examined in the light of the rules relating to unfair competition.[2435]

Article 6(2) TMD2008 must be interpreted as meaning that an 'earlier right' within the meaning of that provision may be granted to a third party in a situation in which the proprietor of the later trade mark has **an even earlier right** recognized by the laws of the Member State in question over the sign registered as a trade mark, to the extent that, under those laws, the proprietor of the trade mark and of the even earlier

2431. CJEU C-112/21 of 2.6.2022 – X/Classic Coach Company a.o., para. 50, with further proof.
2432. CJEU C-112/21 of 2.6.2022 – X/Classic Coach Company a.o., para. 51.
2433. CJEU C-112/21 of 2.6.2022 – X/Classic Coach Company a.o., para. 52.
2434. CJEU C-112/21 of 2.6.2022 – X/Classic Coach Company a.o., para. 53, with reference to CJEU C-482/09 of 22.9.2011 – Budějovický Budvar, para. 32.
2435. CJEU C-112/21 of 2.6.2022 – X/Classic Coach Company a.o., para. 54, with reference to CJEU C-482/09 of 22.9.2011 – Budějovický Budvar, paras 82 et seq.

right may no longer, on the basis of its even earlier right, prohibit the use by the third party of its more recent right.[2436]

It should be noted at the outset that the TMD2008 governs, in principle, not the relationship between the various rights which may be classified as 'earlier rights' within the meaning of Article 6(2) of that directive, but the relationship of those rights with trade marks acquired by registration.[2437]

First, in accordance with Article 1 TMD2008, the TMD2008 applies, in essence, to trade marks which have been the subject of a registration or an application for registration.[2438]

Second, Article 4(4)(b) and (c) and Article 6(2) TMD2008 govern conflicts of registered trade marks or applications for trade marks with earlier rights.[2439]

That finding is supported both by the wording of recital 5 of the TMD2008, which refers to trade marks acquired through use with trade marks acquired by registration, and by Article 9(3) TMD2008, from which it is apparent that, as regards limitation in consequence of acquiescence, that article governs only the relationship of earlier rights with later registered trade marks.[2440]

Consequently, the relationship between the various rights that can be classified as 'earlier rights' within the meaning of Article 6(2) TMD2008 is primarily governed by the domestic law of the Member State concerned.[2441]

Therefore, what matters, for the purposes of the application of Article 6(2) TMD2008, is that the right relied on by the third party is recognized by the laws of the Member State in question and that that right is still protected at the time when it is relied on by its proprietor in order to counter the claims of the proprietor of the trade mark with which it is alleged to conflict, as is apparent from the case law cited above.[2442]

In that context, the fact that the proprietor of the later trade mark has an even earlier right recognized by the law of the Member State concerned over the sign registered as a trade mark may have a bearing on the existence of an 'earlier right' within the meaning of that provision, to the extent that, by relying on that even earlier right, the proprietor of the trade mark is actually able to counter the claim of an earlier right or limit it, which it is, in the present case, for the referring court to determine in accordance with its applicable national law.[2443]

In a situation where a right relied on by a third party is no longer protected under the laws of the Member State in question, it cannot be held that that right constitutes an 'earlier right' recognized by that law, within the meaning of Article 6(2) TMD2008.[2444]

2436. CJEU C-112/21 of 2.6.2022 – X/Classic Coach Company a.o., para. 65.
2437. CJEU C-112/21 of 2.6.2022 – X/Classic Coach Company a.o., para. 57.
2438. CJEU C-112/21 of 2.6.2022 – X/Classic Coach Company a.o., para. 58.
2439. CJEU C-112/21 of 2.6.2022 – X/Classic Coach Company a.o., para. 59.
2440. CJEU C-112/21 of 2.6.2022 – X/Classic Coach Company a.o., para. 60.
2441. CJEU C-112/21 of 2.6.2022 – X/Classic Coach Company a.o., para. 61.
2442. CJEU C-112/21 of 2.6.2022 – X/Classic Coach Company a.o., para. 62.
2443. CJEU C-112/21 of 2.6.2022 – X/Classic Coach Company a.o., para. 63.
2444. CJEU C-112/21 of 2.6.2022 – X/Classic Coach Company a.o., para. 64.

[K] Comparative advertising

As a preliminary point, Article 5(1) and (2) TMD2008 and Article 3a(1) of **Directive 84/450**[2445] must be interpreted as meaning that the proprietor of a registered trade mark is not entitled to prevent the use by a third party of a sign identical with, or similar to, his mark, in a comparative advertisement which satisfies all the conditions, laid down in Article 3a(1) of Directive 84/450, under which comparative advertising is permitted. However, where the conditions required in Article 5(1)(b) TMD2008 to prevent the use of a sign identical with, or similar to, a registered trade mark are met, a comparative advertisement in which that sign is used cannot satisfy the condition, laid down in Article 3a(1)(d) of Directive 84/450, under which comparative advertising is permitted.[2446]

The proprietor of a registered trade mark is not entitled to prevent the use, by a third party, in a comparative advertisement, of a sign similar to that mark in relation to goods or services identical with, or similar to, those for which that mark is registered where such use does not give rise to a likelihood of confusion on the part of the public, and that is so irrespective of whether or not the comparative advertisement satisfies all the conditions laid down in Article 3a of Directive 84/450 under which comparative advertising is permitted.[2447]

A literal interpretation of Directive 84/450[2448] results in a contradiction with Directive 89/104 and cannot therefore be accepted.[2449]

Use by an advertiser, in a comparative advertisement, of a sign identical with, or similar to, a competitor's mark may constitute use within the meaning of Article 5(1) and (2) TMD2008.[2450]

First, Article 5(1) and (2) TMD2008 must be interpreted as covering the use of a sign identical with, or similar to, the trade mark in respect of goods marketed or services supplied by the third party.[2451]

Second, an advertisement in which the advertiser compares the goods and services which he markets with those of a competitor is aimed, evidently, at promoting the goods and services of that advertiser. With such an advertisement the advertiser seeks to distinguish his goods and services by comparing their characteristics with those of competing goods and services. That analysis is confirmed by recital 15 in the preamble to Directive 97/55, in which the Community legislature pointed out that the

2445. Council Directive 84/450/EEC of 10 Sep. 1984 concerning misleading and comparative advertising (OJ 1984 L 250, p. 17).
2446. CJEU C-533/06 of 12.6.2008 – O2 Holdings/Hutchison 3G UK, para. 51; C-487/07 of 18.6.2009 – L'Oréal, para. 54.
2447. CJEU C-533/06 of 12.6.2008 – O2 Holdings/Hutchison 3G UK, para. 69.
2448. Council Directive 84/450/EEC of 10 Sep. 1984 concerning misleading and comparative advertising (OJ 1984 L 250, p. 17), as amended by Directive 97/55/EC of the European Parliament and of the Council of 6 Oct. 1997 (OJ 1997 L 290, p. 18).
2449. CJEU C-112/99 of 25.10.2001 – Toshiba Europe, para. 35.
2450. CJEU C-533/06 of 12.6.2008 – O2 Holdings/Hutchison 3G UK, para. 33.
2451. CJEU C-533/06 of 12.6.2008 – O2 Holdings/Hutchison 3G UK, para. 34.

aim of comparative advertising is to distinguish between the goods and services of the advertiser and those of his competitor.[2452]

Therefore, the use by an advertiser, in a comparative advertisement, of a sign identical with, or similar to, the mark of a competitor for the purposes of identifying the goods and services offered by the latter can be regarded as use for the advertiser's own goods and services for the purposes of Article 5(1) and (2) TMD2008.[2453]

Such use may therefore be prevented, where necessary, by virtue of those provisions.[2454]

However, as is apparent from recitals 2–6 in the preamble to Directive 97/55, the Community legislature was intending to promote comparative advertising, stating, *inter alia*, in recital 2, that comparative advertising 'can also stimulate competition between suppliers of goods and services to the consumer's advantage' and, in recital 5, that it 'may be a legitimate means of informing consumers of their advantage'.[2455]

According to recitals 13–15 in the preamble to Directive 97/55, the Community legislature considered that the need to promote comparative advertising required that the right conferred by the mark be limited to a certain extent.[2456]

Such a limitation of the effects of the mark for the purposes of promoting comparative advertising appears necessary not only in the case of use, by the advertiser, of a competitor's actual mark, but also in the case of use of a sign similar to that mark.[2457]

Under Article 2(2a) of Directive 84/450, 'comparative advertising' means any advertising which explicitly or by implication identifies a competitor or goods or services offered by a competitor.[2458]

According to settled case law, that is a broad definition covering all forms of comparative advertising, so that, in order for there to be comparative advertising, it is sufficient for there to be a statement referring even by implication to a competitor or to the goods or services which he offers.[2459]

The test for determining whether an advertisement is comparative in nature is thus whether it identifies, explicitly or by implication, a competitor of the advertiser or goods or services which the competitor offers.[2460]

Therefore, when the use, in an advertisement, of a sign similar to the mark of a competitor of the advertiser is perceived by the average consumer as a reference to that competitor or to the goods and services which he offers – as in the case in the main

2452. CJEU C-533/06 of 12.6.2008 – O2 Holdings/Hutchison 3G UK, para. 35.
2453. CJEU C-533/06 of 12.6.2008 – O2 Holdings/Hutchison 3G UK, para. 36; C-487/07 of 18.6.2009 – L'Oréal, para. 53.
2454. CJEU C-533/06 of 12.6.2008 – O2 Holdings/Hutchison 3G UK, para. 37; C-487/07 of 18.6.2009 – L'Oréal, para. 53.
2455. CJEU C-533/06 of 12.6.2008 – O2 Holdings/Hutchison 3G UK, para. 38.
2456. CJEU C-533/06 of 12.6.2008 – O2 Holdings/Hutchison 3G UK, para. 39.
2457. CJEU C-533/06 of 12.6.2008 – O2 Holdings/Hutchison 3G UK, para. 40.
2458. CJEU C-533/06 of 12.6.2008 – O2 Holdings/Hutchison 3G UK, para. 41.
2459. CJEU C-533/06 of 12.6.2008 – O2 Holdings/Hutchison 3G UK, para. 42; *see* CJEU C-112/99 of 25.10.2001 – Toshiba Europe, para. 30, 31.
2460. CJEU C-533/06 of 12.6.2008 – O2 Holdings/Hutchison 3G UK, para. 43; *see* CJEU C-112/99 of 25.10.2001 – Toshiba Europe, para. 29.

proceedings – there is comparative advertising within the meaning of Article 2(2a) of Directive 84/450.[2461]

Consequently, in order to reconcile the protection of registered marks and the use of comparative advertising, Article 5(1) and (2) TMD2008 and Article 3a(1) of Directive 84/450 must be interpreted to the effect that the proprietor of a registered trade mark is not entitled to prevent the use, by a third party, of a sign identical with, or similar to, his mark, in a comparative advertisement which satisfies all the conditions, laid down in Article 3a(1) of Directive 84/450, under which comparative advertising is permitted.[2462]

It must, **however**, be pointed out that, where the conditions required under Article 5(1)(b) TMD2008 to prevent the use of a sign identical with, or similar to, a registered mark are met, a comparative advertisement in which that sign is used cannot satisfy the condition, laid down in Article 3a(1)(d) of Directive 84/450, under which comparative advertising is permitted.[2463]

Article 5(1)(a) TMD2008 must be interpreted as meaning that the proprietor of a registered trade mark is entitled to prevent the use by a third party, in a comparative advertisement which does not satisfy all the conditions, laid down in Article 3a(1) of Directive 84/450, under which comparative advertising is permitted, of a sign identical with that mark in relation to goods or services which are identical with those for which that mark was registered, even where such use is not capable of jeopardizing the essential function of the mark, which is to indicate the origin of the goods or services, provided that such use affects or is liable to affect one of the other functions of the mark.[2464]

First, in the case of similarity between the mark and the sign and between the goods or services, the likelihood of confusion constitutes the specific condition for protection. Article 5(1)(b) TMD2008 is thus designed to apply only if, by reason of the identity or similarity both of the marks and of the goods or services which they designate, there exists a likelihood of confusion on the part of the public.[2465]

Second, it is apparent from Article 3a(1)(d) of Directive 84/450 that comparative advertising is not permitted if there is a likelihood of confusion between the advertiser and a competitor or between the advertiser's trade marks, goods or services and those of a competitor.[2466]

In the light of recitals 13–15 of Directive 97/55, the same interpretation must be given to the term 'confusion' used in both Article 5(1)(b) TMD2008 and Article 3a(1)(d) of Directive 84/450.[2467]

Thus, in the case where an advertiser uses, in a comparative advertisement, a sign identical with, or similar to, a competitor's mark, the competitor either does not

2461. CJEU C-533/06 of 12.6.2008 – O2 Holdings/Hutchison 3G UK, para. 44.
2462. CJEU C-533/06 of 12.6.2008 – O2 Holdings/Hutchison 3G UK, para. 45; C-487/07 of 18.6.2009 – L'Oréal, para. 54.
2463. CJEU C-533/06 of 12.6.2008 – O2 Holdings/Hutchison 3G UK, para. 46.
2464. CJEU C-487/07 of 18.6.2009 – L'Oréal, para. 65.
2465. CJEU C-533/06 of 12.6.2008 – O2 Holdings/Hutchison 3G UK, para. 47.
2466. CJEU C-533/06 of 12.6.2008 – O2 Holdings/Hutchison 3G UK, para. 48.
2467. CJEU C-533/06 of 12.6.2008 – O2 Holdings/Hutchison 3G UK, para. 49.

establish the existence of a likelihood of confusion and, consequently, is not entitled to prevent the use of that sign on the basis of Article 5(1)(b) TMD2008, or he establishes the existence of a likelihood of confusion and, consequently, the advertiser cannot challenge such prevention under Article 3a(1) of Directive 84/450, since the advertisement at issue does not satisfy all the conditions laid down in that provision.[2468]

It should be noted at the outset that **comparison lists** such as those at issue in the main proceedings may constitute comparative advertising. Article 2(1) of Directive 84/450 provides that 'advertising' comprises the making of a representation in any form in connection with a trade, business, craft or profession in order to promote the supply of goods or services. Article 2(2a) of Directive 84/450 states that such advertising falls to be treated as comparative where, explicitly or by implication, it identifies a competitor or goods or services offered by a competitor. Those particularly broad definitions mean that the forms which comparative advertising may take are very varied.[2469]

[L] Repair and designs

Article 14 of Directive 98/71/EC[2470] and Article 110 of Regulation (EC) No. 6/2002[2471] must be interpreted as meaning that they do not authorize, by way of derogation from the provisions the TMD2008 and of the CTMR, the producer of vehicle replacement parts and accessories such as wheel caps to apply on his goods a sign which is identical with a trade mark registered by a vehicle manufacture, *inter alia*, for such goods without his authorization, with the argument that the use of the mark thus made is the only possibility to repair the respective vehicle and restore a complex product's original appearance.[2472]

[M] Quality labels

Article 9(1)(a) and (b) CTMR and Article 5(1)(a) and (b) TMD2008 must be interpreted as meaning that they **do not entitle the proprietor** of an individual trade mark consisting of a quality label to oppose the affixing, by a third party, of a sign identical with, or similar to, that mark to products that are neither identical with, nor similar to, the goods or services for which that mark is registered.[2473]

The wording 'in relation to goods or services', which features in those provisions, relates, in principle, to goods or services of a third party who uses a sign identical with

2468. CJEU C-533/06 of 12.6.2008 – O2 Holdings/Hutchison 3G UK, para. 50.
2469. CJEU C-487/07 of 18.6.2009 – L'Oréal, para. 52.
2470. Directive 98/71/EC of the European Parliament and of the Council of 13 Oct. 1998 on the legal protection of designs (OJ L 289, p. 28).
2471. Council Regulation (EC) No. 6/2002 of 12 Dec. 2001 on Community designs (OJ 2002 L 3, p. 1).
2472. CJEU C-500/14 of 6.10.2015 – Ford Motor Company, para. 45.
2473. CJEU C-690/17 of 11.4.2019 – Oko-Text Verlag/Dr. Rudolf Liebe Nachf., para. 43.

the mark. Should the case arise, it can also refer to goods or services of another person on whose behalf the third party is acting.[2474]

On the other hand, that wording does not, in principle, cover goods and services of the proprietor of that mark: they are covered, in Article 9(1)(a) CTMR and Article 5(1)(a) TMD2008, by the expression 'those for which the trade mark is registered'. The requirement for identity 'between the goods or services', referred to in recital 8 of CTMR and in recital 11 of TMD2008, which is contained in Article 9(1)(a) CTMR as well as in Article 5(1)(a) TMD2008, is intended to limit the right of prohibition granted by those provisions to the proprietors of individual trade marks to cases in which there is identity not only between the sign used by the third party and the trade mark but also between the goods marketed and the services supplied by the third party – or by a person on whose behalf that third party is acting – and the goods and services for which the proprietor registered his mark.[2475]

As the Court has already held, use of the sign by the third party to identify the goods of the trade mark proprietor where those goods constitute the actual subject matter of services provided by that third party can, exceptionally, be covered by those provisions. In such a case, that sign is used to identify the origin of the goods that are the subject matter of those services and there is a specific and indissociable link between the goods bearing the trade mark and those services. However, apart from that specific case, Article 9(1)(a) CTMR and Article 5(1)(a) TMD2008 must be interpreted as covering the use of a sign identical to the trade mark in respect of goods marketed or services supplied by the third party that are identical to those for which the trade mark is registered (*see*, to that effect, judgment of 25 January 2007, Adam Opel, C-48/05, EU:C:2007:55, paragraphs 27 and 28).[2476]

The specific case referred to in the preceding paragraph concerns, in particular, situations in which a service provider makes unauthorized use of a sign identical to the trade mark of a manufacturer of goods in order to inform the public that he has specialized or is a specialist in those products.[2477]

In the present case, subject to verification by the referring court, it appears that the affixing by Dr Liebe of a sign allegedly identical to the ÖKO-TEST marks has neither the purpose nor the effect of carrying out, in the same way as ÖKO-Test Verlag or on its behalf, an economic activity consisting in the provision of consumer information and consultancy services. Nor does there appear to be any indication to suggest either that, by affixing that sign, Dr Liebe seeks to present itself to the public as a specialist in the field of product testing or that there is a specific and indissociable link between its economic activity, which consists in the manufacturing and marketing of toothpaste, and that of ÖKO-Test Verlag. On the contrary, it is apparent that the sign that is

2474. CJEU C-690/17 of 11.4.2019 – Oko-Text Verlag/Dr. Rudolf Liebe Nachf., para. 29, with reference to CJEU C-236/08 to C-238/08 of 23.3.2010 – Google France, para. 60.
2475. CJEU C-690/17 of 11.4.2019 – Oko-Text Verlag/Dr. Rudolf Liebe Nachf., para. 30.
2476. CJEU C-690/17 of 11.4.2019 – Oko-Text Verlag/Dr. Rudolf Liebe Nachf., para. 31, with reference to CJEU C-48/05 of 25.1.2007 – Adam Opel, paras 27 et seq.
2477. CJEU C-690/17 of 11.4.2019 – Oko-Text Verlag/Dr. Rudolf Liebe Nachf., para. 32, with reference to CJEU C-179/15 of 3.3.2016 – Daimler/Együd Garage Gépjárműjavító és Értékesítő, para. 28.

identical with, or similar to, those marks is affixed to the toothpaste packaging marketed by Dr Liebe for the sole purpose of drawing consumers' attention to the quality of those toothpastes and thus promoting the sale of Dr Liebe products. Therefore, the situation at issue in the main proceedings differs from the specific case referred to above.[2478]

As regards, next, Article 9(1)(b) CTMR and Article 5(1)(b) TMD2008, which grant the proprietor of the mark specific protection against the use, by a third party, of signs identical with, or similar to, the mark leading to a likelihood of confusion on the part of the public, it is apparent from the wording of those provisions, read in the light of recital 8 of that regulation and recital 11 of that directive, that that protection granted to the proprietor of the trade mark applies only in cases where there is an identity or similarity – not only between the sign used by the third party and the mark – but also between the goods or services covered by that sign, on the one hand, and those covered by the mark, on the other.[2479]

Like the expression 'in relation to goods or services', which appears in Article 9(1)(a) CTMR and Article 5(1)(a) TMD2008, the words 'goods or services covered by ... the sign' referred to in paragraph 1(b) of those articles cover, in principle, the goods marketed or services supplied by the third party. In the absence of any similarity between the goods or services of the third party and those for which the mark is registered, the protection granted by those provisions is not applicable.[2480]

Article 9(1)(b) CTMR and Article 5(1)(b) TMD2008 thus contain, like paragraph 1(a) of those articles, a requirement that the goods or services of a third party, on the one hand, and those of the proprietor of the trade mark, on the other, be comparable. Points (a) and (b) differ fundamentally, in that regard, from point (c) of Article 9(1) CTMR and from Article 5(2) TMD2008, which expressly state that such comparability is not required where the mark has a reputation.[2481]

That difference expressly provided for by the EU legislature between the protection that is granted to proprietors of any individual trade mark and the additional protection that the proprietor enjoys where his mark also has a reputation has been maintained during successive amendments to EU trade mark legislation. Thus, the wording 'in relation to goods or services which are identical with those for which the EU trade mark is registered' and 'in relation to goods or services which are identical with, or similar to, the goods or services for which the trade mark is registered' is now contained in Article 9(2)(a) and (b) of EUTMR and in Article 10(2)(a) and (b) TMD, thus distinguishing the protection afforded by any individual trade mark from that provided for in Article 9(2)(c) EUTMR and in Article 10(2)(c) TMD, which is applicable where the mark has a reputation and a third party uses a sign that 'is identical with, or similar to, the trade mark irrespective of whether it is used in relation to goods or

2478. CJEU C-690/17 of 11.4.2019 – Oko-Text Verlag/Dr. Rudolf Liebe Nachf., para. 33.
2479. CJEU C-690/17 of 11.4.2019 – Oko-Text Verlag/Dr. Rudolf Liebe Nachf., para. 34.
2480. CJEU C-690/17 of 11.4.2019 – Oko-Text Verlag/Dr. Rudolf Liebe Nachf., para. 35, with reference to CJEU C-119/10 of 15.12.2011 – Frisdranken Industrie Winters, paras 31–33.
2481. CJEU C-690/17 of 11.4.2019 – Oko-Text Verlag/Dr. Rudolf Liebe Nachf., para. 36.

services which are identical with, similar to, or not similar to, those for which the trade mark is registered'.[2482]

It follows from all of the foregoing that the proprietor of an individual trade mark that consists of a quality label registered in relation to printed matter and services of conducting tests and providing consumer information and consultancy may, if all the conditions are fulfilled, rely on the right of prohibition set out in Article 9(1)(a) and (b) CTMR and Article 5(1)(a) and (b) TMD2008 against third parties, such as potential competitors, who use a sign identical with, or similar to, that mark in relation to printed matter or services of conducting tests and providing consumer information and consultancy, or in relation to similar goods and services, but that he may not rely on that right against manufacturers of tested consumer products who affix the sign identical with, or similar to, that mark to those consumer products.[2483]

Concerning the argument, that such an interpretation, even though founded on the wording and scheme of CTMR and TMD2008, would unduly reduce the protection of proprietors of individual trade marks consisting of a quality label, such as that at issue in the main proceedings, it should be noted, as the European Commission has indicated in its written observations, that the exclusive right afforded by the mark is not absolute, since the EU legislature has, on the contrary, precisely delimited the scope of that right.[2484]

Furthermore, nothing in the objectives of EU trade mark legislation, such as the objective of contributing to the system of undistorted competition in the Union, supports the conclusion that the purpose of that legislation requires that the proprietor of an individual trade mark consisting of a quality label must be able to oppose, on the basis of Article 9(1)(a) and (b) CTMR or Article 5(1)(a) and (b) TMD2008, the affixing, by the manufacturer of a product, of that label together with the result of the test to which the product was subjected.[2485]

This is particularly true in view of the fact that the EU legislature supplemented the EU trade mark regime by providing in Articles 74a et seq. CTMR, now Articles 83 et seq. EUTMR, for the possibility of registering as an EU certification mark certain signs, including those that are capable of distinguishing the goods or services that are certified by the proprietor of the mark in respect of quality from goods and services that are not so certified. In contrast to an individual trade mark, such a certification mark allows the proprietor to specify in regulations governing use the persons authorized to use the mark.[2486]

In so far as ÖKO-Test Verlag maintains that the affixing of a quality label by Dr Liebe was not covered by the previously concluded licensing agreement, it is lastly necessary to add that the fact that the proprietor of a mark, such as ÖKO-Test Verlag, cannot, with regard to manufacturers whose products it has tested, rely on Article 9(1)(a) and (b) CTMR and Article 5(1)(a) and (b) TMD2008 does not mean that it is

2482. CJEU C-690/17 of 11.4.2019 – Oko-Text Verlag/Dr. Rudolf Liebe Nachf., para. 37.
2483. CJEU C-690/17 of 11.4.2019 – Oko-Text Verlag/Dr. Rudolf Liebe Nachf., para. 38.
2484. CJEU C-690/17 of 11.4.2019 – Oko-Text Verlag/Dr. Rudolf Liebe Nachf., para. 39.
2485. CJEU C-690/17 of 11.4.2019 – Oko-Text Verlag/Dr. Rudolf Liebe Nachf., para. 40, with further proof.
2486. CJEU C-690/17 of 11.4.2019 – Oko-Text Verlag/Dr. Rudolf Liebe Nachf., para. 41.

without legal protection against those manufacturers, but merely that the conflicts between it and those manufacturers must be assessed from the point of view of other rules of law. Those rules may include rules relating to contractual or non-contractual liability, as well as the rules, referred to in the second question, which are set out in Article 9(1)(c) CTMR and Article 5(2) TMD2008.[2487]

Article 9(1)(c) CTMR and Article 5(2) TMD2008 must be interpreted as meaning that they **entitle the proprietor** of an individual trade mark with a reputation, consisting of a quality label, to oppose the affixing, by a third party, of a sign identical with, or similar to, that mark to products that are neither identical with, nor similar to, the goods or services for which that mark is registered, provided that it is established that, by that affixing, the third party takes unfair advantage of the distinctive character or the reputation of the mark concerned or causes detriment to that distinctive character or reputation and provided that, in that case, the third party has not established the existence of a 'due cause', within the meaning of those provisions, in support of such affixing.[2488]

In the present case, Dr. Liebe affixed to its products a sign identical with, or similar to, the ÖKO-TEST marks without ÖKO-Test Verlag's consent. It has some doubts, however, as to whether those marks afford ÖKO-Test Verlag the protection laid down by those provisions. It draws attention to the fact that, for the relevant German public, it is the quality label that has a reputation and not its registration as a trade mark. Additionally, that public perceives the affixing of the sign at issue by Dr. Liebe as the display of a quality label and not as the use of such a label as a trade mark.[2489]

In that regard, it should be recalled that the concept of 'reputation' referred to in Article 9(1)(c) CTMR and Article 5(2) TMD2008 assumes a certain degree of knowledge amongst the relevant public. That public must be determined by reference to the product or service marketed under the trade mark concerned and the degree of knowledge required must be considered to be reached when the trade mark is known by a significant part of that public.[2490]

It follows from those principles that the 'reputation', within the meaning of those provisions, of the ÖKO-TEST marks depends on whether a significant part of the public that ÖKO-Test Verlag targets with its consumer information and consultancy service and its magazine knows the sign of which those marks consist, in this case, the quality label.[2491]

That requirement of knowledge cannot be interpreted as meaning that the public must be aware that the quality label has been registered as a trade mark. It is sufficient that a significant part of the relevant public knows that sign.[2492]

2487. CJEU C-690/17 of 11.4.2019 – Oko-Text Verlag/Dr. Rudolf Liebe Nachf., para. 42.
2488. CJEU C-690/17 of 11.4.2019 – Oko-Text Verlag/Dr. Rudolf Liebe Nachf., para. 53.
2489. CJEU C-690/17 of 11.4.2019 – Oko-Text Verlag/Dr. Rudolf Liebe Nachf., para. 46.
2490. CJEU C-690/17 of 11.4.2019 – Oko-Text Verlag/Dr. Rudolf Liebe Nachf., para. 47, with reference to CJEU C-301/07 of 6.10.2009 – PAGO International, para. 21-24; C-125/14 of 3.9.2015 – Iron & Smith, para. 17.
2491. CJEU C-690/17 of 11.4.2019 – Oko-Text Verlag/Dr. Rudolf Liebe Nachf., para. 48.
2492. CJEU C-690/17 of 11.4.2019 – Oko-Text Verlag/Dr. Rudolf Liebe Nachf., para. 49.

As regards, in particular, Article 9(1)(c), it should also be recalled that it suffices, in order for the proprietor of an EU trade mark to enjoy the protection granted by that provision, that that mark has a reputation in a substantial part of the territory of the European Union, and that part may, in some circumstances, correspond to the territory of a single Member State. If that condition is satisfied, the EU trade mark at issue must be considered to have a reputation in the whole of the European Union.[2493]

The sign of which the ÖKO-TEST marks consist, that is to say, the quality label reproduced in paragraph 11 of the present judgment, is, according to the findings contained in the order for reference, known by a significant part of the relevant public throughout Germany. It follows that the ÖKO-TEST marks enjoy a reputation, within the meaning of Article 9(1)(c) CTMR and of Article 5(2) TMD2008, with the result that ÖKO-Test Verlag enjoys the protection afforded by those provisions.[2494]

It will therefore be for the referring court to examine whether the affixing by Dr. Liebe, of a sign identical with, or similar to, the ÖKO-TEST marks to its products enabled Dr. Liebe to take unfair advantage of the distinctive character or the reputation of those marks or was detrimental to that distinctive character or reputation. Should it find that to be the case, the referring court will, in addition, have to assess whether Dr. Liebe has established, in this case, a 'due cause', within the meaning of Article 9(1)(c) CTMR and of Article 5(2) TMD2008, in relation to the affixing of that sign to those products. In the latter case, it would have to be concluded that ÖKO-Test Verlag does not have the right to prohibit that use on the basis of those provisions.[2495]

[N] Removing the trade mark

Article 5 TMD2008 and Article 9 CTMR must be interpreted as meaning that the proprietor of a mark is entitled to oppose a third party, without his consent, removing all the signs identical to that mark and affixing other signs on the products placed in the customs warehouse, such as in the main proceedings, with a view to importing them or trading them in the EEA where they have never yet been marketed.[2496]

Article 5(1)(1) TMD2008 and Article 9(1)(1) CTMR confer on the proprietor of the registered trade mark an exclusive right, which, according to Article 5(1)(a) and (b) TMD2008 and Article 9(1)(a) and (b) CTMR, entitles the proprietor to prevent all third parties from using, in the course of trade, without his consent, a sign identical to the mark in relation to the goods or services identical to those for which it has been registered of a sign which, because of its identity with, or similarity to, the trade mark and the identity or similarity of the goods or services covered by the trade mark and the sign, there exists a likelihood of confusion on the part of the public, a likelihood of

2493. CJEU C-690/17 of 11.4.2019 – Oko-Text Verlag/Dr. Rudolf Liebe Nachf., para. 50.
2494. CJEU C-690/17 of 11.4.2019 – Oko-Text Verlag/Dr. Rudolf Liebe Nachf., para. 51, with reference to CJEU C-301/07 of 6.10.2009 – PAGO International, para. 27, 29 and 30; C-125/14 of 3.9.2015 – Iron & Smith, para. 51.
2495. CJEU C-690/17 of 11.4.2019 – Oko-Text Verlag/Dr. Rudolf Liebe Nachf., para. 52, with reference to CJEU C-65/12 of 6.2.2014 – Leidseplein Beheer, paras 43 et seq.
2496. CJEU C-129/17 of 25.7.2018 – Mitsubishi Shoji Kaisha a.o./Duma Forklifts a.o., para. 52.

confusion that includes the likelihood of association between the sign and the trade mark.[2497]

As regards the concept of 'use in the course of trade', the Court has already held that the list of types of use that the proprietor of the trade mark may prohibit, contained in Article 5(3) TMD2008 and Article 9(2) CTMR, is not exhaustive, and that it refers exclusively to active behaviour on the part of the third party.[2498]

In the present case, the order for reference states that, without Mitsubishi's consent, Duma and GSI acquire, outside the EEA, Mitsubishi forklift trucks that they bring into EEA territory where they place them under a customs warehousing procedure. Whilst those goods are still under that procedure, they entirely remove the signs identical to the Mitsubishi trade marks, make alterations in order to render them compliant with the standards in force in the European Union, replace the identification plates and serial numbers and affix their own signs, then import them into the EEA, and market them both within and outside the EEA.[2499]

Unlike other cases, the goods concerned in the case in the main proceedings do not therefore bear the marks at issue when they are imported into and marketed in the EEA, after having been placed under the customs warehousing procedure. Also, the third parties do not appear to use in any way at that time the signs identical or similar to the marks at issue, in particular in their commercial communications. The case in the main proceedings is also different from the circumstances envisaged in the judgment *Portakabin*, in which the Court held that, where a reseller, without the consent of the trade mark proprietor, removes the trade mark from the goods and replaces it with a label bearing the reseller's name, with the result that the trade mark of the manufacturer of the goods in question is entirely concealed, the trade mark proprietor is entitled to prevent the reseller from using that mark to advertise that resale, since that adversely affects the essential function of the trade mark.[2500]

Nevertheless, it must be observed, first, that the removal of signs identical to the mark prevents the goods for which that mark is registered from bearing that mark the first time that they are placed on the market in the EEA and, hence, deprives the proprietor of that trade mark of the benefit of the essential right, which is conferred on him to control the initial marketing in the EEA of goods bearing that mark.[2501]

Secondly, the removal of the signs identical to the mark and the affixing of new signs on the goods with a view to their first placing on the market in the EEA adversely affects the functions of the mark.[2502]

As regards the function of the indication of origin, it suffices to recall that the Court has already held that any act by a third party preventing the proprietor of a

2497. CJEU C-129/17 of 25.7.2018 – Mitsubishi Shoji Kaisha a.o./Duma Forklifts a.o., para. 33.
2498. CJEU C-129/17 of 25.7.2018 – Mitsubishi Shoji Kaisha a.o./Duma Forklifts a.o., para. 38, with further proof; *see also* CJEU C-253/20 and C-254/20 of 17.11.2022 – Impexeco/Novartis a.o., para. 44.
2499. CJEU C-129/17 of 25.7.2018 – Mitsubishi Shoji Kaisha a.o./Duma Forklifts a.o., para. 40.
2500. CJEU C-129/17 of 25.7.2018 – Mitsubishi Shoji Kaisha a.o./Duma Forklifts a.o., para. 41, with further references.
2501. CJEU C-129/17 of 25.7.2018 – Mitsubishi Shoji Kaisha a.o./Duma Forklifts a.o., para. 42.
2502. CJEU C-129/17 of 25.7.2018 – Mitsubishi Shoji Kaisha a.o./Duma Forklifts a.o., para. 43.

registered trade mark in one or more Member States from exercising his right to control the first placing of goods bearing that mark on the market in the EEA by its very nature undermines that essential function of the trade mark.[2503]

The referring court wonders whether it makes any difference that goods thus imported or placed on the market can still be identified by the relevant average consumer as originating from the trade mark proprietor, on the basis of their outward appearance or model. It suggests, in effect, that despite the removal of the signs identical to the mark and the affixing of new signs on the forklift trucks, the relevant consumers continue to recognize them as Mitsubishi forklift trucks. In that regard, it must be observed that, while the essential function of the mark may be harmed irrespective of that fact, that fact is likely to accentuate the effects of such harm.[2504]

Moreover, the removal of the signs identical to the mark and the affixing of new signs on the goods precludes the trade mark proprietor from being able to retain customers by virtue of the quality of its goods and affects the functions of investment and advertising of the mark where, as in the present case, the product in question is not still marketed under the trade mark of the proprietor on that market by him or with his consent. The fact that the trade mark proprietor's goods are placed on the market before that proprietor has placed them on that market bearing that trade mark, with the result that consumers will know those goods before being able to associate them with that trade mark, is likely substantially to impede the use of that mark, by the proprietor, in order to acquire a reputation likely to attract and retain consumers, and to serve as a factor in sales promotion or as an instrument of commercial strategy. In addition, such actions deprive the proprietor of the possibility of obtaining, by putting the goods on the EEA market first, the economic value of the product bearing that mark and, therefore, of its investment.[2505]

Thirdly, by infringing the trade mark proprietor's right to control the first placing of goods bearing that mark on the market in the EEA and by adversely affecting the functions of the mark, the removal of the signs identical to the mark and affixing of new signs on the goods by a third party, without the consent of the proprietor, with a view to importing into or placing those goods on the market in the EEA and with the aim of circumventing the proprietor's right to prohibit the importation of those goods bearing its mark, is contrary to the objective of ensuring undistorted competition.[2506]

Finally, it must be held that an operation consisting, on the part of the third party, of removing signs identical to the trade mark in order to affix its own signs involves active conduct on the part of that third party, which, since it is done with a view to importing those goods into the EEA and marketing them there and is therefore carried out in the exercise of a commercial activity for economic advantage, may be regarded as a use in the course of trade.[2507]

2503. CJEU C-129/17 of 25.7.2018 – Mitsubishi Shoji Kaisha a.o./Duma Forklifts a.o., para. 44, with reference to CJEU C-379/14 of 16.7.2015 – TOP Logistics, para. 48.
2504. CJEU C-129/17 of 25.7.2018 – Mitsubishi Shoji Kaisha a.o./Duma Forklifts a.o., para. 45.
2505. CJEU C-129/17 of 25.7.2018 – Mitsubishi Shoji Kaisha a.o./Duma Forklifts a.o., para. 46.
2506. CJEU C-129/17 of 25.7.2018 – Mitsubishi Shoji Kaisha a.o./Duma Forklifts a.o., para. 47.
2507. CJEU C-129/17 of 25.7.2018 – Mitsubishi Shoji Kaisha a.o./Duma Forklifts a.o., para. 48, with further references.

For all of those reasons, it must be held that the trade mark proprietor is entitled, under Article 5 TMD2008 and Article 9 CTMR, to oppose such actions.[2508]

It makes no difference to that conclusion that the removal of the signs identical to the mark and the affixing of new signs took place when the goods were still placed under the customs warehousing procedure, since those operations were carried out for the importing and placing on the market of those goods in the EEA, as is demonstrated, in the case in the main proceedings, by the fact that the importers made alterations to the forklift trucks in order to render them compliant with the standards in force in the European Union and, moreover, by the fact that they are then, at least in part, actually imported and placed on the market in the EEA.[2509]

In that context, it must also be observed that Article 9(4) of Regulation No. 207/2009 [CTMR], as amended by Regulation No. 2015/2424,[2510] which applies to the facts in the main proceedings with effect from 23 March 2016, entitles the proprietor from that date to prevent all third parties from bringing goods, in the course of trade, into the European Union without being released for free circulation there, where those goods, including packaging, come from third countries and bear without authorization a trade mark which is identical to the EU trade mark registered in respect of such goods, or which cannot be distinguished in its essential aspects from that trade mark. That entitlement of the trade mark proprietor lapses only if, during the proceedings to determine whether the registered trade mark has been infringed, evidence is provided by the declarant or the holder of the goods that the proprietor of the registered trade mark is not entitled to prohibit the placing of the goods on the market in the country of final destination.[2511]

[O] Revocation

It is not appropriate to order cessation of the use of the sign in question if it has been established that the trade mark has lost its distinctive character, in consequence of acts or inactivity of the proprietor, so that it has become a common name within the meaning of Article 12(2) TMD2008 and the trade mark has therefore been revoked.[2512]

It follows that the protection of rights that the proprietor of a trade mark derives under the directive in question is not unconditional, since in order to maintain the balance between those interests that protection is limited in particular to those cases in

2508. CJEU C-129/17 of 25.7.2018 – Mitsubishi Shoji Kaisha a.o./Duma Forklifts a.o., para. 49.
2509. CJEU C-129/17 of 25.7.2018 – Mitsubishi Shoji Kaisha a.o./Duma Forklifts a.o., para. 50.
2510. Regulation (EU) 2015/2424 of the European Parliament and of the Council of 16 December 2015 amending Council Regulation (EC) No 207/2009 on the Community trade mark and Commission Regulation (EC) No 2868/95 implementing Council Regulation (EC) No 40/94 on the Community trade mark, and repealing Commission Regulation (EC) No 2869/95 on the fees payable to the Office for Harmonization in the Internal Market (Trade Marks and Designs).
2511. CJEU C-129/17 of 25.7.2018 – Mitsubishi Shoji Kaisha a.o./Duma Forklifts a.o., para. 51.
2512. CJEU C-145/05 of 27.4.2006 – Levi Strauss, para. 37.

which the proprietor shows himself to be sufficiently vigilant by opposing the use of signs by other operators likely to infringe his mark.[2513]

The requirement of vigilant conduct is not confined to trade mark protection, in fact, and may apply in other fields of Community law where an individual seeks to benefit from a right deriving from that legal order.[2514]

A trade mark is liable to revocation if it has become, in consequence of acts or inactivity of the proprietor, the common name in the trade for a product or service in respect of which it has been registered.[2515]

Accordingly, where a trade mark has lost its distinctive character in consequence of acts or inactivity of the proprietor so that it has become a common name within the meaning of Article 12(2) TMD2008, its proprietor can no longer assert the rights conferred on him under Article 5 TMD2008.[2516]

Such inactivity may also take the form of a failure on the part of the proprietor of a mark to have recourse to Article 5 TMD2008 in due time, for the purposes of applying to the competent authority to prevent third parties from using the sign in respect of which there is a likelihood of confusion with that mark, since the purpose of such applications is precisely to preserve the distinctive character of the mark in question.[2517]

Having regard to the considerations set out in paragraphs 29 and 30 of this judgment, it is for the competent national court to establish revocation, if appropriate, linked in particular to such a failure, including in the context of proceedings seeking protection of the exclusive rights conferred by Article 5 TMD2008, and which may have been brought late by the proprietor of the mark. If taking account of revocation for the purposes of Article 12(2) TMD2008 in infringement proceedings were solely a matter for the national laws of the Member States, the consequence for trade mark proprietors might be that protection would vary depending on the applicable law. The objective of 'the same protection under the legal systems of all the Member States' set out in the ninth recital in the preamble to the directive, where it is described as fundamental, would not be attained.[2518]

Accordingly, after revocation in the particular case has been established, the competent national court cannot order cessation of the use of the sign in question, even if, at the time when that sign began to be used, there was a likelihood of confusion between the sign and the mark concerned.[2519]

Article 5(1)(b), the first subparagraph of Article 10(1) and the first subparagraph of Article 12(1) of TMD2008, read in conjunction with recital 6 thereof, must be interpreted as leaving Member States the option of allowing the proprietor of a trade mark whose rights in that mark have been revoked on expiry of the five-year period

2513. CJEU C-145/05 of 27.4.2006 – Levi Strauss, para. 30; C-65/12 of 6.2.2014 – Leidseplein Beheer, para. 42.
2514. CJEU C-145/05 of 27.4.2006 – Levi Strauss, para. 31.
2515. CJEU C-145/05 of 27.4.2006 – Levi Strauss, para. 32.
2516. CJEU C-145/05 of 27.4.2006 – Levi Strauss, para. 33.
2517. CJEU C-145/05 of 27.4.2006 – Levi Strauss, para. 34.
2518. CJEU C-145/05 of 27.4.2006 – Levi Strauss, para. 35.
2519. CJEU C-145/05 of 27.4.2006 – Levi Strauss, para. 36.

from its registration because he or she failed to make genuine use of the mark in the Member State concerned in connection with the goods or services for which it was registered to retain the right to claim **compensation for the injury** sustained as a result of the use by a third party, **before the date on which the revocation took effect**, of a similar sign in connection with identical or similar goods or services that is liable to be confused with his or her trade mark.[2520]

[P] Legal consequences

Where the competent national court finds that the sign in question constituted an infringement of the mark at the time when the sign began to be used, it is for that court to take such measures as proven to be the most appropriate in the light of the circumstances of the case in order to safeguard the proprietor's rights deriving from Article 5(1) TMD2008; such measures may include, in particular, an order to cease use of that sign.[2521]

The Directive provides in Article 5(3) TMD2008 for a non-exhaustive list of measures to guarantee the rights of the proprietor but does not require that such measures take a particular form, and thus the competent national authorities retain a degree of discretion in that regard.[2522]

However, the requirement of genuine and effective protection of the rights which the proprietor derives from the TMD means that the competent national court must take such measures as proven to be the most appropriate in the light of the circumstances of the case in order to safeguard the proprietor's rights and remedy infringements of his mark. In this connection, it should be noted in particular that the order to cease use of the sign in question is indeed a measure which genuinely and effectively safeguards those rights.[2523]

Article 11 The right to prohibit preparatory acts in relation to the use of packaging or other means

Where the risk exists that the packaging, labels, tags, security or authenticity features or devices, or any other means to which the trade mark is affixed, could be used in relation to goods or services and that use would constitute an infringement of the rights of the proprietor of a trade mark under Article 10(2) and (3), the proprietor of that trade mark shall have the right to prohibit the following acts if carried out in the course of trade:

(a) affixing a sign identical with or similar to the trade mark on packaging, labels, tags, security or authenticity features or devices, or any other means on which the mark may be affixed;

2520. CJEU C-622/18 of 26.3.2020 – AR/Cooper International Spirits a.o., para. 48.
2521. CJEU C-145/05 of 27.4.2006 – Levi Strauss, para. 25.
2522. CJEU C-145/05 of 27.4.2006 – Levi Strauss, para. 23.
2523. CJEU C-145/05 of 27.4.2006 – Levi Strauss, para. 24.

(b) offering or placing on the market, or stocking for those purposes, or importing or exporting, packaging, labels, tags, security or authenticity features or devices, or any other means on which the mark is affixed.

Article 12 Reproduction of trade marks in dictionaries

If the reproduction of a trade mark in a dictionary, encyclopaedia or similar reference work, in print or electronic form, gives the impression that it constitutes the generic name of the goods or services for which the trade mark is registered, the publisher of the work shall, at the request of the proprietor of the trade mark, ensure that the reproduction of the trade mark is, without delay, and in the case of works in printed form at the latest in the next edition of the publication, accompanied by an indication that it is a registered trade mark.

Article 13 Prohibition of the use of a trade mark registered in the name of an agent or representative

1. *Where a trade mark is registered in the name of the agent or representative of a person who is the proprietor of that trade mark, without the proprietor's consent, the latter shall be entitled to either or both of the following:*
   (a) to oppose the use of the trade mark by his agent or representative;
   (b) to demand the assignment of the trade mark in his favour.
2. *Paragraph 1 shall not apply where the agent or representative justifies his action.*

Article 14 Limitation of the effects of a trade mark

1. *A trade mark shall not entitle the proprietor to prohibit a third party from using, in the course of trade:*
   (a) the name or address of the third party, where that third party is a natural person;
   (b) signs or indications which are not distinctive or which concern the kind, quality, quantity, intended purpose, value, geographical origin, the time of production of goods or of rendering of the service, or other characteristics of goods or services;
   (c) the trade mark for the purpose of identifying or referring to goods or services as those of the proprietor of that trade mark, in particular, where the use of the trade mark is necessary to indicate the intended purpose of a product or service, in particular as accessories or spare parts.
2. *Paragraph 1 shall only apply where the use made by the third party is in accordance with honest practices in industrial or commercial matters.*
3. *A trade mark shall not entitle the proprietor to prohibit a third party from using, in the course of trade, an earlier right which only applies in a particular locality if that right is recognised by the law of the Member State in question and the use of that right is within the limits of the territory in which it is recognised.*

[A] Principles

Classifying the mark as falling under one specific provision or another of Article 5 TMD2008, as the case may be, is not necessarily determinant as regards the assessment as to whether the use in question is permissible.[2524]

When a third party relies on the requirement of availability to argue its right to use a sign other than that registered by the trade mark proprietor, the relevance of such an argument cannot be assessed under Articles 3 and 12 TMD2008, but must be examined in the light of Article 5 TMD2008, which concerns the protection of the registered mark against use by third parties, as well as of Article 6(1)(b) TMD2008, if the sign in question comes within the scope of that provision.[2525]

Articles 5–7 TMD2008 embody a complete harmonization of the rules relating to the rights conferred by a trade mark and accordingly define the rights of proprietors of trade marks in the Community.[2526]

Article 6(1)(b) TMD2008 does not have a decisive bearing on the interpretation of Article 3(1)(c) TMD2008. Indeed, Article 6(1)(b), which aims, *inter alia*, to resolve the problems posed by registration of a mark consisting wholly or partly of a geographical name, does not confer on third parties the right to use the name as a trade mark but merely guarantees their right to **use** it **descriptively**, that is to say, as an indication of geographical origin, provided that it is used in accordance with honest practices in industrial and commercial matters.[2527]

Article 12 CTMR concerns the limits on the effects of a Community trade mark, whereas Article 7 CTMR relates to the grounds for refusal to register signs as marks.[2528]

Article 6(1)(a) TMD2008 limits in a general way, for the benefit of operators who have a name identical or similar to the registered mark, the right granted by the mark after its registration, that is to say after the existence of the mark's distinctive character has been established. It cannot therefore be taken into account for the purposes of the specific assessment of the distinctive character of the trade mark before the trade mark is registered.[2529]

The Commission pointed out by reference to the drafting history of the Directive that Article 5 of the proposal for a first Council Directive to approximate the laws of the Member States relating to trade marks (OJ 1980 C 351, p. 1) (which became Article 6 TMD2008) laid down the formula, provided he does not use them as a trade mark. However, that formula was replaced in the amended proposal (COM (85) 793 final (OJ 1985 C 351, p. 4)) by the words, provided he uses them in accordance with honest

2524. CJEU C-63/97 of 23.2.1999 – BMW, para. 30.
2525. CJEU C-102/07 of 10.4.2008 – adidas/Marca Mode, para. 26.
2526. CJEU C-59/08 of 23.4.2009 – Copad, para. 40; C-324/08 of 15.10.2009 – Makro Zelfbedieningsgroothandel, para. 20; C-127/09 of 3.6.2010 – Coty Prestige Lancaster Group, para. 27; C-46/10 of 14.7.2011 – Viking Gas, para. 25; C-661/11 of 19.9.2013 – Martin Y Paz Diffusion, para. 54.
2527. CJEU C-108/97 and C-109/97 of 4.5.1999 – Windsurfing Chiemsee, para. 28; C-404/02 of 16.9.2004 – Nichols, para. 32 f.; C-51/10 P of 10.3.2011 – Agencja Wydawnicza Technopol/HABM, para. 59; *see also* CJEU C-48/05 of 25.1.2007 – Adam Opel, para. 42.
2528. CJEU C-51/10 P of 10.3.2011 – Agencja Wydawnicza Technopol/HABM, para. 60.
2529. CJEU C-404/02 of 16.9.2004 – Nichols, para. 33.

industrial or commercial practice. The Commission adds that it is apparent from the statement of reasons for the amended proposal that that substitution was made in the interests of greater clarity.[2530]

In those circumstances, an **expression such as a trade mark** cannot be regarded as appropriate for determining the scope of Article 6 TMD2008.[2531]

Article 12(b) CTMR does **not concern the status of an earlier trade mark** within the meaning of Article 8(2) CTMR. The Court of First Instance therefore did not err in law by holding the view that the argument based on Article 12(b) CTMR was irrelevant.[2532]

[B] Use of a name

> *Take care: Unfortunately, there was a major change in the wording of TMD2008 from 'his own name or address' to 'the name or address of the third party, where that third party is a natural person'.*

With respect to the Community, provision is made for such an exception in Article 6(1)(a) TMD2008, which, essentially, allows third parties to use signs to indicate their own name or address, provided that they use them in accordance with honest practices in industrial or commercial matters.[2533]

A third party may, in principle, rely on the exception provided for in Article 6(1)(a) TMD2008 in order to be entitled to use a sign which is identical or similar to a trade mark for the purpose of indicating his trade name, even if that constitutes a use falling within the scope of Article 5(1) of that directive which the trade mark proprietor may prohibit by virtue of the exclusive rights conferred on him by that provision.[2534]

Unfortunately no longer applicable: The Court has held that that provision is not limited to the names of natural persons.[2535]

[C] Designating indications

That provision draws **no distinction between the possible uses of the indications** referred to in Article 6(1)(b) TMD2008. For such an indication to fall within the scope of that article, it suffices that it is an indication concerning one of the characteristics set out therein, like geographical origin.[2536]

Where a trade mark is registered, *inter alia*, in respect of motor vehicles, the affixing by a third party, without the authorization of the proprietor of the trade mark, of a sign identical to that mark to **scale models** of that make of vehicle, in order

2530. CJEU C-100/02 of 7.1.2004 – Gerolsteiner Brunnen, para. 14.
2531. CJEU C-100/02 of 7.1.2004 – Gerolsteiner Brunnen, para. 15.
2532. CJEU C-3/03 P of 28.4.2004 – Matratzen Concord/OHIM, para. 35; unofficial translation.
2533. CJEU C-245/02 of 16.11.2004 – Anheuser-Busch, para. 77; C-17/06 of 11.9.2007 – Céline, para. 30.
2534. CJEU C-245/02 of 16.11.2004 – Anheuser-Busch, para. 81.
2535. CJEU C-17/06 of 11.9.2007 – Céline, para. 31.
2536. CJEU C-100/02 of 7.1.2004 – Gerolsteiner Brunnen, para. 19.

faithfully to reproduce those vehicles, and the marketing of those scale models do not constitute use of an indication concerning a characteristic of those scale models, within the meaning of Article 6(1)(b) TMD2008.[2537]

Under Article 6(1)(b) TMD2008, the trade mark shall not entitle the proprietor to prohibit a third party from using, in the course of trade, indications concerning the kind, quality, quantity, intended purpose, value, geographical origin, the time of production of goods or of rendering of the service, or other characteristics of goods or services.[2538]

In that regard, whilst this provision is primarily designed to prevent the proprietor of a trade mark from prohibiting competitors from using one or more descriptive terms forming part of his trade mark in order to indicate certain characteristics of their products, its wording is in no way specific to such a situation.[2539]

However, the requirement of availability cannot in any circumstances constitute an independent restriction of the effects of the trade mark in addition to those expressly provided for in Article 6(1)(b) TMD2008. It must be stated in that regard that, in order for a third party to be able to plead the limitations of the effects of the trade mark in Article 6(1)(b) TMD2008 and rely in that respect on the requirement of availability underlying that provision, the indication used by it must, as required by that provision of the Directive, relate to one of the characteristics of the goods marketed or the service provided by that third party.[2540]

One cannot therefore exclude a priori the possibility that that provision might authorize a third party to use a trade mark if such use consists in giving an indication concerning the kind, quality or other characteristics of products marketed by that third party, provided that use is made in accordance with honest practices in industrial or commercial matters.[2541]

However, the affixing of a sign which is identical to a trade mark registered, *inter alia*, in respect of motor vehicles to scale models of that make of vehicle in order to reproduce those vehicles faithfully is not intended to provide an indication as to a characteristic of those scale models, but is merely an element in the faithful reproduction of the original vehicles.[2542]

In general, use of a sign identical with, or similar to, another person's trade mark as a **keyword** for an internet referencing service is not intended to provide an indication of one of the characteristics of the goods or services offered by the third party in that use, with the result that that use does not come within Article 6(1)(b) TMD2008.[2543]

In special circumstances, which must be assessed by the national court, a contrary finding may, however, be necessary. It is, consequently, for the national court to ascertain, on the basis of a full examination of the case before it, whether the third

2537. CJEU C-48/05 of 25.1.2007 – Adam Opel, para. 45.
2538. CJEU C-48/05 of 25.1.2007 – Adam Opel, para. 40.
2539. CJEU C-48/05 of 25.1.2007 – Adam Opel, para. 42.
2540. CJEU C-102/07 of 10.4.2008 – adidas/Marca Mode, paras 47 and 49.
2541. CJEU C-48/05 of 25.1.2007 – Adam Opel, para. 43.
2542. CJEU C-48/05 of 25.1.2007 – Adam Opel, para. 44.
2543. CJEU C-558/08 of 8.7.2010 – Portakabin, para. 60.

party is using descriptive indications for the purposes of Article 6(1)(b) TMD2008. In the course of that assessment, it will have to take account of the fact that the word has been used as a generic name.[2544]

[D] Indications of the intended purpose

According to Article 6(1)(c) TMD2008, the trade mark owner may not prohibit a third party from using the mark in trade where it is necessary to indicate the intended purpose of a product or service, in particular as accessories or spare parts.[2545]

It should be noted that that provision does not lay down criteria for determining whether a given intended purpose of a product falls within its scope, but merely requires that use of the trade mark be **necessary** in order to indicate such a purpose.[2546]

Moreover, since the intended purpose of the products as accessories or spare parts is cited only by way of example, those doubtless being the usual situations in which it is necessary to use a trade mark in order to indicate the intended purpose of a product, the application of Article 6(1)(c) TMD2008 is not limited to those situations. Therefore, it is not always necessary to determine whether a product must be regarded as an accessory or a spare part.[2547]

The situations coming within the scope of Article 6(1)(c) TMD2008 must, however, be limited to those which correspond to the objective of that provision. However, the **objective of Article 6(1)(c)** is to enable providers of goods or services, which are supplementary to the goods or services offered by a trade mark proprietor, to use that mark in order to inform the public of the practical link between their goods or services and those of the proprietor of the mark.[2548]

The use of the trade mark to inform the public that the advertiser repairs and maintains trade marked goods must be held to constitute use indicating the intended purpose of the service within the meaning of Article 6(1)(c) TMD2008. Like the use of a trade mark intended to identify the vehicles which a non-original spare part will fit, the use in question is intended to identify the goods in respect of which the service is provided.[2549]

Furthermore, the use concerned must be held to be necessary to indicate the intended purpose of the service. It is sufficient to note that if an independent trader carries out the maintenance and repair of BMW cars or is in fact a specialist in that field, that fact cannot in practice be communicated to his customers without using the BMW mark.[2550]

2544. CJEU C-558/08 of 8.7.2010 – Portakabin, para. 61.
2545. CJEU C-228/03 of 17.3.2005 – Gillette Company and Gillette Group Finland, para. 30, 39.
2546. CJEU C-228/03 of 17.3.2005 – Gillette Company and Gillette Group Finland, para. 31.
2547. CJEU C-228/03 of 17.3.2005 – Gillette Company and Gillette Group Finland, para. 32; C-558/08 of 8.7.2010 – Portakabin, para. 63.
2548. CJEU C-558/08 of 8.7.2010 – Portakabin, para. 64.
2549. CJEU C-63/97 of 23.2.1999 – BMW, para. 59; *see also* CJEU C-228/03 of 17.3.2005 – Gillette Company and Gillette Group Finland, para. 33.
2550. CJEU C-63/97 of 23.2.1999 – BMW, para. 60; *see also* CJEU C-228/03 of 17.3.2005 – Gillette Company and Gillette Group Finland, para. 33.

Such use of a trade mark is necessary in cases where that information cannot in practice be communicated to the public by a third party without use being made of the trade mark of which the latter is not the owner. That use must **in practice be the only means** of providing such information.[2551]

In that respect, in order to determine whether other means of providing such information may be used, it is necessary to take into consideration, for example, the possible existence of technical standards or norms generally used for the type of product marketed by the third party and known to the public for which that type of product is intended. Those norms, or other characteristics, must be capable of providing that public with comprehensible and full information on the intended purpose of the product marketed by that third party in order to preserve the system of undistorted competition on the market for that product.[2552]

It is for the national court to determine whether, in the circumstances of the case, use of the trade mark is necessary, taking account of the requirements referred to in this judgment and of the nature of the public for which the product marketed is intended.[2553]

Article 6(1)(c) TMD2008 makes no distinction between the possible intended purposes of products when assessing the lawfulness of the use of a trade mark. The criteria for assessing the lawfulness of the use of a trade mark with accessories or spare parts in particular are thus no different from those applicable to other categories of possible intended purposes.[2554]

As a preliminary observation, it should be noted that the use of the Opel logo at issue in the main proceedings cannot be authorized on the basis of Article 6(1)(c) TMD2008. The affixing of that trade mark on Autec's scale models is not designed to indicate the intended purpose of those toys.[2555]

[E] Honest practices in industrial or commercial matters

The provision does specify that that rule applies only in so far as that use by the third party is 'in accordance with honest practices in industrial or commercial matters'.[2556]

The condition requiring use of the trade mark to be made in accordance with honest practices in industrial or commercial matters must be regarded as constituting in substance the expression of a duty to act fairly in relation to the **legitimate interests of the trade mark owner**, similar to that imposed on the reseller where he uses another's trade mark to advertise the resale of products covered by that mark.[2557]

2551. CJEU C-228/03 of 17.3.2005 – Gillette Company and Gillette Group Finland, para. 35, 39.
2552. CJEU C-228/03 of 17.3.2005 – Gillette Company and Gillette Group Finland, para. 36.
2553. CJEU C-228/03 of 17.3.2005 – Gillette Company and Gillette Group Finland, para. 37, 39.
2554. CJEU C-228/03 of 17.3.2005 – Gillette Company and Gillette Group Finland, para. 38, 39.
2555. CJEU C-48/05 of 25.1.2007 – Adam Opel, para. 39.
2556. CJEU C-558/08 of 8.7.2010 – Portakabin, para. 58.
2557. CJEU C-63/97 of 23.2.1999 – BMW, para. 61; C-100/02 of 7.1.2004 – Gerolsteiner Brunnen, para. 24 ff.; C-245/02 of 16.11.2004 – Anheuser-Busch, para. 82; C-228/03 of 17.3.2005 – Gillette Company and Gillette Group Finland, para. 41, 49; C-17/06 of 11.9.2007 – Céline, para. 33; C-558/08 of 8.7.2010 – Portakabin, para. 67.

Just like Article 7 TMD2008, Article 6 TMD2008 seeks to reconcile the fundamental interests of trade mark protection with those of free movement of goods and freedom to provide services in the common market in such a way that trade mark rights are able to fulfil their essential role in the system of undistorted competition which the Treaty seeks to establish and maintain.[2558]

It is essentially the same condition as that laid down by Article 17 of the TRIPS Agreement.[2559]

Specifically, Article 6(1)(b) TMD2008 seeks to ensure that all economic operators have the opportunity to use descriptive indications. That provision therefore gives expression to the requirement of availability.[2560]

Since the case concerns bottled drinks, the circumstances to be taken into account would include in particular the shape and labelling of the bottle in order to assess, more particularly, whether the producer of the drink bearing the indication of geographical origin might be regarded as unfairly competing with the proprietor of the trade mark.[2561]

The mere fact that there exists a **likelihood of aural confusion** between a word mark registered in one Member State and an indication of geographical origin from another Member State is therefore insufficient to conclude that the use of that indication in the course of trade is not in accordance with honest practices. In a Community of fifteen Member States, with great linguistic diversity, the chance that there exists some phonetic similarity between a trade mark registered in one Member State and an indication of geographical origin from another Member State is already substantial and will be even greater after the impending enlargement.[2562]

Account should be taken of the **overall presentation** of the product marketed by the third party, particularly the circumstances in which the mark of which the third party is not the owner is displayed in that presentation, the circumstances in which a distinction is made between that mark and the mark or sign of the third party, and the effort made by that third party to ensure that consumers distinguish its products from those of which it is not the trade mark owner.[2563]

In assessing whether the condition of honest practice is satisfied, account must be taken first of the extent to which the use of the third party's trade name is understood by the relevant public, or at least a significant section of that public, as indicating a link between the third party's goods and the trade mark proprietor or a person authorized

2558. CJEU C-63/97 of 23.2.1999 – BMW, para. 62; C-228/03 of 17.3.2005 – Gillette Company and Gillette Group Finland, para. 29; C-102/07 of 10.4.2008 – adidas/Marca Mode, para. 45; C-558/08 of 8.7.2010 – Portakabin, para. 57; C-500/14 of 6.10.2015 – Ford Motor Company, para. 43.
2559. CJEU C-245/02 of 16.11.2004 – Anheuser-Busch, para. 82.
2560. CJEU C-102/07 of 10.4.2008 – adidas/Marca Mode, para. 46.
2561. CJEU C-100/02 of 7.1.2004 – Gerolsteiner Brunnen, paras 26 et seq.
2562. CJEU C-100/02 of 7.1.2004 – Gerolsteiner Brunnen, para. 25.
2563. CJEU C-228/03 of 17.3.2005 – Gillette Company and Gillette Group Finland, para. 46, *see also* CJEU C-93/16 of 20.7.2017 – Ornua Co-operative/Tindale & Stanton, para. 45.

to use the trade mark, and secondly of the extent to which the third party ought to have been aware of that.[2564]

In that regard, use of the trade mark will not comply with honest practices in industrial or commercial matters where, first, it is done in such a manner that it may give the impression that there is a **commercial connection** between the reseller and the trade mark proprietor.[2565]

Nor may such use **affect** the value of the **trade mark** by taking unfair advantage of its distinctive character or repute.[2566]

Another factor to be taken into account when making the assessment is whether the trade mark concerned enjoys a certain **reputation** in the Member State in which it is registered and its protection is sought, from which the third party might profit in selling his goods.[2567]

In addition, use of the trade mark will not be in accordance with Article 6(1)(c) TMD2008 if it **discredits or denigrates that mark**.[2568]

Finally, where the third party presents its product as an **imitation or replica** of the product bearing the trade mark of which it is not the owner, such use of that mark does not comply with honest practices within the meaning of Article 6(1)(c) TMD2008.[2569]

Moreover, whether the product marketed by the third party has been represented as being of the **same quality** as, or having **equivalent properties** to, the product whose trade mark is being used is a factor which the referring court must take into consideration when it verifies that such use is made in accordance with honest practices in industrial or commercial matters.[2570]

The fact that a third party uses a trade mark of which it is not the owner in order to indicate the intended purpose of its product does not necessarily mean that it is presenting that product as being of the same quality as, or having equivalent properties to, those of the product bearing the trade mark. Whether there has been such a presentation depends on the facts of the case, and it is for the referring court to determine whether it has taken place by reference to the circumstances.[2571]

Consequently, the use of another's trade mark for the purpose of informing the public of the repair and maintenance of goods covered by that mark is authorized on the same conditions[2572] as those applying where the mark is used for the purpose of informing the public of the resale of goods covered by that mark.[2573]

2564. CJEU C-245/02 of 16.11.2004 – Anheuser-Busch, para. 83; C-17/06 of 11.9.2007 – Céline, para. 34; C-558/08 of 8.7.2010 – Portakabin, para. 67.
2565. CJEU C-63/97 of 23.2.1999 – BMW, para. 64; C-228/03 of 17.3.2005 – Gillette Company and Gillette Group Finland, para. 42, 49.
2566. CJEU C-228/03 of 17.3.2005 – Gillette Company and Gillette Group Finland, para. 43, 49; *see also* CJEU C-63/97 of 23.2.1999 – BMW, para. 52.
2567. CJEU C-245/02 of 16.11.2004 – Anheuser-Busch, para. 83.
2568. CJEU C-228/03 of 17.3.2005 – Gillette Company and Gillette Group Finland, para. 44, 49.
2569. CJEU C-228/03 of 17.3.2005 – Gillette Company and Gillette Group Finland, para. 45, 49.
2570. CJEU C-228/03 of 17.3.2005 – Gillette Company and Gillette Group Finland, para. 48, 49.
2571. CJEU C-228/03 of 17.3.2005 – Gillette Company and Gillette Group Finland, para. 47, 49.
2572. *See* Art. 15 'Exceptions of the exhaustion'.
2573. CJEU C-63/97 of 23.2.1999 – BMW, para. 63.

Where a third party that uses a trade mark of which it is not the owner markets **not only a spare part or an accessory but also the product itself** with which the spare part or accessory is intended to be used, such use falls within the scope of Article 6(1)(c) TMD2008 in so far as it is necessary to indicate the intended purpose of the product marketed by the latter and is made in accordance with honest practices in industrial and commercial matters.[2574]

There is nothing in the directive to prevent a third party from relying on Article 6(1)(c) TMD2008 in such a case.[2575]

In certain circumstances, by using in its catalogues the core element of a manufacturer's **distinguishing mark** which is known in specialist circles, a competing supplier does not take unfair advantage of the reputation of that distinguishing mark.[2576]

Use by an advertiser of a sign identical with, or similar to, a trade mark for an **internet referencing service** comes within Article 5(1) TMD2008 where that use does not enable normally informed and reasonably attentive internet users, or enables them only with difficulty, to ascertain whether the goods or services referred to by the ad originate from the trade mark proprietor or from an undertaking economically linked to it or, on the contrary, originate from a third party.[2577]

Thus, the circumstances under which a trade mark proprietor is, pursuant to Article 5(1) TMD2008, entitled to prevent an advertiser from using a sign identical with, or similar to, that trade mark as a keyword may, in the light of the case law, easily correspond to a situation in which the advertiser cannot claim that it is acting in accordance with honest practices in industrial or commercial matters, and cannot therefore validly rely on the exception provided for in Article 6(1) TMD2008.[2578]

In that regard, it must be held, first, that one of the characteristics of this situation lies precisely in the fact that the ad is likely to cause at least a significant section of the target public to establish a link between the goods or services to which it refers and the goods or services of the trade mark proprietor or persons authorized to use that trade mark. Second, in the event that the national court finds that the ad does not enable average internet users, or enables them only with difficulty, to ascertain whether the goods or services referred to by the ad originate from the trade mark proprietor or from a third party, it is unlikely that the advertiser can genuinely claim not to have been aware of the ambiguity thus caused by its ad. It is the advertiser itself, in the context of its professional strategy and with full knowledge of the economic sector in which it operates, which chose a keyword corresponding to another person's trade mark and which, alone or with the assistance of the referencing service provider, designed the ad and therefore decided how it should be presented.[2579]

The advertiser cannot, in principle, claim to have acted in accordance with honest practices in industrial or commercial matters. It is, however, for the national

2574. CJEU C-228/03 of 17.3.2005 – Gillette Company and Gillette Group Finland, para. 51, 53.
2575. CJEU C-228/03 of 17.3.2005 – Gillette Company and Gillette Group Finland, para. 51.
2576. CJEU C-59/05 of 23.2.2006 – Siemens, para. 27.
2577. CJEU C-558/08 of 8.7.2010 – Portakabin, para. 68.
2578. CJEU C-558/08 of 8.7.2010 – Portakabin, para. 69.
2579. CJEU C-558/08 of 8.7.2010 – Portakabin, para. 70.

court to carry out an overall assessment of all the relevant circumstances in order to determine whether there may be evidence to justify a contrary finding.[2580]

It is for the **national court** to carry out an overall assessment of all the relevant circumstances.[2581]

Article 15 Exhaustion of the rights conferred by a trade mark

1. *A trade mark shall not entitle the proprietor to prohibit its use in relation to goods which have been put on the market in the Union under that trade mark by the proprietor or with the proprietor's consent.*
2. *Paragraph 1 shall not apply where there exist legitimate reasons for the proprietor to oppose further commercialisation of the goods, especially where the condition of the goods is changed or impaired after they have been put on the market.*

[A] Principles

Article 7 TMD2008 is intended to reconcile the **interests of trade mark protection and those of free movement of goods** within the Community by making the further commercialization of a product bearing a trade mark possible and preventing opposition by the proprietor of the mark.[2582]

Under the scheme of the TMD2008, the rights conferred by a trade mark are defined by Article 5 TMD2008, while Article 7 TMD2008 contains an important qualification with respect to that definition, in that it provides that the rights conferred by Article 5 do not entitle the proprietor to prohibit the use of the trade mark where the conditions laid down in that provision are satisfied.[2583]

Articles 5–7 TMD2008 embody a complete harmonization of the rules relating to the rights conferred by a trade mark and accordingly define the rights of proprietors of trade marks in the Community.[2584]

In particular, Article 5 TMD2008 confers on the trade mark proprietor exclusive rights which entitle him *inter alia* to prevent any third party from importing goods bearing the mark, offering the goods, or putting them on the market or stocking them for these purposes. Article 7(1) contains an exception to that rule, in that it provides

2580. CJEU C-558/08 of 8.7.2010 – Portakabin, para. 71.
2581. CJEU C-100/02 of 7.1.2004 – Gerolsteiner Brunnen, paras 26 et seq.; C-245/02 of 16.11.2004 – Anheuser-Busch, para. 84; C-228/03 of 17.3.2005 – Gillette Company and Gillette Group Finland, para. 46, 52; C-17/06 of 11.9.2007 – Céline, para. 35; C-558/08 of 8.7.2010 – Portakabin, para. 71.
2582. CJEU C-63/97 of 23.2.1999 – BMW, para. 57; C-16/03 of 30.11.2004 – Peak Holding, para. 37.
2583. CJEU C-355/96 of 16.7.1998 – Silhouette International Schmied/Hartlauer Handelsgesellschaft, para. 34.
2584. CJEU C-59/08 of 23.4.2009 – Copad, para. 40; C-324/08 of 15.10.2009 – Makro Zelfbedieningsgroothandel, para. 20; C-127/09 of 3.6.2010 – Coty Prestige Lancaster Group, para. 27; C-46/10 of 14.7.2011 – Viking Gas, para. 25; C-661/11 of 19.9.2013 – Martin Y Paz Diffusion, para. 54.

that the trade mark proprietor's rights are exhausted where the goods have been put on the market in the EEA by him or with his consent.[2585]

Article 7(1) TMD2008 cannot be interpreted as meaning that the proprietor of a trade mark is entitled, on the basis of that provision alone, to obtain an order restraining a third party from using his trade mark for products which have been put on the market outside the EEA under that mark by the proprietor or with his consent.[2586]

Article 7 TMD2008 is worded in general terms and comprehensively regulates the question of the exhaustion of trade mark rights for products traded in the Community. Therefore, national rules on the subject must be assessed in the light of that article.[2587]

Like any secondary legislation, however, the directive must be interpreted in the light of the Treaty rules on the free movement of goods and in particular Article 36.[2588]

Article 7(1) TMD2008 provides that the rights conferred by a trade mark do not entitle the proprietor to prohibit its use in relation to goods which have been put on the market in the Community under that trade mark by the proprietor or with his consent.[2589]

Trade mark rights are not intended to allow their owners to partition national markets and thus promote the retention of price differences which may exist between Member States. Whilst, in the pharmaceutical market especially, such price differences may result from factors over which trade mark owners have no control, such as divergent rules between the Member States on the fixing of maximum prices, the profit margins of pharmaceutical wholesalers and pharmacies, or the maximum amount of medical expenses which may be reimbursed under sickness insurance schemes, distortions caused by divergent pricing rules in one Member State must be remedied by measures of the Community authorities and not by another Member State introducing measures which are incompatible with the rules on the free movement of goods.[2590]

Article 7 TMD2008, like Article 36 of the Treaty, is intended to reconcile the fundamental interest in protecting trade mark rights with the fundamental interest in

2585. CJEU C-59/08 of 23.4.2009 – Copad, para. 41; C-324/08 of 15.10.2009 – Makro Zelfbedieningsgroothandel, para. 21; C-127/09 of 3.6.2010 – Coty Prestige Lancaster Group, para. 28; C-558/08 of 8.7.2010 – Portakabin, para. 74; C-324/09 of 12.7.2011 – L'Oréal, para. 59; C-46/10 of 14.7.2011 – Viking Gas, para. 26; C-197/21 of 27.10.2022 – Soda-Club (CO2) a.o./MySoda, para. 32; C-175/21 of 17.11.2022 – Harman International Industries/AB, para. 38.

2586. CJEU C-355/96 of 16.7.1998 – Silhouette International Schmied/Hartlauer Handelsgesellschaft, para. 37.

2587. CJEU C-427/93, C-429/93 and C-436/93 of 11.7.1996 – Bristol-Myers Squibb and Others/Paranova, para. 26; C-143/00 of 23.4.2002 – Boehringer Ingelheim and Others (I), para. 17; C-291/16 of 20.12.2017 – Schweppes/Red Paralela, para. 30.

2588. CJEU C-427/93, C-429/93 and C-436/93 of 11.7.1996 – Bristol-Myers Squibb and Others/Paranova, para. 27; C-337/95 of 4.11.1997 – Parfums Christian Dior/Evora, para. 37.

2589. CJEU C-427/93, C-429/93 and C-436/93 of 11.7.1996 – Bristol-Myers Squibb and Others/Paranova, para. 30; *see also* CJEU C-71 to 73/94 of 11.7.1996 – Eurim-Pharm Arzneimittel/Beiersdorf and Others, para. 32; C-349/95 of 11.11.1997 – Loendersloot/Ballantine & Son and Others, para. 23.

2590. CJEU C-71 to 73/94 of 11.7.1996 – Eurim-Pharm Arzneimittel/Beiersdorf and Others, para. 33; C-427/93, C-429/93 and C-436/93 of 11.7.1996 – Bristol-Myers Squibb and Others/Paranova, para. 46; C-232/94 of 11.7.1996 – MPA Pharma/Rhône-Poulenc Pharma, para. 19; C-349/95 of 11.11.1997 – Loendersloot/Ballantine & Son and Others, para. 23; *see also* CJEU C-147/20 of 17.11.2022 – Novartis Pharma/Abacus Medicine, para. 47; C-204/20 of 17.11.2022 – Bayer

the free movement of goods within the common market, so that those two provisions, which pursue the same result, must be interpreted in the same way.[2591]

[B] Consideration of interests

As for the interpretation of Article 36 of the Treaty, prohibitions or restrictions on imports justified on grounds of the protection of industrial and commercial property are authorized by that article, provided they do not constitute a means of arbitrary discrimination or a disguised restriction on trade between Member States.[2592]

The Court's case law shows that Article 36 allows derogations from the fundamental principle of the free movement of goods within the common market only in so far as such derogations are justified in order to safeguard the rights which constitute the specific subject matter of the industrial and commercial property in question.[2593]

As the Court has ruled on numerous occasions, the specific subject matter of trade marks is in particular to guarantee to the proprietor of the trade mark that he has the right to use that trade mark for the purpose of putting a product into circulation for the first time and therefore to protect him against competitors wishing to take advantage of the status and reputation of the trade mark by selling products illegally bearing that mark.[2594]

It follows that the owner of a trade mark protected by the legislation of a Member State cannot rely on that legislation in order to oppose the importation or marketing of

Intellectual Property/kohlpharma, paras 58 and 71; C-224/20 of 17.11.2022 – Merck Sharp & Dohme a.o./Abacus a.o., para. 49; C-253/20 and C-254/20 of 17.11.2022 – Impexeco/Novartis a.o., para. 50.

2591. CJEU C-71 to 73/94 of 11.7.1996 – Eurim-Pharm Arzneimittel/Beiersdorf and Others, para. 27; C-427/93, C-429/93 and C-436/93 of 11.7.1996 – Bristol-Myers Squibb and Others/Paranova, para. 40; C-232/94 of 11.7.1996 – MPA Pharma/Rhône-Poulenc Pharma, para. 13; C-337/95 of 4.11.1997 – Parfums Christian Dior/Evora, para. 53; C-143/00 of 23.4.2002 – Boehringer Ingelheim and Others (I), para. 18; C-291/16 of 20.12.2017 – Schweppes/Red Paralela, para. 35; *see also* CJEU C-63/97 of 23.2.1999 – BMW, para. 57; C-204/20 of 17.11.2022 – Bayer Intellectual Property/kohlpharma, para. 57; C-224/20 of 17.11.2022 – Merck Sharp & Dohme a.o./Abacus a.o., para. 47.

2592. CJEU C-71 to 73/94 of 11.7.1996 – Eurim-Pharm Arzneimittel/Beiersdorf and Others, para. 28; C-232/94 of 11.7.1996 – MPA Pharma/Rhône-Poulenc Pharma, para. 14; *see also* CJEU C-400/09 and C-207/10 of 28.7.2011 – Orifarm, para. 23.

2593. CJEU C-71 to 73/94 of 11.7.1996 – Eurim-Pharm Arzneimittel/Beiersdorf and Others, para. 29; C-427/93, C-429/93 and C-436/93 of 11.7.1996 – Bristol-Myers Squibb and Others/Paranova, para. 42; C-232/94 of 11.7.1996 – MPA Pharma/Rhône-Poulenc Pharma, para. 15; C-379/97 of 12.10.1999 – Upjohn, para. 14.

2594. CJEU 102/77 of 23.5.1978 – Hoffmann-La Roche/Centrafarm, para. 7; C-10/89 of 17.10.1990 – CNL-SUCAL/HAG, para. 14; C-9/93 of 22.6.1994 – IHT Internationale Heiztechnik/Ideal-Standard, para. 33; C-71 to 73/94 of 11.7.1996 – Eurim-Pharm Arzneimittel/Beiersdorf and Others, para. 31; C-427/93, C-429/93 and C-436/93 of 11.7.1996 – Bristol-Myers Squibb and Others/Paranova, para. 44; C-232/94 of 11.7.1996 – MPA Pharma/Rhône-Poulenc Pharma, para. 17; C-349/95 of 11.11.1997 – Loendersloot/Ballantine & Son and Others, para. 22; C-379/97 of 12.10.1999 – Upjohn, para. 15; C-16/03 of 30.11.2004 – Peak Holding, para. 35; C-291/16 of 20.12.2017 – Schweppes/Red Paralela, para. 37; C-197/21 of 27.10.2022 – Soda-Club (CO2) a.o./MySoda, para. 35.

a product which was put on the market in another Member State by him or with his consent.[2595]

[C] Range of application

This principle, known as the exhaustion of rights, applies where the owner of the trade mark in the importing State and the owner of the trade mark in the exporting State are the same or where, even if they are separate persons, they are economically linked. A number of situations are covered: products put into circulation by the same undertaking, by a **licensee**, by a **parent company**, by a **subsidiary** of the same group, or by an **exclusive distributor**.[2596]

There are numerous instances in national case law and Community case law where the trade mark had been assigned to a subsidiary or to an exclusive distributor in order to enable those undertakings to protect their national markets against parallel imports by taking advantage of restrictive approaches to the exhaustion of rights in the national laws of some States.[2597]

Articles 30 and 36[2598] defeat such manipulation of trade mark rights since they preclude national laws which enable the holder of the right to oppose imports.[2599]

In the situations described above, the function of the trade mark is in no way called in question by freedom to import. For the trade mark to be able to fulfil its role, it must offer a guarantee that all goods bearing it have been produced under the control of a single undertaking which is accountable for their quality. In all the cases mentioned, control was in the hands of a single body: the group of companies in the case of products put into circulation by a subsidiary; the manufacturer in the case of products marketed by the distributor; the licensor in the case of products marketed by a licensee. In the case of a licence, the licensor can control the quality of the licensee's products by including in the contract clauses requiring the licensee to comply with his instructions and giving him the possibility of verifying such compliance. The origin which the trade mark is intended to guarantee is the same: it is not defined by reference to the manufacturer but by reference to the point of control of manufacture.[2600]

It must further be stressed that the decisive factor is the **possibility of control** over the quality of goods, not the actual exercise of that control. Accordingly, a national law allowing the licensor to oppose importation of the licensee's products on grounds of poor quality would be precluded as contrary to Articles 30 and 36:[2601] if the licensor tolerates the manufacture of poor quality products, despite having contractual means

2595. CJEU C-427/93, C-429/93 and C-436/93 of 11.7.1996 – Bristol-Myers Squibb and Others/ Paranova, para. 45; C-232/94 of 11.7.1996 – MPA Pharma/Rhône-Poulenc Pharma, para. 18.
2596. CJEU C-9/93 of 22.6.1994 – IHT Internationale Heiztechnik/Ideal-Standard, para. 34; C-352/95 of 20.3.1997 – Phytheron International/Bourdon, para. 21; *see also* CJEU C-291/16 of 20.12.2017 – Schweppes/Red Paralela, para. 44.
2597. CJEU C-9/93 of 22.6.1994 – IHT Internationale Heiztechnik/Ideal-Standard, para. 35.
2598. Articles 28 und 30 EC.
2599. CJEU C-9/93 of 22.6.1994 – IHT Internationale Heiztechnik/Ideal-Standard, para. 36.
2600. CJEU C-9/93 of 22.6.1994 – IHT Internationale Heiztechnik/Ideal-Standard, para. 37; *see also* CJEU C-291/16 of 20.12.2017 – Schweppes/Red Paralela, paras 38 and 43.
2601. Articles 28 und 30 EC.

of preventing it, he must bear the responsibility. Similarly if the manufacture of products is decentralized within a group of companies and the subsidiaries in each of the Member States manufacture products whose quality is geared to the particularities of each national market, a national law which enabled one subsidiary of the group to oppose the marketing in the territory of that State of products manufactured by an affiliated company on grounds of those quality differences would also be precluded. Articles 30 and 36 require the group to bear the consequences of its choice.[2602]

It follows from that case law that the concept of 'economic links', for the purposes of that case law, refers to a substantive, rather than formal, criterion, which is in no way confined to the situations listed in paragraph 44 above and which, in particular, is also fulfilled where, following the division of national parallel trade marks resulting from a territorially limited assignment, the proprietors of those marks coordinate their commercial policies or reach an agreement in order to exercise joint control over the use of those marks, so that it is possible for them to determine, directly or indirectly, the goods to which the trade mark is affixed and to control the quality of those goods.[2603]

Indeed, if such proprietors were permitted to protect their territories against the parallel import of those goods, that would lead to a partitioning of the national markets which is not justified by the purpose of trade mark rights and is, in particular, unnecessary in order to preserve the essential function of the marks concerned.[2604]

Thus, in the circumstances described in paragraph 46 above, it must be held that the product was put on the market in the exporting Member State with the consent of the holder of the trade mark rights protected by the importing Member State, within the meaning of Article 7(1) TMD2008, read in the light of Article 36 TFEU.[2605]

In that regard, it should be specified that the finding that there exist, following the division of national parallel trade marks resulting from a territorially limited assignment, economic links between the proprietors of those trade marks is not conditional upon those proprietors being formally dependent on each other for the purposes of the joint exploitation of those marks, nor is it conditional upon their actually taking advantage of their ability to control the quality of the goods concerned.[2606]

Moreover, although it is true that the Court has previously found that a contract of assignment by itself, that is, where there is no economic link, gives the assignor no means of controlling the quality of the goods marketed by the assignee and to which the latter has affixed the trade mark, it follows precisely from that finding that that is not the case when economic links exist between the assignor and the assignee.[2607]

It is for the national courts to assess whether such economic links exist, taking into account all the relevant circumstances of the case at hand.[2608]

2602. CJEU C-9/93 of 22.6.1994 – IHT Internationale Heiztechnik/Ideal-Standard, para. 38; C-291/16 of 20.12.2017 – Schweppes/Red Paralela, para. 45.
2603. CJEU C-291/16 of 20.12.2017 – Schweppes/Red Paralela, para. 46.
2604. CJEU C-291/16 of 20.12.2017 – Schweppes/Red Paralela, para. 47.
2605. CJEU C-291/16 of 20.12.2017 – Schweppes/Red Paralela, para. 48.
2606. CJEU C-291/16 of 20.12.2017 – Schweppes/Red Paralela, para. 49.
2607. CJEU C-291/16 of 20.12.2017 – Schweppes/Red Paralela, para. 50, with reference to CJEU C-9/93 of 22.6.1994 – IHT Internationale Heiztechnik/Ideal-Standard, paras 41 and 43.
2608. CJEU C-291/16 of 20.12.2017 – Schweppes/Red Paralela, para. 51.

[D] Conditions of the exhaustion

[1] Putting on the market

Article 7(1) TMD2008 must be interpreted as meaning that goods bearing a trade mark cannot be regarded as having been put on the market in the EEA where the proprietor of the trade mark has imported them into the EEA with a view to selling them there or where he has offered them for sale to consumers in the EEA, in **his own shops or those of an associated company**, without actually selling them.[2609]

The wording alone of Article 7(1) TMD2008 does not make it possible to determine whether goods imported into the EEA or offered for sale in the EEA by the proprietor of the trade mark are to be regarded as having been 'put on the market' in the EEA within the meaning of that provision. The interpretation of the provision in question must therefore be sought with regard to the scheme and objectives of the Directive.[2610]

In the present case, it is not disputed that, where he sells goods bearing his trade mark to a third party in the EEA, the proprietor puts those goods on the market within the meaning of Article 7(1) TMD2008.[2611]

A sale which allows the proprietor to realize the economic value of his trade mark exhausts the exclusive rights conferred by the Directive, more particularly the right to prohibit the acquiring third party from reselling the goods.[2612]

On the other hand, where the proprietor imports his goods with a view to selling them in the EEA or offers them for sale in the EEA, he does not put them on the market within the meaning of Article 7(1) TMD2008.[2613]

Such acts do not transfer to third parties the right to dispose of the goods bearing the trade mark. They do not allow the proprietor to realize the economic value of the trade mark. Even after such acts, the proprietor retains his interest in maintaining complete control over the goods bearing his trade mark, in order in particular to ensure their quality.[2614]

Moreover, it should be noted that Article 5(3)(b) and (c) TMD2008, relating to the content of the proprietor's exclusive rights, distinguishes *inter alia* between offering the goods, putting them on the market, stocking them for those purposes and importing them. The wording of that provision therefore also confirms that importing the goods or offering them for sale in the EEA cannot be equated to putting them on the market there.[2615]

In circumstances such as those of the main proceedings, the stipulation, in a contract of sale concluded between the proprietor of the trade mark and an operator

2609. CJEU C-16/03 of 30.11.2004 – Peak Holding, para. 44; *see also* CJEU C-175/21 of 17.11.2022 – Harman International Industries/AB, para. 44.
2610. CJEU C-16/03 of 30.11.2004 – Peak Holding, para. 33.
2611. CJEU C-16/03 of 30.11.2004 – Peak Holding, para. 39.
2612. CJEU C-16/03 of 30.11.2004 – Peak Holding, para. 40.
2613. CJEU C-16/03 of 30.11.2004 – Peak Holding, para. 41.
2614. CJEU C-16/03 of 30.11.2004 – Peak Holding, para. 42.
2615. CJEU C-16/03 of 30.11.2004 – Peak Holding, para. 43.

established in the EEA, of a prohibition on reselling in the EEA does not mean that there is no putting on the market in the EEA within the meaning of Article 7(1) TMD2008 and thus does not preclude the exhaustion of the proprietor's exclusive rights in the event of resale in the EEA in breach of the prohibition.[2616]

Article 7(1) TMD2008 makes Community exhaustion subject either to a putting on the market in the EEA by the proprietor of the trade mark himself or to a putting on the market in the EEA by a third party but with the proprietor's consent.[2617]

In circumstances such as those of the main proceedings, putting on the market in the EEA by the proprietor presupposes a sale of the goods by him in the EEA.[2618]

In the event of such a sale, Article 7(1) TMD2008 does not make exhaustion of the rights conferred by the trade mark subject in addition to the proprietor's consent to further marketing of the goods in the EEA.[2619]

Exhaustion occurs solely by virtue of the putting on the market in the EEA by the proprietor.[2620]

In circumstances, where '**perfume testers**' are made available, without transfer of ownership and with a prohibition on sale, to intermediaries who are contractually bound to the trade mark proprietor for the purpose of allowing their customers to test the contents, where the trade mark proprietor may at any time recall those goods and where the presentation of the goods is clearly distinguishable from that of the bottles of perfume normally made available to the intermediaries by the trade mark proprietor, the fact that those testers are bottles of perfume which bear not only the word 'Demonstration' but also the statement '**Not for Sale**' precludes, in the absence of any evidence to the contrary, which it is for the national court to assess, a finding that the trade mark proprietor impliedly consented to putting them on the market.[2621]

That statement [bottles of perfume presented in packaging including not only the word 'Demonstration' but also the statement 'Not for Sale'], since it clearly reflects the intention of the proprietor of the trade mark concerned that the goods bearing it should not be sold, whether inside or outside the EEA, constitutes, in itself and in the absence of evidence to the contrary, a decisive factor precluding a finding that the proprietor consented to a putting on the market in the EEA within the meaning of Article 7(1) TMD2008.[2622]

A statement 'Not for Sale' such as appears on the packaging of the bottles of perfume testers precludes such a classification, since it clearly reflects the intention of the proprietor of the trade mark concerned that the goods bearing that trade mark should not be sold, whether inside or outside the EEA.[2623]

2616. CJEU C-16/03 of 30.11.2004 – Peak Holding, para. 56.
2617. CJEU C-16/03 of 30.11.2004 – Peak Holding, para. 50.
2618. CJEU C-16/03 of 30.11.2004 – Peak Holding, para. 51.
2619. CJEU C-16/03 of 30.11.2004 – Peak Holding, para. 52.
2620. CJEU C-16/03 of 30.11.2004 – Peak Holding, para. 53.
2621. CJEU C-127/09 of 3.6.2010 – Coty Prestige Lancaster Group, para. 48; *see also* CJEU C-324/09 of 12.7.2011 – L'Oréal, para. 72.
2622. CJEU C-127/09 of 3.6.2010 – Coty Prestige Lancaster Group, paras 42 et seq.
2623. CJEU C-127/09 of 3.6.2010 – Coty Prestige Lancaster Group, para. 45.

As the wording of Article 13(1) CTMR is, in essence, identical to that of Article 7(1) TMD2008, except for the definition of the territory in which the good are to be put on the market, and as there are no other contextual factors or factors linked to the purpose of the provisions requiring them to be interpreted differently, the interpretation in this judgment of Article 7(1) for the purpose of replying to the question for a preliminary ruling referred applies equally for Article 13(1) CTMR.[2624]

Any stipulation, in the **act of sale** effecting the first putting on the market in the EEA, of **territorial restrictions** on the right to resell the goods concerns only the relations between the parties to that act.[2625]

It cannot preclude the exhaustion provided for by the Directive.[2626]

'**Importing**' within the meaning of Article 5(3)(c) TMD2008 and Article 9(2)(c) CTMR, which the trade mark proprietor may oppose in so far as it entails 'using [the mark] in the course of trade' within the meaning of Article 5(1) TMD2008 and Article 9(1) CTMR, therefore requires introduction of those goods into the Community for the purposes of putting them on the market therein.[2627]

In the field of trade marks, placing non-Community goods bearing a mark under a suspensive customs procedure such as that of **external transit** is not, per se, interference with the right of the proprietor of the mark to control the initial marketing in the Community.[2628]

A trade mark proprietor cannot oppose the mere entry into the Community, under the external transit procedure or the customs warehousing procedure, of original goods bearing that mark which had not already been put on the market in the Community previously by that proprietor or with his consent. The trade mark proprietor cannot make the placing of the goods at issue under the external transit procedure or the customs warehousing procedure conditional on the existence, at the time of the introduction of those goods into the Community, of a final destination already specified in a third country, possibly pursuant to a sale agreement.[2629]

The putting on the market in the Community of goods coming from a third country is subject to their release for free circulation within the meaning of Article 24 EC.[2630]

Entry of non-Community goods for customs procedures such as external transit or customs warehousing is distinguishable from placing them under the customs procedure of release for free circulation, which, pursuant to the first paragraph of Article 79 of the Customs Code, confers on non-Community goods the customs status of Community goods.[2631]

2624. CJEU C-127/09 of 3.6.2010 – Coty Prestige Lancaster Group, para. 46.
2625. CJEU C-16/03 of 30.11.2004 – Peak Holding, para. 54.
2626. CJEU C-16/03 of 30.11.2004 – Peak Holding, para. 55.
2627. CJEU C-405/03 of 18.10.2005 – Class International, para. 34.
2628. CJEU C-281/05 of 9.11.2006 – Montex Holdings, para. 21.
2629. CJEU C-405/03 of 18.10.2005 – Class International, para. 50; *see also* CJEU C-281/05 of 9.11.2006 – Montex Holdings, para. 20; C-449/09 of 28.10.2010 – Canon Kabushiki Kaisha, para. 21.
2630. CJEU C-405/03 of 18.10.2005 – Class International, para. 35.
2631. CJEU C-405/03 of 18.10.2005 – Class International, para. 36.

Pursuant to Article 37(2) of the Customs Code, non-Community goods subject to the external transit procedure or the customs warehousing procedure remain under customs supervision until, in particular, their customs status is changed to Community goods. In accordance with Article 91(1)(a) and Article 98(1)(a) of the Customs Code, they are not subject to import duties or to commercial policy measures. In fact, goods coming from third countries and placed under the external transit procedure generally pass through one or more Member States then to be dispatched to a third country. As for non-Community goods placed under the customs warehousing procedure, they are generally stored in Community customs territory while awaiting a final destination, which is not necessarily known at the time of storage.[2632]

On the other hand, non-Community goods released for free circulation become Community goods. They gain the benefit of the free movement of goods pursuant to Article 23(2) EC. In accordance with Article 24 EC and the second paragraph of Article 79 of the Customs Code, they must be covered by formalities in respect of the importation of goods and give rise to the levy of customs duties and, where necessary, the application of commercial policy measures.[2633]

Release for free circulation, a requirement for putting goods on the market in the Community, is therefore only one of the options open to the trader who brings goods into the Community customs territory.[2634]

As long as that option is not chosen and the requirements of the customs-approved treatment or use, other than release for free circulation, under which the goods have been placed are satisfied, the mere physical introduction of those goods into the territory of the Community is not 'importing' within the meaning of Article 5(3)(c) TMD2008 and Article 9(2)(c) CTMR and does not entail 'using [the mark] in the course of trade' within the meaning of Article 5(1) TMD2008 and Article 9(1) CTMR, respectively.[2635]

The trade mark proprietor cannot therefore oppose that introduction pursuant to those provisions or make it conditional on the existence of a final destination already specified in a third country, possibly pursuant to a sale agreement.[2636]

That conclusion is not called into question by Article 58(2) of the Customs Code, under which the choice by the trader concerned of customs-approved treatment or use is not to preclude the imposition of prohibitions or restrictions justified on grounds of, *inter alia*, the protection of industrial and commercial property.[2637]

Article 5 TMD2008 must be interpreted as meaning that the proprietor of a trade mark registered in one or more Member States may oppose a third party placing goods bearing that trade mark under the **duty suspension arrangement after** they have been

2632. CJEU C-405/03 of 18.10.2005 – Class International, para. 37.
2633. CJEU C-405/03 of 18.10.2005 – Class International, para. 38.
2634. CJEU C-405/03 of 18.10.2005 – Class International, para. 43.
2635. CJEU C-405/03 of 18.10.2005 – Class International, para. 44; C-449/09 of 28.10.2010 – Canon Kabushiki Kaisha, para. 18.
2636. CJEU C-405/03 of 18.10.2005 – Class International, para. 45.
2637. CJEU C-405/03 of 18.10.2005 – Class International, para. 46.

introduced into the EEA and **released for free circulation** without the consent of that proprietor.[2638]

The import duties having been paid for the goods at issue in the main proceedings and those having been released for free circulation, those goods have been imported within the meaning of Article 5(3)(c) TMD2008.[2639]

Falling, moreover, within one of the categories of goods referred to in Article 3(1) of Directive 92/12,[2640] the goods at issue, in accordance with Article 5(1) of that directive, also became imported goods within the meaning of that directive as soon as they left the customs arrangement.[2641]

Nevertheless, the doubts which the national court entertains on the question of whether the proprietor of a trade mark can oppose goods, which have thus been released for free circulation without its consent, being placed under the duty suspension arrangement are, in the first place, linked to the fact that, by virtue of the rules set out in Directive 92/12, during that storage for tax purposes the **excise duties are not paid** and consequently the goods concerned cannot yet be released for consumption.[2642]

It follows from the wording of Article 5(3) TMD2008 and also from the case law[2643] that the proprietor of the trade mark is not in any way obliged to wait for the release for consumption of the goods covered by its trade mark to exercise its exclusive right. It can also oppose certain acts committed without its consent, before that release for consumption. Amongst those acts are included, in particular, the import of the goods concerned and their storage for the purpose of putting them on the market.[2644]

On the basis of reading Article 5(3) TMD2008 together with paragraph 1 of that article, it is to be held that the actions of an economic operator consisting of importing into the EU goods without the consent of the proprietor of the trade mark and placing those goods under the duty suspension arrangement, also detaining them in a tax warehouse until the payment of import duties and their release for consumption, must be classified as 'using in the course of trade any sign which is identical with the trade mark in relation to goods ... identical with those for which the trade mark is registered', within the meaning of Article 5(1) TMD2008.[2645]

It is true that, in importing and storing goods bearing a sign identical to another's trade mark for goods identical to those in respect of which that mark is registered, that economic operator does not use that sign in the course of dealings with consumers.

2638. CJEU C-379/14 of 16.7.2015 – TOP Logistics, para. 50.
2639. CJEU C-379/14 of 16.7.2015 – TOP Logistics, para. 35.
2640. Council Directive 92/12/EEC of 25 Feb. 1992 on the general arrangements for products subject to excise duty and on the holding, movement and monitoring of such products (OJ 1992 L 76, p. 1).
2641. CJEU C-379/14 of 16.7.2015 – TOP Logistics, para. 36.
2642. CJEU C-379/14 of 16.7.2015 – TOP Logistics, para. 37.
2643. CJEU C-414/99 to C-416/99 of 20.11.2001 – Zino Davidoff and Levi Strauss, para. 40; C-244/00 of 8.4.2003 – Van Doren + Q, para. 33; C-16/03 of 30.11.2004 – Peak Holding, para. 34.
2644. CJEU C-379/14 of 16.7.2015 – TOP Logistics, para. 38.
2645. CJEU C-379/14 of 16.7.2015 – TOP Logistics, para. 39; *see also* CJEU C-175/21 of 17.11.2022 – Harman International Industries/AB, para. 51.

However, at the risk of depriving the TMD2008 of any useful effect, the terms 'using' and 'in the course of trade' used in paragraph 1 of that article cannot be interpreted as meaning that they refer only to immediate relationships between a trader and a consumer.[2646]

First, concerning the notion of 'using', the Court has previously held[2647] that there is use of a sign identical to the trade mark, within the meaning of Article 5 TMD2008, where the economic operator concerned uses the sign in its own commercial communications.[2648]

That is the case, for example, where an economic operator imports or sends to a warehouse keeper goods bearing a trade mark of which it is not a proprietor with a view to releasing them for marketing. If it were otherwise, the acts of import and of stocking for the purpose of placement on the market, mentioned in Article 5(3) TMD2008 and normally carried out without direct contact with potential consumers, could not be qualified as 'using' within the meaning of that article and could not be prohibited, even though the EU legislature has expressly identified them as being prohibited.[2649]

Concerning the expression 'in the course of trade', it is settled case law[2650] that the use of a sign identical to a trade mark constitutes use in the course of trade where it occurs in the context of commercial activity with a view to economic advantage and not as a private matter.[2651]

That is evidently the case where an economic operator active in the parallel trade of trade marked goods imports and stores such goods.[2652]

By contrast, concerning a warehouse keeper, it must be held that its provision of a warehouse service for goods bearing another's trade mark does not constitute use of a sign identical to that trade mark for goods or services identical or similar to those in respect of which the mark is registered. Inasmuch as such a service provider permits such use by its customers, its role cannot be assessed under the TMD but must be examined, if necessary, from the point of view of other rules of law.[2653]

Regarding the risk of infringement of the functions of the mark by an act of placing goods bearing another's trade mark under the duty suspension, it should be noted that the essential function of the indication of origin serves to identify the goods or services covered by the mark as originating from a particular undertaking, that

2646. CJEU C-379/14 of 16.7.2015 – TOP Logistics, para. 40; *see also* CJEU C-129/17 of 25.7.2018 – Mitsubishi Shoji Kaisha a.o./Duma Forklifts a.o., para. 39.
2647. CJEU C-236/08 to C-238/08 of 23.3.2010 – Google France, para. 56.
2648. CJEU C-379/14 of 16.7.2015 – TOP Logistics, para. 41.
2649. CJEU C-379/14 of 16.7.2015 – TOP Logistics, para. 42.
2650. CJEU C-206/01 of 12.11.2002 – Arsenal Football Club, para. 40; C-48/05 of 25.1.2007 – Adam Opel, para. 18; C-325/06 P of 20.3.2007 – Galileo International Technology and Others/ Commission, para. 32; C-17/06 of 11.9.2007 – Céline, para. 17; C-62/08 of 19.2.2009 – UDV North America, para. 44; C-236/08 to C-238/08 of 23.3.2010 – Google France, para. 50.
2651. CJEU C-379/14 of 16.7.2015 – TOP Logistics, para. 43.
2652. CJEU C-379/14 of 16.7.2015 – TOP Logistics, para. 44.
2653. CJEU C-379/14 of 16.7.2015 – TOP Logistics, para. 45; *see also* CJEU C-119/10 of 15.12.2011 – Frisdranken Industrie Winters, paras 28–35.

undertaking being that under the control of which the goods or services are marketed.[2654]

Any act by a third party preventing the proprietor of a registered trade mark in one or more Member States from exercising his right to control the first placing of the goods bearing that mark on the market in the EEA, by its very nature, undermines that essential function of the trade mark. The importation of products without the consent of the proprietor of the trade mark concerned and the holding of those products in a tax warehouse before their release for consumption in the EU has the effect of depriving the proprietor of that mark of the possibility of controlling the conditions of the first placing on the market within the EEA of products bearing its trade mark. Such acts also adversely affect the function of the trade mark of identifying the undertaking from which the products originate and under whose control the initial placing on the market is organized.[2655]

That analysis is not invalidated by the fact that goods imported and placed under the duty suspension arrangement can subsequently be exported to a third State and thus never be released for consumption in a Member State. In that regard, it is sufficient to note that all goods in free circulation may be exported. That possibility cannot preclude the application of the rules on trade marks to goods imported into the EU. Furthermore, exportation is also itself an act covered by Article 5(3) TMD2008.[2656]

[2] In the EEA

TMD2008 cannot be interpreted as leaving it open to the Member States to provide in their **domestic law** for exhaustion of the rights conferred by a trade mark in respect of products put on the market in third countries.[2657]

Article 7(1) TMD2008 and Article 13(1) CTMR limit exhaustion of the rights conferred on the proprietor of a trade mark to cases where goods are put on the market in the Community. They allow the proprietor to market his products outside the Community without thereby exhausting his rights within it. By making it clear that putting goods on the market outside the Community does not exhaust the proprietor's right to oppose the importation of those goods without his consent, the Community legislature has thus allowed the trade mark proprietor to **control the initial marketing in the Community** of goods bearing the mark.[2658]

Like the rules laid down in Article 6 TMD2008, which set certain limits to the effects of a trade mark, Article 7 TMD2008 states that, in the circumstances which it

2654. CJEU C-379/14 of 16.7.2015 – TOP Logistics, para. 47; *see also* CJEU C-409/12 of 6.3.2014 – Backaldrin Österreich The Kornspitz Company, para. 20; C-689/15 of 8.6.2017 – W.F. Gözze Frottierweberei a.o./Verein Bremer Baumwollbörse, para. 41.

2655. CJEU C-379/14 of 16.7.2015 – TOP Logistics, para. 48, *see also* CJEU C-129/17 of 25.7.2018 – Mitsubishi Shoji Kaisha a.o./Duma Forklifts a.o., para. 44.

2656. CJEU C-379/14 of 16.7.2015 – TOP Logistics, para. 49.

2657. CJEU C-355/96 of 16.7.1998 – Silhouette International Schmied/Hartlauer Handelsgesellschaft, para. 26; C-449/09 of 28.10.2010 – Canon Kabushiki Kaisha, para. 22; *see also* CJEU C-175/21 of 17.11.2022 – Harman International Industries/AB, para. 42.

2658. CJEU C-405/03 of 18.10.2005 – Class International, para. 33; C-129/17 of 25.7.2018 – Mitsubishi Shoji Kaisha a.o./Duma Forklifts a.o., para. 31.

specifies, the exclusive rights conferred by the trade mark are exhausted, with the result that the proprietor is no longer entitled to prohibit use of the mark. Exhaustion is subject first of all to the condition that the goods have been put on the market by the proprietor or with his consent. According to the text of the Directive itself, exhaustion occurs only where the products have been put on the market in the Community (in the EEA since the EEA Agreement entered into force).[2659]

In adopting Article 7 TMD2008, which limits exhaustion of the right conferred by the trade mark to cases where the goods bearing the mark have been put on the market in the Community (in the EEA since the EEA Agreement entered into force), the Community legislature has made it clear that putting such goods on the market outside that territory does not exhaust the proprietor's right to oppose the importation of those goods without his consent and thereby to control the initial marketing in the Community (in the EEA since the EEA Agreement entered into force) of goods bearing the mark. That protection would be devoid of substance if, for there to be exhaustion within the meaning of Article 7, it were sufficient for the trade mark proprietor to hâve consented to the putting on the market in that territory of goods which were identical or similar to those in respect of which exhaustion is claimed.[2660]

Article 7(1) TMD2008 and Article 13(1) CTMR limit exhaustion of the rights conferred on the proprietor of a trade mark to cases where goods are put on the market in the Community. They allow the proprietor to market his products outside the Community without thereby exhausting his rights within it. By making it clear that putting goods on the market outside the Community does not exhaust the proprietor's right to oppose the importation of those goods without his consent, the Community legislature has thus allowed the trade mark proprietor to control the initial marketing in the Community of goods bearing the mark.[2661]

National rules providing for exhaustion of trade mark rights in respect of products put on the market outside the EEA under that mark by the proprietor or with his consent are contrary to Article 7(1) TMD2008, as amended by the EEA Agreement.[2662]

It is of no importance for the application of Article 7 TMD2008 whether or not the product protected by the mark has been manufactured in a non-member country if it has in any event been lawfully put on the market, in the Member State from which it has been imported, by the owner of the mark or with the owner's consent, including marketing by another company in the same group as the owner.[2663]

2659. CJEU C-355/96 of 16.7.1998 – Silhouette International Schmied/Hartlauer Handelsgesellschaft, para. 18; C-16/03 of 30.11.2004 – Peak Holding, para. 36.
2660. CJEU C-173/98 of 1.7.1999 – Sebago and Maison Dubois, para. 21; C-414/99 to C-416/99 of 20.11.2001 – Zino Davidoff and Levi Strauss, para. 33; C-244/00 of 8.4.2003 – Van Doren + Q, para. 26; C-449/09 of 28.10.2010 – Canon Kabushiki Kaisha, para. 23; *see also* CJEU C-175/21 of 17.11.2022 – Harman International Industries/AB, para. 43 and 45.
2661. CJEU C-405/03 of 18.10.2005 – Class International, para. 33.
2662. CJEU C-355/96 of 16.7.1998 – Silhouette International Schmied/Hartlauer Handelsgesellschaft, para. 31; C-173/98 of 1.7.1999 – Sebago and Maison Dubois, paras 13 and 17 and 22; C-414/99 to C-416/99 of 20.11.2001 – Zino Davidoff and Levi Strauss, para. 32; *see also* CJEU C-175/21 of 17.11.2022 – Harman International Industries/AB, para. 42 and 45.
2663. CJEU C-352/95 of 20.3.1997 – Phytheron International/Bourdon, para. 21.

[3] Consent

The concept of consent used in Article 7(1) TMD2008 must be **interpreted uniformly** throughout the Community legal order.[2664]

It appears that consent, which is tantamount to the proprietor's renunciation of his exclusive right under Article 5 TMD2008 to prevent all third parties from importing goods bearing his trade mark, constitutes the decisive factor in the extinction of that right.[2665]

The text of Article 7(1) TMD2008 does not give a direct answer to that question. Nevertheless, the rights conferred by the trade mark are exhausted only in respect of the **individual items** of the product which have been put on the market with the proprietor's consent in the territory there defined. The proprietor may continue to prohibit the use of the mark in pursuance of the right conferred on him by the Directive in regard to individual items of that product which have been put on the market in that territory without his consent.[2666]

If the concept of consent were a matter for the national laws of the Member States, the consequence for trade mark proprietors could be that protection would vary according to the legal system concerned. The objective of the same protection under the legal systems of all the Member States set out in the ninth recital in the preamble to the Directive, where it is described as fundamental, would not be attained.[2667]

On a proper construction of Article 7(1) TMD2008, the consent of a trade mark proprietor to the marketing **within the EEA** of products bearing that mark which have previously been placed on the market outside the EEA by that proprietor or with his consent may be implied, where it is to be inferred from facts and circumstances prior to, simultaneous with or subsequent to the placing of the goods on the market outside the EEA which, in the view of the national court, unequivocally demonstrate that the proprietor has renounced his right to oppose placing of the goods on the market within the EEA.[2668]

According to the very wording of Article 7(1) TMD2008, the Community rule of exhaustion can apply only to goods which have been put on the market in the EEA with the consent of the proprietor of the trade mark concerned. In other words, for the purposes of the extinction of the exclusive rights of the trade mark proprietor laid down

2664. CJEU C-414/99 to C-416/99 of 20.11.2001 – Zino Davidoff and Levi Strauss, paras 37 and 43; C-16/03 of 30.11.2004 – Peak Holding, para. 32.
2665. CJEU C-414/99 to C-416/99 of 20.11.2001 – Zino Davidoff and Levi Strauss, para. 41; C-59/08 of 23.4.2009 – Copad, para. 42; C-324/08 of 15.10.2009 – Makro Zelfbedieningsgroothandel, para. 22; *see also* CJEU C-175/21 of 17.11.2022 – Harman International Industries/AB, para. 46.
2666. CJEU C-173/98 of 1.7.1999 – Sebago and Maison Dubois, para. 19; C-127/09 of 3.6.2010 – Coty Prestige Lancaster Group, para. 31; C-661/11 of 19.9.2013 – Martin Y Paz Diffusion, para. 57; *see also* CJEU C-129/17 of 25.7.2018 – Mitsubishi Shoji Kaisha a.o./Duma Forklifts a.o., para. 32.
2667. CJEU C-414/99 to C-416/99 of 20.11.2001 – Zino Davidoff and Levi Strauss, para. 42.
2668. CJEU C-414/99 to C-416/99 of 20.11.2001 – Zino Davidoff and Levi Strauss, para. 47.

in Article 5 TMD2008, what is important is only the fact that the goods in question have been marketed within the EEA.[2669]

By contrast, as has also been made clear by the Community case law, possible marketing outside the EEA does not have any exhaustive effect in that regard.[2670]

Therefore, in order to ensure the protection of the rights conferred by the trade mark and to make possible the further marketing of goods bearing a trade mark without the proprietor of the trade mark being able to oppose that, it is essential that the proprietor can control the **first placing** of those goods on the market in the EEA, irrespective of the fact that they may have first been marketed outside that area.[2671]

It follows from the above considerations that the purely factual question of whether the goods bearing the trade mark concerned were marketed for the first time within the EEA or outside it is not, as such, relevant for the purposes of the application of the exhaustion rule laid down in Article 7(1) TMD2008.[2672]

In view of its serious effect in extinguishing the exclusive rights of the proprietors of the trade marks in issue in the main proceedings (rights which enable them to control the initial marketing in the EEA), consent must be so expressed that an **intention to renounce** those rights is unequivocally demonstrated.[2673]

Such intention will normally be gathered from an **express statement** of consent. Nevertheless, it is conceivable that consent may, in some cases, be inferred from facts and circumstances prior to, simultaneous with or subsequent to the placing of the goods on the market outside the EEA which, in the view of the national court, unequivocally demonstrate that the proprietor has renounced his rights.[2674]

Consent must be **expressed positively**. The factors taken into consideration in finding implied consent must unequivocally demonstrate that the trade mark proprietor has renounced any intention to enforce his exclusive rights.[2675]

It follows that it is for the trader alleging consent to prove it and not for the trade mark proprietor to demonstrate its absence.[2676]

Consequently, implied consent to the marketing within the EEA of goods put on the market outside that area cannot be inferred from the mere silence of the trade mark proprietor.[2677]

2669. CJEU C-324/08 of 15.10.2009 – Makro Zelfbedieningsgroothandel, para. 30.
2670. CJEU C-324/08 of 15.10.2009 – Makro Zelfbedieningsgroothandel, para. 31.
2671. CJEU C-324/08 of 15.10.2009 – Makro Zelfbedieningsgroothandel, para. 32; C-127/09 of 3.6.2010 – Coty Prestige Lancaster Group, para. 30; C-324/09 of 12.7.2011 – L'Oréal, para. 60; C-379/14 of 16.7.2015 – TOP Logistics, para. 31; C-129/17 of 25.7.2018 – Mitsubishi Shoji Kaisha a.o./Duma Forklifts a.o., para. 32.
2672. CJEU C-324/08 of 15.10.2009 – Makro Zelfbedieningsgroothandel, para. 33.
2673. CJEU C-414/99 to C-416/99 of 20.11.2001 – Zino Davidoff and Levi Strauss, para. 45; C-59/08 of 23.4.2009 – Copad, para. 42; *see also* CJEU C-175/21 of 17.11.2022 – Harman International Industries/AB, para. 46.
2674. CJEU C-414/99 to C-416/99 of 20.11.2001 – Zino Davidoff and Levi Strauss, para. 46; C-324/08 of 15.10.2009 – Makro Zelfbedieningsgroothandel, paras 19 and 23; C-127/09 of 3.6.2010 – Coty Prestige Lancaster Group, paras 37 et seq.; *see also* CJEU C-175/21 of 17.11.2022 – Harman International Industries/AB, para. 47.
2675. CJEU C-414/99 to C-416/99 of 20.11.2001 – Zino Davidoff and Levi Strauss, para. 53.
2676. CJEU C-414/99 to C-416/99 of 20.11.2001 – Zino Davidoff and Levi Strauss, para. 54.
2677. CJEU C-414/99 to C-416/99 of 20.11.2001 – Zino Davidoff and Levi Strauss, para. 55.

There is no distinction being made in principle depending upon whether marketing first occurred outside the EEA or within it.[2678]

Moreover, such a distinction would run counter to the system established by Directive 89/104.[2679]

If the possibility of inferring from certain facts and circumstances the implied consent of the trade mark proprietor were to be limited to only those cases in which the first marketing of the goods in question occurred outside the EEA, that would not be in accordance with either the wording or the objectives of Article 7(1) TMD2008.[2680]

Likewise, implied consent cannot be inferred from the fact that a trade mark proprietor has not communicated his **opposition** to marketing within the EEA or from the fact that the goods do not carry any warning that it is prohibited to place them on the market within the EEA.[2681]

Finally, such consent cannot be inferred from the fact that the trade mark proprietor transferred ownership of the goods bearing the mark without imposing contractual reservations or from the fact that, according to the law governing the contract, the property right transferred includes, in the absence of such reservations, an unlimited right of resale or, at the very least, a right to market the goods subsequently within the EEA.[2682]

A rule of national law which proceeded upon the **mere silence** of the trade mark proprietor would not recognize implied consent but rather deemed consent. This would not meet the need for consent positively expressed required by Community law.[2683]

In so far as it falls to the Community legislature to determine the rights of a trade mark proprietor within the Member States of the Community, it would be unacceptable on the basis of the law governing the contract for marketing outside the EEA to apply rules of law that have the effect of limiting the protection afforded to the proprietor of a trade mark by Articles 5(1) and 7(1) TMD2008.[2684]

With regard to exhaustion of the trade mark proprietor's exclusive rights, it is not relevant:

- that the importer of goods bearing the trade mark is not aware that the proprietor objects to their being placed on the market in the EEA or sold there by traders other than authorized retailers; or
- that the authorized retailers and wholesalers have not imposed on their own purchasers contractual reservations setting out such opposition, even though they have been informed of it by the trade mark proprietor.[2685]

2678. CJEU C-324/08 of 15.10.2009 – Makro Zelfbedieningsgroothandel, para. 28; C-175/21 of 17.11.2022 – Harman International Industries/AB, para. 49.
2679. CJEU C-324/08 of 15.10.2009 – Makro Zelfbedieningsgroothandel, para. 29.
2680. CJEU C-324/08 of 15.10.2009 – Makro Zelfbedieningsgroothandel, para. 34.
2681. CJEU C-414/99 to C-416/99 of 20.11.2001 – Zino Davidoff and Levi Strauss, para. 56.
2682. CJEU C-414/99 to C-416/99 of 20.11.2001 – Zino Davidoff and Levi Strauss, para. 57.
2683. CJEU C-414/99 to C-416/99 of 20.11.2001 – Zino Davidoff and Levi Strauss, para. 58; C-324/08 of 15.10.2009 – Makro Zelfbedieningsgroothandel, para. 19.
2684. CJEU C-414/99 to C-416/99 of 20.11.2001 – Zino Davidoff and Levi Strauss, para. 59.
2685. CJEU C-414/99 to C-416/99 of 20.11.2001 – Zino Davidoff and Levi Strauss, para. 66; C-127/09 of 3.6.2010 – Coty Prestige Lancaster Group, para. 40.

The national rules on the enforceability of sales restrictions against third parties are not, therefore, relevant to the resolution of a dispute between the proprietor of a trade mark and a subsequent trader in the distribution chain concerning the preservation or extinction of the rights conferred by the trade mark.[2686]

Implied consent cannot be inferred:

- from the fact that the proprietor of the trade mark has not communicated to all subsequent purchasers of the goods placed on the market outside the EEA his opposition to marketing within the EEA;
- from the fact that the goods carry no warning of a prohibition on their being placed on the market within the EEA;
- from the fact that the trade mark proprietor has transferred the ownership of the products bearing the trade mark without imposing any contractual reservations and that, according to the law governing the contract, the property right transferred includes, in the absence of such reservations, an unlimited right of resale or, at the very least, a right to market the goods subsequently within the EEA.[2687]

Even in situations where the goods in question were first placed on the market in the EEA by a person having no economic link to the proprietor of the trade mark and without his express consent, the intention to renounce the exclusive rights provided for in Article 5 TMD2008 may result from that proprietor's implied consent.[2688]

In certain circumstances, exhaustion of that exclusive right occurs when the goods are **put on the market by a person with economic links to the proprietor**. This is particularly the case where that person is a licensee.[2689]

The essential function of the trade mark would be jeopardized if, failing any consent on the proprietor's part, that proprietor could not oppose the import of an identical or similar product bearing an identical trade mark or one liable to lead to confusion, which had been manufactured and put into circulation in another Member State by a **third party** having no economic link with that proprietor.[2690]

That analysis cannot be altered by the mere fact that the proprietor's mark and that affixed to the product whose import that proprietor seeks to prohibit originally belonged to the same proprietor, irrespective of whether the division of those marks results from expropriation, and thus an act of public authority, or voluntary contractual assignment, on condition, however, that, notwithstanding their common origin, each of those marks has, from the date of expropriation or assignment, independently

2686. CJEU C-414/99 to C-416/99 of 20.11.2001 – Zino Davidoff and Levi Strauss, para. 65.
2687. CJEU C-414/99 to C-416/99 of 20.11.2001 – Zino Davidoff and Levi Strauss, para. 60; C-127/09 of 3.6.2010 – Coty Prestige Lancaster Group, para. 39.
2688. CJEU C-324/08 of 15.10.2009 – Makro Zelfbedieningsgroothandel, para. 25; *see also* CJEU C-175/21 of 17.11.2022 – Harman International Industries/AB, para. 48.
2689. CJEU C-59/08 of 23.4.2009 – Copad, para. 43; C-324/08 of 15.10.2009 – Makro Zelfbedieningsgroothandel, para. 24; C-127/09 of 3.6.2010 – Coty Prestige Lancaster Group, para. 29; *see also* CJEU C-46/10 of 14.7.2011 – Viking Gas, para. 27.
2690. CJEU C-291/16 of 20.12.2017 – Schweppes/Red Paralela, para. 38.

fulfilled its function, within its own territorial field of application, of guaranteeing that the trade-marked goods originate from one single source.[2691]

That last condition is clearly not satisfied when, following the assignment of some national parallel trade marks to a third party, the proprietor, either acting alone or maintaining his coordinated trade mark strategy with that third party, has actively and deliberately continued to promote the appearance or image of a single global trade mark, thereby generating or increasing confusion on the part of the public concerned as to the commercial origin of goods bearing that mark. By that conduct, which results in the proprietor's trade mark no longer independently fulfilling its essential function within its own territorial field of application, the proprietor has himself compromised or distorted that function. Consequently, he may not rely on the necessity of protecting that function in order to oppose the import of identical goods bearing the same mark originating in another Member State where that mark is now owned by that third party.[2692]

It is for the national courts to assess whether this is the case, taking account of all the features of the individual situation in question.[2693]

In that context, it should none the less be noted that the mere fact that that proprietor continues, following the assignment, to evoke the historical geographical origin of the national parallel trade marks is not sufficient in that regard, even if he no longer holds the rights in respect of the territory in question and seeks to prohibit the import of goods bearing those marks and originating from that territory.[2694]

Article 7(1) TMD2008 must be interpreted as meaning that the consent of the proprietor of a trade mark to the marketing of goods bearing that mark carried out directly in the EEA by a third party who has no economic link to that proprietor may be implied, in so far as such consent is to be inferred from facts and circumstances prior to, simultaneous with or subsequent to the placing of the goods on the market in that area which, in the view of the national court, unequivocally demonstrate that the proprietor has renounced his exclusive rights.[2695]

Article 7(1) TMD2008 is to be interpreted as meaning that **a licensee** who puts goods bearing a trade mark on the market in disregard of a provision in a licence agreement does so without the consent of the proprietor of the trade mark where it is established that the provision in question is included in those listed in Article 8(2) TMD2008.[2696]

The licensor is able to control the quality of the licensee's goods by including in the licence agreement specific provisions requiring the licensee to comply with his instructions and enabling him to check such compliance.[2697]

2691. CJEU C-291/16 of 20.12.2017 – Schweppes/Red Paralela, para. 39, with reference to CJEU C-10/89 of 17.10.1990 – CNL-SUCAL/HAG, paras 17 and 18; C-9/93 of 22.6.1994 – IHT Internationale Heiztechnik/Ideal-Standard, paras 46 to 48.
2692. CJEU C-291/16 of 20.12.2017 – Schweppes/Red Paralela, para. 40.
2693. CJEU C-291/16 of 20.12.2017 – Schweppes/Red Paralela, para. 41.
2694. CJEU C-291/16 of 20.12.2017 – Schweppes/Red Paralela, para. 42.
2695. CJEU C-324/08 of 15.10.2009 – Makro Zelfbedieningsgroothandel, para. 35.
2696. CJEU C-59/08 of 23.4.2009 – Copad, para. 51.
2697. CJEU C-59/08 of 23.4.2009 – Copad, para. 44.

The possibility of control suffices for the trade mark to be able to fulfil its essential function, which is to offer a guarantee that all the goods bearing it have been manufactured under the control of a single undertaking which is responsible for their quality.[2698]

Consequently, where a licensee puts goods bearing the mark on the market, he must, as a rule, be considered to be doing so with the consent of the proprietor of the trade mark, for the purposes of Article 7(1) TMD2008.[2699]

Even though it follows that, in such circumstances, the proprietor of the trade mark cannot plead that the contract was wrongly implemented in order to invoke, in respect of the licensee, the rights conferred on him by the trade mark, the fact remains that the licence agreement does not constitute the absolute and unconditional consent of the proprietor of the trade mark to the licensee putting the goods bearing the trade mark on the market.[2700]

Article 8(2) TMD2008 expressly enables the proprietor of the mark to invoke the rights the trade mark confers on him against a licensee where the latter contravenes certain provisions in the licence agreement.[2701]

In addition, the **list of provisions set out in Article 8(2) TMD2008** is exhaustive.[2702]

Consequently, only the licensee's contravention of one of those clauses precludes exhaustion of the rights conferred by the trade mark on its proprietor, for the purposes of Article 7(1) TMD2008.[2703]

Where a licensee puts luxury goods on the market **in contravention** of a provision in the licence agreement, **but** must **nevertheless be considered** to have done so **with the consent** of the proprietor of the trade mark, the proprietor of the trade mark can rely on such a provision to oppose a resale of those goods on the basis of Article 7(2) TMD2008 only if it can be established that, taking into account the particular circumstances of the case, such resale damages the reputation of the trade mark.[2704]

Where a licensee sells goods to a discount store in contravention of a provision in the licence agreement, such as the one at issue in the main proceedings, a balance must be struck between, on the one hand, the legitimate interest of the proprietor of the trade mark covered by the licence agreement in being protected against a discount store which does not form part of the selective distribution network using that trade mark for commercial purposes in a manner which could damage the reputation of that trade mark and, on the other hand, the discount store's legitimate interest in being able to resell the goods in question by using methods which are customary in its sector of trade.[2705]

2698. CJEU C-59/08 of 23.4.2009 – Copad, para. 45.
2699. CJEU C-59/08 of 23.4.2009 – Copad, para. 46.
2700. CJEU C-59/08 of 23.4.2009 – Copad, para. 47.
2701. CJEU C-59/08 of 23.4.2009 – Copad, para. 48.
2702. CJEU C-59/08 of 23.4.2009 – Copad, para. 49.
2703. CJEU C-59/08 of 23.4.2009 – Copad, para. 50.
2704. CJEU C-59/08 of 23.4.2009 – Copad, para. 59.
2705. CJEU C-59/08 of 23.4.2009 – Copad, para. 56.

Therefore, should the national court find that sale by the licensee to a third party is unlikely to undermine the quality of the luxury goods bearing the trade mark, so that it must be considered that they were put on the market with the consent of the proprietor of the trade mark, it will be for that court to assess, taking into account the particular circumstances of each case, whether further commercialization of the luxury goods bearing the trade mark by the third party, using methods which are customary in its sector of trade, damages the reputation of that trade mark.[2706]

In this respect, it is necessary to take into consideration, in particular, the parties to whom the goods are resold and the specific circumstances in which the luxury goods are put on the market.[2707]

It is apparent from that case law and from the actual wording of Article 7 TMD2008 that the third party who receives that consent and who may therefore invoke the exhaustion of the exclusive right in respect of all the individual items of the goods covered by that consent which it puts on the market in the EEA may no longer invoke such exhaustion once the **consent is withdrawn**.[2708]

It is true, as borne out by the reference by the sixth recital in the preamble to the TMD to the national law on civil liability, that a national court may impose a penalty on the proprietor of a trade mark or order it to pay compensation for the damage suffered if it finds that that proprietor has **unlawfully withdrawn the consent** by which it allowed a third party to use signs which are identical to its marks. However, a finding that there has been such conduct cannot have the effect of prolonging, by a court decision and for an unspecified period, the shared use of those marks where the companies concerned no longer have the joint intention of sharing their use.[2709]

Article 5 TMD2008 precludes a proprietor of trade marks which, in a situation where there has been use shared with a third party, had consented to the use by that third party of signs which are identical to its marks in respect of certain goods in classes for which those marks are registered and which no longer consents to that use, from being deprived of any possibility of asserting the exclusive right conferred upon it by those marks against that third party and of itself exercising that exclusive right in respect of goods which are identical to those of that third party.[2710]

Article 101(1) TFEU must be interpreted as meaning that a **selective distribution system for luxury goods** designed, primarily, to preserve the luxury image of those goods complies with that provision to the extent that resellers are chosen on the basis of objective criteria of a qualitative nature that are laid down uniformly for all potential resellers and applied in a non-discriminatory fashion and that the criteria laid down do not go beyond what is necessary.[2711]

Article 101(1) TFEU must be interpreted as not precluding a contractual clause, such as that at issue in the main proceedings, which prohibits authorized distributors in a selective distribution system for luxury goods designed, primarily, to preserve the

2706. CJEU C-59/08 of 23.4.2009 – Copad, para. 57.
2707. CJEU C-59/08 of 23.4.2009 – Copad, para. 58.
2708. CJEU C-661/11 of 19.9.2013 – Martin Y Paz Diffusion, para. 57.
2709. CJEU C-661/11 of 19.9.2013 – Martin Y Paz Diffusion, para. 61.
2710. CJEU C-661/11 of 19.9.2013 – Martin Y Paz Diffusion, para. 62.
2711. CJEU C-230/16 of 6.12.2017 – Coty Germany/Parfümerie Akzente, para. 36.

luxury image of those goods from using, in a discernible manner, third-party platforms for the internet sale of the contract goods, on condition that that clause has the objective of preserving the luxury image of those goods, that it is laid down uniformly and not applied in a discriminatory fashion, and that it is proportionate in the light of the objective pursued, these being matters to be determined by the referring court.[2712]

Article 4 of Regulation No. 330/2010[2713] must be interpreted as meaning that, in circumstances such as those at issue in the main proceedings, the prohibition imposed on the members of a selective distribution system for luxury goods, which operate as distributors at the retail level of trade, of making use, in a discernible manner, of third-party undertakings for internet sales does not constitute a restriction of customers, within the meaning of Article 4(b) of that regulation, or a restriction of passive sales to end users, within the meaning of Article 4(c) of that regulation.[2714]

[E] Exceptions of the exhaustion

Article 7(2) TMD2008 provides that the owner of a trade mark may oppose the further commercialization of products where there is a legitimate reason for doing so, especially where the **condition of the products has been changed or impaired** since they were put on the market. The use of the word 'especially' shows that the case envisaged is given **only as an example**.[2715]

[1] Conditions of commercialization

The proprietor of a trade mark may not rely on Article 7(2) TMD2008 to oppose the use of the trade mark, by a **reseller** who habitually markets articles of the same kind, but not necessarily of the same quality, as the trade marked goods, in ways customary in the reseller's sector of trade, for the purpose of bringing to the public's attention the further commercialization of those goods, unless it is established that, given the specific circumstances of the case, the use of the trade mark for this purpose seriously damages the reputation of the trade mark.[2716]

The **damage** done **to the reputation of a trade mark** may, in principle, be a legitimate reason, within the meaning of Article 7(2) TMD2008, allowing the proprietor to oppose further commercialization of goods which have been put on the market in the Community by him or with his consent. According to the case law of the Court concerning the repackaging of trade marked goods, the owner of a trade mark has a legitimate interest, related to the specific subject matter of the trade mark right, in being

2712. CJEU C-230/16 of 6.12.2017 – Coty Germany/Parfümerie Akzente, para. 58.
2713. Commission Regulation (EU) No 330/2010 of 20 April 2010 on the application of Article 101(3) of the Treaty on the Functioning of the European Union to categories of vertical agreements and concerted practices.
2714. CJEU C-230/16 of 6.12.2017 – Coty Germany/Parfümerie Akzente, para. 69.
2715. CJEU C-427/93, C-429/93 and C-436/93 of 11.7.1996 – Bristol-Myers Squibb and Others/Paranova, para. 39; C-337/95 of 4.11.1997 – Parfums Christian Dior/Evora, para. 42; C-59/08 of 23.4.2009 – Copad, para. 54; C-46/10 of 14.7.2011 – Viking Gas, para. 36.
2716. CJEU C-337/95 of 4.11.1997 – Parfums Christian Dior/Evora, para. 48.

able to oppose the commercialization of those goods if the presentation of the repackaged goods is liable to damage the reputation of the trade mark.[2717]

Where a reseller makes use of a trade mark in order to bring the public's attention to further commercialization of trade marked goods, a balance must be struck between the legitimate interest of the trade mark owner in being protected against resellers using his trade mark for advertising in a manner which could damage the reputation of the trade mark and the reseller's legitimate interest in being able to resell the goods in question by using advertising methods which are customary in his sector of trade.[2718]

As regards the instant case, which concerns prestigious **luxury goods**, the reseller must not act unfairly in relation to the legitimate interests of the trade mark owner. He must therefore endeavour to prevent his advertising from affecting the value of the trade mark by detracting from the allure and prestigious image of the goods in question and from their aura of luxury.[2719]

In this respect, it is necessary to take into consideration, in particular, the parties to whom the goods are resold and the specific circumstances in which the luxury goods are put on the market.[2720]

However, the fact that a reseller, who habitually markets articles of the same kind but not necessarily of the same quality, uses for trade marked goods the **modes of advertising** which are customary in his trade sector, even if they are not the same as those used by the trade mark owner himself or by his approved retailers, does not constitute a legitimate reason, within the meaning of Article 7(2) TMD2008, allowing the owner to oppose that advertising, unless it is established that, given the specific circumstances of the case, the use of the trade mark in the reseller's advertising seriously damages the reputation of the trade mark.[2721]

For example, such damage could occur if, in an advertising leaflet distributed by him, the reseller did not take care to avoid putting the trade mark in a context which might seriously detract from the image which the trade mark owner has succeeded in creating around his trade mark.[2722]

The fact that the trade mark is used in a **reseller's advertising** in such a way that it may give rise to the impression that there is a commercial connection between the reseller and the trade mark proprietor, and in particular that the reseller's business is affiliated to the trade mark proprietor's distribution network or that there is a special relationship between the two undertakings, may constitute a legitimate reason within the meaning of Article 7(2) TMD2008.[2723]

Such advertising is not essential to the further commercialization of goods put on the Community market under the trade mark by its proprietor or with his consent or,

2717. CJEU C-337/95 of 4.11.1997 – Parfums Christian Dior/Evora, para. 43.
2718. CJEU C-337/95 of 4.11.1997 – Parfums Christian Dior/Evora, para. 44.
2719. CJEU C-337/95 of 4.11.1997 – Parfums Christian Dior/Evora, para. 45; *see also* CJEU C-348/04 of 26.4.2007 – Boehringer Ingelheim and Others (II), para. 43; C-59/08 of 23.4.2009 – Copad, para. 55.
2720. CJEU C-59/08 of 23.4.2009 – Copad, para. 58.
2721. CJEU C-337/95 of 4.11.1997 – Parfums Christian Dior/Evora, para. 46; C-558/08 of 8.7.2010 – Portakabin, para. 79.
2722. CJEU C-337/95 of 4.11.1997 – Parfums Christian Dior/Evora, para. 47.
2723. CJEU C-63/97 of 23.2.1999 – BMW, para. 51.

therefore, to the purpose of the exhaustion rule laid down in Article 7 TMD2008. Moreover, it is contrary to the obligation to act fairly in relation to the legitimate interests of the trade mark owner and it affects the value of the trade mark by taking unfair advantage of its distinctive character or repute. It is also incompatible with the specific object of a trade mark which is, according to the case law of the Court, to protect the proprietor against competitors wishing to take advantage of the status and reputation of the trade mark.[2724]

If, on the other hand, there is no risk that the public will be led to believe that there is a **commercial connection** between the reseller and the trade mark proprietor, the mere fact that the reseller derives an advantage from using the trade mark in that advertisements for the sale of goods covered by the mark, which are in other respects honest and fair, lend an aura of quality to his own business does not constitute a legitimate reason within the meaning of Article 7(2) TMD2008.[2725]

Circumstances in which a trade mark proprietor is, pursuant to Article 5(1) TMD2008, entitled to prohibit use by an advertiser of a sign identical with, or similar to, that trade mark as a **keyword** - that is to say, circumstances in which use of that sign by the advertiser does not enable normally informed and reasonably attentive internet users, or enables them only with difficulty, to ascertain whether the goods or services referred to by the ad originate from the proprietor of that mark or from an undertaking economically linked to it or, on the contrary, originate from a third party - correspond to a situation in which Article 7(2) TMD2008 applies and in which, accordingly, the advertiser cannot rely on the exhaustion rule laid down in Article 7(1) TMD2008.[2726]

The resale by a third party of **second-hand goods**, which had originally been placed on the market under the trade mark by the proprietor of that mark or by a person authorized by him, constitutes a 'further commercialization of the goods' within the meaning of Article 7 TMD2008, and that use of that mark for the purposes of that resale can therefore be prohibited by that proprietor only where there are 'legitimate reasons', within the meaning of Article 7(2), such as to justify his opposition to that commercialization.[2727]

A reseller who sells second-hand BMW cars and who genuinely has specialized or is a specialist in the sale of those vehicles cannot in practice communicate such information to his customers without using the BMW mark. In consequence, such an informative use of the BMW mark is necessary to guarantee the right of resale under Article 7 TMD2008 and does not take unfair advantage of the distinctive character or repute of that trade mark.[2728]

The sale of second-hand goods under a trade mark is a well-established form of business with which the average consumer will be familiar. Therefore, it cannot be held merely on the basis of the fact that an advertiser uses another person's trade mark

2724. CJEU C-63/97 of 23.2.1999 - BMW, para. 52.
2725. CJEU C-63/97 of 23.2.1999 - BMW, para. 53; C-558/08 of 8.7.2010 - Portakabin, paras 80 and 89; C-46/10 of 14.7.2011 - Viking Gas, para. 37.
2726. CJEU C-558/08 of 8.7.2010 - Portakabin, para. 81.
2727. CJEU C-558/08 of 8.7.2010 - Portakabin, para. 76.
2728. CJEU C-63/97 of 23.2.1999 - BMW, para. 54; C-558/08 of 8.7.2010 - Portakabin, para. 90.

with additional wording indicating that the relevant goods are being resold, such as 'used' or 'second-hand', that the ad creates the impression that the reseller and the trade mark proprietor are economically linked or that the ad is seriously detrimental to the reputation of that mark.[2729]

In those circumstances, in which a reseller specializes in the resale of goods under another person's trade mark, the reseller cannot be prohibited from using that mark in order to advertise its resale activities which include – apart from the sale of second-hand goods under that mark – the sale of other second-hand goods, unless the resale of those other goods risks, in the light of their volume, their presentation or their poor quality, seriously damaging the image which the proprietor has succeeded in creating for its mark.[2730]

Where the reseller, without the consent of a trade mark proprietor, removes that trade mark from the goods ('**de-branding**') and replaces it with a label bearing the reseller's name, with the result that the trade mark of the manufacturer of the goods in question is entirely concealed, the trade mark proprietor is entitled to prevent the reseller from using that mark to advertise that resale. In such a case, damage is caused to the essential function of the trade mark, which is to indicate and guarantee the origin of the goods, and the consumer is prevented from distinguishing the goods originating from the proprietor and those originating from the reseller or other third parties.[2731]

Whether advertising may create the impression that there is a commercial connection between the reseller and the trade mark proprietor is a question of fact for the **national court** to decide in the light of the circumstances of each case.[2732]

[2] Adverse effects on the original condition of the product

Under Article 15(2) of Regulation 2017/1001 and Article 15(2) of Directive 2015/2436, the proprietor of a trade mark may provide evidence of legitimate reasons to oppose subsequent commercialization of goods bearing his or her trade mark, especially where the condition of the goods is changed or impaired after they have been put on the market. That ability to oppose, which amounts to a derogation from the fundamental principle of the free movement of goods, has the sole objective of safeguarding rights which form part of the specific subject matter of the mark, as understood in the light of its essential function (*see*, to that effect, judgment of 23 April 2002, Boehringer Ingelheim and Others, C-143/00, EU:C:2002:246, paragraph 28).[2733]

It should be clarified at the outset that the concept of adverse effects on the original condition of the product refers to the condition of the product inside the packaging.[2734]

2729. CJEU C-558/08 of 8.7.2010 – Portakabin, paras 84 and 93.
2730. CJEU C-558/08 of 8.7.2010 – Portakabin, paras 91 and 93.
2731. CJEU C-558/08 of 8.7.2010 – Portakabin, paras 86 and 93.
2732. CJEU C-63/97 of 23.2.1999 – BMW, para. 55; C-558/08 of 8.7.2010 – Portakabin, para. 82.
2733. CJEU C-197/21 of 27.10.2022 – Soda-Club (CO2) a.o./MySoda, para. 34, with reference to CJEU C-143/00 of 23.4.2002 – Boehringer Ingelheim and Others (I), para. 28.
2734. CJEU C-71 to 73/94 of 11.7.1996 – Eurim-Pharm Arzneimittel/Beiersdorf and Others, para. 48; C-427/93, C-429/93 and C-436/93 of 11.7.1996 – Bristol-Myers Squibb and Others/Paranova, para. 58; C-232/94 of 11.7.1996 – MPA Pharma/Rhône-Poulenc Pharma, para. 30.

However, where the parallel importer has added to the packaging an extra article from a source other than the trade mark owner, he must ensure that the origin of the extra article is indicated in such a way as to dispel any impression that the trade mark owner is responsible for it.[2735]

[3] Distribution without packaging

Article 5 TMD2008 and Article 9 CTMR must be interpreted as meaning that the proprietor of a trade mark may, by virtue of the exclusive right conferred by the mark, oppose the resale of goods, on the ground that the person reselling the goods has removed their packaging, where the consequence of that removal is that essential information, such as information relating to the identity of the manufacturer or the person responsible for marketing the cosmetic product, is missing. Where the removal of the packaging has not resulted in the absence of that information, the trade mark proprietor may nevertheless oppose the resale of an unboxed perfume or cosmetic product bearing his trade mark, if he establishes that the removal of the packaging has damaged the image of the product and, hence, the reputation of the trade mark.[2736]

Under Article 6(1) of Directive 76/768, cosmetic products may be marketed only if the container and packaging mention, *inter alia*, the identity of the manufacturer or the person responsible for marketing the product, the composition of the product (content and list of ingredients), the use of the product (function and particular precautions to be observed in use) and preservation of the product (date of minimum durability).[2737]

In the first place, having regard to the wide variety of perfumes and cosmetics, the question whether the removal of the packaging of such goods **harms their image** - and thus the reputation of the trade mark that they bear - must be examined on a case-by-case basis. Where perfumes or cosmetics are displayed without packaging, that may sometimes effectively convey the image of the product as a prestige or luxury product, whilst, in other cases, removing the packaging has precisely the effect of harming that image.[2738]

Such damage may occur when the packaging is as important as, or more important than, the bottle or the container in the presentation of the image of the product created by the trade mark proprietor and his authorized distributors. It may also be the case that the absence of some or all the information required by Article 6(1) of Directive 76/768 harms the product's image. It is for the trade mark proprietor to establish the existence of the constituent elements of such harm.[2739]

In the second place, a trade mark, the essential function of which is to provide the consumer with an assurance as to the **identity of the product's origin**, serves in

2735. CJEU C-427/93, C-429/93 and C-436/93 of 11.7.1996 - Bristol-Myers Squibb and Others/ Paranova, para. 73.
2736. CJEU C-324/09 of 12.7.2011 - L'Oréal, para. 83.
2737. CJEU C-324/09 of 12.7.2011 - L'Oréal, para. 76.
2738. CJEU C-324/09 of 12.7.2011 - L'Oréal, para. 78.
2739. CJEU C-324/09 of 12.7.2011 - L'Oréal, para. 79.

particular to guarantee that all the goods bearing the mark have been manufactured or supplied under the control of a single undertaking which is responsible for their quality.[2740]

When certain information, which is required as a matter of law, such as information relating to the identity of the manufacturer or the person responsible for marketing the cosmetic product, is missing, the trade mark's function of indicating origin is impaired in that the mark is denied its essential function of guaranteeing that the goods that it designates are supplied under the control of a single undertaking which is responsible for their quality.[2741]

In the third and final place, the question of whether or not the offer for sale, or the sale, of trade marked goods without their packaging and thus without certain information required under Article 6(1) of Directive 76/768 is a **criminal offence** under national law does not affect the applicability of EU rules concerning intellectual property protection.[2742]

[4] Removal of identification numbers

Removal of the identification numbers might prove necessary to prevent artificial partitioning of the markets between Member States caused by difficulties for persons involved in parallel trade in obtaining supplies from distributors of the trade mark owner and others for fear of sanctions being imposed by the producers in the event of sales to such persons. Even if such conduct on the part of the producers would be in breach of the Treaty rules on competition, it cannot be excluded that identification numbers have been placed on products by producers to enable them to reconstruct the itinerary of their products, with the purpose of preventing their dealers from supplying persons carrying on parallel trade.[2743]

It must also be acknowledged, however, that for the producers, application of identification numbers may be necessary to comply with a legal obligation, in particular under Directive 89/396/EEC,[2744] or to realize other important objectives which are legitimate from the point of view of Community law, such as the recall of faulty products and measures to combat counterfeiting.[2745]

In those circumstances where identification numbers have been applied for purposes such as those mentioned in the preceding paragraph, the fact that an owner of trade mark rights makes use of those rights to prevent a third party from removing and then reaffixing or replacing labels bearing his trade mark in order to eliminate those numbers does not contribute to artificial partitioning of the markets between

2740. CJEU C-324/09 of 12.7.2011 – L'Oréal, para. 80.
2741. CJEU C-324/09 of 12.7.2011 – L'Oréal, para. 81.
2742. CJEU C-324/09 of 12.7.2011 – L'Oréal, para. 82.
2743. CJEU C-349/95 of 11.11.1997 – Loendersloot/Ballantine & Son and Others, para. 40.
2744. Council Directive 89/396/EEC of 14 Jun. 1989 on indications or marks identifying the lot to which a foodstuff belongs (OJ 1989 L 186, p. 21).
2745. CJEU C-349/95 of 11.11.1997 – Loendersloot/Ballantine & Son and Others, para. 41.

Member States. In such situations, there is no reason to limit the rights which the trade mark owner may rely on under Article 36[2746] of the Treaty.[2747]

Where it is established that the identification numbers have been applied for purposes which are legitimate from the point of view of Community law, but are also used by the trade mark owner to enable him to detect weaknesses in his sales organization and thus combat parallel trade in his products, it is under the Treaty provisions on competition that those engaged in parallel trade should seek protection against action of the latter type.[2748]

[5] Repackaging

Article 9(2) and Article 13 CTMR, and Article 5(1) and Article 7 TMD2008, read in the light of Articles 34 and 36 TFEU, must be interpreted as meaning that the proprietor of the trade mark of a reference medicinal product and the trade mark of a **generic medicinal** product may oppose the placing on the market of a Member State, by a parallel importer, of that generic medicinal product imported from another Member State, where that medicinal product has been repackaged in new outer packaging to which the trade mark of the corresponding reference medicinal product has been affixed, unless, first, the two medicinal products are identical in all respects and, second, the replacement of the trade mark satisfies the conditions laid down in the judgment[2749] *Bristol-Myers Squibb and Others*, in the judgment[2750] *Boehringer Ingelheim and Others*, and in the judgment[2751] *Junek Europ-Vertrieb*.[2752]

As a preliminary point, it should be borne in mind that, under Article 9(1) CTMR and Article 5(1) TMD2008, the registration of a trade mark confers on its proprietor exclusive rights which, under Article 9(2)(a) of that regulation and Article 5(1)(a) of that directive, entitle that proprietor to prevent any third party without its consent from using in the course of trade any sign which is identical with that trade mark in relation to goods or services which are identical with those for which the trade mark was registered.[2753]

Article 9(3) CTMR and Article 5(3) TMD2008 list, non-exhaustively, several types of use which the trade mark proprietor may prohibit.[2754]

In particular, it is apparent from Article 9(3) CTMR and from Article 5(3) TMD2008 that the proprietor may, *inter alia*, prevent all third parties from affixing the

2746. Article 30 EC.
2747. CJEU C-349/95 of 11.11.1997 – Loendersloot/Ballantine & Son and Others, para. 42.
2748. CJEU C-349/95 of 11.11.1997 – Loendersloot/Ballantine & Son and Others, para. 43.
2749. CJEU C-427/93, C-429/93 and C-436/93 of 11.7.1996 – Bristol-Myers Squibb and Others/Paranova, para. 79.
2750. CJEU C-348/04 of 26.4.2007 – Boehringer Ingelheim and Others (II), para. 32.
2751. CJEU C-642/16 of 17.5.2018 – Junek Europ-Vertrieb/Lohmann & Rauscher International, para. 28.
2752. CJEU C-253/20 and C-254/20 of 17.11.2022 – Impexeco/Novartis a.o., para. 74.
2753. CJEU C-253/20 and C-254/20 of 17.11.2022 – Impexeco/Novartis a.o., para. 43.
2754. CJEU C-253/20 and C-254/20 of 17.11.2022 – Impexeco/Novartis a.o., para. 44, with reference to CJEU C-129/17 of 25.7.2018 – Mitsubishi Shoji Kaisha a.o./Duma Forklifts a.o., para. 38.

sign in question to goods or to their packaging and from importing and marketing the goods under that sign.[2755]

The repackaging of a product bearing a mark carried out by a third party without the authorization of the proprietor is likely to create real risks for the guarantee of origin of that product.[2756]

That being so, under Article 13(1) CTMR and Article 7(1) TMD2008, a trade mark is not to entitle the proprietor to prohibit its use in relation to goods which have been put on the market in the European Union under that trade mark by the proprietor or with its consent. These provisions are intended to reconcile the fundamental interest in protecting trade mark rights, on the one hand, with the fundamental interest in the free movement of goods within the internal market, on the other.[2757]

It is necessary to take into account the provisions of secondary EU law laid down in Article 9(2) and Article 13 CTMR, and Article 5(1) and Article 7 TMD2008, since they concern the rights of proprietors of a trade mark and the question of the exhaustion of the rights conferred by that trade mark.[2758]

In that context, it must be borne in mind that although Article 13 CTMR and Article 7 TMD2008, worded in general terms, comprehensively regulate the question of the exhaustion of the rights conferred by a trade mark and although where provision is made for the harmonization of measures necessary to protect the interests referred to in Article 36 TFEU, any national measure relating thereto must be assessed in relation to the provisions of that regulation or that directive and not Articles 34 to 36 TFEU, that regulation and that directive, like any secondary EU legislation, must be interpreted in the light of the TFEU rules on the free movement of goods and of Article 36 TFEU in particular.[2759]

In accordance with the case law of the Court, a trade mark owner which markets in different Member States an identical medicinal product under different trade marks according to the Member State in which the product is marketed also contributes to artificial partitioning of the markets between Member States if it opposes the replacement of the trade mark used in the exporting Member State with that used by that proprietor in the importing Member State, where that replacement is objectively

2755. CJEU C-253/20 and C-254/20 of 17.11.2022 – Impexeco/Novartis a.o., para. 45.

2756. CJEU C-143/00 of 23.4.2002 – Boehringer Ingelheim and Others (I), para. 29; C-348/04 of 26.4.2007 – Boehringer Ingelheim and Others (II), para. 15; C-642/16 of 17.5.2018 – Junek Europ-Vertrieb/Lohmann & Rauscher International, para. 23; C-147/20 of 17.11.2022 – Novartis Pharma/Abacus Medicine, para. 45; C-204/20 of 17.11.2022 – Bayer Intellectual Property/kohlpharma, para. 56; C-224/20 of 17.11.2022 – Merck Sharp & Dohme a.o./Abacus a.o., para. 46; C-253/20 and C-254/20 of 17.11.2022 – Impexeco/Novartis a.o., para. 47.

2757. CJEU C-147/20 of 17.11.2022 – Novartis Pharma/Abacus Medicine, para. 46; C-204/20 of 17.11.2022 – Bayer Intellectual Property/kohlpharma, para. 57; C-224/20 of 17.11.2022 – Merck Sharp & Dohme a.o./Abacus a.o., para. 47; C-253/20 and C-254/20 of 17.11.2022 – Impexeco/Novartis a.o., para. 48, each with reference to CJEU C-291/16 of 20.12.2017 – Schweppes/Red Paralela, para. 35.

2758. CJEU C-253/20 and C-254/20 of 17.11.2022 – Impexeco/Novartis a.o., para. 41.

2759. CJEU C-253/20 and C-254/20 of 17.11.2022 – Impexeco/Novartis a.o., para. 49; C-224/20 of 17.11.2022 – Merck Sharp & Dohme a.o./Abacus a.o., para. 48.

necessary in order for that medicinal product to be marketed in the importing Member State by the parallel importer.[2760]

In the present case, however, the disputes in the main proceedings are characterized by the fact that the medicinal products being traded in parallel are generic medicinal products, whereas the trade marks affixed to the new outer packaging of those medicinal products by the parallel importers concerned are the trade marks of the corresponding reference medicinal products.[2761]

In those circumstances, it is necessary, in the first place, to examine whether those medicinal products may be regarded as being identical, for the purposes of the case law relating to the exhaustion of the trade mark rights, referred to above.[2762]

In that regard, it should be noted, first of all, that Article 10(2)(b) of Directive 2001/83,[2763] as amended by Directive 2004/27,[2764] defines a generic medicinal product as 'a medicinal product which has the same qualitative and quantitative composition in active substances and the same pharmaceutical form as the reference medicinal product, and whose bioequivalence with the reference medicinal product has been demonstrated by appropriate bioavailability studies'.[2765]

Next, as is clear from the wording of the second and third sentences of Article 10(2)(b), the composition of the generic medicinal product may differ from that of the reference medicinal product as regards the pharmaceutical form, the chemical form of the active substance and its excipients.[2766]

Finally, it must be stated that, for medical reasons, it may be contraindicated to replace, during treatment, a medicinal product with an equivalent medicinal product, whether it is a reference medicinal product or a generic medicinal product. That is the case, in particular, with regard to medicinal products with a 'narrow therapeutic margin'.[2767]

In those circumstances, to consider that, where they are therapeutically equivalent, a reference medicinal product and its generic counterpart are identical products for the purposes of the case law referred to above could mislead health professionals and patients as regards the exact composition of the medicinal product concerned, with potentially serious consequences for the health of those patients.[2768]

Therefore, only a medicinal product which is identical in all respects to another medicinal product can be repackaged in new outer packaging bearing the trade mark of the other medicinal product.[2769]

2760. CJEU C-253/20 and C-254/20 of 17.11.2022 – Impexeco/Novartis a.o., para. 57, with reference to CJEU C-379/97 of 12.10.1999 – Upjohn, para. 19 and 38 to 40.
2761. CJEU C-253/20 and C-254/20 of 17.11.2022 – Impexeco/Novartis a.o., para. 58.
2762. CJEU C-253/20 and C-254/20 of 17.11.2022 – Impexeco/Novartis a.o., para. 59.
2763. Directive 2001/83/EC of the European Parliament and of the Council of 6 November 2001 on the Community code relating to medicinal products for human use (OJ 2001 L 311, p. 67).
2764. Directive 2004/27/EC of the European Parliament and of the Council of 31 March 2004 (OJ 2004 L 136, p. 34).
2765. CJEU C-253/20 and C-254/20 of 17.11.2022 – Impexeco/Novartis a.o., para. 60.
2766. CJEU C-253/20 and C-254/20 of 17.11.2022 – Impexeco/Novartis a.o., para. 61.
2767. CJEU C-253/20 and C-254/20 of 17.11.2022 – Impexeco/Novartis a.o., para. 62, corrected version.
2768. CJEU C-253/20 and C-254/20 of 17.11.2022 – Impexeco/Novartis a.o., para. 63.
2769. CJEU C-253/20 and C-254/20 of 17.11.2022 – Impexeco/Novartis a.o., para. 64.

That may be the case, in particular, for a reference medicinal product and a generic medicinal product manufactured by the same entity or by economically linked entities and which, in actual fact, constitute one and the same product marketed under two different sets of rules.[2770]

In such a case, neither the difference in the legal rules applicable to those medicinal products nor the different way in which they are perceived by health professionals or patients can justify the proprietor of the trade marks concerned being able to oppose the replacement of the trade mark which it uses in the exporting Member State by that which it affixes to the medicinal products which it markets in the importing Member State if it is established that that replacement is objectively necessary in order for those medicinal products to be marketed in the latter Member State. Otherwise, the proprietor would be able to contribute to an artificial partitioning of the markets between Member States by marketing an identical medicinal product sometimes as a reference medicinal product and sometimes as a generic medicinal product.[2771]

In the present case, the referring court considers that the generic medicinal product at issue in each of the cases in the main proceedings is identical to the corresponding reference medicinal product.[2772]

Accordingly, it is necessary, in the second place, to examine whether, in circumstances such as those in the main proceedings, the opposition of the trade mark proprietor to the replacement of the trade mark of a generic medicinal product placed on the market in the exporting Member State by that of the corresponding reference medicinal product marketed in the importing Member State constitutes an obstacle to the effective access of the medicinal product concerned to the market of the latter Member State.[2773]

That would be the case if the medicinal product concerned could not be marketed in the importing Member State under its trade mark of origin, thereby making the replacement of that trade mark objectively necessary in order to ensure the free movement of that medicinal product in the internal market.[2774]

In such a situation, the proprietor of a trade mark cannot oppose the replacement of that trade mark by a parallel importer if the latter is able to establish that the circumstances prevailing at the time of marketing the product concerned make it objectively necessary to replace the trade mark of origin by that of the importing Member State for the purpose of placing that product on the market in that Member State and if, moreover, that replacement is carried out in such a way that the legitimate interests of the proprietor are respected, that is to say, under the conditions set out in

2770. CJEU C-253/20 and C-254/20 of 17.11.2022 – Impexeco/Novartis a.o., para. 65.
2771. CJEU C-253/20 and C-254/20 of 17.11.2022 – Impexeco/Novartis a.o., para. 66.
2772. CJEU C-253/20 and C-254/20 of 17.11.2022 – Impexeco/Novartis a.o., para. 67.
2773. CJEU C-253/20 and C-254/20 of 17.11.2022 – Impexeco/Novartis a.o., para. 68.
2774. CJEU C-253/20 and C-254/20 of 17.11.2022 – Impexeco/Novartis a.o., para. 69.

the judgment[2775] *Bristol-Myers Squibb and Others*, in the judgment[2776] *Boehringer Ingelheim and Others*, and in the judgment[2777] *Junek Europ-Vertrieb*.[2778]

Conversely, where the parallel importer is able to market that product under its trade mark of origin by adapting, where appropriate, the packaging in order to satisfy the market requirements of the importing Member State, the condition of necessity referred to above is not satisfied. In such a case, the free movement of goods, which underpins the rule on the exhaustion of trade mark rights in trade between Member States, is not, in essence, threatened and cannot therefore take precedence over the legitimate interests of the trade mark proprietor.[2779]

Furthermore, it should be noted that a Member State cannot, in principle, refuse to grant a parallel import licence for a generic medicinal product where the corresponding reference medicinal product has marketing authorization in that Member State, unless such a refusal is justified by considerations relating to the protection of health and life of humans. Consequently, the condition of necessity referred to above cannot be satisfied where a generic medicinal product corresponds in every respect to the reference medicinal product covered by that authorization, given that, in such a situation, the parallel importer must be regarded as being able to market the generic medicinal product under its mark of origin.[2780]

Finally, the right of a trade mark proprietor to oppose the marketing, under that trade mark, of products repackaged by a parallel importer cannot be limited where the replacement of the trade mark of origin by another trade mark of the proprietor is exclusively motivated by the pursuit of an economic advantage, as is the case, in particular, where an economic operator seeks to take advantage of the reputation of the trade mark of a reference medicinal product or to place a product in a more profitable category.[2781]

Article 10(2) and Article 15 TMD must be interpreted as meaning that the trade mark proprietor is entitled to **oppose** the marketing, by a parallel importer, of a medicinal product repackaged in new outer packaging to which that trade mark is affixed where it is **objectively possible to relabel** the medicinal product concerned in compliance with the requirements provided for in Article 47a of Directive 2001/83 and where the medicinal product thus relabelled could actually access the market of the Member State of importation.[2782]

2775. CJEU C-427/93, C-429/93 and C-436/93 of 11.7.1996 – Bristol-Myers Squibb and Others/ Paranova, para. 79.
2776. CJEU C-348/04 of 26.4.2007 – Boehringer Ingelheim and Others (II), para. 32.
2777. CJEU C-642/16 of 17.5.2018 – Junek Europ-Vertrieb/Lohmann & Rauscher International, para. 28.
2778. CJEU C-253/20 and C-254/20 of 17.11.2022 – Impexeco/Novartis a.o., para. 70, with reference to CJEU C-379/97 of 12.10.1999 – Upjohn, paras 42 et seq.; C-400/09 and C-207/10 of 28.7.2011 – Orifarm, para. 24.
2779. CJEU C-253/20 and C-254/20 of 17.11.2022 – Impexeco/Novartis a.o., para. 71.
2780. CJEU C-253/20 and C-254/20 of 17.11.2022 – Impexeco/Novartis a.o., para. 72, with further proof.
2781. CJEU C-253/20 and C-254/20 of 17.11.2022 – Impexeco/Novartis a.o., para. 73.
2782. CJEU C-204/20 of 17.11.2022 – Bayer Intellectual Property/kohlpharma, para. 68.

Article 9(2) and Article 15 EUTMR must be interpreted as meaning that the proprietor of an EU trade mark is not entitled to oppose the marketing by a parallel importer of a repackaged medicinal product in a new outer packaging bearing that mark, where the **replacement of the anti-tampering device** of the original outer packaging of that medicinal product carried out in accordance with Article 47a(1) of Directive 2001/83 **would leave visible traces** of opening on that packaging and where those traces would cause such strong resistance on the part of a significant proportion of consumers on the market of the Member State of importation or on a substantial part of that market to medicinal products repackaged in that way that it would constitute an obstacle to effective access to that market, which must be established on a case-by-case basis.[2783]

Article 10(2) and Article 15 TMD must be interpreted as meaning that the trade mark proprietor is entitled to **oppose** the marketing, by a parallel importer, of a medicinal product repackaged in new outer packaging to which that trade mark is affixed, where the **visible traces of opening** of the original outer packaging which, where applicable, would result from relabelling of that medicinal product would be clearly attributable to the repackaging thus carried out by that parallel importer, **unless** those traces give rise, on the market of the Member State of importation or on a significant part of that market, to such strong resistance on the part of a significant proportion of consumers to medicinal products repackaged in that way as to constitute a barrier to effective access to that market, which must be established on a case-by-case basis.[2784]

Article 9(2) and Article 15 EUTMR and Article 10(2) and Article 15 TMD, read in conjunction with Articles 34 and 36 TFEU, must be interpreted as meaning that the proprietor of a trade mark is entitled to oppose the marketing, by a parallel importer, of a medicinal product repackaged in **new outer packaging** to which that trade mark is affixed where the **replacement of the anti-tampering device** of the original outer packaging carried out in accordance with Article 47a(1) of Directive 2001/83[2785] would leave visible or tangible traces of that original outer packaging having been opened, provided that:

- there is no doubt that those traces of opening are attributable to the repackaging of that medicinal product by that parallel importer; and
- those traces do not cause, on the market of the Member State of importation or on a substantial part of it, such strong resistance from a significant proportion of consumers to the medicinal products repackaged in that way that it would constitute a barrier to effective access to that market.[2786]

2783. CJEU C-147/20 of 17.11.2022 – Novartis Pharma/Abacus Medicine, para. 74.
2784. CJEU C-204/20 of 17.11.2022 – Bayer Intellectual Property/kohlpharma, para. 86.
2785. Directive 2001/83/EC of the European Parliament and of the Council of 6 November 2001 on the Community code relating to medicinal products for human use (OJ L 311, 28.11.2001, p. 67–128).
2786. CJEU C-224/20 of 17.11.2022 – Merck Sharp & Dohme a.o./Abacus a.o., para. 79.

The concept of 'repackaging', within the meaning of that case law, includes relabelling.[2787]

According to the case law of the Court, the condition in question that packaging be necessary concerns both the actual fact of repackaging the product and the choice between new packaging and relabelling. In so far as the recognition of the right of a parallel trader to market in new packaging a product bearing a trade mark without the authorization of the proprietor of that trade mark amounts to giving the parallel trader a licence normally reserved to the proprietor, namely a licence to affix that trade mark to that new packaging, such repackaging in new packaging constitutes a greater interference with the prerogatives of that proprietor than the marketing of the product in its relabelled original packaging.[2788]

In that regard, it should be borne in mind that, as is apparent from recitals 2 and 3 of Directive 2011/62,[2789] read in conjunction with recital 1 of Delegated Regulation 2016/161,[2790] the EU legislature adopted that directive in order to address the increasing threat to human health constituted by falsified medicinal products by introducing, in Directive 2001/83, measures to prevent the entry of falsified medicinal products in the legal supply chain.[2791]

Directive 2011/62 thus inserted into Article 54 of Directive 2001/83 a point (o) pursuant to which the outer packaging or, where there is no outer packaging, the immediate packaging of medicinal products other than radiopharmaceuticals referred to in Article 54a(1) of that directive must be equipped with safety features enabling wholesale distributors and persons authorized or entitled to supply medicinal products to the public to verify the authenticity of the medicinal product concerned, to identify individual packs and to verify whether the outer packaging of that medicinal product has been tampered with.[2792]

Pursuant to Article 54a(2) of Directive 2001/83, Delegated Regulation 2016/161 establishes the detailed rules for those safety features. Recital 1 of that delegated regulation identifies two types of safety features, namely: (i) a unique identifier and (ii) an anti-tampering device. An anti-tampering device is defined in Article 3(2) of that

2787. CJEU C-224/20 of 17.11.2022 – Merck Sharp & Dohme a.o./Abacus a.o., para. 46, with reference to CJEU C-348/04 of 26.4.2007 – Boehringer Ingelheim and Others (II), para. 28; C-642/16 of 17.5.2018 – Junek Europ-Vertrieb/Lohmann & Rauscher International, para. 30.
2788. CJEU C-147/20 of 17.11.2022 – Novartis Pharma/Abacus Medicine, para. 54; C-204/20 of 17.11.2022 – Bayer Intellectual Property/kohlpharma, para. 65; C-224/20 of 17.11.2022 – Merck Sharp & Dohme a.o./Abacus a.o., para. 56, each with reference to CJEU C-348/04 of 26.4.2007 – Boehringer Ingelheim and Others (II), para. 38.
2789. Directive 2011/62/EU of the European Parliament and of the Council of 8 June 2011 amending Directive 2001/83/EC on the Community code relating to medicinal products for human use, as regards the prevention of the entry into the legal supply chain of falsified medicinal products Text with EEA relevance (OJ L 174, 1.7.2011, p. 74–87).
2790. Commission Delegated Regulation (EU) 2016/161 of 2 October 2015 supplementing Directive 2001/83/EC of the European Parliament and of the Council by laying down detailed rules for the safety features appearing on the packaging of medicinal products for human use (OJ L 32, 9.2.2016, p. 1–27).
2791. CJEU C-147/20 of 17.11.2022 – Novartis Pharma/Abacus Medicine, para. 57; C-224/20 of 17.11.2022 – Merck Sharp & Dohme a.o./Abacus a.o., para. 58.
2792. CJEU C-147/20 of 17.11.2022 – Novartis Pharma/Abacus Medicine, para. 58; C-224/20 of 17.11.2022 – Merck Sharp & Dohme a.o./Abacus a.o., para. 59.

delegated regulation as the safety feature allowing the verification of whether the packaging of a medicinal product has been tampered with.[2793]

More specifically, Article 25(1) of Delegated Regulation 2016/161 requires persons authorized or entitled to supply medicinal products to the public to verify those safety features. In addition, Articles 24 and 30 of that delegated regulation prohibit wholesalers and persons authorized or entitled to supply medicinal products to the public from supplying medicinal products to the public where they have reason to believe that its packaging has been tampered with.[2794]

Furthermore, Article 47a(1) of Directive 2001/83 provides that those safety features may be removed or covered only under strict conditions, intended to guarantee the authenticity of the medicinal product and the absence of any tampering.[2795]

In particular, it is apparent from Article 47a(1)(b) that those conditions include the condition that the safety features in question must be replaced by 'equivalent' safety features. Under that provision, in order to be regarded as such, a safety feature must, *inter alia*, be equally effective in enabling the verification of the authenticity of the medicinal products concerned and their identification, as well as in providing evidence of tampering with them.[2796]

It thus follows from that provision, read in the light of recital 12 of Directive 2011/62, that the EU legislature, which expressly provided for the possibility of 'replacing' the safety features referred to in paragraph 60 of the present judgment, did not intend to prevent the reuse of the original outer packaging, even where that packaging had such features. That interpretation is borne out by Article 34(4) and Article 35(4) of Delegated Regulation 2016/161, pursuant to which an equivalent unique identifier may be affixed both to a repackaged pack, in new packaging, and to a relabelled pack.[2797]

That being so, it follows from Article 47a(1)(b) of Directive 2001/83 that such reuse is possible only on condition that the original safety features can be replaced by features which are equally effective in enabling the verification of the authenticity of the medicinal products concerned, their identification, and in providing evidence of tampering with them, in accordance with the aim of Directive 2011/62, which, as is apparent from recital 29 thereof, is to prevent falsified medicinal products from entering the legal supply chain.[2798]

Pursuant to Article 54a(2) of Directive 2001/83, Delegated Regulation 2016/161 establishes the detailed rules for those safety features. Recital 1 of that delegated regulation identifies two types of safety features, namely: (i) a unique identifier and (ii)

2793. CJEU C-224/20 of 17.11.2022 – Merck Sharp & Dohme a.o./Abacus a.o., para. 60.
2794. CJEU C-147/20 of 17.11.2022 – Novartis Pharma/Abacus Medicine, para. 59; C-224/20 of 17.11.2022 – Merck Sharp & Dohme a.o./Abacus a.o., para. 61.
2795. CJEU C-147/20 of 17.11.2022 – Novartis Pharma/Abacus Medicine, para. 60; C-224/20 of 17.11.2022 – Merck Sharp & Dohme a.o./Abacus a.o., para. 62.
2796. CJEU C-147/20 of 17.11.2022 – Novartis Pharma/Abacus Medicine, para. 61; C-224/20 of 17.11.2022 – Merck Sharp & Dohme a.o./Abacus a.o., para. 63.
2797. CJEU C-147/20 of 17.11.2022 – Novartis Pharma/Abacus Medicine, para. 62; C-224/20 of 17.11.2022 – Merck Sharp & Dohme a.o./Abacus a.o., para. 64.
2798. CJEU C-147/20 of 17.11.2022 – Novartis Pharma/Abacus Medicine, para. 63; C-224/20 of 17.11.2022 – Merck Sharp & Dohme a.o./Abacus a.o., para. 65.

an anti-tampering device. An anti-tampering device is defined in Article 3(2) of that delegated regulation as the safety feature enabling the verification of whether the packaging of a medicinal product has been tampered with.[2799]

In that regard, it should be noted that, under Article 47a(1)(a) of Directive 2001/83, the holder of a manufacturing authorization – authorization that, as is apparent from Article 40(2) of that directive, any actor in the supply chain which packages medicinal products must possess – must verify, before removing or covering either fully or partially the safety features referred to in paragraph 60 of this judgment, that the medicinal product concerned is authentic and that it has not been tampered with.[2800]

Thus, in accordance with Article 47a(1)(b) of Directive 2001/83, a replacement anti-tampering device must make it possible to verify, with the same effectiveness as an original anti-tampering device, that the outer packaging of a medicinal product has not been unlawfully opened between the time at which that medicinal product is repackaged and that at which it is supplied to the public.[2801]

Consequently, the presence on the outer packaging of a medicinal product of possible traces of having been opened is not, in itself, sufficient for the view to be taken that the replacement anti-tampering device is not equivalent, within the meaning of the second paragraph of Article 47a(1)(b) of Directive 2001/83, where there is no doubt, on the part of wholesalers and persons authorized or entitled to supply medicinal products to the public, that those traces of opening are attributable to the repackaging of that medicinal product by a parallel importer. In that regard, the reference on that outer packaging to the repackager provides information to downstream actors in the supply chain as to the possible origin of those traces of opening. That reference, combined with the anti-tampering device and the replacement unique identifier, enables those persons to ensure that the presence of such traces is due to lawful tampering.[2802]

Moreover, since the function of the anti-tampering device is precisely to reveal any opening of the packaging to which it is affixed, the presence of such traces is inevitable. Accordingly, an interpretation different from that in the preceding paragraph would make it impossible, in practice, to relabel a medicinal product, thus rendering redundant Article 47a(1)(b) of Directive 2001/83, read in the light of recital 12 of Directive 2011/62, and Article 34(4) and Article 35(4) of Delegated Regulation 2016/161, which expressly so permit.[2803]

It follows from the foregoing considerations that the fact that the replacement of the anti-tampering device of the original packaging of a medicinal product leaves

2799. CJEU C-147/20 of 17.11.2022 – Novartis Pharma/Abacus Medicine, para. 64.
2800. CJEU C-147/20 of 17.11.2022 – Novartis Pharma/Abacus Medicine, para. 65; C-224/20 of 17.11.2022 – Merck Sharp & Dohme a.o./Abacus a.o., para. 66.
2801. CJEU C-147/20 of 17.11.2022 – Novartis Pharma/Abacus Medicine, para. 66; C-204/20 of 17.11.2022 – Bayer Intellectual Property/kohlpharma, para. 74; C-224/20 of 17.11.2022 – Merck Sharp & Dohme a.o./Abacus a.o., para. 67.
2802. CJEU C-224/20 of 17.11.2022 – Merck Sharp & Dohme a.o./Abacus a.o., para. 68; *see also* CJEU C-147/20 of 17.11.2022 – Novartis Pharma/Abacus Medicine, para. 67; C-204/20 of 17.11.2022 – Bayer Intellectual Property/kohlpharma, paras 75 et seqq.
2803. CJEU C-204/20 of 17.11.2022 – Bayer Intellectual Property/kohlpharma, para. 77; C-224/20 of 17.11.2022 – Merck Sharp & Dohme a.o./Abacus a.o., para. 69.

visible traces of opening on that packaging does not preclude the finding that the new device is equivalent, within the meaning of Article 47a(1)(b) of Directive 2001/83, or, therefore, that that replacement has been carried out in accordance with that Article 47a(1).[2804]

Thus, first, repackaging in new packaging must be regarded as objectively necessary where the anti-tampering device with which the outer packaging of the medicinal product concerned is equipped cannot objectively be replaced by an equivalent device, within the meaning of Article 47a(1)(b) of Directive 2001/83, it being recalled that the presence of traces of opening is, in itself, insufficient to support the inference that the condition of equivalence has not been satisfied.[2805]

In such circumstances, the exercise by the trade mark proprietor of the right conferred by the trade mark to oppose such repackaging would constitute a disguised restriction on trade between Member States, within the meaning of the second sentence of Article 36 TFEU, in that it would contribute, contrary to the purpose of trade mark law, to artificially partitioning national markets within the European Union and thus to promoting the retention of price differences which may exist between Member States.[2806]

That interpretation is supported by the essential function of the trade mark, which is to ensure that the consumer or end user can identify the origin of the product bearing a mark by enabling him or her, without any possibility of confusion, to distinguish it from others which have another origin. That guarantee of origin means that the consumer or end user can be certain that a product bearing a mark offered to him or her has not been subject at a previous stage of marketing to interference by a third party, without the authorization of the trade mark proprietor, in such a way as to affect the original condition of the product.[2807]

Where there is no doubt, in the minds of consumers, that traces of the outer packaging of a medicinal product having been opened are attributable to the repackaging of that product by a parallel importer, the guarantee of origin of that medicinal product is ensured.[2808]

Secondly, the Court has held that the existence on the market of the Member State of importation or on a substantial part of it of such strong resistance from a significant proportion of consumers to relabelled medicinal products that there must be held to be a hindrance to effective market access also constitutes an obstacle to the effective access of a relabelled medicinal product to that market, such as to necessitate repackaging by replacing the packaging. In those circumstances, repackaging of the

2804. CJEU C-147/20 of 17.11.2022 – Novartis Pharma/Abacus Medicine, para. 68; C-224/20 of 17.11.2022 – Merck Sharp & Dohme a.o./Abacus a.o., para. 70.
2805. CJEU C-147/20 of 17.11.2022 – Novartis Pharma/Abacus Medicine, para. 69; C-224/20 of 17.11.2022 – Merck Sharp & Dohme a.o./Abacus a.o., para. 71.
2806. CJEU C-224/20 of 17.11.2022 – Merck Sharp & Dohme a.o./Abacus a.o., para. 72.
2807. CJEU C-204/20 of 17.11.2022 – Bayer Intellectual Property/kohlpharma, para. 80; C-224/20 of 17.11.2022 – Merck Sharp & Dohme a.o./Abacus a.o., para. 73, each with reference to CJEU C-427/93, C-429/93 and C-436/93 of 11.7.1996 – Bristol-Myers Squibb and Others/Paranova, para. 47.
2808. CJEU C-204/20 of 17.11.2022 – Bayer Intellectual Property/kohlpharma, para. 81; C-224/20 of 17.11.2022 – Merck Sharp & Dohme a.o./Abacus a.o., para. 74.

medicinal products in new packaging would not be explicable solely by the attempt to secure a commercial advantage, but would be aimed at securing effective access to the market in question.[2809]

Similarly, if a significant proportion of consumers in the importing Member State are opposed to the idea of acquiring a medicinal product whose outer packaging bears visible traces of being opened which are caused by the replacement of the existing anti-tampering device by an equivalent device carried out in accordance with Article 47a(1) of Directive 2001/83, the effective access of that medicinal product to the market of that Member State must be considered to be hindered and, therefore, its repackaging in new outer packaging must be regarded as necessary for the purposes of its being marketed in that Member State.[2810]

In the circumstances described in the preceding paragraph, the trade mark proprietor's opposition to such repackaging cannot be accepted in so far as it would contribute to artificial partitioning of the markets between Member States.[2811]

However, a parallel importer cannot rely on a general presumption of consumer resistance to relabelled medicinal products whose anti-tampering devices have been replaced. In the light of the considerations set out above, the possible existence of such resistance and its extent must be assessed *in concreto*, taking into account, in particular, the circumstances prevailing in the Member State of importation at the time at which the medicinal product concerned was marketed, and of the fact that traces of opening are visible or, on the contrary, can be detected only after a thorough verification by wholesalers or persons authorized or entitled to supply medicinal products to the public pursuant to their verification obligations under Articles 10, 24 and 30 of Delegated Regulation 2016/161.[2812]

Article 9(2) and Article 15(2) EUTMR and Article 10(2) and Article 15(2) TMD must be interpreted as meaning that the proprietor of a trade mark may oppose the marketing in a Member State by a parallel importer of a medicinal product imported from another Member State which that importer has repackaged in new outer packaging to which he or she has reaffixed the trade mark of the proprietor specific to that product, but not the other trade marks and/or other distinctive signs which appeared on the original outer packaging of that medicinal product, where the presentation of that new outer packaging is in fact liable to **damage the reputation** of the trade mark or where that presentation does not enable normally informed and

2809. CJEU C-147/20 of 17.11.2022 - Novartis Pharma/Abacus Medicine, para. 70; C-204/20 of 17.11.2022 - Bayer Intellectual Property/kohlpharma, para. 82; C-224/20 of 17.11.2022 - Merck Sharp & Dohme a.o./Abacus a.o., para. 75, each with reference to CJEU C-143/00 of 23.4.2002 - Boehringer Ingelheim and Others (I), para. 52.

2810. CJEU C-147/20 of 17.11.2022 - Novartis Pharma/Abacus Medicine, para. 71; C-204/20 of 17.11.2022 - Bayer Intellectual Property/kohlpharma, para. 83; C-224/20 of 17.11.2022 - Merck Sharp & Dohme a.o./Abacus a.o., para. 76.

2811. CJEU C-147/20 of 17.11.2022 - Novartis Pharma/Abacus Medicine, para. 72 C-204/20 of 17.11.2022 - Bayer Intellectual Property/kohlpharma, para. 84; C-224/20 of 17.11.2022 - Merck Sharp & Dohme a.o./Abacus a.o., para. 77.

2812. CJEU C-147/20 of 17.11.2022 - Novartis Pharma/Abacus Medicine, para. 73; C-204/20 of 17.11.2022 - Bayer Intellectual Property/kohlpharma, para. 85; C-224/20 of 17.11.2022 - Merck Sharp & Dohme a.o./Abacus a.o., para. 78.

reasonably attentive consumers, or enables them only with difficulty, to ascertain whether that medicinal product originates from the proprietor of the trade mark or an undertaking economically linked to him or her or, on the contrary, originates from a third party, thus adversely affecting the function of indicating the origin of the mark.[2813]

In the first place, it must be borne in mind that the protection of the trade mark proprietor in relation to the presentation of the new outer packaging in which a medicinal product has been repackaged by the parallel importer of that product is, in principle, ensured by compliance with the condition that the presentation of the repackaged product must not be such as to be liable to damage the reputation of the trade mark or that of its proprietor.[2814]

In that regard, Article 9(2) and Article 15(2) EUTMR and Article 10(2) and Article 15(2) TMD must be interpreted as meaning that the trade mark proprietor may legitimately oppose the further marketing in a Member State of a medicinal product bearing that trade mark and imported from another Member State, where the parallel importer of that product has either repackaged it in new outer packaging to which he or she has reaffixed that mark or affixed a label to the original outer packaging, unless five conditions are fulfilled, including the condition that the presentation of the repackaged product must not be such as to be liable to damage the reputation of the trade mark and of its proprietor.[2815]

The fact that the parallel importer reaffixes to the new outer packaging the trade mark of the proprietor specific to that product, without reproducing the other trade marks and/or the other distinctive signs which appeared on the original outer packaging, is also liable to damage the reputation of the trade mark.[2816]

In the second place, reaffixing the specific trade mark of a product in combination with the parallel importer's trade marks and/or distinctive signs is liable to compromise the function of indicating the origin of that mark.[2817]

In particular, it follows from the Court's case law that a presentation of a product which does not enable normally informed and reasonably attentive consumers, or enables them only with difficulty, to ascertain whether the product originates from the proprietor of the trade mark or an undertaking economically linked to him or her or, on the contrary, originates from a third party adversely affects the function of indicating the origin of the mark.[2818]

In that regard, it should be noted, however, that the function of indicating the origin of the mark is, in principle, guaranteed by compliance with the third of the five conditions set out in the judgment *Boehringer Ingelheim and Others*,[2819] according to

2813. CJEU C-224/20 of 17.11.2022 – Merck Sharp & Dohme a.o./Abacus a.o., para. 130.
2814. CJEU C-224/20 of 17.11.2022 – Merck Sharp & Dohme a.o./Abacus a.o., para. 120, with reference to CJEU C-461/09 P of 9.7.2010 – The Wellcome Foundation, para. 29.
2815. CJEU C-224/20 of 17.11.2022 – Merck Sharp & Dohme a.o./Abacus a.o., para. 121, with reference to CJEU C-348/04 of 26.4.2007 – Boehringer Ingelheim and Others (II), para. 40.
2816. CJEU C-224/20 of 17.11.2022 – Merck Sharp & Dohme a.o./Abacus a.o., para. 124.
2817. CJEU C-224/20 of 17.11.2022 – Merck Sharp & Dohme a.o./Abacus a.o., para. 126.
2818. CJEU C-224/20 of 17.11.2022 – Merck Sharp & Dohme a.o./Abacus a.o., para. 127, with reference to CJEU C-558/08 of 8.7.2010 – Portakabin, para. 34.
2819. CJEU C-143/00 of 23.4.2002 – Boehringer Ingelheim and Others (I).

which the repackager of a product and the name of the product manufacturer must be clearly indicated on the packaging of that product.[2820]

It is in the light of those factors and taking into account the specific circumstances of each case that it is for the referring court to assess whether the reaffixing, to the new outer packaging of a medicinal product, of the proprietor's trade mark specific to that product, without reproducing on that packaging the other trade marks and/or the other distinctive signs which appeared on the original packaging of that medicinal product adversely affects the function of indicating the origin of the mark.[2821]

If the repackaging is carried out in **conditions which cannot affect the original condition of the product inside the packaging**, the essential function of the trade mark as a guarantee of origin is safeguarded. The consumer or end user is not misled as to the origin of the products, and does in fact receive products manufactured under the sole supervision of the trade mark proprietor.[2822]

The reliance by a trade mark owner on his rights as owner in order to prevent an importer from marketing a product which was put on the market in another Member State by the owner or with his consent where that importer has repackaged the product and reaffixed the trade mark without the owner's authorization is being assessed on the basis of the combined provisions of national trade mark law and Article 7 TMD2008, interpreted in the light of Article 36[2823] of the Treaty.[2824]

It is the repackaging of the trade marked pharmaceutical products in itself which is prejudicial to the specific subject matter of the mark, and it is not necessary in that context to assess the actual effects of the repackaging by the parallel importer.[2825]

However, the proprietor may not rely on the rights conferred by the trade mark in order to oppose the marketing under his trade mark of products repackaged by an importer amounts to conferring on the importer certain rights which in normal circumstances are reserved for the trade mark proprietor himself. Consequently, in the interests of the proprietor as owner of the trade mark, and to protect him against any misuse, those rights must be recognized only in so far as the importer also complies with a number of other requirements.[2826]

2820. CJEU C-224/20 of 17.11.2022 – Merck Sharp & Dohme a.o./Abacus a.o., para. 128.
2821. CJEU C-224/20 of 17.11.2022 – Merck Sharp & Dohme a.o./Abacus a.o., para. 129.
2822. CJEU C-400/09 and C-207/10 of 28.7.2011 – Orifarm, para. 25; *see also* CJEU C-427/93, C-429/93 and C-436/93 of 11.7.1996 – Bristol-Myers Squibb and Others/Paranova, para. 67; C-348/04 of 26.4.2007 – Boehringer Ingelheim and Others (II), para. 39.
2823. Article 30 EC.
2824. CJEU C-427/93, C-429/93 and C-436/93 of 11.7.1996 – Bristol-Myers Squibb and Others/Paranova, para. 28.
2825. CJEU C-642/16 of 17.5.2018 – Junek Europ-Vertrieb/Lohmann & Rauscher International, para. 24, with further proof.
2826. CJEU C-400/09 and C-207/10 of 28.7.2011 – Orifarm, para. 26; C-147/20 of 17.11.2022 – Novartis Pharma/Abacus Medicine, para. 49; C-204/20 of 17.11.2022 – Bayer Intellectual Property/kohlpharma, para. 60; C-224/20 of 17.11.2022 – Merck Sharp & Dohme a.o./Abacus a.o., para. 51; C-253/20 and C-254/20 of 17.11.2022 – Impexeco/Novartis a.o., para. 52; *see also* CJEU C-427/93, C-429/93 and C-436/93 of 11.7.1996 – Bristol-Myers Squibb and Others/Paranova, paras 68 et seq.; C-348/04 of 26.4.2007 – Boehringer Ingelheim and Others (II), paras 40 et seq.

Article 9(2) and Article 15 EUTMR and Article 10(2) and Article 15 TMD, read in conjunction with Articles 34 and 36 TFEU, must be interpreted as meaning that a **Member State rule** which requires that medicinal products imported in parallel must, in principle, be repackaged in new packaging and that recourse may be had to relabelling and to the affixing of new safety features to the original outer packaging of those medicinal products only on application and in exceptional circumstances **does not impede the exercise by a trade mark proprietor** of his or her right to oppose the marketing by a parallel importer of a medicinal product repackaged in new outer packaging to which that mark is affixed.[2827]

The trade mark proprietor may oppose the repackaging of a medicinal product by replacement of its outer packaging where the parallel importer is able to reuse the original packaging of that product for the purpose of marketing in the Member State of importation by affixing labels to that packaging, provided that the relabelled medicinal product is able to have effective access to the market concerned.[2828]

However, where the circumstances prevailing at the time of marketing in the importing Member State render repackaging of a medicinal product in new packaging objectively necessary because those circumstances impede the marketing of that medicinal product in its relabelled original outer packaging on the market of that Member State, the trade mark proprietor does not have that power. In such circumstances, a trade mark proprietor's opposition to the repackaging of that medicinal product by replacement of its outer packaging would contribute to artificial partitioning of the markets between the Member States.[2829]

That condition that repackaging be necessary is fulfilled, in particular, if a rule or a practice in the importing Member State prevents a medical product from being marketed in that Member State in the same packaging as that in which that product is marketed in the exporting Member State.[2830]

However, such a rule or practice can justify a restriction on the exercise of the trade mark proprietor's rights only if it complies with EU law.[2831]

Where a rule of a Member State or a practice of its authorities infringes EU law, the obstacle to effective access of the medicinal product concerned to the market of that Member State is due not to the trade mark proprietor's opposition, but to that rule or practice.[2832]

Article 9(2) and Article 15(2) EUTMR and Article 10(2) and Article 15(2) TMD, read in conjunction with Articles 34 and 36 TFEU, must be interpreted as meaning that the Bristol-Myers Squibb condition – according to which the proprietor of a trade mark may legitimately oppose the further marketing in a Member State of a medicinal product bearing that mark and imported from another Member State, where the importer of that medicinal product has repackaged that product and reaffixed that trade

2827. CJEU C-224/20 of 17.11.2022 – Merck Sharp & Dohme a.o./Abacus a.o., para. 107.
2828. CJEU C-224/20 of 17.11.2022 – Merck Sharp & Dohme a.o./Abacus a.o., para. 102.
2829. CJEU C-224/20 of 17.11.2022 – Merck Sharp & Dohme a.o./Abacus a.o., para. 103.
2830. CJEU C-224/20 of 17.11.2022 – Merck Sharp & Dohme a.o./Abacus a.o., para. 104, with reference to CJEU C-348/04 of 26.4.2007 – Boehringer Ingelheim and Others (II), paras 36.
2831. CJEU C-224/20 of 17.11.2022 – Merck Sharp & Dohme a.o./Abacus a.o., para. 105.
2832. CJEU C-224/20 of 17.11.2022 – Merck Sharp & Dohme a.o./Abacus a.o., para. 106.

mark to the packaging and where such repackaging of that medicinal product in new outer packaging is not objectively necessary for the purposes of its being marketed in the Member State of importation – must be satisfied where the trade mark which appeared on the original outer packaging of the medicinal product concerned has been **replaced by a different product name** on the new outer packaging of that medicinal product, provided that the immediate packaging of that product bears that trade mark and/or that new outer packaging refers to that mark.[2833]

In that regard, it must be borne in mind that, under Article 9(1) EUTMR and Article 10(1) TMD, the registration of a trade mark confers on the proprietor exclusive rights which, according to Article 9(2)(a) EUTMR and Article 10(2)(a) TMD, entitle that proprietor to prevent all third parties not having his or her consent from using in the course of trade any sign which is identical with that trade mark in relation to goods or services which are identical with those for which the mark was registered.[2834]

Consequently, it is necessary to examine whether, in circumstances such as those described by the referring court, namely where the trade mark which appears on the original outer packaging of a medicinal product is replaced by a different product name on the new outer packaging of that medicinal product, the parallel importer uses in the course of trade a sign identical with that mark, within the meaning of Article 9(2)(a) and Article 10(2)(a), in relation to the imported medicinal products which he or she wishes to place on the market of a Member State.[2835]

Article 9(3)(a) EUTMR and Article 10(3)(a) TMD provide that the proprietor may prohibit all third parties from affixing the sign in question to the goods or to the packaging of those goods.[2836]

Where a parallel importer indicates on the new outer packaging of an imported medicinal product that that product corresponds to the medicinal product marketed by the proprietor under his or her trade mark and that the blister packs inside that new outer packaging bear that mark, that parallel importer affixes a sign identical to that mark to the packaging of the goods, within the meaning of those provisions.[2837]

Furthermore, where that parallel importer markets, on the market of one Member State, a medicinal product which he or she has imported from another Member State and whose immediate packaging, in the present case those blister packs, bears the trade mark of the proprietor, he or she puts that medicinal product on the market of that first Member State under that sign, within the meaning of Article 9(3)(b) EUTMR and Article 10(3)(b) TMD.[2838]

Therefore, it must be held, that, in circumstances such as those described above, that parallel importer uses in the course of trade a sign identical with the proprietor's trade mark, within the meaning of Article 9 EUTMR and Article 10 TMD, in respect of the medicinal products concerned.[2839]

2833. CJEU C-224/20 of 17.11.2022 – Merck Sharp & Dohme a.o./Abacus a.o., para. 118.
2834. CJEU C-224/20 of 17.11.2022 – Merck Sharp & Dohme a.o./Abacus a.o., para. 110.
2835. CJEU C-224/20 of 17.11.2022 – Merck Sharp & Dohme a.o./Abacus a.o., para. 111.
2836. CJEU C-224/20 of 17.11.2022 – Merck Sharp & Dohme a.o./Abacus a.o., para. 113.
2837. CJEU C-224/20 of 17.11.2022 – Merck Sharp & Dohme a.o./Abacus a.o., para. 114.
2838. CJEU C-224/20 of 17.11.2022 – Merck Sharp & Dohme a.o./Abacus a.o., para. 115.
2839. CJEU C-224/20 of 17.11.2022 – Merck Sharp & Dohme a.o./Abacus a.o., para. 116.

The repackaging of those medicinal products in new outer packaging is liable to affect the functions of the trade mark and, therefore, the proprietor may have a legitimate interest in opposing it.[2840]

[6] Pharmaceutical context

Article 36 of the Treaty must be interpreted as meaning that a trade mark owner may rely on his rights to prevent an importer from marketing a product put on the market in another Member State by the owner or with his consent, where that importer has repackaged the product in new packaging to which the trade mark has been reaffixed, unless:

- it is established that reliance on the trade mark right by the owner, having regard to the marketing system which he has adopted, will contribute to the artificial partitioning of the markets between Member States;
- it is shown that the repackaging cannot adversely affect the original condition of the product;
- the owner of the mark receives prior notice before the repackaged product is put on sale; and
- it is stated on the new packaging by whom the product has been repackaged.[2841]

Nevertheless, a clear indication may be required on the external packaging as to who manufactured the product, since it may indeed be in the manufacturer's interest that the consumer or end user should not be led to believe that the importer is the owner of the trade mark, and that the product was manufactured under his supervision.[2842]

The owner may also require the importer to supply him with a specimen of the repackaged product before it goes on sale, to enable him to check that the repackaging is not carried out in such a way as directly or indirectly to affect the original condition

2840. CJEU C-224/20 of 17.11.2022 – Merck Sharp & Dohme a.o./Abacus a.o., para. 117.

2841. CJEU C-71 to 73/94 of 11.7.1996 – Eurim-Pharm Arzneimittel/Beiersdorf and Others, paras 36 and 70; C-427/93, C-429/93 and C-436/93 of 11.7.1996 – Bristol-Myers Squibb and Others/ Paranova, paras 49 and 79; C-232/94 of 11.7.1996 – MPA Pharma/Rhône-Poulenc Pharma, paras 22 and 50; C-143/00 of 23.4.2002 – Boehringer Ingelheim and Others (I), para. 14; *see also* CJEU C-379/97 of 12.10.1999 – Upjohn, para. 17; C-443/99 of 23.4.2002 – Merck/ Paranova Pharmazeutika, para. 23; C-143/00 of 23.4.2002 – Boehringer Ingelheim and Others (I), para. 32; C-348/04 of 26.4.2007 – Boehringer Ingelheim and Others (II), paras 17 and 21; C-400/09 and C-207/10 of 28.7.2011 – Orifarm, paras 24 and 27; *see also* CJEU C-297/15 of 10.11.2016 – Ferring Lægemidler/Orifarm, para. 16; C-642/16 of 17.5.2018 – Junek Europ-Vertrieb/Lohmann & Rauscher International, paras 26 et seqq.; C-147/20 of 17.11.2022 – Novartis Pharma/Abacus Medicine, para. 50; C-204/20 of 17.11.2022 – Bayer Intellectual Property/kohlpharma, para. 61; C-224/20 of 17.11.2022 – Merck Sharp & Dohme a.o./Abacus a.o., para. 52; C-253/20 and C-254/20 of 17.11.2022 – Impexeco/Novartis a.o., para. 53.

2842. CJEU C-71 to 73/94 of 11.7.1996 – Eurim-Pharm Arzneimittel/Beiersdorf and Others, para. 64; C-427/93, C-429/93 and C-436/93 of 11.7.1996 – Bristol-Myers Squibb and Others/Paranova, para. 74; C-232/94 of 11.7.1996 – MPA Pharma/Rhône-Poulenc Pharma, para. 45; *see also* CJEU 1/81 of 3.12.1981 – Pfizer/Eurim-Pharm, para. 11.

of the product and that the presentation after repackaging is not such as to damage the reputation of the trade mark. Similarly, such a requirement affords the trade mark owner a better possibility of protecting himself against counterfeiting.[2843]

It is, however, not necessary to require that the further express statement be made on the packaging that the repackaging was carried out without the authorization of the trade mark owner, since such a statement could be taken to imply that the repackaged product is not entirely legitimate.[2844]

[7] No pharmaceutical context

Article 36 of the Treaty is to be interpreted as meaning that the owner of trade mark rights may, even if that constitutes a barrier to intra-Community trade, rely on those rights to prevent a third party from removing and then reaffixing or replacing labels bearing the mark which the owner has himself affixed to products he has put on the Community market, unless:

- it is established that the use of the trade mark rights by the owner to oppose the marketing of the relabelled products under that trade mark would contribute to artificial partitioning of the markets between Member States;
- it is shown that the relabelling cannot affect the original condition of the product;
- the presentation of the relabelled product is not such as to be liable to damage the reputation of the trade mark and its owner; and
- the person who relabels the products informs the trade mark owner of the relabelling before the relabelled products are put on sale.[2845]

However, in circumstances such as those in the main proceedings, having regard to the nature of the action of the person carrying out the relabelling, the interests of the trade mark owner, and in particular his need to combat counterfeiting, are given sufficient weight if that person gives him prior notice that the relabelled products are to be put on sale.[2846]

[8] Artificial partitioning of the markets and necessity of the repackaging

The Court's use of the words 'artificial partitioning of the markets' does not imply that the importer must demonstrate that, by putting an identical product on the market in

2843. CJEU C-71 to 73/94 of 11.7.1996 – Eurim-Pharm Arzneimittel/Beiersdorf and Others, para. 69; C-232/94 of 11.7.1996 – MPA Pharma/Rhône-Poulenc Pharma, para. 49; C-427/93, C-429/93 and C-436/93 of 11.7.1996 – Bristol-Myers Squibb and Others/Paranova, para. 78; C-143/00 of 23.4.2002 – Boehringer Ingelheim and Others (I), para. 61; C-349/95 of 11.11.1997 – Loendersloot/Ballantine & Son and Others, para. 30.

2844. CJEU C-71 to 73/94 of 11.7.1996 – Eurim-Pharm Arzneimittel/Beiersdorf and Others, para. 63; C-427/93, C-429/93 and C-436/93 of 11.7.1996 – Bristol-Myers Squibb and Others/Paranova, para. 72; C-232/94 of 11.7.1996 – MPA Pharma/Rhône-Poulenc Pharma, para. 44.

2845. CJEU C-349/95 of 11.11.1997 – Loendersloot/Ballantine & Son and Others, paras 29 and 50.

2846. CJEU C-349/95 of 11.11.1997 – Loendersloot/Ballantine & Son and Others, paras 47 and 49.

varying forms of packaging in different Member States, the trade mark owner deliberately sought to partition the markets between Member States. By stating that the partitioning in question must be artificial, the Court's intention was to stress that the owner of a trade mark may always rely on his rights thereunder in order to oppose the marketing of repackaged products when such action is justified by the need to safeguard the essential function of the trade mark, in which case the resultant partitioning could not be regarded as artificial.[2847]

The trade mark proprietor may oppose the repackaging if it is based solely on the parallel importer's attempt to secure a commercial advantage.[2848]

The national courts must consider whether circumstances in the markets of their own States make **repackaging objectively necessary**.[2849]

The power of the owner of trade mark rights protected in a Member State to oppose the marketing of repackaged products under the trade mark should be limited only in so far as the repackaging undertaken by the importer is necessary in order to market the product in the Member State of importation.[2850]

Reliance on trade mark rights by their owner in order to oppose marketing under that trade mark of products repackaged by a third party would contribute to the partitioning of markets between Member States in particular where the owner has placed an identical pharmaceutical product on the market in several Member States in various forms of packaging, and the product may not, in the condition in which it has been marketed by the trade mark owner in one Member State, be imported and put on the market in another Member State by a parallel importer.[2851]

2847. CJEU C-71 to 73/94 of 11.7.1996 – Eurim-Pharm Arzneimittel/Beiersdorf and Others, paras 47 and 70; C-427/93, C-429/93 and C-436/93 of 11.7.1996 – Bristol-Myers Squibb and Others/Paranova, paras 57 and 79; C-232/94 of 11.7.1996 – MPA Pharma/Rhône-Poulenc Pharma, paras 29 and 50; C-379/97 of 12.10.1999 – Upjohn, para. 18.

2848. CJEU C-143/00 of 23.4.2002 – Boehringer Ingelheim and Others (I), para. 48; C-443/99 of 23.4.2002 – Merck/Paranova Pharmazeutika, para. 27; C-348/04 of 26.4.2007 – Boehringer Ingelheim and Others (II), para. 37; C-147/20 of 17.11.2022 – Novartis Pharma/Abacus Medicine, para. 53; C-204/20 of 17.11.2022 – Bayer Intellectual Property/kohlpharma, para. 64; C-224/20 of 17.11.2022 – Merck Sharp & Dohme a.o./Abacus a.o., para. 55; C-253/20 and C-254/20 of 17.11.2022 – Impexeco/Novartis a.o., para. 56.

2849. CJEU C-349/95 of 11.11.1997 – Loendersloot/Ballantine & Son and Others, para. 38; *see also* CJEU C-297/15 of 10.11.2016 – Ferring Lægemidler/Orifarm, paras 28 et seq.

2850. CJEU C-427/93, C-429/93 and C-436/93 of 11.7.1996 – Bristol-Myers Squibb and Others/Paranova, para. 56; C-349/95 of 11.11.1997 – Loendersloot/Ballantine & Son and Others, para. 36; C-379/97 of 12.10.1999 – Upjohn, para. 18; C-143/00 of 23.4.2002 – Boehringer Ingelheim and Others (I), paras 15 and 33 et seq. and 46; C-443/99 of 23.4.2002 – Merck/Paranova Pharmazeutika, para. 25; C-433/00 of 19.9.2002 – Aventis, para. 26; C-348/04 of 26.4.2007 – Boehringer Ingelheim and Others (II), paras 18 et seq.; C-297/15 of 10.11.2016 – Ferring Lægemidler/Orifarm, para. 17 and 19; *see also* CJEU C-147/20 of 17.11.2022 – Novartis Pharma/Abacus Medicine, para. 51; C-204/20 of 17.11.2022 – Bayer Intellectual Property/kohlpharma, para. 62; C-224/20 of 17.11.2022 – Merck Sharp & Dohme a.o./Abacus a.o., para. 53; C-253/20 and C-254/20 of 17.11.2022 – Impexeco/Novartis a.o., para. 54.

2851. CJEU C-71 to 73/94 of 11.7.1996 – Eurim-Pharm Arzneimittel/Beiersdorf and Others, para. 42; C-427/93, C-429/93 and C-436/93 of 11.7.1996 – Bristol-Myers Squibb and Others/Paranova, para. 52; C-232/94 of 11.7.1996 – MPA Pharma/Rhône-Poulenc Pharma, para. 24; C-349/95 of 11.11.1997 – Loendersloot/Ballantine & Son and Others, para. 35; C-379/97 of 12.10.1999 – Upjohn, para. 19.

The trade mark owner cannot therefore oppose the repackaging of the product in new external packaging, or the modification of the contents of an original external packet, when the packet size used by the owner in the Member State where the importer purchased the product cannot be marketed in the Member State of importation by reason, in particular, of a rule authorizing **packaging only of a certain size** or a national practice to the same effect, sickness insurance rules making the reimbursement of medical expenses depend on the size of the packaging, or well-established medical prescription practices based, *inter alia*, on standard sizes recommended by professional groups and sickness insurance institutions.[2852]

Such an impediment exists, for example, where pharmaceutical products purchased by the parallel importer cannot be placed on the market in the Member State of importation in their original packaging by reason of **national rules or practices relating to packaging**, or where sickness insurance rules make reimbursement of medical expenses depend on a certain packaging or where well-established medical prescription practices are based, *inter alia*, on standard sizes recommended by professional groups and sickness insurance institutions. In that regard, it is sufficient for there to be an impediment in respect of one type of packaging used by the trade mark proprietor in the Member State of importation.[2853]

Where, in accordance with the rules and practices in force in the Member State of importation, the trade mark owner uses many different sizes of packaging in that State, the finding that one of those sizes is also marketed in the Member State of exportation is not enough to justify the conclusion that repackaging is unnecessary. Partitioning of the markets would exist if the importer were able to sell the product in only part of his market.[2854]

The owner may, on the other hand, oppose the repackaging of the product in new external packaging where the importer is able to achieve packaging which may be marketed in the Member State of importation by, for example, affixing to the original external or inner packaging new labels in the language of the Member State of importation, or by adding new user instructions or information in the language of the Member State of importation.[2855]

2852. CJEU C-71 to 73/94 of 11.7.1996 – Eurim-Pharm Arzneimittel/Beiersdorf and Others, para. 43; C-427/93, C-429/93 and C-436/93 of 11.7.1996 – Bristol-Myers Squibb and Others/Paranova, para. 53; C-232/94 of 11.7.1996 – MPA Pharma/Rhône-Poulenc Pharma, para. 25; C-297/15 of 10.11.2016 – Ferring Lægemidler/Orifarm, para. 21.

2853. CJEU C-143/00 of 23.4.2002 – Boehringer Ingelheim and Others (I), para. 47; C-443/99 of 23.4.2002 – Merck/Paranova Pharmazeutika, para. 26.

2854. CJEU C-71 to 73/94 of 11.7.1996 – Eurim-Pharm Arzneimittel/Beiersdorf and Others, para. 44; C-427/93, C-429/93 and C-436/93 of 11.7.1996 – Bristol-Myers Squibb and Others/Paranova, para. 54; C-232/94 of 11.7.1996 – MPA Pharma/Rhône-Poulenc Pharma, para. 26; C-297/15 of 10.11.2016 – Ferring Lægemidler/Orifarm, para. 22.

2855. CJEU C-71 to 73/94 of 11.7.1996 – Eurim-Pharm Arzneimittel/Beiersdorf and Others, para. 45; C-427/93, C-429/93 and C-436/93 of 11.7.1996 – Bristol-Myers Squibb and Others/Paranova, para. 55; C-232/94 of 11.7.1996 – MPA Pharma/Rhône-Poulenc Pharma, para. 27; C-143/00 of 23.4.2002 – Boehringer Ingelheim and Others (I), para. 49; C-443/99 of 23.4.2002 – Merck/Paranova Pharmazeutika, para. 28; *see also* CJEU C-147/20 of 17.11.2022 – Novartis Pharma/Abacus Medicine, para. 55; C-204/20 of 17.11.2022 – Bayer Intellectual Property/kohlpharma, para. 66; C-224/20 of 17.11.2022 – Merck Sharp & Dohme a.o./Abacus a.o., para. 57.

The power of the owner of trade mark rights protected in a Member State to oppose the marketing of repackaged products under the trade mark should be limited only in so far as the repackaging undertaken by the importer is necessary in order to market the product in the Member State of importation.[2856]

The condition that the repackaging of the pharmaceutical product, either by reboxing the product and reapplying the trade mark or by applying a label to the packaging containing the product, be necessary for its further commercialization in the importing Member State, as one of the conditions which, if fulfilled, prevent the proprietor under Article 7(2) TMD2008 from opposing such commercialization, is directed solely at the fact of repackaging and **not at the manner and style of the repackaging**.[2857]

The proprietor can legitimately oppose further commercialization of a pharmaceutical product when the parallel importer has either reboxed the new product and reapplied the trade mark or applied a label to the packaging containing the product, unless five conditions have been fulfilled, including that of establishing that reliance on trade mark rights by the proprietor in order to oppose the marketing of products thus repackaged would contribute to the artificial partitioning of the markets between Member States.[2858]

The change brought about by any repackaging of a trade marked medicinal product may be prohibited by the trade mark proprietor unless the repackaging is necessary in order to enable the marketing of the products imported in parallel and the legitimate interests of the proprietor are also safeguarded.[2859]

That condition that repackaging be necessary is fulfilled if the rules or practices in the importing Member State prevent the product in question from being marketed in that State in the same packaging as that in which those products are marketed in the exporting Member State.[2860]

Conversely, the condition that it be necessary is not fulfilled if repackaging of the product is explicable solely by the parallel importer's attempt to secure a commercial advantage.[2861]

Therefore, the condition that packaging be necessary is directed only at the fact of repackaging the product – and the choice between a new carton and oversticking – for the purposes of allowing that product to be marketed in the importing State and not at the manner or style in which it has been repackaged (*see also* the judgment of the EFTA Court in Case E-3/02 *Paranova v. Merck* [2003] EFTA Court Report 2004, p. 1, paragraphs 41–45).[2862]

2856. CJEU C-71 to 73/94 of 11.7.1996 – Eurim-Pharm Arzneimittel/Beiersdorf and Others, para. 46; C-427/93, C-429/93 and C-436/93 of 11.7.1996 – Bristol-Myers Squibb and Others/Paranova, para. 56; C-232/94 of 11.7.1996 – MPA Pharma/Rhône-Poulenc Pharma, para. 28; C-297/15 of 10.11.2016 – Ferring Lægemidler/Orifarm, para. 18.
2857. CJEU C-348/04 of 26.4.2007 – Boehringer Ingelheim and Others (II), para. 39.
2858. CJEU C-348/04 of 26.4.2007 – Boehringer Ingelheim and Others (II), para. 33.
2859. CJEU C-348/04 of 26.4.2007 – Boehringer Ingelheim and Others (II), para. 35.
2860. CJEU C-348/04 of 26.4.2007 – Boehringer Ingelheim and Others (II), para. 36; C-224/20 of 17.11.2022 – Merck Sharp & Dohme a.o./Abacus a.o., para. 104.
2861. CJEU C-348/04 of 26.4.2007 – Boehringer Ingelheim and Others (II), para. 37.
2862. CJEU C-348/04 of 26.4.2007 – Boehringer Ingelheim and Others (II), para. 38.

Resistance to relabelled pharmaceutical products does not always constitute an impediment to effective market access such as to make replacement packaging necessary, within the meaning of the Court's case law.[2863]

However, there may exist on a market, or on a substantial part of it, such strong resistance from a significant proportion of consumers to relabelled pharmaceutical products that there must be held to be a hindrance to effective market access. In those circumstances, repackaging of the pharmaceutical products would not be explicable solely by the attempt to secure a commercial advantage. The purpose would be to achieve effective market access.[2864]

It is for the national court to determine whether that is the case.[2865]

Replacement packaging of pharmaceutical products is objectively necessary within the meaning of the Court's case law if, without such repackaging, effective access to the market concerned, or to a substantial part of that market, must be considered to be hindered as the result of strong resistance from a significant proportion of consumers to relabelled pharmaceutical products.[2866]

While the trade mark proprietor may oppose the parallel importer's use of replacement packaging, that is conditional on the relabelled pharmaceutical product being able to have effective access to the market concerned.[2867]

[9] Quality of the presentation of the repackaged product

There remains the possibility that the reputation of the trade mark, and thus of its owner, may nevertheless suffer from an **inappropriate presentation** of the repackaged product. In such a case, the trade mark owner has a legitimate interest, related to the specific subject matter of the trade mark right, in being able to oppose the marketing of the product. In assessing whether the presentation of the repackaged product is liable to damage the reputation of the trade mark, account must be taken of the nature of the product and the market for which it is intended.[2868]

In the case of **pharmaceutical products**, that is certainly a sensitive area in which the public is particularly demanding as to the quality and integrity of the product, and the presentation of the product may indeed be capable of inspiring public confidence in

2863. CJEU C-143/00 of 23.4.2002 – Boehringer Ingelheim and Others (I), para. 51; C-443/99 of 23.4.2002 – Merck/Paranova Pharmazeutika, para. 30.
2864. CJEU C-143/00 of 23.4.2002 – Boehringer Ingelheim and Others (I), para. 52; C-443/99 of 23.4.2002 – Merck/Paranova Pharmazeutika, para. 31.
2865. CJEU C-143/00 of 23.4.2002 – Boehringer Ingelheim and Others (I), para. 53; C-443/99 of 23.4.2002 – Merck/Paranova Pharmazeutika, para. 32.
2866. CJEU C-143/00 of 23.4.2002 – Boehringer Ingelheim and Others (I), para. 54; C-443/99 of 23.4.2002 – Merck/Paranova Pharmazeutika, para. 33.
2867. CJEU C-143/00 of 23.4.2002 – Boehringer Ingelheim and Others (I), para. 50; C-443/99 of 23.4.2002 – Merck/Paranova Pharmazeutika, para. 29; C-147/20 of 17.11.2022 – Novartis Pharma/Abacus Medicine, para. 55; C-204/20 of 17.11.2022 – Bayer Intellectual Property/ kohlpharma, para. 66; C-224/20 of 17.11.2022 – Merck Sharp & Dohme a.o./Abacus a.o., para. 57.
2868. CJEU C-71 to 73/94 of 11.7.1996 – Eurim-Pharm Arzneimittel/Beiersdorf and Others, para. 65; C-427/93, C-429/93 and C-436/93 of 11.7.1996 – Bristol-Myers Squibb and Others/Paranova, para. 75; C-232/94 of 11.7.1996 – MPA Pharma/Rhône-Poulenc Pharma, para. 46.

that regard. It follows that defective, poor quality or untidy packaging could damage the trade mark's reputation.[2869]

The requirements to be met by the presentation of a repackaged pharmaceutical product vary according to whether the product is **sold to hospitals or, through pharmacies**, to consumers. In the former case, the products are administered to patients by professionals, for whom the presentation of the product is of little importance. In the latter case, the presentation of the product is of greater importance for the consumer, even if the fact that the products in question are subject to prescription by a doctor may in itself give consumers some degree of confidence in the quality of the product.[2870]

It is for the national court to ascertain, in the light of the above, whether, in particular, the insertion into single external packaging of both original external packaging and **loose blister packs** constitutes an untidy form of packaging liable to damage the reputation of the trade mark. As for the cutting of blister packs, it is for that court to assess in each particular case whether it has been carried out in such a manner that the reputation of the trade mark might suffer.[2871]

The trade mark owner may therefore oppose any repackaging involving a risk of the product inside the package being exposed to **tampering** or to **influences** affecting its original condition. To determine whether that applies, account must be taken of the nature of the product and the method of repackaging.[2872]

As regards pharmaceutical products the repackaging must be regarded as having been carried out in circumstances not capable of affecting the original condition of the product where, for example, the trade mark owner has placed the product on the market in double packaging and the repackaging affects only the **external layer**, leaving the inner packaging intact, or where the repackaging is carried out under the supervision of a public authority in order to ensure that the product remains intact.[2873]

The mere removal of blister packs, flasks, phials, ampoules or inhalers from their original external packaging and their replacement in new external packaging cannot affect the original condition of the product inside the packaging.[2874]

2869. CJEU C-71 to 73/94 of 11.7.1996 – Eurim-Pharm Arzneimittel/Beiersdorf and Others, para. 66; C-427/93, C-429/93 and C-436/93 of 11.7.1996 – Bristol-Myers Squibb and Others/Paranova, para. 75; C-232/94 of 11.7.1996 – MPA Pharma/Rhône-Poulenc Pharma, para. 47; C-348/04 of 26.4.2007 – Boehringer Ingelheim and Others (II), para. 40; *see also* CJEU C-224/20 of 17.11.2022 – Merck Sharp & Dohme a.o./Abacus a.o., para. 122.

2870. CJEU C-71 to 73/94 of 11.7.1996 – Eurim-Pharm Arzneimittel/Beiersdorf and Others, para. 67; C-427/93, C-429/93 and C-436/93 of 11.7.1996 – Bristol-Myers Squibb and Others/Paranova, para. 75; C-232/94 of 11.7.1996 – MPA Pharma/Rhône-Poulenc Pharma, para. 48.

2871. CJEU C-71 to 73/94 of 11.7.1996 – Eurim-Pharm Arzneimittel/Beiersdorf and Others, para. 68.

2872. CJEU C-71 to 73/94 of 11.7.1996 – Eurim-Pharm Arzneimittel/Beiersdorf and Others, para. 49; C-427/93, C-429/93 and C-436/93 of 11.7.1996 – Bristol-Myers Squibb and Others/Paranova, para. 59; C-232/94 of 11.7.1996 – MPA Pharma/Rhône-Poulenc Pharma, para. 31; *see also* CJEU 102/77 of 23.5.1978 – Hoffmann-La Roche/Centrafarm, para. 10.

2873. CJEU C-71 to 73/94 of 11.7.1996 – Eurim-Pharm Arzneimittel/Beiersdorf and Others, para. 50; C-427/93, C-429/93 and C-436/93 of 11.7.1996 – Bristol-Myers Squibb and Others/Paranova, para. 60 f.; C-232/94 of 11.7.1996 – MPA Pharma/Rhône-Poulenc Pharma, para. 32 f.; *see also* CJEU 102/77 of 23.5.1978 – Hoffmann-La Roche/Centrafarm, para. 10.

2874. CJEU C-427/93, C-429/93 and C-436/93 of 11.7.1996 – Bristol-Myers Squibb and Others/Paranova, para. 61; C-232/94 of 11.7.1996 – MPA Pharma/Rhône-Poulenc Pharma, para. 33.

The mere removal of blister packs from their original external packaging and their insertion with one or more original packages into new external packaging or their insertion into another original package cannot affect the original condition of the product inside the packaging.[2875]

As for operations consisting in the fixing of self-stick labels to flasks, phials, ampoules or inhalers, the addition to the packaging of new user instructions or information in the language of the Member State of importation, or the insertion of an extra article, such as a spray, from a source other than the trade mark owner, there is nothing to suggest that the original condition of the product inside the packaging is directly affected thereby.[2876]

As for operations consisting in the fixing of self-stick labels to original external packaging or blister packs, or the addition to the packaging of new user instructions or information in the language of the Member State of importation, there is nothing to suggest that the original condition of the product inside the packaging is directly affected thereby.[2877]

It is for the national court to assess whether that is so, in particular by making a **comparison with the product marketed by the trade mark owner** in the Member State of importation. The possibility of the importer providing certain additional information should not be excluded, however, provided that information does not contradict the information provided by the trade mark owner in the Member State of importation, that condition being met in particular in the case of different information resulting from the packaging used by the owner in the Member State of exportation.[2878]

The original condition of the product inside the packaging might be indirectly affected where, **for example**:

- the external or inner packaging of the repackaged product, or a new set of user instructions or information, omits certain important information or gives inaccurate information concerning the nature, composition, effect, use or storage of the product; or
- the packaging of the repackaged product is not such as to give the product adequate protection.[2879]

It is for the national court to assess whether that is so, in particular by making a comparison with the product marketed by the trade mark owner in the Member State of importation. The possibility of the importer providing certain additional information

2875. CJEU C-71 to 73/94 of 11.7.1996 – Eurim-Pharm Arzneimittel/Beiersdorf and Others, para. 51; C-427/93, C-429/93 and C-436/93 of 11.7.1996 – Bristol-Myers Squibb and Others/Paranova, para. 62 f.; C-232/94 of 11.7.1996 – MPA Pharma/Rhône-Poulenc Pharma, para. 34 f.
2876. CJEU C-427/93, C-429/93 and C-436/93 of 11.7.1996 – Bristol-Myers Squibb and Others/ Paranova, para. 64; *see also* CJEU C-232/94 of 11.7.1996 – MPA Pharma/Rhône-Poulenc Pharma, para. 36.
2877. CJEU C-71 to 73/94 of 11.7.1996 – Eurim-Pharm Arzneimittel/Beiersdorf and Others, para. 55; C-232/94 of 11.7.1996 – MPA Pharma/Rhône-Poulenc Pharma, para. 37.
2878. CJEU C-232/94 of 11.7.1996 – MPA Pharma/Rhône-Poulenc Pharma, para. 38.
2879. CJEU C-71 to 73/94 of 11.7.1996 – Eurim-Pharm Arzneimittel/Beiersdorf and Others, para. 56; C-427/93, C-429/93 and C-436/93 of 11.7.1996 – Bristol-Myers Squibb and Others/Paranova, para. 65.

should not be excluded, however, provided that information does not contradict the information provided by the trade mark owner in the Member State of importation, that condition being met in particular in the case of different information resulting from the packaging used by the owner in the Member State of exportation.[2880]

It is for the national court to determine whether the **cutting of blister packs** or **the reprinting of batch numbers** on them are carried out in such a manner as to exclude any real risk of affecting the original condition of the tablets inside. That will be so in particular where those operations are authorized and supervised by a public authority in order to ensure that the product remains intact.[2881]

The detailed and specific requirements regarding the packaging of the medicinal products which are the subject of a central marketing authorization, which are intended to prevent consumers from being misled and thereby to protect public health, preclude the bundling of the packages of those medicinal products.[2882]

Regulation No. 2309/93[2883] precludes a medicinal product which is the subject of **two separate central marketing authorizations**, one for packs of five items and the other for packs of ten items, from being marketed in a package consisting of two packs of five items which have been joined together and relabelled.[2884]

The condition that the presentation of the pharmaceutical product must not be such as to be liable to damage the reputation of the trade mark and of its proprietor – as a necessary condition for preventing the proprietor, pursuant to Article 7(2) TMD2008, from legitimately opposing further commercialization of a pharmaceutical product, where the parallel importer has either reboxed the product and reapplied the trade mark or applied a label to the packaging containing the product – **is not limited only to cases where the repackaging is defective, of poor quality, or untidy**.[2885]

The Court, in holding that defective, poor quality or untidy packaging could damage the trade mark's reputation, merely referred to certain cases in which inappropriate presentation of the repackaged product is liable to damage the reputation of the trade mark and of its proprietor.[2886]

Accordingly, a repackaged pharmaceutical product could be presented inappropriately and, therefore, damage the trade mark's reputation in particular where the carton or label, while not being defective, of poor quality or untidy, are such as to affect the trade mark's value by detracting from the image of reliability and quality attaching

2880. CJEU C-71 to 73/94 of 11.7.1996 – Eurim-Pharm Arzneimittel/Beiersdorf and Others, para. 57; C-427/93, C-429/93 and C-436/93 of 11.7.1996 – Bristol-Myers Squibb and Others/Paranova, para. 66.
2881. CJEU C-71 to 73/94 of 11.7.1996 – Eurim-Pharm Arzneimittel/Beiersdorf and Others, para. 54.
2882. CJEU C-433/00 of 19.9.2002 – Aventis, para. 25.
2883. Council Regulation (EEC) No 2309/93 of 22 Jul. 1993 laying down Community procedures for the authorization and supervision of medicinal products for human and veterinary use and establishing a European Agency for the Evaluation of Medicinal Products (OJ 1993 L 214, p. 1).
2884. CJEU C-433/00 of 19.9.2002 – Aventis, para. 27.
2885. CJEU C-348/04 of 26.4.2007 – Boehringer Ingelheim and Others (II), para. 44.
2886. CJEU C-348/04 of 26.4.2007 – Boehringer Ingelheim and Others (II), para. 42.

to such a product and the confidence it is capable of inspiring in the public concerned.[2887]

The question whether the fact that a parallel importer:

- fails to affix the trade mark to the new exterior carton ('de-branding'); or
- applies either his own logo or a house-style or a get-up or a get-up used for a number of different products ('co-branding'); or
- positions the additional label so as wholly or partially to obscure the proprietor's trade mark; or
- fails to state on the additional label that the trade mark in question belongs to the proprietor; or
- prints the name of the parallel importer in capital letters,

is liable to damage the trade mark's reputation is a **question of fact** for the national court to decide in the light of the circumstances of each case.[2888]

The fact that a parallel importer does not affix the trade mark to the new exterior carton ('de-branding') or applies either his own logo or a house-style or get-up or a get-up used for a number of different products ('co-branding'), or positions the additional label so as wholly or partially to obscure the proprietor's trade mark, or fails to state on the additional label that the trade mark in question belongs to the proprietor, or prints the name of the parallel importer in capital letters is, in principle, liable to damage the trade mark's reputation.[2889]

However, precisely as with the question of whether advertising is liable to create the impression that there is a commercial connection between the reseller and the trade mark proprietor and, therefore, constitute a legitimate reason within the meaning of Article 7(2) TMD2008, the question of whether the circumstances referred to in the previous paragraph of the present judgment are liable to damage the trade mark's reputation is a question of fact for the national court to decide in the light of the circumstances of each case.[2890]

[10] Indication who repackaged the product

Since it is in the trade mark owner's interest that the consumer or end user should not be led to believe that the owner is responsible for the repackaging, an indication must be given on the packaging of who repackaged the product.[2891]

2887. CJEU C-348/04 of 26.4.2007 – Boehringer Ingelheim and Others (II), para. 43; C-224/20 of 17.11.2022 – Merck Sharp & Dohme a.o./Abacus a.o., para. 122.
2888. CJEU C-348/04 of 26.4.2007 – Boehringer Ingelheim and Others (II), para. 47.
2889. CJEU C-348/04 of 26.4.2007 – Boehringer Ingelheim and Others (II), para. 45; C-224/20 of 17.11.2022 – Merck Sharp & Dohme a.o./Abacus a.o., para. 123.
2890. CJEU C-348/04 of 26.4.2007 – Boehringer Ingelheim and Others (II), para. 46; C-224/20 of 17.11.2022 – Merck Sharp & Dohme a.o./Abacus a.o., para. 125.
2891. CJEU C-71 to 73/94 of 11.7.1996 – Eurim-Pharm Arzneimittel/Beiersdorf and Others, para. 61; C-427/93, C-429/93 and C-436/93 of 11.7.1996 – Bristol-Myers Squibb and Others/Paranova, para. 70; C-232/94 of 11.7.1996 – MPA Pharma/Rhône-Poulenc Pharma, para. 42; C-400/09 and C-207/10 of 28.7.2011 – Orifarm, para. 28.

This indication must be clearly shown on the external packaging of the repackaged product.[2892]

Such an indication, as long as it is printed so as to be comprehensible to a normally attentive person, is such as to avoid the consumer or end user being given the incorrect impression that the product has been repackaged by the proprietor.[2893]

That implies that the national court must assess whether it is printed in such a way as to be understood by a person with normal eyesight, exercising a normal degree of attentiveness.[2894]

Article 7(2) TMD2008 does not allow the proprietor of a trade mark relating to a pharmaceutical product which is the subject of parallel imports to oppose the further marketing of that product in repackaged form on the sole ground that the new packaging indicates as the repackager **not the undertaking which, on instructions, actually repackaged the product** and holds an authorization to do so, but the undertaking which holds the marketing authorization for the product, on whose instructions the repackaging was carried out, and which assumes liability for the repackaging.[2895]

The proprietor of the trade mark has no legitimate interest in requiring that the name of the undertaking which actually repackaged the product should appear on the packaging merely because the repackaging is liable to affect the original condition of the product and might therefore cause harm to his trade mark rights.[2896]

Because the indicated undertaking assumes full responsibility for the repackaging operations, the proprietor can enforce his rights and, where appropriate, obtain compensation if the original condition of the product within the packaging has been affected by the repackaging or the presentation of the repackaged product is liable to damage the reputation of the trade mark. It should be stated that, in such a case, an undertaking which is mentioned as the repackager on the new packaging of a repackaged product will have to answer for any damage caused by the undertaking which actually carried out the repackaging, and cannot avoid liability by arguing, in particular, that that undertaking acted contrary to its instructions.[2897]

The interest of the trade mark proprietor in the preservation of the original condition of the product inside the packaging is sufficiently protected by the requirement that it must be shown that the repackaging cannot affect the original condition of the product. In circumstances such as those of the main proceedings, it is for the holder

2892. CJEU C-71 to 73/94 of 11.7.1996 – Eurim-Pharm Arzneimittel/Beiersdorf and Others, para. 62; C-427/93, C-429/93 and C-436/93 of 11.7.1996 – Bristol-Myers Squibb and Others/Paranova, para. 71; C-232/94 of 11.7.1996 – MPA Pharma/Rhône-Poulenc Pharma, para. 43; *see also* CJEU 102/77 of 23.5.1978 – Hoffmann-La Roche/Centrafarm, para. 12; 1/81 of 3.12.1981 – Pfizer/Eurim-Pharm, para. 11; C-400/09 and C-207/10 of 28.7.2011 – Orifarm, para. 29.
2893. CJEU C-400/09 and C-207/10 of 28.7.2011 – Orifarm, para. 29.
2894. CJEU C-71 to 73/94 of 11.7.1996 – Eurim-Pharm Arzneimittel/Beiersdorf and Others, para. 62; C-427/93, C-429/93 and C-436/93 of 11.7.1996 – Bristol-Myers Squibb and Others/Paranova, para. 71; C-232/94 of 11.7.1996 – MPA Pharma/Rhône-Poulenc Pharma, para. 43.
2895. CJEU C-400/09 and C-207/10 of 28.7.2011 – Orifarm, para. 36.
2896. CJEU C-400/09 and C-207/10 of 28.7.2011 – Orifarm, para. 31.
2897. CJEU C-400/09 and C-207/10 of 28.7.2011 – Orifarm, para. 30.

of the marketing authorization, on whose instructions the repackaging has been carried out and who assumes liability for it, to show that that is the case.[2898]

It is clear from the wording of Article 7(2) TMD2008 that the exception in that provision to the principle of the exhaustion of the rights conferred by the trade mark is limited to the protection of the legitimate interests of the trade mark proprietor, the specific protection of the legitimate interests of consumers being ensured by other legal instruments.[2899]

In any event, even if it were supposed that the interests of the trade mark proprietor coincide, if only partly, with those of the consumer, the fact remains that the indication on the packaging of the product of the undertaking responsible for its repackaging enables the consumer to be sufficiently informed, from the point of view of trade mark law.[2900]

[11] Obligation to notify and to supply

The trade mark owner must be given advance notice of the repackaged product being put on sale. The owner may also require the importer to supply him with a specimen of the repackaged product before it goes on sale, to enable him to check that the repackaging is not carried out in such a way as directly or indirectly to affect the original condition of the product and that the presentation after repackaging is not such as to damage the reputation of the trade mark. Similarly, such a requirement affords the trade mark owner a better possibility of protecting himself against counterfeiting.[2901]

It is not sufficient that the proprietor be notified by other sources, such as the authority which issues a parallel import licence to the importer.[2902]

The notice enables the trade mark owner to check that the repackaging is not carried out in such a way as directly or indirectly to affect the original condition of the product and that the presentation after repackaging is not likely to damage the reputation of the trade mark. Similarly, such a requirement affords the trade mark owner a better possibility of protecting himself against counterfeiting.[2903]

In regard to the period of notice to be given to the proprietor to react to the intended repackaging of the pharmaceutical product bearing its mark, it is self-evident that while, having regard to the purpose of notice to the trade mark proprietor, it is appropriate to allow a reasonable time for it to react to the intended repackaging,

2898. CJEU C-400/09 and C-207/10 of 28.7.2011 - Orifarm, para. 32.
2899. CJEU C-400/09 and C-207/10 of 28.7.2011 - Orifarm, para. 34.
2900. CJEU C-400/09 and C-207/10 of 28.7.2011 - Orifarm, para. 35.
2901. CJEU C-71 to 73/94 of 11.7.1996 - Eurim-Pharm Arzneimittel/Beiersdorf and Others, para. 69; C-232/94 of 11.7.1996 - MPA Pharma/Rhône-Poulenc Pharma, para. 49; C-427/93, C-429/93 and C-436/93 of 11.7.1996 - Bristol-Myers Squibb and Others/Paranova, para. 78; C-349/95 of 11.11.1997 - Loendersloot/Ballantine & Son and Others, para. 30; C-143/00 of 23.4.2002 - Boehringer Ingelheim and Others (I), para. 61; C-348/04 of 26.4.2007 - Boehringer Ingelheim and Others (II), para. 20 and 55.
2902. CJEU C-143/00 of 23.4.2002 - Boehringer Ingelheim and Others (I), para. 64 and 68; C-348/04 of 26.4.2007 - Boehringer Ingelheim and Others (II), para. 55.
2903. CJEU C-427/93, C-429/93 and C-436/93 of 11.7.1996 - Bristol-Myers Squibb and Others/ Paranova, para. 78; C-143/00 of 23.4.2002 - Boehringer Ingelheim and Others (I), para. 61.

consideration must also be given to the parallel importer's interest in proceeding to market the pharmaceutical product as soon as possible after obtaining the necessary licence from the competent authority.[2904]

It is for the national court to assess, in the light of all the relevant circumstances, whether the trade mark proprietor had a reasonable time to react to the intended repackaging. On the basis of the evidence before the Court, a period of fifteen working days seems likely to constitute such a reasonable time where the parallel importer has chosen to give notice to the trade mark proprietor by supplying it simultaneously with a sample of the repackaged pharmaceutical product. That period being purely indicative, it remains open to the parallel importer to allow a shorter time and to the proprietor to ask for a longer time to react than that allowed by the parallel importer.[2905]

Where a parallel importer has failed to give prior notice to the trade mark proprietor concerning a repackaged pharmaceutical product, he infringes that proprietor's rights on the occasion of any subsequent importation of that product, so long as he has not given the proprietor such notice. The sanction for that infringement must be not only proportionate but also sufficiently effective and a sufficient deterrent to ensure that the Directive is fully effective. A national measure under which, in the case of such an infringement, the trade mark proprietor is entitled to claim financial remedies on the same basis as if the goods had been spurious is not in itself contrary to the principle of proportionality. It is for the national court, however, to determine the amount of the financial remedies according to the circumstances of each case, in the light in particular of the extent of damage to the trade mark proprietor caused by the parallel importer's infringement and in accordance with the principle of proportionality.[2906]

In that respect, it must be borne in mind that the Member States are required, within the bounds of the freedom left to them by the third paragraph of Article 249 EC, to choose the most appropriate forms and methods to ensure the effectiveness of directives, in the light of their objective.[2907]

Accordingly, where, as in the case in the main proceedings, Community law does not lay down any specific sanctions where infringements have been committed, it is incumbent on the national authorities to adopt appropriate measures to deal with such a situation. Those measures must be not only proportionate but also sufficiently effective and a sufficient deterrent to ensure that the Directive is fully effective.[2908]

For the trade mark proprietor to be able lawfully to oppose further marketing of a repackaged pharmaceutical product, it is sufficient that one of the conditions set out in paragraph 79 of *Bristol-Myers Squibb and Others*[2909] is not fulfilled.[2910]

2904. CJEU C-143/00 of 23.4.2002 – Boehringer Ingelheim and Others (I), para. 66.
2905. CJEU C-143/00 of 23.4.2002 – Boehringer Ingelheim and Others (I), para. 67.
2906. CJEU C-348/04 of 26.4.2007 – Boehringer Ingelheim and Others (II), para. 64.
2907. CJEU C-348/04 of 26.4.2007 – Boehringer Ingelheim and Others (II), para. 58.
2908. CJEU C-348/04 of 26.4.2007 – Boehringer Ingelheim and Others (II), para. 59; *see also* CJEU C-705/17 of 12.6.2019 – Patent- och registreringsverket/Hansson, para. 38.
2909. CJEU C-427/93, C-429/93 and C-436/93 of 11.7.1996 – Bristol-Myers Squibb and Others/ Paranova.
2910. CJEU C-348/04 of 26.4.2007 – Boehringer Ingelheim and Others (II), para. 60.

It follows that the trade mark owner's right to prevent parallel importation of pharmaceutical products which, while not spurious, have been marketed in breach of the requirement to give prior notice to that proprietor is not different from that enjoyed by the proprietor in respect of spurious goods.[2911]

In both cases, the products ought not to have been marketed on the market concerned.[2912]

Thus, a national measure under which, where a parallel importer has marketed goods which are not spurious without giving prior notice to the trade mark proprietor that proprietor is entitled to claim financial remedies on the same basis as if the goods had been spurious, is not in itself contrary to the principle of proportionality. However, it is for the national court to determine the amount of the financial remedies according to the circumstances of each case, in the light of, in particular, the extent of damage to the trade mark proprietor caused by the parallel importer's infringement and in accordance with the principle of proportionality.[2913]

[12] Relabelling

Article 7(2) TMD2008 must be construed as meaning that the proprietor may legitimately oppose further commercialization of a pharmaceutical product imported from another Member State in its original internal and external packaging with an additional external label applied by the importer, unless:

- it is established that reliance on trade mark rights by the proprietor in order to oppose the marketing of the overstickered product under that trade mark would contribute to the artificial partitioning of the markets between Member States;
- it is shown that the new label cannot affect the original condition of the product inside the packaging;
- the packaging clearly states who overstickered the product and the name of the manufacturer;
- the presentation of the overstickered product is not such as to be liable to damage the reputation of the trade mark and of its proprietor; thus, the label must not be defective, of poor quality, or untidy; and
- the importer gives notice to the trade mark proprietor before the overstickered product is put on sale, and, on demand, supplies him with a specimen of that product.[2914]

It follows from the foregoing that in *Boehringer Ingelheim and Others*,[2915] the Court included in the concept of repackaging the relabelling which was undoubtedly

2911. CJEU C-348/04 of 26.4.2007 – Boehringer Ingelheim and Others (II), para. 61.
2912. CJEU C-348/04 of 26.4.2007 – Boehringer Ingelheim and Others (II), para. 62.
2913. CJEU C-348/04 of 26.4.2007 – Boehringer Ingelheim and Others (II), para. 63.
2914. CJEU C-348/04 of 26.4.2007 – Boehringer Ingelheim and Others (II), para. 32.
2915. CJEU C-143/00 of 23.4.2002 – Boehringer Ingelheim and Others (I).

one of the forms envisaged by the referring court in which the packaging of the medicinal products in question was altered.[2916]

In that regard, it should be borne in mind that the relabelling of the trade marked medicinal products, just like the reboxing of those products, are prejudicial to the specific subject matter of the mark, and it is not necessary in that context to assess the actual effects of the activity performed by the parallel importer.[2917]

The change brought about by any new carton or relabelling of a trade marked medicinal product creates by its very nature real risks for the guarantee of origin which the mark seeks to protect. Such a change may thus be prohibited by the trade mark proprietor unless the new carton or relabelling is necessary in order to enable the marketing of the products imported in parallel and the legitimate interests of the proprietor are also safeguarded.[2918]

It follows that the five requirements set out in *Bristol-Myers Squibb and Others*[2919] in respect of the interpretation of Article 7(2) TMD2008, requirements which, if met, prevent the proprietor from opposing further commercialization of a pharmaceutical product which has been repackaged by the importer, also apply when the repackaging consists in the attachment of a label to the original packaging.[2920]

It is for the national court to assess whether the relabelling is necessary in order to prevent artificial partitioning of the markets between Member States.[2921]

The national court must assess whether the relabelling is necessary to protect the sources of supply of the parallel trade and to enable the products to be marketed on the various markets of the Member States for which they are intended.[2922]

On this point, it must be stated that use by the trade mark owners of their trade mark rights to prevent relabelling for the purposes mentioned by Loendersloot would contribute to artificial partitioning of the markets between Member States if it were established that the use of the original labels would prevent the products in question from being marketed in the Member State of destination because it was contrary to the rules on labelling in force in that State. In such a situation, relabelling would be necessary for the product to be marketed in that State.[2923]

The person carrying out the relabelling must, however, use means which make parallel trade feasible while causing as little prejudice as possible to the specific subject matter of the trade mark right. Thus, if the statements on the original labels comply with the rules on labelling in force in the Member State of destination, but those rules require additional information to be given, it is not necessary to remove and reaffix or

2916. CJEU C-348/04 of 26.4.2007 – Boehringer Ingelheim and Others (II), para. 28; C-642/16 of 17.5.2018 – Junek Europ-Vertrieb/Lohmann & Rauscher International, para. 30; *see also* CJEU C-224/20 of 17.11.2022 – Merck Sharp & Dohme a.o./Abacus a.o., para. 46.
2917. CJEU C-348/04 of 26.4.2007 – Boehringer Ingelheim and Others (II), para. 29.
2918. CJEU C-348/04 of 26.4.2007 – Boehringer Ingelheim and Others (II), para. 30.
2919. C-427/93, C-429/93 and C-436/93 of 11.7.1996 – Bristol-Myers Squibb and Others/Paranova.
2920. CJEU C-348/04 of 26.4.2007 – Boehringer Ingelheim and Others (II), para. 31.
2921. CJEU C-349/95 of 11.11.1997 – Loendersloot/Ballantine & Son and Others, para. 51.
2922. CJEU C-349/95 of 11.11.1997 – Loendersloot/Ballantine & Son and Others, para. 38.
2923. CJEU C-349/95 of 11.11.1997 – Loendersloot/Ballantine & Son and Others, para. 45.

replace the original labels since the mere application to the bottles in question of a sticker with the additional information may suffice.[2924]

The person who carries out the repackaging has to make sure that the reputation of the trade mark, and thus of its owner, may does not suffer from an inappropriate presentation of the repackaged product.[2925]

To assess whether that is the case, the national court must take into account in particular the interest of the trade mark owner in protecting the luxury image of their products and the considerable reputation they enjoy.[2926]

The mere addition on the label of certain information cannot constitute a legitimate reason within the meaning of Article 7(2) TMD2008, provided that the label so altered does not omit important information or give inaccurate information, and its presentation is not liable to damage the reputation of the trade mark and that of its owner.[2927]

Article 13(2) CTMR must be interpreted as meaning that the proprietor of a mark cannot oppose the further commercialization, by a parallel importer, of a **medical device** in its original internal and external packaging where an additional label has been added by the importer, which, by its content, function, size, presentation and placement, does not give rise to a risk to the guarantee of origin of the medical device bearing the mark.[2928]

In that regard, it is clear from the settled case law that the specific purpose of a mark is to guarantee the origin of the product bearing that mark and that a repackaging of that product carried out by a third party without the authorization of the proprietor is likely to create real risks for that guarantee of origin.[2929]

In addition, it must be observed that the Court has held, as regards Article 7(2) TMD1989 the wording of which is equivalent to that of Article 13(2) CTMR, that, under that provision, the trade mark proprietor's opposition to repackaging, in that it constitutes a derogation from free movement of goods, cannot be accepted if the proprietor's exercise of that right constitutes a disguised restriction on trade between Member States within the meaning of the second sentence of Article 36 TFEU.[2930]

2924. CJEU C-349/95 of 11.11.1997 – Loendersloot/Ballantine & Son and Others, para. 46.
2925. CJEU C-427/93, C-429/93 and C-436/93 of 11.7.1996 – Bristol-Myers Squibb and Others/ Paranova, paras 75 and 76; C-71 to 73/94 of 11.7.1996 – Eurim-Pharm Arzneimittel/ Beiersdorf and Others, para. 69; C-232/94 of 11.7.1996 – MPA Pharma/Rhône-Poulenc Pharma, para. 49; C-349/95 of 11.11.1997 – Loendersloot/Ballantine & Son and Others, para. 33; C-143/00 of 23.4.2002 – Boehringer Ingelheim and Others (I), para. 16.
2926. CJEU C-349/95 of 11.11.1997 – Loendersloot/Ballantine & Son and Others, para. 33.
2927. CJEU C-352/95 of 20.3.1997 – Phytheron International/Bourdon, para. 23.
2928. CJEU C-642/16 of 17.5.2018 – Junek Europ-Vertrieb/Lohmann & Rauscher International, para. 39.
2929. CJEU C-642/16 of 17.5.2018 – Junek Europ-Vertrieb/Lohmann & Rauscher International, para. 23, with reference to C-297/15 of 10.11.2016 – Ferring Lægemidler/Orifarm, para. 14.
2930. CJEU C-642/16 of 17.5.2018 – Junek Europ-Vertrieb/Lohmann & Rauscher International, para. 25, with reference to CJEU C-143/00 of 23.4.2002 – Boehringer Ingelheim and Others (I), para. 18; C-348/04 of 26.4.2007 – Boehringer Ingelheim and Others (II), para. 16; also CJEU C-147/20 of 17.11.2022 – Novartis Pharma/Abacus Medicine, para. 47; C-204/20 of 17.11.2022 – Bayer Intellectual Property/kohlpharma, para. 58; C-224/20 of 17.11.2022 – Merck Sharp & Dohme a.o./Abacus a.o., para. 49; C-253/20 and C-254/20 of 17.11.2022 – Impexeco/Novartis a.o., para. 50.

A disguised restriction within the meaning of that provision will exist where the exercise by a trade mark proprietor of its right to oppose repackaging contributes to artificial partitioning of the markets between Member States and where, in addition, the repackaging is done in such a way that the legitimate interests of the proprietor are respected. This means, in particular, that the repackaging must not adversely affect the original condition of the product and must not be such as to harm the reputation of the mark.[2931]

Given that the packaging of the medical device concerned has not been modified and the original presentation of the packaging has not been affected other than by the attachment of a small label, which does not conceal the mark and which designates the parallel importer as responsible for placing it on the market by setting out his details, a barcode and a central pharmacological number, it cannot be held that the attachment of such a label constitutes repackaging.[2932]

Consequently, it cannot, in any event, be held that the attachment of such a label affects the specific purpose of the mark, which is to guarantee the origin of the product that it identifies.[2933]

In those circumstances, the attachment of an additional label, such as that at issue in the case in the main proceedings, by the parallel importer to the original packaging of the medical device, which has not been opened, is not a legitimate reason that justifies the proprietor of the mark opposing the further commercialization of the medical device concerned.[2934]

[13] Replacing the trade mark

It follows that Article 7 TMD2008 is applicable where, after repackaging of the product, the original trade mark is reaffixed. In contrast, that article does not apply where the parallel importer replaces the original trade mark with a different one. In the latter case, the respective rights of the proprietor of the trade marks and of the parallel importer are determined by Articles 30 and 36 of the Treaty.[2935]

In order to determine whether the proprietor of a trade mark may, under national law, prevent a parallel importer of pharmaceutical products from replacing the trade mark used in the Member State of export by that which the proprietor uses in the Member State of import, to assess whether the circumstances prevailing at the time of

2931. CJEU C-642/16 of 17.5.2018 – Junek Europ-Vertrieb/Lohmann & Rauscher International, para. 26, with reference to CJEU C-348/04 of 26.4.2007 – Boehringer Ingelheim and Others (II), paras 17; also CJEU C-147/20 of 17.11.2022 – Novartis Pharma/Abacus Medicine, para. 48; C-204/20 of 17.11.2022 – Bayer Intellectual Property/kohlpharma, para. 59; C-224/20 of 17.11.2022 – Merck Sharp & Dohme a.o./Abacus a.o., para. 50; C-253/20 and C-254/20 of 17.11.2022 – Impexeco/Novartis a.o., para. 51.

2932. CJEU C-642/16 of 17.5.2018 – Junek Europ-Vertrieb/Lohmann & Rauscher International, para. 35.

2933. CJEU C-642/16 of 17.5.2018 – Junek Europ-Vertrieb/Lohmann & Rauscher International, para. 36.

2934. CJEU C-642/16 of 17.5.2018 – Junek Europ-Vertrieb/Lohmann & Rauscher International, para. 37.

2935. CJEU C-379/97 of 12.10.1999 – Upjohn, para. 28.

marketing in the Member State of import make it objectively necessary to replace the original trade mark by that used in the Member State of import in order that the product in question may be marketed in that State by the parallel importer.[2936]

This condition of necessity is satisfied if, in a specific case, the prohibition imposed on the importer against replacing the trade mark hinders effective access to the markets of the importing Member State. That would be the case if the rules or practices in the importing Member State prevent the product in question from being marketed in that State under its trade mark in the exporting Member State. This is so where a rule for the protection of consumers prohibits the use, in the importing Member State, of the trade mark used in the exporting Member State on the ground that it is liable to mislead consumers.[2937]

In contrast, the condition of necessity will not be satisfied if replacement of the trade mark is explicable solely by the parallel importer's attempt to secure a commercial advantage.[2938]

It is for the national courts to determine, in each specific case, whether it was objectively necessary for the parallel importer to use the trade mark used in the Member State of import in order to enable the imported products to be marketed.[2939]

There is no objective difference between reaffixing a trade mark after repackaging and replacing the original trade mark by another which is capable of justifying the condition of artificial partitioning being applied differently in each of those cases.[2940]

There is no reason in principle to distinguish between the situation where a third party reaffixes the trade mark after repackaging the product, and the situation where, after the product has been repackaged, he uses the trade mark affixed to the original packaging by the manufacturer by leaving it visible through new external packaging or by retaining the original external packaging itself.[2941]

In each case, the question is whether, having regard to the essential function of a trade mark, the power of the owner to oppose the use of the trade mark by a third party after the product has been repackaged falls within the specific subject matter of the trade mark right.[2942]

[14] Refilling

Article 15(2) EUTMR and Article 15(2) TMD must be interpreted as meaning that the proprietor of a trade mark who has put on the market, in a Member State, goods bearing that mark and intended to be reused and refilled numerous times is **not** entitled, under

2936. CJEU C-379/97 of 12.10.1999 – Upjohn, para. 46.
2937. CJEU C-379/97 of 12.10.1999 – Upjohn, para. 43; C-297/15 of 10.11.2016 – Ferring Lægemidler/Orifarm, para. 20; C-147/20 of 17.11.2022 – Novartis Pharma/Abacus Medicine, para. 52 and 56; C-204/20 of 17.11.2022 – Bayer Intellectual Property/kohlpharma, para. 63; C-224/20 of 17.11.2022 – Merck Sharp & Dohme a.o./Abacus a.o., para. 54; C-253/20 and C-254/20 of 17.11.2022 – Impexeco/Novartis a.o., para. 55.
2938. CJEU C-379/97 of 12.10.1999 – Upjohn, para. 44.
2939. CJEU C-379/97 of 12.10.1999 – Upjohn, para. 45.
2940. CJEU C-379/97 of 12.10.1999 – Upjohn, para. 37.
2941. CJEU C-71 to 73/94 of 11.7.1996 – Eurim-Pharm Arzneimittel/Beiersdorf and Others, para. 38.
2942. CJEU C-71 to 73/94 of 11.7.1996 – Eurim-Pharm Arzneimittel/Beiersdorf and Others, para. 39.

those provisions, to **oppose** subsequent commercialization of those goods, in that Member State, by a reseller who has **refilled** them and has replaced the label on which the original mark appeared, by another label, while leaving visible the original mark on those goods, unless that new labelling creates a false impression, in the minds of consumers, that there is an economic connection between the reseller and the trade mark proprietor. That likelihood of confusion must be assessed globally in the light of the information appearing on the product and its new labelling and having regard to the distribution practices of the sector concerned and the level of knowledge that consumers have of those practices.[2943]

The question of whether the trade mark proprietor may oppose further commercialization of goods bearing his or her trade mark and, in particular, the steps taken by the reseller concerning the removal of the original labels and the affixing of new labels to those goods, while leaving visible the original mark, must be examined in the light of the legitimate interests of the trade mark proprietor, in particular that of safeguarding the essential function of the trade mark, which is to guarantee the identity of the origin of the marked product to the consumer or end user.[2944]

In so far as it necessarily amounts to a limitation on the fundamental principle of the free movement of goods, the right of the trade mark proprietor to oppose further commercialization of the goods bearing his or her trade mark is not unlimited.[2945]

In the present case, it is common ground that the carbon dioxide cylinders in question were put on the market in the EEA for the first time by the proprietors of the EU and the national trade marks affixed to them.[2946]

According to the case law of the Court of Justice, the sale of a refillable gas bottle by the proprietor of the marks affixed to it exhausts the rights which that proprietor derives from the registration of those marks and transfers to the purchaser the right to use that bottle freely, including the right to exchange it or have it refilled by an undertaking of his or her choice. That right of the purchaser has, as its corollary, the right of competitors of the proprietor of the marks affixed on that bottle to refill and exchange the empty bottles.[2947]

That being so, the activity of a reseller consisting of refilling the cylinders in question, that were returned empty by consumers, and affixing to them its own labels after removing those bearing the original marks, while leaving visible the original mark on the cylinders, is capable of falling within the scope of Article 15(2) EUTMR and Article 15(2) TMD.[2948]

However, under Article 15(2) EUTMR and Article 15(2) TMD, the proprietor of a trade mark is entitled, despite the placing on the market of goods bearing his or her trade mark, to oppose further commercialization of those goods where legitimate

2943. CJEU C-197/21 of 27.10.2022 – Soda-Club (CO2) a.o./MySoda, para. 54.
2944. CJEU C-197/21 of 27.10.2022 – Soda-Club (CO2) a.o./MySoda, para. 36.
2945. CJEU C-197/21 of 27.10.2022 – Soda-Club (CO2) a.o./MySoda, para. 37.
2946. CJEU C-197/21 of 27.10.2022 – Soda-Club (CO2) a.o./MySoda, para. 38.
2947. CJEU C-197/21 of 27.10.2022 – Soda-Club (CO2) a.o./MySoda, para. 39, with reference to CJEU C-46/10 of 14.7.2011 – Viking Gas, para. 35.
2948. CJEU C-197/21 of 27.10.2022 – Soda-Club (CO2) a.o./MySoda, para. 40, with reference to CJEU C-46/10 of 14.7.2011 – Viking Gas, para. 36.

reasons justify such opposition. The situation relating to the alteration or impairment of the condition of goods, which is expressly provided for in those provisions, is given only as an example since those provisions do not provide an exhaustive list of legitimate reasons which may exclude the application of the principle of exhaustion.[2949]

In the context of parallel imports of repackaged pharmaceutical products, the Court has drawn up a list of conditions in order to frame the existence of such reasons in that specific context.[2950]

In a context closer to that at issue in the main proceedings, the Court has held that such a legitimate reason also exists when the use by a third party of a sign identical with, or similar to, a trade mark seriously damages the reputation of that mark or when that use is carried out in such a way as to give the impression that there is a commercial connection between the trade mark proprietor and that third party, and in particular that that third party is affiliated to the proprietor's distribution network or that there is a special relationship between those two persons.[2951]

It follows that a false impression which may arise in the minds of consumers as to whether there is an economic connection between the trade mark proprietor and a reseller is one of the legitimate reasons for which the trade mark proprietor may oppose further commercialization of goods bearing his or her trade mark by a reseller, in particular where that reseller withdraws the label on which the original mark appears and affixes its own label to that product, while leaving visible the original mark engraved on the product. The fact that the measures taken by the reseller for the purposes of further commercialization of the goods in question are located within the Member State in which those goods were initially put on the market is not decisive for the purposes of determining whether the trade mark proprietor's opposition is justified by such a legitimate reason.[2952]

In order to assess whether such a false impression exists, account must be taken of all the circumstances relating to the reseller's activity, such as the way in which the cylinders are presented to consumers following the new labelling and the conditions under which they are sold, in particular the practices of refilling those cylinders which prevail in the sector concerned.[2953]

Although it is for the referring court to assess whether there is a false impression as to the economic connection between the proprietors of the trade marks and the reseller who refilled the cylinders at issue in the main proceedings, the Court may

2949. CJEU C-197/21 of 27.10.2022 – Soda-Club (CO2) a.o./MySoda, para. 41.
2950. CJEU C-197/21 of 27.10.2022 – Soda-Club (CO2) a.o./MySoda, para. 42, with reference to CJEU C-427/93, C-429/93 and C-436/93 of 11.7.1996 – Bristol-Myers Squibb and Others/ Paranova.
2951. CJEU C-197/21 of 27.10.2022 – Soda-Club (CO2) a.o./MySoda, para. 43, with reference to CJEU C-558/08 of 8.7.2010 – Portakabin, paras 79 et seq; C-46/10 of 14.7.2011 – Viking Gas, para. 37.
2952. CJEU C-197/21 of 27.10.2022 – Soda-Club (CO2) a.o./MySoda, para. 44.
2953. CJEU C-197/21 of 27.10.2022 – Soda-Club (CO2) a.o./MySoda, para. 45, with reference to CJEU C-46/10 of 14.7.2011 – Viking Gas, paras 39 et seq.

nevertheless provide that court with all the elements of interpretation under EU law which may be useful to it.[2954]

Thus, it should be noted, in the first place, that the extent of the information appearing on the new labels is of significant importance. The overall impression created by the new label must be assessed in order to determine whether the information relating to the trade mark proprietor, who manufactured the cylinder, and that relating to the reseller, who refilled it, is clear and unambiguous to a consumer, who is reasonably well informed and reasonably observant. That information, presented on the new label, must, in particular, not give the impression that there is an economic connection between the reseller who refilled the cylinder and the proprietor of the original trade mark.[2955]

In the second place, in order to assess the impression created by the new labelling, account must also be taken of the practices in the sector concerned and the question whether consumers are accustomed to the cylinders being refilled by operators other than the proprietor of the original trade mark.[2956]

In that regard, the fact that the product at issue is made up of a cylinder intended to be reused and refilled numerous times, as well as its content, may be relevant for the purposes of determining whether there is such a false impression in the minds of consumers. It is true that account must be taken of the fact that, on account of the functional relationship between a cylinder and its content, the general public is likely to consider that both normally have the same commercial origin. However, if it were impossible to use compressed or liquefied gases independent of the metal containers holding them and if that type of cylinder may, accordingly, be regarded as packaging, those cylinders – in so far as they are intended to be reused and refilled numerous times, according to the logic of recycling – will not necessarily be perceived as having the same commercial origin as the gas which they contain.[2957]

As regards, in particular, the conditions to refill empty cylinders, it must be assumed that a consumer, who goes directly to an operator other than the proprietor of the original mark to have an empty cylinder refilled or to exchange it for a refilled cylinder, will be more readily in a position to be aware that there is no economic connection between that competitor and the trade mark proprietor.[2958]

In the present case, as is apparent from the order for reference and the written observations of the parties to the main proceedings, neither the proprietors of the original trade marks nor the reseller offer their carbon dioxide cylinders directly to consumers since those cylinders are available for sale only in the distributors' shops.[2959]

The absence of direct contact with the reseller may give rise to a likelihood of confusion in the minds of consumers as to the relationship between that reseller and the proprietors of the original trade marks. Such a situation is therefore liable to prevent

2954. CJEU C-197/21 of 27.10.2022 – Soda-Club (CO2) a.o./MySoda, para. 46, with further proof.
2955. CJEU C-197/21 of 27.10.2022 – Soda-Club (CO2) a.o./MySoda, para. 47.
2956. CJEU C-197/21 of 27.10.2022 – Soda-Club (CO2) a.o./MySoda, para. 48.
2957. CJEU C-197/21 of 27.10.2022 – Soda-Club (CO2) a.o./MySoda, para. 49, with further proof.
2958. CJEU C-197/21 of 27.10.2022 – Soda-Club (CO2) a.o./MySoda, para. 50.
2959. CJEU C-197/21 of 27.10.2022 – Soda-Club (CO2) a.o./MySoda, para. 51.

the essential function of the trade mark from being fulfilled, and thus to justify the application of Article 15(2) EUTMR and Article 15(2) TMD.[2960]

In the third place, it follows from the case law of the Court that the fact that the original mark of the cylinder remains visible in spite of the additional labelling affixed by the reseller constitutes a relevant factor in so far as it seems to rule out that the labelling changed the condition of the cylinders by masking their origin.[2961]

Articles 5 and 7 TMD2008 must be interpreted as meaning that the holder of an exclusive licence for the **use of composite gas bottles intended for reuse**, the shape of which is protected as a three-dimensional mark and to which the holder has affixed its own name and logo that are registered both as word and figurative marks, may not prevent those bottles, after consumers have purchased them and consumed the gas initially contained in them, from being exchanged by a third party, on payment, for composite bottles filled with gas which does not come from the holder of that licence, unless that holder is able to rely on a proper reason for the purposes of Article 7(2) TMD2008.[2962]

In that regard, it must be pointed out that the composite bottles, which are intended for reuse a number of times, do not constitute mere packaging of the original product, but have an independent economic value and must be regarded as goods in themselves. When the consumer first purchases such a bottle filled with gas, he must pay not only for that gas but also for the composite bottle, the price of which is higher than that of standard steel gas canisters, in particular on account of their specific technical characteristics, and than the price of the gas which they contain.[2963]

In those circumstances, a balance must be struck between, on the one hand, the legitimate interest on the part of the licensee of the right to the trade mark constituted by the shape of the composite bottle and the proprietor of the marks affixed to that bottle in profiting from the rights attached to those marks and, on the other, the legitimate interests of purchasers of those bottles, in particular the interest in fully enjoying their property rights in those bottles, and the general interest in maintaining undistorted competition.[2964]

As regards the interest of that licensee and proprietor in profiting from the rights attached to those marks, it must be pointed out that the sale of composite bottles allows it to realize the economic value of the marks relating to those bottles. The Court has already held[2965] that a sale which allows the realization of the economic value of a mark exhausts the exclusive rights conferred by the TMD.[2966]

As regards the interests of purchasers of composite bottles, it is common ground that they may not fully enjoy their property rights in those bottles if those rights are restricted by the related trade mark rights even after the sale of those bottles by the

2960. CJEU C-197/21 of 27.10.2022 – Soda-Club (CO2) a.o./MySoda, para. 52.
2961. CJEU C-197/21 of 27.10.2022 – Soda-Club (CO2) a.o./MySoda, para. 53, with reference to CJEU C-46/10 of 14.7.2011 – Viking Gas, para. 41.
2962. CJEU C-46/10 of 14.7.2011 – Viking Gas, para. 42.
2963. CJEU C-46/10 of 14.7.2011 – Viking Gas, para. 30.
2964. CJEU C-46/10 of 14.7.2011 – Viking Gas, para. 31.
2965. CJEU C-16/03 of 30.11.2004 – Peak Holding, para. 40.
2966. CJEU C-46/10 of 14.7.2011 – Viking Gas, para. 32.

proprietor or with his consent. Those purchasers would no longer be free to exercise those property rights, but would be tied to a single gas supplier for the subsequent refilling of those bottles.[2967]

Lastly, to allow the licensee of the trade mark right constituted by the shape of the composite bottle and proprietor of the marks affixed to that bottle to prevent, on the basis of the rights relating to those marks, the bottles from being refilled would unduly reduce competition on the downstream market for the refilling of gas bottles, and would even create the risk of that market being closed off if the licensee and proprietor were to succeed in imposing its bottle because of its specific technical characteristics, the protection of which is not the purpose of trade mark law. That risk is, moreover, increased by virtue of the fact that the cost of the composite bottle is much more than the gas and that the purchaser, in order to regain a free choice of gas supplier, would have to forgo the initial outlay made in purchasing the bottle, the recouping of which requires the bottle to be reused a sufficient number of times.[2968]

It follows from the foregoing that the sale of the composite bottle exhausts the rights that the licensee of the right to the trade mark constituted by the shape of the composite bottle and proprietor of the marks affixed to that bottle derives from those marks and transfers to the purchaser the right to use that bottle freely, including the right to exchange it or have it refilled, once the original gas has been consumed, by an undertaking of his choice, that is to say, not only by that licensee and proprietor but also by one of its competitors. The corollary of that right on the part of the purchaser is the right of those competitors, within the limits set out in Article 7(2) TMD2008, to refill and exchange the empty bottles.[2969]

As regards those limits, it must be borne in mind that, pursuant to Article 7(2) TMD2008, the proprietor of a mark may, despite the putting on the market of goods bearing his mark, oppose further commercialization of those goods where **legitimate reasons** for such opposition exist and especially where the condition of the goods is changed or impaired after they have been put on the market. According to settled case law, the use of the adverb 'especially' in Article 7(2) TMD2008 indicates that alteration or impairment of the condition of goods bearing a mark is given only as an example of what may constitute legitimate reasons.[2970]

The Court has therefore already held[2971] that such a legitimate reason also exists when the use by a third party of a sign identical with, or similar to, a trade mark seriously damages the reputation of that mark or when that use is carried out in such a way as to give the impression that there is a commercial connection between the trade mark proprietor and that third party, and in particular that the third party is affiliated to the proprietor's distribution network or that there is a special relationship between those two persons.[2972]

2967. CJEU C-46/10 of 14.7.2011 – Viking Gas, para. 33.
2968. CJEU C-46/10 of 14.7.2011 – Viking Gas, para. 34, wording corrected.
2969. CJEU C-46/10 of 14.7.2011 – Viking Gas, para. 35.
2970. CJEU C-46/10 of 14.7.2011 – Viking Gas, para. 36.
2971. CJEU C-63/97 of 23.2.1999 – BMW, para. 53; C-558/08 of 8.7.2010 – Portakabin, paras 80 and 89.
2972. CJEU C-46/10 of 14.7.2011 – Viking Gas, para. 37.

Although it is the task of the national court to assess whether, having regard to the circumstances of the case in the main proceedings, such a legitimate reason exists, it is however necessary to provide that court with some guidance in respect of that assessment, in particular as regards the specific matters on which it seeks a ruling from the Court.[2973]

In that connection, it must be stated that, in order to answer the question of whether the commercialization of the composite bottles refilled is carried out in such a way as to give the impression that there is a commercial connection between that undertaking and producer of the bottle which would entitle the producer to oppose that commercialization, it is necessary to take into account the labelling of those bottles and the circumstances in which they are exchanged.[2974]

The labelling of the composite bottles and the circumstances in which they are exchanged must not lead the average consumer who is reasonably well informed and reasonably observant and circumspect to consider that there is a connection between the two undertakings. In order to assess whether such an erroneous impression is precluded, it is necessary to take into account the practices in that sector and, in particular, whether consumers are accustomed to the gas bottles being filled by other dealers. Furthermore, it appears to be reasonable to assume that a consumer who goes directly to a refiller either to exchange his empty gas bottle for a full bottle or to have his own bottle refilled is more readily in a position to be aware that there is no commercial connection.[2975]

As regards the fact that the composite bottles bear word and figurative marks made up of the name and logo of the producer which remain, according to the findings of the national court, visible in spite of the labelling affixed by the refiller to those bottles, it must be pointed out that this constitutes a relevant factor in so far as it seems to rule out that labelling from altering the condition of the bottles by masking their origin.[2976]

[F] Effect of the exhaustion

If the right to prohibit the use of his trade mark in relation to goods, conferred on the proprietor of a trade mark under Article 5 TMD2008, is exhausted once the goods have been put on the market by himself or with his consent, the same applies as regards the right to use the trade mark for the purpose of **bringing to the public's attention the further commercialization** of those goods.[2977]

On a proper interpretation of Articles 5 and 7 TMD2008, when trade marked goods have been put on the Community market by the proprietor of the trade mark or with his consent, a reseller, besides being free to resell those goods, is also free to make

2973. CJEU C-46/10 of 14.7.2011 – Viking Gas, para. 38.
2974. CJEU C-46/10 of 14.7.2011 – Viking Gas, para. 39.
2975. CJEU C-46/10 of 14.7.2011 – Viking Gas, para. 40.
2976. CJEU C-46/10 of 14.7.2011 – Viking Gas, para. 41; *see also* CJEU C-197/21 of 27.10.2022 – Soda-Club (CO2) a.o./MySoda, para. 53.
2977. CJEU C-337/95 of 4.11.1997 – Parfums Christian Dior/Evora, para. 36.

use of the trade mark in order to bring to the public's attention the further commercialization of those goods.[2978]

The purpose of the 'exhaustion of rights' rule is to prevent owners of trade marks from being allowed to partition national markets and thus facilitate the maintenance of price differences which may exist between Member States. Even if the right to make use of a trade mark in order to attract attention to further commercialization were not exhausted in the same way as the right of resale, the latter would be made considerably more difficult, and the purpose of the 'exhaustion of rights' rule laid down in Article 7 TMD2008 would thus be undermined.[2979]

It is contrary to Article 7 TMD2008 for the proprietor of the BMW mark to prohibit the use of its mark by another person for the purpose of informing the public that he has specialized or is a specialist in the **sale of second-hand BMW cars**, provided that the advertising concerns cars which have been put on the Community market under that mark by the proprietor or with its consent and that the way in which the mark is used in that advertising does not constitute a legitimate reason, within the meaning of Article 7(2) TMD2008, for the proprietor's opposition.[2980]

A trade mark proprietor is not entitled to prohibit an advertiser from advertising, on the basis of a keyword identical with, or similar to, that trade mark, which the advertiser has chosen for an internet referencing service without the consent of the proprietor, the resale of second-hand goods originally placed on the market in the EEA under that trade mark by the proprietor or with his consent, unless there are legitimate reasons, within the meaning of Article 7(2) TMD2008, which would justify that proprietor's opposition to such advertising.[2981]

[G] Burden of proof

A rule of evidence according to which exhaustion of the trade mark right constitutes a plea in defence for a third party against whom the trade mark proprietor brings an action, so that the conditions for such exhaustion must, as a rule, be proved by the third party who relies on it, is consistent with Community law and, in particular, with Articles 5 and 7 TMD2008. However, the requirements deriving from the protection of the free movement of goods, enshrined, *inter alia*, in Articles 28 EC and 30 EC, may mean that this rule of evidence needs to be qualified. Accordingly, where a third party succeeds in establishing that there is a real risk of partitioning of national markets if he himself bears that burden of proof, particularly where the trade mark proprietor markets his products in the EEA using an exclusive distribution system, it is for the proprietor of the trade mark to establish that the products were initially placed on the market outside the EEA by him or with his consent. If such evidence is adduced, it is

2978. CJEU C-337/95 of 4.11.1997 – Parfums Christian Dior/Evora, para. 38; C-63/97 of 23.2.1999 – BMW, para. 48; C-558/08 of 8.7.2010 – Portakabin, para. 77.
2979. CJEU C-337/95 of 4.11.1997 – Parfums Christian Dior/Evora, para. 37.
2980. CJEU C-63/97 of 23.2.1999 – BMW, para. 50.
2981. CJEU C-558/08 of 8.7.2010 – Portakabin, para. 78.

for the third party to prove the consent of the trade mark proprietor to subsequent marketing of the products in the EEA.[2982]

A **qualification of the rule of evidence** must be so where that rule would allow the proprietor of the trade mark to partition national markets and thus assist the maintenance of price differences which may exist between Member States.[2983]

Such a qualification of the burden of proof is required in the event of a voluntary division of national parallel trade marks because it is difficult or even impossible for such a trader to prove the existence of economic links between the proprietors of those marks, those links normally resulting from trade agreements or informal arrangements between those proprietors to which that trader does not have access.[2984]

There is a real risk of partitioning of markets, for example, in situations where, as in the main proceedings, the trade mark proprietor markets his products in the EEA using an exclusive distribution system.[2985]

In such situations, if the third party were required to adduce evidence of the place where the goods were first put on the market by the trade mark proprietor or with his consent, the trade mark proprietor could obstruct the marketing of the goods purchased and prevent the third party from obtaining supplies in future from a member of the exclusive distribution network of the proprietor in the EEA, in the event that the third party was able to establish that he had obtained his supplies from that member.[2986]

Accordingly, where a third party against whom proceedings have been brought succeeds in establishing that there is a real risk of partitioning of national markets if he himself bears the burden of proving that the goods were placed on the market in the EEA by the proprietor of the trade mark or with his consent, it is for the proprietor of the trade mark to establish that the products were initially placed on the market outside the EEA by him or with his consent. If such evidence is adduced, it is for the third party to prove the consent of the trade mark proprietor to subsequent marketing of the products in the EEA.[2987]

In situations such as those in the main proceedings,[2988] it is for the **parallel importers** to prove the existence of the conditions that:

2982. CJEU C-244/00 of 8.4.2003 – Van Doren + Q, para. 42.
2983. CJEU C-244/00 of 8.4.2003 – Van Doren + Q, para. 38; *see also* CJEU C-291/16 of 20.12.2017 – Schweppes/Red Paralela, para. 52; C-175/21 of 17.11.2022 – Harman International Industries/AB, para. 50.
2984. CJEU C-291/16 of 20.12.2017 – Schweppes/Red Paralela, para. 53; *see also* CJEU C-175/21 of 17.11.2022 – Harman International Industries/AB, para. 50.
2985. CJEU C-244/00 of 8.4.2003 – Van Doren + Q, para. 39.
2986. CJEU C-244/00 of 8.4.2003 – Van Doren + Q, para. 40.
2987. CJEU C-244/00 of 8.4.2003 – Van Doren + Q, para. 41.
2988. The main proceedings are between manufacturers of pharmaceutical products, on the one hand, and parallel importers and dealers in pharmaceutical products on the other, against which the manufacturers have brought actions for infringement of their trade mark rights on the ground that medicinal products manufactured by them were the subject of parallel importation and marketed in the United Kingdom by the importers after being repackaged and relabelled.

- reliance on trade mark rights by the proprietor in order to oppose the marketing of repackaged products under that trade mark would contribute to the artificial partitioning of the markets between Member States;
- the repackaging cannot affect the original condition of the product inside the packaging;
- the new packaging clearly states who repackaged the product and the name of the manufacturer;
- the presentation of the repackaged product is not such as to be liable to damage the reputation of the trade mark and of its proprietor; thus, the repackaging must not be defective, of poor quality, or untidy; and
- the importer must give notice to the trade mark proprietor before the repackaged product is put on sale and, on demand, supply him with a specimen of the repackaged product, and which, if fulfilled, would prevent the proprietor from lawfully opposing the further commercialization of a repackaged pharmaceutical product.[2989]

As regards the condition that it must be shown that the repackaging cannot affect the original condition of the product inside the packaging, it is sufficient that the parallel importer furnishes evidence that leads to the reasonable presumption that that condition has been fulfilled. This applies, *a fortiori*, also to the condition that the presentation of the repackaged product must not be such as to be liable to damage the reputation of the trade mark and of its proprietor. Where the importer furnishes such initial evidence that the latter condition has been fulfilled, it will then be for the proprietor of the trade mark, who is best placed to assess whether the repackaging is liable to damage his reputation and that of the trade mark, to prove that they have been damaged.[2990]

It is the repackaging of the trade marked medicinal products in itself which is prejudicial to the specific subject matter of the mark, and it is not necessary in that context to assess the actual effects of repackaging by the parallel importer.[2991]

The proprietor can legitimately oppose further commercialization of a pharmaceutical product, where the parallel importer has repackaged the product either by reboxing it and reapplying the trade mark or by applying a label to the original packaging, unless the conditions set out in paragraph 32 of the present judgment[2992] are fulfilled.[2993]

If it were a matter for the national law of the Member States to determine the question of the onus of proving the existence of those conditions, which, if fulfilled, would prevent the proprietor from opposing further commercialization of a repackaged pharmaceutical product, the consequence for trade mark proprietors could be that protection would vary according to the legal system concerned. The objective of 'the

2989. CJEU C-348/04 of 26.4.2007 – Boehringer Ingelheim and Others (II), para. 54.
2990. CJEU C-348/04 of 26.4.2007 – Boehringer Ingelheim and Others (II), para. 54.
2991. CJEU C-348/04 of 26.4.2007 – Boehringer Ingelheim and Others (II), para. 49.
2992. *See* above Art. 15 'Relabelling'.
2993. CJEU C-348/04 of 26.4.2007 – Boehringer Ingelheim and Others (II), para. 50.

same protection under the legal systems of all the Member States' set out in the ninth recital in the preamble to the Directive, and described as 'fundamental', would not be attained.[2994]

In the light of the foregoing, it must be stated that, in situations such as those in the main proceedings, where it is established that the medicinal products which are the subject of parallel importation have been repackaged, it is for the parallel importers to prove the existence of the conditions which, if fulfilled, would prevent the proprietors from lawfully opposing further commercialization of those medicinal products.[2995]

It is for that trader to put forward a body of precise and consistent evidence from which it may be inferred that such economic links exist. It is for the referring court to ascertain whether the facts constitute such evidence.[2996]

[H] Enforcement

Article 15(1) EUTMR, read in combination with the second sentence of Article 36 TFEU, Article 47 of the Charter of Fundamental Rights of the European Union ('the Charter') and Directive 2004/48,[2997] must be interpreted as not precluding a judicial practice by which the operative part of the decision upholding an action for infringement of an EU trade mark is drafted in terms which, owing to their general nature, **leaves it to the authority with competence to enforce that decisio**n to determine the products to which that decision applies, provided that, in the context of the enforcement procedure, the defendant is permitted to contest the determination of the products covered by that procedure and that a court may examine and decide, in compliance with the provisions of Directive 2004/48, which products have in fact been placed on the market in the EEA by the proprietor or with its consent.[2998]

As regards the obligation for Member States to guarantee effective judicial protection in an area covered by EU law, provided for in the second subparagraph of Article 19(1) TEU, it is clear from the settled case law of the Court of Justice that the right to an effective remedy may be invoked solely on the basis of Article 47 of the Charter, without there being a need for the content thereof to be made more specific by other provisions of EU law or by provisions of the domestic law of the Member States, the recognition of that right, in a given case, presupposing, as is apparent from the first paragraph of Article 47 of the Charter, that the person invoking that right is relying on rights or freedoms guaranteed by EU law.[2999]

2994. CJEU C-348/04 of 26.4.2007 – Boehringer Ingelheim and Others (II), para. 51.
2995. CJEU C-348/04 of 26.4.2007 – Boehringer Ingelheim and Others (II), para. 52; C-297/15 of 10.11.2016 – Ferring Lægemidler/Orifarm, para. 23.
2996. CJEU C-291/16 of 20.12.2017 – Schweppes/Red Paralela, para. 54.
2997. Directive 2004/48/EC of the European Parliament and of the Council of 29 April 2004 on the enforcement of intellectual property rights (OJ 2004 L 157, p. 45, corrigendum OJ 2004 L 195, p. 16).
2998. CJEU C-175/21 of 17.11.2022 – Harman International Industries/AB, para. 73.
2999. CJEU C-175/21 of 17.11.2022 – Harman International Industries/AB, para. 32, with further proof.

In addition, it should be recalled, first, that, in accordance with Article 1 thereof, Directive 2004/48 concerns all the measures, procedures and remedies necessary to ensure the enforcement of intellectual property rights and, second, that Article 2(1) of that directive provides that those measures apply to any infringement of those rights as provided for by EU law and/or by the national law of the Member State concerned.[3000]

In accordance with Article 129(3) EUTMR, an EU trade mark court is to apply the rules of procedure that govern an action of the same type relating to a national trade mark in the Member State in which the court is located. It follows that the procedural guarantees available to a defendant to a trade mark infringement action at the stage of the enforcement of a judicial decision must be assessed also with regard to Directive 2004/48.[3001]

In those circumstances, it must be considered that by its sole question the referring court asks, in essence, whether Article 15(1) EUTMR, read in combination with the second sentence of Article 36 TFEU, Article 47 of the Charter and Directive 2004/48, must be interpreted as precluding a judicial practice by which the operative part of the decision upholding an action for the infringement of an EU trade mark is drafted in terms which, owing to their general nature, leaves it to the authority with competence to enforce that decision to determine to which products that decision applies.[3002]

That question should be understood as comprising three parts. The first relates to the exhaustion of the rights conferred by a trade mark and to the requirements flowing from the protection of the free movement of goods. The second part concerns the requirements that must be satisfied, in accordance with Directive 2004/48, by the measures, procedures and remedies necessary to ensure the enforcement of intellectual property rights. The third part concerns the obligation, for the Member States, first, to establish the legal remedies necessary to ensure effective judicial protection in an area covered by EU law and, second, to guarantee the conditions for a fair hearing, in accordance with Article 47 of the Charter.[3003]

The case law relating to the principle that trade mark rights may be exhausted, based on Article 36 TFEU, is intended, like Article 15 EUTMR, to reconcile the fundamental interest in protecting trade mark rights, on the one hand, with the fundamental interest in the free movement of goods within the internal market, on the other, with the result that those two provisions, which have the objective of achieving the same result, must be interpreted in the same way.[3004]

In order to ensure a fair balance between those fundamental interests, the possibility of relying on the exhaustion of the rights conferred by an EU trade mark, as an exception to those rights, is limited in several respects.[3005]

3000. CJEU C-175/21 of 17.11.2022 – Harman International Industries/AB, para. 33.
3001. CJEU C-175/21 of 17.11.2022 – Harman International Industries/AB, para. 34.
3002. CJEU C-175/21 of 17.11.2022 – Harman International Industries/AB, para. 35.
3003. CJEU C-175/21 of 17.11.2022 – Harman International Industries/AB, para. 36.
3004. CJEU C-175/21 of 17.11.2022 – Harman International Industries/AB, para. 40, with reference to CJEU C-291/16 of 20.12.2017 – Schweppes/Red Paralela, para. 35.
3005. CJEU C-175/21 of 17.11.2022 – Harman International Industries/AB, para. 41.

It is clear from Article 15(1) EUTMR, read in the light of Article 36 TFEU and the case law of the Court, that a trader against whom an infringement action is brought by the proprietor of an EU trade mark has the right, for the purposes of its defence, to allege and prove that the products bearing that mark, referred to in the infringement action, were put on the market in the EEA by that proprietor or with its consent. As is clear from the case law referred to in the preceding paragraph of this judgment, that trader must also be able to benefit from a reversal, in its favour, of the burden of proof where the conditions laid down in that regard by the Court of Justice are met.[3006]

However, the trade mark proprietor is required to adopt a marking system for its products that permits it to be established, for each product, whether it was destined for the EEA market.[3007]

In the absence of a provision of EU law whose interpretation could lead to that solution, taking into account, *inter alia*, its wording, its context and the objectives pursued by the legislation of which it is part, a mere finding of the difficulties experienced by a defendant to an infringement action in obtaining information about the original supplier in a parallel distribution network does not amount to a basis in law justifying the imposition of that obligation on the proprietor.[3008]

Moreover, any obligation to that effect would unduly limit the possibility for the proprietor to change, at the last minute, the market destination planned for a given product.[3009]

As regards the second part of the question referred, it must be observed that the procedural aspects of compliance with intellectual property rights, including the exclusive right under Article 9 EUTMR, are governed, in principle, by national law, as harmonized by Directive 2004/48 which, as is clear from Articles 1 to 3 in particular, concerns the measures, procedures and remedies necessary to ensure the enforcement of the intellectual property rights. Therefore, any national procedure relating to an action for the infringement of an EU trade mark must comply with the provisions of that directive.[3010]

However, it must be observed that the procedural aspect that is the specific object of the referring court's question in the present case is not governed by Directive 2004/48, as that directive does not contain any provision concerning the formulation of the operative part of judicial decisions relating to an infringement action. That question therefore raises the principle of procedural autonomy, which is the object of the third part of the question referred.[3011]

As regards the third part of the question, the referring court appears to perceive a causal link between the formulation of the operative part of the decision to be taken to terminate the main proceedings and the alleged difficulties with which the defendant could be confronted at the stage of its enforcement. However, it must be observed that

3006. CJEU C-175/21 of 17.11.2022 – Harman International Industries/AB, para. 52.
3007. CJEU C-175/21 of 17.11.2022 – Harman International Industries/AB, para. 53.
3008. CJEU C-175/21 of 17.11.2022 – Harman International Industries/AB, para. 54.
3009. CJEU C-175/21 of 17.11.2022 – Harman International Industries/AB, para. 55.
3010. CJEU C-175/21 of 17.11.2022 – Harman International Industries/AB, para. 56.
3011. CJEU C-175/21 of 17.11.2022 – Harman International Industries/AB, para. 57.

those difficulties result from the enforcement proceedings, brought after the infringement action.[3012]

It is therefore necessary to examine whether, at the enforcement stage, the limited legal remedies and procedural guarantees that are available to the defendant, under national law, fail to meet the requirements of effective judicial protection imposed by EU law and therefore the unity and effectiveness of that law.[3013]

The principle of the effective judicial protection of individual parties' rights under EU law is a general principle of EU law stemming from the constitutional traditions common to the Member States, which has been enshrined in Articles 6 and 13 of the Convention for the Protection of Human Rights and Fundamental Freedoms, signed in Rome on 4 November 1950, and which is now reaffirmed by Article 47 of the Charter.[3014]

The essence of the right to an effective remedy enshrined in Article 47 of the Charter includes, among other aspects, the possibility, for the person who holds that right, of accessing a court or tribunal with the power to ensure respect for the rights guaranteed to that person by EU law and, to that end, to consider all the issues of fact and of law that are relevant for resolving the case before it.[3015]

Furthermore, the principle of equality of arms, which is a corollary of the very concept of a fair hearing and has the aim of ensuring a balance between the parties to proceedings by guaranteeing that any document submitted to the court may be examined and challenged by any party to the proceedings, is an integral part of the principle of the effective judicial protection of the rights that parties have under EU law, enshrined in Article 47 of the Charter. That principle implies, in particular, that each party must be afforded a reasonable opportunity to present its case, including its evidence, under conditions that do not place it at a substantial disadvantage vis-à-vis its opponent.[3016]

Furthermore, the principle of respect for the rights of the defence is a fundamental principle of EU law. That principle would be infringed if a judicial decision were to be based on facts and documents of which the parties themselves, or one of them, have not been able to take cognizance and in relation to which they have not therefore been able to formulate an opinion.[3017]

According to settled case law, the observance of the rights of the defence in all proceedings initiated against a person and liable to culminate in a measure adversely affecting that person must be guaranteed even in the absence of a specific law.[3018]

3012. CJEU C-175/21 of 17.11.2022 – Harman International Industries/AB, para. 58.
3013. CJEU C-175/21 of 17.11.2022 – Harman International Industries/AB, para. 59.
3014. CJEU C-175/21 of 17.11.2022 – Harman International Industries/AB, para. 60, with further proof.
3015. CJEU C-175/21 of 17.11.2022 – Harman International Industries/AB, para. 61, with further proof.
3016. CJEU C-175/21 of 17.11.2022 – Harman International Industries/AB, para. 62, with further proof.
3017. CJEU C-175/21 of 17.11.2022 – Harman International Industries/AB, para. 63, with further proof.
3018. CJEU C-175/21 of 17.11.2022 – Harman International Industries/AB, para. 64, with further proof.

However, subject to there being EU rules on the matter, such as those laid down in Directive 2004/48, it is, in accordance with the principle of procedural autonomy, for the national legal order of each Member State to establish procedural rules for the remedies, on condition, however, that those rules are not – in situations governed by EU law – less favourable than in similar domestic situations (principle of equivalence) and that they do not make it impossible in practice or excessively difficult to exercise the rights conferred by EU law (principle of effectiveness).[3019]

It would seem, having regard to the information provided in the order for reference, that the relevant provisions of national procedural law do not infringe the principle of equivalence.[3020]

As regards the principle of effectiveness, it must be borne in mind that EU law does not have the effect of requiring Member States to establish remedies other than those established by national law, unless it is apparent from the overall scheme of the national legal system in question that no legal remedy exists that would make it possible to ensure, even indirectly, respect for the rights that individuals derive from EU law, or the sole means of obtaining access to a court is effectively for individuals to break the law.[3021]

In addition, it must be underlined that, in accordance with the Court's case law, every case in which the question arises as to whether a national procedural provision makes the application of EU law impossible or excessively difficult must be analysed by reference to the role of that provision in the procedure, its operation and its particular features, viewed as a whole, before the various national bodies. In that context, it is necessary to take into consideration, where relevant, the principles which lie at the basis of the national legal system, such as the protection of the rights of the defence, the principle of legal certainty and the proper conduct of the proceedings.[3022]

A trader that holds products bearing an EU trade mark placed on the market in the EEA by the proprietor of that trade mark or with its consent derives rights under the free movement of goods, guaranteed by Articles 34 and 36 of the TFEU and Article 15(1) EUTMR, which the national courts must safeguard.[3023]

However, having regard to the principle of procedural autonomy, recognized in the case law cited in paragraph 65 of this judgment, subject to the provisions of Directive 2004/48, EU law cannot preclude a judicial practice according to which the operative part of a decision upholding an action for infringement of an EU trade mark is drafted in general terms, provided that the defendant enjoys the effective judicial protection of the rights that it derives from Articles 34 and 36 TFEU and Article 15(1) EUTMR.[3024]

3019. CJEU C-175/21 of 17.11.2022 – Harman International Industries/AB, para. 65, with further proof.
3020. CJEU C-175/21 of 17.11.2022 – Harman International Industries/AB, para. 66.
3021. CJEU C-175/21 of 17.11.2022 – Harman International Industries/AB, para. 67, with further proof.
3022. CJEU C-175/21 of 17.11.2022 – Harman International Industries/AB, para. 68, with further proof.
3023. CJEU C-175/21 of 17.11.2022 – Harman International Industries/AB, para. 69.
3024. CJEU C-175/21 of 17.11.2022 – Harman International Industries/AB, para. 70.

Therefore, if the national court is required to designate, in the operative part of its decisions upholding an action for infringement of an EU trade mark, by means of a general formulation, the products which were not previously placed on the market in the EEA by the proprietor or with its consent, the defendant should benefit, at the enforcement stage, from all the guarantees of a fair hearing for the purposes of being able effectively to contest the existence of an infringement or threat of an infringement of the exclusive rights of the trade mark proprietor and to challenge the seizure of those items of products in respect of which the trade mark proprietor's exclusive rights have been exhausted and which may therefore freely circulate within the EEA.[3025]

As regards the circumstance mentioned by the referring court that, without access to Harman's database, it is not objectively possible for AB to demonstrate that the products it purchased had been placed on the market in the EEA by Harman or with its consent, it may be necessary even in a case where no exclusive distribution is established, for the competent enforcement authority or, as the case may be, the court with jurisdiction to adjudicate on appeals brought against the acts of that authority, to reverse the burden of proof, to the extent that that authority or court finds, depending on the specific circumstances relating to the marketing of the products concerned, that the rule on the burden of proof is liable to allow the trade mark proprietor to partition national markets and thus assist the maintenance of price differences between Member States.[3026]

Article 16 Use of trade marks

1. *If, within a period of five years following the date of the completion of the registration procedure, the proprietor has not put the trade mark to genuine use in the Member State in connection with the goods or services in respect of which it is registered, or if such use has been suspended during a continuous five-year period, the trade mark shall be subject to the limits and sanctions provided for in Article 17, Article 19(1), Article 44(1) and (2), and Article 46(3) and (4), unless there are proper reasons for non-use.*
2. *Where a Member State provides for opposition proceedings following registration, the five-year period referred to in paragraph 1 shall be calculated from the date when the mark can no longer be opposed or, in the event that an opposition has been lodged, from the date when a decision terminating the opposition proceedings became final or the opposition was withdrawn.*
3. *With regard to trade marks registered under international arrangements and having effect in the Member State, the five-year period referred to in paragraph 1 shall be calculated from the date when the mark can no longer be rejected or opposed. Where an opposition has been lodged or when an objection on absolute or relative grounds has been notified, the period shall be calculated from the date when a decision terminating the opposition proceedings or a ruling on absolute or relative grounds for refusal became final or the opposition was withdrawn.*

3025. CJEU C-175/21 of 17.11.2022 – Harman International Industries/AB, para. 71.
3026. CJEU C-175/21 of 17.11.2022 – Harman International Industries/AB, para. 72.

4. *The date of commencement of the five-year period referred to in paragraphs 1 and 2 shall be entered in the register.*
5. *The following shall also constitute use within the meaning of paragraph 1:*
   (a) use of the trade mark in a form differing in elements which do not alter the distinctive character of the mark in the form in which it was registered, regardless of whether or not the trade mark in the form as used is also registered in the name of the proprietor;
   (b) affixing of the trade mark to goods or to the packaging thereof in the Member State concerned solely for export purposes.
6. *Use of the trade mark with the consent of the proprietor shall be deemed to constitute use by the proprietor.*

[A] Principles

It is incumbent on the Court to give a uniform interpretation of the concept of 'genuine use' as used in Articles 10 and 12 TMD2008.[3027]

It follows both from the requirements of the uniform application of Community law and the principle of equality that the terms of a provision of Community law which make no express reference to the law of the Member States for the purpose of determining its meaning and scope must normally be given an autonomous and uniform interpretation throughout the Community; that interpretation must take into account the context of the provision and the purpose of the legislation in question.[3028]

Article 15 CTMR provides that there is no justification for protecting an earlier mark unless it is put to 'genuine use in the Union in connection with the goods or services in respect of which it is registered'.[3029]

Article 5(1)(b), the first subparagraph of Article 10(1) and the first subparagraph of Article 12(1) of TMD2008, read in conjunction with recital 6 thereof, must be interpreted as leaving Member States the option of allowing the proprietor of a trade mark whose rights in that mark have been revoked on expiry of the five-year period from its registration because he or she failed to make genuine use of the mark in the Member State concerned in connection with the goods or services for which it was registered to retain the right to claim **compensation for the injury** sustained as a result of the use by a third party, **before the date on which the revocation took effect**, of a similar sign in connection with identical or similar goods or services that is liable to be confused with his or her trade mark.[3030]

3027. CJEU C-40/01 of 11.3.2003 – Ansul, para. 31; C-246/05 of 14.6.2007 – Häupl, para. 44; C-149/11 of 19.12.2012 – Leno Merken, para. 28; *see also* CJEU C-445/12 P of 12.12.2013 – Rivella International/OHIM, para. 51.
3028. CJEU C-40/01 of 11.3.2003 – Ansul, para. 26; *see also* CJEU C-714/18 P of 16.7.2020 – ACTC/EUIPO, para. 34.
3029. CJEU C-714/18 P of 16.7.2020 – ACTC/EUIPO, para. 37.
3030. CJEU C-622/18 of 26.3.2020 – AR/Cooper International Spirits a.o., para. 48.

[B] Genuine use

[1] Principles

In the light of the number of marks that are registered and the conflicts that are likely to arise between them, it is essential to maintain the rights conferred by a mark for a given class of goods or services only where that mark has been used on the market for goods or services belonging to that class.[3031]

Article 12(1) TMD2008 must be interpreted as meaning that there is 'genuine use' of a trade mark where the mark is used in accordance with its essential function, which is to guarantee the identity of the origin of the goods or services for which it is registered, in order to create or preserve an outlet for those goods or services; genuine use does not include token use for the sole purpose of preserving the rights conferred by the mark. When assessing whether use of the trade mark is genuine, regard must be had to **all the facts and circumstances** relevant to establishing whether the commercial exploitation of the mark is real, particularly whether such use is viewed as warranted in the economic sector concerned to maintain or create a share in the market for the goods or services protected by the mark, the nature of those goods or services, the characteristics of the market and the scale and frequency of use of the mark.[3032]

In defining the **concept of 'genuine use'** it must first of all be borne in mind that, as the twelfth recital in the preamble to the Directive states, 'all Member States of the Community are bound by the Paris Convention for the Protection of Industrial Property [and that] it is necessary that the provisions of this Directive are entirely consistent with those of the Paris Convention'.[3033]

The Convention simply states, with regard to revocation for lack of use, as follows, at Article 5C(1): 'If, in any country, use of the registered mark is compulsory, the registration may be cancelled only after a reasonable period, and then only if the person concerned does not justify his inaction.'[3034]

As the provisions of the Paris Convention thus contain no guidance for defining the concept of 'genuine use', the scope of that expression must be determined solely on the basis of an analysis of the provisions of the Directive itself.[3035]

3031. CJEU C-495/07 of 15.1.2009 – Silberquelle, para. 19.
3032. CJEU C-40/01 of 11.3.2003 – Ansul, para. 43; C-259/02 of 27.1.2004 – La Mer Technology, para. 27; C-416/04 P of 11.5.2006 – Sunrider/OHIM, para. 70; C-234/06 P of 13.9.2007 – Il Ponte Finanziaria/OHIM, para. 72; C-149/11 of 19.12.2012 – Leno Merken, para. 29; C-141/13 P of 17.7.2014 – Reber Holding/OHIM, para. 29; C-252/15 P of 17.3.2016 – Naazneen/OHIM, para. 56; C-689/15 of 8.6.2017 – W.F. Gözze Frottierweberei a.o./Verein Bremer Baumwollbörse, para. 37; C-194/17 P of 31.1.2019 – Pandalis/EUIPO, para. 83; C-668/17 P of 3.7.2019 – Viridis Pharmaceutical/EUIPO, para. 38 and 41; C-68/19 P of 11.9.2019 – Camomilla/EUIPO, paras 3/12 and 4; C-143/19 P of 12.12.2019 – Der Grüne Punkt – Duales System Deutschland /EUIPO, para. 55 and 62; *see also* CJEU C-514/18 P of 17.10.2019 – Landeskammer für Land- und Forstwirtschaft in Steiermark/EUIPO, para. 36; C-720/18 and C-721/18 of 22.10.2020 – Ferrari/DU, para. 32-34; *see also* CJEU C-714/18 P of 16.7.2020 – ACTC/EUIPO, para. 35.
3033. CJEU C-40/01 of 11.3.2003 – Ansul, para. 32.
3034. CJEU C-40/01 of 11.3.2003 – Ansul, para. 33.
3035. CJEU C-40/01 of 11.3.2003 – Ansul, para. 34.

Next, the eighth recital in the preamble to the Directive states that trade marks 'must actually be used or, if not used, be subject to revocation'. 'Genuine use' therefore means actual use of the mark. That approach is confirmed, *inter alia*, by the Dutch version of the Directive, which uses in the eighth recital the words 'werkelijk wordt gebruikt', and by other language versions such as the Spanish ('uso efectivo'), Italian ('uso effettivo') and English ('genuine use').[3036]

Where use of the mark does not have as its essential **aim the preservation or creation of market share** for the goods or services which it protects, such use must be considered in fact to be intended to defeat any request for revocation. Such use cannot be characterized as genuine within the meaning of the Directive.[3037]

'Genuine use' must therefore be understood to denote use that is not merely token, serving solely to preserve the rights conferred by the mark. Such use must be consistent with the essential function of a trade mark, which is to guarantee the identity of the origin of goods or services to the consumer or end user by enabling him, without any possibility of confusion, to distinguish the product or service from others which have another origin.[3038]

It follows that 'genuine use' of the mark entails use of the mark on the market for the goods or services protected by that mark and not just internal use by the undertaking concerned. The protection the mark confers and the consequences of registering it in terms of enforceability vis-à-vis third parties cannot continue to operate if the mark loses its commercial *raison d'être*, which is to create or preserve an outlet for the goods or services that bear the sign of which it is composed, as distinct from the goods or services of other undertakings. Use of the mark must therefore relate to goods or services already marketed or about to be marketed and for which preparations by the undertaking to secure customers are under way, particularly in the form of **advertising campaigns**. Such use may be either by the trade mark proprietor or, as envisaged in Article 10(3) TMD2008, by a third party with authority to use the mark.[3039]

Finally, when assessing whether there has been genuine use of the trade mark, regard must be had to all the facts and circumstances relevant to establishing whether the commercial exploitation of the mark is real, in particular whether such use is viewed as warranted in the economic sector concerned to maintain or create a share in the market for the goods or services protected by the mark.[3040]

Assessing the circumstances of the case may thus include giving consideration, *inter alia*, to the nature of the goods or service at issue, the characteristics of the market concerned and the scale and frequency of use of the mark. Use of the mark need not,

3036. CJEU C-40/01 of 11.3.2003 – Ansul, para. 35; C-259/02 of 27.1.2004 – La Mer Technology, para. 19; *see also* CJEU C-495/07 of 15.1.2009 – Silberquelle, para. 17.
3037. CJEU C-259/02 of 27.1.2004 – La Mer Technology, para. 26.
3038. CJEU C-40/01 of 11.3.2003 – Ansul, para. 36; C-259/02 of 27.1.2004 – La Mer Technology, para. 19; C-442/07 of 9.12.2008 – Verein Radetzky-Orden, para. 13.
3039. CJEU C-40/01 of 11.3.2003 – Ansul, para. 37; C-259/02 of 27.1.2004 – La Mer Technology, para. 19; C-442/07 of 9.12.2008 – Verein Radetzky-Orden, para. 14; C-668/17 P of 3.7.2019 – Viridis Pharmaceutical/EUIPO, para. 39; *see also* CJEU C-495/07 of 15.1.2009 – Silberquelle, para. 18; C-183/21 of 10.3.2022 – Maxxus Group/Globus Holding, para. 44.
3040. CJEU C-40/01 of 11.3.2003 – Ansul, para. 38; C-259/02 of 27.1.2004 – La Mer Technology, para. 19.

therefore, always be quantitatively significant for it to be deemed genuine, as that depends on the characteristics of the goods or service concerned on the corresponding market.[3041]

Therefore not all evidence of commercial use can be automatically classified as serious use of the mark in question.[3042]

The question of whether use is sufficient to preserve or create market share for those products or services depends on several factors and on a case-by-case assessment which is for the national court to carry out. The characteristics of those products and services, the frequency or regularity of the use of the mark, whether the mark is used for the purpose of marketing all the identical products or services of the proprietor or merely some of them, or evidence which the proprietor is able to provide, are among the factors which may be taken into account.[3043]

Moreover, use of the mark may in some cases be sufficient to establish genuine use within the meaning of the Directive, even if that use is not quantitatively significant. Even **minimal use** can therefore be sufficient to qualify as genuine, on condition that it is deemed to be justified, in the economic sector concerned, for the purpose of preserving or creating market share for the goods or services protected by the mark.[3044]

In addition, use of the mark by a single client which imports the products for which the mark is registered can be sufficient to demonstrate that such use is genuine if it appears that the import operation has a genuine commercial justification for the proprietor of the mark.[3045]

The fact that the proof of use of the earlier trade mark was established only for the sale of products intended for a single customer does not a priori preclude the use being genuine, even though it follows from that situation that the mark was not present in a substantial part of the territory, in which it is protected. The territorial scope of the use is only one of several factors to be taken into account in the determination of whether it is genuine or not.[3046]

In those circumstances, it is not possible to determine a priori, and in the abstract, what quantitative threshold should be chosen in order to determine whether use is genuine or not. A ***de minimis*** rule, which would not allow the national court to appraise all the circumstances of the dispute before it, **cannot** therefore **be laid down**.[3047]

3041. CJEU C-40/01 of 11.3.2003 – Ansul, para. 39; C-259/02 of 27.1.2004 – La Mer Technology, para. 19; C-141/13 P of 17.7.2014 – Reber Holding/OHIM, para. 32.
3042. CJEU C-141/13 P of 17.7.2014 – Reber Holding/OHIM, para. 32; unofficial translation.
3043. CJEU C-259/02 of 27.1.2004 – La Mer Technology, para. 22; C-416/04 P of 11.5.2006 – Sunrider/OHIM, para. 71; *see also* CJEU C-234/06 P of 13.9.2007 – Il Ponte Finanziaria/OHIM, para. 73.
3044. CJEU C-259/02 of 27.1.2004 – La Mer Technology, para. 21.
3045. CJEU C-259/02 of 27.1.2004 – La Mer Technology, para. 24; C-416/04 P of 11.5.2006 – Sunrider/OHIM, para. 72.
3046. CJEU C-416/04 P of 11.5.2006 – Sunrider/OHIM, para. 76; C-149/11 of 19.12.2012 – Leno Merken, para. 30.
3047. CJEU C-259/02 of 27.1.2004 – La Mer Technology, para. 25; C-416/04 P of 11.5.2006 – Sunrider/OHIM, para. 72.

Having established that the other catalogues produced were not dated, the Court of First Instance cannot be criticized for failing to take them into account in its assessment. It must also be observed that the conclusion which the Court of First Instance reached on the evidence available to it falls well within the scope of the assessment of the facts.[3048]

It should also be noted that the need, in order to assess the genuine character of the use of a mark, for an examination which properly takes into account the nature of the goods or services covered and the characteristics of their respective markets and which, therefore, distinguishes several types of goods or services where the latter are of a large range, adequately reflects the **importance of what is at stake** in that assessment. That assessment thus establishes whether the rights of a proprietor of a mark should be revoked and, if so, in respect of which goods or services that revocation is declared.[3049]

In this last respect, it is admittedly important that compliance with the requirement of use which is in fact part of the objective of creating or preserving an outlet for the goods and services in respect of which the mark is registered is ensured so that its proprietor does not remain unduly protected for the goods or services the marketing of which is not genuinely promoted by that mark. It is, however, equally important that the proprietors of marks and, in the case of a collective mark, their members may, in a duly protected manner, make use of their sign in the course of trade.[3050]

Article 12(1) TMD2008 must be interpreted as meaning that a trade mark is put to genuine use by its proprietor where that proprietor provides certain **services connected with the goods previously sold** under that mark, on **condition that those services are provided under that mark**.[3051]

According to the Court's case law, the actual use, by its proprietor, of a trade mark registered in respect of certain goods, for services which are directly connected with the goods previously sold and intended to meet the needs of customers of those goods, is capable of constituting 'genuine use' of that mark, within the meaning of Article 12(1) TMD2008.[3052]

However, it is apparent from that case law that such use presupposes actual use of the trade mark concerned when the services in question are provided. In the absence of use of that mark, there can obviously be no question of 'genuine use' of that mark within the meaning of Article 12(1) TMD2008.[3053]

3048. CJEU C-234/06 P of 13.9.2007 – Il Ponte Finanziaria/OHIM, para. 75; *see also* CJEU C-610/11 P of 26.9.2013 – Centrotherm Systemtechnik/OHIM, para. 44.
3049. CJEU C-143/19 P of 12.12.2019 – Der Grüne Punkt – Duales System Deutschland /EUIPO, para. 72.
3050. CJEU C-143/19 P of 12.12.2019 – Der Grüne Punkt – Duales System Deutschland /EUIPO, para. 73.
3051. CJEU C-720/18 and C-721/18 of 22.10.2020 – Ferrari/DU, para. 64.
3052. CJEU C-720/18 and C-721/18 of 22.10.2020 – Ferrari/DU, para. 62.
3053. CJEU C-720/18 and C-721/18 of 22.10.2020 – Ferrari/DU, para. 63.

[2] Label of quality

Article 15(1) CTMR must be interpreted as meaning that the affixing of an individual EU trade mark, by the proprietor or with his consent, on goods as a label of quality is not a use as a trade mark that falls under the concept of 'genuine use' within the meaning of that provision. However, the affixing of that mark does constitute such genuine use if it guarantees, additionally and simultaneously, to consumers that those goods come from a single undertaking under the control of which the goods are manufactured and which is responsible for their quality. In that case, the proprietor of the mark is entitled to prevent, pursuant to Article 9(1)(b) CTMR, the affixing by a third party of a similar sign on identical goods, if that affixing creates a likelihood of confusion on the part of the public.[3054]

The fact that a mark is used in order to create or preserve an outlet for the goods or services for which it is registered and not for the sole purpose of preserving the rights conferred by the mark is not sufficient to conclude that there is a 'genuine use' within the meaning of Article 15(1) of Regulation No. 207/2009.[3055]

It is equally indispensable that the mark be used in accordance with its essential function.[3056]

As regards **individual marks**, the essential function is to guarantee the identity of origin of the marked goods or services to the consumer or end user by enabling him, without any possibility of confusion, to distinguish the goods or services from others which have another origin. For the trade mark to be able to fulfil its essential role in the system of undistorted competition which the Treaty seeks to establish and maintain, it must offer a guarantee that all the goods or services bearing it have been manufactured or supplied under the control of a single undertaking which is responsible for their quality.[3057]

The requirement, when applying Article 15(1) CTMR, of use in accordance with the essential function of indicating origin reflects the fact that, while a mark may, admittedly, also be used to fulfil other functions, such as that of guaranteeing the quality of that product or service or that of communication, investment or advertising, it is nevertheless subject to the sanctions provided for in that regulation where it has not been used in accordance with its essential function for an uninterrupted period of five years. In that case, the rights of the proprietor of the mark are declared to be revoked, in accordance with the rules laid down in Article 51(1)(a) CTMR, unless he is

3054. CJEU C-689/15 of 8.6.2017 – W.F. Gözze Frottierweberei a.o./Verein Bremer Baumwollbörse, para. 51.
3055. CJEU C-689/15 of 8.6.2017 – W.F. Gözze Frottierweberei a.o./Verein Bremer Baumwollbörse, para. 39.
3056. CJEU C-689/15 of 8.6.2017 – W.F. Gözze Frottierweberei a.o./Verein Bremer Baumwollbörse, para. 40.
3057. CJEU C-689/15 of 8.6.2017 – W.F. Gözze Frottierweberei a.o./Verein Bremer Baumwollbörse, para. 41, with reference to CJEU C-39/97 of 29.9.1998 – Canon Kabushiki Kaisha/Metro-Goldwyn-Mayer, para. 28; C-206/01 of 12.11.2002 – Arsenal Football Club, para. 48; C-409/12 of 6.3.2014 – Backaldrin Österreich The Kornspitz Company, para. 20; *see also* CJEU C-514/18 P of 17.10.2019 – Landeskammer für Land- und Forstwirtschaft in Steiermark/EUIPO, para. 37.

able to invoke proper reasons for failing to make use of the mark in a way that enables it to fulfil its essential function.[3058]

The essential function of the mark should not be confused with the other functions that the mark may fulfil, such as that of guaranteeing quality.[3059]

Where the use of an individual mark, despite certifying the composition or quality of the goods or services, does not guarantee to consumers that the goods or services come from a single undertaking under the control of which they are manufactured or supplied and which, consequently, is responsible for the quality of those goods or services, such use is not made in accordance with the function of indicating origin.[3060]

There is no use in accordance with the essential function of the individual mark where it is affixed on goods for the sole purpose of being a label of quality for those goods and not that of guaranteeing, in addition, that the goods come from a single undertaking under the control of which they are manufactured and which is responsible for their quality.[3061]

In any event, the fact that licence agreements enable the VBB to verify that the licensees use exclusively good-quality cotton fibres cannot constitute such evidence. It implies, at most, that the VBB certifies the quality of the raw material used. As is apparent from Article 66 CTMR and Article 74a, added to that regulation by Regulation No. 2015/2424, such a certification may, depending on the circumstances, suffice for the view to be taken that a mark other than an individual mark fulfils its function as an indication of origin. Indeed, Article 66 provides that a collective mark fulfils its function as an indication of origin where it distinguishes 'the goods or services of the members of the association which is the proprietor of the mark from those of other undertakings' and Article 74a states that a certification mark fulfils that function where it distinguishes 'goods or services which are certified by the proprietor of the mark in respect of material, mode of manufacture of goods or performance of services, quality, accuracy or other characteristics ... from goods and services which are not so certified'. However, the dispute in the main proceedings concerns an individual mark registered for goods. As has been explained in paragraph 41 of the present judgment, such a mark fulfils its function as an indication of origin where its use guarantees to consumers that the goods bearing it come from a single undertaking under the control of which they are manufactured and which is responsible for the quality of those goods, in their finished state and following the manufacturing process.[3062]

3058. CJEU C-689/15 of 8.6.2017 – W.F. Gözze Frottierweberei a.o./Verein Bremer Baumwollbörse, para. 42, with further proof; C-514/18 P of 17.10.2019 – Landeskammer für Land- und Forstwirtschaft in Steiermark/EUIPO, para. 38.

3059. CJEU C-689/15 of 8.6.2017 – W.F. Gözze Frottierweberei a.o./Verein Bremer Baumwollbörse, para. 44.

3060. CJEU C-689/15 of 8.6.2017 – W.F. Gözze Frottierweberei a.o./Verein Bremer Baumwollbörse, para. 45.

3061. CJEU C-689/15 of 8.6.2017 – W.F. Gözze Frottierweberei a.o./Verein Bremer Baumwollbörse, para. 46.

3062. CJEU C-689/15 of 8.6.2017 – W.F. Gözze Frottierweberei a.o./Verein Bremer Baumwollbörse, para. 50.

It is not a use corresponding to the essential function of an individual trade mark if such a trade mark is used in a way which, while **guaranteeing the geographical origin and the characteristics** attributable to that origin of the goods of different manufacturers, does not indicate to consumers that the goods are manufactured under the control of a single undertaking which can be held responsible for their quality.[3063]

The fact that the trade mark proprietor controls whether its members comply with specifications does not alter the fact that the authorization holder, like the trade mark proprietor, is not involved in the production of the goods and that responsibility for their quality remains with the various producers, which in the present case do not form a single undertaking.[3064]

[3] Non-profit use

Article 12(1) TMD2008 is to be construed as meaning that a trade mark is put to genuine use where a non-profit-making association uses the trade mark, in its relations with the public, in announcements of forthcoming events, on business papers and on advertising material and where the association's members wear badges featuring that trade mark when collecting and distributing donations.[3065]

The fact that goods or services are offered on a non-profit-making basis is not decisive.[3066]

The fact that a charitable association does not seek to make profit does not mean that its objective cannot be to create and, later, to preserve an outlet for its goods or services.[3067]

In addition, paid welfare services exist. In modern society, various types of non-profit-making association have sprung up which, at first sight, offer their services free but which, in reality, are financed through subsidies or receive payment in various forms.[3068]

It cannot be ruled out, therefore, that trade marks registered by a non-profit-making association may have a raison d'être, in that they protect the association against the possible use in business of identical or similar signs by third persons.[3069]

As long as the association in question uses the marks of which it is the proprietor to identify and promote the goods or services for which they were registered, it is making an actual use of them which constitutes 'genuine use' within the meaning of Article 12(1) TMD2008.[3070]

3063. CJEU C-514/18 P of 17.10.2019 – Landeskammer für Land- und Forstwirtschaft in Steiermark/ EUIPO, para. 39.
3064. CJEU C-514/18 P of 17.10.2019 – Landeskammer für Land- und Forstwirtschaft in Steiermark/ EUIPO, paras 40 et seq.
3065. CJEU C-442/07 of 9.12.2008 – Verein Radetzky-Orden, para. 24.
3066. CJEU C-442/07 of 9.12.2008 – Verein Radetzky-Orden, para. 16.
3067. CJEU C-442/07 of 9.12.2008 – Verein Radetzky-Orden, para. 17.
3068. CJEU C-442/07 of 9.12.2008 – Verein Radetzky-Orden, para. 18.
3069. CJEU C-442/07 of 9.12.2008 – Verein Radetzky-Orden, para. 19.
3070. CJEU C-442/07 of 9.12.2008 – Verein Radetzky-Orden, para. 20.

Where non-profit-making associations register as trade marks signs which they use to identify their goods or their services, they cannot be accused of not making actual use of those marks when in fact they use them for those goods or services.[3071]

In any event, in accordance with the finding of the Court in paragraph 37 of *Ansul*, and as the Advocate General pointed out in point 30 of his Opinion, use of a trade mark by a non-profit-making association during purely private ceremonies or events, or for the advertisement or announcement of such ceremonies or events, constitutes an internal use of the trade mark and not 'genuine use' for the purposes of Article 12(1) TMD2008.[3072]

It is for the national court to ascertain whether the proprietor has used its trade marks to identify and promote its goods or its services to the general public or whether, on the contrary, it has merely made internal use of them.[3073]

[4] Free of charge use

Even if part of the services for which the earlier mark is registered is offered by the owner of the other trade mark **free of charge**, that does not of itself mean that that commercial company will not seek, by such use of its trade mark, to create or maintain an outlet for those services in the Community, as against the services of other undertakings.[3074]

Articles 10(1) and 12(1) TMD2008 must be interpreted as meaning that, where the proprietor of a mark affixes that mark to items that it gives, free of charge, to purchasers of its goods, it does **not make genuine use** of that mark in respect of the class covering those items.[3075]

The case is different from one in which the proprietor of a mark sells promotional items in the form of souvenirs or other derivative products.[3076]

In such a situation, those items are not distributed in any way with the aim of penetrating the market for goods in the same class. In those circumstances, affixing the mark to those items does not contribute to creating an outlet for those items or to distinguishing, in the interest of the customer, those items from the goods of other undertakings.[3077]

[5] Use for goods that were sold in the past

The fact that a mark is **not used for goods newly available** on the market but for goods that were sold in the past does not mean that its use is not genuine if the proprietor

3071. CJEU C-442/07 of 9.12.2008 – Verein Radetzky-Orden, para. 21.
3072. CJEU C-442/07 of 9.12.2008 – Verein Radetzky-Orden, para. 22.
3073. CJEU C-442/07 of 9.12.2008 – Verein Radetzky-Orden, para. 23.
3074. CJEU C-320/07 P of 12.3.2009 – Antartica/OHIM, para. 29.
3075. CJEU C-495/07 of 15.1.2009 – Silberquelle, para. 22.
3076. CJEU C-495/07 of 15.1.2009 – Silberquelle, para. 13.
3077. CJEU C-495/07 of 15.1.2009 – Silberquelle, para. 21; C-324/09 of 12.7.2011 – L'Oréal, para. 71; C-668/17 P of 3.7.2019 – Viridis Pharmaceutical/EUIPO, para. 40; C-194/17 P of 31.1.2019 – Pandalis/EUIPO, para. 85.

makes actual use of the same mark for component parts that are integral to the make-up or structure of such goods, or for goods or services directly connected with the goods previously sold and intended to meet the needs of customers of those goods.[3078]

Use of the mark may in certain circumstances be genuine for goods in respect of which it is registered that were sold at one time but are no longer available.[3079]

That applies, *inter alia*, where the proprietor of the trade mark under which such goods were put on the market sells parts which are integral to the make-up or structure of the goods previously sold, and for which he makes actual use of the same mark under certain conditions. Since the parts are integral to those goods and are sold under the same mark, genuine use of the mark for those parts must be considered to relate to the goods previously sold and to serve to preserve the proprietor's rights in respect of those goods.[3080]

The same may be true where the trade mark proprietor makes actual use of the mark, under the same conditions, for goods and services which, though not integral to the make-up or structure of the goods previously sold, are directly related to those goods and intended to meet the needs of customers of those goods. That may apply to after-sales services, such as the sale of accessories or related parts, or the supply of maintenance and repair services.[3081]

Article 12(1) of Directive 2008/95 must be interpreted as meaning that a trade mark is **capable** of being put to genuine use by its proprietor when that proprietor resells **second-hand goods** put on the market under that mark.[3082]

It should be noted that it is true that the resale, as such, of a second-hand product bearing a trade mark does not mean that that mark is being 'used' within the meaning of the case law cited above. That mark was used when it was affixed by its proprietor onto the new product when that product was first put on the market.[3083]

However, if the proprietor of the trade mark concerned actually uses that mark, in accordance with its essential function which is to guarantee the identity of the origin of the goods for which it was registered, when reselling second-hand goods, such use is capable of constituting 'genuine use' of that mark within the meaning of Article 12(1) TMD2008.[3084]

Article 7(1) TMD2008 on the exhaustion of the rights conferred by a trade mark confirms that interpretation.[3085]

According to that provision, a trade mark does not entitle the proprietor to prohibit its use in relation to goods which have already been put on the market in the European Union under that trade mark by the proprietor or with his consent.[3086]

3078. CJEU C-40/01 of 11.3.2003 – Ansul, para. 43; C-720/18 and C-721/18 of 22.10.2020 – Ferrari/DU, para. 34.
3079. CJEU C-40/01 of 11.3.2003 – Ansul, para. 40.
3080. CJEU C-40/01 of 11.3.2003 – Ansul, para. 41.
3081. CJEU C-40/01 of 11.3.2003 – Ansul, para. 42.
3082. CJEU C-720/18 and C-721/18 of 22.10.2020 – Ferrari/DU, para. 60.
3083. CJEU C-720/18 and C-721/18 of 22.10.2020 – Ferrari/DU, para. 55.
3084. CJEU C-720/18 and C-721/18 of 22.10.2020 – Ferrari/DU, para. 56.
3085. CJEU C-720/18 and C-721/18 of 22.10.2020 – Ferrari/DU, para. 57.
3086. CJEU C-720/18 and C-721/18 of 22.10.2020 – Ferrari/DU, para. 58.

Accordingly, a trade mark is capable of being put to use in respect of goods already put on the market under that trade mark. The fact that the proprietor of the trade mark cannot prohibit third parties from using his trade mark in respect of goods already put on the market under that mark does not mean that he cannot use it himself in respect of such goods.[3087]

[C] Genuine use of a Community trade mark

A Community trade mark is put to 'genuine use' within the meaning of Article 15(1) CTMR when it is used in accordance with its essential function and for the purpose of maintaining or **creating market share within the Community** for the goods or services covered by it. It is for the referring court to assess whether the conditions are met in the main proceedings, taking account of all the relevant facts and circumstances, including the characteristics of the market concerned, the nature of the goods or services protected by the trade mark and the territorial extent and the scale of the use as well as its frequency and regularity.[3088]

Article 15(1) CTMR must be interpreted as meaning that the **territorial borders** of the Member States should be **disregarded** in the assessment of whether a trade mark has been put to 'genuine use in the Community' within the meaning of that provision.[3089]

The general interpretation of 'genuine use' may be applied by analogy to Community trade marks since, in requiring that the trade mark be put to genuine use, the TMD and the CTMR pursue the same objective.[3090]

Indeed, it follows both from recital 9 to the TMD and from recital 10 to the CTMR that the EU legislature intended to make the preservation of the rights connected to the trade mark conditional upon it actually being used. A Community trade mark which is not used could obstruct competition by limiting the range of signs which can be registered as trade marks by others and by denying competitors the opportunity to use that trade mark or a similar one when putting onto the internal market goods or services which are identical or similar to those covered by the mark in question. Consequently, non-use of a Community trade mark also risks restricting the free movement of goods and services.[3091]

Account must none the less be taken, when applying by analogy to Community trade marks the case law, of the difference between the territorial extent of the protection conferred on national trade marks and that of the protection afforded Community marks, a difference which is in any event apparent from the wording of the provisions relating to the requirement for genuine use which apply to those two types of marks respectively.[3092]

3087. CJEU C-720/18 and C-721/18 of 22.10.2020 – Ferrari/DU, para. 59.
3088. CJEU C-149/11 of 19.12.2012 – Leno Merken, para. 58.
3089. CJEU C-149/11 of 19.12.2012 – Leno Merken, para. 57.
3090. CJEU C-149/11 of 19.12.2012 – Leno Merken, para. 31.
3091. CJEU C-149/11 of 19.12.2012 – Leno Merken, para. 32; C-610/11 P of 26.9.2013 – Centrotherm Systemtechnik/OHIM, para. 54; C-714/18 P of 16.7.2020 – ACTC/EUIPO, para. 35.
3092. CJEU C-149/11 of 19.12.2012 – Leno Merken, para. 33.

Thus, on the one hand, Article 15(1) CTMR provides that '[i]f, within a period of five years following registration, the proprietor has not put the Community trade mark to genuine use in the Community in connection with the goods or services in respect of which it is registered, or if such use has been suspended during an uninterrupted period of five years, the Community trade mark shall be subject to the sanctions provided for in this Regulation, unless there are proper reasons for non-use'. On the other, Article 10 TMD2008 lays down in essence the same rule in respect of national trade marks, whilst providing that they must have been put to genuine use 'in the Member State'.[3093]

That difference between the two sets of trade mark rules as regards the territorial scope of 'genuine use' is also emphasized by Article 42(3) CTMR. That provides that the rule set out in paragraph 2 of Article 42 – namely that where notice of opposition has been given, the applicant for a Community trade mark may require proof that the earlier Community trade mark has been put to genuine use in the Community – is also applicable to earlier national trade marks 'by substituting use in the Member State in which the earlier national trade mark is protected for use in the Community'.[3094]

It should, however, be observed that the territorial scope of the use is not a separate condition for genuine use but one of the factors determining genuine use, which must be included in the overall analysis and examined at the same time as other such factors. In that regard, the phrase 'in the Community' is intended to define the geographical market serving as the reference point for all consideration of whether a Community trade mark has been put to genuine use.[3095]

It is therefore necessary to ascertain what is encompassed by the phrase 'genuine use in the Community' for the purposes of Article 15(1) CTMR.[3096]

There is no reference in the text of Article 15(1) CTMR to the territories of the Member States. However, it is clear from the provision that the Community trade mark must be used in the Community, which means, in other words, that **use of the mark in third States cannot be taken into account.**[3097]

In the absence of further specification in Article 15(1) CTMR, account should be taken of the context of that provision, of the scheme laid down by the legislation in question and of the objectives which that legislation pursues.[3098]

As regards the objectives pursued by the CTMR, if recitals 2, 4 and 6 thereto are read together, it is apparent that the regulation seeks to remove the barrier of territoriality of the rights conferred on proprietors of trade marks by the laws of the Member States by enabling undertakings to adapt their activities to the scale of the Community and carry them out without restriction. The Community trade mark thus enables its proprietor to distinguish his goods and services by identical means throughout the entire Community, regardless of frontiers. On the other hand, undertakings which do not wish to protect their trade marks at Community level may choose

3093. CJEU C-149/11 of 19.12.2012 – Leno Merken, para. 34.
3094. CJEU C-149/11 of 19.12.2012 – Leno Merken, para. 35.
3095. CJEU C-149/11 of 19.12.2012 – Leno Merken, para. 36.
3096. CJEU C-149/11 of 19.12.2012 – Leno Merken, para. 37.
3097. CJEU C-149/11 of 19.12.2012 – Leno Merken, para. 38.
3098. CJEU C-149/11 of 19.12.2012 – Leno Merken, para. 39.

to use national trade marks and are not obliged to apply for registration of their marks as Community marks.[3099]

In order to achieve those objectives, the EU legislature provided, in Article 1(2) CTMR read together with recital 3 thereto, for the Community trade mark to have a unitary character, which results in it enjoying uniform protection and having equal effect throughout the entire area of the Community. It may not, in principle, be registered, transferred or surrendered or be the subject of a decision revoking the rights of its proprietor or declaring it invalid, nor may its use be prohibited, save in respect of the whole Community.[3100]

The purpose of the system of Community trade marks is thus – as can be seen from recital 2 to the CTMR – to offer on the internal market conditions which are similar to those obtaining in a national market. In that context, if it were held that particular significance should be given, in the framework of the Community arrangements for trade marks, to the territories of the Member States, that would frustrate the objectives pursued by the CTMR and would be detrimental to the unitary character of the Community trade mark.[3101]

Admittedly, a systematic examination of the CTMR reveals that reference is made in the wording of certain of its provisions to the territory of one or more Member States. It should be noted, however, that such references are made particularly in relation to national trade marks, in the provisions relating to jurisdiction and procedure in legal actions relating to Community trade marks and in the rules dealing with international registration, whilst the phrase 'in the Community' is generally used in connection with the rights conferred by the Community trade mark.[3102]

It follows from the foregoing considerations that the **territorial borders of the Member States should be disregarded** in the assessment of 'genuine use in the Community' within the meaning of Article 15(1) CTMR.[3103]

That interpretation is not undermined by either the Joint Statement,[3104] according to which 'use which is genuine within the meaning of Article 15 in one country constitutes genuine use in the Community', or the Opposition Guidelines of OHIM which contain in essence the same rule.[3105]

First, regarding the Joint Statement, it is settled case law that, where a statement recorded in Council minutes is not referred to in the wording of a provision of secondary legislation, it cannot be used for the purpose of interpreting that provision.[3106]

3099. CJEU C-149/11 of 19.12.2012 – Leno Merken, para. 40.
3100. CJEU C-149/11 of 19.12.2012 – Leno Merken, para. 41.
3101. CJEU C-149/11 of 19.12.2012 – Leno Merken, para. 42.
3102. CJEU C-149/11 of 19.12.2012 – Leno Merken, para. 43.
3103. CJEU C-149/11 of 19.12.2012 – Leno Merken, para. 44.
3104. Joint Statement No. 10 regarding Art. 15 of Council Regulation (EC) No. 40/94 of 20 Dec. 1993 on the Community trade mark (OJ 1994, L 11, p. 1; also published in the Official Journal of OHIM, 1996, p. 613).
3105. CJEU C-149/11 of 19.12.2012 – Leno Merken, para. 45.
3106. CJEU C-149/11 of 19.12.2012 – Leno Merken, para. 46; *see also* CJEU C-292/89 of 26.2.1991 – Antonissen, para. 18; C-104/01 of 6.5.2003 – Libertel, para. 25; C-402/03 of 10.1.2006 – Skov and Bilka, para. 42; C-356/05 of 19.4.2007 – Farrell, para. 31.

Moreover, the Council and the Commission expressly acknowledged that limitation in the preamble to that Statement, according to which 'since [t]he following statements of the Council and the Commission are not part of the legal text, they are without prejudice to the interpretation of that text by the Court'.[3107]

Second, it is to be noted that the OHIM Guidelines are not binding legal acts for the purpose of interpreting provisions of EU law.[3108]

Nor can the Court accept the submission, made by some of the interested persons to have lodged observations in these proceedings, that the territorial scope of the use of a Community trade mark cannot under any circumstances be limited to the territory of a single Member State. That submission is based on Article 112(2)(a) CTMR pursuant to which it is possible, where the rights of the proprietor have been revoked on grounds of non-use, to convert a Community trade mark into a national trade mark application if 'in the Member State for which conversion is requested, the Community trade mark has been put to use which would be considered to be genuine use under the laws of that Member State'.[3109]

Whilst there is admittedly **some justification** for thinking that a Community trade mark should – because it enjoys more extensive territorial protection than a national trade mark – be used in a **larger area than the territory of a single Member State** in order for the use to be regarded as 'genuine use', it cannot be ruled out that, **in certain circumstances**, the market for the goods or services for which a Community trade mark has been registered is in fact restricted to the territory of **a single Member State**. In such a case, use of the Community trade mark on that territory might satisfy the conditions both for genuine use of a Community trade mark and for genuine use of a national trade mark.[3110]

It is only where a national court finds that, when account is taken of all the facts of the case, use in a Member State was insufficient to constitute genuine use in the Community that it may still be possible to convert the Community trade mark into a national trade mark, applying the exception in Article 112(2)(a) CTMR.[3111]

Some persons also maintain that, even if the borders of the Member States within the internal market are disregarded, the condition of genuine use of a Community trade mark requires that the trade mark should be used in a **substantial part of the Community**, which may correspond to the territory of a Member State. They argue that such a condition follows, by analogy, from case law.[3112]

That argument **cannot be accepted**. First, the cases in question concern the interpretation of provisions relating to the extended protection conferred on trade marks that have a reputation or are well known in the Community or in the Member

3107. CJEU C-149/11 of 19.12.2012 – Leno Merken, para. 47.
3108. CJEU C-149/11 of 19.12.2012 – Leno Merken, para. 48.
3109. CJEU C-149/11 of 19.12.2012 – Leno Merken, para. 49.
3110. CJEU C-149/11 of 19.12.2012 – Leno Merken, para. 50; C-84/17 P, C-85/17 P and C-95/17 P of. 25.7.2018 – Société des produits Nestlé/EUIPO, para. 74.
3111. CJEU C-149/11 of 19.12.2012 – Leno Merken, para. 51.
3112. CJEU C-149/11 of 19.12.2012 – Leno Merken, para. 52; *see also* the cases: CJEU C-375/97 of 14.9.1999 – General Motors, para. 28; C-328/06 of 22.11.2007 – Nuño, para. 17; C-301/07 of 6.10.2009 – PAGO International, para. 27.

State in which they have been registered. However, the requirement for genuine use, which could result in an opposition being rejected or even in the trade mark being revoked, as provided for in particular in Article 51 CTMR, pursues a different objective from those provisions.[3113]

Second, whilst it is reasonable to expect that a Community trade mark should be used in a larger area than a national mark, it is not necessary that the mark should be used in an extensive geographic area for the use to be deemed genuine since such a qualification will depend on the characteristics of the product or service concerned on the corresponding market.[3114]

Since the assessment of whether the use of the trade mark is genuine is carried out by reference to all the facts and circumstances relevant to establishing whether the commercial exploitation of the mark serves to create or maintain market shares for the goods or services for which it was registered, it is impossible to determine a priori, and in the abstract, what territorial scope should be chosen in order to determine whether the use of the mark is genuine or not. A *de minimis* rule, which would not allow the national court to appraise all the circumstances of the dispute before it, cannot therefore be laid down.[3115]

With regard to the use of the Community trade mark at issue in the main proceedings, the Court does not have the factual information necessary to enable it to provide the referring court with more specific guidance as to whether or not there is genuine use of that trade mark. As can be seen from the foregoing considerations, it is **for the referring court** to assess whether the mark in question is used in accordance with its essential function and for the purpose of creating or maintaining market share for the goods or services protected. That assessment must have regard to all the facts and circumstances relevant to the main proceedings, including the characteristics of the market concerned, the nature of the goods or services protected by the trade mark and the territorial extent and the scale of the use as well as its frequency and regularity.[3116]

[D] Genuine use of International Registrations

Article 4(1) of the Madrid Agreement and Article 4(1)(a) of the Protocol relating to that agreement provide that the protection of the mark in each of the Contracting Parties concerned is to be the same as if the mark had been deposited directly with the Office of that Contracting Party.[3117]

3113. CJEU C-149/11 of 19.12.2012 – Leno Merken, para. 53; *see also* CJEU C-125/14 of 3.9.2015 – Iron & Smith, para. 21.
3114. CJEU C-149/11 of 19.12.2012 – Leno Merken, para. 54; *see also* CJEU C-40/01 of 11.3.2003 – Ansul, para. 39.
3115. CJEU C-149/11 of 19.12.2012 – Leno Merken, para. 55; C-125/14 of 3.9.2015 – Iron & Smith, para. 22; *see also* CJEU C-259/02 of 27.1.2004 – La Mer Technology, paras 25 and 27; C-416/04 P of 11.5.2006 – Sunrider/OHIM, paras 72 and 77.
3116. CJEU C-149/11 of 19.12.2012 – Leno Merken, para. 56.
3117. CJEU C-445/12 P of 12.12.2013 – Rivella International/OHIM, para. 41, wording corrected.

Therefore, by virtue of those provisions, 'trade marks registered under international arrangements which have effect in a Member State' for the purposes of Article 8(2)(a)(iii) CTMR are subject to the same system as the 'trade marks registered in a Member State' referred to in Article 8(2)(a)(ii) CTMR.[3118]

Article 42(3) CTMR is intended only to apply the requirement under Article 42(2) of that regulation – that an earlier Community trade mark must have been used within the Community – to earlier national trade marks, in respect of which it is stated that use is required in the territory of a Member State.[3119]

It should be noted that it is clear from the wording of Article 42 CTMR that Article 42(2) applies to earlier Community trade marks, while Article 42(3) applies to earlier national trade marks.[3120]

It should also be noted that those two provisions do not distinguish national trade marks from trade marks which are the subject of an international registration.[3121]

However, the 'earlier national trade marks' mentioned in Article 42(3) CTMR must be understood as being trade marks which have effect in a Member State, regardless of whether they have been registered nationally or internationally.[3122]

Article 42(3) CTMR states that the rules laid down therein are to apply to the 'earlier national trade marks' referred to in Article 8(2)(a) CTMR, but makes no distinction between the four categories of 'earlier trade marks' listed in that latter provision, which include trade marks registered under international arrangements which have effect in a Member State.[3123]

[E] Genuine use of a collective mark

In the absence of any provision to the contrary laid down in Articles 67 to 74 CTMR, Articles 15 and 51 CTMR form part, under Article 66(3) CTMR, of the provisions of that regulation which apply to EU collective marks.[3124]

Consequently, in accordance with Articles 15 and 51, the rights conferred by such a mark on the proprietor are to be declared to be revoked where, within a continuous period of five years, and in the absence of proper reasons for non-use, the mark has not been put to genuine use in the European Union in connection with the goods or services in respect of which it is registered. Where those grounds for revocation of rights exist in respect of only some of the goods or services, the rights in respect of the goods or services concerned are to be declared to be revoked.[3125]

3118. CJEU C-445/12 P of 12.12.2013 – Rivella International/OHIM, para. 42.
3119. CJEU C-445/12 P of 12.12.2013 – Rivella International/OHIM, para. 39.
3120. CJEU C-445/12 P of 12.12.2013 – Rivella International/OHIM, para. 35.
3121. CJEU C-445/12 P of 12.12.2013 – Rivella International/OHIM, para. 36.
3122. CJEU C-445/12 P of 12.12.2013 – Rivella International/OHIM, para. 37.
3123. CJEU C-445/12 P of 12.12.2013 – Rivella International/OHIM, para. 38.
3124. CJEU C-143/19 P of 12.12.2019 – Der Grüne Punkt – Duales System Deutschland /EUIPO, para. 49.
3125. CJEU C-143/19 P of 12.12.2019 – Der Grüne Punkt – Duales System Deutschland /EUIPO, para. 50.

It should be recalled that the essential function of an EU collective mark is to distinguish the goods or services of the members of the association which is the proprietor of the mark from those of other undertakings.[3126]

Thus, unlike an individual mark, a collective mark does not have the function of indicating to the consumer 'the identity of origin' of goods or services in respect of which it is registered, since that function, which seeks to guarantee to the consumer that the goods or services concerned have been manufactured or supplied under the control of a single undertaking which is responsible for their quality, is specific to individual marks.[3127]

It must be noted, in that regard, that Article 66 CTMR by no means requires that manufacturers, producers, suppliers or traders who are affiliated with the association which is the proprietor of an EU collective mark form part of the same group of companies which manufacture or supply the goods or services under unitary control. That regulation does not preclude the members of such an association from being competitors, each of whom uses the collective mark indicating its affiliation with that association, on the one hand, and an individual mark indicating the identity of origin of its goods or services, on the other.[3128]

It also follows from the case law of the Court that there is genuine use of a trade mark where the mark is used in accordance with its essential function, in order to create or preserve an outlet for the goods or services for which it is registered.[3129]

That case law applies, *mutatis mutandis*, to EU collective marks. Indeed, those marks, like individual marks, are part of the course of trade. Their use must therefore, in order to be classified as 'genuine' within the meaning of Article 15(1) CTMR, in fact be part of the objective of the undertakings concerned to create or preserve an outlet for their goods and services.[3130]

It follows that an EU collective mark is put to genuine use where it is used in accordance with its essential function, which is to distinguish the goods or services of members of the association which is the proprietor of the mark from those of other undertakings, in order to create or preserve an outlet for those goods or services.[3131]

More specifically, such a mark is used in accordance with its essential function from the moment when it enables the consumer to understand that the goods or services covered originate from undertakings which are affiliated with the association,

3126. CJEU C-143/19 P of 12.12.2019 – Der Grüne Punkt – Duales System Deutschland /EUIPO, para. 52, with reference to CJEU C-673/15 P to C-676/15 P of 20.9.2017 – The Tea Board/EUIPO, para. 63.
3127. CJEU C-143/19 P of 12.12.2019 – Der Grüne Punkt – Duales System Deutschland /EUIPO, para. 53, with reference to CJEU C-689/15 of 8.6.2017 – W.F. Gözze Frottierweberei a.o./Verein Bremer Baumwollbörse, para. 41.
3128. CJEU C-143/19 P of 12.12.2019 – Der Grüne Punkt – Duales System Deutschland /EUIPO, para. 54.
3129. CJEU C-143/19 P of 12.12.2019 – Der Grüne Punkt – Duales System Deutschland /EUIPO, para. 55, with reference to CJEU C-40/01 of 11.3.2003 – Ansul, para. 43; C-668/17 P of 3.7.2019 – Viridis Pharmaceutical/EUIPO, para. 38.
3130. CJEU C-143/19 P of 12.12.2019 – Der Grüne Punkt – Duales System Deutschland /EUIPO, para. 56.
3131. CJEU C-143/19 P of 12.12.2019 – Der Grüne Punkt – Duales System Deutschland /EUIPO, para. 57.

the proprietor of the mark, and to thereby distinguish those goods or services from those originating from undertakings which are not affiliated.[3132]

It follows that a collective mark is used in accordance with its essential function by the assertion that the relevant public is fully capable of distinguishing between a mark indicating the product's commercial origin and a mark indicating the recovery of the packaging waste of the product itself.[3133]

[F] Period of use

Article 9(1) (b) CTMR, read in conjunction with Articles 15(1) and 51(1)(a) CTMR, must be interpreted as meaning that, **during the period of five years following registration of an EU trade mark,** its proprietor may, if there is a likelihood of confusion, prevent third parties from using in the course of trade a sign identical or similar to his mark in respect of all goods and services identical or similar to those for which that mark has been registered without having to demonstrate genuine use of that mark in respect of those goods or services.[3134]

Article 9(1)(b) CTMR provides that the proprietor of an EU trade mark is to be entitled to prevent all third parties not having his consent from using in the course of trade any sign where, because of its identity with, or similarity to, that mark and the identity or similarity of the goods or services covered by that mark and the sign, there exists a likelihood of confusion on the part of the public.[3135]

Whilst Article 9(1)(b) CTMR is silent as to the use that the proprietor must have made of his EU trade mark in order to be able to rely on the exclusive right conferred by it, Article 15(1) CTMR provides, on the other hand, that if, within a period of five years following registration, the proprietor has not put the EU trade mark to genuine use in the European Union in connection with the goods or services in respect of which it is registered, or if such use has been suspended during an uninterrupted period of five years, that mark is to be subject to the sanctions provided for by the regulation, unless the proprietor can invoke proper reasons for non-use.[3136]

In this connection, Article 51(1)(a) CTMR provides that, in such a situation, and subject to the further points which it lays down, the rights of the proprietor of the EU trade mark are to be declared revoked on application to EUIPO or on the basis of a counterclaim in infringement proceedings. Article 51(2) CTMR adds that, where the grounds for revocation of rights exist in respect of only some of the goods or services for which the mark is registered, the rights of the proprietor are to be declared revoked in respect of those goods or services only.[3137]

3132. CJEU C-143/19 P of 12.12.2019 – Der Grüne Punkt – Duales System Deutschland /EUIPO, para. 58.
3133. CJEU C-143/19 P of 12.12.2019 – Der Grüne Punkt – Duales System Deutschland /EUIPO, para. 60.
3134. CJEU C-654/15 of 21.12.2016 – Länsförsäkringar, para. 29.
3135. CJEU C-654/15 of 21.12.2016 – Länsförsäkringar, para. 22.
3136. CJEU C-654/15 of 21.12.2016 – Länsförsäkringar, para. 23.
3137. CJEU C-654/15 of 21.12.2016 – Länsförsäkringar, para. 24.

In laying down in Articles 15(1) and 51(1)(a) CTMR a rule under which an EU trade mark that has not been used for a period of five years is to be revoked, the EU legislature, as is apparent from recital 10 CTMR, intended to make preservation of the rights connected with an EU trade mark conditional on the mark being actually used. That condition can be explained by the consideration that it would not be justifiable if a mark which is not used were to obstruct competition by limiting the range of signs which can be registered as marks by others and by denying competitors the opportunity to use a sign identical or similar to that mark when putting onto the internal market goods or services which are identical or similar to those covered by the mark in question.[3138]

It is apparent from the wording and purpose of Article 15(1) and Article 51(1)(a) and (2) EUTMR that, until the period of five years following registration of the EU trade mark has expired, the rights of the proprietor cannot be declared to be revoked in respect of either some or all of the goods or services for which the mark is registered. Those provisions thus confer on the proprietor a grace period for beginning genuine use of his mark, during which he may rely on the exclusive rights which the mark confers, pursuant to Article 9(1) CTMR, in respect of all those goods and services, without having to demonstrate such use.[3139]

Therefore, in determining, under Article 9(1)(b) CTMR, whether the goods or services of the alleged infringer are identical or similar to the goods or services covered by the EU trade mark at issue, the extent of the exclusive right conferred by virtue of that provision should be assessed, during the period of five years following registration of the EU trade mark, by having regard to the goods and services as covered by the mark's registration, and not in relation to the use that the proprietor has been able to make of the mark during that period.[3140]

Finally, whilst, from the time that the period of five years following registration of the EU trade mark expires, the extent of that exclusive right may be affected by the finding – made following a counterclaim, or a defence as to the merits, lodged by the third party in infringement proceedings – that the proprietor has at that time not yet begun genuine use of his mark in respect of some or all of the goods and services for which it has been registered, it is, however, not apparent from the order for reference that that is the situation in this instance and that the referring court is seeking explanation in that regard.[3141]

The **'date of the completion of the registration procedure'** within the meaning of Article 10(1) TMD2008 must be determined in each Member State in accordance with the procedural rules on registration in force in that State.[3142]

3138. CJEU C-654/15 of 21.12.2016 – Länsförsäkringar, para. 25, with further proof.
3139. CJEU C-654/15 of 21.12.2016 – Länsförsäkringar, para. 26; C-541/18 of 12.9.2019 – AS/Deutsches Patent- und Markenamt, para. 22; C-622/18 of 26.3.2020 – AR/Cooper International Spirits a.o., para. 37.
3140. CJEU C-654/15 of 21.12.2016 – Länsförsäkringar, para. 27; C-622/18 of 26.3.2020 – AR/Cooper International Spirits a.o., para. 38.
3141. CJEU C-654/15 of 21.12.2016 – Länsförsäkringar, para. 28; CJEU C-622/18 of 26.3.2020 – AR/Cooper International Spirits a.o., para. 40.
3142. CJEU C-246/05 of 14.6.2007 – Häupl, para. 31.

It is first of all necessary to point out that several legal systems are involved when a trade mark is registered internationally, as in the case in the main proceedings. Both the provisions of the Madrid Agreement, which in the main establishes the part of the registration taking place before the International Bureau, and the national legal provisions, which must comply with Community law, in particular TMD2008, apply. In that respect, Article 1 TMD2008 provides that it 'shall apply to every trade mark ... which is the subject of ... an international registration having effect in a Member State'.[3143]

Further, it should be pointed out, as stated in the third recital in the preamble to TMD2008, that the latter is not intended to approximate fully the trade mark laws of the Member States. The fifth recital therein states in that respect that:

> *Member States ... remain free to fix the provisions of procedure concerning the registration, the revocation and the invalidity of trade marks acquired by registration; ... they can, for example, determine the form of trade mark registration and invalidity procedures, decide whether earlier rights should be invoked either in the registration procedure or in the invalidity procedure or in both and, if they allow earlier rights to be invoked in the registration procedure, have an opposition procedure or an ex officio examination procedure or both ....*

It is thus apparent from those recitals in the preamble to the Directive that it does not harmonize the procedural aspect of trade mark registration.[3144]

Account must be taken of those recitals for the purpose of interpreting Article 10(1) TMD2008. In that respect it should be noted that that provision does not determine in an unambiguous manner the beginning of the period of use and therefore the starting point of the five-year period for which it provides. Indeed, its wording defines that starting point in relation to the registration procedure, and thus an area which is not harmonized by the Directive. As submitted by the Commission, that wording makes it possible to adapt that period to the specific features of national procedures.[3145]

It follows that the Member States are free to organize their registration procedure, and, accordingly, they can decide in particular when that procedure is to be regarded as having been completed.[3146]

In the case of international registration, such as that at issue in the main proceedings, it is thus for the Member State for which the registration application has been filed to determine the time at which the registration procedure comes to an end in accordance with its own procedural rules.[3147]

Consequently, the argument that the date of registration corresponds to the 'date of the completion of the registration procedure' within the meaning of Article 10(1) TMD2008 cannot be accepted. That argument is tantamount to interpreting that provision solely in the light of Austrian procedural rules, whereas the determination of

3143. CJEU C-246/05 of 14.6.2007 - Häupl, para. 25.
3144. CJEU C-246/05 of 14.6.2007 - Häupl, para. 26.
3145. CJEU C-246/05 of 14.6.2007 - Häupl, para. 27.
3146. CJEU C-246/05 of 14.6.2007 - Häupl, para. 28.
3147. CJEU C-246/05 of 14.6.2007 - Häupl, para. 29.

the date referred to by that provision may, for the reasons set out in the preceding paragraphs, vary according to national law.[3148]

It is clear from Article 12(1) TMD2008 that the preservation of a trade mark proprietor's right is predicated on the mark being put to genuine use, in any event **before an application for revocation is filed**, and that the commencement or resumption of use of the mark, even if it occurs before the filing of an application for revocation, does not necessarily serve to maintain the rights of the proprietor, if it appears that such commencement or resumption occurred only after he became aware that such an application might be filed.[3149]

It follows from the foregoing that the Directive makes the classification of use of the trade mark as genuine use of the mark consequential on consideration of the circumstances which pertain during the relevant period and which therefore predate the filing of the application for revocation.[3150]

Nevertheless, the Directive does not expressly preclude in assessing the genuineness of use during the relevant period, account being taken, where appropriate, of any circumstances subsequent to that filing. Such circumstances may make it possible to confirm or better assess the extent to which the trade mark was used during the relevant period and the real intentions of the proprietor during that time.[3151]

It is for the national court to determine whether any circumstances subsequent to the filing of the application for revocation confirm the conclusion that the use of the mark was genuine during the relevant period or whether, conversely, they reflect an intention on the part of the proprietor to defeat that claim.[3152]

According to **Article 43(2) CTMR**, the opponent must only prove serious use of the older mark at the applicant's request if this mark has been registered for at least five years at the point of **publication of the application**.[3153]

The legislators of the EU have expressly set a criterion regarding the effective date which is to be assigned for the ascertainment of the admissibility of applications for proof of use, namely the time of the publication of application of the mark, and on which any later introduction of opposition proceedings can have no influence.[3154]

Furthermore, there is no contradiction between Article 43(2) CTMR and the objective of duty of use of the mark, as the parties have further legal remedies to protect themselves in the face of an opposition arising from a mark which becomes due for revocation due to non-use during opposition proceedings. In the case of a Community trade mark, an **application for revocation** due to non-use can namely be applied for at any time - also during the opposition procedure. In the case of a national mark, the application would comply with national regulations which would have to be established by the Member States.[3155]

3148. CJEU C-246/05 of 14.6.2007 - Häupl, para. 30.
3149. CJEU C-259/02 of 27.1.2004 - La Mer Technology, para. 29.
3150. CJEU C-259/02 of 27.1.2004 - La Mer Technology, para. 30.
3151. CJEU C-259/02 of 27.1.2004 - La Mer Technology, para. 31.
3152. CJEU C-259/02 of 27.1.2004 - La Mer Technology, para. 32.
3153. CJEU C-357/12 P of 30.5.2013 - Wohlfahrt/OHIM, para. 30; unofficial translation.
3154. CJEU C-357/12 P of 30.5.2013 - Wohlfahrt/OHIM, para. 31; unofficial translation.
3155. CJEU C-357/12 P of 30.5.2013 - Wohlfahrt/OHIM, para. 32; unofficial translation.

Article 51(1)(a) CTMR must be interpreted as meaning that, **in the case of a counterclaim** for the revocation of rights in an EU mark, the relevant date for the purposes of determining whether the continuous five-year period referred to in that provision has ended is the date on which that counterclaim was filed.[3156]

At the outset, it must be noted that Article 101 CTMR, entitled 'Applicable law', provides, first of all, in paragraph 1, that the EU trade mark courts are to apply the provisions of that regulation. Next, paragraph 2 of that article states that, on all matters not covered by that regulation, an EU trade mark court is to apply its national law, including its private international law. Finally, that article, in paragraph 3, specifies that, unless otherwise provided in that regulation, an EU trade mark court is to apply the rules of procedure governing the same type of action relating to a national trade mark in the Member State in which the court is located.[3157]

As regards revocation, Article 51(1)(a) CTMR provides that the rights of the proprietor of the EU trade mark are to be declared to be revoked, *inter alia*, on the basis of a counterclaim in infringement proceedings if, within a continuous period of five years, the trade mark has not been put to genuine use in the European Union in connection with the goods or services in respect of which it is registered, and there are no proper reasons for non-use.[3158]

That being said, it must be noted, as the referring court stated, that the CTMR does not expressly indicate the relevant date for the purposes of calculating that continuous period of five years.[3159]

Nevertheless, it follows from the provisions of the CTMR laying down the framework of the applicable regime that the date with regard to which it must be determined whether the continuous period of five years has ended is the date on which the application or counterclaim in question was filed.[3160]

In that regard, it must be noted that, pursuant to the first sentence of Article 55(1) CTMR, the EU trade mark is to be deemed not to have had, as from the date of the application for revocation or of the counterclaim, the effects specified in the CTMR, to the extent that the rights of the proprietor have been revoked; the second sentence of that provision states that an earlier date, on which one of the grounds for revocation occurred, may be fixed in the decision at the request of one of the parties.[3161]

It follows from Article 55(1) CTMR that an interpretation of that regulation according to which, in the event of a counterclaim for revocation, the continuous five-year period of non-use laid down in Article 51(1)(a) CTMR must be assessed with regard to the date of the last hearing would be inconsistent with the consequences of revocation provided for in that regulation.[3162]

First, an assessment with regard to the date of the last hearing would lead to the revocation taking effect as from the date, in the course of the proceedings, on which the

3156. CJEU C-607/19 of 17.12.2020 Husqvarna/Lidl Digital International, para. 50.
3157. CJEU C-607/19 of 17.12.2020 Husqvarna/Lidl Digital International, para. 34.
3158. CJEU C-607/19 of 17.12.2020 Husqvarna/Lidl Digital International, para. 35.
3159. CJEU C-607/19 of 17.12.2020 Husqvarna/Lidl Digital International, para. 36.
3160. CJEU C-607/19 of 17.12.2020 Husqvarna/Lidl Digital International, para. 37.
3161. CJEU C-607/19 of 17.12.2020 Husqvarna/Lidl Digital International, para. 38.
3162. CJEU C-607/19 of 17.12.2020 Husqvarna/Lidl Digital International, para. 39.

conditions referred to in Article 51(1)(a) CTMR are fulfilled, even though those conditions were not met at the time the counterclaim was filed.[3163]

In that regard, it must be noted that while Article 55(1) CTMR provides that, exceptionally, the consequences of the revocation may be fixed at a date earlier than that of the counterclaim, it does not provide for such a possibility in respect of a date later than that on which that counterclaim was filed.[3164]

Second, it could be considered that recognizing the merits of a counterclaim as from a date later than the date on which it was filed does not affect the fact that the EU mark is deemed not to have had, as from the date of filing, the effects specified in the regulations on the EU trade mark.[3165]

Nevertheless, an interpretation of the CTMR according to which, where the counterclaim is filed prior to the expiry of the five-year period of non-use, the revocation could have consequences for a period during which the conditions for the establishment of the ground for that revocation, referred to in Article 51(1)(a) CTMR, were not yet met, cannot be accepted.[3166]

Consequently, it is apparent from the consequences of the revocation, as provided for in Article 55(1) CTMR, that it is with regard to the date of the counterclaim that it must be examined whether the continuous five-year period of non-use of the mark, which is one of the circumstances enabling revocation to be established, as referred to in Article 51(1) CTMR, has come to an end. The counterclaim can succeed only if that circumstance has been established as at that date.[3167]

Furthermore, the argument that the relevant date, for the purposes of assessing whether the continuous five-year period of non-use referred to in Article 51(1)(a) CTMR has ended, should be the date of the last hearing before the court hearing the appeal on the merits, on the ground that that interpretation would fulfil the objective of protecting marks only if they are actually used and the objective of procedural economy, cannot be accepted.[3168]

That line of reasoning adopts a criterion which is inconsistent with the one deriving from the relevant provisions of that regulation and is therefore liable to undermine the EU legislature's objective – referred to in recital 3 and Article 1 CTMR – of ensuring the unitary character of the EU mark.[3169]

That unitary character could thus be called into question if the scope of the protection of the mark that its proprietor enjoys under EU law could vary, in the context of counterclaims for revocation, according to the procedural rules of the Member States where those counterclaims are filed.[3170]

3163. CJEU C-607/19 of 17.12.2020 Husqvarna/Lidl Digital International, para. 40.
3164. CJEU C-607/19 of 17.12.2020 Husqvarna/Lidl Digital International, para. 41.
3165. CJEU C-607/19 of 17.12.2020 Husqvarna/Lidl Digital International, para. 42.
3166. CJEU C-607/19 of 17.12.2020 Husqvarna/Lidl Digital International, para. 43.
3167. CJEU C-607/19 of 17.12.2020 Husqvarna/Lidl Digital International, para. 44.
3168. CJEU C-607/19 of 17.12.2020 Husqvarna/Lidl Digital International, para. 45.
3169. CJEU C-607/19 of 17.12.2020 Husqvarna/Lidl Digital International, para. 46.
3170. CJEU C-607/19 of 17.12.2020 Husqvarna/Lidl Digital International, para. 47.

In particular, the merits of a counterclaim for revocation alleging a five-year period of non-use of an EU mark cannot be dependent on the length of the national proceedings.[3171]

To the extent that the questions referred also concern the interpretation of the EUTMR, it must be borne in mind that, as noted above, it is with regard to the date on which the counterclaim is filed that it must be determined whether the continuous five-year period of non-use of the EU mark has ended. Since, in the main proceedings, the CTMR was still applicable when the counterclaim was filed, the questions referred must be answered in the light of that regulation only.[3172]

[G] Use by a third party

Article 15(3) CTMR provides that the genuine use of a trade mark is the use made of that mark by the proprietor or with his consent.[3173]

It follows that it is for the proprietor of the earlier trade mark who has given notice of opposition to furnish proof that he consented to the alleged use of that trade mark by a third party.[3174]

[H] Proper reasons for non-use

Under Article 15(1) CTMR, a trade mark which has not been put to genuine use during the relevant period is subject to the sanctions provided for in that regulation, unless there are proper reasons for non-use.[3175]

Those provisions are essentially the same as those in Article 10(1) and (2)(a) TMD2008.[3176]

It is for the Court to give a **uniform interpretation** to the concept of 'proper reasons for non-use', as referred to in Article 12(1) TMD2008.[3177]

A uniform interpretation must be given to the concept of 'genuine use' of a trade mark as used in Articles 10 and 12 TMD2008. It is apparent from the seventh, eighth and ninth recitals in the preamble to the TMD2008 and from Articles 10–15 thereof that it was the Community legislature's intention that the maintenance of rights in a trade mark be subject to the same condition regarding genuine use in all the Member States, so that the level of protection enjoyed by trade marks does not vary according to the legal system concerned. Since the objective of proper reasons is to make it possible to justify situations in which there is no genuine use of the mark in order to avoid revocation of the mark, their function is thus closely linked to that of genuine use, with

3171. CJEU C-607/19 of 17.12.2020 Husqvarna/Lidl Digital International, para. 48.
3172. CJEU C-607/19 of 17.12.2020 Husqvarna/Lidl Digital International, para. 49.
3173. CJEU C-416/04 P of 11.5.2006 – Sunrider/OHIM, para. 43.
3174. CJEU C-416/04 P of 11.5.2006 – Sunrider/OHIM, para. 44.
3175. CJEU C-234/06 P of 13.9.2007 – Il Ponte Finanziaria/OHIM, para. 81.
3176. CJEU C-234/06 P of 13.9.2007 – Il Ponte Finanziaria/OHIM, para. 83.
3177. CJEU C-246/05 of 14.6.2007 – Häupl, para. 45.

the result that the concept of 'proper reasons' addresses the same need for a uniform interpretation as does the concept of 'genuine use' of the mark.[3178]

Article 12(1) TMD2008 must be interpreted as meaning that obstacles having a direct relationship with a trade mark which make its use impossible or unreasonable and which are **independent of the will of the proprietor** of that mark constitute 'proper reasons for non-use' of the mark.[3179]

It is for the national court or tribunal to assess the facts in the main proceedings in the light of that guidance.[3180]

That provision governs cases in which a mark has been registered but its proprietor has not made use of it. If that is the case during a continuous period of five years, the mark is liable to revocation unless the proprietor can demonstrate proper reasons.[3181]

It must be stated that Article 12(1) TMD2008 does not contain any indication of the nature and characteristics of the 'proper reasons' to which it refers.[3182]

However, the **TRIPS Agreement**, to which the Community is party, also deals, in Article 19(1), with the requirement of use of the mark and the reasons which may justify its non-use. The definition of that concept given there may therefore constitute a factor in the interpretation of the similar concept of proper reasons used in the Directive.[3183]

Thus, under Article 19(1) of the TRIPS Agreement, circumstances arising independently of the will of the owner of the trade mark which constitute an obstacle to the use of the trade mark are to be recognized as valid reasons for non-use.[3184]

It is therefore necessary to determine what kind of circumstances constitute an obstacle to the use of the trade mark within the meaning of that provision. Although, quite often, circumstances arising independently of the will of the owner of the trade mark will at some time hinder the preparations for the use of that mark, the difficulties in question are difficulties which can be overcome in a good many cases.[3185]

In that respect, it should be noted that the eighth recital in the preamble to the Directive states that 'in order to reduce the total number of trade marks registered ... in the Community ... it is essential to require that registered trade marks must actually be used or, if not used, be subject to revocation'. It appears in the light of that recital that it would be contrary to the scheme of Article 12(1) TMD2008 to confer too broad a scope on the concept of proper reasons for non-use of a mark. Achievement of the objective set out in that recital would be jeopardized if any obstacle, however minimal

3178. CJEU C-246/05 of 14.6.2007 – Häupl, para. 44; *see also* CJEU C-252/15 P of 17.3.2016 – Naazneen/OHIM, para. 78.
3179. CJEU C-246/05 of 14.6.2007 – Häupl, para. 55; C-529/17 P of 22.2.2018 – Martín Osete/EUIPO, paras 6/13 and 7.
3180. CJEU C-246/05 of 14.6.2007 – Häupl, para. 55.
3181. CJEU C-246/05 of 14.6.2007 – Häupl, para. 46.
3182. CJEU C-246/05 of 14.6.2007 – Häupl, para. 47.
3183. CJEU C-246/05 of 14.6.2007 – Häupl, para. 48.
3184. CJEU C-246/05 of 14.6.2007 – Häupl, para. 49.
3185. CJEU C-246/05 of 14.6.2007 – Häupl, para. 50.

yet none the less arising independently of the will of the owner of the trade mark, were sufficient to justify its non-use.[3186]

In particular, it does not suffice that 'bureaucratic obstacles', such as those pleaded in the main proceedings, are beyond the control of the trade mark proprietor, since those obstacles must, moreover, have a direct relationship with the mark, so much so that its use depends on the successful completion of the administrative action concerned.[3187]

It must be pointed out, however, that the obstacle concerned need not necessarily make the use of the trade mark impossible in order to be regarded as having a sufficiently direct relationship with the trade mark, since that may also be the case where it makes its use unreasonable. If an obstacle is such as to **jeopardize seriously** the appropriate use of the mark, its proprietor cannot reasonably be required to use it none the less. Thus, for example, the proprietor of a trade mark cannot reasonably be required to sell its goods in the sales outlets of its competitors. In such cases, it does not appear reasonable to require the proprietor of a trade mark to change its corporate strategy in order to make the use of that mark none the less possible.[3188]

It follows that only obstacles having a sufficiently direct relationship with a trade mark making its use impossible or unreasonable, and which arise independently of the will of the proprietor of that mark, may be described as 'proper reasons for non-use' of that mark. It must be assessed on a case-by-case basis whether a change in the strategy of the undertaking to circumvent the obstacle under consideration would make the use of that mark unreasonable. It is the task of the national court or tribunal, before which the dispute in the main proceedings is brought and which alone is in a position to establish the relevant facts, to apply that assessment in the context of the present action.[3189]

In addition, it must be made clear that Article 19(1) of the TRIPS Agreement, to which the European Union is a party and account of which was taken by the Court in the case law set out in the previous paragraph, cites, amongst the examples of valid reasons justifying non-use of a trade mark, government requirements for goods or services covered by that mark.[3190]

The concept of 'proper reasons' mentioned in Article 43 CTMR refers essentially to circumstances unconnected with the proprietor of a trade mark which prevent him from using the mark, rather than to **national legislation** which makes an exception to the rule that a trade mark that has not been used for a period of five years must be revoked, even where such lack of use is intentional on the part of the proprietor of the trade mark.[3191]

3186. CJEU C-246/05 of 14.6.2007 – Häupl, para. 51; *see also* CJEU C-668/17 P of 3.7.2019 – Viridis Pharmaceutical/EUIPO, para. 73.
3187. CJEU C-246/05 of 14.6.2007 – Häupl, para. 52.
3188. CJEU C-246/05 of 14.6.2007 – Häupl, para. 53.
3189. CJEU C-246/05 of 14.6.2007 – Häupl, para. 54; C-668/17 P of 3.7.2019 – Viridis Pharmaceutical/EUIPO, para. 66.
3190. CJEU C-668/17 P of 3.7.2019 – Viridis Pharmaceutical/EUIPO, para. 67.
3191. CJEU C-234/06 P of 13.9.2007 – Il Ponte Finanziaria/OHIM, para. 102.

The argument that the holder of a national registration who opposes a Community trade mark application can rely on an earlier trade mark the use of which has not been established on the ground that, under national legislation, that earlier mark constitutes a '**defensive trade mark**' is therefore incompatible with Article 43(2) and (3) CTMR.[3192]

[I] Use only for part of the products

The **breadth of the categories** of goods or services for which the earlier mark was registered is a key element of the balance between, on the one hand, the maintenance and preservation of the exclusive rights conferred on the proprietor of the earlier mark and, on the other hand, the limitation of those rights in order to prevent a trade mark which has been used in relation to part of the goods or services being afforded extensive protection merely because it has been registered for a wide range of goods or services.[3193]

The assessment of the likelihood of confusion between the contested registration and the earlier national trade mark is **not limited** to the products in the class of the **Nice Classification** for which proof of genuine use of that trade mark has been provided.[3194]

So far as concerns the concept of 'part of the goods or services' referred to in Article 42(2) CTMR, it must be recalled that the Court has held, in the context of the application of Article 43(1) of that regulation, that a subcategory of the goods covered by an application for registration as an EU trade mark must be identified having recourse to a criterion enabling that subcategory to be delimited in a sufficiently precise manner.[3195]

This analysis carried out by the Court in the judgment *OHIM/Kessel medintim* can be transposed to the application of Article 42(2) CTMR since the definition of an independent subcategory of goods or services must be based on the same criteria, whether in relation to a request for restriction of the list of goods or services covered by the application for registration or an opposition, so as to make it possible, in the assessment of the likelihood of confusion, to compare the goods or services at issue, which are defined on the basis of the same criteria.[3196]

It follows, first, that a consumer who wishes to purchase a product or service in a category that has been defined particularly precisely and narrowly, but within which it is not possible to make any significant subdivisions, will associate all the goods or services belonging to that category with the earlier mark, such that that trade mark will fulfil its essential function of guaranteeing the origin of those goods or services. In those circumstances, it is sufficient to require the proprietor of the earlier mark to adduce

3192. CJEU C-234/06 P of 13.9.2007 – Il Ponte Finanziaria/OHIM, para. 103; *see also* CJEU C-445/12 P of 12.12.2013 – Rivella International/OHIM, para. 49.
3193. CJEU C-714/18 P of 16.7.2020 – ACTC/EUIPO, para. 39.
3194. CJEU C-642/17 P of 22.3.2018 – Arrigoni/EUIPO, paras 4/10 et seq. and 5, unofficial transcription.
3195. CJEU C-714/18 P of 16.7.2020 – ACTC/EUIPO, para. 40, with reference to CJEU C-31/14 P of 11.12.2014 – OHIM/Kessel medintim, para. 37.
3196. CJEU C-714/18 P of 16.7.2020 – ACTC/EUIPO, para. 41.

proof of genuine use of that trade mark in relation to part of the goods or services in that homogeneous category.[3197]

Second, with regard to goods or services in a broad category of goods, which may be subdivided into several independent subcategories, it is necessary to require the proprietor of the earlier mark to adduce proof of genuine use of that mark for each of those autonomous subcategories. Indeed, if the proprietor of the earlier mark has registered his trade mark for a wide range of goods or services which he may potentially market, but which he has not done during the period of five years preceding the date of publication of the trade mark application against which it has filed an opposition, his interest in enjoying the protection of the earlier mark for those goods or services cannot prevail over his competitors' interest in registering their trade mark for those goods or services.[3198]

With regard to the relevant criterion or criteria to apply for the purposes of identifying a coherent subcategory of goods or services capable of being viewed independently, the Court has held, in essence, that the criterion of the purpose and intended use of the goods or services at issue is an essential criterion for defining an independent subcategory of goods.[3199]

It is apparent both from the wording of the last sentence of Article 42(2) CTMR that it is important to assess in a concrete manner – principally in relation to the goods for which the proprietor of the earlier mark has furnished proof of use of the earlier mark – whether those goods constitute an independent subcategory in relation to the goods falling within the class of goods concerned, so as to link the goods for which genuine use of the earlier mark has been proved to the category of goods covered by the application for registration of that trade mark.[3200]

Article 12(1) and Article 13 TMD2008 must be interpreted as meaning that a trade mark registered in respect of a **category of goods** and **replacement parts** thereof must be regarded as having been put to 'genuine use' within the meaning of Article 12(1), in connection with all the goods in that category and the replacement parts thereof, if it has been so used only in respect of some of those goods, such as high-priced luxury sports cars, or only in respect of replacement parts or accessories of some of those goods, unless it is apparent from the relevant facts and evidence that a consumer who wishes to purchase those goods will perceive them as an **independent subcategory** of the category of goods in respect of which the mark concerned was registered.[3201]

In the first place, it should be borne in mind that, under Article 12(1) TMD2008, a trade mark is liable to revocation if, within a continuous period of five years, it has not been put to genuine use in the Member State in connection with the goods or services

3197. CJEU C-714/18 P of 16.7.2020 – ACTC/EUIPO, para. 42; C-720/18 and C-721/18 of 22.10.2020 – Ferrari/DU, para. 37.
3198. CJEU C-714/18 P of 16.7.2020 – ACTC/EUIPO, para. 43; C-720/18 and C-721/18 of 22.10.2020 – Ferrari/DU, paras 38 et seq.
3199. CJEU C-714/18 P of 16.7.2020 – ACTC/EUIPO, para. 44, with reference to CJEU C-31/14 P of 11.12.2014 – OHIM/Kessel medintim, para. 39; also CJEU C-720/18 and C-721/18 of 22.10.2020 – Ferrari/DU, para. 40.
3200. CJEU C-714/18 P of 16.7.2020 – ACTC/EUIPO, para. 46; C-720/18 and C-721/18 of 22.10.2020 – Ferrari/DU, para. 41.
3201. CJEU C-720/18 and C-721/18 of 22.10.2020 – Ferrari/DU, para. 53.

in respect of which it is registered, and there are no proper reasons for the non-use of that mark.[3202]

It follows from that case law that the use, by its proprietor, of a registered trade mark in respect of replacement parts forming an integral part of the goods covered by that mark is capable of constituting 'genuine use', within the meaning of Article 12(1) TMD2008, not only for the replacement parts themselves but also for the goods covered by that mark. It is irrelevant in that regard that the registration of that mark covers not only entire goods but also replacement parts thereof.[3203]

In the second place, according to Article 13 TMD2008, where grounds for revocation, such as those provided for in Article 12(1) TMD2008, exist in respect of only some of the goods or services for which that trade mark has been applied for or registered, revocation is to cover those goods or services only.[3204]

It follows from the considerations set out above that the concept of 'particular market segment' is not, as such, relevant to the assessment of whether the goods or services in respect of which the proprietor of a trade mark has used it fall within an independent subcategory of the category of goods or services in respect of which that mark was registered.[3205]

The only relevant question in that regard is whether a consumer who wishes to purchase a product or service falling within the category of goods or services covered by the trade mark in question will associate all the goods or services belonging to that category with that mark.[3206]

Such a situation cannot be excluded on the sole ground that, according to an economic analysis, the various goods or services included within that category belong to different markets, or to different market segments. This is all the more the case where there is a legitimate interest of the proprietor of a trade mark in expanding his range of goods or services for which his trade mark is registered.[3207]

In the present case, in so far as the referring court states that the proprietor of the marks in question in the main proceedings has used those marks for **replacement parts and accessories for 'very high-priced luxury sports cars'**, it must be noted, first, that it follows from the considerations above that the mere fact that the goods in respect of which a mark has been used are sold at a particularly high price and, consequently, may belong to a specific market is not sufficient for them to be regarded as an independent subcategory of the class of goods in respect of which that mark was registered.[3208]

Secondly, it is true that cars referred to as 'sports cars' are high-performance cars and therefore are capable of being used in motor sports. However, this is only one of

3202. CJEU C-720/18 and C-721/18 of 22.10.2020 – Ferrari/DU, para. 31.
3203. CJEU C-720/18 and C-721/18 of 22.10.2020 – Ferrari/DU, para. 35.
3204. CJEU C-720/18 and C-721/18 of 22.10.2020 – Ferrari/DU, para. 36.
3205. CJEU C-720/18 and C-721/18 of 22.10.2020 – Ferrari/DU, para. 42.
3206. CJEU C-720/18 and C-721/18 of 22.10.2020 – Ferrari/DU, para. 43.
3207. CJEU C-720/18 and C-721/18 of 22.10.2020 – Ferrari/DU, para. 44, with reference to CJEU C-714/18 P of 16.7.2020 – ACTC/EUIPO, para. 51.
3208. CJEU C-720/18 and C-721/18 of 22.10.2020 – Ferrari/DU, para. 45.

the possible intended uses for such cars, which are also capable of being used, like any other car, for the transport by road of people and their personal effects.[3209]

Where the goods covered by a mark have several purposes and intended uses – as is often the case – determining whether there exists a separate subcategory of goods by considering in isolation each of the purposes that those goods may have will not be possible since such an approach does not enable independent subcategories to be identified coherently and has the effect of limiting excessively the rights of the proprietor of the mark.[3210]

It follows that the mere fact that the cars in respect of which a mark has been used are referred to as 'sports cars' is not sufficient to consider that they belong to an independent subcategory of cars.[3211]

Thirdly and lastly, the concept of 'luxury', to which the terms 'luxury cars', used by the referring court, refer, could be relevant to several types of cars, so that the fact that cars in respect of which a trade mark has been used are classified as 'luxury cars' is likewise not sufficient for them to be regarded as an independent subcategory of cars.[3212]

It therefore appears, subject to verification by the referring court, that the fact that the company which is the proprietor of the marks in question in the main proceedings has used those marks in respect of replacement parts and accessories for 'very high-priced luxury sports cars' is not sufficient to establish that it has used those marks in respect of only some of the goods covered by them, for the purposes of Article 13 TMD2008.[3213]

However, even if the circumstance that a trade mark has been used for goods classified as 'very high-priced' cannot suffice for those goods to be regarded as an independent subcategory of the goods in respect of which that mark was registered, the fact remains that it is relevant to the assessment of whether that mark has been put to 'genuine use' within the meaning of Article 12(1) TMD2008.[3214]

That circumstance is capable of demonstrating that, despite the relatively low number of product units sold under the trade mark concerned, the use which has been made of that mark has not been token, but constitutes use of that mark in accordance with its essential function, a use which must be classified as 'genuine use' within the meaning of Article 12(1) TMD2008.[3215]

[J] Use of the trade mark in a differing form

Take care: There was a major change in the wording of TMD2008 from 'use of the trade mark in a form differing in elements which do not alter the distinctive

3209. CJEU C-720/18 and C-721/18 of 22.10.2020 – Ferrari/DU, para. 46.
3210. CJEU C-720/18 and C-721/18 of 22.10.2020 – Ferrari/DU, para. 47, with reference to CJEU C-714/18 P of 16.7.2020 – ACTC/EUIPO, para. 51.
3211. CJEU C-720/18 and C-721/18 of 22.10.2020 – Ferrari/DU, para. 48.
3212. CJEU C-720/18 and C-721/18 of 22.10.2020 – Ferrari/DU, para. 49.
3213. CJEU C-720/18 and C-721/18 of 22.10.2020 – Ferrari/DU, para. 50.
3214. CJEU C-720/18 and C-721/18 of 22.10.2020 – Ferrari/DU, para. 51.
3215. CJEU C-720/18 and C-721/18 of 22.10.2020 – Ferrari/DU, para. 52.

character of the mark in the form in which it was registered' to 'use of the trade mark in a form differing in elements which do not alter the distinctive character of the mark in the form in which it was registered, regardless of whether or not the trade mark in the form as used is also registered in the name of the proprietor'.

Under Article 15(2)(a) CTMR, use of the Community trade mark in a form differing in elements which do not alter the distinctive character of the mark in the form in which it was registered also constitutes use within the meaning of Article 15(1).[3216]

Whilst Article 15(1)(2)(a) CTMR thus introduces a degree of flexibility as to the form in which an EU trade mark is used, the fact remains that that provision does not have any effect at all on the assessment of the genuineness of that use, which must be carried out in accordance with the relevant criteria.[3217]

Those provisions are essentially the same as those in Article 10(1) and (2)(a) TMD2008.[3218]

In so far as it does not impose strict conformity between the form in which the trade mark is used and the form in which the mark was registered, the purpose of Article 15(1)(2)(a) CTMR is to allow its proprietor, on the occasion of its commercial exploitation, to make variations in the sign, which, without altering its distinctive character, enable it to be better adapted to the marketing and promotion requirements of the goods or services concerned.[3219]

Probably no longer applicable: In any event, while it is possible to consider a registered trade mark as used where proof is provided of use of that mark in a slightly different form from that in which it was registered, it is not possible to extend, by means of proof of use, the protection enjoyed by a registered trade mark to another registered mark, the use of which has not been established, on the ground that the latter is merely a slight variation on the former.[3220]

Now expressly applicable: Article 10(2)(a) TMD2008 must be interpreted as meaning that the proprietor of a registered trade mark is not precluded from relying, in order to establish use of the trade mark for the purposes of that provision, on the fact that it is used in a form which differs from the form in which it was registered, without the differences between the two forms altering the distinctive character of that trade mark, **even though that different form is itself registered as a trade mark**.[3221]

A fortiori, it must be held that the use of a sign identical to that constituting the earlier mark and itself registered as a trade mark **under a different number** from the

3216. CJEU C-234/06 P of 13.9.2007 – Il Ponte Finanziaria/OHIM, para. 82; C-252/12 of 18.7.2013 – Specsavers International Healthcare, para. 21; C-501/15 P of 11.10.2017 – EUIPO/Cactus, para. 65; C-340/17 P of 29.11.2018 – Alcohol Countermeasure Systems/EUIPO, para. 57; C-668/17 P of 3.7.2019 – Viridis Pharmaceutical/EUIPO, para. 55.
3217. CJEU C-668/17 P of 3.7.2019 – Viridis Pharmaceutical/EUIPO, para. 57.
3218. CJEU C-234/06 P of 13.9.2007 – Il Ponte Finanziaria/OHIM, para. 83.
3219. CJEU C-252/12 of 18.7.2013 – Specsavers International Healthcare, para. 29; C-501/15 P of 11.10.2017 – EUIPO/Cactus, para. 66; C-668/17 P of 3.7.2019 – Viridis Pharmaceutical/EUIPO, para. 56.
3220. CJEU C-234/06 P of 13.9.2007 – Il Ponte Finanziaria/OHIM, para. 86; C-214/09 P of 29.7.2010 – Anheuser-Busch/OHIM, para. 98.
3221. CJEU C-553/11 of 25.10.2012 – Rintisch, para. 30; C-252/12 of 18.7.2013 – Specsavers International Healthcare, paras 27 and 31; C-340/17 P of 29.11.2018 – Alcohol Countermeasure Systems/EUIPO, para. 57.

earlier mark constitutes use of that mark for the purposes of applying the first subparagraph of Article 15(1) CTMR.[3222]

That conclusion is all the more compelling because, as was recalled by the General Court in paragraph 23 of the judgment under appeal, the fundamental condition of genuine use of a trade mark is that, as a consequence of that use, the mark may serve to identify, in the minds of the relevant class of persons, the goods to which it relates as originating from a particular undertaking.[3223]

Still applicable: The arguments which led the Court to interpret Article 10(2)(a) TMD2008 in that way may be applied *mutatis mutandis* to the context of the second subparagraph of Article 15(1)(a) CTMR.[3224]

The assessment of the distinctive elements of the trade mark must precede the examination of genuine use of the trade mark in question since, under Article 15(1), second subparagraph, lit. a CTMR, genuine use means use of the EU trade mark in a form differing in elements which do not alter its distinctive character. The form of use of the trade mark in question must be examined in the light of its distinctive character in order to determine whether that distinctive character is affected.[3225]

In that regard, it must, first, be borne in mind that for a trade mark to possess distinctive character for the purposes of TMD2008, it must serve to identify the product in respect of which registration is applied for as originating from a particular undertaking, and thus to distinguish that product from those of other undertakings.[3226]

The condition of genuine use of a trade mark, within the meaning of Article 15(1) CTMR, may be satisfied where a registered trade mark, which has become **distinctive as a result of the use** of another composite mark of which it constitutes one of the elements, is used only through that other composite mark, or where it is **used only in conjunction with another mark**, and the combination of those two marks is, furthermore, itself registered as a trade mark.[3227]

A situation, in which a word mark is superimposed over a figurative mark, falls within the scope of the second subparagraph of Article 15(1)(a) CTMR, namely, use of the trade mark in a form different from that under which that trade mark was registered.[3228]

Yet, such identification, and thus acquisition of distinctive character, may be as a result both of the use, as part of a registered trade mark, of a component thereof and of the use of a separate mark in conjunction with a registered trade mark. In both cases, it is sufficient that, in consequence of such use, the relevant class of persons actually

3222. CJEU C-340/17 P of 29.11.2018 – Alcohol Countermeasure Systems/EUIPO, para. 58.
3223. CJEU C-340/17 P of 29.11.2018 – Alcohol Countermeasure Systems/EUIPO, para. 59, with reference to CJEU C-12/12 of 18.4.2013 – Colloseum Holding, para. 28.
3224. CJEU C-252/12 of 18.7.2013 – Specsavers International Healthcare, para. 28.
3225. CJEU C-586/15 P of 7.9.2016 – Lotte/EUIPO, para. 30; C-642/15 of 1.12.2016 – Klement, para. 29.
3226. CJEU C-553/11 of 25.10.2012 – Rintisch, para. 19; *see also* CJEU C-468/01 P to C-472/01 P of 29.4.2004 – Procter & Gamble/OHIM (three-dimensional form of tablet I), para. 32; C-64/02 P of 21.10.2004 – OHIM/ERPO MÖBELWERK, paras 33 and 42; C-304/06 P of 8.5.2008 – Eurohypo/OHIM, para. 66; C-311/11 P of 12.7.2012 – Smart Technologies/OHIM, para. 23.
3227. CJEU C-12/12 of 18.4.2013 – Colloseum Holding, para. 36.
3228. CJEU C-252/12 of 18.7.2013 – Specsavers International Healthcare, para. 19.

perceive the product or service, designated exclusively by the mark applied for, as originating from a given undertaking.[3229]

In light of the scheme and purpose of the CTMR and the wording of Article 15(1) CTMR, this conclusion must also be applied in respect of 'genuine use' for the purpose of preserving the rights of the proprietor of a registered trade mark, within the meaning of that provision.[3230]

It is true that the 'use' through which a sign acquires a distinctive character under Article 7(3) CTMR relates to the period before its registration as a trade mark, whereas 'genuine use', within the meaning of Article 15(1) CTMR, relates to a five-year period following registration and, accordingly, 'use' within the meaning of Article 7(3) for the purpose of registration may not be relied on as such to establish 'use' within the meaning of Article 15(1) for the purpose of preserving the rights of the proprietor of the registered trade mark.[3231]

Nevertheless, the 'use' of a mark, in its literal sense, generally encompasses both its independent use and its use as part of another mark taken as a whole or in conjunction with that other mark.[3232]

The criterion of use, which continues to be fundamental, cannot be assessed in the light of different considerations according to whether the issue to be decided is whether use is capable of giving rise to rights relating to a mark or of ensuring that such rights are preserved. If it is possible to acquire trade mark protection for a sign through a specific use made of the sign, that same form of use must also be capable of ensuring that such protection is preserved.[3233]

Therefore, the requirements that apply to verification of the genuine use of a mark, within the meaning of Article 15(1) CTMR, are analogous to those concerning the acquisition by a sign of distinctive character through use for the purpose of its registration, within the meaning of Article 7(3) CTMR.[3234]

Nevertheless, a registered trade mark that is used only as part of a composite mark or in conjunction with another mark must continue to be perceived as indicative of the origin of the product at issue for that use to be covered by the term 'genuine use' within the meaning of Article 15(1) CTMR.[3235]

It follows that the use of the **wordless logo mark with the superimposed word** sign 'Specsavers', even if, ultimately, it amounts to a use as a part of a registered trade

3229. CJEU C-353/03 of 7.7.2005 – Nestlé, para. 30, 32; C-245/06 P of 9.3.2007 – Saiwa/OHIM, para. 43; C-12/12 of 18.4.2013 – Colloseum Holding, para. 27; *see also* CJEU C-24/05 P of 22.6.2006 – Storck/OHIM (light-brown sweet), para. 57.
3230. CJEU C-12/12 of 18.4.2013 – Colloseum Holding, para. 30.
3231. CJEU C-12/12 of 18.4.2013 – Colloseum Holding, para. 31.
3232. CJEU C-12/12 of 18.4.2013 – Colloseum Holding, para. 32; *see also* CJEU C-353/03 of 7.7.2005 – Nestlé, paras 27–30.
3233. CJEU C-12/12 of 18.4.2013 – Colloseum Holding, para. 33.
3234. CJEU C-12/12 of 18.4.2013 – Colloseum Holding, para. 34, *see also* CJEU C-84/17 P, C-85/17 P and C-95/17 P of. 25.7.2018 – Société des produits Nestlé/EUIPO, para. 70.
3235. CJEU C-12/12 of 18.4.2013 – Colloseum Holding, para. 35; C-252/12 of 18.7.2013 – Specsavers International Healthcare, para. 26.

mark or in conjunction with it, may be considered to be a genuine use of the wordless logo mark as such to the extent that that mark as it was registered.[3236]

That conclusion is not affected by the fact that the word sign 'Specsavers' and the combination of the wordless logo with the superimposed word sign 'Specsavers' are also registered as Community trade marks.[3237]

The condition of 'genuine use' in the sense of Article 15(1)(2)(a) CTMR is satisfied even where **only the figurative element of a composite mark is used**, as long as the distinctive character of that mark, as registered, is not altered.[3238]

However, the finding that additions are 'partially' not negligible cannot cause any consequences for the overall impression.[3239]

Article 10(2)(a) TMD2008 must be interpreted as **precluding an interpretation of the national provision** intended to transpose it into domestic law whereby Article 10(2)(a) does not apply to a 'defensive' trade mark which is registered only in order to secure or expand the protection of another registered trade mark that is registered in the form in which it is used.[3240]

[K] Use outside the European Union

Article 351(1) TFEU must be interpreted as allowing a court of a Member State to apply a convention concluded between a Member State of the European Union and a non-Member State before 1 January 1958 or, for States acceding to the European Union, before the date of their accession, such as the Convention of 1892,[3241] which provides that the use of a trade mark registered in that Member State in the territory of the non-Member State must be taken into consideration in order to determine whether that mark has been put to 'genuine use' within the meaning of Article 12(1) TMD2008, until such time as one of the steps referred to in the second paragraph of Article 351 TFEU makes it possible to eliminate any incompatibilities between the TFEU and that convention.[3242]

It is relevant that in so far as Article 12(1) TMD2008 refers to genuine use of a trade mark 'in the Member State concerned', it excludes the taking into consideration of use in a non-Member State, such as the Swiss Confederation.[3243]

However, since the Convention of 1892 was concluded before 1 January 1958, Article 351 TFEU applies. Under the second paragraph of that provision, Member States are required to take all appropriate steps to eliminate the incompatibilities between an agreement concluded before a Member State's accession and the TFEU.[3244]

3236. CJEU C-252/12 of 18.7.2013 – Specsavers International Healthcare, para. 24.
3237. CJEU C-252/12 of 18.7.2013 – Specsavers International Healthcare, para. 25.
3238. CJEU C-501/15 P of 11.10.2017 – EUIPO/Cactus, para. 67.
3239. CJEU C-586/15 P of 7.9.2016 – Lotte/EUIPO, para. 38, unofficial translation.
3240. CJEU C-553/11 of 25.10.2012 – Rintisch, para. 33.
3241. Convention between Switzerland and Germany concerning the Reciprocal Protection of Patents, Designs and Trademarks, signed in Berlin on 13 April 1892.
3242. CJEU C-720/18 and C-721/18 of 22.10.2020 – Ferrari/DU, para. 72.
3243. CJEU C-720/18 and C-721/18 of 22.10.2020 – Ferrari/DU, para. 66.
3244. CJEU C-720/18 and C-721/18 of 22.10.2020 – Ferrari/DU, para. 67.

It follows that the referring court must ascertain whether a possible incompatibility between EU law and the Convention of 1892 can be avoided by interpreting that convention, to the extent possible and in compliance with international law, in such a way that it is consistent with EU law.[3245]

If it is not possible to interpret the Convention of 1892 in such a way that it is consistent with EU law, the Federal Republic of Germany is obliged to take the necessary measures to eliminate the incompatibility of that convention with EU law, where appropriate, by denouncing it. However, pending such elimination, the first paragraph of Article 351 TFEU permits it to continue to apply that convention.[3246]

Admittedly, as the referring court observes, the application of the Convention of 1892 by the Federal Republic of Germany may give rise to difficulties, in so far as a mark registered in Germany, while capable of being maintained in the register only on the basis of genuine use in the territory of the Swiss Confederation, could not be relied on to preclude the registration of an EU trade mark since, in a situation where a request is made for proof of genuine use of that trade mark in the context of opposition proceedings, the proprietor of that trade mark would not be in a position to provide such proof in the territory of the European Union alone.[3247]

However, those difficulties are the inevitable consequence of the incompatibility of the Convention of 1892 with EU law and can be removed only once that incompatibility has been eliminated, which the Federal Republic of Germany is required to do under the second paragraph of Article 351 TFEU.[3248]

[L] Burden of proof

Article 12(1) TMD2008 must be interpreted as meaning that the burden of proof that a trade mark has been put to 'genuine use', within the meaning of that provision, rests on the proprietor of that mark.[3249]

It should be noted that, admittedly, recital 6 of the TMD2008 states, in particular, that Member States should remain free to fix the provisions of procedure concerning the revocation of trade marks acquired by registration.[3250]

However, it cannot be inferred that the question of the burden of proof in respect of genuine use, within the meaning of Article 12(1) TMD2008, in the context of proceedings relating to revocation of a trade mark for non-use constitutes such a procedural provision falling within the competence of Member States.[3251]

3245. CJEU C-720/18 and C-721/18 of 22.10.2020 – Ferrari/DU, para. 68, with further proof.
3246. CJEU C-720/18 and C-721/18 of 22.10.2020 – Ferrari/DU, para. 69, with further proof.
3247. CJEU C-720/18 and C-721/18 of 22.10.2020 – Ferrari/DU, para. 70.
3248. CJEU C-720/18 and C-721/18 of 22.10.2020 – Ferrari/DU, para. 71.
3249. CJEU C-720/18 and C-721/18 of 22.10.2020 – Ferrari/DU, para. 82; C-183/21 of 10.3.2022 – Maxxus Group/Globus Holding, para. 36.
3250. CJEU C-720/18 and C-721/18 of 22.10.2020 – Ferrari/DU, para. 75.
3251. CJEU C-720/18 and C-721/18 of 22.10.2020 – Ferrari/DU, para. 76, with reference to CJEU C-217/13 and 218/13 of 19.6.2014 – Oberbank, para. 66; also CJEU C-183/21 of 10.3.2022 – Maxxus Group/Globus Holding, para. 33.

If the question of the burden of proof in respect of genuine use of a mark in the context of revocation proceedings for non-use of that mark were a matter for the national law of the Member States, the consequence for proprietors of trade marks could be that protection would vary according to the legal system concerned, with the result that the objective of 'the same protection under the legal systems of all the Member States' set out in recital 10 of the TMD2008, where it is described as 'fundamental', would not be attained.[3252]

The Court held, with regard to the revocation of an EU trade mark, that the principle under which it is for the proprietor of the mark to prove genuine use of that mark is in reality merely an application of common sense and requirements of procedural efficacy.[3253]

The Court inferred from this that it is, in principle, for the proprietor of an EU trade mark to which an application for revocation relates to establish genuine use of that mark.[3254]

Those considerations are also valid with regard to proof in respect of genuine use, within the meaning of Article 12(1) TMD2008, of a trade mark registered in a Member State.[3255]

The Court finds that it is the proprietor of the mark at issue which is best placed to adduce evidence in support of the assertion that its mark has been put to genuine use.[3256]

Under Article 43(2) and (3) CTMR, opposition to registration of a **Community trade mark** by the proprietor of an earlier Community or national trade mark must be rejected if that proprietor does not, at the request of the applicant, furnish proof that, during the five-year period preceding the date of publication of the Community trade mark application, the earlier trade mark has been put to genuine use in the Community or in the Member State in which it is protected in connection with the goods or services in respect of which it is registered and which he cites as justification for his opposition, or that there are proper reasons for non-use. Furthermore, Article 56(2) CTMR contains an identical rule for cases involving applications for revocation or for a declaration of nullity of a Community trade mark.[3257]

Articles 42(2) and 57(2) CTMR state specifically that it is **for the proprietor** of the mark to furnish **proof** of genuine use or proper reasons for non-use, failing which the application for a declaration of invalidity is to be rejected.[3258]

3252. CJEU C-720/18 and C-721/18 of 22.10.2020 – Ferrari/DU, para. 77, with reference to CJEU C-217/13 and 218/13 of 19.6.2014 – Oberbank, para. 67; also CJEU C-183/21 of 10.3.2022 – Maxxus Group/Globus Holding, para. 34.
3253. CJEU C-720/18 and C-721/18 of 22.10.2020 – Ferrari/DU, para. 78, with reference to CJEU C-610/11 P of 26.9.2013 – Centrotherm Systemtechnik/OHIM, para. 61; also CJEU C-183/21 of 10.3.2022 – Maxxus Group/Globus Holding, para. 35.
3254. CJEU C-720/18 and C-721/18 of 22.10.2020 – Ferrari/DU, para. 79, with reference to CJEU C-610/11 P of 26.9.2013 – Centrotherm Systemtechnik/OHIM, para. 63.
3255. CJEU C-720/18 and C-721/18 of 22.10.2020 – Ferrari/DU, para. 80.
3256. CJEU C-720/18 and C-721/18 of 22.10.2020 – Ferrari/DU, para. 81, with reference to CJEU C-217/13 and 218/13 of 19.6.2014 – Oberbank, para. 70; also CJEU C-183/21 of 10.3.2022 – Maxxus Group/Globus Holding, para. 35.
3257. CJEU C-234/06 P of 13.9.2007 – Il Ponte Finanziaria/OHIM, para. 100.
3258. CJEU C-610/11 P of 26.9.2013 – Centrotherm Systemtechnik/OHIM, para. 55; *see also* CJEU C-698/17 P of 23.1.2019 – Klement/EUIPO, para. 57.

In that regard, the fact that, unlike Articles 42(2) and 57(2) CTMR, Article 51(1) CTMR does not specify that it is for the proprietor to furnish proof of genuine use or of the presence of proper reasons for non-use cannot be interpreted as meaning that the EU legislature intended that the principle of the burden of proof should not apply in revocation proceedings.[3259]

The absence of specific provision regarding the burden of proof in Article 51(1) CTMR can, moreover, be explained easily given that the purpose of Article 51(1), entitled 'Grounds for revocation', is to set out the grounds for revocation of the mark, which does not require specific provision to be made regarding the issue of the burden of proof.[3260]

Articles 42 and 57 CTMR, by contrast, are essentially procedural provisions. Moreover, the specific purpose of paragraph (2) of each of those articles is to lay down the framework for when a procedural issue is raised by a defendant wishing to question the right of the applicant to bring the proceedings he has initiated.[3261]

It is because of that procedural context, which is specific to opposition and invalidity proceedings and which the EU legislature has laid down in order to settle such procedural issues - that must be resolved prior to the main proceedings of which they are a part - that the proof that the earlier mark has been put to genuine use must be made out by the proprietor of the mark and that, in the absence of such proof, the opposition or invalidity proceedings are to be dismissed.[3262]

By contrast, the fact that any procedural issue of this nature by definition cannot arise in the context of revocation proceedings readily justifies the situation that, although Article 57 CTMR concerns both revocation proceedings and invalidity proceedings, a provision such as Article 57(2) is restricted to invalidity proceedings.[3263]

Third, it is clear that the principle reflected in Articles 42(2) and 57(2) CTMR, under which it is for the proprietor of the earlier mark to prove genuine use of that mark, is in reality merely an application of common sense and requirements of procedural efficacy.[3264]

It is common ground that the proprietor is the best placed - and in some cases the only party able - to furnish specific proof in support of the assertion that he has made genuine use of his mark or set out the proper reasons for non-use of the mark. This includes, *inter alia,* evidence establishing such use, of which Rule 22(4) CTMIR provides a list of **examples, such as packages, labels, price lists, catalogues, invoices, photographs or newspaper advertisements.**[3265]

Thus, it may be inferred from a combined reading of Articles 15, 42(2), 51(1) and 57(2) of CTMR that, in proceedings for revocation of a mark, it is for the proprietor of the mark, and not OHIM of its own motion, to establish genuine use of that mark.[3266]

3259. CJEU C-610/11 P of 26.9.2013 - Centrotherm Systemtechnik/OHIM, para. 56.
3260. CJEU C-610/11 P of 26.9.2013 - Centrotherm Systemtechnik/OHIM, para. 57.
3261. CJEU C-610/11 P of 26.9.2013 - Centrotherm Systemtechnik/OHIM, para. 58.
3262. CJEU C-610/11 P of 26.9.2013 - Centrotherm Systemtechnik/OHIM, para. 59.
3263. CJEU C-610/11 P of 26.9.2013 - Centrotherm Systemtechnik/OHIM, para. 60.
3264. CJEU C-610/11 P of 26.9.2013 - Centrotherm Systemtechnik/OHIM, para. 61.
3265. CJEU C-610/11 P of 26.9.2013 - Centrotherm Systemtechnik/OHIM, para. 62; in regard to undated materials *see* CJEU C-57/14 P of 14.1.2015 - Recaro Holding/OHIM, paras 23–28.
3266. CJEU C-610/11 P of 26.9.2013 - Centrotherm Systemtechnik/OHIM, para. 63.

Similarly, the conclusion in that regard must be that since Rule 40(5) CTMIR provides that proof of genuine use must be made out by the proprietor of the mark, that rule merely specifies a principle relating to the burden of proof which, far from disregarding the CTMR, on the contrary derives from the provisions and scheme of that regulation.[3267]

In those circumstances, the rule that OHIM is to examine facts of its own motion, as laid down in Article 76(1) CTMR, does not apply to the question of proof of genuine use of the mark in revocation proceedings brought before OHIM.[3268]

It follows, *inter alia,* from the foregoing that the conclusion that Article 76(1) CTMR does **not oblige OHIM** to examine of its own motion facts tending to establish genuine use of the mark, revocation of which is sought before it, is well founded in law.[3269]

The Court of First Instance did not err in law in holding that a proprietor of a national registration who opposes a Community trade mark application **cannot**, in order to avoid the burden of proof which rests upon him under Article 43(2) and (3) CTMR, rely on a **national provision** which allows the registration, as trade marks, of signs not intended to be used in trade on account of their purely defensive function in relation to another sign which is being commercially exploited.[3270]

Article 17 Non-use as defence in infringement proceedings

The proprietor of a trade mark shall be entitled to prohibit the use of a sign only to the extent that the proprietor's rights are not liable to be revoked pursuant to Article 19 at the time the infringement action is brought. If the defendant so requests, the proprietor of the trade mark shall furnish proof that, during the five-year period preceding the date of bringing the action, the trade mark has been put to genuine use as provided in Article 16 in connection with the goods or services in respect of which it is registered and which are cited as justification for the action, or that there are proper reasons for non-use, provided that the registration procedure of the trade mark has at the date of bringing the action been completed for not less than five years.

Article 18 Intervening right of the proprietor of a later registered trade mark as defence in infringement proceedings

1. *In infringement proceedings, the proprietor of a trade mark shall not be entitled to prohibit the use of a later registered mark where that later trade mark would not be declared invalid pursuant to Article 8, Article 9(1) or (2) or Article 46(3).*
2. *In infringement proceedings, the proprietor of a trade mark shall not be entitled to prohibit the use of a later registered EU trade mark where that*

3267. CJEU C-610/11 P of 26.9.2013 – Centrotherm Systemtechnik/OHIM, para. 64.
3268. CJEU C-610/11 P of 26.9.2013 – Centrotherm Systemtechnik/OHIM, para. 65.
3269. CJEU C-610/11 P of 26.9.2013 – Centrotherm Systemtechnik/OHIM, para. 66.
3270. CJEU C-234/06 P of 13.9.2007 – Il Ponte Finanziaria/OHIM, para. 101.

later trade mark would not be declared invalid pursuant to Article 53(1), (3) or (4), 54(1) or (2) or 57(2) of Regulation (EC) No 207/2009.

3. *Where the proprietor of a trade mark is not entitled to prohibit the use of a later registered trade mark pursuant to paragraph 1 or 2, the proprietor of that later registered trade mark shall not be entitled to prohibit the use of the earlier trade mark in infringement proceedings, even though that earlier right may no longer be invoked against the later trade mark.*

[A] Principles

Take care: The provision is new in the TMD and might partially change the prior case law.

[B] No need for a latter mark to have been declared invalid beforehand

Probably still applicable: Article 9(1) CTMR must be interpreted as meaning that the exclusive right of the proprietor of a **Community trade mark** to **prohibit all third parties from using**, in the course of trade, signs identical with or similar to its trade mark extends to a third-party proprietor of a later registered Community trade mark, **without the need for that latter mark to have been declared invalid** beforehand.[3271]

Probably still applicable: First of all, it should be noted that Article 9(1) CTMR does not make any distinction on the basis of whether the third party is the proprietor of a Community trade mark or not. Thus, that provision grants the proprietor of a Community trade mark an exclusive right to prevent 'any third party', not having its consent, from using, in the course of trade, any signs liable to infringe its mark.[3272]

Probably still applicable: Consideration should then be given to Article 54 CTMR, concerning limitation in consequence of acquiescence, which states that '[w]here the proprietor of a Community trade mark has acquiesced, for a period of five successive years, in the use of a later Community trade mark ..., he shall no longer be entitled ... either to apply for a declaration that the later trade mark is invalid or to oppose the use of the later trade mark'.[3273]

Probably still applicable: It is apparent from the wording of this provision that, before the limitation in consequence of acquiescence takes effect, the proprietor of a Community trade mark is entitled both to apply to OHIM for a declaration of invalidity of the later Community trade mark and to oppose its use through infringement proceedings before a Community trade mark court.[3274]

Probably still applicable: Finally, it should be pointed out that neither Article 12 CTMR, relating to the limitation of the effects of a Community trade mark, nor any of its other provisions provides for an express limitation of the exclusive right of the

3271. CJEU C-561/11 of 21.2.2013 - Fédération Cynologique Internationale, para. 52; *see also* CJEU C-491/14 of 10.3.2015 - Rosa dels Vents Assessoria, para. 31.
3272. CJEU C-561/11 of 21.2.2013 - Fédération Cynologique Internationale, para. 33; *see also* (concerning Community designs) CJEU C-488/10 of 16.2.2012 - Celaya Emparanza y Galdos Internacional/EUIPO, paras 33 et seq.
3273. CJEU C-561/11 of 21.2.2013 - Fédération Cynologique Internationale, para. 34.
3274. CJEU C-561/11 of 21.2.2013 - Fédération Cynologique Internationale, para. 35.

proprietor of a Community trade mark in favour of the third-party proprietor of a later Community trade mark.[3275]

Probably still applicable: It is thus apparent from the wording and the general approach of Article 9(1) CTMR that the proprietor of a Community trade mark must be able to prevent the proprietor of a later Community trade mark from using that latter trade mark.[3276]

Probably still applicable: That conclusion is not called into question by the fact that the proprietor of a later trade mark also has the benefit of an exclusive right by virtue of Article 9(1) CTMR.[3277]

Probably still applicable: It should be noted in that connection that, as submitted by the European Commission in its observations, the provisions of the Regulation must be interpreted in the light of the priority principle, under which the earlier Community mark takes precedence over the later Community mark.[3278]

Probably still applicable: It is clear from, *inter alia*, Articles 8(1) and 53(1) CTMR that, in the event of a conflict between two marks, the mark registered first is presumed to have met the conditions required to obtain Community protection before the mark registered second.[3279]

Probably still applicable: For the same reason as that set out in paragraphs 39 and 40 of the judgment in Fédération Cynologique Internationale, the provisions of the TMD must be interpreted in the light of the priority principle according to which the earlier trade mark takes priority over the later one, since it follows from Article 4(1) TMD2008 that, in the case of conflict between trade marks, the mark first registered is presumed to fulfil the conditions necessary for obtaining protection before the mark registered subsequently.[3280]

Probably still applicable: Furthermore, it is necessary to reject the argument that the characteristics of the registration procedure for Community trade marks require that, if, at the end of this procedure, the registration of the trade mark is allowed, that mark should confer on its owner a right of use that can be called into question only by an action for invalidity before OHIM or by a counterclaim in infringement proceedings.[3281]

Probably still applicable: It is, admittedly, true that the procedure for the registration of Community trade marks, laid down in Articles 36–45 CTMR, includes a substantive examination that seeks to determine, prior to registration, whether the Community mark fulfils the requirements for protection.[3282]

Probably still applicable: In addition, under this procedure, there is a publication phase in which third parties may submit to OHIM written observations explaining why

3275. CJEU C-561/11 of 21.2.2013 – Fédération Cynologique Internationale, para. 36.
3276. CJEU C-561/11 of 21.2.2013 – Fédération Cynologique Internationale, para. 37.
3277. CJEU C-561/11 of 21.2.2013 – Fédération Cynologique Internationale, para. 38.
3278. CJEU C-561/11 of 21.2.2013 – Fédération Cynologique Internationale, para. 39; *see also* (concerning Community designs) CJEU C-488/10 of 16.2.2012 – Celaya Emparanza y Galdos Internacional/EUIPO, para. 39.
3279. CJEU C-561/11 of 21.2.2013 – Fédération Cynologique Internationale, para. 40.
3280. CJEU C-491/14 of 10.3.2015 – Rosa dels Vents Assessoria, para. 29.
3281. CJEU C-561/11 of 21.2.2013 – Fédération Cynologique Internationale, para. 41.
3282. CJEU C-561/11 of 21.2.2013 – Fédération Cynologique Internationale, para. 42.

the trade mark should not be registered ex officio, as well as an opportunity for owners of earlier trade marks to oppose registration of the trade mark within a period of three months following the publication of the Community trade mark application by putting forward, *inter alia*, the relative grounds for refusal set out in Article 8 CTMR.[3283]

Probably still applicable: However, those circumstances are not conclusive.[3284]

Probably still applicable: First, it must be stated that, despite the safeguards provided by the procedure for registering Community trade marks, it is not entirely inconceivable that a sign that is liable to infringe an earlier Community trade mark may be registered as a Community trade mark.[3285]

Probably still applicable: This may arise, *inter alia*, where the proprietor of the earlier Community trade mark has not filed a notice of opposition under Article 41 CTMR, or where that opposition has not been examined on its merits by OHIM by reason of non-compliance with the procedural requirements laid down by Article 41(3), as indeed was the position in the case in the main proceedings.[3286]

Probably still applicable: Second, the Court has already held,[3287] in the context of Council Regulation (EC) No. 6/2002,[3288] that actions alleging infringement and actions for a declaration of invalidity are distinguished in terms of their object and effects, with the result that the fact that it is possible for the holder of an earlier registered Community design to bring infringement proceedings against the holder of a later registered Community design cannot render the bringing of an application for a declaration of invalidity against the latter before OHIM devoid of all purpose.[3289]

Probably still applicable: That finding may be applied, *mutatis mutandis*, to the context of Community trade marks, in such a way that the possibility for the proprietor of an earlier Community trade mark to bring infringement proceedings against the proprietor of a later registered Community trade mark cannot render either the bringing of an application for a declaration of invalidity before OHIM or the mechanisms for prior control available under the procedure for registering Community trade marks devoid of all purpose.[3290]

Probably still applicable: It is, furthermore, important to emphasize the need to preserve the essential function of the trade mark, which is to guarantee to consumers the origin of the goods.[3291]

Probably still applicable: In that regard, the Court has repeatedly held that the exclusive right under Article 9(1) CTMR was conferred in order to enable the trade

3283. CJEU C-561/11 of 21.2.2013 – Fédération Cynologique Internationale, para. 43.
3284. CJEU C-561/11 of 21.2.2013 – Fédération Cynologique Internationale, para. 44.
3285. CJEU C-561/11 of 21.2.2013 – Fédération Cynologique Internationale, para. 45.
3286. CJEU C-561/11 of 21.2.2013 – Fédération Cynologique Internationale, para. 46.
3287. CJEU C-488/10 of 16.2.2012 – Celaya Emparanza y Galdos Internacional/EUIPO, para. 50.
3288. Council Regulation (EC) No. 6/2002 of 12 Dec. 2001 on Community designs (OJ 2002 L 3, p. 1).
3289. CJEU C-561/11 of 21.2.2013 – Fédération Cynologique Internationale, para. 47.
3290. CJEU C-561/11 of 21.2.2013 – Fédération Cynologique Internationale, para. 48; *see also* CJEU C-226/15 P of 21.7.2016 – Apple and Pear Australia a.o./EUIPO, para. 61.
3291. CJEU C-561/11 of 21.2.2013 – Fédération Cynologique Internationale, para. 49; *see also* CJEU C-206/01 of 12.11.2002 – Arsenal Football Club, para. 51.

mark proprietor to protect his specific interests as proprietor of the mark, that is to say, to ensure that the trade mark can fulfil its own function.[3292]

Probably still applicable: If the proprietor of an earlier trade mark, in order to prevent the use by a third party of a sign that is liable to affect the functions of its trade mark, were required to await the declaration of invalidity of the later Community mark held by that third party, the protection accorded to it by Article 9(1) CTMR would be significantly weakened.[3293]

Probably still applicable: Article 9(1) CTMR must be interpreted as meaning that the exclusive right of the proprietor of a **trade mark** to **prohibit all third parties from using**, in the course of trade, signs identical with or similar to its trade mark extends to a third-party proprietor of a later trade mark, **without the need for that latter mark to have been declared invalid** beforehand.[3294]

Probably still applicable: The considerations set out in paragraphs 49–51 of the judgment in Fédération Cynologique International also apply, *mutatis mutandis*, to Article 5(1) **TMD2008**.[3295]

Probably still applicable: Those considerations concerning the scope of the exclusive right conferred by the Community trade mark are relevant for interpreting the scope of the exclusive right conferred by trade marks that have been registered in a Member State or at the Benelux Office for Intellectual Property, or that have been registered under international arrangements which have effect in a Member State, as harmonized by the TMD.[3296]

Probably still applicable: First, as in the case of Article 9(1) CTMR, Article 5(1) TMD2008 confers an exclusive right on the proprietor of a registered trade mark and gives him the right to prevent 'any third party', where consent has not been given, to use, in the course of trade, signs likely to have an adverse effect on his mark. In that respect, those provisions make no distinction between third parties who are proprietors of a trade mark and those who are not.[3297]

Probably still applicable: A national law, although it does not reproduce verbatim the wording of the TMD or the CTMR relating to the prohibition of 'all third parties' from using, in course of trade, without the consent of the proprietor, signs likely to have an adverse effect on a registered trade mark, prohibits 'third parties' from such use, must be regarded as being worded in a manner analogous to the EU measures at issue. It is for the referring court to apply the national law in a manner consistent with Article 5(1) TMD2008, as interpreted by the Court.[3298]

Probably still applicable: Furthermore, as in the case of Article 54 CTMR, Article 9 TMD2008 provides that:

3292. CJEU C-561/11 of 21.2.2013 – Fédération Cynologique Internationale, para. 50; *see also* CJEU C-487/07 of 18.6.2009 – L'Oréal, para. 58; C-236/08 to C-238/08 of 23.3.2010 – Google France, para. 75; C-278/08 of 25.3.2010 – BergSpechte, para. 29; C-558/08 of 8.7.2010 – Portakabin, para. 26; C-235/09 of 12.4.2011 – DHL Express France, para. 46.
3293. CJEU C-561/11 of 21.2.2013 – Fédération Cynologique Internationale, para. 51.
3294. CJEU C-491/14 of 10.3.2015 – Rosa dels Vents Assessoria, para. 31 [corrected translation].
3295. CJEU C-491/14 of 10.3.2015 – Rosa dels Vents Assessoria, para. 30.
3296. CJEU C-491/14 of 10.3.2015 – Rosa dels Vents Assessoria, para. 22.
3297. CJEU C-491/14 of 10.3.2015 – Rosa dels Vents Assessoria, para. 23.
3298. CJEU C-491/14 of 10.3.2015 – Rosa dels Vents Assessoria, para. 24.

> *the proprietor of an earlier trade mark ... who has acquiesced ... in the use of a later trade mark registered ... for a period of five successive years while being aware of such use shall no longer be entitled ... either to apply for a declaration that the later trade mark is invalid or to oppose the use of the later trade mark.*

It is clear from the wording of that provision that until invalidity in consequence of acquiescence occurs, the proprietor of a trade mark is authorized to request that the later mark be declared invalid or to oppose its use by means of infringement proceedings.[3299]

Probably still applicable: Finally, it should be noted that, as in the case of the CTMR, no provision of the TMD provides for the express limitation of the exclusive right of the proprietor of a trade mark in favour of a third-party proprietor of a later mark.[3300]

Probably still applicable: It is, therefore, clear from the wording of Article 5(1) TMD2008 and from the general approach of that provision that, under the conditions set out therein, the proprietor of a trade mark must be able to prevent its use by the proprietor of a later mark.[3301]

Probably still applicable: That conclusion is not called into question by the fact that the proprietor of a later trade mark also has the benefit of an exclusive right by virtue of the rule set out in Article 5(1) TMD2008.[3302]

SECTION 4 REVOCATION OF TRADE MARK RIGHTS

Article 19 Absence of genuine use as ground for revocation

1. *A trade mark shall be liable to revocation if, within a continuous five-year period, it has not been put to genuine use in the Member State in connection with the goods or services in respect of which it is registered, and there are no proper reasons for non-use.*
2. *No person may claim that the proprietor's rights in a trade mark should be revoked where, during the interval between expiry of the five-year period and filing of the application for revocation, genuine use of the trade mark has been started or resumed.*
3. *The commencement or resumption of use within a three-month period preceding the filing of the application for revocation which began at the earliest on expiry of the continuous five-year period of non-use shall be disregarded where preparations for the commencement or resumption occur only after the proprietor becomes aware that the application for revocation may be filed.*

Article 19 TMD must be interpreted as precluding a procedural rule of a Member State which, in proceedings concerning an application for revocation of a trade mark for non-use, requires the applicant to carry out market research concerning the possible

3299. CJEU C-491/14 of 10.3.2015 – Rosa dels Vents Assessoria, para. 25.
3300. CJEU C-491/14 of 10.3.2015 – Rosa dels Vents Assessoria, para. 26.
3301. CJEU C-491/14 of 10.3.2015 – Rosa dels Vents Assessoria, para. 27.
3302. CJEU C-491/14 of 10.3.2015 – Rosa dels Vents Assessoria, para. 28.

use of that mark by its proprietor and to make in that regard, to the extent possible, substantiated submissions in support of its application.[3303]

Neither Article 16 TMD, relating to the concept of genuine use of a trade mark and the period within which its proprietor must have put it to such use, nor Article 17 TMD, relating to non-use as a defence in infringement proceedings, is of direct relevance for answering the referring court's question. Therefore, the question referred should be answered in the light solely of Article 19 TMD.[3304]

In this connection, it should be pointed out that the question of the burden of proof in respect of genuine use, within the meaning of Article 19(1) TMD, in the context of proceedings relating to revocation of a trade mark for non-use does not constitute a procedural provision falling within the competence of the Member States.[3305]

If that question were a matter for the national law of the Member States, the consequence for proprietors of trade marks could be that protection would vary according to the legal system concerned, with the result that the objective of 'the same protection under the legal systems of all the Member States' set out in recital 10 of the TMD, where it is described as 'fundamental', would not be attained.[3306]

Furthermore, the principle under which it is for the proprietor of the mark to prove genuine use of that mark is in reality merely an application of common sense and of a basic requirement of procedural efficacy. It is the proprietor of the mark at issue which is best placed to adduce evidence in support of the assertion that its mark has been put to genuine use.[3307]

It follows that Article 19 TMD must be interpreted as meaning that the burden of proof that a trade mark has been put to 'genuine use', within the meaning of that provision, rests on the proprietor of that mark.[3308]

It is true that the fact that the applicant, in a given procedure, does not have to bear the burden of proof does not necessarily release that party from the obligation to provide, in its application, a full statement of the facts upon which it bases its claims.[3309]

However, it is clear from Article 19 TMD that an application for revocation of a trade mark on the basis of that provision is founded on the claim that the mark has not been put to genuine use by its proprietor. Such a claim, by its nature, does not lend itself to a more detailed statement.[3310]

In that regard, it must be stated that the national procedural rule contemplated by the referring court goes beyond a mere obligation on the applicant to set out the facts

3303. CJEU C-183/21 of 10.3.2022 – Maxxus Group/Globus Holding, para. 46.
3304. CJEU C-183/21 of 10.3.2022 – Maxxus Group/Globus Holding, para. 31.
3305. CJEU C-183/21 of 10.3.2022 – Maxxus Group/Globus Holding, para. 33, with reference to CJEU C-720/18 and C-721/18 of 22.10.2020 – Ferrari/DU, para. 76.
3306. CJEU C-183/21 of 10.3.2022 – Maxxus Group/Globus Holding, para. 34, with reference to CJEU C-720/18 and C-721/18 of 22.10.2020 – Ferrari/DU, para. 77.
3307. CJEU C-183/21 of 10.3.2022 – Maxxus Group/Globus Holding, para. 35, with reference to CJEU C-720/18 and C-721/18 of 22.10.2020 – Ferrari/DU, paras 78 and 81.
3308. CJEU C-183/21 of 10.3.2022 – Maxxus Group/Globus Holding, para. 36, with reference to CJEU C-720/18 and C-721/18 of 22.10.2020 – Ferrari/DU, para. 82.
3309. CJEU C-183/21 of 10.3.2022 – Maxxus Group/Globus Holding, para. 37.
3310. CJEU C-183/21 of 10.3.2022 – Maxxus Group/Globus Holding, para. 38.

upon which its application is founded. That rule requires the applicant to state and, in the event of challenge, to prove that, before its application was lodged, it carried out market research and that it was unable to establish that the trade mark at issue was put to genuine use.[3311]

Such a rule thus places the burden of proof of use, or non-use, of the trade mark at issue at least partially on the applicant, although, according to the case law cited above, that burden rests exclusively on the proprietor of that mark.[3312]

The risk, mentioned by the referring court, of a proliferation of applications for revocation on the ground of non-use that constitute an abuse cannot result in a different interpretation.[3313]

For the purpose of guarding against such a risk, which, moreover, concerns not only proceedings for revocation of a trade mark for non-use but all judicial proceedings, there are, as the Commission has observed, various appropriate procedural means of deterring abuse of process.[3314]

Those procedural means include the possibility of laying down provisions enabling an application for revocation on the ground of non-use to be dismissed summarily as manifestly inadmissible or manifestly unfounded, or the applicant to be ordered, if its claims are rejected, to pay the costs incurred by the proprietor of the trade mark at issue. It is also **possible to require the applicant to pay a fee** when it brings its action.[3315]

As regards the risk, mentioned by the referring court, of revocation proceedings for non-use of a trade mark being brought solely in order to secure the disclosure of the trade secrets of that mark's proprietor, it is clear from the Court's case law that 'genuine use' of the trade mark, within the meaning of Article 19(1) TMD, entails use of the mark on the market for the goods or services protected by that mark and not just internal use by the undertaking concerned.[3316]

It follows that the evidence of genuine use of a trade mark must relate to use of that mark on the market, which, as such, is not covered by commercial confidentiality.[3317]

Article 20 Trade mark having become generic or misleading indication as grounds for revocation

A trade mark shall be liable to revocation if, after the date on which it was registered:

(a) as a result of acts or inactivity of the proprietor, it has become the common name in the trade for a product or service in respect of which it is registered;

3311. CJEU C-183/21 of 10.3.2022 – Maxxus Group/Globus Holding, para. 39.
3312. CJEU C-183/21 of 10.3.2022 – Maxxus Group/Globus Holding, para. 40.
3313. CJEU C-183/21 of 10.3.2022 – Maxxus Group/Globus Holding, para. 41.
3314. CJEU C-183/21 of 10.3.2022 – Maxxus Group/Globus Holding, para. 42.
3315. CJEU C-183/21 of 10.3.2022 – Maxxus Group/Globus Holding, para. 43.
3316. CJEU C-183/21 of 10.3.2022 – Maxxus Group/Globus Holding, para. 44, with reference to CJEU C-40/01 of 11.3.2003 – Ansul, para. 37.
3317. CJEU C-183/21 of 10.3.2022 – Maxxus Group/Globus Holding, para. 45.

(b) as a result of the use made of it by the proprietor of the trade mark or with the proprietor's consent in respect of the goods or services for which it is registered, it is liable to mislead the public, particularly as to the nature, quality or geographical origin of those goods or services.

[A] Common names

Take care: The article's heading now uses the wording 'become generic'.

While Article 3 TMD2008 specifies the circumstances in which a trade mark is incapable, *ab initio*, of fulfilling its function as an indication of origin, Article 12(2)(a) TMD2008 relates to the situation where the trade mark has become the common name and has therefore lost its distinctive character, with the result that it no longer fulfils that function.[3318]

Article 12(2)(a) TMD2008 addresses the situation where the trade mark is no longer capable of fulfilling its function as an indication of origin.[3319]

Article 12(2)(a) TMD2008 provides that a trade mark is liable to revocation if, after the date on which it was registered, in consequence of acts or inactivity of the proprietor, it has become the common name in the trade for a product or service in respect of which it is registered. Thus, by **balancing the interests** of the proprietor against those of his competitors in the availability of signs, the legislator considered, in adopting this provision, that the loss of that mark's distinctive character can be relied on against the proprietor thereof only where that loss is due to his action or inaction. Therefore, as long as this is not the case, and particularly when the loss of the distinctive character is linked to the activity of a third party using a sign which infringes the mark, the proprietor must continue to enjoy protection.[3320]

Having regard to the considerations set out in paragraphs 29 and 30 of this judgment, it is for the competent national court to establish revocation, if appropriate, linked in particular to such a failure, including in the context of proceedings seeking protection of the exclusive rights conferred by Article 5 TMD2008, and which may have been brought late by the proprietor of the mark. If taking account of revocation for the purposes of Article 12(2) TMD2008 in infringement proceedings were solely a matter for the national laws of the Member States, the consequence for trade mark proprietors might be that protection would vary depending on the applicable law. The objective of 'the same protection under the legal systems of all the Member States' set out in the ninth recital in the preamble to the directive, where it is described as fundamental, would not be attained.[3321]

3318. CJEU C-409/12 of 6.3.2014 – Backaldrin Österreich The Kornspitz Company, para. 22; *see also* CJEU C-371/02 of 29.4.2004 – Björnekulla Fruktindustrier, para. 22.
3319. CJEU C-409/12 of 6.3.2014 – Backaldrin Österreich The Kornspitz Company, para. 19; *see also* CJEU C-371/02 of 29.4.2004 – Björnekulla Fruktindustrier, para. 22; *see also* CJEU C-102/07 of 10.4.2008 – adidas/Marca Mode, para. 24.
3320. CJEU C-145/05 of 27.4.2006 – Levi Strauss, para. 19; C-409/12 of 6.3.2014 – Backaldrin Österreich The Kornspitz Company, para. 32.
3321. CJEU C-145/05 of 27.4.2006 – Levi Strauss, para. 35.

Article 12(2)(a) TMD2008 must be interpreted as meaning that it may be classified as '**inactivity**' within the meaning of that provision if the proprietor of a trade mark does not encourage sellers to make more use of that mark in marketing a product in respect of which the mark is registered.[3322]

Accordingly, where a trade mark has lost its distinctive character in consequence of acts or inactivity of the proprietor so that it has become a common name within the meaning of Article 12(2) TMD2008, its proprietor can no longer assert the rights conferred on him under Article 5 TMD2008.[3323]

Such inactivity may also take the form of a failure on the part of the proprietor of a mark to have recourse to Article 5 in due time, for the purposes of applying to the competent authority to prevent third parties from using the sign in respect of which there is a likelihood of confusion with that mark, since the purpose of such applications is precisely to preserve the distinctive character of the mark in question.[3324]

However, that concept cannot in any way be restricted to that kind of omission, but includes all those by which the proprietor of a trade mark shows that he is not sufficiently vigilant as regards the preservation of the distinctive character of his trade mark. Consequently, in a case in which the sellers of the product made using the material supplied by the proprietor of the trade mark do not generally inform their customers that the sign used to designate the product in question has been registered as a trade mark and thus contribute to the transformation of that trade mark into the common name, that proprietor's failure to take any initiative which may encourage those sellers to make more use of that mark may be classified as inactivity within the meaning of Article 12(2)(a) TMD2008.[3325]

Article 12(2)(a) TMD2008 must be interpreted as meaning that the revocation of a trade mark does not presuppose that it must be ascertained whether there are **other names for a product** for which that trade mark has become the common name in the trade.[3326]

As is apparent from the actual wording of that provision, a trade mark is liable to revocation if, in consequence of acts or inactivity of the proprietor, it has become the common name in the trade for a product or service in respect of which it is registered.[3327]

If such a situation occurs, the possible existence of alternative names for the product or service in question is irrelevant, since it cannot alter the finding that that trade mark has lost its distinctive character as a result of its transformation into the common name in the trade.[3328]

3322. CJEU C-409/12 of 6.3.2014 – Backaldrin Österreich The Kornspitz Company, para. 36.
3323. CJEU C-145/05 of 27.4.2006 – Levi Strauss, para. 33; C-409/12 of 6.3.2014 – Backaldrin Österreich The Kornspitz Company, para. 22.
3324. CJEU C-145/05 of 27.4.2006 – Levi Strauss, para. 34; C-409/12 of 6.3.2014 – Backaldrin Österreich The Kornspitz Company, para. 33.
3325. CJEU C-409/12 of 6.3.2014 – Backaldrin Österreich The Kornspitz Company, para. 34.
3326. CJEU C-409/12 of 6.3.2014 – Backaldrin Österreich The Kornspitz Company, para. 40.
3327. CJEU C-409/12 of 6.3.2014 – Backaldrin Österreich The Kornspitz Company, para. 38.
3328. CJEU C-409/12 of 6.3.2014 – Backaldrin Österreich The Kornspitz Company, para. 39.

Article 12(2)(a) TMD2008 must be interpreted as meaning that, in a case such as that at issue in the main proceedings, a trade mark is liable to revocation in respect of a product for which it is registered if, in consequence of acts or inactivity of the proprietor, that trade mark has become the common name for that product from the **point of view solely of end users** of the product.[3329]

In the case described by the referring court, which remains subject to its factual assessment alone, the end users of the product at issue in the main proceedings, namely the bread rolls known as 'KORNSPITZ', perceive that word sign as the common name for that product and are not, therefore, aware of the fact that some of those bread rolls have been made using a baking mix supplied under the trade mark KORNSPITZ by a particular undertaking.[3330]

As the referring court has also stated, that perception on the part of end users is due, in particular, to the fact that the sellers of the bread rolls made using that mix do not generally inform their customers that the sign 'KORNSPITZ' has been registered as a trade mark.[3331]

The case set out in the order for reference is, in addition, characterized by the fact that the sellers of that finished product do not generally, at the time of sale, offer their customers assistance which includes an indication of the origin of the various goods for sale.[3332]

Clearly, in such a case, the trade mark KORNSPITZ does not, in the trade in respect of the bread rolls known as 'KORNSPITZ', fulfil its essential function as an indication of origin, and, consequently, it is liable to revocation in so far as it is registered for that finished product if the loss of its distinctive character in respect of that product is attributable to acts or inactivity of the proprietor of that trade mark.[3333]

That finding is not contrary to the interpretation of Article 12(2)(a) TMD given by the Court in paragraph 26 of the judgment in *Björnekulla Fruktindustrier*,[3334] according to which, in cases where intermediaries participate in the distribution of a product which is the subject of a registered trade mark, the relevant classes of persons whose views must be taken into account in determining whether that trade mark has become the common name in the trade for the product in question comprise all consumers or end users and, depending on the features of the market concerned, all those in the trade who deal with that product commercially.[3335]

[B] Liability to mislead the public

The conditions for revocation laid down by **Article 12(2)(b) TMD2008** are the **same** as those for the refusal of registration under **Article 3(1)(g) TMD2008.**[3336]

3329. CJEU C-409/12 of 6.3.2014 – Backaldrin Österreich The Kornspitz Company, para. 30.
3330. CJEU C-409/12 of 6.3.2014 – Backaldrin Österreich The Kornspitz Company, para. 23.
3331. CJEU C-409/12 of 6.3.2014 – Backaldrin Österreich The Kornspitz Company, para. 24.
3332. CJEU C-409/12 of 6.3.2014 – Backaldrin Österreich The Kornspitz Company, para. 25.
3333. CJEU C-409/12 of 6.3.2014 – Backaldrin Österreich The Kornspitz Company, para. 26.
3334. CJEU C-371/02 of 29.4.2004 – Björnekulla Fruktindustrier.
3335. CJEU C-409/12 of 6.3.2014 – Backaldrin Österreich The Kornspitz Company, para. 27.
3336. CJEU C-259/04 of 30.3.2006 – Emanuel, para. 53.

A trade mark corresponding to the name of the designer and first manufacturer of the goods bearing that mark is not, by reason of that particular feature alone, liable to revocation on the ground that that mark would mislead the public, within the meaning of Article 12(2)(b) TMD2008, in particular where the goodwill associated with that mark has been assigned together with the business making the goods to which the mark relates.[3337]

Article 21 Revocation relating to only some of the goods or services

Where grounds for revocation of a trade mark exist in respect of only some of the goods or services for which that trade mark has been registered, revocation shall cover those goods or services only.

SECTION 5 TRADE MARKS AS OBJECTS OF PROPERTY

Article 22 Transfer of registered trade marks

1. *A trade mark may be transferred, separately from any transfer of the undertaking, in respect of some or all of the goods or services for which it is registered.*
2. *A transfer of the whole of the undertaking shall include the transfer of the trade mark except where there is agreement to the contrary or circumstances clearly dictate otherwise. This provision shall apply to the contractual obligation to transfer the undertaking.*
3. *Member States shall have procedures in place to allow for the recordal of transfers in their registers.*

Article 23 Rights in rem

1. *A trade mark may, independently of the undertaking, be given as security or be the subject of rights in rem.*
2. *Member States shall have procedures in place to allow for the recordal of rights in rem in their registers.*

Article 24 Levy of execution

1. *A trade mark may be levied in execution.*
2. *Member States shall have procedures in place to allow for the recordal of levy of execution in their registers.*

3337. CJEU C-259/04 of 30.3.2006 – Emanuel, para. 53.

Article 25 Licensing

1. *A trade mark may be licensed for some or all of the goods or services for which it is registered and for the whole or part of the Member State concerned. A licence may be exclusive or non-exclusive.*
2. *The proprietor of a trade mark may invoke the rights conferred by that trade mark against a licensee who contravenes any provision in his licensing contract with regard to:*
   (a) *its duration;*
   (b) *the form covered by the registration in which the trade mark may be used;*
   (c) *the scope of the goods or services for which the licence is granted;*
   (d) *the territory in which the trade mark may be affixed; or*
   (e) *the quality of the goods manufactured or of the services provided by the licensee.*
3. *Without prejudice to the provisions of the licensing contract, the licensee may bring proceedings for infringement of a trade mark only if its proprietor consents thereto. However, the holder of an exclusive licence may bring such proceedings if the proprietor of the trade mark, after formal notice, does not himself bring infringement proceedings within an appropriate period.*
4. *A licensee shall, for the purpose of obtaining compensation for damage suffered by him, be entitled to intervene in infringement proceedings brought by the proprietor of the trade mark.*
5. *Member States shall have procedures in place to allow for the recordal of licences in their registers.*

[A] Territorial rights

The **principle of the independence of trade marks** has led to recognition that a trade mark right may be assigned for one country without at the same time being assigned by its owner in other countries.[3338]

[B] Delimitation agreements

Agreements known as '**delimitation agreements**' are lawful and useful if they serve to delimit, in the mutual interest of the parties, the spheres within which their respective trade marks may be used, and are intended to avoid confusion or conflict between them. That is not to say, however, that such agreements are excluded from the application of Article 85 of the treaty[3339] if they also have the aim of dividing up the market or restricting competition in other ways. As the Court has already stated, the Community system of competition 'does not allow the improper use of rights under any national trade mark law in order to frustrate the Community's law on cartels'.[3340]

3338. CJEU C-9/93 of 22.6.1994 – IHT Internationale Heiztechnik/Ideal-Standard, para. 26.
3339. Article 81 EC.
3340. CJEU 35/83 of 30.1.1985 – BAT Cigaretten-Fabriken/Commission, para. 33.

This may be the case if a claim is based on a trade mark which is liable to be removed from the register due to non-use.[3341]

[C] Invocation of trade mark rights against a licensee

Article 8(2) TMD2008 is to be interpreted as meaning that the proprietor of a trade mark **can invoke** the rights conferred by that trade mark **against a licensee who contravenes** a provision in a licence agreement prohibiting, on grounds of the trade mark's prestige, sales to discount stores such as the ones at issue in the main proceedings, provided it has been established that that contravention, by reason of the situation in the main proceedings, damages the allure and prestigious image which bestows on them an aura of luxury.[3342]

The very wording of Article 8(2) TMD2008 shows that the list set out in it is exhaustive.[3343]

In this respect, it must be noted that that provision contains no adverb, or an expression such as 'especially' or 'in particular', that would allow a finding that the list simply provides guidance.[3344]

Moreover, it must be recalled that it is precisely use of the adverb 'especially' that led the Court to find, by contrast, that the examples given in Article 7(2) TMD2008 provided guidance only.[3345]

As regards provisions in a licence agreement concerning '**the quality of the goods manufactured ... by the licensee**', which that article mentions, it must be recalled that, according to consistent case law, the essential function of the mark is to guarantee the identity of origin of marked goods or services to the consumer or end user by enabling him, without any possibility of confusion, to distinguish the goods or services from others which have another origin. For the trade mark to be able to fulfil its essential role in the system of undistorted competition which the Treaty seeks to establish and maintain, it must offer a guarantee that all the goods or services bearing it have been manufactured or supplied under the control of a single undertaking which is responsible for their quality.[3346]

Therefore, it is precisely where the licensee contravenes provisions in the licence agreement concerning, in particular, the quality of the goods manufactured that Article 8(2) TMD2008 enables the proprietor of the trade mark to invoke the rights that the directive grants him.[3347]

3341. CJEU 35/83 of 30.1.1985 – BAT Cigaretten-Fabriken/Commission, para. 35; no original wording.
3342. CJEU C-59/08 of 23.4.2009 – Copad, para. 37; *see also* CJEU C-376/11 of 19.7.2012 – Pie Optiek, para. 44.
3343. CJEU C-59/08 of 23.4.2009 – Copad, para. 20.
3344. CJEU C-59/08 of 23.4.2009 – Copad, para. 18.
3345. CJEU C-59/08 of 23.4.2009 – Copad, para. 19.
3346. CJEU C-59/08 of 23.4.2009 – Copad, para. 22.
3347. CJEU C-59/08 of 23.4.2009 – Copad, para. 23.

The quality of **luxury goods** is not just the result of their material characteristics but also of the allure and prestigious image which bestows on them an aura of luxury.[3348]

Since luxury goods are high-class goods, the aura of luxury emanating from them is essential in that it enables consumers to distinguish them from similar goods.[3349]

Therefore, an impairment to that aura of luxury is likely to affect the actual quality of those goods.[3350]

The characteristics and conditions of a selective distribution system can, in themselves, preserve the quality and ensure the proper use of such goods.[3351]

Setting up a selective distribution system which, according to the terms of the licence agreement, seeks to ensure that the goods are displayed in sales outlets in a manner that enhances their value, 'especially as regards the positioning, advertising, packaging as well as business policy', contributes to the reputation of the goods at issue and therefore to sustaining the aura of luxury surrounding them.[3352]

It follows that it is conceivable that the sale of luxury goods by the licensee to third parties that are not part of the selective distribution network might affect the quality itself of those goods, so that, in such circumstances, a contractual provision prohibiting such sale must be considered to be falling within the scope of Article 8(2) TMD2008.[3353]

It is for the **national court** having jurisdiction in the matter to examine whether, taking into account the **particular circumstances** of the case before it, contravention by the licensee of a provision such as the one at issue in the main proceedings damages the aura of luxury of the luxury goods, thus affecting their quality.[3354]

In this respect, it is important to take into consideration, in particular, first, the nature of the luxury goods bearing the trade mark, the volumes sold and whether the licensee sells the goods to discount stores that are not part of the selective distribution network regularly or only occasionally and, secondly, the nature of the goods normally marketed by those discount stores, and the marketing methods normally used in that sector of activity.[3355]

Moreover, it should be added that this interpretation of Article 8(2) TMD2008 cannot be called in question by the arguments that a provision in a licence agreement prohibiting sale to discount stores for reasons connected with the prestige of the trade mark may fall within the scope of other provisions than that relating to the 'quality of the goods', provisions, namely those concerning 'the territory in which the trade mark may be affixed' or 'the quality ... of the services provided by the licensee'.[3356]

3348. CJEU C-59/08 of 23.4.2009 – Copad, para. 24.
3349. CJEU C-59/08 of 23.4.2009 – Copad, para. 25.
3350. CJEU C-59/08 of 23.4.2009 – Copad, para. 26.
3351. CJEU C-59/08 of 23.4.2009 – Copad, para. 28.
3352. CJEU C-59/08 of 23.4.2009 – Copad, para. 29.
3353. CJEU C-59/08 of 23.4.2009 – Copad, para. 30.
3354. CJEU C-59/08 of 23.4.2009 – Copad, para. 31.
3355. CJEU C-59/08 of 23.4.2009 – Copad, para. 32.
3356. CJEU C-59/08 of 23.4.2009 – Copad, para. 33.

In this respect, first, it must be held that Article 8(2) TMD2008 must be read in conjunction with paragraph 1 of that article, which refers to '[the territory of] a Member State', so that, for the purpose of those provisions, the concept of 'territory' can only have a geographic scope and cannot, therefore, be interpreted as referring to a group of authorized outlets belonging to a selective distribution network.[3357]

Second, it must be held that it is apparent from the case law of the Court that even though no overriding reason based on the Directive or on general principles of Community law precludes services provided in the context of the retail trade of goods from being covered by the concept of 'services' within the meaning of the Directive, the trade mark must have been registered for those services.[3358]

Article 7(1) TMD2008 is to be interpreted as meaning that **a licensee who puts goods bearing a trade mark on the market in disregard of a provision in a licence agreement does so without the consent** of the proprietor of the trade mark where it is established that the provision in question is included in those listed in Article 8(2) TMD2008.[3359]

[D] Registration of licences

The first sentence of Article 23(1) CTMR must be interpreted as meaning that the licensee may bring proceedings alleging infringement of a Community trade mark which is the subject of the licence, although that licence has not been entered in the Register.[3360]

It follows from the first sentence of Article 23(1) CTMR, according to which '[l]egal acts referred to in Articles 17, 19 and 22 concerning a Community trade mark shall have effects vis-à-vis third parties in all the Member States only after entry in the Register', that the legal acts thus covered are the transfer of the Community trade mark, the creation of rights in rem over that mark and the grant of a licence. Read in isolation, that sentence could be interpreted as meaning that the licensee cannot, if the licence has not been entered in the Register, rely on the rights conferred by that licence vis-à-vis third parties, including the party infringing the trade mark.[3361]

However, in interpreting a provision of EU law, it is necessary to consider not only its wording but also the context in which it occurs and the objectives pursued by the rules of which it is part.[3362]

As regards the context of which the first sentence of Article 23(1) CTMR is part, first of all, that the second sentence of that paragraph qualifies the rule set out in that first sentence as regards 'third parties who have acquired rights' in the trade mark after the date of the legal act in question but who knew of the act at the date on which the rights were acquired. Article 23(2) establishes an exception to that rule in the case of

3357. CJEU C-59/08 of 23.4.2009 – Copad, para. 34.
3358. CJEU C-59/08 of 23.4.2009 – Copad, para. 35.
3359. CJEU C-59/08 of 23.4.2009 – Copad, para. 51; also *see* above Art. 15 'Consent'.
3360. CJEU C-163/15 of 4.2.2016 – Hassan, para. 26.
3361. CJEU C-163/15 of 4.2.2016 – Hassan, para. 18.
3362. CJEU C-163/15 of 4.2.2016 – Hassan, para. 19; also *see* CJEU C-219/11 of 22.11.2012 – Brain Products, para. 13; C-237/15 of 16.7.2015 – PPU, para. 35.

a 'person who acquires the Community trade mark or a right concerning the Community trade mark' by way of transfer of the whole of the undertaking or by any other universal succession. Accordingly, an interpretation of Article 23(1) and (2) CTMR which is both literal and schematic gives support to the idea that it, as a whole, is intended to govern the enforceability of the legal acts referred to in Articles 17, 19 and 22 CTMR in respect of third parties who have, or are likely to have, rights in the Community trade mark.[3363]

Next, section 4 of Title II CTMR, which includes Article 23 CTMR, is entitled 'Community trade marks as objects of property'. Accordingly, all of the articles in that section contain rules relating to the Community trade mark as an object of property. This is the case with regard to Articles 17, 19 and 22 CTMR, as is also apparent from recital 11 thereof. Those articles relate to acts the purpose or effect of which is to create or transfer a right in respect of a trade mark.[3364]

Finally, in the first sentence of Article 22(3) CTMR, the licensee's right to bring proceedings for infringement of a Community trade mark, without prejudice to the provisions of the licensing contract, is subject only to the proprietor's consent thereto.[3365]

It must also be stated that, according to Article 22(5) CTMR, the licence is entered in the Register on request of one of the parties. However, that article, like Article 19 CTMR, does not contain any provision analogous to that of Article 17(6) CTMR, under which '[a]s long as the transfer has not been entered in the Register, the successor in title may not invoke the rights arising from the registration of the Community trade mark'.[3366]

Moreover, Article 17(6) CTMR would serve no useful purpose if Article 23(1) thereof had to be interpreted as precluding reliance, vis-à-vis all third parties, on all of the legal acts referred to in Articles 17, 19 and 22 CTMR as long as they have not been entered in the Register.[3367]

With regard to the purpose of the rule laid down in the first sentence of Article 23(1) CTMR, the lack of effects, vis-à-vis third parties, of the legal acts referred to in Articles 17, 19 and 22 CTMR which have not been entered in the Register is intended to protect a person who has, or may have, rights in a Community trade mark as an object of property. It follows that the first sentence of Article 23(1) CTMR does not apply to a situation, such as that in the main proceedings, in which a third party, by infringing the mark, infringes the rights conferred by the Community trade mark.[3368]

[E] Joint proprietorship

First Council Directive 89/104 and Regulation No. 40/94 must be interpreted as meaning that the question of whether the grant or the termination of a licence to use a

3363. CJEU C-163/15 of 4.2.2016 – Hassan, para. 20.
3364. CJEU C-163/15 of 4.2.2016 – Hassan, para. 21.
3365. CJEU C-163/15 of 4.2.2016 – Hassan, para. 22.
3366. CJEU C-163/15 of 4.2.2016 – Hassan, para. 23.
3367. CJEU C-163/15 of 4.2.2016 – Hassan, para. 24.
3368. CJEU C-163/15 of 4.2.2016 – Hassan, para. 25.

national trade mark or an EU trade mark held in **joint proprietorship** requires a unanimous decision by the joint proprietors or a decision by a majority of them comes within the scope of the applicable national law.[3369]

It should be recalled that, according to Article 5 of First Council Directive 89/104 and Article 9 of Regulation No. 40/94, the trade mark confers an exclusive right on its owner. Article 5 of that regulation states that any natural or legal person, including authorities established under public law, may be the proprietor of an EU trade mark.[3370]

Moreover, it is apparent from Article 8(1) of First Council Directive 89/104 and Article 22(1) of Regulation No. 40/94 that both a national trade mark and an EU trade mark may be licensed, either exclusively or non-exclusively, for all or some of the goods or services for which they are registered.[3371]

It is apparent from Article 16(3) and Article 21(2) of Regulation No. 40/94, which refer to the 'joint proprietors' of an EU trade mark, that such a mark may belong to two or more persons.[3372]

While it is true that First Council Directive 89/104 does not refer to the joint proprietorship of a national trade mark, that omission does not mean that joint proprietorship of such a trade mark is excluded, but that it is governed by national law, under which fall the arrangements for the exercise, by joint proprietors, of the rights conferred by the trade mark, including the right to decide on the grant or the termination of a licence to use it.[3373]

Furthermore, as is apparent from the third and sixth recitals of First Council Directive 89/104, although the purpose of that directive is to approximate the laws of Member States on trade marks in order to abolish existing disparities which may impede the free movement of goods and freedom to provide services, the directive does not seek a full-scale approximation of those laws.[3374]

Regarding Regulation No. 40/94, while recognizing joint proprietorship of an EU trade mark, it does not contain any provision governing the conditions for the exercise, by the joint proprietors of such a mark, of the rights conferred by it, including the right to decide on the grant or the termination of a licence to use it.[3375]

It is apparent from Article 16(1) of Regulation No. 40/94, however, that an EU trade mark as an object of property is to be dealt with as a national trade mark registered in the particular Member State, according to the rules laid down in that article. It follows that, in the absence of a provision in that regulation governing the arrangements for the adoption, by the joint proprietors of an EU trade mark, of the

3369. CJEU C-686/21 of 27.4.2023 – VW/SW a.o., para. 38.
3370. CJEU C-686/21 of 27.4.2023 – VW/SW a.o., para. 31.
3371. CJEU C-686/21 of 27.4.2023 – VW/SW a.o., para. 32.
3372. CJEU C-686/21 of 27.4.2023 – VW/SW a.o., para. 33.
3373. CJEU C-686/21 of 27.4.2023 – VW/SW a.o., para. 34.
3374. CJEU C-686/21 of 27.4.2023 – VW/SW a.o., para. 35, with reference to CJEU C-23/01 of 21.11.2002 – Robelco, para. 33.
3375. CJEU C-686/21 of 27.4.2023 – VW/SW a.o., para. 36.

decision to grant or to terminate a licence to use that mark, those arrangements are governed by the law of that Member State.[3376]

Article 26 The application for a trade mark as an object of property

Articles 22 to 25 shall apply to applications for trade marks.

SECTION 6 GUARANTEE OR CERTIFICATION MARKS AND COLLECTIVE MARKS

Article 27 Definitions

For the purposes of this section, the following definitions apply:

(a) 'guarantee or certification mark' means a trade mark which is described as such when the mark is applied for and is capable of distinguishing goods or services which are certified by the proprietor of the mark in respect of material, mode of manufacture of goods or performance of services, quality, accuracy or other characteristics from goods and services which are not so certified;

(b) 'collective mark' means a trade mark which is described as such when the mark is applied for and is capable of distinguishing the goods or services of the members of an association which is the proprietor of the mark from the goods or services of other undertakings.

Article 28 Guarantee or certification marks

1. *Member States may provide for the registration of guarantee or certification marks.*
2. *Any natural or legal person, including institutions, authorities and bodies governed by public law, may apply for guarantee or certification marks provided that the person does not carry on a business involving the supply of goods or services of the kind certified.*

   Member States may provide that a guarantee or certification mark is not to be registered unless the applicant is competent to certify the goods or services for which the mark is to be registered.
3. *Member States may provide that guarantee or certification marks are not to be registered, or are to be revoked or declared invalid, on grounds other than those specified in Articles 4, 19 and 20 where the function of those marks so requires.*
4. *By way of derogation from Article 4(1)(c), Member States may provide that signs or indications which may serve, in trade, to designate the geographical origin of the goods or services may constitute guarantee or certification marks. Such a guarantee or certification mark shall not entitle the proprietor to prohibit a third party from using in the course of trade such signs or indications, provided that third party uses them in accordance with honest practices in industrial or commercial matters. In particular, such a mark*

3376. CJEU C-686/21 of 27.4.2023 – VW/SW a.o., para. 37.

may not be invoked against a third party who is entitled to use a geographical name.

5. *The requirements laid down in Article 16 shall be satisfied where genuine use of a guarantee or certification mark in accordance with Article 16 is made by any person who has the authority to use it.*

Article 29 Collective marks

1. *Member States shall provide for the registration of collective marks.*
2. *Associations of manufacturers, producers, suppliers of services or traders, which, under the terms of the law governing them, have the capacity in their own name to have rights and obligations, to make contracts or accomplish other legal acts, and to sue and be sued, as well as legal persons governed by public law, may apply for collective marks.*
3. *By way of derogation from Article 4(1)(c), Member States may provide that signs or indications which may serve, in trade, to designate the geographical origin of the goods or services may constitute collective marks. Such a collective mark shall not entitle the proprietor to prohibit a third party from using in the course of trade such signs or indications, provided that third party uses them in accordance with honest practices in industrial or commercial matters. In particular, such a mark may not be invoked against a third party who is entitled to use a geographical name.*

As is clear from the very wording of Article 66(2) CTMR, EU collective marks consisting of signs or indications which may serve, in trade, **to designate the geographical origin** of goods or services constitute EU collective marks within the meaning of paragraph 1 of that article. According to that paragraph, only trade marks that are capable of distinguishing the goods or services of the members of the association which is the proprietor of the trade mark from those of other undertakings may constitute EU collective marks.[3377]

Moreover, Article 4 CTMR, which is applicable to collective marks by virtue of Article 66(3) CTMR, provides, in essence, that only signs that are capable of distinguishing the commercial origin of the goods or services which they designate may constitute EU trade marks.[3378]

The **essential function of an EU collective mark** within the meaning of Article 66(2) CTMR is to indicate the geographical origin of the goods or services offered under such a mark, and not to indicate their commercial origin, that would disregard that essential function.[3379]

That conclusion cannot be called into question by the case law arising from the judgment *Anheuser-Busch v. Budějovický Budvar*,[3380] whereby it submits that an EU collective mark under Article 66(2) CTMR is, by its very nature, incapable of performing a distinguishing function of that kind.[3381]

3377. CJEU C-673/15 P to C-676/15 P of 20.9.2017 – The Tea Board/EUIPO, para. 50.
3378. CJEU C-673/15 P to C-676/15 P of 20.9.2017 – The Tea Board/EUIPO, para. 51.
3379. CJEU C-673/15 P to C-676/15 P of 20.9.2017 – The Tea Board/EUIPO, para. 54.
3380. CJEU C-96/09 P of 29.3.2011 – Anheuser-Busch, para. 147.
3381. CJEU C-673/15 P to C-676/15 P of 20.9.2017 – The Tea Board/EUIPO, para. 55.

While The Tea Board's argument based on Article 67(2) CTMR remains unclear and unsubstantiated, it must be noted that, in its judgment *Anheuser-Busch v. Budějovický Budvar*,[3382] the Court merely held that the essential function of a geographical indication is to guarantee to consumers the geographical origin of the goods and the specific qualities inherent in them. The Court, however, made no assessment of the essential function of EU collective marks within the meaning of Article 66(2) CTMR.[3383]

Secondly, whilst Article 66(2) CTMR constitutes an exception to the absolute ground for refusal under Article 7(1)(c) CTMR, that circumstance is not such as to call into question the fact that the essential function of an EU collective mark under Article 66(2) CTMR is to guarantee the collective commercial origin of the goods sold under that trade mark, and not to guarantee their collective geographical origin.[3384]

Moreover, the derogation in Article 66(2) CTMR from Article 7(1)(c) CTMR is explained by the very nature of the sign covered by the collective marks referred to in that paragraph.[3385]

In that regard, the Court has already held that Article 7(1)(c) CTMR pursues an aim which is in the public interest, namely that descriptive signs or indications relating to the categories of goods or services in respect of which registration is applied for may be freely used by all, including as collective marks or as part of complex or graphic marks. That provision therefore prevents such signs or such indications from being reserved to one undertaking alone because they have been registered as individual trade marks.[3386]

Thus, an EU collective mark falling within Article 66(2) CTMR does not conflict with such a public-interest aim since: (i) in accordance with the last sentence of that paragraph, such a mark does not entitle the proprietor to prohibit a third party from using, in the course of trade, those signs or indications, provided that he uses them in accordance with honest practice in industrial or commercial matters; and (ii) Article 67(2) CTMR requires that the regulations governing use of a mark covered by Article 66(2) authorize any person whose products or services originate from the geographical area concerned to become a member of the association which is the proprietor of the trade mark.[3387]

Thirdly, one cannot rely in support of its argument on Article 13(1)(c) and (d) of Regulation No. 1151/2012[3388] or on Article 22 of the TRIPS Agreement, which relate to the protection of protected geographical indications.[3389]

3382. CJEU C-96/09 P of 29.3.2011 – Anheuser-Busch, para. 147.
3383. CJEU C-673/15 P to C-676/15 P of 20.9.2017 – The Tea Board/EUIPO, para. 56.
3384. CJEU C-673/15 P to C-676/15 P of 20.9.2017 – The Tea Board/EUIPO, para. 57.
3385. CJEU C-673/15 P to C-676/15 P of 20.9.2017 – The Tea Board/EUIPO, para. 58.
3386. CJEU C-673/15 P to C-676/15 P of 20.9.2017 – The Tea Board/EUIPO, para. 59; with reference to CJEU C-108/97 and C-109/97 of 4.5.1999 – Windsurfing Chiemsee, para. 25; C-273/05 P of 19.4.2007 – OHIM/Celltech, para. 75; C-488/16 P of 6.9.2018 – Bundesverband – Souvenir – Geschenke – Ehrenpreise/EUIPO, para. 36.
3387. CJEU C-673/15 P to C-676/15 P of 20.9.2017 – The Tea Board/EUIPO, para. 60.
3388. Regulation (EU) No 1151/2012 of the European Parliament and of the Council of 21 November 2012 on quality schemes for agricultural products and foodstuffs.
3389. CJEU C-673/15 P to C-676/15 P of 20.9.2017 – The Tea Board/EUIPO, para. 61.

It suffices, in that regard, to note that such geographical indications, on the one hand, and EU collective marks consisting of signs or indications which may serve, in trade, to designate the geographical origin of goods and services, on the other hand, are signs which are governed by distinct legal regimes and pursue different aims. Thus, whereas the EU trade mark is, in accordance with Article 4 CTMR, a sign capable of distinguishing the commercial origin of goods or services, a geographical indication is, in accordance with Article 5(2) of Regulation No. 1151/2012, a name that identifies a product originating in a specific geographical area, whose quality, reputation or other characteristic is essentially attributable to its geographical origin, and at least one of the production steps of which take place in the defined geographical area.[3390]

In the light of the foregoing considerations, the General Court did not err in law when it held that the essential function of an EU collective mark is to distinguish the goods or services of the members of the association which is the proprietor of the trade mark from those of other undertakings, and not to distinguish those goods according to their geographical origin.[3391]

It follows that the General Court likewise did not err in law when it held, in essence, that, in the application of Article 8(1)(b) CTMR, where the signs at issue are, on the one hand, collective marks and, on the other hand, individual marks, the possibility that the public might believe that the goods and services covered by the signs at issue have the same geographical origin cannot constitute a relevant criterion for establishing their identity or similarity.[3392]

An extremely wide range of goods and services can be produced or rendered within the same geographical area. By the same token, there is nothing to prevent a region whose geographical name is registered as an EU collective mark under Article 66(2) CTMR from being the source of different raw materials which may be used to make various different products.[3393]

It must be noted, in that regard, that Article 66 CTMR by no means requires that manufacturers, producers, suppliers or traders who are affiliated with the association which is the proprietor of an EU collective mark form part of the same group of companies which manufacture or supply the goods or services under unitary control. That regulation does not preclude the members of such an association from being competitors, each of whom uses the collective mark indicating its affiliation with that association, on the one hand, and an individual mark indicating the identity of origin of its goods or services, on the other.[3394]

Under Article 8(1)(b) CTMR, which is, in the absence of any provision to the contrary in Articles 67 to 74 CTMR, applicable to EU collective marks pursuant to Article 66(3) CTMR, the trade mark applied for is not to be registered if, because of its identity with, or similarity to, the earlier trade mark and the identity or similarity of the

3390. CJEU C-673/15 P to C-676/15 P of 20.9.2017 - The Tea Board/EUIPO, para. 62.
3391. CJEU C-673/15 P to C-676/15 P of 20.9.2017 - The Tea Board/EUIPO, para. 63; C-143/19 P of 12.12.2019 - Der Grüne Punkt - Duales System Deutschland /EUIPO, para. 52.
3392. CJEU C-673/15 P to C-676/15 P of 20.9.2017 - The Tea Board/EUIPO, para. 64.
3393. CJEU C-673/15 P to C-676/15 P of 20.9.2017 - The Tea Board/EUIPO, para. 65.
3394. CJEU C-143/19 P of 12.12.2019 - Der Grüne Punkt - Duales System Deutschland /EUIPO, para. 50.

goods or services covered by the mark applied for and the earlier mark, there exists a **likelihood of confusion** on the part of the public in the territory in which the earlier trade mark is protected.[3395]

Article 30 Regulations governing use of a collective mark

1. *An applicant for a collective mark shall submit the regulations governing its use to the office.*
2. *The regulations governing use shall specify at least the persons authorised to use the mark, the conditions of membership of the association and the conditions of use of the mark, including sanctions. The regulations governing use of a mark referred to in Article 29(3) shall authorise any person whose goods or services originate in the geographical area concerned to become a member of the association which is the proprietor of the mark, provided that the person fulfils all the other conditions of the regulations.*

Article 31 Refusal of an application

1. *In addition to the grounds for refusal of a trade mark application provided for in Article 4, where appropriate with the exception of Article 4(1)(c) concerning signs or indications which may serve, in trade, to designate the geographical origin of the goods or services, and Article 5, and without prejudice to the right of an office not to undertake examination ex officio of relative grounds, an application for a collective mark shall be refused where the requirements of point (b) of Article 27, Article 29 or Article 30 are not satisfied, or where the regulations governing use are contrary to public policy or to accepted principles of morality.*
2. *An application for a collective mark shall also be refused if the public is liable to be misled as regards the character or the significance of the mark, in particular if it is likely to be taken to be something other than a collective mark.*
3. *An application shall not be refused if the applicant, as a result of amendment of the regulations governing use, meets the requirements of paragraphs 1 and 2.*

The argument that the distinctiveness of the earlier mark should, having regard, in particular, to Article 66(2) CTMR, be assessed differently where the earlier mark is an EU collective mark cannot be accepted.[3396]

In that regard, it must be noted that in the absence of any provision to the contrary in Articles 67 to 74 CTMR, Article 7(1)(b) and Article 7(3) CTMR apply to EU collective marks. Consequently, those marks must in any event, whether intrinsically or through use, be distinctive.[3397]

3395. CJEU C-766/18 P of 5.3.2018 – Foundation for the Protection of the Traditional Cheese of Cyprus named Halloumi, para. 59, with reference to CJEU C-673/15 P to C-676/15 P of 20.9.2017 – The Tea Board/EUIPO, para. 46.
3396. CJEU C-766/18 P of 5.3.2018 – Foundation for the Protection of the Traditional Cheese of Cyprus named Halloumi, para. 71.
3397. CJEU C-766/18 P of 5.3.2018 – Foundation for the Protection of the Traditional Cheese of Cyprus named Halloumi, para. 72.

Article 66(2) CTMR is not an exception to that requirement of distinctiveness. While that provision permits, by way of derogation from Article 7(1)(c) CTMR, registration as EU collective marks of signs which may serve to designate the geographical origin of goods or services, it does not, on the other hand, allow the signs thus registered to be devoid of distinctiveness. Where an association applies for registration, as an EU collective mark, of a sign which may designate a geographical origin, it is therefore incumbent on it to ensure that that sign has elements which enable the consumer to distinguish the goods or services of its members from those of other undertakings.[3398]

Therefore, even supposing that the EU collective mark HALLOUMI implicitly refers, as the appellant claims, to the Cypriot geographical origin of the goods covered, that mark must nevertheless still fulfil its essential function, namely to distinguish the goods or services of the members of the association which is the proprietor of that mark from those of other undertakings, and the degree of distinctiveness of that mark is a relevant factor for the purposes of assessing whether there is a likelihood of confusion, within the meaning of Article 8(1)(b) CTMR, between that mark and the mark applied for BBQLOUMI.[3399]

It follows that the General Court did not err in law in assessing the degree of distinctiveness of the earlier mark HALLOUMI and in including that factor in its assessment of the existence of a likelihood of confusion.[3400]

Furthermore, it does not appear that the General Court, in making that assessment, 'deprecated' the distinctiveness of the earlier mark HALLOUMI or that it relied on a premiss of weak distinctiveness which it was for the appellant to rebut. On the contrary, the term 'halloumi', the sole element of which that earlier mark consists, designates a particular type of cheese produced according to a special recipe and that the distinctiveness of such a mark, which is restricted to designating a type of product, is weak. That assessment of the degree of distinctiveness of the earlier mark cannot, in the absence of a specific complaint based on a manifest distortion of the evidence, be challenged before the Court of Justice.[3401]

Article 32 Use of collective marks

The requirements of Article 16 shall be satisfied where genuine use of a collective mark in accordance with that Article is made by any person who has authority to use it.

3398. CJEU C-766/18 P of 5.3.2018 – Foundation for the Protection of the Traditional Cheese of Cyprus named Halloumi, para. 73.
3399. CJEU C-766/18 P of 5.3.2018 – Foundation for the Protection of the Traditional Cheese of Cyprus named Halloumi, para. 74.
3400. CJEU C-766/18 P of 5.3.2018 – Foundation for the Protection of the Traditional Cheese of Cyprus named Halloumi, para. 75.
3401. CJEU C-766/18 P of 5.3.2018 – Foundation for the Protection of the Traditional Cheese of Cyprus named Halloumi, para. 76, with reference to CJEU C-673/15 P to C-676/15 P of 20.9.2017 – The Tea Board/EUIPO, para. 41.

In the absence of any provision to the contrary laid down in Articles 67 to 74 CTMR, Articles 15[3402] and 51 CTMR form part, under Article 66(3) CTMR, of the provisions of that regulation which apply to EU collective marks.[3403]

Article 33 Amendment to the regulations governing use of a collective mark

1. *The proprietor of a collective mark shall submit to the office any amended regulations governing use.*
2. *Amendments to the regulations governing use shall be mentioned in the register unless the amended regulations do not satisfy the requirements of Article 30 or involve one of the grounds for refusal referred to in Article 31.*
3. *For the purposes of this Directive, amendments to the regulations governing use shall take effect only from the date of entry of the mention of those amendments in the register.*

Article 34 Persons entitled to bring an action for infringement

1. *Article 25(3) and (4) shall apply to every person who has the authority to use a collective mark.*
2. *The proprietor of a collective mark shall be entitled to claim compensation on behalf of persons who have authority to use the mark where those persons have sustained damage as a result of unauthorised use of the mark.*

Article 35 Additional grounds for revocation

In addition to the grounds for revocation provided for in Articles 19 and 20, the rights of the proprietor of a collective mark shall be revoked on the following grounds:

(a) the proprietor does not take reasonable steps to prevent the mark being used in a manner that is incompatible with the conditions of use laid down in the regulations governing use, including any amendments thereto mentioned in the register;
(b) the manner in which the mark has been used by authorised persons has caused it to become liable to mislead the public in the manner referred to in Article 31(2);
(c) an amendment to the regulations governing use of the mark has been mentioned in the register in breach of Article 33(2), unless the proprietor of the mark, by further amending the regulations governing use, complies with the requirements of that Article.

Article 36 Additional grounds for invalidity

In addition to the grounds for invalidity provided for in Article 4, where appropriate with the exception of Article 4(1)(c) concerning signs or indications which may

3402. *See* above.
3403. CJEU C-143/19 P of 12.12.2019 – Der Grüne Punkt – Duales System Deutschland /EUIPO, para. 49.

serve, in trade, to designate the geographical origin of the goods or services, and Article 5, a collective mark which is registered in breach of Article 31 shall be declared invalid unless the proprietor of the mark, by amending the regulations governing use, complies with the requirements of Article 31.

CHAPTER 3
Procedures

SECTION 1 APPLICATION AND REGISTRATION

Article 37 Application requirements

1. *An application for registration of a trade mark shall contain at least all of the following:*
   (a) a request for registration;
   (b) information identifying the applicant;
   (c) a list of the goods or services in respect of which the registration is requested;
   (d) a representation of the trade mark, which satisfies the requirements set out in point (b) of Article 3.
2. *The application for a trade mark shall be subject to the payment of a fee determined by the Member State concerned.*

Article 38 Date of filing

1. *The date of filing of a trade mark application shall be the date on which the documents containing the information specified in Article 37(1) are filed with the office by the applicant.*
2. *Member States may, in addition, provide that the accordance of the date of filing is to be subject to the payment of a fee referred to in Article 37(2).*

[A] Principles

Take care: The provision is new in the TMD.

[B] No taking into account hours or minutes

Article 27 CTMR as amended must be interpreted as precluding account being taken not only of the **day** but also of the hour and minute of filing of an application for a

Community trade mark with OHIM for the purposes of establishing that trade mark's priority over a national trade mark filed on the same day, where, according to the national legislation governing the registration of national trade marks, the hour and minute of filing are relevant in that regard.[3404]

First, although the third recital in the preamble to the TMD states that 'it does not appear to be necessary at present to undertake full-scale approximation of the trade mark laws of the Member States', the directive none the less provides for harmonization in relation to substantive rules of central importance in this sphere, that is to say, according to the same recital, the rules concerning the provisions of national law which most directly affect the functioning of the internal market, and that recital does not preclude the harmonization relating to those rules from being complete.[3405]

However, the fifth recital in the preamble to the TMD states, *inter alia*, that the:

> *Member States ... remain free to fix the provisions of procedure concerning the registration, the revocation and the invalidity of trade marks acquired by registration; ... they can, for example, determine the form of trade mark registration and invalidity procedures, decide whether earlier rights should be invoked either in the registration procedure or in the invalidity procedure or in both and, if they allow earlier rights to be invoked in the registration procedure, have an opposition procedure or an ex officio examination procedure or both.*[3406]

It must therefore be held that the TMD does not contain any provisions relating to the procedure for filing or to establishing the date of filing of applications for national trade marks. Since the Member States remain free to determine their own provisions on the subject, those provisions may, consequently, differ from one Member State to another.[3407]

Second, it follows from the second recital in the preamble to the CTMR as amended that the objective of that regulation is the creation of a Community regime for trade marks to which uniform protection is given and which produce their effects throughout the entire area of the EU.[3408]

That Community trade mark system is an autonomous system with its own set of objectives and rules peculiar to it; it applies independently of any national system.[3409]

As an autonomous system which is independent from national systems, the Community trade mark regime has its own rules relating to the procedure for filing an application for a Community trade mark, contained in the CTMR. In particular, Article 27 CTMR as amended contains a specific provision relating to the date of filing of an application for a Community trade mark and does not refer to the provisions of national law in that regard.[3410]

3404. CJEU C-190/10 of 22.3.2012 – Génesis, para. 63.
3405. CJEU C-40/01 of 11.3.2003 – Ansul, para. 32; C-482/09 of 22.9.2011 – Budějovický Budvar, para. 30; C-190/10 of 22.3.2012 – Génesis, para. 32.
3406. CJEU C-190/10 of 22.3.2012 – Génesis, para. 33.
3407. CJEU C-190/10 of 22.3.2012 – Génesis, para. 34.
3408. CJEU C-235/09 of 12.4.2011 – DHL Express France, para. 41; C-190/10 of 22.3.2012 – Génesis, para. 35; C-149/11 of 19.12.2012 – Leno Merken, para. 27.
3409. CJEU C-190/10 of 22.3.2012 – Génesis, para. 36.
3410. CJEU C-190/10 of 22.3.2012 – Génesis, para. 37.

In those circumstances, in order to answer the question referred, it is necessary, first, to determine whether the concept of 'date of filing of a Community trade mark application' contained in Article 27 CTMR as amended should be interpreted as requiring account to be taken not only of the day but also of the hour and minute of filing of that application.[3411]

Second, if the concept of 'date of filing of a Community trade mark application' under Article 27 CTMR as amended is to be interpreted as not requiring account to be taken of the hour and minute of filing of that application, it must be ascertained whether EU law precludes those elements from nevertheless being taken into account under national law for the purposes of establishing a Community trade mark's priority over a national trade mark filed on the same day, where the national legislation governing the registration of that national trade mark considers the hour and minute of filing to be relevant.[3412]

The concept of '**date of filing** of a Community trade mark application' contained in Article 27 CTMR as amended requires the calendar day of filing of an application for a Community trade mark to be taken into account, but does not require the hour and minute of filing to be taken into account.[3413]

It is clear from a comparison of the various language versions of Article 27 CTMR as amended that those versions do display certain differences.[3414]

Thus, the Czech, German, Hungarian, Slovak, Finnish and Swedish versions of that article refer – in both the heading and the main text thereof – to the day of filing ('Den podání', 'Anmeldetag', 'A bejelentés napja', 'Deň podania', 'Hakemispäivä', 'Ansökningsdag'), while the Lithuanian and Polish versions of that article state that the date of filing ('Padavimo data', 'Data zgłoszenia') corresponds to the day ('diena', 'dzień') when the application was filed.[3415]

By contrast, the other language versions simply use the expression 'date of filing' of the Community trade mark application.[3416]

Nevertheless, the differences between those language versions must be placed in perspective since, according to its ordinary meaning, the term 'date' generally designates the day of the month, the month and the year when an act has been adopted or an event has taken place. In the same way, stating the day when an act has been adopted or an event has taken place means, according to its ordinary meaning, that it is also necessary to state the month and the year.[3417]

However, an obligation to state the date or the day does not imply, according to the ordinary meaning, that it is necessary to state the hour and, *a fortiori*, the minute. Therefore, in the absence of any express reference in Article 27 CTMR as amended to the hour and minute of filing of a Community trade mark application, it is apparent that that information was not considered by the Community legislature to be necessary for

3411. CJEU C-190/10 of 22.3.2012 – Génesis, para. 38.
3412. CJEU C-190/10 of 22.3.2012 – Génesis, para. 39.
3413. CJEU C-190/10 of 22.3.2012 – Génesis, para. 54.
3414. CJEU C-190/10 of 22.3.2012 – Génesis, para. 43.
3415. CJEU C-190/10 of 22.3.2012 – Génesis, para. 44.
3416. CJEU C-190/10 of 22.3.2012 – Génesis, para. 45.
3417. CJEU C-190/10 of 22.3.2012 – Génesis, para. 46.

the purposes of establishing the time of filing of a Community trade mark application and hence its priority over another trade mark application.[3418]

That interpretation also follows from the context of Article 27 CTMR as amended. In particular, Rule 5 CTMIR, which details the formalities to be completed by OHIM, by the central industrial property office of a Member State or by the Benelux Trade mark Office upon the filing of an application for a Community trade mark, only establishes an obligation to indicate on the application the date of receipt of that application and not the hour and minute thereof.[3419]

It must be held that if the Community legislature had considered that the hour and minute of filing of a Community trade mark application ought to be taken into account as constituent elements of the 'date of filing' of that application within the meaning of Article 27 CTMR as amended, that information should have been included in CTMIR.[3420]

In that regard, the fact that, according to the information on OHIM's website, the date of filing of a Community trade mark application is that on which the documents referred to in Article 26 CTMR as amended are filed with OHIM, Central European Time (GMT +1), none the less does not permit the conclusion that the hour and minute of filing of that application are relevant for the purposes of establishing that trade mark's priority. That indication of time only allows the date of filing before OHIM to be established.[3421]

The fact that when applications for Community trade marks are submitted by electronic means, OHIM de facto certifies the date and the time of filing of those applications is also irrelevant.[3422]

It is true that, under Article 10(2) of Decision No. EX-11-3 of the President of the Office of 18 April 2011 concerning electronic communication with and by the Office ('Basic Decision on Electronic Communication'), an electronic communication confirming receipt of the – also electronic – Community trade mark application, indicating the date and hour of receipt of that application, is to be issued to the sender. However, it also follows from Article 10(2) that the communication confirming receipt of that application is to include a statement that the date of receipt will be considered to be the filing date provided that a fee is paid in time, and there is no reference in that regard, to the hour of receipt of the application.[3423]

In any event, given that an application for a Community trade mark may be filed, according to Article 25(1) CTMR as amended, with OHIM, with the central industrial property office of a Member State or with the Benelux Trade mark Office (according to preference), if it was necessary to take the hour and minute of filing of an application for a Community trade mark into account, that obligation would have to stem explicitly from provisions of general application and not from the decision of the President of

3418. CJEU C-190/10 of 22.3.2012 – Génesis, para. 47.
3419. CJEU C-190/10 of 22.3.2012 – Génesis, para. 48.
3420. CJEU C-190/10 of 22.3.2012 – Génesis, para. 49.
3421. CJEU C-190/10 of 22.3.2012 – Génesis, para. 50.
3422. CJEU C-190/10 of 22.3.2012 – Génesis, para. 51.
3423. CJEU C-190/10 of 22.3.2012 – Génesis, para. 52.

OHIM relating to the filing of applications for Community trade marks by electronic means.[3424]

EU law precludes **the hour and minute of the filing** of an application for a Community trade mark from being taken into account under national law for the purposes of establishing that Community trade mark's priority over a national trade mark filed on the same day, where the national legislation governing the registration of national trade marks considers the hour and minute of filing to be relevant in that regard.[3425]

In that regard, it is sufficient to note that, as an autonomous system, the Community trade mark regime has its own rules relating to the date of filing of an application for a Community trade mark and does not refer to provisions of national law.[3426]

Accordingly, the date of filing of an application for a Community trade mark may only be established according to the rules of EU law, the approaches adopted by the law of the Member States not having any effect in that regard.[3427]

Indeed, first, it follows from Article 14 read in conjunction with Article 97 CTMR as amended that the applicability of national law is limited to questions which fall outside the scope of the CTMR.[3428]

Second, in a situation such as that at issue in the main proceedings, where a Community trade mark is invoked for the purposes of opposing the registration of a national trade mark, if the date of filing of the application for that Community trade mark were to be established by taking account of provisions of national law, that would in effect undermine the uniform nature of the protection of a Community trade mark. Since the Member States remain free to determine the procedure for filing applications for national trade marks, the extent of the protection given to that Community trade mark might differ from one Member State to another.[3429]

The conclusion that the date of filing of an application for a Community trade mark can only be established according to the rules of EU law is not called into question by Article 32 CTMR as amended according to which a Community trade mark application which has been accorded a date of filing is, in the Member States, to be equivalent to a regular national filing, where appropriate with the priority claimed for the Community trade mark application.[3430]

That provision neither amends the Community concept of the 'date of filing' nor presupposes the secondary application of national law, but simply recognizes that Community trade mark applications filed with OHIM are legally equivalent to those filed with national offices.[3431]

3424. CJEU C-190/10 of 22.3.2012 - Génesis, para. 53.
3425. CJEU C-190/10 of 22.3.2012 - Génesis, para. 62.
3426. CJEU C-190/10 of 22.3.2012 - Génesis, para. 56.
3427. CJEU C-190/10 of 22.3.2012 - Génesis, para. 57.
3428. CJEU C-190/10 of 22.3.2012 - Génesis, para. 58.
3429. CJEU C-190/10 of 22.3.2012 - Génesis, para. 59.
3430. CJEU C-190/10 of 22.3.2012 - Génesis, para. 60.
3431. CJEU C-190/10 of 22.3.2012 - Génesis, para. 61.

Article 39 Designation and classification of goods and services

1. *The goods and services in respect of which trade mark registration is applied for shall be classified in conformity with the system of classification established by the Nice Agreement Concerning the International Classification of Goods and Services for the Purposes of the Registration of Marks of 15 June 1957 ('the Nice Classification').*
2. *The goods and services for which protection is sought shall be identified by the applicant with sufficient clarity and precision to enable the competent authorities and economic operators, on that sole basis, to determine the extent of the protection sought.*
3. *For the purposes of paragraph 2, the general indications included in the class headings of the Nice Classification or other general terms may be used, provided that they comply with the requisite standards of clarity and precision set out in this Article.*
4. *The office shall reject an application in respect of indications or terms which are unclear or imprecise, where the applicant does not suggest an acceptable wording within a period set by the office to that effect.*
5. *The use of general terms, including the general indications of the class headings of the Nice Classification, shall be interpreted as including all the goods or services clearly covered by the literal meaning of the indication or term. The use of such terms or indications shall not be interpreted as comprising a claim to goods or services which cannot be so understood.*
6. *Where the applicant requests registration for more than one class, the applicant shall group the goods and services according to the classes of the Nice Classification, each group being preceded by the number of the class to which that group of goods or services belongs, and shall present them in the order of the classes.*
7. *Goods and services shall not be regarded as being similar to each other on the ground that they appear in the same class under the Nice Classification. Goods and services shall not be regarded as being dissimilar from each other on the ground that they appear in different classes under the Nice Classification.*

[A] Principles

Take care: The provision is new but tries to implement case law.

Pursuant to this, a national mark **protects** the goods covered by the application, and it is up to the applicant to specify his application with regard to the goods which he wants to have protected.[3432]

The registration of a sign as a trade mark must always be applied for in relation to **certain goods or services**. Although the function of the graphic representability requirement is, in particular, to define the mark itself in order to determine the precise subject of the protection afforded by the registered mark,[3433] the extent of that

3432. CJEU C-141/13 P of 17.7.2014 – Reber Holding/OHIM, para. 41; *see also* CJEU C-259/02 of 27.1.2004 – La Mer Technology, para. 20.
3433. *See* CJEU C-273/00 of 12.12.2002 – Sieckmann, para. 48.

protection is determined by the nature and the number of goods and services identified in that application:[3434]

- the TMD must be interpreted as meaning that it requires the goods and services for which the protection of the trade mark is sought to be identified by the applicant with sufficient clarity and precision to enable the competent authorities and economic operators, on that basis alone, to determine the extent of the protection conferred by the trade mark.
- the TMD must be interpreted as meaning that it does not preclude the use of the general indications of the class headings of the Nice Classification to identify the goods and services for which the protection of the trade mark is sought, provided that such identification is sufficiently clear and precise.
- an applicant for a national trade mark who uses all the general indications of a particular class heading of the Nice Classification to identify the goods or services for which the protection of the trade mark is sought must specify whether its application for registration is intended to cover all the goods or services included in the alphabetical list of that class or only some of those goods or services. If the application concerns only some of those goods or services, the applicant is required to specify which of the goods or services in that class are intended to be covered.[3435]

The TMD requires the goods and services for which the protection of the trade mark is sought to be identified by the applicant with **sufficient clarity and precision** to enable the competent authorities and economic operators, on that basis alone, to determine the extent of the protection sought.[3436]

As a preliminary point, it must be observed that there is no provision of the TMD which directly governs the question of the identification of the goods and services concerned.[3437]

However, that observation is not sufficient to support a finding that the determination of goods and services for the purposes of registration of a national trade mark is a matter which does not fall within the scope of the TMD.[3438]

Although it is apparent from recital 6 of the preamble to the TMD that the Member States remain free to fix the provisions of procedure concerning, *inter alia*, the registration of trade marks,[3439] the fact remains that the Court has held[3440] that determination of the nature and content of the goods and services eligible for protection

3434. CJEU C-307/10 of 19.6.2012 – Chartered Institute of Patent Attorneys, para. 37; C-337/12 P to C-340/12 P of 6.3.2014 – Pi-Design/OHIM, para. 57; C-411/13 P of 8.5.2014 – OHIM/Sanco, para. 48; C-480/15 P of 14.4.2016 – KS Sports IPCo/EUIPO, para. 56.
3435. CJEU C-307/10 of 19.6.2012 – Chartered Institute of Patent Attorneys, para. 64.
3436. CJEU C-307/10 of 19.6.2012 – Chartered Institute of Patent Attorneys, para. 49; C-420/13 of 10.7.2014 – Netto Marken-Discount, para. 44.
3437. CJEU C-307/10 of 19.6.2012 – Chartered Institute of Patent Attorneys, para. 38.
3438. CJEU C-307/10 of 19.6.2012 – Chartered Institute of Patent Attorneys, para. 39.
3439. *See* CJEU C-418/02 of 7.7.2005 – Praktiker Bau- und Heimwerkermärkte, para. 30; C-246/05 of 14.6.2007 – Häupl, para. 26.
3440. *See* CJEU C-418/02 of 7.7.2005 – Praktiker Bau- und Heimwerkermärkte, para. 31.

by a registered trade mark is subject not to the provisions on registration procedures but to the substantive conditions for acquiring the right conferred by the trade mark.[3441]

In that regard, recital 8 of the preamble to the TMD emphasizes that attainment of the objectives at which the approximation of the laws of the Member States is aiming requires that the conditions for obtaining and continuing to hold a registered trade mark be, in general, identical in all Member States.[3442]

As regards the requirement of clarity and precision for the identification of the goods and services covered by an application to register a sign as a trade mark, it must be held that the application of certain provisions of the TMD depends to a great extent on whether the goods or services covered by a registered trade mark are indicated with sufficient clarity and precision.[3443]

In particular, the question of whether or not any of the grounds for refusal or invalidity set out in Article 3 TMD2008 apply to the mark must be assessed specifically by reference to the goods or services in respect of which registration is sought.[3444]

Similarly, further grounds for refusal or invalidity concerning conflicts with earlier rights provided for by Article 4(1) TMD2008 presuppose the identity or similarity of the goods or services designated by the two conflicting marks.[3445]

Moreover, the Court has held[3446] that, although it is not necessary to specify in detail the service(s) for which registration is sought, since, to identify those services, it is sufficient to use general wording, the applicant must conversely be required to specify the goods or types of goods to which those services relate by means, for example, of other more specific details. Such details will make it easier to apply the articles of the TMD referred to in the previous paragraphs, without appreciably limiting the protection afforded to the trade mark.[3447]

In that connection, it must be recalled that the entry of the mark in a public register has the aim of making it accessible to the competent authorities and to the public, particularly to economic operators.[3448]

On the one hand, the competent authorities must know with clarity and precision the nature of the signs of which a mark consists in order to be able to fulfil their

3441. CJEU C-307/10 of 19.6.2012 – Chartered Institute of Patent Attorneys, para. 40.
3442. CJEU C-307/10 of 19.6.2012 – Chartered Institute of Patent Attorneys, para. 41; *see also* CJEU C-273/00 of 12.12.2002 – Sieckmann, para. 36; C-363/99 of 12.2.2004 – Koninklijke KPN Nederland, para. 122; C-482/09 of 22.9.2011 – Budějovický Budvar, para. 31.
3443. CJEU C-307/10 of 19.6.2012 – Chartered Institute of Patent Attorneys, para. 42.
3444. CJEU C-307/10 of 19.6.2012 – Chartered Institute of Patent Attorneys, para. 43; *see also* CJEU C-363/99 of 12.2.2004 – Koninklijke KPN Nederland, para. 33; C-239/05 of 15.2.2007 – BVBA Management, Training en Consultancy, para. 31; C-139/16 of 6.7.2017 – Marín a.o./Abadía, para. 24.
3445. CJEU C-307/10 of 19.6.2012 – Chartered Institute of Patent Attorneys, para. 44.
3446. CJEU C-418/02 of 7.7.2005 – Praktiker Bau- und Heimwerkermärkte, paras 49 et seqq.
3447. CJEU C-307/10 of 19.6.2012 – Chartered Institute of Patent Attorneys, para. 45; *see also* CJEU C-420/13 of 10.7.2014 – Netto Marken-Discount, paras 45 and 46.
3448. CJEU C-307/10 of 19.6.2012 – Chartered Institute of Patent Attorneys, para. 46; C-420/13 of 10.7.2014 – Netto Marken-Discount, para. 42; *see also* CJEU C-273/00 of 12.12.2002 – Sieckmann, para. 49; C-49/02 of 24.6.2004 – Heidelberger Bauchemie, para. 28.

obligations in relation to the prior examination of applications for registration and the publication and maintenance of an appropriate and precise register of trade marks.[3449]

On the other hand, economic operators must be able to acquaint themselves, with clarity and precision, with registrations or applications for registration made by their actual or potential competitors, and thus to obtain relevant information about the rights of third parties.[3450]

[B] General indications of the class headings

The TMD does not preclude the use of the **general indications of the class headings** of the Nice Classification to identify the goods and services for which the protection of the trade mark is sought, provided that such identification is sufficiently clear and precise to allow the competent authorities and economic operators to determine the scope of the protection sought.[3451]

The TMD contains no reference to the Nice Classification and, consequently, imposes no obligation or prohibition on Member States with regard to its use for the purposes of registration of national trade marks.[3452]

However, the obligation to use that instrument stems from Article 2(3) of the Nice Agreement which provides that the competent Office of the countries of the Special Union, which encompasses almost all the Member States, is to include in the official documents and publications relating to registrations of marks, the numbers of the classes of the Nice Classification to which the goods or services for which the mark is registered belong.[3453]

Since the Nice Agreement was adopted pursuant to Article 19 of the Paris Convention and the TMD, according to recital 13, was not intended to affect the obligations of the Member States resulting from that Convention, it must be held that that directive does not preclude the competent national authorities from requiring or agreeing that an applicant for a national trade mark should identify the goods and services for which he is seeking the protection conferred by the trade mark by using the Nice Classification.[3454]

However, in order to guarantee the effectiveness of the TMD and the smooth functioning of the system for the registration of trade marks, such identification must meet the requirements of clarity and precision which are laid down by the directive.[3455]

3449. CJEU C-307/10 of 19.6.2012 – Chartered Institute of Patent Attorneys, para. 47; C-420/13 of 10.7.2014 – Netto Marken-Discount, para. 43; *see also* CJEU C-273/00 of 12.12.2002 – Sieckmann, para. 50; C-49/02 of 24.6.2004 – Heidelberger Bauchemie, para. 29.
3450. CJEU C-307/10 of 19.6.2012 – Chartered Institute of Patent Attorneys, para. 48; C-420/13 of 10.7.2014 – Netto Marken-Discount, para. 43; *see also* CJEU C-273/00 of 12.12.2002 – Sieckmann, para. 51; C-49/02 of 24.6.2004 – Heidelberger Bauchemie, para. 30.
3451. CJEU C-307/10 of 19.6.2012 – Chartered Institute of Patent Attorneys, para. 56; C-420/13 of 10.7.2014 – Netto Marken-Discount, para. 49.
3452. CJEU C-307/10 of 19.6.2012 – Chartered Institute of Patent Attorneys, para. 50.
3453. CJEU C-307/10 of 19.6.2012 – Chartered Institute of Patent Attorneys, para. 51.
3454. CJEU C-307/10 of 19.6.2012 – Chartered Institute of Patent Attorneys, para. 52; C-420/13 of 10.7.2014 – Netto Marken-Discount, para. 37.
3455. CJEU C-307/10 of 19.6.2012 – Chartered Institute of Patent Attorneys, para. 53.

In that connection, it must be observed that some of the general indications in the class headings of the Nice Classification are, in themselves, sufficiently clear and precise to allow the competent authorities to determine the scope of the protection conferred by the trade mark, while others are not such as to meet that requirement where they are too general and cover goods or services which are too variable to be compatible with the trade mark's function as an indication of origin.[3456]

It is therefore for the competent authorities to make an assessment on a case-by-case basis, according to the goods or services for which the applicant seeks the protection conferred by a trade mark, in order to determine whether those indications meet the requirements of clarity and precision.[3457]

In order to respect the requirements of **clarity and precision** mentioned above, an applicant for a national trade mark who uses all the **general indications of a particular class heading** of the Nice Classification to identify the goods or services for which the protection of the trade mark is sought must **specify** whether its application for registration is intended to cover all the goods or services included in the alphabetical list of the particular class concerned or only some of those goods or services. If the application concerns only some of those goods or services, the applicant is required to specify which of the goods or services in that class are intended to be covered.[3458]

However, it is important to bear in mind, in the first place, that this does not concern the proprietors of trade marks which have already been registered, but solely applicants for trade marks.[3459]

Communication No 2/12[3460] cannot call into question that case law and thus lead to the scope of protection of trade marks registered before the delivery of the IP Translator judgment for goods or services designated by the general indications of the class headings of the Nice Agreement being limited solely to the goods or services mentioned in the alphabetical list of that class and to that protection being denied, in accordance with Communication No 4/03,[3461] to all the goods and services within that class.[3462]

3456. CJEU C-307/10 of 19.6.2012 – Chartered Institute of Patent Attorneys, para. 54; C-420/13 of 10.7.2014 – Netto Marken-Discount, para. 49.
3457. CJEU C-307/10 of 19.6.2012 – Chartered Institute of Patent Attorneys, para. 55; C-411/13 P of 8.5.2014 – OHIM/Sanco, para. 48; C-420/13 of 10.7.2014 – Netto Marken-Discount, para. 50.
3458. CJEU C-307/10 of 19.6.2012 – Chartered Institute of Patent Attorneys, para. 61; C-141/13 P of 17.7.2014 – Reber Holding/OHIM, para. 40; C-420/13 of 10.7.2014 – Netto Marken-Discount, para. 51; C-501/15 P of 11.10.2017 – EUIPO/Cactus, para. 37; C-121/19 P of 16.9.2020 – Edison/EUIPO, para. 41.
3459. CJEU C-577/14 P of 16.2.2017 – Brandconcern/EUIPO, para. 29, with reference to CJEU C-307/10 of 19.6.2012 – Chartered Institute of Patent Attorneys, para. 61; also CJEU C-501/15 P of 11.10.2017 – EUIPO/Cactus, para. 38 and 45.
3460. Communication No 2/12 of the President of EUIPO, of 20 June 2012, repealing Communication No 4/03 and concerning the use of class headings in lists of goods and services for Community trade mark applications and registrations.
3461. Communication No 4/03 of the President of EUIPO, of 16 June 2003, concerning the use of class headings in lists of goods and services for Community trade mark applications and registrations.
3462. CJEU C-501/15 P of 11.10.2017 – EUIPO/Cactus, para. 39.

The scope of the protection afforded by trade marks that have been registered may not be altered on the basis of a non-binding communication which has no function other than to provide clarification for applicants as to the practices of EUIPO.[3463]

In the second place, the Court of Justice limited itself to specifying the requirements to which new applicants for national trade marks remain subject, who use the general indications of a class in order to identify the goods and services for which protection as a trade mark is sought. Such requirements help to prevent the situation in which it is not possible to determine with certainty the scope of the protection afforded by a trade mark when a trade mark applicant uses all the indications included in the heading of a class.[3464]

That *Brandconcern* judgment did not concern the distinction between, on the one hand, the goods or services appearing in the alphabetical list of a class of the Nice Agreement and, on the other hand, overall and more broadly, goods or services covered by the heading of that class. It was concerned solely with determining whether it was the literal meaning of the relevant class heading that was to be taken into account or, on the contrary, whether it was to be considered that such a heading covered the goods appearing in the alphabetical list of that class. The judgment in *Brandconcern* cannot, therefore, be read as having limited the scope of the registration of earlier trade marks using the heading to solely the goods or services appearing in the alphabetical list of that class.[3465]

It cannot, therefore, be held that the Court of Justice sought to question the validity of the approach set out in Communication No 4/03[3466] as regards trade marks registered before the delivery of that judgment. Consequently, the rule is not applicable to the registration of a trade mark, which took place before the delivery of that judgment.[3467]

Such an approach is moreover consistent with the principles of legal certainty and protection of legitimate expectations.[3468]

Thus, it is apparent from examining the judgments in *IP Translator* – as interpreted by the Court in the *Brandconcern* judgment – and *Praktiker Bau* that the scope of the protection of a trade mark registered before the delivery of those judgments cannot be affected by the authority derived from those judgments in so far as they concern only new applications for registration as EU trade marks.[3469]

3463. CJEU C-501/15 P of 11.10.2017 – EUIPO/Cactus, para. 40.
3464. CJEU C-577/14 P of 16.2.2017 – Brandconcern/EUIPO, para. 30, with reference to CJEU C-307/10 of 19.6.2012 – Chartered Institute of Patent Attorneys, para. 61; C-501/15 P of 11.10.2017 – EUIPO/Cactus, para. 38.
3465. CJEU C-501/15 P of 11.10.2017 – EUIPO/Cactus, para. 42.
3466. Communication No 4/03 of the President of EUIPO, of 16 June 2003, concerning the use of class headings in lists of goods and services for Community trade mark applications and registrations.
3467. CJEU C-577/14 P of 16.2.2017 – Brandconcern/EUIPO, para. 31, with reference to CJEU C-307/10 of 19.6.2012 – Chartered Institute of Patent Attorneys, para. 61; C-501/15 P of 11.10.2017 – EUIPO/Cactus, para. 38.
3468. CJEU C-501/15 P of 11.10.2017 – EUIPO/Cactus, para. 46.
3469. CJEU C-501/15 P of 11.10.2017 – EUIPO/Cactus, para. 48.

An application for registration which does not make it possible to establish whether, by using a particular class heading of the Nice Classification, the applicant intends to cover all or only some of the goods in that class cannot be considered sufficiently clear and precise.[3470]

It must be recalled that the Court has held that it is possible to apply for registration of a mark either in respect of all the goods or services falling within a class or in respect of only some of those goods or services.[3471]

According to the order for reference and to the observations submitted to the Court, there are currently two approaches to the use of the general indications of the class headings of the Nice Classification, namely the approach corresponding to that derived from Communication No. 4/03,[3472] according to which the use of all the general indications listed in the class heading of a particular class constitutes a claim to all the goods or services falling within that particular class, and the literal approach, which seeks to give the terms used in those indications their natural and usual meaning.[3473]

In that regard, most of the parties present at the hearing pointed out, in reply to a question put by the Court, that the existence, in parallel, of those two approaches was liable to affect the smooth functioning of the system for the registration of trade marks in the Union. In particular, it was emphasized that the two approaches may lead to a difference in the extent of the protection of a national trade mark if it is registered in several Member States but also of the protection of the same mark if it is also registered as a Community trade mark. Such a difference might affect, *inter alia*, the outcome of an action for infringement, as such an action may have greater success in the Member States which follow the approach of Communication No. 4/03.[3474]

Moreover, a situation in which the extent of the protection conferred by the trade mark depends on the approach to interpretation adopted by the competent authority and not on the actual intention of the applicant runs the risk of undermining legal certainty both for the applicant and for third-party economic operators.[3475]

Thus, in the case of the main proceedings, it is for the **referring court** to determine whether, when an applicant used all the general indications of the heading of Class 41 of the Nice Classification, the applicant specified in its application whether or not it covered all the services in that class and, in particular, whether or not its application was intended to cover translation services.[3476]

3470. CJEU C-307/10 of 19.6.2012 – Chartered Institute of Patent Attorneys, para. 62; C-420/13 of 10.7.2014 – Netto Marken-Discount, para. 52.
3471. CJEU C-307/10 of 19.6.2012 – Chartered Institute of Patent Attorneys, para. 57; *see also* CJEU C-363/99 of 12.2.2004 – Koninklijke KPN Nederland, para. 112.
3472. Communication No. 4/03 of the President of the Office for Harmonisation in the Internal Market (Trade marks and Designs) (OHIM) of 16.6.2003 concerning the use of class headings in lists of goods and services for Community trade mark applications and registrations (OJ OHIM 2003, p. 1647).
3473. CJEU C-307/10 of 19.6.2012 – Chartered Institute of Patent Attorneys, para. 58.
3474. CJEU C-307/10 of 19.6.2012 – Chartered Institute of Patent Attorneys, para. 59.
3475. CJEU C-307/10 of 19.6.2012 – Chartered Institute of Patent Attorneys, para. 60.
3476. CJEU C-307/10 of 19.6.2012 – Chartered Institute of Patent Attorneys, para. 63.

The **2016 declaration was not intended to add new services to the protection** enjoyed by the contested mark, but to ensure that, following the expiry of the period referred to in the third subparagraph of Article 28(8) CTMR, as amended by Regulation 2015/2424, the services covered by that declaration continue to enjoy such protection even though they are not clearly covered by the literal meaning of the indications included in the headings of Class 35 and 36 of the Nice Agreement.[3477]

It should be observed that, in accordance with the approach set out in the first paragraph of Point IV of Communication No 4/03 and Point V of Communication No 2/12, the designation of the headings of Classes 35 and 36 of the Nice Agreement in the application for the mark was intended to protect that mark for all the services in the alphabetical list for those classes.[3478]

It follows that, at the time of its registration, the protection enjoyed by the contested mark already included the services covered by the 2016 declaration. In that regard, it should be noted that the third subparagraph of Article 28(8) CTMR, as amended by Regulation No. 2015/2424, provides that trade marks such as those at issue in the main proceedings for which no declaration is filed are to be deemed to extend, from 24 September 2016, only to goods or services clearly covered by the literal meaning of the indications included in the heading of the relevant class of the Nice Agreement.[3479]

[C] Services

The concept of '**services**' referred to by the directive, in particular in Article 2 TMD2008, covers services provided in connection with retail trade in goods. For the purposes of registration of a trade mark for such services, it is not necessary to specify the actual service(s) in question. However, details must be provided with regard to the goods or types of goods to which those services relate.[3480]

Under Article 1 TMD2008, the directive applies to 'every trade mark in respect of goods or services'.[3481]

It does not contain a definition of 'services', which Article 50 EC describes as 'normally provided for remuneration'.[3482]

Nor does it specify the conditions to which registration of a trade mark for a service is subject, where such registration is provided for by national legislation.[3483]

In that regard, it should be noted that the fifth recital in the preamble to the directive states that Member States remain free to fix the provisions of procedure concerning the registration of trade marks, in order, for example, to determine the form

3477. CJEU C-653/17 P of 15.5.2019 – VM Vermögens-Management/EUIPO, para. 50.
3478. CJEU C-653/17 P of 15.5.2019 – VM Vermögens-Management/EUIPO, para. 48, with reference to CJEU C-577/14 P of 16.2.2017 – Brandconcern/EUIPO, paras 31 et seq.
3479. CJEU C-653/17 P of 15.5.2019 – VM Vermögens-Management/EUIPO, para. 49.
3480. CJEU C-418/02 of 7.7.2005 – Praktiker Bau- und Heimwerkermärkte, para. 52; C-420/13 of 10.7.2014 – Netto Marken-Discount, para. 33.
3481. CJEU C-418/02 of 7.7.2005 – Praktiker Bau- und Heimwerkermärkte, para. 27.
3482. CJEU C-418/02 of 7.7.2005 – Praktiker Bau- und Heimwerkermärkte, para. 28.
3483. CJEU C-418/02 of 7.7.2005 – Praktiker Bau- und Heimwerkermärkte, para. 29.

of registration procedures. The seventh recital nevertheless emphasizes that attainment of the objectives sought by the approximation of laws requires that the conditions for obtaining a registered trade mark be, in general, identical in all Member States.[3484]

However, determination of the nature and content of the service eligible for protection by a registered trade mark is subject, not to the provisions on registration procedures, but to the substantive conditions for acquiring the right conferred by the trade mark.[3485]

If the concept of 'services' were a matter for the Member States, conditions for the registration of service trade marks could vary according to the national legislation concerned. The objective that acquisition of the right in the trade mark should be subject to 'conditions ... identical' in all Member States would not be attained.[3486]

It therefore falls to the Court to supply a uniform interpretation of the concept of 'services' within the meaning of the directive.[3487]

In that regard, it should be noted that the objective of retail trade is the sale of goods to consumers. That trade includes, in addition to the legal sales transaction, all activity carried out by the trader for the purpose of encouraging the conclusion of such a transaction. That activity consists, *inter alia,* in selecting an assortment of goods offered for sale and in offering a variety of services aimed at inducing the consumer to conclude the above-mentioned transaction with the trader in question rather than with a competitor.[3488]

In addition, it must be pointed out that the explanatory note relating to Class 35, within the meaning of the Nice Agreement, states that that class includes, in particular, the bringing together, for the benefit of others, of a variety of goods, excluding the transport thereof, enabling customers to conveniently view and purchase those goods. Those services may be provided by retail stores, wholesale outlets, through vending machines, mail order catalogues or by means of electronic media, for example, through web sites or television shopping programmes.[3489]

It follows from that explanatory note that the concept of 'retail services' relates to three essential characteristics, namely, first, the purpose of those services is the sale of goods to consumers; secondly, they are addressed to the consumer with a view to enabling him or her to conveniently view and purchase those goods; and, thirdly, they are provided for the benefit of others.[3490]

Accordingly, the concept of 'retail services' covers services which are aimed at the consumer and which consist, on behalf of the businesses occupying a shopping arcade's stores, in bringing together a variety of goods in a range of stores, enabling the consumer to conveniently view and purchase those goods and in offering a variety of

3484. CJEU C-418/02 of 7.7.2005 – Praktiker Bau- und Heimwerkermärkte, para. 30.
3485. CJEU C-418/02 of 7.7.2005 – Praktiker Bau- und Heimwerkermärkte, para. 31.
3486. CJEU C-418/02 of 7.7.2005 – Praktiker Bau- und Heimwerkermärkte, para. 32.
3487. CJEU C-418/02 of 7.7.2005 – Praktiker Bau- und Heimwerkermärkte, para. 33; C-420/13 of 10.7.2014 – Netto Marken-Discount, para. 32.
3488. CJEU C-418/02 of 7.7.2005 – Praktiker Bau- und Heimwerkermärkte, para. 34; C-420/13 of 10.7.2014 – Netto Marken-Discount, para. 33; C-155/18 P to C-158/18 P of 4.3.2020 – Tulliallan Burlington/EUIPO, para. 124.
3489. CJEU C-155/18 P to C-158/18 P of 4.3.2020 – Tulliallan Burlington/EUIPO, para. 125.
3490. CJEU C-155/18 P to C-158/18 P of 4.3.2020 – Tulliallan Burlington/EUIPO, para. 126.

services separate from the act of sale, which seek to ensure that that consumer purchases the goods sold in those stores.[3491]

No overriding reason based on the directive or on general principles of Community law precludes those services from being covered by the concept of 'services' within the meaning of the directive or, therefore, the trader from having the right to obtain, through the registration of his trade mark, protection of that mark as an indication of the origin of the services provided by him.[3492]

That consideration is illustrated by the Explanatory Note to Class 35 of the Nice Classification, according to which that class includes 'the bringing together, for the benefit of others, of a variety of goods ... enabling customers to conveniently view and purchase those goods'.[3493]

[D] Retail services

With regard to the CTMR, it must be observed that OHIM now accepts that the services provided by **retail undertakings** are, as such, eligible for registration as Community trade marks and that they will fall under Class 35 of the Nice Classification (*see* Communication No. 3/01 of the President of [OHIM] of 12 March 2001 concerning the registration of Community trade marks for retail services).[3494]

Moreover, it must be noted that, firstly, all the parties concerned which have submitted observations to the Court have accepted that at least certain services provided in connection with retail trade can constitute services within the meaning of the directive and that, secondly, according the information before the Court, such an analysis underlies a practice now widely adopted in the Member States.[3495]

Consequently, it must be concluded that the concept of 'services' within the meaning of the directive includes services provided in connection with retail trade in goods.[3496]

The question arises as to whether, in the particular case of the retail trade, the concept of 'services' within the meaning of the directive needs further specification.[3497]

In that regard, in the observations submitted to the Court, it was maintained that the services eligible for protection as retail services should be identified in a way which distinguishes them from services which, being closely connected with the sale of goods, could not give rise to registration of a trade mark. It was pointed out, moreover, that the application for registration of the trade mark should specify in detail the service(s) for which the applicant seeks protection.[3498]

3491. CJEU C-155/18 P to C-158/18 P of 4.3.2020 – Tulliallan Burlington/EUIPO, para. 127.
3492. CJEU C-418/02 of 7.7.2005 – Praktiker Bau- und Heimwerkermärkte, para. 35.
3493. CJEU C-418/02 of 7.7.2005 – Praktiker Bau- und Heimwerkermärkte, para. 36.
3494. CJEU C-418/02 of 7.7.2005 – Praktiker Bau- und Heimwerkermärkte, para. 37.
3495. CJEU C-418/02 of 7.7.2005 – Praktiker Bau- und Heimwerkermärkte, para. 38.
3496. CJEU C-418/02 of 7.7.2005 – Praktiker Bau- und Heimwerkermärkte, para. 39; C-420/13 of 10.7.2014 – Netto Marken-Discount, para. 33.
3497. CJEU C-418/02 of 7.7.2005 – Praktiker Bau- und Heimwerkermärkte, para. 40.
3498. CJEU C-418/02 of 7.7.2005 – Praktiker Bau- und Heimwerkermärkte, para. 41.

It is argued that such details are necessary, in particular, to safeguard the essential function of the trade mark, namely, as the guarantee of the identity of the origin of the goods or services covered by the trade mark, and to prevent trade marks for retail services from being afforded over-wide and indeterminate protection.[3499]

The difficulty of the questions thus raised is illustrated by the different answers proposed by the parties which submitted observations and by the information available to the Court regarding the current practices of the Member States.[3500]

For the reasons set out below, there is no need to rely on a definition of 'retail services' for the purposes of the directive which is more restrictive than that which follows from the description contained in paragraph 34 of this judgment.[3501]

It must first be stated that any distinction between the various categories of services provided with the sale of goods which involved a more restrictive definition of 'retail services' would prove artificial in the light of the reality of the important economic sector represented by retail trade. It would inevitably raise difficulties both as regards the general definition of the criteria to be adopted and as regards the application of those criteria in practice.[3502]

Admittedly, a more restrictive definition of 'retail services' would reduce the protection afforded to the proprietor of the trade mark, so that questions concerning the application of Articles 4(1) and 5(1) TMD2008 would arise less often.[3503]

However, that is not sufficient to justify a restrictive interpretation.[3504]

There is nothing to indicate that any problems resulting from the registration of trade marks for retail services could not be resolved on the basis of the two relevant provisions of the directive, as they have been interpreted by the Court. In that regard, it should be recalled that, according to the Court's case law, the likelihood of confusion must be assessed globally, taking into account all the factors relevant to the circumstances of the case. In the context of that global assessment, it is possible to take into consideration, if need be, the particular features of the concept of 'retail services' that are connected with its wide scope, having due regard to the legitimate interests of all interested parties.[3505]

In those circumstances, for the purposes of registration of a trade mark covering services provided in connection with retail trade, it is not necessary to specify in detail the service(s) for which that registration is sought. To identify those services, it is sufficient to use general wording such as 'bringing together of a variety of goods, enabling customers to conveniently view and purchase those goods'.[3506]

However, the applicant must be required to specify the goods or types of goods to which those services relate by means, for example, of particulars such as those contained in the application for registration filed in the main proceedings ('retail trade

3499. CJEU C-418/02 of 7.7.2005 – Praktiker Bau- und Heimwerkermärkte, para. 42.
3500. CJEU C-418/02 of 7.7.2005 – Praktiker Bau- und Heimwerkermärkte, para. 43.
3501. CJEU C-418/02 of 7.7.2005 – Praktiker Bau- und Heimwerkermärkte, para. 44.
3502. CJEU C-418/02 of 7.7.2005 – Praktiker Bau- und Heimwerkermärkte, para. 45.
3503. CJEU C-418/02 of 7.7.2005 – Praktiker Bau- und Heimwerkermärkte, para. 46.
3504. CJEU C-418/02 of 7.7.2005 – Praktiker Bau- und Heimwerkermärkte, para. 47.
3505. CJEU C-418/02 of 7.7.2005 – Praktiker Bau- und Heimwerkermärkte, para. 48.
3506. CJEU C-418/02 of 7.7.2005 – Praktiker Bau- und Heimwerkermärkte, para. 49.

in building, home improvement, gardening and other consumer goods for the do-it-yourself sector').[3507]

Such details will make it easier to apply Articles 4(1) and 5(1) TMD2008 without appreciably limiting the protection afforded to the trade mark. They will also make it easier to apply Article 12(1) TMD2008, which states that '[a] trade mark shall be liable to revocation if, within a continuous period of five years, it has not been put to genuine use in the Member State in connection with the ... services in respect of which it is registered, and there are no proper reasons for non-use'.[3508]

It must be held that, if none of the grounds for refusing registration set out in the TMD preclude it, a sign depicting the layout of the flagship stores of a goods manufacturer may legitimately be registered not only for the goods themselves but also for services falling within one of the classes under the Nice Agreement concerning services, where those services do not form an integral part of the offer for sale of those goods. Certain services, which consist of carrying out, in such stores, demonstrations by means of seminars of the products that are displayed there, can themselves constitute remunerated services falling within the concept of 'service'.[3509]

The provision of services by an economic operator which consist in **bringing together services** so that the consumer can conveniently compare and purchase them may come within the concept of 'services' referred to in Article 2 TMD2008.[3510]

It is unnecessary to examine whether services can, like goods, be the subject of 'retail trade' in the proper sense of the term, since it is clear that there are situations in which a trader selects and offers an assortment of third-party services so that the consumer can choose amongst those services from a single point of contact.[3511]

The services rendered by such a trader can consist, in particular, both of activities designed to allow a consumer conveniently to compare and purchase those services and of advertising services.[3512]

The provision of such bringing together and advertising services can, where appropriate, fall under Class 35 of the Nice Classification. That possibility is supported by the Alphabetical List of the Nice Classification, which includes 'sales (promotion) for third parties' amongst the services in that class.[3513]

The TMD must be interpreted as meaning that it requires an application for registration of a trade mark with respect to a service which consists of bringing together services to be formulated with sufficient clarity and precision so as to allow the competent authorities and other economic operators to know **which services** the applicant intends to bring together.[3514]

3507. CJEU C-418/02 of 7.7.2005 – Praktiker Bau- und Heimwerkermärkte, para. 50; C-501/15 P of 11.10.2017 – EUIPO/Cactus, para. 44.
3508. CJEU C-418/02 of 7.7.2005 – Praktiker Bau- und Heimwerkermärkte, para. 51.
3509. CJEU C-421/13 of 10.7.2014 – Apple, para. 26.
3510. CJEU C-420/13 of 10.7.2014 – Netto Marken-Discount, para. 40.
3511. CJEU C-420/13 of 10.7.2014 – Netto Marken-Discount, para. 34.
3512. CJEU C-420/13 of 10.7.2014 – Netto Marken-Discount, para. 35.
3513. CJEU C-420/13 of 10.7.2014 – Netto Marken-Discount, para. 36.
3514. CJEU C-420/13 of 10.7.2014 – Netto Marken-Discount, para. 53.

In the absence of a sufficiently clear and precise identification of the services which the applicant intends to select and offer to the consumer, it could in particular be difficult, if not impossible, for the competent authorities to carry out a full examination of the application. Where those authorities are not able to deduce from the application which services are referred to by the applicant, they cannot properly examine, in particular, whether the sign which is the subject of the application for registration as a trade mark is descriptive of one or more services which the applicant intends to select and offer.[3515]

A description, according to which the service in question relates, particularly, to 'the bringing together, for the benefit of others, of a variety of services enabling customers conveniently to purchase those services, especially services provided by retail stores, wholesale outlets, through mail order catalogues or by means of electronic media, for example websites or television shopping programmes', allows the competent authorities and economic operators to understand that the application is made in respect of a service which consists in selecting and offering an assortment of services so that the consumer can choose between them from a single point of contact.[3516]

[E] Interpunction

However, a **semicolon** establishes a distinction between two different categories falling within the same class. Thus, the 'jewel boxes in precious metals, their alloys or coated therewith' are not, by definition, 'jewellery' and, consequently, they do not constitute articles falling within the general category of 'jewellery'.[3517]

That difference between the effect of a semicolon and the effect of the word 'including' in a list of goods covered by a particular class is supported by OHIM's Manual of Trade mark Practice. Point 3.4.4 of Part B.3 of that manual states that '[t]he use of commas serves to separate items within a similar category or expression', whereas 'a semi-colon means a separation between expressions'.[3518]

Article 40 Observations by third parties

1. *Member States may provide that prior to registration of a trade mark, any natural or legal person and any group or body representing manufacturers, producers, suppliers of services, traders or consumers may submit to the office written observations, explaining on which grounds the trade mark should not be registered ex officio.*

   Persons and groups or bodies as referred to in the first subparagraph shall not be parties to the proceedings before the office.
2. *In addition to the grounds referred to in paragraph 1 of this Article, any natural or legal person and any group or body representing manufacturers, producers, suppliers of services, traders or consumers may submit to the*

3515. CJEU C-420/13 of 10.7.2014 – Netto Marken-Discount, para. 47.
3516. CJEU C-420/13 of 10.7.2014 – Netto Marken-Discount, para. 45.
3517. CJEU C-97/12 P of 15.5.2014 – Louis Vuitton Malletier/OHIM, para. 96.
3518. CJEU C-97/12 P of 15.5.2014 – Louis Vuitton Malletier/OHIM, para. 97.

office written observations based on the particular grounds on which the application for a collective mark should be refused under Article 31(1) and (2). This provision may be extended to cover certification and guarantee marks where regulated in Member States.

Article 41 Division of applications and registrations

The applicant or proprietor may divide a national trade mark application or registration into two or more separate applications or registrations by sending a declaration to the office and indicating for each divisional application or registration the goods or services covered by the original application or registration which are to be covered by the divisional applications or registrations.

Article 42 Class fees

Member States may provide that the application and renewal of a trade mark is to be subject to an additional fee for each class of goods and services beyond the first class.

SECTION 2 PROCEDURES FOR OPPOSITION, REVOCATION AND INVALIDITY

Article 43 Opposition procedure

1. *Member States shall provide for an efficient and expeditious administrative procedure before their offices for opposing the registration of a trade mark application on the grounds provided for in Article 5.*
2. *The administrative procedure referred to in paragraph 1 of this Article shall at least provide that the proprietor of an earlier trade mark referred to in Article 5(2) and Article 5(3) (a), and the person authorised under the relevant law to exercise the rights arising from a protected designation of origin or geographical indication referred to in Article 5(3)(c) shall be entitled to file a notice of opposition. A notice of opposition may be filed on the basis of one or more earlier rights, provided that they all belong to the same proprietor, and on the basis of part or the totality of the goods or services in respect of which the earlier right is protected or applied for, and may be directed against part or the totality of the goods or services in respect of which the contested mark is applied for.*
3. *The parties shall be granted, at their joint request, a minimum of two months in the opposition proceedings in order to allow for the possibility of a friendly settlement between the opposing party and the applicant.*

In that regard, Rule 17(1) CTMIR makes the commencement of opposition proceedings conditional upon the payment of the opposition fee. That fee must be paid before expiry of the opposition period, failing which the notice of opposition is deemed not to have been entered.[3519]

3519. CJEU C-309/15 P of 8.9.2016 – Real Express/EUIPO, para. 62.

Article 44 Non-use as defence in opposition proceedings

1. *In opposition proceedings pursuant to Article 43, where at the filing date or date of priority of the later trade mark, the five-year period within which the earlier trade mark must have been put to genuine use as provided for in Article 16 had expired, at the request of the applicant, the proprietor of the earlier trade mark who has given notice of opposition shall furnish proof that the earlier trade mark has been put to genuine use as provided for in Article 16 during the five-year period preceding the filing date or date of priority of the later trade mark, or that proper reasons for non-use existed. In the absence of proof to this effect, the opposition shall be rejected.*
2. *If the earlier trade mark has been used in relation to only part of the goods or services for which it is registered, it shall, for the purpose of the examination of the opposition as provided for in paragraph 1, be deemed to be registered in respect of that part of the goods or services only.*
3. *Paragraphs 1 and 2 of this Article shall also apply where the earlier trade mark is an EU trade mark. In such a case, the genuine use of the EU trade mark shall be determined in accordance with Article 15 of Regulation (EC) No 207/2009.*

[A] Principles

Under Article 43(2) and (3) CTMR, opposition to registration of a Community trade mark by the proprietor of an earlier Community or national trade mark must be rejected if that proprietor does not, at the request of the applicant, furnish proof that, during the five-year period preceding the date of publication of the Community trade mark application, the earlier trade mark has been put to genuine use in the Community or in the Member State in which it is protected in connection with the goods or services in respect of which it is registered and which he cites as justification for his opposition, or that there are proper reasons for non-use. Furthermore, Article 56(2) CTMR contains an identical rule for cases involving applications for revocation or for a declaration of nullity of a Community trade mark.[3520]

Article 45 Procedure for revocation or declaration of invalidity

1. *Without prejudice to the right of the parties to appeal to the courts, Member States shall provide for an efficient and expeditious administrative procedure before their offices for the revocation or declaration of invalidity of a trade mark.*
2. *The administrative procedure for revocation shall provide that the trade mark is to be revoked on the grounds provided for in Articles 19 and 20.*
3. *The administrative procedure for invalidity shall provide that the trade mark is to be declared invalid at least on the following grounds:*
   (a) *the trade mark should not have been registered because it does not comply with the requirements provided for in Article 4;*
   (b) *the trade mark should not have been registered because of the existence of an earlier right within the meaning of Article 5(1) to (3).*

3520. CJEU C-234/06 P of 13.9.2007 – Il Ponte Finanziaria/OHIM, para. 100.

4. *The administrative procedure shall provide that at least the following are to be entitled to file an application for revocation or for a declaration of invalidity:*
   (a) *in the case of paragraph 2 and paragraph 3(a), any natural or legal person and any group or body set up for the purpose of representing the interests of manufacturers, producers, suppliers of services, traders or consumers, and which, under the terms of the law governing it, has the capacity to sue in its own name and to be sued;*
   (b) *in the case of paragraph 3(b) of this Article, the proprietor of an earlier trade mark referred to in Article 5(2) and Article 5(3)(a), and the person authorised under the relevant law to exercise the rights arising from a protected designation of origin or geographical indication referred to in Article 5(3)(c).*
5. *An application for revocation or for a declaration of invalidity may be directed against a part or the totality of the goods or services in respect of which the contested mark is registered.*
6. *An application for a declaration of invalidity may be filed on the basis of one or more earlier rights, provided they all belong to the same proprietor.*

Articles 7 and 51 of Regulation No. 40/94 and Article 3 of First Directive 89/104 must be interpreted as meaning that a Community trade mark or a national trade mark **cannot be declared wholly or partially invalid** on the ground that terms used to designate the **goods and services** in respect of which that trade mark was registered **lack clarity and precision.**[3521]

It must be examined, in the first place, whether the lack of clarity and precision of the terms used to designate the goods and services covered by a trade mark constitutes, in itself, an absolute ground for invalidity of a national trade mark or a Community trade mark.[3522]

As regards, first, the provisions of First Directive 89/104, it must be noted that Article 3 of that directive provides a list of the grounds for invalidity which do not include the lack of clarity and precision of the terms used to designate the goods and services covered by the registration of a national trade mark. The seventh recital of that directive states that those grounds for invalidity are listed in an exhaustive manner, even if some of those grounds are optional for the Member States. Consequently, First Directive 89/104 prohibits Member States from introducing grounds for invalidity other than those expressly provided for in that directive.[3523]

As regards, secondly, the provisions of Regulation No. 40/94, it must be noted that Article 7(1) thereof is drafted in almost identical terms to those of Article 3(1) of First Directive 89/104. As regards Article 51(1) of Regulation No. 40/94, subparagraph (a) of that provision refers simply to Article 7 of that regulation, whereas subparagraph (b) provides, as a ground for invalidity, the same ground as that referred to in Article 3(2)(d) of First Directive 89/104. By contrast, the lack of clarity and precision of the terms used to designate the goods and services covered by the registration of a Community trade mark does not appear in those provisions of Regulation No. 40/94.

3521. CJEU C-371/18 of 29.1.2020 – Sky a.o./SkyKick UK a.o., para. 71.
3522. CJEU C-371/18 of 29.1.2020 – Sky a.o./SkyKick UK a.o., para. 55.
3523. CJEU C-371/18 of 29.1.2020 – Sky a.o./SkyKick UK a.o., para. 56, with further proof.

Similarly, Article 96 of Regulation No. 40/94, concerning counterclaims, states that a counterclaim for a declaration of invalidity may only be based on the grounds for invalidity mentioned in that regulation.[3524]

It follows from this that, like Article 3 of First Directive 89/104, Article 7(1) and Article 51(1) of Regulation No. 40/94 must be interpreted as meaning that they provide an exhaustive list of the absolute grounds for invalidity of a Community trade mark.[3525]

Neither Article 3 of First Directive 89/104 nor the above-mentioned provisions of Regulation No. 40/94 provide, among the grounds which they set out, the lack of clarity and precision of the terms used to designate the goods and services covered by the registration of a Community trade mark.[3526]

It follows from the foregoing considerations that the lack of clarity and precision of the terms used to designate the goods or services covered by the registration of a national trade mark or a Community trade mark cannot be considered a ground for invalidity of the national trade mark or Community trade mark concerned, within the meaning of Article 3 of First Directive 89/104 or Articles 7 and 51 of Regulation No. 40/94.[3527]

In any event, it must be added that the judgment *Chartered Institute of Patent Attorneys*[3528] cannot be interpreted as meaning that the Court intended to recognize additional grounds for invalidity, not included in the list in Article 7(1) and Article 51 of Regulation No. 40/94 and Article 3 of First Directive 89/104. The Court stated, in the judgment *Brandconcern v. EUIPO and Scooters India*,[3529] that the judgment *Chartered Institute of Patent Attorneys* provided clarifications only on the requirements relating to new EU trade mark registration applications, and thus does not concern trade marks that were already registered at the date of that latter judgment's delivery.[3530]

In the second place, the Court must examine whether, while not being a ground for the invalidity of a national or a Community trade mark, a lack of clarity and precision of the terms used to designate the goods and services covered by the registration of those trade marks none the less falls within the scope of one of the absolute grounds for invalidity expressly provided for in Article 51 of Regulation No. 40/94, read in conjunction with Article 7 thereof, or in Article 3 of First Directive 89/104.[3531]

Admittedly, the Court held, in the judgment *Sieckmann*,[3532] as regards the requirement of graphic representability, that operators must, with clarity and precision, be able to find out about registrations or applications for registration made by their current or potential competitors and thus to receive relevant information about the rights of third parties. None the less, those considerations apply only in order to

3524. CJEU C-371/18 of 29.1.2020 – Sky a.o./SkyKick UK a.o., para. 57.
3525. CJEU C-371/18 of 29.1.2020 – Sky a.o./SkyKick UK a.o., para. 58.
3526. CJEU C-371/18 of 29.1.2020 – Sky a.o./SkyKick UK a.o., para. 59.
3527. CJEU C-371/18 of 29.1.2020 – Sky a.o./SkyKick UK a.o., para. 60.
3528. CJEU C-307/10 of 19.6.2012 – Chartered Institute of Patent Attorneys.
3529. CJEU C-577/14 P of 16.2.2017 – Brandconcern/EUIPO, paras 29 et seq.
3530. CJEU C-371/18 of 29.1.2020 – Sky a.o./SkyKick UK a.o., para. 61, with further reference to CJEU C-501/15 P of 11.10.2017 – EUIPO/Cactus, para. 38.
3531. CJEU C-371/18 of 29.1.2020 – Sky a.o./SkyKick UK a.o., para. 62.
3532. CJEU C-273/00 of 12.12.2002 – Sieckmann, para. 51.

identify the signs of which a trade mark may consist, and it cannot be inferred from this that such a requirement of clarity and precision should also apply to the terms used to refer to the goods and services in respect of which the trade mark in question has been registered.[3533]

Secondly, it must be determined whether the lack of clarity and precision of the terms used to designate the goods and services in respect of which a trade mark has been registered is capable, in itself, of giving rise to the invalidity of the trade mark concerned on the basis of Article 7(1)(f) of Regulation No. 40/94 and Article 3(1)(f) of First Directive 89/104, on the ground that such a deficiency is contrary to public policy.[3534]

In that regard, it suffices to note that the concept of 'public policy', within the meaning of Article 7(1)(f) of Regulation No. 40/94 and Article 3(1)(f) of First Directive 89/104, cannot be construed as relating to characteristics concerning the trade mark application itself, such as the clarity and precision of the terms used to designate the goods or services covered by that registration, regardless of the characteristics of the sign for which the registration as a trade mark is sought.[3535]

It follows that such a lack of clarity and precision of the terms designating the goods or services covered by a trade mark registration cannot be considered contrary to public policy, within the meaning of those provisions.[3536]

In any event, it must be added, so far as this point is relevant, that, pursuant to Article 50(1) of Regulation No. 40/94 and Article 12 of First Directive 89/104, the rights of the proprietor of a trade mark may be declared to be revoked if, within a continuous period of five years, the trade mark has not been put to genuine use in the territory concerned in connection with the goods or services in respect of which it is registered.[3537]

Article 50(2) of Regulation No. 40/94 and Article 13 of First Directive 89/104 also state that where the grounds for revocation of rights exist in respect of only some of the goods or services for which the trade mark is registered, revocation is to cover those goods or services only.[3538]

It is, therefore, apparent from those provisions that a national or Community trade mark registered for a range of goods and services designated in a manner which lacks clarity and precision is, in any event, capable of being protected only in respect of the goods and services for which it has been put to genuine use.[3539]

3533. CJEU C-371/18 of 29.1.2020 – Sky a.o./SkyKick UK a.o., para. 64.
3534. CJEU C-371/18 of 29.1.2020 – Sky a.o./SkyKick UK a.o., para. 65.
3535. CJEU C-371/18 of 29.1.2020 – Sky a.o./SkyKick UK a.o., para. 66.
3536. CJEU C-371/18 of 29.1.2020 – Sky a.o./SkyKick UK a.o., para. 67.
3537. CJEU C-371/18 of 29.1.2020 – Sky a.o./SkyKick UK a.o., para. 68.
3538. CJEU C-371/18 of 29.1.2020 – Sky a.o./SkyKick UK a.o., para. 69.
3539. CJEU C-371/18 of 29.1.2020 – Sky a.o./SkyKick UK a.o., para. 70.

Article 46 Non-use as defence in proceedings seeking a declaration of invalidity

1. *In proceedings for a declaration of invalidity based on a registered trade mark with an earlier filing date or priority date, if the proprietor of the later trade mark so requests, the proprietor of the earlier trade mark shall furnish proof that, during the five-year period preceding the date of the application for a declaration of invalidity, the earlier trade mark has been put to genuine use as provided for in Article 16 in connection with the goods or services in respect of which it is registered and which are cited as justification for the application, or that there are proper reasons for non-use, provided that the registration process of the earlier trade mark has at the date of the application for a declaration of invalidity been completed for not less than five years.*
2. *Where, at the filing date or date of priority of the later trade mark, the five-year period within which the earlier trade mark was to have been put to genuine use, as provided for in Article 16, had expired, the proprietor of the earlier trade mark shall, in addition to the proof required under paragraph 1 of this Article, furnish proof that the trade mark was put to genuine use during the five-year period preceding the filing date or date of priority, or that proper reasons for non-use existed.*
3. *In the absence of the proof referred to in paragraphs 1 and 2, the application for a declaration of invalidity on the basis of an earlier trade mark shall be rejected.*
4. *If the earlier trade mark has been used in accordance with Article 16 in relation to only part of the goods or services for which it is registered, it shall, for the purpose of the examination of the application for a declaration of invalidity, be deemed to be registered in respect of that part of the goods or services only.*
5. *Paragraphs 1 to 4 of this Article shall also apply where the earlier trade mark is an EU trade mark. In such a case, genuine use of the EU trade mark shall be determined in accordance with Article 15 of Regulation (EC) No 207/2009.*

Article 47 Consequences of revocation and invalidity

1. *A registered trade mark shall be deemed not to have had, as from the date of the application for revocation, the effects specified in this Directive, to the extent that the rights of the proprietor have been revoked. An earlier date, on which one of the grounds for revocation occurred, may be fixed in the decision on the application for revocation at the request of one of the parties.*
2. *A registered trade mark shall be deemed not to have had, as from the outset, the effects specified in this Directive, to the extent that the trade mark has been declared invalid.*

SECTION 3 DURATION AND RENEWAL OF REGISTRATION

Article 48 Duration of registration

1. *Trade marks shall be registered for a period of 10 years from the date of filing of the application.*

2. *Registration may be renewed in accordance with Article 49 for further 10 year-periods.*

Article 49 Renewal

1. *Registration of a trade mark shall be renewed at the request of the proprietor of the trade mark or any person authorised to do so by law or by contract, provided that the renewal fees have been paid. Member States may provide that receipt of payment of the renewal fees is to be deemed to constitute such a request.*
2. *The office shall inform the proprietor of the trade mark of the expiry of the registration at least six months before the said expiry. The office shall not be held liable if it fails to give such information.*
3. *The request for renewal shall be submitted and the renewal fees shall be paid within a period of at least six months immediately preceding the expiry of the registration. Failing this, the request may be submitted within a further period of six months following the expiry of the registration or of the subsequent renewal thereof. The renewal fees and an additional fee shall be paid within that further period.*
4. *Where the request is submitted or the fees paid in respect of only some of the goods or services for which the trade mark is registered, registration shall be renewed for those goods or services only.*
5. *Renewal shall take effect from the day following the date on which the existing registration expires. The renewal shall be recorded in the register.*

The General Court erred in law in determining that Article 47(3) CTMR and the principle of legal certainty preclude the submission, during the further period, of a request for renewal relating to certain classes of goods or services in respect of which an EU trade mark is registered, when a request for renewal concerning other classes of goods or services covered by the same mark has been submitted previously, within the period laid down in the first sentence of that provision.[3540]

On that point, it must be noted that, in paragraph 38 of the judgment under appeal, the General Court considered that '... it is clear from the wording of [Article 47(3)(3) CTMR] and, more specifically, from the expression "failing", that the possibility of submitting a request for renewal after the expiry of the initial period is conditional on no request for renewal having been submitted during that period' and that, 'accordingly, the request for renewal must, as a general rule, be submitted during the initial period and it is only by way of exception, where no request has been submitted during the initial period, that the proprietor of a mark or any person expressly authorised by him may submit such a request during the grace period, in return for the payment of a surcharge ...'.[3541]

It must be pointed out that, in accordance with settled case law, the wording used in one language version of a provision of EU law cannot serve as the sole basis for the interpretation of that provision, or be made to override the other language versions. Provisions of EU law must be interpreted and applied uniformly in the light of the

3540. CJEU C-207/15 P of 22.6.2016 – Nissan Jidosha/EUIPO, para. 58.
3541. CJEU C-207/15 P of 22.6.2016 – Nissan Jidosha/EUIPO, para. 42.

versions existing in all EU languages. Where there is a divergence between the various language versions of an EU legislative text, the provision in question must be interpreted by reference to the general scheme and the purpose of the rules of which it forms part.[3542]

It must be noted in that regard that, according to Article 47(3) CTMR, in the French-language version examined by the General Court in the judgment under appeal, 'la demande de renouvellement est à présenter dans un délai de six mois expirant le dernier jour du mois au cours duquel la période de protection prend fin. Les taxes doivent également être acquittées dans ce délai. À défaut, la demande peut encore être présentée et les taxes acquittées dans un délai supplémentaire de six mois prenant cours le lendemain du jour visé dans la première phrase, sous réserve du paiement d'une surtaxe au cours dudit délai supplémentaire.'[3543]

However, it must be noted that certain language versions of the third sentence of Article 47(3) CTMR differ from the text set out in the preceding paragraph in that they do not use words corresponding to 'à défaut' ('failing this') or any other similar words.[3544]

For example, the German-language version reads: 'der Antrag und die Gebühren können noch innerhalb einer Nachfrist von sechs Monaten nach Ablauf des in Satz 1 genannten Tages eingereicht oder gezahlt werden, sofern innerhalb dieser Nachfrist eine Zuschlagsgebühr entrichtet wird'; the Dutch-language version reads: 'de indiening van de aanvrage en de voldoening van de taksen kunnen nog binnen een extra termijn van zes maanden na het verstrijken van de in de eerste zin genoemde termijn geschieden, tegen betaling van een toeslag binnen deze extra termijn'; the Portuguese-language version reads: 'o pedido pode ainda ser apresentado e as taxas pagas num prazo suplementar de seis meses, a contar do dia seguinte ao referido na primeira frase, sob reserva do pagamento de uma sobretaxa no decurso desse prazo suplementar'; and the Finnish-language version reads: 'hakemus voidaan kuitenkin vielä esittää ja maksut suorittaa kuuden kuukauden lisämääräajan kuluessa, joka alkaa ensimmäisessä virkkeessä tarkoitetun päivän jälkeisenä päivänä, jos mainitun määräajan kuluessa suoritetaan lisämaksu'.[3545]

In any event, it cannot be clearly and unequivocally inferred from the use of the expression 'à défaut' in the French-language version of that provision that a request for renewal of an EU trade mark may be submitted only exceptionally during the further period if no other request to that effect has previously been submitted.[3546]

On the contrary, the wording of Article 47(3)(3) CTMR in all the language versions set out in the preceding paragraphs suggests that the EU legislature made the submission of a request for renewal of an EU trade mark during the further period conditional only upon the payment of an additional fee, which constitutes the only

3542. CJEU C-207/15 P of 22.6.2016 – Nissan Jidosha/EUIPO, para. 43, with further proof.
3543. CJEU C-207/15 P of 22.6.2016 – Nissan Jidosha/EUIPO, para. 44.
3544. CJEU C-207/15 P of 22.6.2016 – Nissan Jidosha/EUIPO, para. 45.
3545. CJEU C-207/15 P of 22.6.2016 – Nissan Jidosha/EUIPO, para. 46.
3546. CJEU C-207/15 P of 22.6.2016 – Nissan Jidosha/EUIPO, para. 47.

factor enabling a request for renewal lodged in those circumstances to be distinguished from a request submitted within the initial six-month period.[3547]

Furthermore, the broad logic of Article 47(3) CTMR is not such as to call that interpretation into question.[3548]

It should be noted in that regard that, in particular, according to Article 47(4) CTMR, where the request for renewal is submitted in respect of only some of the goods or services for which the EU trade mark is registered, registration is to be renewed for those goods or services only, while Article 47(5) CTMR provides that renewal is to take effect from the day following the date on which the existing registration of the trade mark at issue expires, and that the renewal is to be registered.[3549]

It must be held that it is not apparent from those provisions that the submission, during the periods referred to in Article 47(3) CTMR, of requests for renewal of an EU trade mark, staggered over time and relating to different classes of goods or services, is prohibited.[3550]

Furthermore, the objectives pursued by the CTMR support the interpretation that such requests for renewal should be accepted, provided that they are lodged before the further period expires.[3551]

It must be observed in that respect that by providing for the possibility of continuously requesting renewal of the registration of an EU trade mark for periods of 10 years and, in that context, laying down two consecutive periods within which that renewal may be requested pursuant to Articles 46 and 47 CTMR, that regulation aims, in view of the economic importance of the protection conferred by EU trade marks, to facilitate the retention by the proprietors of those trade marks of their exclusive rights.[3552]

It must be noted in that regard that, as is apparent from the Communication from the Commission to the European Parliament, the Council, the European Economic and Social Committee and the Committee of the Regions of 24 May 2011, entitled 'A Single Market for Intellectual Property Rights – Boosting creativity and innovation to provide economic growth, high quality jobs and first class products and services in Europe',[3553] the protection of brand equity stimulates investment in the quality of products and services, particularly in sectors which rely heavily on brands and customers' brand loyalty.[3554]

The pursuit of that aim in the context of the CTMR is also confirmed by the fact that, according to Article 47(2) CTMR, EUIPO must, in good time, inform the proprietor of the EU trade mark, and any person having a registered right in respect of that trade mark, of the expiry of the registration. Moreover, under Article 81 CTMR, the proprietor of an EU trade mark who, in spite of all due care required by the circumstances having

3547. CJEU C-207/15 P of 22.6.2016 – Nissan Jidosha/EUIPO, para. 48.
3548. CJEU C-207/15 P of 22.6.2016 – Nissan Jidosha/EUIPO, para. 49.
3549. CJEU C-207/15 P of 22.6.2016 – Nissan Jidosha/EUIPO, para. 50.
3550. CJEU C-207/15 P of 22.6.2016 – Nissan Jidosha/EUIPO, para. 51.
3551. CJEU C-207/15 P of 22.6.2016 – Nissan Jidosha/EUIPO, para. 52.
3552. CJEU C-207/15 P of 22.6.2016 – Nissan Jidosha/EUIPO, para. 53.
3553. COM(2011) 287 final, p. 5.
3554. CJEU C-207/15 P of 22.6.2016 – Nissan Jidosha/EUIPO, para. 54.

been taken, was unable to comply with a time limit vis-à-vis EUIPO may have his rights re-established, provided that he submits a request within a maximum of one year from expiry of the unobserved time limit.[3555]

It is necessary to examine, in the second place, whether reasons of legal certainty, linked to the erga omnes effect of registering a request for partial renewal of an EU trade mark from the day following the date on which the existing registration of that mark expires, preclude the successive requests for renewal at issue in the present case.[3556]

It is sufficient to note in that respect that the objection thus raised is based on the false premiss that it follows from Article 47(4) and (5) CTMR not only that EUIPO is under an obligation to register a request for partial renewal prior to the expiry of the further period but also that it is impossible for EUIPO to envisage, when registering such a request, information measures that would enable both the rights of proprietors of EU trade marks and the rights of third parties to be safeguarded, instead of the removal of certain classes of goods or services from the register.[3557]

SECTION 4 COMMUNICATION WITH THE OFFICE

Article 50 Communication with the office

Parties to the proceedings or, where appointed, their representatives, shall designate an official address for all official communication with the office. Member States shall have the right to require that such an official address be situated in the European Economic Area.

3555. CJEU C-207/15 P of 22.6.2016 – Nissan Jidosha/EUIPO, para. 55.
3556. CJEU C-207/15 P of 22.6.2016 – Nissan Jidosha/EUIPO, para. 56.
3557. CJEU C-207/15 P of 22.6.2016 – Nissan Jidosha/EUIPO, para. 57.

CHAPTER 4
Administrative Cooperation

Article 51 Cooperation in the area of trade mark registration and administration

The offices shall be free to cooperate effectively with each other and with the European Union Intellectual Property Office in order to promote convergence of practices and tools in relation to the examination and registration of trade marks.

Article 52 Cooperation in other areas

The offices shall be free to cooperate effectively with each other and with the European Union Intellectual Property Office in all areas of their activities other than those referred to in Article 51 which are of relevance for the protection of trade marks in the Union.

CHAPTER 5
Final Provisions

Article 53 Data protection

The processing of any personal data carried out in the Member States in the framework of this Directive shall be subject to national law implementing Directive 95/46/EC.

Article 54 Transposition

1. *Member States shall bring into force the laws, regulations and administrative provisions necessary to comply with Articles 3 to 6, Articles 8 to 14, Articles 16, 17 and 18, Articles 22 to 39, Article 41, Articles 43 to 50 by 14 January 2019. Member States shall bring into force the laws, regulations and administrative provisions to comply with Article 45 by 14 January 2023. They shall immediately communicate the text of those measures to the Commission.*

   When Member States adopt those measures, they shall contain a reference to this Directive or be accompanied by such a reference on the occasion of their official publication. They shall also include a statement that references in existing laws, regulations and administrative provisions to the Directive repealed by this Directive shall be construed as references to this Directive. Member States shall determine how such reference is to be made and how that statement is to be formulated.
2. *Member States shall communicate to the Commission the text of the main provisions of national law which they adopt in the field covered by this Directive.*

Article 55 Repeal

Directive 2008/95/EC is repealed with effect from 15 January 2019, without prejudice to the obligations of the Member States relating to the time limit for the transposition into national law of Directive 89/104/EEC set out in Part B of Annex I to Directive 2008/95/EC.

References to the repealed Directive shall be construed as references to this Directive and shall be read in accordance with the correlation table in the Annex.

Article 56 Entry into Force

This Directive shall enter into force on the twentieth day following that of its publication in the Official Journal of the European Union.

Articles 1, 7, 15, 19, 20, 21 and 54 to 57 shall apply from 15 January 2019.

Article 57 Addressees

This Directive is addressed to the Member States.

Done at Strasbourg, 16 December 2015

For the European Parliament	*For the Council*
The President	*The President*

APPENDICES

APPENDIX 1

Directive 2008/95/EC of the European Parliament and of the Council of 22 October 2008 to Approximate the Laws of the Member States Relating to Trade Marks[3558]

Preamble

[1] *Whereas the trade mark laws at present applicable in the Member States contain disparities which may impede the free movement of goods and freedom to provide services and may distort competition within the common market; whereas it is therefore necessary, in view of the establishment and functioning of the internal market, to approximate the laws of Member States;*

[2] *Whereas it is important not to disregard the solutions and advantages which the Community trade mark system may afford to undertakings wishing to acquire trade marks;*

[3] *Whereas it does not appear to be necessary at present to undertake full-scale approximation of the trade mark laws of the Member States and it will be sufficient if approximation is limited to those national provisions of law which most directly affect the functioning of the internal market;*

[4] *Whereas the Directive does not deprive the Member States of the right to continue to protect trade marks acquired through use but takes them into account only in regard to the relationship between them and trade marks acquired by registration;*

3558. OJ L 299, 8.11.2008, p. 25.

[5] *Whereas Member States also remain free to fix the provisions of procedure concerning the registration, the revocation and the invalidity of trade marks acquired by registration; whereas they can, for example, determine the form of trade mark registration and invalidity procedures, decide whether earlier rights should be invoked either in the registration procedure or in the invalidity procedure or in both and, if they allow earlier rights to be invoked in the registration procedure, have an opposition procedure or an ex officio examination procedure or both; whereas Member States remain free to determine the effects of revocation or invalidity of trade marks;*

[6] *Whereas this Directive does not exclude the application to trade marks of provisions of law of the Member States other than trade mark law, such as the provisions relating to unfair competition, civil liability or consumer protection;*

[7] *Whereas attainment of the objectives at which this approximation of laws is aiming requires that the conditions for obtaining and continuing to hold a registered trade mark are, in general, identical in all Member States; whereas, to this end, it is necessary to list examples of signs which may constitute a trade mark, provided that such signs are capable of distinguishing the goods or services of one undertaking from those of other undertakings; whereas the grounds for refusal or invalidity concerning the trade mark itself, for example, the absence of any distinctive character, or concerning conflicts between the trade mark and earlier rights, are to be listed in an exhaustive manner, even if some of these grounds are listed as an option for the Member States which will therefore be able to maintain or introduce those grounds in their legislation; whereas Member States will be able to maintain or introduce into their legislation grounds of refusal or invalidity linked to conditions for obtaining and continuing to hold a trade mark for which there is no provision of approximation, concerning, for example, the eligibility for the grant of a trade mark, the renewal of the trade mark or rules on fees, or related to the non-compliance with procedural rules;*

[8] *Whereas in order to reduce the total number of trade marks registered and protected in the Community and, consequently, the number of conflicts which arise between them, it is essential to require that registered trade marks must actually be used or, if not used, be subject to revocation; whereas it is necessary to provide that a trade mark cannot be invalidated on the basis of the existence of a non-used earlier trade mark, while the Member States remain free to apply the same principle in respect of the registration of a trade mark or to provide that a trade mark may not be successfully invoked in infringement proceedings if it is established as a result of a plea that the trade mark could be revoked; whereas in all these cases it is up to the Member States to establish the applicable rules of procedure;*

[9] *Whereas it is fundamental, in order to facilitate the free circulation of goods and services, to ensure that henceforth registered trade marks enjoy the same protection under the legal systems of all the Member States; whereas this*

should however not prevent the Member States from granting at their option extensive protection to those trade marks which have a reputation;

[10] *Whereas the protection afforded by the registered trade mark, the function of which is in particular to guarantee the trade mark as an indication of origin, is absolute in the case of identity between the mark and the sign and goods or services; whereas the protection applies also in case of similarity between the mark and the sign and the goods or services; whereas it is indispensable to give an interpretation of the concept of similarity in relation to the likelihood of confusion; whereas the likelihood of confusion, the appreciation of which depends on numerous elements and, in particular, on the recognition of the trade mark on the market, of the association which can be made with the used or registered sign, of the degree of similarity between the trade mark and the sign and between the goods or services identified, constitutes the specific condition for such protection; whereas the ways in which likelihood of confusion may be established, and in particular the onus of proof, are a matter for national Procedural rules which are not prejudiced by the Directive;*

[11] *Whereas it is important, for reasons of legal certainty and without inequitably prejudicing the interests of a proprietor of an earlier trade mark, to Provide that the latter may no longer request a declaration of invalidity nor may he oppose the use of a trade mark subsequent to his own of which he has knowingly tolerated the use for a substantial length of time, unless the application for the subsequent trade mark was made in bad faith;*

[12] *Whereas all Member States of the Community are bound by the Paris Convention for the Protection of Industrial Property; whereas it is necessary that the provisions of this Directive are entirely consistent with those of the Paris Convention; whereas the obligations of the Member States resulting from this Convention are not affected by this Directive; whereas, where appropriate, the second subparagraph of Article 234 of the Treaty is applicable.*

Article 1 – Scope

This Directive shall apply to every trade mark in respect of goods or services which is the subject of registration or of an application in a Member State for registration as an individual trade mark, a collective mark or a guarantee or certification mark, or which is the subject of a registration or an application for registration in the Benelux Trade Mark Office or of an international registration having effect in a Member State.

Article 2 – Signs of which a trade mark may consist

A trade mark may consist of any sign capable of being represented graphically, particularly words, including personal names, designs, letters, numerals, the shape of goods or of their packaging, provided that such signs are capable of distinguishing the goods or services of one undertaking from those of other undertakings.

Article 3 – Grounds for refusal or invalidity

1. *The following shall not be registered or if registered shall be liable to be declared invalid:*
   a. *signs which cannot constitute a trade mark;*
   b. *trade marks which are devoid of any distinctive character;*
   c. *trade marks which consist exclusively of signs or indications which may serve, in trade, to designate the kind, quality, quantity, intended purpose, value, geographical origin, or the time of production of the goods or of rendering of the service, or other characteristics of the goods;*
   d. *trade marks which consist exclusively of signs or indications which have become customary in the current language or in the bona fide and established practices of the trade;*
   e. *signs which consist exclusively of:*
      - *the shape which results from the nature of the goods themselves, or*
      - *the shape of goods which is necessary to obtain a technical result, or*
      - *the shape which gives substantial value to the goods;*
   f. *trade marks which are contrary to public policy or to accepted principles of morality;*
   g. *trade marks which are of such a nature as to deceive the public, for instance as to the nature, quality or geographical origin of the goods or service;*
   h. *trade marks which have not been authorized by the competent authorities and are to be refused or invalidated pursuant to Article 6 ter of the Paris Convention for the Protection of Industrial Property, hereinafter referred to as the 'Paris Convention'.*
2. *Any Member State may provide that a trade mark shall not be registered or, if registered, shall be liable to be declared invalid where and to the extent that:*
   a. *the use of that trade mark may be prohibited pursuant to provisions of law other than trade mark law of the Member State concerned or of the Community;*
   b. *the trade mark covers a sign of high symbolic value, in particular a religious symbol;*
   c. *the trade mark includes badges, emblems and escutcheons other than those covered by Article 6 ter of the Paris Convention and which are of Public interest, unless the consent of the appropriate authorities to its registration has been given in conformity with the legislation of the Member State;*
   d. *the application for registration of the trade mark was made in bad faith by the applicant.*
3. *A trade mark shall not be refused registration or be declared invalid in accordance with paragraph 1 (b), (c) or (d) if, before the date of application for registration and following the use which has been made of it, it has*

acquired a distinctive character. Any Member State may in addition provide that this provision shall also apply where the distinctive character was acquired after the date of application for registration or after the date of registration.

4. *Any Member State may provide that, by derogation from the preceding paragraphs, the grounds of refusal of registration or invalidity in force in that State prior to the date on which the provisions necessary to comply with this Directive enter into force, shall apply to trade marks for which application has been made prior to that date.*

Article 4 – Further grounds for refusal or invalidity concerning conflicts with earlier rights

1. *A trade mark shall not be registered or, if registered, shall be liable to be declared invalid:*
   a. *if it is identical with an earlier trade mark, and the goods or services for which the trade mark is applied for or is registered are identical with the goods or services for which the earlier trade mark is protected;*
   b. *if because of its identity with, or similarity to, the earlier trade mark and the identity or similarity of the goods or services covered by the trade marks, there exists a likelihood of confusion on the part of the public, which includes the likelihood of association with the earlier trade mark.*
2. *'Earlier trade marks' within the meaning of paragraph 1 means:*
   a. *trade marks of the following kinds with a date of application for registration which is earlier than the date of application for registration of the trade mark, taking account, where appropriate, of the priorities claimed in respect of those trade marks;*
      i. *Community trade marks;*
      ii. *trade marks registered in the Member State or, in the case of Belgium, Luxembourg or the Netherlands, at the Benelux Trade Mark Office;*
      iii. *trade marks registered under international arrangements which have effect in the Member State;*

b. *Community trade marks which validly claim seniority, in accordance with the Regulation on the Community trade mark, from a trade mark referred to in (a) (ii) and (iii), even when the latter trade mark has been surrendered or allowed to lapse;*

c. *applications for the trade marks referred to in (a) and (b), subject to their registration;*

d. *trade marks which, on the date of application for registration of the trade mark, or, where appropriate, of the priority claimed in respect of the application for registration of the trade mark, are well known in a Member State, in the sense in which the words 'well known' are used in Article 6 bis of the Paris Convention.*

3. *A trade mark shall furthermore not be registered or, if registered, shall be liable to be declared invalid if it is identical with, or similar to, an earlier Community trade mark within the meaning of paragraph 2 and is to be, or has been, registered for goods or services which are not similar to those for which the earlier Community trade mark is registered, where the earlier Community trade mark has a reputation in the Community and where the use of the later trade mark without due cause would take unfair advantage of, or be detrimental to, the distinctive character or the repute of the earlier Community trade mark.*
4. *Any Member State may furthermore provide that a trade mark shall not be registered or, if registered, shall be liable to be declared invalid where, and to the extent that:*
   a. *the trade mark is identical with, or similar to, an earlier national trade mark within the meaning of paragraph 2 and is to he, or has been, registered for goods or services which are not similar to those for which the earlier trade mark is registered, where the earlier trade mark has a reputation in the Member State concerned and where the use of the later trade mark without due cause would take unfair advantage of, or be detrimental to, the distinctive character or the repute of the earlier trade mark;*
   b. *rights to a non-registered trade mark or to another sign used in the course of trade were acquired prior to the date of application for registration of the subsequent trade mark, or the date of the priority claimed for the application for registration of the subsequent trade mark and that non-registered trade mark or other sign confers on its proprietor the right to prohibit the use of a subsequent trade mark;*
   c. *the use of the trade mark may be prohibited by virtue of an earlier right other than the rights referred to in paragraphs 2 and 4 (b) and in particular:*
      i. *a right to a name;*
      ii. *a right of personal portrayal;*
      iii. *a copyright;*
      iv. *an industrial property right;*
   d. *the trade mark is identical with, or similar to, an earlier collective trade mark conferring a right which expired within a period of a maximum of three years preceding application;*
   e. *the trade mark is identical with, or similar to, an earlier guarantee or certification mark conferring a right which expired within a period preceding application the length of which is fixed by the Member State;*
   f. *the trade mark is identical with, or similar to, an earlier trade mark which was registered for identical or similar goods or services and conferred on them a right which has expired for failure to renew within a period of a maximum of two years preceding application, unless the proprietor of the earlier trade mark gave his agreement for the registration of the later mark or did not use his trade mark;*
   g. *the trade mark is liable to be confused with a mark which was in use abroad on the filing date of the application and which is still in use there, provided that at the date of the application the applicant was acting in bad faith.*

5. *The Member States may permit that in appropriate circumstances registration need not be refused or the trade mark need not be declared invalid where the proprietor of the earlier trade mark or other earlier right consents to the registration of the later trade mark.*
6. *Any Member State may provide that, by derogation from paragraphs 1 to 5, the grounds for refusal of registration or invalidity in force in that State prior to the date on which the provisions necessary to comply with this Directive enter into force, shall apply to trade marks for which application has been made prior to that date.*

Article 5 – Rights conferred by a trade mark

1. *The registered trade mark shall confer on the proprietor exclusive rights therein. The proprietor shall be entitled to prevent all third parties not having his consent from using in the course of trade:*
   aa. *any sign which is identical with the trade mark in relation to goods or services which are identical with those for which the trade mark is registered;*
   ba. *any sign where, because of its identity with, or similarity to, the trade mark and the identity or similarity of the goods or services covered by the trade mark and the sign, there exists a likelihood of confusion on the part of the public, which includes the likelihood of association between the sign and the trade mark.*
2. *Any Member State may also provide that the proprietor shall be entitled to prevent all third parties not having his consent from using in the course of trade any sign which is identical with, or similar to, the trade mark in relation to goods or services which are not similar to those for which the trade mark is registered, where the latter has a reputation in the Member State and where use of that sign without due cause takes unfair advantage of, or is detrimental to, the distinctive character or the repute of the trade mark.*
3. *The following, inter alia, may be prohibited under paragraphs 1 and 2:*
   a. *affixing the sign to the goods or to the packaging thereof;*
   b. *offering the goods, or putting them on the market or stocking them for these purposes under that sign, or offering or supplying services thereunder;*
   c. *importing or exporting the goods under the sign;*
   d. *using the sign on business papers and in advertising.*
4. *Where, under the law of the Member State, the use of a sign under the conditions referred to in 1 (b) or 2 could not be prohibited before the date on which the provisions necessary to comply with this Directive entered into force in the Member State concerned, the rights conferred by the trade mark may not be relied on to prevent the continued use of the sign.*
5. *Paragraphs 1 to 4 shall not affect provisions in any Member State relating to the protection against the use of a sign other than for the purposes of distinguishing goods or services, where use of that sign without due cause takes unfair*

advantage of, or is detrimental to, the distinctive character or the repute of the trade mark.

Article 6 – Limitation of the effects of a trade mark

1. *The trade mark shall not entitle the proprietor to prohibit a third party from using, in the course of trade,*
   a. *his own name or address;*
   b. *indications concerning the kind, quality, quantity, intended purpose, value, geographical origin, the time of production of goods or of rendering of the service, or other characteristics of goods or services;*
   c. *the trade mark where it is necessary to indicate the intended purpose of a product or service, in particular as accessories or spare parts;*

   provided he uses them in accordance with honest practices in industrial or commercial matters.
2. *The trade mark shall not entitle the proprietor to prohibit a third party from using, in the course of trade, an earlier right which only applies in a particular locality if that right is recognized by the laws of the Member State in question and within the limits of the territory in which it is recognized.*

Article 7 – Exhaustion of the rights conferred by a trade mark

1. *The trade mark shall not entitle the proprietor to prohibit its use in relation to goods which have been put on the market in the Community under that trade mark by the proprietor or with his consent.*
2. *Paragraph 1 shall not apply where there exist legitimate reasons for the proprietor to oppose further commercialization of the goods, especially where the condition of the goods is changed or impaired after they have been put on the market.*

Article 8 – Licensing

1. *A trade mark may be licensed for some or all of the goods or services for which it is registered and for the whole or part of the Member State concerned. A license may be exclusive or non-exclusive.*
2. *The proprietor of a trade mark may invoke the rights conferred by that trade mark against a licensee who contravenes any provision in his licensing contract with regard to its duration, the form covered by the registration in which the trade mark may be used, the scope of the goods or services for which the licence is granted, the territory in which the trade mark may be affixed, or the quality of the goods manufactured or of the services provided by the licensee.*

Article 9 – Limitation in consequence of acquiescence

1. *Where, in a Member State, the proprietor of an earlier trade mark as referred to in Article 4 (2) has acquiesced, for a period of five successive years, in the use of a later trade mark registered in that Member State while being aware of such use, he shall no longer be entitled on the basis of the earlier trade mark either to apply for a declaration that the later trade mark is invalid or to oppose the use of the later trade mark in respect of the goods or services for which the later trade mark has been used, unless registration of the later trade mark was applied for in bad faith.*
2. *Any Member State may provide that paragraph 1 shall apply mutatis mutandis to the proprietor of an earlier trade mark referred to in Article 4 (4) (a) or an other earlier right referred to in Article 4 (4) (b) or (c).*
3. *In the cases referred to in paragraphs 1 and 2, the proprietor of a later registered trade mark shall not be entitled to oppose the use of the earlier right, even though that right may no longer be invoked against the later trade mark.*

Article 10 – Use of trade marks

1. *If, within a period of five years following the date of the completion of the registration procedure, the proprietor has not put the trade mark to genuine use in the Member State in connection with the goods or services in respect of which it is registered, or if such use has been suspended during an uninterrupted period of five years, the trade mark shall be subject to the sanctions provided for in this Directive, unless there are proper reasons for non-use.*
2. *The following shall also constitute use within the meaning of paragraph 1:*
   a. *use of the trade mark in a form differing in elements which do not alter the distinctive character of the mark in the form in which it was registered;*
   b. *affixing of the trade mark to goods or to the packaging thereof in the Member State concerned solely for export purposes.*
3. *Use of the trade mark with the consent of the proprietor or by any person who has authority to use a collective mark or a guarantee or certification mark shall be deemed to constitute use by the proprietor.*
4. *In relation to trade marks registered before the date on which the provisions necessary to comply with this Directive enter into force in the Member State concerned:*
   a. *where a provision in force prior to that date attaches sanctions to non-use of a trade mark during an uninterrupted period, the relevant period of five years mentioned in paragraph 1 shall be deemed to have begun to run at the same time as any period of non-use which is already running at that date;*
   b. *where there is no use provision in force prior to that date, the periods of five years mentioned in paragraph 1 shall be deemed to run from that date at the earliest.*

Article 11 – Sanctions for non use of a trade mark in legal or administrative proceedings

1. *A trade mark may not be declared invalid on the ground that there is an earlier conflicting trade mark if the latter does not fulfil the requirements of use set out in Article 10 (1), (2) and (3) or in Article 10 (4), as the case may be.*
2. *Any Member State may provide that registration of a trade mark may not be refused on the ground that there is an earlier conflicting trade mark if the latter does not fulfil the requirements of use set out in Article 10 (1), (2) and (3) or in Article 10 (4), as the case may be.*
3. *Without prejudice to the application of Article 12, where a counter-claim for revocation is made, any Member State may provide that a trade mark may not be successfully invoked in infringement proceedings if it is established as a result of a plea that the trade mark could be revoked pursuant to Article 12 (1).*
4. *If the earlier trade mark has been used in relation to part only of the goods or services for which it is registered, it shall, for purposes of applying paragraphs 1, 2 and 3, be deemed to be registered in respect only of that part of the goods or services.*

Article 12 – Grounds for revocation

1. *A trade mark shall be liable to revocation if, within a continuous period of five years, it has not been put to genuine use in the Member State in connection with the goods or services in respect of which it is registered, and there are no proper reasons for non-use; however, no person may claim that the proprietor's rights in a trade mark should be revoked where, during the interval between expiry of the five-year period and filing of the application for revocation, genuine use of the trade mark has been started or resumed; the commencement or resumption of use within a period of three months preceding the filing of the application for revocation which began at the earliest on expiry of the continuous period of five years of non-use, shall, however, be disregarded where preparations for the commencement or resumption occur only after the proprietor becomes aware that the application for revocation may be filed.*
2. *A trade mark shall also be liable to revocation if, after the date on which it was registered,*
   a. *in consequence of acts or inactivity of the proprietor, it has become the common name in the trade for a product or service in respect of which it is registered;*
   b. *in consequence of the use made of it by the proprietor of the trade mark or with his consent in respect of the goods or services for which it is registered, it is liable to mislead the public, particularly as to the nature, quality or geographical origin of those goods or services.*

Article 13 – Grounds for refusal or revocation or invalidity relating to only some of the goods or services

Where grounds for refusal of registration or for revocation or invalidity of a trade mark exist in respect of only some of the goods or services for which that trade mark has been applied for or registered, refusal of registration or revocation or invalidity shall cover those goods or services only.

Article 14 – Establishment a posteriori of invalidity or revocation of a trade mark

Where the seniority of an earlier trade mark which has been surrendered or allowed to lapse, is claimed for a Community trade mark, the invalidity or revocation of the earlier trade mark may be established a posteriori.

Article 15 – Special provisions in respect of collective marks, guarantee marks and certification marks

1. *Without prejudice to Article 4, Member States whose laws authorize the registration of collective marks or of guarantee or certification marks may provide that such marks shall not be registered, or shall be revoked or declared invalid, on grounds additional to those specified in Articles 3 and 12 where the function of those marks so requires.*
2. *By way of derogation from Article 3 (1) (c), Member States may provide that signs or indications which may serve, in trade, to designate the geographical origin of the goods or services may constitute collective, guarantee or certification marks. Such a mark does not entitle the proprietor to prohibit a third party from using in the course of trade such signs or indications, provided he uses them in accordance with honest practices in industrial or commercial matters; in particular, such a mark may not be invoked against a third party who is entitled to use a geographical name.*

APPENDIX 2
Correlation Table

Directive 2008/95/EC	*This Directive*
Article 1	Article 1
–	Article 2
Article 2	Article 3
Article 3(1)(a) to (h)	Article 4(1)(a) to (h)
–	Article 4(1)(i) to (l)
–	Article 4(2), first sentence
Article 3(2)(a) to (c)	Article 4(2), second sentence
Article 3(2)(d)	Article 4(3)(a) to (c)
Article 3(3), first sentence	Article 4(4), first sentence
–	Article 4(4), second sentence
Article 3(3), second sentence	Article 4(5)
Article 3(4)	–
Article 4(1) and (2)	Article 5(1) and (2)
Article 4(3) and (4)(a)	Article 5(3)(a)
–	Article 5(3)(b)
–	Article 5(3)(c)
Article 4(4)(b) and (c)	Article 5(4)(a) and (b)
Article 4(4)(d) to (f)	–
Article 4(4)(g)	Article 5(4)(c)
Article 4(5) and (6)	Article 5(5) and (6)
–	Article 8
Article 5(1), first introductory sentence	Article 10(1)
Article 5(1), second introductory sentence	Article 10(2), introductory sentence
Article 5(1)(a) and (b)	Article 10(2)(a) and (b)

Directive 2008/95/EC	*This Directive*
Article 5(2)	Article 10(2)(c)
Article 5(3)(a) to (c)	Article 10(3)(a) to (c)
–	Article 10(3)(d)
Article 5(3)(d)	Article 10(3)(e)
–	Article 10(3)(f)
–	Article 10(4)
Article 5(4) and (5)	Article 10(5) and (6)
–	Article 11
–	Article 12
–	Article 13
Article 6(1)(a) to (c)	Article 14(1)(a) to (c), and (2)
Article 6(2)	Article 14(3)
Article 7	Article 15
Article 8(1) and (2)	Article 25(1) and (2)
–	Article 25(3) to (5)
Article 9	Article 9
Article 10(1), first subparagraph	Article 16(1)
–	Article 16(2) to (4)
Article 10(1), second subparagraph	Article 16(5)
Article 10(2)	Article 16(6)
Article 10(3)	–
Article 11(1)	Article 46(1) to (3)
Article 11(2)	Article 44(1)
Article 11(3)	Article 17
Article 11(4)	Articles 17, 44(2) and Article 46(4)
–	Article 18
Article 12(1), first subparagraph	Article 19(1)
Article 12(1), second subparagraph	Article 19(2)
Article 12(1), third subparagraph	Article 19(3)
Article 12(2)	Article 20
Article 13	Article 7 and Article 21
Article 14	Article 6
–	Articles 22 to 24
–	Article 26
–	Article 27
Article 15(1)	Article 28(1) and (3)
Article 15(2)	Article 28(4)
–	Article 28(2) and (5)
–	Articles 29 to 54(1)

Directive 2008/95/EC	*This Directive*
Article 16	Article 54(2)
Article 17	Article 55
Article 18	Article 56
Article 19	Article 57

APPENDIX 3

Register of Cases

File Number	*Date*	*Catchword*	*European Case Law Identifier*	*Page*
21/76	30.10.1976	Bier	EU:C:1976:166	99
102/77	23.5.1978	Hoffmann-La Roche/Centrafarm	EU:C:1978:108	10, 439, 484, 488
1/81	3.12.1981	Pfizer/Eurim-Pharm	EU:C:1981:291	478, 488
306/81	19.5.1983	Verros/Parliament	EU:C:1983:143	70
188/83	9.10.1984	Witte/Parlament	EU:C:1984:309	146
35/83	30.1.1985	BAT Cigaretten-Fabriken/Commission	EU:C:1985:32	560, 561
134/84	4.7.1985	Williams/Rechnungshof	EU:C:1985:297	146
C-10/89	17.10.1990	CNL-SUCAL/HAG	EU:C:1990:359	10, 439, 454
C-292/89	26.2.1991	Antonissen	EU:C:1991:80	523
C-317/91	30.11.1993	Deutsche Renault/AUDI	EU:C:1993:908	312
C-9/93	22.6.1994	IHT Internationale Heiztechnik/Ideal-Standard	EU:C:1994:261	158, 439–441, 454, 560
C-195/91 P	15.12.1994	Bayer/Commission	EU:C:1994:412	47
C-232/94	11.7.1996	MPA Pharma/Rhône-Poulenc Pharma	EU:C:1996:289	9, 438–440, 460, 478–485, 487–489, 493

File Number	*Date*	*Catchword*	*European Case Law Identifier*	*Page*
C-427/93, C-429/93 and C-436/93	11.7.1996	Bristol-Myers Squibb and Others/Paranova	EU:C:1996:282	9, 438–440, 457, 460, 461, 463, 467, 472, 475, 478–490, 492, 493, 497
C-71/94 to 73/94	11.7.1996	Eurim-Pharm Arzneimittel/Beiersdorf and Others	EU:C:1996:286	9, 438, 439, 460, 478–489, 493, 495
C-352/95	20.3.1997	Phytheron International/Bourdon	EU:C:1997:170	440, 449, 493
C-337/95	4.11.1997	Parfums Christian Dior/Evora	EU:C:1997:517	438, 439, 457, 501, 502
C-251/95	11.11.1997	SABEL/Puma, Rudolf Dassler Sport	EU:C:1997:528	16, 179, 283, 284, 290, 291, 294–297, 307, 311, 316
C-349/95	11.11.1997	Loendersloot/Ballantine & Son and Others	EU:C:1997:530	9, 438, 439, 462, 463, 479, 480, 489, 492, 493
C-53/96	16.6.1998	Hermès International/FHT Marketing Choice BV	EU:C:1998:292	12, 147
C-355/96	16.7.1998	Silhouette International Schmied/Hartlauer Handelsgesellschaft	EU:C:1998:374	250, 366, 387, 437, 438, 448, 449
C-151/98 P	28.9.1998	Pharos/Commission	EU:C:1999:563	58
C-39/97	29.9.1998	Canon Kabushiki Kaisha/Metro-Goldwyn-Mayer	EU:C:1998:442	26, 227, 283–286, 289–291, 308, 516

File Number	*Date*	*Catchword*	*European Case Law Identifier*	*Page*
C-63/97	23.2.1999	BMW	EU:C:1999:82	368, 387, 389, 395, 429, 432–435, 437, 439, 458–460, 500, 502
C-87/97	4.3.1999	Consorzio per la tutela del formaggio Gorgonzola	EU:C:1999:115	245
C-108/97 and C-109/97	4.5.1999	Windsurfing Chiemsee	EU:C:1999:230	31, 209, 211, 216–218, 259–262, 429, 568
C-255/97	11.5.1999	Pfeiffer	EU:C:1999:240	141
C-342/97	22.6.1999	Lloyd Schuhfabrik Meyer	EU:C:1999:323	16, 179, 283, 285, 289–291, 294–298, 310, 311, 316
C-173/98	1.7.1999	Sebago and Maison Dubois	EU:C:1999:347	449, 450
C-375/97	14.9.1999	General Motors	EU:C:1999:408	319–321, 331, 524
C-379/97	12.10.1999	Upjohn	EU:C:1999:494	439, 465, 467, 478, 480, 494, 495
C-164/98 P	27.1.2000	DIR International Film and Others/Commission	EU:C:2000:48	80
C-265/97 P	30.3.2000	Coöperatieve Vereniging De Verenigde Bloemenveilingen Aalsmeer/Florimex	EU:C:2000:170	46
C-237/98 P	15.6.2000	Dorsch Consult/Council and Commission	EU:C:2000:321	45
C-425/98	22.6.2000	Marca Mode	EU:C:2000:339	283, 289, 291, 313
C-300/98 and C-392/98	14.12.2000	Dior and Others	EU:C:2000:688	12, 13, 146
C-89/99	13.9.2001	Schieving-Nijstad and Others	EU:C:2001:438	12–14, 146–149

File Number	*Date*	*Catchword*	*European Case Law Identifier*	*Page*
C-383/99 P	20.9.2001	Procter & Gamble/OHIM (Baby-dry)	EU:C:2001:461	181, 182, 189, 190, 209, 211, 219
C-517/99	4.10.2001	Merz & Krell	EU:C:2001:510	9, 170, 220, 221, 259, 260
C-112/99	25.10.2001	Toshiba Europe	EU:C:2001:566	414, 415
C-414/99 to C-416/99	20.11.2001	Zino Davidoff and Levi Strauss	EU:C:2001:617	446, 449–453
C-301/97	22.11.2001	Netherlands/Council	EU:C:2001:621	70
C-446/00 P	13.12.2001	Cubero Vermurie/Commission	EU:C:2001:703	79
C-443/99	23.4.2002	Merck/Paranova Pharmazeutika	EU:C:2002:245	478, 480, 481, 483
C-143/00	23.4.2002	Boehringer Ingelheim and Others (I)	EU:C:2002:246	438, 439, 460, 464, 473, 474, 478–481, 483, 489–491, 493
C-2/00	14.5.2002	Hölterhoff	EU:C:2002:287	391
C-299/99	18.7.2002	Philips	EU:C:2002:377	10, 162, 171, 172, 174, 176, 183, 194, 222–225, 233–235, 259–263, 265
C-104/00 P	19.9.2002	DKV/OHIM	EU:C:2002:506	24, 71, 145, 175, 180
C-433/00	19.9.2002	Aventis	EU:C:2002:510	480, 486
C-184/01 P	7.11.2002	Hirschfeld	EU:C:2002:645	46
C-206/01	12.11.2002	Arsenal Football Club	EU:C:2002:651	9, 10, 17, 314, 366–368, 382, 383, 389–392, 447, 519, 551

File Number	*Date*	*Catchword*	*European Case Law Identifier*	*Page*
C-23/01	21.11.2002	Robelco	EU:C:2002:706	365, 374, 565
C-273/00	12.12.2002	Sieckmann	EU:C:2002:748	157, 162, 164, 165, 167, 191, 580, 582, 583, 596
C-292/00	9.1.2003	Davidoff	EU:C:2003:9	318, 319, 328
C-40/01	11.3.2003	Ansul	EU:C:2003:145	11, 511–514, 520, 525, 527, 555, 576
C-291/00	20.3.2003	LTJ Diffusion	EU:C:2003:169	16, 276, 278, 279, 281, 282, 365
C-244/00	8.4.2003	Van Doren + Q	EU:C:2003:204	446, 449, 503
C-53/01 to C-55/01	8.4.2003	Linde and Others	EU:C:2003:206	162, 174, 176, 183, 188, 193–195, 211, 223, 262
C-104/01	6.5.2003	Libertel	EU:C:2003:244	16, 26, 162–164, 166, 168, 169, 171, 173, 174, 179, 183, 184, 188, 189, 192, 193, 203, 204, 211, 225, 259–261, 277, 523
C-361/01 P	9.9.2003	KIK/OHIM	EU:C:2003:434	42, 44, 46, 69
C-115/02	23.10.2003	Rioglass and Transremar	EU:C:2003:587	401
C-191/01 P	23.10.2003	OHIM/Wrigley	EU:C:2003:579	162, 210, 211

File Number	*Date*	*Catchword*	*European Case Law Identifier*	*Page*
C-408/01	23.10.2003	Adidas-Salomon and Adidas Benelux	EU:C:2003:582	9, 250, 251, 319, 323, 324, 326, 328
C-283/01	27.11.2003	Shield Mark	EU:C:2003:641	162, 164, 166–168
C-100/02	7.1.2004	Gerolsteiner Brunnen	EU:C:2004:11	430, 433, 434, 437
C-259/02	27.1.2004	La Mer Technology	EU:C:2004:50	512–514, 525, 531, 531, 580
C-150/02 P	5.2.2004	Streamserve/OHIM	EU:C:2004:75	73, 211, 218
C-326/01 P	5.2.2004	Telefon & Buch/OHIM	EU:C:2004:72	73, 176, 211, 212, 216, 219
C-363/99	12.2.2004	Koninklijke KPN Nederland	EU:C:2004:86	11, 161, 166, 170, 174–177, 181–185, 210–212, 214, 216, 260, 348, 582, 586
C-265/00	12.2.2004	Campina Melkunie	EU:C:2004:87	174, 175, 181–183, 211, 212
C-218/01	12.2.2004	Henkel	EU:C:2004:88	18, 144, 174, 176, 188, 189, 195, 205, 207, 211, 218, 223, 262
C-369/03 P	19.2.2004	Crama/Commission	EU:C:2004:117	46
C-3/03 P	28.4.2004	Matratzen Concord/OHIM	EU:C:2004:233	16, 73, 77, 179, 283, 179, 295, 296, 300, 301, 307, 312, 313, 430
C-371/02	29.4.2004	Björnekulla Fruktindustrier	EU:C:2004:275	9, 14, 170, 175, 556, 558

File Number	*Date*	*Catchword*	*European Case Law Identifier*	*Page*
C-456/01 P and C-457/01 P	29.4.2004	Henkel/OHIM	EU:C:2004:258	16, 69, 73, 171, 172, 174, 176, 179, 183, 188, 189, 192–195, 202, 262
C-468/01 P to C-472/01 P	29.4.2004	Procter & Gamble/OHIM (Three-dimensional form of tablet I)	EU:C:2004:259	16, 73, 171, 172, 176, 179–181, 188, 189, 193–195, 205, 262, 542
C-473/01 P and C-474/01 P	29.4.2004	Procter & Gamble/OHIM (Three-dimensional form of tablet II)	EU:C:2004:260	16, 73, 171, 172, 176, 179–181, 188, 189, 193–195, 205, 262
C-49/02	24.6.2004	Heidelberger Bauchemie	EU:C:2004:384	162–164, 166, 169, 171, 183, 184, 192, 203, 204, 582, 583
C-445/02 P	28.6.2004	Glaverbel/OHIM	EU:C:2004:393	18, 73, 171, 172, 176, 193, 195, 208, 262
C-329/02 P	16.9.2004	SAT.1 SATELLITENFERNSEHEN/OHIM	EU:C:2004:532	10, 16, 174, 179, 181, 183, 188, 192, 193, 195
C-404/02	16.9.2004	Nichols	EU:C:2004:538	162, 176, 179, 193–196, 209, 259, 262, 429

File Number	*Date*	*Catchword*	*European Case Law Identifier*	*Page*
C-107/03 P	23.9.2004	Procter & Gamble/ OHIM (Form of a soap)	EU:C:2004:554	16, 73, 176, 179, 188, 194. 195, 200, 203, 262
C-192/03 P	5.10.2004	ALCON/OHIM (I)	EU:C:2004:587	15, 73, 175, 185, 186, 311
C-136/02 P	7.10.2004	Mag Instrument/OHIM	EU:C:2004:592	16, 73, 176, 179, 180, 188, 189, 194, 195, 205, 206, 259, 260, 262
C-106/03 P	12.10.2004	VEDIAL/OHIM	EU:C:2004:611	46, 63, 284
C-447/02 P	21.10.2004	KWS Saat/OHIM	EU:C:2004:649	43, 44, 69, 73, 194, 203,
C-64/02 P	21.10.2004	OHIM/ERPO MÖBELWERK	EU:C:2004:645	69, 174–176, 179, 184, 188, 193, 194, 197, 221, 542
C-245/02	16.11.2004	Anheuser-Busch	EU:C:2004:717	9, 12–14, 140, 142, 162, 281, 314, 345, 365, 366, 374, 383, 391, 408–410, 430, 433–435, 437
C-16/03	30.11.2004	Peak Holding	EU:C:2004:759	10, 282, 437, 439, 442–444, 446, 449, 450, 499
C-498/01 P	1.12.2004	OHIM/Zapf	EU:C:2004:760	80
C-325/03 P	18.1.2005	Zuazaga Meabe/OHIM	EU:C:2005:28	46–48

File Number	*Date*	*Catchword*	*European Case Law Identifier*	*Page*
C-228/03	17.3.2005	Gillette Company and Gillette Group Finland	EU:C:2005:177	9, 10, 362, 366, 432–437
C-286/04 P	30.6.2005	Eurocermex/OHIM	EU:C:2005:422	16, 68, 73, 180, 181
C-353/03	7.7.2005	Nestlé	EU:C:2005:432	188, 260, 261, 263, 543
C-418/02	7.7.2005	Praktiker Bau- und Heimwerkermärkte	EU:C:2005:425	283, 581, 582, 587–591
C-37/03 P	15.9.2005	BioID/OHIM	EU:C:2005:547	10, 16, 73, 143, 145, 174, 176, 179, 181–183, 188, 192, 196, 221
C-120/04	6.10.2005	Medion	EU:C:2005:594	10, 277, 283, 285, 296, 297, 300–302, 304–306, 313
C-405/03	18.10.2005	Class International	EU:C:2005:616	273, 401, 403–405, 444, 445, 448, 449
C-512/04 P	1.12.2005	Vitakraft-Werke Wührmann/OHIM	EU:C:2005:736	283, 296, 301
C-66/02	15.12.2005	Italian Republic/ Commission	EU:C:2005:768	70
C-402/03	10.1.2006	Skov and Bilka	EU:C:2006:6	523
C-173/04 P	12.1.2006	Deutsche SiSi-Werke/ OHIM	EU:C:2006:20	143, 145, 146, 174, 176, 179, 183, 188, 192–194, 204–206, 207, 211

File Number	*Date*	*Catchword*	*European Case Law Identifier*	*Page*
C-361/04 P	12.1.2006	Ruiz-Picasso and Others/OHIM	EU:C:2006:25	16–18, 179, 283, 284, 295–297, 299, 300, 312
C-82/04 P	19.1.2006	Audi/OHIM	EU:C:2006:48	80
C-59/05	23.2.2006	Siemens	EU:C:2006:147	436
C-421/04	9.3.2006	Matratzen Concord	EU:C:2006:164	9, 18, 19, 142, 174, 183, 193
C-206/04 P	23.3.2006	Mülhens/OHIM	EU:C:2006:194	73, 283, 284, 296, 298–300
C-259/04	30.3.2006	Emanuel	EU:C:2006:215	143, 162, 171, 244, 245, 558, 559
C-145/05	27.4.2006	Levi Strauss	EU:C:2006:264	8, 11, 285, 311, 312, 352–354, 366, 367, 425–427, 556, 557
C-235/05 P	27.4.2006	L'Oréal/OHIM	EU:C:2006:271	179, 283, 289–293, 295–297, 300, 301, 311, 316
C-508/03	4.5.2006	Commission/United Kingdom	EU:C:2006:287	62
C-416/04 P	11.5.2006	Sunrider/OHIM	EU:C:2006:310	66, 73, 308–310, 512, 514, 525, 534
C-324/05 P	1.6.2006	Plus Warenhandelsgesellschaft/OHIM	EU:C:2006:368	73, 77, 277, 283, 296, 301

File Number	*Date*	*Catchword*	*European Case Law Identifier*	*Page*
C-24/05 P	22.6.2006	Storck/OHIM (light-brown sweet)	EU:C:2006:421	17, 69, 73, 176, 179, 194, 205, 207, 258, 259, 263, 264, 268, 543
C-25/05 P	22.6.2006	Storck/OHIM (gold-coloured sweet wrapper)	EU:C:2006:422	24, 25, 68–70, 73, 172, 176, 179, 194, 205, 207, 208, 261, 269, 270
C-314/05 P	29.6.2006	Creative Technology/ OHIM	EU:C:2006:441	73, 283, 296
C-4/03	13.7.2006	GAT	EU:C:2006:457	158
C-539/03	13.7.2006	Roche Nederland and Others	EU:C:2006:458	158
C-92/06 P	13.7.2006	Soffass/OHIM	EU:C:2006:484	73
C-214/05 P	18.7.2006	Rossi/OHIM	EU:C:2006:494	45, 66, 67, 73
C-108/05	7.9.2006	Bovemij Verzekeringen	EU:C:2006:530	260, 268, 269, 273, 321
C-104/05 P	28.9.2006	El Corte Inglés/ OHIM	EU:C:2006:611	69, 73
C-281/05	9.11.2006	Montex Holdings	EU:C:2006:709	153, 403–405, 444
C-316/05 P	14.12.2006	Nokia	EU:C:2006:789	112, 114, 116–119, 123, 137–139
C-321/03	25.1.2007	Dyson	EU:C:2007:51	142, 143, 161–164, 188

File Number	*Date*	*Catchword*	*European Case Law Identifier*	*Page*
C-48/05	25.1.2007	Adam Opel	EU:C:2007:55	142, 282, 310, 319, 366, 367, 370, 383, 388, 389, 394, 39, 418, 429, 431, 433, 447
C-239/05	15.2.2007	BVBA Management, Training en Consultancy	EU:C:2007:99	142, 176, 178, 179, 184–186, 348–349, 582
C-196/06 P	9.3.2007	Alecansan/OHIM	EU:C:2007:159	73, 283, 296, 308
C-245/06 P	9.3.2007	Saiwa/OHIM	EU:C:2007:160	73, 263, 283, 296, 307, 543
C-29/05 P	13.3.2007	OHIM/Kaul	EU:C:2007:162	26, 48–53, 66, 277
C-432/05	13.3.2007	Unibet	EU:C:2007:163	140
C-171/06 P	15.3.2007	T.I.M.E. ART/OHIM	EU:C:2007:171	73, 283, 284, 289, 293, 296, 299, 300, 310
C-325/06 P	20.3.2007	Galileo International Technology and Others/Commission	EU:C:2007:176	68, 74, 367, 447
C-312/05 P	27.3.2007	TeleTech/OHIM	EU:C:2007:189	74, 77
C-273/05 P	19.4.2007	OHIM/Celltech	EU:C:2007:224	24, 25, 69, 70, 181–183, 211, 568
C-356/05	19.4.2007	Farrell	EU:C:2007:229	523
C-131/06 P	24.4.2007	Castellblanch/OHIM	EU:C:2007:246	51, 74, 283, 296

File Number	*Date*	*Catchword*	*European Case Law Identifier*	*Page*
C-348/04	26.4.2007	Boehringer Ingelheim and Others (II)	EU:C:2007:249	10, 314, 458, 463, 464, 467, 469, 474–476, 478, 480, 482, 484, 486, 487, 489–494, 504, 505
C-412/05 P	26.4.2007	Alcon/OHIM (II)	EU:C:2007:252	10, 14–16, 40, 41, 46, 66, 67, 74, 143, 145, 179, 285, 295, 308
C-334/05 P	12.6.2007	OHIM/Shaker	EU:C:2007:333	74, 179, 283–285, 295–298, 300, 301, 303
C-246/05	14.6.2007	Häupl	EU:C:2007:340	12, 76, 143, 511, 529–531, 534–536, 581
C-17/06	11.9.2007	Céline	EU:C:2007:497	142, 367, 374, 375, 383, 389, 390, 430, 433, 435, 437, 447
C-234/06 P	13.9.2007	Il Ponte Finanziaria/OHIM	EU:C:2007:514	68, 74, 79, 158, 284, 285, 289, 295, 296, 298, 299, 307, 308, 512, 514, 515, 534, 536, 537, 541, 546, 548, 594

File Number	*Date*	*Catchword*	*European Case Law Identifier*	*Page*
C-193/06 P	20.9.2007	Nestlé/OHIM	EU:C:2007:539	79, 174, 283, 285, 295, 296, 300–303
C-371/06	20.9.2007	Benetton Group	EU:C:2007:542	170, 223, 258, 259
C-405/06 P	24.9.2007	Torres/OHIM	EU:C:2007:546	74, 301
C-144/06 P	4.10.2007	Henkel/OHIM	EU:C:2007:577	71, 176, 179–181, 188, 189, 194, 205
C-311/05 P	4.10.2007	Naipes Heraclio Fournier/OHIM	EU:C:2007:572	51, 70
C-301/05 P	11.10.2007	Wilfer/OHIM	EU:C:2007:593	58, 59
C-238/06 P	25.10.2007	Develey Holding/OHIM	EU:C:2007:635	12, 19, 21, 22, 26, 74, 176, 179–181, 188, 194, 205, 349, 350
C-512/06 P	26.10.2007	PTV Planung Transport Verkehr/OHIM	EU:C:2007:649	74, 192
C-328/06	22.11.2007	Nuño	EU:C:2007:704	280, 281, 524
C-212/07 P	13.2.2008	Indorata-Serviços e Gestão	EU:C:2008:83	71, 143, 145, 175, 210
C-243/07 P	15.2.2008	Brinkmann/OHIM	EU:C:2008:94	71, 143, 145
C-102/07	10.4.2008	adidas/Marca Mode	EU:C:2008:217	192, 312, 319, 323, 324, 327, 328, 389, 429, 431, 434, 556
C-344/07 P	11.4.2008	Focus Magazin Verlag/OHIM	EU:C:2008:222	71
C-108/07 P	17.4.2008	Ferrero Deutschland/OHIM	EU:C:2008:234	74, 179, 283, 284, 289–291, 295

File Number	*Date*	*Catchword*	*European Case Law Identifier*	*Page*
C-304/06 P	8.5.2008	Eurohypo/OHIM	EU:C:2008:261	74, 174, 176, 179, 181, 183, 188, 192, 214, 542
C-533/06	12.6.2008	O2 Holdings/Hutchison 3G UK	EU:C:2008:339	276, 283, 285, 288, 334, 367, 370, 374, 389, 390, 414–417
C-497/07 P	27.6.2008	Philip Morris Products/OHIM	EU:C:2008:372	71, 205
C-413/06 P	10.7.2008	Bertelsmann and Sony Corporation of America/Impala	EU:C:2008:392	45
C-488/06 P	17.7.2008	L & D/OHIM	EU:C:2008:420	21, 74, 78, 79, 187, 264, 268, 291, 302, 311
C-514/06	18.9.2008	Armacell Enterprise/OHIM	EU:C:2008:511	20, 21, 71
C-144/07 P	2.10.2008	K-Swiss/OHIM	EU:C:2008:533	59, 60
C-513/07 P	17.10.2008	AGC Flat Glass Europe/OHIM	EU:C:2008:577	71, 75
C-81/08 P	13.11.2008	Cabrera Sánchez/OHIM	EU:C:2008:626	71
C-252/07	27.11.2008	Intel Corporation	EU:C:2008:655	318, 319, 323–327, 329, 332, 333, 335–337, 341, 342
C-20/08 P	9.12.2008	Enercon/OHIM	EU:C:2008:698	43, 44, 46, 74, 205
C-442/07	9.12.2008	Verein Radetzky-Orden	EU:C:2008:696	11, 513, 518, 519
C-57/08 P	11.12.2008	Gateway/OHIM	EU:C:2008:718	71, 74, 283, 284, 289, 292, 296, 327
C-197/07 P	12.12.2008	Aktieselskabet af 21. november 2001/OHIM	EU:C:2008:721	71, 342

File Number	*Date*	*Catchword*	*European Case Law Identifier*	*Page*
C-16/06 P	18.12.2008	Les Éditions Albert René/OHIM	EU:C:2008:739	48, 52, 53, 66, 67, 69, 70, 71, 77, 276, 283, 284, 289, 291, 299, 307, 308
C-495/07	15.1.2009	Silberquelle	EU:C:2009:10	512, 513, 519
C-17/08 P	6.2.2009	MPDV Mikrolab	EU:C:2009:64	71, 74, 176, 180, 348
C-39/08 and C-43/08	12.2.2009	bild digital	EU:C:2009:91	143, 144, 146, 348
C-62/08	19.2.2009	UDV North America	EU:C:2009:111	364, 367, 370, 375, 376, 447
C-320/07 P	12.3.2009	Antartica/OHIM	EU:C:2009:146	324, 325, 332, 341, 342, 519
C-59/08	23.4.2009	Copad	EU:C:2009:260	10, 352, 365, 429, 437, 438, 450, 451, 453–458, 561–563
C-136/08 P	30.4.2009	Japan Tobacco/OHIM	EU:C:2009:282	71, 324, 325, 332, 342
C-398/07 P	7.5.2009	Waterford Wedgwood/OHIM	EU:C:2009:288	71, 283, 290–292
C-565/07	19.5.2009	AMS/OHIM	EU:C:2009:318	30
C-394/08 P	3.6.2009	Zipcar/OHIM	EU:C:2009:334	20, 24, 71, 276, 283, 297, 308
C-529/07	11.6.2009	Chocoladefabriken Lindt & Sprüngli	EU:C:2009:361	251–255
C-542/07 P	11.6.2009	Imagination Technologies/OHIM	EU:C:2009:362	258, 265–267

File Number	*Date*	*Catchword*	*European Case Law Identifier*	*Page*
C-300/08 P	11.6.2009	Leche Celta/OHIM	EU:C:2009:370	71, 283, 296
C-487/07	18.6.2009	L'Oréal	EU:C:2009:378	279, 283, 318, 319, 328, 332–334, 337–339, 347, 374, 382–384, 387, 389, 394, 395, 414–417, 552
C-343/07	2.7.2009	Bavaria	EU:C:2009:415	258
C-302/08	2.7.2009	Zino Davidoff	EU:C:2009:422	153
C-416/08 P	10.7.2009	Apple Computer/OHIM	EU:C:2009:450	71, 74
C-202/08 and C-208/08	16.7.2009	American Clothing Associates/OHIM	EU:C:2009:477	9, 21, 22, 71, 143, 145, 246–249
C-498/07 P	3.9.2009	Aceites del Sur-Coosur/OHIM	EU:C:2009:503	74, 280, 283, 290, 294–296, 299–301
C-478/07	8.9.2009	Budějovický Budvar	EU:C:2009:521	22, 262
C-481/08 P	24.9.2009	Alcon/OHIM	EU:C:2009:579	71, 74
C-520/08 P	24.9.2009	HUP Uslugi Polska	EU:C:2009:582	71, 180
C-78/09 P	24.9.2009	Compagnie des bateaux mouches/OHIM	EU:C:2009:584	71, 186
C-301/07	6.10.2009	PAGO International	EU:C:2009:611	321, 322, 363, 421, 422, 524–525
C-324/08	15.10.2009	Makro Zelfbedieningsgroothandel	EU:C:2009:633	352, 365, 429, 437, 438, 450–454
C-488/08 P and C-489/08 P	4.12.2009	Rath/OHIM	EU:C:2009:754	68, 71

File Number	*Date*	*Catchword*	*European Case Law Identifier*	*Page*
C-494/08 P	9.12.2009	Prana Haus/HABM	EU:C:2009:759	16, 17, 180, 182, 209, 210, 212, 216, 350
C-579/08 P	15.1.2010	Messer Group/OHIM	EU:C:2010:18	71, 79, 283, 290, 291, 294–301, 317
C-398/08 P	21.1.2010	Audi/OHIM	EU:C:2010:29	176, 179, 188, 194, 195, 197–199, 262
C-23/09 P	22.1.2010	ecoblue/OHIM	EU:C:2010:35	68, 71, 78, 290, 294, 296, 305, 306
C-80/09 P	5.2.2010	Mergel a. o./OHIM	EU:C:2010:62	71, 210, 211, 217
C-408/08 P	25.2.2010	Lancôme parfums et beauté & Cie/OHIM	EU:C:2010:92	30, 31, 69, 135, 181, 182
C-193/09 P	4.3.2010	Kaul/OHIM	EU:C:2010:121	43, 71, 145, 284, 285, 292
C-282/09 P	18.3.2010	CFCMCEE/OHIM	EU:C:2010:153	71, 174, 177, 348–350
C-236/08 to C-238/08	23.3.2010	Google France	EU:C:2010:159	10, 104, 279, 328, 339, 367–370, 372–375, 377–385, 392–393, 418, 447, 552
C-278/08	25.3.2010	BergSpechte	EU:C:2010:163	281, 283, 286, 368, 373, 382–384, 392–394, 552

File Number	*Date*	*Catchword*	*European Case Law Identifier*	*Page*
C-91/09	26.3.2010	Eis.de	EU:C:2010:174	368, 373, 384, 392–394
C-332/09 P	23.4.2010	OHIM/Frosch Touristik	EU:C:2010:225	186, 187, 265, 266
C-569/08	3.6.2010	Internetportal und Marketing	EU:C:2010:311	252, 254, 255
C-127/09	3.6.2010	Coty Prestige Lancaster Group	EU:C:2010:313	352, 365, 429, 437, 438, 443, 444, 450–453
C-51/09 P	24.6.2010	Barbara Becker/OHIM	EU:C:2010:368	283, 286, 294, 296, 300, 305, 306
C-558/08	8.7.2010	Portakabin	EU:C:2010:416	281, 283, 286, 368, 373, 374, 382–384, 392–395, 431–438, 458–460, 474, 497, 500, 502, 552
C-461/09 P	9.7.2010	The Wellcome Foundation	EU:C:2010:421	45, 69, 71, 74, 474
C-54/09 P	29.7.2010	Greece/Commission	EU:C:2010:451	79
C-214/09 P	29.7.2010	Anheuser-Busch/OHIM	EU:C:2010:456	26, 27, 69, 541
C-254/09 P	2.9.2010	Calvin Klein/OHIM	EU:C:2010:488	20, 71, 77, 283, 292, 294–297, 301, 327
C-265/09 P	9.9.2010	OHIM/BORCO-Marken-Import Matthiesen	EU:C:2010:508	26, 163, 176, 179, 184, 188, 194, 195, 199, 200, 262

File Number	*Date*	*Catchword*	*European Case Law Identifier*	*Page*
C-48/09 P	14.9.2010	Lego Juris/OHIM	EU:C:2010:516	9, 163, 183, 222–225, 228–231, 233–235
C-559/08 P	16.9.2010	Deepak Rajani/OHIM	EU:C:2010:529	68, 69, 71, 286
C-479/09 P	30.9.2010	Evets/OHIM	EU:C:2010:571	21, 60, 61
C-84/10 P	22.10.2010	Longevity Health Products/OHIM	EU:C:2010:628	71, 74
C-342/09 P	27.10.2010	Victor Guedes/OHIM	EU:C:2010:639	71, 327
C-22/10 P	27.10.2010	Rewe-Zentral/OHIM	EU:C:2010:640	68, 71
C-449/09	28.10.2010	Canon Kabushiki Kaisha	EU:C:2010:651	282, 404, 405, 444, 445, 448, 449
C-204/10 P	23.11.2010	Enercon/OHIM	EU:C:2010:710	74, 296, 297, 301
C-216/10 P	25.11.2010	Lufthansa AirPlus Servicekarten/OHIM	EU:C:2010:719	49, 284, 292, 297, 327
C-585/08 and C-144/09	7.12.2010	Pammer and Hotel Alpenhof	EU:C:2010:740	408
C-92/10 P	13.1.2011	Media-Saturn-Holding /OHIM	EU:C:2011:15	69, 71, 181, 198
C-353/09 P	15.2.2011	Perfetti Van Melle/ OHIM	EU:C:2011:73	40, 71, 74, 179, 283, 286, 294–297, 305, 306
C-349/10 P	2.3.2011	Claro/OHIM	EU:C:2011:105	52
C-51/10 P	10.3.2011	Agencja Wydawnicza Technopol/HABM	EU:C:2011:139	144, 174, 175, 183, 184, 199, 200, 209–212, 215–217, 429
C-369/10 P	14.3.2011	Ravensburger/OHIM	EU:C:2011:148	24, 180, 211
C-370/10 P	14.3.2011	Ravensburger/OHIM	EU:C:2011:149	292, 324, 327

File Number	*Date*	*Catchword*	*European Case Law Identifier*	*Page*
C-388/10 P	24.3.2011	Muñoz Arraiza/OHIM	EU:C:2011:185	40, 41, 68, 71, 77, 78, 301, 302, 312
C-552/09 P	24.3.2011	Ferrero/OHIM	EU:C:2011:177	71, 79, 292, 297, 298, 307, 323–325, 327, 328, 341
C-418/10 P	28.3.2011	Herhof-Verwaltungsgesellschaft/ OHIM	EU:C:2011:187	52, 66, 70, 71, 283, 286, 308
C-96/09 P	29.3.2011	Anheuser-Busch	EU:C:2011:189	32–35, 567, 568
C-235/09	12.4.2011	DHL Express France	EU:C:2011:238	110–115, 137–140, 360, 383, 552, 576
C-429/10 P	16.5.2011	X Technology Swiss/ OHIM	EU:C:2011:307	71
C-5/10 P	16.5.2011	Torresan/OHIM	EU:C:2011:306	71, 186
C-308/10 P	19.5.2011	Union Investment Privatfonds/OHIM	EU:C:2011:327	49, 52, 53, 69
C-317/10 P	16.6.2011	Union Investment Privatfonds/OHIM	EU:C:2011:405	76, 80, 283, 286, 307
C-54/10 P and C-55/10 P	22.6.2011	Agencja Wydawnicza Technopol/HABM	EU:C:2011:416	71, 144, 184, 200, 209, 210, 212
C-56/10 P	22.6.2011	Agencja Wydawnicza Technopol/HABM	EU:C:2011:417	71, 144, 174, 181, 184, 200, 211, 212
C-532/10 P	29.6.2011	adp Gauselmann/OHIM	EU:C:2011:433	68, 71, 75, 283, 294, 296, 297, 300, 301
C-263/09 P	5.7.2011	Edwin/OHIM	EU:C:2011:452	35–38, 40, 45, 70, 74

File Number	*Date*	*Catchword*	*European Case Law Identifier*	*Page*
C-536/10 P	7.7.2011	MPDV Mikrolab/OHIM	EU:C:2011:469	71, 143, 145
C-324/09	12.7.2011	L'Oréal	EU:C:2011:474	10, 102, 104, 107–109, 283, 310, 318, 367–372, 375, 378, 384, 392, 393, 396, 397, 399, 400, 407, 408, 438, 443, 451, 461, 462, 519
C-4/10 and C-27/10	14.7.2011	Bureau national interprofessionnel du Cognac	EU:C:2011:484	245
C-46/10	14.7.2011	Viking Gas	EU:C:2011:485	365, 429, 437, 438, 453, 457, 459, 496, 497, 499–501
C-400/09 and C-207/10	28.7.2011	Orifarm	EU:C:2011:519	439, 467, 475, 478, 487–489
C-546/10 P	13.9.2011	Wilfer/OHIM	EU:C:2011:574	69, 71, 74, 176, 179, 188, 194, 205, 208
C-316/11 P	21.9.2011	Longevity Health Products/OHIM	EU:C:2011:599	68
C-378/11 P	21.9.2011	Longevity Health Products/OHIM	EU:C:2011:600	68

File Number	*Date*	*Catchword*	*European Case Law Identifier*	*Page*
C-323/09	22.9.2011	Interflora	EU:C:2011:604	16, 281, 323, 328, 331–335, 337, 339, 340, 362, 368, 373, 380, 383–386, 389, 392–395
C-482/09	22.9.2011	Budějovický Budvar	EU:C:2011:605	20, 251, 278–280, 314, 351–355, 357, 358, 365, 412, 576, 582
C-344/10 P and C-345/10 P	20.10.2011	Freixenet/OHIM	EU:C:2011:680	176, 188, 194, 195, 205, 207, 208, 262
C-67/11 P	20.10.2011	DTL Corporación/OHIM	EU:C:2011:683	283, 294, 296, 297, 300, 301
C-88/11 P	10.11.2011	LG Electronics/OHIM	EU:C:2011:727	24, 25, 67, 69–71
C-76/11 P	29.11.2011	Tresplain Investments/OHIM	EU:C:2011:790	35, 69, 74
C-446/09 and C-495/09	1.12.2011	Koninklijke Philips Electronics	EU:C:2011:796	153, 402, 407
C-222/11 P	1.12.2011	Longevity Health Products/OHIM	EU:C:2011:803	68, 74
C-45/11 P	7.12.2011	Deutsche Bahn/OHIM	EU:C:2011:808	44, 71, 171
C-119/10	15.12.2011	Frisdranken Industrie Winters	EU:C:2011:837	369, 370, 375, 379, 390, 391, 399, 419, 447
C-462/10 P	13.1.2012	Evropaïki Dynamiki/EEA	EU:C:2012:14	71
C-53/11 P	19.1.2012	OHIM/Nike International	EU:C:2012:27	27, 43, 143, 145
C-488/10	16.2.2012	Celaya Emparanza y Galdos Internacional	EU:C:2012:88	549–551

File Number	*Date*	*Catchword*	*European Case Law Identifier*	*Page*
C-81/11 P	8.3.2012	Longevity Health Products/OHIM	EU:C:2012:132	69, 71, 74
C-90/11 and C-91/11	15.3.2012	Strigl and Securvita	EU:C:2012:147	10, 174, 175, 181, 183, 188, 209, 211, 213–215, 303, 304
C-87/11 P	21.3.2012	Fidelio/OHIM	EU:C:2012:154	68, 72, 74, 175, 349, 350
C-190/10	22.3.2012	Génesis	EU:C:2012:157	8, 21, 111, 351, 576–579
C-354/11 P	22.3.2012	Emram/OHIM	EU:C:2012:167	21, 22, 72, 76, 77, 283, 286, 291, 295, 297, 298, 307, 310
C-523/10	19.4.2012	Wintersteiger	EU:C:2012:220	104, 387
C-307/11 P	26.4.2012	Deichmann/OHIM	EU:C:2012:254	21, 22, 69, 72, 174–176, 179, 188, 191
C-100/11 P	10.5.2012	Helena Rubinstein and L'Oréal/OHIM	EU:C:2012:285	42, 43, 72, 338, 342, 343
C-198/11 P	11.5.2012	LAN Airlines/OHIM	EU:C:2012:289	72
C-453/11 P	14.5.2012	Timehouse/OHIM	EU:C:2012:291	72, 181, 192
C-98/11 P	24.5.2012	Chocoladefabriken Lindt & Sprüngli/OHIM	EU:C:2012:307	22, 145, 176, 179, 189, 205, 269, 271
C-196/11 P	24.5.2012	Formula One Licensing/OHIM	EU:C:2012:314	8, 28
C-307/10	19.6.2012	Chartered Institute of Patent Attorneys	EU:C:2012:361	164, 165, 285, 351, 581–586, 596

File Number	*Date*	*Catchword*	*European Case Law Identifier*	*Page*
C-306/11 P	28.6.2012	XXXLutz Marken/OHIM	EU:C:2012:401	72, 188, 209, 213, 290, 297, 301
C-599/11 P	28.6.2012	TofuTown.com/OHIM	EU:C:2012:403	297
C-311/11 P	12.7.2012	Smart Technologies/OHIM	EU:C:2012:460	72, 176, 179, 180, 188–189, 194, 195, 197, 198, 262, 542
C-376/11	19.7.2012	Pie Optiek	EU:C:2012:502	21, 141, 279, 394, 561
C-96/11 P	6.9.2012	Storck/OHIM	EU:C:2012:537	43, 45, 194, 205, 208, 262
C-327/11 P	6.9.2012	United States Polo/OHIM	EU:C:2012:550	72, 78, 283, 294, 296, 297, 301, 305
C-587/11 P	18.9.2012	Omnicare/OHIM	EU:C:2012:575	30
C-588/11 P	18.9.2012	Omnicare/OHIM	EU:C:2012:576	30
C-624/11 P	27.9.2012	Brighton Collectibles/OHIM	EU:C:2012:598	68, 69, 72
C-649/11 P	3.10.2012	Cooperativa Vitivinícola Arousana, S. Coop. Galega/OHIM	EU:C:2012:603	72, 143, 145
C-611/11 P	10.10.2012	ara/OHIM	EU:C:2012:626	48, 68, 69, 72
C-402/11 P	18.10.2012	Jager & Polacek/OHIM	EU:C:2012:649	52, 61–63
C-553/11	25.10.2012	Rintisch	EU:C:2012:671	189, 307, 308, 541, 542, 544
C-219/11	22.11.2012	Brain Products	EU:C:2012:742	563
C-42/12 P	29.11.2012	Hrbek/OHIM	EU:C:2012:765	68, 70, 72, 283, 290–294, 296, 297
C-149/11	19.12.2012	Leno Merken	EU:C:2012:816	8, 21, 270, 320, 511, 512, 514, 521–525, 576

File Number	*Date*	*Catchword*	*European Case Law Identifier*	*Page*
C-21/12 P	17.1.2013	Abbott Laboratories/OHIM	EU:C:2013:23	68, 71, 72, 175, 176, 179
C-261/12 P	17.1.2013	Annunziata Del Prete/OHIM	EU:C:2013:26	72, 283, 291, 292
C-266/12 P	7.2.2013	Majczak/OHIM	EU:C:2013:73	68, 70, 72, 252
C-561/11	21.2.2013	Fédération Cynologique Internationale	EU:C:2013:91	24, 383, 549–552
C-655/11 P	21.2.2013	Seven for all mankind/OHIM	EU:C:2013:94	74, 78, 283, 290, 297, 301
C-171/12 P	28.2.2013	Carrols/OHIM	EU:C:2013:131	72
C-341/12 P	21.3.2013	Mizuno/OHIM	EU:C:2013:206	68, 72, 301, 302
C-393/12 P	21.3.2013	Foundation for the Protection of the Traditional Cheese of Cyprus named Halloumi/OHIM	EU:C:2013:207	72, 284
C-354/12 P	11.4.2013	ASA/OHIM	EU:C:2013:238	72, 74, 78, 143, 145, 278
C-12/12	18.4.2013	Colloseum Holding	EU:C:2013:253	10, 189, 263, 264, 270, 542, 543
C-268/12 P	8.5.2013	Cadila Healthcare/OHIM	EU:C:2013:296	66, 72, 94
C-294/12 P	14.5.2013	You-Q/OHIM	EU:C:2013:300	70, 72, 74, 79, 292, 328, 341
C-379/12 P	16.5.2013	Arav Holding/OHIM	EU:C:2013:317	21, 72, 78, 291, 306, 312
C-14/12 P	30.5.2013	Shah/OHIM	EU:C:2013:349	72, 74, 77, 79, 284, 290, 291, 293
C-357/12 P	30.5.2013	Wohlfahrt/OHIM	EU:C:2013:356	21, 28, 72, 531
C-381/12 P	6.6.2013	I Marchi Italiani/OHIM	EU:C:2013:371	68, 72, 288, 290, 306, 352, 357, 358
C-346/12 P	13.6.2013	DMK Deutsches Milchkontor	EU:C:2013:397	72, 77

File Number	*Date*	*Catchword*	*European Case Law Identifier*	*Page*
C-320/12	27.6.2013	Malaysia Dairy Industries	EU:C:2013:435	9, 21, 249–252, 254, 256, 328, 351
C-621/11 P	18.7.2013	New Yorker SHK Jeans/OHIM	EU:C:2013:484	48, 49, 55, 56
C-252/12	18.7.2013	Specsavers International Healthcare	EU:C:2013:497	16, 189, 263, 284, 287, 288, 291, 296, 297, 334, 335, 338, 339, 541–544
C-299/12	18.7.2013	Green – Swan Pharmaceuticals CR	EU:C:2013:501	141, 142
C-414/11	18.7.2013	Daiichi Sankyo	EU:C:2013:520	12
C-661/11	19.9.2013	Martin Y Paz Diffusion	EU:C:2013:577	279, 352, 365, 394, 429, 437, 450, 456
C-609/11 P	26.9.2013	Centrotherm Systemtechnik/OHIM	EU:C:2013:592	57, 70
C-120/12 P	3.10.2013	Rintisch/OHIM	EU:C:2013:638	48, 49, 54, 55, 68
C-410/12 P	16.10.2013	medi/OHIM	EU:C:2013:702	28, 72, 74, 143, 145
C-597/12 P	17.10.2013	Isdin/OHIM	EU:C:2013:672	45, 177, 284, 286, 294, 296, 297, 349, 350
C-383/12 P	14.11.2013	Environmental Manufacturing/OHIM	EU:C:2013:741	336, 337
C-49/13	14.11.2013	MF 7	EU:C:2013:767	143
C-524/12 P	14.11.2013	TeamBank/OHIM	EU:C:2013:874	72, 297, 298
C-445/12 P	12.12.2013	Rivella International/OHIM	EU:C:2013:826	21, 511, 525, 526, 537
C-159/13 P	12.12.2013	Fercal – Consultadoria e Serviços/OHIM	EU:C:2013:878	68, 72

File Number	*Date*	*Catchword*	*European Case Law Identifier*	*Page*
C-70/13 P	12.12.2013	Getty Images (US)/OHIM	EU:C:2013:875	68, 69, 71, 72, 144, 146, 175, 181
C-45/13	16.1.2014	Kainz	EU:C:2014:7	99
C-193/13 P	16.1.2014	nfon/OHIM	EU:C:2014:35	72, 76, 78, 284, 290, 294, 297
C-558/12 P	23.1.2014	OHIM/riha WeserGold Getränke	EU:C:2014:22	284, 292, 293
C-422/12 P	30.1.2014	Industrias Alen/OHIM	EU:C:2014:57	68, 72, 77, 297, 300, 301, 317
C-65/12	6.2.2014	Leidseplein Beheer	EU:C:2014:49	279, 281, 318, 328–331, 339, 340, 342, 352, 383, 394, 422, 426
C-98/13	6.2.2014	Blomqvist	EU:C:2014:55	153, 383, 403, 407, 408
C-301/13 P	6.2.2014	El Corte Inglés	EU:C:2014:235	36, 72, 292
C-177/13 P	13.2.2014	Marszałkowski/OHIM	EU:C:2014:183	68, 72, 74, 76, 284, 297, 300, 301
C-479/12	13.2.2014	H. Gautzsch Großhandel	EU:C:2014:75	125, 136, 152, 273
C-337/12 P to C-340/12 P	6.3.2014	Pi-Design/OHIM	EU:C:2014:129	9, 163, 165, 183, 186, 208, 224–226, 229–231, 235, 296, 581
C-409/12	6.3.2014	Backaldrin Österreich The Kornspitz Company	EU:C:2014:130	10, 15, 170, 175, 312, 448, 516, 556–558

File Number	*Date*	*Catchword*	*European Case Law Identifier*	*Page*
C-530/12 P	27.3.2014	OHIM/National Lottery Commission	EU:C:2014:186	36, 37, 39, 43
C-374/13 P	10.4.2014	Metropolis Inmobiliarias y Restauraciones/OHIM	EU:C:2014:270	68, 72, 145, 284, 297, 301
C-412/13 P	10.4.2014	Franz Wilhelm Langguth Erben/OHIM	EU:C:2014:269	68, 69
C-591/12 P	8.5.2014	Bimbo/OHIM	EU:C:2014:305	78, 284, 286, 288, 294, 296, 297, 300, 301, 304–306, 313, 316
C-608/12 P	8.5.2014	Greinwald/HABM	EU:C:2014:394	68, 72
C-411/13 P	8.5.2014	OHIM/Sanco	EU:C:2014:315	74, 308, 581, 584
C-97/12 P	15.5.2014	Louis Vuitton Malletier/OHIM	EU:C:2014:324	26, 63, 72, 79, 172, 176, 179, 189, 194, 205, 208, 209, 592
C-414/13 P	20.5.2014	Reber Holding/OHIM	EU:C:2014:812	72, 74, 76, 79
C-360/12	5.6.2014	Coty Germany	EU:C:2014:1318	95, 98, 101, 104, 109
C-217/13 and 218/13	19.6.2014	Oberbank	EU:C:2014:2012	162, 188, 194, 259–261–263, 265, 268, 273, 274, 311, 314, 545, 546
C-450/13 P	19.6.2014	Donaldson Filtration Deutschland/OHIM	EU:C:2014:2016	30, 45, 176
C-670/13 P	19.6.2014	The Cartoon Network/OHIM	EU:C:2014:2024	45
C-126/13 P	10.7.2014	BSH Bosch und Siemens Hausgeräte/OHIM	EU:C:2014:2065	175, 210, 211

File Number	*Date*	*Catchword*	*European Case Law Identifier*	*Page*
C-325/13 P and C-326/13 P	10.7.2014	Peek & Cloppenburg/OHIM	EU:C:2014:2059	22, 31, 33–35
C-420/13	10.7.2014	Netto Marken-Discount	EU:C:2014:2069	162, 581–584, 586–589, 591, 592
C-421/13	10.7.2014	Apple	EU:C:2014:2070	162, 169, 170, 172, 176, 179, 180, 185, 188, 190, 202, 209, 591,
C-141/13 P	17.7.2014	Reber Holding/OHIM	EU:C:2014:2089	22, 71, 144, 145, 278, 512, 514, 580, 584
C-509/13 P	4.9.2014	Metropolis Inmobiliarias y Restauraciones/OHIM	EU:C:2014:2173	72, 75, 284, 290, 292
C-150/14 P	4.9.2014	Goldsteig Käsereien Bayerwald/OHIM	EU:C:2014:2180	72, 74, 77, 285
C-521/13 P	11.9.2014	Think Schuhwerk/OHIM	EU:C:2014:2222	68, 71, 72, 144, 176, 179, 184, 189, 195, 208,
C-205/13	18.9.2014	Hauck	EU:C:2014:2233	183, 222–225, 228–230, 236, 237, 239, 240
C-308/13 P and C-309/13 P	18.9.2014	Società Italiana Calzature/OHIM	EU:C:2014:2234	69, 180, 295–297, 300–302, 306
C-669/13 P	21.10.2014	Mundipharma/OHIM	EU:C:2014:2308	72, 75, 78, 284, 290, 297, 301

File Number	*Date*	*Catchword*	*European Case Law Identifier*	*Page*
C-466/13 P	22.10.2014	Repsol YPF/OHIM	EU:C:2014:2331	22, 72, 76, 77, 284, 291, 294, 297, 300, 301
C-170/14 P	6.11.2014	Big Line Sas di Graziani Lorenzo/OHIM	EU:C:2014:2361	72, 75, 349
C-581/13 P and C-582/13 P	20.11.2014	Intra-Presse/OHIM	EU:C:2014:2387	20, 45, 52, 72, 74, 75, 324, 327
C-31/14 P	11.12.2014	OHIM/Kessel medintim	EU:C:2014:2436	46, 537, 538
C-368/14 P	11.12.2014	Compagnie des bateaux mooches/OHIM	EU:C:2014:2480	72, 75, 176, 179, 189
C-320/14 P	13.1.2015	Asos/OHIM	EU:C:2015:6	44, 68, 72, 76
C-311/14 P	20.1.2015	Longevity Health Products/OHIM	EU:C:2015:23	68, 72, 74, 76, 77, 284, 297
C-494/13 P	22.1.2015	GRE Grand River Enterprises Deutschland/OHIM	EU:C:2015:49	72, 78
C-420/14 P	5.2.2015	Jyoti Ceramic Industries/OHIM	EU:C:2015:70	297, 300–302
C-370/14 P	12.2.2015	Argo Group International Holdings/OHIM	EU:C:2015:113	68, 69, 72, 76
C-374/14 P	12.2.2015	Walcher Meßtechnik/OHIM	EU:C:2015:101	45, 72, 74
C-414/14 P	26.2.2015	Fundação Calouste Gulbenkian	EU:C:2015:157	65, 67, 69, 70, 284, 290
C-491/14	10.3.2015	Rosa dels Vents Assessoria	EU:C:2015:161	549, 550, 552, 553
C-182/14 P	19.3.2015	MEGA Brands International/OHIM	EU:C:2015:187	45, 72, 77, 297, 300–302
C-622/13 P	30.4.2015	Castel Frères/EUIPO	EU:C:2015:297	30, 134, 181, 189

File Number	*Date*	*Catchword*	*European Case Law Identifier*	*Page*
C-445/13 P	7.5.2015	Voss of Norway/OHIM	EU:C:2015:303	16, 58, 59, 72, 176, 179, 181, 189, 194, 195, 202, 205, 206
C-343/14 P	7.5.2015	Adler Modemärkte/OHIM	EU:C:2015:310	76, 77, 79, 213, 284, 286, 290, 293, 294, 296, 297, 300, 302
C-535/14 P	18.6.2015	Ipatau/Council	EU:C:2015:407	45
C-579/14 P	4.6.2015	Junited Autoglas Deutschland/OHIM	EU:C:2015:374	72, 78
C-147/14	25.6.2015	Loutfi Management Propriété intellectuelle	EU:C:2015:420	284, 288, 294, 295, 297, 298
C-249/14 P	9.7.2015	Pêra-Grave/OHIM	EU:C:2015:459	69, 299
C-580/13	16.7.2015	Coty Germany	EU:C:2015:485	149
C-379/14	16.7.2015	TOP Logistics	EU:C:2015:497	10, 367, 369, 370, 379, 424, 446–448, 451
C-400/14 P	16.7.2015	Basic AG Lebensmittelhandel/ OHIM	EU:C:2015:514	143
C-237/15	16.7.2015	PPU	EU:C:2015:474	563
C-531/14 P	2.9.2015	Giorgis/OHIM	EU:C:2015:547	68, 71, 72
C-125/14	3.9.2015	Iron & Smith	EU:C:2015:539	320–322, 324, 332, 333, 340–342, 363, 421, 422, 525
C-62/15 P	8.9.2015	DTL Corporatión/ OHIM	EU:C:2015:568	43, 45, 52, 69

File Number	*Date*	*Catchword*	*European Case Law Identifier*	*Page*
C-215/14	16.9.2015	Société des Produits Nestlé	EU:C:2015:604	10, 183, 189, 222–225, 233, 259, 260, 263, 264
C-548/14 P	17.9.2015	Arnoldo Mondadori Editore/OHIM	EU:C:2015:624	72, 78, 79, 284, 290, 292, 318, 324, 325, 332
C-500/14	6.10.2015	Ford Motor Company	EU:C:2015:680	141, 352, 365, 417, 434
C-181/15 P	6.10.2015	Marpefa/OHIM	EU:C:2015:678	47
C-270/14 P	15.10.2015	Debonair Trading Internacional/OHIM	EU:C:2015:688	284, 307, 308
C-33/15 P	15.10.2015	Cantina Broglie 1	EU:C:2015:705	28, 45, 72, 74, 144, 278, 301, 302
C-34/15 P	15.10.2015	Cantina Broglie 1	EU:C:2015:704	28, 45, 72, 74, 144, 278, 301, 302
C-20/14	22.10.2015	BGW Beratungs-Gesellschaft Wirtschaft	EU:C:2015:714	192, 211, 214, 215, 277, 288, 294, 296, 300, 302–306
C-17/15 P	26.10.2015	Popp and Zech/OHIM	EU:C:2015:728	43, 72, 78
C-190/15 P	19.11.2015	Fetim/OHIM	EU:C:2015:778	22, 72, 76, 78, 145, 284, 286, 290, 293, 294, 297
C-206/15 P	24.11.2015	Sun Mark and Bulldog Energy Drink/HABM	EU:C:2015:773	57, 58
C-29/15 P	3.12.2015	Verband der Kölnisch-Wasser Hersteller, Köln/OHIM	EU:C:2015:799	68, 72
C-603/14 P	10.12.2015	El Corte Inglés/OHIM	EU:C:2015:807	21, 72, 318, 323, 324, 327

File Number	*Date*	*Catchword*	*European Case Law Identifier*	*Page*
C-278/15 P	14.1.2016	Royal County of Berkshire Polo Club	EU:C:2016:20	78, 176, 348, 350
C-50/15 P	21.1.2016	Hesse/OHIM	EU:C:2016:34	45, 79, 308, 309
C-170/15 P	21.1.2016	Enercon/OHIM	EU:C:2016:53	41, 42, 171
C-374/15 P	28.1.2016	Harper Hygienics/OHIM	EU:C:2016:79	72, 74, 284, 297, 302, 309, 327
C-163/15	4.2.2016	Hassan	EU:C:2016:71	122, 563, 564
C-251/15 P	4.2.2016	Emsibeth/OHIM	EU:C:2016:83	72, 74, 77, 78, 80, 286, 297
C-396/15 P	17.2.2016	Shoe Branding Europe/OHIM	EU:C:2016:95	66, 68, 74, 284, 287, 290, 291, 297, 302
C-346/15 P	25.2.2016	Steinbeck/OHIM	EU:T:2017:164	68, 74
C-487/15 P	25.2.2016	Deutsche Rockwool Mineralwoll/OHIM	EU:C:2016:130	68, 74, 75
C-179/15	3.3.2016	Daimler/Együd Garage Gépjárműjavító és Értékesítő	EU:C:2016:134	114, 279, 370, 378, 380–383, 387, 391, 393, 406, 407, 418
C-440/15 P	3.3.2016	AgriCapital/OHIM	EU:C:2016:144	65, 68, 72
C-476/15 P	15.3.2016	Grupo Bimbo/OHIM	EU:C:2016:165	75
C-99/15	17.3.2016	Liffers/Producciones Mandarina	EU:C:2016:173	120, 121
C-252/15 P	17.3.2016	Naazneen/OHIM	EU:C:2016:178	44, 45, 68, 72, 76, 512, 535
C-474/15 P	7.4.2016	Harper Hygienics/EUIPO	EU:C:2016:263	44, 74, 77, 284, 297
C-475/15 P	7.4.2016	Harper Hygienics/EUIPO	EU:C:2016:264	44, 74, 77, 284, 297

File Number	*Date*	*Catchword*	*European Case Law Identifier*	*Page*
C-479/15 P	14.4.2016	Nanu-Nana Joachim Hoepp/EUIPO	EU:C:2016:276	45, 74, 77, 78
C-480/15 P	14.4.2016	KS Sports IPCo/EUIPO	EU:C:2016:266	44, 78, 143, 144, 278, 308, 310, 348, 581
C-515/15 P	14.4.2016	Roland/EUIPO	EU:C:2016:298	46, 74, 302
C-232/15 P	21.4.2016	ultra air/EUIPO	EU:C:2016:299	74, 75, 175, 176, 179
C-602/15 P	4.5.2016	Monster Energy/EUIPO	EU:C:2016:331	47, 48
C-603/15 P	4.5.2016	Monster Energy/EUIPO	EU:C:2016:332	47, 48
C-636/15 P	11.5.2016	August Storck/EUIPO	EU:C:2016:342	197, 198
C-63/16 P	24.5.2016	Actega Terra/EUIPO	EU:C:2016:348	75
C-639/15 P	26.5.2016	Gat Microencapsulation/EUIPO	EU:C:2016:376	76
C-77/16 P	26.5.2016	Hewlett Packard Development Company/EUIPO	EU:C:2016:373	144
C-94/16 P	15.6.2016	LTJ Diffusion/EUIPO	EU:C:2016:461	75, 76
C-611/15 P	16.6.2016	L'Oréal/EUIPO	EU:C:2016:463	48, 56, 76
C-619/15 P	21.6.2016	Mocek a.o./EUIPO	EU:C:2016:475	75, 77, 78
C-207/15 P	22.6.2016	Nissan Jidosha/EUIPO	EU:C:2016:465	599–602
C-280/15	22.6.2016	Nikolajeva/Multi Protect	EU:C:2016:467	114, 116, 118, 122–125
C-295/15 P	22.6.2016	Matratzen Concord/EUIPO	EU:C:2016:554	72, 76
C-419/15	22.6.2016	Thomas Philipps	EU:C:2016:468	125
C-87/16 P	21.7.2016	Tsujimoto/EUIPO	EU:C:2016:592	72
C-597/14 P	21.7.2016	EUIPO/Grau Ferrer	EU:C:2016:579	55, 56
C-57/15	28.7.2016	United Video Properties	EU:C:2016:611	154, 155
C-237/14 P	6.9.2016	Lidl/EUIPO	EU:C:2016:667	72, 76, 78
C-586/15 P	7.9.2016	Lotte/EUIPO	EU:C:2016:642	81, 542, 544
C-309/15 P	8.9.2016	Real Express/EUIPO	EU:C:2016:671	72, 80, 593
C-223/15	22.9.2016	combit Software/Commit Business Solutions	EU:C:2016:719	20, 112–115, 117, 118, 284, 360, 361

File Number	*Date*	*Catchword*	*European Case Law Identifier*	*Page*
C-442/15 P	22.9.2016	Pensa Pharma/EUIPO	EU:C:2016:720	45, 51, 52, 72, 77
C-285/16 P	13.10.2016	Grupo Bimbo/EUIPO	EU:C:2016:773	75
C-482/15 P	26.10.2016	Westermann Lernspielverlage/EUIPO	EU:C:2016:805	38, 51, 66, 74
C-575/15 P	26.10.2016	Industria de Diseño Textil/EUIPO	EU:C:2016:810	76
C-537/14 P	27.10.2016	Debonair Trading Internacional/EUIPO	EU:C:2016:814	44
C-43/15 P	8.11.2016	BSH Bosch und Siemens Hausgeräte/EUIPO	EU:C:2016:837	28, 68, 69. 72, 76–77, 183, 293, 294
C-361/16 P	8.11.2016	Franmax/EUIPO	EU:C:2016:834	78
C-30/15 P	10.11.2016	Simba Toys/EUIPO	EU:C:2016:849	9, 74, 80, 172, 183, 225, 228, 230, 232, 235, 236
C-297/15	10.11.2016	Ferring Lægemidler/Orifarm	EU:C:2016:857	10, 478, 480–482, 493, 495, 505
C-351/16 P	10.11.2016	100 % Capri Italia/EUIPO	EU:C:2016:866	45, 67, 72, 75, 145
C-389/16 P	15.11.2016	BSH Hausgeräte/EUIPO	EU:C:2016:876	72
C-401/16 P	1.12.2016	Market Watch Franchise & Consulting/EUIPO	EU:C:2016:923	75, 77, 277
C-402/16 P	1.12.2016	Market Watch Franchise & Consulting/EUIPO	EU:C:2016:924	75, 77, 277
C-642/15	1.12.2016	Klement	EU:C:2016:918	45, 74, 79, 542
C-342/16 P	6.12.2016	Novomatic/EUIPO	EU:C:2016:931	45, 70
C-371/16 P	8.12.2016	L'Oréal/EUIPO	EU:C:2016:941	70, 72, 76
C-654/15	21.12.2016	Länsförsäkringar	EU:C:2016:998	150, 151, 528, 529
C-440/16 P	12.1.2017	Staywell Hospitality Group/EUIPO	EU:C:2017:16	295
C-427/15	18.1.2017	NEW WAVE/ALLTOYS	EU:C:2017:18	149

File Number	*Date*	*Catchword*	*European Case Law Identifier*	*Page*
C-367/15	25.1.2017	Stowarzyszenie 'Oławska Telewizja Kablowa'/Stowarzyszenie Filmowców Polskich	EU:C:2017:36	150
C-485/16 P	31.1.2017	Universal Protein Supplements	EU:C:2017:72	36
C-577/14 P	16.2.2017	Brandconcern/EUIPO	EU:C:2017:122	68, 584, 585, 587, 596
C-501/16 P	16.2.2017	Monster Energy/EUIPO	EU:C:2017:140	69, 72, 76
C-502/16 P	16.2.2017	Monster Energy/EUIPO	EU:C:2017:139	69, 72, 76
C-587/16 P	28.2.2017	Skylotec/EUIPO	EU:C:2017:143	75, 76
C-576/16 P	2.3.2017	TVR Italia/EUIPO	EU:C:2017:165	68
C-655/15 P	2.3.2017	Panrico/EUIPO	EU:C:2017:155	44, 46, 69, 72, 77, 78
C-598/14 P	5.4.2017	EUIPO/Szajner a.o.	EU:C:2017:265	36–39, 51
C-71/16 P	4.5.2017	Comercializadora Eloro/EUIPO	EU:C:2017:345	44, 48–50, 55, 56
C-417/16 P	4.5.2017	August Storck/EUIPO	EU:C:2017:340	75, 176, 194, 195, 202, 203, 205, 208, 262
C-421/15 P	11.5.2017	Yoshida Metal Industry/EUIPO	EU:C:2017:360	69, 73, 223, 225, 226, 229, 230, 233
C-639/16 P	11.5.2017	Foodcare/EUIPO	EU:C:2017:367	73, 75
C-437/15 P	17.5.2017	EUIPO/Deluxe Entertainment Services Group	EU:C:2017:380	176–178, 184, 349, 350
C-617/15	18.5.2017	Hummel Holding/Nike a.o.	EU:C:2017:390	9, 95–97, 103
C-37/17 P	31.5.2017	Keil/EUIPO	EU:C:2017:427	73, 175
C-10/17 P	1.6.2017	Polo Club/EUIPO	EU:C:2017:416	74
C-50/17 P	1.6.2017	Universidad Internacional de la Rioja/EUIPO	EU:C:2017:415	44, 75, 77, 290, 294, 297
C-687/16 P	7.6.2017	Capella/EUIPO	EU:C:2017:447	68, 71
C-86/17 P	7.6.2017	Redpur/EUIPO	EU:C:2017:428	73, 77

File Number	*Date*	*Catchword*	*European Case Law Identifier*	*Page*
C-689/15	8.6.2017	W.F. Gözze Frottierweberei a.o./Verein Bremer Baumwollbörse	EU:C:2017:434	244–246, 285, 286, 448, 512, 516, 518, 527
C-23/17 P	15.6.2007	For Tune/EUIPO	EU:C:2017:478	284, 294, 296
C-662/16 P	20.6.2017	Laboratoire de la mer/EUIPO	EU:C:2017:482	20, 75
C-139/16	6.7.2017	Marín a.o./Abadía	EU:C:2017:518	176, 179, 189, 197–199, 211, 216, 217, 582
C-93/16	20.7.2017	Ornua Co-operative/Tindale & Stanton	EU:C:2017:571	111, 114, 115, 284, 295, 297, 322, 328, 359–363, 434
C-84/16 P	26.7.2017	Continental Reifen Deutschland/EUIPO	EU:C:2017:596	44, 45, 73, 78, 284, 293, 294
C-182/16 P	26.7.2017	Meica Ammerländische Fleischwarenfabrik Fritz Meinen/EUIPO	EU:C:2017:600	73, 75, 77, 284, 290, 296, 297, 313
C-471/16 P	26.7.2017	Staatliche Porzellan-Manufaktur Meissen/EUIPO	EU:C:2017:602	44, 65, 324, 325, 332
C-56/16 P	14.9.2017	EUIPO/Instituto dos Vinhos do Douro e do PortoIP	EU:C:2017:693	22, 40
C-158/17 P	20.9.2017	Anton Riemerschmid Weinbrennerei und Likörfabrik/EUIPO	EU:C:2017:701	73, 77, 284, 290
C-673/15 P to C-676/15 P	20.9.2017	The Tea Board/EUIPO	EU:C:2017:702	10, 77, 211, 279, 285, 289, 308, 341, 342, 347, 527, 567–571
C-24/16 and C-25/16	27.9.2017	Nintendo	EU:C:2017:724	21, 105, 106

File Number	*Date*	*Catchword*	*European Case Law Identifier*	*Page*
C-341/16	5.10.2017	Hanssen Beleggingen/Prast Knipping	EU:C:2017:738	94
C-437/16 P	5.10.2017	Wolf Oil/EUIPO	EU:C:2017:737	299, 310
C-501/15 P	11.10.2017	EUIPO/Cactus	EU:C:2017:750	73, 75, 76, 541, 544, 584, 585, 591, 596
C-224/17 P	19.10.2017	Hernández Zamora/EUIPO	EU:C:2017:791	68, 78, 284, 290
C-231/16	19.10.2017	Merck	EU:C:2017:771	101, 104, 110
C-425/16	19.10.2017	Raimund/Aigner	EU:C:2017:776	126–130, 133
C-586/15 P-DEP	9.11.2017	Nestlé Unternehmungen Deutschland/EUIPO	EU:C:2017:855	81
C-520/17 P	30.11.2017	C-cen-tek/EUIPO	EU:C:2017:923	44, 68, 75, 180
C-230/16	6.12.2017	Coty Germany/Parfümerie Akzente	EU:C:2017:941	456, 457
C-468/17 P	13.12.2017	Morton's of Chicago/EUIPO	EU:C:2017:964	40, 74
C-309/15 P-DEP	14.12.2017	MIP Metro Group Intellectual Property/Real Express	EU:C:2017:977	80
C-101/17 P	14.12.2017	Verus/EUIPO	EU:C:2017:979	74
C-499/17 P	14.12.2017	Miguel Torres/EUIPO	EU:C:2017:978	45, 77, 79, 325
C-291/16	20.12.2017	Schweppes/Red Paralela	EU:C:2017:990	9, 286, 287, 438–441, 453, 454, 464, 503, 505, 506
C-559/17 P	11.1.2018	Cafés Pont/EUIPO	EU:C:2018:5	73
C-570/17 P	16.1.2018	Lackmann Fleisch- und Feinkostfabrik/EUIPO	EU:C:2018:11	68, 73, 75
C-536/17 P	17.1.2018	Josel/EUIPO	EU:C:2018:14	22, 74
C-678/16 P	18.1.2018	Monster Energy/EUIPO	EU:C:2018:24	68, 77
C-634/16 P	24.1.2018	EUIPO/European Food	EU:C:2018:30	48–50, 52–54, 68
C-529/17 P	22.2.2018	Martín Osete/EUIPO	EU:C:2018:105	73, 76, 535
C-418/16 P	28.2.2018	mobile.de/EUIPO	EU:C:2018:128	48–50, 52, 55, 56

File Number	*Date*	*Catchword*	*European Case Law Identifier*	*Page*
C-412/16 P and 413/16 P	1.3.2018	Ice Mountain Ibiza/EUIPO	EU:C:2018:140	73, 75, 78, 359
C-560/17 P	13.3.2018	Mediaexpert/EUIPO	EU:C:2018:179	21, 68
C-21/18	14.3.2019	Textilis a.o./Svenskt Tenn	EU:C:2019:199	186, 226–228
C-642/17 P	22.3.2018	Arrigoni/EUIPO	EU:C:2018:219	68, 537
C-651/17	12.4.2018	Grupo Osborne/EUIPO	EU:C:2018:234	68, 73, 77, 78, 290
C-652/17	12.4.2018	Grupo Osborne/EUIPO	EU:C:2018:233	68, 73, 77, 78, 290
C-478/16 P	19.4.2018	EUIPO/Group	EU:C:2018:268	29, 36, 48, 49, 56
C-75/17 P	19.4.2018	Fiesta Hotels & Resorts/EUIPO	EU:C:2018:269	31–35, 51, 74
C-148/17	19.4.2018	Peek & Cloppenburg/Peek & Cloppenburg	EU:C:2018:271	26
C-642/16	17.5.2018	Junek Europ-Vertrieb/Lohmann & Rauscher International	EU:C:2018:322	10, 463, 464, 467, 469, 475, 478, 492–494
C-684/17 P	17.5.2018	Banca Monte dei Paschi di Siena/EUIPO	EU:C:2018:332	71, 79
C-685/17 P	17.5.2018	Banca Monte dei Paschi di Siena/EUIPO	EU:C:2018:331	71, 79
C-30/15 P-DEP2	30.5.2018	Simba Toys/EUIPO	EU:C:2018:353	80
C-85/16 P and C-86/16 P	30.5.2018	Kenzo Tsujimoto/EUIPO	EU:C:2018:349	55, 73, 318, 323, 324, 329, 330
C-519/17 P and C-522/17 P to C-525/17 P	30.5.2018	L'Oréal/EUIPO	EU:C:2018:348	46, 68
C-655/17 P	31.5.2018	Berliner Stadtwerke/EUIPO	EU:C:2018:375	22, 68, 73, 210
C-656/17 P	31.5.2018	Berliner Stadtwerke/EUIPO	EU:C:2018:374	22, 68, 73, 210

File Number	*Date*	*Catchword*	*European Case Law Identifier*	*Page*
C-62/18 P	31.5.2018	Merck/EUIPO	EU:C:2018:373	68, 73
C-32/17 P	6.6.2018	Apcoa Parking Holdings/EUIPO	EU:C:2018:396	22, 68
C-73/18 P	7.6.2018	Cotécnica/EUIPO	EU:C:2018:418	73, 290, 294, 300, 359
C-163/16	12.6.2018	Louboutin a.o./Van Haren Schoenen	EU:C:2018:423	226, 227
C-564/16 P	28.6.2018	EUIPO/Puma	EU:C:2018:509	29, 44, 54, 56, 80, 144, 184, 278, 318, 320, 321
C-118/18 P	28.6.2018	Hochmann Marketing/EUIPO	EU:C:2018:522	22, 146
C-726/17 P	11.7.2018	Tetra Pharm (1997)/EUIPO	EU:C:2018:561	75, 78
C-84/17 P, C-85/17 P and C-95/17 P	25.7.2018	Société des produits Nestlé/EUIPO	EU:C:2018:596	71, 269, 270-272, 524, 543
C-129/17	25.7.2018	Mitsubishi Shoji Kaisha a.o./Duma Forklifts a.o.	EU:C:2018:594	9, 10, 279, 364, 367, 369, 372, 378, 384, 386, 406, 422-425, 447, 448, 450, 451, 463
C-139/17 P	25.7.2018	QuaMa Quality Management/EUIPO	EU:C:2018:608	44, 69, 71, 73, 75
C-488/16 P	6.9.2018	Bundesverband - Souvenir - Geschenke - Ehrenpreise/EUIPO	EU:C:2018:673	22, 44, 73, 75, 211, 216-218, 255, 568
C-547/17 P	6.9.2018	Basic Net/EUIPO	EU:C:2018:682	70, 271, 272
C-136/18 P	6.9.2018	Hansen/EUIPO	EU:C:2018:686	68, 73
C-150/18 P	6.9.2018	El Corte Inglés/EUIPO	EU:C:2018:689	48, 49, 74, 75, 144

File Number	*Date*	*Catchword*	*European Case Law Identifier*	*Page*
C-151/18 P	6.9.2018	El Corte Inglés/EUIPO	EU:C:2018:683	48, 49, 74, 75, 144
C-246/18 P	6.9.2018	Dochirnie pidpryiemstvo Kondyterska korporatsiia 'Roshen'/EUIPO	EU:C:2018:688	68, 73
C-542/17 P	11.9.2018	Allstate Insurance/EUIPO	EU:C:2018:700	74
C-248/18 P	11.9.2018	Moscow Confectionery Factory 'Krasnyiy oktyabr'/EUIPO	EU:C:2018:699	69, 70, 73, 307
C-26/17 P	13.9.2018	Birkenstock Sales/EUIPO	EU:C:2018:714	73, 176, 194, 205, 208
C-411/18 P	3.10.2018	Romantik Hotels & Restaurants/EUIPO	EU:C:2018:823	74, 175, 198, 211
C-326/18 P	4.10.2018	Safe Skies/EUIPO	EU:C:2018:800	74, 187, 265
C-433/17 P	25.10.2018	Enercon/EUIPO	EU:C:2018:860	41, 42, 67
C-48/18 P	13.11.2018	Toontrack Music/EUIPO	EU:C:2018:895	70, 73, 74
C-340/17 P	29.11.2018	Alcohol Countermeasure Systems/EUIPO	EU:C:2018:965	25, 44, 66, 69, 73, 76, 264, 541, 542
C-629/17	6.12.2018	Portugal Ramos Vinhos/Adega Cooperativa de Borba	EU:C:2018:988	209-211, 219, 220
C-370/18	13.12.2018	Uniunea Naţională a Barourilor din România/Holunga	EU:C:2018:1011	143
C-408/18 P	13.12.2018	Senetic/EUIPO	EU:C:2018:1010	73, 207
C-409/18 P	13.12.2018	Senetic/EUIPO	EU:C:2018:1008	73, 207
C-533/18 P	8.1.2019	Emcur Gesundheitsmittel aus Bad Ems/EUIPO	EU:C:2019:2	308, 309
C-463/18 P	15.1.2019	CeramTec/EUIPO	EU:C:2019:18	44, 69, 73
C-553/18 P	15.1.2019	Lion's Head Global Partners/EUIPO	EU:C:2019:21	44, 74, 76-78
C-554/18 P	15.1.2019	Lion's Head Global Partners/EUIPO	EU:C:2019:20	44, 74, 76-78
C-162/17 P	16.1.2019	Republic of Poland/EUIPO	EU:C:2019:27	21, 44, 45, 67, 73, 144, 297, 300
C-698/17 P	23.1.2019	Klement/EUIPO	EU:C:2019:48	69, 205, 546

File Number	*Date*	*Catchword*	*European Case Law Identifier*	*Page*
C-194/17 P	31.1.2019	Pandalis/EUIPO	EU:C:2019:80	44, 73, 285, 512, 519
C-510/18 P	14.2.2019	Prada/EUIPO	EU:C:2019:117	78, 332
C-505/17 P	28.2.2019	Groupe Léa Nature/EUIPO	EU:C:2019:157	44, 69, 73, 79, 297, 300, 302, 305. 323-325
C-733/18 P	19.3.2019	Sevenfriday/EUIPO	EU:C:2019:222	69, 70, 73, 77, 78
C-734/18 P	19.3.2019	Sevenfriday/EUIPO	EU:C:2019:223	69, 70, 73, 77, 78
C-578/17	27.3.2019	Oy Hartwall/Patentti- ja rekisterihallitus	EU:C:2019:261	165-169, 185, 192, 201, 203, 204, 259, 262
C-690/17	11.4.2019	Oko-Text Verlag/Dr. Rudolf Liebe Nachf.	EU:C:2019:317	10, 281, 322, 324, 328, 329, 362, 388, 417-422
C-739/18 P	2.5.2019	Chefaro Ireland/EUIPO	EU:C:2019:356	44, 296, 297
C-653/17 P	15.5.2019	VM Vermögens-Management/EUIPO	EU:C:2019:406	73, 587
C-744/18 P	21.5.2019	Volkswagen/EUIPO	EU:C:2019:437	22, 74
C-780/18 P	22.5.2019	Cuervo y Sobrinos 1882/EUIPO	EU:C:2019:439	44, 73, 76-78, 284
C-822/18 P	4.6.2019	Aldo Supermarkets/EUIPO	EU:C:2019:466	44
C-223/18 P	6.6.2019	Deichmann/EUIPO	EU:C:2019:471	21, 164, 194, 270, 296
C-705/17	12.6.2019	Patent- och registreringsverket/Hansson	EU:C:2019:481	9, 16, 273, 277, 284-286, 290, 294, 297, 311, 313-318, 352, 490
C-795/18 P	20.6.2019	FCA US/EUIPO	EU:C:2019:525	66, 70, 73

File Number	*Date*	*Catchword*	*European Case Law Identifier*	*Page*
C-668/17 P	3.7.2019	Viridis Pharmaceutical/EUIPO	EU:C:2019:557	512, 513, 519, 527, 536, 541
C-99/18 P	4.7.2019	FTI Touristik/EUIPO	EU:C:2019:565	44, 73, 76, 77, 284
C-36/19 P	4.7.2019	Daico International/EUIPO	EU:C:2019:568	60
C-170/19 P	10.7.2019	CheapFlights International/EUIPO	EU:C:2019:581	30
C-819/18 P	11.7.2019	Next design + produktion/EUIPO	EU:C:2019:617	44, 73
C-369/19 P	15.7.2019	Herrero Torres/EUIPO	EU:C:2019:620	91
C-124/18 P	29.7.2019	Red Bull/EUIPO	EU:C:2019:641	69, 166, 169, 192
C-172/18	5.9.2019	AMS Neve a.o./Heritage Audio a.o.	EU:C:2019:674	9, 95, 99, 100-107, 408
C-162/19 P	5.9.2019	Iceland Foods/EUIPO	EU:C:2019:686	69
C-499/19 P	5.9.2019	Lupu/EUIPO	EU:C:2019:683	81
C-68/19 P	11.9.2019	Camomilla/EUIPO	EU:C:2019:711	44, 69, 74, 512
C-124/19 P	11.9.2019	Vitromed/EUIPO	EU:C:2019:713	69, 73, 75, 77, 78
C-104/18 P	12.9.2019	Koton Mağazacilik Tekstil Sanayi ve Ticaret/EUIPO	EU:C:2019:724	10, 46, 249, 251-254
C-541/18	12.9.2019	AS/Deutsches Patent- und Markenamt	EU:C:2019:725	16, 165, 176, 179, 184, 188, 190, 191, 256, 259, 347, 529
C-228/19 P	24.9.2019	ETI Gıda Sanayi ve Ticaret/EUIPO	EU:C:2019:777	74, 76-79
C-426/19 P	24.9.2019	Hesse/EUIPO	EU:C:2019:778	91
C-728/18 P	25.9.2019	EM Research Organization/EUIPO	EU:C:2019:781	44, 65, 69, 73, 75, 145, 180, 212
C-278/19 P	25.9.2019	Mas Que Vinos Global/EUIPO	EU:C:2019:782	44, 73, 76
C-460/19 P	1.10.2019	Stada Arzneimittel/EUIPO	EU:C:2019:803	82
C-293/19 P	2.10.2019	Et Djili Soy Dzhihangir Ibryam/EUIPO	EU:C:2019:814	73, 77

File Number	*Date*	*Catchword*	*European Case Law Identifier*	*Page*
C-586/19 P	7.10.2019	L'Oréal/EUIPO	EU:C:2019:845	79, 91, 92
C-587/19 P	7.10.2019	L'Oréal/EUIPO	EU:C:2019:844	79, 91, 92
C-588/19 P	7.10.2019	L'Oréal/EUIPO	EU:C:2019:843	79, 91, 92
C-589/19 P	7.10.2019	L'Oréal/EUIPO	EU:C:2019:842	79, 91, 92
C-590/19 P	7.10.2019	L'Oréal/EUIPO	EU:C:2019:841	79, 91, 92
C-577/19 P	10.10.2019	KID-Systeme/EUIPO	EU:C:2019:854	82, 84, 86, 88, 92
C-514/18 P	17.10.2019	Landeskammer für Land- und Forstwirtschaft in Steiermark/EUIPO	EU:C:2019:878	512, 516-518
C-582/19 P	22.10.2019	Holzer y Cia/EUIPO	EU:C:2019:891	82, 84, 86, 88, 91
C-613/19 P	24.10.2019	Porsche/EUIPO	EU:C:2019:905	82, 84, 86, 88, 90-92
C-281/18 P	31.10.2019	Repower/EUIPO	EU:C:2019:916	46, 70
C-622/19 P	5.11.2019	Luz Saúde/EUIPO	EU:C:2019:925	82, 84, 86, 88
C-285/19 P	6.11.2019	Geske/EUIPO	EU:C:2019:949	22, 73, 75, 146, 175, 217
C-528/18 P	13.11.2019	Outsource Professional Services/EUIPO	EU:C:2019:961	73, 252, 252
C-659/19 P	19.11.2019	Nonnemacher/EUIPO	EU:C:2019:995	82, 84, 86, 88, 92
C-660/19 P	19.11.2019	Nonnemacher/EUIPO	EU:C:2019:996	82, 84, 86, 88, 92
C-678/19 P	20.11.2019	Retail Royalty/EUIPO	EU:C:2019:994	65, 82, 84, 86, 88, 91, 297
C-678/18	21.11.2019	Procureur-Generaal bij de Hoge Raad der Nederlanden	EU:C:2019:998	149
C-664/19 P	5.12.2019	Agencja Wydawnicza Technopol/EUIPO	EU:C:2019:1048	82, 84, 86, 88, 143
C-783/18 P	12.12.2019	EUIPO/Wajos	EU:C:2019:1073	44, 176, 179, 194, 195, 205, 206

File Number	*Date*	*Catchword*	*European Case Law Identifier*	*Page*
C-143/19 P	12.12.2019	Der Grüne Punkt – Duales System Deutschland /EUIPO	EU:C:2019:1076	76, 289, 512, 515, 526-528, 569, 572
C-713/19 P	12.12.2019	Guiral Broto/EUIPO	EU:C:2019:1080	82, 84, 86
C-714/19 P	12.12.2019	Guiral Broto/EUIPO	EU:C:2019:1085	82, 84, 86
C-715/19 P	12.12.2019	Guiral Broto/EUIPO	EU:C:2019:1086	82, 84, 86
C-696/19 P	19.12.2019	Hauzenberger/EUIPO	EU:C:2019:1116	82, 84, 86, 88, 91
C-371/18	29.1.2020	Sky a.o./SkyKick UK a.o.	EU:C:2020:45	162, 174, 186, 251, 256, 257, 595-597
C-858/19 P	6.2.2020	NHS/EUIPO	EU:C:2020:83	74, 82, 84, 86, 88
C-887/19 P	11.2.2020	Rutzinger-Kurpas/EUIPO	EU:C:2020:91	77, 82, 84, 86, 88, 90
C-823/19 P	13.2.2020	ruwido austria/EUIPO	EU:C:2020:100	82, 84, 86, 88, 91
C-867/19 P	13.2.2020	Confédération nationale du Crédit Mutuel/EUIPO	EU:C:2020:103	82, 84, 86, 88, 90, 92
C-240/18 P	27.2.2020	Constantin Film Produktion/EUIPO	EU:C:2020:118	240-244
C-902/19 P	3.3.2020	Esim Chemicals/EUIPO	EU:C:2020:145	79, 82, 84, 86, 88, 90
C-155/18 P to C-158/18 P	4.3.2020	Tulliallan Burlington/EUIPO	EU:C:2020:151	43, 52, 73, 318, 332, 333, 336, 342, 588, 589
C-328/18 P	4.3.2020	EUIPO/Equivalenza Manufactory	EU:C:2020:156	16, 20, 77, 79, 284, 290, 292, 294-297, 299, 300, 324, 325, 327

File Number	*Date*	*Catchword*	*European Case Law Identifier*	*Page*
C-766/18 P	5.3.2020	Foundation for the Protection of the Traditional Cheese of Cyprus named Halloumi/EUIPO	EU:C:2020:170	77, 284, 286, 289, 290, 297, 312, 570, 571
C-893/19 P	12.3.2020	Roxtec/EUIPO	EU:C:2020:209	75, 82, 84, 86, 88, 90, 91, 233
C-908/19 P	18.3.2020	European Food/EUIPO	EU:C:2020:212	82, 84, 86, 88
C-622/18	26.3.2020	AR/Cooper International Spirits a.o.	EU:C:2020:241	150-152, 427, 511, 529
C-567/18	2.4.2020	Coty Germany/Amazon Services Europe a.o.	EU:C:2020:267	369, 370, 372, 377-382, 396-398, 407
C-26/20 P	21.4.2020	Rezon/EUIPO	EU:C:2020:283	82, 84, 86, 88
C-736/18 P	23.4.2020	Gugler France/EUIPO	EU:C:2020:308	286, 287
C-237/19	23.4.2020	Gömböc Kutató, Szolgáltató és Kereskedelmi/Tulajdon Nemzeti Hivatala	EU:C:2020:296	223, 225, 229-232, 235, 237-240
C-936/19 P	23.4.2020	Rubik's Brand/EUIPO	EU:C:2020:286	
C-14/20 P	23.4.2020	Neoperl/EUIPO	EU:C:2020:287	82, 84, 86, 88, 91
C-608/18 P, C-609/18 P and C-767/18 P	30.4.2020	Republic of Cyprus/EUIPO	EU:C:2020:347	30
C-772/18	30.4.2020	A/B	EU:C:2020:341	367, 371, 372, 375
C-52/20 P	28.5.2020	K.A. Schmersal Holding/EUIPO	EU:C:2020:416	78, 82, 84, 86, 88
C-61/20 P	28.5.2020	Billa/EUIPO	EU:C:2020:408	22, 82, 84, 86, 88, 89
C-74/20 P	28.5.2020	Hänstens Sängar/EUIPO	EU:C:2020:407	82, 84, 86, 88, 90, 92

File Number	*Date*	*Catchword*	*European Case Law Identifier*	*Page*
C-101/20 P	28.5.2020	Currency One/EUIPO	EU:C:2020:406	82, 84, 86, 88, 90
C-72/20 P	4.6.2020	Refan Bulgaria/EUIPO	EU:C:2020:443	82, 84, 86, 88
C-97/20 P	4.6.2020	Société des produits Nestlé/EUIPO	EU:C:2020:442	82, 84, 86, 88, 90, 91
C-115/19 P	11.6.2020	China Construction Bank/EUIPO	EU:C:2020:469	44, 177, 284, 286, 292, 293, 295, 311, 319, 320, 321, 325
C-702/18 P	18.6.2020	Przedsiębiorstwo Produkcyjno-Handlowe 'Primart' Marek Łukasiewicz/EUIPO	EU:C:2020:489	44, 67, 294, 317
C-142/19 P	18.6.2020	Dovgan/EUIPO	EU:C:2020:487	44, 46
C-684/19	2.7.2020	mk advokaten/MBK Rechtsanwälte	EU:C:2020:519	368, 372, 373, 378, 380-382, 406, 407
C-714/18 P	16.7.2020	ACTC/EUIPO	EU:C:2020:573	10, 20, 70, 76, 77, 511, 512, 521, 537-540
C-214/19 P	3.9.2020	achtung!/EUIPO	EU:C:2020:632	175, 176, 179, 189, 190, 210, 350
C-121/19 P	16.9.2020	Edison/EUIPO	EU:C:2020:714	46, 69, 584
C-449/18 P and C-474/18 P	17.9.2020	EUIPO/Messi Cuccittini	EU:C:2020:722	66, 73, 79, 284, 290, 297, 299, 306
C-239/20 P	30.9.2020	Giorgio Armani/EUIPO	EU:C:2020:762	82, 84, 86, 88, 89, 91
C-240/20 P	30.9.2020	Giorgio Armani/EUIPO	EU:C:2020:761	83, 84, 86, 88, 89, 91

File Number	*Date*	*Catchword*	*European Case Law Identifier*	*Page*
C-456/19	8.10.2020	Aktiebolaget Östgötatrafiken/Patent- och registreringsverket	EU:C:2020:813	16, 166, 172, 177, 179, 186, 189, 200, 202-204, 285
C-313/20 P	13.10.2020	Abarca/EUIPO	EU:C:2020:821	83, 84, 86, 88-90
C-386/20 P	21.10.2020	eSky Group IP/EUIPO	EU:C:2020:849	83, 84, 86, 88
C-720/18 and C-721/18	22.10.2020	Ferrari/DU	EU:C:2020:854	512, 515, 520, 521, 538-540, 544-546, 554
C-307/20 P	29.10.2020	Peek & Cloppenburg/EUIPO	EU:C:2020:883	38, 39, 83, 84, 86, 88, 91
C-308/20 P	29.10.2020	Peek & Cloppenburg/EUIPO	EU:C:2020:880	38, 39, 83, 84, 86, 88, 91
C-309/20 P	29.10.2020	Peek & Cloppenburg/EUIPO	EU:C:2020:879	38, 39, 83, 84, 86, 88, 91
C-310/20 P	29.10.2020	Peek & Cloppenburg/EUIPO	EU:C:2020:884	38, 39, 83, 84, 86, 88, 91
C-311/20 P	29.10.2020	Peek & Cloppenburg/EUIPO	EU:C:2020:888	38, 39, 83, 84, 86, 88, 91
C-312/20 P	29.10.2020	Peek & Cloppenburg/EUIPO	EU:C:2020:885	38, 39, 83, 84, 86, 88, 91
C-809/18 P	11.11.2020	EUIPO/John Mills	EU:C:2020:902	12, 308, 343-347
C-446/20 P	12.11.2020	Katjes Fassin/EUIPO	EU:C:2020:910	83, 84, 86, 88, 90
C-418/20 P	26.11.2020	Scorify/EUIPO	EU:C:2020:968	83, 85, 86, 88, 91
C-400/20 P	3.12.2020	Dermavita/EUIPO	EU:C:2020:997	83, 85, 86, 88, 90-92
C-607/19	17.12.2020	Husqvarna/Lidl Digital International	EU:C:2020:1044	532-534

File Number	*Date*	*Catchword*	*European Case Law Identifier*	*Page*
C-404/20 P	17.12.2020	Brands Up/EUIPO	EU:C:2020:1058	83, 85, 86, 88, 91, 143
C-401/20 P	19.1.2021	Leinfelder Uhren München/EUIPO	EU:C:2021:31	83, 85, 86, 88, 90-92
C-626/20 P	28.1.2021	Kaminski/EUIPO	EU:C:2021:83	83, 85, 86, 88, 91
C-600/20 P	11.2.2021	Klose/EUIPO	EU:C:2021:110	83, 85, 86, 88, 91, 143
C-667/20 P	18.3.2021	Laboratorios Ern/EUIPO	EU:C:2021:223	83, 85, 86, 88, 91
C-678/20 P	18.3.2021	Laboratorios Ern/EUIPO	EU:C:2021:224	83, 85, 86, 88, 91
C-639/20 P	23.3.2021	CEDC International/EUIPO	EU:C:2021:227	83, 85, 86, 88
C-681/20 P	24.3.2021	smart things solutions/EUIPO	EU:C:2021:234	83, 85, 86, 88, 91, 144
C-722/20 P	25.3.2021	Ultrasun/EUIPO	EU:C:2021:255	83, 85, 86, 88, 90-92
C-41/21 P	29.4.2021	Allergan Holdings France/EUIPO	EU:C:2021:352	83, 85, 87, 88, 91
C-26/21 P	4.5.2021	Dermavita/EUIPO	EU:C:2021:355	83, 85, 87, 88, 91, 92
C-5/21 P	5.5.2021	Deutsche Post/EUIPO	EU:C:2021:359	83, 85, 87, 88, 90
C-143/21 P	5.5.2021	Production Christian Gallimard/EUIPO	EU:C:2021:360	83, 85, 87, 88
C-48/21 P	12.5.2021	Topcart/EUIPO	EU:C:2021:388	83, 85, 87, 88
C-49/21 P	12.5.2021	Topcart/EUIPO	EU:C:2021:392	83, 85, 87, 88
C-67/21 P	12.5.2021	BSH Hausgeräte/EUIPO	EU:C:2021:391	26, 83, 85, 87, 88, 91, 92, 182
C-59/21 P	18.5.2021	Embutidos Monells/EUIPO	EU:C:2021:396	83, 85, 87, 88, 90, 91

File Number	*Date*	*Catchword*	*European Case Law Identifier*	*Page*
C-93/21 P	20.5.2021	easyCosmetic Swiss/EUIPO	EU:C:2021:408	83, 85, 87, 88
C-109/21 P	2.6.2021	H.R. Participations/EUIPO	EU:C:2021:424	83, 85, 87, 88
C-818/18 P and C-6/19 P	3.6.2021	The Yokohama Rubber/EUIPO	EU:C:2021:431	73, 230
C-114/21 P	22.6.2021	Cinkciarz.pl/EUIPO	EU:C:2021:508	83, 85, 87, 88, 91
C-219/21 P	24.6.2021	Olimp Laboratories/EUIPO	EU:C:2021:522	83, 85, 87, 88, 91, 143
C-185/21 P	29.6.2021	Turk Hava Yollari/EUIPO	EU:C:2021:526	83, 85, 87, 88
C-211/21 P	1.9.2021	12seasons/EUIPO	EU:C:2021:694	85, 87, 88
C-236/21 P	1.9.2021	sprd.net/EUIPO	EU:C:2021:693	21, 83, 85, 87, 88, 91, 143
C-417/21 P	8.9.2021	repowermap.org/EUIPO	EU:C:2021:739	83, 85, 87, 88, 92
C-369/21 P	22.9.2021	Apologistics/EUIPO	EU:C:2021:788	83, 85, 87, 88, 92
C-360/21 P	6.10.2021	FCA Italy/EUIPO	EU:C:2021:841	83, 85, 87, 88
C-415/21 P	10.11.2021	Comercializadora Eloro/EUIPO	EU:C:2021:924	83, 85, 87, 88, 91
C-424/21 P	11.11.2021	Sun Stars & Sons/EUIPO	EU:C:2021:928	83, 85, 87, 88, 91
C-425/21 P	11.11.2021	Sun Stars & Sons/EUIPO	EU:C:2021:927	83, 85, 87, 88, 91
C-465/21 P	12.11.2021	König Ludwig International/EUIPO	EU:C:2021:922	83, 85, 87, 88, 91
C-498/21 P	22.11.2021	Birkenstock IP a.o./EUIPO	EU:C:2021:952	83, 85, 87, 88, 92
C-345/21 P	23.11.2021	Foundation for the Protection of the Traditional Cheese of Cyprus named Halloumi/EUIPO	EU:C:2021:951	83, 85, 87, 88, 90
C-327/21 P	26.11.2021	Giro Travel Company/EUIPO	EU:C:2021:966	83, 85, 87, 88, 90
C-483/21 P	30.11.2021	Health Product Group/EUIPO	EU:C:2021:981	83, 85, 87, 89, 90

File Number	*Date*	*Catchword*	*European Case Law Identifier*	*Page*
C-373/21 P	1.12.2021	Hasbro/EUIPO	EU:C:2021:983	83, 85, 87, 89, 90, 92
C-462/21 P	1.12.2021	Puma/EUIPO	EU:C:2021:982	83, 85, 87, 89, 91, 92
C-473/21 P	8.12.2021	Franz Schröder/EUIPO	EU:C:2021:1001	83, 85, 87, 89
C-474/21 P	8.12.2021	Franz Schröder/EUIPO	EU:C:2021:999	83, 85, 87, 89
C-475/21 P	8.12.2021	Franz Schröder/EUIPO	EU:C:2021:1000	83, 85, 87, 89
C-476/21 P	10.12.2021	Rezon/EUIPO	EU:C:2021:1003	83, 85, 87, 89, 91
C-387/21 P	13.12.2021	Asolo a.o./EUIPO	EU:C:2021:1009	83, 85, 87, 89, 90, 92
C-589/21 P	13.12.2021	Abitron Germany/EUIPO	EU:C:2021:1012	83, 85, 87, 89, 90
C-619/21 P	13.12.2021	Cora/EUIPO	EU:C:2021:1011	83, 85, 87, 89, 90, 92, 145
C-523/21 P	16.12.2021	Innovative Cosmetic Concepts/EUIPO	EU:C:2021:1033	83, 85, 87, 89
C-538/21 P	21.12.2021	Republic of Cyprus/EUIPO	EU:C:2021:1053	83, 85, 87, 89, 91, 92
C-599/21 P	17.1.2022	AM.VI. a.o./EUIPO	EU:C:2022:32	83, 85, 87, 89, 91
C-557/21 P	27.1.2022	Acciona/EUIPO	EU:C:2022:68	83, 85, 87, 89
C-672/21 P	4.2.2022	Eos Products/EUIPO	EU:C:2022:81	83, 85, 87, 89
C-674/21 P	22.2.2022	Residencial Palladium/EUIPO	EU:C:2022:170	83, 85, 87, 89
C-678/21 P	24.2.2022	Sony Interactive Entertainment Europe/EUIPO	EU:C:2022:141	83, 85, 87, 89, 92
C-679/21 P	24.2.2022	Sony Interactive Entertainment Europe/EUIPO	EU:C:2022:109	83, 85, 87, 89, 90, 92

File Number	*Date*	*Catchword*	*European Case Law Identifier*	*Page*
C-183/21	10.3.2022	Maxxus Group/Globus Holding	EU:C:2022:174	513, 545, 546, 554, 555
C-730/21 P	23.3.2022	Collibra/EUIPO	EU:C:2022:208	83, 85, 87, 89
C-529/18 P and 531/18 P	24.3.2022	PJ/EUIPO	EU:C:2022:218	73
C-781/21 P	28.3.2022	Daw/EUIPO	EU:C:2022:234	83, 85, 87, 89, 90, 92
C-743/21 P	31.3.2022	Marina Yachting Brand Management/EUIPO	EU:C:2022:257	83, 85, 87, 89, 90, 92
C-744/21 P	31.3.2022	Henry Cotton's Brand Management/EUIPO	EU:C:2022:256	83, 85, 87, 89, 90, 92
C-761/21 P	31.3.2022	St. Hippolyt Holding/EUIPO	EU:C:2022:249	83, 85, 87, 89
C-762/21 P	31.3.2022	St. Hippolyt Holding/EUIPO	EU:C:2022:255	83, 85, 87, 89
C-784/21 P	5.4.2022	Kappes/EUIPO	EU:C:2022:292	83, 85, 87, 89, 90
C-785/21 P	5.4.2022	Kappes/EUIPO	EU:C:2022:301	83, 85, 87, 89, 90
C-801/21 P	7.4.2022	EUIPO/Indo European Foods	EU:C:2022:295	83, 85, 87, 89, 90, 92-94
C-531/20	28.4.2022	NovaText/Ruprecht-Karls-Universität Heidelberg	EU:C:2022:316	154, 155
C-559/20	28.4.2022	Koch Media/FU	EU:C:2022:317	154, 155
C-65/22 P	6.5.2022	Industria de Diseño Textil/EUIPO	EU:C:2022:369	83, 85, 87, 89, 90
C-103/22 P(I)	17.5.2022	Shanghai Panati/EUIPO	EU:C:2022:399	48
C-466/20	19.5.2022	HEITEC/HEITECH Promotion	EU:C:2022:400	11, 352-359
C-112/21	2.6.2022	X/Classic Coach Company a.o.	EU:C:2022:428	140, 280, 352, 409-413
C-194/22 P	7.6.2022	Magic Box Int. Toys/EUIPO	EU:C:2022:463	83, 85, 87, 89, 90

File Number	*Date*	*Catchword*	*European Case Law Identifier*	*Page*
C-120/22 P	15.6.2022	Republic of Cyprus/EUIPO	EU:C:2022:493	83, 85, 87, 89, 92
C-121/22 P	15.6.2022	Foundation for the Protection of the Traditional Cheese of Cyprus named Halloumi/EUIPO	EU:C:2022:492	83, 85, 87, 89
C-145/22 P	17.6.2022	Lück/EUIPO	EU:C:2022:487	83, 85, 87, 89
C-253/22 P	6.7.2022	Rice/EUIPO	EU:C:2022:546	83, 85, 87, 89, 90
C-187/22 P	11.7.2022	Laboratorios Ern/EUIPO	EU:C:2022:547	83, 85, 87, 89, 90
C-245/22 P(I)	12.7.2022	Cipla Europe/EUIPO	EU:C:2022:549	44, 47, 48
C-247/22 P	14.7.2022	Ignacio Carrasco/EUIPO	EU:C:2022:591	83, 85, 87, 89, 90
C-233/22 P	15.7.2022	Meta Cluster/EUIPO	EU:C:2022:593	83, 85, 87, 92
C-338/22 P	22.9.2022	Hrebenyuk/EUIPO	EU:C:2022:732	83, 85, 87, 89
C-320/22 P	28.9.2022	the airscreen company/EUIPO	EU:C:2022:731	83, 85, 87, 89, 90
C-342/22 P	28.9.2022	Laboratorios Ern/EUIPO	EU:C:2022:730	84, 85, 87, 89
C-575/22 P	10.10.2022	Hochmann Marketing/EUIPO	EU:C:2022:772	82
C-256/21	13.10.2022	KP/TV a.o.	EU:C:2022:786	23, 128, 130-134, 136
C-355/21	13.10.2022	Perfumesco.pl/Procter & Gamble International Operations	EU:C:2022:791	152
C-383/22 P	17.10.2022	SFC/EUIPO	EU:C:2022:799	84, 85, 87, 89
C-446/22 P	20.10.2022	Fidelity National Information Services/EUIPO	EU:C:2022:827	84, 85, 87, 89, 91
C-197/21	27.10.2022	Soda-Club (CO2) a.o./MySoda	EU:C:2022:834	352, 438, 439, 460, 496-499, 501
C-405/22 P	8.11.2022	Mandeley/EUIPO	EU:C:2022:860	84, 85, 87, 89-91
C-337/22 P	16.11.2022	EUIPO/Nowhere	EU:C:2022:908	84, 85, 87, 89, 90, 92-94

File Number	*Date*	*Catchword*	*European Case Law Identifier*	*Page*
C-147/20	17.11.2022	Novartis Pharma/Abacus Medicine	EU:C:2022:891	279, 438, 464, 468-473, 475, 478, 480, 481, 483, 493-495
C-175/21	17.11.2022	Harman International Industries/AB	EU:C:2022:895	438, 442, 446, 448-453, 503, 505-510
C-204/20	17.11.2022	Bayer Intellectual Property/kohlpharma	EU:C:2022:892	279, 438, 439, 464, 467-469, 471-473, 475, 478, 480, 481, 483, 493-495
C-224/20	17.11.2022	Merck Sharp & Dohme a.o./Abacus a.o.	EU:C:2022:893	279, 372, 392, 439, 464, 468-478, 480-484, 487, 492-495
C-253/20 and C-254/20	17.11.2022	Impexeco/Novartis a.o.	EU:C:2022:894	279, 423, 439, 463-467, 475, 478, 480, 493-495
C-577/22 P	29.11.2022	Munich/EUIPO	EU:C:2022:940	84, 85, 87, 89, 90
C-571/22 P	5.12.2022	Unite the Union/EUIPO	EU:C:2022:958	9, 84, 85, 87, 89, 90
C-594/22 P	5.12.2022	Gugler France/EUIPO	EU:C:2022:960	84, 85, 87, 89, 90
C-612/22 P	5.12.2022	Tigercat International/EUIPO	EU:C:2022:959	84, 85, 87, 89, 91

File Number	*Date*	*Catchword*	*European Case Law Identifier*	*Page*
C-148/21 and C-184/21	22.12.2022	Louboutin/Amazon Europe Core a.o.	EU:C:2022:1016	279, 370, 372, 377-380, 392, 393, 397-401
C-702/22 P	1.2.2023	Balaban/EUIPO	EU:C:2023:67	84, 85, 87, 89
C-681/22 P	27.2.2023	Olimp Laboratories/EUIPO	EU:C:2023:128	84, 86, 87, 89
C-605/22 P	8.3.2023	Hijos de Moisés Rodríguez González/EUIPO	EU:C:2023:199	84, 86, 87, 89-91
C-788/22 P	21.3.2023	Louis Vuitton Malletier/EUIPO	EU:C:2023:231	84, 86, 87, 89
C-732/22 P	23.3.2023	G-Core Innovations/EUIPO	EU:C:2023:253	84, 86, 87, 89, 90
C-735/22 P	24.3.2023	Primagran/EUIPO	EU:C:2023:261	84, 86, 87, 89
C-42/23 P	19.4.2023	Mendes/EUIPO	EU:C:2023:325	84, 86, 87, 89
C-628/21	27.4.2023	TB/Castorama Polska a.o.	EU:C:2023:342	150
C-104/22	27.4.2023	Lännen MCE/Berky a.o.	EU:C:2023:343	95, 99-102, 104, 106-109, 407, 408
C-15/23 P	11.5.2023	Heinze/EUIPO	EU:C:2023:407	84, 86, 87, 89, 91
C-654/21	8.6.2023	LM/KP	EU:C:2023:462	30, 31, 128, 131-136
C-38/23 P	13.6.2023	Grupa 'Lew'/EUIPO	EU:C:2023:494	84, 86, 87, 89
C-199/23 P	15.6.2023	Zielonogórski Klub Żużlowy Sportowa/EUIPO	EU:C:2023:560	84, 86, 87, 89, 92
C-77/23 P	27.6.2023	Haskovo Chamber of Commerce and Industry/EUIPO	EU:C:2023:519	84, 86, 88, 89
C-120/23 P	5.7.2023	Suicha/EUIPO	EU:C:2023:539	84, 86, 88-90
C-64/23 P	11.7.2023	Neoperl/EUIPO	EU:C:2023:556	84, 86, 88, 89, 91
C-142/23 P	13.7.2023	Hecht Pharma/EUIPO	EU:C:2023:600	84, 86, 88-91

File Number	*Date*	*Catchword*	*European Case Law Identifier*	*Page*
C-94/23 P	17.7.2023	Puma/EUIPO	EU:C:2023:598	84, 86, 88-91
C-145/23 P	17.7.2023	Puma/EUIPO	EU:C:2023:597	84, 86, 88-91
C-280/23 P	17.7.2023	Canai Technology/EUIPO	EU:C:2023:596	84, 86, 88-90

Index

D

E

J

K

L

O

P

V

W

www.ingramcontent.com/pod-product-compliance
Lightning Source LLC
La Vergne TN
LVHW020649300926
849161LV00004B/869
* 9 7 8 9 4 0 3 5 4 1 2 7 3 *